Corporate Taxation Through the Lens of Mergers & Acquisitions

Corporate Taxation
Through the Lens of
Mergers & Acquisitions

Including Cross-Border Transactions

SECOND EDITION

Samuel C. Thompson, Jr.

PROFESSOR OF LAW, PENN STATE LAW
ARTHUR WEISS DISTINGUISHED FACULTY SCHOLAR
DIRECTOR OF THE CENTER FOR THE STUDY OF MERGERS & ACQUISITIONS

CAROLINA ACADEMIC PRESS
Durham, North Carolina

ISBN 978-1-61163-175-3
LCCN 2016949835

Carolina Academic Press, LLC.
700 Kent Street
Durham, North Carolina 27701
Telephone (919) 489-7486
Fax (919) 493-5668
www.cap-press.com

Printed in the United States of America

Dedication

This book is dedicated to the late Professor Bernard Wolfman, who first introduced me to this subject in his Corporate Tax course in my third year at the University of Pennsylvania School of Law and to the late Professor James S. Eustice who deepened my understanding of this subject in his Advanced Corporate Tax Problems course in the Graduate Tax Program at the NYU School of Law.

Contents

Table of Principal Cases

References are to sections

Preface

I have long thought that the most interesting issues in corporate taxation revolve around the treatment of taxable and tax free mergers and acquisitions. This is particularly true now that a uniform 20% maximum rate applies to long term capital gains and to dividend income. Thus, this book approaches corporate taxation through the lens of the merger and acquisition provisions of Subchapter C of the Internal Revenue Code, which deals with the tax treatment of corporations.

To ensure that the reader has the appropriate background to explore merger and acquisition concepts, Chapter 1 introduces several basic Federal income tax concepts, and Chapter 2 introduces the basic provisions of Subchapter C. The concepts introduced in Chapter 1 include:

- The basic tax treatment of the four principal forms for conducting business: C corporations, S corporations, partnerships, and LLCs;
- The realization and recognition concept;
- The treatment of like kind exchanges;
- The treatment of liabilities, including the *Crane* case;
- The treatment of capital gains and losses;
- The impact of Sections 1231 and 1245 on the disposition of property;
- The cash and accrual accounting methods; and
- The treatment of original issue discount.

Chapter 2 introduces the following provisions of Subchapter C:

- Section 351, which deals with the organization of a corporation;
- Section 301, which deals with the treatment of shareholders on the distribution of property;
- Section 302, which deals with the treatment of shareholders on the redemption of their stock;
- Section 311, which deals with the treatment of the corporation on the distribution of dividends;
- Section 331, which deals with the treatment of shareholders on receipt of a liquidating distribution; and
- Section 336, which deals with the treatment of a corporation that makes a liquidating distribution.

Because of the globalization of business activity, it will be virtually impossible for any law student today who goes into a corporate tax practice to avoid dealing with cross-border issues, and for this reason, this book also introduces many of the issues under the Federal income tax affecting both inbound and outbound cross-border mergers and acquisitions.

I want to thank my research assistants for their excellent help in the preparation of this book. The following students at Penn State Law assisted with the second edition: Zachary Burley, Vasilios Vlahakis, Ying Zeng, and Matt Robida. The following former students assisted with the first edition: Robert Allen Clary, II, a graduate of the University of Miami School of Law and the Graduate Tax Program at the NYU School of Law, Matthew Sgnilek, a graduate of the UCLA School of Law, and Daniel Davis, a graduate of the UCLA School of Law. Finally, I want to thank my lovely wife, Becky Sue, and our son, Tommy, for their love and support.

Samuel C. Thompson, Jr.

Professor of Law and Director Center for the Study of Mergers and Acquisitions

Penn State Law

June 10, 2016

Corporate Taxation
Through the Lens of
Mergers & Acquisitions

Chapter 1

Introduction and Review of Basic Concepts

§ 1.1 Scope of Book

This is a Corporate Tax book that approaches this subject principally through the prism of the Federal income tax treatment of taxable and tax-free mergers and acquisitions (M&A).[1] Although the book discusses virtually every section of subchapter C of the Internal Revenue Code (*i.e.*, § 301 *et seq.*), which governs the tax treatment of "C" or regular corporations, the emphasis is placed on those provisions of subchapter C that have the most impact on M&A transactions. The book is structured for use both by students who have not previously been exposed to Corporate Tax and by those who have.

This approach is justified, at least in part, by the fact that, as discussed more fully below, the maximum rate for individuals on both capital gains and dividends is generally 20%, or 23.8%, when taking into account the Medicare tax on Net Investment Income. Many of the non-M&A related provisions of subchapter C (*e.g.*, § 302, which addresses redemptions) and some of the M&A related provisions (*e.g.*, § 356(a)(2), which addresses the characterization of boot received in a reorganization) draw a distinction between capital gain and dividend income. These distinctions now are largely meaningless, except that if a transaction produces a capital gain the taxpayer usually gets to recover basis, but there is no basis recovery on receipt of a taxable dividend.

The book focuses principally on domestic M&A; however, because of the growing importance of cross-border M&A, the Federal income tax consequences of these transactions are also briefly examined. In this connection, when examining particular transactions, such as taxable asset acquisitions in Chapter 4, the book also examines the Federal income tax consequences under the assumption that a foreign acquiror is acquiring a U.S. target in an inbound acquisition and alternatively that a U.S. acquiror is acquiring a foreign target in an outbound acquisition.

The book is divided into four parts. Part I contains an introduction to business tax principles, to basic corporate tax principles, and to the Federal income tax treatment of taxable and tax-free M&A. Part II focuses on taxable stock and asset acquisitions; Part III focuses on tax-free reorganizations; and Part IV focuses on special topics.

---

1. Many of the sections of this book are based on and modifications of Samuel C. Thompson Jr., Paul R. Wysocki, Robert R. Pluth and Catherine A. Jacobson, *Federal Taxation of Business Enterprises* (1989) [hereinafter cited as "*Federal Taxation of Business Enterprises*"], published with permission.

Part I contains this chapter and Chapters 2 and 3. This chapter contains this introduction to the book and an introduction to fundamental principles affecting business taxation, such as (1) the general treatment of the three principal business forms: the C corporation, the partnership, and the S corporation; (2) the scope of the realization and recognition concepts; (3) the treatment of liabilities in a sale or exchange of property; and (4) an outline of the basic rules under the Code governing the taxation of inbound and outbound transactions. Chapter 2 contains an overview of some fundamental principles of corporate taxation that are important in, but generally not central to, the planning of M&A transactions. The provisions examined in Chapter 2 include the impact of § 351 on the organization of a corporation, the treatment of cash and property distributions at both the shareholder and corporate levels, the effect of redemption transactions, the consequences resulting from a distribution by a corporation of its stock (*i.e.*, stock dividends), and an examination of the basic provisions governing the liquidation of a corporation. Chapter 2 touches on many of the concepts that are examined in detail in a Corporate Tax course, and those students who have already mastered the concepts in Chapter 2 can proceed directly to Chapter 3, which contains an introduction to the Federal income tax aspects of both taxable and tax-free M&A.

Part II contains Chapters 4 and 5, which focus on taxable acquisitions and leveraged buyouts (LBOs). Chapter 4 addresses taxable acquisitions by an acquiring corporation of the assets of a target corporation, and Chapter 5 deals with the taxable acquisition by an acquiring corporation of the stock of a target. Since most LBOs are effectuated as stock acquisitions, issues that arise in such transactions are examined in Chapter 5. Both of these chapters address the treatment of a target's net operating losses (NOLs), and the last sections of each of these chapters briefly addresses the Federal income tax treatment of inbound and outbound acquisitions.

Part III contains Chapters 6 through 10, which focus on tax-free M&A under the reorganization provisions of the Code. Chapter 6 lays the foundation for dealing with acquisitive reorganizations by examining certain fundamental concepts such as the continuity of interest (COI) doctrine, the continuity of business enterprise (COBE) requirement, and the treatment of boot as capital gain or dividend income.

Chapter 7 looks at all forms of tax-free, acquisitive asset reorganizations. In these transactions, an acquiring corporation acquires, either directly or by merger, the assets of a target corporation in exchange for stock of the acquiring corporation or its parent corporation. These transactions are (1) the "(A)" reorganization under § 368(a)(1)(A); (2) the forward subsidiary merger under § 368(a)(2)(D); and (3) the straight and triangular stock for asset "(C)" reorganizations under § 368(a)(1)(C).

Chapter 8 deals with tax-free acquisitive stock reorganizations. In these transactions an acquiring corporation acquires the stock of a target corporation in exchange for stock of the acquiring corporation or its parent corporation. These transactions are (1) the straight and triangular stock for stock "(B)" reorganization under § 368(a)(1)(B), and (2) the reverse subsidiary merger reorganization under § 368(a)(2)(E).

A separate section in Chapters 4 (taxable asset acquisitions), 5 (taxable stock acquisitions), 7 (tax-free asset acquisitions), and 8 (tax-free stock acquisitions) examines for each form of acquisition the impact of the provisions restricting the carryover to post-acquisition periods of pre-acquisition NOLs and other tax attributes. These sections address the impact of § 382, the principal provision limiting the carryover of NOLs, and various collateral provisions, such as (1) § 269, which applies to acquisitions made to avoid taxes, and (2) the § 384 limitation on the ability to use pre-acquisition losses of an acquiring corporation to offset a target's built-in gains.

Chapter 9 focuses on spin-off transactions under § 355 of the Code and the use of such transactions in combination with an acquisitive reorganization. Chapter 10 focuses on the impact of § 367 on cross border acquisitive reorganizations including inversions.

Part IV contains Chapters 11 through 13. Chapter 11 deals with the use of partnerships, including LLCs that are treated as partnerships, and S corporations in acquisition transactions. Chapter 12 introduces some of the issues that can arise in bankruptcy related acquisitions. Finally, Chapter 13 discusses tax policy issues arising in mergers and acquisitions.

Each chapter begins with a brief discussion of the scope of the chapter. Many topics are introduced by a textual discussion of the relevant provisions of the Code and regulations. This introductory material is followed by cases, rulings, notes, and problems that deal with more esoteric issues in the particular area. The issues discussed here are very complex, and the focus is on the basic principles.

§ 1.2 Scope of Chapter

This chapter reviews basic principles of business and corporate taxation that are fundamental to the study of tax aspects of mergers and acquisitions. Sec. 1.3 sets out a general description of the taxation of the three basic forms of conducting business: (1) the C or regular corporation, (2) the partnership, including the limited liability company (LLC), which generally is taxed as partnership or sole proprietorship, and (3) the S corporation. Sec. 1.4 introduces the realization and recognition concept and two principal exceptions to the recognition requirement: the installment sale provision and the like kind exchange provision. Sec. 1.5 introduces the treatment of liabilities in various business settings. Sec. 1.6 briefly reviews the tax treatment of capital gains, and Sec. 1.7 deals with the treatment of the sale of business property under §§ 1231 and 1245. Sec. 1.8 briefly introduces some basic tax accounting concepts that are important in M&A transactions, and Sec. 1.9 sketches out the general principles governing the original discount interest rules. Sec. 1.10 provides a brief introduction to taxable and tax-free M&A. Sec. 1.11 provides a quick overview of the manner in which the U.S. taxes international business transactions, and finally, Sec. 1.12 sets out references.

§ 1.3 General Descriptions of the Three Basic Forms of Business[2]

A. The C Corporation

A subchapter C corporation is a separate taxable entity distinct from its shareholders. Section 11 imposes a tax on the taxable income of a subchapter C corporation. As with any taxpayer, the "taxable income" (*see* § 63) of a corporation is computed by first determining the corporation's "gross income" under Section 61 and then subtracting the allowed deductions. Any dividends distributed by a subchapter C corporation to its shareholders are included in the gross income of the shareholders. *See* § 61(a)(7). Dividends received by shareholders are subject to a separate tax imposed under Section 1 in the case of noncorporate shareholders and under Section 11 in the case of corporate shareholders. Thus, earnings of a business operated as a subchapter C corporation are subject to a corporate level tax and a shareholder level tax.

The corporate tax imposed by Section 11 is equal to (1) 15% of the first $50,000 of taxable income, (2) 25% of the next $25,000 of taxable income, (3) 34% of taxable income in excess of $75,000 but not in excess of $10 million, and (4) 35% of taxable income in excess of $10 million.

The lower 15% and 25% rates are phased out for corporations that have taxable income in excess of $100,000 for any taxable year. *See* § 11(b). This phase out is implemented by imposing an additional tax on income in excess of $100,000 equal to the lesser of (1) 5% of the excess, or (2) $11,750. This $11,750 is the difference between the tax at the 15%, 25% and 34% graduated rates on the first $100,000 of taxable income and the tax on such income at 34%. This means that the benefit of the 15% and 25% rates is completely phased out at $335,000 of taxable income. Thus, any corporation with taxable income between $335,000 and $10 million is subject to a 34% effective rate of tax.

The 34% rate is phased out for corporations with taxable income in excess of $15 million. In such cases, taxable income is increased by an additional amount equal to the lesser of (1) 3% of such excess, or (2) $100,000. *See* § 11(b). Thus, the benefit of the 34% rate is completely recaptured when a corporation's taxable income reaches $18,333,333 (3% of $3,333,333 is $100,000). As discussed in Chapter 13, which addresses policy issues, the 35% maximum corporate rate is one of the highest corporate rates in the world, and as of 2016, there are legislative efforts directed at reducing that rate.

Any operating loss realized by a C corporation can be carried back for 2 years and forward for 20 years. *See* § 172(a) and (b)(1)(A).

As indicated, shareholders are subject to a tax on the receipt of dividends, which are current distributions of cash or property out of a corporation's "earnings and profits," which is similar to retained earnings. *See* §§ 301(a), (c)(1) and 316(a).

---

2. This section is based on a modification of Sec. 2.02 of *Federal Taxation of Business Enterprises,* *supra* note 1.

For individual shareholders, although the maximum individual rate on ordinary income is 39.6% (*see* § 1), the maximum individual rate on capital gains and dividends is generally 20%. *See* § 1(h). However, as a result of the enactment of the Medicare Net Investment Income Tax, which was enacted as part of Obamacare, there is an additional 3.8% tax on net investment income, including dividends and capital gains, of taxpayers with more than a threshold amount of adjusted gross income, generally $250,000. Thus, for many high income taxpayers, the maximum Federal tax on dividends and capital gains will be 23.8%.

Corporate shareholders receive the benefit of a "dividends received deduction" in the amount of 70%, 80%, or 100% of the dividends received. *See* § 243. The purpose of this deduction is to mitigate the effect of multiple corporate level taxes on the same income. However, generally there is no dividends received deduction on dividends received from foreign corporations. Parent corporations generally file consolidated tax returns with their 80%-or-more owned subsidiaries, and the dividends from such subsidiaries are not included in the parent's gross income.

The combined corporate and individual rates currently results in an aggregate maximum tax rate of approximately 50% on the distributed earnings of a subchapter C corporation. This maximum double tax is illustrated as follows:

> Individuals A and B form a corporation (C) as equal shareholders. C earns $20 million of taxable income for the taxable year and pays a corporate tax of $7,000,000 (i.e., 35% of $20 million). C then distributes the $13,000,000 after-tax earnings to A and B as a dividend, and A and B are taxed at a 23.8% rate on the dividend for a tax of $3,094,000. Thus, the combined corporate and shareholder tax on C's $20 million of taxable income is $10,094,000, or approximately 50%.

In addition to being subject to the basic corporate tax under § 11, a corporation may be subject to the alternative minimum tax under § 55. This tax is not examined here.

A subchapter C corporation may be subject to the personal holding company tax under § 541. This tax applies to certain closely held corporations that have a substantial amount of undistributed passive income (*e.g.*, dividends and interest). The accumulated earnings tax under § 531 may apply to a subchapter C corporation that is not a personal holding company and that accumulates earnings for the purpose of avoiding the shareholder tax on dividend distributions. These two penalty taxes, which are not examined here, are not applicable to foreign corporations.

The above analysis does not include the impact of state income taxes on corporate income. As discussed more fully below, the U.S. corporate tax rate is the highest in the industrialized world, and there is significant interest among both Republicans and Democrats in reducing the rate.

The basic tax treatment of the organization, current operation, and liquidation of a C corporation, is introduced in Chapter 2. A C corporation may participate in either a taxable or tax-free acquisition, both of which are introduced in Chapter 3 and explored in detail in later chapters. Tax-free acquisitions are known as reorganizations.

B. The Partnership and the Limited Liability Company

Partnerships may be involved in a merger, acquisition, or joint venture, and therefore, this section introduces some of the basic principles governing partnerships. Subchapter K of the Code, § 701 *et seq.*, governs the taxation of partnerships.

Partnerships for Federal income tax purposes include not only state law partnerships but also certain other alternative entities, such as limited liability companies (LLCs), that under the check-the-box regulations under § 7701 elect or are deemed to elect to be partnerships for Federal income tax purposes. Most multiple member LLCs are treated as partnerships. An election can be made to treat a single member LLC, such as an LLC that is wholly owned by a corporation, as either a corporation or a "disregarded entity." A disregarded entity that is wholly owned by a corporation is taxed as a division of the corporation. Sec. 7.2.I addresses corporate mergers with disregarded entities.

Partnerships (including LLCs that are taxed as partnerships), unlike C corporations, are not subject to Federal income tax. *See* § 701. Each partner includes in gross income her share of the partnership's gross income, whether or not the partnership makes a distribution of cash or property. *See* §§ 702(a) and 706(a). Also, a partner generally deducts from gross income her share of partnership losses to the extent of her basis for her partnership interest. *See* §§ 702 and 704(d). Thus, both taxable income and taxable loss generally pass through the partnership to the partners.

A partner's basis for her partnership interest is increased by her allocable share of partnership income and decreased by her allocable share of partnership losses. *See* § 705. Distributions of cash or other property from a partnership to a partner are generally tax-free to the partner and result in a reduction in the basis of the partner's partnership interest. *See* § 705.

Thus, the fundamental differences between the taxation of partnerships and C corporations are: (1) C corporations are subject to tax but partnerships are not, and (2) partners are taxed on the partnership's income even though the income may not be distributed, but shareholders are taxed only upon the receipt of a distribution from the C corporation. Because of this absence of a double tax, partnerships may be used as an acquisition vehicle in an asset acquisition as discussed briefly in Chapter 11.

The following example illustrates the tax treatment of partnerships:

Corporations *A* and *B* form a partnership (*P*) as equal partners. *P* earns income of $1 million for the taxable year and distributes $500K (K = $1000) of cash to each of *A* and *B*. *A* and *B* each (1) report $500K of gross income from the partnership §§ 702 and 704(a)), (2) increase the basis of their individual partnership interest by the $500K of allocated income (§ 705(a)), (3) receive the $500K of cash tax-free (§ 731), and (4) reduce the basis of their individual partnership interest by $500K (§ 705(a)). Thus, assuming a 35% maximum corporate rate, the $1 million is subject to a tax of

$350,000. In addition, there would be a shareholder tax on the income when it is distributed.

The Code permits flexibility in allocating income, gain, loss deductions, and credits among the partners. *See* § 704(a). This flexibility is much greater than with C or S corporations and is illustrated as follows:

> A and B form partnership P as equal partners. In the fifth year of operation, A and B agree that A has contributed more to the success of the partnership operations than B. As a consequence, A is allocated 75% of the partnership's income for the year, with only 25% going to B. This type of allocation is respected for tax purposes, provided it has substantial economic effect under § 704(b).

C. The S Corporation

An S corporation may be either the target or acquiror in a taxable or tax-free merger or acquisition. Only certain corporations qualify to be treated as S corporations. For example, an S corporation may issue only one class of stock, and it can have no more than 100 shareholders. *See* § 1361(b). An election for subchapter S treatment must be made by the shareholders and the corporation. *See* § 1362. If a business can operate in the form of an S corporation, the tax consequences from regular operations are similar to those of a partnership. Thus, the S corporation is generally not subject to tax, and a shareholder (1) reports her allocable share of the corporation's income or loss, (2) increases the basis for her stock by her allocable share of income, and (3) decreases the basis by her allocable share of any loss. Distributions from S corporations are generally tax-free to the shareholder and result in a reduction in the basis of the shareholder's shares. The operation of an S corporation is illustrated as follows:

> Individuals A and B form an S corporation (S) as equal shareholders. S earns taxable income for its first taxable year of $1 million and distributes $500K to each of A and B. S is not subject to tax. As in the case of a partnership, A and B (1) report $500K of income from S (§ 1366(a)(1)), (2) increase the basis of their shares by $500K (§ 1367(a)), (3) receive a tax-free distribution of the $500K of cash (§§ 1368(a) and (b)), and (4) reduce the basis of their stock by $500K (§ 1367(a)). If the maximum individual rate of 39.6% is applicable, S's $1 million of income is subject to a tax of $396K. Thus, by operating as an S corporation, the combined approximately 50% rate of corporate and shareholder taxes on C corporations is avoided.

An S corporation is subject to tax in two circumstances. First, if an S corporation was previously a C corporation, did not distribute all of its C period earnings and profits, and earns a substantial amount of passive income, a tax may be imposed on the passive income. *See* § 1375. Further, if an S corporation was formerly a C corporation, a tax may be imposed on the disposition by the S corporation of appreciated property held by the C corporation at the time of the conversion from C to S. *See* § 1374.

The provisions of subchapter C apply to S corporations, except where explicitly made inapplicable or where such rules are inconsistent with the rules of subchapter S. *See* § 1371(a). Consequently, the rules governing the transfer of property to C corporations and sales and liquidations of C corporations also generally apply to S corporations.

§ 1.4 Realization and Recognition

A. The Structure of the Statute: Realization and Recognition

See §§ 1001, 1011, 1012, 1015(a) and 1016.

The tax consequences of many merger and acquisition transactions involve a realization event for which the issue is whether the gain or loss is recognized. Section 61(a)(3) provides that gross income includes "gains derived from dealing in property," which includes gains from the sale of stock or assets in a merger or acquisition. The starting point for determining the tax consequences upon the disposition of property is § 1001(a) of the Code, which provides that gain or loss on a sale or other disposition of property shall be the difference between the amount realized and the adjusted basis of the property transferred. The "amount realized" on a sale or other disposition of property is defined in § 1001(b) as "the sum of any money received plus the fair market value of property (other than money) received." Under § 1011, the "adjusted basis" of property for purposes of determining gain or loss is, in general, the taxpayer's cost of the property as provided in § 1012, less depreciation, if any, and plus or minus certain other adjustments, all as provided in § 1016.

Pursuant to § 1001(c), realized gain or loss is "recognized" (*i.e.,* taken into account for tax purposes), except as otherwise provided in the income tax provisions of the Code. The corporate and partnership provisions of the Code contain several exceptions to the general rule of recognition. For example, under § 351 gains or losses realized by a contributing shareholder on the transfer of property to a corporation in exchange for stock may be given nonrecognition treatment, and under § 354 an exchange of stock of a target corporation for stock of an acquiring corporation in a "reorganization" under § 368 qualifies for nonrecognition treatment. Many of these nonrecognition provisions are analogous to the nonrecognition rule of § 1031 for like kind exchanges of property. For this reason, this introductory chapter contains a brief review of § 1031.

To preserve (defer) the gain or loss that is not recognized in a transaction governed by an exception to the rule of recognition, the basis of the property received is, generally, the basis of the property exchanged. This is known, in tax parlance, as a *substituted basis* and is an exception to the cost basis rule of § 1012. *See* §§ 7701(a)(44), (43), and (42) Thus, if a particular transaction is excepted from the rule of recognition, there will also be an exception to the cost basis rule for the property received in the transaction.

The following materials explore some of the aspects of these realization and recognition concepts.

B. The Relationship between Basis and Amount Realized

See §§ 1011 and 1012.

Philadelphia Park Amusement Co. v. United States

United States Court of Claims, 1954
126 F. Supp. 184

[In *Philadelphia Park* the taxpayer had been granted by the City of Philadelphia a franchise to operate a railroad in Fairmount Park. Pursuant to this franchise the taxpayer constructed the Strawberry Bridge over the Schuylkill River at a cost of $381,000. In 1934 the taxpayer deeded the bridge to the City of Philadelphia in exchange for a ten-year extension of the franchise. In 1946 at a time when the franchise had approximately five years to run, the taxpayer abandoned the franchise and began a bus transportation service. The issue involved the determination of the taxpayer's basis for the franchise for purposes of ascertaining the amount of the deductible loss on the abandonment. In analyzing this issue, the court started with an analysis of the 1934 transaction in which the bridge was exchanged for the franchise.]

The gain or loss, whichever the case may have been, should have been recognized, and the cost basis under section 113(a) [now § 1012] of the Code, of the 10-year extension of the franchise was the cost to the taxpayer. The succinct statement in § 113(a) [now § 1012] that "the basis of property shall be the cost of such property" although clear in principle, is frequently difficult in application. One view is that the cost basis of property received in a taxable exchange is the fair market value of the property *given* in the exchange. The other view is that the cost basis of property received in a taxable exchange is the fair market value of the property *received* in the exchange. As will be seen from the cases and some of the Commissioner's rulings the Commissioner's position has not been altogether consistent on this question. The view that "cost" is the fair market value of the property given is predicated on the theory that the cost to the taxpayer is the economic value relinquished. The view that "cost" is the fair market value of the property received is based upon the theory that the term "cost" is a tax concept and must be considered in the light of the designed interrelationship of [the predecessors of §§ 1001, 1011 and 1012] and the prime role that the basis of property plays in determining tax liability. We believe that when the question is considered in the latter context that the cost basis of the property received in a taxable exchange is the fair market value of the property *received* in the exchange.

When property is exchanged for property in a taxable exchange the taxpayer is taxed on the difference between the adjusted basis of the property given in exchange and the fair market value of the property received in exchange. For purposes of determining gain or loss the fair market value of the property received is treated as cash and taxed accordingly. To maintain harmony with the fundamental purpose of these sections, it is necessary to consider the fair market value of the property received as the cost basis to the taxpayer. The failure to do so would result in allowing the taxpayer a stepped-up basis, without paying a tax therefore, if the fair market value of the property received is less than the fair market value of the property given, and the taxpayer would be subjected to a double tax if the fair market value of the property received is more than the fair market value of the property given. By holding that the fair market value of the property received in a taxable exchange is the cost basis, the above discrepancy is avoided and the basis of the property received will equal the adjusted basis of the property given plus any gain recognized, or that should have been recognized, or minus any loss recognized, or that should have been recognized.

Therefore, the cost basis of the 10-year extension of the franchise was its fair market value on August 3, 1934, the date of the exchange. The determination of whether the cost basis of the property received is its fair market value or the fair market value of the property given in exchange therefore, although necessary to the decision of the case, is generally not of great practical significance because the value of the two properties exchanged in an arms-length transaction are either equal in fact, or are presumed to be equal. The record in this case indicates that the 1934 exchange was an arms-length transaction and, therefore, if the value of the extended franchise cannot be determined with reasonable accuracy, it would be reasonable and fair to assume that the value of Strawberry Bridge was equal to the 10-year extension of the franchise. The fair market value of the 10-year extension of the franchise should be established but, if that value cannot be determined with reasonable certainty, the fair market value of Strawberry Bridge should be established and that will be presumed to be the value of the extended franchise. This value cannot be determined from the facts now before us since the case was prosecuted on a different theory.

The taxpayer contends that the market value of the extended franchise or Strawberry Bridge could not be ascertained and, therefore, it should be entitled to carry over the undepreciated cost basis of the bridge as the cost of the extended franchise. * * * If the value of the extended franchise or bridge cannot be ascertained with a reasonable degree of accuracy, the taxpayer is entitled to carry over the undepreciated cost of the bridge as the cost basis of the extended franchise. * * * However, it is only in rare and extraordinary cases that the value of the property exchanged cannot be ascertained with reasonable accuracy. We are presently of the opinion that either the value of the extended franchise or the bridge can be determined with a reasonable degree of accuracy. Although the value of the extended franchise may be difficult or impossible to ascertain because of the nebulous and intangible characteristics inherent in such property, the value of the bridge is subject to more exact measurement. Consideration may be given to expert testimony on the value of comparable bridges, Strawberry Bridge's reproduction cost and its undepreciated cost, as well as other relevant factors.

Therefore, because we deem it equitable, judgment should be suspended and the question of the value of the extended franchise on August 3, 1934, should be remanded to the Commissioner of this court for the taking of evidence and the filing of a report thereon. * * *

C. The Open Transaction Doctrine

See § 1.1001-1(a) (3d sentence).

Burnet v. Logan

Supreme Court of the United States, 1931
283 U.S. 404

Mr. Justice McReynolds delivered the opinion of the Court.

[Mrs. Logan, a cash basis taxpayer, sold her stock in Andrews & Hitchcock Company to Youngstown Sheet & Tube Company for a cash down payment plus 60 cents for each ton of ore to be taken from a mine owned by a subsidiary of Andrews & Hitchcock. The issue was whether Mrs. Logan was required to realize and recognize at the time of sale her share of the amounts to be paid upon the mining of the ore.]

The Commissioner ruled that the obligation of the Youngstown Company to pay 60 cents per ton had a fair market value of $1,942,111.46 on March 11, 1916; that this value should be treated as so much cash and the sale of the stock regarded as a closed transaction with no profit in 1916. He also used this valuation as the basis for apportioning subsequent annual receipts between income and return of capital. His calculations, based upon estimates and assumptions, are too intricate for brief statement. He made deficiency assessments according to the view just stated and the Board of Tax Appeals approved the result.

The Circuit Court of Appeals held that, in the circumstances, it was impossible to determine with fair certainty the market value of the agreement by the Youngstown Company to pay 60 cents per ton. Also, that respondent was entitled to the return of her capital—the value of 250 shares on March 1, 1913, and the assessed value of the interest derived from her mother—before she could be charged with any taxable income. As this had not in fact been returned, there was no taxable income.

We agree with the result reached by the Circuit Court of Appeals.

The 1916 transaction was a sale of stock—not an exchange of property. We are not dealing with royalties or deductions from gross income because of depletion of mining property. Nor does the situation demand that an effort be made to place according to the best available data some approximate value upon the contract for future payments. This probably was necessary in order to assess the mother's estate. As annual payments on account of extracted ore come in they can be readily apportioned first as return of capital and later as profit. The liability for income tax ultimately can be fairly determined without resort to mere estimates, assumptions and speculation. When the profit, if any, is actually realized, the taxpayer will be required to respond.

The consideration for the sale was $2,200,000.00 in cash and the promise of future money payments wholly contingent upon facts and circumstances not possible to foretell with anything like fair certainty. The promise was in no proper sense equivalent to cash. It had no ascertainable fair market value. The transaction was not a closed one. Respondent might never recoup her capital investment from payments only conditionally promised. Prior to 1921 all receipts from the sale of her shares amounted to less than their value on March 1, 1913. She properly demanded the return of her capital investment before assessment of any taxable profit based on conjecture. * * *

From her mother's estate Mrs. Logan obtained the right to share in possible proceeds of a contract thereafter to pay indefinite sums. The value of this was assumed to be $277,164.50 and its transfer was so taxed. Some valuation—speculative or otherwise—was necessary in order to close the estate. It may never yield as much, it may yield more. If a sum equal to the value thus ascertained had been invested in an annuity contract, payments thereunder would have been free from income tax until the owner had recouped his capital investment. We think a like rule should be applied here. The statute definitely excepts bequests from receipts which go to make up taxable income. * * *

The judgments below are

Affirmed.

D. Installment Sales Reporting under § 453[3]

Skim § 453.

In many M&A transactions, a taxpayer sells stock or assets for a debt instrument of the acquiror. Under § 453, if certain conditions are satisfied, the taxpayer may qualify for installment sale treatment, that is, deferred tax treatment, for the payments received on the instrument. The following is a brief summary of the basic elements of § 453, the installment sales provision.

Section 1001(d) allows recognized gain to be reported on the installment method under § 453. This method permits a taxpayer to pay the Federal income tax over the periods during which payments of the sales price are received, thus relieving the taxpayer of the burden of paying taxes on income not yet received.

Section 453(a) provides that income from an installment sale is to be reported on the installment method except as otherwise provided in § 453. Section 453(b)(1) defines an installment sale as a "disposition of property where at least 1 payment is to be received after the close of the taxable year in which the disposition occurs."

The installment method is defined in § 453(c) as a "method under which the income recognized for any taxable year from a disposition is that proportion of the payments received in that year which the gross profit * * * bears to the total contract price." The "gross profit" is equal to the selling price less the adjusted basis of the property sold. Temp. Reg. § 15A.453-1(b)(2)(v).

---

3. This section is based on a modification of Secs. 2.19 and 2.20 of *Federal Taxation of Business Enterprises*, *supra* note 1.

The "selling price" means the gross selling price without any reductions for any mortgage on the property (Temp. Reg. § 15A.453-1(b)(2)(ii)), and the "total contract price" generally equals the selling price. Temp. Reg. § 15A.453-1(b)(2)(iii). These concepts are illustrated in the following example:

> Individual *A* sells stock of a closely held Target Corporation for $10,000 in cash and a note with a face of $90,000, which has adequate stated interest.[4] The note is to be paid in the amount of $10,000 per year during the next nine years. Both the selling price and the total contract price are $100,000. If *A*'s basis for the stock is $40,000, then *A*'s gross profit is $60,000. Consequently, *A* has gain each year equal to that portion of each $10,000 payment that (1) the gross profit ($60,000), bears to (2) the total contract price ($100,000). *A*, therefore, has $6,000 of gain and recovers $4,000 of her $40,000 basis in each of the ten years during which payments are received.

Under § 453(f)(4), installment sale treatment is not available if the evidence of indebtedness is either payable on demand or issued in a readily tradeable form. Prior to the American Jobs Creation Act of 2004 this readily tradeable provision only applied to corporate and government debt. It now applies to all debt without regard to the type of issuer. Also, under § 453(k)(2), a sale of stock or securities that are traded on an established securities market does not qualify for installment sale treatment.

Under § 453(d), installment reporting is automatic for a qualified sale unless the taxpayer elects to apply the general recognition rule. An election out of installment treatment must be made on or before the due date for filing the taxpayer's return for the taxable year in which the installment sale occurs.

Prior to the Installment Sale Revision Act of 1980, installment reporting was not available unless the selling price was fixed and determinable. An installment sale subject to a price contingency thus was not eligible for installment treatment and the taxpayer was required to recognize the total gain in the year of sale. In cases where the payments were determined to have no readily ascertainable fair market value, however, a taxpayer could treat the transaction as open and use the cost recovery method adopted by the Supreme Court in *Burnet v. Logan*, which is set out above. Section 453 now applies to contingent payment sales. *See* Temp. Reg. § 15A.453-1(c).

These regulations set out three basic rules for dealing with contingent payment sales. First, if the contingent sale has a stated maximum selling price, "the taxpayer's basis shall be allocated to payments received and to be received ... by treating the stated maximum selling price as the selling price...." Temp. Reg. § 15A.453.1(c)(2). This principle is illustrated in Example (1) under this regulation:

> *Example (1). A* sells all of the stock of *X* corporation to *B* for $100,000 payable at closing plus an amount equal to 5% of the net profits of *X* for

---

4. The rules regarding original issue discount (OID) under § 1271 *et seq.* and imputed interest under § 483 apply to installment sales. As a consequence, if the instrument fails to provide for the payment of interest at an adequate rate of interest, a portion of the principal payments due under the instrument is recharacterized as interest. This recharacterization reduces the principal amount of the note and the gross profit realized on the sale.

each of the next nine years, the contingent payments to be made annually together with adequate stated interest. The agreement provides that the maximum amount *A* may receive, inclusive of the $100,000 down payment but exclusive of interest, shall be $2,000,000. *A*'s basis in the stock of *X* inclusive of selling expenses, is $200,000. Selling price and contract price are considered to be $2,000,000. Gross profit is $1,800,000, and the gross profit ratio is 9/10 ($1,800,000/$2,000,000). Accordingly, of the $100,000 received by *A* in the year of sale, $90,000 is reportable as gain attributable to the sale and $10,000 is recovery of basis.

Second, if a contingent sale does not have a stated maximum selling price, "but the maximum period over which payments may be received under the contingent sales price agreement is fixed, the taxpayer's basis (inclusive of selling expenses) shall be allocated to the taxable years in which payment may be received under the agreement in equal annual increments." Temp. Reg. § 15A.453-1(c)(3)(i). Thus, if an agreement has neither a stated maximum nor a fixed period, "a question arises whether a sale realistically has occurred or whether, in economic effect, payments received under the agreement are in the nature of rent or royalty income." Temp. Reg. § 15A.453-1(c)(4). If after close scrutiny the arrangement is found to be a sale, the "taxpayer's basis ... shall be recovered in equal annual installments over a period of 15 years...." *Id.*

The benefits of installment sale treatment may be significantly curtailed under § 453A, which imposes an interest charge on certain transactions where the sales price exceeds $150,000 and treats certain pledges of installment notes as sales.

E. Introduction to Like Kind Exchanges

See § 1031.

Section 1031, the like kind exchange provision, provides an exception to the general rule of recognition in § 1001(b). Section 1031 is structured similarly to § 351, which provides for nonrecognition on the contribution of property to a corporation in exchange for stock (*see* Sec. 2.2) and § 354, which provides for nonrecognition on the exchange of stock in one party to a "reorganization," such as a Target Corporation, for stock in another party to the reorganization, such as an Acquiring Corporation (*see* Chapter 6).

The basic outline of § 1031 is described in part in Rev. Rul. 77-297, 1977-2 C.B. 304:

Section 1031(a) of the Code provides that no gain or loss shall be recognized if property held for productive use in trade or business or for investment (not including stock in trade or other property held primarily for sale, nor stocks, bonds, notes, * * * [interest in partnerships], or other securities or evidence of indebtedness or interest) is exchanged solely for property of a like kind to be held either for productive use in trade or business or for investment.

Section 1031(b) of the Code states that if an exchange would be within the provisions of subsection (a) if it were not for the fact that the property received in exchange consists not only of property permitted by such provisions to be received without the recognition of gain, but also of other property or money, then the gain, if any, to the recipient shall be recognized, but in an amount not in excess of the sum of such money and the fair market value of such other property.

The last sentence of § 1031(d) provides that any liability transferred is treated as money received by the taxpayer. The above cited regulations implement this provision.

Under § 1031(c), no loss is recognized on a like kind exchange, and under § 1031(d), the basis of the property received is a substituted basis (*i.e.,* the basis of the property exchanged) decreased by the amount of any money received and increased by the amount of any gain or decreased by the amount of any loss recognized. The basis so determined is allocated among the properties received in accordance with their relative fair market values. The initial substituted basis will include any money paid.

§ 1.5 Treatment of Liabilities

A. Introduction

In most transactions in which the assets of a Target Corporation are being acquired, certain liabilities will also be assumed or the Target Corporation's property will be taken subject to a nonrecourse liability. The following materials introduce the treatment of liabilities.

B. Transfer of Property Subject to a Nonrecourse Liability: Liability Included in § 1001 Amount Realized

See § 1.1000-2.

Crane v. Commissioner
Supreme Court of the United States, 1947
331 U.S. 1

Mr. Chief Justice Vinson delivered the opinion of the Court.

The question here is how a taxpayer who acquires depreciable property subject to an unassumed mortgage, holds it for a period, and finally sells it still so encumbered, must compute her taxable gain.

Petitioner was the sole beneficiary and the executrix of the will of her husband, who died January 11, 1932. He then owned an apartment building and lot subject to a mortgage,[5] which secured a principal debt of $255,000.00 and interest in default of $7,042.50. As of that date, the property was appraised for federal estate tax purposes at a value exactly equal to the total amount of this encumbrance. Shortly after her husband's death, petitioner entered into an agreement with the mortgagee whereby she was to continue to operate the property—collecting the rents, paying for necessary repairs, labor, and other operating expenses, and reserving $200.00 monthly for

---

5. The record does not show whether he was personally liable for the debt.

taxes—and was to remit the net rentals to the mortgagee. This plan was followed for nearly seven years, during which period petitioner reported the gross rentals as income, and claimed and was allowed deductions for taxes and operating expenses paid on the property, for interest paid on the mortgage, and for the physical exhaustion of the building. Meanwhile, the arrearage of interest increased to $15,857.71. On November 29, 1938, with the mortgagee threatening foreclosure, petitioner sold to a third party for $3,000.00 cash, subject to the mortgage, and paid $500.00 expenses of sale.

Petitioner reported a taxable gain of $1,250.00. Her theory was that the "property" which she had acquired in 1932 and sold in 1938 was only the equity, or the excess in the value of the apartment building and lot over the amount of the mortgage. This equity was of zero value when she acquired it. No depreciation could be taken on a zero value.[6] Neither she nor her vendee ever assumed the mortgage, so, when she sold the equity, the amount she realized on the sale was the net cash received, or $2,500.00. This sum less the zero basis constituted her gain, of which she reported half as taxable on the assumption that the entire property was a "capital asset."

The Commissioner, however, determined that petitioner realized a net taxable gain of $23,767.03. His theory was that the "property" acquired and sold was not the equity, as petitioner claimed, but rather the physical property itself, or the owner's rights to possess, use, and dispose of it, undiminished by the mortgage. The original basis thereof was $262,042.50, its appraised value in 1932. Of this value $55,000.00 was allocable to land and $207,042.50 to building. During the period that petitioner held the property, there was an allowable depreciation of $28,045.10 on the building, so that the adjusted basis of the building at the time of sale was $178,997.40. The amount realized on the sale was said to include not only the $2,500.00 net cash receipts, but also the principal amount[7] of the mortgage subject to which the property was sold, both totaling $257,500.00. The selling price was allocable in the proportion, $54,471.15 to the land and $203,028.85 to the building. The Commissioner agreed that the land was a "capital asset," but thought that the building was not. Thus, he determined that petitioner sustained a capital loss of $528.85 on the land, of which 50% or $264.42 was taken into account, and an ordinary gain of $24,031.45 on the building, or a net taxable gain as indicated. * * *

Logically, the first step under [the Code] is to determine the unadjusted basis of the property, under § 113(a)(5), [now § 1014] and the dispute in this case is as to the construction to be given the term "property." If "property," as used in that provision, means the same thing as "equity," it would necessarily follow that the basis of petitioner's property was zero, as she contends. If, on the contrary, it means the land

---

6. This position is, of course, inconsistent with her practice in claiming such deductions in each of the years the property was held. The deductions so claimed and allowed by the Commissioner were in the total amount of $25,500.00.

7. The Commissioner explains that only the principal amount, rather than the total present debt secured by the mortgage, was deemed to be a measure of the amount realized, because the difference was attributable to interest due, a deductible item.

and building themselves, or the owner's legal rights in them, undiminished by the mortgage, the basis was $262,042.50. * * *

We conclude that the proper basis under § 113(a)(5) [now § 1014] is the value of the property, undiminished by mortgages thereon, and that the correct basis here was $262,042.50. The next step is to ascertain what adjustments are required under § 113(b) [now § 1016]. As the depreciation rate was stipulated, the only question at this point is whether the Commissioner was warranted in making any depreciation adjustments whatsoever.

Section 113(b)(1)(B) [now § 1016] provides that "proper adjustment in respect of the property *shall in all cases be made* * * * for exhaustion, wear and tear * * * to the extent allowed (but not less than the amount allowable) * * *." (Italics supplied.) The Tax Court found on adequate evidence that the apartment house was property of a kind subject to physical exhaustion, that it was used in taxpayer's trade or business, and consequently that the taxpayer would have been entitled to a depreciation allowance under § 23(1), [now § 167] except that, in the opinion of that Court, the basis of the property was zero, and it was thought that depreciation could not be taken on a zero basis. As we have just decided that the correct basis of the property was not zero, but $262,042.50, we avoid this difficulty, and conclude that an adjustment should be made as the Commissioner determined. * * *

At last we come to the problem of determining the "amount realized" on the 1938 sale. Section 111(b) [now § 1001(b)] it will be recalled, defines the "amount realized" from "the sale … of property" as "the sum of any money received plus the fair market value of the property (other than money) received," and § 111(a) [now § 1001(a)] defines the gain on "the sale * * * of property" as the excess of the amount realized over the basis. Quite obviously, the word "property," used here with reference to a sale, must mean "property" in the same ordinary sense intended by the use of the word with reference to acquisition and depreciation in § 113, [now § 1016] both for certain of the reasons stated heretofore in discussing its meaning in § 113, and also because the functional relation of the two sections requires that the word mean the same in one section that it does in the other. If the "property" to be valued on the date of acquisition is the property free of liens, the "property" to be priced on a subsequent sale must be the same thing.

Starting from this point, we could not accept petitioner's contention that the $2,500.00 net cash was all she realized on the sale except on the absurdity that she sold a quarter-of-a-million dollar property for roughly one per cent of its value, and took a 99 per cent loss. Actually, petitioner does not urge this. She argues, conversely, that because only $2,500.00 was realized on the sale, the "property" sold must have been the equity only, and that consequently we are forced to accept her contention as to the meaning of "property" in § 113. We adhere, however, to what we have already said on the meaning of "property," and we find that the absurdity is avoided by our conclusion that the amount of the mortgage is properly included in the "amount realized" on the sale.

Petitioner concedes that if she had been personally liable on the mortgage and the purchaser had either paid or assumed it, the amount so paid or assumed would be considered a part of the "amount realized" within the meaning of § 111(b). The cases so deciding have already repudiated the notion that there must be an actual receipt by the seller himself of "money" or "other property," in their narrowest senses. It was thought to be decisive that one section of the Act must be construed so as not to defeat the intention of another or to frustrate the Act as a whole, and that the taxpayer was the "beneficiary" of the payment in "as real and substantial [a sense] as if the money had been paid it and then paid over by it to its creditors."

Both these points apply to this case. The first has been mentioned already. As for the second, we think that a mortgagor, not personally liable on the debt, who sells the property subject to the mortgage and for additional consideration, realizes a benefit in the amount of the mortgage as well as the boot.[8] If a purchaser pays boot, it is immaterial as to our problem whether the mortgagor is also to receive money from the purchaser to discharge the mortgage prior to sale, or whether he is merely to transfer subject to the mortgage — it may make a difference to the purchaser and to the mortgagee, but not to the mortgagor. Or put in another way, we are no more concerned with whether the mortgagor is, strictly speaking, a debtor on the mortgage, than we are with whether the benefit to him is, strictly speaking, a receipt of money or property. We are rather concerned with the reality that an owner of property, mortgaged at a figure less than that at which the property will sell, must and will treat the conditions of the mortgage exactly as if they were his personal obligations. If he transfers subject to the mortgage, the benefit to him is as real and substantial as if the mortgage were discharged, or as if a personal debt in an equal amount had been assumed by another.

Therefore we conclude that the Commissioner was right in determining that petitioner realized $257,500.00 on the sale of this property. * * *

Petitioner contends that the result we have reached taxes her on what is not income within the meaning of the Sixteenth Amendment. If this is because only the direct receipt of cash is thought to be income in the constitutional sense, her contention is wholly without merit. If it is because the entire transaction is thought to have been "by all dictates of common sense * * * a ruinous disaster," as it was termed in her brief, we disagree with her premise. She was entitled to depreciation deductions for a period of nearly seven years, and she actually took them in almost the allowable amount. The crux of this case, really, is whether the law permits her to exclude allowable deductions from consideration in computing gain. We have already showed that, if it does, the taxpayer can enjoy a double deduction, in effect, on the same loss of assets. The Sixteenth Amendment does not require that result any more than does the Act itself.

Affirmed.

---

8. Obviously, if the value of the property is less than the amount of the mortgage, a mortgagor who is not personally liable cannot realize a benefit equal to the mortgage. Consequently, a different problem might be encountered where a mortgagor abandoned the property or transferred it subject to the mortgage without receiving boot. That is not this case.

Questions

Target Corporation sells its plant, for which it has an adjusted basis of $400K, for $200K in cash and the assumption of a nonrecourse liability on the plant of $800K. What is the tax treatment to Target Corporation? What is the purchaser's basis for the plant?

C. The Supreme Court Addresses *Footnote 37* in *Crane*: Liabilities in Excess of Fair Market Value

1. Crane Footnote 37

In footnote 37 of the *Crane* case, which is footnote 8 in the text, the Supreme Court said:

> Obviously, if the value of the property is less than the amount of the mortgage, a mortgagor who is not personally liable cannot realize a benefit equal to the mortgage. Consequently, a different problem might be encountered where a mortgagor abandoned the property or transferred it subject to the mortgage without receiving boot. That is not this case.

The following case addresses the issue in footnote 37. The situation involves a failed tax shelter, which in this situation is an investment in which the value of the property is less than the amount of the outstanding mortgage.

2. The Supreme Court's View

Commissioner v. Tufts

Supreme Court of the United States, 1983
461 U.S. 300

Justice Blackmun delivered the opinion of the Court.

Over 35 years ago, in *Crane v. Commissioner,* this Court ruled that a taxpayer, who sold property encumbered by a nonrecourse mortgage (the amount of the mortgage being less than the property's value), must include the unpaid balance of the mortgage in the computation of the amount the taxpayer realized on the sale. The case now before us presents the question whether the same rule applies when the unpaid amount of the nonrecourse mortgage exceeds the fair market value of the property sold. * * *

We are disinclined to overrule *Crane,* and we conclude that the same rule applies when the unpaid amount of the nonrecourse mortgage exceeds the value of the property transferred. *Crane* ultimately does not rest on its limited theory of economic benefit; instead, we read *Crane* to have approved the Commissioner's decision to treat a nonrecourse mortgage in this context as a true loan. This approval underlies *Crane's* holdings that the amount of the nonrecourse liability is to be included in calculating both the basis and the amount realized on disposition. That the amount of the loan exceeds the fair market value of the property thus becomes irrelevant. * * *

When encumbered property is sold or otherwise disposed of and the purchaser assumes the mortgage, the associated extinguishment of the mortgagor's obligation to repay is accounted for in the computation of the amount realized. * * * Because no difference between recourse and nonrecourse obligations is recognized in calculating basis, *Crane* teaches that the Commissioner may ignore the nonrecourse nature of the obligation in determining the amount realized upon disposition of the encumbered property. He thus may include in the amount realized the amount of the nonrecourse mortgage assumed by the purchaser. The rationale for this treatment is that the original inclusion of the amount of the mortgage in basis rested on the assumption that the mortgagor incurred an obligation to repay. Moreover, this treatment balances the fact that the mortgagor originally received the proceeds of the nonrecourse loan tax-free on the same assumption. Unless the outstanding amount of the mortgage is deemed to be realized, the mortgagor effectively will have received untaxed income at the time the loan was extended and will have received an unwarranted increase in the basis of his property. The Commissioner's interpretation of § 1001(b) in this fashion cannot be said to be unreasonable. * * *

In the specific circumstances of *Crane,* the economic benefit theory did support the Commissioner's treatment of the nonrecourse mortgage as a personal obligation. The footnote in *Crane* acknowledged the limitations of that theory when applied to a different set of facts. *Crane* also stands for the broader proposition, however, that a nonrecourse loan should be treated as a true loan. We therefore hold that a taxpayer must account for the proceeds of obligations he has received tax-free and included in basis. Nothing in either § 1001(b) or in the Court's prior decisions requires the Commissioner to permit a taxpayer to treat a sale of encumbered property asymmetrically, by including the proceeds of the nonrecourse obligation in basis but not accounting for the proceeds upon transfer of the encumbered property. * * *

Question

The facts are the same as at the end of the *Crane* case, except the plant which is subject to a $800K nonrecourse liability has a value of only $500K. Target Corporation transfers the plant to the mortgagee in discharge of the nonrecourse liability.

§ 1.6 Treatment of Capital Gains and Losses

Joint Committee on Taxation Description of Capital Gains

Present Law and Background (JCX-4-98)

PRESENT LAW. In general, gain or loss reflected in the value of an asset is not recognized for income tax purposes until a taxpayer disposes of the asset. On the sale or exchange of capital assets, any gain generally is included in income, and the net capital gain of an individual is taxed at maximum rates lower than the rates applicable to ordinary income. Net capital gain is the excess of the net long-term capital gain for the taxable year over the net short-term capital loss for the year. [§ 1222] Gain or loss is treated as long-term if the asset is held for more than one year [§ 1222]

A capital asset generally means any property except (1) inventory, stock in trade, or property held primarily for sale to customers in the ordinary course of the taxpayer's trade or business, (2) depreciable or real property used in the taxpayer's trade or business, (3) specified literary or artistic property, (4) business accounts or notes receivable, or (5) certain U.S. publications. [§ 1221] In addition, the net gain from the disposition of certain property used in the taxpayer's trade or business is treated as long-term capital gain. [§ 1231] Gain from the disposition of depreciable personal property is not treated as capital gain to the extent of all previous depreciation allowances. [§ 1245] Gain from the disposition of depreciable real property is generally not treated as capital gain to the extent of the depreciation allowances in excess of the allowances that would have been available under the straight-line method of depreciation. [§ 1250]

The maximum rate of tax on the adjusted net capital gain of an individual is [generally] [20] percent. [§ 1(h)] [However, as a result of Obamacare there is a 3.8% Net Investment Income Tax on certain high income individuals, thus taking the maximum rate to 23.8%. Corporations do not get the benefit of a reduced rate on capital gains, and consequently, the maximum corporate rate on capital gains is 35%.]

§ 1.7 Disposition of Property Used in a Trade or Business: § 1231 Gains and Losses; Recapture of Depreciation under § 1245

Section 1231(a) provides for preferred tax treatment for, among other things, sales and exchanges of property used in a trade or business, as defined in § 1231(b). Section 1231(b) defines property used in a trade or business as depreciable property and as real property held for more than one year and used in a trade or business, but only if such property is not inventory, or held primarily for sale, etc. All gains and losses from such dispositions are treated as capital gains and losses if the gains exceed the losses, but are treated as ordinary gains and losses if the losses exceed the gains.

Section 1245 overrides § 1231 and requires that upon the disposition of personal (*i.e.*, non-real property) property with respect to which there has been a depreciation deduction, any gain to the extent of the depreciation is recaptured as ordinary income. Section 1250 applies a similar recapture concept to real property.

Only § 1245 is dealt with here. It can be illustrated as follows: Assume that ten years ago individual A purchased a machine for $100K and that *A* has taken $90K of depreciation. Consequently, under §§ 1011 and 1016(a) the basis of the machine is $10K. *A* sells the machine for $110K, thereby realizing a gain of $100K. In such case, $90K of the gain is recaptured as ordinary income, and the $10K balance is treated as § 1231 gain. Assuming that this is the only disposition of a § 1231 asset during the year, the $10K is capital gain.

§ 1.8 Introduction to Tax Accounting

A. Introduction to the Cash and Accrual Methods

In determining the tax consequences of a transaction it is necessary to consider the method of accounting employed by the taxpayer. The two principal methods of accounting are (1) the cash receipts and disbursement method, and (2) the accrual method. *See* § 446(c). Under the cash method, which is used by most individuals, all items of gross income are included in income for the taxable year in which actually or constructively received and cash expenditures are deducted for the taxable year when actually made. *See* § 1.446-(c)(1)(i).

Under the accrual method, which is required to be used by most businesses, income is included for the taxable year "when all events have occurred which fix the right to receive such income and the amount thereof can be determined with reasonable accuracy," and deductions are allowable for the taxable year in which "all events have occurred which establish the fact of the liability giving rise to such deductions and the amount thereof can be determined with reasonable accuracy." *See* § 1.446-1(c)(1)(ii).

B. The Tension between Expensing and Capitalizing

Section 162 allows a deduction for "ordinary and necessary" business expenses. Section 263, on the other hand, provides that no deduction is allowed for any expenditure for "new buildings or permanent improvements or betterments made to increase the value of any property * * *." Many disputes arise between taxpayers and the Commissioner over whether a particular expenditure is deductible under § 162 or capitalizable under § 263, and as illustrated in the examination of *INDOPOCO* issues in Sec. 5.4.F., many of these disputes have occurred in merger and acquisition transactions. Obviously, in most cases taxpayers argue that an expenditure is immediately deductible and the Commissioner argues that the expenditure must be capitalized. If an expenditure is capitalizable, it generally may be deducted as depreciation or amortization over the life of the asset. However, if the expenditure relates to a nondepreciable asset, such as land or stock, no deduction is allowed. As discussed in Sec. 4.3.C., under § 197, the cost of intangibles, such as goodwill, is amortizable over a period of 15 years.

§ 1.9 Introduction to the Original Issue Discount Rules

A. Introduction

If a debt instrument is issued for an amount (issue price) that is less than the principal amount (stated redemption price at maturity) of the instrument, the difference between the issue price and the stated redemption price at maturity is original issue discount (OID). OID can arise when debt instruments are issued for cash (§ 1273) or for property (§ 1274), such as when a debt instrument is issued in a merger or acquisition transaction. Under § 1272, OID is treated as interest on a yield to maturity basis; this means that there is compounding of interest. Sec. 1.9.B. provides a brief guide to the OID provisions.

B. Guide to the Regulations

Preamble to Proposed Regulations under OID and Imputed Interest Rules
LR 189–84 (April 8, 1986)

Introduction The regulations under sections 163(e), 483, and 1271 through 1275 provide two principal sets of rules: The imputed interest rules and the original issue discount rules. The imputed interest rules are prescribed by sections 1274 and 483, and the original issue discount rules by sections 163(e), 1271, 1272, 1273 and 1275.

The imputed interest rules of sections 1274 and 483 relate to the measurement of interest and principal for tax purposes in a sale or exchange of property (other than publicly traded property) involving deferred payments. [For example, these provisions apply to the sale of stock of a closely held firm for a nontradable note.] For transactions subject to the imputed interest rules, interest will be imputed to the transaction if a minimum amount of interest is not stated. If a transaction states at least the minimum amount of interest, it is said to provide for adequate stated interest. When interest is imputed to a transaction, a portion of the stated principal amount of the debt instrument is recharacterized as interest for tax purposes. The imputed interest rules do not require an increase in the total amount of payments agreed to by the parties to a transaction. These rules merely recharacterize as interest for Federal tax purposes a portion of the payments denominated as principal by the parties. In the case of transactions to which section 1274 applies, imputed interest is treated as original issue discount and is accounted for under those rules. In the case of transactions subject to section 483, imputed interest (and any stated interest) is subject to a new set of rules provided under section 446 and is accounted for under those rules.

In general, under the original issue discount rules, a portion of the original issue discount on a debt instrument is required to be included in income by the holder and deducted from income by the issuer annually without regard to their regular accounting methods. [*See* §§ 1272(a) and 163(e).] The total amount of original issue discount is defined as the difference between the debt instrument's stated redemption price at maturity and its issue price [*See* § 1273(a).] and arises in one of three ways. First, in the case of a debt instrument subject to section 1274 that does not provide for adequate stated interest, [*See* §§ 1274(c)(1) & (2).] interest is imputed and is treated as original issue discount. [*See* § 1274.] [For example, OID would arise on the sale of stock of a closely held corporation for a $10 million note that did not provide for interest; in such case, a portion of the principal of the note would be recharacterized as interest.] Second, in the case of a debt instrument issued for cash, * * * original issue discount arises if the debt instrument is issued for less than its face amount. [*See* §§ 1272(a) & (b).] [For example, OID arises if a corporation sells bonds payable in 10 years, with a face amount of $1,000, and with no interest payable. In such case, the purchaser will pay much less than the face amount so that the difference between the initial purchase price and the face will give the holder an interest rate equal to the required yield to maturity (the required interest rate taking into account compounding of interest) of the debt instrument. The difference between the face and the amount paid is the OID.] * * *

Accounting For Original Issue Discount *In General [See §§ 1272 and 1273.]* Original issue discount is defined as the excess of a debt instrument's stated redemption price at maturity over its issue price. [*See* §§ 1273(a)(1) and (2).] A portion of the original issue discount on a debt instrument is accounted for on a current basis by both the issuer and the holder. The amount of original issue discount that is accounted for on a current basis is the amount that accrues on a constant interest or economic accrual basis, regardless of whether the issuer or holder is an accrual basis taxpayer. [*See* § 1272(a).]

§ 1.10 Introduction to Taxable and Tax Free M&A

Corporate acquisitions of stand-alone (*i.e.,* nonsubsidiary) target corporations fall into two broad categories: (1) taxable acquisitions, and (2) tax-free acquisitive reorganizations under § 368. Within each of these broad categories there can be either taxable or tax-free mergers, stock acquisitions, or asset acquisitions. Leveraged buyouts (LBOs) are taxable stock or asset acquisitions in which a substantial part of the consideration paid in the transaction is either debt or cash raised through the issuance of debt. Thus, LBOs are a subset of taxable acquisitions.

The principal distinguishing feature between a taxable acquisition and a tax-free acquisitive reorganization is the consideration paid by the acquiring corporation. The consideration paid in a taxable acquisition generally consists of cash or debt instruments of the acquiring corporation or a combination of the two. Also, in certain cases, stock may be used in taxable acquisitions. If a substantial portion (and in certain cases all) of the consideration paid by the acquiring corporation consists of its stock or stock of its parent corporation, the acquisition may (assuming certain other conditions are satisfied) qualify as a tax-free acquisitive reorganization.

Chapter 3 discusses in more detail the fundamental Federal income tax concepts associated with both taxable and tax-free mergers and acquisitions.

§ 1.11 Introduction to International Aspects of Business Taxation

This book considers the Federal income tax consequences of various types of merger and acquisition transactions, and the purpose of this section is to provide a general introduction to some of the fundamental concepts of the Federal income tax treatment of (1) outbound corporate transactions, that is, transactions in which a U.S. corporation conducts business operations overseas, and (2) inbound corporate transactions, that is, transactions in which a foreign corporation earns income in the U.S.

The starting point for analyzing the taxation of foreign operations of U.S. taxpayers (that is, outbound transactions) under the Federal income tax, is the worldwide concept embodied in the Code. Under § 61 gross income of a U.S. taxpayer includes all income from whatever source derived. For U.S. domestic corporations, there is no geographic limitation on this inclusion rule. Thus, a U.S. corporation with branch offices in Timbuktu, Mali, and Auckland, New Zealand, that earn income through activities in both Timbuktu and Auckland, is taxed in the U.S. on the income earned from both these sources. *See* Reg. § 1.11-1.

In order to mitigate the potential double tax that can arise in these contexts, the U.S. grants, subject to limitation, a foreign tax-credit for any foreign taxes paid by U.S. taxpayers to foreign jurisdictions.

If rather than operating in Mali through a branch, a U.S. corporation incorporates a Malian Sub that conducts business in Mali and elsewhere, the income of the Malian Sub is not subject to tax in the U.S., unless the income falls within a category of tax-haven income specified in subpart F of the Code. Thus, if a foreign corporation controlled by U.S. shareholders is not subject to current taxation under subpart F, the income of the foreign corporation is deferred from U.S. taxation until the income is repatriated to the U.S. in the form of a current or liquidating distribution. This is known as the deferral principle, and it applies principally to active income earned by a foreign sub.

Because of the deferral system, a domestic parent corporation may have an incentive to sell products to a controlled foreign subsidiary located in a low tax jurisdiction at an artificially low price. The sub could then resell in its jurisdiction at the market price, thereby shifting the bulk of the income from the ultimate sale of the item to the foreign jurisdiction. Section 482, which sets out an arm's length standard for related party sales, is designed to police these types of transactions.

Turning to the manner in which the U.S. taxes foreign persons on U.S. income earned in inbound transactions, the fundamental concept is the source system, which generally provides that foreign corporations are only subject to taxation in the U.S. on their U.S. source income. The income from inbound operations is generally taxed (1) on the basis of withholding for passive U.S. source income (*see* §§ 871, 881, 1441 and 1442), and (2) on the basis of a tax on taxable income of the U. S. business operations of the foreign taxpayer (*see* §§ 871(b) and 882(a)). The withholding rate for passive income is 30% and this is referred to as a gross basis tax. The taxation of the taxable income of U.S. business operations of a foreign corporation is subject to the applicable rates under § 11, which has a maximum rate of 35%. This is referred to as a net basis tax.

These rules governing outbound and inbound transactions may be modified by a tax treaty between the United States and the country in which a U.S. party earns income or a foreign person is resident. The Joint Committee has provided the following basic explanation of the operation of tax treaties:

In addition to the U.S. and foreign statutory rules for the taxation of foreign income of U.S. persons and U.S. income of foreign persons, bilateral income tax treaties limit the amount of income tax that may be imposed by one treaty partner on residents of the other treaty partner. Treaties also contain provisions governing the creditability of taxes imposed by the treaty country in which income was earned in computing the amount of tax owed to the other country by its residents with respect to such income. Treaties further provide procedures under which inconsistent positions taken by the treaty countries with respect to a single item of income or deduction may be mutually resolved by the two countries.

The preferred tax treaty policies of the United States have been expressed from time to time in model treaties and agreements. * * * The Treasury Department, which together with the State Department is responsible for negotiating tax treaties, last published a proposed model income tax treaty in September 1996 (the "U.S. model"). * * *

Many U.S. income tax treaties currently in effect diverge in one or more respects from the U.S. model. These divergences may reflect the age of a particular treaty or the particular balance of interests between the United States and the treaty partner. Staff of Joint Committee on Taxation, *Description and Analysis of Present-Law Rules Relating to International Taxation*, June 30, 1999.

The above is just a brief sketch of the U.S. approach to the taxation of outbound and inbound corporate transactions, and subsequent chapters briefly elaborate on these fundamental principles in the context of specific merger and acquisition transactions. It must be emphasized that these sections merely provide an introduction to and a way to begin thinking about international tax issues. *See* Kuntz and Peroni, *U.S. International Taxation* (1996) and Thompson *International Tax Planning and Policy* (2016).

§ 1.12 Selected References

The domestic corporate tax issues addressed in this book are discussed in greater detail in Chapter 9 of Samuel C. Thompson, Jr, *Mergers, Acquisitions and Tender Offers* (PLI, 2010, Updated semi-annually) [hereinafter Thompson, *Mergers, Acquisitions, and Tender Offers*]. The international issues are addressed in Chapters 21 and 22, and the partnership issues are addressed in Chapter 24. For a discussion of the taxation of corporations, partnerships and S corporations, see Thompson, *Taxation of Business Entities,*(2nd Ed. 2001) [hereinafter *Taxation of Business Entities*].

For a comprehensive treatment of the taxation of corporations and shareholders see the current editions of the following books: Boris I. Bittker and James S. Eustice, *Federal Income Taxation of Corporations and Shareholders* [hereinafter "Bittker and Eustice, *Corporations*"].

For a comprehensive treatment of corporate acquisitions and related transactions see the current editions of Martin D. Ginsburg and Jack S. Levin, *Mergers, Acquisitions and Leveraged Buyouts* [hereinafter "Ginsburg and Levin, *Mergers*"] and Practicing Law Institute, *Tax Strategies for Corporate Acquisitions, Dispositions, Financings, Joint Ventures, Reorganizations and Restructurings* [hereinafter "PLI, *Tax Strategies*"]. *Tax Strategies* is published annually, and is a good source for current developments.

For a comprehensive treatment of international tax aspects of mergers and acquisitions see the current edition of D. Kevin Dolan, *U.S. Taxation of International Mergers, Acquisitions and Joint Ventures* [hereinafter Dolan, *International M&A*]

For a comprehensive treatment of consolidated returns, se the current edition of Dubroff, Blanchard, Broadbent & Duvall, *Federal Income Taxation of Corporations Filing Consolidated Returns* [hereinafter *Consolidated Returns*].

For a discussion of many of the policy aspects of corporate taxation *see* The American Law Institute, *Federal Income Tax Project Subchapter C* (1980) [hereinafter "*ALI 1980 Subchapter C Study*"]; The American Law Institute, *Federal Income Tax Project, Reporter's Study Draft* (1989) [hereinafter "*ALI 1989 Subchapter C Study*"]; The American Law Institute, *Federal Income Tax Project, Integration of Individual and Corporate Income Taxes* (Reporter's Study) (1993) [hereinafter "*ALI 1993 Integration Study*"]; and U.S. Treasury Department Report, *Integration of Individual and Corporate Tax Systems,* (1992) [hereinafter "*Treasury Integration Study*"]. *See also* Samuel C. Thompson, Jr., *Reform of the Taxation of Mergers, Acquisitions and LBOs* (Carolina Academic Press, 1993) [hereinafter "Thompson, *Reform of The Taxation of Mergers, Acquisitions and LBOs*"]. Chapter 1 of this last referred to book cites much of the literature dealing with the taxation of corporate mergers and acquisitions.

Chapter 2

An Overview of Basic Corporate Tax Principles

§ 2.1 Scope

This chapter presents an introduction to several fundamental principles of corporate taxation. Most of these principles are covered in basic courses in Corporate Tax, and this will be a review for many students. However, an understanding of these basic principles is crucial to an ability to work with the advanced issues addressed in subsequent chapters, and it is, therefore, important that the student first master the principles discussed here.

We start at the beginning of the life of a corporation in Sec. 2.2 with an exploration of § 351 and related provisions, which govern the tax treatment on the transfer of property to a corporation. Sec. 2.3 takes a brief look at some of the many issues that can arise in structuring the capital of a corporation. Sec. 2.4 takes a first look at the treatment of dividends, with an examination of the treatment of a distribution of cash by a corporation to individual shareholders; Sec. 2.5 looks at the treatment to the individual shareholders and also to the corporation on the distribution by the corporation of appreciated property. Thus, this section considers the *General Utilities* doctrine and its repeal. As an aside: *General Utilities* was the first case I read in my Corporate Tax course at the University of Pennsylvania Law School, with Professor Wolfman in the Fall of 1970. Sec. 2.6 addresses the treatment of a corporate shareholder upon receipt of a distribution.

Sec. 2.7 looks at the treatment of redemptions of a corporation's stock under § 302, and Sec. 2.8 introduces § 304, which treats certain sales of stock of one controlled corporation to another controlled corporation as a redemption. The purpose of §§ 302 and 304 is to prevent the bailout of corporate earnings at capital gains rates. However, in view of the elimination of the rate differential between capital gains and dividend income (*i.e.*, both are now taxed at 20%), these provisions are of diminished importance. The most important difference is that with capital gains a taxpayer gets a recovery of basis, whereas there is no recovery of basis with a taxable dividend. Sec. 2.9 introduces the treatment of stock dividends under §§ 305–307. The purpose of these provisions is also to prevent the bailout of earnings at capital gains rates, and these provisions are also of diminished importance with the uniform 20% rate on capital gains and dividends. Sec. 2.10 considers the treatment of shareholders and the corporation when the corporation liquidates or is deemed to have sold its assets in a § 338 transaction. Finally, Sec. 2.11 examines the business purpose doctrine as reflected in the *Gregory* case and looks at the step transaction doctrine. These doctrines are important in planning corporate transactions. This chapter does not examine tax-free reorganizations, which are introduced in Chapter 3 and examined in detail in Chapters 6–10.

For a more detailed coverage of these issues *see Taxation of Business Entities supra* Sec. 1.12 and Bittker and Eustice, *Corporations, supra* Sec. 1.12. *See also* Thompson, *Mergers, Acquisitions, and Tender Offers, supra* Sec. 1.12 at Chapter 9.

§ 2.2 Introduction to Federal Income Tax Consequences on the Formation of a Corporation: § 351

A. Contributions Not Involving Liabilities

1. Introduction[1]

> *See* §§ 351, 358, 362, 1032 and 118.

If a taxpayer transfers property to a corporation in exchange for stock, the taxpayer has a realization event and will recognize gain under § 1001 unless § 351(a) provides an exception to the general rule of recognition. Section 351(a), which is similar to the nonrecognition rule for a like kind exchange under § 1031(a), provides:

> No gain or loss shall be recognized if property is transferred to a corporation by one or more persons solely in exchange for stock in such corporation and immediately after the exchange such person or persons are in control (as defined in § 368(c)) of the corporation.

Although, § 351 normally is thought of as applying on the formation of a closely held corporation, as will be seen in Sec. 2.2.C and Sec. 6.19, it can also be used in the acquisition of a publicly-held target corporation.

Pursuant to § 358(a)(1), a shareholder who receives tax-free treatment under § 351(a) substitutes as her basis for the stock received the adjusted basis of the property contributed, that is, the shareholder takes a substituted basis. This is similar to the substituted basis that applies in a like kind exchange under § 1031(d).

The term "property" is not defined for purposes of § 351. The scope of the concept is determined by the case law and IRS rulings, but the term clearly includes such items as cash and various types of intangibles such as patents, trademarks and know-how, at least in situations in which all of the taxpayer's interest in the intangible is transferred to the corporation.

---

1. This section is based on a modification of Sec. 3.02 of *Federal Taxation of Business Enterprises, supra* note 1.

The term "stock" is not defined in the Code. In general, the term refers to common or preferred stock without regard to particular characteristics. However, nonqualified preferred stock as defined in §351(g) does not qualify for nonrecognition treatment under §351(a). *See* §351(g)(1). Nonqualified preferred stock is generally standard preferred stock with a term of no more than 20 years; thus, it has features similar to debt, and it is treated like debt, the treatment of which is discussed below.

Under §351(a), only transferors who end up in "control" of the corporation qualify for nonrecognition treatment on the receipt of stock. Control is defined in §368(c) as ownership of "at least 80 percent of the total combined voting power of all classes of stock entitled to vote and at least 80 percent of the total number of shares of all other classes of stock of the corporation." Control can be held by a single shareholder or by a group of shareholders. The control must exist "immediately after" the exchange.

Section 351 only addresses the tax treatment of the contributing shareholder. Several provisions govern the tax treatment to the corporation. First, §1032 provides that a corporation receives nonrecognition treatment on the issuance of its stock in exchange for property, and §118 provides that a corporation does not have income on the receipt of a contribution to capital, which is a contribution to a corporation in which the corporation does not issue stock in the exchange. Second, a corporation's basis for property received in a §351(a) transaction is a carryover basis pursuant to §362(a), that is, the corporation takes as its basis for the property received, the basis the contributing shareholder had in the property.

If property other than common stock, that is, boot, is distributed in a §351 transaction, §351(b)(1) carves out an exception to the nonrecognition rule. Section 351(b)(1) requires that the gain realized in the transaction be recognized to the extent of the fair market value of the boot received. Section 351(b)(2), however, provides that no loss is recognized.

On a distribution of boot, under §358(a) the shareholder's basis for the stock received is equal to the substituted basis, minus the fair market value of the boot distributed, plus the gain recognized. *See* §358(a)(1)(A) and (B). Under §358(a)(2), the basis of any boot received is the fair market value of such property. Since cash has a basis equal to its face, no basis is allocated to cash. Also, under §362(a), the corporation has a basis in the property received equal to the normal carryover basis plus any gain recognized.

If a corporation issues a debt instrument in the context of a §351 transaction, the instrument is considered "other property" and is, therefore, subject to the boot rules. The same applies to nonqualified preferred stock.

Under §1223(1), the shareholder tacks to the stock received the holding period of any capital assets or §1231 assets transferred to the corporation. For example, if a shareholder transfers to a corporation in a §351 transaction a capital asset for which the shareholder has a long term holding period (*i.e.*, a holding period in excess of a year, §1222), then under §1223(1) the shareholder has a long term holding period for the stock received. Under §1223(2), the corporation takes the shareholder's holding period for the property contributed.

2. Introductory Problems on §§ 351(a) and (b)

1. Corporations *X* and *Y* are planning to form a new joint venture corporation, JV, which will engage in the manufacture and sale of widgets. *X* will contribute to JV a plant, which it has held for several years. The plant has a fair market value of $200M (M = million), and *X*'s adjusted basis for the plant is $90M. *Y* will contribute to JV $200M of cash. JV will issue to each of *X* and *Y*, 100 shares of voting common stock in exchange for the property contributed. Consequently, there will be 200 common shares outstanding with a total initial value of $400M. What are the tax consequences to *X*, *Y*, and JV in this transaction? *See* §§ 351, 358, 362, 1001, 1032, and 1223.

2. The facts are the same as in paragraph 1 above, except the plant contributed by *X* has a fair market value of $225M and to equalize the contributions of the two shareholders, JV distributes to *X* $25M ("boot") of the $200M of cash contributed by *Y*. What are the tax consequences to *X*, *Y*, and JV in this transaction? *See* §§ 351, 358, 362, 1001, 1032, and 1223.

B. Contributions Involving Liability Assumptions

1. Introduction[2]

See §§ 357 and 358(d).

Under the general rule governing the transfer of property subject to a liability as reflected in *Crane*, Sec. 1.5.B., if a shareholder transfers to a corporation in exchange for stock property that is subject to a liability, the shareholder has received not just the stock, but also the release of the liability. The issue presented is whether this release of the liability is boot that can give rise to gain recognition under § 351(b). In this situation, subject to the exceptions discussed below, § 357(a) overrides *Crane* and provides that the release of the liability is not a boot distribution to the shareholder. Therefore, the transaction is within § 351(a), rather than the boot gain rule of §§ 351(b).

Section 358(d) provides that, for purposes of determining the shareholder's basis in her stock, the amount of the liability is treated as "money received." Thus, the assumption of a liability by a corporation generates a downward basis adjustment under § 358(a)(1)(A)(ii).

The operation of these provisions is illustrated as follows. Individual *S* transfers a building to newly formed corporation C in exchange for all of the stock of C. The building has a fair market value of $100K and a basis of $50K. Also, the building is subject to a $20K nonrecourse mortgage. The mortgage has been on the property since it was acquired 10 years ago. Under the principles of *Crane, S* is deemed to receive a $20K cash amount realized as a result of the transfer of the property subject to the $20K mortgage to *C*, and this cash would be recognized under the boot gain

---

2. This section is based on a modification of Sec. 3.10 of *Federal Taxation of Business Enterprises*, *supra* note 1.

rule of § 351(b). However, § 357(a) provides that the transfer of the property subject to the liability is not treated as the receipt by *S* of money or other property. Consequently, *S* has no gain under § 351(b). Under §§ 358(a) and (d), *S*'s basis for her shares is $30K, which is $50K minus the $20K liability.

Section 357(c)(1) provides an exception to the general rule of § 357(a) when the amount of the liability is greater than the basis of the property transferred. This is known as the liability in excess of basis exception to the § 357(a) nonrecognition rule for liabilities. The excess of the aggregate liabilities assumed over the adjusted basis of the assets transferred is treated as gain recognized to the transferor. The character of the gain is dependent upon the character of the assets transferred. Thus, in the above example if the liability was for $80K, *S* would have a $30K gain under § 357(c)(1).

Section 357(c)(3) provides an exception to the liabilities in excess of basis rule in the case of the transfer of accounts payable by a cash basis taxpayer.

Section 357(b)(1) provides an exception to § 357(a) in cases where the transfer of the liabilities to the corporation is for tax avoidance purposes. In such cases, the full amount of the liabilities assumed or transferred is treated as boot distributed.

2. Introductory Problems on Liability Assumptions

See §§ 358(a), 1032, 362(a), 368(c) and 1223(1) and (2).

1. Corporations *X* and *Y* are planning to form a new joint venture corporation, JV, which will engage in the manufacture and sale of widgets. *X* will contribute to JV a plant, which it has held for several years. The plant has a fair market value of $200M (M = million), and *X*'s adjusted basis for the plant is $90M. The plant also is subject to a nonrecourse mortgage in the amount of $25M, which has been on the property for many years. Thus, the net fair market value of *X*'s contribution to JV is $175M. *Y* will contribute to JV $175M of cash. JV will issue to each of *X* and *Y*, 100 shares of voting common stock in exchange for the property contributed. Consequently, there will be 200 common shares outstanding with a total initial value of $350M. What are the tax consequences to *X*, *Y*, and JV in this transaction? *See* §§ 351, 357, 358, 362, 1001, 1032, and 1223.

2. The facts are the same as in paragraph 1 above, except the amount of the mortgage is $100M, *Y* contributes cash of $100M, and the aggregate value of the shares issued is $200M. What are the tax consequences to *X*, *Y*, and JV in this transaction? *See* §§ 351, 357, 358, 362, 1001, 1032, and 1223.

C. Illustration of Use of § 351 in Acquisition of Publicly Held Corporation

Revenue Ruling 74-502

1974-2 C.B. 116

Corporation *Y* wanted to acquire 100-percent control of corporation *X*, which stock is widely held, in a stock-for-stock exchange intended to be nontaxable to the exchanging shareholders under § 351 of the Internal Revenue Code of 1954. Under the laws of the state involved, subject to approval of the board of directors of each corporation and of the proper State authority, and subject to a favorable vote of at least two-thirds of the outstanding stock of the acquired corporation, the acquiring corporation, by operation of law, becomes the owner of all of the outstanding stock of the acquired corporation, except for stock owned by dissenters, on the effective date of the transaction. At such time, those shareholders of the acquired corporation who do not dissent are entitled to receive shares of stock of the acquiring corporation in exchange for their shares of stock of the acquired corporation. Any shareholder of the acquired corporation who dissents is entitled to receive in cash the appraised value of his shares from the acquired corporation.

At a meeting of the shareholders of X (after prior approval of the plan by the X board of directors and the State authority), 70 percent of the outstanding X stock was voted in favor of a plan of acquisition of the X stock by newly formed corporation Y, and two percent was voted against. The remaining 28 percent of the X stock was not voted. On the effective date of the transaction, Y became the owner of all the outstanding X stock by operation of State law except for two percent of such stock which was owned by those X shareholders who exercised their appraisal rights and who received cash from X for their X stock. In exchange for their X stock, the X shareholders, including those who did not vote on the plan but who participated in the exchange because they did not dissent received voting common stock * * * of Y which represented all of the Y stock outstanding after the transaction.

Held, inasmuch as the identity and rights of all the transferors (the nondissenting X shareholders) were defined by state law and the exchange of their X stock for Y stock was by operation of law simultaneous on the effective date of the transaction, the nondissenting X shareholders were in control of Y immediately after the exchange within the meaning of § 351 of the Code. Therefore, under § 351 no gain or loss is recognized to the former X shareholders who exchanged their X stock for Y stock. Those X shareholders who received cash for their X stock are treated as having had such stock redeemed by X with the redemption being subject to the provisions of § 302.

Question

Explain how the elements of § 351 are satisfied in the above transaction.

D. Limitation on Transfer of Built in Losses by the American Jobs Creation Act of 2004

Conference Committee Report to the American Jobs Creation Act of 2004

H.R. Conf. Rep. No. 108-755 (October 2004)
Conference Agreement and Senate Committee Report, S.Rep. No. 108-192

Senate Committee Report

Present Law. Generally, no gain or loss is recognized when one or more persons transfer property to a corporation in exchange for stock and immediately after the exchange such person or persons control the corporation. [§ 351] The transferor's basis in the stock of the controlled corporation is the same as the basis of the property contributed to the controlled corporation, increased by the amount of any gain (or dividend) recognized by the transferor on the exchange, and reduced by the amount of any money or property received, and by the amount of any loss recognized by the transferor. [§ 362]

The basis of property received by a corporation, whether from domestic or foreign transferors, in a tax-free incorporation, reorganization, or liquidation of a subsidiary corporation is the same as the adjusted basis in the hands of the transferor, adjusted for gain or loss recognized by the transferor. [§§ 334(b) and 362(a) and (b)]

Reasons for Change. The Joint Committee on Taxation staff's investigative report of Enron Corporation and other information reveal that taxpayers are engaging in various tax motivated transactions to duplicate a single economic loss and, subsequently, deduct such loss more than once. Congress has previously taken actions to limit the ability of taxpayers to engage in specific transactions that purport to duplicate a single economic loss. However, new schemes that purport to duplicate losses continue to proliferate. In furtherance of the overall tax policy objective of accurately measuring taxable income, the Committee believes that a single economic loss should not be deducted more than once. Thus, the Committee believes that it is generally appropriate to limit a corporation's basis in property acquired in a tax-free transfer to the fair market value of such property. * * *

Explanation of Provision. [See §§ 334 and 362.] * * *

Limitation on transfer of built-in-losses in section 351 transactions. The provision provides that if the aggregate adjusted bases of property contributed by a transferor (or by a control group of which the transferor is a member) to a corporation exceed the aggregate fair market value of the property transferred in a tax-free incorporation, the transferee's aggregate bases of the property is limited to the aggregate fair market value of the transferred property. [§ 362(e)] Under the provision, any required basis reduction is allocated among the transferred properties in proportion to their built-in-loss immediately before the transaction. In the case of a transfer after which the transferor owns at least 80 percent of the vote and value of the stock of the transferee corporation, any basis reduction required by the provision is made to the stock received by the transferor and not to the assets transferred. * * *

Conference Agreement

The conference agreement follows the Senate amendment, with modifications to the limitation on transfer of built-in losses in section 351 transactions. The conference agreement eliminates the provision that requires a basis reduction to be made to stock received by the transferor (rather than to the assets transferred) in the case of a transfer in which the transferor owns at least 80 percent of the vote and value of the stock of the transferee corporation. Thus, the provision that limits the transferee's aggregate basis in the transferred property to the aggregate fair market value of the transferred property generally applies, regardless of the ownership percentage of the transferor in the stock of the transferee corporation.

In addition, the conference agreement permits the transferor and transferee to elect to limit the basis in the stock received by the transferor to the aggregate fair market value of the transferred property, in lieu of limiting the basis in the assets transferred. Such election shall be included with the tax returns of the transferor and transferee for the taxable year in which the transaction occurs and, once made, shall be irrevocable. * * *

§ 2.3 Introduction to Issues Arising in the Capitalization of a Corporation

A. The Difference between Debt and Equity

Treasury Report, Integration of Individual and Corporate Tax Systems

5–6 (January 6, 1992)

CORPORATE CAPITAL STRUCTURE Corporations have three alternatives for financing new investments: (1) issuing new equity, (2) using retained earnings, or (3) issuing debt. There can be important nontax benefits and costs of alternative corporate financing arrangements, and the tax system should avoid prejudicing financial decisions.

The current classical corporate tax system discriminates against equity financing of new corporate investment. Because of the two levels of taxation of corporate profits, the cost of equity capital generally exceeds the cost of debt capital. * * * The lower effective tax rate for debt financed corporate investment than for equity financed corporate investment encourages the use of debt by corporations, assuming nontax factors that affect financing decisions do not change.

If a corporation borrows from an individual to finance an investment, the corporation deducts the interest payments from its taxable income and is therefore not taxed on the investment's pre-tax return to the extent of interest payments, although the lender is taxable on the interest at the individual tax rate. * * *

B. Introduction to Tax Stakes Involved in Debt Equity Issues[3]

This section introduces various tax issues presented when structuring the capital of a corporation. Capitalization issues arise throughout the life cycle of a corporation, from the initial incorporation transaction under § 351, to liquidation, sale or reorganization. Thus, many capitalization issues arise in the context of a merger or acquisition. The bias for debt financing discussed in the above excerpt was mitigated by the 20% maximum rate that now applies to dividends. This change has an impact on many of the issues addressed below. Some of the more important capitalization considerations include:

(1) Under § 351, the contributing shareholders receive nonrecognition treatment on the receipt of common stock in exchange for property. However, the receipt of debt instruments or of nonqualified preferred stock (*see* § 351(g)) is treated as boot. *See* Sec. 2.2.

(2) Interest paid on debt is generally deductible by a corporation in computing its taxable income. *See* § 163. Dividend payments by a corporation with respect to its stock are not deductible. Therefore, capitalizing a corporation with debt is generally favored over equity. If the corporation is too heavily financed with debt, the debt may be recharacterized as equity. This is one of the major tax issues in leverage buyouts (LBOs), which are addressed in Sec. 5.2.D. However, as a result of the 20% rate that now applies to dividends, the bias in favor of debt financing has been reduced.

(3) In general, a corporate shareholder receives a dividend-received deduction with respect to dividends received from domestic corporations. *See* § 243. The deduction is 70%, 80%, or 100% of the dividend. *See* Sec. 2.6. Therefore, a corporate holder may prefer to have the instrument treated as preferred stock rather than debt, whereas a corporate issuer may prefer a debt classification.

(4) The redemption by a corporation of its stock may be treated as either (a) a distribution, which may be a taxable dividend, or (b) a sale or exchange that produces return of capital treatment and a capital gain. *See* § 302 and Sec. 2.7. On the other hand, the redemption of a debt instrument generally gives rise to a return of capital and capital gain. *See* § 1271. For individual shareholders, the difference between capital gain and dividend income is significantly diminished with the 20% maximum uniform rate. However, a redemption that produces a capital gain will give rise to a recovery of basis, but a redemption that is treated as a distribution will produce a fully taxable dividend to the extent of the corporation's earnings and profits. *See* Sec. 2.4.

(5) On the issuance of a debt instrument for cash or property, consideration must be given to the original issue discount provisions. *See* § 1271 *et seq.* and Sec.

---

3. This section is based on a modification of Sec. 4.01 of *Federal Taxation of Business Enterprises*, *supra* note 1.

1.9. The interest on debt instruments with excessive amounts of OID (*i.e.,* applicable high yield discount obligations) may be either disallowed or deferred. *See* § 163(i) and (e)(5). Further, if bonds are issued at a premium, consideration must be given to § 171, which provides for the amortization of bond premium. Also, in any lending transaction between a corporation and either a shareholder or an employee, consideration must be given to the below market loan provisions. *See* § 7872. And loans between commonly controlled entities, such as a domestic parent corporation and its wholly owned foreign subsidiary, are subject to the arm's length standard of § 482.

(6) When stock or debt becomes worthless or is disposed of at a loss, there is a question whether the loss is characterized as a capital or ordinary loss under the rules of §§ 165, 166 or 1244.

(7) Even if debt is treated as debt for Federal income tax purposes, if the debt is used in the acquisition of stock or assets (*i.e.,* corporate acquisition indebtedness), the interest deduction may be disallowed. *See* § 279 and Sec. 5.3.A.2.

(8) The interest deduction with respect to publicly offered debt instruments is generally disallowed if the instruments are not in registered form. *See* § 163(f).

In resolving the issue of whether an interest in a corporation is, for example, (1) debt or equity, (2) stock or a security, (3) preferred stock or debt, or (4) preferred stock or common stock, it is necessary to look at court decisions, and in some situations at the regulations and rulings. The Code generally does not define these terms; however § 351(g)(2) defines nonqualified preferred stock.

In order to promote greater certainty in resolving debt-equity classification issues, Congress enacted § 385 in 1969. Under this section, the Treasury is authorized to promulgate regulations that determine "whether an interest in a corporation is to be treated for purposes of * * * [the Code] as stock or indebtedness (or as in part stock and in part indebtedness." Section 385(b) enumerates the following factors the Treasury may take into account in determining whether an interest in a corporation is stock or indebtedness:

(1) whether there is a written unconditional promise to pay on demand or on a specified date a sum certain in money in return for an adequate consideration in money or money's worth, and to pay a fixed rate of interest,

(2) whether there is subordination to or preference over any indebtedness of the corporation,

(3) the ratio of debt to equity of the corporation,

(4) whether there is convertibility into the stock of the corporation, and

(5) the relationship between holdings of stock in the corporation and holdings of the interest in question.

Although § 385 was enacted in 1969, the Treasury did not promulgate proposed regulations until March 24, 1980. These regulations were amended several times and then withdrawn. Notwithstanding the withdrawal of these regulations, an analysis of them could assist in resolving debt equity issues. Also, in April 2016, in its efforts to curtail inversions, the Treasury issued proposed regulations under Section 385 dealing with the issuance of debt in inversions and related transactions. These regulations are discussed in Secs. 10.11.D and F. For a 2016 analysis of debt-equity issues, *see* Staff of the Joint Committee on Taxation, *Overview of the Tax Treatment of Corporate Debt and Equity* (May 20, 2016).

§ 2.4 Distributions of Cash to Individual Shareholders[4]

A. In General

Section 301 governs the tax treatment to both noncorporate and corporate shareholders on the receipt of a distribution of property from a subchapter C corporation; however, this discussion focuses only on the treatment of individual shareholders. The rules discussed in this and succeeding sections relating to the treatment of distributions also may apply in the context of a merger or acquisition.

Section 301(a) provides that "a distribution of property (as defined in §317(a)) made by a corporation to a shareholder with respect to its stock shall be treated in the manner provided in subsection (c)." The term property is defined in §317(a) as "money, securities and any other property; except that such term does not include stock in the corporation making the distribution (or rights to acquire such stock)." Securities for this purpose are long-term debt obligations of the distributing corporation; thus, the term property includes all types of debt instruments. Under §301(b)(1), the amount of a cash distribution is the amount of the cash, and this discussion focuses only on the treatment of cash.

The term dividend is defined in §316 as any distribution of property (*e.g.*, cash) (1) out of the earnings and profits of a corporation accumulated after February 28, 1913 (accumulated earnings and profits), or (2) out of the earnings and profits of the corporation for the current taxable year (current earnings and profits). Under §316(a)(2), current earnings and profits are calculated "as of the close of the taxable year without diminution by reason of distributions made during the taxable year * * *, [and] without regard to the amount of earnings and profits at the time of the distribution …". Distributions are considered as first made out of the most recently accumulated earnings and profits. A distribution of property is treated as a dividend to the extent of the earnings and profits of the corporation for the year of the distribution and then to the extent of accumulated earnings and profits.

Thus, for a distribution to be a dividend, the distribution must come from the corporation's earnings and profits. The term "earnings and profits," although not de-

---

4. This section is based on a modification of Secs. 9.02 and 9.03 of *Federal Taxation of Business Enterprises*, *supra* note 1.

fined in the Code, refers to the earnings of a corporation after operational expenses and taxes, not to the liquid funds in a corporation. Earnings and profits are positive if the corporation operates at a profit and negative if it operates at a loss, the latter being commonly referred to as a deficit in earnings and profits. Section 312 specifies the effect certain transactions have on earnings and profits. Pursuant to §312(a), earnings and profits are, in general, reduced (but not to a deficit) by the following amounts:

(1) the amount of money distributed,

(2) the principal amount of obligations of the corporation distributed, and

(3) the adjusted basis of property distributed.

Current earnings and profits are the earnings and profits of the current tax year of the corporation. Accumulated earnings and profits are the undistributed earnings and profits of prior tax years. This concept is similar to the financial accounting concept of retained earnings. Unless distributed, current earnings and profits become accumulated earnings and profits at the end of a tax year. Under these rules, accumulated earnings and profits may be positive while current earnings and profits are negative or vice versa. This is illustrated by the following example:

Corporation C has (1) a deficit in its accumulated earnings and profits account of $100K, and (2) current earnings and profits of $10K. C distributes $10K during the current year. The distribution is treated as a dividend because the amount of the distribution does not exceed the current earnings and profits of the distributing corporation. On the other hand, if C distributes the $10K in the following year (at which time the $10K of current earnings has reduced the deficit to $90K), the distribution is not a dividend unless the corporation has current earnings and profits in the year of the distribution.

Tax-exempt income increases earnings and profits because it is money that the corporation has available for distribution to its shareholders. *See* § 1.312-6(b). Although tax-exempt interest is not subject to tax on receipt by the corporation, the tax exempt character does not pass through on distribution. Tax-exempt interest is an example of an item excluded from taxable income but included in earnings and profits. Certain items, such as the excess of accelerated depreciation over straight-line depreciation, reduce taxable income but not earnings and profits. *See* § 312(k).

The computation of earnings and profits is illustrated in the following example. Assume that an accrual basis, calendar year corporation has gross income during calendar year 2005 of $1,000,000, tax exempt income of $10K, operating expenses of $500K (with depreciation computed on a straight line basis), and a tax liability of $250K. The corporation's current earnings and profits are $260K, calculated as follows:

Gross Income	$1,000,000
LESS Operating Expenses	$500,000
= Taxable Income	$500,000
LESS Taxes at assume 50%	$250,000
= Tentative Earnings and Profits	$250,000
PLUS Tax Exempt Interest	$10,000
= Current Earnings and Profits	$260,000

If the corporation distributes cash of $260K during calendar year 2005, the shareholders have a dividend in the amount of $260K.

Any distribution in excess of current earnings and profits is deemed to come out of accumulated earnings and profits as demonstrated by the following example.

C corporation has $260K of current earnings and profits and $400K of accumulated earnings and profits. On the last day of the taxable year, C distributes $500K of cash. Under § 316(b), all of the $500K distribution is treated as a dividend; $260K comes out of current earnings and profits and $240K comes out of accumulated earnings and profits. Under § 312, C's total earnings and profits of $660K are reduced by $500K to $160K all of which is accumulated earnings and profits.

Under § 301(c)(2), any distribution in excess of both current and accumulated earnings and profits is treated as a return of capital to the extent of the shareholder's adjusted basis for her stock. Under § 301(c)(3), any distribution in excess of the adjusted basis is treated as gain from the sale of the stock. This is illustrated as follows: Assume that C corporation has $260K in current earnings and profits, and $400K in accumulated earnings and profits. C distributes $800K to its sole shareholder who has a basis in her stock of $100K. The following results obtain. $260K of the $800K distribution is a dividend from current earnings and profits. The $540K portion of the distribution in excess of current earnings and profits is deemed to be out of accumulated earnings and profits to the extent of $400K. The $140K portion of the distribution in excess of such accumulated earnings and profits is a nontaxable return of capital to the extent of the shareholder's adjusted basis for her stock, which is $100K. The $40K portion in excess of the adjusted basis of the shareholder's stock is treated as gain from the sale of such stock.

These results illustrate that there are four levels of treatment of a distribution in subchapter C:

First Level: A distribution is first deemed to be out of current earnings and profits. *See* § 301(c)(1).

Second Level: A distribution in excess of current earnings and profits is deemed to be out of accumulated earnings and profits. *See* § 301(c)(1).

Third Level: A distribution in excess of both current and accumulated earnings and profits is deemed to be a nontaxable return of capital to the extent of the adjusted basis of the shareholder's stock. *See* § 301(c)(2).

Fourth Level: A distribution in excess of current and accumulated earnings and profits and the adjusted basis of the shareholder's stock normally produces a capital gain. *See* § 301(c)(3).

B. Congress's Explanation of the Maximum 15% [Now 20%] Rate on Dividends Received by Individuals

House Committee Report (H.R. Rep. No. 108-94) to the Jobs and Growth Tax Reconciliation Act of 2003

Reasons For Change. The Committee believes it is important that tax policy be conducive to economic growth. The Committee believes that reducing the individual tax on dividends lowers the cost of capital and will lead to economic growth and the creation of jobs. Economic growth is impeded by tax-induced distortions in the capital markets. Mitigating these distortions will improve the efficiency of the capital markets. In addition, reducing the aggregate tax burden on investments made by corporations will lower the cost of capital needed to finance new investments and lead to increases in aggregate national investment and increases in private sector employment. It is through such investment that the United States' economy can increase output, employment, and productivity. It is through increases in productivity that workers earn higher real wages and all Americans benefit from a higher standard of living. The Committee observes that present law imposes different total tax burdens on income from different investments. The Committee believes that, by placing different tax burdens on different investments, the present system results in economic distortions. The Committee observes that present law distorts individual and corporate financial decisions. The Committee observes that because interest payments on the debt are deductible, present law encourages corporations to finance using debt rather than equity. The Committee believes that the increase in corporate leverage, while beneficial to each corporation from a tax perspective, may place the economy at risk of more bankruptcies during an economic downturn. In addition, the Committee finds that present law, by taxing dividend income at a higher rate than income from capital gains, encourages corporations to retain earnings rather than to distribute them as taxable dividends. If dividends are discouraged, shareholders may prefer that corporate management retain and reinvest earnings rather than pay out dividends, even if the shareholder might have an alternative use for the funds that could offer a higher rate of return than that earned on the retained earnings. This is another source of inefficiency as the opportunity to earn higher pre-tax returns is bypassed in favor of lower pre-tax returns. * * *

Explanation of Provision. Under the provision, [certain] dividends received by an individual shareholder from domestic corporations [and qualified foreign corporations] are taxed at the same rates that apply to net capital gain [which now is subject to a maximum 20% rate]. [*See* § 1(h)(11).] * * *

[Although as noted above, the maximum rate of tax on dividends received by individuals is generally 20 percent, as a result of Obamacare, there is a 3.8% Net Investment Income Tax on certain high income individuals, thus taking the maximum rate to 23.8%, which is also the maximum rate on capital gains.]

§ 2.5 Distribution of Non-Cash Property to Individual Shareholder

A. Treatment of the Shareholder[5]

The treatment of the distributee shareholder on receipt of a distribution of property other than cash is essentially the same as the treatment on the receipt of cash with the following additional rules. First, under § 301(b)(1) the amount of the distribution is the fair market value of the property received. The fair market value is determined as of the date of the distribution. *See* § 301(b)(3). For example, if a corporation distributes to shareholder A property with a fair market value at the time of the distribution of $100K, then the shareholder must account under § 301(c) for a $100K distribution.

Second, under § 301(d), the basis to the shareholder of the property distributed is the fair market value of the property, which in the above case would be $100K. Third, if the property is subject to a liability or in connection with the distribution the shareholder assumes a liability of the corporation, then the amount of the distribution is reduced by the amount of the liability. *See* § 301(b)(2) and § 1.301-1(g). This rule is illustrated as follows. Corporation C distributes property to shareholder S. The property has a fair market value of $100K and is subject to a nonrecourse liability of $60K. Under § 301(b)(2), the amount of the distribution is $40K, which is the fair market value of the property ($100K) less the liability ($60K). If the corporation has sufficient E & P, S has a dividend of $40K under § 301(c)(1). Under § 301(d) S's basis for the property is $100K, the fair market value of the property.

---

5. This section is based on a modification of Sec. 9.02 of *Federal Taxation of Business Enterprises*, *supra* note 1.

B. Treatment of the Corporation on a Distribution of Non-Cash Property: The *General Utilities* Doctrine and Its Repeal

1. The *General Utilities* Doctrine

General Utilities & Operating Co. v. Helvering

Supreme Court of the United States, 1935
296 U.S. 200

Mr. Justice McReynolds delivered the opinion of the Court.

January 1, 1927, petitioner, General Utilities, a Delaware corporation, acquired 20,000 shares (one-half of total outstanding) common stock of Islands Edison Company, for which it paid $2,000. Gillet & Company owned the remainder.

During January 1928, Whetstone, president of Southern Cities Utilities Company, contemplated acquisition by his company of all Islands Edison common stock. He discussed the matter with Lucas, petitioner's president, also with Gillet & Company. The latter concern agreed to sell its holdings upon terms acceptable to all. But Lucas pointed out that the shares which his company held could only be purchased after distribution of them among stockholders, since a sale by it would subject the realized profit to taxation, and when the proceeds passed to the stockholders there would be further exaction. Lucas had no power to sell, but he, Gillet, and Whetstone were in accord concerning the terms and conditions under which purchase of all the stock might become possible — "it being understood and agreed between them that petitioner would make distribution of the stock of the Islands Edison Company to its stockholders and that counsel would prepare a written agreement embodying the terms and conditions of the said sale, agreement to be submitted for approval to the stockholders of the Islands Edison Company after the distribution of said stock by the petitioner."

Petitioner's directors, March 22, 1928, considered the disposition of the Islands Edison shares. Officers reported they were worth $1,122,500, and recommended an appreciation on the books to that figure. Thereupon a resolution directed this change; also "that a dividend in the amount of $1,071,426.25 be and it is hereby declared on the Common Stock of this Company payable in Common Stock to The Islands Edison Company at a valuation of $56.12 1/2 a share, out of the surplus of the Company arising from the appreciation in the value of the Common Stock of The Islands Edison Company held by this Company, viz., $1,120,500.00, the payment of the dividend to be made by the delivery to the stockholders of this Company, pro rata, of certificates for the Common Stock of The Islands Edison Company held by this Company at the rate of two shares of such stock for each share of Company Stock of this Corporation."

Accordingly, 19,090 shares were distributed amongst petitioner's thirty-three stockholders and proper transfers to them were made upon the issuing corporation's books. It retained 910 shares.

After this transfer, all holders of Islands Edison stock sold to Southern Cities Utilities Company at $56.12 1/2 per share. Petitioner realized $46,346.30 net profit on 910 shares and this was duly returned for taxation. There was no report of gain upon the 19,090 shares distributed to stockholders.

The Commissioner of Internal Revenue declared a taxable gain upon distribution of the stock in payment of the dividend declared March 22nd, and made the questioned deficiency assessment. Seeking redetermination by the Board of Tax Appeals, petitioner alleged: "The Commissioner of Internal Revenue has erroneously held that the petitioner corporation made a profit of $1,069,517.25 by distributing to its own stockholders certain capital stock of another corporation which it had theretofore owned." And it asked a ruling that no taxable gain resulted from the appreciation upon its books and subsequent distribution of the shares. Answering, the Commissioner denied that his action was erroneous, but advanced no new basis of support. A stipulation concerning the facts followed; and upon this and the pleadings, the Board heard the cause.

It found: "The respondent has determined a deficiency in income tax in the amount of $128,342.07 for the calendar year 1928. The only question presented in this proceeding for redetermination is whether petitioner realized taxable gain in declaring a dividend and paying it in the stock of another company at an agreed value per share, which value was in excess of the cost of the stock to petitioner." Also: "On March 26, 1928, the stockholders of the Islands Edison Company (one of which was petitioner, owning 910 shares) and the Southern Cities Utilities Company, entered into a written contract of sale of the Islands Edison Company stock. At no time did petitioner agree with Whetstone or the Southern Cities Utilities Company, verbally or in writing, to make sale to him or to the Southern Cities Utilities Company of any of said stock except the aforesaid 910 shares of the Islands Edison Company."

The opinion recites: The Commissioner's "theory is that upon the declaration of the dividend on March 22, 1928, petitioner became indebted to its stockholders in the amount of $1,071,426.25, and that the discharge of that liability by the delivery of property costing less than the amount of the debt constituted income, citing *United States v. Kirby Lumber Co.,* 284 U.S. 1, 52 S.Ct. 4, 76 L.Ed. 131." "The intent of the directors of petitioner was to declare a dividend payable in Islands Edison stock; their intent was expressed in that way in the resolution formally adopted; and the dividend was paid in the way intended and declared. We so construe the transaction, and on authority of *First Savings Bank v. Burnet, supra* [60 App.D.C. 307, 53 F.(2d) 919, 82 A.L.R. 549], we hold that the declaration and payment of the dividend resulted in no taxable income."

The Commissioner asked the Circuit Court of Appeals, Fourth Circuit, to review the Board's determination. He alleged: "The only question to be decided is whether the petitioner [taxpayer] realized taxable income in declaring a dividend and paying it in stock of another company at an agreed value per share, which value was in excess of the cost of the stock."

The court stated: "There are two grounds upon which the petitioner urges that the action of the Board of Tax Appeals was wrong: First, that the dividend declared was in effect a cash dividend and that the respondent realized a taxable income by the distribution of the Islands Edison Company stock to its stockholders equal to the difference between the amount of the dividend declared and the cost of the stock. Second, that the sale made of the Islands Edison Company stock was in reality a sale by the respondent (with all the terms agreed upon before the declaration of the dividend), through its stockholders who were virtually acting as agents of the respondent, the real vendor."

Upon the first ground, it sustained the Board. Concerning the second, it held that, although not raised before the Board, the point should be ruled upon.

"When we come to consider the sale of the stock of the Islands Edison Company we cannot escape the conclusion that the transaction was deliberately planned and carried out for the sole purpose of escaping taxation. The purchaser was found by the officers of the respondent; the exact terms of the sale as finally consummated were agreed to by the same officers; the purchaser of the stock stated that the delivery of all stock was essential and that the delivery of a part thereof would not suffice; the details were worked out for the express and admitted purpose of avoiding the payment of the tax and for the reason that the attorneys for the respondent had advised that unless some such plan was adopted the tax would have to be paid; and a written agreement was to be prepared by counsel for the respondent which was to be submitted to the stockholders; all this without the stockholders, or any of them, who were ostensibly making the sale, being informed, advised or consulted. Such admitted facts plainly constituted a plan, not to use the harsher terms of scheme, artifice or conspiracy, to evade the payment of the tax. For the purposes of this decision it is not necessary to consider whether such a course as is here shown constituted a fraud, it is sufficient if we conclude that the object was to evade the payment of a tax justly due the government.

"The sale of the stock in question was, in substance, made by the respondent company, through the stockholders as agents or conduits through whom the transfer of the title was effected. The stockholders, even in their character as agents, had little or no option in the matter and in no sense exercised any independent judgment. They automatically ratified the agreement prepared and submitted to them."

A judgment of reversal followed.

Both tribunals below rightly decided that petitioner derived no taxable gain from the distribution among its stockholders of the Islands Edison shares as a dividend. This was no sale; assets were not used to discharge indebtedness.

The second ground of objection, although sustained by the court, was not presented to or ruled upon by the Board. * * *

Here the court undertook to decide a question not properly raised. Also it made an inference of fact directly in conflict with the stipulation of the parties and the findings, for which we think the record affords no support whatever. To remand the cause for further findings would be futile. The Board could not properly find anything which would assist the Commissioner's cause.

The judgment of the court below must be reversed. The action of the Board of Tax Appeals is approved.

Reversed.

Note

Why was the distribution in *General Utilities* not treated as a realization and recognition event under the predecessor of § 1001, which was in place at the time of the case? Should a distribution of property by a corporation be treated as a realization and recognition event to the corporation? What is the difference under *General Utilities* between (1) a sale by a corporation of property followed by the distribution of the after-tax proceeds to the shareholders, and (2) a distribution by the corporation of the property to its shareholders followed by a sale of the property by the shareholders? Note that on receipt of a distribution of property the shareholder takes a fair market value basis for the property. *See* § 301(d)

2. The *Court Holding* Doctrine and Its Relationship to *General Utilities*

a. Liquidating Distribution Followed by Sale by Shareholders, Treated as Sale by Corporation

Commissioner v. Court Holding Co.

Supreme Court of the United States, 1945
324 U.S. 331

Mr. Justice Black delivered the opinion of the Court.

An apartment house, which was the sole asset of the respondent corporation, was transferred in the form of a liquidating dividend to the corporation's two shareholders. They in turn formally conveyed it to a purchaser who had originally negotiated for the purchase from the corporation. The question is whether the Circuit Court of Appeals properly reversed the Tax Court's conclusion that the corporation was taxable under § 22 of the Internal Revenue Code for the gain which accrued from the sale. The answer depends upon whether the findings of the Tax Court that the whole transaction showed a sale by the corporation rather than by the stockholders were final and binding upon the Circuit Court of Appeals.

It is unnecessary to set out in detail the evidence introduced before the Tax Court or its findings. Despite conflicting evidence, the following findings of the Tax Court are supported by the record:

The respondent corporation was organized in 1934 solely to buy and hold the apartment building which was the only property ever owned by it. All of its outstanding stock was owned by Minnie Miller and her husband. Between October 1, 1939 and February, 1940, while the corporation still had legal title to the property, negotiations for its sale took place. These negotiations were between the corporation and the lessees of the property, together with a sister and brother-in-law. An oral agreement was reached as to the terms and conditions of sale, and on February 22, 1940, the parties met to reduce the agreement to writing. The purchaser was then advised by the corporation's attorney that the sale could not be consummated because it would result in the imposition of a large income tax on the corporation. The next day the corporation declared a "liquidating dividend," which involved complete liquidation of its assets, and surrender of all outstanding stock. Mrs. Miller and her husband surrendered their stock, and the building was deeded to them. A sale contract was then drawn, naming the Millers individually as vendors, and the lessees' sister as vendee, which embodied substantially the same terms and conditions previously agreed upon. One thousand dollars, which a month and a half earlier had been paid to the corporation by the lessees, was applied in part payment of the purchase price. Three days later, the property was conveyed to the lessees' sister.

The Tax Court concluded from these facts that, despite the declaration of a "liquidating dividend" followed by the transfers of legal title, the corporation had not abandoned the sales negotiations; that these were mere formalities designed "to make the transaction appear to be other than what it was", in order to avoid tax liability. The Circuit Court of Appeals drawing different inferences from the record, held that the corporation had "called off" the sale, and treated the stockholders' sale as unrelated to the prior negotiations.

There was evidence to support the findings of the Tax Court, and its findings must therefore be accepted by the courts. * * * On the basis of these findings, the Tax Court was justified in attributing the gain from the sale to respondent corporation. The incidence of taxation depends upon the substance of a transaction. The tax consequences which arise from gains from a sale of property are not finally to be determined solely by the means employed to transfer legal title. Rather, the transaction must be viewed as a whole, and each step, from the commencement of negotiations to the consummation of the sale, is relevant. A sale by one person cannot be transformed for tax purposes into a sale by another by using the latter as a conduit through which to pass title. To permit the true nature of a transaction to be disguised by mere formalisms, which exist solely to alter tax liabilities, would seriously impair the effective administration of the tax policies of Congress.

It is urged that respondent corporation never executed a written agreement, and that an oral agreement to sell land cannot be enforced in Florida because of the Statute of Frauds, Comp.Gen.Laws of Florida, 1927, vol. 3, Sec. 5779, F.S.A. §725.01. But the fact that respondent corporation itself never executed a written contract is unimportant, since the Tax Court found from the facts of the entire transaction that the executed sale was in substance the sale of the corporation. The decision of the Circuit Court of Appeals is reversed, and that of the Tax Court affirmed.

It is so ordered.

Reversed.

Question

What would have been the treatment in the transaction in *Court Holding* if the Supreme Court had found in *General Utilities* that a distribution of property is a realization event?

b. Liquidating Distribution Followed by Sale by Shareholders Held to Be Bona Fide

United States v. Cumberland Public Service Co.

Supreme Court of the United States, 1950
338 U.S. 451

Mr. Justice Black delivered the opinion of the Court.

A corporation selling its physical properties is taxed on capital gains resulting from the sale. There is no corporate tax, however, on distribution of assets in kind to shareholders as part of a genuine liquidation. The respondent corporation transferred property to its shareholders as a liquidating dividend in kind. The shareholders transferred it to a purchaser. The question is whether, despite contrary findings by the Court of Claims, this record requires a holding that the transaction was in fact a sale by the corporation subjecting the corporation to a capital gains tax.

Details of the transaction are as follows. The respondent, a closely held corporation, was long engaged in the business of generating and distributing electric power in three Kentucky counties. In 1936 a local cooperative began to distribute Tennessee Valley Authority power in the area served by respondent. It soon became obvious that respondent's Diesel-generated power could not compete with TVA power, which respondent had been unable to obtain. Respondent's shareholders, realizing that the corporation must get out of the power business unless it obtained TVA power, accordingly offered to sell all the corporate stock to the cooperative, which was receiving such power. The cooperative refused to buy the stock, but countered with an offer to buy from the corporation its transmission and distribution equipment. The corporation rejected the offer because it would have been compelled to pay a heavy capital gains tax. At the same time the shareholders, desiring to save payment of the corporate capital gains tax, offered to acquire the transmission and distribution equipment and then sell to the cooperative. The cooperative accepted. The corporation transferred the transmission and distribution systems to its shareholders in partial liquidation. The remaining assets were sold and the corporation dissolved. The shareholders then executed the previously contemplated sale to the cooperative.

Upon this sale by the shareholders, the Commissioner assessed and collected a $17,000 tax from the corporation on the theory that the shareholders had been used as a mere conduit for effectuating what was really a corporate sale. Respondent corporation brought this action to recover the amount of the tax. The Court of Claims found that the method by which the stockholders disposed of the property was avowedly chosen in order to reduce taxes, but that the liquidation and dissolution genuinely ended the corporation's activities and existence. The court also found that at no time did the corporation plan to make the sale itself. Accordingly it found as a fact that the sale was made by the shareholders rather than the corporation, and entered judgment for respondent. One judge dissented, believing that our opinion in *Comm'r v. Court Holding Co.*, 324 U.S. 331, 65 S.Ct. 707, 708, 89 L.Ed. 567, required a finding that the sale had been made by the corporation. Certiorari was granted, 338 U.S. 846, 70 S.Ct. 88, to clear up doubts arising out of the *Court Holding Co.* case.

Our *Court Holding Co.* decision rested on findings of fact by the Tax Court that a sale had been made and gains realized by the taxpayer corporation. * * * The Tax Court found that the corporation never really abandoned its sales negotiations, that it never did dissolve, and that the sole purpose of the so-called liquidation was to disguise a corporate sale through use of mere formalisms in order to avoid tax liability. The Circuit Court of Appeals took a different view of the evidence. In this Court the Government contended that whether a liquidation distribution was genuine or merely a sham was traditionally a question of fact. We agreed with this contention, and reinstated the Tax Court's findings and judgment. Discussing the evidence which supported the findings of fact, we went on to say that "the incidence of taxation depends upon the substance of a transaction" regardless of "mere formalisms," and that taxes on a corporate sale cannot be avoided by using the shareholders as a "conduit through which to pass title."

This language does not mean that a corporation can be taxed even when the sale has been made by its stockholders following a genuine liquidation and dissolution. While the distinction between sales by a corporation as compared with distribution in kind followed by shareholder sales may be particularly shadowy and artificial when the corporation is closely held, Congress has chosen to recognize such a distinction for tax purposes. The corporate tax is thus aimed primarily at the profits of a going concern. This is true despite the fact that gains realized from corporate sales are taxed, perhaps to prevent tax evasions, even where the cash proceeds are at once distributed in liquidation. But Congress has imposed no tax on liquidating distributions in kind or on dissolution, whatever may be the motive for such liquidation. Consequently, a corporation may liquidate or dissolve without subjecting itself to the corporate gains tax, even though a primary motive is to avoid the burden of corporate taxation.

Here, on the basis of adequate subsidiary findings, the Court of Claims has found that the sale in question was made by the stockholders rather than the corporation. The Government's argument that the shareholders acted as a mere "conduit" for a sale by respondent corporation must fall before this finding. The subsidiary finding that a major motive of the shareholders was to reduce taxes does not bar this conclusion. Whatever the motive and however relevant it may be in determining whether the transaction was real or a sham, sales of physical properties by shareholders following a genuine liquidation distribution cannot be attributed to the corporation for tax purposes.

The oddities in tax consequences that emerge from the tax provisions here controlling appear to be inherent in the present tax pattern. For a corporation is taxed if it sells all its physical properties and distributes the cash proceeds as liquidating dividends, yet is not taxed if that property is distributed in kind and is then sold by the shareholders. In both instances the interest of the shareholders in the business has been transferred to the purchaser. Again, if these stockholders had succeeded in their original effort to sell all their stock, their interest would have been transferred to the purchasers just as effectively. Yet on such a transaction the corporation would have realized no taxable gain.

Congress having determined that different tax consequences shall flow from different methods by which the shareholders of a closely held corporation may dispose of corporate property, we accept its mandate. It is for the trial court, upon consideration of an entire transaction, to determine the factual category in which a particular transaction belongs. Here as in the *Court Holding Co.* case we accept the ultimate findings of fact of the trial tribunal. Accordingly the judgment of the Court of Claims is affirmed.

Affirmed.

Questions

How do you distinguish the result in *Court Holding* from the result in *Cumberland Service*? What would have been the result in *Cumberland Service* if the Supreme Court had found in *General Utilities* that a distribution is a realization and recognition event?

3. Introductory Note on the Repeal of the *General Utilities* Doctrine

The Tax Reform Act of 1986 essentially repealed the *General Utilities* doctrine for both current distributions by operating corporations and liquidating distributions. Section 311(b) effectuates the repeal for current distributions, and § 336 does the same for liquidating distributions. The materials in this section deal with the repeal of the doctrine under § 311 for current distributions of property, and the materials in Sec. 2.10.D. address the repeal for liquidating distributions.

4. Legislative History of the Repeal of the General Utilities Doctrine by the Tax Reform Act of 1986

General Explanation of Tax Reform Act of 1986
328–346 (1986)

Prior Law *Overview* As a general rule, under prior law (as under present law) corporate earnings from sales of appreciated property were taxed twice, first to the corporation when the sale occurred, and again to the shareholders when the net proceeds were distributed as dividends. At the corporate level, the income was taxed at ordinary rates if it resulted from the sale of inventory or other ordinary income assets, or at capital gains rates if it resulted from the sale of a capital asset held for more than six months. With certain exceptions, shareholders were taxed at ordinary income rates to the extent of their pro rata share of the distributing corporation's current and accumulated earnings and profits.

An important exception to this two-level taxation of corporate earnings was the so-called *General Utilities* rule. The *General Utilities* rule permitted nonrecognition of gain by corporations on certain distributions of appreciated property to their shareholders and on certain liquidating sales of property. Thus, its effect was to allow appreciation in property accruing during the period it was held by a corporation to escape tax at the corporate level. At the same time, the transferee (the shareholder or third-party purchaser) obtained a stepped-up, fair market value basis under other provisions of the Code, with associated additional depreciation, depletion, or amortization deductions. Accordingly, the "price" of a step up in the basis of property subject to the *General Utilities* rule was typically a single capital gains tax paid by the shareholder on receipt of a liquidating distribution from the corporation. * * *

Genesis of the General Utilities rule The precise meaning of *General Utilities* was a matter of considerable debate in the years following the 1935 decision. The essential facts were as follows. General Utilities had purchased 50 percent of the stock of Islands Edison Co. in 1927 for $2,000. In 1928, a prospective buyer offered to buy all of General Utilities' shares in Islands Edison, which apparently had a fair market value at that time of more than $1 million. Seeking to avoid the large corporate-level tax that would be imposed if it sold the stock itself, General Utilities offered to distribute the Islands Edison stock to its shareholders with the understanding that they would then sell the stock to the buyer. The company's officers and the buyer negotiated the terms of the sale but did not sign a contract. The shareholders of General Utilities had no binding commitment upon receipt of the Islands Edison shares to sell them to the buyer on these terms.

General Utilities declared a dividend in an amount equal to the value of the Islands Edison stock, payable in shares of that stock. The corporation distributed the Islands Edison shares and, four days later, the shareholders sold the shares to the buyer on the terms previously negotiated by the company's officers.

The Internal Revenue Service took the position that the distribution of the Islands Edison shares was a taxable transaction to General Utilities. Before the Supreme Court, the Commissioner argued that the company had created an indebtedness to its shareholders in declaring a dividend, and that the discharge of this indebtedness using appreciated property produced taxable income to the company under the holding in *Kirby Lumber Co. v. United States.* Alternatively, he argued, the sale of the Islands Edison stock was in reality made by General Utilities rather than by its shareholders following distribution of the stock. Finally, the Commissioner contended that a distribution of appreciated property by a corporation in and of itself constitutes a realization event. All dividends are distributed in satisfaction of the corporation's general obligation to pay out earnings to shareholders, he argued, and the satisfaction of that obligation with appreciated property causes a realization of the gain.

The Supreme Court held that the distribution did not give rise to taxable income under a discharge of indebtedness rationale. The Court did not directly address the Commissioner's third argument, that the company realized income simply by distributing appreciated property as a dividend. There is disagreement over whether the Court rejected this argument on substantive grounds or merely on the ground it was not timely made. Despite the ambiguity of the Supreme Court's decision, however, subsequent cases interpreted the decision as rejecting the Commissioner's third argument and as holding that no gain is realized on corporate distributions of appreciated property to its shareholders. * * *

Nonliquidating distributions: § 311 Congress subsequently enacted a number of statutory exceptions to the *General Utilities* rule. Under prior law (as under present law), the presumption under *General Utilities* was reversed for nonliquidating distributions: the general rule was that a corporation recognized gain (but not loss) on a distribution of property as a dividend or in redemption of stock. The distributing corporation is treated as if it sold the property for its fair market value on the date of the distribution. A number of exceptions to the general rule were provided. [These exceptions to recognition applied to distributions of appreciated property in the following circumstances:

(1) Distributions to long term noncorporate shareholders who owned at least 10% of the stock;

(2) Distributions of the assets of a trade or business that had been conducted by the corporation for at least five years;

(3) Distributions of the stock of certain subsidiaries; and

(4) Certain distributions to pay death taxes.] * * *

Section 311 also provided under separate rules that a corporation recognized gain on the distribution of encumbered property to the extent the liabilities assumed or to which the property was subject exceeded the distributing corporation's adjusted basis; on the distribution of LIFO inventory, to the extent the basis of the inventory determined under a FIFO method exceeded its LIFO value; and on the distribution of an installment obligation, to the extent of the excess of the face value of the obligation over the distributing corporation's adjusted basis in the obligation. * * *

Reasons For Change. *In general* Congress believed that the *General Utilities* rule, even in its more limited form, produced many incongruities and inequities in the tax system. First, the rule could create significant distortions in business behavior. * * *

Second, the *General Utilities* rule tended to undermine the corporate income tax. Under normally applicable tax principles, nonrecognition of gain is available only if the transferee takes a carryover basis in the transferred property, thus assuring that a tax will eventually be collected on the appreciation. Where the *General Utilities* rule applied, assets generally were permitted to leave corporate solution and to take a stepped-up basis in the hands of the transferee without the imposition of a corporate-level tax.[6] Thus, the effect of the rule was to grant a permanent exemption from the corporate income tax. * * *

Conforming changes to provisions relating to nonliquidating distributions The tax treatment of corporations with respect to nonliquidating distributions of appreciated property historically has been the same as liquidating distributions. In recent years, however, nonliquidating distributions have been subjected to stricter rules than liquidating distributions, and corporations have generally been required to recognize

---

6. The price of this basis step up was, at most, a single, shareholder-level capital gains tax (and perhaps recapture, tax benefit, and other similar amounts). In some cases, moreover, payment of the capital gains tax was deferred because the shareholder's gain was reported under the installment method.

gain as a result of nonliquidating distributions of appreciated property. Consistent with this relationship, the Act generally conforms the treatment of nonliquidating distributions with liquidating distributions. * * *

Explanation of Provisions *Overview* The Act provides that gain or loss generally is recognized by a corporation on liquidating distributions of its property as if the property had been sold at fair market value to the distributee. [*See* § 336.] * * *

The Act also makes certain conforming changes in the provisions relating to nonliquidating distributions of property to shareholders. * * *

Nonliquidating distributions [See §§ 311(a) and (b).] The Act makes certain conforming changes to the provisions relating to nonliquidating distributions of property. For purposes of determining the amount realized on a distribution of property, the fair market value of the property is treated as being no less than the amount of any liability to which it is subject or which is assumed by the shareholder under the principles applicable to liquidating distributions. The prior-law exceptions to recognition that were provided for nonliquidating distributions to ten percent, long-term noncorporate shareholders, and for certain distributions of property in connection with the payment of estate taxes or in connection with certain redemptions of private foundation stock, are repealed. As under prior law, no loss is recognized to a distributing corporation on a nonliquidating distribution of property to its shareholders. * * *

5. Further Elaboration on the Current § 311 Distribution Rule

Section 311(a), which reflects the *General Utilities* doctrine provides that "[e]xcept as provided in subsection (b), no gain or loss [is] recognized to a corporation on the distribution (not in complete liquidation) with respect to its stock, of: (1) its stock (or rights to acquire its stock), or (2) property." In the case of a distribution of appreciated property, but not of loss property, § 311(b)(1) overpowers this general nonrecognition rule by providing that "[i]f: (A) a corporation distributes property (other than an obligation of such corporation) to a shareholder in a distribution to which subpart A applies [the current distribution provisions], and (B) the fair market value of such property exceeds its adjusted basis (in the hands of the distributing corporation), then gain [is] recognized to the distributing corporation as if such property were sold by the distributee at its fair market value."

The gain recognition rule of § 311(b) applies only to distributions to which subpart A applies. Subpart A contains §§ 301 through 307, which deal with the treatment of current distributions of property, redemption transactions, and stock dividends. Therefore, the gain recognition rule does not apply to distributions of stock and securities pursuant to reorganizations, which are governed by §§ 354 through 368.

Under § 311(b)(2), rules similar to the rules of § 336(b) apply for the purposes of determining the effect of a distribution of property, which is subject to a liability. Under § 336(b), the fair market value of property distributed in a liquidating distribution is not treated as less than the amount of the distributed liability. Thus, if a corporation distributes property encumbered by a liability in excess of the basis of the property, gain is recognized in the amount of the excess even though the fair market value of the property is less than the amount of the liability. This is a codification of the principle in the *Tufts* case. *See* Sec. 1.5.C.2.

C. Impact on Computation of Corporation's Earnings and Profits of Distribution of Appreciated Property

In the case of a distribution of property other than cash or debt instruments of the corporation, § 312(a) provides that the earnings and profits to the extent thereof are reduced by the adjusted basis of property. On the other hand, the amount of the distribution to the shareholder under § 301(b) is the fair market value of the property.

This potential difference in treatment at the corporate and shareholder levels of the same distribution of appreciated property is addressed in § 312(b). First, under § 312(b)(1), earnings and profits are increased by the excess of the fair market value over the adjusted basis, thus, taking account of the gain that is realized by the corporation under § 311(b). This increase in earnings and profits is, however, reduced under general principles by the corporate tax liability generated by the distribution.

Second, under § 312(b)(2), the earnings and profits (after the net increase from the gain and the associated tax liability) are reduced under § 312(a)(3) by the fair market value of the property rather than by the adjusted basis.

If a corporation distributes property with an adjusted basis in excess of fair market value, then under § 311(a) no loss is recognized, and under § 312(a), the earnings and profits are reduced by the adjusted basis of the property.

If the property distributed is subject to a liability or the shareholder assumes a liability of the corporation, then under § 312(c) "proper adjustments" are to be made in computing earnings and profits. Under § 1.312-3, the decrease in earnings and profits is reduced by the amount of any such liability.

§ 2.6 Corporation's Distribution of Cash and Property to Corporate Shareholders

The basic rules under §§ 301, 316(a), 311 and 312(a) discussed above in connection with individual shareholders also apply to dividends paid to corporate shareholders. As a consequence, dividends paid to a corporate shareholder can produce more than two levels of tax. For example, if IBM pays a dividend to GM and GM pays the amount to its shareholders, there are three levels of tax: first at the IBM level, second, at the GM level, and third at the GM shareholder level. To help mitigate the effect of these potential multiple levels of tax, corporations are given a dividends received deduction for certain dividends from domestic corporations. The dividends received deduction does not apply to dividends received from a foreign corporation from foreign source income.

Under § 243(a), a corporate shareholder that owns less than 20% of the stock of a domestic distributing corporation is allowed a deduction in an amount equal to 70% of the amount of the dividends received. This is referred to as the 70% deduction for portfolio dividends. Under § 243(c), a corporate shareholder that owns at least 20% but less than 80% of the stock of a domestic distributing corporation is allowed an 80% dividends received deduction. And, for corporations holding at least 80% of the stock of a domestic corporation a 100% deduction applies if the corporations are members of a group filing consolidated returns, which would normally be the case. To qualify as a consolidated group, the parent distributee corporation generally must own at least 80% of the stock of the distributing subsidiary and an election to file consolidated returns must be made. *See* Sec. 5.5.A.3.

§ 2.7 Redemptions of Stock by Corporations: Impact of §§ 302 and 318[7]

A. Introduction

This section briefly addresses redemptions by a corporation of its stock from its shareholders. The purpose is merely to introduce these very complex provisions. As will be seen in Chapter 6, these rules apply in determining if boot paid in a reorganization is treated as a dividend or capital gain under § 356. As indicated, the impact of these provisions has been significantly reduced as a result of the adoption of the 20% maximum uniform rate for both dividends and capital gains.

Redemptions are governed by § 302, which determines whether the distribution is treated as a distribution under § 301 or a capital gain transaction under § 302(a). In defining the scope of redemption transactions, § 317(b) says "stock shall be treated as redeemed by a corporation if the corporation acquires its stock from a shareholder in exchange for property, whether or not the stock so acquired is cancelled, retired, or held as treasury stock." Thus, stock redemptions are transactions in which a corporation purchases its outstanding stock in exchange for cash or property.

Under § 302(a), a redemption of stock is treated as a sale or exchange only if the redemption satisfies one of the four tests set forth in § 302(b): (1) the not equivalent to a dividend test of § 302(b)(1); (2) the substantially disproportionate test of § 302(b)(2); (3) the termination of interest test of § 302(b)(3); or (4) the partial liquidation test of §§ 302(b)(4) and (e). These tests are briefly examined below.

Section 302(d) provides that a redemption that is not treated as a sale or exchange under § 302(a) is "treated as a distribution of property to which § 301 applies." Thus, a redemption that is treated under § 301 is subject to the four levels of treatment discussed above.

---

7. This section is based on a modification of Secs. 11.01 and 11.02 of *Federal Taxation of Business Enterprises, supra* note 1.

A redemption that does not alter the redeemed shareholder's control of the corporation is functionally equivalent to a dividend. For instance, if a sole shareholder has 50 percent of her stock redeemed, the shareholder remains the sole shareholder after the transaction. Consequently, the redemption is economically similar to a dividend. Such a transaction fails to satisfy the requirements of any of the paragraphs in § 302(b) and, therefore, is treated under § 302(d) as a distribution under § 301.

As indicated, § 302(b) covers four types of redemptions. First, § 302(b)(3) treats a redemption that terminates the stock interest of a shareholder as a sale or exchange of the stock. Thus, if a shareholder has all of her shares redeemed, the shareholder has capital gains under § 302(a). However, the determination of whether all of a shareholder's shares are redeemed can become a difficult question, because under constructive ownership rules of § 318, which is discussed below, a shareholder may be deemed to own shares held by certain related parties.

Second, § 302(b)(2) treats as a sale or exchange a redemption after which a shareholder's direct and constructive ownership of the outstanding voting stock is less than 80 percent of her ownership before the redemption. Also, the shareholder must own less than 50 percent of the stock after the redemption. This is known as the "substantially disproportionate" redemption test. Thus, if after the redemption, the shareholder's direct and indirect ownership of shares drops by more than 20% and the shareholder owns less than 50% of the shares, the shareholder has capital gain.

Third, § 302(b)(1) provides that any redemption that is "not essentially equivalent to a dividend" is given sale or exchange treatment. This is a general test as contrasted with the specific tests of §§ 302(b)(3) and (b)(2). In interpreting this test the Supreme Court in *United States v. Davis,* 397 U.S. 301 (1970), held that for § 302(b)(1) to apply, a redemption must result in a "meaningful reduction" of the shareholder's direct and indirect interest in the corporation. In interpreting this meaningful reduction test, the Service has ruled, for example, that a percentage drop from 27% to 22% satisfies the test (*see* Rev. Rul. 76-364, 1976-2 C.B. 91), but a drop from 90% to 60% does not (*see* Rev. Rul. 81-289, 1981-2 C.B. 82).

Fourth, under § 302(b)(4), any redemption of stock of a noncorporate shareholder in a partial liquidation, as defined in § 302(e), of the distributing corporation is given sale or exchange treatment. A partial liquidation includes, for example, certain distributions of an active trade or business.

Redemptions of the stock of closely held corporations present many possibilities for tax avoidance. For instance, shareholder *A* could transfer 50 percent of the stock of one wholly owned corporation *X* to a second wholly owned corporation *Y* and then cause *X* to redeem his remaining 50 percent interest. The redemption on its face would satisfy the termination of interest test of § 302(b)(3). *A* would have received sale or exchange treatment rather than a dividend, although he continued to control, through his exclusive ownership of *Y*, all of the stock of *X*.

The attribution rules of § 318, which, by reason of § 302(c), apply for purposes of § 302, prevent these types of avoidance schemes. Section 318 attributes to certain persons the ownership of stock owned by certain related parties. If, under § 318, a person is the constructive owner of stock held by a related person, the constructively owned stock is taken into consideration in determining if a redemption satisfies any of the tests in § 302(b). *See* § 302(c)(1) and § 1.302-1(a).

In the above hypothetical situation, *A* is treated under § 318(a)(2)(C) as the constructive owner of the *X* stock he transferred to *Y*. Consequently, the redemption of his 50 percent direct stock interest in *X* constitutes a dividend to him because he owns 100 percent of *X* both before and after the redemption.

Subject to certain limitations, § 318 attributes stock ownership (1) from one family member to another, *i.e.*, the family attribution rules, (*see* § 318(a)(1)); (2) from partnerships, corporations, estates and trusts, to the partners, shareholders and beneficiaries, *i.e.*, the attribution-out rules, (*see* § 318(a)(2)); and (3) from partners, shareholders and beneficiaries, to partnerships, corporations, estates and trusts, *i.e.*, the attribution-in rules. *See* § 318(a)(3). The operational rules, set out in § 318(a)(5), provide for multiple attribution in certain cases. Section 318(a)(4) provides that the holder of an option to acquire stock is deemed to own the underlying stock. The rules in § 318 must be studied closely.

Section 318 applies only to those provisions of the Code to which it is expressly made applicable. Section 302(c)(1) provides: "Except as provided in paragraph (2) of this subsection, section 318(a) shall apply in determining the ownership of stock for purposes of this section." Section 302(c)(2) provides an exception to the family attribution rules of § 318(a)(1) (but not to the entity attribution rules of §§ 318(a)(2) and (3)) for determining whether a redemption is a termination of interest under § 302(b)(3). Thus, the family attribution rules can be waived in certain circumstances for purposes of determining if a redemption is treated as a termination of interest under § 302(b)(3). For example, if a father's shares of a corporation are being redeemed in a situation where his son owns the balance of the shares, the father can under certain circumstances waive the attribution rules and receive termination of interest treatment under § 302(b)(3).

Although a stock redemption must fall under one of the paragraphs of § 302(b) to be treated as a sale or exchange, § 302 does not apply to the redemption of debt instruments. Under § 1271(a), redemptions of corporate debt receive sale or exchange treatment.

At the corporate level, a redemption reduces a proportionate amount of E&P, and if a corporation distributes appreciated property in a redemption transaction, the corporation has taxable gain under § 311(b). In general, no deduction is allowed for redemption payments. *See* § 162(k).

B. Illustration of Impact of § 302(b)(1)

Revenue Ruling 76-364

1976-2 C.B. 91

Corporation *X* had outstanding one class of stock consisting of 200,000 shares of common stock each of which was entitled to one vote. *A*, an individual, owned 54,000 shares of *X* common stock (27 percent), each of which was entitled to one vote. Because *A* was retired from business, *A* took no active part in the management of *X*. The remaining 146,000 shares of outstanding *X* common stock (73 percent) were held in equal portions by individuals *B, C,* and *D.* None of the *X* shareholders were related within the meaning of section 318(a)(1) of the Code.

X redeemed for cash 12,160 shares of its stock held by *A.* After the redemption, *A* owned 41,840 shares of the outstanding stock of *X* which represented 22.27 percent of the 187,840 shares then outstanding. The redemption reduced *A's* percentage of ownership and voting rights in *X* from 27 percent to 22.27 percent. This reduction in *A's* percentage ownership in *X* failed to meet the percentage requirement of section 302(b)(2)(C) of the Code. * * *

Rev.Rul. 75-502, 1975-2 C.B. 111, indicates factors to be considered in determining whether a reduction in a shareholder's proportionate interest in a corporation results in a meaningful reduction within the meaning of *Davis.* The factors considered relate to a shareholder's right to vote and exercise control, a shareholder's right to participate in current earnings and accumulated surplus, and a shareholder's right to share in net assets on liquidation.

In the instant case, the fact that *A* failed to meet the requirements of section 302(b)(2) of the Code is not to be taken into consideration in determining whether the redemption meets the requirements of section 302(b)(1) as provided in section 302(b)(5). In determining whether the redemption meets the requirements of section 302(b)(1), it is significant that the redemption, in reducing *A's* interest from 27 percent to 22.27 percent, correspondingly reduced *A's* right to vote, *A's* right to earnings, and *A's* right to share in net assets on liquidation. Moreover, the reduction of *A's* voting rights from 27 percent to 22.27 percent is meaningful in itself in that it caused *A* to go from a position of holding a block of *X* stock that afforded *A* control of *X* if *A* acted in concert with only one other stockholder, to a position where such action was not possible. Thus, under the facts and circumstances of the instant case, the reduction constitutes a meaningful reduction of *A's* interest in *X* within the meaning of *Davis.*

Accordingly, the redemption was not essentially equivalent to a dividend within the meaning of section 302(b)(1) of the Code and, therefore, qualified as an exchange under section 302(a).

C. Illustration: Purchase of Stock Followed by Redemption

Zenz v. Quinlivan

United States Court of Appeals, Sixth Circuit, 1954
213 F.2d 914

GOURLEY, DISTRICT JUDGE.

The appeal relates to the interpretation of Section 115(g) [now § 302(b)] of the Internal Revenue Code and poses the question — Is a distribution of substantially all of the accumulated earnings and surplus of a corporation, which are not necessary to the conduct of the business of the corporation, in redemption of all outstanding shares of stock of said corporation owned by one person *essentially equivalent to the distribution of a taxable dividend under the Internal Revenue Code?*

The District Court answered in the affirmative and sustained a deficiency assessment by the Commissioner of Internal Revenue.

After consideration of the records, briefs and arguments of counsel for the parties, we believe the judgment should be reversed.

* * * Whether a distribution in connection with a cancellation or redemption of stock is essentially equivalent to the distribution of a taxable dividend depends upon the facts and circumstances of each case.

The question stems from the following circumstances:

Appellant is the widow of the person who was the motivating spirit behind the closed corporation which engaged in the business of excavating and laying of sewers. Through death of her husband she became the owner of all shares of stock issued by the corporation. She operated the business until remarriage, when her second husband assumed the management. As a result of a marital rift, separation, and final divorce, taxpayer sought to dispose of her company to a competitor who was anxious to eliminate competition.

Prospective buyer did not want to assume the tax liabilities which it was believed were inherent in the accumulated earnings and profits of the corporation. To avoid said profits and earnings as a source of future taxable dividends, buyer purchased part of taxpayer's stock for cash. Three weeks later, after corporate reorganization and corporate action, the corporation redeemed the balance of taxpayer's stock, purchasing the same as treasury stock which absorbed substantially all of the accumulated earnings and surplus of the corporation.

Taxpayer, in her tax return, invoked [the predecessor of § 302(b)(3)] as constituting a cancellation or redemption by a corporation of all the stock of a particular shareholder, and therefore was not subject to being treated as a distribution of a taxable dividend.

The District Court sustained the deficiency assessment of the Commissioner that the amount received from accumulated earnings and profits was ordinary income since the stock redeemed by the corporation was "at such time and in such manner as to make the redemption thereof essentially equivalent to the distribution of a taxable dividend" under [the predecessor of § 302(b)(1)].

The District Court's findings were premised upon the view that taxpayer employed a circuitous approach in an attempt to avoid the tax consequences which would have attended the outright distribution of the surplus to the taxpayer by the declaration of a taxable dividend.

The rationale of the District Court is dedicated to piercing the external manifestations of the taxpayer's transactions in order to establish a subterfuge or sham.

Nevertheless, the general principle is well settled that a taxpayer has the legal right to decrease the amount of what otherwise would be his taxes or altogether avoid them, by means which the law permits. *Gregory v. Helvering.* [Sec. 2.11.B.] * * * The taxpayer's motive to avoid taxation will not establish liability if the transaction does not do so without it. * * *

The question accordingly presented is not whether the overall transaction, admittedly carried out for the purpose of avoiding taxes, actually avoided taxes which would have been incurred if the transaction had taken a different form, but whether the sale constituted a taxable dividend or the sale of a capital asset. *Chamberlain v. Commissioner of Internal Revenue,* supra.

It is a salutary fact that Section 115(c) [now § 302(b)(3)] is an exception to Section 115(a) [now § 301] that all distributions of earning and profits are taxable as a dividend.

The basic precept underlying the capital gains theory of taxation as distinguished from ordinary income tax is the concept that a person who has developed an enterprise in which earnings have been accumulated over a period of years should not be required to expend the ordinary income tax rate in the one year when he withdraws from his enterprise and realizes his gain.

Common logic dictates that a fair basis of measuring income is not determined upon the profits on hand in the year of liquidation but is properly attributable to each year in which the profits were gained.

We cannot concur with the legal proposition enunciated by the District Court that a corporate distribution can be essentially equivalent to a taxable dividend even though that distribution extinguishes the shareholder's interest in the corporation. To the contrary, we are satisfied that where the taxpayer effects a redemption which completely extinguishes the taxpayer's interest in the corporation, and does not retain any beneficial interest whatever, that such transaction is not the equivalent of the distribution of a taxable dividend as to him. * * *

Since the intent of the taxpayer was to bring about a complete liquidation of her holdings and to become separated from all interest in the corporation, the conclusion is inevitable that the distribution of the earnings and profits by the corporation in payment for said stock was not made at such time and in such manner as to make the distribution and cancellation or redemption thereof essentially equivalent to the distribution of a taxable dividend. * * *

§ 2.8 Redemptions through Related Corporations: Legislative History of § 304

A. Introduction

Section 304 deals with, for example, the purchase by a brother corporation of the stock of its sister corporation from the common controlling shareholder of both corporations. These are known as brother-sister transactions and are subject to the rules of § 304(a)(1). Section 304 also deals with the purchase by a sub of the stock of its parent corporation from the controlling shareholder of the parent. These are referred to as parent-sub transactions and are subject to the rules of § 304(a)(2).

In focusing on the operation of this provision, it is important to keep one's eye on the purpose of this section, which is to prevent the bail out of earnings at capital gains rates in sales of stock of one controlled corporation to another controlled corporation. As we will see, § 304 treats these nominal sales of stock as redemptions that are required to be tested under § 302 to see if the transaction receives capital gain treatment under § 302(a) or distribution treatment under §§ 302(d) and 301. As a result of the 20% maximum rate that now applies to dividends and capital gains, the impact of § 304 has been significantly diminished. As will be seen in Sec. 5.2.B., relating to taxable stock acquisitions, § 304 may apply in what would otherwise be a straight purchase of stock. The following materials provide an introduction to the basic principles in § 304.

B. A Look at § 304 through the Legislative History

THIS SECTION CONTAINS EXCERPTS FROM THE FOLLOWING
COMMITTEE REPORTS: SENATE FINANCE COMMITTEE REPORT TO
THE 1954 CODE; HOUSE CONFERENCE REPORT TO THE TAX EQUITY
AND FISCAL RESPONSIBILITY ACT OF 1982 (TEFRA); HOUSE WAYS AND
MEANS COMMITTEE REPORT TO THE DEFICIT REDUCTION TAX ACT
OF 1984 (DEFRA); HOUSE CONFERENCE REPORT ON THE REVENUE
ACT OF 1987 (1987 ACT), AND CONFERENCE REPORT TO
THE TAXPAYER RELIEF ACT OF 1997 (1997 ACT).

[*General Rule*] * * * The effect of the operation of § 304 is to characterize as redemptions distributions which are cast in the form of sales. The distributions in redemption shall be examined for taxability subject to the rules of § 302 (relating to distributions in redemption of stock). * * *

[*Brother-Sister Redemptions.*] [Section 304(a)(1)] sets forth the new general rule added by this section by providing * * * that in any case in which 1 or more persons who are in control of each of 2 corporations (brother-sister corporations) sell the stock of one of the corporations to another of such corporations the proceeds of such sale shall be considered to be an amount distributed in redemption of the stock of the corporation which purchased the stock. [As explained below in the discussion of the 1997 Act, to the extent the distribution is treated as a § 301 distribution, "the transferor and the acquiring corporation shall be treated in the same manner as if the transferor had transferred the stock so acquired to the acquiring corporation in exchange for stock of the acquiring corporation in a transaction to which § 351 applies, and then the acquiring corporation had redeemed the stock it was treated as issuing in such transaction." *See* § 304(a)(1).]

[This rule can be illustrated as follows. Individual *A*, who owns all the stock of corporations *X* and *Y*, sells 25% of his stock in *X* to *Y* for $100K. The transaction is described in §304(a)(1) and is treated as a redemption of Y's stock. As set forth below, since A is in control of both corporations and has sold stock in one to the other, A is treated as receiving a distribution under §301 because the transaction does not fall within §§302(b)(1), (2), (3), or (4). Thus, the bailout of earnings as capital gains by a sale of stock to a controlled entity is avoided. Since the transaction is treated as a distribution under §301, A is treated as contributing the X stock to Y in a §351 transaction, and Y is treated as issuing its stock to A in the §351 transaction and then immediately redeeming such stock. Under §358, A adds the basis of is contributed shares to his retained shares, and under §362, Y takes A's basis for the X shares acquired.]

[*Parent-Subsidiary Redemptions.*] The general rule of present law, preserved in the parent-subsidiary area, is set forth in [§304(a)(2).] Under this rule, * * * if a subsidiary corporation purchases outstanding stock of its parent the proceeds of such sale shall be considered to be [a distribution in redemption of the parent's stock].

[This rule can be illustrated as follows. Individual A owns all of the stock of corporation P, which owns all of the stock of corporation S. A sells to S 25% of his P stock for $100K. The transaction is described in §304(a)(2) and is treated as a redemption of P's stock. As set forth below, A is treated as receiving a distribution under §301 because the deemed redemption does not fall within §§302(b)(1), (2), (3), or (4). Thus, the bailout of earning as capital gains is avoided.]

[*Application of §302.*] [Section 304(b)] contains special rules for the purpose of applying §302(b) (relating to redemptions of stock treated as exchanges). In the case of any acquisition of stock to which §304(a) applies, determinations as to whether the acquisition is, by virtue of §302(b), to be treated as a distribution in part or full payment in exchange for such stock because such redemption is: (1) not equivalent to a dividend, (2) substantially disproportionate, (3) in complete termination of an interest, [or (4) in partial liquidation] shall be made by reference to the stock of the corporation issuing the stock purchased. [Thus, in an acquisition by a sister corporation of the stock of a brother corporation under §304(a)(1), the §302(b) determination is made with reference to the stock of the brother corporation that is sold. In the acquisition by a subsidiary of stock of a parent, the §302(b) determination is made by reference to the stock of the parent.] In applying §318(a) (relating to constructive ownership of stock) with respect to §302(b) for purposes of this paragraph, §318(a)(2)(C) [and §318(a)(3)(C)] shall be applied without regard to the 50 percent limitation contained therein.

[*Determination of E & P.*] DEFRA provides that [under §304(b)(2)] the amount which is a dividend shall be determined as if the property were distributed by the acquiring corporation to the extent of its earnings and profits and then by the corporation whose stock is acquired (the issuing corporation). The transaction would have no effect on the issuing corporation if earnings and profits of the acquiring corporation equal or exceed the amount treated as a distribution in the hands of the shareholders. If the distribution is in excess of the acquiring corporation's earnings and profits, the amount treated as distributed by the issuing corporation will not exceed the earnings and profits of such corporation.

[*Determination of Control.*] [Section 304(c)] provides that control, for purposes of this section, means the ownership of stock possessing at least 50 percent of the total combined voting power of all classes of stock entitled to vote, or at least 50 percent of the total value of shares of all classes of stock. It is possible under this definition for 4 unrelated shareholders to be in control of a corporation, *i.e.,* 2 shareholders may own 50 percent of the total combined voting power and 2 shareholders own 50 percent of the total value of the shares. [*See* § 304(c)(1).] * * *

[Section 304(c)(3)] provides that the rules of section 318(a) (relating to constructive ownership of stock) shall be applicable for purposes of determining control under [§ 304(c)(1)]. For purposes of the preceding sentence § 318(a)(2)(C) [and § 318(a)(3)(C)] shall be applied without regard to the 50 percent limitation contained therein.

[However, § 304(c)(3)(B), which was amended by DEFRA,] provides a *de minimis* rule [under which] constructive ownership [does] not apply to and from a corporation and a shareholder owning less than 5 percent in value of the stock of the corporation, for purposes of determining whether or not control exists under § 304. * * *

[*Section 351/304 Overlap*] The conference agreement [to TEFRA] extends the anti-bailout rules of § 304 * * * of present law to the use of corporations, including holding companies, formed or availed of to avoid such rules. Such rules are made applicable to a transaction that, under present law, otherwise qualifies as a tax-free incorporation under § 351.

[Under § 304(b)(3),] section 351 generally will not apply to transactions described in § 304. Thus, § 351, if otherwise applicable, will generally apply only to the extent such transaction consists of an exchange of stock for stock in the acquiring corporation. [*See* § 304(b)(3)(A).]

[This provision can be illustrated as follows. Individual *A* owns all of the stock of corporation *X*. The *X* stock has a fair market value of $100K, and *A*'s adjusted basis for the stock is $10K. *A* transfers all of the stock of *X* to newly formed corporation *Y* in exchange for all of *Y*'s stock, which has a value of $75K, plus $25K of cash. In the absence of § 304(b)(3), this transaction would qualify under § 351; *A* would have a $25K capital gain under § 351(b); the $65K balance of *A*'s gain would be nonrecognized under § 351(a); *A*'s basis for his *Y* shares would be $10K under § 358; and *Y*'s basis for the *X* shares would be $35K under § 362(a). As a result of § 304(b)(3)(A), the receipt by *A* of the $25K cash is treated as a distribution governed by the brother-sister rules of § 304(a)(1), and therefore, *A* has a distribution under § 302(d). The distribution is a dividend to the extent of the earning and profits of *Y* and *X*. *See* § 304(b)(2). Otherwise the results are the same.] * * *

§ 2.9 General Description of the Stock Dividend Provisions[8]

A. Introduction

1. Section 305

A corporation may pay to its shareholders a dividend in its stock, such as a common stock dividend paid on common stock or a preferred stock dividend paid on common stock. The treatment of these transactions is governed by §§ 305, 306, and 307. These provisions are in Part I of subchapter C, dealing with the taxation of distributions by corporations.

Section 305(a) sets out the general rule that stock dividends are not included in gross income of the distributee shareholder except as otherwise provided in that section. The general rule of § 305(a) codifies the principles of *Eisner v. Macomber*, 40 S.Ct. 189, 252 U.S. 189, 64 L.Ed. 521 (1920), which held that a common stock dividend on common stock where the common was the only class outstanding could not be taxed under the 16th Amendment. The key to the holding in *Eisner v. Macomber* is that there was no change in the shareholders' proportionate interest in the corporation as a result of the common stock dividend on common stock.

Sections 305(b) and (c) set forth certain exceptions to the general rule of nontaxability in § 305(a). Stock dividends covered by §§ 305(b) and (c) are treated as regular distributions under § 301. Under § 305(c), a redemption premium on preferred stock may be included in income over the term of the preferred similar to the treatment of OID on debt instruments, which is addressed in Chapter 1.

Section 305(b) sets forth five exceptions to the general rule of nontaxability in § 305(a), and in each of these exceptions there is a change in the shareholders' proportionate interest as a result of the distribution:

(1) Distributions which, at the election of the taxpayer-shareholder, are payable either in stock or property (*see* § 305(b)(1));

(2) Distributions having the result of the receipt of property by some shareholders and an increase in the proportionate interest of other shareholders in the corporation's assets or earnings (*see* § 305(b)(2));

(3) Distributions having the result of the receipt of preferred stock by some common stock shareholders and the receipt of common stock by other common stock shareholders (*see* § 305(b)(3));

(4) Distributions on preferred stock other than increases in a conversion ratio to avoid dilution (*see* § 305(b)(4)); and

(5) Distributions of convertible preferred unless it is established that such distribution will not have the effect of a receipt of property by some shareholders

---

8. This section is based on a modification of Secs. 10.01 and 10.02 of *Federal Taxation of Business Enterprises, supra* note 1.

and an increase in the proportionate interest of other shareholders (*see* § 305(b)(5)).

In each of the above distributions, the stock dividend or the increase in proportionate interest is treated as a § 301 distribution. As will be seen in Sec. 6.17, issues under § 305 may arise in reorganization transactions.

Two types of stock dividends are not covered by § 305(b): common stock dividends on common stock and preferred stock dividends on common stock. Thus, these two dividends are tax free under § 305(a); however, preferred stock dividends on common stock are subject to § 306, which is aimed at the abuse known as a preferred stock bail out.

2. Section 306

In its simplest form, the preferred stock bail out can occur, absent § 306, by the shareholders causing a corporation to declare a preferred stock dividend on its outstanding common stock. The preferred is treated as nontaxable under § 305(a) since it is distributed on common. After receipt of the preferred dividend, the stockholders sell it to a third party, possibly an insurance company, claiming a capital gain on the sale. The corporation then exercises a redemption right and redeems the preferred. The end result is that the shareholders get money out of the corporation in the form of capital gains on the sale of the stock, rather than as ordinary dividends. If the preferred had been redeemed directly from the shareholders, they probably would have had a dividend under § 302(d), but a redemption from the purchasing shareholder is treated as a sale or exchange under § 302(a). *Compare Chamberlin v. Commissioner,* 207 F.2d 462 (6th Cir.1953), *cert. denied* 347 U.S. 918, 74 S.Ct. 516, 98 L.Ed. 1073 (1954), with *Rosenberg v. Commissioner,* 36 T.C. 716 (1961).

Both cases, decided under the law prior to § 306, involved a preferred stock dividend followed by sale and redemption. In *Chamberlin* the Sixth Circuit, reversing the Tax Court, held that (1) the transaction was not taxable under the proportionate interest test then applicable to stock dividends, and (2) since the redemption feature was reasonable, the transaction would be taxed in accordance with its form. On the other hand, in *Rosenberg,* the Tax Court held that the shareholders had a dividend because under *Court Holding* principles the sale was made pursuant to a prearranged plan the "net effect [of which] was the realization of a dividend by the shareholders. * * *"

Under § 306, the type of preferred stock dividend in *Chamberland and Rosenberg* is treated as "section 306 stock" under § 306(c)(1)(A), and under § 306(a), the recipient of such a section 306 stock is, in general, taxed at dividend rates on the disposition of such stock, to the extent the recipient would have had a dividend if cash had been distributed in place of the preferred. Obviously, this provision has much less significance as a result of enactment of the maximum 20% rate for dividends and capital gains.

The Senate Report to the 1954 Code gives the following explanation of the definition of section 306 stock in § 306(c):

Section 306(c) sets forth the definition of section 306 stock. [Section 306(c)(1)(A)] provides that section 306 is any stock (other than common stock issued with respect to common stock) distributed to the seller thereof, if by reason of § 305(a) any part of such distribution was not includible in the gross income of the shareholder. Thus, a stock dividend (other than a dividend in common stock issued with respect to common stock) is considered section 306 stock * * *

[Section 306(c)(1)(B)] provides that stock received in connection with a plan of reorganization within the meaning of § 368(a), or in a disposition or exchange to which § 355 applies, is section 306 stock, if the effect of the transaction was substantially the same as the receipt of a stock dividend. The subparagraph also makes it clear that section 306 stock exchanged for section 306 stock shall retain its characteristics. This subparagraph provides that common stock received as a result of a corporate reorganization or separation shall not be considered section 306 stock in any event. Thus, the shareholder is always permitted an opportunity to downgrade preferred stock characterized as section 306 stock in his hands by causing a recapitalization and exchange of such stock for common stock. [Section 306(c)(1)(B) is examined further in Sec. 6.18.B.]

[Section 306(c)(1)(C)] provides that section 306 stock includes stock the basis of which in the hands of the shareholder selling or otherwise disposing of such stock is determined by reference to the basis of section 306 stock. * * *

[Section 306(c)(2)] excepts from the definition of section 306 stock any stock no part of the distribution of which would have been a dividend at the time of distribution if money had been distributed in lieu of the stock. Thus, preferred stock received at the time of original incorporation would not be section 306 stock. Also, stock issued at the time an existing corporation had no earnings and profits would not be section 306 stock.

The Conference Report to the Tax Equity and Fiscal Responsibility Act of 1982 gives the following explanation of § 306(c)(3), which treats certain preferred stock received in a § 351 transaction as section 306 stock:

Another device to bail out earnings is to cause a corporation to issue preferred stock as a nontaxable stock dividend to its shareholders. A sale of the preferred stock at capital gain rates would not dilute the interests of the selling shareholders in future corporate growth while they would receive an amount representing corporate earnings. Preferred stock issued under these circumstances (described as section 306 stock) is tainted under present law so that its subsequent sale or redemption results in ordinary income to the shareholder. This provision does not taint stock of a newly formed corporation issued in a tax-free transaction in exchange for stock in a corporation with earnings and profits. Thus, creation of a holding company issuing both common and preferred stock offers the same bailout opportunity as a preferred stock dividend but does not result in tainted section 306 stock. * * *

Under the conference agreement, § 306 is made applicable to preferred stock acquired in a § 351 exchange if, had money in lieu of stock been received, its receipt would have been a dividend to any extent. [*See* § 306(c)(3).] Thus, if the receipt of cash by the shareholder rather than stock would have caused § 304 as amended by the bill, rather than § 351, to apply to such receipt, some or all of the amount received might have been treated as a dividend. [*See* § 304(b)(3).] In such case, the preferred stock acquired in the exchange will be section 306 stock.

It should be noted that section 306 stock does not arise on the transfer of property other than stock of a controlled corporation to a corporation in a § 351 transaction.

3. Section 307

Under § 307, a portion of the basis of stock on which a nontaxable stock dividend is paid is allocated to the dividend stock.

B. Illustrations of Impact of § 305(b)(2) on Redemption Transactions

1. Periodic Redemption Plan Gives Rise to Stock Dividend to Non-Redeemed Shareholders

Revenue Ruling 78-60

1978-1 C.B. 81

Advice has been requested whether under section 302(a) of the Internal Revenue Code of 1954 the stock redemptions described below qualified for exchange treatment and whether under section 305(b)(2) and (c) the shareholders who experienced increases in their proportionate interests in the redeeming corporation as a result of the stock redemptions will be treated as having received distributions of property to which section 301 applies.

Corporation Z has only one class of stock outstanding. The Z common stock is held by 24 shareholders, all of whom are descendants, or spouses of descendants, of the founder of Z.

In 1975, when Z had 6,000 shares of common stock outstanding, the board of directors of Z adopted a plan of annual redemption to provide a means for its shareholders to sell their stock. The plan provides that Z will annually redeem up to 40 shares of its outstanding stock at a price established annually by the Z board of directors. Each shareholder of Z is entitled to cause Z to redeem two-thirds of one percent of the shareholder's stock each year. If some shareholders choose not to participate fully in the plan during any year, the other shareholders can cause Z to redeem more than two-thirds of one percent of their stock, up to the maximum of 40 shares.

Pursuant to the plan of annual redemption, Z redeemed 40 shares of its stock in 1976. Eight shareholders participated in the redemptions. * * *

Issue 1 None of the redemptions here qualified under section 302(b)(3) of the Code because all of the shareholders who participated in the redemptions continue to own stock of *Z*. Moreover, none of the redemptions qualified under section 302(b)(2) because none of the shareholders who participated in the redemptions experienced a reduction in interest of more than 20 percent, as section 302(b)(2)(C) requires. Therefore, the first question is whether the redemptions were "not essentially equivalent to a dividend" within the meaning of section 302(b)(1). * * *

Several of the shareholders of *Z* experienced reductions in their proportionate interests in *Z* (taking into account constructive stock ownership under section 318 of the Code) as a result of the 1976 redemptions. If their reductions were "meaningful," they are entitled to exchange treatment for their redemptions under section 302(a). Whether the reductions in proportionate interests were "meaningful" depends on the facts and circumstances.

In this case, an important fact is that the 1976 redemptions were not isolated occurrences but were undertaken pursuant to an ongoing plan for *Z* to redeem 40 shares of its stock each year. None of the reductions in proportionate interests experienced by *Z* shareholders as a result of the 1976 redemptions was "meaningful" because the reductions were small and each shareholder has the power to recover the lost interest by electing not to participate in the redemption plan in later years.

Accordingly, none of the 1976 redemptions qualified for exchange treatment under section 302(a) of the Code. All of the redemptions are to be treated as distributions of property to which section 301 applies.

Issue 2 Section 1.305-7(a) of the Income Tax Regulations provides that a redemption treated as a section 301 distribution will generally be treated as a distribution to which sections 305(b)(2) and 301 of the Code apply if the proportionate interest of any shareholder in the earnings and profits or assets of the corporation deemed to have made the stock distribution is increased by the redemption, and the distribution has the result described in section 305(b)(2). The distribution is to be deemed made to any shareholder whose interest in the earnings and profits or assets of the distributing corporation is increased by the redemption.

Section 1.305-3(b)(3) of the regulations provides that for a distribution of property to meet the requirements of section 305(b)(2) of the Code, the distribution must be made to a shareholder in the capacity as a shareholder and must be a distribution to which section 301 [or one of several other specified sections] applies. A distribution of property incident to an isolated redemption will not cause section 305(b)(2) to apply even though the redemption distribution is treated as a section 301 distribution.

Section 305 of the Code does not make the constructive stock ownership rules of section 318(a) applicable to its provisions.

The 16 shareholders of *Z* who did not tender any stock for redemption in 1976 experienced increases in their proportionate interests of the earnings and profits and assets of *Z* (without taking into account constructive stock ownership under section 318 of the Code) as a result of the redemptions. * * * The 1976 redemptions were not isolated but were undertaken pursuant to an ongoing plan of annual stock redemptions. Finally, the 1976 redemptions are to be treated as distributions of property to which section 301 of the Code applies.

Accordingly, * * * the 16 shareholders of Z who did not participate in the 1976 redemptions are deemed to have received stock distributions to which sections 305(b)(2) and 301 of the Code apply. *See* examples (8) and (9) of section 1.305-3(c) of the regulations for a method of computing the amounts of the deemed distributions.

2. Isolated Redemptions from Retired-Shareholder Employees
Revenue Ruling 77-19
1977-1 C.B. 83

Advice has been requested whether under the circumstances described below, past redemptions and a current redemption by a corporation constitute a periodic redemption plan the effect of which is to increase the proportionate interests of certain shareholders within the meaning of section 305(b)(2) and (c) of the Internal Revenue Code of 1954.

Corporation X is a publicly held corporation with 450,000 shares of common stock outstanding. Its stock has been traded over-the-counter, but no active market for X stock currently exists.

Although no formal plan or resolution has been adopted calling for X to redeem shares of its stock, X, over the previous 36 months, has redeemed 20,000 shares of its common stock in 20 separate transactions. The redeeming shareholders have consisted principally of retiring employees of X or the estates of deceased shareholders. Eighteen of these transactions were distributions in redemption of stock within the meaning of section 302(a) of the Code. The remaining two were distributions to which section 301 applied. * * *

In the instant case, all of the redemptions that occurred in the past 36 months were principally from retiring employees of X or the estates of deceased shareholders. Also, the redemptions completely terminated the direct ownership of the redeemed shareholders. * * *

Accordingly, in the instant case the redemptions are not deemed, under section 305(c) of the Code, to result in distributions to which sections 305(b)(2) and 301 apply.

C. Impact of § 305 on Distribution of a Poison Pill
Revenue Ruling 90-11
1990-1 C.B. 10

Issue What are the federal income tax consequences, if any, of a corporation's adoption of a plan as described below, commonly referred to as a "poison pill" plan, which provides the corporation's shareholders with the right to purchase additional shares of stock upon the occurrence of certain events?

Facts X is a publicly held domestic corporation. X's board of directors adopted a plan (the "Plan") that provides the common shareholders of X with "poison pill" rights (the "Rights"). The adoption of the Plan constituted the distribution of a dividend under state law. The principal purpose of the adoption of the Plan was to establish a mechanism by which the corporation could, in the future, provide shareholders with rights to purchase stock at substantially less than fair market value as a means of responding to unsolicited offers to acquire X.

The Rights are rights to purchase a fraction of a share of "preferred stock" for each share of common stock held upon the occurrence of a "triggering event," subject to the restrictions described below. The fractional share of preferred stock has voting, dividend, and liquidation rights that make it the economic equivalent of one common share. Until the issuance of the Rights certificates, as described below, the Rights are not exercisable or separately tradable, nor are they represented by any certificate other than the common stock certificate itself. If no triggering event occurs, the Rights expire *a* years after their creation.

A triggering event is the earlier of the tender offer for, or actual acquisition of, at least *b* percent of X's common stock by an investor or investor group. If X does not redeem the Rights, as described below, by the end of the *c*-day period following a triggering event, it must issue Rights certificates to all persons that held X common stock on the date of the triggering event, including the investor or investor group that caused the triggering event. Once issued, the Rights certificates are tradable separately from the common stock. At any time until *d* days after the actual acquisition by an investor or investor group of at least *b* percent of X's common stock, X can redeem the Rights without shareholder approval (whether or not X has at that time issued Rights certificates, as described above) for *e* cents per Right, which is a nominal amount in relation to the current market value of the share of X common stock.

Upon the issuance of the Rights certificates, the Rights can be exercised but, until a "flip-in" or "flip-over" event, the exercise price is several times the trading price of a share of common stock at the time X adopted the Plan. A flip-in event is either (1) the actual acquisition by an investor or inventors group of *f* percent of X's common stock, or (2) a business combination in which X is the surviving corporation. A flip-over event is a business combination in which X is not the surviving corporation. The occurrence of a flip-in event gives the holder of each Right other than the investor or investor group the right to buy, for *g* dollars, stock of X that has a value substantially greater than *g* dollars. A flip-over event gives the holder of each Right other than the investor or investor group the right to buy, for *g* dollars, stock of the surviving corporation that has a value substantially greater than *g* dollars.

At the time X's board of directors adopted the Plan, the likelihood that the Rights would, at any time, be exercised was both remote and speculative.

Holding The adoption of the Plan by X's board of directors does not constitute the distribution of stock or property by X to its shareholders, an exchange of property or stock (either taxable or nontaxable), or any other event giving rise to the realization of gross income by any taxpayer. This revenue ruling does not address the federal income tax consequences of any redemption of Rights, or of any transaction involving Rights subsequent to a triggering event. * * *

§ 2.10 Liquidations of Corporations

A. Introduction

We now come to the tax consequences of the death of a corporation by liquidation. A corporation's existence may also come to end in a taxable or tax-free merger transaction, and these transactions are first introduced in the next chapter and explored in detail in subsequent chapters. Liquidations can be either tax-free or taxable, and this section first considers the treatment of both the shareholders and the corporation in a taxable liquidation and then focuses on the treatment of both in a tax-free liquidation. Thus, this section focuses on §§ 331–338.

B. General Rule of Shareholder Recognition of Gain or Loss on Complete Liquidation: § 331

The treatment of the distributee shareholder in a complete liquidation is governed by § 331, which provides that amounts distributed in a complete liquidation of a corporation are "treated" as "payment in exchange for the stock." Since these liquidation transactions are treated as exchanges, the rules of § 1001 apply, and the shareholder recognizes a gain or loss, depending upon the amount realized and the adjusted basis of his stock. *See* § 1.331-1(b). The gain or loss is separately calculated on a share-by-share basis; consequently, there may be gain on some shares and loss on others. *See* § 1.331-1(e). Any nonrecourse or recourse liabilities transferred to the shareholder reduce the shareholder's gain recognized.

As demonstrated in Sec. 2.10.D, the distributing corporation recognizes gain and in certain cases loss on the liquidating distribution. A distributee shareholder's basis for the property received in a § 331 liquidation is the fair market value of the property. *See* § 334(a).

Section 331(b) provides that the dividend rules of § 301 do not apply to complete liquidations, except in certain liquidations of personal holding companies. *See* § 316(b)(2)(B). This means that the shareholder is not taxed on any accumulated E&P at dividend rates, but § 1001 sale or exchange treatment controls. This sale or exchange treatment is available only if the corporation is actually liquidating.

C. Non-Taxable Liquidations of Subsidiaries under § 332

Section 332 provides an exception to the general recognition rule of § 331 for certain liquidating distributions. Section 332(a) provides that "[n]o gain or loss shall be recognized on the receipt by a corporation of property distributed in complete liquidation of another corporation." This very broad rule is limited, however, by § 332(b), which provides that a distribution is considered to be in complete liquidation only if the following two requirements are satisfied.

First, under § 332(b)(1), the parent corporation must own stock of the subsidiary meeting the 80% requirement of § 1504(a)(2). Section 1504(a)(2) is satisfied if the parent owns stock of the subsidiary which possesses at least 80% of the total voting power of the stock of the corporation and at least 80% of the total value of the stock of the corporation. Certain nonvoting, limited, preferred stock is not included as stock for purposes of § 1504(a)(2). This 80% stock ownership requirement must be satisfied "on the date of the adoption of the plan of liquidation and at all times until receipt of the property." *See* § 332(b)(1).

Second, the distribution of the property must be either (1) completed within the taxable year (*see* § 332(b)(2)), or (2) one of a series of distributions pursuant to a plan of liquidation that is to be completed within three years after the close of the taxable year during which the first of the series of distributions is made. *See* § 332(b)(3). The Secretary may require a bond or waiver of the statute of limitations in the case of a series of distributions spanning two or more taxable years. *See* § 332(b) (first sentence of flush language).

A liquidation satisfying the conditions of § 332 is treated as a liquidation even though the transaction may be characterized differently (*e.g.,* as a merger) under local law. *See* § 332(b) (second sentence of flush language). Thus, § 332 applies to a transaction in which a less than wholly owned but more than 80% subsidiary is merged into the parent in a nontaxable reorganization where the parent receives all of the subsidiary's assets and the minority shareholders receive the parent's stock. *See* § 332(b) (second sentence of flush language) and § 1.332-2(d) and (e).

As discussed below, under § 337, the liquidating subsidiary generally does not have gain or loss on the liquidation. Under § 334(b)(1), the parent corporation takes a carryover basis (*i.e.,* the sub's basis) for property received in a § 332 liquidation.

If a subsidiary is owned both by a parent corporation that satisfies the 80% stock ownership requirement and also by a minority shareholder or shareholders who own up to 20% of the stock of the subsidiary, then the liquidation of the subsidiary falls within §§ 332 and 334(b) for the parent and within §§ 331 and 334(a) for the minority shareholders.

D. Treatment of the Corporation in a Liquidation Transaction: Partial Repeal of the *General Utilities* Doctrine: §§ 336 and 337

See §§ 336 and 337.

1. The *General Utilities* Doctrine

Review *General Utilities*, Sec. 2.5.B.1., *Court Holding*, Sec. 2.5.B.2.a. and *Cumberland Service*, Sec. 2.5.B.2.b.

2. Impact of Repeal of *General Utilities* on Nonliquidating Distributions

Review the discussion of the repeal of the *General Utilities* doctrine in the General Explanation of the Tax Reform Act of 1986, Sec. 2.5.B.4.

3. The Repeal of the *General Utilities* Doctrine by the Tax Reform Act of 1986

See §§ 336 and 337.

The partial repeal of the *General Utilities* doctrine by the Tax Reform Act of 1986 is implemented in § 311 for nonliquidating distributions and in § 336 for taxable liquidating distributions governed by § 331. Section 337 preserves the *General Utilities* nonrecognition rule for § 332 tax-free sub into parent liquidations. Section 311, which requires that a corporation recognize gain on the non-liquidating distribution of appreciated property, is examined in Sec. 2.5.B.4., and §§ 336 and 337 are examined below.

4. Legislative History of §§ 336 and 337

EXCERPTS FROM (1) GENERAL EXPLANATION OF THE TAX REFORM ACT OF 1986, 328–346 (1987), (2) CONFERENCE REPORT TO THE REVENUE RECONCILIATION ACT OF 1987, 966–969 (1987), AND (3) SENATE FINANCE COMMITTEE REPORT TO THE TECHNICAL AND MISCELLANEOUS REVENUE ACT OF 1988, 67–73 (1988) (TAMRA).

Prior Law [*The General Utilities Rule*] Although the *General Utilities* [*see* Sec. 2.5.B.1] case involved a dividend distribution of appreciated property by an ongoing business, the term "*General Utilities* rule" was often used in a broader sense to refer to the nonrecognition treatment accorded in certain situations to liquidating as well as nonliquidating distributions to shareholders and to liquidating sales. The rule was reflected in Code sections 311, 336, and 337 of prior law: Section 311 governed the treatment of nonliquidating distributions of property (dividends and redemptions), while section 336 governed the treatment of liquidating distributions in kind. Section 337 provided nonrecognition treatment for certain sales of property pursuant to a plan of complete liquidation.

Numerous limitations on the *General Utilities* rule, both statutory and judicial, developed over the years following its codification. Some directly limited the statutory provisions embodying the rule, while others, including the collapsible corporation provisions, the recapture provisions, and the tax benefit doctrine, did so indirectly. * * *

Five years after the decision in *General Utilities,* in a case in which the corporation played a substantial role in the sale of distributed property by its shareholders, the Commissioner successfully advanced the imputed sale argument the Court had rejected earlier on procedural grounds. In *Commissioner v. Court Holding Co.,* [*see* Sec. 2.5.B.2.a] the Court upheld the Commissioner's determination that, in substance, the corporation rather than the shareholders had executed the sale and, accordingly, was required to recognize gain.

In *United States v. Cumberland Public Service Co.,* [*see* Sec. 2.5.B.2.b] the Supreme Court reached a contrary result where the facts showed the shareholders had in fact negotiated a sale on their own behalf. The Court stated that Congress had imposed no tax on liquidating distributions in kind or on dissolution, and that a corporation could liquidate without subjecting itself to corporate gains tax notwithstanding the primary motive is to avoid the corporate tax.

In its 1954 revision of the Internal Revenue Code, Congress reviewed *General Utilities* and its progeny and decided to address the corporate-level consequences of distributions statutorily. It essentially codified the result in *General Utilities* by enacting section 311(a) of prior law, which provided that a corporation recognized no gain or loss on a nonliquidating distribution of property with respect to its stock. Congress also enacted section 336, which in its original form provided for nonrecognition of gain or loss to a corporation on distributions of property in partial or complete liquidation. Although distributions in partial liquidations were eventually removed from the jurisdiction of section 336, in certain limited circumstances a distribution in partial liquidation could, prior to the Act, still qualify for nonrecognition at the corporate level.

Finally, Congress in the 1954 Act provided that a corporation did not recognize gain or loss on a sale of property if it adopted a plan of complete liquidation and distributed all of its assets to its shareholders within twelve months of the date of adoption of the plan (sec. 337). Thus, the distinction drawn in *Court Holding Co.* and *Cumberland Public Service Co.*, between a sale of assets followed by liquidating distribution of the proceeds and a liquidating distribution in kind followed by a shareholder sale, was in large part eliminated. Regulations subsequently issued under section 311 acknowledged that a distribution in redemption of stock constituted a "distribution with respect to * * * stock" within the meaning of the statute. The 1954 Code in its original form, therefore, generally exempted all forms of nonliquidating as well as liquidating distributions to shareholders from the corporate-level tax. * * *

Reasons for Change Congress believed that the *General Utilities* rule, even in its more limited form, produced many incongruities and inequities in the tax system. First, the rule could create significant distortions in business behavior. Economically, a liquidating distribution is indistinguishable from a nonliquidating distribution; yet the Code provided a substantial preference for the former. A corporation acquiring the assets of a liquidating corporation was able to obtain a basis in assets equal to their fair market value, although the transferor recognized no gain (other than possibly recapture amounts) on the sale. The tax benefits made the assets potentially more valuable in the hands of a transferee than in the hands of the current owner. This might induce corporations with substantial appreciated assets to liquidate and transfer their assets to other corporations for tax reasons, when economic considerations might indicate a different course of action. Accordingly, Congress reasoned, the *General Utilities* rule could be at least partly responsible for the dramatic increase in corporate mergers and acquisitions in recent years. Congress believed that the Code should not artificially encourage corporate liquidations and acquisitions, and that repeal of the *General Utilities* rule was a major step towards that goal.

Second, the *General Utilities* rule tended to undermine the corporate income tax. Under normally applicable tax principles, nonrecognition of gain is available only if the transferee takes a carryover basis in the transferred property, thus assuring that a tax will eventually be collected on the appreciation. Where the *General Utilities* rule applied, assets generally were permitted to leave corporate solution and to take a stepped-up basis in the hands of the transferee without the imposition of a corporate-level tax. Thus, the effect of the rule was to grant a permanent exemption from the corporate income tax. * * *

Explanation of Provisions *Overview* The Act provides that gain or loss generally is recognized by a corporation on liquidating distributions of its property as if the property had been sold at fair market value to the distributee. [*See* § 336.] Gain or loss is also recognized by a corporation on liquidating sales of its property. Exceptions are provided for distributions in which an 80-percent corporate shareholder receives property with a carryover basis in a liquidation under section 332, and certain distributions and exchanges involving property that may be received tax-free by the shareholder under subchapter C of the Code. * * * [*See* § 337.]

Distributions in Complete Liquidation [Under Section 336] General Rule [*See* §§ 336(a) and (b).] The Act provides that, in general, gain or loss is recognized to a corporation on a distribution of its property in complete liquidation. The distributing corporation is treated as if it had sold the property at fair market value to the distributee-shareholders. [*See* § 336(a).]

If the distributed property is subject to a liability, the fair market value of the property for this purpose is deemed to be no less than the amount of the liability. [*See* § 336(b).] Thus, for example, if the amount of the liability exceeds the value of the property that secures it, the selling corporation will recognize gain in an amount equal to the excess of the liability over the adjusted basis of the property. [*See also* § 7701(g).] Likewise, if the shareholders of the liquidating corporation assume liabilities of the corporation and the amount of liabilities assumed exceeds the fair market value of the distributed property, the corporation will recognize gain to the extent the assumed liabilities exceed the adjusted basis of the property. However, the provision does not affect, and no inference was intended regarding, the amount realized by or basis of property received by the distributee-shareholders in these circumstances. * * *

[A liquidating corporation recognizes gain on a distribution of § 453 installment note obligations. *See* § 453B(a).]

Tax-Free Reorganizations and Distributions [*See* § 336(c).] The general rule requiring gain or loss recognition on liquidating distributions of property is inapplicable to [distributions in pursuance of a plan of reorganization. *See* § 361(c)(4).]

Limitations on Recognition of Losses [*See* § 336(d).] The Act includes two provisions designed to prevent inappropriate corporate-level recognition of losses on liquidating dispositions of property. In enacting these provisions, Congress did not intend to create any inference regarding the deductibility of such losses under other statutory provisions or judicially created doctrines, or to preclude the application of such provisions or doctrines where appropriate.

Distributions to Related Persons [*See* § 336(d)(1).] Under the first loss limitation rule, a liquidating corporation may not recognize loss with respect to a distribution of property to a related person within the meaning of section 267, unless (i) the property is distributed to all shareholders on a pro rata basis *and* (ii) the property was not acquired by the liquidating corporation in a section 351 transaction or as a contribution to capital during the five years preceding the distribution.

Thus, for example, a liquidating corporation may not recognize loss on a distribution of recently acquired property to a shareholder who, directly or indirectly, owns more than 50 percent in value of the stock of the corporation. Similarly, a liquidating corporation may not recognize a loss on any property, regardless of when or how acquired, that is distributed to such a shareholder on a non-pro rata basis.

Dispositions of Certain Carryover Basis Property Acquired for Tax-Avoidance Purpose [*See* § 336(d)(3).] Under the second loss limitation rule, recognition of loss may be limited if property whose adjusted basis exceeds its value is contributed to a liquidating corporation, in a carryover basis transaction, with a principal purpose of recognizing the loss upon the sale or distribution of the property (and thus eliminating or otherwise limiting corporate level gain). In these circumstances, the basis of the property for purposes of determining loss is reduced, but not below zero, by the excess of the adjusted basis of the property on the date of contribution over its fair market value on such date.

If the adoption of a plan of complete liquidation occurs in a taxable year following the date on which the tax return including the loss disallowed by this provision is filed, except as provided in regulations, the liquidating corporation will recapture the disallowed loss on the tax return for the taxable year in which such plan of liquidation is adopted. In the alternative, regulations may provide for the corporation to file an amended return for the taxable year in which the loss was reported. * * *

Presumption of Tax-Avoidance Purpose in Case of Contributions Within Two Years of Liquidation [*See* § 336(d)(2)(B)(iii).] For purposes of the loss limitation rule, there is a statutory presumption that the tax-avoidance purpose is present with respect to any section 351 transfer or contribution to capital of built-in loss property [after the date two years before] the adoption of the plan of liquidation. [*See* § 336(d)(2)(B)(ii).] Although Congress recognized that a contribution more than two years before the adoption of a plan of liquidation might have been made for such a tax-avoidance purpose, Congress also recognized that the determination that such purpose existed in such circumstances might be difficult for the Internal Revenue Service to establish and therefore as a practical matter might occur infrequently or in relatively unusual cases.

Congress intended that the Treasury Department will issue regulations generally providing that the presumed prohibited purpose for contributions of property within two years of the adoption of a plan of liquidation will be disregarded *unless* there is no clear and substantial relationship between the contributed property and the conduct of the corporation's current or future business enterprises. * * *

Election to Treat Sale or Distribution of Subsidiary Stock as Disposition of Subsidiary's Assets [*See* § 336(e).] The Act generally conforms the treatment of liquidating sales and distributions of subsidiary stock to the prior-law treatment of nonliquidating sales or distributions of such stock; thus, such liquidating sales or distributions are generally taxable at the corporate level. Congress believed it was appropriate to conform the treatment of liquidating and nonliquidating sales or distributions and to require recognition when appreciated property, including stock of a subsidiary, is transferred to a corporate or individual recipient outside the economic unit of the selling or distributing corporation.

However, Congress believed it was appropriate to provide relief from a potential multiple taxation at the corporate level of the same economic gain, which may result when a transfer of appreciated corporate stock is taxed without providing a corresponding step-up in basis of the assets of the corporation. In addition to retaining the election available under section 338(h)(10) of prior law, the Act permits the expansion of the concept of that provision, [(which permits a parent corporation to treat the sale of the stock of a subsidiary as a sale of the subsidiary's assets) *see* Sec. 17.5.], to the extent provided in regulations, to dispositions of a controlling interest in a corporation for which this election is currently unavailable. For example, the election could be made available where the selling corporation owns 80 percent of the value and voting power of the subsidiary but does not file a consolidated return with the subsidiary. Moreover, the Act provides that, under regulations, principles similar to those of section 338(h)(10) may be applied to taxable distributions of controlled corporation stock. * * *

[Liquidations of Subsidiaries under §§ 332 and 337] [General Rules] An exception to the recognition rule is provided for certain distributions in connection with the liquidation of a controlled subsidiary into its parent corporation. Under new section 337 of the Code, no gain or loss is generally recognized with respect to property distributed to a corporate shareholder (an "80-percent distributee") in a liquidation to which section 332 applies. If a minority shareholder receives property in such a liquidation, the distribution to the minority shareholder is treated in the same manner as a distribution in a nonliquidating redemption. Accordingly, gain (but not loss) is recognized to the distributing corporation.

The exception for 80-percent corporate shareholders does not apply where the shareholder is a tax-exempt organization unless the property received in the distribution is used by the organization in an activity, the income from which is subject to tax as unrelated business taxable income (UBTI), immediately after the distribution. * * *

If gain is recognized on a distribution of property in a liquidation described in section 332(a), a corresponding increase in the distributee's basis in the property will be permitted. [*See* § 334(b)(1).]

The Act relocates the provisions of section 332(c) to section 337(b) of the Code. Distributions of property to the controlling parent corporation in liquidations to which section 332 applies in exchange for debt obligations of the subsidiary are treated in the same manner as distributions in exchange for stock of the subsidiary, as under prior law section 332(c).

[Gain is not recognized on the distribution by a subsidiary of § 453 installment-sale obligations in a § 337 liquidation. *See* § 453B(d).]

[The 80% Distributee and Introduction to Mirror Subsidiaries] [Section 337 was amended by the Revenue Reconciliation Act of 1987 to address the mirror subsidiary and related issues. Mirror subsidiary transactions involved attempts to avoid the repeal of *General Utilities* by causing a subsidiary to liquidate into two (or more) intermediate parent corporations (mirror subsidiaries) that were members of the

same affiliated group as the subsidiary and which in the aggregate (but not individually) owned 80% of the subsidiary's stock. The stock of the mirror subsidiaries was owned by the ultimate parent corporation. Wanted assets would be distributed to one of the mirror subsidiaries and unwanted assets would go to the other. Under Reg. § 1.1502-34 of the consolidated return regulations, this type of liquidation is within § 332, and prior to the Revenue Reconciliation Act of 1987, the liquidation arguably was within § 337. Consequently, neither the mirror subsidiaries nor the liquidating subsidiary would recognize gain on the liquidation. The ultimate parent could then dispose of the mirror subsidiary that held unwanted assets. The issues involving mirror subsidiaries arise in stock acquisitions and are addressed in detail in Chapter 5. The following excerpt from the Conference Report to the Revenue Reconciliation Act of 1987 elaborates on the definition of an "80 percent distributee" in § 337(c).]

As under present law [§ 332], gain will not be recognized by a corporation on liquidating distributions to a corporate shareholder directly owning 80 percent (by vote and value) of the stock of the distributing corporation. However, under the conference agreement, gain is recognized on any distribution to a corporation that does not meet the 80-percent test by direct ownership. Thus, for example, the distributing corporation recognizes gain on any distribution to a corporation within an affiliated group filing a consolidated tax return if the distributee would be treated as an 80-percent owner for purposes of section 332 solely by reason of the aggregation rules of section 1.1502-34 of the Treasury Regulations.

Treasury Regulations may provide that gain on a distribution to a less than 80-percent owner within an affiliated group filing a consolidated return may be deferred until a recognition event other than the liquidation itself occurs. (Compare Treas. Reg. sec. 1.1502-14(c)(2)). * * *

Regulatory Authority to Prevent Circumvention of General Utilities Repeal [See § 337(d).] The repeal of the *General Utilities* rule is designed to require the corporate level recognition of gain on a corporation's sale or distribution of appreciated property, irrespective of whether it occurs in a liquidating or nonliquidating context. Congress expected the Treasury Department to issue, or to amend, regulations to ensure that the purpose of the new provisions (including the new subchapter S built-in gain provisions) is not circumvented through the use of any other provision, including the consolidated return regulations or the tax-free reorganization provisions of the Code (part III of subchapter C) or through the use of other pass-through entities such as regulated investment companies (RICs) or real estate investment trusts (REITs). For example, this would include rules to require the recognition of gain if appreciated property of a C corporation is transferred to a RIC or a REIT in a carryover basis transaction that would otherwise eliminate corporate-level tax on the built-in appreciation.

Application of Other Statutory Rules and Judicial Doctrines In providing for recognition of gain on liquidating distributions, Congress did not intend to supersede other existing statutory rules and judicial doctrines, including (but not limited to) sections 1245 and 1250 recapture, the tax benefit doctrine, and the assignment of income doctrine. Accordingly, these rules will continue to apply to determine the character of gain recognized on liquidating distributions where they are otherwise applicable. * * *

E. Introduction to § 338

1. In General

This section briefly introduces § 338, which gives an acquiring corporation in a stock acquisition the ability to elect to treat the transaction as an asset acquisition. This provision is examined in greater detail in Chapter 5, which deals with taxable stock acquisitions.

If an acquiring corporation purchases the stock of a target corporation, there is no change in the basis of the target's assets, unless the acquiring corporation makes an election under § 338 to step up the basis of the assets. If the acquiring corporation makes the § 338 election, the target is deemed to have sold and then repurchased its assets. As a consequence of the deemed sale, the target has a tax liability, and the economic burden of this tax will be borne by the acquiring corporation as the owner of the target's shares. Consequently, as discussed below, unless the target has significant net operating losses to offset the gain, the acquiring corporation will rarely make this election. However, if an acquiring corporation is acquiring the stock of a subsidiary of a consolidated group, it may be beneficial for the acquiring corporation and the selling parent corporation to jointly make what is known as a § 338(h)(10) election.

Section 338, generally, provides that, if the stock of a corporation ("Target") (*see* § 338(d)(2)) is acquired by another corporation ("Purchasing Corporation") (*see* § 338(d)(1)) in a Qualified Stock Purchase (*see* § 338(d)(3)), the Purchasing Corporation may elect to have the Target treated as if it had sold all of its assets (as "Old Target") and then purchased those assets (as "New Target"). *See* § 338(a). Thus, as a result of a § 338 election, the Target recognizes gain or loss with respect to the deemed sale of its assets and takes a fair market value basis for those assets.

The deemed sale of assets by Old Target takes place at the close of the day on which the purchase occurred ("Acquisition Date"). *See* §§ 338(a)(1) and (h)(2). New Target is deemed to purchase those assets ("Acquisition Date Assets") at the beginning of the day after the Acquisition Date. *See* § 338(a)(2).

The regulations set out elaborate rules for determining the deemed sale and purchase price and for allocating the purchase price among the assets sold. These issues are addressed in Chapter 5.

A Purchasing Corporation is a corporation that makes a qualified stock purchase ("Qualified Stock Purchase") of another corporation. *See* § 338(d)(1). A Target is a corporation the stock of which is acquired by purchase in a Qualified Stock Purchase by the Purchasing Corporation. *See* § 338(d)(2).

A Qualified Stock Purchase is defined as any transaction or series of transactions in which a Purchasing Corporation acquires, by purchase, at least 80% of the total combined voting power of all classes entitled to vote and at least 80% of the total number of all other classes of stock (except nonvoting stock which is limited and preferred as to dividends) of the Target during the Acquisition Period. *See* § 338(d)(3). Members of the same affiliated group are treated as one corporation and shares purchased by different members of the group are aggregated in determining if a Qualified Stock Purchase has occurred. *See* § 338(h)(8). Thus, the standard transaction in which an acquiring corporation buys all of the stock of a target corporation would be a Qualified Stock Purchase.

The term "Acquisition Period" is defined as the period of 12 months beginning the first day on which a stock purchase that is part of a Qualified Stock Purchase is made. *See* § 338(h)(1).

The term "Acquisition Date" is defined as the first date on which the Purchaser acquires all of the stock necessary for a Qualified Stock Purchase. *See* § 338(h)(2). After a Qualified Stock Purchase, the Purchasing Corporation may elect the application of § 338 with respect to the transaction. Pursuant to § 338(a)(1), the Target is deemed to have sold all its assets on the Acquisition Date for their fair market value in a single taxable transaction. *See* § 338(g).

As a result of the repeal of the former § 337 by the Tax Reform Act of 1986 (*i.e.,* *General Utilities* repeal), the Target has full gain or loss on the deemed sale of its assets resulting from a § 338 election. Consequently, it is rarely beneficial for the Purchasing Corporation to make a § 338 election. There are three major exceptions to this general rule. First, if a stand-alone Target has net operating losses or other capital losses that can offset the § 338 gain, then it might be beneficial for the Purchasing Corporation to make a § 338 election.

The second exception involves the acquisition of the stock of a subsidiary corporation. This transaction can qualify under § 338(h)(10), which permits a parent corporation that is selling the stock of a subsidiary to elect with the purchasing corporation to treat the transaction as if the subsidiary is selling assets while the subsidiary is a member of the selling parent's consolidated group. As a consequence, the subsidiary's gain on the deemed asset sale is reported in the selling parent's consolidated return and the sub is deemed to be liquidated in a tax-free liquidation under § 332. As a consequence, there is a step-up in the basis of the sub's assets with just a single level of tax (*i.e.,* a tax at the sub level but not at the selling parent level). The parent may agree to such treatment if the basis for the parent's stock in the subsidiary is not significantly higher than the basis of the subsidiary's assets. *See* Sec. 5.5.B.

The third exception involves the acquisition of an S corporation in a situation in which the selling shareholders and the acquiring corporation agree to jointly file an election under the regulations under § 338(h)(10). *See* Sec. 11.8.B.

2. The Kimbell Diamond Doctrine: Purchase of Stock Followed by Liquidation Treated as Purchase of Assets

Kimbell-Diamond Milling Company v. Commissioner

Tax Court of the United States, 1950.14 T.C. 74, *affirmed* 187 F.2d 718
(5th Cir.1951), *cert. denied* 342 U.S. 827 (1951)

[Kimbell-Diamond Milling Company, the petitioner, purchased all the stock of Whaley Mill J. Elevator Co. and then immediately liquidated Whaley. Thus, after the stock acquisition and liquidation, Kimbell-Diamond held Whaley's assets. Kimbell-Diamond's position was that the two steps were separate and that, therefore, the liquidation of Whaley was governed by the predecessor of § 332, which applies to a liquidation of subsidiary corporation into parent corporation. If the transaction were governed by the predecessor of § 332, Kimbell-Diamond would take as its basis for the Whaley assets, Whaley's basis for those assets. *See* predecessor of § 334(b). The Commissioner argued that the two steps should be treated as an acquisition of assets and that Kimbell-Diamond's basis should be its cost of the stock.]

Petitioner argues that the acquisition of Whaley's assets and the subsequent liquidation of Whaley brings petitioner within the provisions of § 112(b)(6) [now § 332] and, therefore, by reason of § 113(a)(15) [now § 334(b)] petitioner's basis in these assets is the same as the basis in Whaley's hands. In so contending, petitioner asks that we treat the acquisition of Whaley's stock and the subsequent liquidation of Whaley as separate transactions. It is well settled that the incidence of taxation depends upon the substance of a transaction. *Commissioner v. Court Holding Co.,* 324 U.S. 331. It is inescapable from petitioner's minutes set out above and from the "Agreement and Program of Complete Liquidation" entered into between petitioner and Whaley, that the only intention petitioner ever had was to acquire Whaley's assets.

We think that this proceeding is governed by the principles of *Commissioner v. Ashland Oil & Refining Co.,* 99 Fed. (2d) 588, certiorari denied, 306 U.S. 661. In that case the stock was retained for almost a year before liquidation. Ruling on the question of whether the stock or the assets of the corporation were purchased, the court stated:

The question remains, however, whether if the entire transaction, whatever its form, was essentially in intent, purpose and result, a purchase by Swiss of property, its several steps may be treated separately and each be given an effect for tax purposes as though each constituted a distinct transaction. * * * And without regard to whether the result is imposition or relief from taxation, the courts have recognized that where the essential nature of a transaction is the acquisition of property, it will be viewed as a whole, and closely related steps will not be separated either at the instance of the taxpayer or the taxing authority. * * *

We hold that the purchase of Whaley's stock and its subsequent liquidation must be considered as one transaction, namely, the purchase of Whaley's assets which was petitioner's sole intention. This was not a reorganization within section 112(b)(6), and petitioner's basis in these assets, both depreciable and nondepreciable, is, therefore, its cost, or $110,721.74 * * *

Note

Section 338 has overridden the *Kimbell-Diamond* doctrine as it applies in the context of a purchase of stock followed by a liquidation. For example, assume that an acquiring corporation purchases all of the stock of a target and then immediately liquidates the target without making a § 338 election. In such case, the liquidation is governed by §§ 332 and 337 and neither the acquiring corporation nor the target have taxable gain. And, the acquiring corporation takes a carry over basis for the assets received. *See* § 334(b).

F. Introduction to the 2013 Regulations under Section 336(e)

Section 336(e) which was enacted in 1986 provides the following exception to the general rule of Section 336(a):

(e) Certain stock sales and distributions may be treated as asset transfers

Under regulations prescribed by the Secretary, if—

(1) a corporation owns stock in another corporation meeting the requirements of section 1504(a)(2) [an 80% test], and

(2) such corporation sells, exchanges, or distributes all of such stock, an election may be made to treat such sale, exchange, or distribution as a disposition of all of the assets of such other corporation, and no gain or loss shall be recognized on the sale, exchange, or distribution of such stock.

Thus, for example, under Section 336(e), a corporation could sell or distribute stock of a sub and have the transaction treated as a sale or distribution of the sub's assets.

On May 15, 2013, the Treasury finally issued regulations (T.D. 9619) under Section 336(e). The preamble to regulations explains:

SUMMARY: This document contains final regulations that provide guidance under section 336(e) of the Internal Revenue Code (Code), which authorizes the issuance of regulations under which an election may be made to treat the sale, exchange, or distribution of at least 80 percent of the voting power and value of the stock of a corporation (target) as a sale of all its underlying assets. These regulations provide the terms and conditions for making such an election and the consequences of the election. These regulations affect domestic corporate sellers (seller), S corporation shareholders, and domestic targets....

Background

Section 336(e) of the Code authorizes the issuance of regulations under which an election may be made to treat the sale, exchange, or distribution of at least 80 percent of the voting power and value of the stock of a corporation (target) as a sale of all its underlying assets. Section 336(e) was enacted as part of *General Utilities* repeal. Similar to an election under section 336(h)(10) available with respect to certain purchases of target stock, section 336(e) is meant to provide taxpayers relief from a potential multiple taxation of the same economic gain that can result when a transfer of appreciated corporate stock is taxed without providing a corresponding step-up in the basis of the assets of the corporation. See H.R. Conf. Rep. No. 841, 99th Cong., 2d Sess., Vol. II, 198, 204 (1986), 1986-3 CB, Vol. 4, 198-207. . . .

Summary of Proposed Regulations

A. In General

Under the proposed regulations, an election under section 336(e) is available for "qualified stock dispositions" of domestic target stock by domestic corporate sellers (seller). The proposed regulations generally adopt the structure and principles established under section 338(h)(10) and the underlying regulations. For example, the proposed regulations generally incorporate the rules of section 338 governing the allocation of consideration in the resulting deemed sale of the target's assets and the determination of target's basis in its underlying assets resulting from such deemed sale. The proposed regulations alter terms or concepts to reflect principles and factual circumstances relevant to section 336(e).

Unlike an election under section 338(h)(10), which is available only if target stock is acquired by a corporate purchaser, the proposed regulations do not require an acquirer of target stock to be a corporation, or even necessarily a purchaser. Also unlike section 338(h)(10), which generally requires that a single purchasing corporation acquire the stock of a target, the proposed regulations permit the aggregation of all stock of a target that is sold, exchanged, and distributed by a seller to different acquirers for purposes of determining whether there has been a qualified stock disposition of a target.

G. Introduction to the 2015 May Department Stores' Final Regulations

In June 2015, the Treasury issued final and temporary regulations dealing with what is known as the May Department Stores' Regulations.[9] These regulations are designed to prevent the avoidance of the recognition of corporate taxable gain on the disposition of appreciated property through the use of a partnership.

The preamble discusses the approach of the 1992 proposed regulations as follows:

After the enactment of sections 311(b) and 337(d), the Treasury Department and the IRS became aware of transactions in which taxpayers used a part-

---

9. Treasury Decision 9722, Partnership Transactions Involving Equity Interests of a Partner (June 29, 2015).

nership to postpone or avoid completely gain generally required to be recognized under section 311(b). In one example of this transaction, a corporation entered into a partnership and contributed appreciated property. The partnership then acquired stock of that corporate partner, and later made a liquidating distribution of this stock to the corporate partner. Under section 731(a), the corporate partner did not recognize gain on the partnership's distribution of its stock. By means of this transaction, the corporation had disposed of the appreciated property it formerly held and had acquired its own stock, permanently avoiding its gain in the appreciated property. If the corporation had directly exchanged the appreciated property for its own stock, section 311(b) would have required the corporation to recognize gain upon the exchange. * * *

The preamble to the 2015 regulations contains the following introduction to the current final and temporary regulations:

Explanation of Provisions

The purpose of these regulations authorized under section 337(d) is to prevent corporate taxpayers from using a partnership to circumvent gain required to be recognized under section 311(b) or section 336(a). * * *

These regulations apply when a partnership, either directly or indirectly, owns, acquires, or distributes Stock of the Corporate Partner[.] Under these regulations, a Corporate Partner ... may recognize gain when it is treated as acquiring or increasing its interest in Stock of the Corporate Partner held by a partnership in exchange for appreciated property in a manner that avoids gain recognition under section 311(b) or section 336(a). * * *

§ 2.11 The Business Purpose and Step Transaction Doctrines

A. Introduction

In planning M&A and other business transactions tax lawyers are often called on to make a judgment whether a transaction that seems to fit squarely within a particular Code section will be taxed in accordance with that section. *Gregory v. Helvering*, which is set out below, demonstrates that even though all of the technical requirements may be satisfied, a transaction may not be governed by a particular section if there is no business purpose for the transaction. Also, we have seen the Service attack transactions on similar grounds in the *Court Holding*, *Cumberland Service* and *Kimbell-Diamond* cases examined earlier in this chapter. The *Esmark* case, which is also set out below, illustrates the limits of the Service's "step transaction" doctrine. Under this doctrine, the Service attempts to integrate several steps of a transaction. Finally, this section introduces the codified economic substance doctrine under § 7701(o).

B. The Business Purpose Doctrine

Gregory v. Helvering

Supreme Court of the United States, 1935

293 U.S. 465, 55 S.Ct. 266, 79 L.Ed. 596

Mr. Justice Sutherland delivered the opinion of the Court.

[**Facts**] Petitioner in 1928 was the owner of all the stock of United Mortgage Corporation. That corporation held among its assets 1,000 shares of the Monitor Securities Corporation. For the sole purpose of procuring a transfer of these shares to herself in order to sell them for her individual profit, and, at the same time, diminish the amount of income tax which would result from a direct transfer by way of dividend, she sought to bring about a "reorganization" under section 112(g) of the Revenue Act of 1928, c. 852, 45 Stat. 791, 816, 818, 26 USCA § 2112(g), set forth later in this opinion. To that end, she caused the Averill Corporation to be organized under the laws of Delaware on September 18, 1928. Three days later, the United Mortgage Corporation transferred to the Averill Corporation the 1,000 shares of Monitor stock, for which all the shares of the Averill Corporation were issued to the petitioner. On September 24, the Averill Corporation was dissolved, and liquidated by distributing all its assets, namely, the Monitor shares, to the petitioner. No other business was ever transacted, or intended to be transacted, by that company. Petitioner immediately sold the Monitor shares for $133,333.33. She returned for taxation, as capital net gain, the sum of $76,007.88, based upon an apportioned cost of $57,325.45. Further details are unnecessary. It is not disputed that if the interposition of the so-called reorganization was ineffective, petitioner became liable for a much larger tax as a result of the transaction.

[**Issue**] The Commissioner of Internal Revenue, being of opinion that the reorganization attempted was without substance and must be disregarded, held that petitioner was liable for a tax as though the United corporation had paid her a dividend consisting of the amount realized from the sale of the Monitor shares. In a proceeding before the Board of Tax Appeals, that body rejected the commissioner's view and upheld that of petitioner. 27 B.T.A. 223. Upon a review of the latter decision, the Circuit Court of Appeals sustained the commissioner and reversed the board, holding that there had been no "reorganization" within the meaning of the statute. 69 F.(2d) 809. Petitioner applied to this court for a writ of certiorari, which the government, considering the question one of importance, did not oppose. We granted the writ.

[**Analysis**] Section 112 of the Revenue Act of 1928 deals with the subject of gain or loss resulting from the sale or exchange of property. Such gain or loss is to be recognized in computing the tax, except as provided in that section. The provisions of the section, so far as they are pertinent to the question here presented, follow:

"Sec. 112 [now § 355(a)] * * * (g) *Distribution of Stock on Reorganization.* If there is distributed, in pursuance of a plan of reorganization, to a shareholder in a corporation a party to the reorganization, stock or securities in such corporation or in another corporation a party to the reorganization, without the surrender by such share-holder of stock or securities in such a corporation, no gain to the distributee from the receipt of such stock or securities shall be recognized. * * *

"(i) [now § 368(a)(1)(D)] *Definition of Reorganization.* As used in this section * * *

"(1) The term 'reorganization' means * * * (B) a transfer by a corporation of all or a part of its assets to another corporation if immediately after the transfer the transferor or its stockholders or both are in control of the corporation to which the assets are transferred. * * *".

It is earnestly contended on behalf of the taxpayer that since every element required by the foregoing subdivision (B) is to be found in what was done, a statutory reorganization was effected; and that the motive of the taxpayer thereby to escape payment of a tax will not alter the result or make unlawful what the statute allows. It is quite true that if a reorganization in reality was effected within the meaning of subdivision (B), the ulterior purpose mentioned will be disregarded. The legal right of a taxpayer to decrease the amount of what otherwise would be his taxes, or altogether avoid them, by means which the law permits, cannot be doubted. * * * But the question for determination is whether what was done, apart from the tax motive, was the thing which the statute intended. The reasoning of the court below in justification of a negative answer leaves little to be said.

When subdivision (B) speaks of a transfer of assets by one corporation to another, it means a transfer made "in pursuance of a plan of reorganization" (section 112(g)) of corporate business; and not a transfer of assets by one corporation to another in pursuance of a plan having no relation to the business of either, as plainly is the case here. Putting aside, then, the question of motive in respect of taxation altogether, and fixing the character of the proceeding by what actually occurred, what do we find? Simply an operation having no business or corporate purpose—a mere device which put on the form of a corporate reorganization as a disguise for concealing its real character, and the sole object and accomplishment of which was the consummation of a preconceived plan, not to reorganize a business or any part of a business, but to transfer a parcel of corporate shares to the petitioner. No doubt, a new and valid corporation was created. But that corporation was nothing more than a contrivance to the end last described. It was brought into existence for no other purpose; it performed, as it was intended from the beginning it should perform, no other function. When that limited function had been exercised, it immediately was put to death.

In these circumstances, the facts speak for themselves and are susceptible of but one interpretation. The whole undertaking, though conducted according to the terms of subdivision (B), was in fact an elaborate and devious form of conveyance masquerading as a corporate reorganization, and nothing else. The rule which excludes from consideration the motive of tax avoidance is not pertinent to the situation, because the transaction upon its face lies outside the plain intent of the statute. To hold otherwise would be to exalt artifice above reality and to deprive the statutory provision in question of all serious purpose.

Judgment affirmed.

Note

The type of transaction in *Gregory* is known generally as a spin-off, that is, a corporation puts part of its assets into a new corporation and then spins off the new corporation to its shareholders. Mrs. Gregory was hoping for tax-free treatment for her spin-off so that she could get capital gain on the subsequent liquidation and sale of the spun-off assets (the Monitor shares). The Court held that although she had literally complied with the statute, she had received a mere dividend taxable as ordinary income, rather than a tax-free spin-off.

A spin-off can be done on a tax-free basis under the current statute provided all of the conditions of §§ 368(a)(1)(D) and 355 are satisfied. Spin-offs are introduced in Chapter 3 and examined in greater detail in Chapter 9. One of the conditions in § 355 is that the transaction "not be used principally as a device for the distribution of earnings and profits * * *." *See* § 355(a)(1)(B).

C. Interrelationship Between Conduit Treatment, Step Transaction and Business Purpose Doctrines

Esmark, Inc. v. Commissioner

Tax Court of the United States, 1988
90 T.C. 171, *affirmed* 886 F.2d 1318 (7th Cir. 1989)

[Mobil arranged with Esmark to purchase the stock of Vickers, a subsidiary of Esmark pursuant to the following arrangement. First, Mobil made a tender offer for part of the stock of Esmark, a publicly-held corporation. Second, Mobil then transferred to Esmark the stock of Esmark it had purchased in the tender offer in exchange for the stock of Vickers. Thus, Esmark redeemed its stock held by Mobil in exchange for the Vickers stock. If the transaction was taxed in accordance with its form (*i.e.,* a tender offer followed by a redemption), then Esmark would not be taxed on the distribution of the stock of Vickers in the redemption from Mobil. As a result of the repeal of the *General Utilities* doctrine by the Tax Reform Act of 1986, this type of distribution now would be subject to tax. The Service challenged the transaction on a variety of grounds, including the following:] * * *

Mobil as a Conduit Respondent's fourth ground for disregarding Mobil's ownership of petitioner's shares is that Mobil was a mere "conduit." The issue raised by respondent is essentially the same as that raised in *Commissioner v. Court Holding Co.,* [Sec. 2.5.B.2.a.], and *Cumberland Public Service Co. v. United States,* [Sec.2.5.B.2.b.]

* * * The existence of a prearrangement does not necessarily signify the presence of a conduit that is to be disregarded. In order to disregard an entity as a conduit, the entity must be a mere intermediary in a transaction where the true "obligation," legal or otherwise, runs between other parties. * * *

The Step-Transaction Doctrine Finally, respondent maintains that Mobil's ownership of the Esmark shares must be disregarded under the step-transaction doctrine. We recently described the step-transaction doctrine as another rule of substance over form that "treats a series of formally separate 'steps' as a single transaction if such steps are in substance integrated, interdependent, and focused toward a particular result." *Penrod v. Commissioner,* 88 T.C. 1415, 1428 (1987). Respondent contends that Mobil's acquisition and subsequent disposition of petitioner's shares were simply steps in an integrated transaction designed to result in Mobil's acquisition of Vickers and petitioner's redemption of its stock.

That Mobil's tender offer was but part of an overall plan is not in dispute. The existence of an overall plan does not alone, however, justify application of the step-transaction doctrine. Whether invoked as a result of the "binding commitment," "interdependence," or "end result" tests, the doctrine combines a series of individually meaningless steps into a single transaction. In this case, respondent has pointed to no meaningless or unnecessary steps that should be ignored.

Petitioner had two objectives: a disposition of its energy business and a redemption of a substantial portion of its stock. Three direct routes to these objectives were available:

First, petitioner could have distributed the Vickers stock to its shareholders in exchange for their shares. The shareholders could then have sold the Vickers stock for cash to interested buyers. *See Commissioner v. Court Holding Co.* and *Cumberland Public Service Co. v. United States, supra.*

Second, petitioner could have sold the Vickers stock for cash and then distributed the cash to its shareholders in exchange for their stock. As appears from our findings (pp. 176–177), however, Mobil might not have been the successful bidder.

Third, the parties could have proceeded as they did, with Mobil purchasing petitioner's stock in a tender offer and exchanging such stock for the Vickers stock. No route was more "direct" than the others. Each route required two steps, and each step involved two of three interested parties. Each route left petitioner, petitioner's shareholders, and the purchaser in the same relative positions. Faced with this choice, petitioner chose the path expected to result in the least tax.

Respondent proposes to recharacterize the tender offer/redemption as a sale of the Vickers shares to Mobil followed by a self-tender. This recharacterization does not simply combine steps; it invents new ones. Courts have refused to apply the step-transaction doctrine in this manner. * * *

Conclusion Although much more might be written about each of respondent's attacks on the form of petitioner's transaction, we have refrained from doing so. Stripped to its essentials, this case is a rematch of the principles expressed in *Gregory v. Helvering,* 293 U.S. 465 (1935), the source of most "substance over form" arguments. * * *

In *Gregory,* the taxpayer's transaction was not "the thing that the statute intended" because a reorganization, as that term was defined in the statute, did not in fact take place. * * *

In this case, in contrast, there were no steps without independent function. Each of the steps—the purchase of petitioner's stock by Mobil and the redemption of that stock by petitioner—had permanent economic consequences. Mobil's tender offer was not a "mere device" having no business purpose; the tender offer was an essential element of petitioner's plan to redeem over 50 percent of its stock. Mobil's ownership, however transitory, must thus be respected, and if Mobil's ownership of petitioner's shares is respected, a "distribution with respect to * * * stock" in fact occurred. * * *

D. Codification of the Economic Substance Doctrine, Section 7701(o)

Staff of Joint Committee on Taxation, Technical Explanation of the Revenue Provisions of the "Reconciliation Act of 2010," As Amended, in Combination with the "Patient Protection and Affordable Care Act"

JCX-18-10, March 21, 2010

Codification of Economic Substance Doctrine * * *

Present Law

* * *

Economic substance doctrine

Courts generally deny claimed tax benefits if the transaction that gives rise to those benefits lacks economic substance independent of U.S. Federal income tax considerations—notwithstanding that the purported activity actually occurred. The Tax Court has described the doctrine as follows:

> The tax law ... requires that the intended transactions have economic substance separate and distinct from economic benefit achieved solely by tax reduction. The doctrine of economic substance becomes applicable, and a judicial remedy is warranted, where a taxpayer seeks to claim tax benefits, unintended by Congress, by means of transactions that serve no economic purpose other than tax savings.[10]

Business purpose doctrine

A common law doctrine that often is considered together with the economic substance doctrine is the business purpose doctrine. The business purpose doctrine involves an inquiry into the subjective motives of the taxpayer ? that is, whether the taxpayer intended the transaction to serve some useful non-tax purpose. In making this determination, some courts have bifurcated a transaction in which activities with non-tax objectives have been combined with unrelated activities having only tax-avoidance objectives, in order to disallow the tax benefits of the overall transaction.[11]

Application by the courts

There is a lack of uniformity regarding the proper application of the economic substance doctrine. Some courts apply a conjunctive test that requires a taxpayer to

---

10. *ACM Partnership v. Commissioner*, 73 T.C.M. at 2215.
11. See, *ACM Partnership v. Commissioner*, 157 F.3d at 256 n.48.

establish the presence of both economic substance (*i.e.*, the objective component) and business purpose (*i.e.*, the subjective component) in order for the transaction to survive judicial scrutiny. A narrower approach used by some courts is to conclude that either a business purpose or economic substance is sufficient to respect the transaction. A third approach regards economic substance and business purpose as "simply more precise factors to consider" in determining whether a transaction has any practical economic effects other than the creation of tax benefits. * * *

Explanation of Provision

The provision clarifies and enhances the application of the economic substance doctrine. Under the provision, new section 7701(o) provides that in the case of any transaction to which the economic substance doctrine is relevant, such transaction is treated as having economic substance only if (1) the transaction changes in a meaningful way (apart from Federal income tax effects) the taxpayer's economic position, and (2) the taxpayer has a substantial purpose (apart from Federal income tax effects) for entering into such transaction. The provision provides a uniform definition of economic substance, but does not alter the flexibility of the courts in other respects.

The determination of whether the economic substance doctrine is relevant to a transaction is made in the same manner as if the provision had never been enacted. Thus, the provision does not change present law standards in determining when to utilize an economic substance analysis.

The provision is not intended to alter the tax treatment of certain basic business transactions that, under longstanding judicial and administrative practice are respected, merely because the choice between meaningful economic alternatives is largely or entirely based on comparative tax advantages. Among these basic transactions are (1) the choice between capitalizing a business enterprise with debt or equity; (2) a U.S. person's choice between utilizing a foreign corporation or a domestic corporation to make a foreign investment; (3) the choice to enter a transaction or series of transactions that constitute a corporate organization or reorganization under subchapter C; and (4) the choice to utilize a related-party entity in a transaction, provided that the arm's length standard of section 482 and other applicable concepts are satisfied. * * *

Conjunctive analysis

The provision clarifies that the economic substance doctrine involves a conjunctive analysis — there must be an inquiry regarding the objective effects of the transaction on the taxpayer's economic position as well as an inquiry regarding the taxpayer's subjective motives for engaging in the transaction. Under the provision, a transaction must satisfy both tests, *i.e.*, the transaction must change in a meaningful way (apart from Federal income tax effects) the taxpayer's economic position and the taxpayer must have a substantial non-Federal-income-tax purpose for entering into such transaction, in order for a transaction to be treated as having economic substance. * * *

Non-Federal-income-tax business purpose

Under the provision, a taxpayer's non-Federal-income-tax purpose for entering into a transaction (the second prong in the analysis) must be "substantial." For purposes of this analysis, any State or local income tax effect which is related to a Federal income tax effect is treated in the same manner as a Federal income tax effect. * * *

Profit potential

Under the provision, a taxpayer may rely on factors other than profit potential to demonstrate that a transaction results in a meaningful change in the taxpayer's economic position or that the taxpayer has a substantial non-Federal-income-tax purpose for entering into such transaction. * * *

Chapter 3

Introduction to Taxable and Tax-Free Mergers and Acquisitions

§ 3.1 Scope

This chapter provides an introduction to both taxable and tax-free acquisitions. Sec. 3.2 introduces taxable stock and asset acquisitions. Taxable asset acquisitions are examined in detail in Chapter 4, and taxable stock acquisitions are examined in detail in Chapter 5.

Sec. 3.2.B. focuses on the Federal income tax treatment of the acquisition of assets of a stand-alone C corporation (*i.e.,* a non-subsidiary regular corporation that is subject to tax under § 11 of the Code), and Sec. 3.2.C. focuses on the Federal income tax treatment of the acquisition of the stock of a stand-alone C corporation. Sec. 3.2.D. examines the Federal income tax treatment of the acquisition of the assets of a consolidated subsidiary, and Sec. 3.2.E. considers the acquisitions of the assets of an S corporation. Sec. 3.2.F. considers the Federal income tax treatment of the acquisition of the stock of a consolidated subsidiary and of an S corporation. Finally, Sec. 3.2.G. discusses issues that can arise when, as part of an asset acquisition, the acquiring corporation acquires the stock of a target's subsidiary.

Sec 3.3 introduces the various forms of reorganization transactions and discusses the tax treatment to the parties to a reorganization. This section starts with a look at the treatment of the parties and then proceeds to examine acquisitive reorganizations, which are the focus of Chapters 6 through 8. Non-acquisitive reorganizations are then examined in Sec. 3.3.E. Finally Sec. 3.4 presents a set of problems that illustrates the principles covered in this chapter for both taxable acquisitions and tax-free reorganizations.

§ 3.2 Introduction to Federal Income Tax Issues in Taxable Asset and Stock Acquisitions[*]

A. Introduction

The following discussion outlines some of the most salient Federal income tax principles in a taxable acquisition of the assets or stock of a target corporation.

---

[*] The author prepared a similar Guide for inclusion as an Appendix to the ABA's Model Asset Acquisition Agreement.

It is generally more advantageous from a Federal income tax standpoint to structure a taxable acquisition of a stand-alone C corporation as a stock acquisition without a §338 election. Overriding business considerations may, however, require that the transaction be structured as an asset acquisition. On the other hand, it is generally advantageous from a Federal income tax perspective to structure as a taxable asset acquisition the acquisition of either (1) the assets of a subsidiary ("consolidated subsidiary") of an affiliated group of corporations filing a consolidated return, or (2) the assets of an S corporation. In many cases, if a §338(h)(10) election is made, the Federal income tax treatment of a taxable stock acquisition of a consolidated subsidiary or of an S corporation will produce essentially the same results as an asset acquisition.

B. Acquisitions of the Assets of a Stand-Alone C Corporation

C corporations are subject to a corporate level tax that can, under §11 of the Code, be as high as 35 percent. The maximum rate on taxable income of less than $10,000,000 is generally 34%. The shareholders of C corporations are subject to a separate tax on the receipt of cash or property distributed by the corporation as dividends, redemption payments, or liquidation payments. Redemption payments can be treated as either capital transactions or distributions, which would constitute dividends to the extent of the corporation's earnings and profits. On the other hand, on the receipt of liquidating distributions, shareholders have capital gain or loss under §331. *See* Sec. 2.10.B. However, under §1(h), both dividends and capital gains received by individual shareholders are subject to a maximum rate of 20%, which with the Medicare tax on Net Investment Income is 23.8%. Thus, on the sale by a stand-alone C corporation of its assets followed by the liquidating distribution of the sales proceeds, a tax is imposed at both the corporate and shareholder levels on any gains realized. The above principles are illustrated in Example 1:

Example 1. All of the stock of Target Corporation (*TC*), a stand-alone C corporation, is owned by individual *A*. *TC* has no net operating losses, capital losses or unused credits. *TC* has a zero adjusted basis for its assets, which have a fair market value of $1,000,000. Acquiring Corporation (*AC*) agrees to purchase all of *TC*'s assets for a cash payment of $1,000,000. The facts are diagramed as follows:

Acquisitions of Assets

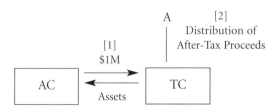

TC has a taxable gain of $1,000,000 (*i.e.*, $1,000,000 amount realized minus -0-adjusted basis for its assets) and incurs a tax of $350,000, which is 35% of $1,000,000. (All the examples in this chapter use a 35% corporate tax rate.) *TC* distributes its after-tax proceeds of $650,000 to *A* who under § 331 realizes a long-term capital gain in that amount (*i.e.*, $650,000 amount realized minus -0- adjusted basis for *A's* stock). *A* has a tax liability of $154,700 on this capital gain, which is 23.8% of $650,000. (All the examples in this chapter use an individual rate of 23.8% on long term capital gains and dividends, reflecting the 20% income tax rate on capital gains and dividends plus the 3.8% Medicare tax on Net Investment Income.) Thus, the total double tax from the sale and distribution is $504,700 (*i.e.*, 50.47% of the $1,000,000 sale price of TC's assets), computed as follows:

[1]	*TC's* TAX	$350,000
[2]	*A's* TAX	$154,700
[3]	TOTAL DOUBLE TAX [1+2]	$504,700

AC has a tax basis of $1,000,000 for the assets acquired from *TC*. Thus, the basis of the assets has been stepped-up from -0- to $1,000,000. *AC* and *TC* are required to allocate the purchase price among the assets sold in accordance with the rules of § 1060, which is designed to force the seller and buyer to allocate purchase price in accordance with the fair market value of the assets sold. *See* Chapter 4. Although the character of *TC's* gain or loss (*i.e.*, capital or ordinary) will depend upon the character of the assets sold, corporations do not receive the benefit of a lower tax rate on capital gains. Under § 197, *AC* can amortize (*i.e.*, deduct for tax purposes) the cost of intangibles, including the cost of goodwill and any covenants not to compete, over a period of 15 years on a straight line basis. *See* Sec. 4.3.C. Under the regulations under § 1060, the cost of the assets is allocated among the seven different asset classes specified in the regulations under § 338(b) (*see* Sec. 4.3.D), with any goodwill or going concern value allocated to class VII.

If *AC* paid for *TC's* assets with a note and the note is distributed by *TC* to *A*, then under § 453(h), *A* might qualify for installment sale treatment upon receipt of the note. *See* Chapter 4. In any event, even if the note qualifies for § 453 treatment in the hands of *TC*, under § 453B(a), upon distribution of the note *TC* will recognize gain.

If *TC* retains some of its assets and distributes the retained assets in the liquidating distribution to *A*, under § 336, which reflects the repeal of the *General Utilities* doctrine (*see* Chapter 2), *TC* realizes any gain (and may realize loss) inherent in the distributed assets. *See* Chapter 2. Gain or loss is also realized under § 336 by *TC* upon the distribution to a liquidating trust or partnership, and the shareholders have gain or loss under § 331 as if their interest in the trust's or partnership's properties were distributed directly to them. *See* Rev. Rul. 69-534, 1969-2, C.B. 48.

Any liabilities of *TC* assumed by *AC* in the transaction are treated as part of *TC's* amount realized on the sale and as part of *AC's* cost basis for the assets. *See Crane*, Sec. 1.5.B.

If instead of acquiring *TC*'s assets for cash or a note, *AC* acquires *TC*'s assets solely in exchange for voting stock of *AC*, then assuming certain other requirements are satisfied (including the distribution by *TC* to *A* of the stock received), the transaction would qualify as a C reorganization. *See* Chapter 8. In such case, *AC*, *TC*, and *A* would have tax-free treatment under §§ 1032, 361 and 354, respectively. Under § 362, *AC* would "carryover" *TC*'s zero basis for the assets received; and under § 358, *A* would "substitute" his zero basis for his *TC* stock as his new basis for the *AC* stock received. If *TC* were to merge into *AC* and the transaction did not qualify as a reorganization under § 368(a)(1)(A) (*see* Chapter 8), then under *West Shore Fuel, Inc. v. United States,* Sec. 4.2.A.2.b., the transaction would be treated as a taxable sale by *TC* of its assets followed by the deemed distribution of the merger consideration in a taxable § 331 transaction at the shareholder level. Thus, there are two levels of tax in such a transaction.

C. Acquisitions of the Stock of a Stand-Alone C Corporation

The double tax that applies on the sale by a stand-alone C corporation of its assets followed by a distribution of the sale proceeds is much higher than the single tax that applies on the sale of the stock of a stand-alone C corporation, assuming the acquiring corporation does not make a § 338 election to step-up the basis of the target's assets. This is illustrated in *Example 2*:

Example 2. The basic facts are as set out in *Example 1*, except that rather than purchasing *TC*'s assets, *AC* purchases from *A* all of *TC*'s outstanding stock for, assume, $1,000,000. The facts are diagramed as follows:

Stock Acquisition

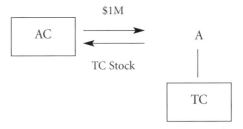

A has a capital gain of $1,000,000 and incurs a tax liability of $238,000 (23.8%). It would not make sense for *AC* to elect under § 338 to step-up the basis of *TC*'s assets because this would trigger a tax liability at the *TC* level. Thus, *TC* will continue to have a zero basis for its assets.

Since *AC* is buying the stock of *TC*, which owns assets with a fair market value of $1,000,000 and a basis of zero, it is likely that in a stock acquisition, *AC* would pay less than $1,000,000 to compensate for the absence of a step-up in basis of the assets.

If *AC* issues solely its voting stock in the acquisition of at least 80% of *TC*'s stock, the transaction might qualify as a tax-free stock for stock (B) reorganization under

§ 368(a)(1)(B). *See* Chapter 8. In such case, *TC*'s exchanging shareholders have non-recognition treatment under § 354 and take a substituted basis for the *AC* stock received, and *AC* has nonrecognition treatment under § 1032 and takes a carryover basis for the *TC* shares under § 362. Since the transaction is not a "purchase," *AC* cannot file a § 338 election.

From a Federal income tax standpoint, on the acquisition of a stand-alone C corporation that does not have losses or credits that can shelter gain, it is more advantageous for the parties to structure the acquisition as a stock acquisition without a § 338 election, and thereby avoid the double tax that would apply in an asset acquisition followed by liquidation and in a stock acquisition with a § 338 election.

Notwithstanding the double tax, there may be sound business reasons for structuring the acquisition of a stand-alone C corporation as an asset acquisition. Probably the principal reason for acquiring such a corporation in a taxable asset acquisition is that this form permits the acquiring corporation to purchase specified assets of the target and to assume specified liabilities. In this regard, the asset acquisition is more flexible than a stock acquisition.

As indicated in Chapter 5, if *TC* is acquired in a taxable reverse subsidiary merger, there is a single level of tax at the shareholder level, and *AC* can, if it chooses, make a § 338 election.

Chapter 5 deals with the impact of the limitations in § 382 on the ability to utilize a target's net operating losses after a stock acquisition.

D. Acquisition of Assets of a Consolidated Subsidiary

The acquisition of the assets of a consolidated subsidiary followed by a liquidating distribution by the consolidated subsidiary to its parent will produce a single level of tax for the selling consolidated group. This is illustrated in *Example 3*:

Example 3. The facts are the same as those set out in *Example 1*, except the stock of *TC* is held by Parent Corporation (*PC*), and *TC* joins with *PC* in filing a consolidated return. Consolidated returns are examined in Chapter 5. *PC*'s basis for its *TC* stock is zero. *AC* purchases *TC*'s assets for $1,000,000 in cash, and *TC* distributes the cash. The facts are diagramed as follows:

Acquisition of Assets of a Subsidiary

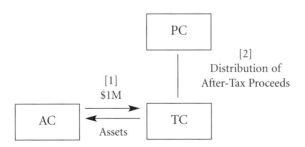

TC's gain is $1,000,000, and the tax for the consolidated group as a result of the sale (assuming no other member of the consolidated group has losses that offset *TC*'s gain) is $350,000 (35%). *TC* then liquidates distributing the after-tax proceeds of $650,000 to *PC*.

Since *PC* owns more than 80% of *TC*'s stock, the liquidation is governed by § 332 (*see* Chapter 2), and *PC* has no gain or loss on receipt of the liquidation proceeds. In fact, in this situation even without § 332, *PC* would have no gain on the liquidation because the basis of its stock in S is increased to $650,000 as a result of the sale. *See* Chapter 5. Under § 337, *TC* has no gain or loss on the § 332 liquidation. *See* Sec. 2.10.C. Thus, there is a single level of tax on the sale of *TC*'s assets followed by the liquidating distribution of the after-tax proceeds. However, if *PC* distributes the after-tax proceeds to its shareholders, those shareholders would be subject to dividend tax on the distribution assuming *PC* has adequate E&P. *See* Chapter 2.

The assets of a consolidated subsidiary can be acquired in a (C) reorganization. *See* Chapter 8. However, if the parent corporation distributes to its shareholders the stock of the acquiring corporation it receives from its subsidiary, the parent will be taxed on any gain inherent in the stock, and the shareholders generally will have a dividend, assuming the parent has adequate E&P. Thus, the parent will have tax-free treatment only if it continues to hold the stock of the acquiring corporation.

E. Acquisition of Assets of an S Corporation

The issues discussed here regarding S corporations are explored in greater detail in Chapter 11. If an S corporation that is not subject to the § 1374 built-in-gains tax, which applies to an S corporation that was previously a C corporation, sells its assets in an asset acquisition followed by a liquidation, there is just one level of tax on the sale and liquidation. Under § 1366, any gain from the sale is taken into account by the shareholders, and under § 1367, the shareholders increase the basis of their shares by the amount of the gain. As a result of the basis increase, the shareholders generally will not have any additional gain on the receipt of the liquidating distribution. These principles are illustrated in *Example 4*:

Example 4. The basic facts are the same as in *Example 1*, except *TC* is an S corporation without any built-in-gain assets. *TC* sells its assets, which have a fair market value of $1,000,000 and a basis of zero, for $1,000,000 in cash. On the sale, S has a taxable gain of $1,000,000, and this gain is taken into account by *TC*'s sole shareholder *A*.

The character of such gain (either ordinary or capital) will depend upon the character of such assets sold to the corporation. Assume that half the gain is ordinary and half is long-term capital gain. In such case, *A*'s tax on the sale would be $319,000, computed as follows:

[1] ORDINARY INCOME	$500,000
[2] MAXIMUM TAX RATE ON ORDINARY INCOME OF INDIVIDUALS, 39.6%, SAY, 40%	40%
[3] TAX ON ORDINARY INCOME	$200,000
[4] CAPITAL GAINS	$500,000
[5] MAXIMUM RATE ON CAPITAL GAINS	23.8%
[6] TAX ON CAPITAL GAINS	$119,000
[7] TOTAL TAX ON ORDINARY INCOME AND CAPITAL GAINS [3+6]	$319,000

Note that even though in the Subchapter S situation, there is a 39.6% maximum rate on the individual shareholder with respect to the ordinary income realized by the S corporation, that ordinary income tax will generally be less than the double tax from operating as a C corporation.

The basis of *A*'s shares in *TC* is increased from -0- to $1,000,000. *TC* distributes the $1,000,000 to *A* in a liquidating distribution. *A* has no gain or loss on receipt of the $1,000,000, because under § 331, *A* is deemed to have sold her shares, in which she has a basis of $1,000,000, for $1,000,000.

AC has a $1,000,000 basis for the assets acquired from *TC*. *AC* and *TC* must allocate the purchase price in accordance with the provisions of § 1060, and under § 197, *AC* may amortize the cost of intangibles, including goodwill, over a period of 15 years.

If *TC* is subject to the built-in-gains tax under § 1374 on the sale of its assets, *TC* will have a corporate level tax on the sale of built-in-gain assets, and the shareholders will be subject to a separate tax on the after-tax proceeds from such sale. Thus, a double tax applies with respect to the built-in-gains.

An S corporation can be acquired in a (C) reorganization (*i.e.,* a stock for asset reorganization) with essentially the same results that apply in the acquisition of the assets of a regular C corporation in a (C) reorganization.

F. Acquisition of (1) Stock of a Consolidated Subsidiary and (2) Stock of an S Corporation

AC purchases the stock of a consolidated subsidiary (*TC*) from Parent Corporation (*PC*) in a transaction described as follows:

Acquisition of Stock of a Subsidiary

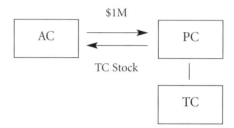

Under § 338(h)(10), *AC* and *PC* can jointly agree to treat the transaction as a sale of assets by *TC*. *See* Chapter 5. As a result of the election, the transaction is treated as follows. First, *TC* is treated as having sold and reacquired its assets, thereby giving *TC* a stepped-up basis for its assets. Second, the gain from the sale is included in *PC*'s consolidated return. Third, under § 332, *PC* is deemed to have received a tax-free liquidating distribution of $1,000,000 from *TC*.

Thus, assuming the basis *PC* has for the stock of *TC* is the same as the basis *TC* has for its assets, the tax treatment to *PC* from the sale of the stock of *TC* with a § 338(h)(10) election should be the same as the tax treatment from the sale by *TC* of its assets followed by a liquidating distribution.

If *AC* purchases the stock of an S corporation there is no adjustment in the basis of *TC*'s assets unless *AC* makes a § 338 election. Under the regulations under § 338(h)(10), *AC* and the selling shareholders of the S corporation may jointly elect to treat the transaction as if the S corporation sold the assets while the stock was held by the selling shareholders. In such case, the selling shareholders (1) report the gain or loss from the sale, (2) adjust the basis of their shares accordingly, and (3) are deemed to have received a liquidating distribution in the amount of the consideration paid for their stock. *See* Sec. 11.8.B. This type of election permits a step-up in basis for the corporation's assets with only a single tax. Thus, assuming the basis the shareholders of an S corporation have in the stock of the corporation equals the basis the corporation has in its assets and the built-in-gains tax is not applicable, the tax treatment to the shareholders from the sale of the stock of the S corporation with a § 338(h)(10) election, should be the same as in a sale by the corporation of its assets followed by a liquidating distribution.

G. Acquisition of Subsidiary as Part of Asset Acquisition

The stock of a subsidiary of a target may be acquired in a transaction in which the assets of the target are acquired. If the acquisition is taxable, *AC* takes a fair market value basis for the stock of the subsidiary, and *AC* and *TC* can jointly file a § 338(h)(10) election to treat the transaction as a taxable asset acquisition as outlined above. If for some reason a § 338(h)(10) election is not filed, *AC* would only make a standard § 338 election if the acquired subsidiary had sufficient NOLs or credits to shelter the tax from the deemed sale of its assets.

If *AC* does not want the risk of acquiring the liabilities that are inherent in an acquisition of a subsidiary's stock, *AC* could either (1) acquire the assets of the subsidiary and the subsidiary could then be liquidated tax-free into *TC* under § 332 (*see* Chapter 2), or (2) have *TC* first liquidate the subsidiary tax-free under § 332 and then acquire the assets of the former subsidiary directly from *TC*.

§ 3.3 Introductory Note on the Current Reorganization Provisions

A. Introduction

This section introduces the broad sweep of the reorganization provisions. Each of the forms of reorganization is introduced, and the treatment of the parties to a reorganization is discussed. Each topic is explored in greater detail in later chapters. The problems in Sec. 3.4 are designed to assist in an understanding of the basic principles.

B. In General

The term "reorganization" is defined in § 368(a)(1) as:

(1) a statutory merger or consolidation (the "(A)") (*see* § 368(a)(1)(A));

(2) a stock for stock acquisition (the "(B)") (*see* § 368(a)(1)(B));

(3) a stock for asset acquisition (the "(C)") (*see* § 368(a)(1)(C));

(4) a transfer of property by one corporation to another, including a split-up of a single corporation into two or more corporations (the "(D)") (*see* § 368(a)(1)(D));

(5) a recapitalization (the "(E)") (*see* § 368(a)(1)(E));

(6) a mere change in form (the "(F)") (*see* § 368(a)(1)(F)); and

(7) certain transfers by corporations in connection with bankruptcy reorganizations (the "(G)") (*see* § 386(a)(1)(G)).

Section 368(a)(2) provides special rules relating to the reorganizations defined in § 368(a)(1), and §§ 368(a)(2)(D) and (E) set out the forward and reverse subsidiary merger reorganizations discussed below. Section 368 says nothing about the treatment of the taxpayers involved in a reorganization; it merely describes those transactions that are reorganizations. The tax treatment to the various taxpayers is governed by §§ 354 through 362 and 381 to 383. The (G) bankruptcy reorganization and mergers between investment companies (*see* §368(a)(2)(F)) are not discussed here. However, the (G)reorganization is examined in Chapter 12.

Basically, reorganization transactions are shifts in corporate ownership in which the exchanging stockholder or security holder has a continuing interest in the corporation and has not merely been cashed out.

For example, an acquiring corporation may acquire the stock of a target corporation by issuing its own stock to the target's shareholders. The target's former shareholders then have a continuing interest in the target's assets, even though the direct ownership of the target has passed to the acquiring corporation. Such a transaction might qualify as a stock for stock (B) reorganization. In a (B), the target's shareholders receive nonrecognition under § 354 and take a substituted basis (*i.e.,* an exchanged basis under § 7701(a)(44)) for the stock received under § 358. On the other hand, the acquiring corporation has non-recognition treatment under § 1032 upon the issuance of its stock and takes a carryover basis under § 362(b) for the target's stock (*i.e.,* a transferred basis under § 7701(a)(43)). The reorganization provisions thus provide an exception to the recognition rule of § 1001 and the cost basis rule of § 1012.

In the discussion below, the tax treatment to the various taxpayers involved in a reorganization is outlined, and this is followed by an examination of the types of reorganizations.

C. Tax Treatment to the Taxpayers Involved in a Reorganization

Section 354(a)(1) gives shareholders and security holders nonrecognition treatment upon an exchange, pursuant to a "plan of reorganization," of stock or securities in a corporation that is a "party to a reorganization," provided the exchange is "solely" for stock or securities in such corporation or in another corporation that is a party to a reorganization. The term "plan of reorganization" is not defined in the statute; the regulations say, however, that the plan must be "adopted" by each of the corporate parties thereto. *See* § 1.368-3(a). The term "party to a reorganization" is defined in § 368(b) to include all of the corporations involved in a reorganization under § 368(a).

Section 354(a)(2)(A) limits the nonrecognition treatment for security holders to cases in which the principal amount of the securities received is equal to the principal amount surrendered. In the event cash or other property (boot) is received or the principal amount of the securities received exceeds the principal amount of the securities surrendered, then under § 356 the exchanging shareholder or security holder recognizes the gain realized to the extent of the boot and the fair market value of the excess principal amount of the securities received. *See* §§ 356(a)(1) and 356(d)(1) and (2)(A) and (B). Under §356(a)(2), any gain recognized with respect to stock may be treated as a dividend, to the extent of the shareholder's pro rata share of the accumulated earnings and profits, if the exchange "has the effect of the distribution of a dividend." The issue of whether gain is treated as a dividend is examined in Chapter 6; however, in view of the 20% maximum rate that now applies to dividends and capital gains, this issue may be of little practical significance. No loss is recognized. *See* §356(c). Also, under §354(a)(2)(C), nonqualified preferred stock received in a reorganization is generally treated as boot. The scope of §354 is examined further in Chapter 6.

Under §358, the exchanging shareholder or security holder who receives non-recognition treatment under §354 or partial nonrecognition treatment under §356 takes the stock or securities received at a substituted basis, decreased by the amount of any boot received and increased by any gain recognized. The basis of the boot, other than money, is the fair market value thereof. *See* §358(a)(2).

For example, assume that individual *S* owns all the stock of target corporation (*TC*). The stock has a value of $1 million, and *S*'s basis is $500K. *TC* merges into acquiring corporation (*AC*) in a transaction that qualifies as an (A) reorganization under §368(a)(1)(A). *S* surrenders his *TC* stock and receives *AC* stock with a value of $1 million. Under §354, *S* has nonrecognition treatment, and under §358, *S* takes a substituted basis of $500K for the *AC* stock. Assume, on the other hand, that *S* receives $900K of *AC* stock and $100K of cash (boot). The transaction still constitutes an (A) reorganization; however, *S* has a recognized gain of $100K under §356(a)(1), and the gain might be treated as a dividend under §356(a)(2). *See* Chapter 6. *S*'s basis under §358(a) for his *AC* stock is $500K (*i.e.*, the basis of his *TC* stock ($500K), minus the cash received ($100K), plus the gain recognized ($100K)). Since the value of his *AC* stock is $900K, *S* has deferred $400K of his gain.

On the corporate side of the ledger, §1032 provides for nonrecognition treatment upon the issuance of stock by a corporation. Also, no gain is recognized by a corporation upon the issuance of its securities. *See* §1.61-12(c)(1). Under §362(b), the acquiring corporation's basis for stock or assets received is a carryover basis, increased by the amount of any gain recognized by the transferor.

If a corporation (the target) that is a "party to a reorganization" exchanges its property solely for stock of another corporation (the acquiring corporation) that is a party to the reorganization, then under §361(a), the target corporation does not recognize any gain or loss. Under §358, the basis to the target corporation of the stock or securities it receives from the acquiring corporation is a substituted basis, decreased by the boot received and increased by the gain recognized.

Under §361(b), if the target corporation receives both stock and boot, the target recognizes the gain realized to the extent of the boot, unless the boot is distributed pursuant to the plan of reorganization. Under §361(c), the target does not recognize gain or loss on the distribution of stock of the acquiring corporation. Section 361 is explored in detail in Chapter 6.

Pursuant to §357(a), liabilities transferred from a target to an acquiring corporation generally do not constitute boot. *See* §357(b) and (c).

For example, where *TC* merges into *AC* with *TC*'s shareholder, *S,* receiving *AC* stock, *TC* has nonrecognition treatment under § 361(a). *AC* has nonrecognition under § 1032 upon the issuance of its stock and takes a carryover basis under § 362(b) for *TC*'s assets (*i.e.,* if *TC*'s basis for its assets was $200K, *AC*'s basis would be $200K).

Section 381 provides that in reorganizations in which the target's assets are transferred to the acquiring corporation, the target corporation's tax attributes (*e.g.,* earnings and profits and net operating losses) carry over to the acquiring corporation after the reorganization. This same rule applies for subsidiary liquidations under § 332 in which the parent takes a carryover basis under § 334(b)(1) for the assets received. Section 381 is examined in Chapter 8.

Section 382 limits the amount of a target's net operating losses that can be deducted after a reorganization. Also, § 382 limits the carryover of capital losses and certain credits. Section 382 is discussed in Chapters 5, 7, and 8.

The reorganizations under § 368 can be broadly categorized into acquisitive reorganizations and non-acquisitive reorganizations. Acquisitive reorganizations can be subdivided into asset reorganizations, which are transactions in which an acquiring corporation acquires the assets of a target corporation and stock reorganizations, which are transactions in which an acquiring corporation acquires the stock of a target corporation. The following sections give a brief introduction to acquisitive and non-acquisitive reorganizations.

D. Introduction to § 368 Acquisitive Reorganizations[*]

1. In General

Section 368 defines seven types of acquisitive reorganization transactions. Four of these reorganizations involve the acquisition of a target's assets and three involve the acquisition of a target's stock.

2. Asset Reorganizations

a. The Direct Merger under § 368(a)(1)(A)

The "(A)" reorganization under § 368(a)(1)(A) is a merger of a target directly into an acquiror with the target's shareholders receiving stock in the acquiror. In the merger all of the target's assets and liabilities pass over to the acquiror by operation of the state merger law. For private letter ruling purposes, to satisfy the continuity of interest requirement (*i.e.,* that a substantial portion of the consideration be in stock) at least 40% of the consideration paid in an (A) must be stock of the acquiror.[1] Thus, under

---

[*] Excerpt from Thompson, *Impact of Code Section 367 and the European Union's 1990 Council Directive on Tax-Free Cross-Border Mergers and Acquisitions,* Section II.A., 66 Univ. Of Cincinnati L. Rev. 1193 (1998).

1. Rev. Proc. 77-37, 1977-2 C.B. 568, Sec. 3.02, and Treas. Reg. § 1.368-1(e)(2)(u), Exp. 1.

the Service's view, up to 60% of the consideration paid can be non-stock consideration, *i.e.*, boot. The transaction can be diagramed as follows:

Direct "(A)" Merger Reorganization under § 368(a)(1)(A)

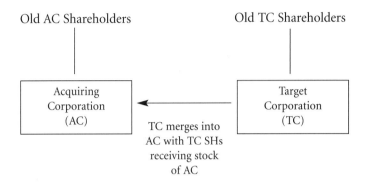

When the Dust Settles

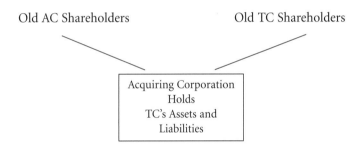

Under § 354, the target's shareholders have tax-free treatment on the receipt of the acquiror's common stock,[2] and under § 358 they take a substituted basis for the acquiror's stock, thereby deferring their gain. Any boot received is subject to tax under § 356 as either a dividend or capital gain.

The target has tax-free treatment under § 361, and the acquiror has tax-free treatment under § 1032 and takes a carryover basis for the target's assets under § 362(b). Under § 381, other tax attributes carryover to the acquiror.

b. Forward Subsidiary Merger under § 368(a)(2)(D)

A § 368(a)(2)(D) reorganization is a merger of a target into a subsidiary (Acquiring Subsidiary) of the acquiring corporation (Acquiring Parent). The Acquiring Subsidiary

---

2. As a result of an amendment to § 354 by the Taxpayer Relief Act of 1997, the target's shareholders will not receive tax-free treatment on the receipt of the acquiror's "nonqualified preferred stock." This applies for all forms of reorganization transactions.

must acquire substantially all of the target's assets and for private letter ruling purposes, to satisfy the continuity of interest requirement, at least 40% of the consideration paid must be stock of the Acquiring Parent. This transaction may be diagramed as follows:

Forward Subsidiary Merger Reorganization under § 368(a)(2)(D)

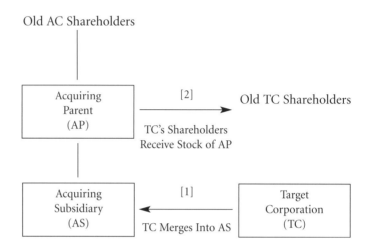

When the Dust Settles

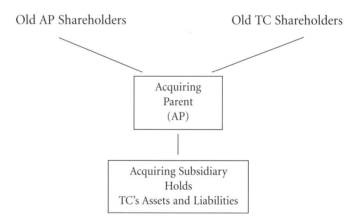

The target has tax-free treatment under § 361. The target's shareholders have tax-free treatment under § 354 on the receipt of stock of the Acquiring Parent and take a substituted basis for the stock under § 358. Both the Acquiring Sub and the Acquiring Parent have tax-free treatment under § 1032 and the regulations thereunder, and under § 362(b) the Acquiring Subsidiary takes a carryover basis for the target's assets. Also, under § 381, the Acquiring Subsidiary carries-over the target's other tax attributes.

c. Direct Stock for Asset Reorganization under § 368(a)(1)(C)

In this "(C)" reorganization, an acquiring corporation acquires substantially all of a target's assets in exchange solely for voting stock of the acquiror. The acquiror acquires specified assets of the target and assumes specified liabilities pursuant to an asset acquisition agreement. In certain limited circumstances the acquiror can pay up to 20% boot. The target must liquidate,[3] thereby distributing to the shareholders the stock received from the acquiror. The transaction can be diagramed as follows:

Direct "(C)" Stock for Asset Reorganization under § 368(a)(1)(C)

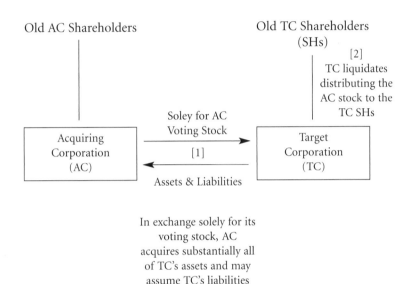

When the Dust Settles

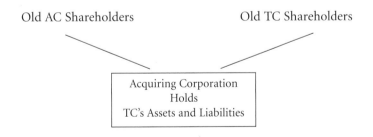

The target has tax-free treatment under § 361. The target's shareholders have tax-free treatment under § 354 and take a substituted basis under § 358 for the acquiror's stock they receive. The acquiror has tax-free treatment under § 1032 and takes a carry-over basis for the target's assets under § 362(b). Also, under § 381, the acquiror carries-over the target's other tax attributes.

---

3. § 368(a)(2)(H).

d. Triangular Stock for Asset Reorganization under § 368(a)(1)(C)

The triangular (C) reorganization is essentially the same as the direct (C) reorganization described above, except the acquisition is made by an Acquiring Subsidiary, and the consideration paid is voting stock of the Acquiring Parent. This form of transaction shields the Acquiring Parent's assets from any of the target's liabilities assumed by the Acquiring Subsidiary. The transaction can be diagramed as follows:

Triangular "(C)" Stock for Asset Reorganization under § 368(a)(1)(C)

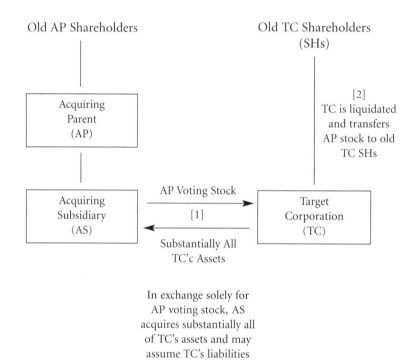

When the Dust Settles

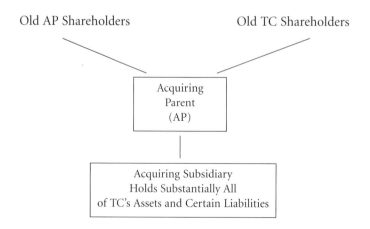

The tax treatment to the target and the target's shareholders is the same as in the (C) reorganization. Both the Acquiring Parent and Acquiring Subsidiary have tax-free treatment. Under § 362(b), the Acquiring Subsidiary takes a carry-over basis for the target's assets, and under § 381 the Acquiring Subsidiary carries-over the target's other tax attributes.

e. Summary of Asset Reorganizations

The four asset reorganizations are (1) the direct (A) merger, (2) the forward triangular merger, (3) the stock for asset (C) reorganization, and (4) the triangular stock for asset (C) reorganization. In each of these transactions the target's assets are transferred to the acquiror or an Acquiring Subsidiary.

3. Stock Reorganizations

a. Reverse Subsidiary Merger under § 368(a)(2)(E)

In the reverse triangular merger under § 368 (a)(2)(E), an Acquiring Subsidiary merges into the target, with the target's shareholders receiving voting stock of the Acquiring Parent in exchange for at least 80% of the target's stock. The balance of the target's stock may be acquired for boot. When the dust settles, the target has become a wholly-owned subsidiary of the Acquiring Parent. The transaction can be diagramed as follows:

Reverse Subsidiary Merger under § 368(a)(2)(E)

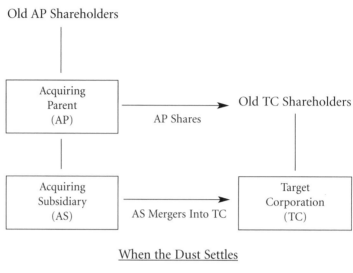

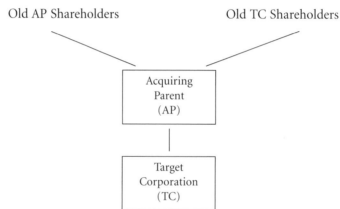

In this transaction the target's shareholders receive tax-free treatment under § 354 on receipt of stock of the acquiror, and the Acquiring Subsidiary, the target, and the Acquiring Parent also have nonrecognition treatment. The Acquiring Parent takes a carry-over basis for the target's stock.

b. Stock for Stock Reorganization under § 368(a)(1)(B)

In this "(B)" reorganization an acquiring corporation acquires in exchange solely for its voting stock at least 80% of the stock of a target. No boot can be used in the transaction. The acquiror will acquire the stock of the target pursuant to either (1) a stock acquisition agreement, or (2) in the case of a publicly held target, an exchange offer that is subject to regulation under the tender offer rules of the Securities Exchange Act of 1934. After the exchange the target is a subsidiary of the acquiror. The transaction may be diagramed as follows:

Stock for Stock "(B)" Reorganization under § 368(a)(1)(B)

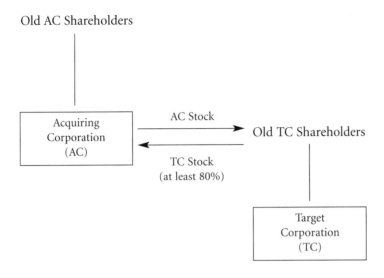

When the Dust Settles

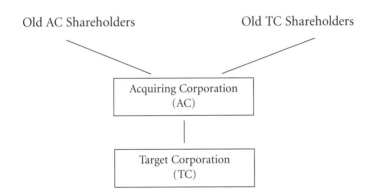

Under § 354 the target's shareholders have tax-free treatment. Under § 1032 the acquiror has tax-free treatment, and under § 362(b) the acquiror takes a carry-over basis for the target's stock.

c. Triangular (B) Reorganization under § 368(a)(1)(B)

This triangular (B) reorganization is the same as the direct (B), except an Acquiring Subsidiary acquires the target's stock in exchange for stock of the Acquiring Parent. This transaction can be diagramed as follows:

Triangular (B) Reorganization under § 368(a)(1)(B)

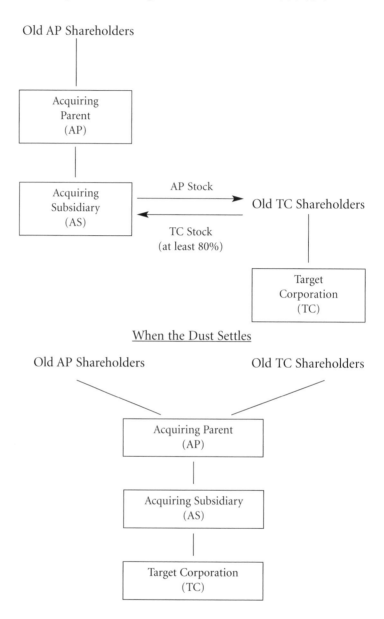

d. Summary of Stock Reorganizations

The three stock reorganizations are (1) the reverse subsidiary merger under §368(a)(2)(E), (2) the stock for stock (B) reorganization under §368(a)(1)(B), and (3) the triangular stock for stock (B) reorganization under § 368 (a)(1)(B). In each of these transactions, the target ends up as a subsidiary of the acquiror or Acquiring Subsidiary, and assuming only voting stock consideration is paid, the target's shareholders have tax-free treatment under §354.

4. Summary of Acquisitive Reorganizations

These seven forms of acquisitive reorganizations can be subdivided into four asset reorganizations and three stock reorganizations:

Asset Reorganizations: The (A) merger reorganization, the straight and triangular (C) stock for asset reorganizations, and the forward subsidiary merger reorganization under § 368(a)(2)(D). Each of these asset reorganizations is explored in Chapter 7.

Stock Reorganizations: The straight and triangular (B) stock for stock reorganization and the reverse subsidiary merger under § 368(a)(2)(E). Each of these stock reorganizations is explored in Chapter 8.

After each of these reorganizations, the assets or stock acquired may be pushed down to a subsidiary of the acquiring corporation. *See* § 368(a)(2)(C).

E. The Non-Acquisitive Reorganizations

1. The (D) Reorganization

a. Introduction

In a (D) reorganization under § 368 (a)(1)(D), a corporation (the "distributing corporation") transfers all or part of its assets to another corporation (the "controlled corporation"), and immediately after the transfer, the distributing corporation or its shareholders, or a combination thereof, are in control of the controlled corporation. The distribution by the distributing corporation to its shareholders of stock or securities of the controlled corporation must qualify under §§ 354, 355 or 356. In addition, as illustrated in the *Gregory* case, which is set out in Sec. 2.11.B., the transaction must have a business purpose.

b. The Nondivisive (D)

The (D) reorganization contemplated by § 354 is a transaction in which the distributing corporation (1) transfers "substantially all" of its assets to the controlled corporation, and (2) distributes pursuant to the plan of reorganization the stock or securities and other property received as well as its other properties. Thus, the distributing corporation is stripped of its assets and liquidated. *See* § 354(b). This type of transaction is known as a nondivisive (D) and can be diagramed as follows:

Nondivisive (D) under §§ 368(a)(1)(D) and 354(b)

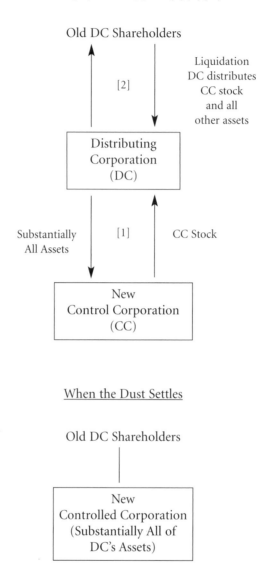

The distributing corporation receives nonrecognition under §§ 351 and 361 on the transfer of the assets to the controlled corporation and receives nonrecognition under § 361 on the distribution of the stock and securities of the controlled corporation. The controlled corporation receives nonrecognition under § 1032 on the issuance of its stock and takes a carryover basis for the assets under § 362. The shareholders of the distributing corporation receive nonrecognition treatment under § 354 and take a carryover basis under § 358.

Sec. 4.2.B. examines the nondivisive D reorganization in the context of what would otherwise be a taxable asset acquisition.

c. The Divisive (D): Spin-Offs, Split-Offs and Split-Ups

Section 355 encompasses divisive (D) reorganizations under § 368 (a)(1)(D) in which there is a breakup of a corporation into two or more corporations. Divisive (D) reorganizations generally fall into three broad categories: spin-offs, split-offs and split-ups. In a spin-off, a distributing corporation transfers part of its assets to a controlled corporation in exchange for stock and then distributes to its shareholders the stock of the controlled corporation in a pro rata distribution. Thus, the shareholders continue their same pro rata interest but in two corporations rather than one. In a split-off, stock of the distributing corporation is redeemed in exchange for stock of the controlled corporation. In a split-up, the distributing corporation contributes its assets to two or more controlled corporations and then liquidates, distributing the stock to its shareholders. Section 355 applies not only to (D) reorganizations; it also applies to distributions of the stock of existing subsidiaries. In order for a transaction to fit within § 355, the following basic requirements must be satisfied:

(A) The distributing corporation must distribute to its shareholders or security holders "solely" stock or securities of the controlled corporation (*see* § 355(a)(1)(A) and 355(a)(2)); the distribution need not be pro rata. If boot is distributed, § 356 will apply (*see* § 356(a) and (b));

(B) The transaction must not be a "device" for the distribution of E & P (*see* § 355(a)(1)(B));

(C) A separate active trade or business that has been conducted for at least five years must continue to be conducted after the distribution by each of the distributing and controlled corporations (*see* § 355(a)(1)(C) and 355(b)); and

(D) The distributing corporation must distribute all of the stock or securities of the controlled corporation or an amount of stock of the controlled corporation amounting to control, provided that in the latter case it is established that the retention of stock or securities of the controlled corporation is not for tax avoidance purposes (*see* § 355(a)(1)(D)).

For transactions that fall within § 355, the shareholders or security holders of the distributing corporation receive nonrecognition treatment on receipt of the stock or securities of the controlled corporation. *See* § 355(a). Thus, § 355 is analogous to § 354, which gives nonrecognition treatment for reorganizations other than the divisive (D). In the event boot is distributed in a § 355 transaction, gain is recognized to the extent of the boot. *See* § 356(a)(1). The gain recognized is generally treated as a dividend. *See* §§ 356(a)(2) and 356(b).

At the corporate level, the distributing corporation generally has nonrecognition treatment under § 355(c) or § 361(c) (in the case of a (D) reorganization) on the distribution of stock or securities of the controlled corporation. However, the distributing corporation has gain recognition in the case of certain distributions to new shareholders (§ 355(d)) and distributions followed by an acquisition of the distributing corporation or the controlled corporation (§ 355(e)).

The divisive (D) and § 355 are explored in Chapter 9. A divisive (D) spin-off is diagramed as follows:

Divisive Spin-Off under §§ 368(a)(1)(D) and 355

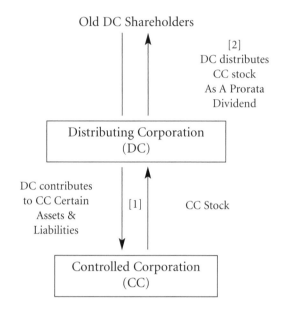

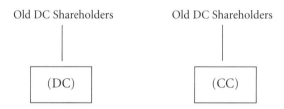

2. The (E) Recapitalization

The (E) reorganization is a recapitalization of a corporation; that is, a restructuring of the capital of a single corporation. For example, if the shareholders of a corporation exchange their common stock for new common stock, the transaction may constitute a recapitalization. The shareholders receive non-recognition treatment under § 354 and take a substituted basis under § 358. The corporation has nonrecognition treatment under § 1032 upon the issuance of its stock. The recapitalization is not examined further here.

3. The (F) Mere Change in Form

The (F) reorganization is a "mere change in identity, form, or place of organization." For instance, a New York corporation reincorporates in Virginia. Under § 381(b)(3), post-reorganization net operating losses can be carried back to a former corporation only in an (F). The (F) reorganization is not examined further here.

§ 3.4 Introductory Problems on Reorganizations and Taxable Acquisitions

The following problems are designed to illustrate the basic operation of both the provisions governing reorganizations and the provisions governing taxable acquisitions.

Individuals *A* and *B* each own 50 percent of the outstanding stock of target corporation (*TC*). *A*'s basis for his stock is $50K, and *B*'s basis is $150K. The value of *TC*'s stock is $200K, and, consequently, *A*'s and *B*'s shares are each worth $100K. The fair market value of *TC*'s assets is $220K, and the adjusted basis thereof is $100K. *TC* has liabilities of $20K and E & P of $100K. Acquiring corporation (*AC*) is interested in acquiring *TC* in a nontaxable reorganization.

(a) What result to *A, B, TC* and *AC*, if *TC* merges into *AC* in a transaction in which *A* and *B* each receive voting stock of *AC* with a fair market value of $100K? *See* §§ 368(a)(1)(A), 368(b), 354, 356, 357, 358, 361, 362, and 1032. What if the merger consideration is cash?

(b) What if *AC* forms a subsidiary (*AC-S*) by transferring *AC* voting stock to it, and *TC* merges into *AC-S* with *A* and *B* receiving the *AC* stock? Focus only on the treatment of *A* and *B* and *AC-S*'s basis for the *TC* assets. What if *AC-S* merges into *TC*? Focus only on the treatment of *A* and *B. See* §§ 368(a)(1)(A), (a)(2)(D), (a)(2)(E), 368(b), 368(c), 354, 357, 358, 361, 362, and 1032. What if in each case the merger consideration is cash?

(c) What result to *A, B, TC* and *AC*, if *AC* acquires the stock of *TC* from *A* and *B* in exchange for $200K of voting stock of *AC* ? What result if *AC-S* makes the acquisition using *AC* voting stock? Focus only on the treatment of *A* and *B* and *AC-S*'s basis for the *TC* stock. *See* §§ 368(a)(1)(B), 368(b), 368(c), 354, 357, 358, 361, 362, and 1032. What result if the consideration paid in each case is cash?

(d) What results to *A, B, TC* and *AC* if *AC* acquires the assets and liabilities of *TC* in exchange for $200K of voting stock of *AC*, and *TC* is then liquidated? Suppose *AC-S* makes the acquisition using $200K of *AC* voting stock? *See* §§ 368(a)(1)(C), (a)(2)(B), 368(b), 354, 356, 357, 358, 361, 362, and 1032. What result if the consideration paid in each case is cash?

(e) In general, what result if after the transactions described in (a) through (d) above, the acquiring corporation contributes the stock or assets acquired to a subsidiary of the acquiring corporation? *See* §§ 368(a)(2)(C), 368(b), 351, 354, 357, 358, 361, 362, and 1032.

(f) Assume *A* and *B* disagree on selling out to *AC*, and they decide to split-up and go their separate ways. In general, is there any way *TC* can be divided down the middle into two corporations in a nontaxable division? *See* §§ 368(a)(1)(D), 368(b), 351, 355, 357, 358, 361, 362, and 1032.

(g) Assume that *A* is quite old and would like very much to pull out of the business and that his son *B* is young and wants to continue. In general, what result if *A* turns in his common stock for a new issue of preferred stock that pays a 12% dividend, and *B* thereby becomes the only common shareholder? *See* §§ 368(a)(1)(E), 368(b), 354, 357, 358, and 1032. What is the effect of § 354 (a)(2)(C) relating to nonqualified preferred stock? Is the preferred § 306 stock? *See* §§ 305(a) and 306(c).

(h) In general, what result if *TC* changes its state of incorporation? *See* §§ 368(a)(1)(F), 354, 357, 358, 361, 362, and 1032.

Chapter 4

Taxable Asset Acquisitions: Including the Treatment of Net Operating Losses

§ 4.1 Scope

This chapter deals with taxable asset acquisitions, including the treatment of net operating losses in such transactions. Sec. 4.2 addresses issues of concern to both the acquiring corporation and the target corporation, such as the structure of the transaction. Sec. 4.3 deals with issues of concern primarily to the acquiring corporation and its shareholders, and Sec. 4.4 deals with issues of concern principally to the target corporation and its shareholders. Sec. 4.5 deals with planning for the utilization of the target's net operating losses, and Sec. 4.6 presents summary problems. Sec. 4.7 discusses the Federal income tax treatment of cross border taxable asset acquisitions. To give the student a practical experience in dealing with these transactions, Sec. 4.8 contains selected provisions from a sample asset acquisition agreement. As a starting point, the student should read this agreement.

For a more detailed discussion of taxable asset acquisitions, *see* Ginsburg and Levin, Mergers, *supra* Sec. 1.12. *See also* the most recent edition of the PLI, *Tax Strategies, supra* Sec. 1.12; and Thompson, *Mergers, Acquisitions, and Tender Offers, supra* Sec. 1.12 at Chapter 9.

§ 4.2 Issues of Concern to Both the Acquiring Corporation and the Target Corporation

A. Structure of the Transaction

1. Direct Purchase by Acquiring Corporation of Target's Assets

State business corporation laws generally require the approval of the stockholders and the board of directors of the target corporation for a sale of "all or substantially all" of the target's assets. Under Delaware law, a simple majority of the board of directors and a majority of the outstanding shares entitled to vote are necessary to effectuate such a transaction. *See* Delaware Business Corporation Law § 271. The approval of the acquiring corporation's shareholders is not needed for an asset acquisition; the acquiring corporation can, therefore, act on a resolution of its board of directors.

A purchase of assets is usually effectuated by a purchase agreement, sometimes labeled *Asset Purchase Agreement,* that specifies the assets to be acquired and the liabilities to be assumed by the acquiring corporation. Sec. 4.8 contains selected provisions from a sample asset acquisition agreement. Usually the target is liquidated after the sale and the proceeds are distributed to the target's shareholders.

There can be several major problems with effectuating a transaction as a purchase of assets. Separate documents of conveyance might have to be prepared for the transfer of the target's assets. Releases must be obtained for any covenants that prohibit sale of the target's assets, and the bulk sales act may have to be complied with. If the acquiring corporation assumes any of the target's liabilities, separate assumption documents might have to be prepared. Even if the target's liabilities are not assumed, the acquiring corporation may nonetheless be held responsible for the target's liabilities under the *de facto* merger doctrine or similar successor liability principles. Finally, there may be transfer and sales taxes imposed on the transaction.

In order to insulate the acquiring corporation's assets from the target's liabilities, the acquisition can be made by a subsidiary of the acquiring corporation.

Because of the repeal of former § 337 by the Tax Reform Act of 1986 (*see* Chapter 2), a target corporation has complete recognition on the sale of its assets. If, however, the consideration received by the target is stock of the acquiring corporation, the transaction might qualify as a tax-free asset reorganization under § 368(a)(1)(C). *See* Chapter 7.

Under § 336 the target recognizes gain and in certain cases loss on the distribution of any retained property. *See* Sec. 2.10. The target has no gain or loss on the distribution of cash.

The shareholders have capital gain or loss under § 331 on the receipt of the liquidation proceeds. The treatment of any installment obligations received by the target on the sale of its assets and distributed to the shareholders is discussed in Sec. 4.4.D.2.

The acquiring corporation takes a fair market value basis under § 1012 for the assets acquired. The basis is allocated among the assets in accordance with the rules of § 1060, which are discussed in Sec. 4.3.D. The target's tax attributes, such as basis and net operating losses, do not carryover to the acquiring corporation, but stay with the target.

Because of the double tax that arises on the sale by a C corporation of its assets followed by liquidation, the taxable asset acquisition form is not the preferred acquisition technique. This is particularly so in the case of the acquisition of a stand-alone target corporation that does not have net operating losses (NOLs) that can offset its gain. Because the target's shareholders ultimately bear the economic burden of the double tax, it can be assumed that they generally will insist upon a sale of their target stock, rather than a sale by the target of its assets. As pointed out in Chapter 5, the target level tax can be avoided in a stock acquisition.

If the target is a subsidiary in a consolidated group of corporations, the parent corporation may be indifferent between selling the target's stock and selling its assets. This is because the basis adjustment to the subsidiary's stock required by

§ 1503(e) (*see* Sec. 5.5.A.7.c) may give the parent a basis for the subsidiary's stock that approximates the subsidiary's basis for its assets. Consequently, the same amount of gain will arise on a sale of the target's assets that would arise on a sale of the target's stock by the parent. Also, the liquidation of the target after the sale of its assets is tax-free to the parent under § 332 and to the subsidiary under § 337. *See* Chapter 2.

2. Forward Cash Merger

a. Introduction

As demonstrated by the *West Shore Fuel* case below, a merger of the target corporation into the acquiring corporation or into a subsidiary of the acquiring corporation is treated for tax purposes as a purchase of the target's assets followed by the liquidation of the target, unless the transaction qualifies as a reorganization under § 368(a)(1)(A) or § 368(a)(2)(D). In this transaction, a tax applies both at the target level and the target shareholder level.

In order to qualify as a reorganization, a substantial portion of the consideration must consist of stock of the acquiring corporation. Thus, if the consideration is cash or notes or a combination of the two, the merger will be treated as a taxable asset acquisition.

This type of transaction is referred to as either a taxable forward merger in the case of a merger of the target directly into the acquiring corporation or a taxable forward subsidiary merger of the target in the case of a merger into a subsidiary of the acquiring corporation. Normally the target will merge into a subsidiary of the acquiring corporation in order to insulate the acquiring parent's assets from the target's liabilities.

The merger must be approved by the board of directors and the shareholders of the target. *See, e.g.,* Delaware Business Corporation Law § 251. If no stock of the acquiring corporation is issued, the acquiring corporation's shareholders generally need not approve the merger. *See, e.g.,* Delaware Business Corporation Law § 251. As a result of the merger, the target's assets and liabilities are, by operation of law, transferred to the acquiring corporation. Thus, one advantage of the merger is that there is no need to separately transfer the target's assets and liabilities; the major disadvantage is that all of the target's liabilities pass to the acquiring corporation.

b. Illustration of a Taxable Forward Subsidiary Merger
West Shore Fuel, Inc. v. United States

United States Court of Appeals, Second Circuit, 1979
598 F.2d 1236

Oakes, Circuit Judge:

[The target corporation (Old American) merged into the acquiring corporation (New American). Pursuant to the merger, the shareholders of Old American received cash and notes of New American. The issue was whether the merger should be viewed as a purchase by New American of the stock of Old American or of the assets of Old American. Under §453, as it then applied, the taxpayers (shareholders of Old American) would be entitled to installment sale treatment only if the merger was viewed as a stock acquisition.]

* * * The issue * * * is whether [New American] was the "purchaser" of the taxpayers' stock. Resolution of that question depends on the proper characterization of the underlying corporate transaction. The taxpayers argue that because the transaction took the form of a merger under state law, [New American] was the direct purchaser of the taxpayers' stock. But the United States District Court held that in substance the underlying transaction was a sale of [Old American's] assets to [New American] for its cash and notes, followed by a liquidation in which the taxpayers as stockholders of [Old American] received the cash and notes as a liquidating distribution. * * * We agree with this interpretation and consequently affirm the judgment of the district court dismissing the taxpayers' suits for a refund of income taxes.

Background * * *

We agree with the court below and with the Commissioner that the transaction here, although carried out through the medium of a merger, in substance was a sale of assets coupled with a liquidation, not a direct sale of stock by shareholders to New American. We will assume, as taxpayers contend, that this transaction qualified under New York law, * * * as a statutory merger and did not consist of a sale, exchange, or other disposition of assets. * * * We nevertheless conclude that as a matter of federal law, the transaction was a sale of assets, not a sale of stock. As Judge Curtin pointed out, [New American] did not make any tender offers to individual shareholders, and individual shareholders could not elect whether to sell or retain their stock but could only vote for or against the plan of merger and liquidation. Once shareholders owning two-thirds of the outstanding shares voted in favor of the plan, under New York law an individual shareholder had only a right to receive a liquidation distribution. When the transaction was completed New American held the assets of Old American but not its shares, Old American no longer existed as a separate corporate entity, and New American had absorbed Old American's business. Even more important, perhaps, if the transaction had been a simple sale of stock, New American need not have assumed Old American's liabilities. * * *

Notes and Questions

1. *West Shore Fuel* illustrates the use of a state merger statute to effectuate an acquisition of a target's assets. There, Oswego Shipping, the parent (*AC-P*), formed Oswego Steamship, the acquiring subsidiary (*AC-S*), for the purpose of making the acquisition of American Steamship, the target (*TC*). *TC* was then merged into *AC-S*, with *TC*'s shareholders receiving cash and notes. Although the transaction was a merger under state law, it was not a tax-free merger under §368(a)(1)(A), because *TC*'s shareholders did not have a "continuity of interest" in *TC*'s assets through a stock interest in *AC-P* or *AC-S*. The continuity of interest doctrine is explored in detail in Sec. 4.2.

2. State precisely the tax impact of the transaction in *West Shore Fuel* on each of *AC-P, AC-S, TC* and *TC*'s shareholders. *See, e.g.,* Rev. Rul. 69-6, 1969-1 C.B. 104.

3. Under the present § 453(h) (*see* Sec. 4.4.D.2), shareholders of a target may receive installment sale treatment upon receipt, as a liquidating distribution from a target corporation, of notes of an acquiring corporation that purchased the target's assets.

3. Sub's Use of Parent's Stock in a Taxable Asset Acquisition or Taxable Forward Subsidiary Merger

a. Section 1032 Generally Not Applicable to Sub's Sale of Parent's Stock

Revenue Ruling 70-305
1970-1 C.B. 169

S, a wholly owned domestic subsidiary of domestic corporation *P*, purchased shares of *P*'s stock on the open market and sold the stock to outside interests at a gain. *S* received dividends from *P* prior to the sale of the stock.

HELD, the stock of *P* held by *S* is not treasury stock and the sale of such stock is not to be treated as a sale by the corporation of its own capital stock pursuant to the provisions of section 1032 of the Internal Revenue Code of 1954. The sale of such stock to outside interests is a transaction resulting in a gain or loss.

The dividends, however, will be treated as prescribed by section 243 of the Code, pertaining to dividends received by corporations. * * *

b. Exception for Immediate Disposition by Sub of Parent's Stock in Taxable Acquisition

Preamble to Notice of Proposed [Now Final] Rule Making on Guidance under § 1032
(REG-106221-98) (September 23, 1998)

Background Section 1032(a) provides that no gain or loss shall be recognized to a corporation on the receipt of money or other property in exchange for stock (including treasury stock) of such corporation. No gain or loss shall be recognized by a corporation with respect to any lapse or acquisition of an option to buy or sell its stock (including treasury stock).

Before the enactment of section 1032 in 1954, Treasury regulations provided that "where a corporation deals in its own shares as it might in the shares of another corporation, the resulting gain or loss is to be computed in the same manner as though the corporation were dealing in the shares of another." (Treas. Reg. 111 § 29.22(a)-15 (1934)).

As applied, this regulation resulted in the recognition of gain or loss on the disposition by a corporation of its treasury stock, even though the corporation would not have recognized gain or loss on the disposition of newly issued shares. *See, e.g.,*

Firestone Tire & Rubber Co. v. Commissioner, 2 T.C. 827 (1943). This disparity of treatment gave rise to tax avoidance possibilities. A corporation expecting a gain upon disposition of treasury shares might avoid such gain by canceling its treasury shares and issuing new stock, whereas a corporation might produce a fictitious loss by purchasing its own shares and reselling them at a lower price.

Congress enacted section 1032(a) in 1954 to eliminate this potential disparity between the tax treatment of a disposition by a corporation of its treasury stock and a disposition of newly issued stock. H.R. No. 1337, 83d Cong., 2d Sess. 268 (1954).

Rev. Rul. 74-503 (1974-2 C.B. 117) considers the tax consequences of a parent corporation's transfer to its subsidiary of its own treasury stock in a transaction to which section 351 applies. The ruling states that "[t]he transfer of [parent] stock was not for the purpose of enabling [the subsidiary corporation] to acquire property by the use of such stock." Rev. Rul. 74-503 holds that, since the basis of previously unissued parent stock in the hands of the parent corporation is zero, the basis of the parent corporation's treasury stock in the hands of the parent corporation is also zero. Accordingly, under the transferred basis rule of section 362(a), the subsidiary corporation's basis of the treasury stock of the parent corporation is also zero (the zero basis result).

Section 1.1032-2(b), applicable to certain triangular reorganizations occurring on or after December 23, 1994, eliminates gain recognition in certain cases when an acquiring corporation (S) acquires property or stock of another corporation (T) in exchange for stock of the corporation (P) in control of S. [*See* Chapter 26.] Section 1.1032-2(b) provides that, "For purposes of §1.1032-1(a), in the case of a forward triangular merger, a triangular C reorganization, or a triangular B reorganization (as described in §1.358-6(b)), P stock provided by P to S, or directly to T or T's shareholders on behalf of S, pursuant to the plan of reorganization is treated as a disposition by P of its own stock for T's assets or stock, as applicable." Section 1.1032-2(c) provides that S must recognize gain or loss on its exchange of P stock if S did not receive the P stock pursuant to the plan of reorganization. * * *

Explanation of Provisions Some of the concerns that ultimately led to the enactment of section 1032 are present where a subsidiary corporation holds the stock of a parent corporation. For example, a parent corporation could place treasury stock in a subsidiary corporation in order to attempt to recognize losses if the price of the parent corporation stock goes down, or could sell shares directly if the price rises. *See* Rev. Rul. 74-503 (2974-2 C.B. 117). The zero basis result limits such planning opportunities.

These tax avoidance possibilities are not present, however, in transactions where one corporation transfers its own stock to another corporation pursuant to a plan by which the second corporation immediately transfers the stock of the first corporation to acquire money or other property. The risk of selective loss recognition does not arise where the stock of the parent corporation is used immediately by the subsidiary corporation to acquire money or other property and therefore does not have sufficient time to depreciate in value. This concept is reflected in Rev. Rul. 74-

503, which provides a factual carve-out for transfers of parent corporation stock made for the purpose of enabling a subsidiary corporation to acquire property. Also, the IRS and the Treasury have not applied the zero basis result in such integrated transactions, regardless of whether such a disposition of stock is part of a tax-free reorganization or is part of the taxable acquisition. *See* §§ 1502-13(f)(6)(ii) and 1.1032-2(b). These proposed regulations provide that no gain or loss is recognized in certain taxable transactions where one corporation immediately disposes of the stock of another corporation pursuant to a plan to acquire money or other property. The IRS and Treasury believe that, in such transactions, the nonapplicability of the zero basis result avoids inappropriate gain recognition and is consistent with the purposes of section 1032. No inference is intended regarding the applicability of the zero basis result to transactions outside of the scope of these proposed regulations.

If the conditions of these proposed regulations are satisfied, no gain or loss is recognized on the disposition of the stock of one corporation (the issuing corporation) by another corporation (the acquiring corporation). The proposed regulations apply if, pursuant to a plan to acquire money or other property, (1) the acquiring corporation acquires stock of the issuing corporation directly or indirectly from the issuing corporation in a transaction in which, but for this section, the basis of the stock of the issuing corporation in the hands of the acquiring corporation would be determined with respect to the issuing corporation's basis in the issuing corporation's stock under section 362(a); (2) the acquiring corporation immediately transfers the stock of the issuing corporation to acquire money or other property; and (3) no party receiving stock of the issuing corporation from the acquiring corporation receives a substituted basis in the stock of the issuing corporation within the meaning of section 7701(a)(42). For purposes of this section, "property" includes services. See § 1.1032-1. * * *

B. Shareholder Overlap Problem: Potential Nondivisive (D) Reorganization

1. Introduction

If shareholders of the target are also shareholders of the acquiring corporation, care must be taken to ensure that the transaction is not treated as a nondivisive "(D)" reorganization under §§ 368(a)(1)(D) and 354(b). *See* Sec. 3.3.E.1.b. Basically, if shareholders of the target own at least 50% of the stock of the acquiring corporation (*see* § 368(a)(2)(H)), the transaction may be treated as a nondivisive (D) reorganization, with the following effects. First, under § 361 the target would not have gain or loss, and under § 362 the acquiring corporation would take a carryover basis for the target's assets. The target's shareholders who receive cash or other property would have gain and possibly dividends under § 356.

This overlap problem is similar to the § 304 overlap problem that can arise in a stock acquisition. *See* Chapters 2 and 5.

2. 1984 Amendment to the Control Requirement in the Nondivisive (D)

See §§ 368(a)(1)(D) and (2)(H).

The Senate Finance Committee's Report on the Deficit Reduction Tax Bill of 1984

207–209 (1984)

Present Law Under section 368(a)(1)(D), a transfer by a corporation of all or a part of its assets to a corporation controlled immediately after the transfer by the transferor or one or more of its shareholders is generally treated as a D reorganization if, among other things, stock or securities of the controlled corporation are distributed pursuant to the plan of reorganization in a transaction qualifying under sections 354, 355, or 356. A D reorganization may involve the acquisition of substantially all of the assets of a corporation (an acquisitive or nondivisive transaction) or the division of an existing corporation (a divisive transaction). For purposes of a D reorganization, the term "control" is defined as the ownership of stock possessing at least 80 percent of the total combined voting power of all classes of stock entitled to vote and at least 80 percent of the total number of shares of all other classes of stock of the corporation. No attribution rules are explicitly made applicable.

If a nondivisive transaction qualifies as a D reorganization, generally no gain or loss is recognized by the transferor corporation or its shareholders. [*See* §§ 361 and 354.] The acquiring corporation's basis in the assets acquired from the transferor corporation is generally the same as it was in the hands of the transferor corporation. [*See* § 362.] If boot (*i.e.*, money or other property other than stock or securities of the transferee corporation) is distributed to the shareholders of the transferor corporation, then any gain realized by such shareholders is recognized, but in an amount not in excess of the sum of such money and the fair market value of such other property. [*See* § 356.] If the distribution of the boot has the effect of a dividend, it is treated by the shareholder as a dividend to the extent of his or her pro rata share of the corporation's undistributed earnings and profits.[1]

Liquidation and contribution to a related corporation. In general, under section 331, amounts distributed to a shareholder in complete liquidation of a corporation are treated as full payment in exchange for the shareholder's stock. If the stock is a capital asset in the hands of the shareholder, a complete liquidation will result in capital gain or loss, the shareholder's basis in the property received in the taxable liquidation is the fair market value of the property at the time of the distribution. * * *

The Internal Revenue Service has taken the position, and a number of cases have held, that a liquidation followed by a contribution of a substantial part of the distrib-

---

1. The IRS takes the position that for purposes of determining dividend equivalency, a boot distribution is treated as having been made by the acquired corporation (*i.e.*, the transferor) rather than by the acquiring corporation. Rev. Rul. 75-83, 1975-1, C.B. 112. *See also Shimberg v. United States,* 577 F.2d 283 (5th Cir.1978). But see *Wright v. United States,* 482 F.2d 600 (8th Cir.1973).

uted properties to a corporation controlled by the shareholders of the liquidating corporation can constitute a D reorganization. In such cases, the transferee corporation's basis in acquired assets is the same as the basis in the transferor corporation's hands prior to the transfer. Further, the transferee corporation inherits tax attributes of the transferor corporation, which would generally disappear in the case of a liquidation. If money or property (other than stock or securities in the transferee corporation) is distributed to the shareholders of the transferor corporation, the shareholders may be treated as having received a dividend rather than a payment in exchange for stock.[2]

Sale of stock to commonly controlled corporation. Under present law, a sale of stock in one corporation by a shareholder to a commonly controlled corporation is generally treated under section 304 as a redemption rather than as a sale to an independent third party. A distribution in redemption of stock is generally treated by the shareholders as in part or full payment in exchange for the stock if (1) it is not essentially equivalent to a dividend, (2) it is substantially disproportionate with respect to the shareholder, (3) it is in complete termination of the shareholder's interest, or (4) certain other requirements are satisfied. Distributions in redemption of a shareholder's stock that are not treated as in part or full payment in exchange for the stock are treated as dividends to the extent of undistributed earnings and profits.

For purposes of section 304, the term control means the ownership of stock possessing at least 50 percent of the total combined voting power of all classes of stock entitled to vote, or at least 50 percent of the total value of shares of all classes of stock. Attribution rules apply for purposes of determining ownership of stock.

Reasons for Change Liquidation-reincorporation transactions (*i.e.,* transactions involving the liquidation of a corporation coupled with a transfer of its operating assets to a new corporation in which the shareholders of the transferor corporation have a substantial stock interest) that are not treated as reorganizations can be used to accomplish a bail-out of earnings and profits at capital gains rates. Further, these transactions can be used by a shareholder (or group of shareholders) to obtain a step-up in the basis of assets that are held in corporate solution largely at the cost of a shareholder-level capital gains tax without a significant change in ownership.

The D reorganization provisions generally envision the continuation of the transferor corporation's business in a corporation in which the transferor corporation or its shareholders have a substantial interest. In many transactions, the liquidating corporation's business is being continued by a related corporation. However, the control requirement that applies in the case of a D reorganization has in some instances prevented the Service from successfully asserting that these transactions constitute D reorganizations.

Also, the D reorganization provisions and section 304 both operate to prevent the bail-out of earnings and profits at capital gains rates. Further, both apply to transactions in which property is transferred from one corporation to another corporation in a transaction in which money or other property is received by common shareholders.

---

2. *See, e.g., James Armour, Inc.,* 43 TC 295 (1965).

Nonetheless, the control requirement under section 304 is a 50-percent requirement. Further, attribution rules apply for purposes of determining stock ownership under section 304. The committee believes that the control test in the case of the D reorganization provisions should more closely conform to that of section 304.

The absence of explicit attribution rules to determine ownership of stock for purposes of the control requirement may enable taxpayers to bail-out earnings and profits at capital gains rates by transferring assets to a corporation controlled by a related person rather than to a corporation controlled by them.

Explanation of Provision Under the bill, in the case of a transaction otherwise qualifying as a nondivisive D reorganization, the transferor corporation or its shareholders are treated as having control of the transferee corporation if the transferor corporation or its shareholders own stock possessing at least 50 percent of the total combined voting power of all classes of stock entitled to vote and at least 50 percent of the total number of shares of all other classes of stock of the corporation. [*See* § 368(a)(2)(H).] Further, the constructive ownership of stock rules contained in section 318(a), modified, are applicable for purposes of determining whether the transferor corporation or its shareholders are in control of the transferee corporation. * * *

[The Conference adopted the above provision except that control is defined as the ownership, directly or indirectly, of stock possessing at least 50 percent of the total combined voting power of all classes of stock entitled to vote, or at least 50 percent of the total value of all shares of all classes of stock. The Conference Report says that the conferees do not intend that "recharacterization as a D reorganization * * * be the exclusive means for the Service to challenge liquidation-reincorporation and similar transactions. For example, it is not intended that this provision supersede or otherwise replace the various doctrines that have been developed by the Service and the courts to deal with such transactions. *See, e.g.,* Rev. Rul. 61-156 * * * *Telephone Answering Service* * * * and *Smothers.*"]

3. Illustration of Purported Taxable Purchase of Assets that is Treated as Reorganization

Revenue Ruling 61-156

1961-2 C.B. 62

Advice has been requested whether the transaction described below should be treated, for Federal income tax purposes, as a sale of corporate assets to a newly organized corporation followed by the liquidation of the "selling" corporation under [former] section 337 and [section] 331 of the Internal Revenue Code of 1954, or whether the transaction should be treated as a reorganization within the meaning of section 368 of the Code.

Within a 12-month period following the adoption of a plan of complete liquidation, a corporation sold substantially all of its assets to a new corporation formed by the management of the selling corporation. The "purchasing" corporation paid 18,000x dollars for the assets as follows:

(a) 2,025*x* dollars in shares of its stock equal to 45 percent of all the shares to be issued,

(b) 4,975*x* dollars in long-term notes, and

(c) 11,000*x* dollars in cash obtained through a first mortgage borrowing on the assets acquired.

Immediately thereafter, the new corporation sold shares of its stock, equal to 55 percent of all the shares to be issued, to the public through underwriters.

The "selling" corporation was then completely liquidated, paying off its funded and unfunded liabilities and distributing the balance of its assets, including the 45 percent stock interest in the purchasing corporation, the long-term notes, and cash to its shareholders. As a result of the transaction, the business enterprise continued without interruption in the corporate form with a substantial continuing stock interest on the part of those persons who were shareholders in the selling corporation.

Section 1.331-1(c) of the Income Tax Regulations provides as follows:

A liquidation which is followed by a transfer to another corporation of all or part of the assets of the liquidating corporation or which is preceded by such a transfer may, however, have the effect of the distribution of a dividend or of a transaction in which no loss is recognized and gain is recognized only to the extent of "other property." *See* sections 301 and 356.

In this case, if the issuance of stock to the new investors is disregarded, there is clearly a mere recapitalization and reincorporation coupled with a withdrawal of funds. The withdrawal would be treated either under section 356(a) of the Code as "money or other property" received in connection with a reorganization exchange of stock for stock, or under section 301 of the Code as an unrelated distribution to the shareholders.

The issuance of stock to new investors can be disregarded as being a separate transaction, since even without it the dominant purpose—to withdraw corporate earnings while continuing the equity interest in substantial part in a business enterprise conducted in corporate form—was fully achieved. The issuance of stock to new investors was not needed to implement the dominant purpose and, therefore, the rest of the transaction was not fruitless without it and so dependent on it.

The transaction was shaped so as to make it essentially "a device whereby it has been attempted to withdraw corporate earnings at capital gains rates by distributing all the assets of a corporation in complete liquidation and promptly reincorporating" them. *See* Conference Report No. 2543, 83d Cong., to accompany H.R. 8300 (Internal Revenue Code of 1954), page 41.

It was not intended by Congress that such a device should obtain the benefits of [former] section 337 [which provided generally for non-recognition on the sale by a corporation of its assets] and avoid dividend taxation. In substance there was no reality to the "sale" of corporate assets or to the "liquidation" of the selling corporation, since each was only a formal step in a reorganization of the existing corporation. The entire transaction was consummated pursuant to a plan of reorganization which readjusted interests in property continuing in a modified corporate form. Sections 1.368-1(b) and 1.368-2(g) of the regulations.

The newly formed "purchasing" corporation was utilized to effect, in substance, a recapitalization [*see* § 368(a)(1)(E)] and a change in identity, form, or place of organization of the "selling" corporation [*see* § 368(a)(1)(F)] and, at the same time, to withdraw accumulated earnings from the corporate enterprise for the benefit of the shareholders, while they nevertheless continued a substantial equity interest in the enterprise.

The fact that the shareholders of the "selling" corporation own only 45 percent of the stock of the "purchasing" corporation because of the public stock offering does not dispose of the reorganization question. A surrender of voting control, or ownership of less than 50 percent of the stock of a newly-formed corporation, does not in itself mark a discontinuity of interest. In *John A. Nelson Co. v. Helvering*, 296 U.S. 374, (1936), [Sec. 6.2.B.3.] the Supreme Court of the United States held that there was a "reorganization" even though the shareholders of the acquired corporation received less than half of the stock of the acquiring corporation and received only nonvoting preferred stock therein. It is necessary only that the shareholders continue to have a definite and substantial equity interest in the assets of the acquiring corporation.

In view of the foregoing, it is held that the transaction here described constitutes a reorganization within the meaning of sections 368(a)(1)(E) and (F) of the Code. No gain or loss is recognized to the "selling" corporation on the exchange of property, as provided by section 361 of the Code. The basis of the assets in the hands of the "purchasing" corporation will be the same as in the hands of the "selling" corporation, as provided in section 362(b) of the Code. No gain or loss is recognized under section 354 of the Code on the exchange of the stock of the "selling" corporation for stock of the "purchasing" corporation pursuant to the plan of reorganization.

With regard to the stockholders' withdrawal of money and other property from the corporate solution, it is necessary to determine whether such withdrawal is to be treated as "boot" received as part of the consideration for their stock in the "selling" corporation in accordance with section 356(a) of the Code or as a separate dividend distribution taxable in accordance with the provisions of section 301 of the Code. See sections 1.301-1(1) and 1.331-1(c) of the regulations and *J. Robert Bazley v. Commissioner.* [Sec. 6.7.C.] * * *

[I]t is concluded that the distribution to stockholders of the "selling" corporation of the cash, long-term notes, and other assets should be treated as a distribution under section 301 of the Code. * * *

4. The All Cash (D) Reorganization Regulations

Preamble to Final Regulations on All Cash (D) Reorganizations under Sections 368(a)(1)(D) and 354(b)(1)(B)

TD 9475, December 18, 2009

SUMMARY: This document contains final regulations under section 368 of the Internal Revenue Code (Code). The regulations provide guidance regarding the qualification of certain transactions as reorganizations described in section 368(a)(1)(D) where no stock and/or securities of the acquiring corporation is issued and distributed in the transaction. This document also contains final regulations under section 358 that provide guidance regarding the determination of the basis of stock or securities in a reorganization described in section 368(a)(1)(D) where no stock and/or securities of the acquiring corporation is issued and distributed in the transaction. * * *

BACKGROUND

The Code provides general nonrecognition treatment for reorganizations specifically described in section 368(a). Section 368(a)(1)(D) describes as a reorganization a transfer by a corporation (transferor corporation) of all or a part of its assets to another corporation (transferee corporation) if, immediately after the transfer, the transferor corporation or one or more of its shareholders (including persons who were shareholders immediately before the transfer), or any combination thereof, is in control of the transferee corporation; but only if stock or securities of the controlled corporation are distributed in pursuance of a plan of reorganization in a transaction that qualifies under section 354, 355, or 356.

Section 354(a)(1) provides that no gain or loss shall be recognized if stock or securities in a corporation that is a party to a reorganization are, in pursuance of the plan of reorganization, exchanged solely for stock or securities in such corporation or in another corporation that is a party to the reorganization. Section 354(b)(1)(B) provides that section 354(a)(1) shall not apply to an exchange in pursuance of a plan of reorganization described in section 368(a)(1)(D) unless the transferee corporation acquires substantially all of the assets of the transferor corporation, and the stock, securities, and other properties received by such transferor corporation, as well as the other properties of such transferor corporation, are distributed in pursuance of the plan of reorganization.

Further, section 356 provides that if section 354 or 355 would apply to an exchange but for the fact that the property received in the exchange consists not only of property permitted by section 354 or 355 without the recognition of gain or loss but also of other property or money, then the gain, if any, to the recipient shall be recognized, but not in excess of the amount of money and fair market value of such other property. Accordingly, in the case of an acquisitive transaction, there can only be a distribution to which section 354 or 356 applies where the target shareholder(s) receive at least some property permitted to be received by section 354.

On December 19, 2006, the IRS and Treasury Department published a notice of proposed rulemaking (REG-125632-06) in the Federal Register (71 FR 75898) that included regulations under section 368 (the Temporary Regulations) providing guidance regarding whether the distribution requirement under sections 368(a)(1)(D) and 354(b)(1)(B) is satisfied if there is no actual distribution of stock and/or securities. The Temporary Regulations provide that the distribution requirement will be satisfied even though no stock and/or securities is actually issued in the transaction if the same persons or persons own, directly or indirectly, all of the stock of the transferor and transferee corporations in identical proportions. In such cases, the transferee will be deemed to issue a nominal share of stock to the transferor in addition to the actual consideration exchanged for the transferor's assets. The nominal share is then deemed distributed by the transferor to its shareholders and, when appropriate, further transferred through chains of ownership to the extent necessary to reflect the actual ownership of the transferor and transferee corporations. The IRS and Treasury Department issued the Temporary Regulations in response to taxpayer requests regarding whether certain acquisitive transactions can qualify as reorganizations described in section 368(a)(1)(D) where no stock of the transferee corporation is issued and distributed in the transaction pending a broader study of issues related to acquisitive section 368(a)(1)(D) reorganizations in general. In the notice of proposed rule making, the IRS and Treasury Department requested comments on the Temporary Regulations as well as on several broader issues discussed below relating to acquisitive section 368(a)(1)(D) reorganizations.

On February 27, 2007, the IRS and Treasury Department published a clarifying amendment to the Temporary Regulations (REG-157834-06) in the Federal Register (72 FR 9284-9285) providing that the deemed issuance of the nominal share of stock of the transferee corporation in a transaction otherwise described in section 368(a)(1)(D) does not apply if the transaction otherwise qualifies as a triangular reorganization described in section 1.358-6(b)(2) or section 368(a)(1)(G) by reason of section 368(a)(2)(D). * * *

Explanation of Provisions

These final regulations retain the rules of the Temporary Regulations, but make certain modifications to the Temporary Regulations in response to comments received. * * *

Meaningless Gesture Doctrine

Notwithstanding the requirement in section 368(a)(1)(D) that "stock or securities of the corporation to which the assets are transferred are distributed in a transaction which qualifies under section 354, 355, or 356", the IRS and the courts have not required the actual issuance and distribution of stock and/or securities of the transferee corporation in circumstances where the same person or persons own all the stock of the transferor corporation and the transferee corporation. In such circumstances, the IRS and the courts have viewed an issuance of stock by the transferee corporation to be a "meaningless gesture" not mandated by sections 368(a)(1)(D) and 354(b). *See James Armour, Inc. v. Commissioner,* 43 T.C. 295, 307 (1964); *Wilson v. Commissioner,* 46 T.C. 334 (1966); Rev. Rul. 70-240, 1970-1 CB 81. In the notice of proposed rulemaking, the IRS and Treasury Department requested comments on whether the meaningless gesture doctrine is inconsistent with the distribution requirement in sections 368(a)(1)(D) and 354(b)(1)(B), especially in situations in which the cash consideration received equals the full fair market value of the property transferred such that there is no missing consideration for which the nominal share of stock deemed received and distributed could substitute. * * *

[T]hese final regulations retain the rules of the Temporary Regulations which are based in part on the meaningless gesture doctrine. In addition, consistent with the IRS and Treasury Department's view of such transactions and in response to comments, the final regulations provide that if no consideration is received, or the value of the consideration received in the transaction is less than the fair market value of the transferor corporation's assets, the transferee corporation will be treated as issuing stock with a value equal to the excess of the fair market value of the transferor corporation's assets over the value of the consideration actually received in the transaction. The final regulations further provide that if the value of the consideration received in the transaction is equal to the fair market value of the transferor corporation's assets, the transferee corporation will be deemed to issue a nominal share (discussed in this preamble) of stock to the transferor corporation in addition to the actual consideration exchanged for the transferor corporation's assets.

Issuance of Nominal Share

As described in this preamble, if the same person or persons own, directly or indirectly, all of the stock of the transferor and transferee corporations in identical proportions in a transaction otherwise described in section 368(a)(1)(D), the transferee will be deemed to issue a nominal share of stock to the transferor in addition to the actual consideration exchanged for the transferor's assets. The nominal share is then deemed distributed by the transferor to its shareholders and, when appropriate, further transferred through the chains of ownership to the extent necessary to reflect the actual ownership of the transferor and transferee corporations. * * *

The IRS and Treasury Department have carefully considered the comments regarding the nominal share concept and believe that it is preferable to an approach that simply deems the statutory requirements satisfied because the nominal share also provides a useful mechanism with respect to stock basis consequences to the exchanging shareholder. * * *

Basis Allocation

While the IRS and Treasury Department believe that all of the normal tax consequences occur from the issuance of a nominal share in a transaction described in these final regulations, commentators have noted that such consequences are unclear with respect to the allocation of basis in the shares of the stock or securities surrendered when the consideration received in the transaction consists solely of cash. * * *

The IRS and Treasury Department agree with the commentators that the basis in the shares of the stock surrendered should be preserved in the basis of the stock of the transferee in a transaction described in these final regulations. * * * Accordingly, the regulations under section 1.358-2(a)(2)(iii) are amended to provide that in the case of a reorganization in which the property received consists solely of non-qualifying property equal to the value of the assets transferred (as well as a nominal share described in these final regulations), the shareholder or security holder may designate the share of stock of the transferee to which the basis, if any, of the stock or securities surrendered will attach. * * *

C. Use of Partnership or S Corporation as Acquisition Vehicle

In a purchase of assets, individual owners of the acquisition entity can avoid the corporate tax on future operating profits by using either a partnership or an S corporation as the acquisition vehicle. If a partnership or S corporation is used, the individual owners will receive the direct benefit of the write-off of the acquisition cost, subject to the basis limitation (§704(d) or §1366(d)), the at risk rules (§465), and the passive loss rules (§469). *See* Chapter 11.

§4.3 Issues of Concern Principally to the Acquiring Corporation and Its Shareholders

A. Structuring the Capital of the Acquiring Corporation

Care must be taken in structuring the capital of the acquiring corporation, particularly if the transaction is highly leveraged, such as in an LBO. Because most LBOs of stand-alone targets are structured as stock acquisitions, this issue is addressed in Sec. 5.3.A.

B. Treatment of Covenants Not to Compete

1. Introduction

When the stock or assets of a business is sold, the seller often enters into a covenant not to compete, and a portion of the purchase price is allocated to the covenant. Assuming the allocation is bona fide, the seller has ordinary income for the amounts attributable to the covenant, and the purchaser has a deduction which is generally amortized as provided under §197, which is discussed in Sec. 4.3.C.

If an allocation to a covenant is not bona fide, the Service might attempt to allocate the amount paid for the covenant to the property sold (for instance, stock). In such case, the seller has a larger gain, which is capital gain in the case of assets like stock. The purchaser, on the other hand, has a higher cost for the asset. If the asset is non-depreciable, such as stock, the purchaser does not receive a deduction for that cost. If the asset is goodwill in an asset sale a deduction would be allowed under §197 as discussed in Sec. 4.3.C.

2. Illustration: Is the Covenant Bona Fide?

Revenue Ruling 77-403

1977-2 C.B. 302

Advice has been requested concerning the Federal income tax treatment of a payment for a covenant not to compete under the circumstances described below.

P, whose primary business was managing rental property, purchased a newly-constructed rental building from S, a real estate developer, for 12x dollars. P made a cash payment to S of 2x dollars and assumed an existing 10x dollar mortgage on the property. P made an additional cash payment to S of 3x dollars for a covenant not to compete under which S is obligated for a specified time not to participate directly or indirectly in the construction, purchase or management of competing property within a specified distance from the building. S had constructed and sold many buildings but did not have personnel capable of managing rental property, had never managed rental property, and, irrespective of the existence of the covenant, did not intend to construct, purchase or manage rental property. At the time that the covenant was executed, the area specified therein contained no buildings suitable for competing with the property purchased by P. Additionally, construction of such a building within the specified time was unlikely.

Section 1012 of the Internal Revenue Code of 1954 provides, in part, that the basis of property is the cost of the property.

Whether a payment for a covenant not to compete made in connection with the purchase of real property is part of the cost of the property or is the cost of a separate asset depends on whether the covenant has any demonstrable value. In determining whether the covenant has any demonstrable value, the facts and circumstances in the particular case must be considered. The relevant factors include: (1) whether in the absence of the covenant the covenantor would desire to compete with the covenantee; (2) the ability of the covenantor to compete effectively with the covenantee in the activity in question; and (3) the feasibility, in view of the activity and market in question, of effective competition by the covenantor within the time and area specified in the covenant. See Schulz v. Commissioner, 294 F.2d 52 (9th Cir. 1961).

Although S and P characterized the 3x dollar payment as consideration for a covenant not to compete, under the circumstances S's obligation not to construct, purchase or manage a competing property has no demonstrable value. Therefore, the 3x dollar payment is part of the cost of the real property rather than the cost of a separate asset. If the covenant not to compete did have a demonstrable value, the amount characterized as a payment for that covenant would be regarded as the cost of an asset separate from the real property only to the extent it did not exceed the demonstrable value of the covenant.

Accordingly, the 3x dollar payment must be added to P's basis in the real property pursuant to section 1012 of the Code, and it may not be amortized over the duration of the covenant.

C. Amortization of Goodwill and Certain Other Intangibles Including Covenants Not to Compete; Legislative History of § 197

House Report to the Revenue Reconciliation Act of 1993
322–339 (1993)

Present Law In determining taxable income for Federal income tax purposes, a taxpayer is allowed depreciation or amortization deductions for the cost or other basis of intangible property that is used in a trade or business or held for the production of income if the property has a limited useful life that may be determined with reasonable accuracy. Treas. Reg. sec. 1.167(a)-(3). These Treasury Regulations also state that no depreciation deductions are allowed with respect to goodwill.

The U.S. Supreme Court recently held that a taxpayer able to prove that a particular asset can be valued, and that the asset has a limited useful life which can be ascertained with reasonable accuracy, may depreciate the value over the useful life regardless of how much the asset appears to reflect the expectancy of continued patronage. However, the Supreme Court also characterized the taxpayer's burden of proof as "substantial" and stated that it "often will prove too great to bear." *Newark Morning Ledger Co. v. United States*, 507 U.S. 546, 61 U.S.L.W. 4313 at 4320, 4319 (April 20, 1993).

Reasons for Change The Federal income tax treatment of the costs of acquiring intangible assets is a source of considerable controversy between taxpayers and the Internal Revenue Service. Disputes arise concerning (1) whether an amortizable intangible asset exists; (2) in the case of an acquisition of a trade or business, the portion of the purchase price that is allocable to an amortizable intangible asset; and (3) the proper method and period for recovering the cost of an amortizable intangible asset. These types of disputes can be expected to continue to arise, even after the decision of the U.S. Supreme Court in *Newark Morning Ledger Co. v. United States, supra.*

It is believed that much of the controversy that arises under present law with respect to acquired intangible assets could be eliminated by specifying a single method and period for recovering the cost of most acquired intangible assets and by treating acquired goodwill and going concern value as amortizable intangible assets. It is also believed that there is no need at this time to change the Federal income tax treatment of self-created intangible assets, such as goodwill that is created through advertising and other similar expenditures.

Accordingly, the bill requires the cost of most acquired intangible assets, including goodwill and going concern value, to be amortized ratably over a [15]-year period. It is recognized that the useful lives of certain acquired intangible assets to which the bill applies may be shorter than [15] years, while the useful lives of other acquired intangible assets to which the bill applies may be longer than [15] years.

Explanation of Provision In general [See § 197(a).] The bill allows an amortization deduction with respect to the capitalized costs of certain intangible property (defined as a "section 197 intangible") that is acquired by a taxpayer and that is held by the taxpayer in connection with the conduct of a trade or business or an activity engaged in for the production of income. The amount of the deduction is determined by amortizing the adjusted basis (for purposes of determining gain) of the intangible ratably over a [15]-year period that begins with the month that the intangible is acquired. No other depreciation or amortization deduction is allowed with respect to a section 197 intangible that is acquired by a taxpayer. [Under the financial accounting rules there is no amortization deduction for good will.]

In general, the bill applies to a section 197 intangible acquired by a taxpayer regardless of whether it is acquired as part of a trade or business. In addition, the bill generally applies to a section 197 intangible that is treated as acquired under section 338 of the Code. The bill generally does not apply to a section 197 intangible that is created by the taxpayer if the intangible is not created in connection with a transaction (or series of related transactions) that involves the acquisition of a trade or business or a substantial portion thereof.

Except in the case of amounts paid or incurred under certain covenants not to compete (or under certain other arrangements that have substantially the same effect as covenants not to compete) and certain amounts paid or incurred on account of the transfer of a franchise, trademark, or trade name, the bill generally does not apply to any amount that is otherwise currently deductible (*i.e.*, not capitalized) under present law. * * *

Definition of section 197 intangible [See § 197(c).] In general. The term "section 197 intangible" is defined as any property that is included in any one or more of the following categories: (1) goodwill and going concern value; (2) certain specified types of intangible property that generally relate to workforce, information base, know-how, customers, suppliers, or other similar items; (3) any license, permit, or other right granted by a governmental unit or an agency or instrumentality thereof; (4) any covenant not to compete (or other arrangement to the extent that the arrangement has substantially the same effect as a covenant not to compete) entered into in connection with the direct or indirect acquisition of an interest in a trade or business (or a substantial portion thereof); and (5) any franchise, trademark, or trade name.

Certain types of property, however, are specifically excluded from the definition of the term "section 197 intangible." [*See* § 197(e).] The term "section 197 intangible" does not include: (1) any interest in a corporation, partnership, trust, or estate; (2) any interest under an existing futures contract, foreign currency contract, notional principal contract, interest rate swap, or other similar financial contract; (3) any interest in land; (4) certain computer software; (5) certain interests in films, sound recordings, video tapes, books, or other similar property; (6) certain rights to receive tangible property or services; (7) certain interests in patents or copyrights; (8) any interest under an existing lease of tangible property; (9) any interest under an existing indebtedness (except for the deposit base and similar items of a financial institution); (10) a franchise to engage in any professional sport, and any item acquired in connection with such a franchise; and (11) certain transaction costs.

In addition, the Treasury Department is authorized to issue regulations that exclude certain rights of fixed duration or amount from the definition of a section 197 intangible.

Goodwill and going concern value [See §§ 197(d)(1)(A) and (B).]

For purposes of the bill, goodwill is the value of a trade or business that is attributable to the expectancy of continued customer patronage, whether due to the name of a trade or business, the reputation of a trade or business, or any other factor.

In addition, for purposes of the bill, going concern value is the additional element of value of a trade or business that attaches to property by reason of its existence as an integral part of a going concern. Going concern value includes the value that is attributable to the ability of a trade or business to continue to function and generate income without interruption notwithstanding a change in ownership. Going concern value also includes the value that is attributable to the use or availability of an acquired trade or business (for example, the net earnings that otherwise would not be received during any period were the acquired trade or business not available or operational).

*Workforce, information base, know-how, customer-based intangibles, supplier-based intangibles and other similar items * * **

Know-how. [*See* § 197(d)(1)(C)(iii).] The term "section 197 intangible" includes any patent, copyright, formula, process, design, pattern, know-how, format, or other similar item. For this purpose, the term "section 197 intangible" is to include package designs, computer software, and any interest in a film, sound recording, videotape, book, or other similar property, except as specifically provided otherwise in the bill. * * *

Licenses, permits, and other rights granted by governmental units. [*See* § 197(d)(1)(D).] The term "section 197 intangible" also includes any license, permit, or other right granted by a governmental unit or any agency or instrumentality thereof (even if the right is granted for an indefinite period or the right is reasonably expected to be renewed for an indefinite period). Thus, for example, the capitalized cost of acquiring from any person a liquor license, a taxi-cab medallion (or license), an airport landing or takeoff right (which is sometimes referred to as a slot), a regulated airline route, or a television or radio broadcasting license is to be amortized over the [15]-year period specified in the bill. * * *

Covenants not to compete and other similar arrangements. [*See* §§ 197(d)(1)(E), (f)(1)(B) and (f)(3).] The term "section 197 intangible" also includes any covenant not to compete (or other arrangement to the extent that the arrangement has substantially the same effect as a covenant not to compete; hereafter "other similar arrangement") entered into in connection with the direct or indirect acquisition of an interest in a trade or business (or a substantial portion thereof). For this purpose, an interest in a trade or business includes not only the assets of a trade or business, but also stock in a corporation that is engaged in a trade or business or an interest in a partnership that is engaged in a trade or business.

Any amount that is paid or incurred under a covenant not to compete (or other similar arrangement) entered into in connection with the direct or indirect acquisition of an interest in a trade or business (or a substantial portion thereof) is chargeable to capital account and is to be amortized ratably over the [15]-year period specified in the bill. In addition, any amount that is paid or incurred under a covenant not to compete (or other similar arrangement) after the taxable year in which the covenant (or other similar arrangement) was entered into is to be amortized ratably over the remaining months in the [15]-year amortization period that applies to the covenant (or other similar arrangement) as of the beginning of the month that the amount is paid or incurred.

For purposes of this provision, an arrangement that requires the former owner of an interest in a trade or business to continue to perform services (or to provide property or the use of property) that benefit the trade or business is considered to have substantially the same effect as a covenant not to compete to the extent that the amount paid to the former owner under the arrangement exceeds the amount that represents reasonable compensation for the services actually rendered (or for the property or use of property actually provided) by the former owner. As under present law, to the extent that the amount paid or incurred under a covenant not to compete (or other similar arrangement) represents additional consideration for the acquisition of stock in a corporation, such amount is not to be taken into account under this provision but, instead, is to be included as part of the acquirer's basis in the stock.

[The Conference Report adds the following explanation of Section 197(f)(1)(B):]

The conference agreement contains a technical correction conforming the statute to both the House and Senate committee reports regarding the amortization of covenants not to compete. The correction provides that a covenant not to compete (or other arrangement to the extent such arrangement has substantially the same effect as a covenant not to compete) shall not be considered to have been disposed of or to have become worthless until the disposition or worthlessness of all interests in the trade or business or substantial portion thereof that was directly or indirectly acquired in connection with such covenant (or other arrangement).

Thus, for example, in the case of an indirect acquisition of a trade or business (*e.g.*, through the acquisition of stock that is not treated as an asset acquisition), it is clarified that a covenant not to compete (or other arrangement) entered into in connection with the indirect acquisition cannot be written off faster than on a straight-line basis over 15 years (even if the covenant or other arrangement expires or otherwise becomes worthless) unless all the trades or businesses indirectly acquired (*e.g.*, acquired through such stock interest) are also disposed of or become worthless.

Franchises, trademarks, and trade names. [*See* § 197(d)(1)(F).] * * *

Exceptions to the definition of a section 197 intangible. [*See* § 197(e).] *In general.* The bill contains several exceptions to the definition of the term "section 197 intangible." Several of the exceptions contained in the bill apply only if the intangible property is not acquired in a transaction (or series of related transactions) that involves the acquisition of assets which constitute a trade or business or a substantial portion of a trade or business. It is anticipated that the Treasury Department will exercise its regulatory authority to require any intangible property that would otherwise be excluded from the definition of the term "section 197 intangible" to be taken into account under the bill under circumstances where the acquisition of the intangible property is, in and of itself, the acquisition of an asset which constitutes a trade or business or a substantial portion of a trade or business.

The determination of whether acquired assets constitute a substantial portion of a trade or business is to be based on all of the facts and circumstances, including the nature and the amount of the assets acquired as well as the nature and amount of the assets retained by the transferor. It is not intended, however, that the value of the assets acquired relative to the value of the assets retained by the transferor is determinative of whether the acquired assets constitute a substantial portion of a trade or business.

For purposes of the bill, a group of assets is to constitute a trade or business if the use of such assets would constitute a trade or business for purposes of section 1060 of the Code (*i.e.*, if the assets are of such a character that goodwill or going concern value could under any circumstances attach to the assets). In addition, the acquisition of a franchise, trademark or trade name is to constitute the acquisition of a trade or business or a substantial portion of a trade or business.

In determining whether a taxpayer has acquired an intangible asset in a transaction (or series of related transactions) that involves the acquisition of assets that constitute a trade or business or a substantial portion of a trade or business, only those assets acquired in a transaction (or a series of related transactions) by a taxpayer (and persons related to the taxpayer) from the same person (and any related person) are to be taken into account. In addition, any employee relationships that continue (or covenants not to compete that are entered into) as part of the transfer of assets are to be taken into account in determining whether the transferred assets constitute a trade or business or a substantial portion of a trade or business.

Interests in a corporation, partnership, trust, or estate. [*See* § 197(e)(1)(A).] The term "section 197 intangible" does not include any interest in a corporation, partnership, trust, or estate. Thus, for example, the bill does not apply to the cost of acquiring stock, partnership interests, or interests in a trust or estate, whether or not such interests are regularly traded on an established market. * * *

Certain interests in patents or copyrights. [*See* § 197(e)(4)(C).] The term "section 197 intangible" does not include any interest in a patent or copyright which is not acquired in a transaction (or a series of related transactions) that involves the acquisition of assets which constitute a trade or business or a substantial portion of a trade or business.

If a depreciation deduction is allowed with respect to an interest in a patent or copyright and the interest is not a section 197 intangible, then the amount of the deduction is to be determined in accordance with regulations to be promulgated by the Treasury Department. * * *

Interests under leases of tangible property. [*See* § 197(e)(5)(A).] The term "section 197 intangible" does not include any interest as a lessor or lessee under an existing lease of tangible property (whether real or personal). * * *

Interests under indebtedness. [*See* § 197(e)(5)(B).] The term "section 197 intangible" does not include any interest (whether as a creditor or debtor) under any indebtedness that was in existence on the date that the interest was acquired. Thus, for example, the value of assuming an existing indebtedness with a below-market interest rate is to be taken into account under present law rather than under the bill. In addition, the premium paid for acquiring the right to receive an above-market rate of interest under a debt instrument may be taken into account under section 171 of the Code, which generally allows the amount of the premium to be amortized on a yield-to-maturity basis over the remaining term of the debt instrument. This exception for interests under existing indebtedness does not apply to the deposit base and other similar items of a financial institution. * * *

Certain transaction costs. [*See* § 197(e)(8).] The term section 197 intangible does not include the amount of any fees for professional services, and any transaction costs, incurred by parties to a transaction with respect to which any portion of the gain or loss is not recognized under part III of subchapter C. This provision addresses a concern that some taxpayers might attempt to contend that the [15]-year amortization provided by the provision applies to any such amounts that may be required to be capitalized under present law but that do not relate to any asset with a readily identifiable useful life.[3] The exception is provided solely to clarify that section 197 is not to be construed to provide [15]-year amortization for any such amounts. No inference is intended that such amounts would (but for this provision) be properly characterized as amounts eligible for such [15]-year amortization, nor is any inference intended that any amounts not specified in this provision should be so characterized. In addition, no inference is intended regarding the proper treatment of professional fees or transaction costs in other circumstances under present law.

Regulatory authority regarding rights of fixed term or duration. [*See* § 197(e)(4)(D).] * * *

Exception for certain self-created intangibles. [*See* § 197(c)(2).] The bill generally does not apply to any section 197 intangible that is created by the taxpayer if the section 197 intangible is not created in connection with a transaction (or a series of related transactions) that involves the acquisition of assets which constitute a trade or business or a substantial portion thereof. * * *

Special rules. Determination of adjusted basis. The adjusted basis of a section 197 intangible that is acquired from another person generally is to be determined under the principles of present law that apply to tangible property that is acquired from an-

---

3. *See, e.g., INDOPCO, Inc. v. Commissioner,* 112 S.Ct. 1039 (1992). [*See* 5.4.F.]

other person. Thus, for example, if a portion of the cost of acquiring an amortizable section 197 intangible is contingent, the adjusted basis of the section 197 intangible is to be increased as of the beginning of the month that the contingent amount is paid or incurred. This additional amount is to be amortized ratably over the remaining months in the [15]-year amortization period that applies to the intangible as of the beginning of the month that the contingent amount is paid or incurred.

Treatment of certain dispositions of amortizable section 197 intangibles. [*See* § 197(f)(1).] Special rules apply if a taxpayer disposes of a section 197 intangible that was acquired in a transaction or series of related transactions and, after the disposition, the taxpayer retains other section 197 intangibles that were acquired in such transaction or series or related transactions. First, no loss is to be recognized by reason of such a disposition. Second, the adjusted bases of the retained section 197 intangibles that were acquired in connection with such transaction or series of related transactions are to be increased by the amount of any loss that is not recognized.

Treatment of certain nonrecognition transactions. [*See* § 197(f)(2).] If any section 197 intangible is acquired in a transaction to which section 332, 351, 361, 721, 731, 1031, or 1033 of the Code applies (or any transaction between members of the same affiliated group during any taxable year for which a consolidated return is filed), the transferee is to be treated as the transferor for purposes of applying this provision with respect to the amount of the adjusted basis of the transferee that does not exceed the adjusted basis of the transferor.* * *

Treatment of amortizable section 197 intangible as depreciable property. [*See* § 197(f)(7).] For purposes of chapter 1 of the Internal Revenue Code, an amortizable section 197 intangible is to be treated as property of a character which is subject to the allowance for depreciation provided in section 167. * * *

Treatment of certain amounts that are properly taken into account in determining the cost of property that is not a section 197 intangible. [*See* § 197(f)(8).] The bill does not apply to any amount that is properly taken into account under present law in determining the cost of property that is not a section 197 intangible. Thus, for example, no portion of the cost of acquiring real property that is held for the production of rental income (for example, an office building, apartment building or shopping center) is to be taken into account under the bill (*i.e.*, no goodwill, going concern value or any other section 197 intangible is to arise in connection with the acquisition of such real property). Instead, the entire cost of acquiring such real property is to be included in the basis of the real property and is to be recovered under the principles of present law applicable to such property.

Modification of purchase price allocation and reporting rules for certain asset acquisitions. [*See* §§ 1060 and 338(b).] Sections 338(b)(5) and 1060 of the Code authorize the Treasury Department to promulgate regulations that provide for the allocation of purchase price among assets in the case of certain asset acquisitions. Under regulations that have been promulgated pursuant to this authority, the purchase price of an acquired trade or business must be allocated among the assets of the trade or business using the "residual method." * * *

Under the residual method specified in the Treasury regulations, all assets of an acquired trade or business are divided into [several different classes as discussed in connection with the examination below of Section 1060.] * * *

General regulatory authority. [*See* § 197(g).] The Treasury Department is authorized to prescribe such regulations as may be appropriate to carry out the purposes of the bill including such regulations as may be appropriate to prevent avoidance of the purposes of the bill through related persons or otherwise. It is anticipated that the Treasury Department will exercise its regulatory authority where appropriate to clarify the types of intangible property that constitute section 197 intangibles. * * *

D. Allocation of Purchase Price under § 1060

See § 1060 and the regulations.

1. The Basic Rules Governing Allocation of Purchase Price to Assets
Preamble to Temporary Regulations under § 1060
Treasury Decision 8215 (7/15/88)

Introduction For tax purposes, the sale of a going trade or business for a lump sum amount is viewed as a sale of each individual asset rather than a single capital asset. [*See Williams v. McGowan, infra* Sec. 4.4.B.] Both the purchaser and the seller must allocate the purchase price for the acquisition among the assets transferred. The seller must allocate the purchase price among the assets to determine the amount and character of its realized gain or loss on the sale. The purchaser's allocation determines its basis in each asset and will affect its amount of allowable depreciation, cost depletion, or amortization deductions, its realized gain or loss on a subsequent sale of those assets, and may have other tax consequences.

Section 1060(a) provides that in the case of an applicable asset acquisition, the seller and the purchaser each must allocate the consideration among the assets transferred in the same manner as the amounts are allocated under section 338(b)(5) (relating to certain stock purchases treated as asset acquisitions). [*See* Sec. 5.3.D.] Thus, the seller and the purchaser are required to allocate consideration under the residual method in order to make the respective determinations of the amount of gain or loss from the transfer of each asset and the basis in each asset acquired.

Prior to the enactment of section 1060, there was considerable controversy between taxpayers and the Internal Revenue Service concerning the allocation of the purchase price among assets of a going business. The controversy principally was due to the difficulty in establishing the value of goodwill and going concern value. Section 1060, by mandating the application of the residual method of allocation as prescribed in the regulations under section 338(b)(5), alleviates this controversy since the residual method does not require a separate determination of the value of goodwill and going concern value. Instead, under the residual method any "premium" paid in excess of the total fair market value of the purchased assets (other than goodwill or going concern value) is treated as payment for goodwill or going concern value. The mandatory application of the residual method of allocation also eliminates disparities in purchase price allocations that existed, prior to the enactment of section 1060, between asset purchases and stock purchases treated as asset purchases under section 338.

Section 1060(b) requires the seller and the purchaser to report certain information in connection with an applicable asset acquisition. The information reporting requirements are intended to encourage compliance with the substantive rules of section 1060. * * *

Subsequent Adjustments to Consideration Section 1.1060-1T(f) provides rules for the allocation of increases or decreases in consideration of either the purchaser or seller that occur after the purchase date. Increases in consideration are allocated among the assets in accordance with the general allocation rules set forth in § 1.1060-1T(d), subject to the limitation rules contained in § 1.1060-1T(e). Thus, in general, the aggregate amount of consideration allocated to an asset may not exceed the asset's fair market value on the purchase date, except for assets in the nature of goodwill and going concern value.

The rule for decreases in consideration is similar to the one for increases, except that decreases are allocated to assets in the reverse of the order in which consideration is allocated under § 1.1060-1T(d). Thus, as a general rule, decreases are allocated first among assets in the nature of goodwill and going concern value to the extent of the consideration previously allocated to them, and then as a decrease in the consideration previously allocated to other acquired assets. * * *

The regulations provide a special rule analogous to § 1.338(b)-3T(g) for allocating an increase (or decrease) in consideration that directly relates to the income produced by a particular intangible asset, such as a patent, copyright, or secret process ("contingent income assets"), as long as the increase (or decrease) in consideration is related to such contingent income asset and does not relate to other assets. Subject to the fair market value and other limitations in § 1.1060-1T(e), the increase (or decrease) in consideration is first allocated to the contingent income asset and then to other assets. * * *

2. Requirement of Consistent Treatment and Reporting of Employment and Other Payments by 10% Shareholders
House Report to Revenue Reconciliation Act of 1990
100–104 (1990)

Present Law. Special allocation and information reporting rules apply to applicable asset acquisitions (sec. 1060). * * *

Taxpayers required to report consistent positions. Courts apply different standards in determining whether a party to a sale of a business can assert an allocation of consideration to assets that is inconsistent with the allocation contained in a written agreement. The Third Circuit has held that a party to a contract allocating a portion of the purchase price to a covenant not to compete can "challenge the tax consequences of his agreement as construed by the Commissioner only by adducing proof which in an action between the parties to the agreement would be admissible to alter that construction or to show its unenforceability because of mistake, undue influence, fraud, duress, etc." *Commissioner v. Danielson,* 378 F.2d 771, 775 (3d Cir.), *cert. denied,* 389 U.S. 858 (1967). In a similar situation, the Second Circuit required the parties to adduce "strong proof" in order to refute the price assigned by the sale contract to a covenant not to compete. *See Ullman v. Commissioner,* 264 F.2d 305, 308 (2d Cir.1959).

Reasons for Change The allocation of consideration among the assets transferred in a transaction continues to be a troublesome area of the tax law in those situations in which the existing reporting and allocation rules do not apply. It is believed that extending the rules to certain situations to which they do not currently apply will tend to reduce controversies between the IRS and taxpayers. In addition, extending the rules may diminish some of the "whipsaw" potential that results when the parties' allocations for tax reporting purposes are inconsistent. * * *

Finally, it is believed it is appropriate to bind the parties to a transaction to any written agreement they reach regarding the allocation of the consideration to, or fair market value of, any of the specific asset(s) transferred. In such cases, it is believed that taxpayers should not be allowed to take positions that are inconsistent with their written agreements.

Explanation of Provisions * * * In addition, the bill provides that where a person holds at least 10 percent of the value of an entity (immediately before the transaction) and both transfers an interest in the entity and, in connection therewith, enters into an employment contract, covenant not to compete, royalty or lease agreement or other agreement with the transferee, such person and the transferee must report information concerning the transaction at such time and in such manner as the Secretary may require. [*See* § 1060(e).] These reporting rules apply regardless of whether the transaction constitutes an applicable asset acquisition within the meaning of section 1060 or whether, in the case of a stock purchase, a section 338 election is made. In determining whether a person holds at least 10 percent of an entity, the constructive ownership rules of section 318 (or similar principles in cases involving interests other than stock) will apply. In addition, the reporting rules will apply if a person who is related to the 10-percent owner (within the meaning of section 267(b) or section 707(b)(1)) enters into the agreement with the transferee.

Taxpayers required to report consistent positions. The bill provides that a written agreement regarding the allocation of consideration to, or the fair market value of, any of the assets in an applicable asset acquisition will be binding on both parties for tax purposes, unless the parties are able to refute the allocation or valuation under the standards set forth in the *Danielson* case. [*See* § 1060(f).] The parties are bound only with respect to the allocations or valuations actually provided in the agreement. Thus, the parties are bound to any written partial allocation or valuation. It is intended that the Secretary may require reporting regarding any such agreements.

It is not intended to restrict in any way the ability of the IRS to challenge the taxpayers' allocation to any asset or to challenge the taxpayers' determination of the fair market value of any asset by any appropriate method, particularly where there is a lack of adverse tax interests between the parties.

3. The 1999 Proposed Regulations under § 1060

Preamble to Proposed Regulations

August 10, 1999, 64 F.R. 43462 [Treasury Decision 8940, Feb. 13, 2001, finalized these regulations substantially in the form discussed here.]

Background* * * Section 1060 was added by section 641 of the Tax Reform Act of 1986, Public Law 99-514 (100 Stat. 2282). Section 1060 requires both the buyer and the seller of a trade or business to allocate their consideration paid or received to the assets under the same residual method prescribed by the section 338 regulations. [*See* Chapter 5.] Also as part of the 1986 act, miscellaneous changes were made to section 338. * * *

Sections 338 and 1060 were amended by section 11323 of the Omnibus Budget Reconciliation Act of 1990, Public Law 101-508 (104 Stat. 1388-464). The amendments add certain reporting requirements under sections 338 and 1060. In addition, a provision was added to section 1060 under which parties are bound by written agreements as to allocations or fair market values. The legislative history indicates that the parties are so bound unless the parties can refute the agreement under the standards set forth in [*Danielson, supra*] (by presenting proof which in an action between the parties would be admissible to alter that construction or to show its unenforceability because of mistake, undue influence, fraud, duress, etc.). See, H.R. Ways and Means Comm., 101st Cong., 2d Sess. (Print No. 101-37, Oct. 15, 1990), at 79. * * *

Section 1060 was again amended by section 13261(e) of the Omnibus Budget Reconciliation Act of 1993, Public Law 103-66 (107 Stat. 539). This amendment made changes to section 1060 to conform the rules for actual asset acquisitions to the amortization of intangibles under section 197. In addition, the legislative history to section 197 suggested that the residual method should be altered to accommodate section 197 intangibles. See, H.R. Rep. 111, 103d Cong., 1st Sess. 760 (May 23, 1993). * * *

Section 1060(a) requires a purchaser and a seller to allocate basis for any applicable asset acquisition in the same manner as amounts are allocated to such assets under section 338(b)(5). [*See* Chapter 5.] Section 1060(c) defines an applicable asset acquisition as any transfer of assets that constitute a trade or business where the transferee's basis is determined wholly by reference to the consideration paid for the assets.

Section 338(b)(5) authorizes the Secretary to issue regulations prescribing how the deemed purchase price is to be allocated among the assets. Final and temporary regulations under sections 338(b) and 1060, as amended, implement this authority. The regulations generally require that the basis of the acquired (or deemed acquired) assets will be determined using a five class residual method. [As seen below, this has been modified to Seven Classes.] Class I consists of cash and cash equivalents; Class II consists of certificates of deposit, U.S. Government securities, readily marketable stock or securities, and foreign currency; Class III includes all assets not included in

Class I, Class II, Class IV, or Class V; Class IV consists of section 197 intangible assets except those in the nature of goodwill and going concern value; and Class V consists of section 197 intangible assets in the nature of goodwill and going concern value. The total allocable basis is first decreased by the amount of Class I assets. Any remaining amount is allocated proportionally to Class II assets to the extent of their fair market value. Any remaining amount is then allocated first to Class III assets and then to Class IV assets in the same manner as to Class II assets. Finally, any remaining amount is allocated to the Class V assets. * * *

Reasons for Change * * * Number *and Content of Classes* The seven classes under the proposed regulations [under both §§ 338 and 1060] are as follows: Class I, cash and cash equivalents; Class II, actively traded personal property as defined in section 1092(d), certificates of deposit, and foreign currency; Class III, accounts receivable, mortgages, and credit card receivables which arise in the ordinary course of business; Class IV, stock in trade of the taxpayer or other property of a kind which would properly be included in the inventory of taxpayer if on hand at the close of the taxable year, or property held by the taxpayer primarily for sale to customers in the ordinary course of his trade or business; Class V, all assets not in Class I, II, III, VI, or VII; Class VI, all section 197 intangibles except goodwill or going concern value; and Class VII, goodwill and going concern value. * * * [These seven classes are explored in greater detail in the discussion of § 338 in Sec.5.3.D.]

Explanation of Provisions. * * * Overview *of Changes. The proposed regulations are intended to clarify the treatment of, and provide consistent rules (where possible) for, both deemed and actual asset acquisitions under sections 338* [*see* Chapter 5] *and 1060.* * * * The proposed regulations also attempt to provide similar treatment, when appropriate, for deemed and actual asset acquisitions by stating the relevant concepts once in the regulations under section 338 and cross-referencing those rules in § 1.1060-1 of the proposed regulations. * * *

Section 1.1060-1. Definition of Trade or Business. Section 1060 applies to the direct or indirect transfer of a trade or business. * * *

The proposed regulations clarify that an applicable asset acquisition can occur even if the trade or business is transferred from seller to purchaser in a series of related transactions and that the residual method must be applied once to all of the assets transferred in a series of related transactions. The proposed regulations also incorporate the principles of the anti-abuse rule from § 1.338-1(c) of the proposed regulations to determine which assets must be included for purposes of applying the residual method. * * *

Transaction Costs. Under the current regulations, consideration is allocated to each asset to the extent of that asset's fair market value as long as there is sufficient consideration to provide full allocation of basis to each asset in the class. The fair market value limitation and the residual allocation method of the current regulations do not permit costs associated with specific assets to be allocated to those assets. For example, if a purchaser incurred costs to acquire an asset and section 1060 did not apply to the acquisition, the basis of that asset would be increased to reflect those costs. However, the fair market value limitation under the current regulations would limit a purchaser's basis in the asset to its fair market value. The proposed regulations allow the buyer and seller to adjust their allocation of consideration to particular assets for costs incurred which are specifically identified with those assets. Thus, the total amount the seller allocates to an asset for which it incurs specifically identifiable costs would be less than its fair market value and, for the buyer, greater than its fair market value. The parties are not allowed to apportion costs associated generally with the overall transaction to specific assets. A similar rule is not necessary, and therefore not included, under section 338, because the underlying transaction is a stock sale. Any costs associated with a deemed asset sale are of the type generally associated with the overall sale of stock and, therefore, the parties would not be allowed to apportion those costs to specific assets under the rule.

Written Allocation Agreements. After the current regulations were adopted, Congress amended section 1060 to provide that a written agreement allocating purchase price is binding on both parties. *See* section 1060(a). The legislative history indicates that parties must report consistent with their agreed-upon allocations, unless the parties are able to refute the agreement under the standards set forth in [*Danielson, supra*]. The proposed regulations incorporate the Danielson standard by reference.

E. Treatment of the Target's Liabilities

New York State Bar Association Tax Section, Report on the Federal Income Tax Treatment of Contingent Liabilities in Taxable Asset Acquisition Transactions

Tax Notes 885 (November 19, 1990)*

PRECEDENTS AND AUTHORITIES REGARDING THE TAX TREATMENT OF LIABILITIES IN ASSET ACQUISITION TRANSACTIONS

Before describing the precedents relating to contingent liabilities, it is useful to consider the precedents in the area of fixed liabilities, which are relatively well settled.

Rules Governing Fixed Liabilities *Treatment of Seller*. A Seller of property whose fixed liability is assumed in connection with a transfer of property realizes income in the amount of the liability. [*See Crane,* Chapter 1.] (No distinction is intended to be made herein between the Purchaser's "assumption" of a liability of the Seller as contrasted with the Purchaser's acquiring the Seller's property "subject to" a liability encumbering the property.) This conclusion holds true whether the liability is recourse or nonrecourse.

In the case of a Seller that uses the cash method of accounting, the assumption of a deductible liability that has accrued but not been paid (and therefore not previously

---

* Published with permission of TAX NOTES.

been deducted) triggers the deduction on the premise that the Purchaser's assumption is tantamount to the Seller's payment of the liability. * * *

Treatment of Purchaser The Purchaser treats an assumed fixed liability as a cost of the acquired property and accordingly includes such amount in its tax basis. To the extent the liability assumed is a deductible item as to the Seller, the Purchaser is not entitled to a deduction based on the character of the assumed liability; which is accorded the same treatment as a nondeductible item. Due to the reflection of the liability in the basis of the acquired asset, the Purchaser may, of course, obtain a deduction through its recovery of basis (via amortization, depreciation, cost of goods sold, etc.). * * *

Rules Governing Contingent Liabilities. *Treatment of Seller.* While precedents are sparse (and perhaps contradictory in the section 338 setting), * * * it is reasonably clear that the Seller does not recognize net income by reason of the Purchaser's assumption of a contingent liability. The approach taken by present law is not wholly clear, but some insight can be gained from *James M. Pierce Corp. v. Commissioner.* At issue in *Pierce* was the tax treatment of an unearned subscription reserve where the newspaper business to which the reserve related had been sold. The reserve represented subscription amounts that had been received but not yet included in income under the taxpayer's method of accounting. The Tax Court held that the unrecovered balance of the reserve was required to be included in income at the time of the acquisition. The Court of Appeals for the Eighth Circuit agreed that recapture of the reserve was required, but went on to hold that an offsetting deduction was permitted since the reduction in cash consideration to the Seller by reason of the liability assumption amounted to a *de facto* (deductible) payment by the Seller.

The logic of *Pierce* was adhered to in *Commercial Security Bank v. Commissioner,* in which the "accrued business liabilities" (largely interest expense) of a cash method bank were held deductible against the accrued interest receivables triggered into income upon sale of a banking business, again based on the notion that assumption of the liabilities was the functional equivalent of payment thereof. * * *

While no authority expressly so holds, it seems likely that the Seller would have income upon the assumption of a nondeductible contingent liability (e.g., a contingent liability for federal taxes, or an obligation to pay a fine to a governmental entity). It is not believed that the assumption of such contingent liabilities occurs commonly.

Treatment of Purchaser. The treatment of the Purchaser who assumes a contingent liability is not altogether clear. Three alternatives appear possible:

Alternative 1: Purchaser deducts the amount of the liability when it becomes fixed, applying the all-events test, as well as other limiting provisions such as sections 404 or 461(h).

Alternative 2: Purchaser includes the amount of the liability in its cost basis for the acquired assets, but only as the liability is satisfied, similar to the treatment of contingent purchase price amounts.

Alternative 3: Purchaser (i) includes the amount of the liability in income upon its assumption thereof, (ii) includes the amount of the liability in the tax basis of the acquired assets currently, and (iii) deducts the amount of the liability when it is satisfied.

Alternative 2 has the greatest, but not uniform, support. Alternative 1 is supported by selected decisions. There is little direct support for Alternative 3. * * *

The section 1060 regulations do not specifically address the treatment of contingent liabilities. The regulations simply define the Purchaser's consideration as its cost for the acquired assets and the Seller's consideration as the amount realized under section 1001(b). Similarly, the subsequent adjustment rules defer to "applicable principles of tax law." As regards the Purchaser, subsequent adjustments in purchase price are required to be allocated among the acquired assets employing the residual allocation rule. * * *

F. General Capitalization Requirement and Potential Deductibility of Startup expenses under § 195

Revenue Ruling 99-23

1999-1 C.B. 998

Issue When a taxpayer acquires the assets of an active trade or business, which expenditures will qualify as investigatory costs that are eligible for amortization as start-up expenditures under § 195? * * *

Law and Analysis Section 195(a) provides that, except as otherwise provided in § 195, no deduction is allowed for start-up expenditures.

Section 195(b) provides that start-up expenditures may, at the election of the taxpayer, be [deduced as follows:

(A) the taxpayer shall be allowed a deduction for the taxable year in which the active trade or business begins in an amount equal to the lesser of—

(i) the amount of start-up expenditures with respect to the active trade or business, or

(ii) $5,000, reduced (but not below zero) by the amount by which such start-up expenditures exceed $50,000, and

(B) the remainder of such start-up expenditures shall be allowed as a deduction ratably over the 180-month period [15-years, which also applies under Section 197] beginning with the month in which the active trade or business begins.]

Section 195(c)(1) defines "start-up expenditure," in part, as any amount (A) paid or incurred in connection with investigating the creation or acquisition of an active trade or business, and (B) which, if paid or incurred in connection with the operation of an existing active trade or business (in the same field as the trade or business referred to in subparagraph (A)), would be allowable as a deduction for the taxable year in which paid or incurred. Thus, in order to qualify as start-up expenditures under § 195(c)(1), a taxpayer's "investigatory costs" must satisfy the requirements in both §§ 195(c)(1)(A) and (B). In addition, the term "start-up expenditure" does not include any amount with respect to which a deduction is allowable under § 163(a), 164, or 174. * * *

Note

In general, the costs incurred by an acquiring corporation in making an acquisition are required to be capitalized under § 263. *See* Sec. 5.4.F., which addresses various capitalization issues arising under the *INDOPCO* case and the Treasury's new approach to resolving such issues.

§ 4.4 Issues of Concern Principally to Target Corporation and Its Shareholders

A. Repeal of *General Utilities* Doctrine and Former § 337

In view of the repeal of the *General Utilities* doctrine and of former § 337, the target has complete recognition of gain and loss on the sale of its assets, except that under § 336(d)(2), the target does not recognize loss with respect to certain contributed property. *See* Chapter 2, which examines in detail the repeal of the *General Utilities* doctrine.

If a non-subsidiary target retains some of its assets and distributes them to the shareholders in final liquidation, the target recognizes gain and in certain cases loss on the liquidating distribution. *See* § 336 and Sec. 2.10.D. If the target is a subsidiary and the liquidation is governed by § 332, then under § 337 the target has no gain or loss on the distribution of property to its parent, and the parent takes a carryover basis for the property under § 334(b). *See* Secs. 2.10.C. and D.

B. Computation and Character of Target's Gain or Loss on the Sale of Assets of a Business

Williams v. McGowan

United States Court of Appeals, Second Circuit, 1945
152 F.2d 570

L. Hand, Circuit Judge.* * * [The taxpayer, Williams, sold his sole proprietorship, which consisted of several assets, including inventory and fixtures. The issue was the character of the gain on the sale: capital, ordinary or split between capital and ordinary.]

[I]n this instance the section [the predecessor of § 1221] itself furnishes the answer. It starts in the broadest way by declaring that all "property" is "capital assets," and then makes three exceptions. The first is "stock in trade * * * or other property of a kind which would properly be included in the inventory"; next comes "property held * * * primarily for sale to customers"; and finally, property "used in the trade or business of a character which is subject to * * * allowance for depreciation." In the face of this language, although it may be true that a "stock in trade," taken by itself, should be treated as a "universitas facti," by no possibility can a whole business be so treated; and the same is true as to any property within the other exceptions. Congress plainly did mean to comminute the elements of a business; plainly it did not regard the whole as "capital assets."

As has already appeared, Williams transferred to the Corning Company "cash," "receivables," "fixtures" and a "merchandise inventory." "Fixtures" are not capital because they are subject to a depreciation allowance [see § 1231(b)]; the inventory, as we have just seen, is expressly excluded. * * * There can of course be no gain or loss in the transfer of cash; and, although Williams does appear to have made a gain of $1072.71 upon the "receivables," the point has not been argued that they are not subject to a depreciation allowance. That we leave open for decision by the district court, if the parties cannot agree. The gain or loss upon every other item should be computed as an item in ordinary income.

Judgment reversed.

[Dissenting opinion deleted.]

Question

What is the character of gain from the sale of goodwill?

C. Allocation of Purchase Price under § 1060

The rules of § 1060 regarding allocation of purchase price apply also to the target corporation and its shareholders. Under § 1060(e) 10% shareholders are required to report to the IRS with respect to such items as covenants not to compete and employment contracts. *See* Sec. 4.3.D.

D. Treatment of the Target's Shareholders: Including Installment Sales

1. Capital Gain or Loss under § 331

Under § 331, the target's shareholders have capital gain or loss upon receipt of a liquidating distribution, and under § 334(a) they take a fair market value basis for the property received. *See* Chapter 2.

2. Installment Sale Treatment under § 453(h)

a. Introduction

Under § 453(h), the shareholders may under certain circumstances qualify for installment sale treatment, which is discussed generally in Sec. 1.4.D., on the receipt of installment obligations of the acquiring corporation that are distributed by the target corporation.

Although the target's shareholders may qualify for installment sale treatment, the target recognizes gain with respect to the installment obligation upon the distribution of the obligation to the shareholders, unless the distribution is to a parent corporation under §§ 332 and 337. *See* §§ 453B(a) and (d).

The following excerpt from the final regulations under § 453(h) elaborate on this treatment.

b. The 1998 Final Regulations under § 453(h)

Preamble to Final Regulations

Treasury Decision 8762, 63 F.R. 4168, January 28, 1998

Explanation of Provisions. *Overview of Provisions.* Prior to the Installment Sales Revision Act of 1980, a shareholder recognized gain or loss on receipt of an installment obligation that was distributed by a liquidating corporation in exchange for the shareholder's stock. Gain could not be reported under the installment sale provisions of section 453 as payments were received on the obligation distributed by the corporation in the liquidation.

As enacted by the Installment Sales Revision Act of 1980 and amended by the Tax Reform Act of 1986, section 453(h) provides a different treatment for certain installment obligations that are distributed in a complete liquidation to which section 331 applies. Under section 453(h), a shareholder that does not elect out of the installment method treats the payments under the obligation, rather than the obligation itself, as consideration received in exchange for the stock. The shareholder then takes into account the income from the payments under the obligation using the installment method. In this manner, the shareholder generally is treated as if the shareholder sold the shareholder's stock to an unrelated purchaser on the installment method.

This treatment under section 453(h) applies generally to installment obligations received by a shareholder (in exchange for the shareholder's stock) in a complete liquidation to which section 331 applies if (a) the installment obligations are qualifying installment obligations, i.e., the installment obligations are acquired in respect of a sale or exchange of property by the corporation during the 12-month period beginning on the date a plan of complete liquidation is adopted, and (b) the liquidation is completed within that 12-month period. However, an installment obligation acquired in a sale or exchange of inventory, stock in trade, or property held for sale in the ordinary course of business qualifies for this treatment only if the obligation arises from a single bulk sale of substantially all of such property attributable to a trade or business of the corporation. If an installment obligation arises from both a sale or exchange of inventory, etc., that does not comply with the requirements of the preceding sentence and a sale or exchange of other assets, the portion of the installment obligation that is attributable to the sale or exchange of other assets is a qualifying installment obligation. * * *

E. Golden Parachute Payments under § 280G

If the executives of the target receive severance payments in connection with the sale of the assets of a publicly held target, such payments may be subject to the golden parachute rules of § 280G. Golden parachute issues arise principally in the context of stock acquisitions and for that reason this issue is addressed in detail in Chapter 5.

F. Consequence of Keeping the Corporation Alive

If the target's shareholders decide to have a target that is a C corporation hold the proceeds of the sale and invest the proceeds in passive investments, the C corporation may become a personal holding company (PHC). PHCs are certain closely held C corporations that have substantial amounts of passive income. *See* §§ 541 *et seq.* and Chapter 12 of *Taxation of Business Entities, supra* Sec. 1.12.

The PHC tax can be avoided by converting the C to an S, but this can present problems that are not addressed here. *See* Chapter 15 of *Taxation of Business Entities, supra* Sec. 1.12.

§ 4.5 Planning for the Utilization of Target's Net Operating Losses

A. In General

In a taxable asset acquisition, the target's losses do not pass over to the acquiring corporation; they stay with the target and can be utilized to shelter the gain realized by the target on the sale of its assets. If the target is a subsidiary in a consolidated group, any net operating losses of the group can be utilized to offset the gain realized by the target. *See* Chapter 5.

Thus, provisions limiting the utilization of net operating loss carryovers such as §§ 382 and 269, have no applicability to taxable acquisitions of the target's assets. The following ruling addresses situations in which a loss corporation makes a taxable acquisition of assets.

B. The Applicability of Libson Shops or § 269 to Purchase by Loss Company of Profitable Company

Revenue Ruling 63-40

1963-1 C.B. 46

Advice has been requested whether either the rationale of the decision in *Libson Shops, Inc. v. Koehler*, 353 U.S. 382 (1957), or the provisions of section 269 of the Internal Revenue Code of 1954 [*See* Sec. 4.5.] prevent the use of a net operating loss carryover under the circumstances described below.

1. The *M* corporation was organized in 1947 by three individuals who owned an equal number of shares of its authorized and outstanding stock. From the date of its incorporation until the early part of 1958 it was engaged in the fabrication and sale, through distributors, of household light steel products. The business was successful during its early years of operation. However, commencing in 1953 it sustained losses in each of its taxable years and over the period ending December 31, 1957, had accumulated substantial net operating losses.

In 1958 *M* corporation purchased for cash, at fair market value, all of the assets of *N* corporation, which had a history of successful operation of drive-in restaurants. *M* and *N* were unrelated corporations and none of the shareholders of *M* corporation owned, directly or indirectly, any stock of *N* corporation. The funds for the cash purchase were derived in part from *M* corporation's own business assets and in part from an equal contribution to its capital of cash by its three stockholders. Shortly thereafter, *M* corporation discontinued its former business activity, sold the assets connected therewith, and engaged exclusively in the business of operating the chain of drive-in restaurants formerly operated by the *N* corporation.

Under the facts presented, neither section 269 nor section 382 of the Code is applicable and the sole question raised is whether the rationale of the *Libson Shops* decision bars the allowance of the net operating loss deduction attributable to losses incurred prior to the acquisition of the new business activity for *M* corporation's taxable year ended December 31, 1958.

In cases, like the one discussed above, arising under section 122 of the Internal Revenue Code of 1939 or section 172 of the 1954 Code in which losses have been incurred by a single corporation and there has been little or no change in the stock ownership of the corporation during or after the period in which the losses were incurred, the Internal Revenue Service will not rely on the rationale of the *Libson Shops* decision to bar the corporation from using losses previously incurred by it solely because such losses are attributable to a discontinued corporate activity. Accordingly since there was no change in stock ownership in *M* corporation either before the discontinuance of its former business activity or after the commencement of its new business activity, a net operating loss deduction is allowable for its taxable year ended December 31, 1958.

However, if there is more than a minor change in stock ownership of a loss corporation which acquires a new business enterprise, the Service may continue to contest the deductibility of the carryover of the corporation's prior losses against income of the new business enterprise. * * *

Notes

1. The principle in the above ruling should also apply if the loss corporation acquires the stock of a profitable target and then makes a §338 election.

2. If the loss corporation acquires a target's stock and does not make a §338 election, §384 may disallow the use of the loss corporation's net operating loss carryovers against the post-acquisition built-in gains generated by the target's assets. Section 384 is examined in Sec. 5.11.

§ 4.6 Summary Problems on Asset Acquisitions

The stock of Target Corporation (*TC*), a C corporation, is owned by five individual shareholders (*A, B, C, D,* and *E*), who each own 20% of the stock. Each shareholder has a low basis for her shares. *TC* owns manufacturing assets and associated liabilities and rental real property and associated liabilities. Both the manufacturing assets and the real property are substantially appreciated, and there is significant goodwill associated with the manufacturing assets. *TC* has substantial earnings and profits. Acquiring Corporation (*AC*) has proposed to acquire, for $250K in cash and $250K in *AC* notes, *TC*'s manufacturing assets and certain fixed and contingent liabilities. After the sale, it is planned that *TC* will distribute the cash and notes received to its shareholders and continue to operate the real property. What result to *AC, TC,* and *TC*'s shareholders? *See* §§ 302(b)(4) and 302(e).

a. What result, if after the sale *TC* liquidates, distributing the cash, notes and real property to its shareholders?

b. What result if *AC* purchases all of *TC*'s assets for $500K of cash, $500K of notes, and the assumption of certain designated liabilities? *TC* then pays its retained liabilities and liquidates, distributing the cash and notes to its shareholders?

c. What result in b. above, if *TC* continues to operate as an investment company?

d. What result in b. above, if *TC* has one million in NOL carryovers? Also, what if instead of liquidating, *TC* purchases the assets of another business?

e. What result in b. above, if instead of a purchase by *AC* of *TC*'s assets, *TC* merges into a subsidiary of *AC*?

f. What result in e. above, if *TC* merges into *AC*?

g. What result in b. above, if *AC* is a newly-formed corporation and individual *E* owns 25% of the stock of *AC*? What if *E* owns 60% of the stock of *AC*?

h. What result in b. above, if in addition to the purchase of *TC*'s assets, *AC* enters into a covenant not to compete with each of *TC*'s shareholders? Pursuant to the covenant, each shareholder receives $100K and agrees not to compete with any of *TC*'s businesses for a period of five years.

i. Both *TC* and *AC* incurred expenses for in house and outside attorneys and for investment bankers on the transaction. What is the treatment of these fees? What is the treatment of these expenses if the deal is aborted?

§ 4.7 Introduction to Federal Income Tax Consequences of Cross Border Taxable Asset Acquisitions

A. Introduction

This section briefly introduces some of the many issues that can arise under the Internal Revenue Code in connection with (1) the acquisition by a foreign acquiring corporation or its wholly owned U.S. subsidiary of the U.S. assets of a U.S. target in a taxable asset acquisition (*i.e.*, inbound asset acquisitions), and (2) the acquisition by a U.S. acquiring corporation or its wholly owned foreign subsidiary of the foreign assets of a foreign target in a taxable asset acquisition (*i.e.*, outbound asset acquisitions). If the foreign acquiror acquires the assets of the U.S. target directly, the foreign acquiror will be conducting a business through a U.S branch, and if the U.S. acquiror acquires the assets of the foreign target directly, then the U.S. acquiror will be conducting business through a foreign branch. In the case of the outbound asset acquisition through a foreign subsidiary, it is assumed that the U.S. acquiror will transfer in a § 351 transaction appreciated property to the foreign subsidiary that is making the taxable asset acquisition. For a more in depth coverage of these issues see the references in Sec. 1.12.

B. Inbound Asset Acquisitions

1. Treatment of U.S. Shareholders

The U.S. shareholders of the U.S. target will have the same tax treatment on the receipt of the consideration from the foreign acquiror or its U.S. sub that they would have on receipt of the same consideration in a wholly domestic asset acquisition. However, if they receive notes from the foreign acquiror, then there may be a withholding tax imposed by the foreign acquiror's home country on the interest payments on the notes. For example, as will be seen in the discussion of outbound asset acquisitions, if a foreign person holds notes of a U.S issuer, the interest payments on the notes are subject to a 30% withholding tax under §§ 871 or 881 of the Code, and many countries have similar provisions. However, if there is a treaty between the U.S. and the other country, the withholding tax may be reduced or eliminated. For example, the U.S. Model treaty provides for a zero withholding tax on interest payments.

2. Direct Acquisition of U.S. Target's Assets by Foreign Acquiror: Inbound Branch Operations

a. Introduction

The foreign acquiror is subject to the same tax treatment on the acquisition of assets that applies to a U.S. acquiror, that is, the foreign acquiror will take a cost basis for the assets acquired, will be subject to the allocation rules under § 1060, and will get the benefit of the amortization deduction under § 197. The next section addresses the tax consequences of operating the target's business as a U.S. branch.

b. U.S. Taxation of Branch Operations

Joint Committee on Taxation, Description and Analysis of Present-Law Rules Relating to International Taxation

June 30, 1999

Income From A U.S. Business. The United States taxes on a net basis the income of foreign persons that is "effectively connected" with the conduct of a trade or business in the United States (§§ 871(b) and 882). Any gross income earned by the foreign person that is not effectively connected with the person's U.S. business is not taken into account in determining the rates of U.S. tax applicable to the person's income from such business (§§ 871(b)(2) and 882(a)(2)).

U.S. trade or business. A foreign person is subject to U.S. tax on a net basis if the person is engaged in a U.S. trade or business. [Thus, a foreign corporation operating in the U.S. through a branch is subject to U.S. taxation on the income of the branch.] In this regard, partners in a partnership * * * are treated as engaged in the conduct of a trade or business within the United States if the partnership, estate, or trust is so engaged (§ 875).

The question of whether a foreign person is engaged in a U.S. trade or business has generated a significant body of case law. Basic issues involved in the determination include whether the activity constitutes business rather than investing, whether sufficient activities in connection with the business are conducted in the United States, and whether the relationship between the foreign person and persons performing functions in the United States with respect to the business is sufficient to attribute those functions to the foreign person. * * *

Effectively-connected income. A foreign person that is engaged in the conduct of a trade or business within the United States is subject to U.S. net-basis taxation on the income that is "effectively connected" with such business. Specific statutory rules govern the determination of whether income is so effectively connected (§ 864(c)).

In the case of U.S.-source capital gain or loss and U.S.-source income of a type that would be subject to gross basis U.S. taxation, the factors taken into account in determining whether the income, gain, deduction, or loss is effectively connected with a U.S. trade or business include whether the amount is derived from assets used in or held for use in the conduct of the U.S. trade or business and whether the activities of the trade or business were a material factor in the realization of the amount (§ 864(c)(2)). * * *

Foreign-source income of a foreign person that is effectively connected with the conduct of a trade or business in the United States may also be taxed by the United States, subject to a credit for any foreign income taxes (§§ 864(c)(4) and 906). However, only specific types of foreign-source income are considered to be effectively connected with a U.S. trade or business (§ 864(c)(4)(A)). Foreign-source income of a type not specified generally is exempt from U.S. tax. * * *

[**FIRPTA**] Gains of a foreign individual or foreign corporation on the disposition of U.S. real property interests are taxed on a net basis under FIRPTA, even if they are not otherwise effectively connected with a U.S. trade or business. Similarly, rental and other income from U.S. real property may be taxed, at the election of the taxpayer, on a net basis at graduated rates (§§ 871(d) and 882(d)).

[**The Branch Profits Tax**] A U.S. corporation owned by foreign persons is subject to U.S. income tax on its net income. In addition, the earnings of the U.S. corporation are subject to a second tax [a gross basis tax], this time at the shareholder level, when dividends are paid. [W]hen the shareholders are foreign, the second-level tax is imposed at a flat rate and collected by withholding. Similarly, * * *, interest payments made by a U.S. corporation to foreign creditors are subject to a U.S. withholding tax in certain circumstances. Pursuant to the branch tax provisions, the United States taxes foreign corporations engaged in a U.S. trade or business on amounts of U.S. earnings and profits that are shifted out of, or amounts of interest deducted by, the U.S. branch of the foreign corporation. The branch level taxes are comparable to these second-level taxes. In addition, where a foreign corporation is not subject to the branch profits tax as the result of a treaty, it may be liable for withholding tax on actual dividends it pays to foreign shareholders.

The United States imposes a tax of 30 percent on a foreign corporation's "dividend equivalent amount" (§ 884(a)). The "dividend equivalent amount" generally is the earnings and profits of a U.S. branch of a foreign corporation attributable to its income effectively connected with a U.S. trade or business (§ 884(b)). * * *

In arriving at the dividend equivalent amount, a branch's effectively connected earnings and profits are adjusted to reflect changes in a branch's U.S. net equity (*i.e.*, the excess of the branch's assets over its liabilities, taking into account only amounts treated as connected with its U.S. trade or business) (§ 884(b)). The first adjustment reduces the dividend equivalent amount to the extent the branch's earnings are reinvested in trade or business assets in the United States (or reduce U.S. trade or business liabilities). The second adjustment increases the dividend equivalent amount to the extent prior reinvested earnings are considered remitted to the home office of the foreign corporation.

Interest paid by a U.S. trade or business of a foreign corporation generally is treated as if paid by a U.S. corporation and therefore is subject to U.S. 30-percent withholding tax (if the interest is paid to a foreign person) (§ 884(f)(1)(A)). Certain "excess interest" of a U.S. trade or business of a foreign corporation is treated as if paid by a U.S. corporation to a foreign parent and, therefore, is subject to U.S. 30-percent withholding tax (§ 884(f)(1)(B)). For this purpose, excess interest is the excess of the interest deduction allowed with respect to the U.S. trade or business over the amount of interest paid by such trade or business.

[**Impact of Tax Treaties on Branch Operations**] *Business Profits Attributable To A Permanent Establishment.* Under the U.S. model, one treaty country may not tax the business profits of an enterprise of a qualified resident of the other treaty country, unless the enterprise carries on business in the first country through a permanent establishment situated there. In that case, the business profits of the enterprise may be taxed in the first country on profits that are attributable to that permanent establishment. The U.S. model describes in detail the characteristics relevant to determine whether a place of business is a permanent establishment. The term includes a place of management, a branch, an office, a factory, a workshop, a mine, an oil or gas well, a quarry, or any other place of extraction of natural resources.

The U.S. model provides that the business profits to be attributed to the permanent establishment include only the profits derived from the assets or activities of the permanent establishment. * * *

3. Acquisition of U.S. Target's Assets by U.S. Sub of Foreign Acquiror: Inbound U.S. Subsidiary Operations

a. Introduction

On the acquisition of the U.S. target's assets, the U.S. subsidiary has the same treatment as any other U.S. acquiror, and the U.S. subsidiary will be subject to Federal income tax on its worldwide income just like any other U.S. corporation. However, a 30% gross basis tax, subject to treaty modification, applies to the payment of dividends, interest and royalties by the U.S. sub to its foreign parent. The following section elaborates on the principles governing the operations of U.S. subs of foreign parent corporations.

If the foreign acquiror transfers foreign property to the U.S. subsidiary, the transaction is governed by § 351; however, the foreign acquiror is not in any event subject to capital gains tax on such a transfer.

b. U.S. Taxation of U.S. Subsidiary

Joint Committee on Taxation, Description and Analysis of Present-Law Rules Relating to International Taxation

June 30, 1999

[**Basic Income Tax.** As indicated the U.S. sub is subject to Federal income tax on its worldwide income.]

Gross-Basis Taxation *Withholding tax.* In the case of U.S.-source interest, dividends, rents, royalties, or other similar types of income (known as fixed or determinable, annual or periodical gains, profits and income), the United States generally imposes a flat 30-percent tax on the gross amount paid to a foreign person if such income or gain is not effectively connected with the conduct of a U.S. trade or business (§§ 871(a) and 881). This tax generally is collected by means of withholding by the person making the payment to the foreign person receiving the income (§§ 1441 and 1442). Accordingly, the 30-percent gross-basis tax generally is referred to as a withholding tax. In most instances, the amount withheld by the U.S. payor is the final tax liability of the foreign recipient and, thus, the foreign recipient files no U.S. tax return with respect to this income.

The United States generally does not tax capital gains of a foreign corporation that are not connected with a U.S. trade or business. * * *

Although payments of U.S.-source interest that is not effectively connected with a U.S. trade or business generally are subject to the 30-percent withholding tax, there are significant exceptions to that rule. For example, interest from certain deposits with banks and other financial institutions is exempt from tax (§§ 871(i)(2)(A) and 881(d)). * * * An additional exception is provided for certain interest paid on portfolio obligations (§§ 871(h) and 881(c)). Portfolio interest generally is defined as any U.S.-source interest * * *, not effectively connected with the conduct of a U.S. trade or business, (1) on an obligation that satisfies certain registration requirements or specified exceptions thereto, and (2) that is not received by a 10-percent shareholder (§ 871(h)). * * * [This portfolio interest exception permits U.S. corporations to issue bonds in the Euro Market without any withholding obligation.]

Pursuant to an applicable tax treaty, the 30-percent gross-basis tax imposed on foreign persons may be reduced or eliminated. * * *

Dividends. The U.S. model permits taxation of dividends by the residence country of the payor, but limits the rate of such tax in cases in which the dividends are beneficially owned by a resident of the other treaty country. In such cases, the U.S. model allows not more than a 5-percent gross-basis tax if the beneficial owner is a company that owns directly at least 10 percent of the payor's voting stock, and not more than a 15-percent gross-basis tax in any other case. * * *

Interest and royalties. The U.S. model generally allows no tax to be imposed by a treaty country on interest or royalties arising in that country and beneficially owned by a resident of the other treaty country. * * *

C. Outbound Asset Acquisitions

1. Introduction

In this transaction, the U.S. acquiror ends up conducting the acquired business operations of the foreign target directly as a branch or indirectly through a foreign subsidiary. The U.S. is not concerned with the tax consequences to the foreign target or its foreign shareholders in the asset acquisition. The discussion below first focuses on foreign branch operations and then foreign subsidiary operations. In the case of foreign subsidiary operations, the discussion focuses first on the treatment of the transfer by the U.S. acquiror of appreciated property to the foreign sub in a § 351 transaction (*see* Sec. 2.2). Such a transaction might occur for purposes of integrating business operations.

2. Direct Acquisition of Foreign Target's Assets by U.S. Acquiror: Outbound Branch Operations

Joint Committee on Taxation, Description and Analysis of Present-Law Rules Relating to International Taxation

June 30, 1999

Foreign Operations Conducted Directly. The tax rules applicable to U.S. persons that control business operations in foreign countries depend on whether the business operations are conducted directly (through a foreign branch, for example) or indirectly (through a separate foreign corporation). A U.S. person that conducts foreign operations directly includes the income and losses from such operations on the person's U.S. tax return for the year the income is earned or the loss is incurred. Detailed rules are provided for the translation into U.S. currency of amounts with respect to such foreign operations. The income from the U.S. person's foreign operations thus is subject to current U.S. tax. However, the foreign tax credit may reduce or eliminate the U.S. tax on such income. * * *

Foreign Tax Credit Rules *In general.* Because the United States taxes U.S. persons on their worldwide income, Congress enacted the foreign tax credit in 1918 to prevent U.S. taxpayers from being taxed twice on their foreign source income: once by the foreign country where the income is earned and again by the United States. The foreign tax credit generally allows U.S. taxpayers to reduce the U.S. income tax on their foreign income by the foreign income taxes they pay on that income. The foreign tax credit does not operate to offset U.S. income tax on U.S.-source income.

A credit against U.S. tax on foreign income is allowed for foreign taxes paid or accrued by a U.S. person (§ 901). In addition, a credit is allowed to a U.S. corporation for foreign taxes paid by certain foreign subsidiary corporations and deemed paid by the U.S. corporation upon a dividend received by, or certain other income inclusions of, the U.S. corporation with respect to earnings of the foreign subsidiary (the "deemed-paid" or "indirect" foreign tax credit) (§ 902). [This deemed paid credit is considered further in connection with the discussion of foreign operations through foreign subsidiaries.]

The foreign tax credit provisions of the Code are elective on a year-by-year basis. In lieu of electing the foreign tax credit, U.S. persons generally are permitted to deduct foreign taxes (§ 164(a)(3)). * * *

A foreign tax credit limitation, which is calculated separately for various categories of income, is imposed to prevent the use of foreign tax credits to offset U.S. tax on U.S.-source income. Detailed rules are provided for the allocation of expenses against U.S.-source and foreign-source income. Special rules apply to require the allocation of foreign losses in one category of income for a taxable year to offset foreign income in the other categories for such year and to require the recharacterization of foreign income for a year subsequent to a foreign loss year from one income category to another or from foreign source to U.S. source (§ 904(f)).

The amount of creditable taxes paid or accrued (or deemed paid) in any taxable year which exceeds the foreign tax credit limitation is permitted to be carried back to the two immediately preceding taxable years and carried forward to the first five succeeding taxable years, and credited in such years to the extent that the taxpayer otherwise has excess foreign tax credit limitation for those years (§ 904(c)). For purposes of determining excess foreign tax credit limitation amounts, the foreign tax credit separate limitation rules apply. * * *

Foreign tax credit limitation. A premise of the foreign tax credit is that it should not reduce the U.S. tax on a taxpayer's U.S.-source income but should only reduce the U.S. tax on the taxpayer's foreign-source income. Permitting the foreign tax credit to reduce U.S. tax on U.S. income would in effect cede to foreign countries the primary right to tax income earned from U.S. sources.

In order to prevent foreign taxes from reducing U.S. tax on U.S.-source income, the foreign tax credit is subject to an overall limitation and a series of separate limitations. Under the overall limitation, the total amount of the credit may not exceed the same proportion of the taxpayer's U.S. tax which the taxpayer's foreign-source taxable income bears to the taxpayer's worldwide taxable income for the taxable year (§ 904(a)). In addition, the foreign tax credit limitation is calculated separately for [certain passive] categories of income (§ 904(d)). Under these separate limitations, the total amount of the credit for foreign taxes on income in each category may not exceed the same proportion of the taxpayer's U.S. tax which the taxpayer's foreign-source taxable income in that category bears to the taxpayer's worldwide taxable income for the taxable year. * * *

3. Acquisition of Foreign Target's Assets by Foreign Sub of U.S. Acquiror: Outbound Operations through a Foreign Sub

a. Introduction

As in the direct acquisition by the U.S acquiror, the U.S. is not concerned with the tax treatment of the foreign target or of its foreign shareholders.

In this transaction, we start by assuming that the U.S. acquiror transfers property to the foreign sub in a § 351 transaction and that the foreign sub then makes the acquisition of the foreign target's assets. The income of foreign corporations is generally not subject to taxation in the U.S., and consequently, when U.S. taxpayers transfer property to a foreign corporation, the property is moving outside of the taxing jurisdiction of the U.S. This is a reflection of the deferral regime, which generally subjects income of foreign corporations to Federal income tax only when the income is repatriated to U.S. shareholders in the form of dividends or liquidation distributions. As will be seen below, there are many exceptions to this deferral principle.

Given the nonrecognition treatment available under § 351 and the applicability of the deferral principle, a U.S. person could transfer appreciated property outside the U.S. taxing jurisdiction and the foreign corporation could then sell the appreciated property thereby avoiding the Federal income tax until the proceeds are repatriated.

As illustrated below, in addressing this problem, § 367 denies § 351 nonrecognition treatment for the transfer of certain types of property to a foreign corporation.

b. Transfer by U.S. Acquiror of Property to Foreign Sub
General Explanation of the Tax Reform Act of 1984
420–430 (1984)

Prior Law Certain transfers of appreciated property, in the course of a corporate organization, reorganization, or liquidation, can be made without recognition of gain to the corporation involved or its shareholders. [*See, e.g.,* § 351.] Under prior law, however, if the transfer was made out of the United States (an "outbound transfer"), a foreign corporation was not considered a corporation unless, pursuant to a request filed no later than the close of the 183rd day after the beginning of the transfer, the taxpayer established to the satisfaction of the Internal Revenue Service (IRS) that the exchange did not have the avoidance of Federal income taxes as one of its principal purposes (prior-law sec. 367(a)). Because corporate status is essential to a tax-free organization, reorganization, or liquidation, the failure to obtain a favorable ruling resulted in the recognition of gain realized by the participating corporation and shareholders. This rule prevented the tax-free removal of appreciated assets from the U.S. tax jurisdiction prior to their sale without IRS review.

The types of tax-free exchanges that were subject to post-transaction clearance by the IRS were contributions of property to the capital of a controlled corporation (sec. 351), corporate reorganizations (§§ 354, 355, 356, and 361) [*see* Chapter 6], and liquidations of subsidiary corporations (sec. 332) [*see* Chapter 2]. The prior statute authorized the Secretary to provide exceptions to the post-transaction ruling requirements. * * *

Reasons for Change The Congress originally enacted the special rules for nonrecognition transactions involving foreign corporations specifically to prevent avoidance of U.S. tax by transferring appreciated property outside the United States. [§ 367] Although this provision generally worked well over the years, a series of Tax Court cases threatened to weaken it. * * *

Explanation of Provision The Act restructures the rules governing outbound transfers. Under the general rule, a foreign corporation is not considered a corporation for purposes of determining the extent to which gain is recognized on an outbound transfer. [§ 367(a)] A general exception is provided for transfers of property for use in the active conduct of a trade or business outside of the United States. [§ 367(a)(3)] Transfers of stock, securities, or partnership interests may qualify for the exception. The Secretary of the Treasury, however, by regulations, may provide for recognition of gain in cases of transfers of property for use in the active conduct of a trade or business outside the United States. It was intended that the Secretary use this regulatory authority to provide for recognition in cases of transfers involving potential tax avoidance. The Act also authorizes the Secretary to designate other transfers that are excepted from the general rule of recognition. In addition, the Act imposes a notification requirement with respect to transfers of property outside the United States.

Certain categories of tainted assets (similar to those in the IRS guidelines) are ineligible for the active trade or business exception [*e.g.*, inventory]. The active trade or business exception to the general rule is also inapplicable to the incorporation of certain foreign branches in circumstances where the branch has operated at a loss. Special rules are provided for the transfer of intangibles (*e.g.*, patents, know-how, or similar items), under which the taxpayer is treated as receiving income over the useful life of the intangible in an amount reflecting reasonable payments contingent upon the productivity, use, or disposition of the intangible. * * *

c. Outbound Operations Conducted through a Foreign Subsidiary

Joint Committee on Taxation, Description and Analysis of Present-Law Rules Relating to International Taxation

June 30, 1999

Foreign Operations Conducted through a Foreign Corporation *In general.* Income earned by a foreign corporation from its foreign operations generally is subject to U.S. tax only when such income is distributed to any U.S. persons that hold stock in such corporation. Accordingly, a U.S. person that conducts foreign operations through a foreign corporation generally is subject to U.S. tax on the income from those operations when the income is repatriated to the United States through a dividend distribution to the U.S. person. The income is reported on the U.S. person's tax return for the year the distribution is received, and the United States imposes tax on such income at that time. The foreign tax credit may reduce the U.S. tax imposed on such income.

A variety of complex anti-deferral regimes impose current U.S. tax on income earned by a U.S. person through a foreign corporation. Detailed rules for coordination among the anti-deferral regimes are provided to prevent the U.S. person from being subject to U.S. tax on the same item of income under multiple regimes.

The Code sets forth the following anti-deferral regimes: the controlled foreign corporation rules of subpart F (§§ 951–964); the passive foreign investment company rules (§§ 1291–1298); * * * the personal holding company rules (§§ 541–547); [and] the accumulated earnings tax rules (§§ 531–537)[.] * * *.

Controlled Foreign Corporations. *General rules.* U.S. 10-percent shareholders of a controlled foreign corporation (a "CFC") are required to include in income for U.S. tax purposes currently certain income of the CFC (referred to as "subpart F income"), without regard to whether the income is distributed to the shareholders (§ 951(a)(1)(A)). In effect, the Code treats the U.S. 10-percent shareholders of a CFC as having received a current distribution of their pro rata shares of the CFC's subpart F income. In addition, the U.S. 10-percent shareholders of a CFC are required to include in income for U.S. tax purposes their pro rata shares of the CFC's earnings to the extent invested by the CFC in U.S. property (§ 951(a)(1)(B)). The amounts included in income by the CFC's U.S. 10-percent shareholders under these rules are subject to U.S. tax currently. The U.S. tax on such amounts may be reduced through foreign tax credits.

For this purpose, a U.S. 10-percent shareholder is a U.S. person that owns 10 percent or more of the corporation's stock (measured by vote) (§ 951(b)). A foreign corporation is a CFC if U.S. 10-percent shareholders own more than 50 percent of such corporation's stock (measured by vote or by value) (§ 957). [Thus, a wholly-owned foreign sub of a U.S. parent corporation is clearly a CFC.] * * *

Earnings and profits of a CFC that have been included in income by the U.S. 10-percent shareholders are not taxed again when such earnings are actually distributed to such shareholders (§ 959(a)(1)). Similarly, previously-taxed earnings are not included in income by the U.S. 10-percent shareholders in the event that such earnings are invested by the CFC in U.S. property (§ 959(a)(2)). * * *

Subpart F income. In general. Subpart F income typically is passive income or income that is relatively movable from one taxing jurisdiction to another. Subpart F income consists of foreign base company income (defined in § 954), insurance income (defined in § 953), and certain income relating to international boycotts and other violations of public policy (defined in § 952(a)(3)-(5)). Subpart F income does not include income of the CFC that is effectively connected with the conduct of a trade or business within the United States (on which income the CFC is subject to current U.S. tax) (§ 952(b)).

The subpart F income of a CFC is limited to its current earnings and profits (§ 952(c)). * * *

Pursuant to a *de minimis* rule, generally none of a CFC's income for a taxable year is treated as foreign base company income or subpart F insurance income if the CFC's gross foreign base company income and gross subpart F insurance income total less than the lesser of 5 percent of the CFC's gross income or $1 million (§ 954(b)(3)(A)). Pursuant to a full inclusion rule, if more than 70 percent of a CFC's gross income is foreign base company income and/or subpart F insurance income, generally all of the CFC's income is treated as foreign base company income or subpart F insurance income (whichever is appropriate) (§ 954(b)(3)(B)). Under an elective exception for income that is subject to high foreign taxes, foreign base company income and subpart F insurance income generally do not include items of income received by the CFC that the taxpayer establishes were subject to an effective foreign tax rate greater than 90 percent of the maximum U.S. corporate tax rate (§ 954(b)(4)).

Foreign base company income. Foreign base company income includes five categories of income: foreign personal holding company income, foreign base company sales income, foreign base company services income, foreign base company shipping income, and foreign base company oil related income (§ 954(a)). In computing foreign base company income, income in these five categories is reduced by allowable deductions properly allocable to such income (§ 954(b)(5)).

Foreign personal holding company income. One major category of foreign base company income is foreign personal holding company income (§ 954(c)). For subpart F purposes, foreign personal holding company income generally consists of the following: (1) dividends, interest, royalties, rents and annuities; (2) net gains from the sale or exchange of (a) property that gives rise to the preceding types of income, (b) property that does not give rise to income, and (c) interests in trusts, partnerships, and REMICS; (3) net gains from commodities transactions; (4) net gains from foreign currency transactions; (5) income that is equivalent to interest; (6) income from notional principal contracts; and (7) payments in lieu of dividends. * * *

Foreign base company sales and services income. Foreign base company income also includes foreign base company sales and services income. Foreign base company sales income generally consists of sales income of a CFC located in a country that is neither the origin nor the destination of the goods with respect to sales of property purchased from or sold to a related person (§ 954(d)). Foreign base company services income consists of income from services performed outside the CFC's country of incorporation for or on behalf of a related party (§ 954(e)). * * *

For purposes of the subpart F rules, a related person is defined as any individual, corporation, trust, or estate that controls or is controlled by the CFC, or any individual, corporation, trust, or estate that is controlled by the same person or persons that control the CFC (§ 954(d)(3)). Control with respect to a corporation means ownership of more than 50 percent of the corporation's stock (by vote or value). Control with respect to a partnership, trust, or estate means ownership of more than 50 percent of the value of the beneficial interests of the partnership, trust, or estate. Indirect and constructive ownership rules apply. * * *

Treatment of investments in U.S. property. As discussed above, the U.S. 10-percent shareholders of a CFC generally are subject to U.S. tax currently on their *pro rata* shares of the CFC's subpart F income. In addition, the U.S. 10-percent shareholders of a CFC are subject to U.S. tax currently on their *pro rata* shares of the CFC's earnings to the extent invested by the CFC in U.S. property.

A shareholder's current income inclusion with respect to a CFC's investment in U.S. property for a taxable year is the shareholder's *pro rata* share of an amount equal to the lesser of (1) the CFC's average investment in U.S. property for such year, to the extent that such investment exceeds the foreign corporation's earnings and profits that were previously taxed on that basis, or (2) the CFC's current or accumulated earnings and profits, reduced by distributions during the year and by earnings that have been taxed previously as earnings invested in U.S. property (§§ 956 and 959). An income inclusion is required only to the extent that the amount so calculated exceeds the amount of the CFC's earnings that have been previously taxed as subpart F income (§§ 951(a)(1)(B) and 959).

The U.S. property held (directly or indirectly) by a CFC must be measured as of the close of each quarter in the taxable year (§ 956(a)). The amount taken into account with respect to any property is the property's adjusted basis as determined for purposes of reporting the CFC's earnings and profits, reduced by any liability to which the property is subject.

For purposes of § 956, U.S. property generally is defined to include tangible property located in the United States, stock of a U.S. corporation, an obligation of a U.S. person, and the right to use certain intellectual property in the United States (§ 956(c)(1)). Specified exceptions are provided for, among other things, obligations of the United States, U.S. bank deposits, certain export property, certain trade or business obligations, stock or debt of certain unrelated U.S. corporations, and certain deposits or receipts of collateral or margin by, and certain repurchase or reverse re-purchase agreement transactions entered into by or with, a securities or commodities dealer in the ordinary course of the dealer's business (§ 956(c)(2)).

Passive Foreign Investment Companies. *General rules.* The Tax Reform Act of 1986 established an anti-deferral regime applicable to U.S. persons that hold stock in a passive foreign investment company (a "PFIC"). A U.S. shareholder of a PFIC generally is subject to U.S. tax, plus an interest charge that reflects the value of the deferral of tax, upon receipt of a distribution from the PFIC or upon a disposition of PFIC stock. However, if a "qualified electing fund" election is made, the U.S. shareholder is subject to U.S. tax currently on the shareholder's *pro rata* share of the PFIC's total earnings; a separate election may be made to defer payment of such tax, subject to an interest charge, on income not currently received by the shareholder. In addition, with respect to PFIC stock that is marketable, electing shareholders currently take into account as income (or loss) the difference between the fair market value of their PFIC stock as of the close of the taxable year and their adjusted basis in such stock (subject to certain restrictions).

Constructive ownership rules apply in determining whether a U.S. person owns stock in a PFIC (§ 1298(a)). Under these rules, a U.S. person generally is treated as owning such person's proportionate share of PFIC stock (1) owned by a partnership, trust or estate of which the person is a partner or beneficiary, (2) owned by a cor-poration of which the person is a 50-percent or greater shareholder (measured by value), or (3) owned by another PFIC of which the person is a shareholder.

Qualification as a PFIC. A foreign corporation is a PFIC if (1) 75 percent or more of its gross income for the taxable year consists of passive income, or (2) 50 percent or more of the average assets of the corporation consists of assets that produce, or are held for the production of, passive income (§ 1297(a)). The 50-percent PFIC asset test generally is applied using fair market value for purposes of measuring the PFIC's assets (§ 1297(f)). * * *

Deemed-Paid Foreign Tax Credit U.S. corporations owning at least 10 percent of the voting stock of a foreign corporation are treated as if they had paid a share of the foreign income taxes paid by the foreign corporation in the year in which that cor-poration's earnings and profits become subject to U.S. tax as dividend income of the U.S. shareholder (§ 902(a)). This is the "deemed-paid" or "indirect" foreign tax credit. A U.S. corporation may also be deemed to have paid taxes paid by a second, third, fourth, fifth, or sixth-tier foreign corporation, if certain requirements are satisfied (§ 902(b)). Foreign taxes paid below the third tier are eligible for the deemed credit only with respect to taxes paid in taxable years during which the payor is a CFC. For-eign taxes paid below the sixth tier are not eligible for the deemed-paid credit. In ad-dition, a deemed-paid credit generally is available with respect to subpart F inclusions (§ 960(a)). Moreover, a deemed-paid credit generally is available with respect to in-clusions under the PFIC provisions by U.S. corporations meeting the requisite own-ership threshold (§§ 1291(g) and 1293(f)).

The amount of foreign tax eligible for the indirect credit is added to the actual dividend or inclusion (the dividend or inclusion is said to be "grossed-up") and is included in the U.S. corporate shareholder's income; accordingly, the shareholder is treated as if it had received its proportionate share of pre-tax profits of the foreign corporation and paid its proportionate share of the foreign tax paid by the foreign corporation (§ 78)).

For purposes of computing the deemed-paid foreign tax credit, dividends (or other inclusions) are considered made first from the post-1986 pool of all the distributing foreign corporation's accumulated earnings and profits (§ 902(c)(6)(B)). Accumulated earnings and profits for this purpose include the earnings and profits of the current year undiminished by the current distribution (or other inclusion) (§ 902(c)(1)). Dividends in excess of the accumulated pool of post-1986 undistributed earnings and profits are treated as paid out of pre-1987 accumulated profits and are subject to the ordering principles of pre-1986 Act law (§ 902(c)(6)).

Transfer Pricing Rules [Since a U.S. controlled foreign corporation is generally not subject to U.S. taxation, there may be an incentive for a U.S. parent of the sub to sell products to the sub at low prices, which the sub in turn will sell to third parties at the market price. This is particularly so if the sub is operating in a low-tax jurisdiction, because the low intercompany price has the effect of minimizing the amount of high taxed U.S. taxable income and maximizing the amount of low taxed foreign income. This structure works only if the income of the sub is not subpart F income and thereby includible in the parent's income. Transfer pricing issues can also arise in the context of inbound transactions and completely foreign to foreign transactions. Section 482 places a restraint on the ability of taxpayers to engage in such schemes.]

In the case of a multinational enterprise that includes at least one U.S. corporation and at least one foreign corporation, the United States taxes all of the income of the U.S. corporation, but only so much of the income of the foreign corporation as is determined to have sufficient nexus to the United States. The determination of the amount that properly is the income of the U.S. member of a multinational enterprise and the amount that properly is the income of a foreign member of the same multinational enterprise thus is critical to determining the amount of income the United States may tax (as well as the amount of income other countries may tax).

Due to the variance in tax rates and tax systems among countries, a multinational enterprise may have a strong incentive to shift income, deductions, or tax credits among commonly controlled entities in order to arrive at a reduced overall tax burden. Such a shifting of items between commonly controlled entities could be accomplished by setting artificial transfer prices for transactions between group members. * * *

Under § 482, the Secretary of the Treasury is authorized to redetermine the income of an entity subject to U.S. taxation, when it appears that an improper shifting of income between that entity and a commonly controlled entity in another country has occurred. This authority is not limited to reallocations of income between different taxing jurisdictions; it permits reallocations in any common control situation, including reallocations between two U.S. entities. However, it has significant application to multinational enterprises due to the incentives for taxpayers to shift income to obtain the benefits of significantly different effective tax rates.

Section 482 grants the Secretary of the Treasury broad authority to allocate income, deductions, credits, or allowances between any commonly controlled organizations, trades, or businesses in order to prevent evasion of taxes or clearly to reflect income. * * *

One method for addressing [transfer pricing issues] is through the advance pricing agreement ("APA") procedure. An APA is an advance agreement establishing an approved transfer pricing methodology entered into between the taxpayer, the Internal Revenue Service, and a foreign tax authority. * * *

§ 4.8 Sample Asset Acquisition Agreement: Selected Provisions

Sample Asset Acquisition Agreement*

ASSETS ACQUISITION AGREEMENT, dated as of March 3, 1996 between Acquiring Corporation, Inc., a Delaware corporation (the Acquiring Corporation) and Selling Corporation, Inc., a Delaware corporation (the Selling Corporation).

Comment

In acquisitions of closely held corporations it is common to include principal shareholders as parties to the transaction.

* * *

WHEREAS

A. The Selling Corporation is engaged in the business of manufacturing widgets.

B. Subject only to the limitations and exclusions contained in this Agreement and on the terms and conditions hereinafter set forth, the Acquiring Corporation will purchase certain assets of the Selling Corporation and will assume certain liabilities of the Selling Corporation.

NOW, THEREFORE, in consideration of the recitals and of the respective covenants, representations, warranties and agreements herein contained, and intending to be legally bound hereby, the parties hereto hereby agree as follows:

Article I
Purchase and Sale and Closing

§ 1.1 *Agreement to Sell.* At the Closing hereunder (as defined in Section 1.8 thereof) and except as otherwise specifically provided in this Section 1.1, the Selling Corporation shall grant, sell, convey, assign, transfer and deliver to the Acquiring Corporation, upon and subject to the terms and conditions of this

---

* This agreement is adapted from Appendix O of Thompson, *Statutory Supplement and Documentary Appendices to Business Planning for Mergers and Acquisitions* (2nd Ed. 2001).

Agreement, all right, title and interest of the Selling Corporation in and to (a) the assets specified in Section 1.2 (the Assets), and (b) the name "SELLING CORPORATION, INC." and all goodwill associated therewith, each free and clear of all mortgages, liens, pledges, security interests, charges, claims, restrictions and encumbrances of any nature whatsoever.

§ 1.2   *Included Assets.* The Assets shall include without limitation the following assets, properties and rights used directly or indirectly by the Selling Corporation in the conduct of its business, except as otherwise expressly set forth in Section 1.3 hereof:

   (a)   all the land, structures, improvements and fixtures and all water lines, rights of way, uses, licenses, easements, hereditament, tenements and appurtenances belonging or appertaining thereto;

   (b)   all machinery, equipment, tools, vehicles, furniture, furnishings, leasehold improvements, goods, and other tangible personal property;

   (c)   all cash or cash equivalents in transit, in hand or in bank accounts;

   (d)   all prepaid items, unbilled costs and fees, and accounts, notes and other receivables;

   (e)   all supplies and inventories and office and other supplies;

   (f)   to the extent permitted by applicable law, all rights under any written or oral contract, agreement, lease, plan, instrument, registration, license, certificate of occupancy, other permit or approval of any nature, or other document, commitment, arrangement, undertaking, practice or authorization;

   (g)   all rights under any patent, trademark, service mark, trade name or copyright, whether registered or unregistered, and any applications therefore;

   (h)   all technologies, methods, formulations, data bases, trade secrets, know-how, inventions and other intellectual property used in the Selling Corporation or under development;

   (i)   all computer software (including documentation and related object and source codes);

   (j)   all rights or choices in action arising out of occurrences before or after the Closing, including without limitation all rights under express or implied warranties relating to the Assets;

   (k)   all assets and properties reflected on the Closing Balance Sheet as defined in Section 1.7; and

   (l)   all information, files, records, data, plans, contracts and recorded knowledge, including customer and supplier lists, related to the foregoing.

§ 1.3   *Excluded Assets.* Notwithstanding the foregoing, the Assets shall not include any of the following:

(a) the corporate seals, certificates of incorporation, minute books, stock books, tax returns, books of account or other records having to do with corporate organization of the Selling Corporation;

(b) the rights which accrue or will accrue to the Selling Corporation under this Agreement;

(c) the rights to any of the Selling Corporation's claims for any federal, state, local, or foreign tax refunds; or

(d) the assets, properties or rights set forth on SCHEDULE 1.3.

§ 1.4 *Agreement to Purchase.* At the Closing hereunder, the Acquiring Corporation shall purchase the Assets from the Selling Corporation, upon and subject to the terms and conditions of this Agreement and in reliance on the representations, warranties and covenants of the Selling Corporation contained herein, in exchange for the Purchase Price (hereinafter defined in Section 1.5 hereof). In addition, the Acquiring Corporation shall assume at the Closing and agree to pay, discharge or perform, as appropriate, certain liabilities and obligations of the Selling Corporation only to the extent and as provided in Section 1.6 of this Agreement. Except as specifically provided in Section 1.6 hereof, Purchaser shall not assume or be responsible for any liabilities or obligations of the Selling Corporation.

§ 1.5 *The Purchase Price.*

(a) *Purchase Price,* The Purchase Price shall be an amount equal to:

(1) $____ (the Base Amount);

(2) (i) less, the amount, if any, by which the Net Assets (hereinafter defined) on the Closing Date as reflected on the Closing Balance Sheet (hereinafter defined) is less than the Net Assets on the balance sheet for the period ending December 31, 1995 (the 1995 Balance Sheet);

(ii) *plus,* the amount, if any, by which the Net Assets on the Closing Date as reflected on the Closing Balance Sheet exceeds the Net Assets on the 1995 Balance Sheet (the amount determined under 1.5(a)(2) is referred to as the Adjustment Amount).

Net Assets as of a given date shall mean the net book value of all assets which would have been included in the Assets if the Closing had taken place on such date without regard to any other assets reflected on the balance sheet which would not be included in the Assets if the Closing had taken place on such date. ***

(b) *Payment of Purchase Price.* On the Closing Date the Acquiring Corporation shall pay the Selling Corporation the Base Amount payable by wire transfer of immediately available funds to such account as the Selling Corporation shall designate. Upon the determination of the Adjustment Amount either the Acquiring Corporation shall promptly pay to the Selling Corporation or the Selling Corporation shall promptly pay to the Acquiring Corporation, as the case may be, the Adjustment Amount payable by wire transfer of immediately available funds to such account as the payee shall designate. Pending resolution and payment of the Adjustment Amount, the Selling Corporation will not distribute any of the Base Amount to the shareholders as a liquidating distribution or otherwise.

(c) *Allocation of Purchase Price.* The Purchase Price and the liabilities assumed by the Acquiring Corporation in accordance with Section 1.6 hereof and any non-recourse liabilities to which any Assets is subject (together, the "Total Consideration) as finally determined shall be allocated among the Assets acquired hereunder as described on SCHEDULE 1.5(c) hereof. The parties agree to follow the allocation in SCHEDULE 1.5(c) in any and all filings and reports, made and positions taken, with the Internal Revenue Service and any other taxing authority, including the reports required to be filed pursuant to Section 1060 of the Internal Revenue Code of 1986, as amended. The Selling Corporation and the Acquiring Corporation will collaborate in the preparation of IRS Form 8594 and will both timely file such form in a consistent manner. The Selling Corporation and the Acquiring Corporation each hereby further covenant and agree that it will not take a position on any income tax return, before any governmental agency charged with the collection of any income tax, or in any judicial proceeding that is in any way inconsistent with the terms of this Section 1.5(c).

§ 1.6 *Assumption of Liabilities.*

(a) *Assumed Liabilities.* At the Closing hereunder and except as otherwise specifically provided in this Section 1.6, the Acquiring Corporation shall assume and agree to pay, discharge or perform, as appropriate, the following liabilities and obligations of the Selling Corporation:

   (i) all liabilities and obligations of the Selling Corporation existing as of the 1995 Balance Sheet Date but only if and to the extent that the same are accrued or reserved for on the 1995 Balance Sheet and remain unpaid and undischarged on the Closing Date;

   (ii) all liabilities and obligations of Selling Corporation arising in the regular and ordinary course of its business between (the 1995 Balance Sheet Date) and the Closing Date, to the extent that the same remain unpaid and undischarged on the Closing Date and are accrued or reserved for on the Closing Balance Sheet; and

   (iii) all liabilities and obligations of the Selling Corporation in respect of the agreements contracts, commitments and leases which are specifically identified in any list called for by paragraphs of the representations and warranties, except that the Acquiring Corporation shall not assume or agree to pay, discharge or perform any:

      (A) liabilities or obligations of the aforesaid character existing as of the 1995 Balance Sheet Date, and which under generally accepted accounting principles should have been accrued or reserved for on a balance sheet or the notes thereto as a liability or obligation, if and to the extent that the same were not accrued or reserved for on the 1995 Balance Sheet;

(B) liabilities or obligations of the aforesaid thereafter existing as of the Closing Date, and which under generally accepted accounting principles should have been accrued or reserved for on a balance sheet or the notes thereto as a liability or obligation, if and to the extent that the same were not accrued or reserved for on the Closing Balance Sheet; or

(C) liabilities or obligations arising out of any breach by the Selling Corporation of any provision of any agreement, contract, commitment or lease referred to in this paragraph (C), including but not limited to liabilities or obligations arising out of the Selling Corporation's failure to perform any agreement, contract, commitment or lease in accordance with its terms prior to the Closing, but excluding however any liability arising out of the assignment to the Acquiring Corporation of such agreements, contracts, commitments or lease in violation of the terms thereof to the extent that the agreement, contract, commitment or lease is listed on SCHEDULE 1.6 hereof.

(b) *Retained Liabilities.* In no event, however, shall the Acquiring Corporation assume or incur any liability or obligation under this Section 1.6 or otherwise in respect of any of the following:

(i) any product liability or similar claim for injury to person or property, regardless of when made or asserted, which arises out of or is based upon any express or implied representation, warranty, agreement or guarantee made by the Selling Corporation, or alleged to have been made by the Selling Corporation, or which is imposed or asserted to be imposed by operation of law, in connection with any service performed or product sold or leased by or on behalf of the Selling Corporation on or prior to the Closing, including without limitation any claim relating to any product delivered in connection with the performance of such service and any claim seeking recovery for such service and any claim seeking recovery for consequential damage, lost revenue or income;

Comment

This provision is designed to make sure the Acquiring Corporation does not assume any liabilities of the Selling Corporation for defective products sold or services provided before the closing. Notwithstanding this provision, the Acquiring Corporation may, under state successor liability laws, be liable to the injured party.

* * *

(ii) any federal, state or local income or other tax (A) payable with respect to the business, assets, properties or operations of the Selling Corporation or the Shareholders of the Selling Corporation or any member of any affiliated group of which either is a member for any period prior to the Closing Date, or (B) incident to or arising as a consequence of the negotiation or consummation by the Selling Corporation or its shareholders or any member of any affiliated group of which either is a member of this Agreement and the transactions contemplated hereby;

Comment

In an asset acquisition, the target is responsible for its Federal income tax liability.

* * *

(iii) any liability or obligation under or in connection with the assets excluded from the Assets under Section 1.3.

(iv) any liability or obligation arising prior to or as a result of the Closing to any employees, agents or independent contractors of the Selling Corporation, whether or not employed by the Acquiring Corporation after the Closing, or under any benefit arrangement with respect thereto; or

(v) any liability or obligation of the Selling Corporation or any of its shareholders arising or incurred in connection with the negotiation, preparation and execution of this Agreement and the transactions contemplated hereby and fees and expenses of counsel, accountants and other experts.

§ 1.7 *Closing Financial Statements.* Not later than 60 days after the Closing Date, the Selling Corporation shall cause to be prepared the balance sheet of its business at the Closing Date (the Closing Balance Sheet) and the related statement of income, changes in financial position, and notes of the business for the period from the 1995 Balance Sheet Date until the Closing Date, in accordance with generally accepted accounting principles consistently applied by the Selling Corporation in accordance with past practice for the financial statements described in Section ___ of the representations and warranties. Such balance sheet shall specifically identify all assets reflected thereon which are not included in the Assets and all liabilities reflected thereon which are not assumed by the Acquiring Corporation hereunder.

The Selling Corporation shall cause, its independent accountants (Seller's Auditors), to review such financial statements in accordance with standard procedures of the accounting profession. Seller's Auditors shall specify the Adjustment Amount. [The parties may elaborate on these procedures].

Any dispute which may arise between the Selling Corporation and the Acquiring Corporation as to such financial statements or the proper amount of the Adjustment Amount shall be resolved in the following manner. [The parties here will set out the dispute resolution mechanism.]

§ 1.8 *Closing.* * * * The Closing (the Closing) of the sale and purchase of the Assets shall take place at 10:00 A.M., local time, on, ____ at the offices of the attorneys for Acquiring Corporation or on such other date as may be mutually agreed upon in writing by the Acquiring Corporation and the Selling Corporation. The date of the Closing is sometimes herein referred to as the "Closing Date."

§ 1.9 *Items to be Delivered at Closing.* At the Closing, subject to the terms and conditions here in contained:

(a) The Selling Corporation shall deliver to the Acquiring Corporation the following:

(i) such bills of sale with covenants of warranty assignments, endorsements, and other good and sufficient instruments and documents of conveyance and transfer in form reasonably satisfactory to the Acquiring Corporation and its counsel as shall be necessary and effective to transfer and assign to, and vest in, the Acquiring Corporation all of the Selling Corporation's right, title and interest in and to the Assets, including without limitation, (A) good and valid title in and to all of the Assets owned by the Selling Corporation, (B) good and valid leasehold interests in and to all of the Assets leased by the Selling Corporation as leasee, and (C) all of the Selling Corporations rights under all agreements, contracts, commitments, leases, plans, bids, quotations, proposals, instruments and other documents included in the Assets to which Seller is a party or by which it has rights on the Closing Date; and

(ii) all of the agreements, contracts, commitments, leases, plans, bids, quotations, proposals, instruments, computer programs and software, databases whether in the form of computer tapes or otherwise, related object and source codes, manuals and guidebooks, price books and price lists, customer and subscriber lists, supplier lists, sales records, files, correspondences, legal opinions, rulings issued by governmental entities, and other documents, books, records, papers, files, office supplies and data belonging to the Selling Corporation which are part of the Assets. * * *

§ 1.10 *Third Party Consents.* To the extent that the Selling Corporation's rights under any agreement, contract, commitment, lease, or other Asset to be assigned to the Acquiring Corporation hereunder may not be assigned without the consent of another person which has not been obtained, this Agreement shall not constitute an agreement to assign the same if an attempted assignment would constitute a breach thereof or be unlawful, and the Selling Corporation, at its expense, shall use its best efforts to obtain any such required consent(s) as promptly as possible. * * *

§ 1.11 *Change in Name.* * * *

Article II
Representation and Warranties

§ 2.1 *Representations and Warranties of the Selling Corporation.*

Comment

The representations and warranties of the Selling Corporation in an asset acquisition will be extensive because the acquiror wants to be sure of what it is buying. With respect to Federal, state, local and foreign taxes (even though Federal income taxes do not carry over to the Acquiring Corporation), the Acquiring Corporation will want to know that the Selling Corporation has paid its taxes. Therefore, the Acquiring Corporation will seek representations from the Selling Corporation to the effect that, unless specifically disclosed otherwise: (1) the Selling Corporation has filed all required returns, (2) such returns reflect all amounts due, (3) the Selling Corporation has paid all taxes shown on the returns, and (3) no governmental authority is asserting a tax deficiency against the Selling Corporation. These representations may be qualified by a materiality or knowledge standard.

* * *

§ 2.2 *Representations and Warranties of the Acquiring Corporation.*

Comment

The representations and warranties of the Acquiring Corporation will be dependant upon the consideration being paid. If cash is paid, there may be simple representations and warranties relating to organization, standing and authority to act. If the Acquiring Corporation issues its securities, so that the shareholders of the Selling Corporation are making an investment in the Acquiring Corporation, more complete representations will be required.

* * *

Article III
Covenants Relating to Conduct of Business

§ 3.1 *Covenants by the Selling Corporation.*

Comment

The covenants made here by the Selling Corporation relate to the operation of the Selling Corporation from the date of the signing of the acquisition agreement to the date of the closing. They will relate to such things as the requirement to operate the business in the normal course and not to pay extraordinary dividends or make major acquisitions or divestitures.

* * *

§ 3.2 *Covenants of Acquiring Corporation.*

Comment

Since the acquisition is for cash, the Acquiring Corporation generally will not make any covenants here. However, if the consideration is securities of the Acquiring Corporation, it would make covenants similar to those made by the Selling Corporation.

Article IV
Additional Agreements

§ 4.1 *Additional Agreements of the Selling Corporation.*

Comment

Depending on the circumstances, the Selling Corporation would undertake to perform certain tasks such as not to shop the company to another person.

* * *

§ 4.2 *Additional Agreements of Acquiring Corporation.*

Comment

In a cash deal, there will probably be no additional agreements by the Acquiring Corporation. ***

Article V
Conditions to Acquiring Corporation's Obligations

Comment

The conditions to closing for the Acquiring Corporation would include such items as the requirement that all of the representations of the Selling Corporation be true and accurate both at the signing and the closing. Also, since the Acquiring Corporation is acquiring "substantially all" of the assets of the Selling Corporation, under state corporate law, the transaction is contingent upon the approval of the shareholders of the Selling Corporation, and this approval should be one of the conditions to closing.

* * *

Article VI
Survival of Representations; Indemnity; Set-Off

Comment

In asset and stock acquisition agreements for closely-held Selling Corporations, it is common for the representations, warranties and other agreements to survive the closing. This will give the Acquiring Corporation protection if it discovers a misrepresentation after the closing. Also, in acquisitions of closely held corporations, it is common for the shareholders of the Selling Corporation to indemnify the Acquiring Corporation for any losses resulting from any material misrepresentation.

* * *

Article VII
Termination

Comment

The termination provision in an asset acquisition agreement would normally provide a right to terminate (1) with mutual consent, (2) upon material breach, and (3) if the transaction does not close before a drop-dead date. The termination provision may give the parties the right to recover damages in the event of a termination.

* * *

Article VIII
General Provisions

Comment

The general provisions of an asset acquisition agreement would cover such things as notices and governing law.

* * *

Chapter 5

Taxable Stock Acquisitions and LBOs: Including Treatment of Net Operating Losses

§ 5.1 Scope

This chapter deals with taxable stock acquisitions and leveraged buyouts (LBOs). This chapter also considers the treatment of a target's net operating losses (NOLs) after a stock acquisition. Sec. 5.2 addresses issues of concern to both the acquiring corporation and a stand-alone target corporation in a stock acquisition, including the structure of the transaction. Sec. 5.3 addresses issues of concern principally to the acquiring corporation and its shareholders, such as the § 338 election. Sec. 5.4 deals with issues of concern principally to the target corporation and its shareholders. Sec. 5.5 examines planning for the acquisition of a target corporation that is a subsidiary of a consolidated group, and this section introduces several of the basic principles in the consolidated return regulations. Sec. 5.6 provides an introduction to mirror subsidiaries and the disallowance of loss rule in the consolidated return regulations, as amended after the *Rite Aid* decision. Sec. 5.7 sets out various considerations in planning for the utilization of a target's net operating losses, and Sec. 5.8 deals with the impact of § 382 on the carryover of a target's NOLs. Sec. 5.9 addresses some of the basic principles under the consolidated return regulations impacting the utilizations of a target's NOLs, and Sec. 5.10 deals with the impact of § 269 on the utilization of such losses. Sec. 5.11 discusses the effect of § 384 on the utilization of an acquiring corporation's NOLs as an offset to a target's pre-acquisition built-in gains. Sec. 5.12 deals with the CERT limitation on the carryback of losses after LBOs. Sec. 5.13 provides summary problems on the use of NOLs. Sec. 5.14 contains an introduction to some of the issues that can arise in a cross border taxable stock acquisition, and Sec 5.15 contains selected provisions of a sample stock acquisition agreement.

For a more detailed discussion of these issues, *see* Ginsburg and Levin, *Mergers, supra* Sec. 1.12; Bittker and Eustice, *Corporations, supra* Sec. 1.12; *Consolidated Returns, supra* Sec. 1.12; and PLI, *Tax Strategies, supra* Sec. 1.12. *See also* Thompson, *Mergers, Acquisitions, and Tender Offers, supra* Sec. 1.12 at Chapter 9.

§ 5.2 Acquisition of Stand-Alone Target: Issues of Concern to Both the Acquiring Corporation and the Target Corporation

A. Structure of the Transaction

1. Direct Stock Purchase of Target's Stock for Cash

The purchase of stock for cash is the most straightforward form of acquisition. Each selling shareholder makes his own independent decision whether to sell, and there are no corporate approvals (other than a resolution of the board of directors of the acquiring corporation) required for the transaction. Moreover, there are no filing requirements under the federal securities laws, unless the target firm is a reporting company, that is, a publicly-held corporation under the Securities Exchange Act of 1934 (the "1934 Act").

A tender offer for the stock of a reporting target is subject to certain reporting and disclosure rules contained in §§ 14(d), (e) and (f) of the 1934 Act. These provisions are referred to as the Williams Act amendments. Basically, they require any person making a tender offer for stock registered under the 1934 Act to make certain disclosures prior to the tender, if as a result of the tender the person would be the beneficial owner of more than five percent of the target's stock. Disclosures are also required, under § 13(d) of the Williams Act if as a result of open market purchases of the target's stock, the purchaser would own more than five percent of the stock.

2. Purchase of Target's Stock in Exchange for Stock or Securities of Acquiror

The purchase of a publicly-held target's stock in exchange for the acquiror's stock or securities is subject to the same Williams Act requirements as a cash tender offer. In addition, the acquiror's stock or securities are subject to the registration requirements of § 5 of the Securities Act of 1933 (the "1933 Act").

A stock-for-stock acquisition may be treated as a nontaxable reorganization under § 368(a)(1)(B). *See* Chapter 8. The purchase of a closely-held target corporation's stock in exchange for the acquiror's stock or securities may qualify for an exemption from the registration requirements of § 5 of the 1933 Act. The principal exception is under Reg D, which encompasses the private offering exemption. Stock or securities received by a target's shareholders in a Reg D offering can be resold under Rule 144 or in a registered offering.

3. Reverse Triangular (or Subsidiary) Cash Merger to Deal with Recalcitrant Shareholders

Revenue Ruling 73-427

1973-2 C.B. 301

Advice has been requested concerning the Federal income tax treatment of the transaction described below.

Corporation P wanted to acquire all of the outstanding stock of corporation Y for cash and thereby become the sole shareholder of Y. Pursuant to the plan of acquisition, P was only able to purchase 97.9 percent of the outstanding stock of Y for cash. In order to complete the acquisition, P, as part of the same plan, acquired the remaining 2.1 percent of the outstanding stock of Y in the following manner.

P transferred to S, a wholly owned subsidiary formed solely to effectuate the acquisition, $5x$ dollars (solely to satisfy capital requirements of state law) and $10x$ shares of P stock in exchange for $10x$ shares of S stock. Pursuant to the applicable state laws, S was merged with and into Y, with Y acquiring all the assets of S (the $5x$ dollars and the $10x$ shares of P stock). Y distributed the $10x$ shares of P stock received in the merger to the minority shareholders of Y in exchange for their stock, and by operation of state law the S stock held by P was automatically converted into Y stock. Y, as part of the plan, returned the $5x$ dollars to P.

The result of the entire plan described above was that P acquired all of the stock of Y partly in exchange for cash and partly in exchange for P voting stock, with Y becoming a wholly owned subsidiary of P. This result is not negated because part of the acquisition was cast in the form of a redemption by Y of its stock from the minority shareholders of Y in exchange for the P stock received by Y in the merger of S into Y. Therefore, the transaction will be treated for Federal income tax purposes as though P transferred its stock directly to the minority shareholders of Y in exchange for their Y stock. Furthermore, the transitory existence of S, and therefore the transactions described above involving S, will be disregarded.

Accordingly, it is held as follows:

1. No gain or loss will be recognized to P upon the receipt of the Y stock from the minority shareholders of Y in exchange for P stock under section 1032(a) of the Internal Revenue Code of 1954.

2. No gain or loss is realized by S or Y as a result of the transactions described above.

3. Gain or loss is realized and recognized to the minority shareholders of Y upon the receipt by them from P of P stock in exchange for their Y stock under section 1001. Gain or loss is also realized and recognized by those former shareholders of Y who received cash from P in exchange for their Y stock under section 1001.

4. The $5x$ dollars transferred by P to S to satisfy capital requirements and which was returned to P by Y is disregarded and results in no tax consequences.

The same results would obtain if:

1. *P* actually received *Y* stock in exchange for the *S* stock rather than, as in the instant case, the *S* stock held by *P* being converted into *Y* stock by operation of law;

2. no stock of *P* was transferred to *S* and the *Y* stock held by the minority shareholders of *Y* was converted into *P* stock by operation of law; or

3. the 5*x* dollars transferred to *S* to satisfy capital requirements was not returned to *P* by *Y*. In such case the 5*x* dollars is a contribution by *P* to the capital of *Y*. * * *

Note and Question

1. Rev. Rul. 90-95, 1990-2 C.B. 67, which is set out below in the materials governing § 338, also holds that a taxable reverse subsidiary merger is treated as a taxable stock acquisition. *See* Sec. 5.3.D.2.

2. What result in the above ruling if *Y* had merged into *S*? *See West Shore Fuel, supra* Sec. 4.2.A.2.b.

4. Liquidation of Target under § 332 after Acquisition by Acquiring Corporation

After the acquisition by an acquiring corporation of the stock of a target, the target may be liquidated or merged into the acquiror under § 332. *See* Chapter 2.

Section 332 provides an exception to the general recognition rule of § 331 for liquidating distributions. Section 332(a) provides that "[n]o gain or loss shall be recognized on the receipt by a corporation of property distributed in complete liquidation of another corporation." This very broad rule is limited, however, by § 332(b) which provides that a distribution is considered to be in complete liquidation only if the following two requirements are satisfied.

First, under § 332(b)(1), the parent corporation must own stock of the subsidiary meeting the 80% requirement of § 1504(a)(2). Section 1504(a)(2) is satisfied if the parent owns stock of the subsidiary which possesses at least 80% of the total voting power of the stock of the corporation and at least 80% of the total value of the stock of the corporation. Certain nonvoting, limited, preferred stock is not included as stock for purposes of § 1504(a)(2). Section 1504(a)(2) is addressed below in the discussion of consolidated returns. This 80% stock ownership requirement must be satisfied "on the date of the adoption of the plan of liquidation and at all times until receipt of the property." *See* § 332(b)(1).

Second, the distribution of the property must be either (1) completed within the taxable year (*see* § 332(b)(2)), or (2) one of a series of distributions pursuant to a plan of liquidation that is to be completed within three years after the close of the taxable year during which the first of the series of distributions is made. *See* § 332(b)(3). The Secretary may require a bond or waiver of the statute of limitations in the case of a series of distributions spanning two or more taxable years. *See* § 332(b) (first sentence of flush language).

A liquidation satisfying the conditions of § 332 is treated as a liquidation even though the transaction may be characterized differently (*e.g.,* as a merger) under local law. *See* § 332(b) (second sentence of flush language). Also, § 332 applies to a transaction in which a less than wholly owned but more than 80% subsidiary is merged into the parent in a nontaxable reorganization where the parent receives all of the subsidiary's assets and the minority shareholders receive the parent's stock. *See* § 332(b) (second sentence of flush language) and § 1.332-2(d) and (e).

Under § 337, the liquidating subsidiary generally does not have gain or loss on the liquidation. *See* Chapter 2. Under § 334(b)(1), the parent corporation takes a carryover basis for property received in a § 332 liquidation.

If a subsidiary is owned both by a parent corporation that satisfies the 80% stock ownership requirement and also by a minority shareholder or shareholders who own up to 20% of the stock of the subsidiary, then the liquidation of the subsidiary falls within §§ 332 and 334(b) for the parent and within §§ 331 and 334(a) for the minority shareholders.

5. Direct (i.e., Non-Triangular) Reverse Merger

Revenue Ruling 78-250

1978-1 C.B. 83

Corporation *X* had outstanding only common stock, which was owned 65 percent by individual *A,* president and a director of *X.* The balance of the *X* stock was widely held.

For various business reasons, *X* desired to operate without any ownership of its stock by the public. Under a plan to eliminate the minority stock interests, a new corporation, *Y,* was formed by *A* who received all of the *Y* stock in exchange for *A*'s *X* stock on a share-for-share basis. Upon approval of a plan of merger by the shareholders of both corporations, *Y* was then merged with and into *X* under applicable state law. In the merger each share of *A*'s *Y* stock was converted into a share of *X* stock and the minority shareholders of *X* received cash in exchange for their *X* stock, in an amount equal in value to the stock exchanged.

In Rev. Rul. 67-448, 1967-2 C.B. 144, [*see* Sec. 8.2.I.2] a series of inter-related steps involving the transitory existence of a newly created corporation is disregarded and the transaction is treated for Federal income tax purposes as the mere exchange by a corporation of shares of its voting stock for the outside minority stock interest in its subsidiary, which transaction qualified as a reorganization under section 368(a)(1)(B) of the Internal Revenue Code of 1954. See also Rev. Rul. 73-427, [*see* Sec. 5.2.A.3], which disregards the creation and elimination of a corporation in an integrated transaction.

In the instant case, the net result of the overall plan is that the minority shareholders of *X* received cash from *X* for their shares, after which they were no longer shareholders.

Accordingly, the creation of *Y* followed by the merger of *Y* into *X* with *A* exchanging *X* stock for *Y* stock, with the minority shareholders receiving cash and the conversion of the *Y* stock into *X* stock is disregarded for Federal income tax purposes. Rev. Rul. 73-427. The transaction is treated as if *A* never transferred any *X* stock, with the net effect that the minority shareholders of *X* received cash in exchange for their stock. Such cash is treated as received by the minority shareholders as distributions in redemption of their *X* stock subject to the provisions and limitations of section 302 of the Code. [*See* Chapter 2.]

B. Overlap Problem: If Shareholders of Target Corporation Own Stock of Acquiring Corporation, Ensure that the Transaction Does Not Qualify as a § 304 Redemption

See §§ 304, 302 and 301.

1. Background on Section 304

See Chapter 2.

2. Illustration of the Interaction between § 304(a)(1) and § 302 in the Stock Acquisition Context

Zimmerman v. Commissioner

Tax Court of the United States, 1985
49 TCM 1616

Memorandum Opinion

PANUTHOS, SPECIAL TRIAL JUDGE: * * *

The issue for decision is whether the proceeds of petitioners' sale of stock in Custom Met, Inc. to Rogers Metal Processing, Ltd. are ordinary income or whether petitioners properly treated the proceeds as long term capital gain.

[Donald Zimmerman owned 66 2/3% of the stock of Custom Met, and his son Jonathan owned 33 1/3% of the stock. Also, Donald owned 80% of the stock of Rogers Metal and Jonathan owned 5%; unrelated parties owned the 15% balance.]

* * * In August of 1980, by a resolution adopted by all the directors of Rogers Metal, 100 percent of the issued and outstanding stock of Custom Met, was acquired by Rogers Metal for $35,824.14.

Donald and Jonathan Zimmerman each treated the sale of stock in Custom Met to Rogers Metal as a long term capital gain on their 1980 income tax returns. * * *

Generally, sale of stock in a corporation to a related corporation (other than a subsidiary) is treated as a redemption if the terms of section 304(a) are met. One of the tests to be met under section 304(a)(1) is whether one or more persons are in control of each of the two corporations. Under section 304(c)(2) the attribution rules of section 318 apply in determining control. Since Donald Zimmerman owned 66 2/3 percent of all stock in Custom Met, and his son Jonathan Zimmerman owned 33 1/3 percent of Custom Met Stock, under the attribution rules of section 318 the stock held by each of them is attributed to the other. Prior to the sale of the stock, both Donald and Jonathan Zimmerman were in control of Custom Met. [*See* § 304(c).] Thus, section 304(a)(1) recasts the stock sale as a redemption.

In examining the transaction under section 302(b), section 304(b)(1) states that any determination made under section 302(b) must be made with reference to the stock of the "issuing corporation." The issuing corporation is Custom Met. * * * Whether the distribution by Rogers Metal is treated as payment in exchange for stock or a dividend depends upon the application of section 302(a) and (b). The attribution rules of section 318(a) apply in determining ownership of stock for purposes of section 302. Sec. 302(c). *United States v. Davis.*

Section 302(a) provides that a distribution of property to a shareholder by a corporation in redemption of stock will be treated as an exchange of such stock if the redemption falls within one of the four categories enumerated in section 302(b). * * * If the redemption fails to qualify in any of the categories, then the redemption is treated as a dividend distribution to the extent of corporate earnings and profits. Sections 301 and 302(d). * * *

Petitioners claim eligibility only under section 302(b)(1) which states that a redemption will be treated as an exchange if it is not essentially equivalent to a dividend. Resolution of this issue depends upon the facts of each case. * * * Petitioners assert that acquisition of the stock in Custom Met by Rogers Metal was motivated by strong business reasons and was an attempt to protect their joint investment interests. They contend that their primary purpose was not to avoid payment of taxes. This is, however, no longer the critical inquiry under section 302(b)(1). As the Supreme Court has plainly stated, the business purpose behind a redemption is irrelevant in determining whether the redemption is essentially equivalent to a dividend. *United States v. Davis, supra* at 312. * * * (1973).

According to *Davis,* the relevant inquiry is instead whether the corporate distribution of property results in a meaningful reduction of a shareholder's proportionate interest in the corporation. In the instant case, there has been no meaningful reduction of petitioners' proportionate interests in Custom Met. After application of the attribution rules, each petitioner is attributed with ownership of 85 percent of stock in Custom Met. Although there were three other minority shareholders and petitioners no longer had total control, a reduction in interest of only 15 percent is not a meaningful reduction where no real threat is posed to petitioners' control of Custom Met, the corporation. In reality, petitioners' control of Custom Met is essentially unaltered. * * *

Decisions will be entered for the respondent.

C. Possible Use of § 351 for Nonrecognition Treatment for Shareholders who are to Continue as Shareholders in the Acquiring Corporation

1. Background on the Overlap between § 351 and the Reorganization Provisions

See Revenue Ruling 84-44, *infra* Sec. 6.19.C.

2. Illustration: The Service's Initial Ruling: The National Starch Transaction: Combination § 351 and Reverse Subsidiary Taxable Merger

Private Letter Ruling 7839060

June 28, 1978

This is in reply to a letter dated January 6, 1978, requesting a ruling concerning the Federal income tax consequences of a proposed transaction * * *.

Parent was organized in 1977 as a wholly-owned subsidiary of Corp. X, a publicly-traded foreign corporation. * * *.

* * * Target had outstanding 6,563,030 shares of $.50 par value common stock, which were widely-held and publicly traded. A and B, who are husband and wife, together own 944,436 shares of Target common stock.

Parent wishes to acquire Target by way of an exchange offer ("Exchange Offer") and a merger, and accordingly the following plan is proposed.

Parent and certain Target shareholders who so elect will form a new corporation ("Newco"). Newco in turn will form a new wholly-owned subsidiary of Newco ("Sub"). Sub will be organized solely to participate in this transaction and will be nominally capitalized. Parent will transfer to Newco approximately $484,000,000 in cash in exchange for 1,000 shares of Newco voting common stock. * * *. Shareholders of Target who elect to accept the Exchange Offer will transfer their Target common stock to Newco in exchange for Newco preferred stock on a share-for-share basis. Such shareholders will be required to tender all their shares to Newco.

Immediately after the issuance by Newco of its stock to Parent and to the shareholders of Target who accept the Exchange Offer, Sub will be merged into Target (the "Merger"). Under the terms of the Merger, each share of common stock of Target (other than shares held by Newco) will be converted into the right to receive $73.50 in cash. Shares of common stock of Target acquired by Newco in the Exchange Offer will be cancelled and each share of common stock of Sub will be converted into common stock of Target, which will be the surviving corporation. Shareholders of Target will have statutory rights to dissent to the Merger and receive the appraised value of their stock in cash. * * *

Based solely on the information submitted and on the representations set forth above, it is held as follows:

(1) No gain or loss will be recognized to Target shareholders who accept the Exchange Offer upon the transfer of their shares of Target common stock to Newco solely in exchange for Newco preferred stock [provided such stock is not nonqualified preferred stock under §351(g)] or to Parent on its transfer of cash or cash and an irrevocable letter of credit to Newco in exchange for Newco common stock, as described above (section 351(a) of the Internal Revenue Code of 1954).

(2) The basis of the Newco preferred stock received by the Target shareholders who accept the Exchange Offer will be the same as the basis of the Target common stock surrendered in exchange therefore (section 358(a)(1)). * * *

(6) For Federal income tax purposes, the formation of Sub, the merger of Sub into Target and the distribution of cash to the shareholders of Target who do not accept the Exchange Offer will be disregarded. The effect of the transaction will be viewed as an acquisition by Newco for cash of all the outstanding common stock of Target held by nondissenting shareholders who do not accept the Exchange Offer. No gain or loss will be recognized to Newco, Sub or Target as a result of the acquisition (Rev. Rul. 73-427, [see Sec. 5.2.A.3]).

(7) As provided in section 1001, gain or loss will be realized and recognized by the nondissenting Target shareholders who do not accept the Exchange Offer on the purchase of their Target common stock measured by the difference between the amount received and the adjusted basis of the Target common stock surrendered as determined under section 1011. * * *

(8) Where cash is received by a dissenting Target shareholder from Target, as described above, the cash will be treated as received by the dissenting shareholders as a distribution in redemption of his Target stock, subject to the provisions and limitations of section 302. * * *

Notes and Questions

1. What are the principal tax stakes in the above private ruling? Is the ruling a road map for avoiding the constraints in the reorganization provisions? What result in the above transaction if the stock issued to the target's shareholders is nonqualified preferred stock within §351(g)? *See* Chapter 2. Can §351 be used to accomplish what cannot be accomplished under §368? *See* Sec. 6.19.

2. The Service has blessed the use of §351 in this manner. *See* Rev. Rul. 84-44 and Sec. 6.19.C.

3. As illustrated in Sec. 5.2.D., this type of transaction can also be used in a management buy out to give the purchasing managers tax-free treatment for their target shares.

D. Principal Parties in Leveraged Buyout*

The stock or assets of a target corporation may be acquired in a leveraged buyout (LBO). These are acquisition transactions in which a substantial part of the acquisition price is paid either in debt or in cash raised by the issuance of debt. The principal source of repayment of the debt is the target's assets and earnings. LBOs take a variety of forms, but the following parties are present in most LBOs.

Shareholders of the Target Corporation Some (but not necessarily all) of the shareholders of the target corporation want to receive cash or notes in exchange for their target stock. The tax objective of these shareholders generally is to receive capital gain rather than dividend income with respect to the consideration received because they will recover basis if they have capital gain. However, if the shareholders have a low basis for their shares, they likely would be indifferent between capital gain and dividends given the maximum 20% rate. The shareholders generally prefer installment sale treatment under § 453 (*see* Sec. 1.4.D) with respect to any notes they receive.

Management of the Target Corporation Some of the senior employees of the target corporation, who may be shareholders of the target corporation, may become major shareholders of the continuing corporation. In some transactions, the target corporation continues in existence, and, in other transactions, the stock or assets of the target corporation are purchased by the acquiring corporation. The managers may also convert some of their stock in the target corporation to cash or notes. The tax objective of the management generally is to receive capital gain treatment rather than dividend treatment (to permit recovery of basis) on any of the stock of the target corporation that is cashed out and installment sale treatment with respect to any notes they receive in exchange for their stock. Also, they want nonrecognition treatment on receipt of the stock of the acquiring corporation in exchange for stock of the target corporation. This treatment may be obtained through the use of § 351. *See* Sec. 5.2.C.2. Finally, the managers are looking for capital gain rather than dividend income on the later sale of their shares in the leveraged corporation.

Venture Capitalist A venture capital group contributes equity capital to the acquiring corporation (or the continuing target corporation). The venture capitalist is looking to realize substantial appreciation on its equity, and if the venture capitalist is a corporation, it will want the benefit of the dividends received deduction under § 243.

Financial Institution A financial institution, such as an insurance company or bank, provides the debt financing for the acquisition. It may also receive an equity interest in the leveraged corporation in the form of common stock, convertible debt, options or warrants. The tax objectives of the financial institution are to receive (1) nonrecognition treatment on the repayment of the principal of its loans, (2) nonrecognition treatment on the conversion of its preferred stock or debt into common stock, (3) the

---

* Based on § 35:09 of *Federal Taxation of Business Enterprises, supra,* Chapter 1, note 1, with permission.

benefit of the dividends received deduction under § 243, and (4) capital gain on any redemption of its preferred stock or common stock and on the final sale of its equity.

The financial institution is also particularly concerned that the interest on the debt used in the acquisition be deductible for Federal income tax purposes. If the debt is classified as equity, interest payments constitute nondeductible dividends and redemption payments may constitute dividends to the holder under § 302. As a result of the denial of the interest deduction, the target would have less after-tax income to service the debt.

Acquiring Corporation The principal tax objectives of the acquiring corporation (or the continuing target corporation) are to maximize its deductions for depreciation, amortization of intangibles, covenants not to compete and similar items, and interest. If the target corporation has net operating losses (NOLs), the acquiring corporation may want to utilize these NOLs.

Target Corporation The principal tax objective of the target corporation is to minimize the taxes required to be paid as a result of the LBO. As a result of the repeal of the *General Utilities* doctrine, if a stand-alone target has appreciated assets and no NOLs, it is generally better to effectuate the transaction as a stock sale without a § 338 election. *See* Sec. 5.3.D. The cost of the immediate tax at the target corporation level generally exceeds the present value of the tax benefits associated with the stepped up basis for the assets. The tax burden associated with an asset sale is imposed on the target corporation and derivatively its shareholders.

Thus, under current law, most LBOs involving a stand-alone target corporation are effectuated as either a direct acquisition of the target's stock pursuant to a stock purchase agreement, or a taxable reverse subsidiary merger. *See* Sec. 5.2.A.

Employee Stock Option Plan An employee stock option plan (ESOP) may be used in an LBO. The ESOP, which is a tax-qualified retirement plan, purchases part of the target's stock and holds the stock for the benefit of the target's employees. The ESOP generally borrows its acquisition price from a bank or other financial institution. The loan is repaid by tax deductible contributions made to the ESOP by the target. Thus, the use of an ESOP may permit a portion of the purchase price to be paid with tax deductible payments.

E. Introductory Problems on Structuring Stock Acquisitions

1. Target Corporation (*TC*) is publicly held with only common stock outstanding. *TC*'s assets are substantially appreciated. Acquiring Corporation (*AC*) is planning to make a cash tender offer for 70% of the stock of *TC*. If this tender offer is successful, *AC* then wants to eliminate the 30% minority held shares of *TC* by some sort of transaction that will force those shareholders to sell for cash. What advice do you have for *AC*?

2. The facts are the same as in Question 1, except individual *A*, the president and 15% shareholder of *TC*, is opposed to *AC*'s transaction unless he can receive tax-free treatment. Can you structure a transaction in which (1) *AC* and *A* strike a deal that gives *A* nonrecognition treatment for his shares; (2) *AC* makes

its cash tender offer; and (3) the non-tendering shareholders of *TC* are forced to sell for cash?

3. Target Corporation (*TC*) is a closely held firm, with five shareholders (*A, B, C, D,* and *E*) each owning 20% of *TC*'s stock. *TC* has appreciated assets. *A, B, C,* and *D* want to sell their shares to Acquiring Corporation, but *E* has no interest in selling. Can you structure a transaction in which all of the *TC* shareholders will be forced to sell their shares in a transaction that will be treated as a stock acquisition?

4. The facts are the same as in Question 3, except *A* wants to buy out the other shareholders for cash. *B, C,* and *D* are willing to sell but *E* is not. Venture Capitalist (*VC*) will provide all of the funds in exchange for an 80% interest in *TC*. *A* would have a 20% interest. Can you structure a transaction in which (1) *A* gets nonrecognition treatment with respect to his shares of *TC*, (2) *B, C, D,* and *E* are forced to take cash for their shares, and (3) *VC* and *A* own, directly or indirectly, 80% and 20%, respectively, of the stock of *TC*? What if state law requires that *TC* be owned directly by its shareholders (*VC* and *A*) and not as a subsidiary of a holding company?

§ 5.3 Acquisition of Stand-Alone Target: Issues of Concern Principally to the Acquiring Corporation and Its Shareholders

A. Structuring of the Capital of the Acquiring Corporation or of the Continuing Target Corporation

1. Debt/Equity Structure of Acquiring Corporation or Continuing Target Corporation*

One of the principal objectives of a leveraged buyout is to ensure that the acquisition debt is treated as debt for Federal income tax purposes, so that the designated interest payments are deductible as interest, and the repayment of the principal qualifies as a return of capital. If the debt is classified as equity, interest payments constitute nondeductible dividends and redemption payments may constitute dividends to the holder under § 302. In view of the withdrawal of the regulations under § 385, the determination of whether an interest in a corporation is debt or equity is made under the so called facts and circumstances test.

One of the leading cases on the characterization of an instrument as debt or equity is *Fin Hay Realty Co. v. United States*, 398 F.2d 694 (3rd Cir. 1968).

In order to increase the equity base of the acquiring corporation and thereby reduce the debt equity ratio, preferred stock may be issued to the financial institution in lieu

---

* Based on § 35:04 of *Federal Taxation of Business Enterprises, supra,* Chapter 1, note 1, with permission.

of debt. In capitalizing the corporation in this manner, the parties want to ensure that the preferred stock is in fact stock and not debt.

Other debt/equity issues, such as the treatment of original issue discount on the issuance of certain debt instruments, are explored in Chapter 2. The treatment of preferred stock issued with a redemption premium is also addressed in Chapter 2. Section 279, which disallows the deduction of interest on certain corporate acquisition indebtedness, is examined in Sec. 5.3.A.2.

2. Impact of § 279: Disallowance of Interest on Certain Corporate Acquisition Indebtedness*

a. Introduction

In general, § 279 disallows an interest deduction to the issuing corporation with respect to its corporate acquisition indebtedness to the extent interest paid or incurred on the indebtedness exceeds $5,000,000 during the taxable year, reduced by certain other interest costs.

Corporate acquisition indebtedness means any obligation evidenced by a bond, debenture, note, certificate, or other evidence of indebtedness, if:

(1) The obligation is issued to acquire stock or substantially all of the assets of another corporation;

(2) The obligation is subordinated to the claims of trade creditors, or expressly subordinated to any substantial amount of unsecured indebtedness (whether outstanding or subsequently issued);

(3) The obligation is convertible into stock of the issuing corporation, or is part of an investment unit, such as a note with a detachable warrant; and

(4) The issuing corporation's debt to equity ratio exceeds 2:1, or the projected earnings do not exceed 3 times the annual interest paid or incurred. *See* § 279(b).

The $5,000,000 allowable interest deduction on corporate acquisition indebtedness is reduced by interest paid or incurred on indebtedness that is not corporate acquisition indebtedness (such as senior debt) that is issued to buy stock or substantially all of the assets of a corporation. *See* § 279(a).

b. Legislative History of § 279

Senate Report to the Tax Reform Act of 1969
137–140 (1969)

* * * Although the problem of distinguishing debt from equity is a long-standing one in the tax laws, it has become even more significant in recent years because of

---

* Based on § 35:05 of *Federal Taxation of Business Enterprises, supra* Chapter 1, note 1, with permission.

the increased level of corporate merger activities and the increasing use of debt for corporate acquisition purposes.

There are a number of factors which make the use of debt for corporate acquisition purposes desirable, including the fact that the acquiring company may deduct the interest on the debt but cannot deduct dividends on stock. A number of the other factors which make the use of bonds or debentures desirable are also the factors which tend to make a bond or debenture more nearly like the equity than debt. For example, the fact that a bond is convertible into stock tends to make it more attractive since the convertibility feature will allow the bondholder to participate in the future growth of the company. The fact that a bond is subordinated to other creditors of the corporation makes it more attractive to the corporation since it does not impair its general credit position.

Although it is possible to substitute debt for equity without a merger this is much easier to bring about at the time of the merger. * * *

The committee agrees with the House that in many cases the characteristics of an obligation issued in connection with a corporate acquisition make the interest in the corporation which it represents more nearly like a stockholder's interest than a creditor's interest, even though the obligation is labeled as debt. In view of the increasing use of debt for corporate acquisition purposes and the fact that the substitution of debt for equity is most easily accomplished in this situation, the committee also agrees with the House that it is appropriate to take action in this bill to provide rules for resolving, in a limited context, the ambiguities and uncertainties which have long existed in our tax law in distinguishing between a debt interest and an equity interest in a corporation. * * *

* * * [T]he House bill and the committee amendments * * * provide specific rules for determining whether an obligation constitutes debt or equity insofar as the allowability of the interest deduction is concerned in the corporate acquisition context. It is provided that a corporation is not to be allowed in interest deduction * * * with respect to certain types of indebtedness * * * which it issues as consideration for the acquisition of stock in another corporation, or the acquisition of assets of another corporation. * * *

The types of indebtedness to which the limitation on the interest deduction provided under the House bill and the committee amendments apply are obligations which meet each of three tests, namely, the subordination test, the convertibility test and the debt-equity or interest coverage test. * * *

* * * [T]he committee amendments provide that the subordination test is to be satisfied if the obligation either is subordinated to the claims of trade creditors of the issuing corporation generally or is expressly subordinated in right of payment to any substantial amount of the corporation's unsecured indebtedness (whether outstanding or subsequently issued). [See § 279(b)(2).] * * *

Under the convertibility test * * *, it is required that the obligation either must be directly or indirectly convertible into the stock of the issuing corporation or the obligation must be part of an investment unit or other arrangement which also includes an option to acquire, directly or indirectly, stock of the issuing corporation. Thus, the convertibility test is satisfied if warrants to purchase the stock of the corporation are issued in conjunction with the obligation. [*See* § 279(b)(3).]

The debt-equity and interest coverage limits—which generally are to be applied as of the last day of a taxable year in which an obligation is issued for the specified acquisition purposes—would be exceeded * * * either if the debt-equity ratio of the issuing corporation was in excess of 2 to 1 or if the annual interest expenses to be paid by the issuing corporation on its total indebtedness was not covered at least three times over by its projected earnings. [*See* § 279(b)(4).] * * *

B. Treatment of Covenants Not to Compete and Similar Items

See Secs. 4.3.B. and C.

C. Reporting Requirement under § 1060(e) with Respect to Covenants Paid to 10% Shareholders

See Sec. 4.3.D.2.

D. Possibility of Making a § 338 Election

See § 338 and the regulations.

1. Introduction to Section 338[*]

As explained in Chapters 2 and 3, § 338 generally provides that if the stock of a corporation ("Target") (*see* § 338(d)(2)) is acquired by another corporation ("Purchasing Corporation") (*see* § 338(d)(1)) in a Qualified Stock Purchase (*see* § 338(d)(3)), the Purchasing Corporation may elect (or may be deemed to elect under certain consistency rules which have a limited application) to have the Target treated as if it had sold all of its assets (as "Old Target") and then purchased those assets at fair market value (as "New Target"). *See* § 338(a). The deemed sale of assets by Old Target takes place at the close of the day on which the purchase occurred ("Acquisition Date"). *See* §§ 338(a)(1) and (h)(2). New Target is deemed to purchase those assets ("Acquisition Date Assets") at the beginning of the day after the Acquisition Date. *See* § 338(a)(2).

Section 338(b) sets forth the framework for determining the aggregate amount of New Target's deemed purchase price of Old Target's assets ("adjusted grossed-up basis") and allocating this amount among New Target's acquisition date assets. A

---

[*] This section is based on § 33:02 of *Federal Taxation of Business Enterprises, supra,* Chapter 1, note 1, with permission.

Purchasing Corporation is a corporation that makes a qualified stock purchase (Qualified Stock Purchase) of another corporation. *See* § 338(d)(1). A Target is a corporation the stock of which is acquired by purchase in a Qualified Stock Purchase by the Purchasing Corporation. *See* § 338(d)(2).

A Qualified Stock Purchase is defined as any transaction or series of transactions in which a Purchasing Corporation acquires, by purchase, at least 80% of the total combined voting power of all classes entitled to vote and at least 80% of the total number of all other classes of stock (except nonvoting stock which is limited and preferred as to dividends) of the Target during the Acquisition Period. *See* § 338(d)(3). Members of the same affiliated group are treated as one corporation and shares purchased by different members of the group are aggregated in determining if a Qualified Stock Purchase has occurred. *See* § 338(h)(8).

The term "Acquisition Period" is defined as the period of 12 months beginning the first day on which a stock purchase that is part of a Qualified Stock Purchase is made. *See* § 338(h)(1).

The term "Acquisition Date" is defined as the first date on which the Purchaser acquires all of the stock necessary for a Qualified Stock Purchase. *See* § 338(h)(2).

After a Qualifying Stock Purchase, the Purchasing Corporation may elect (or may under certain limited circumstances be deemed to have elected) the application of § 338 with respect to the transaction. Pursuant to § 338(a)(1), the Target is deemed to have sold all its assets on the Acquisition Date for their fair market value in a single taxable transaction. *See* § 338(g).

The above concepts are illustrated as follows: Assume that corporation P purchases 5% of the stock of corporation T on February 1, 2003 and that P purchases another 30% of T's stock on June 1, 2003. Assume further that P purchases another 50% of T's stock on March 15, 2004. P makes a Qualified Stock Purchase of T as of March 15, 2004. The acquisition period commences on June 1, 2003 despite the earlier purchase. The Acquisition Date is March 15, 2004, the first date on which P is considered to have made a Qualified Stock Purchase. P may elect under § 338(g) to treat T as if it sold and then reacquired its assets on the Acquisition Date. Any gain or loss the Target recognizes is reported on the Target's final return filed for the taxable year that ends on the Acquisition Date.

As a result of the repeal of the former § 337 by the Tax Reform Act of 1986 (*i.e.*, *General Utilities* repeal), the Target has full gain or loss on the deemed sale of its assets resulting from a § 338 election. Consequently, it is rarely beneficial for the Purchasing Corporation to make a § 338 election. There are two major exceptions to this general rule. First, if a stand-alone Target has net operating losses or other capital losses that can offset the § 338 gain, then it might be beneficial for the Purchasing Corporation to make a § 338 election. The utilization of a Target's net operating and net capital losses in a § 338 deemed sale is not limited under § 382. *See* § 382(h)(1)(C) and Sec. 5.8.C.3.m. The second exception involves the acquisition of the stock of a subsidiary corporation. This transaction can qualify under § 338(h)(10), which is examined below in Sec. 5.5.B.

2. Taxable Reverse Subsidiary Merger Treated as Qualified Stock Acquisition

Revenue Ruling 90-95
1990-2 C.B. 67

Issues.(1) If a corporation organizes a subsidiary solely for the purpose of acquiring the stock of a target corporation in a reverse subsidiary cash merger, is the corporation treated on the occurrence of a merger as having acquired the stock of the target in a qualified stock purchase under section 338 of the Internal Revenue Code?

(2) If the corporation makes a qualified stock purchase of the target stock and immediately liquidates the target as part of a plan to acquire the assets of the target, is the corporation treated as having made an asset acquisition pursuant to the *Kimbell-Diamond* [*see* Sec. 2.10.E.2] doctrine or a section 338 qualified stock purchase followed by a liquidation of the target?

Facts. *Situation 1. P,* a domestic corporation, formed a wholly owned domestic subsidiary corporation, *S,* for the sole purpose of acquiring all of the stock of an unrelated domestic target corporation, *T,* by means of a reverse subsidiary cash merger. Prior to the merger, *S* conducted no activities other than those required for the merger.

Pursuant to the plan of merger, *S* merged into *T* with *T* surviving. The shareholders of *T* exchanged all of their *T* stock for cash from *S.* Part of the cash used to carry out the acquisition was received by *S* from *P;* the remaining cash was borrowed by *S.* Following the merger, *P* owned all of the outstanding *T* stock.

Situation 2. The facts are the same as in *Situation 1,* except that *P* planned to acquire *T*'s assets through a prompt liquidation of *T.* State law prohibited *P* from owning the stock of *T.* Pursuant to the plan, *T* merged into *P* immediately following the merger of *S* into *T.* The merger of *T* into *P* satisfied the requirements for a tax-free liquidation under section 332 of the Code. The liquidation was not motivated by the evasion or avoidance of federal income tax.

Law and Analysis. In *Kimbell-Diamond Milling Co. v. Commissioner* [*see* Sec. 2.10.E.2], * * * the court held that the purchase of the stock of a target corporation for the purpose of obtaining its assets through a prompt liquidation should be treated by the purchaser as one transaction, namely, a purchase of the target's assets with the purchaser receiving a cost basis in the assets. Old section 334(b)(2) of the Code was added in 1954 to codify the principles of *Kimbell-Diamond.* * * *

In 1982, Congress repealed old section 334(b)(2) of the Code and enacted section 338. Section 338 was "intended to replace any nonstatutory treatment of a stock purchase as an asset purchase under the *Kimbell-Diamond* doctrine." * * * [S]tock purchase or asset purchase treatment generally results whether or not the target is liquidated, merged into another corporation, or otherwise disposed of by the purchasing corporation. *See* section 1.338-4T(d) *Question and Answer 1.* [T]emporary Income Tax Regulations. * * *

Question and Answer 3 of section 1.338-4T(d) of the temporary regulations provides that the parent of the subsidiary corporation in a reverse subsidiary cash merger is considered to have made a qualified stock purchase of the target if the subsidiary's existence is properly disregarded under the step-transaction doctrine and the requirements of a qualified stock purchase are satisfied. A subsidiary used to acquire target stock in a reverse subsidiary cash merger is ordinarily disregarded for federal income tax purposes if it was formed solely for the purpose of acquiring the stock and did not conduct any activities other than those required for the merger. *See* Rev. Rul. 73-427, [*supra* Sec. 5.2.A.3.] * * *

In *Situations 1 and 2,* the step-transaction doctrine is properly applied to disregard the existence of *S* for federal income tax purposes. *S* had no significance apart from *P*'s acquisition of the *T* stock. *S* was formed for the sole purpose of enabling *P* to acquire the *T* stock, and *S* did not conduct any activities that were not related to that acquisition. Accordingly, the transaction is treated as a qualified stock purchase of *T* stock by *P*.

In *Situation 2,* the step-transaction doctrine does not apply to treat the stock acquisition and liquidation as an asset purchase. Section 338 of the Code replaced the *Kimbell-Diamond* doctrine and governs whether a corporation's acquisition of stock is treated as an asset purchase. Under section 338, asset purchase treatment turns on whether a section 338 election is made (or is deemed made) following a qualified stock purchase of target stock and not on whether the target's stock is acquired to obtain the assets through a prompt liquidation of the target. The acquiring corporation may receive stock purchase treatment or asset purchase treatment whether or not the target is subsequently liquidated. A qualified stock purchase of target stock is accorded independent significance from a subsequent liquidation of the target regardless of whether a section 338 election is made or deemed made. This treatment results even if the liquidation occurs to comply with state law. Accordingly, in *Situation 2,* the acquisition is treated as a qualified stock purchase by *P* of *T* stock followed by a tax-free liquidation of *T* into *P*.

Holdings. (1) In *Situations 1 and 2,* P is treated as having acquired stock of *T* in a qualified stock purchase under section 338 of the Code.

(2) In *Situation 2,* P is treated as having acquired stock of *T* in a qualified stock purchase under section 338 followed by a liquidation of *T* into *P,* rather than having made an acquisition of assets pursuant to the *Kimbell-Diamond* doctrine.

3. Introduction to Consistency Requirements of 1992 Proposed Regulations

Preamble to Proposed Regulations under § 338

CO-111-90 (January 14, 1992)

The [prior law] consistency rules. The consistency rules of sections 338(e) and (f), as implemented by the current temporary regulations, apply whenever a purchasing corporation ("P") makes a qualified stock purchase ("QSP") of a target corporation

("*T*") from a selling group ("*S* group"). The current consistency rules prevent *P* from selectively acquiring a stepped-up basis in particular *T* assets and preserving *T*'s corporate attributes (including a carryover basis in other *T* assets) by acquiring *T*'s stock. These rules apply broadly to transactions involving *P* or any member of *P*'s affiliated group and *T* or any member of *T*'s affiliated group ("*T* affiliates").

Under the asset consistency rules of § 1.338-4T(f) of the temporary regulations, if *P* does not make a section 338 election for *T* and, during *T*'s consistency period, any member of the *P* group acquires an asset of *T* or a *T* affiliate (a "tainted asset"), the District Director generally may deem *P* to have made a section 338 election for *T*. If the District Director imposes a deemed election for *T*, the *P* group is, in effect, treated as having acquired all of *T*'s assets and the tainted asset in a taxable asset acquisition.

If a deemed election is not made, the *P* group is treated as having made an "affirmative action carryover election." Under an affirmative action carryover election, the *P* group's basis in the tainted asset equals the *S* group's basis in the asset (a carryover basis). * * *

P may avoid a deemed election for *T* by making a "protective carryover basis election" and, as under an affirmative action carryover election, taking a carryover basis in the tainted asset. * * *

The stock consistency rules of § 1.338-4T(e), require the *P* group to treat consistently the QSP of *T* and any QSP of a *T* affiliate made during *T*'s consistency period. If *P* makes a section 338 election for *T*, the *P* group is deemed to make a section 338 election for any *T* affiliate purchased during *T*'s consistency period and after *T*'s acquisition date. Conversely, if *P* does not make (or is not deemed to make) a section 338 election for *T*, the *P* group cannot make a section 338 election for any *T* affiliate purchased during *T*'s consistency period. * * *

The proposed [now adopted] consistency rules. In general. The proposed [now adopted] regulations [§ 1. 338-8] adopt a narrower set of consistency rules than those contained in the temporary regulations. [These modified consistency rules were adopted in view of the repeal of the *General Utilities* doctrine, which insures taxation of corporate gains.] Under the proposed regulations, the consistency rules generally apply only if *T* is a subsidiary in a consolidated group. The consistency rules also apply in certain limited cases where *T* pays dividends eligible for a 100 percent dividends received deduction.

The proposed [now adopted] regulations also simplify the consistency and mitigation rules. For example, the proposed regulations eliminate the District Director's and Commissioner's discretion in applying the rules. They also eliminate the affirmative action carryover, protective carryover, offset prohibition, and regular exclusion elections.

Unlike the temporary regulations, the proposed [now adopted] regulations allow *P* to make an election under section 338 for *T* without being deemed to have made a section 338 election for any *T* affiliate.

Asset consistency. In general. The proposed [now adopted] regulations apply the consistency rules in the context of consolidated groups to prevent acquisitions from being structured to take advantage of the investment adjustment rules [*see* Sec. 5.5]. If the consistency rules did not apply in such a case, *P* could acquire assets from *T* with a stepped-up basis in the assets, and then acquire the *T* stock at no additional tax cost to the *S* group.

Example. *S* and *T* file a consolidated return. *S* has a $100x basis in the *T* stock, which has a fair market value of $200x. On January 1, 1993, *T* sells an asset to *P* and recognizes $100x of gain. Under § 1.1502-32 [*see* Sec. 5.5], *S*'s basis in the *T* stock is increased from $100x to $200x. On March 1, 1993, *S* sells the *T* stock to *P* for $200x and recognizes no gain or loss.

The consistency rules of the proposed [now adopted] regulations apply to the transaction because *T*'s gain on the asset sale is reflected under § 1.1502-32 in *S*'s basis in the *T* stock. However, under the proposed regulations, the District Director no longer has the discretion to impose a deemed section 338 election for *T*. Instead, under [the present § 1.338-8(a)(2)], *P* takes a carryover basis in any asset acquired from *T*. (This is referred to as the carryover basis rule.) Thus, *P* is no longer forced to make protective carryover basis elections in connection with every stock acquisition in order to assure the tax treatment it anticipated.

Direct acquisitions. The carryover basis rule generally applies to direct acquisitions of assets from *T* by *P* during *T*'s consistency period. A direct acquisition is one in which the asset is owned by *P* both immediately after the asset is sold by *T* and on *T*'s acquisition date.

The carryover basis rule also applies to assets acquired directly from lower-tier *T* affiliates or certain conduits if gain from the sale is reflected under § 1.1502-32 in the basis of the *T* stock. In addition, the carryover basis rule applies to assets acquired by an affiliate of *P*, rather than by *P*. * * *

4. Preamble from the Final Consistency Regulations
Preamble to Treasury Decision 8515
1994-1 C.B. 89

The Consistency Rules. The final regulations adopt the consistency rules of the proposed regulations with several minor modifications. [§ 1. 338-8]

Carryover basis rule. * * * For purposes of simplification and administrative convenience, the consistency rules in the final regulations apply in a more limited set of circumstances than in the temporary regulations. Adopting the suggested modifications, however, would substantially complicate the regulations. In addition, the carryover basis rule generally will apply only when the stock sale is contemplated at the time of the asset sale. For these reasons, the suggestions have not been adopted.

Affiliated groups. The final regulations apply the consistency rules in certain cases where dividends qualifying for a 100 percent dividends received deduction may be used in conjunction with asset dispositions to achieve a result similar to that available under the consolidated return investment adjustment rules. This provision applies only to amounts treated as dividends under general tax principles. The substance-over-form, step-transaction, and similar principles continue to apply to treat certain amounts that are dividends in form as payments by P for the T stock. *See, e.g., Commissioner v. Waterman Steamship Corp.*, 430 F.2d 1185 (5th Cir. 1970), *cert. denied*, 401 U.S. 939 (1971).

As discussed in more detail below, these regulations also permit section 338(h)(10) elections to be made for certain targets that are members of affiliated, non-consolidated groups. * * *

Anti-abuse rules. Some commentors requested that the anti-abuse rules of § 1.338-4(j) be narrowed and that these rules and the indirect acquisition rule of § 1.338-4(f) be stated as general principles. The Treasury Department and the Service believe that the anti-abuse and indirect acquisition rules are necessary to protect the final consistency rules. Further, no statement of general principle has been identified that provides adequate guidance to distinguish the cases described in the proposed regulations from those not described. Accordingly, these rules have been retained with minor modifications.

5. The 1999 Proposed Regulations Dealing with Issues Other than Consistency

Preamble to Proposed Regulations

[This excerpt provides basic guidance to the very complex § 338 regulations. When making a § 338 election it is obviously necessary to review and consider all of the potentially applicable provisions in these regulations. The final regulations are similar to these proposed regulations.]

Current Regulations. Section 338 allows certain purchasers of stock to treat the stock purchases as purchases of assets. A purchasing corporation can elect to treat a stock acquisition as an asset acquisition if it acquires 80 percent of the total voting power and 80 percent of the total value of the stock of a target corporation (not taking into account certain preferred stock) by purchase within a 12-month period. If a purchasing corporation makes a section 338 election, the target is treated as if it (as old target) sold all of its assets at the close of the acquisition date at fair market value in a single transaction and (as new target) purchased all of the assets as of the beginning of day after the acquisition date.

If a purchasing corporation acquires the stock of a target corporation in a qualified stock purchase and makes a section 338(g) election (i.e., makes a general section 338 election, not a section 338(h)(10) election), old target's gain or loss from the deemed asset sale is included in old target's final return unless old target is a member of a consolidated group or is an S corporation. * * *

In the case of a section 338(g) election, old target's total amount realized for the assets it is deemed to sell (aggregate deemed sale price or ADSP) is the sum of (a) the purchasing corporation's grossed-up basis in recently purchased target stock; (b) the liabilities of new target; and (c) other relevant items. This is the amount to be allocated among the assets sold for purposes of determining gain or loss on the assets. The liabilities referred to in (b) are those liabilities assumed by new target, but the amount thereof taken into account in ADSP is determined as if old target had sold its assets to an unrelated person for consideration that included the liabilities. The liabilities include any tax liability resulting from the deemed asset sale. * * *

New target's adjusted grossed-up basis in the assets it is deemed to purchase (AGUB) is the sum of (a) the purchasing corporation's grossed-up basis in recently purchased target stock; (b) the purchasing corporation's basis in nonrecently purchased target stock; (c) the liabilities of new target; and (d) other relevant items. This is the amount to be allocated among the assets sold for purposes of determining the purchaser's basis in the assets. * * *

Section 338(b)(5) authorizes the Secretary to issue regulations prescribing how the deemed purchase price is to be allocated among the assets. Final and temporary regulations under sections 338(b) and 1060, as amended, implement this authority. [As discussed in Sec. 4.3.F, relating to § 1060, the final regulations generally require that the basis of the acquired (or deemed acquired) assets will be determined using the following seven class residual method:

> Number *and Content of Classes* The seven classes * * * [under both §§ 338 and 1060] are as follows: Class I, cash and cash equivalents; Class II, actively traded personal property as defined in section 1092(d), certificates of deposit, and foreign currency; Class III, accounts receivable, mortgages, and credit card receivables which arise in the ordinary course of business; Class IV, stock in trade of the taxpayer or other property of a kind which would properly be included in the inventory of taxpayer if on hand at the close of the taxable year, or property held by the taxpayer primarily for sale to customers in the ordinary course of his trade or business; Class V, all assets not in Class I, II, III, VI, or VII; Class VI, all section 197 intangibles except goodwill or going concern value; and Class VII, goodwill and going concern value.]

Reasons for Change *In General.* * * *[T]he current regulations have proven problematic in three major respects: first, in their statement of tax accounting rules and their relationship to tax accounting rules for asset purchases outside of section 338, second, in the effects of the allocation rules, and, third, in their lack of a statement of a complete model for the deemed asset sale (and, in the case of section 338(h)(10) elections, the deemed liquidation) from which one can determine the tax consequences not specifically set forth in the regulations. * * *

Explanation of Provisions. *Overview of Changes.* The proposed regulations are intended to clarify the treatment of, and provide consistent rules (where possible) for, both deemed and actual asset acquisitions under sections 338 and 1060. * * * The changes made by the proposed regulations have four major components: organization of the regulations; clarification and modification of the accounting rules applicable to deemed and actual asset acquisitions; modifications to the residual method mandated for allocating consideration and basis; and miscellaneous revisions to the current regulations. These changes are [not discussed further here.] * * *

7. Merger of Target into Sister Sub after Qualified Stock Purchase of Target under § 338

See Sec. 6.2.F.3.

8. Introductory Problems on § 338

Target Corporation (*TC*) is closely held and has the following assets:

ASSET	ADJUSTED BASIS	FAIR MARKET VALUE
Cash	$100K	$100K
Equipment	$50K	$100K
Investment Securities	$50K	$100K
Patents	0	$100K
Goodwill	0	?

1. *TC* also has $100K of liabilities. *TC* has always been profitable and expects to remain so. *TC*'s tax rate is 33 1/3%. Acquiring Corporation (*AC*) purchases all of *TC*'s stock for $400K in cash and makes a § 338 election. What are the consequences of the election? Is it advisable for *AC* to make a § 338 election?

2. If the transaction in Question 1 is restructured as a purchase by *AC* of all of *TC*'s assets and the assumption of its $100K liability, how much should *AC* pay in cash?

3. Acquiring Corporation (*AC*) purchases for cash 20% of the outstanding stock of Target Corporation (*TC*) on each of January 1, 2016, March 1, 2016, November 1, 2016, January 15, 2017 and February 1, 2017. Has *AC* made a qualified stock purchase and if so, when?

4. Assume that *AC* has made a qualified stock purchase of the stock of *TC*. *TC* has appreciated assets and has always been profitable. What result if five months before making the qualified stock purchase, *AC* had purchased a division from *TC* for cash? What result if five months before making the qualified stock purchase of *TC*, *AC* had purchased from *TC* all of the stock of *TS*, a subsidiary of *TC*, and *AC* had made a § 338 election for *TS*?

5. *AC* makes a qualified stock purchase of *TC* for $100K in cash. *TC*'s only asset is the stock of its wholly owned subsidiary *TS*. *TC*'s basis for the stock of *TS* is zero. *TS* has operating assets with a basis of zero. What result to *TC* and *TS*, if *AC* makes a § 338 election? Assume that *TC* has operating assets other than the stock of *TS*. Can *AC* make a § 338 election for *TS* but not *TC*?

E. Capitalization of Stock Acquisition Expenses

Under § 263, the expenses incurred by the acquiring corporation in acquiring the stock of a target generally have to be capitalized, and since stock is not an amortizable asset, there is no amortization deduction for those costs under § 197 (*see* Sec. 4.3.C) or otherwise. As indicated in Chapter 4, in an asset acquisition the acquiring corporation receives an amortization deduction for the cost of intangibles under § 197.

Although the § 195 deduction for startup expenses does not apply in a stock acquisition, it is possible that an acquiring corporation may be allowed a deduction for analogous expenses in a stock acquisition under the Treasury's capitalization initiative. *See* Sec. 5.4.F.

§ 5.4 Issues of Concern Principally to Target and Its Shareholders

A. Treatment of Covenants Not to Compete

See Sec. 4.3.B.

B. Reporting Required under § 1060(e) with Respect to Covenants Paid to 10% Shareholders

See Sec. 4.3.D.2.

C. § 453 Treatment of Receipt of Installment Obligations

See § 453 and Chapter 2.

D. Golden Parachute Payments

See §§ 280G and 4999.

General Explanation of the Deficit Reduction Act of 1984
199–200 (1984)

Prior Law. Prior law generally permitted a taxpayer a deduction for all the ordinary and necessary expenses paid or incurred during the taxable year in carrying on a trade or business. Generally, reasonable compensation for salaries or other compensation for personal services actually rendered qualifies as ordinary and necessary trade or business expenses, as did other items. Compensation paid to an individual generally is treated as ordinary income, taxable at a rate of up to 50 percent.

Reasons for Change. In recent years, there has been a large volume of activity involving acquisitions and attempted acquisitions of corporations by other taxpayers. In many instances, the "target" corporation has resisted being taken over. In other cases, acquisitions have gone forward on a "friendly" basis. In both situations, however, arrangements were often made to provide substantial payments to top executives and other key personnel of the target corporation in connection with any acquisition that might occur.

In many "hostile" takeover situations, the Congress believed that such arrangements, commonly called "golden parachutes," were designed in part to dissuade an interested buyer, by increasing the cost of the acquisition, from attempting to proceed with the acquisition. If the takeover did not occur, the target's executives and other key personnel would more likely retain their positions, so the golden parachute could have had an effect of helping to preserve the jobs of such personnel. Where no takeover had yet commenced but the corporation viewed itself as an unwilling potential target, the Congress believed that golden parachutes were oftentimes entered into to discourage potential buyers from becoming interested. It was the view of Congress that to the extent golden parachutes had the desired effect in either such a case, they hindered acquisition activity in the marketplace and, as a matter of policy, should be strongly discouraged.

In other situations, the Congress was concerned that the existence of such arrangements tended to encourage the executives and other key personnel involved to favor a proposed takeover that might not be in the best interests of the shareholders or others. * * *

Explanation of Provisions.*General rules.* Under the Act, no deduction is allowed for "excess parachute payments." [*See* § 280G(a).] Furthermore, if any such payment is made by the acquiring company, or a shareholder of the acquired or the acquiring company, Congress did not intend that it be treated as part of the acquiring company's purchase price for the acquired company, or as increasing the shareholder's basis in his stock in the acquired or acquiring company.

Finally, a nondeductible 20-percent excise tax is imposed on the recipient of any excess parachute payment. [*See* § 4999.] * * *

E. Greenmail Payments

See § 5881.

House Report to the Revenue Act of 1987

1086–1087 (1987)

Reasons for Change.* * * The committee believes that taxpayers should be discouraged from realizing short-term profits by acquiring stock in a public tender offer and later being redeemed by the corporation in an effort by the corporation to avert the hostile takeover.

Explanation of Provisions.* * * [U]nder the bill a person who receives "greenmail" is subject to a non-deductible 50-percent excise tax on any gain realized on such receipt. [*See* § 5881(a).] Greenmail is defined as any amount paid by a corporation in redemption of its stock if such stock has been held by the shareholder for less than two years and the shareholder (or any related person or person acting in concert with the shareholder) made or threatened a public tender offer for stock in the corporation during that period.

F. Deductibility of Investment Banking and Other Expenses in M&A

1. Deductibility by Target of Expenses in Friendly Transaction the Supreme Court's View

INDOPCO, Inc. v. C.I.R.

Supreme Court of the United States, 1992
503 U.S. 79

JUSTICE BLACKMUN delivered the opinion of the Court.

In this case we must decide whether certain professional expenses incurred by a target corporation in the course of a friendly takeover are deductible by that corporation as "ordinary and necessary" business expenses under § 162(a) of the federal Internal Revenue Code.

I

Most of the relevant facts are stipulated. Petitioner INDOPCO, Inc., formerly named National Starch and Chemical Corporation and hereinafter referred to as National Starch, is a Delaware corporation that manufactures and sells adhesives, starches, and specialty chemical products. In October 1977, representatives of Unilever United States, Inc., also a Delaware corporation (Unilever), expressed interest in acquiring National Starch, which was one of its suppliers, through a friendly transaction. National Starch at the time had outstanding over 6,563,000 common shares held by approximately 3700 shareholders. The stock was listed on the New York Stock Exchange. Frank and Anna Greenwall were the corporation's largest shareholders and owned approximately 14.5% of the common. The Greenwalls, getting along in years and concerned about their estate plans, indicated that they would transfer their shares to Unilever only if a transaction tax-free for them could be arranged.

Lawyers representing both sides devised a "reverse subsidiary cash merger" that they felt would satisfy the Greenwalls' concerns. Two new entities would be created — National Starch and Chemical Holding Corp. (Holding), a subsidiary of Unilever, and NSC Merger, Inc., a subsidiary of Holding that would have only a transitory existence. In an exchange specifically designed to be tax-free under § 351 of the Internal Revenue Code, 26 U.S.C. § 351, Holding would exchange one share of its nonvoting preferred stock for each share of National Starch common that it received from National Starch shareholders. Any National Starch common that was not so exchanged would be converted into cash in a merger of NSC Merger, Inc., into National Starch. [This transaction is explored further in Sec. 5.2.C.2.]

In November 1977, National Starch's directors were formally advised of Unilever's interest and the proposed transaction. At that time, Debevoise, Plimpton, Lyons & Gates, National Starch's counsel, told the directors that under Delaware law they had a fiduciary duty to ensure that the proposed transaction would be fair to the shareholders. National Starch thereupon engaged the investment banking firm of Morgan Stanley & Co., Inc., to evaluate its shares, to render a fairness opinion, and generally to assist in the event of the emergence of a hostile tender offer.

Although Unilever originally had suggested a price between $65 and $70 per share, negotiations resulted in a final offer of $73.50 per share, a figure Morgan Stanley found to be fair. Following approval by National Starch's board and the issuance of a favorable private ruling from the Internal Revenue Service that the transaction would be tax-free under § 351 for those National Starch shareholders who exchanged their stock for Holding preferred, the transaction was consummated in August 1978.[1]

Morgan Stanley charged National Starch a fee of $2,200,000, along with $7,586 for out-of-pocket expenses and $18,000 for legal fees. The Debevoise firm charged National Starch $490,000, along with $15,069 for out-of-pocket expenses. National Starch also incurred expenses aggregating $150,962 for miscellaneous items—such as accounting, printing, proxy solicitation, and Securities and Exchange Commission fees—in connection with the transaction. No issue is raised as to the propriety or reasonableness of these charges.

On its federal income tax return for its short taxable year ended August 15, 1978, National Starch claimed a deduction for the $2,225,586 paid to Morgan Stanley, but did not deduct the $505,069 paid to Debevoise or the other expenses. Upon audit, the Commissioner of Internal Revenue disallowed the claimed deduction and issued a notice of deficiency. Petitioner sought redetermination in the United States Tax Court, asserting, however, not only the right to deduct the investment banking fees and expenses but, as well, the legal and miscellaneous expenses incurred.

The Tax Court, in an unreviewed decision, ruled that the expenditures were capital in nature and therefore not deductible under § 162(a) in the 1978 return as "ordinary and necessary expenses." The court based its holding primarily on the long-term benefits that accrued to National Starch from the Unilever acquisition. The United States Court of Appeals for the Third Circuit affirmed, upholding the Tax Court's findings that "both Unilever's enormous resources and the possibility of synergy arising from the transaction served the long-term betterment of National Starch." In so doing, the Court of Appeals rejected National Starch's contention that, because the disputed expenses did not "create or enhance * * * a separate and distinct additional asset," *see Commissioner v. Lincoln Savings & Loan Assn.*, 403 U.S. 345, 354, 91 S.Ct. 1893, 1899, 29 L.Ed.2d 519 (1971), they could not be capitalized and therefore were deductible under § 162(a). 918 F.2d, at 428–431. We granted certiorari to resolve a perceived conflict on the issue among the Courts of Appeals.

II

Section 162(a) of the Internal Revenue Code allows the deduction of "all the ordinary and necessary expenses paid or incurred during the taxable year in carrying

---

1. Approximately 21% of National Starch common was exchanged for Holding preferred. The remaining 79% was exchanged for cash.

on any trade or business." In contrast, § 263 of the Code allows no deduction for a capital expenditure—an "amount paid out for new buildings or for permanent improvements or betterments made to increase the value of any property or estate." The primary effect of characterizing a payment as either a business expense or a capital expenditure concerns the timing of the taxpayer's cost recovery: While business expenses are currently deductible, a capital expenditure usually is amortized and depreciated over the life of the relevant asset, or, where no specific asset or useful life can be ascertained, is deducted upon dissolution of the enterprise. * * *

The Court * * * has examined the interrelationship between the Code's business expense and capital expenditure provisions. In so doing, it has had occasion to parse § 162(a) and explore certain of its requirements. For example, in *Lincoln Savings,* we determined that, to qualify for deduction under § 162(a), "an item must (1) be 'paid or incurred during the taxable year,' (2) be for 'carrying on any trade or business,' (3) be an 'expense,' (4) be a 'necessary' expense, and (5) be an 'ordinary' expense." * * *

National Starch contends that the decision in *Lincoln Savings* * * * announced an exclusive test for identifying capital expenditures, a test in which "creation or enhancement of an asset" is a prerequisite to capitalization, and deductibility under § 162(a) is the rule rather than the exception. We do not agree, for we conclude that National Starch has overread *Lincoln Savings.*

In *Lincoln Savings,* we were asked to decide whether certain premiums, required by federal statute to be paid by a savings and loan association to the Federal Savings and Loan Insurance Corporation (FSLIC), were ordinary and necessary expenses under § 162(a), as Lincoln Savings argued and the Court of Appeals had held, or capital expenditures under § 263, as the Commissioner contended. We found that the "additional" premiums, the purpose of which was to provide FSLIC with a secondary reserve fund in which each insured institution retained a pro rata interest recoverable in certain situations, "serv[e] to create or enhance for Lincoln what is essentially a separate and distinct additional asset." * * *

Lincoln Savings stands for the simple proposition that a taxpayer's expenditure that "serves to create or enhance * * * a separate and distinct" asset should be capitalized under 263. It by no means follows, however, that *only* expenditures that create or enhance separate and distinct assets are to be capitalized under § 263. * * *

III

* * *

Although petitioner attempts to dismiss the benefits that accrued to National Starch from the Unilever acquisition as "entirely speculative" or "merely incidental," the Tax Court's and the Court of Appeals' findings that the transaction produced significant benefits to National Starch that extended beyond the tax year in question are amply supported by the record. * * *

In addition to * * * anticipated resource-related benefits, National Starch obtained benefits through its transformation from a publicly held, freestanding corporation into a wholly owned subsidiary of Unilever. * * *

Courts long have recognized that expenses such as these, " 'incurred for the purpose of changing the corporate structure for the benefit of future operations are not ordinary and necessary business expenses.' " * * * Deductions for professional expenses thus have been disallowed in a wide variety of cases concerning changes in corporate structure. Although support for these decisions can be found in the specific terms of § 162(a), which require that deductible expenses be "ordinary and necessary" and incurred "in carrying on any trade or business," courts more frequently have characterized an expenditure as capital in nature because "the purpose for which the expenditure is made has to do with the corporation's operations and betterment, sometimes with a continuing capital asset, for the duration of its existence or for the indefinite future or for a time somewhat longer than the current taxable year." The rationale behind these decisions applies equally to the professional charges at issue in this case.

IV

The expenses that National Starch incurred in Unilever's friendly takeover do not qualify for deduction as "ordinary and necessary" business expenses under § 162(a). The fact that the expenditures do not create or enhance a separate and distinct additional asset is not controlling; the acquisition-related expenses bear the indicia of capital expenditures and are to be treated as such. * * *

Questions

What is the treatment of an investment banker's fees incurred by a target corporation in an acquisition of the target's stock? What if the fees are incurred by a target in the sale of all of its assets? What if the fees are incurred by an acquiring corporation in an acquisition of the target's stock, on the one hand, and assets on the other?

2. The Treasury's Initiative to Resolve INDOPCO Capitalization Issues

a. Notice of Proposed Rule Making Regarding Capitalization Issues
Preamble to Reg-125638-01
January 17, 2002

Guidance Regarding Deduction and Capitalization of Expenditures * * *

Summary This document describes and explains rules and standards that the IRS and Treasury Department expect to propose in 2002 in a notice of proposed rulemaking that will clarify the application of section 263(a) of the Internal Revenue Code to expenditures incurred in acquiring, creating, or enhancing certain intangible assets or benefits.* * *

Supplementary Information The IRS and Treasury Department are reviewing the application of section 263(a) of the Internal Revenue Code to expenditures that result in taxpayers acquiring, creating, or enhancing intangible assets or benefits. This document describes and explains rules and standards that the IRS and Treasury Department expect to propose in 2002 in a notice of proposed rulemaking. A fundamental purpose of section 263(a) is to prevent the distortion of taxable income through current deduction of expenditures relating to the production of income in future taxable years. See *Commissioner v. Idaho Power Co.*, 418 U.S. 1, 16 (1974). Thus, the Supreme Court has held that expenditures that create or enhance separate and distinct assets or produce certain other future benefits of a significant nature must be capitalized under section 263(a). *See INDOPCO, Inc. v. Commissioner*, 503 U.S. 79 (1992); *Commissioner v. Lincoln Savings & Loan Ass'n*, 403 U.S. 345 (1971).

The difficulty of translating general capitalization principles into clear, consistent, and administrable standards has been recognized for decades. See *Welch v. Helvering*, 290 U.S. 111, 114–15 (1933). * * * The IRS and Treasury Department are concerned that the current level of uncertainty and controversy is neither fair to taxpayers nor consistent with sound and efficient tax administration.

Recently, much of the uncertainty and controversy in the capitalization area has related to expenditures that create or enhance intangible assets or benefits. To clarify the application of section 263(a), the forthcoming notice of proposed rulemaking will describe the specific categories of expenditures incurred in acquiring, creating, or enhancing intangible assets or benefits that taxpayers are required to capitalize. In addition, the forthcoming notice of proposed rulemaking will recognize that many expenditures that create or enhance intangible assets or benefits do not create the type of future benefits for which capitalization under section 263(a) is appropriate, particularly when the administrative and record keeping costs associated with capitalization are weighed against the potential distortion of income.

To reduce the administrative and compliance costs associated with section 263(a), the forthcoming notice of proposed rulemaking is expected to provide safe harbors and simplifying assumptions including a "one-year rule," under which expenditures relating to intangible assets or benefits whose lives are of a relatively short duration are not required to be capitalized, and "de minimis rules," under which certain types of expenditures less than a specified dollar amount are not required to be capitalized. The IRS and Treasury Department are also considering additional administrative relief, for example, by providing a "regular and recurring rule," under which transaction costs incurred in transactions that occur on a regular and recurring basis in the routine operation of a taxpayer's trade or business are not required to be capitalized.

The proposed standards and rules described in this document will not alter the manner in which provisions of the law other than section 263(a) (*e.g.*, sections 195, 263(g), 263(h), or 263A) apply to determine the correct tax treatment of an item. Moreover, these standards and rules will not address the treatment of costs other than those to acquire, create, or enhance intangible assets or benefits, such as costs to repair or improve tangible property. The IRS and Treasury Department are considering separate guidance to address these other costs.

The following discussion describes the specific expenditures to acquire, create, or enhance intangible assets or benefits for which the IRS and Treasury Department expect to require capitalization in the forthcoming notice of proposed rulemaking. The IRS and Treasury Department anticipate that other expenditures to acquire, create, or enhance intangible assets or benefits generally will not be subject to capitalization under section 263(a).

Amounts Paid to Acquire Intangible Property. *Amounts paid to acquire financial interests.* Under the expected regulations, capitalization will be required for an amount paid to purchase, originate, or otherwise acquire a security, option, any other financial interest described in section 197(e)(1), or any evidence of indebtedness. For a discussion of related transaction costs see section C of this document.

For example, a financial institution that acquires portfolios of loans from another person or originates loans to borrowers would be required to capitalize the amounts paid for the portfolios or the amounts loaned to borrowers.

Amounts paid to acquire intangible property from another person. Under the expected regulations, capitalization will be required for an amount paid to another person to purchase or otherwise acquire intangible property from that person. For a discussion of related transaction costs see section C of this document.

For example, an amount paid to another person to acquire an amortizable section 197 intangible from that person would be capitalized. Thus, a taxpayer that acquires a customer base from another person would be required to capitalize the amount paid to that person in exchange for the customer base. On the other hand, a taxpayer that incurs costs to create its own customer base through advertising or other expenditures that create customer goodwill would not be required to capitalize such costs under this rule.

Amounts Paid to Create or Enhance Certain Intangible Rights or Benefits. *12-month rule.* The IRS and Treasury Department expect to propose a 12-month rule applicable to expenditures paid to create or enhance certain intangible rights or benefits. Under the rule, capitalization under section 263(a) would not be required for an expenditure described in the following paragraphs 2 through 8 unless that expenditure created or enhanced intangible rights or benefits for the taxpayer that extend beyond the earlier of (i) 12 months after the first date on which the taxpayer realizes the rights or benefits attributable to the expenditure, or (ii) the end of the taxable year following the taxable year in which the expenditure is incurred. * * *

Prepaid items. Subject to the 12-month rule, the IRS and Treasury Department expect to propose a rule that requires capitalization of an amount prepaid for goods, services, or other benefits (such as insurance) to be received in the future.

For example, a taxpayer that prepays the premium for a 3-year insurance policy would be required to capitalize such amount under the rule. * * *

Transaction Costs. The IRS and Treasury Department expect to propose a rule that requires a taxpayer to capitalize certain transaction costs that facilitate the taxpayer's acquisition, creation, or enhancement of intangible assets or benefits described above (regardless of whether a payment described in sections A or B of this document is made). In addition, this rule would require a taxpayer to capitalize transaction costs that facilitate the taxpayer's acquisition, creation, restructuring, or reorganization of a business entity, an applicable asset acquisition within the meaning of section 1060(c), or a transaction involving the acquisition of capital, including a stock issuance, borrowing, or recapitalization. However, this rule would not require capitalization of employee compensation (except for bonuses and commissions that are paid with respect to the transaction), fixed overhead (*e.g.*, rent, utilities and depreciation), or costs that do not exceed a specified dollar amount, such as $5,000. * * *

The IRS and Treasury Department are considering alternative approaches to minimize uncertainty and to ease the administrative burden of accounting for transaction costs. For example, the rules could allow a deduction for all employee compensation (including bonuses and commissions that are paid with respect to the transaction), be based on whether the transaction is regular or recurring, or follow the financial or regulatory accounting treatment of the transaction. * * *

For example, under the rule described above, a taxpayer would be required to capitalize legal fees in excess of the threshold dollar amount paid to its outside attorneys for services rendered in drafting a 3-year covenant not to compete because such costs would not have been incurred but for the creation of the covenant not to compete. Similarly, the rule would require a taxpayer to capitalize legal fees in excess of the threshold dollar amount paid to its outside attorneys for services rendered in defending a trademark owned by the taxpayer.

Conversely, a taxpayer that originates a loan to a borrower in the course of its lending business would not be required to capitalize amounts paid to secure a credit history and property appraisal to facilitate the loan where the total amount paid with respect to that loan does not exceed the threshold dollar amount. The taxpayer also would not be required to capitalize the amount of salaries paid to employees or overhead costs of the taxpayer's loan origination department.

In addition, the rule would require a corporate taxpayer to capitalize legal fees in excess of the threshold dollar amount paid to its outside counsel to facilitate an acquisition of all of the taxpayer's outstanding stock by an acquirer. *See, e.g., INDOPCO, Inc. v. Commissioner*, 503 U.S. 79 (1992). However, the rule would not require capitalization of the portion of officers' salaries that is allocable to time spent by the officers negotiating the acquisition. *Cf. Wells Fargo & Co. v. Commissioner*, 224 F.3d 874 (8th Cir. 2000).

The rule also would not require capitalization of post-acquisition integration costs or severance payments made to employees as a result of an acquisition transaction because such costs do not facilitate the acquisition. * * *

b. Final Capitalization Regulations
Final Regulations Addressing Amounts Paid for Intangibles
Treasury Decision 9107, January 5, 2004

Explanation of Provisions. *Format of the Final Regulations.* The final regulations modify the format of the proposed regulations. The final regulations retain in § 1.263(a)-4 the rules requiring capitalization of amounts paid to acquire or create intangibles and amounts paid to facilitate the acquisition or creation of intangibles.

However, the rules requiring capitalization of amounts paid to facilitate an acquisition of a trade or business, a change in the capital structure of a business entity, and certain other transactions are contained in a new § 1.263(a)-5. Dividing the rules into two sections enabled the IRS and Treasury Department to apply some of the simplifying conventions in the proposed regulations to certain acquisitions of tangible assets in § 1.263(a)-5, while limiting the application of § 1.263(a)-4 to costs of acquiring and creating intangibles. The format of the final regulations contained in §§ 1.446-5 and 1.167(a)-3 is essentially unchanged from the format of the proposed version of these regulations.

*Explanation and Summary of Comments Concerning § 1.263(a)-4.General principle of capitalization.*The final regulations identify categories of intangibles for which capitalization is required. As in the proposed regulations, the final regulations provide that an amount paid to acquire or create an intangible not otherwise required to be capitalized by the regulations is not required to be capitalized on the ground that it produces significant future benefits for the taxpayer, unless the IRS publishes guidance requiring capitalization of the expenditure. If the IRS publishes guidance requiring capitalization of an expenditure that produces future benefits for the taxpayer, such guidance will apply prospectively. * * *

The final regulations change the general principle of capitalization in three respects from the proposed regulations. First, § 1.263(a)-4 of the final regulations does not include the rule requiring capitalization of amounts paid to facilitate a "restructuring or reorganization of a business entity or a transaction involving the acquisition of capital, including a stock issuance, borrowing, or recapitalization." As noted above, the rules requiring taxpayers to capitalize amounts paid to facilitate these types of transactions are now contained in § 1.263(a)-5.

Second, the final regulations eliminate the word "enhance" from portions of the general principle. Commentators expressed concerns that the use of the term "enhance" would require capitalization in unintended circumstances. For example, if a taxpayer acquires goodwill as part of the acquisition of a trade or business, future expenditures to maintain the reputation of the trade or business arguably could constitute amounts paid to "enhance" the acquired goodwill. The final regulations remove the word "enhance" in favor of more specifically identifying the types of enhancement for which capitalization is appropriate. For example, the final regulations modify the proposed regulations to provide that a taxpayer must capitalize an amount paid to "upgrade" its rights under a membership or a right granted by a government agency.

Third, the final regulations eliminate the use of, and the definition of, the term "intangible asset" that was contained in the proposed regulations. This change was made in an effort to aid readability. The final regulations simply identify categories of "intangibles" for which amounts are required to be capitalized.

The final regulations clarify that nothing in § 1.263(a)-4 changes the treatment of an amount that is specifically provided for under any other provision of the Code (other than section 162(a) or 212) or regulations thereunder. Thus, where another section of the Code (or regulations under that section) prescribes a specific treatment of an amount, the provisions of that section apply and not the rules contained in these final regulations. * * *

The general definition of a separate and distinct intangible asset in paragraph (b)(3) of the final regulations is unchanged from the proposed regulations, except to clarify that a separate and distinct intangible asset must be intrinsically capable of being sold, transferred, or pledged (ignoring any restrictions imposed on assignability) separate and apart from a trade or business. * * *

In addition, the application of the separate and distinct intangible asset definition to specific intangibles has been further limited in the final regulations. The final regulations provide that an amount paid to create a package design, computer software or an income stream from the performance of services under a contract is not treated as an amount that creates a separate and distinct intangible asset. * * *

Transaction costs. In General. The final regulations require taxpayers to capitalize amounts that facilitate the acquisition or creation of an intangible. The proposed regulations provide that an amount facilitates a transaction if it is paid "in the process of pursuing the transaction." Some commentators questioned whether amounts paid to investigate a transaction constitute amounts paid in the process of pursuing the transaction. The IRS and Treasury Department believe that it is inappropriate to distinguish amounts paid to investigate the acquisition or creation of an intangible from other amounts paid in the process of acquiring or creating an intangible. To clarify that investigatory costs are within the scope of the rule, the final regulations provide that amounts facilitate a transaction if they are paid in the process of "investigating or otherwise pursuing the transaction." In addition, the final regulations clarify that an amount paid to determine the value or price of an intangible is an amount paid in the process of investigating or otherwise pursuing the transaction.

The proposed regulations provide that, in determining whether an amount is paid to facilitate a transaction, the fact that the amount would (or would not) have been paid "but for" the transaction is "not relevant." The IRS and Treasury Department believe that the fact that the amount would or would not have been paid "but for" the transaction is a relevant factor, but not the only factor, to be considered. Accordingly, the final regulations revise this rule to provide that the fact that the amount would (or would not) have been paid "but for" the transaction is a relevant but not a "determinative" factor. * * *

Commentators expressed concern that the rules in the proposed regulations requiring taxpayers to capitalize amounts paid in the process of pursuing certain agreements could be interpreted very broadly to require taxpayers to capitalize amounts that should be treated as deductible costs of sustaining or expanding the taxpayer's business. To address this concern, the final regulations add a rule providing that an amount is treated as not paid in the process of investigating or otherwise pursuing the creation of a contract right if the amount relates to activities performed before the earlier of the date the taxpayer begins preparing its bid for the contract or the date the taxpayer begins discussing or negotiating the contract with another party to the contract. An example is provided in the final regulations illustrating the application of the rule.

Simplifying Conventions. The final regulations retain the simplifying conventions applicable to employee compensation, overhead, and *de minimis* costs, with several modifications. * * *

Explanation and Summary of Comments Concerning § 1.263(a)-5. In general. Section 1.263(a)-5 contains rules requiring taxpayers to capitalize amounts paid to facilitate the acquisition of a trade or business, a change in the capital structure of a business entity, and certain other transactions. The types of transactions covered by § 1.263(a)-5 are more clearly identified than in paragraph (b)(1)(iii) of the proposed regulations. Section 1.263(a)-5 applies to acquisitions of an ownership interest in an entity conducting a trade or business only if, immediately after the acquisition, the taxpayer and the entity are related within the meaning of section 267(b) or 707(b). Other acquisitions of an ownership interest in an entity are governed by the rules contained in § 1.263(a)-4, and not the rules contained in § 1.263(a)-5. Similar to the § 1.263(a)-4 final regulations, the § 1.263(a)-5 regulations clarify that an amount facilitates a transaction if it is paid in the process of "investigating or otherwise pursuing the transaction" and that an amount paid to determine the value or price of a transaction is an amount paid in the process of investigating or otherwise pursuing that transaction. In addition, the fact that an amount would (or would not) have been paid "but for" the transaction is a relevant, but not determinative, factor in evaluating whether an amount is paid to facilitate a transaction.

Acquisition of assets constituting a trade or business. As explained in the preamble to the proposed regulations, the proposed regulations (and the simplifying conventions in the proposed regulations) apply only to amounts paid to acquire (or facilitate the acquisition of) intangibles acquired as part of a trade or business and do not apply to amounts paid to acquire (or facilitate the acquisition of) tangible assets acquired as part of a trade or business. The preamble to the proposed regulations further notes that the IRS and Treasury Department were considering the application of the rules in the proposed regulations to tangible assets acquired as part of a trade or business in order to provide a single administrable standard in these transactions. To avoid the application of one set of rules to intangible assets acquired in the acquisition of a trade or business and a different set of rules to the tangible assets acquired in the acquisition, the final regulations under § 1.263(a)-5 provide a single set of rules for amounts paid to facilitate an acquisition of a trade or business, regardless of whether the transaction is structured as an acquisition of the entity or as an acquisition of assets (including tangible assets) constituting a trade or business. * * *

Special rules for certain costs. * * * **Costs of Asset Sales.** The final regulations provide that an amount paid to facilitate a sale of assets does not facilitate a transaction other than the sale, regardless of the circumstances surrounding the sale. This modifies the rule in the proposed regulations, which requires capitalization of amounts paid to facilitate a sale of assets where the sale is required by law, regulatory mandate, or court order and the sale itself facilitates another capital transaction. Several commentators argued that costs to dispose of assets are properly viewed as costs to facilitate the sale, and not costs to facilitate a subsequent transaction. The IRS and Treasury Department have adopted this suggestion and revised the rule in the final regulations.

Mandatory Stock Distributions. The final regulations modify the rules in the proposed regulations relating to government mandated divestitures of stock. The proposed regulations provide that capitalization is not required for a distribution of stock by a taxpayer to its shareholders if the divestiture is required by law, regulatory mandate, or court order, except in cases where the divestiture itself facilitates another capital transaction. The final regulations eliminate the exception. In addition, the final regulations clarify that costs to organize an entity to receive the divested properties or to facilitate the transfer of certain divested properties to a distributed entity also are not required to be capitalized under section 263(a). *See* sections 248 and 709. An example has been added to the final regulations illustrating this rule.

Bankruptcy Reorganization Costs. * * *

Simplifying conventions. In general, the simplifying conventions applicable to transactions described in § 1.263(a)-5 are similar to the simplifying conventions applicable to acquisitions or creations of intangibles governed by § 1.263(a)-4. * * *

Special rules for certain acquisitive transactions. The final regulations contain a "bright line date" rule and an "inherently facilitative" rule intended to aid the determination of amounts paid to facilitate certain acquisitive transactions. The final regulations modify the bright line date rule provided in the proposed regulations. Under the final regulations, an amount (that is not an inherently facilitative amount) facilitates the transaction only if the amount relates to activities performed on or after the earlier of (i) the date on which a letter of intent, exclusivity agreement, or similar written communication is executed by representatives of the acquirer and the target or (ii) the date on which the material terms of the transaction are authorized or approved by the taxpayer's board of directors (or other appropriate governing officials). Where board approval is not required for a particular transaction, the bright line date for the second prong of the test is the date on which the acquirer and the target execute a binding written contract reflecting the terms of the transaction.

Many comments were received concerning the bright line dates. Some commentators noted that any bright line date is inappropriate and that the determination should be based on all of the facts and circumstances surrounding the transaction. As discussed in the preamble to the proposed regulations, the IRS and Treasury Department continue to believe that a bright line rule is necessary to eliminate the subjectivity and controversy inherent in this area. Further, the IRS and Treasury Department believe that the bright line rule is within the scope of the authority of the IRS and Treasury Department to prescribe rules necessary to enforce the requirements of section 263(a), and that the bright line rule, as modified in these final regulations, serves as an appropriate and objective standard for determining the point in time at which amounts paid in certain acquisitive transactions must be capitalized.

Some commentators who agreed with the use of a bright line date rule to improve administrability of section 263(a) suggested that the bright line date should be the date the taxpayer's board of directors approves a transaction. The date of the board of directors approval may, in some cases, be the date determined under the rule contained in the final regulations. However, the IRS and Treasury Department believe that an earlier date is more appropriate where the parties have mutually agreed to pursue a transaction, notwithstanding the fact that the parties are not bound to complete the transaction. Accordingly, the rule requires capitalization if the parties execute a letter of intent, exclusivity agreement, or similar written communication. The term *similar written communication* in the rule is not intended to include a confidentiality agreement.

The board of directors approval date contemplated by the rule is not the date the board authorizes a committee (or management) to explore the possibility of a transaction with another party. Additionally, the board of directors approval date contemplated by the rule is not intended to be the date the board ratifies a shareholder vote in favor of the transaction.

Some commentators suggested that the final regulations clarify how the bright line date rule applies to a target that puts itself up for auction. These commentators noted that, under the proposed regulations, submission of a bid by a bidder could trigger the bright line date for the target, even if the target has not made any decision regarding the bid. Under the final regulations, submission of a bid by a bidder does not trigger the bright line date for the target because the first part of the test requires execution by both the acquirer and the target and the second part of the test is applied independently by the acquirer and the target. The final regulations include an example illustrating the application of the rule in this case.

The final regulations specifically identify the types of transactions to which the bright line date and inherently facilitative rules apply. Some commentators suggested that the final regulations extend the rule to apply not only to acquisitive transactions, but to spin-offs, stock offerings, and acquisitions of individual assets that do not constitute a trade or business. The IRS and Treasury Department believe that the bright line test is not suitable for these transactions and that amounts paid in the process of investigating or otherwise pursuing these transactions are appropriately capitalized.

Regarding the inherently facilitative rule contained in the proposed regulations, several commentators suggested that the rule be deleted or changed to a rebuttable presumption that the identified amounts are capital. The final regulations do not adopt this suggestion. The IRS and Treasury Department believe that the list of inherently facilitative amounts properly identifies certain types of costs that are capital regardless of when they are incurred. In addition, a rebuttable presumption would not provide the certainty sought by the regulations. However, the final regulations modify the list of inherently facilitative amounts to more clearly identify the types of costs considered inherently facilitative. For example, the proposed regulations treat "amounts paid for activities performed in determining the value of the target" as inherently facilitative costs. Commentators expressed concerns that this language would require taxpayers to capitalize all due diligence costs. The final regulations tighten this category to include amounts paid for "securing an appraisal, formal written evaluation, or fairness opinion related to the transaction." General due diligence costs are intended to be addressed by the bright line test, not the inherently facilitative rules.

Some commentators questioned whether the regulations are intended to affect the treatment of an expenditure under section 195. As a result of section 195(c)(1)(B), the regulations are relevant in determining whether an expenditure constitutes a start-up expenditure within the meaning of section 195. An amount cannot constitute a start-up expenditure within the meaning of section 195(c)(1)(B) if the amount is a capital expenditure under section 263(a). Accordingly, amounts required to be capitalized under the final regulations do not constitute start-up expenditures within the meaning of section 195(c)(1). Conversely, amounts that are not required to be capitalized under the final regulations may constitute start-up expenditures within the meaning of section 195(c)(1) provided the other requirements of that section are met.

*Hostile takeover defense costs.*The IRS and Treasury Department decided that the rules in the proposed regulations for amounts paid to defend against a hostile takeover attempt are unnecessary. The hostile transaction rule in the proposed regulations does not permit taxpayers to deduct costs that otherwise would have been capitalized under the regulations. For example, the hostile transaction rule does not apply to any inherently facilitative costs or to costs that facilitate another capital transaction (for example, a recapitalization or a proposed merger with a white knight). Other amounts that a target would pay in defending against a hostile acquisition would not be capitalized under the final regulations either because the costs would not be paid in investigating or otherwise pursuing the transaction with the hostile acquirer (for example, costs to seek an injunction against the acquisition) or would relate to activities performed before the bright line dates (while the transaction is hostile, the target will not execute any agreements with the acquirer and the target's board of directors will not authorize the acquisition). Thus, the IRS and Treasury Department believe the hostile transaction rule in the proposed regulations is unnecessary and could cause needless controversy over when a transaction changes from hostile to friendly. Accordingly, the final regulations do not contain any special rules related to hostile acquisition attempts. The final regulations contain an example illustrating how the regulations apply in the context of a hostile acquisition attempt.

Documentation of success-based fees. Under the proposed regulations, a payment that is contingent on the successful closing of an acquisition facilitates the acquisition except to the extent that evidence clearly demonstrates that some portion of the payment is allocable to activities that do not facilitate the acquisition. The final regulations retain the success-based fee rule, but extend it to all transactions to which § 1.263(a)-5 applies, instead of just acquisitive transactions. In addition, the final regulations eliminate the "clearly demonstrates" standard in favor of a rule providing that success-based fees facilitate a transaction except to the extent the taxpayer maintains sufficient documentation to establish that a portion of the fee is allocable to activities that do not facilitate the transaction. The regulations require that this documentation consist of more than a mere allocation between activities that facilitate the transaction and activities that do not facilitate the transaction. [As indicated below, the IRS has issued a Rev. Proc. that gives taxpayers another option for dealing with success fees.]

*Treatment of capitalized costs.*The final regulations provide that amounts required to be capitalized by an acquirer in a taxable acquisitive transaction are added to the basis of the acquired assets in an asset transaction or to the basis of the acquired stock in a stock transaction. Amounts required to be capitalized by the target in an acquisition of its assets in a taxable transaction are treated as a reduction of the target's amount realized on the disposition of its assets.

The final regulations do not address the treatment of amounts required to be capitalized in certain other transactions to which § 1.263(a)-5 applies (for example, amounts required to be capitalized in tax-free transactions, costs of a target in a taxable stock acquisition and stock issuance costs). The IRS and Treasury Department intend to issue separate guidance to address the treatment of these amounts and will consider at that time whether such amounts should be eligible for the 15-year safe harbor amortization period described in § 1.167(a)-3. * * *

c. I.R.S. 70-30 Option for Treatment of Success Fees in M&A Transactions

Rev. Proc. 2011-29
(May 2, 2011)

SECTION 1. PURPOSE

This revenue procedure provides a safe harbor election for allocating success-based fees paid in business acquisitions or reorganizations described in § 1.263(a)-5(e)(3) of the Income Tax Regulations. In lieu of maintaining the documentation required by § 1.263(a)-5(f), this safe harbor permits electing taxpayers to treat 70 percent of the success-based fee as an amount that does not facilitate the transaction. The remaining portion of the fee must be capitalized as an amount that facilitates the transaction.

SECTION 2. BACKGROUND

.01 Section 263(a)(1) of the Internal Revenue Code and § 1.263(a)-2(a) provide that no deduction shall be allowed for any amount paid out for property having a useful life substantially beyond the taxable year. In the case of an acquisition or reorganization of a business entity, costs that are incurred in the process of acquisition and that produce significant long-term benefits must be capitalized. *INDOPCO, Inc. v. Commissioner*, 503 U.S. 79, 89–90 (1992); Woodward v. Commissioner, 397 U.S. 572, 575–576 (1970).

.02 Under § 1.263(a)-5, a taxpayer must capitalize an amount paid to facilitate a business acquisition or reorganization transaction described in § 1.263(a)-5(a). An amount is paid to facilitate a transaction described in § 1.263(a)-5(a) if the amount is paid in the process of investigating or otherwise pursuing the transaction.

.03 Section 1.263(a)-5(f) provides that an amount that is contingent on the successful closing of a transaction described in § 1.263(a)-5(a) ("success-based fee") is presumed to facilitate the transaction. A taxpayer may rebut the presumption by maintaining sufficient documentation to establish that a portion of the fee is allocable to activities that do not facilitate the transaction.

.04 A taxpayer's method for determining the portion of a success-based fee that facilitates a transaction and the portion that does not facilitate the transaction is a method of accounting under § 446.

.05 The Internal Revenue Service and the Treasury Department are aware that the treatment of success-based fees continues to be the subject of controversy between taxpayers and the Service. In particular, numerous disagreements have arisen regarding the type and extent of documentation required to establish that a portion of a success-based fee is allocable to activities that do not facilitate a business acquisition or re-organization transaction described in § 1.263(a)-5(e)(3) ("covered transaction"). The Service and the Treasury Department expect that much of this controversy can be eliminated by providing taxpayers a simplified method for allocating a success-based fee paid in a covered transaction between facilitative and non-facilitative activities. Accordingly, this revenue procedure provides a safe harbor election for allocating a success-based fee between activities that facilitate a covered transaction and activities that do not facilitate a covered transaction.

SECTION 3. SCOPE

This revenue procedure applies to a taxpayer that—

(1) pays or incurs a success-based fee for services performed in the process of investigating or otherwise pursuing a transaction described in § 1.263(a)-5(e)(3); and

(2) makes the safe harbor election described in section 4 of this revenue procedure.

SECTION 4. SAFE HARBOR ELECTION

.01 The Service will not challenge a taxpayer's allocation of a success-based fee between activities that facilitate a transaction described in § 1.263(a)-5(e)(3) and activities that do not facilitate the transaction if the taxpayer—

(1) treats 70 percent of the amount of the success-based fee as an amount that does not facilitate the transaction;

(2) capitalizes the remaining 30 percent as an amount that does facilitate the transaction; and

(3) attaches a statement to its original federal income tax return for the taxable year the success-based fee is paid or incurred, stating that the taxpayer is electing the safe harbor, identifying the transaction, and stating the success-based fee amounts that are deducted and capitalized.

.02 An election under this revenue procedure applies only to the transaction for which the election is made and, once made, is irrevocable. The election applies with respect to all success-based fees paid or incurred by the taxpayer in the transaction for which the election is made.

.03 An election under this revenue procedure for any transaction does not constitute a change in method of accounting for success-based fees generally. Accordingly, a §481(a) adjustment is neither permitted nor required. * * *

d. Treatment of Amounts that Facilitate Certain Tax-Free and Taxable Acquisitions

Notice 2004-18
I.R.B. 2004-11, February 19, 2004

* * * The Service and Treasury Department are aware that there is continuing controversy as to the proper treatment of certain costs that facilitate certain tax-free and taxable transactions and other restructurings and that are required to be capitalized under §263(a) and §1.263(a)-5. The Service and Treasury Department also are aware that, under current law, capitalized costs that facilitate tax-free and taxable transactions that are similar may be treated differently. For example, §1.263(a)-5(g)(2) provides that the acquirer's capitalized transaction costs that facilitate a taxable asset acquisition increase the basis of the acquired assets. Some commentators, however, have expressed differing views as to how an acquirer's capitalized transaction costs that facilitate a tax-free asset acquisition are treated. In addition, the Service and Treasury Department are aware that, under current law, similar costs may be treated differently depending on which party incurs the costs. Commentators have suggested that capitalized transaction costs incurred by an acquirer and target to facilitate a tax-free stock acquisition may be treated differently.

To reduce the prospect of future controversy, the Service and Treasury Department intend to propose regulations to address the treatment of amounts that facilitate certain tax-free and taxable transactions and other restructurings and that are required to be capitalized under §263(a) and §1.263(a)-5. The Service and Treasury Department intend to develop a set of rules that are clear and administrable.

The Service and Treasury Department are considering the treatment of capitalized costs that facilitate the following transactions:

(1) Tax-free asset acquisitions and dispositions (for example, reorganizations under §368(a)(1)(A), (C), (D), (G));

(2) Taxable asset acquisitions and dispositions (*see* §1.263(a)-5(g) for the treatment of certain transaction costs in taxable asset acquisitions);

(3) Tax-free stock acquisitions and dispositions (for example, reorganizations under §368(a)(1)(B));

(4) Taxable stock acquisitions and dispositions (*see* §1.263(a)-5(g) for the treatment of certain transaction costs in taxable stock acquisitions);

(5) Tax-free distributions of stock (for example, distributions of stock to which §305(a) or §355(a) applies);

(6) Tax-free distributions of property (for example, distributions to which §§332 and 337 apply);

(7) Taxable distributions of property (for example, distributions to which §§ 331 and 336 apply and distributions of stock to which § 311 applies);

(8) Organizations of corporations, partnerships, and entities that are disregarded as separate from their owner (for example, transfers described in § 351 or § 721);

(9) Corporate recapitalizations (for example, reorganizations under § 368 (a)(1)(E));

(10) Reincorporations of corporations in a different state (for example, in a reorganization under § 368(a)(1)(F)); and

(11) Issuances of stock.

There are specific issues raised by each of these types of transactions. The Service and Treasury Department previously have requested comments more generally on the treatment of capitalized costs that facilitate certain of these transactions. In this Notice, the Service and Treasury Department request additional comments, including comments focusing on the following issues.

ISSUES ON WHICH COMMENTS ARE REQUESTED.

Treatment of capitalized costs. Section 263(a) and the regulations thereunder require that certain amounts that facilitate the transactions listed above be capitalized. The Service and Treasury Department request comments regarding whether the particular capitalized costs that facilitate transactions for which the Service and Treasury Department are considering guidance should (a) increase the basis of a particular asset or assets (and, if the basis of multiple assets should be increased, the methodology for allocating the costs among the assets), (b) be treated as giving rise to a new asset the basis of which may not be amortized, (c) be treated as giving rise to a new asset the basis of which may be amortizable, (d) reduce an amount realized, or (e) be treated as an adjustment to equity. To the extent that capitalized costs should be treated as giving rise to a new asset the basis of which may be amortizable, the Service and Treasury Department request comments regarding the appropriate amortizable useful life. For example, an appropriate amortizable useful life might be 15 years, a useful life consistent with that afforded to certain intangibles under § 1.167(a)-3(b) and § 197. Additionally, if such costs are treated as giving rise to a new, amortizable asset, the Service and Treasury Department also request comments as to the treatment of such costs if a specific event (e.g., a liquidation) occurs prior to the expiration of the amortization period.

Consistent treatment of capitalized costs that facilitate similar taxable and tax-free transactions. The regulations promulgated under § 263(a) provide rules regarding the treatment of amounts that facilitate a taxable acquisition of stock and assets and a taxable disposition of assets. The Service and Treasury Department request comments regarding whether, as a policy matter, capitalized costs that facilitate a tax-free transaction should be treated in the same manner as the capitalized costs that facilitate a similar taxable transaction.

Consistent treatment of all capitalized costs that facilitate a transaction. The Service and Treasury Department request comments regarding whether, as a policy matter, capitalized costs that facilitate a transaction, regardless of the type of cost and the party to the transaction that incurs such cost, should be treated similarly.

§ 5.5 Planning for the Acquisition of a Target that Is a Subsidiary in a Consolidated Group

A. Introduction to Consolidated Return Issues Generally

1. Purpose

The purpose of this introduction is to discuss several of the basic provisions relating to the filing of consolidated returns. An understanding of these basic principles is absolutely necessary to an understanding of how the consolidated return provisions operate in M&A transactions. The consolidated return regulations are very complex, and the purpose of this discussion is only to present an introduction to these regulations. Obviously, in addressing any issue involving consolidated returns, it is necessary to review the current applicable regulations.

2. The Statutory Structure of the Consolidated Return Provisions

The statutory structure of these provisions is short; merely authorizing the filing of a consolidated return (§ 1501), directing the Secretary to promulgate the regulations (§ 1502), providing that the tax is determined in accordance with the regulations (§ 1503), and defining an affiliated group of corporations (§ 1504). On the other hand, the regulations are voluminous.

Under § 1501 an "affiliated group of corporations [has] the privilege of making a consolidated return * * *." The term "affiliated group" is defined in § 1504, which is discussed in the next section. If the privilege is elected, the affiliated group files a single federal income tax return rather than separate returns for each corporation. Section 1501 also requires as a condition for filing a consolidated return "that all corporations which at any time during the taxable year have been members of the affiliated group consent to all the consolidated return regulations prescribed under section 1502 prior to the last day prescribed by law for filing such a return." This section further provides that the "making of a consolidated return shall be considered as such consent."

Section 1502 directs the Secretary of Treasury to

> * * * prescribe such regulations as he may deem necessary in order that the tax liability of any affiliated group of corporations making a consolidated return and of each corporation in the group, both during and after the period of affiliation, may be returned, determined, computed, assessed, collected, and adjusted, in such manner as clearly to reflect the income tax liability and the various factors necessary for the determination of such liability, and in order to prevent avoidance of such tax liability.

3. Definition of Affiliated Group in § 1504

a. Legislative History of § 1504(a)

General Explanation of Deficit Reduction Tax Act of 1984
170–173 (1984)

Reasons for Change * * * The Congress was aware that * * * corporations were filing consolidated returns under circumstances in which a parent corporation's interest in the issuing corporation accounted for less than 80 percent of the real equity value of such corporation. Further, the Congress was aware that this may have permitted certain unwarranted tax benefit transfers. * * *

Explanation of Provisions *Affiliated group [See §§ 1504(a)(1) and (2).]* Under the Act, the definition of the term "affiliated group" is amended for all purposes of subtitle A. Under the amended definition, 2 corporations do not qualify as an affiliated group (and, among other things, are therefore not eligible to elect to file, or continue to file, a consolidated return) unless 1 owns, directly, stock (1) possessing at least 80 percent of the total voting power of all classes of stock, and (2) having a fair market value equal to at least 80 percent of the total value of all outstanding stock, of such other corporation. For this purpose, as described below, certain preferred stock is to be disregarded. Similar rules apply in determining whether any other corporation is, or continues to be, a member of the group.

Preferred stock and employer securities [See § 1504(a)(4).] [C]ertain stock is to be disregarded in testing for affiliated group status. The stock to be disregarded is stock which (1) is not entitled to vote, (2) is limited and preferred as to dividends and does not participate in corporate growth to any significant extent, (3) has redemption and liquidation rights that do not exceed the stock's paid-in capital and/or par value (except for a reasonable redemption premium), and (4) is not convertible into any other class of stock. * * *

Regulations [See § 1504(a)(5).] * * * Authority is also provided for the Secretary to prescribe regulations necessary or appropriate to carry out the purposes of the provision including, but not limited to, regulations: (1) which treat warrants, obligations convertible into stock, and other similar interests as stock, and stock (like "puttable" stock) as not stock; and (2) which treat options to acquire or sell stock as having been exercised. * * *

b. Elaboration on §§ 1504(a) and (b)

Under § 1504(a), an "affiliated group" means a chain of "includible corporations" with a common parent. The 80% vote and value test for stock ownership must be met with respect to each includible corporation except the common parent. For example, assume that Parent Corporation owns 85% of Subsidiary 1's only class of stock, and Subsidiary 1 owns 70% of Subsidiary 2's only class of stock, with the balance held by the public. In such case, Parent and Subsidiary 1 are members of an affiliated group, but not Subsidiary 2.

The term "includible corporation" is defined in § 1504(b) to mean "any corporation" except, *inter alia*, (1) corporations exempt from tax, (2) insurance companies, (3) foreign corporations, and (4) S corporations. Thus, for example, if in the above example, Parent Corporation also owned 100% of the stock of Foreign Sub, Foreign Sub would not be a member of the affiliated group. As will be seen this means that Parent Corporation is going to be subject to taxation on dividends received from Foreign Sub.

4. Computation of Consolidated Taxable Income and Consolidated Tax Liability

The starting point in computing the tax liability of a consolidated group for a taxable year is to compute the consolidated taxable income. This section discusses the computation of consolidated taxable income in a simple situation in which the group does not have any intercompany transactions, distributions or other special circumstances. Under § 1.1502-11, "consolidated taxable income" is computed by adding the "separate taxable income" of each member and the group's "consolidated" items. The separate taxable income is computed under -12 (only the section of the § 1502 regulations is referred to hereafter) in accordance with the general rules applicable in computing the taxable income of a corporation that is not filing consolidated returns. Separate taxable income under -12 includes a "case in which the determination [of separate taxable income] results in an excess of deductions over gross income." Consequently, if a member has a separate operating loss, the loss is technically the member's separate taxable income.

Once the separate taxable income of each member and the consolidated items of the group are computed, the items are aggregated to arrive at the consolidated taxable income. (*See* -11.) For example, assume that in the above example of the Parent Corporation Subsidiary 1 consolidated group, the separate taxable incomes are as follows:

Member	Separate Taxable Income (Loss)
Parent Corporation	$100K
Subsidiary 1	($50K)

The consolidated taxable income of the group is, therefore, $50K.

After the consolidated taxable income is computed, the consolidated tax liability is computed under -2. Under -2, the group receives credit against the liability for, *inter alia,* its consolidated foreign tax credit (-4), and its consolidated estimated tax payments (-5). Thus, the basic methodology of filing consolidated returns is similar to the methodology of preparing a return for a non-affiliated corporation.

5. Intercompany Transactions

In many situations the different members of a consolidated group will engage in transactions with each other, such as a sale of property from one member to another or a distribution by a subsidiary of appreciated property to a parent corporation. At a subsequent time the property that is exchanged between members may be disposed of outside the consolidated group. This type of transaction is referred to in the regulations as an "intercompany transaction" and is defined in -13(b)(1)(i) as "a transaction between corporations that are members of the same consolidated group immediately after the transaction." Reg. § 1.1502-13(a)(2) gives the following general description of intercompany transactions:

> *Separate entity and single entity treatment.* Under this section, the selling member (S) and the buying member (B) are treated as separate entities for some purposes but as divisions of a single corporation for other purposes. The amount and location of S's intercompany items and B's corresponding items are determined on a separate entity basis (separate entity treatment). For example, S determines its gain or loss from a sale of property to B on a separate entity basis, and B has a cost basis in the property. The timing, and the character, source, and other attributes of the intercompany items and corresponding items, although initially determined on a separate entity basis, are redetermined under this section to produce the effect of transactions between divisions of a single corporation (single entity treatment). For example, if S sells land to B at a gain and B sells the land to a nonmember, S does not take its gain into account until B's sale to the nonmember.

Reg. § 1.1502-13(f) treats distributions by a sub to a parent of a consolidated group (*i.e.*, an intercompany distribution) as an intercompany transaction. This provision is examined below.

6. Introduction to the Investment Adjustment System

In *Ilfeld v. Hernandes*, 292 U.S. 62 (1934), the taxpayer-parent deducted the operating losses attributable to its consolidated subsidiaries in computing its consolidated tax liability. The parent was not required to reduce the basis of the subsidiaries' stock by the amount of the losses. Consequently, upon liquidation of the subsidiaries the parent claimed a second loss under the predecessor of § 331. The Supreme Court, however, disallowed the double deduction.

Under the present consolidated return regulations, a parent generally must reduce the basis of a subsidiary's stock by the amount of the subsidiary's operating losses and must increase the basis by the amount of the subsidiary's income. The basis may be reduced below zero, creating an "excess loss account" for the subsidiary's stock. Conceptually this is similar to a negative basis for the subsidiary's stock. If a subsidiary's stock for which there is an excess loss account is sold, the parent must include in income the amount of the excess loss account. These rules are discussed below.

Also discussed below are the rules under -20, which disallow loss on the disposition of the stock of a subsidiary in mirror subsidiary type transactions. These regulations were revised in 2002 as a result of the *Rite Aide* case, which is also discussed.

On November 12, 1992, the Treasury issued Proposed Regulations revising the investment adjustment system of the consolidated returns regulations, including the rules governing earnings and profits and excess loss accounts. *See* Notice of Proposed Rulemaking, CO-30-92, November 12, 1992. The proposed regulations were adopted with modifications in 1994, and the following sections briefly introduce both the prior and the current regulations.

7. The Prior Investment Adjustment System

a. In General

The prior investment adjustment system is described as follows in the preamble to the proposed regulations:

Preamble to Proposed Regulations on Investment Adjustments
CO-30-92 (Nov. 12, 1992)

The [prior] investment adjustment system (§§ 1.1502-19, 1.1502-32, and 1.1502-33) combines single entity and separate entity treatment of subsidiaries in consolidated groups. Unlike a single corporation with divisions, a consolidated group must determine gain or loss from the disposition of a subsidiary's stock, and each subsidiary must maintain a separate earnings and profits account. These requirements reflect the group's treatment as a collection of separate entities. The investment adjustment system was developed to modify the separate entity treatment of subsidiaries in favor of single entity treatment.

Under [prior] § 1.1502-32, an owning member (P) must adjust its basis in the stock of a subsidiary (S) to reflect S's earnings and profits, whether positive or negative (E & P). P's basis is also reduced by the amount of any dividends distributed by S to P, if the distributed E & P is deemed to be reflected in P's basis in S's stock (*e.g.*, if S's E & P arose in a prior consolidated return year and is reflected in stock basis through investment adjustments). To the extent reductions exceed P's basis in S's stock, they result in an excess loss account in the stock. P must include its excess loss account in income under current § 1.1502-19, generally when S's stock is sold to a nonmember or becomes worthless. These rules reflect the treatment of P and S as a single entity by causing P's basis (or excess loss account) in S's stock to reflect amounts recognized by S and taken into account in determining consolidated taxable income, and S's distributions to P.

Under [prior] § 1.1502-33, P must adjust its E & P account to reflect the adjustments to its basis in S's stock. As a result, S's E & P is currently "tiered up" to P's E & P through the investment adjustment system. If P is also a subsidiary, P's E & P (which includes S's E & P) is also tiered up through the investment adjustment system and ultimately reflected in the E & P of the common parent. Each member retains its own E & P, however, including its share of the E & P of lower tier members.

P's stock basis and E & P adjustments are generally determined separately for each share of S's stock and are limited to the share's "allocable part" of S's E & P. For example, if the group owns 80 percent of S's only class of stock, only 80 percent of S's E & P tiers up.

The [prior] rules are expressed as a series of complex, mechanical adjustments. The purposes of the investment adjustment system are not articulated in the regulations, and tax policy concerns with respect to stock basis adjustments (*e.g.,* to prevent overstatement of stock basis) often conflict with those for E & P adjustments (*e.g.,* to prevent understatement of E & P). As a result, the current rules do not easily accommodate changes in the tax law, particularly those giving rise to the growing disparity between taxable income and E & P.

b. The Woods Investment Problem

Woods Investment Co. v. Commissioner, 85 T.C. 274 (1985), acq., 1986-1 C.B.1, dealt with the determination of the basis for a parent of the stock of a consolidated sub at the time the parent sold the stock. The Sub had used accelerated depreciation in computing its taxable income, which was included in the consolidated return. However, pursuant to the consolidated return regulations then in effect, the parent computed the basis for its shares of the sub using the straight-line method of depreciation. The court held that the basis of stock of the sub was to be determined by reference to E & P computed on a straight-line basis under § 312(k). As a result, the basis reductions computed on straight-line depreciation were less than the subsidiary's losses. Consequently, on the sale of stock of the sub, the parent, in essence, realized what amounted to a double loss (one passed through from the subsidiary's operation and a second on the sale of the stock of the subsidiary). The amount of the double loss is the difference between accelerated and straight-line depreciation. As will be seen below, this discontinuity has now been eliminated.

c. Section 1503(e)(1)(A) Response to Woods Investment

The preamble to the proposed regulations explains the congressional reaction to *Woods Investment*:

Preamble to Proposed Regulations on Investment Adjustments
CO-30-92 (Nov. 12, 1992)

Section 1503(e)(1)(A) was enacted in 1987 to overrule *Woods* and reverse the effects of sections 312(k) and (n) on stock basis adjustments. Under section 1503(e)(1)(A), stock basis adjustments must generally be determined without regard to section 312(k) and (n) for purposes of determining gain or loss on dispositions of subsidiary stock after December 15, 1987. * * *

Because section 1503(e)(1)(A) does not apply for purposes of tiering up S's E & P, adjustments to stock basis and to E & P have been delinked. Thus, two separate systems are currently required—one for determining stock basis and the other for determining E & P.

Congress expected that the principles of section 1503(e)(1) would be incorporated into the investment adjustment system. The legislative history states:

[T]he committee does not believe that the consequences of a disposition of stock in a member of the group should be more favorable than if the operations of the subsidiary had been conducted (and the assets had been owned) directly by the parent corporation. The amendments made by this provision are intended to prevent this result, and the committee expects that appropriate modifications will be made not only to the basis adjustment rules, but to other provisions of the consolidated return regulations, in furtherance of this objective. H.R.Rep. No. 391 (Part 2), 100th Cong., 1st Sess. 1089 (1987).

8. General Approach of the Proposed and Final Regulations

a. The Preamble to the Proposed Regulations

The preamble says the following about the general approach of the Proposed Regulations:

Preamble to Proposed Regulations on Investment Adjustments

CO-30-92 (Nov. 12, 1992)

The proposed rules represent a comprehensive revision of the investment adjustment system, as well as a revision of the related consolidated return rules for the determination and adjustment of P's basis in S's stock. * * *

In connection with the revision of the investment adjustment system, several methods for adjusting stock basis and E & P were considered, and the policies underlying the [prior] system were reexamined. For example, consideration was given to conforming basis and partial conforming basis regimes. Under a conforming basis regime, the basis of a subsidiary's stock would conform to the net asset basis of the subsidiary (generally, the basis of its assets, minus its liabilities). Under a partial conforming basis regime, changes in stock basis would be measured by changes in the member's net asset basis.

Each system has significant sources of complexity and presents significant policy issues. The Treasury Department and the Service concluded that the greatest simplification would be achieved by adopting, to the extent feasible, the existing principles for adjusting the basis of partnership interests (section 705) and stock in S corporations (section 1367). The adjustments under these other systems are similar to the adjustments under the current investment adjustment system, and groups therefore should be familiar with the approach. Additional modifications have been adopted to simplify operation of the current rules and to correct anomalies. * * *

The proposed rules delink stock basis adjustments from E & P adjustments. Separating these systems prevents policies specific to one system from distorting the other. Stock basis adjustments and E & P continue to tier up, but under separate systems.

In general, P's stock basis adjustments are measured by reference to S's taxable income rather than S's E & P. As in the case of partnerships and S corporations, the rules also take into account tax-exempt income and expenditures that are not deductible or chargeable to capital account.

Because the proposed rules conform the investment adjustment system to recent Code amendments under section 1503(e), the Treasury Department and the Service anticipate that the proposed rules will not materially alter the investment adjustments of most subsidiaries as determined under current law. * * *

b. Preamble from the Final Investment Adjustment Regulations
Preamble to Treasury Decision 8560
(August 15, 1994)

The Proposed and Final Regulations. The final regulations retain the general approach of the proposed regulations, delinking stock basis adjustments from E&P adjustments and operating through uniform rules of general application rather than through mechanical rules. However, numerous changes have been made to clarify the regulations and to conform their style to that of other recent consolidated return regulations.

Delinking Stock Basis and E&P The investment adjustment system of the [prior] regulations requires an owning member (P) to adjust its basis in the stock of a subsidiary (S) to reflect S's current E&P (or E&P deficit). P's basis is also generally reduced by the amount of any dividend distributions by S to P. The adjustments have the effect of treating P and S as a single entity. To the extent E&P includes amounts such as tax-exempt interest income, the adjustments prevent the income from being taxed indirectly on the disposition of S's stock.

After S's E&P is taken into account by P in adjusting its basis in S's stock, the stock basis adjustment is taken into account to adjust P's own E&P. This adjustment ensures that S's E&P is taken into account by P for purposes of further stock basis adjustments if P is not the common parent, and for distributions by P to nonmembers.

The [prior] regulations were adopted in 1966. It was appropriate at that time to link stock basis and E&P adjustments because the modifications to taxable income required to compute E&P were generally also necessary to compute stock basis. Differences between taxable income and E&P have substantially increased since 1966, however, and many changes in the rules for determining E&P are not appropriate to the determination of stock basis. The resulting confusion and conflict is evidenced by recent cases examining the investment adjustment system. [*See Woods Investment*, Sec. 5.5.A.7.b.]

Section 1503(e) corrects many investment adjustment distortions resulting from the divergence of taxable income and E&P. It requires P to redetermine its basis in S's stock under modified rules at the time the stock is disposed of. The modifications eliminate the original rationale for a system linking stock basis to E&P. Moreover, because the modifications are not generally integrated into the investment adjustment regulations, significant complexity has resulted.

The proposed regulations comprehensively revise the investment adjustment system by delinking stock basis adjustments from E&P adjustments. Stock basis adjustments are determined by reference to a modified computation of S's taxable income, rather than to S's E&P. S's E&P continues to tier up to P, but under a separate E&P adjustment system. Separating the stock basis and E&P adjustment systems implements the intent of section 1503(e) and prevents policies specific to one system from distorting the other. * * *

Most commentators, * * *, agreed that delinking stock basis and E&P is appropriate.

The E&P system is fundamentally concerned with measuring dividend paying capacity, while the investment adjustment system is concerned with measuring consolidated taxable income. The [prior] system is overly complex because it provides different rules for different sources of E&P, the effect of many transactions on E&P is uncertain, and the E&P rules are already overridden by temporary consolidated return regulations and later enacted Code provisions. * * *

Because the proposed regulations delink stock basis and E&P determinations, the policies influencing the development of E&P rules no longer affect the unrelated and potentially conflicting policies for stock basis adjustments. Section 1503(e) already mandates separate computations for purposes of adjusting stock basis and E&P, and the growing disparity between taxable income and E&P may preclude taxpayers from relying on E&P guidance in many instances. *See, e.g.,* section 1503(e)(1)(B). Consequently, the best approach to the investment adjustment system is to begin the computation with taxable income or loss and make adjustments. Compare the systems for adjusting the basis of partnership interests (section 705) and stock in S corporations (section 1367).

The final regulations retain the approach of the proposed regulations. Investment adjustments are determined by reference to (i) taxable income or loss, (ii) tax-exempt income, (iii) noncapital, nondeductible expenses, and (iv) distributions.

9. Basis Adjustment Rules under Reg. § 1.1502-32

a. Background

The preamble to the Proposed Regulations explains the general operation of the investment adjustment rules as follows:

Preamble to Proposed Regulations on Investment Adjustments

CO-30-92 (Nov. 12, 1992)

Under the proposed [now final] rules, P's stock basis adjustments with respect to S's stock are determined by reference to S's taxable income or loss, certain tax-exempt and noncapital, nondeductible items, and distributions. As under the current system, a positive adjustment increases, and a negative adjustment decreases, P's basis in S's stock. If a negative adjustment exceeds P's basis, the excess is referred to as P's excess loss account.

Section 1.1502-32(a) describes the basic purposes of the stock basis adjustment rules as reflecting the treatment of P and S as a single entity. Thus, stock basis adjustments prevent items recognized by S from being recognized a second time on P's disposition of S's stock. In addition, even if the adjustments are not necessary to prevent duplication of S's items (e.g., the items are attributable to unrealized loss of S that is reflected in P's cost basis for S's stock), the adjustments have the effect of causing P to recapture the items. (But *see* § 1.1502-20 [Sec. 13.7.F], disallowing certain stock losses to implement the repeal of the *General Utilities* doctrine.)

Amount of adjustment The adjustment is the net amount (treating income and gain items as increases and losses, deductions, and distributions as decreases) of S's:

(i)   Taxable income or tax loss;

(ii) Tax-exempt income;

(iii) Noncapital, nondeductible expenses; and

(iv) Distributions with respect to S's stock.

b. Stock Basis under Reg. § 1.1502-32(b)(2)

Reg. § 1.1502-32(b)(2) provides the following rules for determining stock basis:

Stock basis. P's basis in S's stock is increased by positive adjustments and decreased by negative adjustments under this paragraph (b)(2).

c. Amount of the Adjustment under Reg. § 1.1502-32(b)(2)

Reg. § 1.1502-32(b)(2) provides the following rules for determining the amount of the adjustment:

Amount of adjustment. * * * The amount of the adjustment, determined as of the time of the adjustment, is the net amount of S's:

(i)   Taxable income or tax loss;

(ii) Tax-exempt income;

(iii) Noncapital, nondeductible expenses; and

(iv) Distributions with respect to S's stock.

d. Operating Rules under Reg. § 1.1502-32(b)(3)(i)

A variety of operating rules are set forth in Reg. § 1.1502-32(b)(3)(i) regarding a subsidiary's taxable income and tax loss:

> (i) Taxable income or loss. S's taxable income or loss is consolidated taxable income (or loss) determined by including only S's items of income, gain, deduction, and loss taken into account in determining consolidated taxable income (or loss), treating S's deductions and losses as taken into account to the extent they are absorbed by S or any other member. For this purpose:

> (A) To the extent that S's deduction or loss is absorbed in the year it arises or is carried forward and absorbed in a subsequent year (*e.g.*, under section 172, 465, or 1212), the deduction or loss is taken into account under paragraph (b)(2) of this section in the year in which it is absorbed.

(B) To the extent that S's deduction or loss is carried back and absorbed in a prior year (whether consolidated or separate), the deduction or loss is taken into account under paragraph (b)(2) of this section in the year in which it arises and not in the year in which it is absorbed.

e. Determining the Amount of an Excess Loss Account under Reg. § 1.1502-32(a)(2)(ii)

Reg. § 1.1502-32(a)(2)(ii) provides the following rules for determining the amount of an excess loss account:

Excess loss account. Negative adjustments under this section may exceed P's basis in S's stock. The resulting negative amount is P's excess loss account in S's stock. *See* § 1.1502-19 for rules treating excess loss accounts as negative basis, and treating references to stock basis as including references to excess loss accounts.

f. Illustration: Taxable Income

The following examples are based on the following basic facts set forth in Reg. 1.1502-32(b)(5)(i):

Examples — (i) In general. For purposes of the examples in this section, unless otherwise stated, P owns all of the only class of S's stock, the stock is owned for the entire year, S owns no stock of lower-tier members, the tax year of all persons is the calendar year, all persons use the accrual method of accounting, the facts set forth the only corporate activity, preferred stock is described in section 1504(a)(4), all transactions are between unrelated persons, and tax liabilities are disregarded.

Reg. § 1.1502-32(b)(5) *Example 1* gives the following illustration of the investment adjustment system when a subsidiary has taxable income:

Example 1. Taxable income. (a) Current taxable income. For Year 1, the P group has $100 of taxable income when determined by including only S's items of income, gain, deduction, and loss taken into account. Under paragraph (b)(1) of this section, P's basis in S's stock is adjusted under this section as of the close of Year 1. Under paragraph (b)(2) of this section, P's basis in S's stock is increased by the amount of the P group's taxable income determined by including only S's items taken into account. Thus, P's basis in S's stock is increased by $100 as of the close of Year 1. * * *

g. Illustration: Tax Loss

Reg. § 1.1502-32(b)(5) Example 2 gives the following illustration of the investment adjustment system when a subsidiary has a tax loss:

Example 2. Tax loss. (a) Current absorption. For Year 2, the P group has a $50 consolidated net operating loss when determined by taking into account only S's items of income, gain, deduction, and loss. S's loss is absorbed by the P group in Year 2, offsetting P's income for that year. Under paragraph (b)(3)(i)(A) of this section, because S's loss is absorbed in the year it arises, P has a $50 negative adjustment with respect to S's stock. Under paragraph (b)(2) of this section, P reduces its basis in S's stock by $50. Under paragraph (a)(3)(ii) of this section, if the decrease exceeds P's basis in S's stock, the excess is P's excess loss account in S's stock. * * *

h. Illustration: Distribution

Reg. § 1.1502-32(b)(5) Example 5, gives the following illustration of the treatment of a distribution by S to P:

> *Example 5.* Distributions. (a) Amounts declared and distributed. For Year 1, the P group has $120 of consolidated taxable income when determined by including only S's items of income, gain, deduction, and loss taken into account. S declares and makes a $10 dividend distribution to P at the close of Year 1. Under paragraph (b) of this section, P increases its basis in S's stock as of the close of Year 1 by a $110 net amount ($120 of taxable income, less a $10 distribution).
>
> (b) Distributions in later years. The facts are the same as in paragraph (a) of this Example 5, except that S does not declare and distribute the $10 until Year 2. Under paragraph (b) of this section, P increases its basis in S's stock by $120 as of the close of Year 1, and decreases its basis by $10 as of the close of Year 2. (If P were also a subsidiary, the basis of its stock would also be increased in Year 1 to reflect P's $120 adjustment to basis of S's stock; the basis of P's stock would not be changed as a result of S's distribution in Year 2, because P's $10 of tax-exempt dividend income under paragraph (b)(3)(ii) of this section would be offset by the $10 negative adjustment to P's basis in S's stock for the distribution.)

10. Earnings and Profits under Prop. Reg. § 1.1502-33

a. Purpose and Effect of E & P Tiering Rules

The preamble to the Proposed Regulations gives the following explanation of the purpose and effect of the [prior and current] E & P tiering rules:

Preamble to Proposed Regulations on Investment Adjustments
CO-30-92 (Nov. 12, 1992)

A principal effect of the current investment adjustment system is to consolidate a group's E & P in the E & P account of the common parent. Because of the stock ownership requirements under section 1504, the common parent is typically the only member of a group whose stock is held largely by nonmembers. Therefore, to determine whether distributions to nonmembers should be characterized as dividends, the group's E & P must be consolidated in the common parent.

The proposed rules establish a separate system for adjusting and tiering up E & P. Consequently, anomalies resulting from the interdependence of stock basis adjustments and E & P adjustments are eliminated. For example, if S sustains an E & P deficit and a corresponding tax loss, P's basis in S's stock is not reduced to reflect the E & P deficit under the current rules until the tax loss is absorbed. Because the stock basis adjustment is deferred, the current linked system automatically defers the tiering up of the E & P deficit. The E & P result is incorrect because the group's E & P, determined on a single entity basis, should be reduced to reflect S's E & P deficit when the deficit is sustained.

The proposed [and final] rules provide for separately adjusting the basis of S's stock for E & P purposes to determine P's E & P on the disposition of S's stock. Separate stock basis adjustments for E & P purposes are necessary to avoid duplicating E & P. For example, if S earns $100 of E & P that tiers up and increases P's E & P by $100, P should not have another $100 of E & P if it subsequently sells S's stock for an additional $100 because of S's earnings.

b. Guiding Principles under Reg. § 1.1502-33(a)(1)

Reg. § 1.1502-33(a)(1) sets forth the purpose of the regulations:

(a) In general — (1) *Purpose.* This section provides rules for adjusting the earnings and profits of a subsidiary (S) and any member (P) owning S's stock. These rules modify the determination of P's earnings and profits under applicable rules of law, including section 312, by adjusting P's earnings and profits to reflect S's earnings and profits for the period that S is a member of the consolidated group. The purpose for modifying the determination of earnings and profits is to treat P and S as a single entity by reflecting the earnings and profits of lower-tier members in the earnings and profits of higher-tier members and consolidating the group's earnings and profits in the common parent. References in this section to earnings and profits include deficits in earnings and profits.

c. The Tiering Rules under Prop. Reg. § 1.1502-33(b)(1)

Reg. § 1.1502-33(b)(1) sets forth the general rule for tiering up E & P:

(b) Tiering up earnings and profits — (1) *General rule.* P's earnings and profits are adjusted under this section to reflect changes in S's earnings and profits in accordance with the applicable principles of § 1.1502-32, consistently applied, and an adjustment to P's earnings and profits for a tax year under this paragraph (b)(1) is treated as earnings and profits of P for the tax year in which the adjustment arises. Under these principles, for example, the adjustments are made as of the close of each consolidated return year, and as of any other time if a determination at that time is necessary to determine the earnings and profits of any person. Similarly, S's earnings and profits are allocated under the principles of § 1.1502-32(c), and the adjustments are applied in the order of the tiers, from the lowest to the highest.

d. Illustration of Tiering Rules

The following example of the tiering rules is based on the following facts which are set out in § 1502-33(b)(3)(i):

> (3) Examples — (i) *In general.* For purposes of the examples in this section, unless otherwise stated, P owns all of the only class of S's stock, the stock is owned for the entire year, S owns no stock of lower-tier members, the tax year of all persons is the calendar year, all persons use the accrual method of accounting, the facts set forth the only corporate activity, preferred stock is described in section 1504(a)(4), all transactions are between unrelated persons, and tax liabilities are disregarded.

Reg. § 1.1502-33(b)(3)(ii) Example (1) illustrates the tiering rules:

> *Example 1. Tier-up and distribution of earnings and profits.* (a) Facts. P forms S in Year 1 with a $100 contribution. S has $100 of earnings and profits for Year 1 and no earnings and profits for Year 2. During Year 2, S declares and distributes a $50 dividend to P.
>
> (b) *Analysis.* Under paragraph (b)(1) of this section, S's $100 of earnings and profits for Year 1 increases P's earnings and profits for Year 1. P has no additional earnings and profits for Year 2 as a result of the $50 distribution in Year 2, because there is a $50 increase in P's earnings and profits as a result of the receipt of the dividend and a corresponding $50 decrease in S's earnings and profits under section 312(a) that is reflected in P's earnings and profits under paragraph (b)(1) of this section.
>
> (c) *Distribution of current earnings and profits.* The facts are the same as in paragraph (a) of this Example 1, except that S distributes the $50 dividend at the end of Year 1 rather than during Year 2. Under paragraph (b)(1) of this section, P's earnings and profits are increased by $100 (S's $50 of undistributed earnings and profits, plus P's receipt of the $50 distribution). Thus, S's earnings and profits increase by $50 and P's earnings and profits increase by $100. * * *

e. Allocation of Tax Liability in Computing Earnings and Profits

Section 1552 and the regulations thereunder set forth rules for determining the impact of the group's tax liability on the computation of earnings and profits. Section 1552 provides three formulas for allocating the tax liability among members of the group, and also provides for an allocation in accordance with any method selected by the group and approved by the Secretary. Absent an election, the first option applies. This option apportions the tax liability among the members in accordance with the following formula:

$$\frac{\text{Member's Portion of Consolidated Taxable Income}}{\text{Group's Consolidated Taxable Income}} \times \text{Group's Tax Liability}$$

Section 1.1552-1(b), which determines the effect of an allocation, provides that each member's earnings and profits are reduced by the amount of the tax liability allocated to it. If another member has paid the liability, the payment is treated as a "distribution with respect to stock, a contribution to capital, or a combination thereof."

The following excerpt from the preamble to the proposed regulations explains the purpose and effect of these allocation provisions:

Preamble to Proposed Regulations on Investment Adjustments
CO-30-92 (Nov. 12, 1992)

E & P is generally reduced for federal taxes, and each member must adjust its E & P for an allocable part of the tax liability of the group, determined under section 1552. The current E & P rules also permit groups to allocate additional amounts. For example, if P has $100 of income and S has $100 of loss, the group's consolidated taxable income is $0 and nothing is allocated under section 1552. Current § 1.1502-33(d) provides elective methods by which P may be treated as incurring a liability to S in recognition of P's income offsetting S's loss.

The elective allocation methods of current § 1.1502-33(d) are retained under the proposed rules but are rewritten to improve comprehension. Although these rules are the most complex feature of the current E & P rules, they are retained because the Treasury Department and the Service understand that groups rely on them for non-tax purposes, such as ratemaking for public utilities. * * *

11. Excess Loss Accounts under Reg. § 1.1502-19

a. Purpose and Effect of Excess Loss Accounts

The preamble to the Proposed Regulations gives the following general description of the purpose and effect of the excess loss account (ELA) rules:

Preamble to Proposed Regulations on Investment Adjustments
CO-30-92 (Nov. 12, 1992)

The excess loss account (ELA) rules are an extension of the rules for adjusting stock basis. P's basis in S's stock is reduced as the group absorbs S's losses and as S makes distributions to P. The reductions are not limited to the group's basis in S's stock and, to the extent reductions exceed stock basis, they result in an ELA with respect to P's S stock. P's ELA is included in its income when P disposes of the stock, and the income is generally treated as gain from the sale of the stock.

An ELA ordinarily arises with respect to a share of S's stock only if S's losses and distributions are funded with capital not reflected in the basis of the share. The reductions may be funded by creditors or by other shareholders, including other members.

b. General Description of the Rules

The preamble to the Proposed Regulations gives the following general description of the operation of the rules:

Preamble to Proposed Regulations on Investment Adjustments

CO-30-92 (Nov. 12, 1992)

The proposed rules revise and simplify the current rules by applying principles. In general, an ELA is treated as negative basis for computational purposes, to eliminate the need for special ELA rules paralleling the basis rules of the Code. Similarly, the rules of the Code are generally used to determine the timing for inclusion of an ELA in income. For example, if S has an ELA in T's stock and distributes the stock to P in a transaction to which section 355 applies, section 358 eliminates S's ELA (instead, P's basis in T's stock is an allocable part of P's basis in S's stock), and section 355 provides that any gain realized by S from the disposition of T's stock is not recognized. Although P's ELA in S's stock is generally included in income when P or S becomes nonmembers of the group, a special exception is provided if they cease to be members by reason of the acquisition of the entire group. Unlike the current rules, the proposed rules do not provide special investment adjustments to prevent income attributable to preacquisition ELAs from increasing the E & P or the stock basis of members of the acquiring group. An ELA is merely one form of built-in gain to the acquiring group, and built-in gain is more generally addressed by § 1.1502-20.

c. Determining the Amount of an Excess Loss Account

See Sec. 5.A.9. above.

d. General Rule of Income Recognition

Reg. § 1.1502-19(b)(1) provides the general rule of income realization for an excess loss account (ELA):

> (b) Excess loss account taken into account as income or gain—(1) *General rule.* If P is treated under this section as disposing of a share of S's stock, P takes into account its excess loss account in the share as income or gain from the disposition. Except as provided in paragraph (b)(4) of this section, the disposition is treated as a sale or exchange for purposes of determining the character of the income or gain.

Dispositions of stock are defined broadly in Reg. § 1.1502-19(c) to include transfers, deconsolidations and worthlessness.

e. Illustration

The following example is based on the following facts set out in § 1.1502-19(g):

> (g) Examples. For purposes of the examples in this section, unless otherwise stated, P owns all 100 shares of the only class of S's stock and S owns all 100 shares of the only class of T's stock, the stock is owned for the entire year, T owns no stock of lower-tier members, the tax year of all persons is the calendar year, all persons use the accrual method of accounting, the facts set forth the only corporate activity, all transactions are between unrelated persons, and tax liabilities are disregarded. * * *

Reg. § 1.1502-19(g) Example (1) gives the following illustration of the recognition of an ELA upon the sale of stock of a subsidiary:

> *Example 1. Taxable disposition of stock.* (a) *Facts.* P has a $150 basis in S's stock, and S has a $100 basis in T's stock. For Year 1, P has $500 of ordinary income, S has no income or loss, and T has a $200 ordinary loss. S sells T's stock to a nonmember for $60 at the close of Year 1.
>
> (b) *Analysis.* Under paragraph (c) of this section, the sale is a disposition of T's stock at the close of Year 1 (the day of the sale). Under § 1.1502-32(b), T's loss results in S having a $100 excess loss account in T's stock immediately before the sale. Under paragraph (b)(1) of this section, S takes into account the $100 excess loss account as an additional $100 of gain from the sale. Consequently, S takes into account a $160 gain from the sale in determining the group's consolidated taxable income. Under § 1.1502-32(b), T's $200 loss and S's $160 gain result in a net $40 decrease in P's basis in S's stock as of the close of Year 1, from $150 to $110. * * *

f. The Validity of the § 1.1502-19 Excess Loss Regulations

Covil Insulation Co. v. Commissioner

Tax Court of the United States, 1975

65 T.C. 364

Opinion * * *

[T]he current earnings or losses of each member of the consolidated group enter into the computation of consolidated income, section 1.1502-11, Income Tax Regs. The losses of one affiliate may offset the profits of another and thus serve to reduce or eliminate consolidated income. Losses of a subsidiary may be utilized in this matter without limitation, even if the amount of utilized losses exceeds the group's basis in the affiliate's stock. As a result, the group's tax liability may be distorted since the tax losses may exceed the economic losses. This distortion is eliminated, however, through the vehicle of compensating adjustments to the group's basis in the affiliate's stock.

[Former] Section 1.1502-32, Income Tax Regs., entitled "Investment adjustment," and [former] section 1.1502-19, Income Tax Regs., entitled "Excess losses," deal with this problem. Under section 1.1502-32, Income Tax Regs., the impact of the subsidiary's losses (and gains) is reflected in annual adjustments to the group's basis in the subsidiary's stock. The adjustments are of two kinds: positive and negative. Generally, the subsidiary's undistributed earnings and profits, which contribute to consolidated income, necessitate a positive adjustment which increases the group's basis in the stock. Losses of the subsidiary used to reduce the group's consolidated income require negative adjustments which decrease the group's basis in that stock. The adjustments are netted at the end of each taxable year. If the net negative adjustment exceed the group's basis in the stock, an "excess loss account"—a negative basis for the stock—results. Sec. 1.1502-32(e)(1), Income Tax Regs.

When all of the subsidiary's stock is disposed of, the members of the affiliated group owning the stock are required to include the balance of the "excess loss account" in income. *See* sec. 1.1502-19(a)(1). The income, in most cases is taxable as gain from the sale or exchange of stock. However, where, as in the instant case, the subsidiary is insolvent, the income is treated as ordinary income. Sec. 1.1502-19(a)(2).

The term "disposed of" or "disposition" is given a rather broad meaning. * * *

The group is thus able to reduce its consolidated income by loss deductions which are in excess of its true economic losses. It may be that these losses are temporary and the subsidiary will create enough earnings and profits later to eliminate the excess loss account. If, however, the stock is disposed of prior to the subsidiary's economic turnaround, the utilized excess losses are the practical equivalent of an "amount realized" in excess of the group's investment and are logically includible in consolidated income. Sec. 1.1502-19(a).

The 1968 Consolidated Income Petitioner concedes that its Imesco stock was worthless in 1968, that Imesco could not pay its debts at the end of that year, that Imesco was insolvent within the meaning of applicable regulations, and that these regulations, if valid, would require the excess loss account of $118,661.01 to be included in the consolidated income for 1968. But petitioner contends that section 1.1502-32(e), requiring a parent corporation filing a consolidated return to reduce its basis in its subsidiary's stock to a figure below zero is invalid. Petitioner also challenges the validity of section 1.1502-19(a), Income Tax Regs., requiring the parent to include in income the amount of the excess loss account upon a disposition of the subsidiary's stock. * * *

We think the challenged regulations reflect a permissible exercise of the rulemaking power granted by section 1502. Indeed, the facts of this case amply demonstrate their reasonableness. Petitioner's investment in Imesco was only $45,005, comprised of the $5 paid to acquire Imesco's stock and the $45,000 indebtedness which petitioner capitalized. Yet Imesco's losses, allowed as deductions in computing the tax results of the consolidated group, far exceeded that investment. * * *

The disputed regulations require this difference [between the investment and the loss, *i.e.*, the ELA] to be included in petitioner's income for 1968. In so providing, the regulations merely bring the tax results in line with the economic results of petitioner's ownership of Imesco's stock. The regulation might have been drafted to limit the deductible losses to petitioner's basis in Imesco's stock, but such a regulation would be unnecessarily cumbersome where the loss situation is expected to be temporary. We cannot say that the excess loss account provisions of the regulations are not a permissible alternative technique for limiting the tax deduction to the amount of the group's economic [loss]. * * *

12. Treatment of Cash and Property Distributions

Reg. § 1.1502-13(f)(2)(1) provides that paragraph (f)(2) "provides rules for intercompany transactions to which section 301 applies (intercompany distributions"). -13(f)(2)(ii) sets out the following rule for the "distributee member:"

(f) *Stock of members*—* * * (2) *Intercompany distributions to which section 301 applies*—* * *

(ii) *Distributee member.* An intercompany distribution is not included in the gross income of the distributee member (B). However, this exclusion applies to a distribution only to the extent there is a corresponding negative adjustment reflected under § 1.1502-32 in B's basis in the stock of the distributing member (S). For example, no amount is included in B's gross income under section 301(c)(3) from a distribution in excess of the basis of the stock of a subsidiary that results in an excess loss account under § 1.1502-32(a) which is treated as negative basis under § 1.1502-19. B's dividend received deduction under section 243(a)(3) is determined without regard to any intercompany distributions under this paragraph (f)(2) to the extent they are not included in gross income. * * *

Thus, a distribution which results in a negative adjustment to the distributee's basis for the distributor's shares is excluded from gross income. -13(f)(2)(iii) provides the following rule for the "distributing member:"

(iii) *Distributing member.* The principles of section 311(b) apply to S's loss, as well as gain, from an intercompany distribution of property. Thus, S's loss is taken into account under the matching rule if the property is subsequently sold to a nonmember. However, section 311(a) continues to apply to distributions to nonmembers (for example, loss is not recognized).

Thus, if a distributor distributes property both gain and loss are recognized; however, the gain or loss is only taken into account under the matching rule that comes into effect if the property is sold to a nonmember.

The dividend exclusion and property distribution rules are illustrated in Example 1 of -13(f)(7):

(7) *Examples.* The application of this section to intercompany transactions with respect to stock of members is illustrated by the following examples.

Example 1. Dividend exclusion and property distribution. (a) *Facts.* S owns land with a $70 basis and $100 value. On January 1 of Year 1, P's basis in S's stock is $100. During Year 1, S declares and makes a dividend distribution of the land to P. Under section 311(b), S has a $30 gain. Under section

301(d), *P's* basis in the land is $100. On July 1 of Year 3, *P* sells the land to *X* for $110.

(b) *Dividend elimination and stock basis adjustments.* Under paragraph (b)(1) of this section, *S's* distribution to *P* is an intercompany distribution. Under paragraph (f)(2)(ii) of this section, *P's* $100 of dividend income is not included in gross income. Under § 1.1502-32, *P's* basis in *S's* stock is reduced from $100 to $0 in Year 1.

(c) *Matching rule and stock basis adjustments.* Under the matching rule (treating *P* as the buying member and *S* as the selling member), *S* takes its $30 gain into account in Year 3 to reflect the $30 difference between *P's* $10 gain taken into account and the $40 recomputed gain. Under § 1.1502-32, *P's* basis in *S's* stock is increased from $0 to $30 in Year 3. * * *

13. Summary Problems on Basic Consolidated Return Principles

1. *P* and *S*, both newly organized corporations, file a consolidated return. *S* has only common stock outstanding, and *P* owns 90 percent of the common. *P's* basis for the common is $40K. In the first year of operations, *S* has a separate taxable loss of $20K and *P* has separate taxable income of $230K.

    a. What is the group's consolidated taxable income and tax liability (assuming 35 percent rate)? *See* §§ 1.1502-11, -12 and -2.

    b. What is *P's* basis for the *S* common, and what are *P's* and *S's* earnings and profits at the beginning of the second year?

    c. Same questions as in (a) and (b) above, except that instead of $20K loss for the year, *S* had a $100K loss. At the beginning of the second year *P* sold the stock of *S* for $75K. What result to *P*?

2. At the beginning of 2017, *P* sold to its wholly owned subsidiary, *S*, a parcel of land for which *P* had an adjusted basis of $50K. The selling price to *S* was $100K. One year later *S* sold the land to a third party for $125K. Both *P* and *S* hold the land for investment. *P* and *S* file a consolidated return. What result from the transactions?

B. Planning for the § 338(h)(10) Election

1. Introduction

See also Sec. 5.3.D.

Preamble to Temporary Regulations under § 338(h)(10)

Treasury Decision 8065 (March 15, 1986)

Explanation of Provisions *Introduction.* Section 338, generally, provides that, if the stock of a corporation ("target") is acquired by another corporation ("purchasing corporation") in a qualified stock purchase, the purchase corporation may elect (or may be deemed to elect under certain consistency rules) to have the target treated as if it had sold all of its assets (as "old target") and then purchased those assets (as "new target"). * * * Section 338(h)(9) now provides that old target is not treated as a member of an affiliated group with respect to the deemed sale of its assets, except as otherwise provided in section 338(h)(10). Thus, even if consolidated returns are filed by the selling group and by the purchasing group, the general rule is that any gain that target must recognize * * * is reported by target on its final return which is a separate return referred to as a "deemed sale return." Section 338(h)(10) provides that, under regulations, if the target is a member of a selling consolidated group ("selling group") and section 338(h)(10) is elected, old target is treated as having sold all of its assets to new target in a single transaction. Gain or loss is recognized by old target on the deemed sale of its assets but, except as provided by regulations, no gain or loss is recognized upon the sale or exchange of old target stock to the purchasing corporation. Old target, then, is treated as having sold all of its assets in a single taxable transaction while a member of the selling consolidated group. * * * Thus, if section 338(h)(10) is elected, the selling consolidated group directly bears any income tax on the deemed sale of target's assets instead of target initially bearing that tax on a separate return.

Under the document, the section 338(h)(10) transaction is characterized as if old target sells all of its assets at the close of the acquisition date and then immediately liquidates under section 332. * * *

Consequences of Election. The following consequences obtain when an election is made for a section 338(h)(10) target:

1. Old target recognizes gain or loss as if, while a member of the selling group, it sold in a single taxable transaction all of its assets at the close of the acquisition date. * * *

2. Gain or loss from the sale or deemed sale of the stock of a section 338(h)(10) target or target affiliate to the purchaser by the selling group is ignored for all purposes of chapter 1 of the Code.

3. Old target is deemed to have liquidated under section 332 at the close of the acquisition date but after the deemed asset sale. Thus, attributes listed in section 381, such as net operating loss carryovers, carry over from target to the transferee in the deemed liquidation. * * *

2. Requirement of Consistent Treatment in § 338(h)(10) Election

See § 338(h)(10)(C).

House Report to Revenue Reconciliation Act of 1990

102 (1992)

Explanation of Provisions It is intended that the reporting and allocation rules of section 1060 not apply in any case in which a stock purchase is treated as an asset purchase under section 338. Thus, except as noted below, section 1060 is inapplicable even if an actual asset purchase of the same assets would constitute an applicable asset acquisition.

The bill provides that in the case of a stock purchase where a section 338(h)(10) election is made, the purchasing corporation and the selling consolidated group must report information with respect to the consideration received in the transaction at such times and in such manner as may be provided in regulations promulgated under section 338. [*See* § 338(h)(10)(C).] The reporting rules apply regardless of whether the transaction constitutes an applicable asset acquisition within the meaning of section 1060.

3. The 1999 Proposed Regulations: The § 338(h)(10) for a Consolidated Sub

Preamble to Proposed Regulations

August 10, 1999, 64 F.R. 43462 [Treasury Decision 8940, Feb. 13, 2001, finalized these regulations substantially in the form discussed here.]

Explanation of Provisions * * * Section *1.338(h)(10)-1 Deemed Asset Sale and Liquidation. Model.* The proposed regulations explain the effects of the section 338(h)(10) election on the parties involved. The proposed regulations discuss the effects of the section 338(h)(10) election on the purchasing corporation, the effects on new target, the effects on old target, and the effects on old target's shareholders (including non-selling shareholders).

As with the rest of the proposed regulations, proposed § 1.338(h)(10)-1 describes the model on which taxation of the section 338(h)(10) election is based. Under the proposed regulations, old target is treated as transferring all of its assets by sale to an unrelated person. Old target recognizes the deemed sale gain while a member of the selling consolidated group, or owned by the selling affiliate, or owned by the S corporation shareholders (both those who actually sell their shares and any who do not). Old target is then treated as transferring all of its assets to members of the selling consolidated group, the selling affiliate, or S corporation shareholders and ceasing to exist. If target is an S corporation, the deemed asset sale and deemed liquidation are considered as occurring while it is still an S corporation. The proposed regulations treat all parties concerned as if the fictions the section 338(h)(10) regulations deem to occur actually did occur, or as closely thereto as possible. The structure of this model should help taxpayers answer any questions not explicitly addressed by the proposed regulations. Also, old target generally is barred by the proposed regulations from obtaining any tax benefit from the section 338(h)(10) election that it would not obtain if it actually sold its assets and liquidated.

The treatment of S corporation targets which own one or more qualified subchapter S subsidiaries (as defined in section 1361(b)(3)) is also addressed, as is the treatment of tiered targets (*i.e.*, the order of their deemed asset sales and deemed liquidations).

Deemed Liquidation. The current regulations provide that, when a section 338(h)(10) election is made, old target is deemed to sell all of its assets and distribute the proceeds in complete liquidation. The term *complete liquidation* is generally considered to be a term of art in tax law. The proposed regulations instead provide that old target transferred all of its assets to members of the selling consolidated group, the selling affiliate, or S corporation shareholders and ceased to exist, making it clear that the transaction following the deemed asset sale does not automatically qualify as a distribution in complete liquidation under either section 331 or 332. This is meant to clarify any inference one might draw from previous regulations that section 332 treatment is automatic under section 338(h)(10) in the case of an affiliated or consolidated group. For example, if S owns all of the stock of T, T is insolvent because of its indebtedness to S, P acquires T from S in a qualified stock purchase, and, as a condition of the sale, S cancels the debt owed it by T, and P and S make a section 338(h)(10) election for target, T's deemed liquidation would not qualify under section 332 because S would not be considered to receive anything in return for its stock in T. Rev. Rul. 68-602, 1968-2 C.B. 135. * * *

C. Introductory Problems on Impact of §338 on Acquisition of Subsidiaries

1. Parent Corporation (*PC*) organized Subsidiary Corporation (*SC*) on January 1, 2016 and contributed $100K to *SC*. *PC* and *SC* file consolidated returns and are on the calendar year. During 2016, *SC* had a separate taxable loss of $150K, all of which was deducted by *PC* on the consolidated return. *SC* had a deficit in E & P for the year of $100K. The $50K difference was attributable to accelerated depreciation. On January 1, 2017, *PC* sells the stock of *SC* for $200K in cash. How much gain or loss does *PC* realize and recognize on the sale?

2. The facts are the same as in Question 1, except during 2016, *SC* realized a separate taxable loss of $60K, and had a deficit in earnings and profits of $50K. The $10K difference was attributable to accelerated depreciation. *SC* has a $40K basis for its assets. *AC* is considering the purchase of *SC*'s stock or assets for $200K.

    a. What result to *AC, SC,* and *PC,* if *SC* sells its assets for $200K and then liquidates?

    b. What result to *AC, SC,* and *PC,* if *AC* purchases the stock of *SC* for $200K and the parties file a §338(h)(10) election?

    c. What result to *AC, SC,* and *PC,* if *AC* purchases the stock of *SC* for $200K, and *AC* then makes a regular §338 election for *SC*?

D. Treatment of Dividend from Sub before Parent Sells Sub's Stock

Litton Industries, Inc. v. Commissioner

Tax Court of the United States, 1987
89 T.C. 1086

CLAPP, JUDGE:

After concessions, the issue for decision is whether Litton Industries received a $30,000,000 dividend from Stouffer Corporation, its wholly owned subsidiary, or whether that sum represented proceeds from the sale of Stouffer stock to Nestle Corporation.

Opinion The issue for decision is whether the $30,000,000 dividend declared by Stouffer on August 23, 1972, and paid to its parent, Litton by means of a negotiable promissory note was truly a dividend for tax purposes or whether it should be considered part of the proceeds received by Litton from the sale of all of Stouffer's stock on March 1, 1973. If, as petitioner contends, the $30,000,000 constitutes a dividend, petitioner may deduct 85 percent of that amount as a dividend received credit pursuant to section 243(a), as that section read during the year at issue. However, if the $30,000,000 represents part of the selling price of the Stouffer stock, as contended by respondent, the entire amount will be added to the proceeds of the sale and taxed to Litton as additional capital gain. Respondent's approach, of course produces the larger amount of tax dollars.

The instant case is substantially governed by *Waterman Steamship Corp. v. Commissioner*, 50 T.C. 650 (1968), revd. 430 F.2d 1185 (5th Cir.1970), cert. denied 401 U.S. 939 (1971). Respondent urges us to follow the opinion of the Fifth Circuit, which in substance adopted the position of Judge Tannenwald's dissent (concurred in by three other judges) from our Court-reviewed opinion. If we hold for respondent, we must overrule our majority opinion in Waterman Steamship. Petitioner contends that the reasoning of the Fifth Circuit in Waterman Steamship should not apply since the facts here are more favorable to petitioner. Additionally, petitioner points out that several business purposes were served by the distribution here which provide additional support for recognition of the distribution as a dividend. For the reasons set forth below, we conclude that the $30,000,000 distribution constituted a dividend which should be recognized as such for tax purposes. We believe that the facts in the instant case lead even more strongly than did the facts in *Waterman Steamship* to the conclusion that the $30,000,000 was a dividend. Accordingly, we hold that the Stouffer distribution to Litton was a dividend within the meaning of section 243(a).

In many respects, the facts of this case and those of *Waterman Steamship* are parallel. The principal difference, and the one which we find to be most significant, is the timing of the dividend action. In *Waterman Steamship*, the taxpayer corporation received an offer to purchase the stock of two of its wholly-owned subsidiary corporations, Pan-Atlantic and Gulf Florida, for $3,500,000 cash. The board of directors of Waterman Steamship rejected that offer but countered with an offer to sell the two subsidiaries for $700,000 after the subsidiaries declared and arranged for payments of dividends to Waterman Steamship amounting in the aggregate to $2,800,000. Negotiations between the parties ensued, and the agreements which resulted therefrom included, in specific detail, provisions for the declaration of a dividend by Pan-Atlantic to Waterman Steamship prior to the signing of the sales agreement and the closing of that transaction. Furthermore, the agreements called for the purchaser to loan or otherwise advance funds to Pan-Atlantic promptly in order to pay off the promissory note by which the dividend had been paid. Once the agreement was reached, the entire transaction was carried out by a series of meetings commencing at 12 noon on January 21, 1955, and ending at 1:30 p.m. the same day. At the first meeting the board of directors of Pan-Atlantic met and declared a dividend in the form of a promissory note in the amount of $2,799,820. The dividend was paid by execution and delivery of the promissory note. At 12:30 p.m., the board of directors of the purchaser's nominee corporation ('Securities') met and authorized the purchase and financing of Pan-Atlantic and Gulf Florida. At 1 p.m., the directors of Waterman authorized the sale of all outstanding stock of Pan-Atlantic and Gulf Florida to Securities. Immediately following that meeting, the sales agreement was executed by the parties. The agreement provided that the purchaser guaranteed prompt payment of the liabilities of Pan-Atlantic and Gulf Florida including payment of any notes given by either corporation as a dividend.

Finally at 1:30 p.m., the new board of directors of Pan-Atlantic authorized the borrowing of sufficient funds from the purchaser personally and from his nominee corporation to pay off the promissory note to Waterman Steamship, which was done forthwith. As the Fifth Circuit pointed out, "By the end of the day and within a ninety minute period, the financial cycle had been completed. Waterman had $3,500,000, hopefully tax-free, all of which came from Securities and McLean, the buyers of the stock." This Court concluded that the distribution from Pan-Atlantic to Waterman was a dividend. The Fifth Circuit reversed, concluding that the dividend and sale were one transaction.

The timing in the instant case was markedly different. The dividend was declared by Stouffer on August 23, 1972, at which time the promissory note in payment of the dividend was issued to Litton. There had been some general preliminary discussions about the sale of Stouffer, and it was expected that Stouffer would be a very marketable company which would sell quickly. However, at the time the dividend was declared, no formal action had been taken to initiate the sale of Stouffer. It was not until 2 weeks later that Litton publicly announced that Stouffer was for sale. There ensued over the next 6 months many discussions with various corporations, investment banking houses, business brokers, and underwriters regarding Litton's disposition of Stouffer through sale of all or part of the business to a particular buyer, or through full or partial public offerings of the Stouffer stock. All of this culminated on March 1, 1973, over 6 months after the dividend was declared, with the purchase by Nestle of all of Stouffer's stock. Nestle also purchased the outstanding promissory note for $30,000,000 in cash.

In the instant case, the declaration of the dividend and the sale of the stock were substantially separated in time in contrast to *Waterman Steamship* where the different transactions occurred essentially simultaneously. In *Waterman Steamship*, it seems quite clear that no dividend would have been declared if all of the remaining steps in the transaction had not been lined up in order on the closing table and did not in fact take place. Here, however, Stouffer declared the dividend, issued the promissory note and definitely committed itself to the dividend before even making a public announcement that Stouffer was for sale. * * *

Since the facts here are distinguishable in important respects and are so much stronger in petitioner's favor, we do not consider it necessary to consider further the opinion of the Fifth Circuit in *Waterman Steamship.*

The term "dividend" is defined in section 316(a) as a distribution by a corporation to its shareholders out of earnings and profits. The parties have stipulated that Stouffer had earnings and profits exceeding $30,000,000 at the time the dividend was declared. This Court has recognized that a dividend may be paid by a note. Based on these criteria, the $30,000,000 distribution by Stouffer would clearly constitute a dividend if the sale of Stouffer had not occurred. We are not persuaded that the subsequent sale of Stouffer to Nestle changes that result merely because it was more advantageous to Litton from a tax perspective. * * *

Under these facts, where the dividend was declared 6 months prior to the sale of Stouffer, where the sale was not prearranged, and since Stouffer had earnings and profits exceeding $30,000,000 at the time the dividend was declared, we cannot conclude that the distribution was merely a device designed to give the appearance of a dividend to a part of the sales proceeds. In this case the form and substance of the transaction coincide; it was not a transaction entered into solely for tax reasons, and it should be recognized as structured by petitioner.

On this record, we hold that for Federal tax purposes Stouffer declared a dividend to petitioner on August 23, 1972, and, subsequently, petitioner sold all of its stock in Stouffer to Nestle for $75,000,000.

Decision will be entered under Rule 155.

Problems

Parent Corporation (*PC*) owns 70% of the stock of Target Corporation (*TC*), and *PC* has a basis of $70K for this stock. *TC* has operating assets with a value of $100K and cash of $100K. *TC* has $200K of E & P. The value of all of *TC*'s stock is $200K, and the value of the stock held by *PC* is $140K. Acquiring corporation (*AC*) has offered to purchase the stock of *TC* held by *PC* for $140K.

(a) What would be the tax impact on *PC* if it sold the *TC* stock to *AC* for $140K, assuming a 34% corporate tax rate?

(b) Suppose instead that *PC* countered with an offer to first cause *TC* to distribute as a dividend to its shareholders the $100K in cash *TC* holds, with PC receiving its $70K ratable share of this cash. *PC* would then sell to *AC* for $70K, the shares *PC* owns in the stripped-down *TC*, which has $100K of operating assets only. *AC* accepted the offer. What is the tax impact on *PC* upon receipt of the dividend and the sale of the stock?

(c) How can *PC* ensure that the transaction in (b) will be taxed in accordance with its form?

(d) What is the impact on the above transaction of § 1059, which reduces basis in stock on the receipt of certain extraordinary dividends?

§ 5.6 Mirror Subsidiaries, Related Transactions, and the Disallowance of Loss Consolidated Return Regulations[*]

A. In General

As discussed in Chapter 2, the Tax Reform Act of 1986 authorizes the Treasury to promulgate regulations as "may be necessary or appropriate to carry out the purposes" of §§ 336 and 337. *See* § 337(d). The authority includes (1) regulations to ensure that the general recognition rule of § 336 is not circumvented through the use of any provision of law or regulations (including the consolidated return regulations and the reorganization provisions), or through the use of a regulated investment company, real estate investment trust or tax exempt entity, and (2) regulations providing for coordination of the liquidation provisions with the provisions relating to taxation of foreign corporations and their shareholders.

Prior to the Revenue Act of 1987 (RA 1987), several corporate transactions arguably avoided a corporate level tax on a disposition of part of a target corporation's assets following the acquisition of the target corporation. Thus, these transactions could avoid the effect of the repeal of the *General Utilities* doctrine. The four basic transactions were: (1) the mirror subsidiary acquisition, (2) the son of mirrors, (3) the § 304 sale, and (4) the § 355 spin-off transaction. The RA 1987 eliminates the tax advantages of the mirror subsidiary acquisition (*see* Sec. 5.6.B), the § 304 sale (*see* Chapter 2) and the § 355 spin-off transaction. *See* Chapter 9. The regulations under the consolidated return provisions eliminate the use of the son of mirrors transactions and other variants of the mirror. These regulations are introduced below.

B. The Prototypical Mirror

Prior to the RA 1987, a typical mirror transaction was structured on the assumption that the transaction qualified as a § 337 liquidation of a controlled subsidiary. Section 337(a) provides that "[n]o gain or loss [is] recognized to the liquidating corporation

---

[*] Based on §§ 14:17 to 14:28 of *Federal Taxation of Business Enterprises, supra* Chapter 1, note 1, with permission.

on the distribution to the 80-percent distributee of any property in a complete liquidation to which section 332 applies." *See* Chapter 2. The following example illustrates a standard mirror subsidiary transaction. Assume that a target corporation had two divisions, each having assets with a fair market value of $10 million and an adjusted basis of $1 million. The acquiring corporation planned to purchase the target's stock for $20 million and wanted to sell Division No. 2. In order to avoid gain on the proposed sale of Division No. 2, the acquiring corporation, prior to the purchase of target's stock, formed two subsidiaries, Sub 1 and Sub 2 and capitalized each with $10 million. Subs 1 and 2 each purchased $10 million of target's stock, and target then liquidated distributing the assets of Division 1 to Sub 1 and the assets of Division 2 to Sub 2. Under the stock aggregation rules in § 1.1502-34 of the consolidated return regulations, the liquidation of the target qualified as a liquidation under § 332. Consequently, neither Subs 1 and 2 nor the target recognized gain on the liquidation. In addition, Subs 1 and 2 took a carryover basis under § 334(b) for the assets received. After the liquidation, the acquiring corporation sold the stock of Sub 2 for $10 million, and recognized no gain or loss because the acquiring corporation's basis for the stock of Sub 2 was $10 million.

Prior to the RA 1987, it was uncertain whether the Treasury would promulgate regulations under its general regulatory authority of § 337(d) to repeal or limit the stock aggregation rules of the consolidated return regulations in order to deny § 337 liquidation treatment for the target corporation. If the liquidation of the target corporation did not qualify as a liquidation under § 332, then the target would recognize gain or loss on the liquidating distribution. An amendment to § 337(c) by the RA 1987 eliminates the mirror subsidiary transaction.

The amendment provides that the determination of whether a parent is an "80% distributee" and, therefore, qualifies for § 337 nonrecognition treatment is made without regard to the consolidated return regulations.

C. The Son of Mirror Transaction

Notice 87-14

1987-1 C.B. 445

* * * The Internal Revenue Service intends to promulgate regulations affecting certain adjustments to the basis of the stock of a subsidiary that is a member of an affiliated group of corporations filing a consolidated return. In general, the adjustments affected are among those made pursuant to the investment adjustment provisions of the consolidated return regulations (section 1.1502-32 of the Income Tax Regulations). The investment adjustment regulations provide for certain positive or negative adjustments to the basis of the stock of a subsidiary based generally on the subsidiary's earnings and profits. The adjustments to stock basis are intended to reflect changes in a group's investment in the stock of a subsidiary, so that income or loss previously included in a group's consolidated taxable income is not reflected a second time on the sale of a subsidiary's stock.

The regulations to be promulgated will affect the adjustment to stock basis in certain cases where one or more members have acquired stock of a target with a built-in gain asset, that is, an asset that at the time of the acquisition of target stock has a fair market value in excess of its adjusted basis. In general, the adjustment to stock basis will not reflect built-in gains that are recognized by target on sales of, or by reason of distributions of, its assets. Thus, in cases where a target's stock is sold, the regulations will prevent recognition of losses that are attributable to the subsidiary's recognition of built-in gains. * * *

D. Anti-Mirror Regulations: Disallowance of Loss on Dispositions of Subsidiaries*

1. Introduction and Purpose

This section introduces the purposes and scope of (1) the basic disallowance of loss rule as originally reflected in § 1.1502-20 and as of March 7, 2002 reflected in § 1.337(d)-2T, and (2) the allowable loss exception to the disallowance of loss rule. The discussion refers to the preambles of the following disallowance of loss regulations:

(1) The 1990 initial Regulations (T.D. 8294, March 9, 1990),

(2) The 1990 Proposed Regulations (CO-93-90 Nov. 20, 1990),

(3) The 1991 Final Regulations (T.D. 8364 Sept. 19, 1991), and

(4) The 2002 Final and Temporary Regulations (T.D. 8984, March 7, 2002).

The preamble to the 1990 initial Regulations explains that the principal purpose of the repeal of the *General Utilities* doctrine by the Tax Reform Act of 1986 was to "require the payment of a corporate level tax in a transaction that results in a stepped-up basis to the new owner" and that the investment adjustment rules in the consolidated return Regulations are inconsistent with the repeal of the *General Utilities* doctrine because in certain cases they can be used to "obtain a stepped-up basis in corporate assets without the payment of corporate level tax." As will be seen below, the 1991 Final Regulations were replaced in 2002 with new Final and Temporary Regulations as a result of the decision in the *Rite Aid* case, which held that the loss duplication provisions of the disallowance of loss rule were invalid.

2. Investment Adjustments Inconsistent with Repeal of General Utilities

The preamble to the 1990 initial Regulations gives the following example and explanation of how the investment adjustment Regulations can undermine the purposes behind the repeal of the *General Utilities* doctrine:

> Corporation S has one asset with a basis of 0 and a value of $100. Corporation P buys all the stock of S for $100 and P and S elect to file consolidated returns. S then sells the asset for $100 and recognizes gain of $100.

---

* Based on §§ 4:17 to 14:28 of *Federal Taxation of Business Enterprises, supra* Chapter 1, Note 1, with permission.

Under the investment adjustment rules, P's basis in the stock of S is increased to $200 because the sale of the asset generated $100 of earnings and profits to S. This basis increase permits P to recognize a loss of $100 if P sells the S stock, thus offsetting the gain on the sale of the asset.

The increase in the basis of P's stock in S is inconsistent with the repeal of the *General Utilities* doctrine. The failure to require the P group to fully account for S's recognized built-in gain in effect permits the elimination of corporate-level tax on the gain, because the increase in P's basis for the S stock is attributable to S's recognition of built-in gain (gain already reflected in P's cost basis for the S stock) and not to earnings that increase S's value. Moreover, P's loss does not represent an economic loss of either P or S. * * *

3. Loss Disallowance Rule

After surveying various ways of dealing with this type of problem the preamble to the initial Regulations explains the purpose and effect of the adoption of the loss disallowance rule:

> The regulations retain the present investment adjustment rules, but disallow any loss on the sale or other disposition by a member of the stock of a subsidiary. This loss disallowance rule eliminates the possibility that gain recognized on the disposition or consumption of an acquired subsidiary's built-in gain assets can be offset by a loss at the parent level created by an investment adjustment caused by the subsidiary's recognition of built-in gain.

The disallowance of loss rule is examined in Sec. 5.6.D.5.

4. Economic Losses

The preamble to the 1990 Proposed Regulations explains that the initial Regulations were heavily criticized because they would have disallowed deductions of real economic losses:

> Virtually all commentators criticized § 1.1502-20 for disallowing loss on the sale of subsidiary stock when the loss results from the subsidiary's decline in value rather than from investment adjustments attributable to recognition of built-in-gain. The commentary centered on Example (6) in the preamble, which provided the following illustration:
>
> Corporation S has one asset with a basis of $0 and a value of $100. Corporation P buys all the stock of S for $100 and P and S elect to file consolidated returns. S's asset declines in value and is sold for $0. Because S's sale of its asset results in no gain or loss, P's basis in S remains $100. P then sells S for $0 and recognizes a loss of $100. The loss is disallowed by the loss disallowance rule.
>
> The preamble states that, while it may be argued that loss should be allowed under these facts, an exception would require appraisals of assets (including assets of any lower tier subsidiary) and tracing of built-in-gains and losses, thus imposing the very compliance and administrative burdens on taxpayers and the Internal Revenue Service that the loss disallowance rule was designed

to avoid. The commentators maintained that disallowance of loss in this situation is unwarranted because the parent corporation has realized an economic loss. * * *

The preamble to the Proposed Regulations goes on to explain that the Proposed Regulations now allow real economic losses:

> The Treasury Department and the Internal Revenue Service have determined, however, that the loss disallowance rule can be modified, consistent with implementation of *General Utilities* repeal, to permit loss to a limited extent. The modifications to the rule are intended to distinguish loss of unrealized built-in-gain from both loss attributable to recognized built-in-gain and loss duplication. In order to avoid tracing, the modified rule necessarily operates by the use of presumptions.

Economic losses are allowed under the allowable loss rule. *See* Sec. 5.6.D.6.

5. General Loss Disallowance Rule under § 1.1502-20(a)

Under the general rule of § 1.1502-20(a) as adopted in the 1991 Final Regulations, no deduction was allowed for any loss recognized by a member of a consolidated group on the disposition of the stock of a subsidiary. The term disposition is defined as "any event in which gain or loss is recognized, in whole or in part."

The 1991 Final Regulations had numerous examples illustrating the operation of the loss disallowance rule, including the following two examples:

> **Example (1).** *Loss attributable to recognized built-in-gain. P* buys all the stock of *T* for $100, and *T* becomes a member of the *P* group. *T* has an asset with a basis of $0 and a value of $100. *T* sells the asset for $100. Under the investment adjustment system, *P*'s basis in the *T* stock increases to $200. Five years later, *P* sells all the *T* stock for $100 and recognizes a loss of $100. Under [the loss disallowance rule], no deduction is allowed to *P* for the $100 loss.

> **Example (2).** *Effect of post-acquisition appreciation. P* buys all the stock of *T* for $100, and *T* becomes a member of the *P* group. *T* has an asset with a basis of $0 and a value of $100. *T* sells the asset for $100. Under the investment adjustment system, *P*'s basis in the *T* stock increases to $200. *T* reinvests the proceeds of the sale in an asset that appreciates in value to $180. Five years after the sales, *P* sells all the stock of *T* for $180 and recognizes a $20 loss. Under [the loss disallowance rule], no deduction is allowed to *P* for the $20 loss. *See* § 1.1502-20(a)(5), Examples (1) and (2).

6. Allowable Losses under § 1.1502-20(c): Allowing Economic Losses

The preamble to the 1991 Final Regulations gave the following introduction to the Allowable Loss Rule, the purpose of which was to permit a parent to deduct economic losses on the disposition of the stock of a subsidiary:

> Section 1.1502-20(c) allows loss to the extent it exceeds an amount determined by a formula: (i) E & P from extraordinary gain dispositions (extra-

ordinary gain factor); (ii) positive investment adjustments in excess of the amount described in (i) (positive adjustment factor); and (iii) duplicated loss (loss duplication factor). The formula is designed to protect against the elimination of corporate level tax while permitting economic loss to the extent feasible without tracing. [See § 1.1502-20(c)(1).]

The 1991 Final Regulations contain several illustrations of the allowable loss rule including the following:

> **Example (1).** *Allowed loss attributable to lost built-in-gain.* (i) Individual *A* forms *T*. *P* buys all the stock of *T* from *A* for $100, and *T* becomes a member of the *P* group. *T* has a capital asset with a basis of $0 and a value of $100. The value of the asset declines, and *T* sells the asset for $40. Under the investment adjustment system, *P*'s basis in the *T* stock increases to $140. *P* then sells all the stock of *T* for $40 and recognizes a loss of $100.
>
> (ii) The amount of the $100 loss disallowed under [the loss disallowance rule] may not exceed the amount determined under, [the allowable loss rule]. The $40 of *T*'s earnings and profits is from an extraordinary gain disposition * * *. Because this amount is the only amount described in paragraph (c)(1), of this section, the amount of *P*'s $100 loss that is disallowed under [the loss disallowance rule] is limited to $40. *See* § 1.1502-20(c)(4), Example (1).

Thus, in the above example the parent corporation is allowed its economic loss of $60, which is the difference between what the parent paid for the stock of the subsidiary and the value of such stock at the time of the sale. This loss is not attributable to built-in gain.

7. Treasury's Reaction to Rite Aid

Notice 2002-11

2002-7, I.R.B. 526

This Notice sets forth the Internal Revenue Service's position with respect to the opinion of the U.S. Court of Appeals for the Federal Circuit in *Rite Aid Corp, supra*, and the loss disallowance rules that apply to sales of stock of a member of a consolidated group.

In *Rite Aid*, the Federal Circuit held that the duplicated loss component of § 1.1502-20, which disallows certain losses on sales of stock of a member of a consolidated group, was an invalid exercise of regulatory authority. The Internal Revenue Service believes that the court's analysis and holding were incorrect.

Nevertheless, the Service has decided that the interests of sound tax administration will not be served by continuing to litigate the validity of the loss duplication factor of § 1.1502-20. Moreover, because of the interrelationship in the operation of all of the loss disallowance factors, the Service has decided that new rules governing loss disallowance on sales of stock of a member of a consolidated group should be implemented.

Accordingly, the Service intends to promulgate interim regulations that, prospectively from the date of their issuance, will require consolidated groups to determine the allowable loss on a sale or disposition of subsidiary stock under an amended § 1.337(d)-2 instead of under § 1.1502-20. * * * The Service and Treasury are undertaking a broader study of the regulatory provisions necessary to implement § 337(d) in the context of affiliated groups filing consolidated returns and will request comments in conjunction with the issuance of the interim regulations.

It is the Service's position that the *Rite Aid* opinion implicates only the loss duplication aspect of the loss disallowance regulation and that the authority to prescribe consolidated return regulations conferred on the Secretary is limited only by the requirement that the Secretary, in his discretion, has determined such rules necessary clearly to reflect consolidated tax liability.

8. Preamble to 2002 New Loss Disallowance Rules

Preamble to Final and Temporary Regulations

Treasury Decision 8984 (March 2, 2002)

Summary This document contains regulations under sections 337(d) and 1502. These regulations permit certain losses recognized on sales of subsidiary stock by members of a consolidated group. These regulations apply to corporations filing consolidated returns, both during and after the period of affiliation, and also affect purchasers of the stock of members of a consolidated group. * * *

Explanation of Provisions. This Treasury decision adds §§ 1.337(d)-2T, 1.1502-20T(i), and 1.1502-32T(b)(4)(v), as described below.

For dispositions and deconsolidations of subsidiary stock on or after March 7, 2002, * * * this Treasury decision provides that § 1.337(d)-2T, and not § 1.1502-20, governs the amount of loss allowable on such sales, or the amount of basis reduction required on such deconsolidations, of subsidiary stock. In substantial part, § 1.337(d)-2T restates the current § 1.337(d)-2, with certain modifications. As described above, as currently in effect, § 1.337(d)-2 permits recognition of loss only where a consolidated group disposes of its entire equity interest in a member of the group to persons not related to any member of the consolidated group within the meaning of section 267(b) or section 707(b)(1) (applying the language "10 percent" instead of "50 percent"). Section 1.337(d)-2T eliminates those restrictions. * * *

9. The 2002 Regulations under § 1.337(d)-2T

§ 1.337(d)-2T Loss limitation window period (temporary).

(a) Loss disallowance—(1) General rule. No deduction is allowed for any loss recognized by a member of a consolidated group with respect to the disposition of stock of a subsidiary.

(2) Definitions. For purposes of this section:

(i) The definitions in § 1.1502-1 apply.

(ii) Disposition means any event in which gain or loss is recognized, in whole or in part.

(3) Coordination with loss deferral and other disallowance rules. For purposes of this section, the rules of § 1.1502-20(a)(3) apply, with appropriate adjustments to reflect differences between the approach of this section and that of § 1.1502-20.

(b) Basis reduction on deconsolidation—(1) General rule. If the basis of a member of a consolidated group in a share of stock of a subsidiary exceeds its value immediately before a deconsolidation of the share, the basis of the share is reduced at that time to an amount equal to its value. If both a disposition and a deconsolidation occur with respect to a share in the same transaction, paragraph (a) of this section applies and, to the extent necessary to effectuate the purposes of this section, this paragraph (b) applies following the application of paragraph (a) of this section.

(2) Deconsolidation. Deconsolidation means any event that causes a share of stock of a subsidiary that remains outstanding to be no longer owned by a member of any consolidated group of which the subsidiary is also a member.

(3) Value. Value means fair market value.

(c) Allowable Loss—(1) Application. This paragraph (c) applies with respect to stock of a subsidiary only if a separate statement entitled "§ 1.337(d)-2T(c) statement" is included with the return in accordance with paragraph (c)(3) of this section.

(2) General rule. Loss is not disallowed under paragraph (a)(1) of this section and basis is not reduced under paragraph (b)(1) of this section to the extent the taxpayer establishes that the loss or basis is not attributable to the recognition of built-in gain on the disposition of an asset (including stock and securities). Loss or basis may be attributable to the recognition of built-in gain on the disposition of an asset by a prior group. For purposes of this section, gain recognized on the disposition of an asset is built-in gain to the extent attributable, directly or indirectly, in whole or in part, to any excess of value over basis that is reflected, before the disposition of the asset, in the basis of the share, directly or indirectly, in whole or in part, after applying section 1503(e) and other applicable provisions of the Internal Revenue Code and regulations.

(3) Contents of statement and time of filing. The statement required under paragraph (c)(1) of this section must be included with or as part of the taxpayer's return for the year of the disposition or deconsolidation and must contain:

(i) The name and employer identification number (E.I.N.) of the subsidiary.

(ii) The amount of the loss not disallowed under paragraph (a)(1) of this section by reason of this paragraph (c) and the amount of basis not reduced under paragraph (b)(1) of this section by reason of this paragraph (c).

(4) Example. The principles of paragraphs (a), (b), and (c) of this section are illustrated by the examples in §§ 1.337(d)-1(a)(5) and 1.1502-20(a)(5) (other than Examples 3, 4, and 5) and (b), with appropriate adjustments to

reflect differences between the approach of this section and that of § 1.1502-20, and by the following example. For purposes of the examples in this section, unless otherwise stated, the group files consolidated returns on a calendar year basis, the facts set forth the only corporate activity, and all sales and purchases are with unrelated buyers or sellers. The basis of each asset is the same for determining earnings and profits adjustments and taxable income. Tax liability and its effect on basis, value, and earnings and profits are disregarded. Investment adjustment system means the rules of § 1.1502-32.

Example. Loss offsetting built-in gain in a prior group.

(i) P buys all the stock of T for $50 in Year 1, and T becomes a member of the P group. T has 2 assets. Asset 1 has a basis of $50 and a value of $0, and asset 2 has a basis of $0 and a value of $50. T sells asset 2 during Year 3 for $50, and recognizes a $50 gain. Under the investment adjustment system, P's basis in the T stock increased to $100 as a result of the recognition of gain. In Year 5, all of the stock of P is acquired by the P1 group, and the former members of the P group become members of the P1 group. T then sells asset 1 for $0, and recognizes a $50 loss. Under the investment adjustment system, P's basis in the T stock decreases to $50 as a result of the loss. T's assets decline in value from $50 to $40. P then sells all the stock of T for $40 and recognizes a $10 loss.

(ii) P's basis in the T stock reflects both T's unrecognized gain and unrecognized loss with respect to its assets. The gain T recognizes on the disposition of asset 2 is built-in gain with respect to both the P and the P1 groups for purposes of paragraph (c)(2) of this section. In addition, the loss T recognizes on the disposition of asset 2 is built-in loss with respect to the P and P1 groups for purposes of paragraph (c)(2) of this section. T's recognition of the built-in loss while a member of the P1 group offsets the effect on T's stock basis of T's recognition of the built-in gain while a member of the P group. Thus, P's $10 loss on the sale of the T stock is not attributable to the recognition of built-in gain, and the loss is therefore not disallowed under paragraph (c)(2) of this section.

(iii) The result would be the same if, instead of having a $50 built-in loss in asset 2 when it becomes a member of the P group, T has a $50 net operating loss carryover and the carryover is used by the P group.

(d) *Successors.* For purposes of this section, the rules and examples of § 1.1502-20(d) apply, with appropriate adjustments to reflect differences between the approach of this section and that of § 1.1502-20.

(e) *Anti-avoidance rules.* For purposes of this section, the rules and examples of § 1.1502-20(e) apply, with appropriate adjustments to reflect differences between the approach of this section and that of § 1.1502-20.

(f) *Investment adjustments.* For purposes of this section, the rules and examples of § 1.1502-20(f) apply, with appropriate adjustments to reflect differences between the approach of this section and that of § 1.1502-20.

(g) Effective dates. This section [generally] applies with respect to dispositions and deconsolidations on or after March 7, 2002. * * *

10. The American Jobs Creation Act of 2004 Clarification of the Rite Aid Decision

The Senate's JOBS Act of 2003 contains the following provision that would amend Section 1502 with regard to the *Rite Aide* case. The provision was enacted by the American Jobs Creation Act of 2004.

Reasons For Change. The Committee is concerned that Treasury Department resources might be unnecessarily devoted to defending challenges to consolidated return regulations on the mere assertion by a taxpayer that the result under the consolidated return regulations is different than the result for separate taxpayers. The consolidated return regulations offer many benefits that are not available to separate taxpayers, including generally rules that tax income received by the group once and attempt to avoid a second tax on that same income when stock of a subsidiary is sold. The existing statute authorizes adjustments to clearly reflect the income of the group and of the separate members of the group, during and after the period of affiliation. The Committee believes that this standard, which is stated in the present law statute, should be reiterated.

Explanation of Provision. The bill confirms that, in exercising its authority under section 1502 to issue consolidated return regulations, the Treasury Department may provide rules treating corporations filing consolidated returns differently from corporations filing separate returns.

Thus, under the statutory authority of section 1502, the Treasury Department is authorized to issue consolidated return regulations utilizing either a single taxpayer or separate taxpayer approach or a combination of the two approaches, as Treasury deems necessary in order that the tax liability of any affiliated group of corporations making a consolidated return, and of each corporation in the group, both during and after the period of affiliation, may be determined and adjusted in such manner as clearly to reflect the income-tax liability and the various factors necessary for the determination of such liability, and in order to prevent avoidance of such liability. *Rite Aid* is thus overruled to the extent it suggests that the Secretary is required to identify a problem created from the filing of consolidated returns in order to issue regulations that change the application of a Code provision. The Secretary may promulgate consolidated return regulations to change the application of a tax code provision to members of a consolidated group, provided that such regulations are necessary to clearly reflect the income tax liability of the group and each corporation in the group, both during and after the period of affiliation.

The bill nevertheless allows the result of the *Rite Aid* case to stand with respect to the type of factual situation presented in the case. That is, the legislation provides for the override of the regulatory provision that took the approach of denying a loss on a deconsolidating disposition of stock of a consolidated subsidiary to the extent the subsidiary had net operating losses or built in losses that could be used later outside the group.

Retaining the result in the *Rite Aid* case with respect to the particular regulation section 1.1502-20(c)(1)(iii) as applied to the factual situation of the case does not in any way prevent or invalidate the various approaches Treasury has announced it will apply or that it intends to consider in lieu of the approach of that regulation, including, for example, the denial of a loss on a stock sale if inside losses of a subsidiary may also be used by the consolidated group, and the possible requirement that inside attributes be adjusted when a subsidiary leaves a group.

11. Introductory Problems on the 2002 Disallowance of Loss Rule

1. Parent Corporation (*PC*) forms Subsidiary Corporation (*SC*) on January 1, 2016 by contributing to *SC* $100K in cash. *PC* and *SC* file consolidated returns. For calendar year 2016, *SC* has a separate taxable loss of $50K, all of which is deducted by *PC* on the consolidated return. *SC* also had a deficit of $50K in its E & P for the year. What result if on January 1, 2017, *PC* sells all of the stock of *SC* for $30K?

2. The facts are the same as in Question 1, except that on January 1, 2017, *PC* sells all of the stock of *SC* to Acquiring Corporation (*AC*) for $100K. What result to *PC*? *SC* is included in *AC*'s consolidated return, which is filed on a calendar year basis. For 2017, *SC* breaks even, except for the sale of one of its two divisions for $50K. The division had a basis of $25K, and therefore, *SC* had a taxable gain from the sale of $25K. *SC* had E & P of $25K from this disposition. On January 1, 2005, *AC* sells the stock of *SC* for $60K. What result to *AC*?

3. The facts are the same as in Question 2, except *SC* did not sell its division. What result to *AC* if on January 1, 2018, *AC* sells all of *SC*'s stock for $60K?

§5.7 Planning for the Utilization of the Target's Net Operating Losses and Other Attributes

In a stock acquisition of a target, the net operating losses (NOLs) and other tax attributes of the target stay with the target unless a §338 election is made. *See* Sec. 5.8.C. Thus, if after the acquisition of all of the stock of a target, no §338 election is made, the target's tax attributes continue even though there has been a change in control of the target. If a §338 election is made, as a result of the deemed sale and reacquisition of the target's assets, the target's attributes no longer exist, and the target has a new basis for its assets.

As will be seen below, any pre-acquisition net operating loss carryovers and capital loss carryovers of the target can be utilized to offset any gain realized by the target as a result of the §338 election. *See* §382(h)(1)(C). In view of the repeal of the *General Utilities* doctrine, it generally is beneficial to make a §338 election for a non-subsidiary target only if the target has sufficient net operating losses to offset the §338 gain.

Assuming a §338 election is not made, several provisions govern the utilization of the target's pre-acquisition net operating loss carryovers, capital loss carryovers, foreign tax credit carryovers and excess credits. The most important provisions governing the utilization of these items are §§ 382 and 383. Section 382 limits the deductibility of a target's pre-acquisition net operating loss carryovers, and § 383 provides similar limitations for a target's capital loss carryovers, foreign tax credit carryovers and excess credits. The discussion here focuses only on the post-acquisition deductibility of a target's pre-acquisition net operating loss carryovers under § 382. Rules similar to those of § 382 apply for purposes of § 383.

Section 382 can be illustrated by the following example. Target corporation (*TC*) has $200K of net operating losses that are available to be carried over and utilized to reduce future taxable income of *TC*. Acquiring corporation (*AC*) purchases all of the stock of *TC* for $500K. Under § 382, after the acquisition of *TC*'s stock by *AC*, *TC*'s NOLs can be utilized in any tax year after the acquisition only in an amount equal to the long term tax-exempt rate, say 8 percent, times the purchase price of *TC*'s stock ($500K). *TC*'s $200K of NOLs, therefore, can only be utilized to the extent of $40K (8 percent of $500K) in each taxable year after the acquisition. Thus, § 382 limits the deductibility of a target's NOL carryover after the acquisition of the target.

Section 382 also applies in an acquisition of a loss corporation in tax-free asset reorganizations (*see* Sec. 7.9) and in tax-free stock acquisitions. *See* Sec. 8.7. Most of the § 382 principles discussed in this chapter also apply to tax-free asset and stock reorganizations. Section 382 has no role in a taxable asset acquisition, because there is no limit on the ability of the target to utilize its losses to offset its gains, and the losses do not carry over to the acquiring corporation.

The following materials also examine the potential impact of § 269, which deals with acquisitions made to avoid income tax, on acquisitions of loss corporations. *See* Sec. 5.10.

In addition to the rules of §§ 382 and 269, if as a result of the acquisition of the target's stock the target becomes a subsidiary in a new consolidated group, special rules under the consolidated return regulations apply for determining the deductibility of the target's pre-acquisition net operating loss carryovers in the new group's consolidated return. These special rules, principally the separate return limitation year (SRLY) rules and the built-in deduction rules, are discussed in Sec. 5.9.C. This section also discusses the rules governing the determination of the net operating losses attributable to a target that is a subsidiary of a consolidated group at the time of its acquisition by the acquiring corporation. Also, this section discusses the carryback of post-acquisition net operating losses to the target's pre-acquisition years. The impact of the consolidated return provisions on acquisitions of loss corporations in tax-free asset reorganizations and tax-free stock acquisitions is examined in Secs. 7.10 and 8.7, respectively.

§ 5.8 The Impact of § 382 on the Carryover of a Target's NOLs after an Acquisition

A. Introduction to the Scope and Purpose of § 382

The General Explanation of the Tax Reform Act of 1986
288–325 (1986)

Prior Law *Overview.* In general, a corporate taxpayer is allowed to carry a net operating loss ("NOL(s)") forward for deduction in a future taxable year, as long as the corporation's legal identity is maintained. After certain nontaxable asset acquisitions in which the acquired corporation goes out of existence, the acquired corporation's NOL carryforwards are inherited by the acquiring corporation. [*See* § 381.] Similar rules apply to tax attributes other than NOLs, such as net capital losses and unused tax credits. [*See* § 381.] Historically, the use of NOL and other carryforwards has been subject to special limitations after specified transactions involving the corporation in which the carryforwards arose (referred to as the "loss corporation"). [*See* former § 382.] Prior law also provided other rules that were intended to limit tax-motivated acquisitions of loss corporations. [*See e.g.* § 269.]

The operation of the special limitations on the use of carryforwards turned on whether the transaction that caused the limitations to apply took the form of a taxable sale or exchange of stock in the loss corporation or one of certain specified tax-free reorganizations in which the loss corporation's tax attributes carried over to a corporate successor. [*See* former § 382.] After a purchase (or other taxable acquisition) of a controlling stock interest in a loss corporation, NOL and other carryforwards were disallowed unless the loss corporation continued to conduct its historical trade or business. [*See* former § 382.] In the case of a tax-free reorganization, NOL and other carryforwards were generally allowed in full if the loss corporation's shareholders received stock representing at least 20 percent of the value of the acquiring corporation. [*See* former § 382.] * * *

Acquisitions to evade or avoid income tax. The Secretary of the Treasury was authorized to disallow deductions, credits, or other allowances following an acquisition of control of a corporation or a tax-free acquisition of a corporation's assets if the principal purpose of the acquisition was tax avoidance (sec. 269). This provision applied in the following cases:

(1) where any person or persons acquired (by purchase or in a tax-free transaction) at least 50 percent of a corporation's voting stock, or stock representing 50 percent of the value of the corporation's outstanding stock;

(2) where a corporation acquired property from a previously unrelated corporation and the acquiring corporation's basis for the property was determined by reference to the transferor's basis; and

(3) where a corporation purchased the stock of another corporation in a transaction that qualified for elective treatment as a direct asset purchase (sec. 338), a sec-

tion 338 election was not made, and the acquired corporation was liquidated into the acquiring corporation (under sec. 332).

Treasury regulations under section 269 provided that the acquisition of assets with an aggregate basis that is materially greater than their value (*i.e.,* assets with built-in losses), coupled with the utilization of the basis to create tax-reducing losses, is indicative of a tax-avoidance motive (Treas. Reg. sec. 1.269-3(c)(1)). [Section 269 is still part of the Code. *See* Sec. 5.10.]

Consolidated return regulations. To the extent that NOL carryforwards were not limited by the application of [former] section 382 or section 269, after an acquisition, the use of such losses might be limited under the consolidated return regulations. In general, if an acquired corporation joined the acquiring corporation in the filing of a consolidated tax return by an affiliated group of corporations, the use of the acquired corporation's pre-acquisition NOL carryforwards against income generated by other members of the group was limited by the "separate return limitation year" ("SRLY") rules (Treas. Reg. sec. 1.1502-21(c)). An acquired corporation was permitted to use pre-acquisition NOLs only up to the amount of its own contribution to the consolidated group's taxable income. [The SRLY rules continue although under a modified form. *See* Sec. 5.9.C.] Section 269 was available to prevent taxpayers from avoiding the SRLY rules by diverting income-producing activities (or contributing income-producing assets) from elsewhere in the group to a newly acquired corporation (*see* Treas. Reg. sec. 1.269-3(c)(2), to the effect that the transfer of income-producing assets by a parent corporation to a loss subsidiary filing a separate return may be deemed to have tax avoidance as a principal purpose).

Applicable Treasury regulations provided rules to prevent taxpayers from circumventing the SRLY rules by structuring a transaction as a "reverse acquisition" (defined in regulations as an acquisition where the "acquired" corporation's shareholders end up owning more than 50 percent of the value of the "acquiring" corporation) (Treas. Reg. sec. 1.1502-75(d)(3)). [The reverse acquisition rules continue and are examined in Sec. 5.10.C, in connection with tax-free asset reorganizations.] Similarly, under the "consolidated return change of ownership" ("CRCO") rules, if more than 50 percent of the value of stock in the common parent of an affiliated group changed hands, tax attributes (such as NOL carry-forwards) of the group were limited to use against post-acquisition income of the members of the group (Treas. Reg. sec. 1.1502-21(d)). [The Treasury has eliminated the CRCO rules. *See* Sec. 5.9.F.]

Treasury regulations also prohibited the use of an acquired corporation's built-in losses to reduce the taxable income of other members of an affiliated group (Treas. Reg. sec. 1.1502-15). Under the regulations, built-in losses were subject to the SRLY rules. In general, built-in losses were defined as deductions or losses that economically accrued prior to the acquisition but were recognized for tax purposes after the acquisition, including depreciation deductions attributable to a built-in loss (Treas. Reg. sec. 1.1502-15(a)(2)). The built-in loss limitations did not apply unless, among other things, the aggregate basis of the acquired corporation's assets (other than cash, marketable securities, and goodwill) exceeded the value of those assets by more than

15 percent. [The built-in-loss rules continue although under a proposed modified form. *See* Sec. 5.9.E.]

Allocation of income and deductions among related taxpayers. The Secretary of the Treasury was authorized to apportion or allocate gross income, deductions, credits, or allowances, between or among related taxpayers (including corporations), if such action was necessary to prevent evasion of tax or to clearly reflect the income of a taxpayer (sec. 482). Section 482 could apply to prevent the diversion of income to a loss corporation in order to absorb NOL carryforwards.

Libson Shops doctrine. In *Libson Shops v. Koehler,* 353 U.S. 382 (1957) (decided under the 1939 Code), the U.S. Supreme Court adopted a test of business continuity for use in determining the availability of NOL carryovers. The court denied NOL carryovers following the merger of 16 identically owned corporations (engaged in the same business at different locations) into one corporation, on the ground that the business generating post-merger income was not substantially the same business that incurred the loss (three corporations that generated the NOL carryovers continued to produce losses after the merger).

There was uncertainty whether the *Libson Shops* doctrine had continuing application as a separate nonstatutory test under the 1954 Code. Compare *Maxwell Hardware Co. v. Commissioner,* 343 F.2d 713 (9th Cir.1965) (holding that *Libson Shops* is inapplicable to years governed by the 1954 Code) with Rev. Rul. 63-40, 1963-1 C.B. 46, as modified by T.I.R. 773 (October 13, 1965) (indicating that *Libson Shops* may have continuing vitality where, inter alia, there is a shift in the "benefits" of an NOL carryover). * * *

Reasons for Change.* * * Preservation *of the averaging function of carryovers.* The primary purpose of the special limitations is the preservation of the integrity of the carryover provisions. The carryover provisions perform a needed averaging function by reducing the distortions caused by the annual accounting system. If, on the other hand, carryovers can be transferred in a way that permits a loss to offset unrelated income, no legitimate averaging function is performed. With completely free transferability of tax losses, the carryover provisions become a mechanism for partial recoupment of losses through the tax system. Under such a system, the Federal Government would effectively be required to reimburse a portion of all corporate tax losses. Regardless of the merits of such a reimbursement program, the carryover rules appear to be an inappropriate and inefficient mechanism for delivery of the reimbursement. * * *

General approach. After reviewing various options for identifying events that present the opportunity for a tax benefit transfer (*e.g.,* changes in a loss corporation's business), it was concluded that changes in a loss corporation's stock ownership continue to be the best indicator of a potentially abusive transaction. Under the Act, the special limitations generally apply when shareholders who bore the economic burden of a corporation's NOLs no longer hold a controlling interest in the corporation. In such a case, the possibility arises that new shareholders will contribute income-producing assets (or divert income opportunities) to the loss corporation, and the corporation will obtain greater utilization of carryforwards than it could have had there been no change in ownership.

To address the concerns described above, the Act adopts the following approach: After a substantial ownership change, rather than reducing the NOL carryforward itself, the earnings against which an NOL carryforward can be deducted are limited. [*See* § 382.] This general approach has received wide acceptance among tax scholars and practitioners. This "limitation on earnings" approach is intended to permit the survival of NOL carryforwards after an acquisition, while limiting the ability to utilize the carryforwards against unrelated income. * * *

For purposes of determining the income attributable to a loss corporation's assets, the Act prescribes an objective rate of return on the value of the corporation's equity * * *

Annual limitation. The annual limitation on the use of pre-acquisition NOL carryforwards is the product of the prescribed rate and the value of the loss corporation's equity immediately before a proscribed ownership change. The average yield for long-term marketable obligations of the U.S. government was selected as the measure of a loss corporation's expected return on its assets.

The rate prescribed by the Act [that is, the long term tax exempt rate] is higher than the average rate at which loss corporations actually absorb NOL carryforwards. * * *

B. Outline of § 382 and the Regulations

Preamble to Temporary Regulations under § 382

Treasury Decision 8149 (Aug. 5, 1987)

* * * After an ownership change occurs with respect to a loss corporation, section 382 limits the amount of taxable income against which NOL carryforwards and certain unrealized built-in losses of the corporation may be applied. The limitation is applied annually and is equal to a prescribed percentage rate, multiplied by the value of the stock of the loss corporation immediately before the ownership change. * * *

In general, an ownership change occurs if the percentage of stock of a loss corporation owned by one or more "5-percent shareholders" has increased by more than 50 percentage points over the lowest percentage of such stock that was owned by those persons at any time during the testing period. The determination whether an ownership change has occurred is made by adding together the separate increases in percentage ownership of each 5-percent shareholder whose percentage ownership interest in the loss corporation has increased over such shareholder's lowest percentage ownership interest at any time during the testing period. The testing period (described below) generally is the three-year period that precedes any date on which the loss corporation is required to make the determination of whether an ownership change has occurred.

Under the temporary regulations, the determination whether an ownership change has occurred is generally made as of the close of any date (a "testing date") on which there is an owner shift (described below), an equity structure shift (described below), or a transaction in which an option (or other similar interest) is acquired by a 5-percent shareholder (or a person who would be a 5-percent shareholder if the option were exercised). * * *

In general, in determining whether an ownership change has occurred, all transactions (whether related or unrelated) occurring during the testing period that affect the stock ownership of any 5-percent shareholder whose percentage of stock ownership has increased as of the close of the testing date are taken into account. * * *

The determination of the percentage ownership interest of any shareholder is made on the basis of the relative fair market value of the loss corporation stock owned by the shareholder to the total fair market value of the outstanding stock of the loss corporation. In general, all stock of the loss corporation, except certain preferred stock described in section 1504(a)(4), is taken into account. * * *

C. Methodology for Approaching Problems under § 382[*]

This section provides a basic guide to the structure of § 382; obviously, in addressing an issue under § 382, it is necessary to consult all of the current authorities relating to the issue.

There are three major issues in § 382: (1) identification of a loss corporation; (2) determining whether an ownership change of the loss corporation has occurred, and (3) applying the "Section 382 limitation" to a loss corporation that has experienced an ownership change. Each of these issues is addressed below. The italicized terms are defined in the Code of Regulations.

1. First: Is Target a Loss Corporation?

The first task in approaching questions under § 382 is to determine whether the target corporation is a *Loss Corporation*, that is, a corporation that is entitled to utilize a NOL carryover under § 172 or that has a *Net Unrealized Built-In Loss. See* § 382(k)(1).

a. Net Unrealized Built-In Loss

A Net Unrealized Built-In Loss exists if the aggregate fair market value of a *Loss Corporation's* assets (other than cash, etc.) immediately before an *Ownership Change* is less than the aggregate adjusted basis of such assets by an amount greater than the lesser of 15% of the fair market value of such assets or $10,000,000. *See* § 382(h)(3)(B)(i). This concept is illustrated in the following example from the Conference Report to the Tax Reform Act of 1986 (TRA 1986):

> *Example 25.* L corporation owns two assets: asset X, with a basis of $150 and a value of $50 (a built-in loss asset), and asset Y, with a basis of zero and a value of $50 (a built-in gain asset, described below). L has a net unrealized

---

[*] Based on Appendix 51A of Federal Taxation of Business Enterprises, supra Chapter 1, note 1, with permission.

built-in loss of $50 (the excess of the aggregate bases of $150 over the aggregate value of $100).

b. Net Unrealized Built-In Gain

If the target is a Loss Corporation but does not have a *Net Unrealized Built-In Loss,* determine whether it has a *Net Unrealized Built-In Gain.* A *Net Unrealized Built-In Gain* exists if the fair market value of the assets (other than cash, etc.) immediately before the *Ownership Change* exceeds the aggregate adjusted basis of such assets at such time by an amount greater than the lesser of 15% of the fair market value of the *Loss Corporation's* assets immediately before the *Ownership Change* or $10,000,000. *See* § 382(h)(3)(A)(i). As noted in Sec. 5.8.C.3, if there is a *Net Unrealized Built-In Gain,* the *Section 382 Limitation* is increased.

c. Old and New Loss Corporations

If the target is a *Loss Corporation* and there is an *Ownership Change* as defined in Sec. 5.8.C.2., then the *Loss Corporation* becomes the *Old Loss Corporation* (*see* § 382(k)(2)) and the corporation that survives the *Ownership Change* becomes the *New Loss Corporation. See* § 382(k)(3).

d. Annual Information Statement

Under the regulations, the *Loss Corporation* is required to file an annual infor-mation statement with its return indicating whether a *Testing Date* (a date for testing for an *Ownership Change*) has occurred during the taxable year and whether an *Ownership Change* has occurred on any of the *Testing Dates. See* Temp. Reg. § 1.382-2T(a)(2). The preamble to the Temporary Regulations explains this requirement as follows:

> On each testing date, the loss corporation is required to determine both the stock ownership and the changes in the stock ownership during the testing period for only the following four categories of persons: (1) any individual shareholder who has a direct ownership interest of five percent or more in the loss corporation, (2) any entity with a direct ownership interest of five percent or more in the loss corporation, (3) any entity with an indirect own-ership interest of five percent or more in the loss corporation, and (4) any individual who has an indirect ownership interest of five percent or more in the loss corporation, through any one of the entities described above. [*See* Temp. Reg. § 1.382-2T(a)(2).]

2. Second: Has an Ownership Change Occurred?

If the target corporation is a *Loss Corporation,* the second step is to determine whether the proposed acquisition will result in an *Ownership Change. See* § 382(g)(1). An *Ownership Change* occurs if immediately after (1) an *Owner Shift Involving a 5-Percent Shareholder* or (2) an *Equity Structure Shift,* there has been an increase by more than 50 percentage points in (A) the percentage of stock of the *New Loss Corporation* owned by one or more *5-Percent Shareholders,* over (B) the lowest percentage of stock of the *Old Loss Corporation* owned by such *5-Percent Shareholders* at any time during the *Testing Period.*

a. Testing Period

The preamble to the Temporary Regulations under § 382 gives the following explanation of the *Testing Period* (*see* § 382(i)):

> The testing period is generally the three-year period ending on any testing date. Because a new testing period begins on the day following any ownership change, however, a loss corporation is not required to take into account transactions occurring on or before the date of the most recent ownership change in determining whether a subsequent ownership change has occurred. [*See* Temp. Reg. § 1.382-2T(d).]

b. 5-Percent Shareholders

Identify each *5-Percent Shareholder,* that is, any person holding 5 percent or more of the stock of the *Loss Corporation* at any time during the *Testing Period. See* § 382(k)(7). Special rules are provided for determining stock ownership of publicly held corporations and stock ownership by certain entities. The preamble to the Temporary Regulations discusses the presumptions concerning stock ownership set forth in the regulations.

> The temporary regulations provide the loss corporation with an ability to establish the identity of its 5-percent shareholders under two different rules that are designed to reduce the burdens of compliance with section 382. With respect to loss corporation stock that is described in Rule 13d-11(d) of Regulation 13D-G, promulgated under the Securities and Exchange Act of 1934 ("registered stock"), a loss corporation may rely on the existence or absence of filings under Schedules 13D and 13G as of a date to identify the corporation's shareholders (both individuals and entities) who have a direct ownership interest of five percent or more. * * *

> The second part of the rule provides the loss corporation with an ability to determine shifts in the indirect ownership of its stock without regard to the actual identity of the ultimate beneficial owners of the loss corporation. Under this rule, a loss corporation may rely on a statement, signed under penalties of perjury, by any entity with a five percent or more ownership interest in the loss corporation, to establish the extent, if any, to which the ownership interests of any such entity's owners have changed as of the testing date. [*See* Temp. Reg. § 1.382-2T(k)(1).]

c. Aggregation Rule

Apply the aggregation rule, which treats all stock owned by shareholders of a corporation who are not *5-Percent Shareholders* as one *5-Percent Shareholder. See*

§ 382(g)(4). The preamble to the Temporary Regulations discusses this aggregation concept.

> Aggregation rules are applied under the temporary regulations to all stock ownership by (1) public shareholders (persons who directly own less than five percent of loss corporation stock) and (2) owners of any first tier entity (or higher tier entity) who each indirectly own less than five percent of the stock of the loss corporation. Under the temporary regulations, stock owned by any such group of persons generally is treated as being owned by a separate 5-percent shareholder (referred to in the temporary regulations as a "public group"). In general, therefore, all of the stock of a widely held loss corporation is treated as owned by a single 5-percent shareholder. [*See* Temp. Reg. § 1.382-2T(j)(1).]

The § 382 regulations provide that stock held by members of a group acting pursuant to a plan may be aggregated. *See* Reg. § 1.382-3(a)(1). The preamble to the Proposed Regulations gives the following explanation.

> For purposes of section 382 and the regulations thereunder, the temporary regulations define the term "entity" as "any corporation, estate, trust, association, company, partnership, or similar organization." Consequently where an entity is or becomes a 5-percent shareholder, a loss corporation is required to identify changes in ownership by that entity that occur during the testing period.

> An identifiable shift in the ownership of a loss corporation also occurs when a group of persons acting pursuant to a plan acquires five percent or more of the stock of the loss corporation. The temporary regulations are amended to make clear that the definition of the term "entity" includes a group of persons acting pursuant to a plan. [*See* Prop. Reg. § 1.382-3(a)(1).]

This regulation has been finalized.

d. Segregation Rule

Apply the segregation rules set out in the Temporary Regulations. *See* Temp. Reg. § 1.382-2T(j)(2). The preamble to the Temporary Regulations explains these rules as follows:

> As a result of various types of transactions enumerated in the regulations, the public shareholders of a loss corporation may be segregated into two or more separate groups (also referred to in the temporary regulations as "public groups"), each of which is treated as a separate 5-percent shareholder (regardless of whether the group owns as much as five percent of loss corporation stock). For example, public shareholders who receive loss corporation stock as the result of an equity structure shift [*i.e.* a tax-free reorganization] or any other transaction to which section 1032 applies are segregated and treated separately from the public shareholders that owned stock of the loss corporation prior to the transaction. Thus, for example, public shareholders who

receive stock of a widely held corporation in a new stock issuance are segregated from the public shareholders who own stock prior to the transaction, and the group of public shareholders that acquire stock in the offering is treated as a separate 5-percent shareholder whose percentage stock ownership has increased. [*See* Temp. Reg. § 1.382-2T(j)(2).]

e. Attribution Rules

Apply the attribution rules of § 382(l)(3)(A), which (1) treat family members as one person, (2) attribute stock held by a corporation, partnership, trust or estate out to the shareholders, partners, and beneficiaries, (3) do not attribute any stock from an owner to an entity, and (4) treat the holder of an option as holding the stock underlying the option if the application results in an *Ownership Change.*

The preamble to the Temporary Regulations gives the following explanation of the general attribution rules:

> The principal modification to the constructive ownership rules requires attribution of stock from a corporation to its shareholders without regard to the 50 percent stock ownership limitation in section 318(a)(2)(C). A second significant modification to the constructive ownership rules is that stock attributed from an entity to its owners is not treated as owned by the entity. Accordingly, loss corporation stock owned, directly or constructively, by an entity is attributed to all of its owners and is not treated as owned by the entity. [*See* Temp. Reg. § 1.382-2T(h).]

The preamble also discusses the option attribution rule.

> Subject to certain exceptions provided in the temporary regulations, the owner of an option is treated as owning the underlying stock if such treatment would cause an ownership change. [*See* Temp. Reg. § 1.382-2T(h)(4).]

f. Four Categories of 5-Percent Shareholders

The preamble to the Temporary Regulations under § 382 explains that the regulations identify four categories of 5-percent shareholders:

> First, an individual who has either a direct ownership interest or an indirect ownership interest (by virtue of an ownership interest in any one entity) in loss corporation stock of at least five percent is a 5-percent shareholder. Second, the direct shareholders of the loss corporation (both individuals and entities) who own less than five percent of loss corporation stock (referred to in the temporary regulations as "public shareholders"), as described further below, are aggregated together as a group that is a single 5-percent shareholder. Third, the owners (other than individual 5-percent shareholders referred to above) of an entity that has a five percent or more direct or indirect ownership interest in the loss corporation are also generally aggregated together as a group that is a separate 5-percent shareholder. Finally, as discussed further below, the temporary regulations provide a mechanism to segregate

the groups of shareholders referred to above into two or more separate groups following certain enumerated transactions, with each such group being a 5-percent shareholder. [*See* Temp. Reg. § 1.382-2T(g).]

g. Definition of Owner Shift

The preamble to the Temporary Regulations under § 382 explains that the regulations have the following definition of *Owner Shift:*

> An owner shift is defined as any change in the ownership of the stock of the loss corporation that affects the percentage of stock owned (directly and by attribution) by any person who is a 5-percent shareholder. Thus, an owner shift includes (but is not limited to) the following transactions: (1) a purchase or disposition of loss corporation stock by a 5-percent shareholder; (2) a section 351 exchange that affects the percentage of stock owned by a 5-percent shareholder; (3) a decrease in the outstanding stock of a loss corporation (*e.g.,* by virtue of redemption) that affects the percentage of stock owned by a 5-percent shareholder; (4) an issuance of loss corporation stock that affects the percentage of stock owned by a 5-percent shareholder; and (5) an equity structure shift [*i.e.,* a tax-free reorganization] that affects the percentage of stock owned by a 5-percent shareholder.

> Under the temporary regulations, transfers of stock between persons who are not 5-percent shareholders generally are not taken into account. [*See* Temp. Reg. § 1.382-2T(e).]

h. Determining Percentage of Loss Corporation Stock Owned

In determining the percentage of the *Loss Corporation's* stock acquired by *5-Percent Shareholders,* focus on *Value* (*see* § 382(k)(6)(C)), but generally disregard fluctuations in *Value* (*see* § 382(l)(3)(D)). Also, except as provided in regulations, disregard nonvoting, limited preferred stock described in § 1504(a)(4). *See* § 382(k)(6)(A).

i. Owner-Shift Involving a 5-Percent Shareholder

Determine whether there is an *Owner Shift Involving a 5-Percent Shareholder,* that is, any change (purchase, redemption, etc.) in the ownership of stock of a *Loss Corporation* that affects the percentage of stock of such corporation owned by a *5-Percent Shareholder* before or after such change. *See* § 382(g)(2).

j. Equity Structure Shift

Determine whether there has been an *Equity Structure Shift,* that is, generally an acquisitive reorganization, recapitalization or, pursuant to regulations, a taxable reorganization type transaction. *See* § 382(g)(3). *Equity Structure Shifts* are explored in Sec. 5.9.B.

k. Ownership Change: Increase of More than 50 Percentage Points Resulting from Owner Shift or Equity Structure Shift

If there has been either an *Owner Shift Involving a 5-Percent Shareholder* or an *Equity Structure Shift,* determine whether there has been an increase by more than 50 percentage points in the percentage of stock of the *New Loss Corporation* owned by one or more *5-Percent Shareholders,* over the lowest percentage of stock of the *Old Loss Corporation* owned by *5-Percent Shareholders* at any time during the *Testing Period. See* § 382(g)(1). If such an increase has occurred, then there has been an *Ownership Change.*

(i)   In making this determination, consider only the stock of those *5-Percent Shareholders* whose percentage ownership has increased during the *Testing Period.* See Conference Report at II-73.

(ii)   The *Testing Period* is the 3-year period ending on the day of any *Owner Shift Involving a 5-Percent Shareholder* or *Equity Structure Shift. See* § 382(i)(1).

(iii) Disregard stock acquired by death, gift, etc. *See* § 382(l)(3)(B).

(iv) In the case of an *Equity Structure Shift* or subsequent transaction, apply the aggregation rule for *Less Than 5-Percent Shareholders* separately for the target and acquiring corporation. *See* § 382(g)(4)(B)(i).

(v)   A series of transactions that includes both *Owner Shifts Involving 5-Percent Shareholders* and *Equity Structure Shifts* may constitute an *Ownership Change.*

(vi) In the case of an *Equity Structure Shift* or subsequent transaction, a proportionate acquisition rule applies for post-reorganization purchases of the survivor's stock. *See* § 382(g)(4)(B)(ii).

l. Example of Ownership Change in a Stock Acquisition

The following example of an ownership change from the Conference Report to the TRA 1986 illustrates both the aggregation rule and the attribution out rule:

> *Example 15.* — L corporation is publicly traded; no shareholder owns as much as five percent. P corporation is publicly traded; no shareholder owns as much as five percent. On January 1, 1988, P corporation purchases 100 percent of L corporation stock on the open market. The L stock owned by P is attributed to the shareholders of P, all of whom are less-than-5-percent shareholders who are treated as a single, separate 5-percent shareholder. Accordingly, there has been an ownership change of L, because the percentage of stock owned by the P shareholders after the purchase (100 percent) has increased by more than 50 percentage points over the lowest percentage of L stock owned by that group at any time during the testing period * * *.

3. Third: Determine the § 382 Limitation

If there has been an Ownership Change with respect to a *Loss Corporation,* the third step is to determine the *Section 382 Limitation.* Under this rule, the amount of taxable income of the *New Loss Corporation* for any *Post-Change Year* that may be offset by *Pre-Change Losses* may not exceed the *Section 382 Limitation. See* § 382(a).

a. Pre-Change Losses

Determine the *Pre-Change Losses*, which means the (1) NOL carryforward of the *Old Loss Corporation* to the taxable year ending with the *Ownership Change* or in which the *Change Date* occurs, and (2) the NOLs of the *Old Loss Corporation* for the taxable year in which the *Ownership Change* occurs to the extent that the loss is allocable to the period in such year on or before the *Change Date. See* § 382(d)(1).

b. Change Date

Where the last component of an *Ownership Change* is an *Owner Shift Involving a 5-Percent Shareholder,* the *Change Date* is the date on which such shift occurs, and where such last component is an *Equity Structure Shift,* the *Change Date* is the date of the reorganization. *See* § 382(j).

c. Post-Change Year

A *Post-Change Year* is any taxable year ending after the *Change Date. See* § 382(d)(2).

d. Section 382 Limitation

The *Section 382 Limitation* for any *Post-Change Year* is generally an amount equal to (A) the *Value* of the *Old Loss Corporation,* multiplied by (B) the *Long Term Tax Exempt Rate. See* § 382(b)(1).

e. Value of Old Loss Corporation

The *Value* of the *Old Loss Corporation* is generally the value of the stock of the corporation including nonvoting, limited preferred stock described in § 1504(a)(4) immediately before the *Ownership Change. See* §§ 382(e)(1) and 382(k)(5).

(i) Certain capital contributions to the *Old Loss Corporation* are disregarded in determining *Value. See* § 382(l)(1)(A).

(ii) If the *New Loss Corporation* has substantial non-business assets, the *Value* of the *Old Loss Corporation* may be reduced. *See* § 382(l)(4)(A).

(iii) Value is determined after certain corporate contractions, such as redemptions. *See* § 382(e)(2). If the target is acquired in an LBO that amounts to a redemption, the value of the target's stock may be the post-LBO value.

f. Long Term Tax Exempt Rate

The Long Term Tax Exempt Rate is published by the IRS monthly and is determined under principles similar to those in § 1274(d). Generally it is the highest rate in effect for the three-month period ending with the calendar month in which the *Change Date* occurs. *See* § 382(f).

g. Illustration of Computation of § 382 Limitation

The computation of the Section 382 Limitation is illustrated as follows:

> If there has been an *Ownership Change* with respect to an *Old Loss Corporation* that has (1) a *Pre-Change Loss* of $10 million dollars, and (2) a *Value* (*i.e.* fair market value of the stock immediately before the *Ownership Change*) of $25M, and (3) the *Long Term Tax Exempt Rate* is 10%, then the *Section 382 Limitation* for any *Post-Change Year* is $2.5 million (*i.e.*, $25 million *Value* multiplied by the *Long Term Tax-Exempt Rate*). Thus, under the general limitation rule of 382(a), the amount of the taxable income of the *New Loss Corporation* for any *Post-Change Year* that can be offset by *Pre-Change Losses* (*i.e.*, $10 million) cannot exceed $2.5 million.

h. Excess § 382 Limitation

If the *Section 382 Limitation* for a *Post-Change Year* exceeds the taxable income of the *New Loss Corporation* for such year that is offset by *Pre-Change Losses*, then the excess is added to the *Section 382 Limitation* for the next year. *See* § 382(b)(2).

i. Pre-Change Date Income

The *Section 382 Limitation* does not apply to the portion of the *Loss Corporation's* taxable income that is allocable to the period before the *Change Date*. *See* § 382(b)(3)(A).

j. Continuity of Business Enterprise

If the *New Loss Corporation* does not satisfy the continuity of business enterprise requirement for the two-year period after the *Change Date*, the *Section 382 Limitation* for any *Post-Change Year* is zero. *See* § 382(c).

k. Net Unrealized Built-In Loss

If the *Old Loss Corporation* has a *Net Unrealized Built-In Loss,* any *Recognized Built-In Loss* for any *Recognition Period Taxable Year* (*i.e.,* any taxable year within the 5-year Recognition Period) is subject to limitation in the same manner as if such loss were a *Pre-Change Loss.* See §§ 382(h)(1)(B) and 382(h)(7).

l. Net Unrealized Built-In Gain

If the *Old Loss Corporation* has a *Net Unrealized Built-In Gain,* the *Section 382 Limitation* for any *Recognition Period Taxable Year* is increased by any *Recognized Built-In Gain,* for such taxable year. *See* § 382(h)(1)(A)(i).

m. Section 338 Election

If a § 338 election is made with respect to the *Old Loss Corporation, the Section 382 Limitation* for such year is in effect increased by the built-in gains resulting from the election. *See* § 382(h)(1)(C). Thus, the NOLs can shelter the § 338 gains.

4. Fourth: Collateral Considerations

Under the fourth step, consideration must be given to the following:

Special rules apply (1) in the case of Title II and similar cases (*see* § 382(l)(5)) and (2) to certain insolvency transactions (*see* § 382(l)(6)). These rules are considered in Chapter 12. Also, special rules apply for coordinating § 382 with the alternative minimum tax (*see* § 382(l)(7)).

The Treasury has broad regulatory authority under § 382 including authority to deal with NOL partnerships. *See* § 382(m).

Section 269 and the SRLY and CRCO rules of the consolidated return regulations are to continue to apply. Conf. Rep. at II-194. The § 269 rules are covered in Sec. 5.10, and the SRLY rules are addressed in Sec. 5.9.C. The CRCO rules have been repealed. *See* Sec. 5.9.F. Proposed Regulations have been promulgated dealing with the application of § 382 in the context of an acquisition of a group of loss corporations. *See* Prop. Reg. §§ 1.1502-90 to -98 and § 1.382-5. Prop. Reg. §§ 1.502-90 to -98 deal with the acquisition of loss corporations that are members of consolidated groups. These rules are introduced in Sec. 5.9.H. Prop. Reg. § 1.382-5, which deals with the acquisition of loss corporations that are not part of a consolidated group, is not addressed here.

§ 5.9 Effect of Consolidated Return Regulations on Utilization of a Target's NOLs[*]

A. Introduction

The consolidated return regulations contain an elaborate set of rules governing the computation of items such as consolidated net operating loss carryovers and carrybacks after acquisitions of new members of a group and after the disposition of old members of a group. On January 29, 1991 the Treasury promulgated Proposed Regulations (CO-78-90, Jan. 29, 1991) under the consolidated return provisions which, *inter alia*, coordinate these Regulations with § 382. Section 382 limits the amount of losses that can be utilized after an ownership change to an amount equal to the value of the loss corporation multiplied by the long term tax exempt rate. The legislative history to the TRA 1986 clarifies that the limitations on the utilization of losses contained in the consolidated return regulations continue to apply.

---

[*] Based on §§ 52.08–52:14 of *Federal Taxation of Business Enterprises, supra* Chapter 1, note 1, with permission.

This and succeeding sections consider the effect of the consolidated return regulations on acquisitions and dispositions of members of a consolidated group. The effect of the consolidated return regulations on regular operations is discussed in Sec. 5.5.A. The anti-mirror disallowance of loss rule is discussed in Sec. 5.6. The consolidated return regulations are extremely complex and the following sections of this chapter merely introduce the topics.

In examining the effect of the consolidated return regulations on acquisitions, the issues may be separated into the following categories:

1. The effect on the taxable year of a corporation that becomes a member of a consolidated group as a result of an acquisition (*see* Sec. 5.9.B);

2. The effect of the revised "weak form" separate return limitation year (SRLY) rules on the ability of members of a consolidated group to use preacquisition NOLs of the new member in a consolidated return year (*see* Sec. 5.9.C);

3. The effect of the reverse acquisition rule in the application of the SRLY rules. This issue arises in reorganization transactions and is addressed in Secs. 7.10. and 8.7;

4. The limitation on the utilization of built in losses (*see* Sec. 5.9.D);

5. The carryover and carryback of consolidated NOLs and net capital losses to separate return years (*see* Sec. 5.9.G); and

6. The rules dealing with the interface between consolidated return Regulations and § 382 (*see* Sec. 5.9.H).

B. Taxable Years of New Members of Consolidated Group

Each new member of a consolidated group must adopt the taxable year of the common parent of the consolidated group. *See* § 1.1502-76(a). The income of the common parent for the entire taxable year and the income of each subsidiary for the portion of the year during which it is a member of the consolidated group is included in the consolidated return for the year. *See* § 1.1502-76(b)(1). A newly acquired subsidiary (or its former consolidated group) is required to file a separate return for the portion of its taxable year prior to the acquisition. *See* § 1.1502-76(b)(2).

C. Separate Return Limitation Year (SRLY) Rules

1. Introduction to the Strong Form and Weak Form SRLY Rules

Prior to the adoption of final regulations in 1999, the SRLY rules applied whenever, for example, all of the stock of a target corporation with net operating losses was acquired by an acquiring corporation, and the target thereby became a member of the acquiring corporation's consolidated group. In such case, under § 1.1502-21(c), the net operating loss carryovers of the target that arose in a separate return limitation year (a SRLY, that is, years before the acquisition) could be included in the consolidated net operating loss (CNOL) deductions of the acquiring corporation's consolidated group only to the extent of the aggregate of the consolidated taxable income of the group determined by taking into account only the target's items of income, gain, deduction and loss ("income items").

Thus, under this, if as a result of a taxable stock acquisition, a target corporation that had a net operating loss carryover (NOL) became a member of a consolidated group, any NOLs of the target allowed after the application of § 382 could be utilized only to offset the aggregate of the post-acquisition separate taxable income of the target. The NOL carryovers from the SRLYs of the target could not be utilized by other members of the consolidated group. This rule is known here as the Strong Form Separate Return Limitation Year (SRLY) rule. The purpose of the rule, which was adopted prior to the adoption of the current limitation on losses under § 382, was to permit pre-acquisition NOL carryovers of a new member of a group to be offset only the post-acquisition income of that member and not the income of other members.

As indicated below in the discussion of the 1999 amendments, this Strong Form SRLY rule was replaced with a Weak Form SRLY rule. This Weak Form SRLY rule (-21(c)) applies only where the transaction giving arise to the target becoming a member of the acquiring corporation's group does not overlap with limitation on losses under § 382. Thus, for example, if an acquiring corporation purchases all of a target's stock in one transaction, the transaction would be subject to both the limitation on losses under § 382 and the SRLY rules, and as a consequence of this overlap the SRLY rules do not apply.

2. Introduction to the Regulations

Preamble to Treasury Decision 8823

64 F.R. 36092, July 2 1999

Summary: * * * The regulations provide rules for computing the limitation with respect to separate return limitation year (SRLY) losses, and the carryover or carryback of losses to consolidated and separate return years. The regulations also eliminate the application of the SRLY rules in certain circumstances in which the rules of section 382 of the Internal Revenue Code also apply. * * *

Operation of the Proposed and Temporary Regulations. * * *

Elimination or Retention of SRLY. The preliminary issue considered in finalizing these regulations was the extent, if any, to which the SRLY rules should be retained. The comments were divided about whether to retain or eliminate SRLY. Some commentators asserted that the amendment to section 382 in 1986 adequately addressed Congressional concerns regarding loss trafficking. Therefore, it was argued, the SRLY rules should be eliminated because they have become superfluous, add unwarranted complexity to the consolidated return system, and are easily avoided. Other commentators asserted that the SRLY rules should be retained because in their view, policing loss trafficking is incidental to SRLY's function of resolving a single entity/separate entity conflict in applying the consolidated return regulations. A third group suggested a middle position by urging the elimination of SRLY only in those circumstances in which the rules of section 382 also apply. * * *

The Overlap Rule. The Treasury and the IRS believe that limitations on the extent to which a consolidated group can use attributes arising in a separate return limitation year remain necessary. However, the Treasury and the IRS remain concerned about complexity in applying the current SRLY rules, particularly with respect to situations where both the SRLY rules and section 382 apply. As described above, the SRLY limitation is based on the member's (or subgroup's) actual contribution to consolidated taxable income. The section 382 limitation is based on the expected income generation of the member (or subgroup) determined with reference to its value on the change date. On balance, the Treasury and the IRS believe that the simultaneous or proximate imposition of a section 382 limitation reasonably approximates a corresponding SRLY limitation. Accordingly, these regulations generally eliminate the SRLY limitation in circumstances in which its application overlaps with that of section 382. * * *

3. Illustration of the Overlap Rule

Reg § 1.1502-21(g)

(g) *Overlap with section 382*(1) *General rule.* The limitation provided in paragraph (c) [the SRLY limitation] of this section does not apply to net operating loss carryovers * * * when the application of paragraph (c) of this section results in an overlap with the application of section 382. * * *

(2) *Definitions*(i) *Generally.* For purposes of this paragraph (g), the definitions and nomenclature contained in section 382, the regulations thereunder, and §§ 1.1502-90 through 1.1502-99 apply.

(ii) *Overlap.* (A) An overlap of the application of paragraph (c) [the SRLY limitation] of this section and the application of section 382 with respect to a net operating loss carryover occurs if a corporation becomes a member of a consolidated group (the SRLY event) within six months of the change date of an ownership change giving rise to a section 382(a) limitation with respect to that carryover (the section 382 event).

(B) If an overlap described in paragraph (g)(2)(ii)(A) of this section occurs with respect to net operating loss carryovers of a corporation whose SRLY event occurs within the six month period beginning on the date of a section 382 event, then an overlap is treated as also occurring with respect to that corporation's net operating loss carryover that arises within the period beginning with the section 382 event and ending with the SRLY event. * * *

(3) *Operating rules.*(i) *Section 382 event before SRLY event.* If a SRLY event occurs on the same date as a section 382 event or within the six month period beginning on the date of the section 382 event, paragraph (g)(1) of this section applies beginning with the tax year that includes the SRLY event.

(ii) *SRLY event before section 382 event.* If a section 382 event occurs within the period beginning the day after the SRLY event and ending six months after the SRLY event, paragraph (g)(1) of this section applies starting with the first tax year that begins after the section 382 event.

(4) *Subgroup rules.* In general, in the case of a net operating loss carryover for which there is a SRLY subgroup and a loss subgroup (as defined in § 1.1502-91(d)(1)), the principles of this paragraph (g) apply to the SRLY subgroup, and not separately to its members. However, paragraph (g)(1) of this section applies—

(i) With respect to a carryover described in paragraph (g)(2)(ii)(A) of this section only if—

(A) All members of the SRLY subgroup with respect to that carryover are also included in a loss subgroup with respect to that carryover; and

(B) All members of a loss subgroup with respect to that carryover are also members of a SRLY subgroup with respect to that carryover; and

(ii) With respect to a carryover described in paragraph (g)(2)(ii)(B) of this section only if all members of the SRLY subgroup for that carryover are also members of a SRLY subgroup that has net operating loss carryovers described in paragraph (g)(2)(ii)(A) of this section that are subject to the overlap rule of paragraph (g)(1) of this section.

(5) *Examples.* The principles of this paragraph (g) are illustrated by the following examples:

Example 1. Overlap — Simultaneous Acquisition. (i) Individual A owns all of the stock of P, which in turn owns all of the stock of S. P and S file a consolidated return. In Year 2, B, an individual unrelated to Individual A, forms T which incurs a $100 net operating loss for that year. At the beginning of Year 3, S acquires T.

(ii) S's acquisition of T results in T becoming a member of the P group (the SRLY event) and also results in an ownership change of T, within the meaning of section 382(g), that gives rise to a limitation under section 382(a) (the section 382 event) with respect to the T carryover.

(iii) Because the SRLY event and the change date of the section 382 event occur on the same date, there is an overlap of the application of the SRLY rules and the application of section 382.

(iv) Consequently, under this paragraph (g), in Year 3 the SRLY limitation does not apply to the Year 2 $100 net operating loss. * * *

D. The Lonely Parent Rule

A separate return year of a common parent is not a SRLY (*see* § 1.1502-1(f)(2)(i)) and, therefore, there are no limitations in the consolidated return regulations on the utilization of the net operating loss carryovers of a parent that accrued prior to an acquisition of a profitable corporation by the parent or by a member of its group. This is generally known as the lonely parent rule. Also, note that in this transaction, the § 382 limitation is not applicable, because there is not an ownership change with respect to the parent.

Thus, if a parent corporation of a consolidated group that has NOLs acquires all the stock of a target corporation, the SRLY rules do not apply and therefore the NOLs of the acquiring group can be utilized to offset postacquisition income of the target corporation. This type of transaction may, however, be subject to the § 384 limitation. *See* Sec. 5.11.

E. Limitation on Built-In Losses

Regulation § 1.1502-15 of the consolidated return regulations limits the use of deductions that have economically accrued in a SRLY but are recognized in a consolidated return year. *See* § 1.1502-15. These deductions, are referred to as built-in losses because they were built-in at the time the loss corporation became a member of the consolidated group. The term built-in loss is defined to mean net unrealized built in loss under § 382(h)(3). *See* -15(a). This limitation on built-in losses does not apply if there is an overlap with Section 382.

F. Carryover and Carry Back to Separate Return Years

The rules discussed here are contained principally in Reg. § 1.1502-21(b). Only the basic principles are covered here.

A consolidated net operating loss (CNOL) (that is a loss arising in a consolidated return year) may be carried over or back to a separate return year of a member in the following two situations:

(1) If a member of a consolidated group leaves the group, the portion of the CNOL attributable to the member is apportioned to the member (apportioned loss) and generally is carried over to the separate return years of the departing member (*see* Reg. § 1.1502-21(b)(2)(ii)); and

(2) If a member of a consolidated group was not a member of the group during any of the preceding three years, the CNOL attributable to the member and which is apportioned to the member (apportioned loss) generally may be carried back to the separate return years of the member. *See* Reg. § 1.1502-21(b)(2)(i).

Under § 1.1502-21(b)(2)(iv), the portion of a CNOL attributable to a member or a group is an amount equal to the CNOL of the group multiplied by the following fraction:

Separate NOL of Member / Separate NOLs of All Members

G. Interface between § 382 and the Consolidated Return Regulations

This section briefly outlines the provisions of Reg. §§ 1.1502-90 to 1.1502-98, which deal with the application of § 382 to the acquisition of a consolidated group of corporations that has a consolidated net operating loss.

Reg. §§ 1.1502-90 to 1.1502-98 generally provide that an ownership change and the Section 382 limitation (*see* Sec. 5.8) are determined for a loss group (or *loss subgroup*) on a single entity basis and not for members separately. *See* Reg. § 1.1502-91(a)(1). A loss group is generally a consolidated group that is entitled to use a net operating loss that did not arise in a separate return limitation year (SRLY). *See* Reg. § 1.1502-91(c). A loss subgroup exists if two or more corporations which become members of a group (1) were affiliated with each other in another group, (2) bear a relationship to each other described in § 1504(a)(1) (*i.e.*, 80% control) through a loss group parent immediately after they become members of the group, and (3) at least one of the members carries over a net operating loss that did not arise in a SRLY with respect to the former group. *See* Reg. § 1.1502-91(d). The loss subgroup concept is illustrated in the following example in Reg. § 1.1502-91(d)(7), Example (1):

> *Example 1. Loss subgroup.* (i) P owns all the L stock and L owns all the L1 stock. The P group has a consolidated net operating loss arising in Year 1 that is carried to Year 2. On May 2, of Year 2, P sells all the stock of L to A, and L and L1 thereafter file consolidated returns. A portion of the Year 1 consolidated net operating loss is apportioned under § 1.1502-21(b) [*see* Sec. 5.9.F] to each of L and L1, which they carry over to Year 2. * * *

> (ii) L and L1 compose a loss subgroup * * * because (A) They were affiliated with each other in the P group (the former group), (B) They bear a relationship described in Section 1504(a)(1) to each other through a loss subgroup parent (L) immediately after they became members of the L group, and (C) At least one of the members * * * carries over a net operating loss to the L group (the current group) that did not arise in a SRLY with respect to the P group. * * * L is the loss subgroup parent of the L loss subgroup.

If a loss group or a loss subgroup experiences an ownership change under § 382 and Reg. § 1.1502-92, then the amount of the consolidated taxable income for any post-change year that may be offset by pre-change consolidated (or subgroup) attributes may not exceed the consolidated (or subgroup) Section 382 limitation for such year as determined in Reg. § 1.1502-93. *See* Reg. § 1.1502-91(a)(1).

Reg. § 1.1502-92 provides that a loss group or a loss subgroup has an ownership change if the loss group's common parent or the loss subgroup's common parent, as the case may be, has an ownership change under § 382(g). *See* Reg. § 1.1502-92(b)(1)(i) and (ii). This is known as the parent change method and is illustrated in the following example from Reg. § 1.1502-92(b)(2), *Example (1)*:

> *Example 1. Loss group—ownership change of the common parent.* (a) A owns all the L stock. L owns 80 percent and B owns 20 percent of the L1 stock. For Year 1, the L group has a consolidated net operating loss that resulted from the operations of L1 and that is carried over to Year 2. The value of the L stock is $1000. The total value of the L1 stock is $600 and the value of the L1 stock held by B is $120. The L group is a loss group under § 1.1502-91(c)(1) because of its net operating loss carryover from Year 1. On August 15, Year 2, A sells 51 percent of the L stock to C. * * *

> (b) * * * [S]ection 382 and the regulations thereunder are applied to L to determine whether it (and therefore the L loss group) has an ownership change with respect to its net operating loss carryover from Year 1 attributable to L1 on August 15, Year 2. The sale of the L stock to C causes an ownership

change of L under § 1.382-2T and of the L loss group under paragraph (b)(1)(i) of this section. The amount of consolidated taxable income of the L loss group for any post-change taxable year that may be offset by its pre-change consolidated attributes (that is, the net operating loss carryover from Year 1 attributable to L1) may not exceed the consolidated section 382 limitation for the L loss group for the taxable year.

Under Reg. § 1.1502-93, if there is an ownership change the consolidated Section 382 limitation or the subgroup Section 382 limitation for any post-change year is an amount equal to the value of the loss group or of the loss subgroup multiplied by the long-term exempt rate. *See* Reg. § 1.1502-93. Subject to certain adjustments the value of the loss group or the loss subgroup is the value immediately before the ownership change of the stock of each member, other than stock that is owned directly or indirectly by another member. The following example in Reg. § 1.1502-93(b)(3), Example (1), illustrates these principles:

> *Example 1. Basic case.* (i) L, L1, and L2 compose a loss group. L has outstanding common stock, the value of which is $100. L1 has outstanding common stock and preferred stock that is described in section 1504(a)(4). L owns 90 percent of the L1 common stock, and A owns the remaining 10 percent of the L1 common stock plus all the preferred stock. The value of the L1 common stock is $40, and the value of the L1 preferred stock is $30. L2 has outstanding common stock, 50 percent of which is owned by L and 50 percent by L1. The L group has an ownership change. * * *
>
> (ii) * * * [T]he L group does not include the value of the stock of any member that is owned directly or indirectly by another member in computing its consolidated section 382 limitation. Accordingly, the value of the stock of the loss group is $134, the sum of the value of (a) The common stock of L ($100), (b) The 10 percent of the L1 common stock ($4) owned by A, and (3) The L1 preferred stock ($30) owned by A.

Thus, in the above example, since the value of the loss group stock is $134, assuming the long-term tax exempt rate is 10%, the consolidated Section 382 limitation would be $13.4. Consequently, the loss group of L, L1 and L2 could utilize on an annual basis up to $13.4 of their consolidated net operating loss after an ownership change.

§ 5.10 The Impact of § 269 on the Utilization of Target's NOLs*

A. Introduction to § 269

Section 269(a) provides that if any person acquires, directly or indirectly, control of a corporation, or if any corporation acquires, directly or indirectly, property of

---

* Based on §§ 52:02 to 52:05 of *Federal Taxation of Business Enterprises, supra* Chapter 1, note 1, with permission.

an unrelated corporation in a carryover basis transaction, and the principal purpose of the acquisition of control or of the property is the evasion or avoidance of federal income tax by securing the benefit of a deduction, credit or other allowance (tax benefit) which the person would otherwise not have enjoyed, then the Internal Revenue Service may disallow the tax benefit. Control for purposes of § 269(a)(1) is defined as the ownership of stock possessing at least 50% of the total combined voting power of all classes of stock entitled to vote or at least 50% of the total value of shares of all classes of stock of the corporation. *See* § 269(a). The Service may disallow a tax benefit in whole or in part. *See* § 269(c).

The acquisition of control element in § 269 could apply to both taxable stock acquisitions and tax-free acquisitive stock for stock reorganizations. *See* Chapter 8. The acquisition of property element could apply to tax-free asset reorganizations (*see* Chapter 7), but not to taxable asset acquisitions. *See* Sec. 3.5.

Under § 269(b), the Service may disallow tax benefits where (1) there is a qualified stock purchase, within the meaning of § 338(d)(3), of a target corporation by an acquiring corporation; (2) a § 338 election is not made; (3) the target corporation is liquidated pursuant to a plan of liquidation adopted not more than two years after the acquisition date; and (4) the principal purpose of the liquidation is the "evasion or avoidance of Federal income tax by securing [a tax benefit] which the acquiring corporation would not otherwise enjoy." This provision is designed to prevent an acquiring corporation from directly utilizing a target corporation's losses by liquidating the target corporation.

Section 382 significantly curtails the ability of a loss corporation to utilize its NOLs after an ownership change. *See* Sec. 5.8.

B. Relationship between § 269 and § 382

Preamble to Proposed Regulations under § 1.269-7

Adopted by Treasury Decision 8388 (Dec. 31, 1991)

The amendments to sections 382 and 383 of the Code by the 1986 Act do not alter the continuing application of section 269 to acquisitions made for the principal purpose of evasion or avoidance of Federal income tax. Conference Report at II-194. Accordingly, the proposed regulations address the application of section 269 in situations in which section 382 or 383 also apply.

The proposed regulations provide, in general, that section 269 of the Code may be applied to disallow a deduction, credit, or other allowance the use or amount of which is limited or reduced under section 382 or 383 and the regulations thereunder. Nevertheless, because the limitations on the use of a deduction, credit, or other allowance under section 382(a) or 383 may significantly reduce the value of the deduction, credit, or other allowance to an acquirer, the proposed regulations provide that the application of these limitations following an acquisition is relevant to the determination of whether, for purposes of section 269, the principal purpose of the acquisition was to evade or avoid Federal income taxes by securing the benefit of the deduction, credit, or other allowance. [*See* § 1.269-7.] * * *

§ 5.11 Impact of § 384 on Utilization of Acquiring Corporation's NOL against Target's Built-In Gains

A. The 1987 Act

House Ways and Means Report on the Revenue Act of 1987
1092–1094 (1987)

Present Law. Special limitations apply to the use of net operating loss carry-forwards (NOLs) following an ownership change of the loss corporation generally, when there has been an increase of more than 50 percentage points in ownership of a loss corporation by certain persons (sec. 382). [*See* Sec. 5.8.] * * *

If a loss corporation does not experience an ownership change, the use of its losses may be limited [but only in certain limited circumstances.]

Section 269 of the Code may also limit the use of a loss corporation's losses in certain situations where there is a principal purpose of evasion or avoidance of Federal income tax. *See, e.g. Briarcliff Candy Corporation,* 54 T.C.M. 667 (1987).

Reasons for Change. * * * Although section 269 of the Code applies where the principal purpose of an acquisition is evasion or avoidance of Federal income tax, some taxpayers may take the position that section 269 does not apply to a particular transaction. The committee understands that in some instances, loss corporations may effectively be paid to "launder" built-in gains or to take over "burnt-out" tax shelter or similar property. The committee is concerned that the "principal purpose" test of section 269 and its other restrictions may not be adequate to deter some taxpayers from taking positions that the Internal Revenue Service may lack the resources to challenge in all cases. Therefore, the committee believes that a bright-line test in addition to the rules of section 269 is desirable.

Explanation of Provisions. * * * The bill provides that loss corporations will be precluded from using their losses to shelter built-in gains of an acquired company recognized within 5 years of the acquisition. Built-in gains for this purpose includes any item of income which is attributable to periods before the acquisition date. For example, built-in gains for this purpose include so-called "phantom" gains on property for which depreciation had been taken prior to the acquisition. * * *

B. The 1988 Act

House Ways and Means Committee Report on Technical and Miscellaneous Revenue Act of 1988

410–414 (1988)

Present Law. The 1987 Act limited a corporation's ability to offset gains that accrued prior to a merger or acquisition against preacquisition losses [*see* § 384(c)(3)] of a second corporation. Under one rule (the "stock acquisition rule"), if a gain corporation (one with a net unrealized built-in gain in excess of a *de minimis* threshold amount) becomes a member of an affiliated group, income of the corporation attributable to recognized built-in gains cannot be offset by preacquisition losses of other members of the group. [*See* § 384(a)(1).] Under a second rule (the "asset acquisition rule"), if the assets of a gain corporation are acquired by another corporation in a tax-free subsidiary liquidation under section 332 or in a tax-free reorganization, the income of the acquiring corporation attributable to recognized built-in gains of the gain corporation may not be offset by preacquisition losses of the acquiring corporation, or of members of its affiliated group. [The asset acquisition rule is also discussed in Sec. 7.12.] [*See* § 384(a)(1).]

An exception to both the stock acquisition rule and the asset acquisition rule is provided for preacquisition losses of a corporation (or affiliated group of corporations) that has held more than 50 percent of the gain corporation's stock for five years or longer. [*See* § 384(b).]

A recognized built-in gain is defined as any gain recognized during the five-year period beginning on the acquisition date, except to the extent the taxpayer establishes that the gain accrued after the acquisition date. [*See* § 384(c)(1)(A).] Items of income attributable to periods before the acquisition date are also treated as recognized built-in gain. [*See* § 384(c)(1)(B).]

A preacquisition loss is defined as any net operating loss carry-forward to the taxable year in which the acquisition date occurs (or any built-in loss recognized during the recognition period), and the portion of any loss incurred in the taxable year of the acquisition allocable to the period before the acquisition date. [*See* § 384(c)(3).]

Except as provided in regulations, the terms "net unrealized built-in gain", "net unrealized built-in loss", "recognized built-in loss", "recognition period", and "recognition period taxable year" have the same respective meanings as when used in section 382(h), except that the acquisition date shall be taken into account in lieu of the change date. [*See* § 384 (c)(8).]

Explanation of Provision. *Events triggering limitation.* The bill provides that the stock acquisition rule applies if one corporation acquires (directly or indirectly) control of another corporation and either corporation is a gain corporation. [*See* §§ 384(a)(1), (2) and (c)(4).] Control is defined as stock representing 80 percent of the vote and value of a corporation within the meaning of section 1504(a)(2). [*See*

§ 384(c)(5).] The asset acquisition rule applies if either the acquired or the surviving corporation is a gain corporation. [*See* §§ 384(a)(1), (2) and (c)(4).]

Application to successor corporations. The bill clarifies that the limitation applies to any successor corporation to the same extent it applied to its predecessor. [*See* § 384(c)(7).]

For example, assume that corporation L, which has net operating loss carryovers, acquires control of corporation G, which has net unrealized built-in gain in excess of the *de minimis* threshold. The two corporations subsequently file a consolidated return. Under the stock acquisition rule, income attributable to G's recognized built-in gains may not be offset by L's preacquisition losses during the subsequent five-year recognition period. If G is liquidated into L under section 332 within five years after the acquisition, income attributable to G's recognized built-in gains may not be offset by L's preacquisition losses during the remainder of the five-year period. The same result would occur if L merged downstream into G. * * *

As under the Act, the limitations of section 384 apply independently of and in addition to the limitations of section 382.

Treatment of affiliated corporations (including definition of preacquisition loss). The bill clarifies that (except to the extent provided in regulations and subject to the successor rule described above) all corporations which are members of the same affiliated group immediately before the acquisition date shall be treated as one corporation. [*See* § 384(c)(6).]

Thus, for example, the determination of whether the *de minimis* threshold for built-in gain or loss is satisfied is to be made on an affiliated group basis, unless regulations provide otherwise.

In addition, if a corporation becomes a member of an affiliated group and subsequently merges with another member, although any gains or losses which were limited under section 384 as a result of the stock acquisition rule when the corporation became a member of the group will continue to be limited, gains or losses accruing after the date of affiliation and before the merger will not be preacquisition gains or losses with respect to the merger. * * *

Common control exception. The bill modifies the exception from the limitation for more than 50-percent ownership over a five-year period in two respects. [*See* § 384(b)(1).]

First, the exception applies in any case where the gain corporation and the corporation with the preacquisition loss were members of the same "controlled group" at all times during the five-year period. * * *

Second, the bill provides that if the gain corporation was not in existence throughout this five-year period, the exception is applied by substituting the period of its existence. * * *

Conforming amendment to rules relating to net operating loss carryovers and carrybacks. The bill provides that, if a taxpayer is prevented from using a preacquisition loss against a recognized built-in gain under this provision, the gain is not taken into account in applying the rules relating to carryovers and carrybacks of net operating losses, excess credits, and capital losses. Thus, the loss (or credit) carryover is not reduced when it cannot be used by reason of this provision. [*See* §384(c)(1).]

The bill also provides ordering rules, similar to those provided under section 382, in the case of losses that are subject to limitation under section 384 because they cannot be used to offset built-in gains. [*See* §384(c)(2).]

Application of section 382 definitions with respect to net unrealized built-in gain, net unrealized built-in loss, etc. Under section 382 of the Code, net unrealized built-in gain or net unrealized built-in loss is treated as zero if the amount of such gain or loss is not greater than [the lesser of 15 percent] of the fair market value of the assets of the corporation [or $10,000,000]. This * * * threshold also applies for purposes of section 384. [*See* §384(c)(8).]

The portion of the bill that contains technical corrections to the 1986 Act amends section 382 to provide that, for purposes of determining whether the [15%] percent threshold has been met, there shall not be taken into account cash or cash items, or any marketable security which has a value which does not substantially differ from adjusted basis, except to the extent provided in regulations. * * * It is recognized that the taxpayer may have a different interest with respect to the threshold for purposes of section 382 than for purposes of section 384. It is expected that regulations may apply any prophylactic rules where there is a potential for taxpayer manipulation in accordance with the purposes of the particular provision for purposes of which the threshold is being applied. * * *

§5.12 Limitation on Carryback of Losses after LBOs: The Cert Provision

See §172(h).

Senate Finance Committee Report to the Revenue Reconciliation Act of 1989

Present Law A corporation that incurs net operating losses (NOLs) generally can carry the NOLs back 3 taxable years and forward 15 taxable years (sec. 172). Carrying the NOLs back against prior taxable income allows a corporation to recognize currently the benefit of those losses by obtaining a refund of Federal income taxes paid in prior years.

Reasons for Change The committee believes that the ability of corporations to carry back NOLs that are created by certain debt-financed transactions is contrary to the purpose of the NOL carryback rule. Specifically, the purpose of the rule is to allow corporations to smooth out the swings in taxable income that result from business cycle fluctuations and unexpected financial reverses. The committee believes that when a corporation is involved in certain debt-financed transactions, the underlying nature of the corporation is substantially altered. In addition, the committee believes that the interest expense associated with such transactions does not have a sufficient nexus with prior period operations to justify a carryback of NOLs attributable to such expense. Therefore, the committee believes that it is inappropriate to permit a corporation to carry back an NOL generated by such a transaction to a year prior to the year in which such transaction occurred.

Explanation of Provision *In general.* The ability of C corporations to obtain refunds of taxes paid in prior years by carrying back NOLs is limited in cases where the losses are created by interest deductions allocable to certain corporate equity-reducing transactions.

Corporate equity reduction transaction. A corporate equity reduction transaction ("CERT") means either a major stock acquisition or an excess distribution. A major stock acquisition is an acquisition by a corporation (or any group of persons acting in concert with such corporation) of at least 50 percent of the vote or value of the stock of another corporation. All acquisitions made during any 24-month period are aggregated for these purposes. A major stock acquisition does not include an acquisition where the acquiring corporation has made a section 338 election * * *.

An excess distribution is the excess of the aggregate distributions and redemptions made by a corporation during the taxable year with respect to its stock (other than stock described in section 1504(a)(4)), over 150 percent of the average of such distributions and redemptions for the preceding 3 taxable years. * * *

Limitation of net operating loss carryback. If a C corporation has an NOL in the taxable year in which it is involved in a CERT or in the following 2 taxable years, the corporation may be limited in its ability to carry back some portion of the loss. A C corporation is treated as being involved in a CERT if it is either the acquired or acquiring corporation, or successor thereto (in the case of a major stock acquisition) or the distributing or redeeming corporation, or successor thereto (in the case of an excess distribution). Any portion of an NOL that cannot be carried back due to the operation of this provision may be carried forward to the corporation's future taxable years, as otherwise provided under present law. * * *

Examples. The operation of the provision may be illustrated by the following examples.

(1) Profitable corporation P, a calendar year C corporation, is capitalized with $150 million of debt and $50 million of equity. P's annual interest expense has been $15 million for the past 3 years. P has paid a 1% annual dividend to its shareholders, or an average of $.5 million, for each of the past 3 years. On January 1, 1990, P borrows $50 million and distributes the proceeds to its shareholders. Due to increased interest deductions of $5 million, P incurs an NOL in 1990 of $4 million.

P was involved in a CERT in 1990 because P made an excess distribution to its shareholders (*i.e.*, the $50 million distribution exceeds 150% of the average $.5 million dividend). The portion of P's $4 million NOL that is limited under the provision is the lesser of (1) P's interest expense that is allocable to the CERT ($5 million), or (2) the excess of P's interest expense in 1990 ($20 million) over P's average interest expense for the past 3 years ($15 million), or $5 million. Thus, P would not be able to carry back the $4 million NOL to any taxable year prior to 1990. In addition, if P has NOLs in 1991 and 1992 due to interest deductions allocable to the 1990 CERT, a similar computation would be made in each of those years and P may be limited in its ability to carry back the losses to pre-1990 taxable years. If P has income in subsequent years, however, P would be able to use the NOLs to offset that income. * * *

§ 5.13 Summary Problems on the Utilization of NOLs after a Taxable Stock Acquisition

Statement of Facts

Loss corporation (*LC*) was organized on January 1, 2014 and has been engaged in the business of manufacturing and selling widgets since that time. *LC* is a calendar year, accrual basis taxpayer. The original capital contribution to *LC* was $500K in cash. *LC* has incurred an operating loss of $100K in each of its calendar years 2014, 2015 and 2016. It is now (January 1, 2017) projected that *LC* will break even in calendar year 2017 and have $100K of taxable income in each of its calendar years subsequent to 2014. The adjusted basis of *LC*'s assets as of the close of business on December 31, 2016 was $200K, and the fair market value of both its assets and its stock at that time was estimated to be $500K. *LC* has only common stock outstanding and *LC* has no liabilities.

Profitable Corporation (*PC*), a publicly held corporation, has been operating for many years on a profitable basis. For the past several years, *PC* has had approximately $100K of taxable income, and it is projected that *PC* will continue to have approximately $100K of taxable income in the succeeding several years. *PC*'s tax rate is 33 1/3%. The adjusted basis of *PC*'s assets is $500K and the fair market value of both its assets and stock is $800K. *PC* is a calendar year, accrual basis taxpayer and has no liabilities. The long-term tax exempt rate is 10%.

1. *PC Acquires the Stock of LC in a Taxable Purchase; LC is Not Liquidated*

Prior to the transaction described below, the stock of *LC* was owned by individual A, the initial organizer of *LC*. As of the close of business on December 31, 2016, *PC* purchased 100% of the stock of *LC* for $500K in cash. *PC* plans to operate *LC* as a wholly-owned subsidiary. *LC* will continue to be engaged in the business of manufacturing and selling widgets. *PC* and *LC* will file consolidated returns. *PC* does not file a § 338 election.

a. What is the impact, if any, of § 382 on *LC*'s net operating loss carryover? Suppose *LC*'s widget business is terminated and it goes into the real estate business?

b. What is the potential impact, if any, of § 269 on *LC*'s net operating loss carryovers?

c. What is the potential impact, if any, of § 384?

d. What will be the impact of the rules under the consolidated return regulations, including the SRLY rules, on the utilization by the *PC-LC* consolidated group of *LC*'s $300K of net operating loss carryovers? As noted in the basic fact statement, it is projected that *LC* will break even in 2017 and have $100K of taxable income in each subsequent year. On the other hand, *PC* is expected to have approximately $100K of taxable income in 2017 and following years.

e. Suppose *PC* had net operating loss carryovers from its years prior to 2017. Would those losses be subject to the limitation under the consolidated return regulations? Under § 384?

f. What result if PC files a § 338 election with respect to LC? Should it file a § 338 election?

2. *Taxable Purchase; LC Is Then Liquidated*

After purchasing *LC*'s stock on December 31, 2016, *PC* immediately liquidates *LC*. *PC* does not file a § 338 election.

a. What is the impact, if any, of §§ 382, 269, and 384?

b. What is the impact, if any, of the SRLY limitation?

c. What is the impact, if any, of § 381 on *LC*'s net operating loss carryovers as a result of the liquidation of *LC* into *PC*? *See* §§ 332, 334(b)(1), and 381(a)(1). *See* Sec. 7.8.

3. *Taxable Purchase by LC of PC's Stock Followed by Sale of PC's Assets*

Acquiring Corporation (AC) is interested in acquiring *PC*'s assets. The parties have tentatively agreed on a sale price of $800K; however, *PC*'s shareholders would like to avoid, or at least reduce, the corporate level tax on the sale of *PC*'s assets that would result from the repeal of the *General Utilities* doctrine. Since the basis of *PC*'s assets is $500K, *PC*'s taxable gain on the sale would be $300K, and its tax liability would be $100K. As a consequence, after liquidation of *PC,* its shareholders would only receive $700K (*i.e.,* $800K sales proceeds less, $100K tax liability.) One of the investment bankers working on the deal has suggested that the following transaction be structured. First, *LC* purchases the stock of *PC* for $750K and *LC* and *PC* file consolidated returns. This puts $50K more cash into the hands of *PC*'s shareholders. Second, *LC* causes *PC* to sell its assets to *AC* for $800K, and *LC*'s NOLs are used to offset PC's $300K gain. Thus, the repeal of *General Utilities* is avoided. Third, *PC* is then liquidated distributing the $800K in cash to *LC*. Under § 332, *LC* has no gain or loss on the liquidation. *LC* has a net economic gain of $50K (*i.e.,* $800K liquidation proceeds minus $750K purchase price for *PC*'s stock). Assuming the transaction could withstand attack by the Service under the step transaction doctrine, does the transaction produce the expected results?

§ 5.14 Introduction to Federal Income Tax Consequences of Cross Border Taxable Stock Acquisitions

A. Introduction

This section briefly addresses some of the Federal income tax issues that can arise when (1) a foreign acquiring corporation purchases the stock of a domestic target corporation (inbound stock acquisition), and (2) a U.S. acquiring corporation purchases the stock of a foreign target (outbound stock acquisition). The acquiring corporation can purchase the stock of the target directly or through a wholly owned subsidiary located in the U.S. in the case of an inbound stock acquisition or in the foreign country in the case of an outbound stock acquisition. The principal issues faced in these transactions are the tax treatment of the stock acquisition, and the tax treatment of the dividends or interest paid on the debt or equity capital of the target to its new parent, the acquiring corporation. The treatment of these issues is governed by both the Code and any tax treaty that may be applicable. The issues are similar to those discussed in Sec. 4.7 in connection with cross border taxable asset acquisitions. Sec. 4.7 should be reviewed before proceeding here.

B. Inbound Stock Acquisitions

1. General Principles

The tax treatment to the U.S. selling shareholders is essentially the same as in the case of a sale to a domestic acquiror. The foreign acquiring corporation (FAC) or its domestic acquiring sub (DAS) will take a cost basis for the U.S. target's (USTC) stock, and unless USTC has significant NOLs it is unlikely that FAC or DAS would make a § 338 election. If USTC were a member of a consolidated group, then FAC or DAS would want to file a § 338(h)(10) election.

If the acquisition is made by DAS, then FAC will have to determine the capital structure of DAS. Under § 881 the U.S. imposes a 30% withholding tax on U.S. source dividends, interest, royalties and "other fixed or determinable" income from U.S. sources paid by either USTC or DAS to FAC, which is the foreign parent. USTC or DAS is required to withhold the 30%. *See* § 1442. This 30% tax is referred to as a gross basis tax because it is imposed on the gross payment.

Although the 30% gross basis tax applies to both dividend and interest payments, if FAC is resident in a country that has a tax treaty with the U.S., the treaty likely will provide for a lower withholding rate on cross border dividend and interest payments flowing between the U.S. and the treaty partner. Under the U.S. Model Treaty the maximum withholding rate on interest is zero, and the maximum withholding rate on dividends paid to a corporate shareholder that holds at least 10% of the stock of the paying corporation (which is the case with FAC) is 5%.

The zero withholding rate on interest could cause FAC to capitalize DAS with significant debt, so that the interest received from DAS by FAC would not be subject to any U.S. tax. This type of transaction is referred to as interest stripping and as is seen in the next section, § 163(j) puts a limit on the ability to strip interest in this type of situation.

2. Introduction to the Earnings Stripping Rules

House Report to the Revenue Reconciliation Act of 1989

Present Law In many cases, U.S. taxpayers are related to, and share common economic interests with, persons that are effectively exempt from U.S. tax. For example, a U.S. corporation may be a wholly owned subsidiary of a foreign corporation that is not subject to U.S. tax. * * *

Interest expenses of a U.S. corporate taxpayer are generally deductible, whether or not the interest is paid to a related party or a tax-exempt entity. When a related tax-exempt person receives interest from a taxpayer, however, the Code provides rules to protect the U.S. tax base. * * *

The committee understands that the tax laws of several industrialized countries include limitations on the deduction of excessive amounts of interest paid to related foreign (*i.e.* tax-exempt) parties. For example, interest paid by a French corporation to a foreign related party that is a manager of the French corporation is generally not deductible to the extent that the principal amount of debt exceeds 150 percent of the corporation's capital. * * *

Reasons for Change The committee believes, as a general matter, that it is appropriate to limit the deduction for interest that a taxable person pays or accrues to a tax-exempt entity whose economic interests coincide with those of the payor. To allow an unlimited deduction for such interest permits significant erosion of the tax base. Allowance of unlimited deductions permits an economic unit that consists of more than one legal entity to contract with itself at the expense of the government. The payment of deductible interest that is tax-free to a related party is sometimes referred to as "earnings stripping." When a U.S. corporation that is consistently profitable before substantial interest deductions pays interest to its tax-exempt foreign parent, those interest deductions may greatly reduce or even eliminate) U.S. tax on a source basis. Absent deductions for related party interest, the United States would collect both a corporate tax on the U.S. corporation's profits and, in most cases, a withholding tax on dividends it pays to its parent. The committee believes that a limitation on the ability to "strip" earnings out of this country through interest payments in lieu of dividend distributions is appropriate. The committee believes that the uncertainty of present law (particularly the debt-equity distinction) may allow taxpayers to take aggressive positions that inappropriately erode the U.S. tax base. * * *

Explanation of Provisions The bill provides that certain interest paid or accrued by a corporation to related tax-exempt parties is not deductible. [*See* § 163(j).] The bill defines interest paid to related tax-exempt parties as "disqualified interest," and denies deductions for disqualified interest to the extent that the excess (if any) of the payor corporation's total interest expense over its total interest income is greater than 50 percent of adjusted taxable income. Adjusted taxable income means taxable income computed without regard to either net interest expense or NOL carryovers. * * *

C. Outbound Taxable Stock Acquisition

Assuming all of the selling shareholders are foreign persons, they will not be subject to U.S. taxation. The domestic acquiring corporation (DAC) or its foreign acquiring sub (FAS) will take a cost basis for the foreign target's (FT) stock. Assuming that FT does not conduct business in the U.S., DAC or FAS may want to file a § 338 election. In such case, FT would take a fresh basis for its assets without incurring any U.S. tax, and presumably the § 338 election would not trigger taxable gain in FT's country of operation. FT will be a controlled foreign corporation (CFC), and therefore, any subpart F income (*i.e.*, passive income and certain tax haven income) of FT will be imputed to DAC. If FT has no subpart F income, DAC will not be taxed on FT's earnings until those earnings are repatriated to the U.S. *See* Sec 4.7.

If FAS make the acquisition, then DAC will have to determine the capital structure of FAS. The capital structure would be determined by the internal laws of the country in which FAS is organized and by any treaty between the U.S. and such country. The internal laws of most countries have a gross basis tax on interest and dividends from sources in the country, subject to reduction by tax treaty.

Subject to certain limitations, DAC will qualify for a foreign tax credit on any withholding tax on interest or dividends received from FT or FAS. *See* § 901 *et seq.* Also, since DAC will hold more than 10% of the stock of FT or FAS, under § 902, DAC will receive a deemed paid credit for the underlying foreign corporate taxes paid by FAS and FT with respect to the earnings out of which the dividends are paid.

§ 5.15 Sample Stock Acquisition Agreement: Selected Provision

Sample Stock Purchase Agreement[*]

STOCK PURCHASE AGREEMENT, dated as of March 3, 2003 between Acquiring Corporation, Inc., a Delaware corporation (the Acquiring Corporation), and the individuals named in Exhibit 1 attached hereto (the Selling Shareholders), being all of the shareholders of Target Corporation, Inc., a Delaware Corporation (the Target Corporation).

WITNESSETH

WHEREAS, the Selling Shareholders own the shares of common stock, [insert par value as stated in the Target Corporation's charter], of the Target Corporation

---

[*] This agreement is adapted from Appendix N of Thompson, *Statutory Supplement and Documentary Appendices to Business Planning for Mergers and Acquisitions* (2nd Ed., 2001).

(the Stock), as set forth in Exhibit 1, being all of the outstanding shares of such common stock;

WHEREAS, the Selling Shareholders desire to sell, and the Acquiring Corporation desires to purchase, the Stock pursuant to this Agreement; and

WHEREAS, it is the intention of the parties hereto that, upon consummation of the purchase and sale of the Stock pursuant to this Agreement, the Acquiring Corporation shall own all of the outstanding shares of capital stock of the Target Company;

NOW, THEREFORE, IT IS AGREED:

Article I
Sale of Stock and Closing

§ 1.1 *Sale of Stock.* Subject to the terms and conditions herein stated, the Selling Shareholders agree to sell, assign, transfer and deliver to the Acquiring Corporation on the Closing Date, and the Acquiring Corporation agrees to purchase from each Selling Shareholder on the Closing Date, the number of shares of Stock set forth opposite the name of such Selling Shareholder on Exhibit 1 attached hereto. The certificates representing the Stock shall be duly endorsed in blank, or accompanied by stock powers duly executed in blank, by the Selling Shareholders transferring the same, with signatures guaranteed by a domestic commercial bank or trust company, with all necessary transfer tax and other revenue stamps, acquired at the Selling Stockholder's expense, affixed and cancelled. Each Selling Shareholder agrees to cure any deficiencies with respect to the endorsement of the certificates representing the Stock owned by such Selling Shareholder or with respect to the stock power accompanying any such certificate.

§ 1.2 *Price.* In full consideration for the purchase by the Acquiring Corporation of the Stock, the Acquiring Corporation shall pay to the Selling Shareholders on the Closing Date an aggregate of $____, by official bank checks in New York funds payable to the order of each of the Selling Shareholders, such checks to be in the amounts set forth in Exhibit 1 attached hereto.

§ 1.2 *Closing.* (a) The sale referred to in Section 1.1 shall take place at 10:00 A.M. at the offices of [Name and Address of the Acquiring Corporation's counsel] on, ____ 2003, or at such other time and date (not later than, ____ 2003) as the parties hereto shall by written instrument designate. Such time and date are herein referred to as the "Closing Date".* * *

Article II
Representation and Warranties

§ 2. *Representations of the Selling Shareholders.* The Selling Stockholders represent, warrant and agree, jointly and severally except as otherwise indicated, as follows:

§ 2.1(a) *Ownership of Stock.* Each Selling Shareholder is the lawful owner of the number of shares of Stock listed opposite the name of such Selling Shareholder in Exhibit 1 hereto, free and clear of all liens, encumbrances, restrictions and claims of every kind; each Selling Shareholder has full legal right, power and authority to enter into this Agreement and to sell, assign, transfer and convey the shares of Stock so owned by such Selling Shareholder pursuant to this Agreement; the delivery to the Acquiring Corporation of the Stock pursuant to the provisions of this Agreement will transfer to the Acquiring Corporation, valid title thereto, free and clear of all liens, encumbrances, restrictions and claims of every kind. Each Selling Shareholder is a resident or incorporated under the laws of the state set forth opposite such Selling Shareholder's name in Exhibit 1.

Comment

The Selling Shareholders will generally be required by the Acquiring Corporation to make certain representations about the status of the business and operation of the Target Corporation. In the acquisition of a closely-held firm, the representations relating to the Target Corporation are likely to be much more extensive than the representations in a public deal.

* * *

§ 2.1(b) *Absence of Undisclosed Liabilities.* The Target Corporation has no liabilities or obligations, either direct or indirect, matured or unmatured or absolute, contingent or otherwise, except:

(i) those liabilities or obligations set forth on the balance sheet of the Target Corporation for its last fiscal year and not herefore paid or discharged;

(ii) liabilities arising in the ordinary course of business under any agreement, contract, commitment, lease or plan specifically disclosed on the Disclosure Schedule or not required to be disclosed because of the term or amount involved; and

(iii) those liabilities or obligations incurred, consistently with past business practice, in or as a result of the normal and ordinary course of business since the end of the last fiscal year. * * *

For purposes of this Agreement, the term "liabilities" shall include, without limitation, any direct or indirect indebtedness, guaranty, endorsement, claim, loss, damage, deficiency, cost, expense, obligation or responsibility, fixed or unfixed, known or unknown, asserted or unasserted, choate or inchoate, liquidated or unliquidated, secured or unsecured.

§ 2.1(c) *Completeness of Disclosure.* No representation or warranty by the Selling Shareholders in this Agreement nor any certificate, schedule, statement, document or instrument furnished or to be furnished to the Acquiring Corporation pursuant hereto, or in connection with the negotiation, execution or performance of this Agreement, contains or will contain any untrue statement of a material fact or omits or will omit to state a material fact required to be stated herein or therein or necessary to make any statement herein or therein not misleading.

§ 2.2 *Representations and Warranties of The Acquiring Corporation.*

Comment

The representations and warranties of the Acquiring Corporation will depend upon the type of consideration paid. If cash is paid, there may be simple representations relative to organization, standing and power. If the Acquiring Corporation is issuing its securities so that the Selling Shareholders are making an investment in the Acquiring Corporation, more complete representations are appropriate.***

Article III
Covenants Relating to Conduct of Business

§ 3.1 *Covenants of The Selling Shareholders*

Comment

The covenants made here by the Selling Shareholders may relate to the operations of the Target Corporation prior to closing.* * *

§ 3.2 *Covenants of the Acquiring Corporation.*

Comment

Since the purchase is for cash, the Acquiring Corporation has no covenants here. If the Acquiring Corporation were issuing its securities, the Acquiring Corporation would normally undertake significant covenants.* * *

Article IV
Additional Agreements

§ 4.1 *Additional Agreements of Selling Shareholders.*

Comment

Depending on the circumstances, the Selling Shareholders may agree to perform certain other actions between the signing and closing. The Selling Shareholders may also covenant not to cause the Target Corporation or its officers and directors to directly or indirectly solicit, initiate or encourage other acquisition proposals.* * *

§ 4.2 *Additional Agreements of Acquiring Corporations.*

Comment

Since the consideration is cash, the Acquiring Corporation may not have elaborate undertakings. However, the Acquiring Corporation should undertake to use all reasonable efforts to promptly comply with all legal requirements. * * *

Article V
Conditions to Acquiring Corporation's Obligations

§ 5.1 *Conditions to Acquiring Corporation's Obligations.* The purchase of the Stock by the Acquiring Corporation on the Closing Date is conditioned upon satisfaction, on or prior to such date, of the following conditions:

§ 5.1(a) *Opinion of the Selling Shareholders' Counsel.* The Stockholders shall have furnished the Acquiring Corporation with a favorable opinion, dated the Closing Date, of, the counsel to the Selling Shareholders, in form and substance satisfactory to the Acquiring Corporation and its counsel, to the effect set forth in Exhibit 2 attached hereto. * * *

§ 5.1(c) *No Material Adverse Change.* Prior to the Closing Date, there shall be no material adverse change in the assets or liabilities, the business or condition, financial or otherwise, the results of operations, or prospects of the Target Corporation and its subsidiaries, whether as a result of any legislative or regulatory change, revocation of any license or rights to do business, fire, explosion, accident, casualty, labor trouble, flood, drought, riot, storm, condemnation or act of God or other public force or otherwise, and the Selling Stockholders shall have delivered to the Acquiring Corporation a certificate, dated the Closing Date, to such effect.

Article VI
Survival of Representations; Indemnity; Set Off

§ 6.1 *Survival of Representations.* The respective representations and warranties and other covenants and agreements of the Selling Shareholders and the Acquiring Corporation contained in this Agreement or in any schedule attached hereto shall survive the purchase and sale of the Stock contemplated hereby.

§ 6.2 *Indemnification.* (a) The Selling Shareholders agree, jointly and severely, to indemnity and hold the Acquiring Corporation and its officers, directors and agents harmless from damages, losses or expenses (including, without limitation, reasonable counsel fees and expenses) in excess of $25,000 in the aggregate, suffered or paid, directly or indirectly, through application of the Target Corporation's or the Acquiring Corporation's assets, as a result of or arising out of the failure of any representation or warranty made by the Selling Shareholders in this Agreement or in any scheduled attached hereto to be true and correct in all respects as of the date of this Agreement and as of the Closing Date. * * *

Chapter 6

Fundamental Reorganization Concepts

§ 6.1 Scope

This chapter, which is divided into eight parts, addresses several fundamental concepts concerning reorganizations. Part A, which deals with concepts relating to the reorganization definition in § 368, looks at (1) the continuity of interest doctrine (including the regulations) in Sec. 6.2; (2) the continuity of business enterprise doctrine (including the regulations) in Sec. 6.3; (3) the meaning of solely for voting stock in Sec. 6.4; (4) the definition of control in Sec. 6.5; (5) the meaning of the "plan of reorganization" in Sec. 6.6; and (6) the ever-present business purposes doctrine in Sec. 6.7.

Part B, which deals with concepts relating to the exchanging stockholders and security holders, examines (1) the meaning of "securities exchanged" in Sec. 6.8; (2) the treatment of warrants in Sec. 6.9; (3) the treatment of a swap of securities for securities in Sec. 6.10; and (4) the determination of the shareholder's basis in Sec. 6.11.

Part C, which deals with concepts relating to treatment of boot under § 356, examines (1) the requirement of a reorganization as a condition for § 356 treatment and the treatment of nonqualified preferred stock as boot in Sec. 6.12, and (2) the impact of the *Clark* case in determining whether a distribution has the effect of the distribution of the dividend in Sec. 6.13.

Part D, which deals with concepts relating to the treatment of the target corporation, examines (1) the treatment of the target corporation upon the receipt and distribution of stock, securities, and boot in Sec. 6.14, and (2) the impact of the treatment of liabilities in Sec. 6.15.

Part E, which deals with concepts relating to the acquiror, examines the carryover basis rule in Sec. 6.16. Part F, which focuses on the impact of stock dividends and § 306 stock, examines the impact of § 305 in Sec. 6.17 and the impact of § 306 in Sec. 6.18. Finally, Part G, surveys (1) various overlap issues between § 351 and the reorganization provisions in Sec. 6.19 and (2) issues with the E and F reorganizations in Sec. 6.20.

Chapters 7–10 build on the principles discussed in this chapter, with (1) Chapter 7 focusing on asset reorganizations (*i.e.*, the A, the direct and triangular C, and the forward subsidiary merger reorganizations); (2) Chapter 8 focusing on stock reorganizations (*i.e.*, the direct and triangular B and the reverse subsidiary merger reorganizations); Chapter 9 focusing on spinoffs, and Chapter 10 focusing on cross border acquisitive reorganizations, including inversions.

These issues are covered in greater detail in Bittker and Eustice, *Corporations, supra* Sec. 1.12, and Ginsburg and Levin, *Mergers, supra* Sec. 1.12. *See also* the most recent edition of PLI, *Tax Strategies, supra* Sec. 1.12; and Thompson, *Mergers, Acquisitions, and Tender Offers, supra* Sec. 1.12 at Chapter 9.

Part A:
Concepts Relating to Reorganization Definition: § 368

§ 6.2 Introduction to Reorganizations and to the Concept of Continuity of Interest

A. Introduction

1. The Law Prior to the 1918 Act

Marr v. United States

Supreme Court of the United States, 1925
268 U.S. 536

MR. JUSTICE BRANDEIS delivered the opinion of the Court.

Prior to March 1, 1913, Marr and wife purchased 339 shares of the preferred and 425 shares of the common stock of the General Motors Company of New Jersey [GM, N.J.] for $76,400. In 1916, [GM, NJ was reincorporated in Delaware and] they received in exchange for this stock 451 shares of the preferred and 2,125 shares of the common stock of the General Motors Corporation of Delaware which (including a small cash payment) had the aggregate market value of $400,866.57. The difference between the cost of their stock in the New Jersey corporation and the value of the stock in the Delaware corporation was $324,466.57. The Treasury Department ruled that this difference was gain or income under the Act of September 8, 1916. * * *

* * * Marr contends that, since the new corporation was organized to take over the assets and continue the business of the old, and his capital remained invested in the same business enterprise, the additional securities distributed were in legal effect a stock dividend; and that under the rule of *Eisner v. Macomber,* 252 U.S. 189, applied in *Weiss v. Stearn,* 265 U.S. 242, he was not taxable thereon as income, because he still held the whole investment. The government insists that identity of the business enterprise is not conclusive; that gain in value resulting from profits is taxable as income, not only when it is represented by an interest in a different business enterprise or property, but also when it is represented by an essentially different interest in the same business enterprise or property; that, in the case at bar, the gain actually made is represented by securities with essentially different characteristics in an essentially different corporation; and that, consequently, the additional value of the new securities, although they are still held by the Marrs, is income under the rule applied in *United States v. Phellis,* 257 U.S. 156, 42 S.Ct. 63, 66 L.Ed. 180; *Rockefeller v. United States,* 257 U.S. 176, 42 S.Ct. 68, 66 L.Ed. 186; and *Cullinan v. Walker,* 262 U.S. 134, 43 S.Ct. 495, 67 L.Ed. 906. In our opinion the government is right.

In each of the five cases named, as in the case at bar, the business enterprise actually conducted remained exactly the same. In *United States v. Phellis,* in *Rockefeller v. United States* and in *Cullinan v. Walker,* where the additional value in new securities distributed was held to be taxable as income, there had been changes of corporate identity. That is, the corporate property, or a part thereof, was no longer held and operated by the same corporation; and,after the distribution, the stockholders no longer owned merely the same proportional interest of the same character in the same corporation. In *Eisner v. Macomber* and in *Weiss v. Stearn,* where the additional value in new securities was held not to be taxable, the identity was deemed to have been preserved. In *Eisner v. Macomber* the identity was literally maintained. There was no new corporate entity. The same interest in the same corporation was represented after the distribution by more shares of precisely the same character. It was as if the par value of the stock had been reduced, and three shares of reduced par value stock had been issued in place of every two old shares. That is, there was an exchange of certificates but not of interests. In *Weiss v. Stearn* a new corporation had, in fact, been organized to take over the assets and business of the old. Technically there was a new entity; but the corporate identity was deemed to have been substantially maintained because the new corporation was organized under the laws of the same state, with presumably the same powers as the old. There was also no change in the character of securities issued. By reason of these facts, the proportional interest of the stockholder after the distribution of the new securities was deemed to be exactly the same as if the par value of the stock in the old corporation had been reduced, and five shares of reduced par value stock had been issued in place of every two shares of the old stock. Thus, in *Weiss v. Stearn,* as in *Eisner v. Macomber,* the transaction was considered, in essence, an exchange of certificates representing the same interest, not an exchange of interests.

In the case at bar, the new corporation is essentially different from the old. A corporation organized under the laws of Delaware does not have the same rights and powers as one organized under the laws of New Jersey. Because of these inherent differences in rights and powers, both the preferred and the common stock of the old corporation is an essentially different thing from stock of the same general kind in the new. But there are also adventitious differences, substantial in character. A 6 per cent nonvoting preferred stock is an essentially different thing from a 7 per cent voting preferred stock. A common stock subject to the priority of $20,000,000 preferred and a $1,200,000 annual dividend charge is an essentially different thing from a common stock subject only to $15,000,000 preferred and a $1,050,000 annual dividend charge. The case at bar is not one in which after the distribution the stockholders have the same proportional interest of the same kind in essentially the same corporation.

Affirmed.

2. A Review of the Legislative History of the Current Reorganization Provisions

Excerpt from Chapman v. Commissioner

United States Court of Appeals, First Circuit, 1980

618 F.2d 856

One exception to [the general rule of recognition in § 1001(c)] appears in Section 354(a)(1), which provides that gain or loss shall not be recognized if stock or securities in a corporation are, in pursuance of the plan of reorganization, exchanged solely for stock or securities in another corporation which is a party to the reorganization. This exception does not grant a complete tax exemption for reorganizations, but rather defers the recognition of gain or loss until some later event such as a sale of stock acquired in the exchange. [*See* § 358.] Section 354(a)(1) does not apply to an exchange unless the exchange falls within one of the six categories of "reorganization" defined in Section 368(a)(1).[1] * * *

[The initial predecessor of the reorganization provisions was enacted in 1918 and was comprehensively revised in 1924.]

The 1924 Code defined reorganization, in part, as "a merger or consolidation (including the acquisition by one corporation of at least a majority of the voting stock and at least a majority of the total number of shares of all other classes of stock of another corporation, or substantially all the properties of another corporation)." Although the statute did not specifically limit the consideration that could be given in exchange for stock or assets, courts eventually developed the so-called "continuity of interest" doctrine, which held that exchanges that did not include some quantum of stock as consideration were ineligible for reorganization treatment for lack of a continuing property interest on the part of the acquiree's shareholders.

Despite this judicial development, sentiment was widespread in Congress that the reorganization provisions lent themselves to abuse, particularly in the form of so-called "disguised sales." In 1934, the House Ways and Means Committee proposed abolition of the stock-acquisition and asset-acquisition reorganizations which had appeared in the parenthetical section of the 1924 Act quoted above. The Senate Finance Committee countered with a proposal to retain these provisions, but with "restrictions designed to prevent tax avoidance." One of these restrictions was the requirement that the acquiring corporation obtain at least 80 percent, rather than a bare majority, of the stock of the acquiree. The second requirement was stated in the Senate Report as follows: "the acquisition, whether of stock or of substantially all the properties, must be in exchange solely for the voting stock of the acquiring corpo-

---

1. In the tax practice, these six categories are referred to by their alphabetic designations in the 1954 Code: hence, an (A) reorganization is a statutory merger or consolidation, a (B) reorganization is a stock-for-stock acquisition, a (C) reorganization is a stock-for-assets acquisition, a (D) reorganization is a corporate transfer of assets to a controlled corporation, an (E) reorganization is a recapitalization, and an (F) reorganization is a mere change in identity, form, or place of organization. * * *

ration." The Senate amendments were enacted as Section 112(g)(1) of the Revenue Act of 1934, 48 Stat. 680, which provided in pertinent part:

> "(1) The term 'reorganization' means (A) a statutory merger or consolidation, or (B) the acquisition by one corporation in exchange solely for all or a part of its voting stock: of at least 80 per centum of the voting stock and at least 80 per centum of the total number of shares of all other classes of stock of another corporation; or of substantially all the properties of another corporation * * *."

Congress revised this definition in 1939 in response to the Supreme Court's decision in *United States v. Hendler*, 303 U.S. 564, 58 S.Ct. 655, 82 L.Ed. 1018 (1938), which held that an acquiring corporation's assumption of the acquiree's liabilities in an asset-acquisition was equivalent to the receipt of "boot" by the acquiree. Since virtually all asset-acquisition reorganizations necessarily involve the assumption of the acquiree's liabilities, a literal application of the "solely for * * * voting stock" requirement would have effectively abolished this form of tax-free reorganization. In the Revenue Act of 1939, Congress separated the stock-acquisition and asset-acquisition provisions in order to exempt the assumption of liabilities in the latter category of cases from the "solely for * * * voting stock" requirement. Section 112(g)(1) of the revised statute then read, in pertinent part, as follows:

> "(1) the term 'reorganization' means (A) a statutory merger or consolidation, or (B) the acquisition by one corporation, in exchange solely for all or a part of its voting stock, of at least 80 per centum of the voting stock and at least 80 per centum of the total number of shares of all other classes of stock of another corporation, or (C) the acquisition by one corporation, in exchange solely for all or a part of its voting stock, of substantially all the properties of another corporation, but in determining whether the exchange is solely for voting stock the assumption by the acquiring corporation of a liability of the other, or the fact that property acquired is subject to liability, shall be disregarded * * *."

The next major change in this provision occurred in 1954. In that year, the House Bill, H.R. 8300, would have drastically altered the corporate reorganization sections of the Tax Code, permitting, for example, both stock and "boot" as consideration in a corporate acquisition, with gain recognized only to the extent of the "boot." The Senate Finance Committee, in order to preserve the familiar terminology and structure of the 1939 Code, proposed a new version of Section 112(g)(1), which would retain the "solely for * * * voting stock" requirement, but alter the existing control requirement to permit so-called "creeping acquisitions." Under the Senate Bill, [in a (B) reorganization] it would no longer be necessary for the acquiring corporation to obtain 80 percent or more of the acquiree's stock in one "reorganization." The Senate's proposal permitted an acquisition to occur in stages; a bloc of shares representing less than 80 percent could be added to earlier acquisitions, regardless of the consideration given earlier, to meet the control requirement. * * *

At the same time the Senate was revising the (B) provision, (while leaving intact the "solely for * * * voting stock" requirement), it was also rewriting the (C) provision to explicitly permit up to 20 percent of the consideration in an asset acquisition to take the form of money or other nonstock property. The Senate revisions of subsections (B) and (C) were ultimately passed, and have remained largely unchanged since 1954. Proposals for altering the (B) provision to allow "boot" as consideration have been made, but none has been enacted.

[In 1954 Congress also added the triangular (C) and the over-and-down under § 368(a)(2)(C). The triangular (B) was added in 1964; the forward subsidiary merger under § 368(a)(2)(D) was added in 1968; and the reverse subsidiary merger under § 368(a)(2)(E) was added in 1970.]

As this history shows, Congress has had conflicting aims in this complex and difficult area. On the one hand, the 1934 Act evidences a strong intention to limit the reorganization provisions to prevent forms of tax avoidance that had proliferated under the earlier revenue acts. This intention arguably has been carried forward in the current versions through retention of the "solely for * * * voting stock" requirement in (B), even while the (C) provision was being loosened. On the other hand, both the 1939 and 1954 revisions represented attempts to make the reorganization procedures more accessible and practical in both the (B) and (C) areas. * * *

3. Introduction to Reorganizations

Reorganization concepts were first introduced in Chapter 3. As indicated there, the starting point in approaching the reorganization provisions is the term "reorganization," which is defined in § 368(a)(1) as:

(1) a statutory merger or consolidation (the "(A)") (*see* § 368(a)(1)(A));

(2) a voting stock for stock acquisition (the "(B)") (*see* § 368(a)(1)(B));

(3) a voting stock for asset acquisition (the "(C)") (*see* § 368(a)(1)(C));

(4) a transfer of property by one corporation to another, including a split-up of a single corporation into two or more corporations (the "(D)") (*see* § 368(a)(1)(D));

(5) a recapitalization (the "(E)") (*see* § 368(a)(1)(E));

(6) a mere change in form (the "(F)") (*see* § 368(a)(1)(F)); and

(7) certain transfers by corporations in connection with bankruptcy reorganizations (the "(G)") (*see* § 368(a)(1)(G)). *See* Chapter 12.

Section 368(a)(2) adds two other reorganizations, and also provides special rules relating to the reorganizations defined in § 368(a)(1). The two reorganizations defined in § 368(a)(2) are:

(1) the merger of the target into a subsidiary of the acquiror (the "forward subsidiary merger") (*see* § 368(a)(2)(D)); and

(2) the merger of a subsidiary of the acquiror into the target (the "reverse subsidiary merger") (*see* § 368(a)(2)(E)).

Each of these forms of reorganization is diagrammed and illustrated in Chapter 3.

Section 368 says nothing about the treatment of the taxpayers involved in a reorganization; it merely describes those transactions that are reorganizations. The tax treatment to the various taxpayers is governed by §§ 354 through 362 and 381 to 383. Mergers between investment companies are not discussed here. *See* § 368(a)(2)(F). The (G) re-organization is examined in Chapter 12, which deals with bankruptcy restructurings.

Basically, reorganization transactions are shifts in corporate ownership in which the exchanging stockholder or security holder has a continuing interest in the surviving corporation and has not merely been cashed out. This continuing interest element is referred to as the continuity of interest requirement, and it is examined in detail in this section.

4. Introduction to the Tax Treatment to the Taxpayers Involved in a Reorganization

Section 354(a)(1) gives shareholders and security holders nonrecognition treatment upon an exchange, pursuant to a "plan of reorganization," of stock or securities in a corporation that is a "party to a reorganization," provided the exchange is "solely" for stock or securities in such corporation or in another corporation that is a party to a reorganization. *See* § 1.354-1(a). The term "plan of reorganization" is not defined in the statute; the regulations say, however, that the plan must be "adopted" by each of the corporate parties thereto. *See* § 1.368-3(a) and Sec. 6.6. The term "party to a re-organization" is defined in § 368(b) to include all of the corporations involved in a reorganization under § 368(a). *See* Sec. 6.2.G.

Section 354(a)(2)(A) limits the nonrecognition treatment for security holders to cases in which the principal amount of the securities received is equal to the principal amount surrendered. *See* Sec. 6.8. In the event cash or other property (boot) is received or the principal amount of the securities received exceeds the principal amount of the securities surrendered, then under § 356 the exchanging shareholder or security holder recognizes the gain realized to the extent of the boot and the fair market value of the excess principal amount of the securities received. *See* §§ 356(a)(1) and 356(d)(1) and (2)(A) and (B). *See* Sec. 6.12. Under § 356(a)(2), any gain recognized with respect to stock may be treated as a dividend, to the extent of the shareholder's pro rata share of the accumulated earnings and profits, if the exchange "has the effect of the distri-bution of a dividend." *See* Sec. 6.13. As a result of the uniform maximum rate of 20% that now applies to dividends and capital gains, § 356(a)(2) has very little practical significance. There is no difference between capital gain and dividend income even with respect to basis recovery, because there is no recovery of basis under § 356(a). No loss is recognized. *See* § 356(c). Also, under § 354(a)(2)(C), nonqualified preferred stock received in a reorganization is generally treated as boot. *See* Sec. 6.12.B.

Under § 358, the exchanging shareholder or security holder who receives non-recognition treatment under § 354 or partial nonrecognition treatment under § 356 takes the stock or securities received at a substituted basis, decreased by the amount of any boot received and increased by any gain recognized. The basis of the boot, other than money, is the fair market value thereof. *See* § 358(a)(2) and Sec. 6.11.

For example, assume that individual *S* owns all the stock of target corporation (*TC*). The stock has a value of $1 million, and *S*'s basis is $500K. *TC* merges into ac-quiring corporation (*AC*) in a transaction that qualifies as an (A) reorganization under § 368(a)(1)(A). *S* surrenders his *TC* stock and receives *AC* stock with a value of $1 million. Under § 354, *S* has nonrecognition treatment, and under § 358, *S* takes a substituted basis of $500K for the *AC* stock. Assume, on the other hand, that *S* receives $900K of *AC* stock and $100K of cash (boot). The transaction still constitutes an (A) reorganization; however, *S* has a recognized gain of $100K under § 356(a)(1), and the gain might be treated as a dividend under § 356(a)(2). *S*'s basis under § 358(a) for his *AC* stock is $500K (*i.e.*, the basis of his *TC* stock ($500K), minus the cash received ($100K), plus the gain recognized ($100K)). Since the value of his *AC* stock is $900K, *S* has deferred $400K of his gain.

On the corporate side of the ledger, § 1032 provides for nonrecognition treatment upon the issuance of stock by a corporation. Also, no gain is recognized by a corporation upon the issuance of its securities. *See* § 1.61-12(c)(1). Under § 362(b), the acquiring corporation's basis for stock or assets received is a carryover basis, increased by the amount of any gain recognized by the transferor. *See* Sec. 6.16.

If a corporation (the target), that is a "party to a reorganization", exchanges its property solely for stock of another corporation (the acquiring corporation), that is a party to the reorganization, then under § 361(a), the target corporation does not recognize any gain or loss. *See* Sec. 6.14. Under § 358, the basis to the target corporation of the stock or securities it receives from the acquiring corporation is a substituted basis, decreased by the boot received and increased by the gain recognized.

Under § 361(b), if the target corporation receives both stock and boot, the target recognizes the gain realized to the extent of the boot, unless the boot is distributed pursuant to the plan of reorganization. Under § 361(c), the target does not recognize gain or loss on the distribution of stock of the acquiring corporation.

Pursuant to § 357(a), liabilities transferred from a target to an acquiring corporation generally do not constitute boot. *See* § 357(b) and (c) and Sec. 6.15.

For example, where *TC* merges into *AC* with *TC*'s shareholder, *S*, receiving *AC* stock, *TC* has nonrecognition treatment under § 361(a). *AC* has nonrecognition under § 1032 upon the issuance of its stock, and takes a carryover basis under § 362(b) for *TC*'s assets (*i.e.*, if *TC*'s basis for its assets was $200K, *AC*'s basis would be $200K).

Section 381 provides that in reorganizations in which the target's assets are transferred to the acquiring corporation, the target corporation's tax attributes (*e.g.*, earnings and profits and net operating losses) carry over to the acquiring corporation after the reorganization. This same rule applies for subsidiary liquidations under § 332 in which the parent takes a carryover basis under § 334(b)(1) for the assets received. Section 381 is examined in connection with the examination of asset reorganizations in Chapter 7.

Section 382 limits the amount of a target's net operating losses that can be deducted after a reorganization. Also, § 382 limits the carryover of capital losses and certain credits. Section 382 is discussed in Chapters 5, 7, and 8.

The reorganizations under § 368 can be broadly categorized into acquisitive reorganizations and non-acquisitive reorganizations. Acquisitive reorganizations can be subdivided into asset reorganizations, which are transactions in which an acquiring corporation acquires the assets of a target corporation and stock reorganizations, which are transactions in which an acquiring corporation acquires the stock of a target corporation. Asset reorganizations are examined in Chapter 7 and stock reorganizations are examined in Chapter 8.

5. Introduction to the Continuity of Interest Doctrine

The regulations under § 1.368-1 and -2 refer in several places to the requirement that the transferor in a reorganization or its shareholders must have a continuity of interest in the assets transferred. This means that the target corporation or its shareholders must have, as a result of the reorganization, an ownership interest in the acquiring corporation. There is no reference in § 368 to continuity of interest; the concept was judicially developed. The stock for stock (B) reorganization, the stock for asset (C) reorganization, and the reverse subsidiary merger under § 368(a)(2)(E), have their own statutorily mandated continuity of interest requirements, in that the acquiring corporation must use its own or its parent's voting stock in making the acquisition. None of the other forms of reorganization have this voting stock requirement, and, consequently, the cases that have developed the concept are still important.

6. The Service's Private Ruling Policy on Reorganizations and Related Transactions

In many reorganization transactions, the parties may desire a private letter ruling from the IRS on the transaction. However, the IRS generally does not issue private rulings on reorganization and related issues, and prior to seeking a ruling the attorney should consult the current "No Rulings" Revenue Procedure of the IRS, which identifies those issues on which the IRS will not or generally will not rule. The IRS's current "no ruling" revenue procedure is normally the third revenue procedure issued each year, such as Rev. Proc. 2016-3.

B. What Type of Interest Satisfies the Continuity of Interest Requirement

1. Short-Term Notes Do Not Provide Continuity of Interest: The (C) before the Solely for Voting Stock Requirement

Pinellas Ice & Cold Storage Co. v. Commissioner

Supreme Court of the United States, 1933
287 U.S. 462

Mr. Justice McReynolds delivered the opinion of the Court.

Petitioner, a Florida corporation, made and sold ice at St. Petersburg. Substantially the same stockholders owned the Citizens' Ice & Cold Storage Company, engaged in like business at the same place. In February, 1926, Lewis, general manager of both companies, began negotiations for the sale of their properties to the National Public Service Corporation. Their directors and stockholders were anxious to sell, distribute the assets, and dissolve the corporations. The prospective vendee desired to acquire the properties of both companies, but not of one without the other.

In October 1926, agreement was reached and the vendor's directors again approved the plan for distribution and dissolution. In November 1926, petitioner and the National Corporation entered into a formal written contract conditioned upon a like one by the Citizens' Company. This referred to petitioner as "vendor" and the National Corporation as "purchaser." [The consideration was $400,000 in cash and $1,000,000 in short-term notes due within six months.] * * *

The Commissioner of Internal Revenue determined that the petitioner derived taxable gain exceeding $500,000 and assessed it accordingly under the Revenue Act of 1926. The Board of Tax Appeals and the Circuit Court of Appeals approved this action.

The facts are not in controversy. The gain is admitted; but it is said this was definitely exempted from taxation by section 203, [now § 361(b)(2)] Revenue Act of 1926.

Counsel for the petitioner maintain—

The record discloses a "reorganization" to which petitioner was party and a preliminary plan strictly pursued. The Florida West Coast Ice Company acquired substantially all of petitioner's property in exchange for cash and securities which were promptly distributed to the latter's stockholders. Consequently, under section 203, the admitted gain was not taxable.

The Board of Tax Appeals held that the transaction in question amounted to a sale of petitioner's property for money and not an exchange for securities within the true meaning of the statute. It, accordingly and as we think properly, upheld the Commissioner's action.

The "vendor" agreed "to sell," and the "purchaser" agreed "to purchase," certain described property for a definite sum of money. Part of this sum was paid in cash; for the balance the purchaser executed three promissory notes, secured by the deposit of mortgage bonds, payable, with interest, in about forty-five, seventy-five, and one hundred and five days, respectively. These notes—mere evidence of obligation to pay the purchase price—were not securities within the intendment of the act and were properly regarded as the equivalent of cash. It would require clear language to lead us to conclude that Congress intended to grant exemption to one who sells property and for the purchase price accepts well secured, short-term notes (all payable within four months), when another who makes a like sale and receives cash certainly would be taxed. We can discover no good basis in reason for the contrary view and its acceptance would make evasion of taxation very easy. In substance the petitioner sold for the equivalent of cash; the gain must be recognized.

The court below held that the facts disclosed failed to show a "reorganization" within the statutory definition. And, in the circumstances, we approve that conclusion. But the construction which the court seems to have placed upon clause A, paragraph (h)(1), section 203 (26 USCA § 934(h)(1), cls. (A, B), [now § 368(a)(1)] we think is too narrow. It conflicts with established practice of the tax officers and, if passed without comment, may produce perplexity.

The court said: "It must be assumed that in adopting paragraph (h) [now § 368(a)(1)] Congress intended to use the words 'merger' and 'consolidation' in their ordinary and accepted meanings. Giving the matter in parenthesis the most liberal construction, it is only when there is an acquisition of substantially all the property of another corporation in connection with a merger or consolidation that a reorganization takes place. Clause (B) of the paragraph removes any doubts as to the intention of Congress on this point."

The paragraph in question directs: "The term 'reorganization' means (A) a merger or consolidation (including the acquisition by one corporation of at least a majority of the voting stock and at least a majority of the total number of shares of all other classes of stock of another corporation, or substantially all the properties of another corporation)." The words within the parenthesis may not be disregarded. They expand the meaning of "merger" or "consolidation" so as to include some things which partake of the nature of a merger *or* consolidation but are beyond the ordinary and commonly accepted meaning of those words so as to embrace circumstances difficult to delimit but which in strictness cannot be designated as either merger or consolidation. But the mere purchase for money of the assets of one company by another is beyond the evident purpose of the provision, and has no real semblance to a merger or consolidation. Certainly, we think that to be within the exemption the seller must acquire an interest in the affairs of the purchasing company more definite than that incident to ownership of its short-term purchase-money notes. This general view is adopted and well sustained in *Cortland Specialty Co. v. Commissioner of Internal Revenue* (C.C.A.) 60 F.(2d) 937, 939, 940. It harmonizes with the underlying purpose of the provisions in respect of exemptions and gives some effect to all the words employed.

The judgment of the court below is affirmed.

Questions

Who is the taxpayer in *Pinellas*? What was the lower court's narrower reading of the statute which the Supreme Court in *Pinellas* rejects? The Court said the "seller must acquire an interest in the affairs of the purchasing company more definite than that incident to ownership of its short-term purchase-money notes." What type of interest would meet such a requirement? What result in *Pinellas* under the current statute? Does *Pinellas* have any continuing vitality with respect to the (C) reorganization? The (A) reorganization? The forward subsidiary merger under § 368(a)(2)(D)? The reverse subsidiary merger under § 368(a)(2)(E)?

2. Interest Must be "Definite and Material" and "Substantial Part of Value of the Thing Transferred": Cash and Common Received in a (C) Before the Solely for Voting Stock Requirement

Helvering v. Minnesota Tea Co.

Supreme Court of the United States, 1935
296 U.S. 378, 56 S.Ct. 269, 80 L.Ed. 284 (Minnesota Tea I)

Mr. Justice McReynolds delivered the opinion of the Court.

Respondent, a Minnesota corporation with three stockholders, assailed a deficiency assessment for 1928 income tax, and prevailed below. The Commissioner seeks reversal. He claims the transaction out of which the assessment arose was not a reorganization within section 112, par. (i)(1)(A), Revenue Act, 1928. [Now § 368(a)(1)(A).] * * *

July 14, 1928, respondent caused Peterson Investment Company to be organized, and transferred to the latter real estate, investments, and miscellaneous assets in exchange for the transferee's entire capital stock. The shares thus obtained were immediately distributed among the three stockholders. August 23, 1928, it transferred all remaining assets to Grand Union Company in exchange for voting trust certificates, representing 18,000 shares of the transferee's common stock, and $426,842.52 cash. It retained the certificates; but immediately distributed the money among the stockholders, who agreed to pay $106,471.73 of its outstanding debts. Although of opinion that there had been reorganization, the Commissioner treated as taxable gain the amount of the assumed debts upon the view that this amount of the cash received by the company was really appropriated to the payment of its debts.

The matter went before the Board of Tax Appeals upon the question whether the Commissioner ruled rightly in respect of this taxable gain. Both parties proceeded upon the view that there had been reorganization. Of its own motion, the Board questioned and denied the existence of one. It then ruled that the corporation had realized taxable gain amounting to the difference between cost of the property transferred and the cash received, plus the value of the 18,000 shares; $712,195.90.

The Circuit Court of Appeals found there was reorganization within the statute, and reversed the Board. It concluded that the words, "the acquisition by one corporation of * * * substantially all the properties of another corporation," plainly include the transaction under consideration. Also, that clause (B), § 112(i)(1) [now § 368(a)(1)], first introduced by Revenue Act of 1924, and continued in later statutes, did not narrow the scope of clause (A). Further, that reorganization was not dependent upon dissolution by the conveying corporation. And, finally, that its conclusions find support in treasury regulations long in force. * * *

[In *Pinellas* we said that] "we think that to be within the exemption the seller must acquire an interest in the affairs of the purchasing company more definite than that incident to ownership of its short-term purchase-money notes." And we now add that this interest must be definite and material; it must represent a substantial part of the value of the thing transferred. This much is necessary in order that the result accomplished may genuinely partake of the nature of merger or consolidation.

Gregory v. Helvering, Sec. 2.7.B., revealed a sham; a mere device intended to obscure the character of the transaction. We, of course, disregarded the mask and dealt with realities. The present record discloses no such situation; nothing suggests other than a bona fide business move.

The transaction here was no sale, but partook of the nature of a reorganization, in that the seller acquired a definite and substantial interest in the purchaser.

True it is that the relationship of the taxpayer to the assets conveyed was substantially changed, but this is not inhibited by the statute. Also, a large part of the consideration was cash. This, we think, is permissible so long as the taxpayer received an interest in the affairs of the transferee which represented a material part of the value of the transferred assets.

Finally, it is said the transferor was not dissolved, and therefore the transaction does not adequately resemble consolidation. But dissolution is not prescribed, and we are unable to see that such action is essential to the end in view. * * *

We think the court below rightly decided there was a reorganization. It reversed the Board of Tax Appeals, and remanded the cause for further proceedings, and its judgment must be affirmed.

Questions

Who is the taxpayer here? Following its decision in *Pinellas,* the Court here again rejects the narrower reading of § 203(h)(1)(A) of the 1924 and 1926 Acts as encompassing only mergers or consolidations. Thus, the Court sanctions the asset acquisition reorganization. The Court goes on to add to what it said in *Pinellas,* that in order to constitute a reorganization the interest acquired must be "definite and material; it must represent a substantial part of the value of the thing transferred." What is a "definite and material" interest? What is a "substantial part" of the thing transferred? How much cash (boot) could be paid before breaking a reorganization? Does *Minnesota Tea I* have any continuing vitality for the (C) reorganization? The (A) reorganization? The (B) reorganization? The forward subsidiary merger under § 368(a)(2)(D)? The reverse subsidiary merger under § 368(a)(2)(E)? How would the transaction be treated under the current statute?

3. Nonvoting Preferred Carries Continuity of Interest in a (C) before the Solely for Voting Stock Requirement

John A. Nelson Co. v. Helvering

Supreme Court of the United States, 1935
296 U.S. 374

Mr. Justice McReynolds delivered the opinion of the Court.

The petitioner contests a deficiency income assessment made on account of alleged gains during 1926. It claims that the transaction out of which the assessment arose was reorganization within the statute. Section 203, Revenue Act, 1926, [now § 361] * * * relied upon. * * *

In 1926, under an agreement with petitioner, the Elliott-Fisher Corporation organized a new corporation with 12,500 shares non-voting preferred stock and 30,000 shares of common stock. It purchased the latter for $2,000,000 cash. This new corporation then acquired substantially all of petitioner's property, except $100,000, in return for $2,000,000 cash and the entire issue of preferred stock. Part of this cash was used to retire petitioner's own preferred shares, and the remainder and the preferred stock of the new company went to its stockholders. It retained its franchise and $100,000, and continued to be liable for certain obligations. The preferred stock so distributed, except in case of default, had no voice in the control of the issuing corporation.

The Commissioner, Board of Tax Appeals, and the court all concluded there was no reorganization. This, we think, was error.

The court below thought the facts showed "that the transaction essentially constituted a sale of the greater part of petitioner's assets for cash and the preferred stock in the new corporation, leaving the Elliott-Fisher Company in entire control of the new corporation by virtue of its ownership of the common stock."

True, the mere acquisition of the assets of one corporation by another does not amount to reorganization within the statutory definition. *Pinellas, Ice & Cold Storage Co. v. Commissioner of Internal Revenue*, 287 U.S. 462, 53 S.Ct. 257, 77 L.Ed. 428, so affirmed. But where, as here, the seller acquires a definite and substantial interest in the affairs of the purchasing corporation, a wholly different situation arises. The owner of preferred stock is not without substantial interest in the affairs of the issuing corporation, although denied voting rights. The statute does not require participation in the management of the purchaser; nor does it demand that the conveying corporation be dissolved. A controlling interest in the transferee corporation is not made a requisite by section 203(h)(1)(A) [now § 368(a)(1)] (26 U.S.C.A. § 112 note) * * *.

Finally, as has been pointed out in the *Minnesota Tea Case,* paragraph (h)(1)(B) was not intended to modify the provisions of paragraph (h)(1)(A). It describes a class. Whether some overlapping is possible is not presently important.

The judgment below must be reversed.

Questions

Who is the taxpayer here? The Supreme Court here holds that nonvoting preferred constitutes a "definite and substantial interest in the affairs of the purchasing corporation." The preferred amounted to only 38% of the total consideration. Is the nonvoting preferred in *John A. Nelson* that much different from the notes in *Pinellas*? Suppose the preferred had been redeemable at the option of the corporation? Does *John A. Nelson* have any continuing vitality with respect to the (C) reorganization? The (A) reorganization? The (B)? The forward subsidiary merger under § 368(a)(2)(D)? The reverse subsidiary merger under § 368(a)(2)(E)?

4. Receipt of Stock and Bonds in a (B) before the Solely for Voting Stock Requirement: Bonds Are Securities

Helvering v. Watts

Supreme Court of the United States, 1935
269 U.S. 387

MR. JUSTICE MCREYNOLDS delivered the opinion of the Court.

These causes involved deficiency assessments for income tax against the three respondents for the year 1924.

They were the sole stockholders of United States Ferro Alloys Corporation, herein Ferro Alloys, and the causes, alike in all essential particulars, were dealt with below in one opinion.

The respondents maintain that they exchanged all stock of Ferro Alloys for shares of Vanadium Corporation of America and bonds of Ferro Alloys guaranteed by Vanadium; that these two corporations were parties to a reorganization, and that under section 203(b)(2), [now §354] Revenue Act 1924, 43 Stat. 256 (26 U.S.C.A. §112 note), no taxable gain resulted. The Commissioner insists that the transaction was a sale of all the stock of the Ferro Alloys, and therefore taxable gain resulted. * * *

In December, 1924, respondents owned all the stock of Ferro Alloys Corporation. They exchanged this with the Vanadium Corporation for stock of the latter valued at $30 per share and for $1,161,184.50 mortgage bonds of Ferro Alloys guaranteed by Vanadium. Ferro Alloys continued to conduct business until its dissolution in 1928. Article 1574 of Treasury Regulations 65 provided that under the Act of 1924 no gain or loss shall be recognized to the shareholders from the exchange of stock made in connection with the reorganization, if two or more corporations reorganize; for example, by either the sale of the stock of B to A, or the acquisition by A of a majority of the total number of shares of all other classes of stock of B.

The transaction here involved is within the description of reorganization recognized by the Treasury Regulation above quoted. And if the regulation can be taken as properly interpreting the statute, the challenged judgment must be affirmed.

The court below recites the history of the Treasury Regulation above quoted, and concludes that, in view of the re-enactment of the paragraph to which it refers without change, Congress intended to approve the regulation as written.

The Commissioner here maintains that the definition of reorganization found in section 203(h)(1)(A), Revenue Act 1924, [now §368(a)(1)] * * * should be limited to transactions which partake of the nature of mergers or consolidations, and that here the Vanadium merely made an investment in Ferro Alloys stock and obtained only the rights of a stockholder therein. It is also urged that an exchange of stocks for bonds results in a substantial change of position and that such bonds are "other property" within the meaning of the statute, and, as such, subject to tax. Much of the argument presented is the same as the one considered in the *Minnesota Tea Com-*

pany Case, and it need not be again followed in detail. The bonds, we think, were securities within the definition, and cannot be regarded as cash, as were the short-term notes referred to in *Pinellas*. * * *

The judgment of the court below must be affirmed.

Questions

What result if the transaction had been structured as an (A) reorganization? What was the mix of consideration here? How would the transaction be treated under the current statute?

5. Acquiring Corporation Acquires Stock of Target in Exchange for 25% Stock and 75% Cash Consideration in (B) Reorganization Prior to Enactment of Solely for Voting Stock Requirement

Miller v. Commissioner of Internal Revenue

United States Court of Appeals, Sixth Circuit, 1936
84 F.2d 415

SIMONS, CIRCUIT JUDGE.

The review here sought is of orders of the Board of Tax Appeals sustaining deficiencies determined by the respondent in the taxes of the petitioners for the year 1928. In that year the petitioner A.L. Miller and Mrs. Hawk's decedent, Henry C. Hawk, then the majority stockholders of the Enquirer-News Company, a newspaper publishing corporation of Battle Creek, Mich., transferred all of their stock in that corporation to Federated Publications, Inc., for a consideration partly in cash and partly in stock of the purchasing company, which at the same time acquired all of the minority stock of the Enquirer-News Company. [Only 25% of the consideration paid by the acquiring corporation was stock of the acquiring corporation.] Concededly gain was derived by the petitioners through the transaction. Whether gain is to be recognized upon the stock exchanged as well as on that sold for cash is the question to be decided, and this in turn depends upon whether the transaction was a sale, or, within the applicable statute, a merger or reorganization.

The taxes here involved are governed by section 112 of the Revenue Act of 1928 [now §1001]. Subsection (a) declares the general rule that upon the sale or exchange of property the entire amount of the gain or loss shall be recognized except as thereinafter provided. By subsection (b)(3) [now §354] no gain or loss is recognized if stock or securities in a corporation which is a party to a reorganization are, in pursuance of the plan of reorganization, exchanged solely for stock or securities in another corporation which is a party to the reorganization. Subsection (i)(1) [now §368(a)(1)], in so far as here applicable, defines the term "reorganization" to mean: "(A) a merger or consolidation (including the acquisition by one corporation of at least a majority of the voting stock and at least a majority of the total number of shares of all other classes of stock of another corporation, or substantially all the properties of another corporation), or * * *."

It is not disputed that Federated Publications, Inc., acquired all of the stock of the Enquirer-News Company, so that the transaction is within the literal wording of the parenthetical clause of subsection (i)(1). But this, says the respondent, is not enough, for every acquisition of a majority of stock of one corporation by another does not constitute reorganization within the purview of the statute. Only those acquisitions satisfy the statute which partake of the nature of a merger or consolidation, but for some reason do not come entirely within the precise definition of those terms. * * *

The Supreme Court has of course, neither in the *Minnesota Tea Company* nor in companion cases, defined what is meant by a "definite and material interest," or "a substantial part of the value of the thing transferred," which it considers necessary in order that the result accomplished may genuinely partake of the nature of merger or consolidation. Manifestly, it could not be precise, for in the final analysis each case must rest upon its own peculiar facts. However, a controlling interest in the transferee corporation is not requisite. *Nelson Company v. Helvering*, supra. It was there held also that the owner of preferred stock is not without substantial interest in the affairs of the issuing corporation, although denied voting rights, for the statute does not require participation in the management of the purchaser. In the present case we find that the petitioners acquired an interest in the transferee of the value of $125,000. * * * It will therefore be seen that the petitioners acquired an interest in the new corporation almost equal to 50 percent of the interest they had in the old company, and exactly equal to 25 percent of the value of the total number of shares transferred. It is idle to say that this is not a substantial part of the value of the thing transferred, or does not constitute a definite and material interest in the affairs of the purchasing company. In the commonly accepted legal sense, a substantial interest is something more than a merely nominal interest, and, in respect to corporations, a definite and material interest is an interest beyond what is usually referred to as represented by "qualifying shares."

We attach no importance to the fact that some of the stockholders in the transferring corporation acquired no interest in the transferee. This is certainly not a test by which the effectuation of a merger or consolidation is to be determined, for it will rarely result when reorganizations, even in their strict literal sense, are undertaken that all stockholders will approve. It is almost universal experience that some nonassenting stock must be acquired otherwise than through the mechanics of the consolidation plan. * * * The transaction between the two corporations was a merger or consolidation within the statute.

The orders of the Board of Tax Appeals are set aside.

Questions

What is the treatment of the transaction in *Miller* under the current statute? Does the holding in *Miller* have any continuing significance for the (B) reorganization? The (C)? The (A)? The forward subsidiary merger under § 368(a)(2)(D)? The reverse subsidiary merger under § 368(a)(2)(E)?

6. Receipt of Cash and Bonds in a (C) Before the Solely for Voting Stock Requirement

Le Tulle v. Scofield

United States Supreme Court, 1940
308 U.S. 415

MR. JUSTICE ROBERTS delivered the opinion of the Court.

* * * The Gulf Coast Irrigation Company was the owner of irrigation properties. Petitioner was its sole stockholder. He personally owned certain lands and other irrigation properties. November 4, 1931, the Irrigation Company, the Gulf Coast Water Company, and the petitioner, entered into an agreement which recited that the petitioner owned all of the stock of the Irrigation Company; described the company's properties, and stated that, prior to conveyance to be made pursuant to the contract, the Irrigation Company would be the owner of certain other lands and irrigation properties. These other lands and properties were those which the petitioner individually owned. The contract called for a conveyance of all the properties owned, and to be owned, by the Irrigation Company for $50,000 in cash and $750,000 in bonds of the Water Company, payable serially over the period January 1, 1933, to January 1, 1944. The petitioner joined in this agreement as a guarantor of the title of the Irrigation Company and for the purpose of covenanting that he would not personally enter into the irrigation business within a fixed area during a specified period after the execution of the contract. Three days later, at a special meeting of stockholders of the Irrigation Company, the proposed reorganization was approved, the minutes stating that the taxpayer, "desiring also to reorganize his interest in the properties," had consented to be a party to the reorganization. The capital stock of the Irrigation Company was increased and thereupon the taxpayer subscribed for the new stock and paid for it by conveyance of his individual properties.

The contract between the two corporations was carried out November 18, with the result that the Water Company became owner of all the properties then owned by the Irrigation Company including the property theretofore owned by the petitioner individually. Subsequently all of its assets, including the bonds received from the Water Company, were distributed to the petitioner. The company was then dissolved. The petitioner and his wife filed a tax return as members of a community in which they reported no gain as a result of the receipt of the liquidating dividend from the Irrigation Company. The latter reported no gain for the taxable year in virtue of its receipt of bonds and cash from the Water Company. The Commissioner of Internal Revenue assessed additional taxes against the community, as individual taxpayers, by reason of the receipt of the liquidating dividend, and against the petitioner as transferee of the Irrigation Company's assets in virtue of the gain realized by the company on the sale of its property. The tax was paid and claims for refund were filed. [Petitioner] alleged that the transaction constituted a tax-exempt reorganization as defined by the Revenue Act. * * *

The respondent's contention that the transaction amounted merely to a sale of assets by the petitioner and the Irrigation Company and did not fall within the statutory definition of a tax-free reorganization was overruled by the District Court and judgment was entered for the petitioner.

The respondent appealed. * * *

The Circuit Court of Appeals [reversed]. * * *

[W]e are of opinion that the transaction did not amount to a reorganization and that, therefore, the petitioner cannot complain, as the judgment must be affirmed on the ground that no tax-free reorganization was effected within the meaning of the statute.

Section 112(i) [now § 368(a)(1)] provides, so far as material: "(1) The term 'reorganization' means (A) a merger or consolidation (including the acquisition by one corporation of at least a majority of the voting stock and at least a majority of the total number of shares of all other classes of stock of another corporation, or substantially all the properties of another corporation) * * *.

As the court below properly stated, the section is not to be read literally, as denominating the transfer of all the assets of one company for what amounts to a cash consideration given by the other a reorganization. We have held that where the consideration consists of cash and short term notes the transfer does not amount to a reorganization within the true meaning of the statute, but is a sale upon which gain or loss must be reckoned. We have said that the statute was not satisfied unless the transferor retained a substantial stake in the enterprise and such a stake was thought to be retained where a large proportion of the consideration was in common stock of the transferee, or where the transferor took cash and the entire issue of preferred stock of the transferee corporation. And, where the consideration is represented by a substantial proportion of stock, and the balance in bonds, the total consideration received is exempt from tax under Sec. 112(b)(4) and 112(g).

In applying our decision in the *Pinellas* case, supra, the courts have generally held that receipt of long term bonds as distinguished from short term notes constitutes the retention of an interest in the purchasing corporation. There has naturally been some difficulty in classifying the securities involved in various cases.

We are of opinion that the term of the obligations is not material. Where the consideration is wholly in the transferee's bonds, or part cash and part such bonds, we think it cannot be said that the transferor retains any proprietary interest in the enterprise. * * *

Questions

Who are the taxpayers here? What is the difference between the bonds in *Le Tulle* and the nonvoting preferred in *John A. Nelson*? In which of the following situations is the interest more definite and material: (1) target corporation sells its assets for $1 million of long-term bonds of the acquiring corporation, and (2) target sells its assets for $500K of cash and $500K of nonvoting preferred of the acquiring corporation? Does *Le Tulle* have any continuing vitality for the (C) reorganization? The (A) reorganization?

7. Bankrupt Corporation: Noteholders Exchange Notes for Stock
Helvering v. Alabama Asphaltic Limestone Co.

Supreme Court of the United States, 1942
315 U.S. 179

Mr. Justice Douglas delivered the opinion of the Court.

Respondent in 1931 acquired all the assets of Alabama Rock Asphalt, Inc., pursuant to a reorganization plan consummated with the aid of the bankruptcy court. In computing its depreciation and depletion allowances for the year 1934, respondent treated its assets as having the same basis which they had in the hands of the old corporation. The Commissioner determined a deficiency, computed on the price paid at the bankruptcy sale. The Board of Tax Appeals rejected the position of the Commissioner. 41 B.T.A. 324. The Circuit Court of Appeals affirmed. 5 Cir., 119 F.2d 819. We granted the petition for certiorari. * * *

The answer to the question turns on the meaning of that part of § 112(i)(1) of the Revenue Act of 1928 [now § 368(a)(1)], which provides: "The term 'reorganization' means (A) a merger or consolidation (including the acquisition by one corporation of * * * substantially all the properties of another corporation) * * *."

The essential facts can be stated briefly. The old corporation was a subsidiary of a corporation which was in receivership in 1929. Stockholders of the parent had financed the old corporation taking unsecured notes for their advances. Maturity of the notes was approaching and not all of the noteholders would agree to take stock for their claims. Accordingly a creditors' committee was formed late in 1929 and a plan of reorganization was proposed to which all the noteholders, except two, assented. The plan provided that a new corporation would be formed which would acquire all the assets of the old corporation. The stock of the new corporation, preferred and common, would be issued to the creditors in satisfaction of their claims. Pursuant to the plan involuntary bankruptcy proceedings were instituted in 1930. The appraised value of the bankrupt corporation's assets was about $155,000. Its obligations were about $838,000, the unsecured notes with accrued interest aggregating somewhat over $793,000. The bankruptcy trustee offered the assets for sale at public auction. They were bid in by the creditors' committee for $150,000. The price was paid by $15,000 in cash, by agreements of creditors to accept stock of a new corporation in full discharge of their claims, and by an offer of the committee to meet the various costs of administration, etc. Thereafter respondent was formed and acquired all the assets of the bankrupt corporation. It does not appear whether the acquisition was directly from the old corporation on assignment of the bid or from the committee. Pursuant to the plan respondent issued its stock to the creditors of the old corporation-over 95% to the noteholders and the balance to small creditors. Nonassenting creditors were paid in cash. Operations were not interrupted by the reorganization and were carried on subsequently by substantially the same persons as before.

* * * On the basis of the continuity of interest theory as explained in the *Le Tulle* case it is now earnestly contended that a substantial ownership interest in the trans-

feree company must be retained by the holders of the ownership interest in the transferor. * * *

We conclude, however, that it is immaterial that the transfer shifted the ownership of the equity in the property from the stockholders to the creditors of the old corporation. Plainly the old continuity of interest was broken. Technically that did not occur in this proceeding until the judicial sale took place. For practical purposes, however, it took place not later than the time when the creditors took steps to enforce their demands against their insolvent debtor. In this case, that was the date of the institution of bankruptcy proceedings. From that time on they had effective command over the disposition of the property. * * *

That conclusion involves no conflict with the principle of the *Le Tulle* case. A bondholder interest in a solvent company plainly is not the equivalent of a proprietary interest, even though upon default the bondholders could retake the property transferred. The mere possibility of a proprietary interest is of course not its equivalent. But the determinative and controlling factors of the debtor's insolvency and an effective command by the creditors over the property were absent in the *Le Tulle* case.

Nor are there any other considerations which prevent this transaction from qualifying as a "reorganization" within the meaning of the Act. The *Pinellas* case makes plain that "merger" and "consolidation" as used in the Act includes transactions which "are beyond the ordinary and commonly accepted meaning of those words". 287 U.S. page 470, 53 S.Ct. page 260, 77 L.Ed. 428. Insolvency reorganizations are within the family of financial readjustments embraced in those terms as used in this particular statute.

Questions

What were the tax stakes in *Alabama Asphaltic*? What side of the reorganization transaction is *Alabama Asphaltic* concerned with? If a holder of short-term notes of a target corporation exchanges his notes for stock of an acquiring corporation in a transaction in which the acquiring corporation acquires the stock or assets of the target in a bona fide reorganization, will the exchanging noteholder receive nonrecognition treatment? Suppose the target is on the verge of bankruptcy?

8. Receipt of Bonds in an (A)

Roebling v. Commissioner

United States Court of Appeals, Third Circuit, 1944
143 F.2d 810

KALODNER, DISTRICT JUDGE.

This appeal presents three questions: (1) Whether the transaction hereafter stated between a lessor corporation and a lessee corporation constituted a "statutory merger", within the meaning of Sec. 112(g)(1)(A) of the Revenue Act of 1938, [now §368(a)(1)]; (2) whether the doctrine of "continuity of interest" as enunciated in *Le Tulle v. Scofield,* applies to a "statutory merger", and (3) whether under the facts a "continuity of interest" actually existed.

On May 10, 1937, the directors of South Jersey and of Public Service Electric and Gas Company adopted a "Plan of Reorganization" under which it was proposed that the former company be merged into the latter in accordance with the statutes of New Jersey. This plan provided that the stockholders of South Jersey (other than Public Service Electric and Gas Company) should exchange, dollar for dollar, their stock in South Jersey for 8% one hundred years first mortgage bonds of Public Service Electric and Gas Company. These bonds were to be issued under a prior mortgage of Public Service Electric and Gas Company dated August 1, 1924, and under a supplemental indenture later to be executed. It was expressly provided in the "Agreement of Merger" executed on the same day: "The capital stock of the Public Service Electric and Gas Company * * * will not be changed by reason of this agreement." Also, the stock of South Jersey held by Public Service Electric and Gas Company was not to participate in the exchange but was to be delivered up and cancelled. * * *

The "Agreement of Merger" was consummated pursuant to its provisions. In accordance therewith the taxpayer received in exchange for his 166 shares of stock in South Jersey, $16,600, principal amount of 8% bonds which on November 25, 1938, had a fair market value of $34,777.

The Commissioner determined that the difference between the basis of the taxpayer's stock in South Jersey and the fair market value of the bonds received in exchange therefor must be recognized as taxable income in 1938 and he asserted a deficiency which the Tax Court sustained, so far as it was based upon this item.

The issues presented here arise by reason of taxpayer's contention (1) that the merger of South Jersey into Public Service Electric and Gas Co. was a "true statutory merger" under the laws of the state of New Jersey and therefore the exchange of stock for bonds was not a taxable event under Sec. 112 of the Revenue Act of 1938; [now § 368(a)(1)]; (2) that since there was a "true statutory merger" the "continuity of interest" doctrine in the *Le Tulle v. Scofield* case is inapplicable and (3) that in any event a "continuity of interest" actually existed in the instant case.

As to the taxpayer's first two contentions, which may be considered together: The admitted fact that the merger of the two corporations was a "true statutory merger" under the New Jersey law is not dispositive of the question as to whether there was a "statutory merger" here within the meaning of Sec. 112(g)(1)(A) [now § 368(a)(1).] It is well-settled that a State law cannot alter the essential characteristics required to enable a taxpayer to obtain exemption under the provisions of a Federal Revenue Act.

* * * [W]e cannot subscribe to the taxpayer's contention that under Sec. 112(g)(1)(A) [now § 368(a)(1)] of the Revenue Act of 1938 the requirements of New Jersey law supersede the "continuity of interest" test as applied in *Le Tulle v. Scofield* and the numerous other decisions.

The taxpayer's remaining contention that the requisite "continuity of interest" is present under the peculiar facts in this case is premised on a rather novel theory. He urges that "prior to the merger, the stockholders of South Jersey had *no proprietary interest* in its properties in any real sense", and that in sanctioning the merger "the decision of the New Jersey courts recognized that the stock in the lessor companies was substantially equivalent to a perpetual 8% bond." * * *

In view of the incontrovertible facts the taxpayer's argument that the stockholders in South Jersey had *no* proprietary interest is without basis.

Finally, it is equally clear that when the stockholders of South Jersey exchanged their stock in that corporation for the long-term bonds of Public Service Electric and Gas Company, they surrendered their proprietary interest and simply became creditors of Public Service. They no longer owned any of the former property of South Jersey and they had no proprietary interest in the property of Public Service. * * *

For the reasons stated the decision of the Tax Court of the United States is affirmed.

Questions

Roebling specifically holds that the continuity of interest requirement enunciated in *Le Tulle v. Scofield* and its predecessors, which dealt principally with asset acquisitions, is applicable to mergers under the (A) reorganization. What is the practical effect of this holding? How would this transaction be treated under today's statute?

9. Determination of Whether Stock Represents a Substantial Part of Assets Transferred in an (A)

Southwest Natural Gas Co. v. Commissioner

United States Court of Appeals, Fifth Circuit, 1951
189 F.2d 332, cert. denied 342 U.S. 860 (1951)

RUSSELL, CIRCUIT JUDGE.

* * * [The question is] whether a merger of Peoples Gas & Fuel Corporation with the taxpayer, effected in accordance with the laws of Delaware, was a sale, as asserted by the Commissioner, or a "reorganization" within the terms of Section 112(g) of the Internal Revenue Code, [now § 368(a)(1)] as contended by the taxpayer * * *.

* * * [The Tax] Court held that literal compliance with the provisions of a state law authorizing a merger would not in itself effect a "reorganization" within the terms applicable under Internal Revenue Statutes; that the test of continuity of interest was nevertheless applicable; and that the transaction in question did not meet this test. * * *

* * * [W]e think, that the accomplishment of a statutory merger does not *ipso facto* constitute a "reorganization" within the terms of the statute here involved. This has been expressly held by the Court of Appeals for the Third Circuit in a well considered opinion, supported by numerous authorities cited. *Roebling v. Commissioner,* 143 F.2d 810. * * *

It is thus clear that the test of "continuity of interest" announced and applied by these cited authorities, supra, must be met before a statutory merger may properly be held a reorganization within the terms of Section 112(g)(1)(A) [now § 368(a)(1)(A).] Each case must in its final analysis be controlled by its own peculiar facts. While no precise formula has been expressed for determining whether there has been retention of the requisite interest, it seems clear that the requirement of continuity of interest consistent with the statutory intent is not fulfilled in the absence of a showing: (1) that the transferor corporation or its shareholders retained a substantial proprietary stake in the enterprise represented by a material interest in the affairs of the transferee corporation, and, (2) that such retained interest represents a substantial part of the value of the property transferred.

Among other facts, the Tax Court found that under the merger all of Peoples' assets were acquired by the petitioner in exchange for specified amounts of stock, bonds, cash and the assumption of debts. There was a total of 18,875 shares common stock of Peoples' entitled to participate under the agreement of merger. The stockholders were offered Option A and Option B. The holders of 7,690 of such shares exercised Option B of that agreement and received $30.00 in cash for each share, or a total of $230,700.00. In respect to the stock now involved, the stockholders who exercised Option A, the holders of 59.2 per cent of the common stock received in exchange 16.4 per cent of petitioner's outstanding common stock plus $340,350.00 principal amount of six per cent mortgage bonds (of the market value of 90 per cent of principal), which had been assumed by petitioner in a prior merger, and $17,779.59 cash. The 16.4 per cent of the common stock referred to was represented by 111,850 shares having a market value of $5,592.50, or five cents per share, and represented the continuing proprietary interest of the participating stockholders in the enterprise. This was less than one per cent of the consideration paid by the taxpayers.

We think it clear that these and other facts found by the Tax Court find substantial support in the evidence, and the conclusion of the Tax Court that they failed to evidence sufficient continuity of interest to bring the transaction within the requirements of the applicable statute is correct.

The decision of the Tax Court is *Affirmed*.

Questions

What was the mix of consideration paid by the acquiring corporation in *Southwest Natural Gas Co.*? How much stock of the acquiring corporation is needed to constitute a "substantial part of the value of the property transferred"?

10. Receipt of Pass Book Savings Accounts on Merger of Savings and Loan Association

Paulsen v. Commissioner

United States Supreme Court, 1985
469 U.S. 131

JUSTICE REHNQUIST delivered the opinion of the Court.

Commerce Savings and Loan Association of Tacoma, Wash., merged into Citizens Federal Savings and Loan Association of Seattle in July 1976. Petitioners Harold and Marie Paulsen sought to treat their exchange of stock in Commerce for [passbook savings accounts and time certificates of deposit] in Citizens as a tax-free reorganization under 26 U.S.C. §§ 354(a)(1) and 368(a)(1)(A). The Court of Appeals for the Ninth Circuit, disagreeing with the Court of Claims and other Courts of Appeals, reversed a decision of the Tax Court in favor of petitioners. We granted certiorari, to resolve these conflicting interpretations of an important provision of the Internal Revenue Code. * * *

These shares are the association's only means of raising capital. Here they are divided into passbook accounts and certificates of deposit. In reality, these shares are hybrid instruments having both equity and debt characteristics. They combine in one instrument the separate characteristics of the guaranty stock and the savings accounts of stock associations like Commerce.

The Citizens shares have several equity characteristics. The most important is the fact that they are the only ownership instrument of the association. Each share carries in addition to its deposit value a part ownership interest in the bricks and mortar, the goodwill, and all the other assets of Citizens. Another equity characteristic is the right to vote on matters for which the association's management must obtain shareholder approval. The shareholders also receive dividends rather than interest on their accounts; the dividends are paid out of net earnings, and the shareholders have no legal right to have a dividend declared or to have a fixed return on their investment. The shareholders further have a right to a pro rata distribution of any remaining assets after a solvent dissolution.

These equity characteristics, however, are not as substantial as they appear on the surface. * * *

In our view, the debt characteristics of Citizens' shares greatly outweigh the equity characteristics. The face value of petitioners' passbook accounts and certificates of deposit was $210,000. Petitioners have stipulated that they had a right to withdraw the face amount of the deposits in cash, on demand after one year or at stated intervals thereafter. Their investment was virtually risk free and the dividends received were equivalent to prevailing interest rates for savings accounts in other types of savings institutions. The debt value of the shares was the same as the face value, $210,000; because no one would pay more than this for the shares, the incremental value attributable to the equity features was, practically, zero. Accordingly, we hold that petitioners' passbook accounts and certificates of deposit were cash equivalents.

Petitioners have failed to satisfy the continuity-of-interest requirement to qualify for a tax-free reorganization. In exchange for their guaranty stock in Commerce, they received essentially cash with an insubstantial equity interest. Under *Minnesota Tea Co.*, their equity interest in Citizens would have to be "a substantial part of the value of the thing transferred." Assuming an arm's-length transaction in which what petitioners gave up and what they received were of equivalent worth, their Commerce stock was worth $210,000 in withdrawable deposits and an unquantifiably small incremental equity interest. This retained equity interest in the reorganized enterprise, therefore, is not a "substantial" part of the value of the Commerce stock which was given up. We agree with the Commissioner that the equity interests attached to the Citizens shares are too insubstantial to satisfy *Minnesota Tea Co.* The Citizens shares are not significantly different from the notes that this Court found to be the mere "equivalent of cash" in *Pinellas & Cold Storage Ice Co.* The ownership interest of the Citizens shareholders is closer to that of the secured bondholders in *Le Tulle v. Scofield*, than to that of the preferred stockholders in *John A. Nelson Co. v. Helvering.* The latter case involved a classic ownership instrument-preferred stock carrying voting rights only in the event of a dividend default—which we held to represent "a definite and substantial interest in the affairs of the purchasing corporation." * * *

C. The Service's Prior Ruling Policy Requirement on Continuity of Interest

Revenue Procedure 77-37

1977-2 C.B. 568 § 3.02

.02 The "continuity of interest" requirement of section 1.368-1(b) of the Income Tax Regulations is satisfied if there is continuing interest through stock ownership in the acquiring or transferee corporation (or a corporation in "control" thereof within the meaning of section 368(c) of the Code) on the part of the former shareholders of the acquired or transferor corporation which is equal in value, as of the effective date of the reorganization, to at least 50 percent of the value of all of the formerly outstanding stock of the acquired or transferor corporation as of the same date. It is not necessary that each shareholder of the acquired or transferor corporation receive in the exchange stock of the acquiring or transferee corporation, or a corporation in "control" thereof, which is equal in value to at least 50 percent [Treas. Regs. § 1.368-1(e)(2)(v), Example 1 now requires only a 40% continuity of interest] of the value of his former stock interest in the acquired or transferor corporation, so long as one or more of the shareholders of the acquired or transferor corporation have a continuing interest through stock ownership in the acquiring or transferee corporation (or a corporation in "control" thereof) which is, in the aggregate, equal in value to at least 50 percent [now 40%] of the value of all of the formerly outstanding stock of the acquired or transferor corporation. * * *

Questions

What is the testing date for determining whether the continuity of interest test is satisfied? What if at the time a merger is agreed to by the boards of the target and the acquiror, the consideration to be paid is $50 million in cash and 200 million shares of AC with an aggregate trading value of $50 million? At the time of the closing, the 200 million shares have an aggregate value of $25 million. What types of reorganizations are covered by the above rule? Does the 40% continuity rule affect the (A), the (B), the (C), the forward subsidiary merger under § 368(a)(2)(D), and the reverse subsidiary merger under § 368(a)(2)(E)? In 1934 Congress added the "solely for voting stock" requirement for the (B) and the (C), and when Congress adopted the reverse subsidiary merger under § 368(a)(2)(E) in 1970 it included an 80% voting stock requirement. Thus, the (B), the (C), and the (a)(2)(E) have their own statutory continuity of interest rules. Is it sensible to have (1) a 40% continuity requirement for the (A) and the (a)(2)(D), (2) a solely for voting stock requirement for a (B), (3) a solely for voting stock requirement, subject to the 20% boot relaxation rule, for a (C), and (4) an 80% voting stock requirement for the (a)(2)(E)?

D. An Illustration of the 50% [Now 40%] Continuity Requirement

Revenue Ruling 66-224

1966-2 C.B. 114

Corporation *X* was merged under state law into corporation *Y*. Corporation *X* had four stockholders (*A, B, C, D*), each of whom owned 25 percent of its stock. Corporation *Y* paid *A* and *B* each $50,000 in cash for their stock of corporation *X*, and *C* and *D* each received corporation *Y* stock with a value of $50,000 in exchange for their stock of corporation *X*. There are no other facts present that should be taken into account in determining whether the continuity of interest requirement of section 1.368-1(b) of the Income Tax Regulations has been satisfied, such as sales, redemptions or other dispositions of stock prior to or subsequent to the exchange which were part of the plan of reorganization.

Held, the continuity of interest requirement of section 1.368-1(b) of the regulations has been satisfied. [Treas. Regs. § 1.368-1(e)(2)(v), Example 1 now requires only a 40% continuity of interest.] It would also be satisfied if the facts were the same except corporation *Y* paid each stockholder $25,000 in cash and each stockholder received corporation *Y* stock with a value of $25,000.

E. Impact of Prior Purchase of Target's Stock

1. Acquiror Purchases 85% of Target's Stock after which Target's Assets Are Acquired by Acquiror's Subsidiary in Exchange for Subsidiary's Stock and Cash

YOC Heating Corp. v. Commissioner

Tax Court of the United States, 1973

61 T.C. 168

[On September 14, 1961, Reliance purchased approximately 85% of the stock of Old Nassau. Reliance later purchased a small number of the shares of Old Nassau. Reliance formed a subsidiary, New Nassau, and New Nassau offered to purchase the assets of Old Nassau under terms pursuant to which the shareholders of Old Nassau (including Reliance) would receive either cash or stock of New Nassau. All of the minority shareholders of Old Nassau elected to receive cash and Reliance elected to receive stock of New Nassau. The purchase of assets of Old Nassau was completed on July 3, 1962, nine months after the first purchase by Reliance of Old Nassau's shares. Old Nassau was later liquidated. New Nassau incurred an operating loss during its first six months of operation.] * * *

Reliance's purpose in purchasing the stock of Old Nassau was to acquire the underlying assets of that corporation through the vehicle of New Nassau. The organization of New Nassau, the transfer of all the assets of Old Nassau to New Nassau, and the accompanying transfer to Reliance of the stock of New Nassau in exchange for the stock of Old Nassau and the payments by New Nassau to minority shareholders of Old Nassau were each steps in a single plan to accomplish that purpose.

The resolution of the issues presented in this case will depend upon the proper characterization of the following transactions:

(1) The purchase by Reliance from unrelated sellers of more than 85 percent of the common stock of Old Nassau.

(2) The organization of New Nassau.

(3) The transfer to New Nassau by Old Nassau of all its assets and the assumption by New Nassau of all of Old Nassau's liabilities against the issuance of common stock of New Nassau or the payment of cash to the shareholders of Old Nassau.

The first question raised by this series of transactions is the basis to New Nassau of the assets it acquired from Old Nassau. Respondent contends that the transaction whereby New Nassau acquired all the assets of Old Nassau constituted a reorganization within the meaning of section 368(a)(1)(F) or, alternatively, section 368(a)(1)(D). The acquired assets would then retain the same basis in the hands of New Nassau as they had in the hands of Old Nassau. Sec. 362(b). Petitioner (New Nassau) claims a higher basis in those assets equal to the cost of the Old Nassau stock purchased during the series of transactions summarized above, either under section 334(b)(2), the *Kimbell-Diamond* doctrine [Sec. 2.10.E.2], or the broader principle sometimes referred to as the "integrated transaction" doctrine. * * *

For the purpose of determining petitioner's basis in the assets acquired from Old Nassau, it is immaterial whether the transaction herein qualifies as a reorganization under clause (D) or clause (F) of section 368(a)(1). * * *

In view of the foregoing, we hold that a comparison of the stock ownership of Old Nassau immediately prior to the inception of the series of transactions involved herein with the situation which obtained immediately after the transfer by Old Nassau of its assets and liabilities to New Nassau clearly reveals that the control requirements of a (D) reorganization were not satisfied.

By a parity of reasoning rooted in the judicial "continuity of interest" principle applicable to reorganizations rather than in the specific statutory definition of "control" contained in section 368(c), there was likewise no (F) reorganization. *Helvering v. Southwest Corp.*, 315 U.S. 194 (1942); *Hyman H. Berghash*, 43 T.C. 743 (1965), affd. 361 F.2d 257 (C.A. 2, 1966). Compare *May B. Kass*, 60 T.C. 218 (1973), on appeal (C.A. 3, July 16, 1973). Compare also *Casco Products Corp.*, 49 T.C. 32 (1967), where the intention was from the outset to acquire stock and not assets.

Since there was no (D) or (F) reorganization, there can be no carryover of Old Nassau's basis under section 362(b). Likewise, in the absence of an (F) reorganization, the carryback of petitioner's net operating loss to the prior taxable years of Old Nassau is not permitted. Sec. 381(b)(3).

Having concluded that the assets and liabilities of Old Nassau were acquired by New Nassau other than by way of a reorganization or a liquidation of Old Nassau, it remains for us to determine how that acquisition should be characterized. Under all the circumstances, we conclude that such acquisition was by way of purchase with an accompanying step up in basis to petitioner and we so hold. We posit our holding on the "integrated transaction" doctrine in terms of the application of that principle generally and not in terms of the narrower *Kimbell-Diamond* doctrine. * * *

2. Sidewise Mergers after a § 338 Qualified Stock Purchase: Overriding YOC Heating

a. The Preamble to the Proposed Regulations

Preamble to Proposed Regulations under Section 338(i)

CO-62-94 (February 17, 1995)

Background This document proposes guidance [now finalized] as to the treatment of transfers of target assets to another corporation after a qualified stock purchase of target stock, if a section 338 election is not made for the target. It addresses the effect of section 338 on the result in *YOC Heating v. Commissioner* and similar cases.

Under § 1.368-1(b), for a transfer of assets to be pursuant to a reorganization within the meaning of section 368, there must be a continuity of interest in the target's business enterprise on the part of those persons who, directly or indirectly, were the owners of the enterprise prior to the reorganization.

In *YOC Heating v. Commissioner*, 61 T.C. 168 (1973), a corporation bought 85 percent of a target corporation's stock for cash and notes. As part of the same plan, the target subsequently transferred its assets to a newly formed subsidiary of the purchaser and dissolved. The purchaser received additional stock of its subsidiary in exchange for the purchaser's target stock and the minority shareholders received cash in exchange for their target stock.

The Tax Court, viewing the stock purchase and asset acquisition as an integrated transaction in which the purchaser acquired all of the target's assets for cash and notes, held there was insufficient continuity of interest to qualify the asset transfer as a reorganization under section 368 because the shareholders of the target before the stock purchase received no stock in the acquiring entity. As a result, the subsidiary received a cost basis in the target's assets.

In addition to *YOC Heating*, there are other cases in which courts have denied reorganization treatment and have given the transferee a stepped-up basis in the target's assets following the purchase of the target's stock and the merger of the target into the purchaser or a related corporation. *See, e.g., Russell v. Commissioner*, 832 F.2d 349 (6th Cir. 1987), *aff'g Cannonsburg Skiing Corp. v. Commissioner*, T.C. Memo 1986-150 (corporation purchased target stock and then target merged into purchaser); *Security Industrial Insurance Co. v. United States*, 702 F.2d 1234 (5th Cir. 1983) (corporation purchased stock of targets and then targets merged into purchaser, which then transferred the target assets to a subsidiary of the purchaser); *South Bay Corporation v. Commissioner*, 345 F.2d 698 (2d Cir. 1965) (individual purchased stock in two targets and then targets merged into a third corporation owned by the individual); *Superior Coach of Florida v. Commissioner*, 80 T.C. 895 (1983) (individual purchased target stock and then target merged into another corporation controlled by the individual); *Estate of McWhorter v. Commissioner*, 69 T.C. 650 (1978), aff'd, 590 F.2d 340 (8th Cir. 1978) (corporation purchased target stock and then target merged into purchaser); and *Kass v. Commissioner*, 60 T.C. 218 (1973), aff'd, 491 F.2d 749 (3d Cir. 1974) (corporation purchased target stock and then target merged into purchaser).

The *YOC Heating* court's analysis of the transaction as, in substance, a taxable asset acquisition by the subsidiary is consistent with generally applied federal income tax principles. For example, in *Kimbell-Diamond Milling Co. v. Commissioner*, [Sec. 2.7.D], an acquiring corporation's purchase of a target corporation's stock followed by the liquidation of the target was treated for federal income tax purposes as, in substance, a direct purchase of the target's assets by the acquiring corporation. The Tax Court's characterization in *Kimbell-Diamond* was based on a finding that the acquiring corporation intended to obtain the target's assets rather than its stock. As a result, the acquiring corporation's basis in the target's assets was determined by reference to the purchase price of the target's stock.

In 1954, Congress codified principles derived from *Kimbell-Diamond* by enacting former section 334(b)(2) of the Internal Revenue Code of 1954, which created an objective test that permitted a stock purchase followed by liquidation of the target to be treated as an asset acquisition. S. Rep. No. 1622, 83d Cong., 2d Sess. 257 (1954).

In 1982, Congress repealed section 334(b)(2) and replaced it with section 338, which provides that, if a corporation makes a qualified stock purchase (QSP) of the stock of a target, the purchasing corporation may elect to have the target treated as having sold all of its assets at the close of the acquisition date in a single transaction and as a new corporation that purchased all such assets at the beginning of the following day. Section 338 was "intended to replace any nonstatutory treatment of a stock purchase as an asset purchase under the *Kimbell-Diamond* doctrine." [*See* Chapter 2.] H.R. Conf. Rep. No. 760, 97th Cong., 2d Sess. 467, 536 (1982), 1982-2 C.B. 600, 632.

Under section 338(i), the IRS and Treasury are authorized to prescribe such regulations as may be necessary or appropriate to carry out the purposes of section 338. The IRS and Treasury believe that the result in *YOC Heating* is inconsistent with the legislative intent behind section 338. As a result of the enactment of section 338, an intragroup merger or similar transaction following a QSP generally should not be treated as part of an overall asset acquisition. The qualified stock purchase must be accorded its intended effect. Cf. Rev. Rul. 90-95, 1990-2 C.B. 67 [Sec. 5.3.D.2.] (applying sections 332 and 334 to a merger of the target into the purchasing corporation following a QSP). If a section 338 election is not made, in a subsequent intragroup merger or similar transaction, the target assets generally should preserve their historic basis maintained in the qualified stock purchase. The IRS and Treasury believe that applying the reorganization rules to the target and purchasing group in mergers and similar transactions following a QSP is the simplest and most effective means of achieving the congressional intent in repealing the *Kimbell-Diamond* doctrine.

Explanation Of Provisions Proposed § 1.338-3(d) applies to the transfer of target assets to the purchasing corporation or another member of the same affiliated group as the purchasing corporation (the transferee) following a QSP of target stock, if the purchasing corporation does not make a section 338 election for the target.

As noted above, for the transfer of target assets to be pursuant to a reorganization within the meaning of section 368, there must be a continuity of interest in the target's business enterprise on the part of those persons who, directly or indirectly, were the owners of the enterprise prior to the reorganization. *See* 1.368-1(b). The proposed regulations generally provide that, by virtue of the application of section 338, the purchasing corporation's target stock acquired in the QSP represents an interest on the part of a person who was an owner of the target's business enterprise prior to the transfer that can be continued in a reorganization for the purpose of determining whether the continuity of interest requirement is satisfied. A corollary provision enables the transfer to satisfy the requirements for an acquisitive reorganization under section 368(a)(1)(D).

Notwithstanding the general rule above, the proposed regulations provide that sections 354, 355, 356 and 358 do not apply to any person other than the purchasing corporation or another member of the same affiliated group as the purchasing corporation unless the transfer of target assets is pursuant to a reorganization under generally applicable rules without regard to the provisions of the proposed regulations. The legislative history of section 338 does not indicate any intent to eliminate the continuity of interest requirement generally and allow reorganization treatment to shareholders receiving stock in acquisitions where the overall consideration does not preserve continuity of interest. The rules provided in the proposed regulations reconcile Congress' concerns in enacting section 338 with general reorganization principles. * * *

b. Preamble to the Final Regulations
Treasury Decision 8940
(Feb. 13, 2001)

Summary This document contains final regulations relating to deemed and actual asset acquisitions under sections 338 and 1060. The final regulations affect sellers and buyers of corporate stock that are eligible to elect to treat the transaction as a deemed asset acquisition. The final regulations also affect sellers and buyers of assets that constitute a trade or business. * * *

Transactions After QSPs

Since 1995, the regulations under section 338 have provided special rules that apply, by virtue of section 338, to certain transfers of target assets following a QSP of the target's stock if a section 338 election is not made for the target. These provisions modify the normal operation of the continuity of interest requirement under section

368 and the interpretation of the term shareholder for purposes of section 368(a)(1)(D), as applied to certain taxpayers. These rules were adopted to effectuate Congressional intent, in replacing former section 334(b)(2) with section 338, that the deemed sale results provided by section 338 not be available through transactions within the purchasing group after the acquisition. In the final regulations, these rules are located at § 1.338-3(d).

The 1995 amendments did not provide any special rule to modify the application of the statutory requirements for reorganizations under section 368(a)(1)(C). However, the considerations that justify the modified application of the continuity of interest rule and the shareholder definition for "D" reorganizations also justify an analogous modification of the "solely for voting stock" requirement for post-acquisition "C" reorganizations. Accordingly, the final regulations provide that consideration other than voting stock issued in connection with a QSP is ignored in determining whether a subsequent transfer of assets by the target corporation to a member of its new affiliated group satisfies the solely for voting stock requirement of a "C" reorganization. *See* § 1.338-3(d)(4). * * *

Question

Acquiring Corporation (*AC*) acquires all of the stock of Target Corporation (*TC*) in a qualified stock purchase under § 338. To rationalize the corporate structure, *AC* immediately causes *TC* to merge into *Sub*, a previously existing wholly-owned subsidiary of *AC*. In the merger, *Sub* issues to *AC* additional *Sub* stock. What result to *AC*, *TC*, and *Sub*?

F. Pre- and Post-Reorganization Sales and Redemptions

1. Recent Changes to the Continuity of Interest Regulations on Pre- and Post-Reorganization Sales

Excerpt from Thompson and Sayed, 1998 Developments in the Federal Income Taxation of Mergers and Acquisitions: The Year of M&A

51 Univ. of Southern Cal. School of Law Inst on Fed Tax,
Major Tax Planning for 1999 at 1-6–1-36 (1999)

Introduction On January 23, 1998, the U.S. Treasury Department issued final regulations dealing with the continuity of interest (COI) requirement (Final COI Regs.).[2] These regulations also contain amendments to the continuity of business enterprise (COBE) requirement (Final COBE Regs.), which are addressed in Sec. 6.3. In addition on August 30, 2000, the Treasury promulgated final regulations addressing the impact

---

2. T.D. 8760 (January 23, 1998).

of certain redemptions and extraordinary dividends on the COI requirement (Redemption COI Regs.)[3] This section provides a guide to the Final COI Regulations. The next section addresses the Redemption COI Regulations.

Purpose of the COI Requirement The preamble to the Final COI Regs. gives the following explanation of the purpose of the COI requirement:

> The purpose of the continuity of interest requirement is to prevent transactions that resemble sales from qualifying for nonrecognition of gain or loss available to corporate reorganizations. ***

> The COI requirement was applied first to reorganization provisions that did not specify that P [the acquiring corporation] exchange a proprietary interest in P for a proprietary interest in T [the target corporation]. Supreme Court cases imposed the COI requirement to further Congressional intent that tax-free status be accorded only to transactions where P exchanges a substantial proprietary interest in P for a proprietary interest in T held by the T shareholders rather than to transactions resembling sales. *See LeTulle v. Scofield*, 308 U.S. 415 (1940) [Sec. 6.2.B.6.]; *Helvering v. Minnesota Tea Co.*, 296 U.S. 378 (1935) [Sec. 6.2.B.2.]; *Pinellas Ice & Cold Storage Co. v. Commissioner*, 287 U.S. 462 (1933) [Sec. 6.2.B.1]. *See 2 also Cortland Specialty Co. v. Commissioner*, 60 F.2d 937 (2d Cir. 1932), *cert. denied* 288 U.S. 599 (1933).

Problem with Post-Reorganization Sales The preamble to the Final COI Regs. gives the following explanation of the development of the law governing the impact on the COI requirement of post-reorganization sales of P stock by the shareholders of T:

> None of the Supreme Court cases establishing the COI requirement addressed the issue of whether sales by former T shareholders of P stock received in exchange for T stock in the potential reorganization cause the COI requirement to fail to be satisfied. Since then, however, some courts have premised decisions on the assumption that sales of P stock received in exchange for T stock in the potential reorganization may cause the COI requirement to fail to be satisfied. *McDonald's Restaurants of Illinois, Inc. v. Commissioner*, 688 F.2d 520 (7th Cir. 1982); *Penrod v. Commissioner*, 88 T.C. 1415 (1987); *Heintz v. Commissioner*, 25 T.C. 132 (1955), *nonacq.*, 1958-2 C.B. 9; *Estate of Elizabeth Christian v. Commissioner*, 57 T.C.M. (CCH) 1231 (1989). The apparent focus of these cases is on whether the T shareholders intended on the date of the potential reorganization to sell their P stock and the degree, if any, to which P facilitates the sale. Based on an intensive inquiry into nearly identical facts, some of these cases held that as a result of the subsequent sale the potential reorganization did not satisfy the COI requirement; others held that satisfaction of the COI requirement was not adversely affected by the subsequent sale.

---

3. T.D. 8898 (August 30, 2000).

The Treasury's Reaction to Post-Reorganization Sales The preamble to the Final COI Regs. gives the following explanation of the change in policy with regard to post-reorganization sales:

> The IRS and Treasury Department have concluded that the law as reflected in these cases does not further the principles of reorganization treatment and is difficult for both taxpayers and the IRS to apply consistently.

> Therefore, consistent with Congressional intent and the Supreme Court precedent which distinguishes between sales and reorganizations, the final regulations focus the COI requirement generally on exchanges between the T shareholders and P. Under this approach, sales of P stock by former T shareholders generally are disregarded.

> The final regulations will greatly enhance administrability in this area by both taxpayers and the government. The regulations will prevent "whipsaw" of the government, such as where the former T shareholders treat the transaction as a tax-free reorganization, and P later disavows reorganization treatment to step up its basis in the T assets based on the position that sales of P stock by the former T shareholders did not satisfy the COI requirement. *See, e.g., McDonald's Restaurants, supra.* In addition, this approach will prevent unilateral sales of P stock by former majority T shareholders from adversely affecting the section 354 nonrecognition treatment expected by former minority T shareholders.

General Explanation of the New Approach The preamble to the Final COI Regs. gives the following explanation of the new approach of these regulations:

> *** The final regulations provide that the COI requirement is satisfied if in substance a substantial part of the value of the proprietary interest in the target corporation (T) is preserved in the reorganization. A proprietary interest in T is preserved if, in a potential reorganization, it is exchanged for a proprietary interest in the issuing corporation (P), it is exchanged by the acquiring corporation for a direct interest in the T enterprise, or it otherwise continues as a proprietary interest in T. The issuing corporation means the acquiring corporation (as the term is used in section 368(a)), except that, in determining whether a reorganization qualifies as a triangular reorganization (as defined in Sec. 1.358-6(b)(2)), the issuing corporation means the corporation in control of the acquiring corporation. However, a proprietary interest in T is not preserved if, in connection with the potential reorganization, it is acquired by P for consideration other than P stock * * *. All facts and circumstances must be considered in determining whether, in substance, a proprietary interest in T is preserved.

> *Rationale for the COI Regulations*

> The proposed and final regulations permit former T shareholders to sell P stock received in a potential reorganization to third parties without causing the reorganization to fail to satisfy the COI requirement.

Continuing Impact of Step Transactions The Final COI Regs. amend Reg. § 1.368-1(a) to provide:

> In determining whether a transaction qualifies as a reorganization under section 368(a), the transaction must be evaluated under relevant provisions of law, including the step transaction doctrine. *But see* Secs. 1.368-2 (f) and (k) and 1.338-2(c)(3).

The preamble to the Final COI Regs. gives the following explanation of the purpose of this sentence:

> In soliciting comments on the effect upon COI of dispositions of T stock prior to a potential reorganization, the preamble to the proposed COI regulations specifically requests comments on *King Enterprises, Inc. v. United States*, 418 F.2d 511 (Ct. Cl. 1969) [Sec. 7.2.C.] (COI requirement satisfied where, pursuant to a plan, P acquires the T stock for 51 percent P stock and 49 percent debt and cash, and T merges upstream into P), and *YOC Heating Corp. v. Commissioner*, 61 T.C. 168 (1973) [Sec.3 6.2.E.1.] (COI requirement not satisfied where, pursuant to a plan, P acquires 85 percent of the T stock for cash and notes, and T merges into P's newly formed subsidiary with minority shareholders receiving cash). Consistent with these cases, where the step transaction doctrine applies to link T stock purchases with later acquisitions of T, the final regulations provide that a proprietary interest in T is not preserved if, in connection with the potential reorganization, it is acquired by P for consideration other than P stock. Whether a stock acquisition is made in connection with a potential reorganization will be determined based on the facts and circumstances of each case. *See generally* Sec. 1.368-1(a).

General COI Rule in Final COI Regs *Preservation of COI* The Final COI Regs. amend Reg. § 1.368-1(e)(1)(i) to set forth guidance on the preservation of proprietary interests, and the preamble to the Final COI Regs. elaborates on this provision as follows:

> Commentators requested clarification of whether P must actually furnish stock to T shareholders that own T stock which was not acquired in connection with a potential reorganization. The final regulations provide that a proprietary interest in T is preserved if it is exchanged by the acquiring corporation (which may or may not also be P) for a direct interest in the T enterprise, or otherwise continues as a proprietary interest in T.

Pre-Reorganization Sales of T Stock and Post-Reorganization Sales of P Stock The Final COI Regs. amend § 1.368-1(e)(1)(i) to provide rules regarding pre-reorganization sales of T stock and post-reorganization sales of P stock, and the preamble to the Final COI Regs. elaborates on the rule regarding pre-organization and post-reorganization sales of T stock as follows:

> The proposed COI regulations do not specifically address the effect upon COI of dispositions of T stock prior to a potential reorganization, but ask for comments on that issue. The IRS and Treasury Department believe that issues concerning the COI requirement raised by dispositions

of T stock before a potential reorganization correspond to those raised by subsequent dispositions of P stock furnished in exchange for T stock in the potential reorganization. As requested by commentators, the final regulations apply the rationale of the proposed COI regulations to transactions occurring both prior to and after a potential reorganization. *Cf. J.E. Seagram Corp. v. Commissioner*, 104 T.C. 75 (1995) (sales of T stock prior to a potential reorganization do not affect COI if not part of the plan of reorganization). The final regulations provide that, for COI purposes, a mere disposition of T stock prior to a potential reorganization to persons not related to P is disregarded and a mere disposition of P stock received in a potential reorganization to persons not related to P is disregarded. * * *

Related Person Acquisitions The Final COI Regs set out a related party acquisitions rule in Reg. § 1.368-1(e)(2)(i), and the preamble to the Final COI Regs. gives the following explanation of the origin and purpose of this provision:

> The proposed COI regulations provide that "[i]n determining whether [COI is satisfied], all facts and circumstances must be considered, including any plan or arrangement for the acquiring corporation or its successor corporation (or a person related to the acquiring corporation or its successor corporation within the meaning of section 707(b)(1) or 267(b) (without regard to section 267(e)) to redeem or acquire the consideration provided in the reorganization." The final regulations provide a more specific rule that a proprietary interest in T is not preserved if, in connection with a potential reorganization, a person related (as defined below) to P acquires, with consideration other than a proprietary interest in P, T stock or P stock furnished in exchange for a proprietary interest in T in the potential reorganization. The IRS and Treasury Department believe, however, that certain related party acquisitions preserve a proprietary interest in T and therefore, the rule includes an exception to the related party rule. Under this exception, a proprietary interest in T is preserved to the extent those persons who were the direct or indirect owners of T prior to the potential reorganization maintain a direct or indirect proprietary interest in P. *See, e.g.,* Rev. Rul. 84-30 (1984-1 C.B. 114). * * *

The Final COI Regs. provide a definition of related person in Reg. § 1.368-1(e)(3), and the preamble to the Final COI Regs. gives the following explanation of this provision:

> Commentators stated that the proposed COI regulations' rule, which employs sections 707(b)(1) and 267(b) to define persons related to P, is too broad. In response, the final regulations adopt a narrower related person definition which has two components in order to address two separate concerns.
>
> First, the IRS and Treasury Department were concerned that acquisitions of T or P stock by a member of P's affiliated group were no different in sub-

stance from an acquisition or redemption by P, because of the existence of various provisions in the Code that permit members to transfer funds to other members without significant tax consequences. Accordingly, Sec. 1.368-1(e)(3)(i)(A) includes as related persons corporations that are members of the same affiliated group under section 1504, without regard to the exceptions in section 1504(b).

Second, because the final regulations take into account whether, in substance, P has redeemed the stock it exchanged for T stock in the potential reorganization, the final regulations treat two corporations as related persons if a purchase of the stock of one corporation by another corporation would be treated as a distribution in redemption of the stock of the first corporation under section 304(a)(2) (determined without regard to Sec. 1.1502-80(b)).

Because the final regulations focus generally on the consideration P exchanges, related persons do not include individual or other noncorporate shareholders. Thus, the IRS will no longer apply the holdings of *South Bay Corporation v. Commissioner*, 345 F.2d 698 (2d Cir. 1965), and *Superior Coach of Florida, Inc. v. Commissioner*, 80 T.C. 895 (1983), to transactions governed by these regulations. * * *

Acquisition by Partnerships The Final COI Regs. add a rule in Reg. § 1.368-1(e)(4) regarding acquisitions by partnerships.

Successors and Predecessors The Final COI Regs. add Reg. § 1.368-1(e)(5) regarding successors and predecessors.

Conforming Amendment to Section 338 Regulations The preamble to the Final COI Regs. gives the following explanation of a conforming amendment to Reg. § 1.338-2(c)(3):

Transactions Following a Qualified Stock Purchase

As stated above, these final regulations focus the COI requirement generally on exchanges between the T shareholders and P. Accordingly, the language of Sec. 1.338-[3(d)] is conformed to these final COI regulations to treat the stock of T acquired by the purchasing corporation in the qualified stock purchase as though it was not acquired in connection with the transfer of the T assets.

Under this regulation a sidewise merger of a target acquired in a qualified stock purchase by an acquiring parent into a sister subsidiary is generally not taxable. [*See* Sec. 6.2.F.2.]

Effect on Other Authorities and Other Documents The preamble to the Final COI Regs. makes it clear that these regulations do not apply to reorganizations under Section 368(a)(1)(D) and to distributions under Section 355:

Effect on Other Authorities

The IRS and Treasury Department continue to study the role of the COI requirement in section 368(a)(1)(D) reorganizations and section 355 transactions. Therefore, these final COI regulations do not apply to section 368(a)(1)(D) reorganizations and section 355 transactions. *See* Sec. 1.355-2(c). These COI regulations apply solely for purposes of determining whether the COI requirement is satisfied. No inference should be drawn from any provision of this regulation as to whether other reorganization requirements are satisfied, for example, whether P has issued solely voting stock for purposes of section 368(a)(1)(B) or (C).

The preamble to the Final COI Regs. says the following concerning the effect on other documents:

Effect on Other Documents

Rev. Proc. 77-37 (1977-2 C.B. 568) [Sec. 6.2.C.] and Rev. Proc. 86-42 (1986-2 C.B. 722) will be modified to the extent inconsistent with these regulations.

Rev. Rul. 66-23 (1966-1 C.B. 67) is hereby obsoleted because it indicates that a plan or arrangement in connection with a potential reorganization for disposition of stock to unrelated persons does not satisfy the COI requirement. * * *

Examples Reg. § 1.368-1(e)(6) contains nine examples of the rules set out in the Final COI Regs. * * *

2. Elaboration on Post-Reorganization Redemptions by Acquiror

Revenue Ruling 99-58

1999-52 I.R.B. 701

Issue What is the effect on continuity of interest when a potential reorganization is followed by an open market reacquisition of P's stock?

Facts T merges into P, a corporation whose stock is widely held, and is publicly and actively traded. P has one class of common stock authorized and outstanding. In the merger, T shareholders receive 50 percent common stock of P and 50 percent cash. Viewed in isolation, the exchange would satisfy the continuity of interest requirement of § 1.368-1(e) of the Income Tax Regulations. However, in an effort to prevent dilution resulting from the issuance of P shares in the merger, P's pre-existing stock repurchase program is modified to enable P to reacquire a number of its shares equal to the number issued in the acquisition of T. The number of shares repurchased will not exceed the total number of P shares issued and outstanding prior to the merger. The repurchases are made following the merger, on the open market, through a broker for the prevailing market price. P's intention to repurchase shares was announced prior to the T merger, but the repurchase program was not a matter negotiated with T or the T shareholders. There was not an understanding between the T shareholders and P that the T shareholders' ownership of P stock would be transitory. Because of the mechanics of an open market purchase, P does not know the identity of a seller of P stock, nor does a former T shareholder who receives P stock in the merger and subsequently sells it know whether P is the buyer. Without regard to the repurchase program, a market exists for the newly-issued P stock held by the former T shareholders. During the time P undertakes its repurchase program, there are sales of P stock on the open market, which may include sales of P shares by former T shareholders.

Law And Analysis Requisite to a reorganization under the Internal Revenue Code is a continuity of interest as described in § 1.368-1(e). Section 1.368-1(b). The general purpose of the continuity of interest requirement is "to prevent transactions that resemble sales from qualifying for nonrecognition of gain or loss available to corporate reorganizations." Section 1.368-1(e)(1)(i). To achieve this purpose, the regulation provides that a proprietary interest in the target corporation is not preserved to the extent that, "in connection with the potential reorganization, … stock of the issuing corporation furnished in exchange for a proprietary interest in the target corporation in the potential reorganization is redeemed." *Id.* However, for purposes of the continuity requirement, "a mere disposition of stock of the issuing corporation received in the potential reorganization to persons not related … to the issuing corporation is disregarded." *Id.* The regulation provides that all facts and circumstances will be considered in determining whether, in substance, a proprietary interest in the target corporation is preserved.

Under the facts set forth above, continuity of interest is satisfied. There was not an understanding between the T shareholders and P that the T shareholders' ownership of the P shares would be transitory. Further, because of the mechanics of an open market repurchase, the repurchase program does not favor participation by the former T shareholders. Therefore, even if it could be established that P has repurchased P shares from former T shareholders in the repurchase program, any such purchase would be coincidental. The merger and the stock repurchase together in substance would not resemble a sale of T stock to P by the former T shareholders and, thus, the repurchase would not be treated as "in connection with" the merger. Under the facts presented, a sale of P stock on the open market by a former T shareholder during the repurchase program will have the same effect on continuity of interest as a mere disposition to persons not related to P.

Holding Under the facts presented, the open market repurchase of shares through a broker has no effect on continuity of interest.

3. Final Regulations Addressing Pre-Reorganization Distributions and Redemptions by Target

See § 1.368-1(e)(1)(ii) and Example 9 of § 1.368-1(e)(6)

Treasury Decision 8898

I.R.B. 2000-38, 276 (September 18, 2000)

Summary This document contains final regulations providing guidance regarding the continuity of interest requirement for corporate reorganizations. The final regulations affect corporations and their shareholders. The final regulations provide that distributions and redemptions by a target corporation prior to a potential reorganization are taken into account for continuity of interest purposes to the extent that the consideration received by the target shareholder in the redemption or distribution is treated as other property or money under section 356 of the Internal Revenue Code, or to the extent that the consideration would be treated as other property or money if the target shareholder also had received stock of the issuing corporation in exchange for stock owned by the shareholder in the target corporation. * * *

The regulations provide that a proprietary interest in T (other than one held by P) is not preserved to the extent that consideration received prior to a potential reorganization, either in a redemption of T stock or in a distribution with respect to T stock, is treated as other property or money received in the exchange for purposes of section 356 or would be so treated if the T shareholder also had received stock of P in exchange for stock owned by the shareholder in T. In determining whether consideration is treated as other property or money under section 356 received in an exchange for a proprietary interest in T, taxpayers should consider all facts, circumstances, and relevant legal authorities.

The regulations posit for COI purposes that each T shareholder receives some P stock in exchange for T stock. Section 356 generally does not apply to a T shareholder who does not receive any P stock in exchange for T stock in a reorganization. *See* Rev. Rul. 74-515 (1974-2 C.B. 118). Solely for purposes of determining whether the COI requirement is satisfied, however, the regulations deem each T shareholder to have received some P stock in exchange for T stock (without ascribing any value to that stock). The regulations thus use the same criterion for determining whether COI is satisfied, regardless of whether a T shareholder receives any P stock. These final regulations do not offer safe harbors or special rules for the transactions about which commentators expressed concern. Unlike the temporary regulations, however, the final regulations do not automatically take all pre-reorganization redemptions and extraordinary distributions in connection with the reorganization into account for COI purposes.

Stock Repurchase Programs Example 8 of § 1.368-1(e)(6) illustrates the effect on COI of a general stock repurchase program. In the example, P repurchases a small percentage of its stock after a reorganization, as part of a preexisting stock repurchase program. COI is satisfied because the redemption of a small percentage of P stock was not in connection with the merger. In response to comments received, the IRS and Treasury Department issued further guidance on the effect of a stock repurchase program on COI in Rev. Rul. 99-58 (1999-52 I.R.B. 701) [Sec. 6.2.F.2]. Because Example 8 suggests a more restrictive approach to COI than was intended in this context, Example 8 is removed by this Treasury decision.

Effect on Other Authorities These COI regulations apply solely for purposes of determining whether the COI requirement is satisfied. No inference should be drawn from any provision of this regulation as to whether other reorganization requirements are satisfied, or as to the characterization of a related transaction.

Effect on Other Documents The following publications do not apply to the extent they are inconsistent with these regulations:

Rev. Proc. 77-37 (1977-2 C.B. 568) [Sec. 6.2.C.]

Rev. Proc. 86-42 (1986-2 C.B. 722). * * *

G. Remote Continuity

1. Party to the Reorganization; Remote Continuity; The Groman and Bashford Doctrines

One of the conditions for nonrecognition treatment for the exchanging shareholder or security holder under §354(a) and for the target corporation under §361(a) is that each corporation involved in the transaction be a "party to the reorganization," as defined in §368(b).

In *Groman v. Commissioner*, 302 U.S. 82 (1937) [Sec. 6.2.G.2.a.], *infra*, and *Helvering v. Bashford*, 302 U.S. 454 (1938) *infra*, the Supreme Court held that in a transaction in which a subsidiary used its parent's stock in the acquisition of a target corporation, the parent's stock did not count for continuity of interest purposes because the parent was not a "party to the reorganization." The *Groman* and *Bashford* doctrines have been overruled for certain triangular reorganizations by amendments to the definition of "party to the reorganization" in §368(b). The amendments include, for instance, the parent in a triangular (C) as a party to the reorganization. The *Groman* and *Bashford* doctrines are of continuing validity where not overridden by statute or regulations. As will be seen in Sec. 6.3.D., the doctrines have been partially overruled in the new continuity of business enterprise regulations.

2. The Early Anti-Triangular Reorganization Cases

a. Acquisition of Stock of Target in Exchange for (1) Stock of Acquiring Parent, (2) Stock of Acquiring Sub, and (3) Cash

Groman v. Commissioner

Supreme Court of the United States, 1937
302 U.S. 82, 58 S.Ct. 108, 82 L.Ed. 63

MR. JUSTICE ROBERTS delivered the opinion of the Court.

Glidden [the acquiring parent] organized Ohio [the acquiring sub] and became the owner of all its common stock but none of its preferred stock.

[T]he shareholders of Indiana [the target corporation] transferred their stock to Ohio and received therefore a total consideration of $1,207,016 consisting of Glidden prior preference stock valued at $533,980, shares of the preferred stock of Ohio valued at $500,000, and $153,036 in cash. Indiana then transferred its assets to Ohio and was dissolved.

As a result of the reorganization petitioner received shares of Glidden stock, shares of Ohio stock, and $17,293 in cash. In his return for 1929 he included the $17,293 as income received but ignored the shares of Glidden and of Ohio as stock received in exchange in a reorganization. The respondent ruled that Glidden was not a party to a reorganization within the meaning of the Revenue Act, treated the transaction as a taxable exchange to the extent of the cash and shares of Glidden, and determined a deficiency of $7,420. * * *

The question is whether that portion of the consideration consisting of prior preference shares of Glidden should be recognized in determining petitioner's taxable gain. The decision of this question depends upon whether Glidden's stock was that of a party to the reorganization for, if so, the statute declares gain or loss due to its receipt shall not be included in the taxpayer's computation of income for the year in which the exchange was made.

If section 112(i)(2) [now § 368(b)] is a definition of a party to a reorganization and excludes corporations not therein described, Glidden was not a party since its relation to the transaction is not within the terms of the definition. It was not a corporation resulting from the reorganization; and it did not acquire a majority of the shares of voting stock and a majority of the shares of all other classes of stock of any other corporation in the reorganization. The Circuit Court of Appeals thought the section was intended as a definition of the term party as used in the act and excluded all corporations not specifically described. It therefore held Glidden could not be considered a party to the reorganization. * * *

It is argued, however, that Ohio was the alter ego of Glidden; that in truth Glidden was the principal and Ohio its agent; that we should look at the realities of the situation, disregard the corporate entity of Ohio, and treat it as Glidden. But to do so would be to ignore the purpose of the reorganization sections of the statute, which, as we have said, is that where, pursuant to a plan, the interest of the stockholders of a corporation continues to be definitely represented in substantial measure in a new or different one, then to the extent, but only to the extent, of that continuity of interest, the exchange is to be treated as one not giving rise to present gain or loss. If cash or "other property," that is, property other than stock or securities of the reorganized corporations, is received, present gain or loss must be recognized. Was not Glidden's prior preference stock "other property" in the sense that its ownership represented a participation in assets in which Ohio, and its shareholders through it, had no proprietorship? Was it not "other property" in the sense that *qua* that stock the shareholders of Indiana assumed a relation toward the conveyed assets not measured by a continued substantial interest in those assets in the ownership of Ohio, but an interest in the assets of Glidden a part of which was the common stock of Ohio? These questions we think must be answered in the affirmative. To reject the plain meaning of the term "party," and to attribute that relation to Glidden, would be not only to disregard the letter but also to violate the spirit of the Revenue Act.

We hold that Glidden was not a party to the reorganization and the receipt of its stock by Indiana's shareholders in exchange, in part, for their stock was the basis for computation of taxable gain to them in the year 1929.

The judgment is affirmed.

Mr. Justice Black took no part in the consideration or decision of this case.

b. Acquisition of Three Targets by Consolidation with Target's Shareholders Receiving (1) Stock of Acquiring Parent, (2) Stock of Acquiring Sub, and (3) Cash

Helvering v. Bashford

Supreme Court of the United States, 1938
302 U.S. 454

Mr. Justice Brandeis delivered the opinion of the Court.

Atlas Powder Company [the acquiring parent] desired to eliminate the competition of three concerns — Peerless Explosives Company, Union Explosives Company, and Black Diamond Powder Company. Deeming it unwise to do so by buying either their stock or their assets, Atlas conceived and consummated a plan for consolidating the three competitors into a new corporation [the acquiring sub], with Atlas to get a majority of its stock. To this end holders of the stock of the three companies were duly approached by individuals who represented Atlas; their agreements to carry out the plan were obtained; the new corporation was formed and became the owner practically of all the stock, and all the assets of the three competitors; Atlas became the owner of all the preferred stock and 57 percent of the common stock of the new corporation; and in exchange for the stock in the three companies each of the former stockholders received some common stock in the new company, some Atlas stock, and some cash which Atlas supplied.

Bashford, one of the stockholders in Peerless, received in exchange for his stock 2,720.08 shares of the common stock of the new corporation, $25,306.67 in cash, 625 shares of Atlas preferred, and 1,344 shares of Atlas common. In his income tax return for the year 1930 he included all the cash, but did not include the gain on stock of either the new corporation or Atlas. The Commissioner concedes that gain on the stock in the new corporation was properly omitted, since the new company was a "reorganization" of Peerless. He insists that the Atlas stock should have been included, as it was "other property" on which gain was taxable under section 112(c)(1) of the Revenue Act of 1928, [now § 354] since Atlas was not "a party to the reorganization." The Board of Tax Appeals (33 B.T.A. 10) held that Atlas was "a party to the reorganization," and hence that gain on its stock was properly omitted by Bashford. * * *

Applying the rule here, we hold likewise that the [Atlas] stock was "other property" and Bashford, therefore, liable on the deficiency assessment; because the Atlas Powder Company was not "a party to the reorganization." * * *

Any direct ownership by Atlas of Peerless, Black Diamond, and Union was transitory and without real substance; it was part of a plan which contemplated the immediate transfer of the stock or the assets or both of the three reorganized companies to the new Atlas subsidiary. Hence, under the rule stated, the [factual] distinctions are not of legal significance. The difference in the degree of stock control by the parent company of its subsidiary and the difference in the method or means by which that control was secured are not material. The participation of Atlas in the reorganization of its competitors into a new company which became a subsidiary did not make Atlas "a party to the reorganization." The continuity of interest required by the rule is lacking.

Reversed.

Questions

In both *Groman* and *Bashford* the Board of Tax Appeals held that the parent corporation (Glidden in *Groman* and Atlas in *Bashford*) was a party to a reorganization and that, consequently, its stock was not boot in the reorganization. What result under the current statute if *S*, a wholly owned subsidiary of *P*, acquires *T* in a merger in which the consideration paid by *S* is 50% *S* stock and 50% *P* stock? In *Bashford*, Atlas only owned 57% of the new corporation. Would it be possible under the current statute for the parent in a triangular reorganization to own only 57% of the stock of the subsidiary?

H. Use of Contingent or Escrow Stock in a Reorganization

1. General Principles

Revenue Ruling 84-42

1984-1 C.B. 194, Sec. 2 Procedure

.01 Section 3.03 of Rev.Proc. 77-37 is amplified to read as follows: In transactions under sections 368(a)(1)(A), 368(a)(1)(B), 368(a)(1)(C), 368(a)(1)(D), 368(a)(1)(E), and 351 of the Code, it is not necessary that all the stock which is to be issued in exchange for the requisite stock or property, be issued immediately provided (1) that all the stock will be issued within 5 years from the date of transfer of assets or stock for reorganizations under sections 368(a)(1)(A), 368(a)(1)(C), 368(a)(1)(D), and 368(a)(1) (E), or within 5 years from the date of the initial distribution in the case of transactions under sections 368(a)(1)(B), and 351; (2) there is a valid business reason for not issuing all the stock immediately, such as difficulty in determining the value of one or both of the corporations involved in the transaction; (3) the maximum number of shares which may be issued in the exchange is stated; (4) at least 50 percent of the maximum number of shares of each class of stock which may be issued is issued in the initial distribution; (5) the agreement evidencing the right to receive stock in the future prohibits assignment (except by operation of law) or if the agreement does not prohibit assignment, the right must not be evidenced by negotiable certificates of any kind and must not be readily marketable; (6) such right can give rise to the receipt only of additional stock of the corporation making the underlying distribution; (7) such stock issuance will not be triggered by an event the occurrence or nonoccurrence of which is within the control of shareholders; (8) such stock issuance will not be triggered by the payment of additional tax or reduction in tax paid as a result of a Service audit of the shareholders or the corporation either (a) with respect to the reorganization or section 351 transaction in which the contingent stock will be issued, or (b) when the reorganization or section 351 transaction in which the contingent stock will be issued, or (c) when the reorganization or section 351 transaction in which the escrowed stock will be issued involves persons related within the meaning of section 267(c)(4) of the Code; and (9) the mechanism for the calculation of the additional stock to be issued is objective and readily ascertainable. Stock issued as compensation, royalties or any other consideration other than in exchange for stock or assets will not be considered to have been received in the exchange. Until the final distribution of the total number of shares of stock to be issued in the exchange is made, the interim basis of the stock of the issuing corporation received in the exchange by the shareholders (not including that portion of each share representing interest) will be determined, pursuant to section 358(a), as though the maximum number of shares to be issued (not including that portion of each share representing interest) has been received by the shareholders.

In connection with item 3.03(8) above, the Service reserves the right to refuse to rule if, based on all the facts and circumstances of a case, it is determined that the principal purpose of the triggering mechanism is the reduction in federal income taxes (*see* section 3.02(1) of Rev.Proc. 84-22, 1984-13 I.R.B. 18).

.02 Section 3.06 of Rev.Proc. 77-37 is amplified to read as follows: In transactions under section 368(a)(1)(A), 368(a)(1)(B), 368(a)(1)(C), 368(a)(1)(D), 368(a)(1)(E), and 351 of the Code, a portion of the stock issued in exchange for the requisite stock or property may be placed in escrow by the exchanging shareholders, or may be made subject to a condition pursuant to the agreement, or plan of reorganization or of the transaction, for possible return to the issuing corporation under specified conditions provided (1) there is a valid business reason for establishing the arrangement; (2) the stock subject to such arrangement appears as issued and outstanding on the balance sheet of the issuing corporation and such stock is legally outstanding under applicable state law; (3) all dividends paid on such stock will be distributed currently to the exchanging shareholders; (4) all voting rights of such stock (if any) are exercisable by or on behalf of the shareholders or their authorized agent; (5) no shares of such stock are subject to restrictions requiring their return to the issuing corporation because of death, failure to continue employment, or similar restrictions; (6) all such stock is released from the arrangement within 5 years from the date of consummation of the transaction (except where there is a bona fide dispute as to whom the stock should be released); (7) at least 50 percent of the number of shares of each class of stock issued initially to the shareholders (exclusive of shares of stock to be issued at a later date as described in .01 above) is not subject to the arrangement; (8) the return of stock will not be triggered by an event the occurrence or nonoccurrence of which is within the control of shareholders; (9) the return of stock will not be triggered by the payment of additional tax or reduction in tax paid as a result of a Service audit of the shareholders or the corporation either (a) with respect to the reorganization or section 351 transaction in which the escrowed stock will be issued, or (b) when the reorganization or section 351 transaction in which the escrowed stock will be issued involves persons related within the meaning of section 267(c)(4) of the Code; and (10) the mechanism for the calculation of the number of shares of stock to be returned is objective and readily ascertainable.

In connection with item 3.06(9) above, the Service reserves the right to refuse to rule if, based on all the facts and circumstances of a case, it is determined that the principal purpose of the triggering mechanism is the reduction in federal income taxes (*see* section 3.02(1) of the Rev. Proc. 84-22, 1984-13 I.R.B. 18).

2. Applicability of Imputed Interest Rules to Contingent Payouts
Solomon v. Commissioner
United States Circuit Court of Appeals, Second Circuit, 1977
570 F.2d 28

Mansfield, Circuit Judge: * * * The only question before us is whether [former] § 483 of the Internal Revenue Code, which requires that a portion of deferred payments received on account of the sale or exchange of property must be treated as interest rather than capital, applies to a "non-taxable corporate reorganization," *see* §§ 354(a)(1), 368(a)(1)(B), so as to render part of those shares interest income [where shares of the acquiring corporation (Whittaker) are received after the date of acquisition pursuant to a contingent payout arrangement]. [This type of transaction is now subject to the contingent interest rules of §§ 1274 and 1275. *See* Sec. 1.9.]

The Tax Court held that § 483 was applicable. We affirm.

Discussion [Former] § 483 provides in pertinent part that in the case of any contract for the sale or exchange of property under which any payment constituting part or all of the sales price is deferred for more than one year after the sale or exchange without providing for payment of any interest or of adequate interest on the deferred payment or payments, a portion of each payment received by the seller more than six months after the date of the sale or exchange shall be treated as unstated interest. * * *

* * * [W]e agree with the Commissioner that the purpose of § 483 [and presumably the purpose of §§ 1274 and 1275 do] not conflict with the purpose underlying the Code's corporate reorganization provisions. * * * The purpose of § 483 * * * is to end an abuse whereby ordinary interest income was being converted into capital gain; the legislative history indicates that Congress intended its solution to encompass all transactions with certain objective characteristics, whether or not they were consciously designed to avoid taxes. The transaction before us may be taxed so as to give effect to both of these purposes and without any eventual tax overlap. A finding that this transaction constituted only "a readjustment of continuing interest in property under modified corporate forms" does not foreclose implementation of Congress' prophylactic solution to the problem of unstated interest. Taxation of the interest portion does not conflict with maintenance of the tax-free status of the portion received in an exchange of capital assets. * * *

I. The Signing Date Regulations
Proposed Amendments of Regulations (REG-129706-04)
(August 10, 2004)

[The proposed regulations have been finalized as Treas. Reg. § 1.368-1(e)(2), and this section merely introduces the basic concepts.]

Background. * * * In a transaction in which the shareholders of the target corporation receive both money and acquiring corporation stock, commentators have expressed concern that the transaction could fail to satisfy the COI requirement as a result of a decline in the value of the acquiring corporation's stock between the date the parties agree to the terms of the transaction (the signing date) and the date the transaction closes. Commentators have noted that attempts to mitigate this concern have led to complexity in structuring transactions intended to qualify as reorganizations. These proposed regulations provide guidance to help address those concerns.

Explanation of Provisions. The IRS and Treasury Department believe that there are certain cases in which the determination of whether the COI requirement is satisfied should be made by reference to the signing date value of the issuing corporation stock to be issued in the transaction. In these cases, the target corporation shareholders generally can be viewed as being subject to the economic fortunes of the issuing corporation as of the signing date. Therefore, these proposed regulations [now finalized in Treas. Reg. § 1.368-1(e)(2) provide that in determining whether the COI requirement is satisfied, the consideration to be exchanged for the proprietary interests in the target corporation is valued as of the end of the last business day before the first date there is a binding contract to effect the potential reorganization, provided the consideration to be provided to the target corporation shareholders is fixed in such contract and includes only stock of the issuing corporation and money.

For this purpose, a binding contract is an instrument enforceable under applicable law against the parties to the instrument. The IRS and Treasury Department understand that tender offers are a frequent acquisition vehicle. Because the terms of a tender offer that is subject to section 14(d) of the Securities and Exchange Act of 1934 [15 U.S.C. 78n(d)(1)] and the regulations promulgated thereunder are fixed in a manner similar to those of a binding contract, these proposed regulations provide that such a tender offer, even if not pursuant to a binding contract, will be treated as a binding contract for purposes of these regulations.

The proposed regulations provide that the presence of a condition outside the control of the parties shall not prevent an instrument from being a binding contract. For example, the fact that the completion of a tender offer is subject to a shareholder vote or the target shareholders tendering a sufficient amount of target stock will be considered a condition outside the control of the parties.

Finally, these proposed regulations provide that consideration is fixed if the contract states the exact number of shares of the issuing corporation and the exact amount of money, if any, to be exchanged for the proprietary interests in the target corporation. * * *

§ 6.3 The Continuity of Business Enterprise Doctrine

A. Introduction to the Current Regulations

See § 1.368-1(d).

Preamble Regulations under § 1.368-1(d)

Treasury Decision 7745 (December 29, 1980)

Summary This document contains final regulations clarifying the continuity of business enterprise requirement for corporate reorganizations. The continuity of business enterprise requirement is fundamental to the notion that tax-free reorganizations merely readjust continuing interests in property. Recent developments involving the availability of tax-free reorganization treatment for certain mutual fund transactions require clarification, in general, of the continuity of business enterprise requirement. * * *

General Description Of Regulations The regulation sets forth certain basic concepts underlying the continuity of business enterprise requirement. Continuity of business enterprise requires that the transferee (*P*) either continue the transferor's (*T*'s) historic business or use a significant portion of *T*'s historic business assets. *P* is not required to continue *T*'s business. However, there must be significant use of *T*'s historic business assets in *P*'s business.

The facts of the examples in the regulation are based, in large part, upon administrative rulings and judicial opinions. *Example* (1), which is based on *Lewis v. Commissioner,* 176 F.2d 646 (1st Cir. 1949), shows that continuity of business enterprise requires only that *P* continue one of the significant lines of *T*'s business. *Example* (2), which is based on *Atlas Tool Co. v. Commissioner,* 70 T.C. 86 (1978), *aff'd* 614 F.2d 860 (3d Cir. 1980), *cert. denied,* 449 U.S. 836 (1980), shows that continuity of business enterprise may exist even if *P*'s use of *T*'s assets differs from *T*'s use of those assets.

Example (3) shows that stocks and bonds acquired following the sale of *T*'s historic business as part of a plan of reorganization are not *T*'s historic business assets. Compare *Lester J. Workman,* T.C. Memo 1977-378.

The facts in *example* (4) are a variation of those in Rev. Rul. 63-29, 1963-1 C.B. 77, although the example reaches a different result. This transaction is not a mere purchase by *T* of *P* stock because *T* receives third party notes which are not cash equivalents. *Example* (5) shows that a disposition of *T*'s assets by *P* does not differ in result from a disposition of those assets by *T*. * * *

Overall Policy Considerations * * * The courts have long recognized that a tax-free reorganization presupposes that T's shareholders retain a material proprietary interest in P (continuity of interest). A necessary corollary to this continuity of interest requirement is that the interest retained represents a link to T's business or its business assets. The continuity of business enterprise requirement ensures that tax-free reorganizations effect only a readjustment of the T shareholders' continuing interest in T's property under a modified corporate form. *See,* § 1.368-1(b). Absent such a link between T's shareholders and T's business or assets there would be no reason to require T's shareholders to retain a continuing stock interest in P. If the shareholders' link to T's business or its assets is broken by, for example, a sale of T's business to an unrelated party as part of the overall plan of reorganization, the interest received in P is no different than an interest in any corporation. An exchange of stock without a link to the underlying business or business assets resembles any stock for stock exchange and, as such, is a taxable event. * * *

"Historic" concept based on step transaction principles The regulation requires a continuing link between T's shareholders and T's business or assets. The examples in the regulation illustrate that the transfer of sale proceeds is not sufficient. It follows that it is not sufficient to transfer assets acquired with the sale proceeds as part of a plan of reorganization. * * *

B. Sale of Assets in Anticipation of Reorganization

1. Sale by Target before a (C) Reorganization

Revenue Ruling 79-434

1979-2 C.B. 155

Issue Does the transfer by a corporation, previously engaged in a manufacturing business, of its assets (cash and short-term Treasury notes) for stock of a regulated investment company qualify as a reorganization under section 368(a)(1) of the Internal Revenue Code?

Facts Corporation *X*, a corporation engaged in manufacturing, sold all of its assets to unrelated corporation *Z* for $1,000x cash. This sale was made in anticipation of *X*'s acquisition by corporation *Y*, an open-end diversified investment company that qualifies as a regulated investment company as that term is defined in section 851 of the Code. Pursuant to an agreement between *X* and *Y*, *X* transferred all of its assets (cash and short-term Treasury notes that *X* had purchased with the proceeds from the sale of its assets) to *Y* in return for 1,000 shares of *Y*. As provided in the agreement, *X* dissolved after the transfer and distributed the stock of *Y* to its shareholders, individuals *A* and *B*, in exchange for their *X* stock.

Law And Analysis A tax-free reorganization assumes that "the new enterprise, the new corporate structure, and the new property are substantially continuations of the old [ones] still unliquidated." Section 1.1002-1(c). [A] transaction that in substance is a mere purchase by one corporation of stock in another corporation is not a reorganization.

Holding The transfer of cash or short-term Treasury notes for stock does not qualify as a reorganization under section 368(a)(1) of the Code because in substance it represents a purchase by *X* of the shares of *Y* prior to *X*'s liquidation.

The fair market value of the *Y* stock distributed by *X* to its shareholders in complete liquidation will be treated as in full payment in exchange for their *X* stock under section 331 of the Code. Gain or loss is recognized to the shareholders of *X* under section 1001.

2. Sale by Target before a (B) Reorganization
Revenue Ruling 81-92
1981-1 C.B. 133

Issue Does the acquisition by one corporation of all of the stock of another corporation solely in exchange for voting stock of the acquiring corporation qualify as a tax-free reorganization under section 368(a)(1)(B) if the acquired corporation's assets consist solely of cash that it realized from the sale of assets it previously used in its manufacturing business?

Facts *T*, a corporation engaged in manufacturing, sold all of its assets for cash to *Z*, an unrelated corporation. The sale was made as part of a plan of reorganization in which *P*, a corporation engaged in the manufacture of products different than those previously manufactured by *T*, acquired all of the outstanding stock in *T* from *T*'s shareholders, in exchange solely for *P* voting stock. *T*, as a wholly owned subsidiary of *P*, then used the cash realized on the sale of its manufacturing assets to engage in a business entirely unrelated to its previous manufacturing business.

Law And Analysis * * * Section 1.368-1(d) of the regulations provides, in general, that the continuity of business enterprise requirement of section 1.368-1(b) is satisfied if the transferee in a corporate reorganization either (i) continues the transferor's historic business or (ii) uses a significant portion of the transferor's historic business assets in a business. Because the continuity of business enterprise requirement must be met for a transaction to qualify as a reorganization, section 1.368-1(d) is applicable to a transaction intended to qualify as a tax free reorganization under section 368(a)(1)(B) of the Code. *See* section 1.368-1(d)(1)(iii). Therefore, the transferee corporation must continue the transferor's historic business, or continue to use a significant portion of the transferor's historic business assets, in modified corporate form as a subsidiary of the transferee corporation for the transaction to qualify under section 368(a)(1)(B).

Holding In the instant transaction, the acquisition by *P* of the *T* stock solely for *P*'s voting stock does not qualify as a tax-free reorganization under section 368(a)(1)(B) since *P* did not continue *T*'s historic (the manufacturing) business or use a significant portion of *T*'s historic business assets (those used in the manufacturing business) in a business conducted as a subsidiary of *P* after the transaction.

Accordingly, gain or loss is realized and recognized to the former shareholders of *T* upon the receipt by them from *P* of the *P* voting stock in exchange for their *T* stock under section 1001 of the Code.

3. Acquisition of Investment Company in a (C) Reorganization
Revenue Ruling 87-76
1987-2 C.B. 84

Issue Are the requirements of section 1.368-1(d) of the Income Tax Regulations, relating to continuity of business enterprise, satisfied under the circumstances described below?

Facts *T* is a corporation engaged in the investment business since 1975. From its inception, *T*'s investment practice has been to maintain approximately one-third of the value of its investment portfolio in diversified corporate stock purchased primarily for equity growth, one-third in corporate stock purchased with a view to maximizing current income, and the remaining one-third in general corporate bonds purchased with a view to producing steady, predictable returns of income. *T* has no other significant assets, tangible or intangible.

P is a diversified open-end management investment company whose investment policy since it was organized in 1978 has been to attract investors who wish to participate in a managed portfolio consisting exclusively of high grade municipal bonds, the income from which is exempt from federal income tax.

In 1982, *P* acquired substantially all of T's assets in exchange solely for shares of P voting common stock in a transaction intended to qualify as a reorganization described in section 368(a)(1)(C) of the Internal Revenue Code. Pursuant to the plan of reorganization, *T* was required, prior to the reorganization, to sell its entire portfolio of corporate stock and bonds, and reinvest the proceeds therefrom in municipal bonds that were subject to *P*'s approval. * * *

Law And Analysis * * * In the present situation, the transaction does not meet the asset continuity test since all of *T*'s historic assets, the portfolio of corporate stocks and bonds, were, as part of the plan of reorganization, sold before the transaction was consummated, and the proceeds were reinvested in municipal bonds. Consequently, the issue is whether *P* will continue *T*'s historic business.

Section 1.368-1(d)(3)(i) of the regulations provides that the fact that the acquiring corporation is in the same line of business as the acquired corporation tends to establish the requisite continuity, but is not alone sufficient. * * *

Holding The continuity of business enterprise requirement of section 1.368-1(d) of the regulations is not met upon the transfer to *P* of all of *T*'s assets consisting of municipal bonds *T* purchased with the proceeds from the sale of its historic business assets. Accordingly, the transaction does not qualify as a reorganization under section 368(a)(1)(C) of the Code.

C. Changes to Continuity of Business Enterprise Regulations and Related Remote Continuity of Interest Rules

Excerpt from Thompson and Sayed, 1998 Developments in the Federal Income Taxation of Mergers and Acquisitions: The Year of M&A

51 Univ. of Southern Cal Sch of Law Inst on Fed Tax,
Major Tax Planning for 1999 at 1-55–1-73 (1999)

Introduction The Final COI Regs. also contain amendments to the continuity of business enterprise (COBE) requirement (Final COBE Regs). [TD 8760, Jan 28, 1998] This section provides a guide to the basic principles in the Final COBE Regs. The Final COBE Regs. also amend the remote continuity of interest rules and this amendment is also discussed here.

Purpose of the COBE Requirement The preamble to the Final COBE Regs. gives the following explanation of the purpose of the COBE requirement:

> The COBE requirement is fundamental to the notion that tax-free reorganizations merely readjust continuing interests in property. In Sec. 1.368-1(d), as effective prior to these final regulations, COBE generally required the acquiring corporation to either continue a significant historic T business or use a significant portion of T's historic business assets in a business. However, a valid reorganization may qualify as tax-free even if the acquiring corporation does not directly carry on the historic T business or use the historic T assets in a business. *See* section 368(a)(2)(C). *See also* Rev. Rul. 68-261 (1968-1 C.B. 147); Rev. Rul. 81-247 (1981-1 C.B. 87).

General Treatment Of T Assets Held By Members of a Qualified Group The preamble to the Final COBE Regs. gives the following general description of the rule set out in the regulations:

> Consistent with the view that the acquiring corporation need not directly conduct the T business or use the T assets, the final regulations provide rules under which, in an otherwise qualifying corporate reorganization, the assets and the businesses of the members of a qualified group of corporations are treated as assets and businesses of the issuing corporation. Accordingly, in the final regulations, COBE requires that the issuing corporation either continue T's historic business or use a significant portion of T's historic business assets in a business.

> A qualified group is one or more chains of corporations connected through stock ownership with the issuing corporation, but only if the issuing corporation owns directly stock meeting the requirements of section 368(c) in at least one of the corporations, and stock meeting the requirements of section 368(c) in each of the corporations is owned directly by one of the other corporations.

The Qualified Group Rule Reg. § 1.368-1(d)(4) which deals with qualified groups was added by the Final COBE Regs., and the preamble to the Final COBE Regs. gives the following explanation of the qualified group definition:

> The proposed COBE regulations define the qualified group using a control test based on section 368(c). The IRS and Treasury Department received comments suggesting the replacement of the section 368(c) definition of control by the affiliated group definition of control stated in section 1504, without regard to section 1504(b). However, because section 368 generally determines control by reference to section 368(c), the final regulations retain the approach of the proposed COBE regulations.

The Partnership Rule The Final COBE Regs. added Reg. § 1.368(d)(4)(iii) relating to the treatment of the push down of a target's assets to a partnership, and the preamble to the Final COBE Regs. gives the following explanation of the partnership rule:

> In determining whether COBE is satisfied, the proposed COBE regulations aggregate the interests of the members of a qualified group. In addition, the proposed COBE regulations attribute a business of a partnership to a corporate transferor partner if the partner has a sufficient nexus with that partnership business. However, the proposed COBE regulations only consider the transferor partner's interest in the partnership business, and do not aggregate this interest with interests in the partnership held by other members of the qualified group.

> In response to comments requesting a partnership aggregation rule, the final regulations, through a system of attribution, aggregate the interests in a partnership business held by all the members of a qualified group. The final regulations provide rules under which a corporate partner may be treated as holding assets of a business of a partnership. Additionally, P is treated as holding all the assets, and conducting all the businesses of its qualified group. Furthermore, in certain circumstances, P will be treated as conducting a business of a partnership. Once the relevant T businesses and T assets are attributed to P, COBE is tested under the general rule of the final COBE regulations. *See* Sec. 1.368-1(d)(1).

Relationship of the Qualified Group Rule and Partnership Rule to the Remote Continuity of Interest Doctrine The preamble to the Final COBE Regs. addresses the relationship of the qualified group rule and partnership rule to the remote continuity of interest rule set out in the *Groman* and *Bashford* cases [Sec. 6.2.G.]:

> The judicial continuity of interest doctrine historically included a concept commonly known as remote continuity of interest. Commonly viewed as arising out of *Groman v. Commissioner*, 302 U.S. 82 (1937), and *Helvering v. Bashford*, 302 U.S. 454 (1938), remote continuity of interest focuses on the link between the T shareholders and the former T business assets following the reorganization. In Sec. 1.368-1(d), as effective prior to these final regulations, COBE focuses on the continuation of T's business, or the use of T's business assets, by the acquiring corporation. Section 1.368-1(d), as revised herein, expands this concept by treating the issuing corporation as conducting

a T business or owning T business assets if these activities are conducted by a member of the qualified group or, in certain cases, by a partnership that has a member of the qualified group as a partner.

The proposed COBE regulations separately address COBE (Sec. 1.368-1(d)) and remote continuity of interest (Sec. 1.368-1(f)). The IRS and Treasury Department believe the COBE requirements adequately address the issues raised in *Groman* and *Bashford* and their progeny. Thus, these final regulations do not separately articulate rules addressing remote continuity of interest.

Regulatory Extension of the Statutory Override of the *Groman* and *Bashford* Doctrines Code Section 368(a)(2)(C) permits the post-reorganization transfer by the acquiring corporation of a target's stock or assets to a subsidiary. These are known as post-reorganization push-down transactions. The Final COBE Regs. extend this statutory provision in Reg. § 1.368-2(k), and the preamble to the Final COBE Regs. gives the following explanation of this provision:

> Section 1.368-2(k) of the final regulations states that a transaction otherwise qualifying under section 368(a)(1) (A), (B), (C), or (G) (where the requirements of sections 354(b)(1) (A) and (B) are met) shall not be disqualified by reason of the fact that part or all of the acquired assets or stock acquired in the transaction are transferred or successively transferred to one or more corporations controlled in each transfer by the transferor corporation. Control is defined under section 368(c). The final regulations also provide a rule for transfers of assets following a reorganization qualifying under section 368(a)(1)(A) by reason of section 368(a)(2)(E). No inference is to be drawn as to whether transactions not described in Sec. 1.368-2(k) otherwise qualify as reorganizations.

In a related amendment the Final COBE Regs. amended Reg. § 1.368-2(f), relating to the definition of party to a reorganization, and the preamble to the Final COBE Regs. gives the following explanation of this provision:

> The final regulations also provide that, if a transaction otherwise qualifies as a reorganization, a corporation remains a party to the reorganization even though stock or assets acquired in the reorganization are transferred in a transaction described in Sec. 1.368-2(k). *See* Section 1.368-2(f). Furthermore, if a transaction otherwise qualifies as a reorganization, a corporation shall not cease to be a party to the reorganization solely because acquired assets are transferred to a partnership in which the transferor is a partner if the COBE requirement is satisfied.

The Final COBE Regs. and the Step Transaction Doctrine The preamble to the Final COBE Regs. provides the following guidance on the application of the step transaction doctrine:

> The proposed COBE regulations are limited in their application to COBE and remote continuity of interest. The rules of the proposed COBE regulations provide that for certain reorganizations, transfers of acquired assets

or stock among members of the qualified group, and in certain cases, transfers of acquired assets to partnerships, do not disqualify a transaction from satisfying the COBE and remote continuity of interest requirements. The preamble to the proposed COBE regulations states that these rules do not address any other issues concerning the qualification of a transaction as a reorganization.

Comments suggest that the proposed COBE regulations are ambiguous as they could be interpreted to mean that a transfer of stock or assets to a qualified group member after an otherwise tax-free reorganization would be given independent significance and the step transaction doctrine would not apply. Under such an interpretation, the potential reorganization would not be recast as a taxable acquisition or another type of reorganization. To eliminate this ambiguity, Sec. 1.368-1(a) of the final regulations provides that, in determining whether a transaction qualifies as a reorganization under section 368(a), the transaction must be evaluated under relevant provisions of law, including the step transaction doctrine. Section 1.368-1(d) of the final regulations is limited to a discussion of the COBE requirement, and does not address satisfaction of the explicit statutory requirements of a reorganization, which is the subject of Sec. 1.368-2. However, Sec. 1.368-2(k) of the final regulations does provide guidance in this regard, extending the application of section 368(a)(2)(C) to certain successive transfers.

The Limits of the Final COBE Regs. The preamble to the Final COBE Regs. Discusses the limits of the regulations as follows:

> The proposed COBE regulations, applying only to the COBE and remote continuity of interest requirements, are limited to transactions otherwise qualifying for reorganization treatment under section 368(a)(1) (A), (B), (C), or (G) (where the requirements of sections 354(b)(1) (A) and (B) are met). The IRS and Treasury Department received comments stating that the final regulations should apply to reorganizations qualifying under section 368(a)(1) (D) or (F) or to transactions qualifying under section 355.

> The final regulations do not limit the application of Sec. 1.368-1(d) to the transactions enumerated in section 368(a)(2)(C). The COBE provisions in the final regulations apply to all reorganizations for which COBE is relevant.

> Section 1.368-2(k)(1) of the final regulations, however, is limited in its application to the transactions described in section 368(a)(2)(C), and does not apply in determining whether a reorganization qualifies under section 368(a)(1)(D), section 368(a)(1)(F), or section 355. The IRS and Treasury Department believe that further study is needed prior to extending Sec. 1.368-2(k)(1) to one or more of these provisions. * * *

§ 6.4 The Meaning of Solely for Voting Stock: An Introduction

Helvering v. Southwest Consolidated Corporation

Supreme Court of the United States, 1942

315 U.S. 194

Mr. Justice Douglas delivered the opinion of the Court.

[The assets of a financially troubled corporation were acquired in exchange for cash, the acquiring corporation's voting stock and Class A and B warrants. The issue was whether the transaction qualified as a reorganization under clause (B) of § 112(g)(1) of the 1934 Act, which is a predecessor of the current (C) reorganization. The 1934 Act amended the reorganization definition to require that "solely voting stock" be used in a stock for stock and a stock for asset acquisition.]

[C]lause (B) of § 112(g)(1) of the 1934 Act effects an important change as respects transactions whereby one corporation acquires substantially all of the assets of another. The continuity of interest test is made much stricter. Congress has provided that the assets of the transferor corporation must be acquired in exchange "solely" for "voting stock" of the transferee. "Solely" leaves no leeway. Voting stock plus some other consideration does not meet the statutory requirement. Congress, however, in 1939 amended clause (B) of § 112(g)(1) by adding, "but in determining whether the exchange is solely for voting stock the assumption by the acquiring corporation of a liability of the other, or the fact that property acquired is subject to a liability, shall be disregarded." That amendment was made to avoid the consequences of *United States v. Hendler,* [*see* Sec. 4.15.A] * * * But with that exception, the requirements of § 112(g)(1)(B) are not met if properties are acquired in exchange for a consideration other than, or in addition to, voting stock. Under that test this transaction fails to qualify as a "reorganization" under clause (B).

In the first place, security holders of the old company owning $440,000 face amount of obligations were paid off in cash. * * *

In the second place, the warrants which were issued were not "voting stock". Whatever rights a warrant holder may have "to require the obligor corporation to maintain the integrity of the shares" covered by the warrants, he is not a shareholder.

* * * Accordingly, the acquisition in this case was not made "solely" for voting stock. And it makes no difference that in the long run the unexercised warrants expired and nothing but voting stock was outstanding. The critical time is the date of the exchange. In that posture of the case it is no different than if other convertible securities had been issued, all of which had been converted within the conversion period.

Reversed.

Questions and Notes

In general, what impact does *Southwest Consolidated* have on the interpretation of the phrase "solely for voting stock"? In a (B) reorganization, can the acquiring corporation pay cash in lieu of fractional shares? *See* Rev. Rul. 66-365, Sec. 8.2.F.1. What about paying the shareholders reorganization expenses? *See* Rev. Rul. Sec. 8.2.F.3. As a general proposition in planning a (B) or (C), the cautious tax advisor should be sure that there is no hidden boot. The solely for voting stock issue is examined further in Chapter 8.

§6.5 Definition of Control in §368(c)

A. Introduction

Revenue Ruling 76-223

1976-1 C.B. 103

Advice has been requested whether the transaction described below satisfies the "control" requirements of section 368(c) of the Internal Revenue Code of 1954.

For valid business reasons corporation *X* desired to acquire the stock of corporation *Y* in a transaction within the meaning of section 368(a)(1)(B) of the Code. *Y* had 81 shares of voting common stock and 19 shares of non-voting preferred stock outstanding. *X* did not want to acquire any of the outstanding preferred stock of *Y* in the proposed transaction. Therefore, as a part of the overall plan and prior to the consummation of the acquisition, the charter of *Y* was amended to permanently give voting rights to holders of the preferred stock of *Y*, on a one vote per share basis, the same right attributable to the voting common stock. Subsequently, *X* acquired 81 shares of *Y* voting common stock solely in exchange for shares of *X* voting stock. There was no plan to later amend *Y*'s charter and thereby revoke the voting rights of holders of *Y* preferred stock.

Immediately after the transaction by which *X* acquired 81 shares of the voting common stock of *Y* in exchange for voting stock of *X*, *X* owned 81 percent of the total combined voting power of all classes of the stock of *Y* entitled to vote. The exchange of non-voting preferred for voting preferred resulted in a permanent change in the rights of preferred shareholders prior to the acquisition of the voting common stock. Thus, there were no classes of nonvoting stock of *Y* outstanding at the time of the acquisition.

Accordingly, in the instant case, the control requirements of section 368(c) of the Code have been satisfied and the transaction qualifies as a reorganization within the meaning of section 368(a)(1)(B). Furthermore, no gain or loss is recognized under section 1036 upon the exchange of the *Y* nonvoting preferred stock for *Y* voting preferred stock pursuant to the amendment of *Y*'s charter.

B. Obama Administration's Proposed Modification of the "Control" Concept

U.S. Treasury, General Explanations of the Administration's Fiscal Year 2017 Revenue Proposals

February 2016

CONFORM CORPORATE OWNERSHIP STANDARDS

Current Law

For tax-free transfers of assets to controlled corporations in exchange for stock [§ 351], tax-free distributions of controlled corporations [§ 355], and tax-free corporate reorganizations [§ 368(c)], "control" is defined in section 368 as the ownership of 80 percent of the voting stock and 80 percent of the number of shares of all other classes of stock of the corporation. The section 368 control test also is incorporated by cross-reference in other sections of the Code relating to discharge of indebtedness income, non-deductibility of interest on corporate acquisition indebtedness, installment obligations, qualified small business stock, and qualifying as an S corporation. In contrast, the "affiliation" test under section 1504 for permitting two or more corporations to file consolidated returns is the direct or indirect ownership by a parent corporation of at least 80 percent of the total voting power of another corporation's stock and at least 80 percent of the total value of the corporation's stock. Several other Code provisions, including rules relating to tax-free parent-subsidiary liquidations, and qualified stock purchases and dispositions incorporate by cross-reference the affiliation test.

Prior to 1984, the affiliation test required ownership of 80 percent of the voting stock and 80 percent of the number of shares of all other classes of stock of the corporation, similar to the control test. Congress amended the affiliation test in 1984 in response to concerns that corporations were filing consolidated returns under circumstances in which a parent corporation's interest in the issuing corporation accounted for less than 80 percent of the equity value of such corporation. In 1986, the affiliation test became the ownership standard for tax free parent-subsidiary liquidations and qualified stock purchases and dispositions. In 2006, the Code was amended to provide that the affiliation test applies to determine whether a distributing or controlled corporation satisfied the active trade or business requirement for a tax-free distribution of subsidiary stock.

Reasons for Change

By carefully allocating voting power among the shares of a corporation, taxpayers can manipulate the control test in order to qualify or not qualify, as desired, a transaction as tax-free (for example, a transaction could be structured to avoid tax-free treatment to recognize a loss). In addition, the absence of a value component allows corporations to retain control of a corporation but to "sell" a significant amount of the value of the corporation tax-free. Congress amended the affiliation test in 1984 to address similar concerns regarding the manipulation of the vote and value of affiliated corporations. A uniform ownership test for corporate transactions will also reduce complexity currently caused by these inconsistent tests.

Proposal

The proposal would conform the control test under section 368 with the affiliation test under section 1504. Thus, "control" would be defined as the ownership of at least 80 percent of the total voting power and at least 80 percent of the total value of stock of a corporation. For this purpose, stock would not include certain preferred stock that meets the requirements of section 1504(a)(4).

§ 6.6 Plan of Reorganization

A "plan of reorganization" is one of the conditions for nonrecognition treatment both for the exchanging stockholder or security holder under § 354(a) and for the target corporation under § 361(a). Although the term is not defined in the Code, § 1.368-2(g) says that a plan of reorganization "has reference to a consummated transaction specifically defined as a reorganization under § 368(a)(1)." This regulation goes on to say that the term is "not to be construed as broadening the definition of reorganization * * * but is to be taken as limiting the nonrecognition of gain or loss to such exchanges or distributions as are directly a part of the [reorganization] transaction * * *." Reflecting the business purpose doctrine of *Gregory v. Helvering, see* Sec. 2.11.B, the regulation further provides that "the transaction or series of transactions, embraced in a plan of reorganization must not only come within the specific language of section 368(a), but * * * must be undertaken for reasons germane to the continuance of the business of the corporation * * *." Although it is possible that a plan of reorganization need not be in any particular form and need not be in writing, *see C.T. Investment Co. v. Commissioner,* 88 F.2d 582 (8th Cir. 1937), it is advisable to have the "plan of reorganization" reflected in the corporate records. Indeed, § 1.368-3, which specifies the records to be kept with respect to a reorganization, says that "the plan of reorganization must be adopted by each of the corporation's parties thereto and the adoption must be shown by the acts of its duly constituted responsible officers, and appear upon the official records of the corporation."

§ 6.7 Business Purpose, Step Transaction, and Economic Substance Doctrines

A. In General

The regulations under § 368 make it clear that in order to constitute a reorganization a transaction must have a business purpose. Specifically, the regulations say that to be a reorganization a transaction (1) must be required by the "business exigencies" (*see* § 1.368-1(b)), (2) must satisfy "both the terms of the specifications [of the reorganization provisions] and their underlying assumptions and purposes" (*id.*), (3) must be an "ordinary and necessary incident of the conduct of the enterprise" (*see* § 1.368-1(c)); (4) must not be a "mere device that puts on the form of a reorganization" but that has "no business or corporate purpose" (*id.*), and (5) must be "undertaken for reasons germane to the continuance of the business of the corporation" (*see* § 1.368-1(g)).

B. Business Purpose in the (D) before § 355

Review *Gregory v. Helvering, supra* Sec. 2.11.B.

C. Business Purpose in a Recapitalization

Bazley v. Commissioner

Supreme Court of the United States, 1947
331 U.S. 737

Mr. Justice Frankfurter delivered the opinion of the Court.

* * * In *Bazley* the Commissioner of Internal Revenue assessed an income tax deficiency against the taxpayer for the year 1939. Its validity depends on the legal significance of the recapitalization in that year of a family corporation in which the taxpayer and his wife owned all but one of the Company's one thousand shares. These had a par value of $100. Under the plan of reorganization the taxpayer, his wife, and the holder of the additional share were to turn in their old shares and receive in exchange for each old share five new shares of no par value, but of a stated value of $60, and new debenture bonds, having a total face value of $400,000, payable in ten years but callable at any time. Accordingly, the taxpayer received 3,990 shares of the new stock for the 798 shares of his old holding and debentures in the amount of $319,200. At the time of these transactions the earned surplus of the corporation was $855,783.82. * * *

The Commissioner charged to the taxpayer as income the full value of the debentures. The Tax Court affirmed the Commissioner's determination, against the taxpayer's contention that as a "recapitalization" the transaction was a tax-free "reorganization" and that the debentures were "securities in a corporation a party to a reorganization," "exchanged solely for stock or securities in such corporation" "in pursuance of a plan of reorganization," and as such no gain is recognized for income tax purposes. Internal Revenue Code, §§ 112(g)(1)(E) * * * The Tax Court found that the recapitalization had "no legitimate corporate business purpose" and was therefore not a "reorganization" within the statute. The distribution of debentures, it concluded, was a disguised dividend, taxable as earned income under §§ 22(a) and 115(a) and (g) [now § 301]. The Circuit Court of Appeals for the Third Circuit, sitting en banc, affirmed, two judges dissenting. * * *

It was not the purpose of the reorganization provision to exempt from payment of a tax what as a practical matter is realized gain. Normally, a distribution by a corporation, whatever form it takes, is a definite and rather unambiguous event. It furnishes the proper occasion for the determination and taxation of gain. But there are circumstances where a formal distribution, directly or through exchange of securities, represents merely a new form of the previous participation in an enterprise, involving no change of substance in the rights and relations of the interested parties one to another or to the corporate assets. As to these, Congress has said that they are not to be deemed significant occasions for determining taxable gain. * * *

No doubt there was a recapitalization of the Bazley corporation in the sense that the symbols that represented its capital were changed, so that the fiscal basis of its operations would appear very differently on its books. But the form of a transaction as reflected by correct corporate accounting opens questions as to the proper application of a taxing statute; it does not close them. * * *

What have we here? No doubt, if the Bazley corporation had issued the debentures to Bazley and his wife without any recapitalization, it would have made a taxable distribution. [*See* § 301.]

The Commissioner, the Tax Court and the Circuit Court of Appeals agree that nothing was accomplished that would not have been accomplished by an outright debenture dividend. * * * A "reorganization" which is merely a vehicle, however elaborate or elegant, for conveying earnings from accumulations to the stockholders is not a reorganization under § 112 [now § 368]. This disposes of the case as a matter of law, since the facts as found by the Tax Court bring them within it. * * *

Questions

1. *Bazley* was decided prior to the adoption of §§ 354(a)(2) and 356(d)(2)(B) in 1954. What result under the current statute if a Court were to find that the transaction in *Bazley* constituted a reorganization?

2. Individual *A* is the sole shareholder of corporation *X*. *X* has substantial E & P. *A* exchanges half of his stock for newly issued debentures of *X* in a transaction that purports to qualify as a recapitalization. *A* realizes no gain or loss on the transaction because the adjusted basis of his stock equals the fair market value of the debentures. Does *A* have a dividend? *See* § 356 and § 1.301-1(l).

D. Reincorporations and Step Transactions

Revenue Ruling 96-29

1996-1 C.B. 50

Issue Do the transactions described below qualify as reorganizations under § 368(a)(1)(F) of the Internal Revenue Code?

Facts *Situation 1.* Q is a manufacturing corporation all of the common stock of which is owned by twelve individuals. One class of nonvoting preferred stock, representing 40 percent of the aggregate value of Q, is held by a variety of corporate and noncorporate shareholders. Q is incorporated in state M. Pursuant to a plan to raise immediate additional capital and to enhance its ability to raise capital in the future by issuing additional stock, Q proposes to make a public offering of newly issued stock and to cause its stock to become publicly traded. Q entered into an underwriting agreement providing for the public offering and a change in its state of incorporation. The change in the state of incorporation was undertaken, in part, to enable the corporation to avail itself of the advantages that the corporate laws of state N afford to public companies and their officers and directors. In the absence of the public offering, Q would not have changed its state of incorporation. Pursuant to the underwriting agreement, Q changed its place of incorporation by merging with and into R, a newly organized corporation incorporated in state N. The shares of Q stock were converted into the right to receive an identical number of shares of R stock. Immediately thereafter, R sold additional shares of its stock to the public and redeemed all of the outstanding shares of nonvoting preferred stock. The number of new shares sold was equal to 60 percent of all the outstanding R stock following the sale and redemption.

Situation 2. W, a state M corporation, is a manufacturing corporation all of the stock of which is owned by two individuals. W conducted its business through several wholly owned subsidiaries. The management of W determined that it would be in the best interest of W to acquire the business of Z, an unrelated corporation, and combine it with the business of Y, one of its subsidiaries, and to change the state of incorporation of W. In order to accomplish these objectives, and pursuant to an overall plan, W entered into a plan and agreement of merger with Y and Z. In accordance with the agreement, Z merged with and into Y pursuant to the law of state M, with the former Z shareholders receiving shares of newly issued W preferred stock in exchange for their shares of Z stock. Immediately following the acquisition of Z, W changed its place of organization by merging with and into N, a newly organized corporation incorporated in state R. Upon W's change of place of organization, the holders of W common and preferred stock surrendered their W stock in exchange for identical N common and preferred stock, respectively.

Law and Analysis Section 368(a)(1)(F) provides that a reorganization includes a mere change in identity, form, or place of organization of one corporation, however effected. This provision was amended by the Tax Equity and Fiscal Responsibility Act of 1982, Pub.L. No. 97-248, in order to limit its application to one corporation. Certain limitations contained in § 381(b), including those precluding the corporation acquiring property in a reorganization from carrying back a net operating loss or a net capital loss for a taxable year ending after the date of transfer to a taxable year of the transferor, do not apply to reorganizations described in § 368(a)(1)(F) "in recognition of the intended scope of such reorganizations as embracing only formal changes in a single operating corporation." H.R.Rep. No. 760, 97th Cong., 2d Sess. 540, 541 (1982). Although a change in the place of organization usually must be effected through the merger of one corporation into another, such a transaction qualifies as a reorganization under § 368(a)(1)(F) because it involves only one operating corporation. The 1982 amendment of § 368(a)(1)(F) thus overruled several cases in which a merger of two or more operating corporations could be treated as a reorganization under § 368(a)(1)(F). *See, e.g., Estate of Stauffer v. Commissioner,* 403 F.2d 611 (9th Cir.1968); *Associated Machine, Inc. v. Commissioner,* 403 F.2d 622 (9th Cir.1968); and *Davant v. Commissioner,* 366 F.2d 874 (5th Cir.1966).

A transaction does not qualify as a reorganization under § 368(a)(1)(F) unless there is no change in existing shareholders or in the assets of the corporation. However, a transaction will not fail to qualify as a reorganization under § 368(a)(1)(F) if dissenters owning fewer than 1 percent of the outstanding shares of the corporation fail to participate in the transaction. Rev. Rul. 66-284, 1966-2 C.B. 115.

The rules applicable to corporate reorganizations as well as other provisions recognize the unique characteristics of reorganizations qualifying under § 368(a)(1)(F). In contrast to other types of reorganizations, which can involve two or more operating corporations, a reorganization of a corporation under § 368(a)(1)(F) is treated for most purposes of the Code as if there had been no change in the corporation and, thus, as if the reorganized corporation is the same entity as the corporation that was in existence prior to the reorganization. *See* § 381(b); § 1.381(b)-1(a)(2); *see also* Rev. Rul. 87-110, 1987-2 C.B. 159; Rev. Rul. 80-168, 1980-1 C.B. 178; Rev. Rul. 73-526, 1973-2 C.B. 404; Rev. Rul. 64-250, 1964-2 C.B. 333.

In Rev. Rul. 69-516, 1969-2 C.B. 56, the Internal Revenue Service treated as two separate transactions a reorganization under § 368(a)(1)(F) and a reorganization under § 368(a)(1)(C) undertaken as part of the same plan. Specifically, a corporation changed its place of organization by merging into a corporation formed under the laws of another state and immediately thereafter, it transferred substantially all of its assets in exchange for stock of an unrelated corporation. The ruling holds that the change in place of organization qualified as a reorganization under § 368(a)(1)(F).

Accordingly, in *Situation 1*, the reincorporation by Q in state N qualifies as a reorganization under § 368(a)(1)(F) even though it was a step in the transaction in which Q was issuing common stock in a public offering and redeeming stock having a value of 40 percent of the aggregate value of its outstanding stock prior to the offering.

In *Situation 2*, the reincorporation by W in state N qualifies as a reorganization under § 368(a)(1)(F) even though it was a step in the transaction in which W acquired the business of Z.

Holding On the facts set forth in this ruling, in each of *Situations 1 and 2*, the reincorporation transaction qualifies as a reorganization under § 368(a)(1)(F), notwithstanding the other transactions effected pursuant to the same plan.

Effect on Other Revenue Rulings Rev. Rul. 79-250, 1979-2 C.B. 156, addressed a similar issue on facts that are substantially similar, in all material respects, to those of *Situation 2*. The ruling holds that a merger of Z with and into Y in exchange for the stock of W qualifies as a reorganization under § 368(a)(1)(A) by reason of § 368(a)(2)(D), even though W is reincorporated in another state immediately after the merger. The ruling also holds that the reincorporation qualifies as a reorganization under § 368(a)(1)(F). Rev. Rul. 79-250 did not apply the step transaction doctrine in order to combine the two transactions, stating that the merger and the subsequent reincorporation were separate transactions because "the economic motivation supporting each transaction is sufficiently meaningful on its own account, and is not dependent upon the other transaction for its substantiation."

Although the holding of Rev. Rul. 79-250 is correct on the facts presented therein, in order to emphasize that central to the holding in Rev. Rul. 79-250 is the unique status of reorganizations under § 368(a)(1)(F) and that Rev. Rul. 79-250 is not intended to reflect the application of the step-transaction doctrine in other contexts, Rev. Rul. 79-250 is modified. * * *

E. Codified Economic Substance Doctrine

See Sec. 2.11.D.

Part B:
Concepts Relating to Exchanging Stockholders and Security Holders under §§ 354 and 358

§ 6.8 Meaning of "Securities Exchanged" under § 354

A. Exchange of Short-Term Notes for Debentures

Neville Coke & Chemical Co. v. Commissioner

United States Court of Appeals, Third Circuit, 1945
148 F.2d 599, *cert. denied* 326 U.S. 726 (1945)

GOODRICH, CIRCUIT JUDGE.

[Upon the recapitalization of a financially troubled corporation, the holder of short-term notes received debentures and stock in exchange therefor. The issue was whether the noteholder received nonrecognition treatment under a predecessor of § 354(a)(1).]

There is no gain or loss recognized if "stock or securities in a corporation * * * are * * * exchanged solely for stock or securities in such corporation * * *." Were the notes of Davison, which the taxpayer had in its possession, and which it exchanged for debentures and shares of stock issued by the reorganized debtor, "securities" within the wording of the statute? No question has been raised as to the sufficiency of the evidence of obligations issued by the reorganized debtor to qualify under the description of "stock or securities", and the problem is limited to the consideration of what the taxpayer turned in, that is, the notes above mentioned.

What then are "securities" within the meaning of the section? The taxpayer makes a tentative argument that the word ought to be taken in its common, accepted interpretation and that interpretation includes evidence of indebtedness, but he goes on to admit that the Supreme Court has read into the term a meaning differing radically from common interpretation.

It is to be noted that the phrase "stock or securities" appears twice in § 112(b)(3) [now § 354(a)]. Once it refers to what a party turns into a corporation being reorganized. The second appearance of the phrase relates to what a recipient takes from the reorganized company as a result of the transaction. We have no reason for thinking that the phrase has a different meaning in either of the two instances and the argument by the taxpayer that it does differ fails to convince us * * *.

[The court went on to hold that the notes surrendered were not securities.]

Questions

What is the significance of *Neville Coke*? Could an open account trade creditor get nonrecognition treatment upon the extinguishment of the obligations in exchange for the debtor's common stock?

B. Exchange of Bonds for Stock: Are Bonds Securities?

Revenue Ruling 59-98

1959-1 C.B. 76

Advice has been requested whether the exchange of bonds and accrued interest thereon for stock of the corporation which issued such bonds is a recapitalization under the terms of section 368(a)(1)(E) of the Internal Revenue Code of 1954 and whether such bonds constitute "securities" within the meaning of section 354(a)(1) of the Code.

In 1957, the corporation here involved, which had been in serious financial difficulties for several years, exchanged newly issued common stock for all its outstanding first mortgage bonds and the accrued unpaid interest thereon, so that after the exchange the former bondholders owned 40 percent of the common stock outstanding. The bonds surrendered had been issued in 1946 and had originally been payable in from three to ten years, the average time to maturity at issuance being six and one-half years. The corporation had not deducted any of the unpaid interest, either in its computation of income or in its computation of earnings and profits. Before the bonds were surrendered none of the bondholders owned any of the common stock. The exchange of stock for bonds was arranged in order to bring the corporation out of the financial difficulties which had made it unable to pay the principal and interest of the bonds when due. The fair market value of the stock issued for each bond was substantially less than the principal amount of the bond. All of the bonds were purchased at issuance by various individuals as investments.

Section 354(a)(1) of the Code states, in part, that no gain or loss shall be recognized if *securities* in a corporation a party to a reorganization are, in pursuance of a plan of reorganization, exchanged solely for stock in such corporation. Section 368(a)(1)(E) states that a "reorganization" includes a *recapitalization.*

[S]ince in the instant case the bonds were secured by a mortgage on the corporate property, since they had an average life of six and one-half years when issued, and since they were purchased for investment purposes by persons other than the stockholders, it is held that these bonds constitute securities for purposes of subchapter C, chapter 1, of the Code. Thus the change in the capital structure of the corporation constitutes a recapitalization and, therefore, a reorganization as defined in section 368(a)(1)(E) of the Code. Accordingly, under section 354(a) of the Code, no gain or loss is recognized to the bondholders from the exchange of the mortgage bonds, together with the unpaid accrued interest thereon, for capital stock of the corporation.

Note

As indicated in the ruling, "securities" are long term debt instruments. Although there are no hard and fast rules, in attempting to structure a security it would be prudent to provide for an average life of at least six and one half years as set forth in the ruling.

C. Treatment of Debt Instrument with Two Year Term Remaining

Revenue Ruling 2004-78
I.R.B. 2004-31, July 13, 2004

Issue. Under the circumstances described below, whether a debt instrument issued by the acquiring corporation in a reorganization in exchange for a security of the target corporation is a security within the meaning of §354 of the Internal Revenue Code.

Facts. On January 1, 2004, Target Corporation issues debt instruments with a stated maturity date of January 1, 2016. On the issue date, the debt instruments provide for a market rate of interest and are securities within the meaning of §354. Target Corporation has outstanding one class of common stock. On January 1, 2014, pursuant to state law, Target Corporation merges into Acquiring Corporation in a transaction that qualifies as a reorganization under §368(a)(1)(A). In the merger, the Target Corporation stockholders exchange their Target Corporation common stock for Acquiring Corporation common stock. Also in the merger, the Target Corporation security holders exchange their Target Corporation securities for Acquiring Corporation debt instruments with terms identical to those of the Target Corporation securities (including the maturity date), except that the interest rate is changed (for example, to reflect differences in creditworthiness between Target Corporation and Acquiring Corporation). The modification of the interest rate is a significant modification under §1.1001-3 of the Income Tax Regulations.

Law and Analysis. Section 368(a)(1)(A) provides, in part, that the term "reorganization" includes a statutory merger. Section 368(b) provides that the term "party to a reorganization" includes a corporation resulting from a reorganization and both corporations, in the case of a reorganization resulting from the acquisition by one corporation of stock or properties of another corporation.

Section 354(a)(1) provides, in part, that no gain or loss shall be recognized if securities in a corporation that is a party to a reorganization are, in pursuance of the plan of reorganization, exchanged solely for securities in such corporation or in another corporation that is a party to the reorganization.

Section 1.368-1(b) sets forth the general rule that, upon an exchange, gain or loss must be recognized if the new property differs materially in kind or extent from the old property. The regulation then explains that the purpose of the reorganization provisions is to except from the general rule certain exchanges incident to readjustments of corporate structures that are required by business exigencies and that effect only a readjustment of continuing interests in property under modified corporate forms. Congress has recognized that when a taxpayer receives stock or securities in exchange for stock or securities owned by the taxpayer incident to a readjustment of a corporate structure, the new stock or securities are treated as taking the place of the stock or securities exchanged therefor. See H.R. Rep. No. 704, at 13–14 (1933).

Neither § 354 nor the regulations under § 354 define the term "securities." Under case law, an instrument with a term of less than five years generally is not a security. See, e.g., Pinellas Ice & Cold Storage Co. v. Commissioner, 287 U.S. 462 (1933) (holding that short-term notes payable within four months were not securities within the meaning of the reorganization provisions); Lloyd-Smith v. Commissioner, 116 F.2d 642 (2d Cir.), cert. denied, 313 U.S. 588 (1941) (holding that two-year notes were not securities); Neville Coke & Chemical Co., 148 F.2d 599 (3d Cir.), cert. denied, 326 U.S. 726 (1945) (holding that three, four, and five-year notes were not securities).

Under the foregoing authorities, an instrument with a term of two years generally would not qualify as a security. However, because the debt instruments of the Acquiring Corporation are issued in the reorganization in exchange for securities of the Target Corporation and bear the same terms (other than interest rate) as the securities of the Target Corporation, the debt instruments of the Acquiring Corporation represent a continuation of the security holder's investment in the Target Corporation in substantially the same form. Therefore, the debt instruments of the Acquiring Corporation exchanged for the securities of the Target Corporation are securities within the meaning of § 354.

Holding. Under the circumstances described above, a debt instrument issued by the acquiring corporation in a reorganization in exchange for a security of the target corporation is a security within the meaning of § 354.

§ 6.9 Treatment of Warrants under § 354

A. The Standard View

William H. Bateman v. Commissioner

Tax Court of the United States, 1963
40 T.C. 408 (First Issue)

OPINION

SCOTT, JUDGE: * * *

The issues for decision are:

(1) Should gain to petitioners be recognized under the provisions of section 356(a)(1) of the Internal Revenue Code of 1954 to the extent of the fair market value of common stock purchase warrants of the Symington Wayne Corp. which were received by William H. Bateman in addition to common stock of that corporation in exchange for common stock of the Wayne Pump Co. upon its merger into Symington Wayne Corp.? * * *

Respondent contends the stock purchase warrants are neither stock nor securities within the meaning of section 354(a)(1), but rather constitute other property within the meaning of section 356. Respondent asserts the distribution of the warrants has the effect of a dividend within the meaning of section 356(a)(2) and that the amount of the fair market value of the warrants on March 12, 1958, should be taxed to petitioner as a dividend. * * *

Respondent, in his regulations, [says] that section 354(a)(1) applies only where stock is surrendered for stock, securities are surrendered for securities, or securities are surrendered for stock and securities * * *. We think that respondent's regulations correctly interpret section 354(a)(2)(B) as making section 354(a)(1) inapplicable if only stock is surrendered and stock and securities are received * * *. We will therefore confine our consideration to whether the warrants constitute stock within the meaning of section 354(a)(1).

In *Helvering v. Southwest Corp.*, 315 U.S. 194 (1942) [Sec. 6.4.], warrants to purchase voting stock were held not to be voting stock. In *E.P. Raymond*, 37 B.T.A. 423 (1938), we held stock purchase warrants to be securities and in so doing apparently accepted as a fact that these securities were not stock * * *. In the instant case a payment was required before the warrant holder would be entitled to receive stock and the warrants did not entitle the holder to any dividends or other rights of stockholders until exercised with the required payments to receive the stock. The provisions of the warrants here involved are not distinguishable in any material respect from those involved in *Helvering v. Southwest Corp., supra*. We, therefore, hold that the stock purchase warrants did not constitute stock. If they were securities, section 354(a)(1) is made inapplicable to this exchange by the provisions of section 354(a)(2)(B) and the fair market value of the warrants is recognized as gain to the extent provided in section 356 just as it would be if the warrants were not securities but were "other property." * * *

Questions

Could the receipt of stock warrants in a reorganization give rise to boot dividend treatment under §356? *See* §317(a). Are warrants securities for purposes of §354?

B. Final Regulations Regarding Treatment of Warrants as Securities in Corporate Reorganizations

Excerpt from Thompson and Sayed, 1998 Developments in the Federal Income Taxation of Mergers and Acquisitions: The Year of M&A

51 Univ. of Southern Cal Sch of Law Inst on Fed Tax,
Major Tax Planning for 1999 at 1-74–1-77 (1999)

Introduction On January 5, 1998, the Treasury issued final regulations that in certain instances provide for nonrecognition of gain or loss on the receipt, in pursuance of a reorganization, of rights [*i.e.*, warrants] to acquire stock of a corporation that is a party to the reorganization.[4]

Background and Proposed Regulations The preamble to the final regulations explains the background of the problem and the approach of the proposed regulations:

> In general, sections 354, 355, and 356 provide for nonrecognition of gain or loss, in whole or in part, to a stockholder or security holder on the exchange of stock or securities of parties to a reorganization and in pursuant of a plan of reorganization.

> The proposed regulations would extend the nonrecognition rule of sections 354, 355, and 356 to certain rights to acquire stock. Thus, for purposes of sections 354, 355, and 356, the proposed regulations would treat rights to acquire stock issued by a corporation that is a party to a reorganization as securities of the corporation with no principal amount. The preamble to the proposed regulations provided that, for this purpose, the term rights to acquire stock issued by that corporation would have the same meaning as the term has in sections 305(d) (1) and 317(a). In addition, the preamble stated that the proposed regulations would have no effect on other Internal Revenue Code rules that pertain to securities, including sections 83 and 421 through 424 and the regulations thereunder.

Final Reg §1.354-1(e) And Reg §1.355-1(c), Relating to Tax-Free Treatment Upon Receipt of Warrants Subsection (e) of Reg. §1.354-1 now reads as follows:

> Except as provided in §1.356-6T [relating to nonqualified preferred stock] for purposes of section 354, the term securities includes rights issued by a party to the reorganization to acquire its stock. For purposes of this section and section 356(d)(2)(B), a right to acquire stock has no principal amount. For this purpose, rights to acquire stock has the same meaning as it does

---

4. T.D. 8752 (Jan. 5, 1998).

under sections 305 and 317(a). Other Internal Revenue Code provisions governing the treatment of rights to acquire stock may also apply to certain exchanges occurring in connection with a reorganization. *See*, for example, sections 83 and 421 through 424 and the regulations thereunder.

A similar amendment is made to Reg. §1.355-1(c).

Final Reg. §1.356-3(b) And (c), Relating to the Treatment of Warrants as Not Boot Subsection (b) of Reg. §1.356-3, relating to the treatment of securities as other property, is amended to read as follows:

> Except as provided in §1.356-6T [relating to nonqualified preferred stock] for purposes of this section, a right to acquire stock that is treated as a security for purposes of section 354 or 355 has no principal amount. Thus, such right is not other property when received in a transaction to which section 356 applies (regardless of whether securities are surrendered in the exchange).

If warrants were treated as having a principal amount, then nonrecognition treatment on receipt of warrants would be available under Sections 354(a)(2) and Sections 356(b) and (d) only if such warrants were exchanged for securities (including warrants) of an equal principal amount. Gain would be recognized to the extent of the fair market value of the excess principal amount received. This result is avoided by treating the warrants treated as securities with a zero principal amount.

Illustration of the Treatment of Warrants Examples 7, 8 and 9 of Reg §1.356-3(c) illustrate the operation of this warrant rule. [Read these examples.] * * *

It is interesting to note that, under the regulations, warrants qualify for nonrecognition treatment but they do not count for continuity of interest purposes. Since the Supreme Court had held that warrants are not stock, the best way to permit warrants to qualify for non-recognition treatment in otherwise valid reorganizations and spin-offs was to define warrants as securities with no principal amount.

§6.10 Treatment of Exchanging Shareholders under §354(a)(2)

A. Substitution of Acquiror's Convertible Securities for Target's Convertible Securities: Treatment under §354(a)(2)

Revenue Ruling 79-155
1979-1 C.B. 153

Issues (1) Will changes, negotiated as part of a plan of reorganization, in terms of the securities of *T*, the acquired corporation in a reorganization under section 368(a)(1)(A) and (a)(2)(D) of the Internal Revenue Code of 1954, constitute a taxable exchange to the *T* security holders? * * *

Facts Corporation *T*, incorporated in state *A*, had outstanding one class of common stock and 8 percent convertible securities in the principal amount of 50,000*x* dollars with a maturity date of July 1, 1995. The terms of the securities contained a provision that they were convertible into *T* common stock, but did not impart to the holders thereof any rights or liabilities as shareholders of *T*. The security holders owned no *T* stock.

In order to have the stock of *T* owned by a holding company, and to enable joint sharing of the liability for the convertible securities, corporation *P* and its wholly-owned subsidiary, *S*, were incorporated in state *A* to effect a merger of *T* into *S*.

Pursuant to the laws of state *A, T* merged into *S* in exchange for the stock of *P*, and *S* received all of the assets of *T* and assumed all of *T*'s liabilities. The shareholders of *T* exchanged their *T* stock for *P* common stock. If *T* had merged into *P* the merger would have been a reorganization under section 368(a)(1)(A) of the Code.

As part of the plan of reorganization, negotiations were entered into with the *T* security holders, whose consent was a precondition to the merger. An agreement was reached pursuant to which *P* and *S* became jointly and severally liable for the convertible securities; the securities became convertible into *P* common stock; the security holders obtained the right to convert the securities into *S* common stock if *P* disposed of its *S* stock, although there was no plan on the part of *P* to do so; the interest rate on the securities was increased to 9 percent; the maturity date was changed to July 1, 1990; and the *T* security holders consented to the merger. The principal amount of the outstanding securities remained unchanged. * * *

Law and Analysis *Issue (1).* Under section 368(a)(2)(D) of the Code the acquisition by *S* in exchange for stock of *P*, of substantially all of the properties of *T*, which in the transaction is merged into *S*, will not be disqualified under section 368(a)(1)(A) provided the transaction would qualify under section 368(a)(1)(A) if the merger had been into *P* and no stock of *S* is used in the transaction.

The transaction in the instant case is a reorganization as defined in section 368(a)(2)(D) of the Code. The convertible debentures of *T* do not confer upon the holders thereof rights or liabilities as shareholders of *S* unless and until *P* divests itself of its *S* stock and subsequently the security holders elect to convert their securities into *S* stock. Moreover, there was no intention on the part of *P* to divest itself of its *S* stock at the time of the merger. Thus, *S* stock is not deemed to have been issued upon the merger of *T* into *S*. *See* Rev. Rul. 69-91, 1969-1 C.B. 106. Further, no gain or loss is recognized to *T* upon the assumption by *P* and *S* of the liability for the convertible securities. *See* section 357 and section 1.368-2(b)(2) of the Income Tax Regulations. *See also* Rev. Rul. 73-257, 1973-1 C.B. 189.

Under section 1001 of the Code and section 1.1001-1(a) of the regulations, unless otherwise provided in subtitle A of the Code, the gain or loss realized from the exchange of property for other property differing materially either in kind or in extent is treated as income or as loss sustained.

Under section 354(a)(1) and (a)(2) of the Code no gain or loss shall be recognized if securities in a corporation of a party to a reorganization are, in pursuance of the plan of reorganization, exchanged solely for securities in such corporation or in another corporation a party to the reorganization if the principal amount of any securities received does not exceed the principal amount of any such securities surrendered.

When the changes in the terms of outstanding securities are so material as to amount virtually to the issuance of a new security, the income tax consequences will follow as if the new security were actually issued. *See* Rev. Rul. 73-160, 1973-1 C.B. 365.

In this instant case, the convertible securities of *T,* an operating company, became the joint and several obligations of *P* and *S,* a holding company and an operating company, respectively, and became accompanied by a right of conversion into stock of *P.* The addition of *P* as an obligor, the change in conversion rights from the right to convert into the stock of an operating company, *T,* to the right to convert into the stock of a holding company, *P,* the increase in the interest rate, and the earlier maturity date, are, taken together, material changes that would otherwise constitute an exchange subject to recognition of gain or loss under section 1001 of the Code. However, section 354(a)(1) and (a)(2) applies to the transaction since it qualified as a reorganization under section 368(a)(1)(A) and (a)(2)(D) and since the securities deemed to be exchanged were of the same principal amount. * * *

B. Proposed Modification to § 356(a)(2)

Section 444 of the Tax Simplification Bill of 1991

pp. 100–101 (1991)

Present Law Under present law, gain is recognized by a shareholder or securityholder in a reorganization (or distribution under sec. 355) only to the extent property other than stock or securities of the corporation or of a party to the reorganization are received. For purposes of this rule, the fair market value of the excess of the principal amount of any securities received over the principal amount of any securities surrendered is treated as other property. If the principal amount of the securities received and the principal amount of the securities surrendered is the same, no amount of the securities received is treated as other property.

Also, under present law, a certain portion of the stated redemption price at maturity of a security may be treated as interest (referred to as "original issue discount" or "OID"), rather than principal. Also, in certain limited circumstances, a portion of a payment designated as principal may be treated as interest (under sec. 483).

It is unclear under present law whether the OID rules apply for purposes of determining the principal amount of a security for purposes of the nonrecognition rules described above.

Reasons for Simplification The provision promotes simplification by conforming the rules for determining gain where securities are exchanged in a corporate reorganization with other rules in the Code allocating amounts in a debt instrument between principal and interest.

Explanation of Provision The bill provides that for purposes of determining the amount of gain recognized to a securityholder in a reorganization (or a sec. 355 distribution), the excess of the issue price (as defined in secs. 1273 and 1274) of the securities received over the adjusted issue price of the securities surrendered would be treated as other property. If securities are received and none surrendered, the entire issue price is treated as other property. If the issue price of the securities received does not exceed the adjusted issue price of the securities surrendered, then no amount of the securities is treated as other property. These rules apply both to security holders using the cash method and the accrual method of accounting.

The adjusted issue price of a security surrendered means the issue price of the security, increased by the OID previously included in the gross income of any holder of the security (determined without regard to the special rule for subsequent holders), or decreased by the amount of bond premium which would have been allowed as a deduction (or offset) if the bond had always been held by the original holder. Where section 1273(b)(4) applies to a security, the stated redemption price is reduced by the amount of the redemption price which is treated as interest (for example, under sec. 483).

The provision is not intended to create any inference as to the proper treatment of these transactions under present law.

The following examples illustrate the application of this provision:

Example (1). — Assume that a publicly traded security with a stated principal amount of $1,000 and a fair market value of $800 is issued by a corporation in a reorganization to a security holder in exchange for a security with a stated principal amount of $600 and an adjusted issue price of $500. Under the bill, the amount of the excess issue price, or $300, is treated as "other property" for purposes of section 356.

Example (2). — Assume that a publicly traded security with a stated principal amount of $1,000 and a fair market value of $1,200 is issued by a corporation in a reorganization to a security holder in exchange for a security with a stated principal amount and an adjusted issue price of $1,000. Under the bill, the amount of the excess issue price, or $200, is treated as "other property" for purposes of section 356. * * *

Note

This proposal has not been enacted, presumably because the provision does not work properly. How should the provision be revised?

§6.11 Section 358 Substituted Basis for Target Shareholders and Security Holders

A. The Basic Rules

Revenue Ruling 85-164

1985-2 C.B. 117

Issue May a transferor determine the bases and holding periods of stock * * * received in a transfer under section 351 of the Internal Revenue Code by designating the specific property to be exchanged for particular stock * * *? * * *

Law and Analysis * * * Section 358(a)(1) of the Code and section 1.358-1 of the Income Tax Regulations provide that in the case of an exchange to which section 351 applies in which only non-recognition property is received, the basis of all of the stock * * * received in the exchange shall be the same as the basis of all property exchanged therefor. Section 358(b)(1) directs that, under regulations prescribed by the Secretary, the basis determined under subsection (a)(1) shall be allocated among the properties permitted to be received without the recognition of gain or loss.

Section 1.358-2(a) of the regulations prescribes rules for the allocation of basis among nonrecognition property received in corporate reorganization exchanges governed by sections 354, 355, 356 and 371(b). In general, these rules allow limited tracing of the basis of old stock * * * into new only with respect to (i) persons who owned stock * * * of more than one class * * * before the exchange and (ii) corporate recapitalizations under section 368(a)(1)(E). In all other cases, including exchanges under section 351, section 1.358-2(b)(2) provides that the basis of property transferred shall be allocated among all the stock * * * received in proportion to the fair market values of the stock of each class. * * *

Section 1223(1) and section 1.1223-1(a) of the regulations require that, in determining the period for which a taxpayer has held property received in an exchange, there shall be included the period for which he held the property exchanged if (i) in the taxpayer's hands the property received has the same basis in whole or in part as the property exchanged and (ii) for exchanges after March 1, 1954, the property exchanged was at the time of exchange a capital asset as defined in section 1221 or property used in a trade or business as described in section 1231.

Rev. Rul. 62-140, 1962-2 C.B. 181, holds that a share of stock received in exchange for a debenture and a cash payment had a split holding period. The portion of each share received attributable to ownership of the debenture was treated as including the period for which the taxpayer held the debenture and the portion of each share received attributable to the cash payment was treated as held beginning with the date following the date of acquisition.

Rev. Rul. 68-55, 1968-1 C.B. 140, holds that when property is transferred to a corporation under §351(a) of the Code each asset must be considered transferred separately in exchange for a proportionate share of each of the various categories of the total consideration received.

In the instant case, *A* formed *Y* by transferring all of the business assets of the sole proprietorship to *Y* in exchange solely for all of *Y*'s stock. * * * *Y* will continue to carry on the business that *A* conducted, and *A* will remain in control of *Y*. The transfer, therefore, is subject to section 351 of the Code, with the bases and holding periods of the *Y* stock * * * in the hands of *A* determined under sections 358 and 1223 of the Code respectively.

Holding *A* may not determine the bases and holding periods of the *Y* stock * * * received by designating specific property to be exchanged for particular stock * * * Under §§ 1.358-1 and 1.358-2(b)(2) of the regulations, the aggregate basis of the property transferred is allocated among the stock * * * received in proportion to the fair market values of each class. The holding period of the *Y* stock * * * received by *A* is determined by referring to the assets deemed exchanged for each portion of the stock * * *

Note and Question

1. If boot is received and the transaction is governed by § 356, the exchanging shareholder's or security holder's basis for the stock or securities received is the basis of the stock or securities exchanged (1) decreased by the money received and the fair market value of the non-cash boot received (§ 358(a)(1)(A)), and (2) increased by the amount of the gain or the dividend (§ 358(a)(1)(B)). The basis of non-cash boot is the fair market value of such boot. *See* § 356(a)(2).

2. What result under § 358 if shareholder *A*, who has a basis for her shares of $50K, exchanges those shares for stock of an acquiring corporation with a value of $100K, plus cash of $25K? The transaction is an (A) reorganization.

B. Final Regulations on Stock Basis under § 358 in Reorganizations and Related Transactions

Preamble to Final and Temporary Regulations under § 358
RIN — 1545-BC05, Jan. 23, 2006

SUMMARY: This document contains final regulations under section 358 that provide guidance regarding the determination of the basis of stock or securities received in exchange for, or with respect to, stock or securities in certain transactions. This document also contains temporary regulations under section 1502 that govern certain basis determinations and adjustments of subsidiary stock in certain transactions involving members of a consolidated group. * * *

BACKGROUND.

Section 358(a)(1) of the Internal Revenue Code (Code) generally provides that the basis of property received pursuant to an exchange to which section 351, 354, 355, 356, or 361 applies is the same as that of the property exchanged, decreased by the fair market value of any other property (except money) received by the taxpayer, the amount of any money received by the taxpayer, and the amount of loss to the taxpayer which was recognized on such exchange, and increased by the amount which was treated as a dividend, and the amount of gain to the taxpayer which was recognized on such exchange (not including any portion of such gain which was treated as a dividend). Section 358(b)(1) provides that, under regulations prescribed by the Secretary, the basis determined under section 358(a)(1) must be allocated among the properties received in the exchange or distribution.

On May 3, 2004, the IRS and Treasury Department published a notice of proposed rulemaking (REG-116564-03) in the Federal Register (69 FR 24107) that included regulations under section 358 (the proposed regulations) providing guidance regarding the determination of the basis of shares or securities received in a reorganization described in section 368 and a distribution to which section 355 applies. The proposed regulations adopt a tracing method pursuant to which the basis of each share of stock or security received in a reorganization under section 368 is traced to the basis of each surrendered share of stock or security, and each share of stock or security received in a distribution under section 355 is allocated basis from a share of stock or security of the distributing corporation. In the course of developing the proposed regulations, the IRS and Treasury Department considered whether a tracing method or an averaging method should be used to determine the basis of stock and securities received in such transactions. The proposed regulations' adoption of the tracing method is based on the view of the IRS and Treasury Department that, in light of the carryover basis rule of section 358, a reorganization is not an event that justifies averaging the bases of exchanged stock or securities that have been purchased at different times and at different prices. Moreover, the adoption of the tracing method reflects the concern of the IRS and Treasury Department that averaging the bases of exchanged blocks of stock or securities may inappropriately limit the ability of taxpayers to arrange their affairs and may afford opportunities for the avoidance of certain provisions of the Code.

Under the proposed regulations, the basis of each share of stock or security received in an exchange to which section 354, 355, or 356 applies is generally the same as the basis of the share or shares of stock or security or securities exchanged therefor. In the case of a distribution to which section 355 applies, the proposed regulations provide that the basis of each share of stock or security of the distributing corporation is allocated between the share of stock or security of the distributing corporation and the share of stock or security received with respect to such share of stock or security of the distributing corporation in proportion to their fair market values.

If a shareholder or security holder is unable to identify which particular share (or portion of a share) of stock or security is exchanged for, or received with respect to, a particular share (or portion of a share) of stock or security, the proposed regulations permit the shareholder or security holder to designate which share or security is received in exchange for, or in respect of, which share or security. Such designation, however, must be consistent with the terms of the exchange or distribution and must be made on or before the first date on which the basis of a share or security received is relevant, for example, the date on which a share or security received is sold, or is transferred in an exchange described in section 351 or section 721 or a reorganization described in section 368. * * *

EXPLANATION OF PROVISIONS.

These final regulations retain the tracing method of the proposed regulations, but make several modifications to the proposed regulations in response to the comments received. * * *.

Part C:
Concepts Relating to Treatment of Boot under § 356

§ 6.12 Issues under § 356

A. Reorganization: A Condition to § 356 Treatment

Turnbow v. Commissioner

Supreme Court of the United States, 1961
368 U.S. 337, 82 S.Ct. 353, 7 L.Ed.2d 326

MR. JUSTICE WHITTAKER delivered the opinion of the Court.

* * * Specifically the question presented is whether, in the absence of a "reorganization," as that term is defined in [§ 368(a)(1)(B)] and used in § [354], the gain on an exchange of stock for stock *plus cash* is to be recognized in full, or, because of the provisions of § [356(a)(1)], is to be recognized only to the extent of the cash.

The facts are simple and undisputed. Petitioner owned all of the 5,000 shares of outstanding stock of International Dairy Supply Company ("International"), a Nevada corporation. In 1952, petitioner transferred all of the International stock to Foremost Dairies, Inc. ("Foremost"), a New York corporation, in exchange for 82,375 shares (a minor percentage) of Foremost's common (voting) stock of the fair market value of $15 per share or $1,235,625 *plus cash* in the amount of $3,000,000. Petitioner's basis in the International stock was $50,000, and his expenses in connection with the transfer were $21,933.06. Petitioner therefore received for his International stock property and money of a value exceeding his basis and expenses by $4,163,691.94.

In his income tax return for 1952, petitioner treated his gain as recognizable only to the extent of the cash he received. The Commissioner concluded that the whole of the gain was recognizable and accordingly proposed a deficiency. * * *

There is no dispute between the parties about the fact that the transaction involved was not a "reorganization," as defined in § [368(a)(1)(B)], because "the acquisition by" Foremost was not "in exchange *solely* for * * * its voting stock," but was partly for such stock and partly for cash * * *.

But petitioner contends that § [356(a)(1)] authorizes the indulging of assumptions, contrary to the actual facts, hypothetically to supply the missing elements that are necessary to make the exchange a "reorganization." * * * To the contrary, we think that an actual "reorganization," as defined in § [368] and used in § [354] must exist before § [356(a)(1)] can apply thereto.

Affirmed.

Questions

What result in the transaction if the taxpayer had received 90% voting stock and 10% cash? Suppose he sold 10% of his stock for cash, and six months later exchanged the balance for the acquiror's voting stock?

B. Treatment of Nonqualified Preferred Stock as Boot

Preamble to Proposed (Now Final) Regulations under § 1.356-7

REG-105089-99 (January 26, 2000)

Summary This document contains proposed regulations providing guidance relating to nonqualified preferred stock. [*See* § 1.356-7.] The proposed [now adopted] regulations address the effective date of the definition of nonqualified preferred stock and the treatment of nonqualified preferred stock and similar preferred stock received by shareholders in certain reorganizations and distributions. This document also provides notice of a public hearing on these proposed regulations. * * *

Background This document contains proposed amendments to the Income Tax Regulations (26 CFR part 1) under sections 354, 355, 356, and 1036 of the Internal Revenue Code (the Code). Section 1014 of the Taxpayer Relief Act of 1997 (TRA of 1997), Public Law 105-34, enacted on August 5, 1997, amended sections 351, 354, 355, 356, and 1036 of the Code. As amended, these sections, in general, provide that nonqualified preferred stock (as defined in section 351(g)(2)) (NQPS) received in an exchange or distribution will not be treated as stock or securities but, instead, will be treated as "other property" or "boot." As a result, the receipt of NQPS in a transaction occurring after the NQPS provisions are effective will, unless a specified exception applies, result in gain (or, in some instances, loss) recognition. Section 351(g)(4) provides authority to issue regulations to carry out the purposes of these provisions.

Section 351(g)(2)(A) defines NQPS as preferred stock if (1) the holder has the right to require the issuer or a related person to redeem or purchase the stock, (2) the issuer or a related person is required to redeem or purchase the stock, (3) the issuer or a related person has the right to redeem or purchase the stock and, as of the issue date, it is more likely than not that such right will be exercised, or (4) the dividend rate on the stock varies in whole or in part (directly or indirectly) with reference to interest rates, commodity prices, or other similar indices. Factors (1), (2), and (3) above will cause an instrument to be NQPS only if the right or obligation may be exercised within 20 years of the date the instrument is issued and such right or obligation is not subject to a contingency which, as of the issue date, makes remote the likelihood of the redemption or purchase.

These rights or obligations do not cause preferred stock to be NQPS in certain circumstances described in section 351(g)(2)(C). * * *

The NQPS provisions also provide certain exceptions to the treatment of NQPS as boot. Under sections 354(a)(2)(C), 355(a)(3)(D), and 356(e)(2), NQPS is treated as stock, and not other property, in cases where the NQPS is received in exchange for, or in a distribution with respect to, NQPS. As a result, the receipt of NQPS in exchange for NQPS will not result in gain or loss recognition.

Under prior law, preferred stock generally did not constitute boot in a reorganization or in a distribution under section 355 of the Code. The legislative history of the NQPS provisions indicates that Congress was concerned about nonrecognition transactions in which a secure preferred stock instrument is received in exchange for common stock or riskier preferred stock. The committee reports state that

> [c]ertain preferred stocks have been widely used in corporate transactions to afford taxpayers non-recognition treatment, even though the taxpayers may receive relatively secure instruments in exchange for relatively risky investments, and that [t]he Committee believes that when such preferred stock instruments are received in certain transactions, it is appropriate to view such instruments as taxable consideration, since the investor has often obtained a more secure form of investment.

H.R. Rep. No. 148, 105th Cong., 1st Sess. 472 (1997); S. Rep. 33, 105th Cong., Sess. (1997). * * *

Explanation of Provisions The proposed regulations address three technical issues relating to the question of whether certain preferred stock instruments qualify as NQPS. * * *

The second issue addressed by the proposed regulations is the treatment of NQPS received in a reorganization in exchange for (or in a distribution with respect to) preferred stock that is not NQPS solely because, at the time the original stock was issued, a redemption or purchase right was not exercisable until after a 20-year period beginning on the issue date, or a redemption or purchase right was exercisable within a 20-year period but was subject to a contingency which made remote the likelihood of the redemption or purchase, or, in the case of an issuer's right to redeem or purchase stock described in section 351(g)(2)(A)(iii), was unlikely to be exercised within a 20-year period beginning on the issue date (or because of any combination of these reasons). To illustrate, assume that after June 8, 1997, T issues preferred stock to X that permits the holder to require T to redeem the stock on demand, but not before the stock is held for 22 years. Assume that seven years later, the T stock is exchanged in a reorganization for P preferred stock with substantially identical terms that permits the holder to require P to redeem the stock after 15 years.

Technically, this transaction could be viewed as a taxable exchange because X is receiving P stock that meets the definition of NQPS in exchange for T stock that is not NQPS (QPS). However, the IRS and Treasury believe that nonrecognition treatment is appropriate because the P stock represents a continuation of the original investment in the T stock.

The proposed regulations provide a rule that treats the P stock received in such transactions as QPS if the P stock is substantially identical to the T preferred stock surrendered (or the T stock on which a distribution is made). The substantially identical requirement is necessary to ensure that this rule does not permit the NQPS provisions to be circumvented through exchanges of QPS for more secure NQPS. * * *

Under this rule, the P stock received will continue to be treated as QPS in subsequent transactions, and similar principles will apply to those transactions. For example, if the P stock is later exchanged in a reorganization for substantially identical stock of another acquiring corporation, the acquiring corporation stock will also be treated as QPS. However, if the P stock is later exchanged for stock described in section 351 (g)(2) that is not substantially identical, the receipt of the stock will be treated as boot. * * *

Note

As indicated in *Southwest Consolidated*, Sec. 6.4, *supra*, warrants do not count for continuity of interest purposes, but as indicated in Sec. 6.9, *supra*, warrants qualify for non-recognition treatment. On the other hand, as indicated in *Nelson*, Sec. 6.2.B.3., *supra*, non-qualified preferred stock when paid as consideration to the former target shareholders counts for continuity of interest purposes, but as indicated above, such stock does not qualify for non-recognition treatment. It is interesting to note that in a merger in which 50% of the consideration paid by the acquiror to the former target shareholders consists of non-qualified preferred stock and 50% of the consideration consists of warrants, the transaction will be a good reorganization because the non-qualified preferred stock satisfies the continuity of interest requirement, but half of the consideration will be taxed because the non-qualified preferred stock does not qualify for non-recognition treatment.

§ 6.13 Determination of Whether a Distribution Has the "Effect" of the Distribution of a Dividend

See § 368(a)(2).

A. The Supreme Court Decision

Commissioner v. Clark

Supreme Court of the United States, 1989
489 U.S. 726

JUSTICE STEVENS delivered the opinion of the Court.

This is the third case in which the Government has asked us to decide that a shareholder's receipt of a cash payment in exchange for a portion of his stock was taxable as a dividend. In the two earlier cases, *Commissioner v. Estate of Bedford*, 325 U.S. 283, 65 S.Ct. 1157, 89 L.Ed. 1611 (1945), and *United States v. Davis*, 397 U.S. 301, 90 S.Ct. 1041, 25 L.Ed.2d 323 (1970), we agreed with the Government largely because the transactions involved redemptions of stock by single corporations that did not "result in a meaningful reduction of the shareholder's proportionate interest in the corporation." In the case we decide today, however, the taxpayer in an arm's-length transaction exchanged his interest in the acquired corporation for less than 1% of the stock of the acquiring corporation and a substantial cash payment. The taxpayer held no interest in the acquiring corporation prior to the reorganization. Viewing the exchange as a whole, we conclude that the cash payment is not appropriately characterized as a dividend. We accordingly agree with the Tax Court and with the Court of Appeals that the taxpayer is entitled to capital gains treatment of the cash payment.

[**Background**] In determining tax liability under the Internal Revenue Code of 1954, gain resulting from the sale or exchange of property is generally treated as capital gain, whereas the receipt of cash dividends is treated as ordinary income. The Code, however, imposes no current tax on certain stock-for-stock exchanges. In particular, § 354(a)(1) provides, subject to various limitations, for nonrecognition of gain resulting from the exchange of stock or securities solely for other stock or securities, provided that the exchange is pursuant to a plan of corporate reorganization and that the stock or securities are those of a party to the reorganization. 26 U.S.C. § 354(a)(1).

Under § 356(a)(1) of the Code, if such a stock-for-stock exchange is accompanied by additional consideration in the form of a cash payment or other property—something that tax practitioners refer to as "boot"—"then the gain, if any, to the recipient shall be recognized, but in an amount not in excess of the sum of such money and the fair market value of such other property." 26 U.S.C. § 356(a)(1). That is, if the shareholder receives boot, he or she must recognize the gain on the exchange up to the value of the boot. Boot is accordingly generally treated as a gain from the sale or exchange of property and is recognized in the current tax year.

Section 356(a)(2), which controls the decision in this case, creates an exception to that general rule. It provided in 1979:

> "If an exchange is described in paragraph (1) but has the effect of the distribution of a dividend, then there shall be treated as a dividend to each distributee such an amount of the gain recognized under paragraph (1) as is not in excess of his ratable share of the undistributed earnings and profits of the corporation accumulated after February 28, 1913. The remainder, if any, of the gain recognized under paragraph (1) shall be treated as gain from the exchange of property." 26 U.S.C. § 356(a)(2) (1976 ed.).

Thus, if the "exchange * * * has the effect of the distribution of a dividend," the boot must be treated as a dividend and is therefore appropriately taxed as ordinary income to the extent that gain is realized. In contrast, if the exchange does not have "the effect of the distribution of a dividend," the boot must be treated as a payment in exchange for property and, insofar as gain is realized, accorded capital gains treatment. The question in this case is thus whether the exchange between the taxpayer and the acquiring corporation had "the effect of the distribution of a dividend" within the meaning of § 356(a)(2).

The relevant facts are easily summarized. For approximately 15 years prior to April 1979, the taxpayer was the president of Basin Surveys, Inc. (Basin). In January 1978, he became sole shareholder in Basin, a company in which he had invested approximately $85,000. The corporation operated a successful business providing various technical services to the petroleum industry. In 1978, N.L. Industries, Inc. (NL), a publicly owned corporation engaged in the manufacture and supply of petroleum equipment and services, initiated negotiations with the taxpayer regarding the possible acquisition of Basin. On April 3, 1979, after months of negotiations, the taxpayer and NL entered into a contract.

The agreement provided for a "triangular merger," whereby Basin was merged into a wholly owned subsidiary of NL. In exchange for transferring all of the outstanding shares in Basin to NL's subsidiary, the taxpayer elected to receive 300,000 shares of NL common stock and cash boot of $3,250,000, passing up an alternative offer of 425,000 shares of NL common stock. The 300,000 shares of NL issued to the taxpayer amounted to approximately 0.92% of the outstanding common shares of NL. If the taxpayer had instead accepted the pure stock-for-stock offer, he would have held approximately 1.3% of the outstanding common shares. The Commissioner and the taxpayer agree that the merger at issue qualifies as a reorganization under §§ 368(a)(1)(A) and (a)(2)(D).

Respondents filed a joint federal income tax return for 1979. As required by § 356(a)(1), they reported the cash boot as taxable gain. In calculating the tax owed, respondents characterized the payment as long-term capital gain. The Commissioner on audit disagreed with this characterization. In his view, the payment had "the effect of the distribution of a dividend" and was thus taxable as ordinary income up to $2,319,611, the amount of Basin's accumulated earnings and profits at the time of the merger. The Commissioner assessed a deficiency of $972,504.74.

Respondents petitioned for review in the Tax Court, which, in a reviewed decision, held in their favor. 86 T.C. 138 (1986). The court started from the premise that the question whether the boot payment had "the effect of the distribution of a dividend" turns on the choice between "two judicially articulated tests." *Id.,* at 140. Under the test advocated by the Commissioner and given voice in *Shimberg v. United States,* 577 F.2d 283 (CA5 1978), cert. denied, 439 U.S. 1115, 99 S.Ct. 1019, 59 L.Ed.2d 73 (1979), the boot payment is treated as though it were made in a hypothetical redemption by the acquired corporation (Basin) immediately *prior* to the reorganization. Under this test, the cash payment received by the taxpayer indisputably would have been treated as a dividend. [*See* § 302 and Chapter 10.] The second test, urged by the taxpayer and finding support in *Wright v. United States,* 482 F.2d 600 (CA8 1973), proposes an alternative hypothetical redemption. Rather than concentrating on the taxpayer's pre-reorganization interest in the acquired corporation, this test requires that one imagine a pure stock-for-stock exchange, followed immediately by a *post*-reorganization redemption of a portion of the taxpayer's shares in the acquiring corporation (NL) in return for a payment in an amount equal to the boot. Under § 302 of the Code, which defines when a redemption of stock should be treated as a distribution of dividend, NL's redemption of 125,000 shares of its stock from the taxpayer in exchange for the $3,250,000 boot payment would have been treated as capital gain. [*See* § 302(b)(2) and Chapter 10.]

The Tax Court rejected the pre-reorganization test favored by the Commissioner because it considered it improper "to view the cash payment as an isolated event totally separate from the reorganization." 86 T.C., at 151. Indeed, it suggested that this test requires that courts make the "determination of dividend equivalency fantasizing that the reorganization does not exist." The court then acknowledged that a similar criticism could be made of the taxpayer's contention that the cash payment should be viewed as a post-reorganization redemption. It concluded, however, that since it was perfectly clear that the cash payment would not have taken place without the reorganization, it was better to treat the boot "as the equivalent of a redemption *in the course of implementing the reorganization*," than "as having occurred *prior to and separate from the reorganization*." *Id.*, at 152 (emphasis in original).

The Court of Appeals for the Fourth Circuit affirmed. 828 F.2d 221 (1987). Like the Tax Court, it concluded that although "[s]ection 302 does not explicitly apply in the reorganization context," *id.*, at 223, and although § 302 differs from § 356 in important respects, *id.*, at 224, it nonetheless provides "the appropriate test for determining whether boot is ordinary income or a capital gain," *id.*, at 223. Thus, as explicated in § 302(b)(2), if the taxpayer relinquished more than 20% of his corporate control and retained less than 50% of the voting shares after the distribution, the boot would be treated as capital gain. However, as the Court of Appeals recognized, "[b]ecause § 302 was designed to deal with a stock redemption by a single corporation, rather than a reorganization involving two companies, the section does not indicate which corporation [the taxpayer] lost interest in." Thus, like the Tax Court, the Court of Appeals was left to consider whether the hypothetical redemption should be treated as a pre-reorganization distribution coming from the acquired corporation or as a post-reorganization distribution coming from the acquiring corporation. It concluded:

> "Based on the language and legislative history of § 356, the change-in-ownership principle of § 302, and the need to review the reorganization as an integrated transaction, we conclude that the boot should be characterized as a post-reorganization stock redemption by N.L. that affected [the taxpayer's] interest in the new corporation. Because this redemption reduced [the taxpayer's] N.L. holdings by more than 20%, the boot should be taxed as a capital gain." *Id.*, at 224–225.

This decision by the Court of Appeals for the Fourth Circuit is in conflict with the decision of the Fifth Circuit in *Shimberg v. United States*, 577 F.2d 283 (1978), in two important respects. In *Shimberg*, the court concluded that it was inappropriate to apply stock redemption principles in reorganization cases "on a wholesale basis." In addition, the court adopted the pre-reorganization test, holding that "§ 356(a)(2) requires a determination of whether the distribution would have been taxed as a dividend if made prior to the reorganization or if no reorganization had occurred."

To resolve this conflict on a question of importance to the administration of the federal tax laws, we granted certiorari.

[**Analysis**] We agree with the Tax Court and the Court of Appeals for the Fourth Circuit that the question under § 356(a)(2) whether an "exchange * * * has the effect of the distribution of a dividend" should be answered by examining the effect of the exchange as a whole. We think the language and history of the statute, as well as a commonsense understanding of the economic substance of the transaction at issue, support this approach.

The language of § 356(a) strongly supports our understanding that the transaction should be treated as an integrated whole. Section 356(a)(2) asks whether "*an exchange is described in paragraph* (1)" that "has the effect of the distribution of a dividend." (Emphasis supplied.) The statute does not provide that boot shall be treated as a dividend if its payment has the effect of the distribution of a dividend. Rather, the inquiry turns on whether the "exchange" has that effect. Moreover, paragraph (1), in turn, looks to whether "the property received in *the exchange* consists not only of property permitted by section 354 or 355 to be received without the recognition of gain but also of other property or money." (Emphasis supplied.) Again, the statute plainly refers to one integrated transaction and, again, makes clear that we are to look to the character of the exchange as a whole and not simply its component parts. Finally, it is significant that § 356 expressly limits the extent to which boot may be taxed to the amount of gain realized in the reorganization. This limitation suggests that Congress intended that boot not be treated in isolation from the overall reorganization.

Our reading of the statute as requiring that the transaction be treated as a unified whole is reinforced by the well-established "step-transaction" doctrine, a doctrine that the Government has applied in related contexts. * * *

Viewing the exchange in this case as an integrated whole, we are unable to accept the Commissioner's pre-reorganization analogy. The analogy severs the payment of boot from the context of the reorganization. Indeed, only by straining to abstract the payment of boot from the context of the overall exchange, and thus imagining that Basin made a distribution to the taxpayer independently of NL's planned acquisition, can we reach the rather counterintuitive conclusion urged by the Commissioner—that the taxpayer suffered no meaningful reduction in his ownership interest as a result of the cash payment. We conclude that such a limited view of the transaction is plainly inconsistent with the statute's direction that we look to the effect of the entire exchange. * * *

The post-reorganization approach adopted by the Tax Court and the Court of Appeals is, in our view, preferable to the Commissioner's approach. Most significantly, this approach does a far better job of treating the payment of boot as a component of the overall exchange. Unlike the pre-reorganization view, this approach acknowledges that there would have been no cash payment absent the exchange and also that, by accepting the cash payment, the taxpayer experienced a meaningful reduction in his potential ownership interest.

Once the post-reorganization approach is adopted, the result in this case is pellucidly clear. Section 302(a) of the Code provides that if a redemption fits within any one of the four categories set out in § 302(b), the redemption "shall be treated as a distribution in part or full payment in exchange for the stock," and thus not regarded as a dividend. As the Tax Court and the Court of Appeals correctly determined, the hypothetical post-reorganization redemption by NL of a portion of the taxpayer's shares satisfies at least one of the subsections of § 302(b). In particular, the safe harbor provisions of subsection (b)(2) provide that redemptions in which the taxpayer relinquishes more than 20% of his or her share of the corporation's voting stock and retains less than 50% of the voting stock after the redemption shall not be treated as distributions of a dividend. Here, we treat the transaction as though NL redeemed 125,000 shares of its common stock (*i.e.*, the number of shares of NL common stock foregone in favor of the boot) in return for a cash payment to the taxpayer of $3,250,000 (*i.e.*, the amount of the boot). As a result of this redemption, the taxpayer's interest in NL was reduced from 1.3% of the outstanding common stock to 0.9%. Thus, the taxpayer relinquished approximately 29% of his interest in NL and retained less than a 1% voting interest in the corporation after the transaction, easily satisfying the "substantially disproportionate" standards of § 302(b)(2). We accordingly conclude that the boot payment did not have the effect of a dividend and that the payment was properly treated as capital gain. * * *

Note and Questions

1. In Rev. Rul. 74-515, 1974-2 C.B. 118, which was issued before the *Clark* decision, the Service said that it would apply § 302 principles in making the dividend determination under § 356(a)(2). *Clark* confirms this approach and sets forth the methodology for applying § 302 principles. State precisely the holding in *Clark*. As a result of the maximum uniform 20% rate that applies to capital gains and dividends, § 356(a)(2) is of little practical significance.

2. Individuals *A* and *B* each own 50% of the stock of target corporation (*TC*). Both have a basis of $10K for their stock. Acquiring corporation (*AC*) acquires *TC* in a merger by issuing $100K of *AC* stock and paying $100K in cash. The $100K of *AC* stock amounts to 1% of the outstanding *AC* stock after the merger. What is the treatment of the $100K boot in each of the following cases?

   a. *A* and *B* each receive $50K of the stock and $50K of cash?

   b. *A* receives $100K of *AC* stock, and *B* receives $100K of cash?

   c. *A* receives $75K of cash and $25K of *AC* stock, and *B* receives $75K of *AC* stock and $25K of cash?

3. The facts are the same as in Question 2, except the $100K of *AC* stock amounts to 50% of the outstanding stock of *AC* after the merger. Same questions as in 2a–2c.

4. Note that in view of the uniform 20% maximum rate applicable to capital gains and dividends of individuals, there may not be a significant difference between having boot characterized as a dividend or capital gain. However, with a capital gain designation, there is a recovery of basis, which is not the case with a dividend characterization.

B. The Service's Position

Revenue Ruling 93-61

1993-2 C.B. 118

This revenue ruling revokes Rev.Rul. 75-83, 1975-1 C.B. 112.

Law and Analysis Section 354(a) of the Internal Revenue Code provides that no gain or loss shall be recognized if stock or securities in a corporation a party to a reorganization are exchanged solely for stock or securities in such corporation or in another corporation a party to the reorganization. If section 354 would apply to the exchange except for the receipt of money or property other than stock or securities in a corporate party to the reorganization, referred to as boot, section 356(a)(1) provides that the recipient shall recognize gain, but in an amount not in excess of the sum of the money and the fair market value of the other property. Under section 356(a)(2), if an exchange described in section 356(a)(1) has the effect of the distribution of a dividend, the shareholder must treat the gain recognized on the exchange as a dividend to the extent of the distributee's ratable share of the undistributed earnings and profits of the corporation accumulated after February 28, 1913.

In Rev. Rul. 75-83, *X* corporation merged into *Y* corporation in a reorganization under section 368(a)(1)(A) of the Code. The sole shareholder of *X* corporation received shares of *Y* corporation stock and a note, which was treated as boot under section 356(a)(1). To determine whether the exchange had the effect of the distribution of a dividend under section 356(a)(2), the Service treated the distribution as though it were made by the acquired corporation (*X*) and not the acquiring corporation (*Y*). Therefore, the Service concluded that the exchange had the effect of a dividend under section 356(a)(2).

In *Commissioner v. Clark*, [Sec. 6.13.A.], the sole shareholder of a target corporation exchanged his target stock for stock of an acquiring corporation and cash. The Supreme Court applied the dividend equivalency rules for redemptions contained in section 302 of the Code to determine whether the boot payment had the effect of a dividend distribution under section 356(a)(2). At issue was whether the boot payment should be treated as if it were made (i) by the target corporation in a hypothetical section 302 redemption of a portion of the shareholder's target stock prior to and separate from the reorganization exchange, or (ii) by the acquiring corporation in a hypothetical section 302 redemption of the acquiring stock that the shareholder would have received in the reorganization exchange if there had been no boot distribution. The Court concluded that the treatment of a boot distribution is determined "by examining the effect of the exchange as a whole," 489 U.S. 726, 737, and held that the second approach better tested the effect of the payment of boot as a component in the overall exchange.

Holding In an acquisitive reorganization, the determination of whether boot is treated as a dividend distribution under section 356(a)(2) of the Code is made by comparing the interest the shareholder actually received in the acquiring corporation in the reorganization exchange with the interest the shareholder would have received in the acquiring corporation if solely stock had been received.

Effect On Other Rulings Rev. Rul. 75-83 is revoked. * * *

C. Application of § 318 Attribution Rules under § 356(a)(2)

House Conference Report to the Tax Equity and Fiscal Responsibility Act of 1982

544 (1982)

Present Law To determine whether a shareholder is entitled to sale or exchange treatment on a stock redemption, stock held by related parties is attributed to the shareholder in determining whether the shareholder's interest in the corporation was terminated or significantly reduced. [*See* §§ 302(c) and 318.] The attribution rules do not apply to some transactions that are economically equivalent to straight stock redemptions and that offer an equivalent opportunity to bail out earnings. For example, * * * a shareholder exchanging stock in a reorganization for property other than stock or securities may have dividend consequences if the transaction has the effect of the distribution of a dividend. For this purpose, attribution rules do not apply. * * *

The conference agreement extends the ownership attribution rules * * * in determining whether the receipt of property in a reorganization has the effect of a dividend. * * * [*See* § 356(a)(2).]

D. Cash for Fractional Shares

Revenue Procedure 77-41

1977-2 C.B. 574

Rev. Rul. 77-37, 1977-2 C.B. 568, contains operating rules for the issuance of advance rulings as to matters within the jurisdiction of the Reorganization Branch of the Internal Revenue Service. Rev. Proc. 77-37 is amplified to include the following:

A ruling will usually be issued under section 302(a) of the Code that cash to be distributed to shareholders in lieu of fractional share interests arising in corporate reorganizations, stock splits, stock dividends, conversion of convertible stocks, and other similar transactions will be treated as having been received in part or full payment in exchange for the stock redeemed if the cash distribution is undertaken solely for the purpose of saving the corporation the expense and inconvenience of issuing and transferring fractional shares, and is not separately bargained-for consideration. The purpose of the transaction giving rise to the fractional share interests, the maximum amount of cash that may be received by any one shareholder, and the percentage of the total consideration that will be cash are among the factors that will be considered in determining whether a ruling is to be issued.

Rev. Proc. 73-35, 1973-2 C.B. 490, calls for the submission of certain information with requests for rulings under section 302 of the Code. This information need not be supplied with requests for rulings with respect to redemptions of fractional share interests. However, Rev.Proc. 72-3, 1972-1 C.B. 698, and section 601.201 of the Statement of Procedural Rules (26 CFR 601.201 (1977)), which contain the procedures to be followed for the issuance of ruling letters, should be complied with.

Rev. Proc. 77-37 is amplified and Rev. Proc. 73-35 is modified.

E. No Dividend Where Boot Paid in Respect of Securities

Revenue Ruling 71-427

1971-2 C.B. 183

The shareholders of *X,* a solvent corporation, approved a plan of reorganization in order to eliminate outstanding debt in the form of debentures, which qualified as securities under section 354(a)(1) of the Code. Pursuant to the plan, the debenture holders exchanged their securities for common stock of *X* and cash in a transaction which qualified as a reorganization (recapitalization) under section 368(a)(1)(E) of the Code.

* * * [T]he receipt of the cash payment in addition to the stock of *X* results in the recognition of gain under section 356(a) of the Code to the former holders of the debentures who realized a gain, but in an amount not in excess of the cash received. Section 356(a)(2) of the Code providing for dividend treatment is not applicable to the recognized gain since the distributees received the cash payment as creditors, and not as shareholders of *X.* Thus, any recognized gain will be treated as a gain from the exchange of property under section 356 of the Code. However, losses, if any, from the exchange described above, will not be recognized pursuant to section 356(c) of the Code.

F. Determination of E & P under § 356(a)(2)

Which corporation's E & P is counted for purposes of § 356(a)(2)? Is it the target's? The acquiror's? Or both? Suppose there is a (D) reorganization with boot? The Tax Court's position is that only the transferor's E & P is considered. *See American Manufacturing Co. v. Commissioner,* 55 T.C. 204 (1970) and *Atlas Tool Co. v. Commissioner,* 70 T.C. 86 (1978) (both of which dealt with (D) reorganizations). The Fifth Circuit has held that in a (D) reorganization the E & P of both the distributing and the controlled corporations are counted for purposes of § 356(a)(2). *See Davant v. Commissions,* 366 F.2d 874 (1967).

Part D:
Concepts Relating to Treatment of
Target under §§ 361 and 357

§ 6.14 Treatment of Target Corporation upon Receipt and Distribution of Stock, Securities, and Boot

A. General Principles

See § 361.

Technical Corrections Provisions of House Miscellaneous Revenue Bill of 1988

371–373 (1988)

Present Law The Tax Reform Act of 1984 generally required that all property received by a corporation in a "C" reorganization be distributed. In addition, that Act provided that a corporation must recognize gain on the distribution of appreciated property to its shareholders in a nonliquidating distribution. The 1986 Act made a series of amendments to the reorganization provisions attempting to conform those provisions with changes made by the 1984 Act. However, numerous technical problems with the 1986 amendments have arisen. The bill responds to these technical problems with a complete revision of the 1986 amendments.

Explanation of Provision *Treatment of reorganization exchange.* The bill restores the provisions of section 361, relating to the nonrecognition treatment of an exchange pursuant to a plan of reorganization, as in effect prior to the amendments made by the 1986 Act. Thus, as under prior law, gain or loss will generally not be recognized to a corporation which exchanges property, in pursuance of the plan of reorganization, for stock and securities in another corporation a party to the reorganization. [*See* § 361(a).] However, as under prior law, gain will be recognized to the extent the corporation receives property other than such stock or securities and does not distribute the other property pursuant to the plan of reorganization.[5] [*See* § 361(b).]

The bill amends prior law by providing that transfers of property to creditors in satisfaction of the corporation's indebtedness in connection with the reorganization are treated as distributions pursuant to the plan of reorganization for this purpose.[6] [*See* § 361(b)(3).] The Secretary of the Treasury may prescribe regulations necessary to prevent tax avoidance by reason of this provision. This amendment is not intended to change in any way the definition of a reorganization within the meaning of section 368.

Treatment of distributions in reorganizations. The bill also conforms the treatment of distributions of property by a corporation to its shareholders in pursuance of a

---

5. This could occur, for example, where liabilities are assumed in a transaction to which section 357(b) or (c) applies.

6. This overrules the holding in *Minnesota Tea Company v. Helvering*, 302 U.S. 609 (1938).

plan of reorganization to the treatment of nonliquidating distributions (under section 311). Under the bill, the distributing corporation generally will recognize gain, but not loss, on the distribution of property in pursuance of the plan of reorganization. [*See* § 361(c).] However, no gain will be recognized on the distribution of "qualified property". [*See* § 361(c)(2)(B).] For this purpose, "qualified property" means (1) stock (or rights to acquire stock) in, or the obligation of, the distributing corporation and (2) stock (or rights to acquire stock) in, or the obligation of, another corporation which is a party to the reorganization and which were received by the distributing corporation in the exchange.[7] [*See* § 361(c)(2)(B).] The bill also provides that the transfer of qualified property by a corporation to its creditors in satisfaction of indebtedness is treated as a distribution pursuant to the plan of reorganization.[8] [*See* § 361(c)(3).]

Basis. The bill clarifies that the basis of property received in an exchange to which section 361 applies, other than stock or securities in another corporation a party to the reorganization, is the fair market value of the property at the time of the transaction (pursuant to section 358(a)(2)). [*See* § 358(f).] Thus the distributing corporation will recognize only post-acquisition gain on any taxable disposition of such property received pursuant to the plan of reorganization. Of course, the other corporation will recognize gain or loss on the transfer of its property under the usual tax principles governing the recognition of gain or loss.

B. Protection of *General Utilities* Repeal upon Mergers with RICs or REITs

Treasury Decision 8872

February 7, 2000

Summary This document contains temporary regulations that apply with respect to the net built-in gain of C corporation assets that become assets of a Regulated Investment Company [RIC] or Real Estate Investment Trust [REIT] by the qualification of a C corporation as a RIC or REIT or by the transfer of assets of a C corporation to a RIC or REIT in a carryover basis transaction. The regulations generally require the corporation to recognize gain as if it had sold the assets transferred or converted to RIC or REIT assets at fair market value and immediately liquidated. The regulations permit the transferee RIC or REIT to elect, in lieu of liquidation treatment, to be subject to the rules of section 1374 of the Internal Revenue Code and the regulations thereunder. * * *

Background Sections 631 and 633 of the Tax Reform Act of 1986 (the 1986 Act) (Public Law 99-514), as amended by sections 1006(e) and (g) of the Technical and

---

7. For analysis that acquiring corporation voting stock held by the acquired corporation in a Type C reorganization is transferred to the acquiring corporation in exchange for the same stock, see Rev. Rul. 78-47, 1978-1 C.B. 113.

8. These amendments are not intended to affect the treatment of any income from the discharge of indebtedness arising in connection with a corporate reorganization.

Miscellaneous Revenue Act of 1988 (the 1988 Act) (Public Law 100-647), amended the Code to repeal the *General Utilities* doctrine. The 1986 Act amended sections 336 and 337 of the Code, generally requiring corporations to recognize gain when appreciated property is distributed in connection with a complete liquidation. Section 337(d) directs the Secretary to prescribe regulations as may be necessary to carry out the purposes of *General Utilities* repeal, including rules to "ensure that such purposes shall not be circumvented * * * through the use of a regulated investment company [RIC], a real estate investment trust [REIT], or a tax exempt entity * * *." The transfer of the assets of a C corporation to a RIC or REIT could result in permanently removing the built-in gain inherent in those assets from the reach of the corporate income tax because RIC and REIT income is not subject to a corporate-level income tax if such income is distributed to the RIC or REIT shareholders.

Accordingly, on February 4, 1988, the IRS issued Notice 88-19 *(1988-1 C.B. 486)*. Notice 88-19 announced that the IRS intended to promulgate regulations under the authority of section 337(d) with respect to transactions or events that result in the ownership of C corporation assets by a RIC or REIT with a basis determined by reference to the corporation's basis (a carryover basis). * * *

Explanation of Provisions These regulations implement Notice 88-19 by providing that when a C corporation (1) qualifies to be taxed as a RIC or REIT, or (2) transfers assets to a RIC or REIT in a carryover basis transaction, the C corporation is treated as if it sold all of its assets at their respective fair market values and immediately liquidated, unless the RIC or REIT elects to be subject to tax under section 1374. [§ 1.337(d)-5T] Any resulting net built-in gain is recognized by the C corporation and the bases of the assets in the hands of the RIC or REIT are generally adjusted to their fair market values to reflect the recognized net built-in gain. The regulations do not permit a C corporation to recognize a net built-in loss, and, in this case, the carryover bases of the assets in the hands of the RIC or REIT are preserved.

If the RIC or REIT elects to be subject to treatment under section 1374, its built-in gain, and the corporate-level tax imposed on that gain, is subject to rules similar to the rules applying to the net income of foreclosure property of REITs. * * *

Note

A similar recognition rule applies upon the transfer of substantially all of the assets of a C corporation to a tax exempt entity and upon the conversion of a C corporation to a tax exempt entity. *See* § 1.337(d)-4.

§ 6.15 Treatment of Liabilities

A. The Genesis of the Problem: The Supreme Court Holds that Liabilities Assumed Are Boot in a Reorganization

United States v. Hendler

Supreme Court of the United States, 1938. 303 U.S. 564

Under [the predecessor of § 361], gains are not taxed if one corporation, pursuant to a "plan of reorganization" exchanges its property "solely for *stock* or *securities,* in another corporation a party to the reorganization." But, when a corporation not only receives "stock or securities" in exchange for its property, but also receives "other property or money" in carrying out a "plan of reorganization,"

(1) If the corporation receiving such other property or money *distributes* it in pursuance of the plan of reorganization, no gain to the corporation shall be recognized from the exchange, but

(2) If the corporation receiving such other property or money *does not distribute* it in pursuance of the plan of reorganization, the gain, if any, to the corporation shall be recognized [taxed]. * * *

In this case, there was a merger or "reorganization" of the Borden Company and the Hendler Creamery Company, Inc., resulting in gains of more than six million dollars to the Hendler Company, Inc., a corporation of which respondent is transferee. The Court of Appeals, believing there was an exemption under [the predecessor of § 361], affirmed the judgment of the District Court holding all Hendler gains non-taxable.

This controversy between the government and respondent involves the assumption and payment—pursuant to the plan of reorganization—by the Borden Company of $534,297.40 bonded indebtedness of the Hendler Creamery Co., Inc. We are unable to agree with the conclusion reached by the courts below that the gain to the Hendler Company, realized by the Borden Company's payment, was exempt from taxation under [the predecessor of § 361].

It was contended below and it is urged here that since the Hendler Company did not actually receive the money with which the Borden Company discharged the former's indebtedness, the Hendler Company's gain of $534,297.40 is not taxable. The transaction, however, under which the Borden Company assumed and paid the debt and obligation of the Hendler Company is to be regarded in substance as though the $534,297.40 had been paid directly to the Hendler Company. The Hendler Company was the beneficiary of the discharge of its indebtedness. Its gain was as real and substantial as if the money had been paid it and then paid over by it to its creditors. The discharge of liability by the payment of the Hendler Company's indebtedness constituted income to the Hendler Company and is to be treated as such.[9]

---

9. *Old Colony Trust Co. v. Commissioner,* 279 U.S. 716, 729.

[The predecessor of 361] provides no exemption for gains — resulting from corporate "reorganization" — neither received as "stocks or securities," nor received as "money or other property" and distributed to stockholders under the plan of reorganization. In *Minnesota Tea Co. v. Helvering*, 302 U.S. 609, 58 S.Ct. 393, 394, 82 L.Ed. 474, it was said that this exemption "contemplates a distribution to stockholders, and not payment to creditors." The very statute upon which the taxpayer relies provides that "If the corporation receiving such other property or money does not distribute it in pursuance of the plan of reorganization, the gain, if any, to the corporation shall be recognized [taxed]. * * * "

Since this gain or income of $534,297.40 of the Hendler Company was neither received as "stock or securities" nor distributed to its stockholders "in pursuance of the plan of reorganization" it was not exempt and is taxable gain as defined in the 1928 Act. This $534,297.40 gain to the taxpayer does not fall within the exemptions of §112, and the judgment of the court below is

Reversed.

Questions

What is the relationship between *Hendler* and *Crane* (*see* Sec. 1.5.B)?

B. Reaction to *Hendler*

In response to the *Hendler* case, Congress (1) provided in §357(a) that liabilities are to be disregarded in a §361 transaction, and (2) provided in the definition of the (C) reorganization that the transfer of the target's liabilities to the acquiror is to be disregarded in determining whether the acquisition is "solely for voting stock." Section 357(a) does not apply, however, if the transfer of the liabilities is for tax avoidance purposes (*see* §357(b)) or if the liabilities exceed basis in a (D) reorganization to which §361 applies (*see* §357(c)(1)(B)). Section 1.368-2(d)(1) says that, although an assumption of a target's liabilities will not prevent the transaction from qualifying as a (C), an assumption may in some cases "so alter the character of the transaction as to place the transaction outside the purposes and assumptions of the reorganization provisions." *See Wortham Machinery Co., infra.*

C. Discharge of Intercorporate Debt in an (A) Reorganization

Revenue Ruling 72-464

1972-2 C.B. 214

Advice has been requested whether, under the circumstances described below, the acquisition of assets in exchange for stock and assumption of liabilities pursuant to a plan of reorganization under section 368(a)(1)(A) of the Internal Revenue Code of 1954 results in the recognition of gain to either the acquired or the acquiring corporation.

In a prior transaction, unrelated to the present statutory merger, *X* corporation purchased from certain banks, at a cost of $20,000, outstanding notes of *Y* corporation in the unpaid face amount of $25,000. *Y* subsequently merged with and into *X* in a transaction qualifying as a reorganization under section 368(a)(1)(A) of the Code. In the merger, *X* transferred solely its stock. *X* received all of *Y*'s assets and assumed all of *Y*'s liabilities. The liabilities assumed included *Y*'s obligation to pay *X* the $25,000 for the *Y* notes, which was also their fair market value. * * *

The statutory merger of *Y* into *X* is a reorganization within the meaning of section 368(a)(1)(A) of the Code. *X* and *Y* are each a party to this reorganization within the meaning of section 368(b) of the Code.

The question presented is whether *Y* should be viewed as transferring a portion of its assets to *X* in satisfaction of its indebtedness on the notes. And, if so viewed, whether any gain or loss realized by *X* or *Y* on the transaction would fall outside of the nonrecognition provisions of sections 361(a) and 1032(a) of the Code. * * *

[T]he extinguishment of the debt in the instant case is incident to the statutory merger because the termination of the debtor-creditor relationship was merely a consequence of *X* and *Y* achieving a readjustment of their corporate structures. Accordingly, sections 357(a) and 361(a) of the Code prevent *Y* from recognizing any gain or loss on the satisfaction of its indebtedness. * * *

However, *X*, the acquiring corporation, will recognize gain on the satisfaction of the indebtedness of *Y* purchased at market discount. Such gain will be $5,000, the difference between the adjusted basis of the notes in the hands of *X* and the face amount of the notes. * * *

In addition, the basis of the assets received in satisfaction of the indebtedness will be determined under section 362(b) of the Code so that such property takes a carryover basis equal to the transferor's basis. * * *

Part E:
Concepts Relating to Treatment of Acquiror

§6.16 Increase Basis by Amount of Transferor's Gain Recognized, Not Its Shareholders' Gain Recognized

Schweitzer & Conrad, Inc. v. Commissioner

Tax Court of the United States, 1940
41 B.T.A. 533

Mellott: [The petitioner, the acquiring corporation, acquired the assets of Illinois, the target, in a (C) reorganization in which Illinois shareholders recognized gain. The issue was whether the petitioner could, under the predecessor of §362(b), increase the basis of Illinois' assets by the amount of such gain.]

Section 113(a)(7) [now §362(b)] of the Revenue Act of 1932, *supra*, provides that the basis of the transferee corporation "shall be the same as it would be in the hands of the transferor, increased in the amount of gain or decreased in the amount of loss recognized to the transferor * * *." Petitioner urges that the word "transferor" should be construed to mean "transferor *or its stockholders* ", and has attempted to show by reference to the legislative history of the section that Congress intended, when it used the word "transferor", to cover both the transferor corporation and its stockholders. * * *

* * * Nonrecognition of gain to the transferor corporation and nonrecognition of gain to both the transferor or transferee corporations are two different things. When the reorganization provisions of the statute provide for the nonrecognition of gain to the transferor, they usually provide a method by which the Government will realize a tax from the transferee. In other words, these provisions merely result in a postponement or deferment of the tax, and not its forfeiture by the Government. Provisions relating to the basis of the transferee, such as section 113(a)(7) [now §362(b)], must be read in this light; and in providing that the basis of the transferee is to be the basis in the hands of the transferor it is apparent that Congress intended that the transferee should take the assets subject to the income tax which might properly have been assessed to the transferor corporation but for the provisions of section 112(d)(1) [now §361]. * * *

Problem

Target corporation, *TC*, has assets with a basis of $10K and a fair market value of $100K. *TC*'s shareholder, *A*, has a basis of $50K for the stock of *TC*. Pursuant to the merger of *TC* into *AC*, *A* receives $75K of *AC* stock and $25K of cash. What is the tax treatment to the parties, and, specifically, what is *AC*'s basis for *TC*'s assets?

Part F:
Concepts Relating to Impact of Stock Dividends and § 306 Preferred Stock in Reorganizations

§ 6.17 Impact of § 305 in the Context of Reorganizations

A. In General

Under §305, which is examined generally in Sec. 2.9, a distribution of a stock dividend in certain circumstances gives rise to taxable dividend treatment. This dividend treatment may arise in the context of reorganizations, particularly if preferred stock is issued with a redemption premium. However, if the preferred stock issued in a reorganization is nonqualified preferred stock, which is treated as boot, the recipient shareholder will have gain under §356 on receipt of the preferred. *See* Sec. 6.12.B. Presumably the recipient would have additional income under §305(c) if the preferred has an unreasonable redemption premium. The ruling in the following section illustrates this §305(c) issue in the context of acquisitive reorganizations. The same principles apply to each form of acquisitive reorganization. *See* Chapters 7 and 8.

B. Illustration of Impact of § 305 in Acquisitive Reorganizations: Redeemable Preferred Issued in a "B" Reorganization

The following ruling deals with the treatment of redemption premiums on preferred stock under § 305(c). Although § 305(c) has been amended to make it parallel with the original issue discount provisions, the principles discussed in the ruling should still apply, certainly with respect to preferred stock that is not nonqualified preferred stock and possibly with respect to nonqualified preferred stock, assuming § 305(c) applies to such stock. Under the amended § 305(c), a premium is reasonable only if it does not exceed the *de minimis* rule of § 1273(a)(3). *See* § 305(c)(1).

Revenue Ruling 81-190
1981-2 C.B. 84

Issue Is the redemption premium reasonable, for purposes of section 305(b)(4) and (c) of the Internal Revenue Code, when a class of stock created for issuance in a reorganization between two widely held corporations is intended to have a 10 percent [now a *de minimis*] redemption premium, but as a result of an unanticipated market fluctuation it actually has a redemption premium in excess of 10 percent of the issue price? * * *

In this situation, there was a redemption premium of only 10 percent at the time the terms of reorganization were agreed to by the managements of *X* and *Y* and at the time the prospectus was submitted to the S.E.C. Moreover, it was reasonably anticipated by an independent advisor possessing relevant expertise that the redemption premium at the time of issue would not exceed 10 percent of the issue price of the preferred stock. The increase in the redemption premium to 21 percent arose from an event that was found not to have been reasonably foreseeable. This event caused the fair market value of the *X* preferred stock to be less on the date of exchange than it was on the date the terms for the transaction were agreed to.

* * * The essential facts are that here: (i) when the agreement was made, a redemption premium in excess of 10 percent was not bargained for, it was not intended that the redemption premium exceed the amount of a typical call premium, and it was not reasonably foreseeable that it would exceed such amount; and (ii) subsequently, when the size of the redemption premium was foreseeable, business constraints made it no longer possible for the terms of the stock to be renegotiated.

Holding The difference between the redemption price and issue price of the *X* preferred stock is a reasonable redemption premium. Therefore, the redemption premium will not be treated as a distribution of property to which section 301 of the Code applies by virtue of the application of section 305(b)(4) and (c).

§6.18 Impact of §306 in the Context of Reorganizations

A. In General

Under §306, preferred stock that does not give rise to dividend treatment under §305 may produce dividend income upon sale. *See* Sec. 2.9. Section 306(c), which defines §306 stock, provides in §306(c)(1)(B) that in certain cases preferred stock issued in a reorganization may be treated as §306 stock. Nonqualified preferred stock is generally treated as boot, *See* Sec. 6.12.B. If the receipt of such stock produces a taxable gain, the stock will presumably not also be §306 stock. The materials in this section introduce this topic and illustrate the application of the rules in acquisitive reorganizations. The principles are the same for each form of acquisitive reorganization. *See* Chapters 7 and 8. In view of the uniform 15% maximum that now applies to capital gains and dividends, §306 has little practical significance.

B. Introduction to §306(c)(1)(B)

Section 306(c)(1)(B) provides that §306 stock includes stock that is not common stock that is received tax free in a reorganization or a §355 distribution, "but only to the extent that either the effect of the transaction was substantially the same as the receipt of a stock dividend, or the stock was received in exchange for section 306 stock." The attribution rules of §318 apply in determining whether the effect of the transaction is substantially the same as the receipt of a stock dividend. *See* §306(c)(4).

Section 1.306-3(d) sets out a cash substitution test for determining whether preferred stock (presumably preferred stock that is not nonqualified preferred) issued in a reorganization or §355 distribution is §306 stock. Section 306 stock arises "if cash received in lieu of [the preferred] would have been a dividend under section 356(a)(2) or would have been treated as a distribution to which section 301 applies by virtue of section 356(b) or section 302(d)." The regulations give the following examples of this provision:

Example (1). Corporation *A*, having only common stock outstanding, is merged in a statutory merger (qualifying as a reorganization under section 368(a)) with Corporation *B*. Pursuant to such merger, the shareholders of Corporation *A* received both common and preferred stock in Corporation *B*. The preferred stock received by such shareholders is section 306 stock.

Example (2). *X* and *Y* each own one-half of the 2,000 outstanding shares of preferred stock and one-half of the 2,000 outstanding shares of common stock of Corporation *C*. Pursuant to a reorganization within the meaning of section 368(a)(1)(E) (recapitalization) each shareholder exchanges his preferred stock for preferred stock of a new issue which is not substantially different from the preferred stock previously held. Unless the preferred stock exchanged was itself section 306 stock the preferred stock received is not section 306 stock.

The first example does not give any reasons for its conclusion that the preferred received in the merger is §306 stock. This regulation may be based on the automatic dividend rule of the *Bedford* case and Rev. Rul. 56-220, both of which have been rejected by *Clark*, Sec. 6.13

C. Illustration of Impact of §306(c)(1)(B) in an Acquisitive Reorganization

Revenue Ruling 88-100
1988-2 C.B. 46

Issue If preferred stock of an acquired corporation that is not "section 306 stock" is exchanged in an acquisitive reorganization for an acquiring corporation's preferred stock of equal value and with terms not substantially different, is the preferred stock issued "section 306 stock" within the meaning of section 306(c)(1)(B) of the Internal Revenue Code? [Note that since this is an exchange of preferred for substantially similar preferred, the newly issued preferred is not nonqualified preferred. *See* §354(a)(1)(C)(i) and Sec. 6.12.B.]

Facts *X*, a publicly held corporation, had outstanding a single class of common stock. *Y*, also a publicly held corporation, had outstanding for many years one class of common stock and one class of preferred stock. None of the *Y* preferred stock was "section 306 stock" within the meaning of section 306(c) of the Code. *A*, an individual, owned ten shares of *Y* common stock and ten shares of *Y* preferred stock, which *A* had held for at least ten years. *A* owned no *X* stock.

Y merged into *X* in a transaction qualifying as a reorganization under section 368(a)(1)(A) of the Code. Each share of *Y* common stock was exchanged for one share of *X* common stock of equal value. Each share of *Y* preferred stock was exchanged for one share of newly issued *X* preferred stock of equal value. The terms of the new *X* preferred stock were not substantially different from those of the *Y* preferred stock. *X* had no plan to redeem its newly issued preferred stock. *A* realized gain on the exchange. *Y* had sufficient earnings and profits so that if *Y* had distributed an amount of cash equal to the value of the *X* preferred stock actually exchanged in the transaction, the cash distribution would have been taxed as a dividend.

Law and Analysis Section 306(c)(1)(B) of the Code provides that the term "section 306 stock" includes stock which is not common stock and which was received pursuant to a tax-free reorganization, but only to the extent that either the effect of the transaction was substantially the same as the receipt of a stock dividend, or the stock was received in exchange for "section 306 stock."

Section 1.306-3(d) of the Income Tax Regulations provides that, ordinarily, "section 306 stock" includes stock which is not common stock received in pursuance of a plan of reorganization if cash received in lieu of such stock would have been treated as a dividend under section 356(a)(2) of the Code or would have been treated as a distribution to which section 301 applies by virtue of section 356(b) or section 302(d).

An exception to the application of the "cash in lieu of" test is provided by *Example (2)* of section 1.306-3(d) of the regulations ("*Example (2)*"). *Example (2)* deals with a recapitalization under section 368(a)(1)(E) of the Code in which preferred stock was exchanged for preferred stock of a new issue. The new stock was not substantially different from the preferred stock previously held. *Example (2)* states that unless the preferred stock exchange was itself "section 306 stock" the preferred stock received is not "section 306 stock." * * *

In the instant situation, the issuance of the *X* preferred stock in exchange for *Y* preferred stock of equal value and with terms not substantially different does not have the effect of the distribution of the earnings and profits of *X* or *Y*. The receipt of *X* preferred stock left the former *Y* preferred shareholders in no better position to convert corporate earnings into capital gains on a disposition of the stock than they had been in before. As the *Y* preferred stock was not "section 306 stock," the *X* preferred stock is not "section 306 stock," pursuant to the exception to the "cash in lieu of" test provided by *Example (2)*. * * *

D. Impact of § 306(b)(4) on § 306(c)(1)(B) Determination: Widely Held Target

Revenue Ruling 89-63

1989-1 C.B. 90

Law and Analysis Section 306(a) of the Code concerns the treatment of the amount realized on the disposition or redemption of section 306 stock (as defined in section 306(c)). Section 306(b)(4) provides in part that section 306(a) shall not apply if it is established to the satisfaction of the Secretary that the distribution and the disposition or redemption of the section 306 stock was not in pursuance of a plan having as one of its principal purposes the avoidance of federal income tax.

In Rev. Rul. 56-116, two widely held corporations, *X* and *Y*, were merged in a reorganization qualifying under section 368(a)(1)(A) of the Code. In the merger, both preferred and common stock of *X* were issued in exchange for the common stock of *Y*. There was a business reason for issuing both preferred and common stock of *X* in exchange for the *Y* common stock. The management of *X* had no intention of redeeming any of the preferred stock issued in connection with the merger, except as required under the provisions of purchase fund and sinking fund agreements.

That ruling holds that the *X* preferred stock issued in connection with the merger is section 306 stock, but it concludes without full explanation that section 306(a)(1) of the Code does not apply to the proceeds of the disposition of such stock, unless the disposition is in anticipation of redemption. * * *

Rev. Rul. 57-212 reasons that Rev. Rul. 56-116 stands for the proposition that section 306(b)(4) of the Code provides relief from section 306(a)(1) on the disposition of section 306 stock issued by a widely held corporation unless the disposition was in anticipation of redemption. * * *

Upon reconsideration, the Service has concluded that the fact that the section 306 stock is issued by a corporation whose stock is widely held is not sufficient grounds for the application of section 306(b)(4) of the Code. Thus, in such circumstances, relief from the provisions of section 306(a) should not be automatic. * * *

Note

If the preferred stock that is issued is nonqualified preferred, the § 306 issue will presumably not be reached, because the recipient will be taxed on receipt of the preferred. Thus, this ruling apparently only applies to preferred that is not nonqualified preferred. The Service should issue advice on the proper application of §§ 305 and 306 to nonqualified preferred issued in reorganization.

Part G:
Concepts Relating to (1) the Overlap between § 351 and Reorganization Provisions, and (2) the E and F Reorganizations

§ 6.19 Survey of Issues Involving Overlap with § 351

A. Incorporation in Anticipation of Reorganization

Revenue Ruling 70-140
1970-1 C.B. 73

Advice has been requested whether the provisions of section 351 of the Internal Revenue Code of 1954 apply to the transfer of property under the circumstances described below.

All the outstanding stock of X corporation was owned by A, an individual. A also operated a similar business in the form of a sole proprietorship on the accrual basis of reporting income. Pursuant to an agreement between A and Y, an unrelated corporation, A transferred all the assets of the sole proprietorship to X in exchange for additional shares of X stock. A then transferred all his X stock to Y solely in exchange for voting common stock of Y, which was widely held. * * *

Section 368(a)(1)(B) of the Code provides, in part, that the term reorganization includes the acquisition by one corporation, in exchange solely for all or a part of its voting stock, of stock of another corporation if, immediately after the acquisition, the acquiring corporation has control of such other corporation.

The two steps of the transaction described above were part of a prearranged integrated plan and may not be considered independently of each other for Federal income tax purposes. The receipt by A of the additional stock of X in exchange for the sole proprietorship assets is transitory and without substance for tax purposes since it is apparent that the assets of the sole proprietorship were transferred to X for the purpose of enabling Y to acquire such assets without the recognition of gain to A.

Section 351 of the Code is not applicable to the transfer of the sole proprietorship assets to *Y* inasmuch as *A* was not in control of *Y* immediately after the transfer. The sole proprietorship cannot be a party to a reorganization within the meaning of section 368(b) of the Code. Thus, the transfer of the sole proprietorship assets to *X* is treated as a sale by *A* of the assets to *Y* followed by a transfer of these assets by *Y* to the capital of *X*.

Accordingly, that portion of the stock of *Y* received by *A* equal to the fair market value of the sole proprietorship assets is treated as an amount received from the sale of those assets. Gain or loss is recognized to *A* as provided in sections 1001 and 1002 of the Code. The exchange by *A* of all the outstanding stock of *X*, solely for voting common stock of *Y*, other than the *Y* stock received in payment for the sole proprietorship assets, is a reorganization within the meaning of section 368(a)(1)(B) of the Code.

B. Use of § 351 to Preserve Separate Existences of Target and Acquiror

Revenue Ruling 76-123

1976-1 C.B. 94

Advice has been requested concerning the treatment for Federal income tax purposes of the transaction described below.

Individual *A* owned all the stock of *X* corporation, which was incorporated in State *O*. Individual *B*, who is unrelated to *A*, owned all the stock of *Y* corporation, which was incorporated in State *P*. *A* and *B* determined that the businesses operated by *X* and *Y* could be improved if their interests in *X* and *Y* were combined while at the same time preserving the separate corporate existence of *X* and *Y*. *A* and *B* also decided that the laws of State *P* were more favorable to the operation of the combined enterprise. To carry out their plan, *A* and *B* transferred all of their stock in *X* and *Y* to a newly organized corporation, *Z*, incorporated in State *P*, in exchange for, respectively, 60 percent and 40 percent of all of the outstanding stock of *Z*. In addition, *B* received from *Z* 10x dollars in cash. The consideration received by *A* and *B* was in each case equal to the fair market value of the stock exchanged. As part of this plan, *X* then distributed all of its assets to *Z* in complete liquidation, and *Y* remained as a wholly owned subsidiary of *Z*.

Section 351(a) of the Internal Revenue Code of 1954 provides, in general, for the nonrecognition of gain or loss on the transfer by one or more persons of property to a corporation solely in exchange for stock or securities in such corporation if, immediately after the exchange, such person or persons are in control of the corporation to which the property was transferred.

Section 351(c) of the Code provides that, for purposes of determining control under section 351, the fact that any corporate transferor distributes part or all of the stock that it receives in the exchange to its shareholders holders will not be taken into account.

Section 351(b) of the Code provides, in part, that if section 351(a) would apply to an exchange but for the fact that money is received in addition to the stock received, then any gain recognized will not exceed the amount of money received. Section 368(c) of the Code provides that the term "control" means the ownership of stock possessing at least 80 percent of the total combined voting power of all classes of stock entitled to vote and at least 80 percent of the total number of shares of each of the other classes of stock of the corporation.

Section 368(a)(1)(B) of the Code provides, in part, that the term "reorganization" means the acquisition by one corporation, in exchange solely for shares of its voting stock, of the outstanding stock of another corporation if, immediately after the transaction, the acquiring corporation has control of such other corporation.

Section 368(a)(1)(C) of the Code provides, in part, that a reorganization is the acquisition by one corporation, in exchange solely for all or a part of its voting stock, of substantially all of the properties of another corporation, but in determining whether the exchange is solely for stock, the assumption by the acquiring corporation of a liability of the other, or the fact that property acquired is subject to a liability, is disregarded.

In Rev. Rul. 67-274, 1967-2 C.B. 141, Sec. 7.3.B. a corporation, pursuant to a plan of reorganization, acquired all the outstanding stock of another corporation from the shareholders in exchange for voting stock of the acquiring corporation and thereafter, as part of the same plan, the acquiring corporation completely liquidated the acquired corporation. Rev. Rul. 67-274 holds that under these circumstances the acquisition of the stock of the acquired corporation and its liquidation by the acquiring corporation are part of the overall plan of reorganization and may not be considered independently of each other for Federal income tax purposes. Rev. Rul. 67-274 concludes that the transaction is not an acquisition of the stock of the acquired corporation qualifying as a reorganization under section 368(a)(1)(B) of the Code but is an acquisition of the assets of the acquired corporation qualifying as a reorganization under section 368(a)(1)(C).

Rev. Rul. 68-357, 1968-2 C.B. 144, holds that section 351 of the Code applies where, as part of an overall plan to consolidate the operations of five businesses, an individual and three corporations transfer property to a corporation that they control immediately after the transfers within the meaning of section 368(c) even though the transfers of property by the corporations are reorganizations within the meaning of section 368(a)(1)(C).

The transfer by A of A's X stock to Z and, as part of the overall transaction, the liquidation of X by Z are interdependent steps in an overall reorganization plan the substance of which is treated for Federal income tax purposes as an acquisition by Z of all of the assets of X solely in exchange for Z voting stock in a transaction qualifying as a reorganization under section 368(a)(1)(C) of the Code, followed by a distribution by X of the Z stock to A in exchange for all of A's X stock. Accordingly, no gain or loss is recognized by X upon the exchange of its property solely for Z stock as provided by section 361(a), and no gain or loss is recognized to A on the exchange of A's X stock solely for voting stock of Z as provided in section 354(a).

Furthermore, the transfer by *X* of its property to *Z* in liquidation and the transfer by *B* of *B's* *Y* stock to *Z* is a transaction within the provisions of section 351(a) of the Code since *X* and *B* are in control of *Z* immediately after the exchanges within the meaning of section 368(c). Pursuant to section 351(c) the distribution by *X* of the *Z* stock to *A* does not violate the control requirement of section 368(c). Accordingly, no loss is recognized to *B* and no gain is recognized to *B* in excess of the 10x dollars received by *B*, as provided in section 351(b), upon the exchange of *B's* *Y* stock solely for cash and voting stock of *Z*. See Rev. Rul. 68-357.

Rev. Rul. 68-349, 1968-2 C.B. 143, holds that the transfer of property by an individual to a newly formed corporation does not qualify under section 351 of the Code where another corporation simultaneously transfers all of its property to the new corporation for the purpose of qualifying the individual's transfer under section 351. Rev. Rul. 68-349 states that the organization of the new corporation is considered under the circumstances to be merely a continuation of the transferor corporation. Rev. Rul. 68-349 is distinguishable from the instant case in that *Z* was not employed solely for the purpose of enabling *B* to transfer *B's* *Y* stock without the recognition of gain and was not merely a continuation of *X*. *Z* was organized to enable *X* to be reincorporated in State *P*. Further, the transfer by *B* of his *Y* stock to *Z* effected the combination of *A's* and *B's* former business interests in the form of affiliated corporations.

Rev. Rul. 68-349 is distinguished.

C. Combination Triangular Reorganization and Purported §351: Determination of Control

Revenue Ruling 84-44

1984-1 C.B. 105

Issue Under the facts described below, does section 351 of the Internal Revenue Code apply to the transfer of assets from *Y* to *P* in exchange for *P* stock?

Facts *X*, *Y* and *P* were unrelated corporations. In a transaction qualifying as a reorganization under sections 368(a)(1)(A) and (a)(2)(D) of the Code, *X* was merged into *S*, a wholly owned subsidiary of *P*. In the transaction, the shareholders of *X* received shares of *P* stock in exchange for their shares of *X* stock. At the same time, as part of an overall plan, *Y* transferred part (but less than substantially all) of its assets to *P* in exchange for *P* stock. While *Y* did not have the requisite control of *P* to qualify its transfer of assets within the provisions of section 351, *Y* together with the former shareholders of *X* were in control of *P* within the meaning of section 368(c) of the Code.

Law and Analysis Section 368(a)(2)(D) of the Code provides that the acquisition by one corporation, in exchange for stock of a corporation which is in control of the acquiring corporation, of substantially all of the properties of another corporation shall not disqualify the transaction under section 368(a)(1)(A) if no stock of the acquiring corporation is used in the transaction and the transaction would have qualified as a reorganization under section 368(a)(1)(A) had the merger been into the controlling corporation.

Section 351(a) of the Code provides that no gain or loss will be recognized if property is transferred to a corporation solely in exchange for its stock and immediately after the exchange the transferors are in control of the corporation (as defined in section 368(c)).

Although *P* stock was used as the consideration in the merger of *X* into *S*, the shareholders of *X* did not transfer any property to *P*. Therefore, since *P* is not the transferee of the stock of *X*, the *P* stock received by the shareholders of *X* is not taken into account with the *P* stock received by *Y* in determining whether the requirements of section 351 of the Code have been met. The only assets received by *P* were transferred by *Y*, and since *Y* was not in control of *P* immediately after the transfer, the transaction does not qualify under section 351. Additionally, since *P* is not the transferee of the *X* assets, the receipt of *P* stock by *X* upon the transfer of its assets to *S* cannot be aggregated with the *P* stock received by *Y* in determining whether the 80 percent control requirement of section 351 could be met by *X* and *Y*.

The instant case should be compared with Rev. Rul. 68-357, 1968-2 C.B. 144, and Rev. Rul. 76-123, 1976-1 C.B. 94. In those rulings, stock received by individual transferors was aggregated with stock received in reorganizations for purposes of the control requirement of section 351 of the Code when the transfers were to the same corporation.

Holding Since the control requirement of section 351 of the Code was not met by *Y*, any gain or loss realized by *Y* on the exchange will be recognized as provided by section 1001 of the Code. No gain or loss is recognized to *P* under section 1032(a) upon the exchange with *Y* of *P* stock for assets of *Y*.

Effect on Other Revenue Ruling Rev. Rul. 68-357 and Rev. Rul. 76-123 are distinguished.

D. Use of § 351 to Avoid Continuity of Interest Requirements

Revenue Ruling 84-71

1984-2 C.B. 106

The Internal Revenue Service has reconsidered Rev. Rul. 80-284, 1980-2 C.B. 117, and Rev. Rul. 80-285, 1980-2 C.B. 119, in which transfers that satisfied the technical requirements of section 351(a) of the Internal Revenue Code were nevertheless held to constitute taxable exchanges because they were part of larger acquisitive transactions that did not meet the continuity of interest test generally applicable to acquisitive reorganizations.

In Rev. Rul. 80-284, fourteen percent of *T* corporation's stock was held by *A*, president and chairman of the board, and eighty-six percent by the public. *P*, an unrelated, publicly held corporation wished to purchase the stock of *T*. All the *T* stockholders except *A* were willing to sell the *T* stock for cash. *A* wished to avoid recognition of gain.

In order to accommodate these wishes, the following transactions were carried out as part of an overall plan. *First, P* and *A* formed a new corporation, *S.P.* transferred cash and other property to *S* in exchange solely for all of *S*'s common stock; *A* transferred *T* stock to *S* solely in exchange for all *S*'s preferred stock. These transfers were intended to be tax-free under section 351 of the Code. *Second, S* organized a new corporation, *D,* and transferred to *D* the cash it had received from *P* in exchange for all the *D* common stock. *Third, D* was merged into *T* under state law. As a result of the merger, each share of *T* stock, except those shares held by *S,* were surrendered for cash equal to the stock's fair market value and each share of *D* stock was converted into *T* stock.

Rev. Rul. 80-284 concluded that if a purported section 351 exchange is an integral part of a larger transaction that fits a pattern common to acquisitive reorganizations, and if the continuity of shareholder interest requirement of section 1.368-1(b) of the Income Tax Regulations is not satisfied with respect to the larger transaction, then the transaction as a whole resembles a sale and the exchange cannot qualify under section 351 because that section is not intended to apply to sales. Rev. Rul. 80-285 reached a similar conclusion with respect to an asset, rather than stock, acquisition in which a purported section 351 exchange was also part of a larger acquisitive transaction.

Upon reconsideration, the Service has concluded that the fact that "larger acquisitive transactions," such as those described in Rev. Rul. 80-284 and Rev. Rul. 80-285, fail to meet the requirements for tax-free treatment under the reorganization provisions of the Code does not preclude the applicability of section 351(a) to transfers that may be described as part of such larger transactions, but also, either alone or in conjunction with other transfers, meet the requirements of section 351(a).

Effect on Other Revenue Rulings Rev. Rul. 80-284 and Rev. Rul. 80-285 are revoked.

E. Use of § 351 in Acquisition of Publicly-Held Corporation in a Compulsive § 351

Normally § 351 is utilized in the formation of small closely-held corporations. As Rev. Rul. 74-502, Sec. 2.2.C., illustrates, § 351 also may be used in the acquisition of a publicly-held target firm.

F. Use of § 351 in Horizontal Double Dummy

Section 351, which provides for tax-free treatment on certain transfers of property to a corporation in exchange for stock, is discussed in Chapter 7. Section 351 can also be used (as a substitute for a reorganization) in effectuating certain tax-free acquisitions. In one form of acquisitive Section 351 transaction the shareholders of a target corporation transfer their stock in the target to a newly formed holding company in exchange for common stock of the holding company. Simultaneously the shareholders of the acquiror transfer their stock in the acquiror to the holding company in exchange for common stock of the holding company. The shareholders of the acquiror end up with more than 50% of the stock of the holding company, but together the shareholders of the target and the acquiror must own at least 80% of the stock of the holding company. The transaction may be effectuated by causing the holding company to form two subs and have one of the subs merge into the acquiror while the other sub merges into the target in two reverse subsidiary mergers with the shareholders of the target and acquiror receiving stock of the holding company. This is known as the "horizontal double dummy" and was used in the 2005 acquisition by Oracle of Seibel. This transaction can be diagramed as follows:

Acquisitive Section 351 Transaction

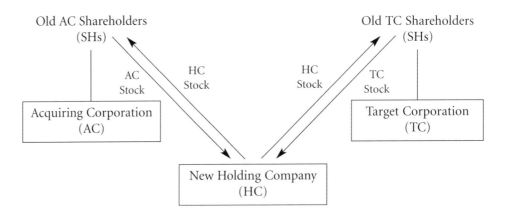

When the Dust Settles

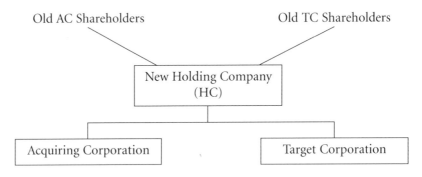

In this transaction the shareholders of target and acquiror receive nonrecognition under Section 351 and take a substituted basis for their holding company shares under Section 358. Holding company has nonrecognition under Section 1032 and takes a carryover basis for the stock of target and acquiror under Section 362. The tax attributes of both the acquiror and the target continue, and unless the shareholders of target are in control of the holding company, the target's NOLs are limited by Section 382.

Although there is no revenue ruling directly on point, the conclusion that the transaction falls within §351 can reasonably be deduced from the following authorities: Rev. Rul. 73-123, Sec. 6.19.B.; Rev. Rul. 84-44, Sec. 6.19.C.; and Rev. Rul. 84-71, Sec. 6.19.D.

G. The Triple Drop and Check, Two 351s Followed by a Nondivisive (D) Reorganization, Rev. Rul. 2015-10

Rev. Rul. 2015-10

Internal Revenue Bulletin: 2015-21 (May 26, 2015)

ISSUE

Is a transaction in which (1) a parent corporation transfers all of the interests in its limited liability company that is taxable as a corporation to its subsidiary (first subsidiary) in exchange for additional stock, (2) the first subsidiary transfers all of the interests in the limited liability company to its subsidiary (second subsidiary) in exchange for additional stock, (3) the second subsidiary transfers all of the interests in the limited liability company to its subsidiary (third subsidiary) in exchange for additional stock, and (4) the limited liability company elects to be disregarded as an entity separate from its owner for federal income tax purposes effective after it is owned by the third subsidiary, properly treated for federal income tax purposes as two transfers of stock in exchanges governed by § 351 of the Internal Revenue Code (Code) followed by a reorganization under § 368(a)(1)(D) of the Code?

FACTS

P, a domestic corporation, owns all of the interests in LLC, a domestic limited liability company that elected pursuant to § 301.7701-3(c) of the Procedure and Administration Regulations to be an association taxable as a corporation for federal income tax purposes effective on its date of formation. P also owns all of the stock of S1. S1 owns all of the stock of S2, which owns all of the stock of S3. S3 owns all of the stock of S4. S1, S2, and S3 are each holding companies that are domestic corporations. For valid business purposes, and as part of a plan:

(a) P will transfer all of the interests in LLC to S1 in exchange for additional shares of voting common stock of S1 (P's transfer).

(b) S1 will transfer all of the interests in LLC to S2 in exchange for additional shares of voting common stock of S2 (S1's transfer).

(c) S2 will transfer all of the interests in LLC to S3 in exchange for additional shares of voting common stock of S3 (S2's transfer).

(d) LLC will elect pursuant to § 301.7701-3(c) to be disregarded as an entity separate from its owner for federal income tax purposes, effective no sooner than one day after S2's transfer (LLC's election).

Following the transaction, S3 will, through LLC, continue to conduct the business conducted by LLC prior to the transaction.

LAW

Section 351(a) provides that no gain or loss will be recognized if property is transferred to a corporation by one or more persons solely in exchange for stock in such corporation and immediately after the exchange such person or persons are in control (as defined in § 368(c)) of the corporation.

Section 368(c) defines "control" to mean the ownership of stock possessing at least 80 percent of the total combined voting power of all classes of stock entitled to vote and at least 80 percent of the total number of shares of all other classes of stock of the corporation.

Section 301.7701-3(a) provides that a business entity that is not classified as a corporation under § 301.7701-2(b)(1), (3), (4), (5), (6), (7), or (8) (eligible entity) can elect its classification for federal income tax purposes. An eligible entity with at least two members can elect pursuant to § 301.7701-3(c) to be classified as either an association (and thus a corporation under § 301.7701-2(b)(2)) or a partnership, and an eligible entity with a single owner can elect to be classified as an association or to be disregarded as an entity separate from its owner.

Section 301.7701-3(g)(1)(iii) provides that if an eligible entity classified as an association elects pursuant to § 301.7701-3(c) to be disregarded as an entity separate from its owner, the following is deemed to occur: the association distributes all of its assets and liabilities to its single owner in liquidation of the association.

Section 301.7701-3(g)(2)(i) provides that the tax treatment of a change in the classification of an entity for federal income tax purposes by an election pursuant to § 301.7701-3(c) is determined under all relevant provisions of the Internal Revenue Code and general principles of tax law, including the step transaction doctrine.

Section 368(a)(1)(D) provides that the term "reorganization" includes a transfer by a corporation of all or a part of its assets to another corporation if immediately after the transfer the transferor, or one or more of its shareholders (including persons who were shareholders immediately before the transfer), or any combination thereof, is in control of the corporation to which the assets are transferred; but only if, in pursuance of the plan, stock or securities of the corporation to which the assets are transferred are distributed in a transaction which qualifies under § 354, 355, or 356.

Section 354(a) provides, in general, that no gain or loss will be recognized if stock or securities in a corporation a party to a reorganization are, in pursuance of the plan of reorganization, exchanged solely for stock or securities in such corporation or in another corporation a party to the reorganization.

Section 368(b)(2) provides that "a party to a reorganization" includes both corporations, in the case of a reorganization resulting from the acquisition by one corporation of stock or property of the other.

Section 354(b)(1) provides, in general, that § 354(a) will not apply to an exchange in pursuance of a plan of reorganization under § 368(a)(1)(D) unless (A) the corporation to which the assets are transferred acquires substantially all of the assets of the transferor of such assets; and (B) the stock, securities, and other properties received by such transferor, as well as the other properties of such transferor, are distributed in pursuance of the plan of reorganization.

Section 368(a)(2)(H) provides that for purposes of determining whether a nondivisive transaction qualifies under § 368(a)(1)(D), the term "control" has the meaning given such term by § 304(c).

Section 304(c)(1) provides that "control" means the ownership of stock possessing at least 50 percent of the total combined voting power of all classes of stock entitled to vote, or at least 50 percent of the total value of shares of all classes of stock. If a person (or persons) is in control (within the meaning of the preceding sentence) of a corporation, which in turn owns at least 50 percent of the total combined voting power of all stock entitled to vote of another corporation or owns at least 50 percent of the total value of the shares of all classes of stock of another corporation, then such person (or persons) will be treated as in control of such other corporation.

Section 304(c)(3) provides, in part, that § 318(a) relating to constructive ownership of stock will apply for purposes of determining control under § 304 and that paragraph (2)(C) of § 318(a) will be applied by substituting "5 percent" for "50 percent."

As modified by § 304(c)(3), § 318(a)(2)(C) provides that if 5 percent or more in value of the stock in a corporation is owned, directly or indirectly, by or for any person, such person will be considered as owning the stock owned, directly or indirectly, by or for such corporation, in that proportion which the value of the stock such person so owns bears to the value of all the stock in such corporation.

In Rev. Rul. 67-274, 1967-2 C.B. 141, pursuant to a plan of reorganization, corporation Y acquired all of the stock of corporation X in exchange for voting stock of Y. Thereafter, X completely liquidated into Y. The ruling concludes that the two steps will not constitute a reorganization under § 368(a)(1)(B) followed by a liquidation under § 332, but instead will be considered a single acquisition of X's assets in a reorganization under § 368(a)(1)(C).

ANALYSIS

A transfer of property may be respected as a § 351 exchange even if it is followed by subsequent transfers of the property as part of a prearranged, integrated plan. See Rev. Rul. 77-449, 1977-2 C.B. 110, amplified by Rev. Rul. 83-34, 1983-1 C.B. 79, and Rev. Rul. 83-156, 1983-2 C.B. 66; see also Rev. Rul. 2003-51, 2003-1 C.B. 938. However, a transfer of property in an exchange otherwise described in § 351 will not qualify as a § 351 exchange if, for example, a different treatment is warranted to reflect the substance of the transaction as a whole. See Rev. Rul. 54-96, 1954-1 C.B. 111; Rev. Rul. 70-140, 1970-1 C.B. 73.

Under the facts of this revenue ruling, even though P's transfer is part of a series of transactions undertaken as part of a prearranged, integrated plan involving successive transfers of the LLC interests, P's transfer satisfies the formal requirements of § 351, including the requirement that P control S1 within the meaning of § 368(c) immediately after the exchange, and an analysis of the transaction as a whole does not dictate that P's transfer be treated other than in accordance with its form in order to reflect the substance of the transaction. Accordingly, P's transfer is respected as a § 351 exchange, and no gain or loss is recognized by P. Similarly, § 351 applies to S1's transfer, and no gain or loss is recognized by S1.

With regard to S2's transfer and LLC's election, if an acquiring corporation acquires all of the stock of a target corporation in an exchange otherwise qualifying as a § 351 exchange, and as part of a prearranged, integrated plan, the target corporation thereafter transfers its assets to the acquiring corporation in liquidation, the transaction is more properly characterized as a reorganization under § 368(a)(1)(D), to the extent it so qualifies. See Rev. Rul. 67-274; see also Rev. Rul. 2004-83, 2004-2 C.B. 157. Accordingly, under the circumstances described above, S2's transfer and LLC's election are more properly characterized as a reorganization under § 368(a)(1)(D) than as a § 351 exchange followed by a § 332 liquidation.

HOLDING

A transaction in which (1) a parent corporation transfers all of the interests in its limited liability company that is taxable as a corporation to the first subsidiary in exchange for additional stock, (2) the first subsidiary transfers all of the interests in the limited liability company to the second subsidiary in exchange for additional stock, (3) the second subsidiary transfers all of the interests in the limited liability company to the third subsidiary in exchange for additional stock, and (4) the limited liability company elects to be disregarded as an entity separate from its owner for federal income tax purposes effective after it is owned by the third subsidiary, is properly treated for federal income tax purposes as two transfers of stock in exchanges governed by § 351 followed by a reorganization under § 368(a)(1)(D).

Note

See also, Rev. Rul. 2015-9, I.R.B. 2015-21 (May 26, 2015), which addressed the following issue, which is similar to the issue in Rev. Rul. 2015-10 above:

ISSUE

Is a transaction in which (1) a domestic corporation transfers all of the stock of its foreign operating subsidiary to its foreign holding company subsidiary in exchange for additional stock, (2) the foreign operating subsidiary and three foreign subsidiaries of the foreign holding company transfer substantially all of their assets to a newly-formed foreign subsidiary of the foreign holding company in exchange for stock of the new subsidiary, and (3) the subsidiaries that transfer their assets are liquidated, properly treated for federal income tax purposes as a transfer of the foreign operating subsidiary's stock in an exchange governed by § 351 of the Internal Revenue Code (Code) followed by reorganizations under § 368(a)(1)(D) of the Code? * * *

The ruling holds:

HOLDING

A transaction in which (1) a domestic corporation transfers all of the stock of its foreign operating subsidiary to its foreign holding company subsidiary in exchange for additional stock, (2) the foreign operating subsidiary and three foreign subsidiaries of the foreign holding company transfer substantially all of their assets to a newly-formed foreign subsidiary of the foreign holding company in exchange for stock of the new subsidiary, and (3) the subsidiaries that transfer their assets are liquidated, is properly treated for federal income tax purposes as a transfer of the foreign operating subsidiary's stock in an exchange governed by § 351 followed by reorganizations under § 368(a)(1)(D).

§ 6.20 Survey of Issues Involving the E, Recapitalization, and F, Mere Change in Form Reorganizations

A. No Continuity of Interest or Continuity of Business Enterprise in an E or F Reorganization

Preamble to Final Regulations Eliminating Continuity of Interest and of Business Enterprise for E and F Reorganizations

Treasury Decision 9182, February 25, 2005

SUMMARY: This document contains final regulations regarding reorganizations under section 368(a)(1)(E) and section 368(a)(1)(F) of the Internal Revenue Code. The regulations affect corporations and their shareholders.

BACKGROUND AND EXPLANATION OF PROVISIONS. * * *

Generally, a transaction must satisfy the continuity of interest and continuity of business enterprise requirements to qualify as a reorganization under section 368(a). The notice proposed amending § 1.368-1(b) to provide that a continuity of interest and a continuity of business enterprise are not required for a transaction to qualify as a reorganization under section 368(a)(1)(E) (E reorganization) or section 368(a)(1)(F) (F reorganization). The notice also proposed amending § 1.368-2 to include rules regarding the requirements for a transaction to qualify as an F reorganization and regarding the effects of an F reorganization.

The IRS and Treasury Department have received oral comments urging that the rule providing that the continuity of interest and continuity of business enterprise requirements do not apply to E and F reorganizations be finalized quickly. For the reasons expressed in the preamble to the proposed regulations, this Treasury decision adopts that rule for transactions on or after February 25, 2005. The IRS and Treasury Department continue to study the other issues addressed in the notice of proposed rulemaking, and welcomes further comment on those issues.

EFFECT ON OTHER DOCUMENTS

The following publications are obsolete as of February 25, 2005: Rev. Rul. 69-516 (1969-2 C.B. 56); Rev. Rul. 77-415 (1977-2 C.B. 311); Rev. Rul. 77-479 (1977-2 C.B. 119); and Rev. Rul. 82-34 (1982-1 C.B. 59).

B. 2015 Final Regulations on the F Reorganization

Reorganizations under Section 368(a)(1)(F); Section 367(a) and Certain Reorganizations under Section 368(a)(1)(F)

Treasury Decision 9739, October 13, 2015

SUMMARY: This document contains final regulations that provide guidance regarding the qualification of a transaction as a corporate reorganization under section

368(a)(1)(F) by virtue of being a mere change of identity, form, or place of organization of one corporation (F reorganization). This document also contains final regulations relating to F reorganizations in which the transferor corporation is a domestic corporation and the acquiring corporation is a foreign corporation (an outbound F reorganization) [*See* Chapter 10.] These regulations will affect corporations engaging in transactions that could qualify as F reorganizations (including outbound F reorganizations) and their shareholders. * * *

Background

Introduction

This Treasury decision contains final regulations (the Final Regulations) that amend 26 CFR part 1 under sections 367 and 368 of the Internal Revenue Code (Code). These Final Regulations provide guidance relating to the qualification of transactions as F reorganizations and the treatment of outbound F reorganizations.

In general, upon the exchange of property, gain or loss must be recognized if the new property differs materially, in kind or extent, from the old property. See § 1.1001-1(a); § 1.368-1(b). The purpose of the reorganization provisions of the Code is to except from the general rule of section 1001 certain specifically described exchanges that are required by business exigencies and effect only a readjustment of continuing interests in property under modified corporate forms. See § 1.368-1(b). These exchanges, described in sections 354, 356, and 361, must be made in pursuance of a plan of reorganization. See § 1.368-1(c).

Section 368(a)(1) describes several types of transactions that constitute reorganizations. One of these, described in section 368(a)(1)(F), is "a mere change in identity, form, or place of organization of one corporation, however effected" (a Mere Change). One court has described the F reorganization as follows:

[The F reorganization] encompass[es] only the simplest and least significant of corporate changes. The (F)-type reorganization presumes that the surviving corporation is the same corporation as the predecessor in every respect, except for minor or technical differences. For instance, the (F) reorganization typically has been understood to comprehend only such insignificant modifications as the reincorporation of the same corporate business with the same assets and the same stockholders surviving under a new charter either in the same or in a different State, the renewal of a corporate charter having a limited life, or the conversion of a U.S.-chartered savings and loan association to a State-chartered institution.

Although the statutory description of an F reorganization is short, and courts have described F reorganizations as simple, questions have arisen regarding the requirements of F reorganizations. In particular, when a corporation changes its identity, form, or place of incorporation, questions have arisen as to what other changes (if any) may occur, either before, during, or after the Mere Change, without affecting the status of the Mere Change (that is, what other changes are compatible with the Mere Change). These questions can become more pronounced if the transaction intended to qualify as an F reorganization is composed of a series of steps occurring over a period of days or weeks. Moreover, changes in identity, form, or place of organization are often undertaken to facilitate other changes that are difficult to effect in the corporation's current form or place of organization. * * *

Mere Change * * *

Like other types of reorganizations, an F reorganization generally involves, in form, two corporations, one (a Transferor Corporation) that transfers (or is deemed to transfer) assets to the other (a Resulting Corporation). However, the statute describes an F reorganization as being with respect to "one corporation" and provides for treatment that differs from that accorded other types of reorganizations in which assets are transferred from one corporation to another (Asset Reorganizations). "[A]n F reorganization is treated for most purposes of the Code as if the reorganized corporation were the same entity as the corporation in existence before the reorganization." Thus, the tax treatment accorded an F reorganization is more consistent with that of a single continuing corporation in that (1) the taxable year of the Transferor Corporation does not close and includes the operations of the Resulting Corporation for the remainder of the year [see § 381(b) and (b)(1)], and (2) the Resulting Corporation's losses may be carried back to taxable years of the Transferor Corporation [see § 381(b) and (b)(3)].

Because an F reorganization must involve "one corporation," and continuation of the taxable year and loss carrybacks from the Resulting Corporation to the Transferor Corporation are allowed, the statute cannot accommodate transactions in which the Resulting Corporation has preexisting activities or tax attributes. See H. Rep. Conf. Rep't. 97-760, 97th Cong., 2d Sess., at pp. 540–41 (1982). Accordingly, the 2004 Proposed Regulations did not allow for more than *de minimis* activities or very limited assets or tax attributes in the Resulting Corporation from sources other than the Transferor Corporation. This is one of the principal distinctions between F reorganizations and Asset Reorganizations. The proposed rule was consistent with the historical interpretation of the statute in this regard. * * *

Explanation of Revisions * * *

[T]he Final Regulations are based on the premise that it is appropriate to treat the Resulting Corporation in an F reorganization as the functional equivalent of the Transferor Corporation and to give its corporate enterprise roughly the same freedom of action as would be accorded a corporation that remains within its original corporate shell. The Final Regulations provide that a transaction that involves an actual or deemed transfer of property by a Transferor Corporation to a Resulting Corporation is a Mere Change that qualifies as an F reorganization if six requirements are satisfied (with certain exceptions). * * *

The F Reorganization Requirements and Certain Exceptions

[First Two Requirement:] Resulting Corporation Stock Issuances and Identity of Stock Ownership

[T]he *first* and the *second* requirements of the Final Regulations reflect the Supreme Court's holding in *Helvering v. Southwest Consolidated Corp*, supra, that a transaction that shifts the ownership of the proprietary interests in a corporation cannot qualify as a Mere Change. Thus, the Final Regulations provide that a transaction that involves the introduction of a new shareholder or new equity capital into the corporation "in the bubble" does not qualify as an F reorganization. * * *

[T]he first requirement in the Final Regulations is that immediately after the Potential F Reorganization, all the stock of the Resulting Corporation must have been distributed (or deemed distributed) in exchange for stock of the Transferor Corporation in the Potential F Reorganization. * * *

[T]he *second* requirement is that, subject to certain exceptions, the same person or persons own all the stock of the Transferor Corporation at the beginning of the Potential F Reorganization and all of the stock of the Resulting Corporation at the end of the Potential F Reorganization, in identical proportions.

Notwithstanding these requirements and also consistent with the Proposed Regulations, the Final Regulations allow the Resulting Corporation to issue a *de minimis* amount of stock not in respect of stock of the Transferor Corporation, to facilitate the organization or maintenance of the Resulting Corporation. * * *

[Third and Fourth Requirements] Resulting Corporation's Assets or Attributes and Liquidation of Transferor Corporation

[T]he *third* requirement (limiting the assets and attributes of the Resulting Corporation immediately before the transaction) and the *fourth* requirement (requiring the liquidation of the Transferor Corporation) * * * reflect the statutory mandate that an F reorganization involve only one corporation. Although the Final Regulations generally require the Resulting Corporation not to hold any property or have any tax attributes immediately before the Potential F Reorganization, * * *, the Resulting Corporation is allowed to hold a *de minimis* amount of assets to facilitate its organization or preserve its existence (and to have tax attributes related to these assets), and the Resulting Corporation is allowed to hold proceeds of borrowings undertaken in connection with the Potential F Reorganization. * * *

[Fifth Requirement] One Section 381(a) Acquiring Corporation, One Section 381(a) Transferor Corporation

The *fifth* requirement under the Final Regulations is that immediately after the Potential F Reorganization, no corporation other than the Resulting Corporation may hold property that was held by the Transferor Corporation immediately before the Potential F Reorganization, if such other corporation would, as a result, succeed to and take into account the items of the transferor corporation described in section 381(c). * * *

Chapter 7

Tax-Free Asset Acquisitions: The (A) Reorganization, the Forward Subsidiary Merger Reorganization, the Straight and Triangular (C) Reorganizations; Including Treatment of Net Operating Losses

§7.1 Scope

This chapter deals with the various types of asset reorganizations, that is, transactions in which an acquiring corporation or a subsidiary of the acquiring corporation acquires either directly or by merger the assets of a target corporation in exchange for stock of the acquiring corporation. Sec. 7.2 addresses the straight (A) reorganization under §368(a)(1)(A) in which the target mergers directly into the acquiring corporation. Sec. 7.3 deals with the straight (C) reorganization under §368(a)(1)(C) in which the acquiring corporation acquires the assets of the target in exchange for voting stock of the acquiring corporation. Sec. 7.4 examines the triangular (C) under §368(a)(1)(C) in which a subsidiary of the acquiring corporation acquires the assets of a target corporation in exchange for stock of its parent. Sec. 7.5 sets out the representations required by the Service in a private letter ruling request on a straight or triangular (C) reorganization. Sec. 7.6 deals with the forward subsidiary merger under §368(a)(2)(D) in which a target corporation merges into a subsidiary of the acquiring corporation. Sec. 7.7 presents summary problems on these forms of asset reorganizations.

Sec. 7.8 deals with the carryover rules under §381. Sec. 7.9 examines the impact of §382 on the utilization of a target's net operating losses. Sec. 7.10 deals with the impact of the consolidated return regulations on the use of a target's net operating losses, and Sec. 7.11 addresses the impact of §269 on the utilization of such losses. Sec. 7.12 deals with the impact of §384 on the ability of an acquiring loss corporation to offset its losses against the income of a profitable target. Sec. 7.13 presents summary problems on the utilization of NOLs after an asset reorganization.

Finally, to illustrate a forward subsidiary merger, which is the most common of these asset reorganizations, Sec. 7.14 contains excerpts from the merger agreement

411

pursuant to which British Telcom (BT), a publicly held U.K. company, was going to acquire MCI, a publicly held U.S. target. In this transaction, which was aborted, MCI was going to merge into a U.S. subsidiary of BT, and the MCI shareholders were going to receive stock of BT and cash. As will be seen in Chapter 10, this type of transaction can qualify for tax-free treatment under the reorganization provisions, provided certain conditions in § 367 are satisfied.

For a more detailed discussion of these issues, *see* Ginsburg and Levin, *Mergers, supra* Sec. 1.12; and Bittker and Eustice, *Corporations, supra* Sec. 1.12. *See also* the most recent edition of PLI, *Tax Strategies, supra* Sec. 1.12; and Thompson, *Mergers, Acquisitions, and Tender Offers, supra* Sec. 1.12 at Chapter 9.

§ 7.2 The Straight (A) Reorganization: Statutory Merger or Consolidation

A. Introduction

The (A) reorganization has been a part of the tax law since the adoption of the first reorganization statute in 1918. Section 368(a)(1)(A) does not say much about the (A); it merely states that a "statutory merger or consolidation" is a reorganization. There is no solely for voting stock requirement as in the (B), the (C) and the (a)(2)(E), nor is there a "substantially all" requirement as in the (C), the (a)(2)(D), and the (a)(2)(E). The regulations, however, make it clear that the statutory merger or consolidation must be "effected pursuant to the corporation laws of the United States or a State or Territory or the District of Columbia." *See* § 1.368-2(b)(1). Although a merger under foreign law does not constitute an (A), such a merger might qualify, for instance, as a (C) or a § 354(b) nondivisive (D) reorganization. *See, e.g.,* Rev. Rul. 67-326, 1967-2 C.B. 143, holding that prior to the enactment of § 368(a)(2)(D), a forward subsidiary merger of the target into the acquiring subsidiary in exchange for voting stock of the acquiring parent was a triangular (C).

Notwithstanding the absence of a formal voting stock or a similar requirement, the Supreme Court has made it clear that in order to qualify as an (A), there must be a "continuity of interest." The leading cases dealing with the continuity of interest doctrine, beginning with the Supreme Court's decision in *Pinellas,* are collected in Sec. 6.2. These cases have a continuing impact on reorganizations, particularly on the (A) since it has no statutorily imposed voting stock requirement. The forward subsidiary merger under § 368(a)(2)(D) is the only other acquisitive reorganization that does not have a statutorily mandated voting stock requirement.

The regulations under § 368 reflect in several places the continuity of interest requirement, and the Service's current ruling policy on continuity of interest is set out in Sec. 6.2.C. Before proceeding with the study of the (A), the reader should master the materials on continuity of interest in Sec. 6.2. In addition to satisfying the continuity of interest requirement, the continuity of business enterprise doctrine, examined in Sec. 6.3 and the business purpose doctrine, examined in Sec. 6.7, must be satisfied.

By way of summary, the tax treatment to the parties in an (A) is as follows:

(1) The target has nonrecognition treatment under §361. Under §357(a), liabilities assumed by the acquiror are not boot to the target.

(2) The acquiror has nonrecognition treatment upon the issuance of its stock or securities under §1032 and §1.61-12.

(3) The acquiror takes a carryover basis for the target's assets under §362(b).

(4) The target's tax attributes, other than basis, carry over to the acquiror in accordance with the principles in §§381, 382, and 383. *See* Sec. 7.8.

(5) The target's shareholders receive nonrecognition treatment under §354 and boot gain treatment under §356. The fair market value of any excess principal amount of securities received is treated as boot under §§354(a)(2) and 356(d). Under §356(a)(2), the shareholders' gain is treated as a dividend to the extent of their pro rata share of the accumulated E & P if the boot has the effect of a distribution of a dividend. *See* Sec. 6.13. for a full exploration of §356(a)(2) and the Supreme Court's decision in *Clark*.

(6) The target's shareholders take a substituted basis under §358 for the stock or securities received.

One of the principal nuances in the (A) involves transactions in which a corporation acquires part of a target's stock prior to a merger. Such transactions are commonly referred to as "two step acquisitions." The leading authorities dealing with this type of transaction are set out below: In *King Enterprises* (Sec. 7.2.C.) the acquiror acquired the target's stock for both cash and stock and then merged the target upstream. Sec. 7.2.D. sets out Rev. Rul. 2001-46, which deals with the treatment of a reverse subsidiary merger that does not qualify as a reorganization under §368(a)(2)(E) and which is followed by an upstream merger into the acquriror. This ruling, which relies in part on the *King Enterprises* case, holds that the transaction is an (A) reorganization. In *Kass* (Sec. 7.2.E.) the acquiror acquired a portion of the target's stock by purchase and then merged the target upstream. The interface between the reorganization provisions and the liquidation provisions in an upstream merger of a less than 80% owned subsidiary is examined in Sec. 7.2.F. Rev. Rul. 70-223 (Sec. 7.2.G.) deals with a downstream merger of the acquiror into the target after the acquiror purchases the target's stock. Sec. 7.2.H. addresses the question of whether a divisive transaction can qualify as (A); this is a different question than whether an (A) can follow a spinoff, which is addressed in Chapter 9. Sec. 7.2.I. deals with mergers with disregarded entities. Sec. 7.2.J. addresses the impact of §§305 and 306 in an (A). Finally, Sec. 7.2.K. sets out the representations required in a ruling request under §368(a)(1)(A).

The combination of a tax-free spin-off under §355 followed by an (A) is addressed in Chapter 9, which looks at spin-offs and their use in acquisitive reorganizations. That chapter examines, *inter alia,* the leading case dealing with this type of transaction: *Morris Trust.*

B. The Continuity of Interest Requirement

See generally Sec. 6.2.*See* § 3.02 Revenue Procedure 77-37 in Sec. 6.2.C.

C. The Step Transaction Doctrine: Broken (B) Followed by Upstream Merger Equals an (A)

King Enterprises, Inc. v. United States

United States Court of Claims 1969

418 F.2d 511

PER CURIAM:

[King Enterprises, Inc. was one of 11 shareholders of Tenco. The stock of Tenco was sold pursuant to a "Purchase and Sale Agreement."]

Pursuant to the Agreement providing for the sale of their Tenco stock to Minute Maid, the Tenco shareholders received a total consideration consisting of $3,000,000 in cash, $2,550,000 in promissory notes and 311,996 shares of Minute Maid stock valued at $5,771,926. Petitioner's share of the total consideration consisted of $281,564.25 in cash, $239,329.40 in promissory notes, and 29,282 shares of Minute Maid stock valued at $541,717. The Minute Maid stock received by Tenco stockholders represented 15.62 percent of the total outstanding Minute Maid shares, and constituted in excess of 50 percent of the total consideration received.

On December 10, 1959, the Minute Maid directors approved the November 24th recommendation of its general counsel to merge the company's four subsidiaries, including Tenco, into the parent company, and authorized that the merger be submitted to its stockholders for approval at a meeting scheduled for February 1960. Minute Maid's annual report to stockholders announced the merger plan about December 3, 1959. On January 5, 1960, Minute Maid requested a ruling from the Commissioner of Internal Revenue whether in the event of the proposed Tenco merger the basis of Tenco assets in Minute Maid's hands would be determined under [former] section 334(b)(2) of the Internal Revenue Code of 1954 [the predecessor of § 338]. This was approved by the Commissioner by ruling of February 25, 1960 that "Under the provisions of [former] section 334(b)(2) that basis of the property received by Minute Maid upon the complete liquidation of Tenco will be determined by reference to the adjusted basis of the Tenco stock in the hands of Minute Maid." On April 30 and May 2, 1960, in accordance with the applicable state laws, Tenco and certain other subsidiaries were merged into Minute Maid.

On its income tax return for the fiscal year ended June 30, 1960, petitioner reported the cash and notes received as dividend income, subject to the 85 percent intercorporate dividends received deduction. The value of the Minute Maid stock received by petitioner was not reported, it being petitioner's position that such stock was received in connection with a nontaxable corporate reorganization. The District Director of Internal Revenue assessed a deficiency on the ground that the gain portion of the total consideration received (cash, notes, and Minute Maid stock) constituted taxable capital gain from the sale of a capital asset. Petitioner paid the deficiency, then sued here.

Petitioner contends that the transfer by the Tenco stockholders of their Tenco stock to Minute Maid in exchange for Minute Maid stock, cash and notes, followed by the merger of Tenco into Minute Maid, were steps in a unified transaction qualifying as a reorganization under section 368(a)(1)(A) of the 1954 Code. Consequently, petitioner continues, the Minute Maid stock was received by it pursuant to the plan of reorganization and is nontaxable as such, while the cash and notes received constitute a dividend distribution to which the 85 percent intercorporate dividends received deduction is applicable. The Government asserts that the transfer of Tenco stock to Minute Maid was an independent sales transaction: therefore, the entire gain realized by petitioner on the payment to it of cash, notes and Minute Maid stock is taxable as gain from the sale of a capital asset.

The Reorganization Issue The threshold issue is whether the transfer of Tenco stock to Minute Maid is to be treated for tax purposes as an independent transaction of sale, or as a transitory step in a transaction qualifying as a corporate reorganization. Significant tax consequences turn on which characterization is determined to be proper.

It is not disputed that there was a Type A reorganization in April 1960 when Tenco and Minute Maid were merged in accordance with state law. Nor does the Government dispute that Minute Maid continued the business of Tenco following the merger, or that the former Tenco shareholders had a continuity of interest in the enterprise by virtue of their ownership of stock in Minute Maid received in the exchange. The disagreement centers on whether the initial exchange of stock was a step in a unified transaction pursuant to a "plan of reorganization."

The underlying theory of the petitioner's claim is that the tax consequences of business transactions are properly determined by their substance and not by the form in which they are cast. Thus petitioner views the substance of the transaction under review to be an acquisition by Minute Maid of Tenco's assets in exchange for transferring Minute Maid stock, cash and notes to Tenco's stockholders * * * The value of the Minute Maid stock received, which exceeded 50 percent of the total consideration, constituted a sufficient continuity of interest to support a Type A reorganization. Petitioner concludes, therefore, that the net result of the entire transaction is a reorganization, not to be altered by splitting the entire transaction into its component transitory steps. * * *

In support of its position that the step transaction doctrine is inapplicable to the facts of this case the Government correctly points out that there was no binding commitment for the merger of Tenco to follow the acquisition of its stock. Defendant erroneously concludes, however, that the absence of such a commitment here renders the step transaction doctrine inapplicable. * * *

In the alternative, the Government asserts that the step transaction doctrine has no application to this case because the merger of Tenco into Minute Maid was not the intended end result from the outset. Although the appropriate standard is invoked, defendant's assertion is inconsistent with the inferences to be drawn from the record.

* * * The record reveals that, prior to the acquisition of Tenco stock, the officers of Minute Maid considered merging its existing subsidiaries into the parent in order to eliminate some of the general ledgers and extra taxes, and to bring about other savings. In fact, the merger of subsidiaries as a money-saving device was Mr. Speeler's (Minute Maid's vice president and general counsel) pet idea, which he discussed with Minute Maid's President Fox before the initial agreement with Tenco.

Shortly after the stock acquisition, Minute Maid instituted steps to consummate the merger of Tenco into Minute Maid. The proposed merger was motivated by a desire to avoid additional income tax on intercorporate dividends, to eliminate duplicate costs in the approximate amount of $50,000, and to obtain a stepped-up basis for stock in foreign corporations and other assets owned by Tenco. The potential step-up in basis for the foreign stock was estimated at $750,000 and the step-up for Tenco's other assets, although unable to be precisely ascertained, was considerable and probably sufficient as a justification for the merger independent of the other assigned reasons.

Minute Maid applied for on January 5, 1960, and received on February 25, 1960, a ruling by the Internal Revenue Service that Minute Maid's basis in property received upon the complete liquidation of Tenco would be determined under [former] section 334(b)(2) by reference to the adjusted basis of Tenco stock in Minute Maid's hands. Subsequently, on April 30 and May 2, 1960, in accordance with applicable state laws, Tenco and certain other subsidiaries were merged into Minute Maid.

No express intention on the part of Minute Maid to effect a merger of Tenco surfaces in the record until after the initial agreement to exchange stock. It strains credulity, however, to believe other than that the plan to merge was something more than inchoate, if something less than announced, at the time of such exchange. * * *

The operative facts in this case clearly justify the inference that the merger of Tenco into Minute Maid was the intended result of the transaction in question from the outset, the initial exchange of stock constituting a mere transitory step. Accordingly, it is concluded that the initial exchange and subsequent merger were steps in a unified transaction qualifying as a Type A reorganization, and that petitioner received its Minute Maid stock pursuant to the plan of reorganization shown by the facts and circumstances above to have existed.

Questions

What is the precise holding of *King Enterprises*? What impact did the court's holding that the transaction was an (A) reorganization have on the Service's ruling that the upstream merger was governed by former § 334(b)(2)? What would have been the result if there had been a mere liquidation as opposed to an upstream merger? *Compare American Potash, infra* Sec. 7.3.H.2.

D. Failed § 368(a)(2)(E) Reverse Subsidiary Followed by Upstream Merger

Revenue Ruling 2001-46

2001-42 I.R.B. 321

Issue Under the facts described below, what is the proper tax treatment if, pursuant to an integrated plan, a newly formed wholly owned subsidiary of an acquiring corporation merges into a target corporation, followed by the merger of the target corporation into the acquiring corporation?

Facts Situation (1). Corporation X owns all the stock of Corporation Y, a newly formed wholly owned subsidiary. Pursuant to an integrated plan, X acquires all of the stock of Corporation T, an unrelated corporation, in a statutory merger of Y into T (the "Acquisition Merger"), with T surviving. In the Acquisition Merger, the T shareholders exchange their T stock for consideration, 70 percent of which is X voting stock and 30 percent of which is cash. Following the Acquisition Merger and as part of the plan, T merges into X in a statutory merger (the "Upstream Merger"). Assume that, absent some prohibition against the application of the step transaction doctrine, the step transaction doctrine would apply to treat the Acquisition Merger and the Upstream Merger as a single integrated acquisition by X of all the assets of T. Also assume that the single integrated transaction would satisfy the non-statutory requirements of a reorganization under § 368.

Situation (2). The facts are the same as in Situation (1) except that in the Acquisition Merger the T shareholders receive solely X voting stock in exchange for their T stock, so that the Acquisition Merger, if viewed independently of the Upstream Merger, would qualify as a reorganization under § 368(a)(1)(A) by reason of § 368(a)(2)(E).

Law Section 338(a) provides that if a corporation makes a qualified stock purchase and makes an election under that section, then the target corporation (i) shall be treated as having sold all of its assets at the close of the acquisition date at fair market value and (ii) shall be treated as a new corporation which purchased all of its assets as of the beginning of the day after the acquisition date. Section 338(d)(3) defines a qualified stock purchase as any transaction or series of transactions in which stock (meeting the requirements of § 1504(a)(2)) of one corporation is acquired by another corporation by purchase during a 12-month acquisition period. Section 338(h)(3) defines a purchase generally as any acquisition of stock, but excludes acquisitions of stock in exchanges to which § 351, § 354, § 355 or § 356 applies.

Rev. Rul. 90-95 [Sec. 5.3.D.2] (Situation 2), holds that the merger of a newly formed wholly owned domestic subsidiary into a target corporation with the target corporation shareholders receiving solely cash in exchange for their stock, immediately followed by the merger of the target corporation into the domestic parent of the merged subsidiary, will be treated as a qualified stock purchase of the target corporation followed by a § 332 liquidation of the target corporation. As a result, the parent's basis in the target corporation's assets will be the same as the basis of the assets in the target corporation's hands. The ruling explains that even though "the step-transaction doctrine is properly applied to disregard the existence of the [merged subsidiary]," so that the first step is treated as a stock purchase, the acquisition of the target corporation's stock is accorded independent significance from the subsequent liquidation of the target corporation and, therefore, is treated as a qualified stock purchase regardless of whether a § 338 election is made.

Section 1.338-3(d) of the Income Tax Regulations incorporates the approach of Rev. Rul. 90-95 into the regulations by requiring the purchasing corporation (or a member of its affiliated group) to treat certain asset transfers following a qualified stock purchase (where no § 338 election is made) independently of the qualified stock purchase. In the example in § 1.338-3(d)(5), the purchase for cash of 85 percent of the stock of a target corporation, followed by the merger of the target corporation into a wholly owned subsidiary of the purchasing corporation, is treated (other than by certain minority shareholders) as a qualified stock purchase of the stock of the target corporation followed by a § 368 reorganization of the target corporation into the subsidiary. As a result, the subsidiary's basis in the target corporation's assets is the same as the basis of the assets in the target corporation's hands.

Section 368(a)(1)(A) defines the term "reorganization" as a statutory merger or consolidation. Section 368(a)(2)(E) provides that a transaction otherwise qualifying under § 368(a)(1)(A) shall not be disqualified by reason of the fact that stock of a corporation (controlling corporation), which before the merger was in control of the merged corporation, is used in the transaction if (i) after the transaction, the corporation surviving the merger holds substantially all of its properties and the properties of the merged corporation, and (ii) in the transaction, former shareholders of the surviving corporation exchange, for an amount of voting stock of the controlling corporation, an amount of stock in the surviving corporation which constitutes control of such corporation.

In Rev. Rul. 67-274 [Sec. 7.3.B.] Corporation Y acquires all of the stock of Corporation X in exchange for some of the voting stock of Y and, thereafter, X completely liquidates into Y. The ruling holds that because the two steps are parts of a plan of reorganization, they cannot be considered independently of each other. Thus, the steps do not qualify as a reorganization under § 368(a)(1)(B) followed by a liquidation under § 332, but instead qualify as an acquisition of X's assets in a reorganization under § 368(a)(1)(C).

Analysis Situation (1). Because of the amount of cash consideration paid to the T shareholders, the Acquisition Merger could not qualify as a reorganization under § 368(a)(1)(A) and § 368(a)(2)(E). If the Acquisition Merger and the Upstream Merger in Situation (1) were treated as separate from each other, as were the steps in Situation (2) of Rev. Rul. 90-95 the Acquisition Merger would be treated as a stock acquisition that is a qualified stock purchase, because the stock is not acquired in a § 354 or § 356 exchange. The Upstream Merger would qualify as a liquidation under § 332.

However, if the approach reflected in Rev. Rul 67-274 were applied to Situation (1), the transaction would be treated as an integrated acquisition of T's assets by X in a single statutory merger (without a preliminary stock acquisition). Accordingly, unless the policies underlying § 338 dictate otherwise, the integrated asset acquisition in Situation (1) is properly treated as a statutory merger of T into X that qualifies as a reorganization under § 368(a)(1)(A). *See King Enterprises* [Sec. 7.2.C.] (in a case that predated § 338, the court applied the step transaction doctrine to treat the acquisition of the stock of a target corporation followed by the merger of the target corporation into the acquiring corporation as a reorganization under § 368(a)(1)(A)); *J.E. Seagram Corp* (same). Therefore, it is necessary to determine whether the approach reflected in Rev. Rul. 90-95 applies where the step transaction doctrine would otherwise apply to treat the transaction as an asset acquisition that qualifies as a reorganization under § 368(a).

Rev. Rul. 90-95 and § 1.338-3(d) reject the approach reflected in Rev. Rul. 67-274 where the application of that approach would treat the purchase of a target corporation's stock without a § 338 election followed by the liquidation or merger of the target corporation as the purchase of the target corporation's assets resulting in a cost basis in the assets under § 1012. The rejection of step integration in Rev. Rul. 90-95 and § 1.338-3(d) is based on Congressional intent that § 338 "replace any nonstatutory treatment of a stock purchase as an asset purchase under the Kimbell-Diamond doctrine." H.R. Rep. No. 760, 97th Cong., 2d Sess. 536 (1982). (In *Kimbell-Diamond* [Chapter 2], the court held that the purchase of the stock of a target corporation for the purpose of obtaining its assets through a prompt liquidation should be treated by the purchaser as a purchase of the target corporation's assets with the purchaser receiving a cost basis in the assets.) Rev. Rul. 90-95 and § 1.338-3(d) treat the acquisition of the stock of the target corporation as a qualified stock purchase followed by a separate carryover basis transaction in order to preclude any nonstatutory treatment of the steps as an integrated asset purchase.

The policy underlying § 338 is not violated by treating Situation (1) as a single statutory merger of T into X because such treatment results in a transaction that qualifies as a reorganization under § 368(a)(1)(A) in which X acquires the assets of T with a carryover basis under § 362, and does not result in a cost basis for those assets under § 1012. Thus, in Situation (1), the step transaction doctrine applies to treat the Acquisition Merger and the Upstream Merger not as a stock acquisition that is a qualified stock purchase followed by a § 332 liquidation, but instead as an acquisition of T's assets through a single statutory merger of T into X that qualifies as a reorganization under § 368(a)(1)(A). Accordingly, a § 338 election may not be made in such a situation.

Situation (2). Situation (2) differs from Situation (1) only in that the Acquisition Merger, if viewed independently of the Upstream Merger, would qualify as a reorganization under § 368(a)(1)(A) by reason of § 368(a)(2)(E). This difference does not change the result from that in Situation (1). The transaction is treated as a single statutory merger of T into X that qualifies as a reorganization under § 368(a)(1)(A) without regard to § 368(a)(2)(E).

Holding Under the facts presented, if, pursuant to an integrated plan, a newly formed wholly owned subsidiary of an acquiring corporation merges into a target corporation, followed by the merger of the target corporation into the acquiring corporation, the transaction is treated as a single statutory merger of the target corporation into the acquiring corporation that qualifies as a reorganization under § 368(a)(1)(A).

Application Pursuant to § 7805(b)(8), the Service will not apply the principles of this revenue ruling to challenge a taxpayer's position with respect to the treatment of a multi-step transaction, one step of which, viewed independently, is a qualified stock purchase if:

(1) a timely (including extensions) and valid (without regard to whether there was a qualified stock purchase under the principles of this revenue ruling) election under § 338(h)(10) or § 338(g) (Election) is or was filed with respect to the acquisition of the stock of the target corporation; and

(2) either

(a) the acquisition date for the target corporation is on or before September 24, 2001; or

(b) the acquisition of stock of the target corporation meeting the requirements of § 1504(a)(2) by the purchasing corporation is pursuant to a written agreement that (subject to customary conditions) is binding on September 24, 2001, and at all times thereafter until the acquisition date; and

(3) such taxpayer does not take a position for U.S. tax purposes that is inconsistent with the treatment of the acquisition as a qualified stock purchase with respect to which the Election was made.

Further, the Service and the Treasury are considering whether to issue regulations that would reflect the general principles of this revenue ruling, but would allow taxpayers to make a valid election under § 338(h)(10) with respect to a step of a multi-step transaction that, viewed independently, is a qualified stock purchase if such step is pursuant to a written agreement that requires, or permits the purchasing corporation to cause, a § 338(h)(10) election in respect of such step to be made. The Service and the Treasury request comments regarding the adoption of such an approach.

Effect on Other Documents. Rev. Rul. 67-274 is amplified and Rev. Rul. 90-95 is distinguished.

E. Purchase of a Portion of Target's Stock Followed by Upstream Merger with Minority Shareholders Receiving Parent's Stock

Kass v. Commissioner

Tax Court of the United States, 1973
60 T.C. 218

Dawson, Judge: * * *

Opinion The only issue for decision is whether petitioner, a minority shareholder of an 84-percent-owned subsidiary, must recognize gain upon the receipt of the parent's stock pursuant to a statutory merger of the subsidiary into the parent.* * *

For a period greater than 6 months prior to 1965, petitioner had owned 2,000 shares of common stock of Atlantic City Racing Association (herein called ACRA). Her basis in the stock was $1,000. The stock in her hands was a capital asset.

ACRA was a New Jersey corporation which was * * * engaged in the business of operating a racetrack. * * *

Track Associates, Inc. (herein called TRACK), is a New Jersey corporation which was formed on November 19, 1965. The total authorized capital stock of TRACK consisted of 500,000 shares of common stock. Its original capitalization consisted of 202,577 shares. Over 50 percent of the original issue was acquired by the Levy family and 8 percent was acquired by the Casey family. The remaining stock went to 18 other individuals. The Levys and the Caseys were also minority shareholders (whether computed separately or as a group) in ACRA. Their purpose in forming TRACK was to gain control over ACRA's racetrack business. They wanted to do away with ACRA's cumbersome capital structure and institute a new corporate policy with regard to capital improvements and higher purses for the races. Control was to be gained by establishing TRACK and then by (1) having TRACK purchase at least 80 percent of the stock of ACRA and (2) subsequently merging ACRA into TRACK.

The Levys acquired 48,300 shares of TRACK stock (out of the total original capitalization of 202,577 shares) in exchange for stock of ACRA. The Caseys acquired 3,450 shares in exchange for their ACRA stock. Together the Levys and Caseys purchased an additional 70,823 shares of TRACK stock as part of the original capitalization.

On December 1, 1965, TRACK offered to purchase the stock of ACRA at $22 per share, subject to the condition that at least 405,000 shares (slightly more than 80 percent of ACRA's outstanding shares) be tendered. As a result of this tender offer, which terminated on February 11, 1966, 424,764 shares of ACRA stock were received and paid for by TRACK. A total of 29,486 shares of ACRA stock were not tendered.[1]

---

1. All 506,00 shares of ACRA stock can be accounted for as follows 51,750 (10.23 percent) were transferred to TRACK upon formation; 424,764 (83.95 percent) were purchased by TRACK following the tender offer; 29,486 (5.82 percent) remained in the hands of the minority shareholders such as the petitioner.

The board of directors of TRACK approved a plan of liquidation providing for the liquidation of ACRA by way of merger into TRACK. * * *

The merger having taken place, the remaining shares of ACRA that were not sold pursuant to the tender offer or the dissenting shareholder provisions were exchanged for TRACK stock, 1 for 1. The petitioner exchanged 2,000 shares of ACRA stock, with a fair market value at the time of $22 per share, for 2,000 shares of TRACK stock. She did not report any capital gain in connection with this transaction.

Petitioner contends that the merger of ACRA into TRACK, although treated at least in part as a liquidation at the corporate level, is at her level, the shareholder level, (1) a true statutory merger and (2) a section 368(a)(1)(A) reorganization, occasioning no recognition of gain on the ensuing exchange. In support of this she cites *Madison Square Garden Corp.,* 58 T.C. 619 (1972). Respondent, on the other hand, argues that the purchase of stock by TRACK and the liquidation of ACRA into TRACK, which took the form of a merger, must be viewed at all levels as an integrated transaction; that the statutory merger does not qualify as a reorganization because it fails the continuity-of-interest test; and that, as a consequence, petitioner falls outside of section 354(a)(1) and must recognize gain pursuant to section [§ 1001].

The problems presented by these facts are somewhat complex. * * * Put another way, does the merger of ACRA into TRACK fall under section 368(a)(1)(A), thus placing the exchange of petitioner's ACRA stock for TRACK stock within the applicable non-recognition provision?

Respondent does not take the position that a statutory merger, such as the one we have here, can never qualify for reorganization-nonrecognition status. He admits that "Theoretically, it is possible for TRACK to get a stepped-up basis in 83.95 percent of the assets of ACRA per [former] section 334(b)(2), IRC [the predecessor of § 338] upon a section 332, IRC liquidation of ACRA into TRACK and at the same time allow nonrecognition reorganization treatment to minority shareholders." Rather, his position is simply that the merger in question fails to meet the time-honored continuity-of-interest test. We agree with this and so hold.

[Former] section 334(b)(2) and the reorganization provisions might apply to the same transaction only in certain cases where the continuity-of-interest test is met. See sec. § 332 (last sentence, last independent clause); sec. 1.332-2(d) and (e), Income Tax Regs. Reorganization treatment is appropriate when the parent's stock ownership in the subsidiary was not acquired as a step in a plan to acquire assets of the subsidiary: the parent's stockholding can be counted as contributing to continuity-of-interest, so that since such holding represented more than 80 percent of the stock of the subsidiary, the continuity-of-interest test would be met. Reorganization treatment is inappropriate when the parent's stock ownership in the subsidiary was purchased as the first step in a plan to acquire the subsidiary's assets in conformance with the provisions of [former] section 334(b)(2). The parent's stockholding could not be counted towards continuity-of-interest, so in the last example there would be a continuity-of-interest of less than 20 percent. (Less than 20-percent continuity would be significantly less continuity-of-interest than that allowed in *John A. Nelson Co. v. Helvering,* 296 U.S. 374 (1935).) In short, where the parent's stock interest is "old and cold," it may contribute to continuity-of-interest. Where the parent's interest is not "old and cold," the sale of shares by the majority of shareholders actually detracts from continuity-of-interest. * * *

[Petitioner argues that] assuming that the continuity-of-interest test is applied, it is met where all 16 percent of the stockholders of ACRA exchanged their stock for a total of 35 percent of the stock of TRACK. The 16-percent figure (really 16.04 percent) is the sum of the percentage of ACRA stock transferred to TRACK at the time of TRACK's formation (10.22 percent) plus the percentage of ACRA stock exchanged for TRACK stock following the statutory merger (5.82 percent). Fortunately, we need not engage in a game of percentages since the continuity figure argued for by petitioner, 16 percent, is not "tantalizingly" high. The plain fact that more than 80 percent of the shareholders of ACRA sold out for cash is sufficient to prevent this merger from meeting the quantitative test expressed in the *Southwest Natural Gas Co. v. Commissioner,* 189 F.2d 332, 334 (C.A.5, 1951), affirming 14 T.C. 81 (1950):

While no precise formula has been expressed for determining whether there has been retention of the requisite interest, it seems clear that the requirement of continuity of interest consistent with the statutory intent is not fulfilled in the absence of a showing: (1) that the transferor corporation or its shareholders retained a substantial proprietary stake in the enterprise represented by a material interest in the affairs of the transferee corporation, and, (2) *that such retained interest represents a substantial part of the value of the property transferred.* [Emphasis added.]

The two Supreme Court cases on point are *John A. Nelson Co. v. Helvering,* [Chapter 6], and *Helvering v. Minnesota Tea Co.,* [Chapter 6].

Finally, we emphasize that the petitioner is not any worse off than her fellow shareholders who sold their stock. She could have also received money instead of stock had she chosen to sell or to dissent from the merger. The nonrecognition of a realized gain is always an important matter. We hold that petitioner is not entitled to such favorable treatment in this case.

Reviewed by the Court.

Decision will be entered for the respondent.

Questions

1. What result to the taxpayer if she had participated with the Caseys and Levys in organizing TRACK? Should the ACRA stock that the Levys and Caseys contributed to TRACK have been included in determining the continuity of interest?

2. What is the significance of (1) the last sentence of § 332(b), and (2) § 1.332-2(d) and (e)? Suppose *P* has always owned 90% of the stock of *S*, and individual *A* owns the 10% balance. *S* has assets with a value of $100K and a basis of $50K. *S* merges upstream into *P*, with *A* receiving *P* stock. What result to *P, S* and *A*? What

result to *P, S* and *A* if, pursuant to the merger, *P* transfers $10K of cash to *A* in cancellation of his shares?

3. Acquiring corporation, *AC*, purchases 85% of the stock of target, *TC, AC* then forms a new subsidiary, *AC-S*, and *TC* merges into *AC-S*. In the merger, *AC* receives additional stock of *AC-S* in exchange for its stock of *TC* and the minority shareholders of *TC* receive cash for their stock. What result to each of the parties?

F. Upstream Merger of Less than 80% Subsidiary

General Counsel Memorandum 39404

April 15, 1982

Issues 1. Does the statutory merger of S into P result in sufficient continuity of interest to constitute a "reorganization" within the meaning of section 368(a)(1)(A) if P owns a 70 percent "old and cold" stock interest in S?

2. If the statutory merger does qualify as an "A" reorganization, does P recognize gain or loss on the transaction?

Conclusion 1. The proposed revenue ruling concludes that the merger does not qualify as a reorganization because the continuity of interest requirement is not satisfied. The transaction is viewed instead as a complete liquidation of S, and P is required to recognize gain or loss pursuant to section 331(a)(1) on the receipt of the assets of S. The proposed ruling is based on G.C.M. 31228, * * * A-629558 (May 14, 1959).

Upon reconsideration we believe G.C.M. 31228 is in error. We are therefore unable to concur in the proposed ruling. The conversion of P's indirect stock interest in S into a direct interest in the S assets should be viewed as preserving continuity of interest for purposes of section 368(a)(1)(A). It is only in those cases in which the receipt of solely voting stock is required that the conversion of an indirect interest into a direct interest will cause the transaction to fail to qualify as a reorganization. G.C.M. 31228 is revoked. * * *

2. In view of our conclusion that the merger qualifies as a reorganization under section 368(a)(1)(A), we conclude that no gain or loss will be recognized to either P or S as a result of the transaction. The basis of the S assets in the hands of P is determined by section 362(b). The exchange of the minority shareholders' S stock is governed by sections 354 or 356. * * *

Nonrecognition to Parent Corporation The Service has argued on at least two occasions that although an upstream merger could qualify as a reorganization, the parent's acquisition is not tax-free, because there is no provision that literally provides nonrecognition treatment to exchanges by a corporation of stock in another corporation for property of such other corporation. [*Contrast* §§ 354 and 1032.] * * *

We do not believe the absence of a section 1032 exchange preceding the merger [is necessary]. Such an exchange is a purely formal transaction, an "idle act", * * * so that to insist upon it as a condition for nonrecognition would serve only to set a trap for the unwary. Moreover, the strict requirement of a stock-for-stock exchange [under §354] would be contrary to the characterization of the transaction in Rev. Rul. 58-93. * * *

G. Downstream Merger of Acquiring Corporation into Target after Purchase of Target's Stock

Revenue Ruling 70-223

1970-1 C.B. 79

* * * Corporation *X* purchased all of the outstanding stock of corporation *Y* within a 12-month period. Within two years of the last stock purchase *X* was merged into *Y*. *Y*'s assets had an adjusted basis to *Y* greater than the cost of the *Y* stock to *X*. Some of these assets, if disposed of by sale or by liquidation, would be subject to the provisions of sections 47, 1245, and 1250 of the Code.

There are good business reasons for combining the businesses of *X* and *Y*. In this case it was decided to merge *X* into *Y* rather than liquidate *Y* in order to obtain the more favorable tax treatment afforded by the reorganization provisions of the Code.

Section 368(a)(1)(A) of the Code defines a statutory merger or consolidation as a reorganization. Section 362 of the Code provides that the basis of property acquired by a corporation in connection with a reorganization, will be the same as the basis in the hands of the transferor.

Since *X* may accomplish its desired objective of combining the two businesses by either liquidating *Y* or by merging into *Y*, it may choose whichever form it desires for the transaction.

Accordingly, it is held that the merger of *X* into *Y* is a reorganization within the meaning of section 368(a)(1)(A) of the Code provided it complies with the laws of the states of incorporation of *X* and *Y*.

Questions and Note

1. Acquiror, *AC*, has 10,000 shares outstanding with a fair market value of $100 per share, for a total fair market value of $1M. Target Corporation, *TC*, has 1,000 shares outstanding with a fair market value of $100 per share, for a total fair market value of $100K. *TC*'s only asset is a building with a basis of $10K. *AC* purchases 80% of the stock of *TC* (800 shares) for $80K and then merges *TC* into it in a transaction in which the minority shareholders of *TC* receive in exchange for their 200 shares of *TC* stock, 200 shares of *AC*'s stock. What result to *TC*, *AC*, and the minority shareholders of *TC*? Suppose that instead of an upstream merger, *AC* merged into *TC* with the shareholders of *AC* exchanging their 1,000 shares of *AC* for 1,000 shares of *TC*. What result to *AC*, *TC*, the *AC* shareholders and the minority shareholders of *TC*? Is there any economic difference between the two transactions? Is the difference in tax treatment sound? Suppose the upstream merger took place 2 1/2 years after the purchase?

2. Is the position of Rev. Rul. 70-223 consistent with the Tax Court's position in *Kass*? Is it sound tax policy for a downstream merger to qualify as an (A) reorganization when an upstream merger involving the same corporations would not?

H. Merger Cannot Be Divisive

Revenue Ruling 2000-5
2000-5 I.R.B. 436

Issues Whether a transaction in which (1) a target corporation "merges" under state law with and into an acquiring corporation and the target corporation does not go out of existence, or (2) a target corporation "merges" under state law with and into two or more acquiring corporations and the target corporation goes out of existence, qualifies as a reorganization under §368(a)(1)(A) of the Internal Revenue Code?

Facts *Situation (1).* A target corporation transfers some of its assets and liabilities to an acquiring corporation, retains the remainder of its assets and liabilities, and remains in existence following the transaction. The target corporation's shareholders receive stock in the acquiring corporation in exchange for part of their target corporation stock and they retain their remaining target corporation stock. The transaction qualifies as a merger under state X corporate law.

Situation (2). A target corporation transfers some of its assets and liabilities to each of two acquiring corporations. The target corporation liquidates and the target corporation's shareholders receive stock in each of the two acquiring corporations in exchange for their target corporation stock. The transaction qualifies as a merger under state X corporate law.

Discussion The purpose of the reorganization provisions of the Code is to provide tax-free treatment to certain exchanges incident to readjustments of corporate structures made in one of the specified ways described in the Code. Section 1.368-1(b) of the Income Tax Regulations. In 1921, Congress defined a reorganization as including "... a merger or consolidation (including the acquisition by one corporation ... of substantially all the properties of another corporation)." In 1934, Congress separated this rule into two distinct provisions. In the predecessor of current §368(a)(1)(C), an "acquisition by one corporation ... of substantially all the properties of another corporation" continued to be a reorganization where payment was effectuated with the acquiror's voting stock. In the predecessor of current §368(a)(1)(A), the terms "merger or consolidation" were qualified by requiring that they be "statutory" mergers and consolidations. The word "statutory" was added to the definition of a reorganization so that the definition "will conform more closely to the general requirements of [state] corporation law." *See* H. R. Rep. No. 704, 73d Cong., 2d Sess. 14 (1934).

Historically, corporate law merger statutes have operated to ensure that "[a] merger ordinarily is an absorption by one corporation of the properties and franchises of another whose stock it has acquired. The merged corporation ceases to exist, and the merging corporation alone survives." *Cortland Specialty Co. v. Commissioner, 60 F.2d 937, 939 (2d Cir. 1932), cert. denied, 288 U.S. 599 (1933);* for other cases that describe mergers as requiring that the target corporation transfer its assets and cease to exist, *see, e.g., Vulcan Materials Company v. U.S., 446 F.2d 690, 694 (5th Cir. 1971), cert. denied, 404 U.S. 942 (1971); Fisher v. Commissioner, 108 F.2d 707, 709 (6th Cir. 1939), cert. denied, 310 U.S. 627 (1939).* Thus, unlike 368(a)(1)(C), in which Congress included a "substantially all the properties" requirement, it was not necessary for Congress to explicitly include a similar requirement in § 368(a)(1)(A) because corporate law merger statutes contemplated an acquisition of the target corporation's assets by the surviving corporation by operation of law.

Compliance with a corporate law merger statute does not by itself qualify a transaction as a reorganization. *See, e.g., Southwest Natural Gas Co. v. Commissioner, 189 F.2d 332 (5th Cir. 1951), cert. denied, 342 U.S. 860 (1951)* (holding that a state law merger was not a reorganization under 368(a)(1)(A)); *Roebling v. Commissioner, 143 F.2d 810 (3d Cir. 1944), cert. denied, 323 U.S. 773 (1944)* (same holding). In addition to satisfying the requirements of business purpose, continuity of business enterprise and continuity of interest, in order to qualify as a reorganization under § 368(a)(1)(A), a transaction effectuated under a corporate law merger statute must have the result that one corporation acquires the assets of the target corporation by operation of the corporate law merger statute and the target corporation ceases to exist. The transactions described in Situations (1) and (2) do not have the result that one corporation acquires the assets of the target corporation by operation of the corporate law merger statute and the target corporation ceases to exist. Therefore, these transactions do not qualify as reorganizations under § 368(a)(1)(A).

In contrast with the operation of corporate law merger statutes, a divisive transaction is one in which a corporation's assets are divided among two or more corporations. Section 355 provides tax-free treatment for certain divisive transactions, but only if a number of specific requirements are satisfied. Congress intended that § 355 be the sole means under which divisive transactions will be afforded tax-free status and, thus, specifically required the liquidation of the acquired corporation in reorganizations under both §§ 368(a)(1)(C) and 368(a)(1)(D) in order to prevent these reorganizations from being used in divisive transactions that did not satisfy § 355. *See* S. Rep. No. 1622, 83d Cong., 2d Sess. 274 (1954); S. Rep. No. 169, 98th Cong., 2d Sess. 204 (1984). No specific liquidation requirement was necessary for statutory mergers because corporate law merger statutes contemplated that only one corporation survived a merger. The transaction described in Situation (1) is divisive because, after the transaction, the target corporation's assets and liabilities are held by both the target corporation and acquiring corporation and the target corporation's shareholders hold stock in both the target corporation and acquiring corporation. The transaction described in Situation (2) is divisive because, after the transaction, the target corporation's assets and liabilities are held by each of the two acquiring corporations and the target corporation's shareholders hold stock in each of the two acquiring corporations.

Holding The transactions described in Situations (1) and (2) do not qualify as reorganizations under § 368(a)(1)(A). However, the transactions described in Situations (1) and (2) possibly may qualify for tax-free treatment under other provisions of the Code. * * *

I. Mergers with Disregarded Entities

Reg. § 1.368-2(b)(1) generally permits a merger of a corporation into a disregarded entity that is a branch of a corporation to qualify as an A reorganization, assuming all of the other conditions for an A reorganization are satisfied. Reg. § 1.368-2(b)(1)(i) defines the terms "disregarded entity," "combining entity," and "combining unit" as follows:

> (A) *Disregarded entity.* A disregarded entity is a business entity * * * that is disregarded as an entity separate from its owner for Federal income tax purposes. Examples of disregarded entities include a domestic single member limited liability company that does not elect to be classified as a corporation for Federal income tax purposes[.] * * *

> (B) *Combining entity.* A combining entity is a business entity that is a corporation * * * that is not a disregarded entity.

> (C) *Combining unit.* A combining unit is composed solely of a combining entity and all disregarded entities, if any, the assets of which are treated as owned by such combining entity for Federal income tax purposes [*i.e.*, the assets of the disregarded entity constitutes, in essence, a branch of the combining entity.]

Reg. § 1.368-2(b)(1)(ii) addresses the concepts of a "statutory merger" and "consolidation" as follows:

> (ii) *Statutory merger or consolidation generally.* For purposes of section 368(a)(1)(A), a statutory merger or consolidation is a transaction effected pursuant to the statute or statutes [note the statutes need not be domestic corporation statutes, see below] necessary to effect the merger or consolidation, in which transaction, as a result of the operation of such statute or statutes, the following events occur simultaneously at the effective time of the transaction—

> > (A) All of the assets (other than those distributed in the transaction) and liabilities (except to the extent such liabilities are satisfied or discharged in the transaction or are nonrecourse liabilities to which assets distributed in the transaction are subject) of each member of one or more combining units (each a transferor unit) become the assets and liabilities of one or more members of one other combining unit (the transferee unit); and

> > (B) The combining entity of each transferor unit ceases its separate legal existence for all purposes; provided, however, that this requirement will be satisfied even if, under applicable law, after the effective time of the transaction, the combining entity of the transferor unit (or its officers, directors, or agents) may act or be acted against, or a member of the transferee unit (or its officers, directors, or agents) may act or be acted against in the name of the combining entity of the transferor unit, pro-

vided that such actions relate to assets or obligations of the combining entity of the transferor unit that arose, or relate to activities engaged in by such entity, prior to the effective time of the transaction, and such actions are not inconsistent with the requirements of paragraph (b)(1)(ii)(A) of this section.

Example 2 of Reg. § 1.368-2(b)(1)(iii) illustrates a merger of a target into a branch-disregarded entity of the acquiror:

> *Example 2. Merger of a target corporation into a disregarded entity in exchange for stock of the owner.* (i) *Facts.* Under State W law, Z [the target corporation] merges into X [a domestic LLC that is a disregarded entity wholly owned by corporation Y, the acquiror]. Pursuant to such law, the following events occur simultaneously at the effective time of the transaction: all of the assets and liabilities of Z become the assets and liabilities of X and Z's separate legal existence ceases for all purposes. In the merger, the Z shareholders exchange their stock of Z for stock of Y.
>
> (ii) *Analysis.* The transaction satisfies the requirements of paragraph (b)(1)(ii) of this section because the transaction is effected pursuant to State W law and the following events occur simultaneously at the effective time of the transaction: all of the assets and liabilities of Z, the combining entity and sole member of the transferor unit, become the assets and liabilities of one or more members of the transferee unit that is comprised of Y, the combining entity of the transferee unit, and X, a disregarded entity the assets of which Y is treated as owning for Federal income tax purposes, and Z ceases its separate legal existence for all purposes. Accordingly, the transaction qualifies as a statutory merger or consolidation for purposes of section 368(a)(1)(A).

The theory is that the merger into the branch-disregarded entity is, in substance, a merger into the corporate owner of the disregarded entity.

On the other hand, the merger of a corporation into a disregarded entity that is not a branch of a corporation cannot qualify as a reorganization. The theory is that the merger into the non-branch-disregarded entity is like a merger into a sole proprietorship or partnership, which cannot qualify as an A reorganization.

J. Regulations Permitting Foreign Mergers

Preamble to Proposed Regulations, REG-117969-00

(January 5, 2005)

See Reg § 1.368-2(b)(1)(ii).

[Many of the principles in these Proposed Regulations have been adopted as Final Regulations.]

Background and Explanation of Provisions. Before 1934, the term *merger*, as used in the reorganization provisions, included statutory mergers as well as other combinations of corporate entities. In 1934, Congress amended the definition of a reorganization to provide separately for *statutory mergers or consolidations* and for the other types of transactions previously included in the definition of a *merger*. There is no indication in the legislative history of the 1934 changes to the definition of a reorganization that Congress intended to exclude transactions effected under foreign law.

In 1935, Treasury regulations interpreted the term *statutory merger* under the revised provision to mean a merger or consolidation effected pursuant to the corporation laws of a State or Territory or the District of Columbia. The requirement that the transaction be effected under domestic law remains in place, with minor variations. The Treasury Department and IRS believe that this interpretation is reasonable; nevertheless, the Treasury Department and IRS believe that a reexamination is warranted in light of the purposes of the statute and changes in domestic and foreign law since 1935.

The states have revised their laws to offer a greater variety of business entities and greater flexibility in effecting business combinations. Accordingly, the Treasury Department and IRS thought it advisable to define a merger or consolidation functionally, to supplement the reference to state law. Accordingly, the Treasury Department and IRS developed and proposed such a functional definition in 2003. See Notice of Proposed Rulemaking (REG-126485-01, 2003-9 I.R.B. 542, 68 FR 3477), cross-referencing temporary regulations (TD 9038, 2003-9, I.R.B. 524, 68 FR 3384) (January 24, 2003) [*see* Sec. 7.2.I].

Many foreign jurisdictions now have merger or consolidation statutes that operate in material respects like those of the states, i.e., all assets and liabilities move by operation of law. The Treasury Department and IRS believe that transactions effected pursuant to these statutes should be treated as reorganizations if they satisfy the functional criteria applicable to transactions under domestic statutes.

This document proposes a revised definition of a statutory merger or consolidation. The previously proposed definition of a statutory merger required that it be a transaction effected "pursuant to the laws of the United States or a State or the District of Columbia."

See REG-126485-01 (2003-9 I.R.B. 542, 68 FR 3477). The new proposed definition contained in this document replaces the quoted language with "pursuant to the statute or statutes necessary to effect the merger or consolidation." *See* Reg § 1.368-2(b)(1)(ii)] This proposed [now adopted] change would allow a transaction effected pursuant to the statutes of a foreign jurisdiction or of a United States possession to qualify as a statutory merger or consolidation under section 368(a)(1)(A), provided it otherwise qualifies as a reorganization. The phrase *statute or statutes* is not intended to prevent transactions effected pursuant to legislation from qualifying as mergers or consolidations where such legislation is supplemented by administrative or case law. * * *

K. Section 305 and 306 Issues Arising in an (A) Reorganization

If the target's shareholders receive both common and preferred, the preferred may be treated as § 306 stock if it in not "nonqualified preferred stock." Section 306 is examined generally in Chapter 2, and the impact of § 306 on acquisitive reorganizations is considered in Sec. 6.18. Also, Sec. 6.17 considers the impact of § 305.

L. Representations Required in a Ruling Request under § 368(a)(1)(A)

Excerpt from Revenue Procedure 86-42, § 7.01
1986-2 C.B. 722

[Although as noted in Sec. 6.2.A.6, the IRS generally does not issue private letter rulings on reorganization transactions, the following ruling guidelines can be helpful in structuring a deal.]

Legend: Acquiring = The surviving transferee corporation in a merger (or the new corporation formed in a consolidation)

Target = The transferor corporation

1. THE FAIR MARKET VALUE OF THE ACQUIRING STOCK AND OTHER CONSIDERATION RECEIVED BY EACH TARGET SHAREHOLDER WILL BE APPROXIMATELY EQUAL TO THE FAIR MARKET VALUE OF THE TARGET STOCK SURRENDERED IN THE EXCHANGE.

2. [**NOTE: IN VIEW OF THE AMENDMENTS TO THE CONTINUITY OF INTEREST REGULATION DISCUSSED IN CHAPTER 6, THIS REPRESENTATION NO LONGER IS APPLICABLE UNLESS THE SALE IS TO THE ACQUIROR OR CERTAIN RELATED PARTIES TO IT.**] THERE IS NO PLAN OR INTENTION BY THE SHAREHOLDERS OF TARGET WHO OWN 1 PERCENT OR MORE OF THE TARGET STOCK, AND TO THE BEST OF THE KNOWLEDGE OF THE MANAGEMENT OF TARGET, THERE IS NO PLAN OR INTENTION ON THE PART OF THE REMAINING SHAREHOLDERS OF TARGET TO SELL, EXCHANGE, OR OTHERWISE DISPOSE OF [TO THE ACQUIROR] A NUMBER OF SHARES OF ACQUIRING STOCK RECEIVED IN THE TRANSACTION THAT WOULD REDUCE THE TARGET SHAREHOLDERS' OWNERSHIP OF ACQUIRING STOCK TO A NUMBER OF SHARES HAVING A VALUE, AS OF THE DATE OF THE TRANSACTION, OF LESS THAN 50 PERCENT OF THE VALUE OF ALL OF THE FORMERLY OUTSTANDING STOCK OF TARGET AS OF THE SAME DATE. FOR PURPOSES OF THIS REPRESENTATION, SHARES OF TARGET STOCK EXCHANGED FOR CASH OR OTHER PROPERTY, SURRENDERED BY DISSENTERS, OR EXCHANGED FOR CASH IN LIEU OF FRACTIONAL SHARES OF ACQUIRING STOCK WILL BE TREATED AS OUTSTANDING TARGET STOCK ON THE DATE OF THE TRANSACTION. MOREOVER, SHARES OF TARGET STOCK AND SHARES OF ACQUIRING STOCK HELD BY TARGET SHAREHOLDERS AND OTHERWISE SOLD, REDEEMED, OR DISPOSED OF PRIOR OR SUBSEQUENT TO THE TRANSACTION WILL BE CONSIDERED IN MAKING THIS REPRESENTATION. (Alternatively, for publicly traded

companies, submit the above representation substituting "5 percent" for "1 percent" where it appears.)

3. ACQUIRING HAS NO PLAN OR INTENTION TO REACQUIRE ANY OF ITS STOCK ISSUED IN THE TRANSACTION.

4. ACQUIRING HAS NO PLAN OR INTENTION TO SELL OR OTHERWISE DISPOSE OF ANY OF THE ASSETS OF TARGET ACQUIRED IN THE TRANSACTION, EXCEPT FOR DISPOSITIONS MADE IN THE ORDINARY COURSE OF BUSINESS OR TRANSFERS DESCRIBED IN SECTION 368(a)(2)(C) OF THE INTERNAL REVENUE CODE.

5. THE LIABILITIES OF TARGET ASSUMED BY ACQUIRING AND THE LIABILITIES TO WHICH THE TRANSFERRED ASSETS OF TARGET ARE SUBJECT WERE INCURRED BY TARGET IN THE ORDINARY COURSE OF ITS BUSINESS.

6. FOLLOWING THE TRANSACTION, ACQUIRING WILL CONTINUE THE HISTORIC BUSINESS OF TARGET OR USE A SIGNIFICANT PORTION OF TARGET'S HISTORIC BUSINESS ASSETS IN A BUSINESS.

7. ACQUIRING, TARGET, AND THE SHAREHOLDERS OF TARGET WILL PAY THEIR RESPECTIVE EXPENSES, IF ANY, INCURRED IN CONNECTION WITH THE TRANSACTION.

8. THERE IS NO INTERCORPORATE INDEBTEDNESS EXISTING BETWEEN TARGET AND ACQUIRING THAT WAS ISSUED, ACQUIRED, OR WILL BE SETTLED AT A DISCOUNT.

9. NO TWO PARTIES TO THE TRANSACTION ARE INVESTMENT COMPANIES AS DEFINED IN SECTION 368(a)(2)(F)(iii) AND (iv) OF THE INTERNAL REVENUE CODE.

10. TARGET IS NOT UNDER THE JURISDICTION OF A COURT IN A TITLE 11 OR SIMILAR CASE WITHIN THE MEANING OF SECTION 368(a)(3)(A) OF THE INTERNAL REVENUE CODE.

11. THE FAIR MARKET VALUE OF THE ASSETS OF TARGET TRANSFERRED TO ACQUIRING WILL EQUAL OR EXCEED THE SUM OF THE LIABILITIES ASSUMED BY ACQUIRING PLUS THE AMOUNT OF LIABILITIES, IF ANY, TO WHICH THE TRANSFERRED ASSETS ARE SUBJECT.

12. If the transaction also meets the definition of a reorganization under section 368(a)(1)(D) of the Code, submit the following:

THE TOTAL ADJUSTED BASIS OF THE ASSETS OF TARGET TRANSFERRED TO ACQUIRING WILL EQUAL OR EXCEED THE SUM OF THE LIABILITIES ASSUMED BY ACQUIRING, PLUS THE AMOUNT OF LIABILITIES, IF ANY, TO WHICH THE TRANSFERRED ASSETS ARE SUBJECT.

§7.3 The Straight (C) Reorganization

A. Introductory Note

The stock-for-asset (C) reorganization has been a part of the tax law since the 1921 Act. Many of the cases that developed the parameters of the continuity of interest doctrine were (C) transactions. *See* Sec. 6.2. There are three basic requirements to qualify as a straight (C). First, the acquiring corporation must acquire "substantially all of the properties" of the target. The "substantially all" requirement has been in the statute since the 1921 Act. Second, the consideration paid by the acquiring corporation must be "solely" its voting stock. The voting stock requirement was added by the 1934 Act. In determining whether the transaction is solely for voting stock, "the assumption by the acquiring corporation of a liability of the [target], or the fact that property acquired is subject to a liability, shall be disregarded." *See* § 357(a). This qualification was added in 1939 to devitalize the Supreme Court's decision in *Hendler*. *See* Sec. 6.15.A. Third, the target must distribute the acquiring corporation's stock or securities pursuant to the plan of reorganization. *See* § 368(a)(2)(G). This requirement was added by the Deficit Reduction Act of 1984.

The regulations say that although an assumption of liabilities does "not prevent an exchange from being solely for voting stock * * *, it may, however, in some cases, so alter the character of the transaction as to place the transaction outside the purposes and assumptions of the reorganization provisions." *See* § 1.368-2(d). This regulation further says:

Section 368(a)(1)(C) does not prevent consideration of the effect of an assumption of liabilities on the general character of the transaction but merely provides that the requirement that the exchange be solely for voting stock is satisfied if the only additional consideration is an assumption of liabilities. * * *

The solely for voting stock requirement in a (C) is relaxed by § 368(a)(2)(B), the "boot relaxation" provision. This provision was added in 1954, and the Senate Report to the 1954 Code explains:

Paragraph (2)(B) provides that where one corporation acquires substantially all the property of another (subsection (a)(1)(C)) if at least 80 percent of the fair market value of all the property of the other corporation is acquired solely for voting stock, the remainder of the property acquired may be acquired for cash or other property without disqualifying the transaction as a reorganization. For this purpose only, a liability assumed or to which the property is subject, is considered other property. For example, corporation A has assets worth $100,000 and $10,000 in liabilities. Corporation Y acquires $98,000 worth of assets subject to a liability of $10,000. In exchange for these assets, corporation Y transfers its own voting stock, assumes the $10,000 liability, and pays $8,000 cash. This transaction is a reorganization even though a part of the assets of corporation A is acquired for cash. On the other hand, if the assets of corporation A, worth $100,000, were subject to $50,000 in liabilities, an acquisition of all of the assets subject to the liabilities could only be in exchange for voting stock because the liabilities alone are in excess of 20 percent of the fair market value of the property. Thus, only the rule of subsection (a)(1)(C) could be applicable.

The boot relaxation rule is illustrated in § 1.368-2(d)(3).

If a transaction meets the definition of both a (C) and a (D), § 368(a)(2)(A) provides that the transaction is considered a (D). This provision was added by the 1954 Code. The Senate Report explains:

> Paragraph (2) of subsection (a) lists three special rules which modify existing law. It is provided that if a transaction meets the description, both of an acquisition of assets for stock (subsec. (a)(1)(C)) and also meets the description of a transfer to a controlled corporation (subsec. (a)(1)(D)) it shall be treated as described only in subsection (a)(1)(D).

> Your committee intends by this rule to insure that the tax consequences of the distribution of stocks or securities to shareholders or security holders in connection with divisive reorganizations will be governed by the requirements of section 355 relating to distribution of stock of a controlled corporation.

The Senate Finance Committee Report to the Deficit Reduction Act of 1984 gives the following explanation of the distribution requirement:

Reasons for Change Prior to 1934, Federal statutes provided for reorganization treatment only in the case of a transaction qualifying as a merger or consolidation under state law. The C reorganization provisions were added to the Code because uniform merger or consolidation statutes had not been enacted in all states, and the Congress believed that for Federal tax purposes substantially similar transactions should be treated consistently without regard to state law. Thus, the provisions were intended to apply to transactions that are acquisitive in nature and resemble statutory mergers or consolidations.

Different provisions are intended to apply to divisive transactions. The committee is concerned that since a distribution by the transferor corporation of all its assets is not required in connection with a C reorganization, and after such a reorganization the transferor may be able to engage in an active trade or business and not merely serve as a holding company for its shareholders' interests in the acquiring corporation, transactions that are somewhat divisive in nature can qualify as reorganization without qualifying under the provisions generally applicable to divisive transactions.* * *

Explanation of Provision Except as otherwise provided by regulations, an acquisition by one corporation, in exchange solely for all or a part of its voting stock (or in exchange solely for all or a part of the voting stock of a corporation which is in control of the acquiring corporation), of substantially all of the properties of another corporation, is treated as a C reorganization only if the transferor corporation distributes all of its assets (less those retained to meet claims), including consideration received from the acquiring corporation and any retained assets, within 12 months of the acquisition. [See § 368(a)(2)(G).]

Under the bill, the Secretary may prescribe regulations providing exceptions to the distribution requirement. The committee intends that the regulations will provide that a distribution will not be required if substantial hardship, such as the loss of a valuable nontransferable charter, will result. The committee anticipates that any such regulations will impose appropriate conditions so that the abuses intended to be corrected by the bill will not be present.

The Secretary is also directed to prescribe regulations under section 312 providing, among other things, for the allocation of earnings and profits between the acquiring corporation and the transferor corporation in situations in which one corporation owns 80 percent or more of the stock of the transferor corporation before the transaction. * * *

[The Conference follows the above principles except that the distribution must be pursuant to the plan of reorganization (rather than within 12 months of the acquisition).]

The basic tax treatment to the parties in a (C) is as follows:

(1) The acquiring corporation receives nonrecognition treatment, under § 1032 and § 1.61-12(c), upon the issuance of its stock and securities.

(2) Under § 362(b), the acquiring corporation takes a carryover basis for the target's assets. The carryover basis is increased by any gain recognized by the target but not by the gain recognized by the target's shareholders. *See Sweitzer,* Sec. 6.16.

(3) The target has nonrecognition treatment under § 361(a) for any stock or securities of the acquiring corporation it receives. There is no analogue in § 361 to the excess principal amount of securities rule in § 354(a)(2). Under § 361(b), the target generally must distribute any boot it receives in order to qualify for nonrecognition. The treatment of the target under § 361 is explored in Sec. 6.14. The boot dividend rule of § 356(a)(2) does not apply to the target. Liabilities transferred to the acquiring corporation are not treated as boot. *See* § 357(a).

(4) The target takes a substituted basis under § 358 for the stock or securities received.

(5) The target has nonrecognition under § 361(c) upon the distribution of the stock or securities received.

(6) The target's shareholders receive nonrecognition treatment under § 354 and have boot gain or boot dividend treatment under § 356. *See* Sec. 6.13.

(7) The target's shareholders take a substituted basis under § 358.

Sec. 7.3.B explores the scope of the (C). Sec. 7.3.C. looks at the "substantially all" requirement. Sec. 7.3.D. considers strip-down transactions followed by (C) reorganizations. These transactions are more limited in the (C) than in the (A) or (B), and as a consequence, it is not practical to combine a spin-off under § 355 with a (C) reorganization. Sec. 7.3.E. deals with liability assumptions. Sec. 7.3.F. considers the solely for voting stock requirement. Many of the rulings that deal with the solely for voting stock requirement in a (B) also apply in a (C). *See* Sec. 8.2. Sec. 7.3.G. considers the boot relaxation provision. Sec. 6.3.H. examines "creeping (C)" reorganizations and the repeal of the *Bausch & Lomb* doctrine. The creeping (C) should be compared with the creeping (A) and creeping (B). *See,* e.g., *King Enterprises* and *Kass, supra* Sec. 7.2.C. and E. (creeping (As)) and *Chapman infra* Sec. 8.2.B (creeping (Bs)). Sec. 7.3.I. addresses issues under §§ 305 and 306 that can arise in (C) reorganizations. Finally, the representations required for a ruling request under both the straight and triangular (C) reorganizations under § 368(a)(1)(C) are set out in Sec. 7.5, after the examination of triangular (C)s.

B. The Scope of the (C): Acquisition of Target Followed by Liquidation

Revenue Ruling 67-274
1967-2 C.B. 141

Pursuant to a plan of reorganization, corporation *Y* acquired all of the outstanding stock of corporation *X* from the *X* shareholders in exchange solely for voting stock of *Y.* Thereafter *X* was completely liquidated as part of the same plan and all of its assets were transferred to *Y* which assumed all of the liabilities of *X. Y* continued to conduct the business previously conducted by *X.* The former shareholders of *X* continued to hold 16 percent of the fair market value of all the outstanding stock of *Y.* * * *

Under the circumstances of this case the acquisition of *X* stock by *Y* and the liquidation of *X* by *Y* are part of the overall plan of reorganization and the two steps may not be considered independently of each other for Federal income tax purposes. See Revenue Ruling 54-96, C.B. 1954-1, 111, as modified by Revenue Ruling 56-100, C.B. 1956-1, 624. The substance of the transaction is an acquisition of assets to which section 368(a)(1)(B) of the Code does not apply.

Accordingly, the acquisition by *Y* of the outstanding stock of *X* will not constitute a reorganization within the meaning of section 368(a)(1)(B) of the Code but will be considered an acquisition of the assets of *X* which in this case is a reorganization described in section 368(a)(1)(C) of the Code. * * *

Questions and Note

What is the significance of this ruling? What difference does it make whether the transaction is a (C) or alternatively a (B) followed by a § 332 liquidation in which the parent takes a § 334(b)(1) basis for the new subsidiary's assets? *See* § 381.

In Rev. Rul. 72-405, 1972-2 C.B. 217 the Service, following Rev. Rul. 67-274 above, held that a forward subsidiary merger under § 368(a)(2)(D) followed by a liquidation was a (C).

C. What Constitutes "Substantially All"

1. In General

Revenue Ruling 57-518

1957-2 C.B. 253

* * * The *M* and *N* corporations were engaged in the fabrication and sale of various items of steel products. For sound and legitimate business reasons, *N* corporation acquired most of *M* corporation's business and operating assets. Under a plan of reorganization, *M* corporation transferred to *N* corporation (1) all of its fixed assets (plant and equipment) at net book values, (2) 97 percent of all its inventories at book values, and (3) insurance policies and other properties pertaining to the business. In exchange therefore, *N* corporation issued shares of its voting common stock to *M* corporation.

The properties retained by *M* corporation include cash, accounts receivable, notes, and three percent of its total inventory. The fair market value of the assets retained by *M* was roughly equivalent to the amount of its liabilities. *M* corporation proceeded to liquidate its retained properties as expeditiously as possible and applied the proceeds to its outstanding debts. The property remaining after the discharge of all its liabilities was turned over to *N* corporation, and *M* corporation was liquidated. * * *

The specific question presented is what constitutes "substantially all of the properties" as defined in [section 368(a)(1)(C)] of the Code. The answer will depend upon the facts and circumstances in each case rather than upon any particular percentage. Among the elements of importance that are to be considered in arriving at the conclusion are the nature of the properties retained by the transferor, the purpose of the retention, and the amount thereof. In *Milton Smith, et al. v. Commissioner*, 34 B.T.A. 702, acquiescence, page 7, this Bulletin, withdrawing nonacquiescence, C.B. XV-2, 46 (1936), a corporation transferred 71 percent of its gross assets. It retained assets having a value of $52,000, the major portion of which was in cash and accounts receivable. It was stated that the assets were retained in order to liquidate liabilities of approximately $46,000. Thus, after discharging its liabilities, the outside figure of assets remaining with the petitioner would have been $6,000, which the court stated was not an excessive margin to allow for the collection of receivables with which to meet its liabilities. No assets were retained for the purpose of engaging in any business or for distribution to stockholders. In those circumstances, the court held that there had been a transfer of "substantially all of the assets" of the corporation. The court very definitely indicated that a different conclusion would probably have been reached if the amount retained was clearly in excess of a reasonable amount necessary to liquidate liabilities. Furthermore, the court intimated that transfer of all of the net assets of a corporation would not qualify if the percentage of gross assets transferred was too low. Thus, it stated that, if a corporation having gross assets of $1,000,000 and liabilities of $900,000 transferred only the net assets of $100,000, the result would probably not come within the intent of Congress in its use of the words "substantially all."

[In t]he instant case, of the assets not transferred to the corporation, no portion was retained by *M* corporation for its own continued use inasmuch as the plan of reorganization contemplated *M's* liquidation. Furthermore, the assets retained were for the purpose of meeting liabilities, and these assets, at fair market values, approximately equaled the amount of such liabilities. Thus, the facts in this case meet the requirements established in the case of *Milton Smith, supra.*

The instant case is not in conflict with I.T. 2373, C.B. VI-2 19 (1927), which holds that, where one corporation transferred approximately three-fourths of its properties to another corporation for a consideration of bonds and cash, it did not dispose of "substantially all the properties" owned by it at the time and, therefore, no corporate reorganization took place, so that the transaction constituted an exchange of property resulting in a gain or loss to the transferor for income tax purposes. I.T. 2372, *supra,* is obsolete to the extent that it implies that a corporate reorganization could have occurred where there was no continuity of interest. However, that ruling is still valid with regard to its discussion of the question of what constitutes "substantially all of the properties." From the facts as stated in that case, it appears that a major part of the 25 percent of the assets retained were operating assets, and it does not appear that they were retained for the purpose of liquidating the liabilities of the corporation. On the contrary, it seems likely that the corporation may have contemplated continuation of its business or the sale of the remainder of its operating assets to another purchaser. As a result, I.T. 2373, *supra,* is clearly distinguishable from the instant case.

Accordingly, since the assets transferred by *M* to *N* constitute "substantially all" of the assets of the transferor corporation within the meaning of that statutory phrase, the acquisition by *N* corporation, in exchange solely for part of its voting common stock, of the properties of *M* corporation pursuant to the plan will constitute a reorganization within the purview of section 368(a)(1)(C) of the Code. No gain or loss is recognized to the transferor as a result of the exchange of its property for common stock of the transferee under section 361 of the Code; and no gain or loss is recognized to the shareholders of *M* corporation, under section 354(a)(1) of such Code, as the result of their receipt of *N* common stock.

I.T. 2373, C.B. VI-2, 19 (1927), distinguished.

2. Service's Ruling Policy

Excerpt from Revenue Procedure 77-37

1977-2 C.B. 568

Sec. 3. Operating Rules for Issuing Ruling Letters .01 The "substantially all" requirement of sections 354(b)(1)(A), 368(a)(1)(C), 368(a)(2)(B)(i), 368(a)(2)(D), and 368(a)(2)(E)(i) of the Code is satisfied if there is a transfer (and in the case of a surviving corporation under section 368(a)(2)(E)(i), the retention) of assets representing at least 90 percent of the fair market value of the net assets and at least 70 percent of the fair market value of the gross assets held by the corporation immediately prior to the transfer. All payments to dissenters and all redemptions and distributions (except for regular, normal distributions) made by the corporation immediately preceding the transfer and which are part of the plan of reorganization will be considered as assets held by the corporation immediately prior to the transfer.

Problems

1. Target (*TC*) has $100K of assets and $40K of liabilities. Acquiror (*AC*) proposes to acquire $60K of *TC*'s assets and none of its liabilities solely in exchange for *AC* voting stock. *TC* will use the $40K of retained assets to discharge its $40K of liabilities and will then liquidate, distributing the *AC* voting stock. Will this transaction qualify as a (C) reorganization under the Service's ruling policy? If not, what amount of *TC*'s assets would *AC* have to acquire, assuming *AC* refuses to take over any of the liabilities? In such case what result to *TC*?

2. Assume that three separate target corporations (*TC*) have the following assets and liabilities:

TC	Assets	Liabilities
TC # 1	$100K	-0-
TC # 2	$100K	$10K
TC# 3	$100K	$50K

What is the minimum amount of assets of each *TC* that can be acquired by an acquiring corporation in exchange for its voting stock and still have the transaction qualify as a (C) reorganization under the Service's ruling policy? Assuming all the assets and liabilities of each *TC* are acquired, what is the maximum amount of cash that can be paid under the boot relaxation rule of §368(a)(2)(B)?

3. Sale of Part of Assets to Unrelated Party Prior to the Transaction
Revenue Ruling 88-48
1988-1 C.B. 117

Issue If a transferor corporation sold 50 percent of its historic assets to unrelated parties for cash and immediately afterwards transferred to an acquiring corporation all of its assets (including the cash from the sale), did the subsequent transfer meet the "substantially all" requirement of section 368(a)(1)(C) of the Internal Revenue Code?

Facts *X* and *Y* were unrelated corporations that for many years were engaged in the hardware business. *X* operated two significant lines of business, a retail hardware business and a wholesale plumbing supply business. *Y* desired to acquire and continue to operate *X*'s hardware business but did not desire to acquire the other business. Accordingly, pursuant to an overall plan, the following steps were taken. First, in a taxable transaction, *X* sold its entire interest in the plumbing supply business (constituting 50 percent of its total historic business assets) to purchasers unrelated to either *X* or *Y* or their shareholders. Second, *X* transferred all of its assets, including the cash proceeds from the sale, to *Y* solely for *Y* voting stock and the assumption of *X*'s liabilities. Finally, in pursuance of the plan of reorganization, *X* distributed the *Y* stock (the sole asset *X* then held) to the *X* shareholders in complete liquidation.

Except for the issue relating to the "substantially all" requirement, the transfer of assets from *X* to *Y* constituted a corporate reorganization within the meaning of section 368(a)(1)(C) of the Code.

Law and Analysis * * * Section 368(a)(1)(C) of the Code is intended to accommodate transactions that are, in effect, mergers, but which fail to meet the statutory requirements that would bring them within section 368(a)(1)(A). *See* S.Rep. No. 558, 73d Cong., 2d Sess. 16, 17 (1939), 1939-1 C.B. (Pt. 2) 586, 598.

Congress intended that transactions that are divisive in nature not qualify under section 368(a)(1)(C) of the Code, but, instead, be subject to the tests under section 368(a)(1)(D). *See* S.Rep. No. 1622, 83d Cong., 2d Sess. 274 (1954). The enactment of section 368(a)(2)(G) indicates the continuing interest in furthering this underlying objective of preventing divisive "C" reorganizations.

Rev. Rul. 57-18, 1957-C.B. 253, concerns whether, in a "C" reorganization, assets may be retained to pay liabilities. The ruling states that what constitutes "substantially all" for purposes of section 368(a)(1)(C) of the Code depends on the facts and circumstances in each case. Rev. Rul. 57-518 exemplifies the Service's longstanding position that where some assets are transferred to the acquiring corporation and other assets retained, then the transaction may be divisive and so fail to meet the "substantially all" requirement of section 368(a)(1)(C). *See also* Rev. Rul. 78-47, 1978-1 C.B. 113.

In the present situation, 50 percent of the *X* assets acquired by *Y* consisted of cash from the sale of one of *X*'s significant historic businesses. Although *Y* acquired substantially all the assets *X* held at the time of transfer, the prior sale prevented *Y* from acquiring substantially all of *X*'s historic business assets. The transaction here at issue, however, was not divisive. The sale proceeds were not retained by the transferor corporation or its shareholders, but were transferred to the acquiring corporation. Moreover, the prior sale of the historic business assets was to unrelated purchasers, and the *X* shareholders retained no interest, direct or indirect, in these assets. Under these circumstances, the "substantially all" requirement of section 368(a)(1)(C) was met because all of the assets of *X* were transferred to *Y*.

Holding The transfer of all of its assets by *X* to *Y* met the "substantially all" requirement of section 368(a)(1)(C) of the Code, even though immediately prior to the transfer *X* sold 50 percent of its historic business assets to unrelated parties for cash and transferred that cash to *Y* instead of the historic assets. * * *

D. Strip Down of Target Prior to the (C): Spin-Offs and Dividends

1. Spin-Off Prior to a (C)

Helvering v. Elkhorn Coal Co.

United States Court of Appeals, Fourth Circuit, 1937
95 F.2d 732, *cert. denied* 305 U.S. 605

PARKER, CIRCUIT JUDGE.

This is a petition to review a decision of the Board of Tax Appeals holding profit realized by the Elkhorn Coal & Coke Company upon a transfer of certain mining properties to the Mill Creek Coal & Coke Company to be nontaxable. The ground of the decision was that the transfer was made pursuant to a plan of reorganization within the meaning of section 203(h)(1)(A) of the Revenue Act of 1926 [now § 368(a)(1)(C).]

Prior to December 18, 1925, the Elkhorn Coal & Coke Company, to which we shall hereafter refer to as the old company, owned certain coal mining properties in West Virginia and certain stocks in other mining companies engaged in business in that state. It was closely associated with the Mill Creek Coal & Coke Company, which owned neighboring property; and a majority of the directorate of both corporations consisted of the same persons. Early in December 1925, a plan was formed whereby the old company was to transfer its mine, mining plant, and mining equipment at Mayberry, W.Va., to the Mill Creek Company in exchange for 1,000 shares of the capital stock of that company. This exchange was accomplished on December 31, 1925, at which time, it is stipulated, the stock received by the old company had a fair market value of $550,000 which is in excess of the deficiency asserted by the Commissioner. There is no contention that the transfer by the old company was to a corporation controlled by it or by its stockholders and therefore within the nonrecognition provision of section 203(h)(1)(B) [now § 368(a)(1)(D)] of the act; but the argument of the taxpayer is that the transfer was of all the properties of one corporation for the stock of another, and therefore within the nonrecognition provision of section 203(h)(1)(A) [now § 368(a)(1)(C).]

The contention that the transfer in question was of all the properties of the old company depends upon the legal conclusion to be drawn from certain evidentiary facts relating to the prior organization of another corporation and the transfer to it of all the property of the old company which was not to be transferred to the Mill Creek Company. These facts, which were found by the Board and are undisputed, are as follows: At the time that the transfer to the Mill Creek Company was decided upon, the officers of the old company caused another corporation to be organized under the name of the Elkhorn Coal Company, which we shall refer to as hereafter as the new company, and on December 18, 1925, transferred to it, in exchange for 6,100 shares of its stock, all of the property of the old company which was not to be transferred to the Mill Creek Company except certain accounts, which were transferred to the new company on December 28, 1931, in consideration of its assuming the liabilities of the old company. The 6,100 shares of stock in the new company were promptly distributed by the old company as a dividend to its stockholders. This left the old company owning only the property which was to be transferred to the Mill Creek Company under the plan and which was transferred to that company on December 31st, as mentioned in the preceding paragraph. Following that transfer and the receipt by the old company of the 1,000 shares of the stock of the Mill Creek Company pursuant thereto, the new company proceeded to place itself in the same position relative to the stockholders of the old company that the old company had occupied, and then to wind up its affairs. It accomplished that result in the following manner: On January 22, 1926, it exchanged 1,440 shares of its capital stock for the 7,540 shares of the outstanding capital stock of the old company, making the exchange with the stockholders of that company. This gave those who had been stockholders in the old company the same interest in the new company that they had had in the old, and gave to the new company the ownership of all of the stock in the old. The

1,000 shares of stock received from the Mill Creek Company were then transferred to the new company and the old company was dissolved. No business whatever was done by the old company after the transfer of assets to the Mill Creek Company on December 31st; and no reason appears for the organization of the new company except to provide a transferee to take over and hold the assets which were not to be transferred to the Mill Creek Company so that the transfer to that company when made would be a transfer of all the assets of the old company.

The Board was of opinion that all of these transactions were carried through pursuant to prearranged plan. * * * The Board thought, however, with five members dissenting, that because the transfers from the old company to the new were genuine and were separate and distinct from the transfer to the Mill Creek Company, the latter must be treated as a transfer of substantially all of the properties of the corporation within the meaning of the reorganization statute. * * *

A careful consideration of the evidentiary facts discloses no purpose which could have been served by the creation of the new company and the transfer of the assets to it, except to strip the old company of all of its properties which were not to be transferred to the Mill Creek Company, in anticipation of that transfer. The creation of the new company and its acquisition of the assets of the old was not a corporate reorganization, therefore, within the meaning of the statute or within any fair meaning of the term "reorganization." It did not involve any real transfer of assets by the business enterprise or any rearranging of corporate structure, but at most a mere shifting of charters, having no apparent purpose except the avoidance of taxes on the transfer to the Mill Creek Company which was in contemplation.

Under such circumstances we think that the decision in *Gregory v. Helvering* * * * is controlling. * * * The court said: "In these circumstances, the facts speak for themselves and are susceptible of but one interpretation. The whole undertaking, though conducted according to the terms of subdivision (B), was in fact an elaborate and devious form of conveyance masquerading as a corporate reorganization, and nothing else. The rule which excludes from consideration the motive of tax avoidance is not pertinent to the situation, because the transaction upon its face lies outside the plain intent of the statute. To hold otherwise would be to exalt artifice above reality and to deprive the statutory provision in question of all serious purpose."

We do not see how that case can be distinguished from this. If the property which was to be transferred to Mill Creek had been transferred to a new company created for the purpose and had been by that company transferred to Mill Creek, no one would contend that there was a distinction; and certainly there is no difference in principle between creating a subsidiary to take and convey the property to the intended transferee and creating a subsidiary to take over the other assets and having the old company make the transfer. In either case, the apparent reorganization is a mere artifice; and it can make no difference which of the affiliated corporations makes the transfer of assets which it is desired to bring within the nonrecognition provisions of the statute.

It is suggested in the opinion of the Board that the case before us is analogous to that which would have been presented if the old company, prior to the transfer to

Mill Creek, had distributed to its stockholders all of the assets except those destined for such transfer; but the distinction is obvious. In the case supposed, the business enterprise would have definitely divested itself of the property distributed. Here it did not divest itself of the property at all, but merely made certain changes in the legal papers under which it enjoyed corporate existence. No rule is better settled than that in tax matters we must look to substance and not to form; and no one who looks to substance can see in the mere change of charters, which is all that we have here, any reason for permitting a transfer of a part of the corporate assets to escape the taxation to which it is subject under the statute.

Congress has seen fit to grant nonrecognition of profit in sale or exchange of assets only under certain conditions, one of which is that one corporation shall transfer "substantially all" of its properties for stock in another. If nonrecognition of profit can be secured by the plan adopted in this case, the exemption is broadened to cover all transfers of assets for stock, whether "substantially all" or not, if only the transferor will go to the slight trouble and expense of getting a new charter for his corporation and making the transfer of assets to the new corporation thus created in such way as to leave in the old only the assets to be transferred at the time the transfer is to be made. We do not think the statutory exemption may be thus broadened by such an artifice.

For the reasons stated, the decision of the Board will be reversed, and the cause will be remanded to it for further proceedings in accordance with this opinion.

Reversed.

[Dissenting Opinion deleted.]

Questions

What were the precise facts in *Elkhorn Coal?* What was the holding? What is the significance of *Elkhorn Coal* under the current (C) reorganization?

2. Payment of Dividends before and after the (C)

Revenue Ruling 74-457

1974-2 C.B. 122

Pursuant to a plan of reorganization corporation *Y* agreed to acquire the assets of corporation *X* in exchange solely for *Y* voting stock and the assumption by *Y* of *X*'s liabilities, with the exchange to take place on September 29, 1973. *Y* was an existing corporation in which neither *X* nor its shareholders owned any stock. On September 5, 1973, *X* declared a regular quarterly cash dividend payable on September 25, 1973, to its shareholders. After paying the dividend *X* transferred all of its assets to *Y* on September 29, 1973, in exchange solely for *Y* voting stock and the assumption by *Y* of *X*'s liabilities.

Held, the cash used by *X* to pay the regular quarterly dividend prior to the reorganization exchange is not taken into account in determining whether *Y* acquired "substantially all of the properties" of *X* within the meaning of section 368(a)(1)(C) of the Internal Revenue Code of 1954.

However, if payment of the dividend occurs after the reorganization exchange, both the cash to pay the dividend and the amount of the liability for payment of the dividend will be taken into account in determining whether *Y* acquired "substantially all the properties" of *X*.

3. Acquisition of Assets of Newly Formed Controlled Corporation That Is Spun Off under § 355

Revenue Ruling 2003-79

I.R.B. 2003-29, July 1, 2003

ISSUE. Whether the acquisition by an unrelated corporation of all the assets of a newly formed controlled corporation following the distribution of the stock of the controlled corporation by a distributing corporation will satisfy the requirement of § 368(a)(1)(C) of the Internal Revenue Code that substantially all of the properties of the acquired corporation be acquired where the assets of the controlled corporation represent less than substantially all of the assets that the distributing corporation held before it formed the controlled corporation.

FACTS. D, a domestic corporation, directly conducts Business X and Business Y. D's assets are equally divided between the two businesses. A, a domestic corporation unrelated to D, conducts Business X and wishes to acquire D's Business X, but not D's Business Y.

To accomplish the acquisition, D and A agree to undertake the following steps in the following order: (i) D will transfer its Business X assets to C, a newly formed domestic corporation, in exchange for 100 percent of the stock of C, (ii) D will distribute the C stock to D's shareholders, (iii) A will acquire all the assets of C in exchange solely for voting stock of A, and (iv) C will liquidate. Apart from the question of whether the acquisition of C's assets by A will satisfy the requirement of § 368(a)(1)(C) that the acquiring corporation acquire substantially all of the properties of the acquired corporation, steps (i) and (ii) together meet all the requirements of § 368(a)(1)(D), step (ii) meets all the requirements of § 355(a), and steps (iii) and (iv) together meet all the requirements of § 368(a)(1)(C).

LAW. Section 355 provides that if certain requirements are met, a corporation may distribute stock and securities in a controlled corporation to its shareholders and security holders without causing the distributees to recognize gain or loss.

Section 368(a)(1)(C) defines a reorganization to include the acquisition by one corporation, in exchange solely for all or a part of its voting stock, of substantially all of the properties of another corporation.

Section 368(a)(1)(D) defines a reorganization to include a transfer by a corporation of all or a part of its assets to another corporation if immediately after the transfer the transferor, or one or more of its shareholders (including persons who were shareholders immediately before the transfer), or any combination thereof, is in control of the corporation to which the assets are transferred; but only if, in pursuance of the plan, stock or securities of the corporation to which the assets are transferred are distributed in a transaction that qualifies under § 354, 355, or 356.

In *Helvering v. Elkhorn Coal Co.*, 95 F.2d 732 (4 th Cir. 1937), *cert. denied*, 305 U.S. 605, *rehg denied*, 305 U.S. 670 (1938), Elkhorn Coal, in anticipation of being acquired by Mill Creek, transferred part of its operating assets to a newly formed subsidiary and distributed the subsidiary's stock to Elkhorn Coal's shareholders. The court concluded that the distribution of subsidiary stock prevented the subsequent acquisition from qualifying under a predecessor of § 368(a)(1)(C) because, as a result of the distribution, Mill Creek did not acquire substantially all of Elkhorn Coal's historical assets.

In *Commissioner v. Mary Archer W. Morris Trust*, 367 F.2d 794 (4 th Cir. 1966), *aff'g* 42 T.C. 779 (1964), the taxpayer, in anticipation of a merger with a national bank, contributed its insurance business to a new subsidiary and distributed the subsidiary's stock to its shareholders. The divestiture was necessary to comply with national banking laws. The court held that the distribution satisfied the requirements for nonrecognition under § 355(a) and, therefore, that the contribution qualified as a reorganization under § 368(a)(1)(D).

In Rev. Rul. 68-603, 1968-2 C.B. 148, the Internal Revenue Service announced that it would follow the decision in *Mary Archer W. Morris Trust* to the extent it held that (1) the active business requirements of § 355(b)(1)(A) were satisfied even though the distributing corporation, immediately after the spin-off, merged into the unrelated acquiring corporation, (2) the control immediately after requirement of § 368(a)(1)(D) implies no limitation upon a reorganization of the transferor corporation (the distributing corporation) after the distribution of the stock of the controlled corporation, and (3) there was a business purpose for the spin-off and the merger.

Rev. Rul. 98-27, 1998-1 C.B. 1159, states that the Service will not apply any formulation of the step transaction doctrine to determine whether the distributed corporation was a controlled corporation immediately before a distribution under § 355(a) solely because of any post-distribution acquisition or restructuring of the distributed corporation, whether prearranged or not. The holding of Rev. Rul. 98-27 is based on § 1012(a) and § 1012(c) of the Taxpayer Relief Act of 1997 (the "1997 Act"), Pub. L. No. 105-34, 111 Stat. 788, 916-17. Section 1012(c) amended the control requirements of § 368(a)(1)(D) and 351 to provide that, generally for transactions seeking qualification after August 5, 1997, under either provision and § 355, the shareholders of the distributing corporation must own stock possessing more than 50 percent of the voting power and more than 50 percent of the total value of the controlled corporation's stock immediately after the distribution. *See* §§ 368(a)(2)(H) and 351(c). Section 1012(a) amended § 355 by adding subsection (e), which provides rules for the recognition of gain on certain distributions of stock or securities of a controlled corporation in connection with acquisitions of stock representing a 50 percent or greater interest in the distributing corporation or any controlled corporation.

The Conference Report accompanying the 1997 Act states, in part, that:

> The ... bill does not change the present-law requirement under section 355
> that the distributing corporation must distribute 80 percent of the voting

power and 80 percent of each other class of stock of the controlled corporation. It is expected that this requirement will be applied by the Internal Revenue Service taking account of the provisions of the proposal regarding plans that permit certain types of planned restructuring of the distributing corporation following the distribution, and to treat similar restructurings of the controlled corporation in a similar manner. Thus, the 80-percent control requirement is expected to be administered in a manner that would prevent the tax-free spin-off of a less-than-80-percent controlled subsidiary, but would not generally impose additional restrictions on post-distribution restructurings of the controlled corporation if such restrictions would not apply to the distributing corporation.

H.R. Rep. No. 105-220, at 529–30 (1997); 1997-4 C.B. 1457, at 1999–2000.

Section 6010(c)(2) of the Internal Revenue Service Restructuring and Reform Act of 1998 (the "1998 Act"), P.L. 105-206, 1998-3 C.B. 145, amended § 1012(c) of the 1997 Act to provide that, in the case of a § 368(a)(1)(D) or § 351 transaction that is followed by a § 355 transaction, solely for purposes of determining the tax treatment of any transfer of property by the distributing corporation to the controlled corporation, the fact that the shareholders of the distributing corporation dispose of part or all of the controlled corporation's stock after the § 355 distribution shall not be taken into account in determining whether the control requirement of either § 368(a)(1)(D) or § 351 has been satisfied.

The Senate Report accompanying the 1998 Act contains three examples in which distributing corporation D transfers appreciated business X to newly created subsidiary C in exchange for at least 85 percent of the C stock and then distributes its C stock to the D shareholders. As part of the same plan, C then merges into unrelated acquiring corporation A. Each example concludes that if the distribution satisfies the requirements of § 355, the control immediately after requirement will be satisfied solely for purposes of determining the tax treatment of the transfer of business X by D to C. *See* S. Rep. No. 105-174, at 173–176 (1998); 1998-3 C.B. 537, at 709–712.

ANALYSIS. Section 1012 of the 1997 Act, as amended by 6010(c) of the 1998 Act, evidences the intention of Congress that a corporation formed in connection with a distribution that qualifies for nonrecognition under § 355 will be respected as a separate corporation for purposes of determining (i) whether the corporation was a controlled corporation immediately before the distribution and (ii) whether a pre-distribution transfer of property to the controlled corporation satisfies the requirements of § 368(a)(1)(D) or § 351, even if a post-distribution restructuring causes the controlled corporation to cease to exist. *See* Rev. Rul. 98-44, 1998-2 C.B. 315; Rev. Rul. 98-27, *supra*; S. Rep. No. 105-174, *supra*. Therefore, the controlled corporation should also be considered independently from the distributing corporation in determining whether an acquisition of the controlled corporation will qualify as a reorganization under § 368. Accordingly, in determining under § 368(a)(1)(C) whether an acquiring corporation has acquired substantially all of the properties of a newly formed controlled corporation, reference should be made solely to the properties held by the controlled corporation immediately following the distributing corporation's transfer of properties to the controlled corporation, rather than to the properties held by the distributing corporation immediately before its formation of the controlled corporation.

Hence, the acquisition by A of all the properties held by C immediately after the distribution will satisfy the requirement of § 368(a)(1)(C) that A acquire substantially all the properties of C. This result obtains even though an acquisition by A of the same properties from D would have failed this requirement if D had retained Business X, contributed Business Y to C, and distributed the stock of C. *See Helvering v. Elkhorn Coal Co., supra.*

HOLDING. The acquisition by an unrelated corporation of all the assets of a newly formed controlled corporation following the distribution of the stock of the controlled corporation by a distributing corporation will satisfy the requirement of § 368(a)(1)(C) that substantially all of the properties of the acquired corporation be acquired where the assets of the controlled corporation represent less than substantially all of the assets that the distributing corporation held before it formed the controlled corporation.

E. Assumption of Liabilities: Assumption of Target's Obligation to Warrant Holders and Holders of Stock Options

Revenue Ruling 68-637

1968-2 C.B. 158

Advice has been requested whether the assumption of outstanding unexercised stock warrants and outstanding employee stock options under the circumstances described below violates the "solely for all or a part of its voting stock" requirement of section 368(a)(1)(C) of the Internal Revenue Code of 1954.

Pursuant to a plan of reorganization, *X* corporation acquired all the assets of *Y* corporation in exchange for some of *X*'s voting stock. Prior to this transaction *Y* had issued stock warrants to certain investors and had granted options to certain employees to purchase shares of its stock. Pursuant to the plan of reorganization, *X* agreed to substitute its stock for that of *Y* under the terms of the stock warrants and options issued by the latter. *X* accordingly agreed that upon the exercise of any of the warrants or stock options outstanding as of the date of exchange, it would issue to the warrant and option holders that number of shares of *X* voting stock that they would have been entitled to receive had they exercised the warrants or options immediately prior to the exchange. Following the acquisition, *X* continued to conduct the business previously conducted by *Y.*

The question presented is whether the agreement by *X* to substitute its stock for that of *Y* under the terms of the stock warrants and options issued by the acquired corporation constitutes nonqualifying consideration under the definition contained in section 368(a)(1)(C) of the Code. * * *

The arrangements under which *Y* was obligated to issue its stock to the holders of the warrants and options constitute a contractual liability of *Y*. Thus, the undertaking by *X* to discharge *Y*'s obligation by substituting its own stock for that of *Y* was no different than the assumption of a liability under any other executory contract of *Y* and such assumption is to be disregarded as provided in section 368(a)(1)(C) of the Code.

Accordingly, the assumption of *Y*'s outstanding warrants and outstanding employee stock options by *X* and the substitution of the latter corporation's stock thereunder pursuant to a transaction otherwise qualifying under section 368(a)(1)(C) of the Code, does not violate the "solely for all or a part of its voting stock" requirement of this section of the Code.

F. Solely for Voting Stock Requirement

1. Acquiring Corporation Pays Reorganization Expenses of Target and Its Shareholders

Revenue Ruling 76-365
1976-2 C.B. 110

Advice has been requested whether the payment of expenses, under the circumstances described below, violates the solely for voting stock requirement of section 368(a)(1)(C) of the Internal Revenue Code of 1954.

All of the stock of corporation *X* was owned by *A*, an individual. Pursuant to a plan of reorganization, *Y*, a corporation whose stock is widely held, acquired all the assets of *X* in exchange for *Y* voting common stock and the assumption by *Y* of all of the liabilities of *X* in a transaction intended to qualify as a reorganization under section 368(a)(1)(C) of the Code. Prior to this transaction, at the same time that *Y* made its offer, five other corporations made unsuccessful offers to acquire all the assets and liabilities of *X*.

In order to evaluate the acquisition offers of the prospective acquiring corporations, *X* independently hired a financial consultant and an accountant to ascertain the value of the stock of each of the prospective acquiring corporations and was solely liable for the expenses incurred. The fees of these individuals for their services totaled 6*x* dollars. As part of the plan of reorganization described above, *Y* made direct cash payments in the total amount of 6*x* dollars to the consultant and the accountant in satisfaction of the appraisal and accounting expenses incurred by *X*.

[The ruling discusses Rev. Rul. 73-54, *supra*.]

In the present case, the expenses of *X* incurred to evaluate the acquisition offer of *Y* are expenses solely and directly related to the plan of reorganization, but those expenses of *X* incurred to evaluate the acquisition offers of the five unsuccessful corporations were not expenses solely and directly related to the plan of reorganization by which *Y* acquired all the assets of *X* and do not constitute valid reorganization expenses within the meaning of Rev. Rul. 73-54. However, the payment of these unrelated expenses should be treated as an assumption of liability of the acquired corporation under section 368(a)(1)(C) of the Code. The unrelated expenses constitute preexisting obligations of *X*, the nature and amount of which were not determined and fixed in the reorganization in question. * * *

Accordingly, under the facts of this case, *Y*'s payment of the reorganization expenses incurred does not violate the solely for voting stock requirement of section 368(a)(1)(C) of the Code. Such payment by *Y* is viewed as a payment of two separate types of expenses, those expenses that are solely and directly related to the reorganization, and, those expenses that are treated as liabilities of *X* assumed by *Y* pursuant to the plan of reorganization.

2. Prior Purchase of Target's Stock by Person Related to Acquiror
Revenue Ruling 85-138
1985-2 C.B. 122

Issue Whether the acquisition of substantially all the properties of *X* by *S1* under the facts described below meets the requirements of a reorganization pursuant to section 368(a)(1)(C) of the Internal Revenue Code.

Facts Corporation *P* owned all the stock of corporation *S1* and corporation *S2*. It was *P*'s desire that *S1* acquire substantially all the properties of *X*, a corporation unrelated by stock ownership to *P*, *S1* or *S2*. In order to eliminate any possible adverse minority interest in *X*, and pursuant to a plan adopted by *P*, *P* caused *S2* to purchase with *S2*'s own cash some of the shares of outstanding voting stock of *X*. *S2*, along with the other shareholders of *X*, then approved an agreement between *P* and *X* under which *X* transferred substantially all its properties to *S1* in exchange for voting stock of *P* and the assumption by *S1* of all of *X*'s liabilities. [It was intended that this transaction qualify as a triangular (C).] The liabilities assumed by *S1* were in excess of twenty percent of the fair market value of *X*'s assets. Subsequent to this exchange, *X* was dissolved and the *P* stock was distributed to the shareholders of *X* (including *S2*) in exchange for the surrender and cancellation of all the *X* stock.

Law and Analysis [Under § 368(a)(2)(B)], if nonqualifying consideration such as cash is furnished by the acquiring corporation, liabilities of the acquired corporation assumed by the acquiring corporation are added to cash paid in order to determine whether 80 percent of the fair market value of the assets of the acquired corporation are exchanged solely for voting stock. In the instant case, *S1*'s assumption of *X* liabilities in excess of 20 percent of the fair market value of *X* assets effectively precludes the application of the boot relaxation rule of section 368(a)(2)(B) of the Code. As a result, if *S1* is deemed to have exchanged partly *P* voting stock and partly cash for substantially all the assets of *X*, the transaction will not qualify as a reorganization under section 368(a)(1)(C) of the Code.

In Rev. Rul. 69-48, 1969-1 C.B. 106, corporation *P* purchased for cash nineteen percent of the stock of corporation *X* and acquired an option to purchase an additional thirty percent as part of a plan for *P*'s wholly-owned subsidiary, *S*, to acquire the assets of *X*.

Under the option agreement, *P* was able to vote the optioned stock as well as the stock it had purchased outright. Twenty-two months later, *P* voted for the transfer of *X's* assets to *S* in exchange for *P* voting stock and the assumption by *S* of *X's* liabilities. After the transfer of its assets, *X* was liquidated. Rev. Rul. 69-48 concludes that *P's* cash purchase of *X* stock violated the "solely for voting stock" requirement of section 368(a)(1)(C) because it was an integral step in the plan to acquire substantially all of *X's* assets.

In the present case, *S2's* prearranged cash purchase of *X* shares was an integral step in the plan for *S1* to acquire substantially all the assets of *X*. Therefore, as in Rev. Rul. 69-48, the consideration for the acquisition of *X's* properties by *S1* is deemed to consist of cash in addition to the voting stock of *P* and the assumption of liabilities by *S1* permitted under section 368(a)(1)(C) of the Code.

Holding The transaction does not qualify as a reorganization defined in section 368(a)(1)(C) of the Code. Compare Rev. Rul. 85-139 wherein the same conclusion is reached in a purported reorganization under section 368(a)(1)(B).

Questions and Note

1. Does the transaction in the ruling satisfy the continuity of interest requirement? How does the continuity of interest requirement relate to the solely for voting stock requirement?

2. *See also* Rev. Rul. 85-139, *infra,* Sec. 8.2.E.

G. The Boot Relaxation Rule: Acquiring Corporation Pays Off Target's Dissenters

Revenue Ruling 73-102

1973-1 C.B. 186

Advice has been requested whether, under the circumstances described below, the "solely for voting stock" requirement of section 368(a)(1)(C) of the Internal Revenue Code is satisfied.

For valid business reasons, *X* corporation entered into a plan of reorganization with unrelated *Y* corporation. Pursuant to the plan, *X* transferred all of its assets to *Y* in exchange for *Y* voting stock and the assumption by *Y* of the *X* liabilities, including liabilities to pay claims of dissenting shareholders.

Under the plan, *Y* paid 50*x* dollars to dissenting *X* shareholders in satisfaction of their claims, based on the fair market value of their *X* stock surrendered. The dissenting shareholders surrendered all their *X* stock for cash in the transaction. The fair market value of the gross assets transferred by *X* to *Y* was 2,000*x* dollars. The amount of the liabilities assumed by *Y* (other than the liability to pay dissenting shareholders) was 150*x* dollars. * * *

The payment by *Y* of 50*x* dollars to dissenting shareholders of *X* in satisfaction of their claims was, in substance, the same as if *Y* had exchanged cash plus voting stock for the properties of X. Therefore, this cash payment is not a payment by Y of an assumed liability, but is additional consideration paid by Y in the exchange for the properties acquired by Y. Thus, the acquisition of the X property for the Y voting stock and cash cannot qualify under section 368(a)(1)(C) of the Code unless section 368(a)(2)(B) of the Code applies.

For purposes of section 368(a)(2)(B) of the Code, Y constructively paid a total of 200x dollars in money to X (liabilities assumed in the amount of 150x dollars, plus 50x dollars paid to the dissenting shareholders). Therefore, Y received property of X having a fair market value of 1,800x dollars (gross assets in the amount of 2,000x dollars, less 200x dollars in money constructively paid to X) solely for voting stock of Y, which represents 90 percent of the fair market value of all of the X property.

Accordingly, in the instant case, since at least 80 percent of all the property of X was acquired solely for voting stock of Y, it is held that the transaction qualifies as a reorganization under sections 368(a)(1)(C) and (a)(2)(B) of the Code. Under section 361(b)(1)(A) of the Code, no gain is recognized to X upon the constructive receipt and distribution of 50x dollars to the dissenting shareholders. Under section 361(b)(2) of the Code, no loss is recognized to X. The cash received by the dissenting shareholders will be treated as a constructive distribution to them by X in redemption of their X stock subject to the provisions and limitations of section 302 of the Code.

H. The Creeping (C)

1. The Bausch & Lomb Doctrine and Its Repeal

a. The Service's Prior Position on Pre-Transaction Stock Ownership in Target by Acquiror: The Bausch & Lomb Doctrine

Revenue Ruling 54-396
1954-2 C.B. 147

M Corporation owned 79 percent of the outstanding capital stock of N Corporation. This stock had been acquired by M Corporation by a cash consideration in prior years. M and N Corporations entered into an agreement whereby shares of common stock of M were issued in exchange for all the properties and assets of N, subject to its liabilities. N Corporation was liquidated and the shares of M received by it in exchange for its assets were distributed to its stockholders pro rata. Thereafter, the business of both corporations was conducted by M.

The question presented is whether the transaction qualifies as a reorganization under the provisions of section 112(g)(1)(C) of the Internal Revenue Code of 1939 [now § 368(a)(1)(C)]. * * *

Under the Revenue Act of 1934, the later revenue acts, and the Internal Revenue Code of 1939, however, it was made clear that, except in cases where clause (A) or clause (D) of section 112(g)(1), *supra,* is applicable, the question whether an acquisition of stock or assets of another corporation constitutes a "reorganization" must stand or fall on its full compliance with clause (B) or clause (C) of section 112(g)(1), irrespective of the element of merger.

The language of section 112(g)(1)(C) of the Internal Revenue Code, which is controlling in the instant case, defines a reorganization as the acquisition by one corporation, in exchange solely for all or part of its voting stock, of substantially all the properties of another corporation. Under the circumstances presented, the M corporation, already the owner of 79 percent of N Corporation stock, acquired only the remaining 21 percent of the assets of N through the exchange of stock. The remaining 79 percent of the assets were acquired by M as a liquidating dividend in exchange for the stock of N which had been acquired by cash purchase in prior years.

Accordingly, it is held that the transaction in the instant case does not qualify as a reorganization within the purview of section 112(g)(1)(C) of the Internal Revenue Code. It is further held that the minority stockholders effected a taxable exchange within the meaning of section 112(a) of the Code, and a taxable gain or loss resulted to M Corporation upon the liquidation of N as provided in section 115(c) of the Code. * * *

Note

The position in Rev. Rul. 54-396 was sustained in the *Bausch & Lomb* opinion, which is discussed below.

b. Preamble to the to the Proposed Regulations Repealing the Bausch & Lomb Doctrine

Preamble to Proposed Regulations Reg-115086-98
(June 14, 1999)

Summary: This document contains proposed regulations relating to the solely for voting stock requirement in certain corporate reorganizations under section 368(a)(1)(C) of the Internal Revenue Code. The proposed regulations provide that prior ownership of a portion of a target corporation's stock by an acquiring corporation generally will not prevent the solely for voting stock requirement in a "C" reorganization of the target corporation and the acquiring corporation from being satisfied. * * *

Background: * * * These regulations propose to reverse the IRS's longstanding position that the acquisition of assets of a partially controlled subsidiary does not qualify as a tax-free reorganization under section 368(a)(1)(C).

The Bausch & Lomb Doctrine The IRS's position that the acquisition of assets of a partially controlled subsidiary does not qualify as a tax-free reorganization under section 368(a)(1)(C) is articulated in Rev. Rul. 54-396 (1954-2 C.B. 147). This position subsequently was sustained in litigation in Bausch & Lomb Optical Co. v. Commissioner, 30 T.C. 602 (1958), aff'd, 267 F.2d 75 (2d Cir.), cert. denied, 361 U.S. 835 (1959) (the *Bausch & Lomb* doctrine). In Rev. Rul. 54-396, a parent corporation owning 79 percent of the stock of a subsidiary as the result of a prior unrelated cash purchase acquires all of the assets of the subsidiary in exchange for a block of the parent's voting stock. The block of the parent's stock that has been transferred to the subsidiary is then distributed in liquidation pro rata to its shareholders. The ruling concludes that the transaction does not qualify as a "C" reorganization under the 1939 Internal Revenue Code, but rather is a taxable liquidation of the subsidiary. The rationale of the revenue ruling is that the acquisition violates the solely for voting stock requirement, because the parent corporation acquires only 21 percent of the subsidiary's assets in exchange for the parent's voting stock, while the remaining 79 percent of the subsidiary's assets is acquired as a liquidating distribution in exchange for the previously held stock of the subsidiary.

In Bausch & Lomb (which had nearly identical facts to Rev. Rul. 54-396), the parent corporation, Bausch & Lomb, owned 79.9 percent of the stock of Riggs Optical Company. In order to acquire the assets of Riggs, Bausch & Lomb exchanged shares of its voting stock for all of the Riggs assets. Pursuant to a prearranged plan, Riggs subsequently was dissolved and distributed its only asset, the Bausch & Lomb shares, pro rata to its shareholders. The Tax Court and the Second Circuit Court of Appeals sustained the Commissioner's contention that the acquisition of the Riggs assets and the dissolution of Riggs should be viewed together as part of a single plan, and that the surrender by Bausch & Lomb of its Riggs stock constituted nonstock consideration in violation of the "C" reorganization requirements.

The Solely for Voting Stock Requirement The "C" reorganization first appeared in 1921 when a tax-free reorganization was defined as a merger or consolidation "including the acquisition by one corporation ... of substantially all of the properties of another corporation." Revenue Act of 1921, section 202(c)(2), 42 Stat. 227, 230. The statutory language failed to limit the type of permissible consideration, arguably allowing an acquisition for cash to qualify as a merger.

In 1934, Congress restricted the permissible consideration in an acquisition of a target's stock or assets (in other than a statutory merger or consolidation) to voting stock. Revenue Act of 1934, section 112(g)(1), 48 Stat. 680, 705. The stated purpose for this limitation was to "remove the danger that taxable sales [could] be cast into the form of a reorganization." *See* H.R. Rep. No. 704, 73d Cong., 2d Sess. 12-14 (1934), 1939-1 C.B. (Part 2) 554, 563-565; S. Rep. No. 558, 73d Cong., 2d Sess. 16-17 (1934), 1939-1 C.B. (Part 2) 586, 598–599.

Reasons for Change: The legislative history of the "C" reorganization provisions provides that the purpose of the solely for voting stock requirement in section 368(a)(1)(C) is to prevent transactions that resemble sales from qualifying for non-recognition of gain or loss available to corporate reorganizations. The IRS and Treasury Department have concluded that a transaction in which the acquiring corporation converts an indirect ownership interest in assets to a direct interest in those assets does not resemble a sale and, thus, have concluded that Congress did not intend to disqualify a transaction from qualifying under section 368(a)(1)(C) merely because the acquiring corporation has prior ownership of a portion of a target corporation's stock. Because the judicial doctrine of continuity of interest arose from similar concerns, the regulations under 1.368-1(e)(1)(i) reach a similar conclusion with respect to the continuity of interest doctrine.

Moreover, the taxable treatment of the "upstream" "C" reorganization under the Bausch & Lomb doctrine contrasts with the tax-free treatment of the "upstream" "A" reorganization under section 368(a)(1)(A). *See* also Rev. Rul. 57-278 (1957-1 C.B. 124) (Bausch & Lomb does not apply to an asset acquisition by a newly formed corporation in exchange for its parent's stock, even though prior to the acquisition the parent already owned 72 percent of the transferor's stock). In the "upstream" "A" reorganization, the indirect interest of the parent in the assets of its subsidiary (i.e., the target corporation) is converted into a direct interest in the subsidiary's assets. An exchange is deemed to occur for purposes of section 354 even if, in form, one does not occur. The IRS and Treasury Department have concluded that the "upstream" reorganization under section 368(a)(1)(C) (i.e., the Bausch & Lomb transaction) should not be treated differently from the "upstream" "A" reorganization solely because the acquiring corporation already owns stock in the target corporation. Accordingly, the IRS and Treasury Department have concluded that the Bausch & Lomb doctrine does not further the principles of reorganization treatment.

Explanation of Provisions The proposed regulations provide that preexisting ownership of a portion of a target corporation's stock by an acquiring corporation generally will not prevent the solely for voting stock requirement in a "C" reorganization from being satisfied. If the boot relaxation rule applies, the sum of (i) the money or other property that is distributed in pursuance of the plan of reorganization to the shareholders of the target corporation other than the acquiring corporation and to the creditors of the target corporation pursuant to section 361(b)(3), and (ii) the assumption of all the liabilities of the target corporation (including liabilities to which the properties of the target corporation are subject), cannot exceed 20 percent of the value of all of the properties of the target corporation. In this regard, the proposed regulations provide that if, in connection with a potential "C" reorganization of a target corporation into an acquiring corporation, the acquiring corporation acquires the target corporation's stock for consideration other than its own voting stock (or voting stock of a corporation in control of the acquiring corporation if such stock is used in the acquisition of the target corporation's properties), whether from a shareholder of the target corporation or from the target corporation itself, such consideration will be treated as money or other property exchanged by the acquiring corporation for the target corporation's assets. Accordingly, the requirements of section 368(a)(1)(C) will not be satisfied unless the transaction can qualify under the boot relaxation rule of section 368(a)(2)(B). The determination of whether there has been an acquisition in connection with a potential "C" reorganization of a target corporation's stock for consideration other than an acquiring corporation's own voting stock (or voting stock of a corporation in control of the acquiring corporation if such stock is used in the acquisition of the target corporation's properties) will be made on the basis of all of the facts and circumstances. * * *

c. Preamble to the Final Regulations
Treasury Decision 8885
(May 18, 2000)

Summary This document contains final regulations relating to the solely for voting stock requirement in certain corporate reorganizations under section 368(a)(1)(C). The final regulations provide that a prior acquisition of a target corporation's stock by an acquiring corporation generally will not prevent the solely for voting stock requirement in a "C" reorganization of the target corporation and the acquiring corporation from being satisfied. * * *

Explanation of Revisions and Summary of Comments * * * A comment was received requesting that the IRS reconsider its position in *Rev. Rul. 69-294 (1969-1 C.B. 110)*, where the *Bausch & Lomb* doctrine was applied to disqualify a purported section 368(a)(1)(B) reorganization that followed a tax-free section 332 liquidation. In *Rev. Rul. 69-294*, X owned all of the stock of Y and Y owned 80 percent of the stock of Z. Y completely liquidated into X in a section 332 liquidation. As part of the plan, X (now owning 80 percent of the stock of Z) acquired the minority 20 percent stock interest in Z in exchange for X voting stock in a purported "B" reorganization. The ruling holds that the exchange with the 20 percent minority shareholders was not a "B" reorganization. The rationale is that although the acquisition from the minority shareholders was "solely for voting stock," the liquidation of Y, as part of the same plan, resulted in X acquiring 80 percent of the Z stock in exchange for Y stock surrendered back to Y on the liquidation of Y and not solely in exchange for X voting stock.

The commentator's suggestion is beyond the scope of this regulation's project, which relates to "C" reorganizations. In light of these regulations, however, the IRS and Treasury Department may reconsider Rev. Rul. 69-294. * * *

2. Disqualified Creeping (B) Followed by Liquidation
American Potash & Chemical Corp. v. United States
United States Court of Claims, 1968
399 F.2d 194

LARAMORE, JUDGE.

* * * The only issue before the court is the determination of the basis of depreciable assets upon which the deduction is based. Taxpayer argues that a cost basis is appropriate, and defendant contends that a carryover basis is required. Defendant has moved for summary judgment.

The facts are not in dispute. Taxpayer is engaged in the production and sale of industrial and agricultural chemicals. Between September 1954 and November 1955, Potash acquired all of the outstanding stock of Western Electrochemical Company (hereinafter referred to as Wecco) in exchange for 66,662 shares of its voting stock and $466.12 in cash paid for fractional shares. * * *

Between September 28, 1954 and November 3, 1954, Potash acquired 48 percent of the Wecco stock in exchange for 33,367 shares of Potash plus $466.12 in cash. On November 30, 1955 Potash acquired the remaining 52 percent of Wecco stock in exchange for 33,295 shares of Potash. * * *

Plaintiff admits that both of these stock acquisitions were to further its ultimate purpose-obtaining the Wecco assets—and that if it could not have obtained the remaining 52 percent ownership it would have sold the 48 percent interest acquired in 1954.

Potash did not acquire either 80 percent of the total combined voting power of all voting stock or 80 percent of the total number of shares of all other classes of stock during any 12-month period between September 1954 and November 1955.

For seven months, from December 1, 1955 to June 30, 1956, Wecco was operated by Potash. * * * On June 30, 1956, Wecco was completely liquidated, and all of its assets were distributed to (and its liabilities were assumed by) Potash. * * *

For 1957, 1958, 1959 and 1960 fiscal tax years Potash computed its depreciation deduction for the depreciable assets received from Wecco on an adjusted basis of $7,085,551. This was its "cost" of the depreciable assets. * * * Immediately prior to the liquidation Wecco's basis in these assets was $3,788,779.

On audit of Potash's 1956 and 1957 tax returns the Internal Revenue Service determined that the correct basis of these assets was $3,788,779, the basis in the hands of Wecco prior to the liquidation. * * *

For the purpose of this motion, both plaintiff and defendant agree that the stock acquisition of Wecco and its liquidation were undertaken for the purpose of obtaining the Wecco assets, *i.e.,* plaintiff purchased the stock to reach the assets.

The government, in support of its motion for summary judgment, argues that, as a matter of law, a carryover basis is required because either the entire transaction was a reorganization under section 368(a)(1)(C) of the Internal Revenue Code of 1954, 68A Stat. 120, or alternatively, if the stock acquisition can be separated from the liquidation, the assets received in the liquidation are subject to a carryover basis under sections 332 and 334 as assets received by a parent (Potash) in the process of liquidating its wholly-owned subsidiary (Wecco). Plaintiff argues that the transaction cannot be termed a reorganization. * * *

* * * We find that the facts do not establish that this transaction was a reorganization. * * *

* * * Defendant concludes that a C reorganization has occurred and, therefore, a carryover basis is required for the assets. * * *

Before a transaction can be classified as a C reorganization three basic factors must be present. These are (a) an acquiring corporation gives *stock* to another corporation, and (b) receives *in exchange* for that stock (c) substantially all of the *properties* of the transferor corporation.

Defendant argues that taxpayer has not *purchased* Wecco's stock for cash and liquidated but has *exchanged* its stock for Wecco stock and then liquidated Wecco pursuant to its plan and intent to obtain Wecco's assets. * * *

We note that defendant admits, and we agree, that the form of this transaction — a transfer of Potash stock to the shareholders of Wecco in return for the stock of Wecco — resembles, and would seem to invoke the provisions of, section 368(a)(1)(B), if any reorganization provision were applicable. Without question, the basis transaction was a stock for stock exchange (B reorganization) rather than a stock for asset exchange (C reorganization). Potash transferred stock to, and received stock from, the Wecco shareholders. It did not transfer stock to the Wecco corporation in return for a transfer by the corporation of its assets.

In our view the transaction does not meet the requirements of a B reorganization but only because control of Wecco was not obtained by a series of stock for stock exchanges within a 12-month period (as is required by the applicable regulations [*see* Sec. 6.2.A]. This is an aspect of the attainment of stock control by "creeping acquisitions" rather than a single stock for stock exchange.

The creeping acquisition of control problem arose under the 1939 Code in a B reorganization when an acquiring corporation owned some stock of the corporation to be acquired but less than control. To resolve any lingering doubts about the validity of classifying successive stock for voting stock exchanges as a B reorganization, the 1954 Code specifically approved its use in the context of a B reorganization.

By its regulation (Reg.§ 1.368-2(c)), which echoes S.Rep. No. 1622, supra, the government provided:

Such an acquisition [B reorganization] is permitted tax-free in a single transaction or in a series of transactions taking place *over a relatively short period of time such as 12 months*. [Emphasis added.]

The infirmity, in this case, is that the entire transaction took place over a period of 14 months, and plaintiff never obtained control within any 12-month period. Defendant has not urged that this was a B reorganization. Were this a B reorganization which was complete when the stock for stock exchange resulted in control, we would be faced with a problem which has faced many other courts, i.e., whether the postreorganization liquidation was an integral step of the overall plan to obtain the assets and, therefore, a carryover basis is appropriate for the assets received in the process of liquidation. The liquidation is denied independent tax significance, and a carryover basis is imposed. We will discuss the post-reorganization liquidation problem in more detail at a later point. Insofar as the facts of this case are concerned, Potash did not obtain control within a 12-month period, and we find that a B reorganization did not occur.

Defendant argues that despite its form (stock for stock) the entire transaction should be tested as a C reorganization because plaintiff has stated that it intended to obtain Wecco's assets. This position is premised on our integrating and collapsing the several transactions which began with the first acquisition in 1954 and ended with the assets received in the June 1956 liquidation into a "single transaction". That "single transaction," defendant argues, is a reorganization when measured against the provisions of section 368(a)(1)(C). Plaintiff's intent, as mentioned above, is relevant to the existence of a plan to obtain the assets and is an important factor when we are faced with denying independent tax significance to a liquidation which follows a reorganization. It does not establish that a reorganization occurred, or that *stock* was, in fact, *exchanged for assets* as is required in a C reorganization.

The issue before the court is whether we can transform a stock for stock exchange which does not itself qualify as a B reorganization, into a C-type stock for asset exchange by finding that the subsequent liquidation and distribution of the assets of the acquired corporation had no tax significance and that Potash, therefore, exchanged its stock with the Wecco corporation for the Wecco assets. The issue before us is not whether a liquidation which follows a valid B reorganization is to be given independent tax significance. In this case we are faced with the more basic problem; *i.e.*, finding if a reorganization occurred. We cannot find any decision which has transformed a non-qualifying B-type exchange into a valid C reorganization by concluding that a subsequent liquidation of the acquired corporation was without significance. Defendant has not urged that this transaction was anything other than a C reorganization. Courts have concluded, under comparable circumstances, that the property received in the post-reorganization (qualifying) liquidation was property received in connection with a transaction which separately qualified as a B reorganization. Other courts have concluded that an assets transfer was a mere change in the identity or form of the corporation and, therefore, a reorganization occurred. (Both of these possibilities will be explored at a later point.)

Defendant would have us create a C reorganization out of the substructure of an unqualified B-type exchange and a subsequent liquidation. We find that there was no reorganization to which we might attach the liquidation and that the liquidation itself does not transform the non-qualifying B-type exchange into a valid C reorganization. * * *

Corporations may choose between a stock for stock exchange or a stock for asset exchange to effect a combination. Typically, in a C reorganization the transferor corporation is divested of its assets (and usually is liquidated). A B reorganization results in the acquisition of a subsidiary.

One important reason for choosing a B rather than a C exchange is that gradual exchanges of stock may be accomplished in a B "creeping" reorganization. The acquisition of assets in a C reorganization should be accomplished in a single exchange transaction. In addition, the transferor corporation in a C reorganization must obtain stockholder approval before transferring its assets. In a B reorganization, however, each stockholder can, independently, exchange his stock for the stock offered by the acquiring corporation.

There is no evidence that Potash or Wecco could have obtained the approval of Wecco shareholders, and the presence of a dissenting majority during the first series of acquisitions would seem to imply that Potash could not have chosen a C reorganization. Potash states that it was *forced* to seek the Wecco assets by an acquisition of stock because it could not otherwise obtain the assets.

The practical merger aspect of a C reorganization precludes multiple stock for asset exchanges. A creeping asset acquisition is not permissible in a C reorganization as it would be impermissible in a statutory merger. * * *

Questions and Note

1. *King Enterprises,* Sec. 7.2.C., held that a broken (B) followed by an upstream merger of the target into the acquiror qualified as an (A). *American Potash* holds that a broken (B) followed by a liquidation of the target into the acquiror does not qualify as a (C). Can you reconcile these two decisions? If not, which decision is correct and why?

2. The court in *American Potash* went on to hold that the *Kimbell-Diamond* doctrine [*see* Sec. 2.10.E.2] is not dead and that, consequently, the plaintiff took a stepped-up basis for the target's assets even though the transaction did not satisfy former § 334(b)(2).

I. Sections 305 and 306 Issues Arising in (C) Reorganizations

See Secs. 6.17 and 6.18 for a discussion of issues under
§§ 305 and 306 arising in acquisitive reorganizations.

§ 7.4 The Triangular (C) Reorganization

A. Legislative History of the Triangular (C) and § 368(a)(2)(C)

The first legislative override of the *Groman* and *Bashford* doctrines (*see* Sec. 6.2.G.2) came in the 1954 Code, with the addition of the parenthetical clause to § 368(a)(1)(C), allowing triangular (C) reorganizations, and the addition of § 368(a)(2)(C), allowing the assets acquired in an (A) or (C) reorganization to be dropped into a subsidiary of the acquiring corporation. The term "party to the reorganization" in § 368(b) was amended to include the parent of an acquiring corporation as a party to the reorganization. These amendments were discussed as follows in the Senate Report to the 1954 Code:

Subparagraph (C) of subsection (a)(1) corresponds to section 112(g)(1)(C) of the 1939 Code relating to the acquisition by one corporation, without the recognition of gain or loss, of substantially all of the properties of another corporation in exchange for part or all of the voting stock of the acquiring corporation. The rule of this subparagraph is intended to modify the rule of *Groman v. Commissioner* (302 U.S. 82) and *Helvering v. Bashford* (302 U.S. 454). Under subparagraph (C) a corporation may acquire substantially all the properties of another corporation solely in exchange of the voting stock of a corporation which is in control of the acquiring corporation.

For example, corporation P owns all the stock of corporation A. All the assets of corporation W are transferred to corporation A solely in exchange for the voting stock of corporation P. Such a transaction constitutes a reorganization under subparagraph C. * * *

Subparagraph (C) of paragraph (2) provides that if one corporation acquires all, or substantially all, of the assets of another corporation in a reorganization qualifying under section 368(a)(1)(A) or (C), the acquisition will not fail to be a reorganization merely because the acquiring corporation transfers some or all of these assets to a corporation controlled by it. This subparagraph is intended to give further clarification in the area treated in the *Groman* and *Bashford* cases, supra.

Subsection (b) of section 368 defines a "party to a reorganization." It reinstates existing law as now appearing in section 112(g)(2), and in addition provides (with respect to the area of the *Groman* and *Bashford* cases, supra) that the corporation controlling the acquiring corporation is also a party to the reorganization when the stock of such controlling corporation is used to acquire assets. It also provides that a corporation remains a party to the reorganization although it transfers all or part of the assets acquired to a controlled subsidiary.

B. Introduction

The basic issues presented in a straight (C) are also present in a triangular (C). *See* Sec. 7.3. Certain additional problems are presented below. Section 1.368-2(d) says that the subsidiary cannot use any of its stock in the acquisition. Thus, the boot relaxation rule does not extend to stock of the subsidiary. Query: what is the reason for this rule?

C. Transfer of Target's Assets to Remote Subsidiary

Revenue Ruling 64-73
1964-1 C.B. 142

L corporation owns 100 percent of the outstanding stock of corporation *M. M* owns 100 percent of the outstanding stock of corporation *N. L* entered into an agreement with *X,* an unrelated corporation, under which *L* acquired all of the assets of *X,* solely in exchange for *L* voting stock. Some of the *X* assets were transferred from *X* to *N,* and the remaining *X* assets were transferred to *L.* Neither the assets which were transferred to *N* nor the assets transferred to *L* constituted substantially all of *X*'s assets, but together they constituted all of *X*'s assets. * * *

In applying specific statutory relief to certain factual situations previously governed by the *Groman* and *Bashford* cases [*see* Sec. 6.2.G] Congress indicated its desire to remove the continuity-of-interest problem from the section 368(a)(1)(C) reorganization area. Having modified the continuity-of-interest rule where assets move to a corporation directly controlled by the parent in exchange for the parent's stock, there is no sound reason to assume the Congress intended to have the *Groman-Bashford* rule apply where the assets are caused to be transferred by the parent to a wholly-owned subsidiary of a corporation controlled by the parent corporation. * * *

Accordingly, it is held that the transaction described in the instant case constitutes a reorganization as defined in section 368(a)(1)(C) of the Code.

Question

Is the Service here repudiating its victories in *Groman* and *Bashford?*

D. Acquiring Parent Cannot Assume Target's Liabilities

Revenue Ruling 70-107

1970-1 C.B. 78

Corporation *X* owned all of the stock of corporation *Y.* Pursuant to a plan of reorganization intended to meet the requirements of section 368(a)(1)(C) of the Internal Revenue Code of 1954, *Y* directly acquired all the assets of corporation *Z* using voting stock of *X* previously transferred to it. Part of the liabilities of *Z* were assumed by *Y* and part were assumed by *X.*

Held, in view of the assumption by *X* of some of *Z*'s liabilities, the exchange does not meet the "solely for voting stock" requirement of section 368(a)(1)(C) of the Code because that section provides in part that in determining whether the exchange is solely for voting stock the assumption *by the acquiring corporation* of a liability of the other shall be disregarded. Since *X* (the parent of *Y*) is not the acquiring corporation, its assumption of *Z*'s liabilities will not be disregarded.

Questions

What is the specific holding of this ruling? Is the holding overly formalistic? Is it sound from a policy perspective? Recall that the language in the definition of the (C) that allows an acquiring corporation to assume the target's liabilities without running afoul of the solely for voting stock requirement was a response to the Supreme Court's decision in *Hendler. See* Sec. 6.15.A.

E. Triangular (C) Followed by a Push-Up of Substantially All of Target's Assets; Acquiring Subsidiary Assumes Target's Liabilities

Proposed Revenue Ruling Attached to GCM 39102

(December 21, 1983)

Issue Does the following transaction qualify as a reorganization under I.R.C. § 368(a)(1)(C)?

Facts Corporation *X* is engaged in the businesses of manufacturing men's shoes and women's shoes through its two divisions. Corporation *P*, unrelated to *X*, is also engaged in the business of manufacturing women's shoes.

As part of a plan to acquire the assets of *X, P* organized *S* as a wholly owned subsidiary. Then, under a contract between *X* and *S, X* transferred substantially all of
its assets to *S* in exchange for *P* voting stock and the assumption by *S* of *X*'s liabilities
that were primarily related to the men's shoe manufacturing business. The assumption
by *S* of the liabilities of *X* constituted more than 20 percent of the total consideration
received by *X* in exchange for its assets. Next, *X* distributed the *P* voting stock to its
shareholders in exchange for their *X* stock and dissolved. Finally, as part of the plan
and in order to facilitate the more efficient management of the women's shoes manufacturing businesses as one unit, *S* distributed the women's shoe manufacturing
business to *P*. The women's shoe manufacturing division before the transaction represented at least 90 percent of the fair market value of the net assets of *X* and at least
70 percent of the gross assets of *X*.

Law and Analysis * * *The first question presented is whether *P* or *S* is the "acquiring" corporation for purposes of section 368(a)(1)(C) of the Code in view of the
"push-up" by *S* to *P* of the women's shoe manufacturing business. * * *

* * * It is well established that, in the absence of a more compelling rule of law,
the substance of a transaction, rather than its form controls for federal income tax
purposes. *See Commissioner v. Court Holding Company,* 324 U.S. 331 (1945); Higgins
v. Smith, 308 U.S. 473 (1940). It is concluded in view of the relative magnitude of
the women's shoe manufacturing business transferred from *S* to *P* as part of the overall
plan, that, in substance, *P* is the "acquiring" corporation of *X*'s assets to *S* under the
contract.

The second question presented is whether the assumption of liabilities by *S* will be
considered to violate the "solely for voting stock" requirement of section 368(a)(1)(C).

Rev. Rul. 70-107, 1970-1 C.B. 78, holds that an assumption of the acquired corporation's liabilities by the parent corporation in a parenthetical "C" reorganization
will not be disregarded in determining whether the solely for voting stock requirement
is satisfied because the parent corporation is not an acquiring corporation within the
meaning of section 368(a)(1)(C). Thus, under Rev. Rul. 70-107, *P*'s acquisition of
the *X* assets does not qualify as a reorganization under section 368(a)(1)(C) because
the liabilities of *X* were assumed by *S*, which is not the "acquiring corporation."

The conclusion of Rev. Rul. 70-107 rests on the language of section 368(a)(1)(C)
which implies that only the actual acquiring corporation may assume liabilities. However, this interpretation does not accord with the legislative history underlying that
provision. * * *

In addition, Rev. Rul. 70-107 artificially distinguishes between triangular mergers
under section 368(a)(1)(A) and (a)(2)(D), in which the liabilities of the acquired
corporation may be assumed by either parent or subsidiary or both, *see* Rev. Rul. 73-
257, 1973-1 C.B. 189, and between practical mergers under section 368(a)(1)(C).

Therefore, the Service has concluded that Rev. Rul. 70-107 is no longer correct.
An assumption of liabilities by any party to the reorganization exchange will be disregarded in determining whether the solely for voting stock requirement is met.

Rev. Rul. 73-257 further concludes that the parent corporation in a transaction qualifying under sections 368(a)(1)(A) and (a)(2)(D) of the Code is a "party to the exchange" as such term is used in section 357(a) of the Code. As such, the assumption by the parent of target liabilities was not treated as the receipt of money or other property and the exchange of assets was treated as within the terms of section 361(a). Similarly, *P* and *S* in this case will both be treated as parties to the exchange for purposes of section 357(a).

Holding The transaction is viewed as an acquisition of *X* assets by *P* in a reorganization that qualifies under section 368(a)(1)(C). The assumption by *S* of *X* liabilities does not violate the solely for voting stock requirement.

Effect on Other Rulings

Rev. Rul. 70-107 is revoked.

F. Dealing with the Zero Basis Problem

1. Background on the Problem

a. Introduction to the Problem: Illustration of Interactions among §§ 358, 362 and 1032

Revenue Ruling 74-503, Revoked by Revenue Ruling 2006-2

1974-2 C.B. 117

[Even though Rev. Rul. 74-503 has been revoked by Rev Rul. 2006-2, it is helpful to understand the position taken in Rev. Rul. 74-503.] Advice has been requested as to the basis of the stock acquired in the transaction described below.

X corporation transferred shares of its treasury stock (with a fair market value of $3,000x and purchased by X several years previously from its shareholders for $2,000x) to Y in exchange for newly issued shares of Y stock (with a fair market value of $3,000x) which constituted 80 percent of the only outstanding class of stock of Y. The transfer of X stock was not for the purpose of enabling Y to acquire property by the use of such stock. No gain or loss was recognized to X under section 351(a) (and section 1032(a)) of the Internal Revenue Code of 1954. No gain or loss was recognized to Y under section 1032(a).

Section 358(a) of the Code provides, in part, rules for determining the basis of property received by a transferor in a transaction to which section 351 applies. However, section 358(e) provides that section 358(a) does not apply to property acquired by a corporation by the exchange of its stock as consideration in whole or in part for the transfer of property to it. Therefore, section 358(a) is not applicable in determining the basis of the Y stock received by X in the transaction.

Section 1.1032-1(d) of the Income Tax Regulations provides:

> (d) For basis of property acquired by a corporation in connection with a transaction to which section 351 applies or in connection with a reorganization, see section 362. For basis of property acquired by a corporation in a

transaction to which section 1032 applies but which does not qualify under any other non-recognition provision, see section 1012.

Section 362(a) of the Code provides, in part, that the basis to a corporation of property acquired in a section 351 transaction will be the same as it would be in the hands of the transferor, increased in the amount of gain recognized to the transferor on such transfer.

Pursuant to section 1.1032-1(d) of the regulations, the basis of the stock of X received by Y and the basis of the stock of Y received by X will be determined under section 362(a) of the Code since the transaction also qualifies, for purposes of determining basis, under section 351.

Therefore, the basis of the X treasury stock received by Y will be the same as it was in the hands of X immediately prior to the exchange. In addition, the basis of the newly issued stock of Y received by X will be the same as it was in the hands of Y immediately prior to the exchange.

The basis of previously unissued stock in the hands of the corporation issuing it in a transaction to which section 362 of the Code applies is zero. However, in order to ascertain the basis of the stock received by Y, a determination must be made as to the basis of the X treasury stock.

In Firestone Tire & Rubber Company, 2 T.C. 827 (1943), acq., 1945 C.B. 3, withdrawing nonacq., 1944 C.B. 38, the taxpayer-corporation purchased shares of its common stock for cash in the open market and held them as treasury shares. At a later date, it exchanged these shares in a nontaxable reorganization described under the predecessor of section 368(a)(1)(B) of the 1954 Code for all the stock of S corporation. Section 113(a)(7) of the Revenue Act of 1936 (the predecessor of section 362(b) of the 1954 Code) provided that the basis of shares acquired in a reorganization exchange by the transferee for the *issuance* of its own shares was the same as the transferor's basis of the shares received. The taxpayer-corporation contended that the exchange of its treasury stock for all the stock of S corporation was not an *issuance* since it had purchased the treasury stock in the open market for cash.

The Tax Court of the United States in *Firestone* relied on two interrelated propositions for its decision. The first was the pre-1954 Code rule that a corporation dealing in its shares as it might in the shares of another corporation must recognize gain or loss on the disposition of its treasury stock. The second, as a necessary corollary to the first, was that a corporation has a basis in its treasury stock equal to the amount paid therefore.

The validity of these propositions was abolished for post-1954 Code years by the enactment of section 1032(a) of the Code, effective with respect to taxable years beginning after December 31, 1953, and ending after August 16, 1954. Section 1032(a) expressly provides nonrecognition treatment for a corporation upon the disposition of its treasury stock. It was intended to remove the uncertainties under prior law relating to whether a corporation was "dealing" in its own shares, and to eliminate any distinction between treasury stock and previously unissued stock. See *H.Rep. No.*

1337, 83rd Cong.2d Sess. 268; *S.Rep. No. 1622,* 83rd Cong.2d Sess., 426. Among the reasons for this provision were the tax avoidance possibilities of the prior law, under which a corporation expecting a gain upon disposition of treasury shares might avoid such gain by cancelling its treasury shares and issuing "new" stock, whereas a corporation might produce a fictitious loss by purchasing its own shares and reselling them at a lower price.

The enactment of section 317(b) of the Code, which makes it clear that a "redemption" of stock can occur whether such stock is cancelled or held as treasury stock, is further evidence of Congress' intention to eliminate the formalistic distinctions that had existed under pre-1954 Code law with respect to treasury stock. *See S.Rep. No. 1622,* at page 252.

Therefore, the *Firestone* decision is not applicable under the 1954 Code. Thus, under the 1954 Code, a corporation's treasury stock is no different than its previously unissued stock, the purchase of such treasury stock being merely a part of the capital transaction which began when such stock was first issued.

Accordingly, the basis of the *X* treasury stock received by *Y* is zero and the basis of the newly issued *Y* stock received by *X* is zero.

Rev. Rul. 62-217, 1962-2 C.B. 59 (which refers to the "cost basis" of treasury stock), Rev. Rul. 70-117, 1970-1 C.B. 30 (which holds that premiums paid by a corporation on life insurance policies used to fund the cost of a stock purchase agreement do not represent ordinary and necessary business expenses of the taxpayer but are in the nature of amounts paid for the acquisition of a corporation asset (treasury stock)), and Rev. Rul. 70-305, 1970-1 C.B. 169 (which holds, in part, that the sale of stock of a parent corporation held by a subsidiary corporation, which was acquired by the subsidiary in a transaction described in section 304(a)(2), can result in a loss), are hereby modified to remove any implication that for tax purposes a corporation's treasury stock held by it has a cost basis rather than a zero basis.

Questions

What are the grounds for the holding in the ruling that *X*'s basis for the *Y* stock is determined under §362(a)? Corporation *P,* an operating corporation, transfers newly issued *P* stock to a newly formed subsidiary, *S,* in exchange for *S* stock in a §351 transaction. What is *S*'s basis for the *P* stock and *P*'s basis for the *S* stock? What result to *S* if it uses the *P* stock to purchase a building for $100K? Suppose *P* used its own stock to purchase the building, and then transferred the building to *S*? Are the transactions functional equivalents? Are they taxed the same? Should they be? Is the ruling correct in holding that, because of §1032, a corporation cannot have a basis in its stock?

b. The Problems with Zero Basis and Potential Recognition of Gain on the Issuance by Acquiring Subsidiary of Its Parent's Stock

Under the principle set out in Rev. Rul. 74-503, *supra* Sec. 7.4.F.1.a. when an acquiring parent contributes its stock to an acquiring subsidiary for use by the subsidiary in a triangular acquisition of the (B), (C), (a)(2)(D) or (a)(2)(E) type, the parent receives a substituted basis of zero for the subsidiary's stock (*see* § 358(a)) and the subsidiary receives a carryover basis of zero for the parent's stock (*see* § 362(a)). Both corporations are protected from recognition on the exchanges by § 1032. When the subsidiary uses the parent's stock in the acquisition, the subsidiary (or the surviving target in a reverse (a)(2)(E)) takes a carryover basis for the target's stock or assets received. (*See* § 362(b) parenthetical phrase and § 358(e) parenthetical phrase; see *also* Senate Report to the 1968 Act, III. *Basis of Properties or Stock Acquired in a Reorganization with Stock of a Parent, infra,* Sec. 7.4.F.1.c.) There is no provision in the Code, however, that gives the parent a reciprocal carryover basis for the subsidiary's (or surviving target's) stock. Thus, the parent's basis for such stock would be zero. Furthermore, there is no Code section that gives the subsidiary nonrecognition treatment on the issuance of the parent's stock; § 1032 only protects the subsidiary from recognition on the issuance of its own stock. The Service's response to these problems is set out below. *See also* Rev. Rul. 74-503, *supra,* Sec. 7.4.F.1.a.

c. Revocation of Revenue Ruling 74-503 by Revenue Ruling 2006-2

Revenue Ruling 2006-2 Revoking Revenue Ruling 74-503

IRB 2006-2 (January 9, 2006)

In Rev. Rul. 74-503, 1974-2 C.B. 117, corporation X transferred shares of its treasury stock to corporation Y in exchange for newly issued shares of Y stock. In the exchange, X obtained 80 percent of the only outstanding class of Y stock. Rev. Rul. 74-503 concludes that the basis of the X treasury stock received by Y is zero and the basis of the newly issued Y stock received by X is zero.

Rev. Rul. 74-503 states that X's basis in the Y stock received in the exchange is determined under § 362(a) of the Internal Revenue Code. This conclusion is incorrect. Accordingly, Rev. Rul. 74-503, 1974-2 C.B.117, is revoked, effective December 20, 2005. The other conclusions in the ruling, including the conclusions that X's basis in the Y stock received in the exchange and Y's basis in the X stock received in the exchange are zero, are under study. * * *

d. Legislative History of Amendments to §§ 358 and 362 Relating to Basis to Acquiring Sub for Target's Stock or Assets in a Triangular Reorganization

Senate Report to the 1968 Act

1968-2 C.B. 851–852

Basis of Properties or Stock Acquired in a Reorganization With Stock of Parent * * * While under present law the carryover basis rule specifically applies to properties or stock acquired by the issuance of stock of the *acquiring* corporation in the case of type A, B, and C reorganizations, no mention is made of the basis rule to apply in these types of reorganizations where the properties or stock are acquired with the stock of the parent corporation (or with treasury stock of the acquiring corporation). The committee agrees with the House that the same basis rules should apply where the properties or stock are acquired with the parent's stock (or with treasury stock of the acquiring corporation) as where they are obtained by the issuance of new stock of the acquiring corporation and that this should be specified in the tax laws.

Explanation of provision. For the reasons given above the bill amends present law in two respects to provide that the carryover basis rule is to apply in the case of type A, B, and C reorganizations where the properties or stock are acquired with the stock of the parent of the acquiring corporation (or with treasury stock of the acquiring corporation).

The first of these amendments (sec. 2(a) of the bill) amends the provision of present law providing the substituted basis rule (sec. 358) to expand the exception in present law which provides that this substituted basis rule does not apply to property acquired by a corporation in exchange for its stock of securities. The bill expands the statutory language under this exception to the substituted basis rule to cover cases where the acquisition is made with the stock of the parent of the acquiring corporation (or with treasury stock of the acquiring corporation). [A correlative change is made to the second sentence of §362(b).]

Both of these amendments also apply when the stock of the parent corporation used in the acquisition was originally purchased (whether before or after the date of enactment of this provision) by the subsidiary.

e. The Service's Response to the Problem
Preamble to Proposed Regulations under §§ 1032 and 358
(January 2, 1981)

Background This document contains proposed amendments to the Income Tax Regulations (26 CFR Part 1) under sections 358 and 1032 of the Internal Revenue Code of 1954. These amendments provide rules for a transaction in which a controlled corporation (S) acquires stock or property in exchange for stock of its parent corporation (P) in a triangular corporate reorganization. These amendments also provide rules for a triangular reorganization in which the controlled corporation (S) is merged into a surviving corporation (T).

General Statement of Purpose *Acquisition of Subsidiary Using Parent's Stock.* The proposed amendment provides rules to apply whenever S uses P stock to acquire stock or property in a triangular reorganization under section 368. In these transactions, two questions are present. First, whether S recognizes gain by the use of P stock and, second, whether any adjustment is made to the basis of S stock owned by P to reflect S's acquisition of property.

In the case of a two-party reorganization where P directly acquires the property or stock of another corporation (T), section 1032(a) provides that no gain or loss is recognized to P on the receipt of property in exchange for its stock. In addition, under section 368(a)(2)(C), P may transfer the acquired property to S. In such a case, P's basis in its S stock is adjusted under section 358 to reflect the transfer of the acquired property to S.

Congress has also provided that a reorganization may qualify under section 368(a)(1) where S directly acquires the property in exchange for P stock. However, there is no explicit statutory rule regarding the recognition of gain or loss by S as a result of using P's stock and there is no provision for an adjustment to the basis of the S stock owned by P to reflect the property acquired by S.

The proposed amendment adds §§ 1.358-6 and 1.1032-2 to provide rules to resolve these problems. In general, the rules provide for the same results that would occur if P acquires T's stock or property in a two-party reorganization and then transferred the acquired property and any assumed liabilities to S in a tax-free transfer.

The rules do not provide for an increase in P's basis in its S stock to reflect the transfer of property by P to S that is subsequently transferred to T or distributed to T's shareholders in the reorganization. The reason for this treatment is that if P had acquired T's property in a two-party reorganization in exchange for P stock and other property and had transferred T's property to S, P would not have received an increase in the basis of its S stock to reflect the transfer of property to T. Consequently, P is not entitled to an increase in the basis of its S stock to reflect the transfer of its property to S, if S subsequently transfers the property to T. However, as in a two-party reorganization, if T recognizes gain attributable to the transfer of the property to it, then P's basis in its S stock is increased by the amount of the gain. *See* section 362(b).

The rules also provide that P's basis in its S stock is decreased by the fair market value of any consideration provided in exchange for T's property in the reorganization that is not furnished by P in the reorganization. The reason for this treatment is to preserve in P's basis in its S stock any unrealized appreciation in T's property. If P had acquired T's property in a two-party reorganization and then had transferred T's property to S, P's basis in its S stock would be increased by the basis in T's property. Consequently, any unrealized appreciation in T's property would be preserved in P's basis in its S stock. In order to reach the same result where S directly acquires T's property in a reorganization exchange for P stock, it is necessary to reduce P's basis in its S stock by the fair market value of any consideration not furnished by P in the reorganization.

Merger of Subsidiary into Surviving Corporation. Proposed § 1.358-6 also provides rules for determining the basis of T stock acquired by P in the case of the merger of S into T in a reorganization that qualifies under section 368(a)(1)(A) by reason of the application of section 368(a)(2)(E). In general, the rules provide for the same results that would occur if P acquired T's property in exchange for P stock and then transferred the acquired property and any assumed liabilities back to T in a tax-free transfer. Under these rules, P will have a uniform basis in the T stock (of each class) owned by it after the reorganization (including any T stock owned by P before the reorganization). This treatment is consistent with the results that would occur if P had acquired T's property in the merger and then transferred the property back to T. These rules are designed to parallel the basis rules on forward triangular reorganizations. In addition, by providing for an asset basis they avoid the problems that are inherent in determining the basis of stock held by T's previous shareholders.

f. Final Regulations Dealing with Triangular Reorganizations under §§ 1.358-6 and 1.1032-2

Preamble to Final Regulations on Basis Adjustments in Triangular Reorganizations

Treasury Decision 8648 (December 20, 1995)

Overview The final regulations adopt the over-the-top model contained in the proposed regulations. Subject to certain modifications, the model generally adjusts a controlling corporation's (P's) basis in the stock of its controlled corporation (S or T) as a result of certain triangular reorganizations as if P had acquired the T assets (and any liabilities assumed or to which the T assets were subject) directly from T in a transaction in which P's basis in the T assets was determined under section 362(b), and P then had transferred the T assets (and liabilities) to S in a transaction in which P's basis in the S or T stock was adjusted under section 358. * * *

The final regulations also provide a special rule that treats S's use of P's stock provided by P pursuant to the plan of reorganization as a disposition of those shares by P.

The final regulations apply only for the purpose of determining P's basis in its S or T stock following a transaction that otherwise qualifies as a reorganization within the meaning of section 368. They do not address issues concerning the qualification of a transaction as a reorganization. * * *

The proposed regulations adjusted basis as a result of a reverse triangular merger to reflect the amount of T stock received in the transaction. Comments on the proposed regulations questioned how an adjustment based on the amount of T stock received in the transaction would apply in the case in which P owns T stock before the transaction.

In response to these comments, the final regulations allow P to treat its T stock as acquired in the transaction or not, without regard to the form of the transaction. Thus, P may retain its basis in the T stock owned before the transaction, or may determine its basis in that stock as an allocable portion of T's net asset basis. The regulations require no explicit election. Instead, it is assumed P will pick the higher basis. This rule applies only for determining basis, and not for qualifying the transaction as a reverse triangular merger. *See* Rev. Rul. 74-564, 1974-2 C.B. 124.

The Treasury and the IRS continue to study issues relating to restructurings involving related parties and cross-ownership, and welcome comments and suggestions on these issues.

Net Negative Adjustment Under the proposed regulations, P's basis adjustment was reduced by the fair market value of consideration not provided by P, and by the amount of liabilities assumed by S or to which T assets are subject. These reductions did not result in a net negative basis adjustment to P's basis in its S stock before the transaction. This limitation did not apply, however, where P and S, or P and T, as applicable, were members of a consolidated group following the triangular reorganization. In the consolidated context, the negative adjustments could result in a net negative adjustment to P's basis in its S stock before the transaction, even if the adjustment resulted in an excess loss account under § 1.1502-19.

Some comments on the proposed regulations argued against reducing P's basis in its S stock before the transaction by a net negative adjustment in the consolidated context. Other comments, however, agreed that it is appropriate not to limit the net negative adjustment in this context.

The Treasury and the IRS continue to believe that the proposed regulations reach the correct result. Therefore, the final regulations adopt the rules as proposed. * * *

Application of Section 1032 The proposed regulations under section 1032 generally provided that P stock provided by P to S, or directly to T or T's shareholders on behalf of S, pursuant to the plan of reorganization would be treated as a disposition by P of shares of its own stock for T assets or stock, as applicable. Thus, no gain or loss was recognized on the use of such P stock in the transaction. S, however, recognized gain or loss on its use of P stock if S did not receive the stock from P as part of the plan of reorganization. This rule did not apply in the case of a reverse triangular merger; section 361 provides nonrecognition treatment for S's use of P stock in such a case. To clarify this treatment, a cross-reference has been added to the final regulations.

Comments to the proposed regulations requested that they be expanded to cover P debt, warrants and options provided by P to S, or directly to T or T's shareholders on behalf of S, pursuant to the plan of reorganization. Comments also requested that the rule be extended to taxable transactions.

The issues raised in these comments are beyond the scope of this project. However, the Treasury and the IRS are studying issues relating to the scope of section 1032 and welcome comments and suggestions. * * *

g. 1998 Regulations Addressing Zero Basis Problem in a Taxable Acquisition

In 1998 the Treasury issued regulations that give a sub tax-free treatment under § 1032 on the issuance of its parent's stock in a taxable acquisition. *See* § 1.1032-3. One of the conditions of this treatment is that the sub immediately dispose of the parent's stock in exchange for money or other property.

§ 7.5 Representations Required in a Ruling Request under § 368(a)(1)(C)

Excerpt from Revenue Procedure 86-42

§ 7.05, 1986-2 C.B. 722

[Although as noted in Sec. 6.2.A.6., the IRS generally does not issue private letter rulings on reorganization transactions, the following ruling guidelines can be helpful in structuring a deal.]

[In addition to the following representations, the parties are required to give representations 1 through 11 that are required for rulings under § 368(a)(1)(A). *See* Sec. 7.2.L.]

3. ACQUIRING WILL ACQUIRE AT LEAST 90 PERCENT OF THE FAIR MARKET VALUE OF THE NET ASSETS AND AT LEAST 70 PERCENT OF THE FAIR MARKET VALUE OF THE GROSS ASSETS HELD BY TARGET IMMEDIATELY PRIOR TO THE TRANSACTION. FOR PURPOSES OF THIS REPRESENTATION, AMOUNTS PAID BY TARGET TO DISSENTERS, AMOUNTS USED BY TARGET TO PAY ITS REORGANIZATION EXPENSES, AMOUNTS PAID BY TARGET TO SHAREHOLDERS WHO RECEIVE CASH OR OTHER PROPERTY, AND ALL REDEMPTIONS AND DISTRIBUTIONS (EXCEPT FOR REGULAR, NORMAL DIVIDENDS) MADE BY TARGET IMMEDIATELY PRECEDING THE TRANSFER WILL BE INCLUDED AS ASSETS OF TARGET HELD IMMEDIATELY PRIOR TO THE TRANSACTION. * * *

6. TARGET WILL DISTRIBUTE THE STOCK, SECURITIES, AND OTHER PROPERTY IT RECEIVES IN THE TRANSACTION, AND ITS OTHER PROPERTIES, IN PURSUANCE OF THE PLAN OF REORGANIZATION. * * *

12. ACQUIRING DOES NOT OWN, DIRECTLY OR INDIRECTLY, NOR HAS IT OWNED DURING THE PAST FIVE YEARS, DIRECTLY OR INDIRECTLY, ANY STOCK OF TARGET. * * *

§ 7.6 Forward Subsidiary Merger under § 368(a)(2)(D)

See Reg.§ 1.368-2(b)(2).

A. Legislative History of the Forward Subsidiary Merger

In 1968, § 368(a)(2)(D), which allows a forward triangular merger, was added. Also, § 358(e) was amended to change the word "issuance" to "exchange" and to add a parenthetical clause dealing with triangular reorganizations. The operation of these provisions was discussed as follows in the Senate Report:

Explanation of provision. The bill (sec. 1) permits a corporation which is a controlled subsidiary of another corporation (*i.e.,* the parent holds 80 percent of the voting shares and 80 percent of the total number of shares of all other classes of stock of the subsidiary) to acquire tax free all the assets of a third corporation in a statutory merger in which stock of the *parent* corporation is exchanged for the stock of the transferor corporation. The amendment (new subparagraph (D) in sec. 368(a)(2)) provides that if a parent corporation controls a subsidiary corporation (*i.e.,* has the 80-percent control referred to above), then the acquisition of substantially all the properties of a corporation merged (in a statutory merger) into the subsidiary in exchange for the stock of the parent corporation is not to be disqualified as a type A reorganization if two conditions are met: (1) the merger insofar as the tax laws are concerned would have qualified as a type A reorganization had the merger been made into the parent instead of into the subsidiary, and (2) no stock of the subsidiary is used in the transaction. In addition, the definition of "a party to a reorganization" is modified to include a parent corporation in the case described (by adding a new sentence to sec. 368(b)).

The amendment does not alter or modify the present requirements of "business purpose" or "continuity of enterprise." It modifies the present "continuity of interest" requirement but only in that it permits the use of the stock of the parent in making the acquisition, instead of the stock of the subsidiary.

The amendment applies whether or not the parent corporation is formed immediately before the merger, in anticipation of the merger, or after preliminary steps were taken to merge directly.

B. Introductory Note

In order to qualify under Section 368(a)(2)(D), the following basic conditions must be satisfied:

(1) The acquiring subsidiary must acquire "substantially all" of the target's properties.

(2) The consideration paid by the acquiring subsidiary must be stock of the acquiring parent, and cannot be stock of the acquiring subsidiary.

(3) The target must be merged into the acquiring subsidiary.

(4) The transaction must be such that it would have qualified as an (A) merger if the target had merged into the acquiring parent.

The "substantially all" test is the same as the one that applies in the (C). *See* § 1.368-2(b)(2) and Sec. 7.3.C. The regulations say that the test of whether the transaction would have qualified as an (A) if the target had merged into the acquiring parent "means that the general requirements of a reorganization under § 368(a)(1)(A) (such as a business purpose, continuity of business enterprise and continuity of interest) must be met in addition to the special requirements under § 368(a)(2)(D)." *See* § 1.368-2(b)(2). *See* Chapter 6 for an exploration of business purpose, continuity of business enterprise and continuity of interest. This regulation further says that it is "not relevant whether the merger * * * could have been effected pursuant to State or Federal corporation law."

Although the acquiring subsidiary cannot issue its own stock, it may issue other boot, as long as the continuity of interest test is satisfied. *See* § 1.368-2(b)(2). The acquiring parent may assume all or a part of the target's liabilities. *Id.* Finally, § 368(a)(2)(D) applies without respect to the time the acquiring subsidiary is formed. *Id.*

The following materials amplify the (a)(2)(D).

C. Drop Down after Subsidiary Merger

Revenue Ruling 72-576

1972-2 C.B. 217

Corporation *Y*, a wholly owned subsidiary of Corporation *X*, acquired, pursuant to a statutory merger, the assets of Corporation *W*, an unrelated corporation, in exchange for stock of *X*, and the assumption by *Y* of the liabilities of *W*. The merger, in and of itself, otherwise qualified as a reorganization described in sections 368(a)(1)(A) and (a)(2)(D) of the Code.

Immediately following the merger of *W* into *Y*, and as part of the same plan of reorganization, *Y* transferred the newly acquired assets of *W* to its wholly owned subsidiary, Corporation *Z*.* * *

The Code places no restriction on the application of section 368(a)(2)(C) of the Code to a reorganization that otherwise qualifies as a reorganization under sections 368(a)(1)(A) and (a)(2)(D) of the Code. Accordingly, the acquisition by *Y* of the assets of *W* in exchange for the stock of *X* and the assumption by *Y* of the liabilities of *W* will not be disqualified as a reorganization described in sections 368(a)(1)(A) and (a)(2)(D) by reason of the subsequent transfer by *Y* of the assets of *W* to *Z*.

D. The Parent Can Assume Liabilities of the Target

Revenue Ruling 73-257

1973-1 C.B. 189

Corporation *Y*, a wholly owned subsidiary of corporation *X*, desired to acquire all of the assets of corporation *Z*, an unrelated corporation. This acquisition was effectuated by the merging of *Z* into *Y* in exchange for stock of *X*, pursuant to the laws of the state of *A*, in which all three corporations were incorporated. No stock of *Y* was used in the transaction. In the merger *Y* received substantially all of the assets of *Z* and assumed most of the liabilities of *Z*, while *X*, for a bona fide business purpose, assumed the remaining liabilities of *Z*. All of *Z*'s outstanding liabilities at the time of the merger had been incurred in the ordinary course of its business. If *Z* had been merged into X, the merger would have qualified under the provisions of section 368(a)(1)(A) of the Code as a statutory merger.* * *

The transaction described above meets the requirements of section 368(a)(2)(D) of the Code, but a question arises regarding the assumption of some of Z's liabilities by X.

By way of analogy section 368(a)(1)(C) of the Code permits only the "acquiring corporation" to assume the liabilities of the acquired corporation. See Rev. Rul. 70-107, 1970-1 C.B. 78. In contrast, neither section 368(a)(1)(A) nor section 368(a)(2)(D) of the Code contains a limitation on which a corporation (the acquiring corporation or its parent) may assume such liabilities in a statutory merger. There is no provision in either section 368(a)(1)(A) or section 368(a)(2)(D) of the Code that would prohibit both the acquiring corporation and its parent from assuming the liabilities of the acquired corporation (although section 368(a)(2)(D) of the Code does prohibit the issuance of stock of both the parent and the subsidiary).

Accordingly, liabilities of Z may be assumed by both X and Y without disqualifying the reorganization under section 368(a)(2)(D) of the Code and thus the merger of Z into Y meets the requirements of sections 368(a)(1)(A) and (a)(2)(D) of the Code.

Since the transaction meets the definition of a reorganization under sections 368(a)(1)(A) and (a)(2)(D) of the Code, the question arises as to whether the assumption of the liabilities by X should be treated as if money or other property were received by Z from X, resulting in the recognition of gain to Z under section 361(b) of the Code, or whether section 357(a) of the Code is applicable preventing the recognition of gain by Z.* * *

Since the term "a party to a reorganization" applies to X under section 368(a)(2)(D) of the Code, by virtue of section 368(b) of the Code, X must also be considered a "party to the exchange" as such term is used in section 357(a) of the Code. Thus, since subsections (b) and (c) of section 357 of the Code are not applicable to the transaction, section 357(a) of the Code applies.

Accordingly, the assumption by X of liabilities of Z will not be treated as the receipt of money or other property by Z by virtue of section 357(a) of the Code. Thus, the exchange by Z of substantially all of its assets in return for X stock is within the provisions of section 361(a) of the Code and no gain or loss will be recognized to Z on the exchange.

Note

In Rev. Rul. 70-224, 1970-1 C.B. 79, the Service held that an acquiring corporation may assume the target's liabilities even though, pursuant to § 368(a)(2)(C), the target's assets are dropped into a subsidiary of the acquiring corporation after a (C) reorganization. Rev. Rul. 70-107, *supra*, Sec. 7.4.D., holds that an acquiring parent in a triangular (C) may not assume the target's liabilities. Rev. Rul. 73-257 holds that an acquiring parent in an (a)(2)(D) forward subsidiary merger can assume the target's liabilities. Can these rulings be reconciled?

E. Creation of a Holding Company

Revenue Ruling 77-428

1977-2 C.B. 117

Advice has been requested whether the transactions described in *Situation 1* and *Situation 2*, below, qualify as reorganizations under section 368(a)(1)(A) of the Internal Revenue Code of 1954 by reason of section 368(a)(2)(D) and section 368(a)(2)(E), respectively.

Situation 1. *P* is a corporation chartered under state law that has been engaged in the commercial banking business for a number of years. *P*, for good business reasons, decided that its business activities could be expanded if its banking business were conducted by a corporation whose stock was owned by another corporation. The other corporation could then engage in related nonbanking activities, such as selling insurance to borrowers, and leasing personal property, activities that could not be engaged in directly by *P* under state law. To accomplish this, *P* caused corporation *S1* to be organized as a wholly owned subsidiary. *S1* then caused corporation *S2* to be organized as a wholly owned subsidiary. Other than the cash received from *P* to satisfy capitalization requirements, the only asset of *S1* was the stock of *S2*, and the only asset of *S2* was the cash received from *S1* to satisfy capitalization requirements.

Pursuant to a plan of merger, *P* merged with and into *S2* under the applicable state laws with *S2* being the surviving corporation. On the effective date of the merger, each share of *P* stock held by the *P* shareholders was exchanged for a share of newly issued *S1* stock. Thus, as a result of the merger, all of the assets and business of *P* became the assets and business of *S2*, the *P* shareholders became the shareholders of *S1*, and *S1* then engaged in the nonbanking activities described above. * * * Section 1.368-2(b)(2) of the Income Tax Regulations provides that [section 368(a)(2)(D)] applies whether or not the controlling corporation (or the acquiring corporation) is formed immediately before the merger, in anticipation of the merger, or after preliminary steps have been taken to merge directly into the controlling corporation.

While section 1.368-2(b)(2) of the regulations does not specifically provide for the formation of *both* the controlling and acquiring corporation, or for the acquiring of a related corporation, there is nothing in the legislative history of the enactment of section 368(a)(2)(D) of the Code to indicate that section was not intended to apply where such was the case.

Accordingly, the merger of *P* with and into *S2* qualifies as a reorganization under section 368(a)(1)(A) of the Code by reason of section 368(a)(2)(D) even though *S1* and *S2* were newly organized corporations and even though a related corporation was acquired in the transaction. See Rev. Rul. 72-274, 1972-1 C.B. 97, in which a similar transaction was treated as a reorganization under section 368(a)(1)(A) by reason of section 368(a)(2)(D).

Section 2. The facts are the same as in *Situation 1* except that *S2* merged with and into *P* under the applicable state laws with *P* being the surviving corporation. On the effective date of the merger the *S2* stock held by *S1* was converted, pursuant to state law, into stock of *P* and each outstanding share of *P* stock not held by *S1* exchanged for a share of *S1* stock. Thus, as a result of the merger *P* became a wholly owned subsidiary of *S1* and the former *P* shareholders became the shareholders of *S1*. After the merger, *P* held all of its assets and all the assets of *S2*.* * *

The committee reports, *H.R.Rep. No. 91-1778*, 91st Cong., 2nd Sess. (1970), and *S.Rep. No. 91-1533*, 91st Cong., 2nd Sess. (1970), 1971-1 C.B. 622, indicate that section 368(a)(2)(E) of the Code was enacted to allow as a tax-free reorganization a transaction identical to a transaction described in section 368(a)(2)(D) except that the surviving corporation was the acquired rather than the acquiring corporation. Since, as concluded in *Situation 1*, a corporation may form first- and second-tier subsidiaries and then merge into the second-tier subsidiary under section 368(a)(2)(D), a reverse merger of the second-tier subsidiary into the "grandparent" is permissible under section 368(a)(2)(E).

Accordingly, the merger of *S2* with and into *P* qualifies as a reorganization within the meaning of section 368(a)(1)(A) of the Code by reason of section 368(a)(2)(E) even though *S1* and *S2* were newly organized corporations and a related corporation was acquired in the transaction.

F. Tender Offer Followed by a Forward Subsidiary Merger: The Step Transaction Doctrine in *Seagram*

J.E. Seagram Corp. v. Commissioner

United States Tax Court, 1995
104 T.C. 75

Opinion. NIMS, *Judge:* * * * [T]he only issue for decision is whether petitioner is entitled to a short-term capital loss in the amount of $530,410,896. * * *

Background Petitioner [JES] is a Delaware corporation with its principal place of business at 800 Third Avenue, New York, New York. [JES is a wholly owned subsidiary of a Canadian corporation, SCL.] * * *

The Dome Tender Offer On May 6, 1981, Dome Petroleum Ltd. (Dome) commenced a tender offer for approximately 20 percent of the common stock of Conoco, Inc. (Conoco), a Delaware corporation engaged in the oil and gas industry as an "integrated oil company". * * *

JES/Conoco Discussions Between May 29 and June 17, 1981, SCL conducted extensive negotiations with Conoco concerning proposals for it to acquire directly from Conoco, and/or through open-market purchases, between 18 percent and 35 percent of the common stock of Conoco. * * *

The JES Tender Offer On June 18 and 19, 1981, JES purchased 143,800 shares of Conoco in open market purchases on the NYSE. On June 25, 1981, JES Holdings,

Inc. (JES Tenderor), a wholly owned subsidiary of JES, initiated a tender offer for the purchase of up to 35 million shares (40.76 percent of the 85,864,538 shares outstanding on such date) of Conoco for $73 per share (the JES tender offer).* * * On June 30, 1981, the Conoco board of directors recommended that Conoco shareholders reject the JES tender offer on the ground that it was not "in the best interests of [Conoco] and its subsidiaries."

The DuPont/Conoco Agreement On June 24, 1981, Edward G. Jefferson, chairman and chief executive officer of E.I. DuPont de Nemours & Co. (DuPont), called [Conoco] to determine whether there was any constructive role DuPont might play in light of public reports. * * *

On July 6, 1981, DuPont Holdings, Inc. (DuPont Tenderor), a wholly owned subsidiary of DuPont, signed an agreement with Conoco (the DuPont/Conoco agreement or, alternatively, the agreement). The DuPont/Conoco agreement provided that DuPont Tenderor would offer (the DuPont tender offer) to exchange for each share of Conoco common stock at least either (i) 1.6 shares of DuPont common stock, or (ii) $87.50 in cash. The agreement also provided that "As promptly as practicable following the consummation or termination of the Offer, * * * [Conoco] shall be merged into * * * [DuPont Tenderor] in accordance with the Delaware General Corporation Law" (the merger), and DuPont Tenderor would thereby acquire any Conoco shares not acquired in the tender offer. * * *

The obligation of DuPont Tenderor to accept shares for exchange was not conditioned upon the consummation of the merger. The consummation of the merger was subject to, among other conditions, DuPont shareholder approval, Federal antitrust review, the absence of an injunction prohibiting the merger, and the condition that a majority of Conoco common shareholders approve the merger if required under the Delaware General Corporation Law.

The Mobil Tender Offer On July 17, 1981, Mobil Corp. (Mobil) initiated a tender offer for the purchase of up to 43,500,000 shares (51 percent) of Conoco for $90 per share (the Mobil tender offer). * * *

The Tender Offer Competition On July 12, 1981, JES Tenderor increased its tender offer to include the purchase of up to 44,350,000 Conoco shares (slightly over 51 percent of the outstanding Conoco shares not already owned by JES) and increased its offering price from $73 to $85 in cash per Conoco common share. * * *

On July 14, 1981, DuPont Tenderor announced an increase in the cash price of its tender offer from $87.50 to $95 per Conoco common share and in the number of shares of DuPont common stock offered from 1.6 to 1.7 shares per Conoco share. * * *

Tax counsel [for Dupont] concluded that

> It is our opinion that the Offer and the Merger should, if the Merger is consummated, be treated by the Internal Revenue Service or the courts as a single integrated transaction (with exchanges pursuant to the Offer treated as part of the Merger transaction) and that, accordingly, exchanges of Conoco Shares for DuPont Shares and cash pursuant to the Offer and the Merger

should be treated for federal income tax purposes as exchanges pursuant to a plan of "reorganization" within the meaning of Section 368(a)(1)(A) and (a)(2)(D) of the Code. * * *

The DuPont tender offer commenced on July 15, 1981, when DuPont's registration statement was declared effective by the Securities and Exchange Commission (SEC). Under the heading "Purpose of the Offer; the Option; Plans for Merger and Control of Conoco", the offering prospectus stated, in part, that

The purpose of the Offer and the Merger is to acquire the entire equity interest in Conoco. The Offer is being made pursuant to the Agreement which provides that following consummation of the Offer Conoco will be merged into * * * [DuPont Tenderor]. * * * The Merger requires the approval of a majority of the outstanding Conoco Shares. * * * If, as a result of the Offer and the acquisition of Conoco Shares pursuant to the Option, * * * [DuPont Tenderor] is the holder of a majority of the Conoco Shares, the Merger could be adopted regardless of the votes of any other Conoco stockholders * * *

On July 23, 1981, JES Tenderor increased its tender offer price from $85 to $92 in cash per Conoco common share. * * *

On July 27, 1981, Mobil increased its tender offer from $90 to $105 in cash per Conoco common share, and DuPont announced an increase in the cash portion of its tender offer from 40 percent of the outstanding Conoco shares to 45 percent of said shares (which was approved by the DuPont board of directors on July 29, 1981).* * *

On July 28, 1981, DuPont announced that its continuing preliminary count indicated that as of the close of business on July 27, 1981, at least 38,700,000 Conoco shares had been tendered pursuant to the DuPont tender offer. On July 29, 1981, DuPont announced that its preliminary count indicated that as of the close of business on July 28, more than 48 million Conoco shares (56 percent of those outstanding) had been tendered pursuant to the DuPont tender offer. This announcement noted that tendered shares were subject to withdrawal until midnight August 4, 1981

Also on July 29, JES issued a press release which stated, in part, that [JES] charged this morning that any decision by DuPont's Board of Directors to increase the cash portion of the DuPont offer for Conoco common stock is likely to destroy any possibility of an Internal Revenue Service Ruling that the stock portion of the offer is not fully taxable. * * * *

* * [JES] emphasized that the risk of full taxability is especially relevant in light of DuPont's announcement this morning that the cash portion of its offer is fully subscribed. Because of this oversubscription, shareholders who have not yet tendered their shares will receive only DuPont stock if they tender to DuPont, while shareholders who have already tendered may receive DuPont stock even though they elected to receive cash.

* * * [JES] further noted that shareholders who prefer to receive $92 in cash rather than DuPont stock with a value of $77.78 (based on last night's close) for their Conoco

shares continue to have the opportunity to do so by tendering to [JES]. Any tenders previously made to DuPont or Mobil are not irrevocable and may still be withdrawn.

On August 1, 1981, at 1 p.m., the withdrawal rights with respect to shares tendered to JES expired. Immediately thereafter, JES Tenderor began buying tendered Conoco shares. As of midnight on August 1, 1981, JES Tenderor had received tenders of more than 15,500,000 Conoco shares.

On August 3, 1981, Mobil increased its tender offer from $105 to $115 in cash per Conoco common share. On the same day, DuPont Tenderor announced a reduction from 51 percent to 41 percent in the minimum percentage of outstanding shares of Conoco common stock required to be tendered by Conoco shareholders in order to be accepted for payment.

On August 4, 1981, DuPont Tenderor announced that the Justice Department had terminated the Hart-Scott-Rodino waiting period. On the same day, DuPont Tenderor increased the cash price of its tender offer from $95 to $98 per Conoco share.

Mobil also announced on August 4, 1981, that it was raising its tender offer consideration to $120 in cash per Conoco share.

On August 5, 1981, JES Tenderor extended the expiration date of its tender offer, which was scheduled to expire on August 5, to August 7, 1981.

Litigation Between the Competitors [was resolved in favor of Conoco and DuPont]. ＊ ＊ ＊

The Outcome At midnight on August 4, 1981, the withdrawal period for shares tendered to DuPont Tenderor expired. On August 5, 1981, DuPont Tenderor began purchasing Conoco common shares tendered for cash. A press release issued on that day stated that

The DuPont Company has been tendered a significant majority of the outstanding shares of Conoco Inc., and will move forward as rapidly as possible to effect a merger of the two companies.

Also on August 5, 1981, DuPont Tenderor exercised the option to purchase 15,900,000 Conoco shares directly from Conoco at a price of $87.50 per share. DuPont Tenderor paid $79,500,000 in cash and a 1-year note of DuPont in the principal amount of $1,311,750,000 for the Conoco shares purchased pursuant to the option. ＊ ＊ ＊

On August 7, 1981, the JES tender offer expired with approximately 28 million Conoco shares (32 percent of the Conoco shares outstanding at the commencement of the DuPont tender offer) having been tendered to JES Tenderor for cash at $92 per share. JES Tenderor ultimately purchased 24,625,750 shares of Conoco for $92 per share and 3,113,025 shares for $91.35 per share, with an aggregate cost of $2,557,738,302.25.

Because Mobil never received tenders for 51 percent of Conoco's shares, under the terms of its tender offer, it did not purchase any of the Conoco shares tendered to it.

JES Tenderor and DuPont Tenderor were acting independently of one another and pursuant to competing tender offers.

JES' Tender of Its Conoco Shares A press release dated August 11, 1981, announced that the board of directors of SCL had authorized the exchange of the Conoco shares held by JES Tenderor pursuant to the terms of the DuPont tender offer. The release quoted JES chairman and chief executive officer Edgar Bronfman as stating:

This is an appropriate time to congratulate the management and Board of DuPont on the success of their offer for Conoco. While Seagram would have been delighted to win 51 percent of Conoco, we are pleased at the prospect of becoming a large stockholder of the combined DuPont and Conoco. We believe it will be a very strong company, with a fine future.

On August 17, 1981, JES Tenderor tendered its shares of Conoco in exchange for shares of DuPont common stock on the basis of an exchange ratio of 1.7 shares of DuPont for each Conoco share. JES Tenderor formally elected to receive DuPont stock in exchange for its Conoco stock and received 47,400,377 shares of DuPont common stock. On the exchange date, the mean high and low per share price of DuPont common stock traded on the NYSE was $43. The schedule-13D filed by JES with the SEC upon the exchange of the Conoco shares for DuPont shares stated, in part, that

The purpose of the exchange of the Conoco Shares for the DuPont Shares is to enable * * * [JES] to obtain a substantial equity interest in DuPont. Based upon publicly available information, * * * [JES] believes that it will be the largest DuPont shareholder. Accordingly, * * * [JES] may seek representation on DuPont's Board of Directors.

The Merger On August 17, 1981, the common shareholders of DuPont approved the planned merger [between Dupont and Conoco] and the issuance of additional DuPont common shares. The merger was voted in favor of by 75.3 percent of the outstanding DuPont shares and was voted against by 5.9 percent of the outstanding DuPont shares.

On September 30, 1981, Conoco merged into DuPont Tenderor. The merger was approved by a shareholder vote in which 99,100,246 Conoco shares (97 percent) were voted in favor and 89,889 Conoco shares (less than 0.1 percent) were voted against the merger. The 5,491,896 Conoco shares (6 percent of the shares outstanding at the commencement of the DuPont tender offer) not tendered were exchanged for DuPont stock pursuant to the merger. Neither petitioner, JES, nor JES Tenderor commenced any legal action with respect to the merger.

Immediately following the merger, JES Tenderor owned 20.2 percent of the outstanding common stock of DuPont. Thereafter, petitioner purchased additional shares of DuPont common stock and increased its interest in DuPont to 24.5 percent, which interest it has maintained to date. Petitioner's total cost for this stock was approximately $2,892,297,000 and its total market value, as of January 31, 1992, was approximately $7,635,300,000.

Summary of Conoco Share Trades * * * DuPont treated the tender offer and merger as a tax-free reorganization for Federal income tax purposes and filed its tax return for its 1981 taxable year accordingly. DuPont and Conoco advised former Conoco shareholders who had exchanged their stock for DuPont stock in either the exchange portion of the tender offer or the merger that they had no taxable gain or loss.

When the dust had settled at the completion of the Conoco-DuPont merger on September 30, 1981, approximately 78 percent of the Conoco stock had changed hands for cash pursuant to the competing JES and DuPont tender offers, yet approximately 54 percent of the Conoco equity (in addition to the optioned shares) remained in corporate solution in the form of DuPont shares received in exchange for Conoco shares.

Petitioner tendered each share of Conoco stock, for which it had paid about $92 per share, in exchange for 1.7 shares of DuPont stock, each share of which had a mean market value on the August 17, 1981, tender date of about $43 or approximately $73.10 for each 1.7-share unit. * * *

The amount of the loss petitioner claims to have realized (whether or not recognizable) upon the exchange of Conoco stock for DuPont stock was $530,410,896.

Discussion The ultimate issue for decision is whether, for tax purposes, petitioner had a recognized loss upon the exchange of its Conoco stock for DuPont stock. Whether such a loss is to be recognized depends upon the effect to be given section 354(a)(1) under the above facts. * * *

Thus, if DuPont, DuPont Tenderor, and Conoco were parties to a reorganization, and if the statutory merger of Conoco into DuPont Tenderor was in pursuance of a plan of reorganization, then no loss is to be recognized by petitioner upon the exchange of its Conoco stock for DuPont stock.

Petitioner challenges the validity of the putative reorganization on several grounds, discussed subsequently, whereas respondent argues in support of the reorganization. While petitioner basically questions the existence of the kind of plan of reorganization envisioned by the statute, petitioner does not challenge the status of DuPont, DuPont Tenderor, and Conoco as parties to a reorganization, assuming that in fact there was one.

In form, at least, DuPont's acquisition of Conoco (during the course of which petitioner effected the aforementioned exchange) was what the commentators Bittker and Eustice have called a "creeping multistep merger"; that is, a merger which is in their words "the culminating step in a series of acquisition transactions, all looking to the ultimate absorption of the target company's properties when control has been obtained by the acquiring corporation." * * * [citing, *inter alia King Enterprises,* Sec. 7.2.C.]

There appears to be no dispute that the merger of Conoco into DuPont Tenderor complied with the requirements of Delaware law, thus meeting the description of a "reorganization" in section 368(a)(1)(A) in that there was a "statutory merger or consolidation", and that the exchange of DuPont common stock by DuPont Tenderor for Conoco common stock fits within the provisions of section 368(a)(2)(D). Petitioner maintains, however, that the exchange of its Conoco common stock for DuPont common stock was not done in pursuance of a plan of reorganization, as required by section 354, and that therefore a loss is to be recognized on the exchange.

We first address the question of whether Conoco's merger into DuPont was pursuant to a plan of reorganization, as contemplated by section 354(a)(1). Simply stated, petitioner claims that DuPont's tender offer and the subsequent merger squeezing out the remaining Conoco shareholders were separate and independent transactions. Consequently, petitioner argues that the exchange of Conoco stock for DuPont stock pursuant to DuPont's tender offer rather than pursuant to the merger could not have been in pursuance of a plan of reorganization, as section 354 requires.

Petitioner argues at length that (1) the DuPont tender offer had independent significance from the DuPont-Conoco merger in that the tender offer had a separate business motive apart from the merger; separate and permanent legal, economic, and business consequences; and a strategically critical role in the contest for control of Conoco; (2) there were material conditions and contingencies which could have been serious impediments to the consummation of the merger; (3) the tender offer was a legally binding contract that closed prior to the merger and irrespective of whether the subsequent merger would ever close; and (4) the tender offer, not the merger, was the essential transaction by which DuPont obtained control of Conoco. We can agree with most of these assertions, and yet disagree with petitioner's conclusion that there was no reorganization. Since petitioner's points are all variations on a single theme, we will deal with them together as a single issue.

Petitioner insists that the DuPont tender offer was a legally binding contract that closed prior to the merger and irrespective of whether the subsequent merger would even be consummated. Petitioner argues that the tender offer was "plainly not a 'step' engaged in by DuPont for tax planning reasons. Rather the tender offer was the essential transaction by which DuPont obtained control of Conoco."

Petitioner asks us to apply the rationale of [*Esmark*, Sec. 2.11.C.] to sustain the argument that the DuPont tender offer, standing alone, controls the outcome of this case. However, *Esmark, Inc.* did not involve a reorganization, so the facts of that case are not apposite. Furthermore, the result in *Esmark, Inc.* is antithetical to petitioner's position in this case.

Esmark, Inc. involved a series of related transactions culminating in a tender offer and redemption of a part of the taxpayer's stock in exchange for certain property. The Commissioner, seeking to apply the step transaction doctrine, sought to recharacterize the tender offer/redemption as a sale of assets followed by a self-tender. While it is true that we held that each of the preliminary steps leading to the tender offer/redemption had an independent function, we also held that the form of the overall transaction coincided with its substance, and was to be respected. In the case before us, petitioner would have us respect the independent significance of DuPont's tender offer, but disregard the overall transaction, which included the merger. That result would, of course, be inconsistent as an analogy with the result in *Esmark, Inc.* We therefore decline petitioner's request that we apply *Esmark, Inc.* to the facts of this case.

Petitioner makes much of the fact that there were significant contingencies that might have prevented the completion of the merger even after the tender offer had closed, citing in support, among other cases, [*Dunlap & Associates*]. But the facts of *Dunlap & Associates, Inc.* are far from apposite to those of this case. * * *

The fatal defect in petitioner's "contingencies" argument, however, is that whatever the contingencies (and *any* contemplated merger involving public companies like DuPont and Conoco is bound to be fraught with contingencies), the merger *did* in fact take place, just as contemplated in the DuPont/Conoco agreement.

As respondent correctly states in her memorandum of law in opposition to petitioner's motion for summary judgment and in support of respondent's motion for summary judgment (respondent's memorandum), taxation depends on actual events, not on what might have happened. * * * As discussed *infra*, DuPont had an indisputable legal obligation to complete the merger with Conoco, notwithstanding the possibility of intervening legal impediments, or contingencies, which in fact, never materialized.

The concept of "plan of reorganization", as described in § 1.368-2(g), quoted above, is one of substantial elasticity. * * *

The DuPont/Conoco agreement was the definitive vehicle spelling out the inter-related steps by which DuPont would acquire 100 percent of Conoco's stock. * * * As we have previously noted, the agreement originally provided that the obligation of DuPont Tenderor to accept shares for exchange was, among other things, subject to the condition that at least 51 percent of Conoco's outstanding shares be tendered. Due to the exigencies created by the competing tender offers of petitioner and Mobil, DuPont subsequently found it expedient to reduce the 51-percent minimum to 41 percent. However, on August 5, 1981, DuPont Tenderor exercised the option provided in the agreement to buy 15,900,000 authorized but unissued Conoco shares, which would give DuPont an absolute majority of Conoco shares.* * *

Petitioner argues that DuPont had a "plan" to engage in a series of transactions that "ultimately may include a reorganization", but not a "plan of reorganization". For reasons already discussed, we disagree. We hold that, because DuPont was contractually committed to undertake and complete the second step merger once it had undertaken and completed the first step tender offer, these carefully integrated transactions together constituted a plan of reorganization within the contemplation of section 354(a).

Petitioner also argues that even if the DuPont tender offer and merger were to be treated as an integrated transaction, the merger does not qualify as a reorganization because it fails the "continuity of interest" requirement. * * * [This portion of the opinion is deleted because it is no longer an issue in view of the amendments to the continuity of interest regulations dealing with pre- and post-reorganization sales of stock. *See* Sec. 6.2.F.] * * *

For the reasons stated in this opinion, we hold that a loss cannot be recognized by petitioner on its exchange of Conoco stock for DuPont stock, made pursuant to the DuPont-Conoco plan of reorganization.

G. Combination (a)(2)(D) and Purported § 351

See Rev. Rul. 84-44, Sec. 6.19.C.

H. Treatment of Target's Securities in an (a)(2)(D)

See Rev. Rul. 79-155, Sec. 6.10.A.

I. Push Up of Target's Assets after a Forward Subsidiary Reorganization

With respect to the question of whether assets acquired by the acquiring corporation subsidiary in a forward triangular reorganization can be "pushed up" to the acquiring parent, *see* Pvt.Ltr.Rulings 8104127, Oct. 30, 1980; 8018030, Feb. 5, 1980; and 7943037, July 25, 1979. These rulings are discussed in Cook & Coalson, *The "Substantially All of the Properties" Requirement in Triangular Reorganizations—A Current Review*, 35 Tax Lawyer 303 (1982). *See also* Pvt.Ltr.Rul. 8206062, November 10, 1981, which allows a push up to the acquiring parent in the case of a formation of a holding company structure. The parties represented that the acquiring subsidiary would push up less than 90% of the fair market value of its net assets and less than 70% of the fair market value of its gross assets.

J. Pushdown of Stock of Acquiring Sub after a Forward Subsidiary Merger

Revenue Ruling 2001-24

I.R.B. 2001-22, (May 3, 2001)

Issue Whether a controlling corporation's transfer of the acquiring corporation's stock to another subsidiary controlled by the controlling corporation as part of the plan of reorganization, following the merger of the acquired corporation with and into the acquiring corporation, will cause the transaction to fail to qualify as a reorganization under §§ 368(a)(1)(A) and 368(a)(2)(D) of the Internal Revenue Code.

Facts Pursuant to a plan of reorganization, corporation X merges with and into corporation S, a newly organized wholly owned subsidiary of P, a corporation unrelated to X, in a transaction intended to qualify as a reorganization under §§ 368(a)(1)(A) and 368(a)(2)(D). S continues the historic business of X following the merger. Following the merger and as part of the plan of reorganization, P transfers the S stock to S1, a pre-existing, wholly owned subsidiary of P. Without regard to P's transfer of the S stock to S1, X's merger with and into S qualifies as a reorganization under §§ 368(a)(1)(A) and 368(a)(2)(D).

Law and Analysis Section 368(a)(1)(A) provides that the term reorganization includes a statutory merger or consolidation. Pursuant to § 368(a)(2)(D), the acquisition by one corporation, in exchange for stock of a corporation (the "controlling corporation") that is in control (as defined in § 368(c)) of the acquiring corporation, of substantially all of the properties of another corporation (the "merged corporation") shall not disqualify a transaction under § 368(a)(1)(A) if—

(i) no stock of the acquiring corporation is used in the transaction, and

(ii) in the case of a transaction under § 368(a)(1)(A), such transaction would have qualified under § 368(a)(1)(A) had the merger been into the controlling corporation.

Section 368(b) provides that a party to a reorganization qualifying under §§ 368(a)(1)(A) and 368(a)(2)(D) includes the merged corporation, the acquiring corporation, and the controlling corporation.

Section 368(a)(2)(C) provides that a transaction otherwise qualifying under §§ 368(a)(1)(A), (1)(B), or (1)(C) is not disqualified by reason of the fact that part or all of the assets or stock which were acquired in the transaction are transferred to a corporation controlled (as defined by § 368(c)) by the corporation acquiring such assets or stock.

Under § 1.368-2(f) of the Income Tax Regulations, if a transaction otherwise qualifies as a reorganization, a corporation remains a party to a reorganization even though the stock or assets acquired in the reorganization are transferred in a transaction described in § 1.368-2(k). Section 1.368-2(k)(1) restates the general rule contained in § 368(a)(2)(C) but permits the assets or stock acquired in the reorganization to be successively transferred to one or more corporations controlled (as defined under § 368(c)) in each transfer by the transferor corporation without disqualifying the reorganization. Additionally, § 1.368-2(k)(2) provides that a transaction qualifying under §§ 368(a)(1)(A) and 368(a)(2)(E) is not disqualified by reason of the fact that part or all of the stock of the surviving corporation is transferred or successively transferred to one or more corporations controlled in each transfer by the transferor corporation, or because part or all of the assets of the surviving corporation or the merged corporation are transferred or successively transferred to one or more corporations controlled in each transfer by the transferor corporation.

To qualify as a reorganization under § 368(a), a transaction must satisfy the continuity of business enterprise requirement. Section 1.368-1(d)(1) requires that the issuing corporation, in this case P, must either continue the target corporation's historic business or use a significant portion of the target's historic business assets in a business in order for a reorganization to satisfy the continuity of business enterprise requirement. The underlying policy of this rule is to ensure that reorganizations are limited to readjustments of continuing interests in property under modified corporate form. Pursuant to § 1.368-1(d)(4), the issuing corporation (the controlling corporation in the case of a § 368(a)(2)(D) reorganization) is treated as holding all of the businesses and assets of all of the members of its qualified group. Section 1.368-1(d)(4)(ii) defines a qualified group as one or more chains of corporations connected through stock ownership with the issuing corporation, but only if the issuing corporation owns directly stock meeting the requirements of § 368(c) in at least one other corporation, and stock meeting the requirements of § 368(c) in each of the corporations (except the issuing corporation) is owned directly by one of the other corporations. Therefore, the issuing corporation is treated as directly holding the businesses and assets of second-tier and lower-tier subsidiaries that are part of the qualified group.

In applying these requirements to the facts, the continuity of business enterprise requirement is satisfied. Because S and S1 are members of P's qualified group, P will be treated as directly holding the businesses and assets of S. Therefore, because S will continue X's historic business following the merger, the transaction will satisfy the continuity of business enterprise requirement of § 1.368-1(d).

The remaining issue is whether P's transfer of the S stock to S1 as part of the plan of reorganization causes P to fail to control S for purposes of § 368(a)(2)(D) and causes P to fail to be a party to the reorganization. Section 368(a)(2)(C) and § 1.368-2(k) do not specifically address P's transfer of the stock of S to S1 following an otherwise qualifying reorganization under §§ 368(a)(1)(A) and 368(a)(2)(D), because assets and not stock were acquired in the reorganization. If the transaction were recast under the step transaction doctrine so that X's assets were viewed as being acquired by a second-tier subsidiary of P, the transaction would not qualify as a reorganization under §§ 368(a)(1)(A) and 368(a)(2)(D) because P would not control S. For the reasons set forth below, the transaction will not be recast under the step transaction doctrine.

The legislative history of § 368(a)(2)(E) suggests that forward and reverse triangular mergers should be treated similarly. *See* S. Rep. No. 1533, 91st Cong., 2d Sess. 2 (1970). As discussed above, pursuant to § 1.368-2(k)(2), a controlling corporation in a merger that qualifies under §§ 368(a)(1)(A) and 368(a)(2)(E) may transfer the stock (or assets) of the surviving corporation to a controlled subsidiary without causing the transaction to fail to qualify as a reorganization under §§ 368(a)(1)(A) and 368(a)(2)(E). The concept that forward and reverse triangular mergers should be treated similarly supports permitting P to transfer the S stock to S1 without causing the transaction to fail to qualify as a reorganization under §§ 368(a)(1)(A) and 368(a)(2)(D). This concept also is reflected in the continuity of business enterprise regulations under § 1.368-1(d), which do not distinguish between § 368(a)(2)(D) and § 368(a)(2)(E) reorganizations and do not differentiate between whether stock or assets are acquired.

Section 368(a)(2)(C) does not preclude this transaction from qualifying as a reorganization under §§ 368(a)(1)(A) and 368(a)(2)(D) because of the stock transfer. By its terms, § 368(a)(2)(C) is a permissive rather than an exclusive or restrictive section. *See, e.g.,* § 1.368-2(k); Rev. Rul. 64-73, 1964-1 C.B. 142. Further, § 368(a)(2)(C) and § 1.368-2(k) similarly do not cause P to fail to be treated as a party to the reorganization. *See* Rev. Rul. 64-73.

Accordingly, for the reasons set forth above, P's transfer of the S stock to S1 as part of the plan of reorganization, following the merger of X with and into S, will not cause P to be treated as not in control of S for purposes of § 368(a)(2)(D). Additionally, P will be treated as a party to the reorganization.

Holding A controlling corporation's transfer of the acquiring corporation's stock to a subsidiary controlled by the controlling corporation as part of the plan of reorganization, following the merger of the acquired corporation with and into the acquiring corporation, will not cause the transaction to fail to qualify as a reorganization under §§ 368(a)(1)(A) and 368(a)(2)(D).

K. Sale of 50% of Target's Assets after a Forward Subsidiary Merger

Revenue Ruling 2001-25

I.R.B. 2001-22 (May 7, 2001)

Issue On the facts below, does a merger fail to qualify as a tax-free reorganization under §§ 368(a)(1)(A) and 368(a)(2)(E) of the Internal Revenue Code if, immediately after the merger and as part of a plan that includes the merger, the surviving corporation sells a portion of its assets to an unrelated party?

Facts P is a manufacturing corporation organized under the laws of state A. T is also a manufacturing corporation organized under the laws of state A. P organizes corporation S as a wholly owned state A subsidiary of P, and S merges with and into T in a statutory merger under the laws of state A. In the merger, the shareholders of T holding 90 percent of the T stock exchange their T stock for voting stock of P. The remaining shareholders of T receive $y cash for their T stock. Immediately after the merger and as part of a plan that includes the merger, T sells 50 percent of its operating assets for $z cash to X, an unrelated corporation. After the sale of the assets to X, T retains the sales proceeds. Without regard to the requirement that T hold substantially all of the assets of T and S, the merger satisfies all the other requirements applicable to reorganizations under §§ 368(a)(1)(A) and 368(a)(2)(E).

Law and Analysis Section 368(a)(1)(A) states that the term—reorganization—means a statutory merger or consolidation. Section 368(a)(2)(E) provides that a transaction otherwise qualifying under § 368(a)(1)(A) will not be disqualified by reason of the fact that stock of a corporation (the "controlling corporation") that before the merger was in control of the acquiring corporation is used in the transaction, if (1) after the transaction, the corporation surviving the merger holds substantially all of its properties and of the properties of the merged corporation (other than stock of the controlling corporation distributed in the transaction), and (2) in the transaction, former shareholders of the surviving corporation exchanged, for an amount of voting stock of the controlling corporation, an amount of stock in the surviving corporation that constitutes control of such corporation.

Section 1.368-2(j)(3)(iii) of the Income Tax Regulations provides that, for purposes of § 368(a)(2)(E), "[t]he term 'substantially all' has the same meaning as in section 368(a)(1)(C)."

Rev. Rul. 88-48, 1988-1 C.B. 117, holds that the requirement of § 368(a)(1)(C) that the acquiring corporation acquire "substantially all" of the properties of a target corporation is satisfied when immediately prior to the target corporation's transfer of assets to the acquiring corporation, the target corporation sells 50 percent of its historic assets to unrelated parties for cash and immediately transfers that cash, along with its other properties, to the acquiring corporation.

Section 368(a)(2)(E) uses the term "holds" rather than the term "acquisition" as do §§ 368(a)(1)(C) and 368(a)(2)(D) because it would be inapposite to require the surviving corporation to "acquire" its own properties. The "holds" requirement of § 368(a)(2)(E) does not impose requirements on the surviving corporation before and after the merger that would not have applied had such corporation transferred its properties to another corporation in a reorganization under § 368(a)(1)(C) or a reorganization under §§ 368(a)(1)(A) and 368(a)(2)(D).

In this case, T's post-merger sale of 50 percent of its operating assets for cash to X prevents T from holding substantially all of its historic business assets immediately after the merger. As in Rev. Rul. 88-48, however, the sales proceeds continue to be held by T. Therefore, the post-acquisition sale of 50 percent of T's operating assets where T holds the proceeds of such sale along with its other operating assets does not cause the merger to violate the requirement of § 368(a)(2)(E) that the surviving corporation hold substantially all of its properties after the transaction.

Accordingly, the merger qualifies as a reorganization under §§ 368(a)(1)(A) and 368(a)(2)(E), notwithstanding the sale by T of a portion of its assets to X immediately after the merger and as part of a plan that includes the merger.

Holding On the facts above, a merger qualifies as a tax-free reorganization under §§ 368(a)(1)(A) and 368(a)(2)(E), notwithstanding the fact that the surviving corporation sells a portion of its assets to an unrelated party immediately after the merger and as part of a plan that includes the merger.

L. Dealing with the Zero Basis Problem

See §§ 1.1032-2 and 1.358-6(a). *See* § 7.4.F.

M. Representations Required in a Ruling Request under § 368(a)(2)(D)

Excerpt from Revenue Procedure 86-42

§ 7.02, 1986-2 C.B. 722

[Although as noted in Sec. 6.2.A.6., the IRS generally does not issue private letter rulings on reorganization transactions, the following ruling guidelines can be helpful in structuring a deal.]

[In addition to the following representations, the parties are required to give representations 1, 2, 9, 10 and 11 that are required for rulings under § 368(a)(1)(A). *See* Sec. 7.2.L.]

.02 Section 368(a)(1)(A) and (a)(2)(D) mergers:

Legend: Parent   =   The controlling corporation
           Sub   =   The acquiring corporation
           Target   =   The transferor corporation

* * *

3. SUB WILL ACQUIRE AT LEAST 90 PERCENT OF THE FAIR MARKET VALUE OF THE NET ASSETS AND AT LEAST 70 PERCENT OF THE FAIR MARKET VALUE OF THE GROSS ASSETS HELD BY TARGET IMMEDIATELY PRIOR TO THE TRANSACTION. FOR PURPOSES OF THIS REPRESENTATION, AMOUNTS PAID BY TARGET TO DISSENTERS, AMOUNTS PAID BY TARGET TO SHAREHOLDERS WHO RECEIVE CASH OR OTHER PROPERTY, TARGET ASSETS USED TO PAY ITS REORGANIZATION EXPENSES, AND ALL REDEMPTIONS AND DISTRIBUTIONS (EXCEPT FOR REGULAR, NORMAL DIVIDENDS) MADE BY TARGET IMMEDIATELY PRECEDING THE TRANSFER, WILL BE INCLUDED AS ASSETS OF TARGET HELD IMMEDIATELY PRIOR TO THE TRANSACTION.

4. PRIOR TO THE TRANSACTION, PARENT WILL BE IN CONTROL OF SUB WITHIN THE MEANING OF SECTION 368(c) OF THE INTERNAL REVENUE CODE.

5. FOLLOWING THE TRANSACTION, SUB WILL NOT ISSUE ADDITIONAL SHARES OF ITS STOCK THAT WOULD RESULT IN PARENT LOSING CONTROL OF SUB WITHIN THE MEANING OF SECTION 368(c) OF THE INTERNAL REVENUE CODE.

6. PARENT HAS NO PLAN OR INTENTION TO REACQUIRE ANY OF ITS STOCK ISSUED IN THE TRANSACTION.

7. PARENT HAS NO PLAN OR INTENTION TO LIQUIDATE SUB; TO MERGE SUB WITH AND INTO ANOTHER CORPORATION; TO SELL OR OTHERWISE DISPOSE OF THE STOCK OF SUB; OR TO CAUSE SUB TO SELL OR OTHERWISE DISPOSE OF ANY OF THE ASSETS OF TARGET ACQUIRED IN THE TRANSACTION, EXCEPT FOR DISPOSITIONS MADE IN THE ORDINARY COURSE OF BUSINESS OR TRANSFERS DESCRIBED IN SECTION 368(a)(2)(C) OF THE INTERNAL REVENUE CODE.

8. THE LIABILITIES OF TARGET ASSUMED BY SUB AND THE LIABILITIES TO WHICH THE TRANSFERRED ASSETS OF TARGET ARE SUBJECT WERE INCURRED BY TARGET IN THE ORDINARY COURSE OF ITS BUSINESS.

9. FOLLOWING THE TRANSACTION, SUB WILL CONTINUE THE HISTORIC BUSINESS OF TARGET OR USE A SIGNIFICANT PORTION OF TARGET'S BUSINESS ASSETS IN A BUSINESS.

10. PARENT, SUB, TARGET, AND THE SHAREHOLDERS OF TARGET WILL PAY THEIR RESPECTIVE EXPENSES, IF ANY, INCURRED IN CONNECTION WITH THE TRANSACTION.

11. THERE IS NO INTERCORPORATE INDEBTEDNESS EXISTING BETWEEN PARENT AND TARGET OR BETWEEN SUB AND TARGET THAT WAS IS-SUED, ACQUIRED, OR WILL BE SETTLED AT A DISCOUNT. * * *

15. NO STOCK OF SUB WILL BE ISSUED IN THE TRANSACTION.

§ 7.7 Summary Problems on Straight and Triangular Acquisitive Asset Reorganizations

Target corporation (*TC*) has 100 common shares outstanding (its only stock), which is owned as follows:

	No. of Shares	Adjusted Basis
Individual *A*	40	20K
Corporation *X*	40	20K
Individual *B*	20	10K

TC has two different divisions: (1) a widget division, which has plant and equipment with a value of $55K and a basis of $35K, and (2) a wodget division, which has plant and equipment with a value of $55K and a basis of $75K. *TC* has cash of $20K and liabilities of $30K, represented by 10-year debentures. There is no OID on the debentures. *A* owns $10K of the debentures and the balance is owned by a bank (*Y*). *A* has a basis of $9K for his debentures and *Y* has a basis of $18K. The debentures have a fair market value of $30K.

The total fair market value of *TC*'s assets is $130K and the net value is $100K, as follows:

Assets	Fair Market Value	Adjusted Basis
Cash	$20K	$20K
Widget Division	$55K	$35K
Wodget Division	$55K	$75K
Total Assets	$130K	

Less

	Liabilities	
	Debentures	$30K

Net Value $100K

The value of *TC*'s stock is also $100K. *TC* has accumulated E & P of $50K.

Acquiring corporation (*AC*) is a large conglomerate whose stock is traded on the New York Stock Exchange. *AC* wants to acquire *TC* principally for the purpose of getting into the widget business, which *AC* thinks is about to take off. *AC* wants *A*, who is also an employee of *TC*, to enter into a long-term employment agreement.

What are the tax consequences to each of the parties under each of the following basic asset transactions and the modifications thereof?

TC merges into *AC* with the shareholders of *TC* receiving in exchange for their *TC* stock on a pro rata basis (1) $50K of *AC* nonvoting common, (2) $25K of cash, and

(3) *AC* debentures with a face and value of $25K. There is no OID on *AC*'s debentures. Also, *AC* issues its debentures with a face and value of $30K in exchange for the *TC* debentures held by *A* and *Y*?

Consider each of the following modifications separately.

a. Suppose the *AC* debentures issued in exchange for the *TC* debentures have a face of $36K and a value of $30K?

b. Suppose that instead of the *AC* debentures issued in exchange for the *TC* stock, *AC* issues its nonvoting preferred?

c. Suppose that instead of receiving the consideration on a pro rata basis it was received by the shareholders as follows:

Shareholders	AC Stock	AC Debentures	Cash	Total
A	$10K	$20K	$10K	$40K
B	$5K	$5K	$10K	$20K
X	$35K	-0-	$5K	$40K
	$50K	$25K	$25K	$100K

d. Suppose that instead of a direct merger of *TC* into *AC*, *AC* forms a new subsidiary (*AC-S*) and transfers to *AC-S* the consideration specified in the basic transaction. *TC* then merges into *AC-S*?

e. Suppose *AC* purchases the *TC* stock held by *X* for cash of $40K and immediately thereafter merges *TC* upstream with *A* receiving *AC* voting common and *B* receiving $20K in *AC* debentures?

f. Suppose that prior to the merger of *TC* into *AC*, *TC* redeems *B*'s stock for $20K in cash and then *TC* merges into *AC* with *A* receiving $40K of *AC* nonvoting preferred and *X* receiving $40K of *AC* debentures?

g. Suppose that instead of a merger of *TC* into *AC*, *AC* acquires all of *TC*'s assets and assumes *TC*'s liability to its debenture holders in exchange for the consideration specified in the basic transaction, and *TC* immediately liquidates, transferring the consideration to its shareholders?

h. Suppose that in the transaction in g. above, the consideration paid is $100K of *AC* voting common?

i. Suppose that in the transaction in g. above, the consideration is $130K of *AC* voting common and *AC* does not take over *TC*'s liability? *TC* utilizes $30K of the *AC* stock to discharge its obligation to its debenture holders?

j. Suppose that prior to the acquisition, *TC* distributes the wodget business subject to $15K of the liabilities to *X* in redemption of its *TC* stock. *AC* then acquires the remaining assets of *TC* solely for *AC* voting common stock? Suppose instead *TC* mergers into *AC* with *TC* shareholders receiving *AC* voting stock and *TC* debenture holders receiving *AC* debentures?

l. Suppose *AC* purchases the *TC* stock held by *B* for $20K in cash, and shortly thereafter *AC* acquires all of *TC*'s assets subject to its liabilities for $100K in *AC* voting common stock. *TC* is then liquidated? Suppose the acquisition of

TC is made by *AC-S,* in exchange solely for *AC* voting common stock and *TC* is liquidated?

n. *AC* is a mutual fund. In order to give the *TC* shareholders shares in *AC* on a tax free basis, *AC* proposes that (1) *TC* sell its assets for cash, (2) *TC* pay off its debentures with cash, (3) *AC* then acquire *TC*'s assets, which will be only $100K of cash, for $100K of *AC* shares, and (4) *TC* liquidate, distributing the *AC* shares to *A, B* and *X?*

§ 7.8 The § 381 Carryover Rules

A. The General Carryover Rules of § 381(a)

Section 381(a) provides that in the types of transactions specified below the acquiring corporation shall succeed to and take into account, as of the close of the date of distribution or transfer, the items of the distributor or transferor corporation specified in § 381(c), subject to the conditions and limitations specified in § 381(b) and (c). As will be seen below, one of these items is the net operating loss carryovers of the distributor or transferor corporation.

Section 381(a) covers certain nontaxable liquidations and reorganizations. It covers the liquidation of a subsidiary into its parent in a liquidation governed by § 332 in which the parent takes a carryover basis for the subsidiary's assets under § 334(b)(1). *See* the discussion of § 332 in Chapter 2 and § 381(a)(1).

The reorganizations which are covered by § 381(a) are (1) mergers under § 368(a)(1)(A); (2) forward triangular mergers under § 368(a)(2)(D); (3) the direct and triangular acquisition of assets for voting stock under § 368(a)(1)(C); (4) the nondivisive (D) under § 368(a)(1)(D) and § 354(b); and (5) mere changes in form under § 368(a)(1)(F). *See* § 381(a)(2). Thus § 381 applies to the acquisitive asset reorganizations discussed in this chapter. The Service has held that a stock for stock B reorganization under § 368(a)(1)(B) followed by a liquidation will be treated, for purposes of §§ 381 and 382, as a stock for assets C reorganization under § 368(a)(1)(C). *See* Rev. Rul. 67-274, *supra* Sec. 7.3.B.

Section 381 does not apply to divisive reorganizations under § 368(a)(1)(D) and 355. *See* § 1.381(a)-1(b)(3). Consequently, in Revenue Ruling 56-373, 1956-2 C.B. 217, the Service held that in a non-pro rata split-up of one corporation into two with the two shareholders going their separate ways with different corporations, the net operating loss does not carry over to either corporation. Also, in Revenue Ruling 77-133, 1977-1 C.B. 96, the Service held that when a parent splits off a new subsidiary in a non-pro rata distribution with one of the two shareholders taking the subsidiary and the other shareholder retaining the stock of the parent, the net operating loss of the parent will stay with the parent.

Also, § 381 does not apply to a § 351 organization transaction. Consequently, if a corporation with a net operating loss carryover forms a subsidiary and transfers the assets of a division to it, the net operating losses associated with the division will not pass to the new corporation but will stay with the parent.

B. Definition of "Acquiring Corporation"

As indicated above, § 381(a) provides that the "acquiring corporation" shall succeed to the net operating losses of the distributor or transferor corporation. The regulations set forth several rules for determining the acquiring corporation. *See* § 1.381(a)-1(b)(2).

There can be only one acquiring corporation under § 381. The parent in a § 332 liquidation is treated as the acquiring corporation. In a reorganization covered by § 381(a)(2), the corporation which pursuant to the plan of reorganization "ultimately acquires, directly or indirectly, all of the assets transferred by the transferor" is generally the acquiring corporation. If the assets of the transferor are disbursed among several transferee corporations so that no one corporation "ultimately acquires all of the assets" of the transferor, the corporation that made the direct acquisition from the transferor will be treated as the acquiring corporation even though it retains none of the assets. Whether a corporation acquired all of a transferor's assets is a question of fact. The regulations give four examples illustrating these rules.

The first example involves a triangular C reorganization under § 368(a)(1)(C) where a parent ("AC-P") forms a subsidiary to which it transfers its voting stock and the subsidiary ("AC-S") acquires the assets of the target in exchange for the parent's stock. The regulation holds that the subsidiary, AC-S, is the acquiring corporation. *See* § 1.381(a)-1(b)(2)(ii), Example 1. The second example involves a C reorganization in which the target's assets are dropped down under § 368(a)(2)(C) to a subsidiary. The regulation holds that the subsidiary is the acquiring corporation. *See* § 1.381(a)-1(b)(2)(ii), Example 2. The third example involves a C reorganization in which half the assets of the target are dropped down to a subsidiary and half are retained by the parent. The regulation holds that the parent is the acquiring corporation. *See* § 1.381(a)-1(b)(2)(ii), Example 3. In the fourth example there is a C reorganization in which the target's assets are dropped into two separate subsidiaries. The regulation holds that the parent is the acquiring corporation although it retains none of the target's assets. *See* § 1.381(a)-1(b)(2)(ii), Example 4.

C. The Operating Rules of § 381(b)

Section 381(b) sets forth certain operating rules governing reorganizations covered by § 381(a) other than the (F) (mere change in form) reorganization.

Section 381(b)(1), the first operating rule, provides that the taxable year of the distributor or transferor (hereafter the "target") corporation ends on the date of the distribution or transfer. Section 381(b)(2) provides that the date of the distribution or transfer (hereafter the "acquisition date") is the date on which the distribution or transfer is complete, except that under the regulations such date may be the date when "substantially all of the property has been distributed or transferred" if the target has ceased operations and is in the process of liquidating. The regulations require the filing of a joint statement by the acquiring corporation and the target in a case in which the tax year is to end on the date of the transfer of substantially all the target's assets. *See* § 1.381(b)-1(b). A target may retain a reasonable amount of assets in order to discharge debts without violating the "substantially all" requirement.

Under Section 381(b)(3), the acquiring corporation may not carry back a net operating loss or net capital loss arising in a taxable year after the acquisition date to a prior taxable year of the target. § 1.381(c)-1(b).

Any postacquisition losses of the acquiring corporation may be carried back to preacquisition years of the acquiring corporation. *See* § 1.381(c)(1)-1(b). As a planning matter if two corporations are going to be merged and the target has had taxable income in prior years while the acquiring corporation has not, it might be advisable to structure the transaction so that the target is the surviving corporation. In this way, any postacquisition losses could be carried back and offset against preacquisition taxable income.

D. The (F) Reorganization and the Nonapplicability of the § 381(b) Operating Rules

As indicated above, the operating rules of § 381(b) do not apply to the F reorganization under § 368(a)(1)(F), *i.e.,* "a mere change in identity, form, or place of organization, however affected." *See* Chapter 3. Consequently, in the case of an F, the taxable year of the distributor or transferor corporation (the "Old corporation") will not end on the date of the distribution or transfer (*compare* § 381(b)(1)) and an operating loss or net capital loss incurred by the corporation acquiring the property of the Old corporation (the "New corporation") may be carried back to the prior tax years of the Old corporation (*compare* § 381(b)(3)).

E. Carryover Items under § 381(c)

Section 381(c) specifies twenty-five items which will carry over from the target to the acquiring corporation under § 381(a). Such items include, *inter alia:*

(1) net operating losses (*see* § 381(c)(1));

(2) earnings and profits (*see* § 381(c)(2));

(3) capital loss carryovers (*see* § 381(c)(3));

(4) accounting methods (*see* § 381(c)(4));

(5) depreciation methods (*see* § 381(c)(6)); and

(6) the § 453 installment sale method (*see* § 381(c)(8)).

The regulations provide that § 381 does not apply to any tax attribute that is not specified in § 381(c). Also the regulations say that no inference is to be drawn from § 381 as to whether any tax attribute that is not specified should be taken into account by the acquiring corporation. *See* § 1.381(a)-1(b)(3).

F. Section 381(c)(1) Limitations on Carryover of Net Operating Losses

Three basic rules governing net operating loss carryovers are provided in §381(c)(1): the *first year rule* of §381(c)(1)(A); the *first year limitation rule* of §381(c)(1)(B); and the *loss year ordering rule* of §381(c)(1)(C). There is a full carryover of net operating losses even though the acquiring corporation does not acquire 100 percent of the target's assets. For instance, in a §332 subsidiary liquidation of an 80 percent owned subsidiary, although the parent only receives 80 percent of the subsidiary's assets, all of subsidiary's net operating losses carry over to the parent. *See* §1.381(c)(1)-1(c)(2). In addition to the rules of §381(c), net operating losses may be limited by §382. *See* Sec. 7.9.

The first year rule. Section 381(c)(1)(A) provides that the first year of the acquiring corporation to which a target's net operating losses may be carried is the first taxable year ending after the acquisition date.

The first year limitation rule. Under §381(c)(1)(B), the amount of a target's net operating losses which can be carried over to the first taxable year of the acquiring corporation is limited by the following formula (where X = maximum allowable losses):

$$\frac{X}{\text{Acquiring Corporation's Taxable Income for First Taxable Year}} = \frac{\text{Number of Days in First Taxable Year After the Acquisition Date}}{\text{Total Number of Days in First Taxable Year}}$$

This limitation is applied to the aggregate of the target's loss carryovers without regard to the year in which they arose. *See* §1.381(c)-1(c)(2).

This formula can be illustrated by the following examples. Assume that an acquiring corporation on a calendar year makes an acquisition of a target on December 31. The target has a $100,000 net operating loss carryover and none of this NOL is limited by §382. In the first year ending after the acquisition the acquiring corporation has $150,000 of taxable income before taking into account the net operating loss deduction. In such case the limitation on the target's carryovers would be $150,000, *i.e.*:

$$\frac{X}{\$150,000} = \frac{365}{365}$$

Consequently, all of the target's loss carryovers would be deducted in the first year after the acquisition.

Assume that the facts are the same as in the above example, except the acquisition is made on July 1. In such a case the first year limitation would be approximately $75,000, *i.e.*:

$$\frac{X}{\$150,000} = \frac{182}{365}$$

Consequently, only $75,000 of the target's loss carryovers could be used in the first year. Also, under §381(b), the target has a short taxable year running from January 1 to June 30 and this is counted as one of the carryover years under §172.

The loss year ordering rules. If both the acquiring corporation and the target have net operating loss carryovers, then pursuant to §381(c)(1)(C), any loss year of the target ending on or before the acquiring corporation's loss year shall be treated as having arisen in a year prior to the acquiring corporation's loss year.

If the acquisition occurs on any day other than the last day of the acquiring corporation's tax year, and the acquiring corporation has a loss for such year, then such loss shall be deemed to have arisen in two tax years; the pre-acquisition part year and the post-acquisition part year. The loss for the preacquisition part year will be deemed to have occurred after any loss year of the target.

§7.9 Impact of §382 on the Utilization of the Target's Net Operating Losses

A. Introduction

In each of the forms of acquisitive asset reorganizations, the target's net operating loss carryovers pass over to the acquiring corporation under §381, as discussed in Sec. 7.8. The losses, however, are subject to limitation under §382. Also, limitations similar to those of §382 apply to capital loss carryovers, foreign tax credit carryovers, and excess credits under §383. Only the rules of §382 are discussed here.

Many of the provisions of §382 governing acquisitive asset reorganizations are the same as those that apply to the taxable acquisition of a target's stock. The legislative background to §382 and the impact of §382 generally and in taxable stock acquisitions is explored in Sec. 5.8. The purpose of this section is to introduce those provisions of §382 that apply specifically to acquisitive asset reorganizations. The applicability of §382 to acquisitive stock reorganizations is considered in Sec. 8.7.

B. Applicability of §382 to Equity Structure Shifts

An *Ownership Change* under §382 occurs if immediately after (1) an *Owner Shift Involving a 5% Shareholder,* or (2) any *Equity Structure Shift,* there has been an increase by more than 50 percentage points in (A) the percentage of stock of the *Loss Corporation* owned by one or more *5 Percent Shareholders,* over (B) the lowest percentage of stock of the *Loss Corporation* owned by the *5 Percent Shareholders* at any time during the 3 year *Testing Period, See* Sec. 3.8.

An *Equity Structure Shift* means any reorganization under §368, except that the term does not include (1) any §368(a)(1)(D) (split-up) or (G) (bankruptcy) reorganization unless the requirements of § 354(b)(1) (relating to transfer of substantially all the assets) are met, and (2) any § 368(a)(1)(F) (mere change in form) reorganization. *See* § 382(g)(3)(A). The term encompasses both acquisitive asset reorganizations, acquisitive stock reorganizations and also recapitalizations. The term also means, to the extent provided in regulations, any taxable reorganization-type transactions, public offerings and similar transactions. *See* § 382(g)(3)(B).

The Conference Report to the Tax Reform Act of 1986 (p. 177) gives the following example of an *Ownership Change* that results from a tax-free merger of a *Loss Corporation* into a profitable corporation:

> *Example 8.* On January 1, 1988, L corporation (a loss corporation) is merged (in a transaction described in section 368(a)(1)(A)) into P corporation (not a loss corporation), with P surviving. Both L and P are publicly traded corporations with no shareholder owning five percent or more of either corporation or the surviving corporation. In the merger, L shareholders receive 30 percent of the stock of P. There has been an ownership change of L, because the percentage of P stock owned by the former P shareholders (all of whom are less-than-5-percent shareholders who are treated as a separate, single 5-percent shareholder) after the equity structure shift (70 percent) has increased by more than 50 percentage points over the lowest percentage of L stock owned by such shareholders at any time during the testing period (0 percent prior to the merger). If, however, the former shareholders of L had received at least 50 percent of the stock of P in the merger, there would not have been an ownership change of L.

As a result of the *Ownership Change* in the above example, L's losses, which carry over to P under § 381, are subject to the § 382 Limitation. Thus, if the value of L's stock is $10 million and the long-term tax-exempt rate is 10%, L's losses could be utilized only to the extent of $1 million each year. *See* Sec. 5.8.C.

§ 7.10 Impact of Consolidated Return Regulations on Utilization of a Target's NOLs[*]

A. Introduction

If as a result of an asset reorganization, a loss corporation becomes a member of a new consolidated group, the rules discussed in Chapter 5 relating to the following provisions of the consolidated return regulations apply:

(1) the taxable year rules (*see* Sec. 5.9.B);

(2) the separate return limitation year (SRLY) rules, which will not apply where there is an overlap with § 382 (*see* Sec. 5.9.C);

---

[*] Based on § 52.10 of *Federal Taxation of Business Enterprises, supra* Chapter 1, note 1, with permission.

(3) the built-in loss rules, which will not apply where there is an overlap with § 382 (*see* Sec. 5.9.E);

(4) the carryover and carryback rules (*see* Sec. 5.9.F); and

(5) the consolidated return/§ 382 interface rules (*see* Sec. 9.9.G).

The following sections discuss the application of the SRLY rules in asset reorganizations and the reverse acquisition rules.

B. Reverse Acquisitions in Acquisitive Asset Reorganizations*

The NOLs of a common parent corporation are not SRLYs. *See* § 1.1502-1(f)(3). Consequently, a consolidated group of corporations that has NOLs may acquire a profitable corporation without affecting the utilization of the losses, except to the extent that § 384 applies. *See* Sec. 5.12. Thus, for example, if a loss group and a profitable group are combined in a stock for asset (C) reorganization, the parties may contemplate having the common parent of the loss group act as the acquiring corporation. Thus, even though the loss group may be the smaller group and the shareholders of the profitable group may own the majority of the shares of the combined entity, the loss corporation could act as the acquiring corporation in order to avoid the SRLY rules.

In order to guard against the circumvention of the SRLY rules by having the loss corporation become the common parent in this type of situation, the consolidated return regulations incorporate the concept of a reverse acquisition. *See* § 1.1502-75(d)(3); § 1.1502-1(f)(3). A reverse acquisition occurs in an acquisitive asset reorganization if "substantially all of the assets of the [acquired] corporation [are transferred] in exchange for stock of the [acquiring] corporation" and the shareholders of the target corporation end up owning more than 50% of the fair market value of the stock of the acquiring corporation as a result of the acquisition. *See* § 1.1502-75(d)(3). In such circumstances, the acquired corporation is treated as the acquiring corporation for purposes of applying the SRLY rules and for determining which consolidated group continues in existence. *See* § 1.1502-75(d)(3); § 1.1502-1(f)(3).

The application of the reverse acquisition rule in the context of an (A) reorganization is illustrated in the following example from the regulations:

> [A]ssume that corporations P and S comprised group PS (P being the common parent), that P was merged into corporation T (the common parent of a group composed of T and corporation U), and that the shareholders of P immediately before the merger, as a result of owning stock in P, own 90 percent of the fair market value of T's stock immediately after the merger. The group of which P was the common parent is treated as continuing in existence with T and U being added as members of the group, and T taking the place of P as the common parent. *See* § 1.1502-75(d)(3).

---

* Based on § 52:11 of *Federal Taxation of Business Enterprises, supra* Chapter 1, note 1, with permission.

Similar principles apply in the straight and triangular (C) reorganizations and in the forward triangular merger under § 368(a)(2)(D). Also, the reverse acquisition rule applies to acquisitive stock reorganizations. *See* Sec. 8.7.

The reverse acquisition rule seems to have little significance since the transaction giving rise to a reverse acquisition would normally be subject to § 382, and as a result, the SRLY rules would not apply.

§ 7.11 Impact of § 269 on Utilization of Target's NOLs: Transactions Involving Acquisitions of Property

Section 269 is discussed generally and in the context of taxable stock acquisitions in Sec. 3.10. The principles discussed there also apply to acquisitions of a loss corporation in an acquisitive asset reorganization because § 269 specifically applies to carryover basis acquisitions of property. *See* § 269(a).

§ 7.12 Impact of § 384 on Utilization of Preacquisition NOLs of Either Target or Acquiror

See § 384.

A. Introduction and Background

See Sec. 5.11.

B. Applicability to Acquisitive Asset Reorganizations

House Ways and Means Report on the Technical and Miscellaneous Revenue Act of 1988

The 1987 Act limited a corporation's ability to offset gains that accrued prior to a merger or acquisition against preacquisition losses of a second corporation. * * * [Under the asset acquisition rule,] if the assets of a gain corporation are acquired by another corporation in a tax-free subsidiary liquidation under section 332 or in a tax-free reorganization, the income of the acquiring corporation attributable to recognized built-in gains of the gain corporation may not be offset by preacquisition losses of the acquiring corporation, or of members of its affiliated group. * * *

Explanation of Provision * * * The asset acquisition rule applies if either the acquired or the surviving corporation is a gain corporation. * * *

§ 7.13 Summary Problems on Utilization of NOLs after an Acquisitive Asset Reorganization

A. Statement of Facts

Loss corporation (*LC*) was organized on January 1, 2014, and has been engaged in the business of manufacturing and selling widgets since that time. *LC* is a calendar year, accrual basis taxpayer. The original capital contribution to *LC* was $500K in cash. *LC* has incurred an operating loss of $100K in each of its calendar years 2014, 2015 and 2016. It is now (January 1, 2017) projected that *LC* will break even in calendar year 2017 and have $100K of taxable income in each of its calendar years subsequent to 2017. The adjusted basis of *LC*'s assets as of the close of business on December 31, 2016 was $200K, and the fair market value of both its assets and its stock at that time was estimated to be $250K. *LC* has only common stock outstanding, all of which is owned by individual A.

Profitable Corporation (*PC*) has been operating for many years on a profitable basis. For the past several years, *PC* has had approximately $500K of taxable income, and it is projected that *PC* will continue to have approximately $500K of taxable income in the succeeding several years. *PC*'s tax rate is 33 1/3%. Its stock has a value of $2 million, and only common is outstanding. *PC* is a calendar year, accrual basis taxpayer. The long-term tax-exempt rate is 10%.

1. LC Merges Into PC

As of December 31, 2017, *LC* merges into *PC* in a nontaxable merger under § 368(a)(1)(A). The consideration paid is stock of *PC* with a value of $250K.

a. What is the impact, if any, of § 381 on this transaction?

b. What is the potential impact, if any, of § 382 on this transaction?

c. What is the impact, if any, of § 269 on this transaction?

d. What is the potential impact, if any, of § 384 on this transaction?

e. Suppose that in calendar year 2017 *PC* incurs a net operating loss of $100K, all of which is attributable to the former assets of *LC*. Could *PC* carry back that loss against its taxable income of 2016? *See* § 1.381(c)(1)-1(b).

f. Suppose *PC* was a loss corporation and *LC* was a profitable corporation, could a post-merger 2017 loss be carried back to a former year of *LC*? *See* § 381(b)(3).

2. PC Acquires LC in a Triangular (C) Reorganization or a Triangular Forward Subsidiary Merger under § 368(a)(2)(D)

As of December 31, 2016, *PC-S*, a newly formed subsidiary of *PC*, acquires all of the assets of *LC* in either a triangular subsidiary asset acquisition under § 368(a)(1)(C) or a forward subsidiary merger under § 368(a)(2)(D). The consideration paid is voting common stock of *PC* with a value of $250K. *PC* and *PC-S* file consolidated returns.

a. What is the impact, if any, of § 381 on this transaction?

b. What is the impact, if any, of § 382 on this transaction?

c. What is the impact, if any, of the consolidated return regulations on this transaction?

d. Suppose *LC* was a profitable corporation prior to the acquisition by *PC-S*, and after the acquisition *PC-S* incurred net operating losses. Could *PC-S* carry back those losses to the prior years of *LC*?

e. What is the impact, if any, of § 384 on this transaction?

§ 7.14 Sample Merger Agreement for a Forward Subsidiary Merger under § 368(a)(2)(E): BT's Acquisition of MCI*

British Telecommunications PLC and MCI Communications Corporation Merger Agreement

November 3, 1996

AGREEMENT AND PLAN OF MERGER, dated as of November 3, 1996 (this "Agreement"), among BRITISH TELECOMMUNICATIONS plc, a public limited company incorporated under the laws of England and Wales ("BT"), MCI COMMUNICATIONS CORPORATION, a Delaware corporation ("MCI"), and TADWORTH CORPORATION, a Delaware corporation and a wholly owned subsidiary of BT ("Merger Sub").

W I T N E S S E T H:

WHEREAS, the respective Boards of Directors of BT, MCI and Merger Sub have each determined that the Merger is in the best interests of their respective shareholders and have approved the Merger upon the terms and subject to the conditions set forth in this Agreement, whereby each issued and outstanding share of common stock, par value $.10 per share, of MCI ("MCI Common Stock"), other than shares owned directly or indirectly by BT or by MCI, will be converted into the right to receive ordinary shares of BT represented by American Depositary Shares of BT ("BT ADSs"), each representing ten ordinary shares of 25p each of BT ("BT Ordinary Shares") and evidenced by American Depositary Receipts ("BT ADRs") and cash [Many shares of foreign issuers trade as ADS.];

WHEREAS, in order to effectuate the foregoing, MCI, upon the terms and subject to the conditions of this Agreement and in accordance with the General Corporation Law of the State of Delaware (the "DGCL"), will merge with and into Merger Sub (the "Merger") [This is a forward subsidiary merger.]; ***

---

* This agreement is adapted from Appendix R of Thompson, *Statutory Supplement and Documentary Appendices to Business Planning for Mergers and Acquisitions* (2nd Ed. 2001).

WHEREAS, for United States Federal income tax purposes, it is intended that the Merger shall qualify as a reorganization under the provisions of Section 368(a) of the Internal Revenue Code of 1986, as amended (the "Code") and that this Agreement constitute a plan of reorganization within the meaning of Section 1.368-2(g) of the income tax regulations promulgated under the Code. [This is a forward subsidiary merger reorganization under Section 368(a)(2)(D).]

NOW, THEREFORE, in consideration of the foregoing and the respective representations, warranties, covenants and agreements set forth herein, and intending to be legally bound hereby, the parties hereto agree as follows:

Article I
The Merger

1.1. *The Merger.* Upon the terms and subject to the conditions set forth in this Agreement, and in accordance with the DGCL, MCI shall be merged with and into Merger Sub at the Effective Time. Following the Merger, the separate corporate existence of MCI shall cease and Merger Sub shall continue as the surviving corporation (the "Surviving Corporation"). ***

1.8. *Effect on Capital Stock.* As of the Effective Time, by virtue of the Merger and without any action on the part of the holders of (i) any shares of MCI Common Stock, (ii) any shares of Class A Common Stock, par value $.10 per share, of MCI ("MCI Class A Common Stock") or (iii) any shares of common stock, par value $.01 per share, of Merger Sub:

(a) Cancellation *of Treasury Stock and BT-Owned Stock.* Each share of MCI Common Stock that is owned by MCI as treasury stock and each share of MCI Common Stock and each share of MCI Class A Common Stock that are owned by BT or any wholly owned Subsidiary of BT (together, in each case, with the associated Right) shall automatically be cancelled and retired and shall cease to exist and no stock of BT or *** other consideration shall be delivered in exchange therefore.

(b) *Conversion of MCI Common Stock.* *** [E]ach issued and outstanding share of MCI Common Stock (other than shares to be cancelled in accordance with Section 1.8(a)) together with the associated Right shall be converted into the right to receive 0.54 BT ADSs (the "Stock Consideration") and $6.00 in cash (the "Cash Consideration" and, collectively with the Stock Consideration, the "Merger Consideration"). ***

Article II
Exchange Of Certificates

2.1. *Exchange Fund.* At the Effective Time, (a) BT shall issue to and deposit with BT's United States depositary (the "ADR Depositary"), for the benefit of the holders of shares of MCI Common Stock converted in accordance with Article I, BT Ordinary Shares in an amount sufficient to permit the ADR Depositary to issue BT ADRs representing the number of BT ADSs issuable pursuant to Section 1.8 and (b) the Surviving Corporation shall deposit with such bank or trust company as may be designated by BT and be reasonably acceptable to MCI (the "Exchange Agent") cash in the amount required to be exchanged for shares of MCI Common Stock in the Merger pursuant to Section 1.8 and any cash in lieu of fractional BT ADSs. ***

2.14. *Shares of Dissenting Stockholders.* Notwithstanding anything in this Agreement to the contrary, any shares of MCI Common Stock that are outstanding immediately prior to the Effective Time and that are held by stockholders who shall not have voted in favor of the Merger or consented thereto in writing and who shall have demanded properly in writing appraisal for such shares in accordance with Section 262 of the DGCL (collectively, the "Dissenting Shares") shall not be converted into or represent the right to receive the Merger Consideration. Such stockholders shall be entitled to receive payment of the appraised value of such shares of MCI Common Stock held by them in accordance with the provisions of Section 262 of the DGCL ***.

Article III
Representations And Warranties

3.1. *Representations and Warranties of MCI.* Except as set forth in the MCI Disclosure Schedule ***, MCI represents and warrants to BT as follows: ***

(l) *Vote Required.* The affirmative vote of the holders of a majority of the outstanding shares of MCI Common Stock and the affirmative vote of the holders of a majority of the outstanding shares of MCI Class A Common Stock, each voting as a separate class (the "Required MCI Votes"), are the only votes of the holders of any class or series of MCI capital stock necessary to approve this Agreement and the transactions contemplated hereby ***.

Article V
Additional Agreements

5.1. *Preparation of Disclosure Documents; MCI Stockholder and BT Shareholder Meetings.* * * *

Article VI
Conditions Precedent

6.1. *Conditions to Each Party's Obligation to Effect the Merger.* The obligations of MCI, BT and Merger Sub to effect the Merger are subject to the satisfaction or waiver on or prior to the Closing Date of the following conditions:

(a) *Stockholder Approvals.* ***

6.2. *Additional Conditions to Obligations of BT and Merger Sub.* The obligations of BT and Merger Sub to effect the Merger are subject to the satisfaction of, or waiver by BT, on or prior to the Closing Date of the following additional conditions: ***

(c) *Tax Opinion.* BT shall have received the opinion of Shearman & Sterling, counsel to BT, to the effect that, on the basis of the facts, representations and assumptions set forth in such opinion (i) the Merger will be treated for United States Federal income tax purposes as a reorganization within the meaning of Section 368(a) of the Code, (ii) each of MCI, BT and Merger Sub will be a party to that reorganization within the meaning of Section 368(b) of the Code and (iii) no gain or loss will be recognized on the exchange of shares of MCI Common Stock for the Merger Consideration, except that gain, if any, shall be recognized to the extent of the Cash Consideration received, which opinion shall be dated on or about the date that is two Business Days prior to the date the Proxy Statement/Prospectus is first mailed to stockholders of MCI and which shall not have been withdrawn or modified in any material respect as of the Closing Date. The issuance of such opinion shall be conditioned on receipt of representation letters from each of MCI and BT. The specific provisions of each such representation letter shall be in form and substance satisfactory to Shearman & Sterling and Simpson Thacher & Bartlett, and each such representation letter shall be dated on or before the date of such opinion and shall not have been withdrawn or modified in any material respect as of the Closing Date. * * *

Chapter 8

Tax-Free Stock Acquisitions: The Straight and Triangular (B) Reorganizations and the Reverse Subsidiary Merger Reorganization under § 368(a)(2)(E); Including Treatment of Net Operating Losses

§ 8.1 Scope

This chapter introduces tax-free stock reorganizations under § 368(a)(1)(B) and the reverse subsidiary merger under § 368(a)(2)(E). Sec. 8.2 deals with the straight (B) in which the acquiring corporation acquires the stock of the target corporation in return for the acquiring corporation's voting stock. Sec. 8.3 deals with the triangular (B) reorganization in which a subsidiary of the acquiring corporation acquires the stock of the target in exchange for voting stock of the acquiring corporation. Sec. 8.4 sets out the representations the Service requires in issuing a private letter ruling on a straight or triangular (B) reorganization. Sec. 8.5 deals with the reverse subsidiary merger under § 368(a)(2)(E). This transaction has the effect of a stock acquisition and, therefore, is considered together with the (B) reorganization. Sec. 8.6 presents summary problems on these forms of acquisitive stock reorganizations. In addition to these stock reorganizations, the stock of a target may be acquired in a transaction governed by § 351, which is examined in Sec. 2.2 and in Sec. 6.19.

Sec. 8.7 deals with the impact of § 382, the consolidated return regulations, and § 269 on the utilization of the target's net operating losses after a stock reorganization. Sec. 8.8 deals with the impact of § 384 on the utilization of an acquiring corporation's pre-acquisition NOLs against the target's pre-acquisition built-in gains. Sec. 8.9 presents summary problems on the utilization of NOLs after a stock reorganization. Finally, as an illustration of a reverse subsidiary merger under § 368(a)(2)(E), which is the most common form of stock reorganization, Sec. 8.10 sets out the merger agreement in the originally structured acquisition by Time, Inc. of Warner, Inc. to form Time Warner.

For a more detailed discussion of the issues discussed here, see *Ginsburg and Levin, Mergers, supra Sec. 1.12,* and *Bittker and Eustice, Corporations, supra Sec. 1.12. See also* the most recent edition of *PLI, Tax Strategies, supra Sec. 1.12;* and Thompson, *Mergers, Acquisitions, and Tender Offers, supra* Sec. 1.12 at Chapter 9.

§ 8.2 The Straight (B) Reorganization

A. Introduction

There are two basic requirements for a straight (B) reorganization under § 368(a)(1)(B). First, an acquiring corporation must acquire a target's stock in exchange "solely for all or a part of the [acquiring corporation's] voting stock." Second, the acquiring corporation must, immediately after the acquisition, have control (within the meaning of § 368(c)) of the target. In determining whether control exists "immediately after," it does not matter "(whether or not [the] acquiring corporation had control immediately before the acquisition)." This parenthetical, which allows a creeping (B), was added to the definition of the (B) by the 1954 Code. The Senate Report to the 1954 Code explains:

> Under section 112(g)(1)(B), of existing law, one corporation can acquire enough stock of another to get control of the second corporation solely for its own voting stock tax free. However, there is doubt as to whether the existing statute permits such an acquisition tax free when the acquiring corporation already owns some of the voting stock of the other corporation. This doubt is removed by your committee's bill and paragraph (B) of subsection (a)(1) permits such an acquisition tax free (in a single transaction or in a series of transactions taking place over a relatively short period of time such as 12 months). For example, corporation A purchased 30 percent of the common stock of corporation W (the only class of stock outstanding) for cash in 1939. On March 1, 1955, corporation A offers to exchange its own voting stock, for all of the stock of corporation W tendered within 6 months from the date of the offer. Within the 6 months period corporation A acquires an additional 60 percent of the stock of W for its own voting stock. As a result of the 1955 transactions, corporation A will own 90 percent of all of corporation W's stock. No gain or loss is recognized with respect to the exchanges of the A stock for the W stock. For this purpose it is immaterial whether such exchanges occurred before corporation A acquired control of W (80 percent) or after such control was acquired. If corporation A had acquired 80 percent of corporation W's stock for cash in 1939, it could likewise acquire some or all of the remainder of such stock solely in exchange for its own voting stock without recognition of gain or loss.

Section 1.368-2(c) repeats almost verbatim the above language. *See American Potash* Sec. 7.3.H.2. for an example of a nonqualifying creeping (B).

The following is a summary of the basic tax treatment to the parties in a (B):

(1) The acquiring corporation has nonrecognition treatment under § 1032 upon the issuance of its stock.

(2) The acquiring corporation takes a carryover basis under § 362(b) for the stock of the target. If the target is publicly held, statistical sampling may be used to

determine the bases of the target shareholder's shares. *See* Rev. Rul. 81-70, 1981-1 C.B. 389.

(3) The target's shareholders have nonrecognition treatment under § 354(a) upon the exchange of their target stock for the stock of the acquiring corporation. Since the acquiror cannot pay any boot, § 356 does not come into play.

(4) The target's shareholders take a substituted basis under § 358 for the stock received.

The (B) has been in the tax law in various forms since the Revenue Act of 1921. The "solely for voting stock" requirement was added by the 1934 Act. Thus, unlike the (A), the (B) has a statutorily mandated continuity of interest requirement.

The leading case dealing with the meaning of "solely for voting stock" is *Southwest Consolidated,* which is set out in Sec. 6.4. The determination of whether the consideration paid consists solely of voting stock is one of the most important issues in a (B). Most of the topics covered in this section relate in some respect to the solely for voting stock requirement.

Sec. 8.2.B. addresses the fundamental question of whether boot is permissible in a (B). This section sets out the First Circuit's decision in *Chapman,* which directly addressed this issue in the acquisition by ITT of Hartford Insurance. Sec. 8.2.C. examines the treatment of the acquisition by the acquiror of the target's securities as part of a (B) reorganization. Sec. 8.2.D. deals with a situation in which the shareholder of an acquiror purchases stock of a target prior to the acquisition by the acquiror of the balance of the target's stock in a purported (B), and Sec. 8.2.E. addresses this issue when a subsidiary of an acquiring corporation purchases part of a target's stock. Sec. 8.2.F. considers various situations in which boot flows directly from the acquiror to the target's shareholders. Sec. 8.2.G. deals with the effect of pre-reorganization payments (*i.e.,* dividends and redemptions) by the target to its shareholders. Sec. 8.2.H. examines the hybrid (B): that is, various types of subsidiary acquisitions that are treated as (B)'s. Sec. 8.2.I. deals with the push up of a target's assets after a (B). Sec. 8.2.J. considers the impact of §§ 305 and 306 in a (B). The representations required in a ruling request dealing with both the straight and triangular (B) are set forth in Sec. 8.4.

The potential use of a (B) reorganization in connection with a spin-off under § 355 is examined in Chapter 9. This is a variation of the *Morris Trust* type of transaction, which is also addressed in Chapter 9.

B. Can There Be Boot in a (B)? The First Circuit's View of ITT-Hartford

Chapman v. Commissioner

United States Court of Appeals, First Circuit, 1980
618 F.2d 856

Levin H. Campbell, Circuit Judge.

* * * We must decide whether the requirement of Section 368(a)(1)(B) that the acquisition of stock in one corporation by another be solely in exchange for voting stock of the acquiring corporation is met where, in related transactions, the acquiring corporation first acquires 8 percent of the acquiree's stock for cash and then acquires more than 80 percent of the acquiree in an exchange of stock for voting stock. The Tax Court agreed with the taxpayers that the latter exchange constituted a valid tax-free reorganization. *Reeves v. Commissioner,* 71 T.C. 727 (1979).

[ITT purchased for cash 8% of the stock of Hartford. ITT then proposed to acquire the balance of the stock of Hartford in a (B) reorganization. In order to get a ruling from the IRS to the effect that the stock-for-stock acquisition would qualify as a (B), ITT was required to sell the 8% of the stock that it had purchased to an independent third party before beginning a stock-for-stock exchange. Otherwise the IRS would have viewed the cash purchase as integrated with the stock-for-stock exchange, thereby violating the solely for stock requirement. ITT sold the stock to an Italian bank, Mediobanca, and the IRS ruled that the prior purchase would not be integrated with the stock-for-stock exchange. ITT then completed the stock-for-stock exchange.

After completion of the transaction, the IRS later revoked its ruling on the grounds that ITT and Mediobanca had an understanding that Mediobanca would tender its Hartford shares in the stock-for-stock exchange. The IRS, therefore, treated the stock-for-stock exchange as a taxable transaction on grounds that ITT had acquired Hartford's stock partially for cash and partially for stock.]

* * * For purposes of this motion, the taxpayers conceded that questions of the merits of the revocation of the IRS rulings were not to be considered; the facts were to be viewed as though ITT had not sold the shares previously acquired for cash to Mediobanca. The taxpayers also conceded, solely for purposes of their motion for summary judgment, that the initial cash purchases of Hartford stock had been made for the purpose of furthering ITT's efforts to acquire Hartford.

The Issue. * * * The single issue raised on this appeal is whether "the acquisition" in this case complied with the requirement that it be "solely for * * * voting stock." It is well settled that the "solely" requirement is mandatory; if any part of "the acquisition" includes a form of consideration other than voting stock, the transaction will not qualify as a (B) reorganization. *See Helvering v. Southwest Consolidated Corp.,* 315 U.S. 194, 198, 62 S.Ct. 546, 550, 86 L.Ed. 789 (1942) [Sec. 6.4.] ("'Solely' leaves no leeway. Voting stock plus some other consideration does not meet the statutory requirement"). The precise issue before us is thus how broadly to read the term "acquisition." The Internal Revenue Service argues that "the acquisition * * * of stock of another corporation" must be understood to encompass the 1968–69 cash purchases as well as the 1970 exchange offer. If the IRS is correct, "the acquisition" here fails as a (B) reorganization. The taxpayers, on the other hand, would limit "the acquisition" to the part of a sequential transaction of this nature which meets the requirements of subsection (B). They argue that the 1970 exchange of stock for stock was itself an "acquisition" by ITT of stock in Hartford solely in exchange for ITT's voting stock, such that after the exchange took place ITT controlled Hartford. Taxpayers contend that the earlier cash purchases of 8 percent, even if conceded to be part of the same acquisitive plan, are essentially irrelevant to the tax-free reorganization otherwise effected.

The Tax Court accepted the taxpayers' reading of the statute, effectively overruling its own prior decision in *Howard v. Commissioner,* 24 T.C. 792 (1955), *rev'd on other grounds,* 238 F.2d 943 (7th Cir.1956). The plurality opinion stated its "narrow" holding as follows:

> We hold that where, as is the case herein, 80 percent or more of the stock of a corporation is acquired in one transaction,[18] in exchange for which only voting stock is furnished as consideration, the 'solely for voting stock' requirement of section 368(a)(1)(B) is satisfied.

71 T.C. at 741. The plurality treated as "irrelevant" the 8 percent of Hartford's stock purchased for cash, although the opinion left somewhat ambiguous the question whether the 8 percent was irrelevant because of the 14-month time interval separating the transactions or because the statute was not concerned with transactions over and above those mathematically necessary to the acquiring corporation's attainment of control.

For reasons set forth extensively in section III of this opinion, we do not accept the position adopted by the Tax Court. Instead we side with the Commissioner on the narrow issue presented in this appeal, that is, the correctness of taxpayers' so-called "second" argument premised on an assumed relationship between the cash and stock transactions. As explained below, we find a strong implication in the language of the statute, in the legislative history, in the regulations, and in the decisions of other courts that cash purchases which are concededly "parts of" a stock-for-stock exchange must be considered constituent elements of the "acquisition" for purposes of applying the "solely for * * * voting stock" requirement of Section 368(a)(1)(B). We believe the presence of non-stock consideration in such an acquisition, regardless of whether such consideration is necessary to the gaining of control, is inconsistent with treatment of the acquisition as a nontaxable reorganization. It follows for purposes of taxpayers' second argument — which was premised on the assumption that the cash transactions were part of the 1970 exchange offer reorganization — that the stock transfers in question would not qualify for nonrecognition of gain or loss. * * *

18. In determining what constitutes 'one transaction,' we include all the acquisitions from shareholders which were clearly part of the same transaction."

Having summarized in advance our holding, and its intended scope, we shall now revert to the beginning of our analysis, and, in the remainder of this opinion, describe the thinking by which we reached the result just announced. We begin with the words of the statute itself. The reorganization definitions contained in Section 368(a)(1) are precise, technical, and comprehensive. They were intended to define the exclusive means by which nontaxable corporate reorganizations could be effected. In examining the language of the (B) provision, we discern two possible meanings. On the one hand, the statute could be read to say that a successful reorganization occurs whenever Corporation X exchanges its own voting stock for stock in Corporation Y, and, immediately after the transaction, Corporation X controls more than 80 percent of Y's stock. On this reading, purchases of shares for which any part of the consideration takes the form of "boot" should be ignored, since the definition is only concerned with transactions which meet the statutory requirements as to consideration and control. To take an example, if Corporation X bought 50 percent of the shares of Y, and then almost immediately exchanged part of its voting stock for the remaining 50 percent of Y's stock, the question would arise whether the second transaction was a (B) reorganization. Arguably, the statute can be read to support such a finding. In the second transaction, X exchanged only stock for stock (meeting the "solely" requirement), and after the transaction was completed X owned Y (meeting the "control" requirement).

The alternative reading of the statute — the one which we are persuaded to adopt — treats the (B) definition as prescriptive, rather than merely descriptive. We read the statute to mean that the entire transaction which constitutes "the acquisition" must not contain any nonstock consideration if the transaction is to qualify as a (B) reorganization. In the example given above, where X acquired 100 percent of Y's stock, half for cash and half for voting stock, we would interpret "the acquisition" as referring to the entire transaction, so that the "solely for * * * voting stock" requirement would not be met. We believe if Congress had intended the statute to be read as merely descriptive, this intent would have been more clearly spelled out in the statutory language.

We recognize that the Tax Court adopted neither of these two readings. [T]he Tax Court purported to limit its holding to cases, such as this one, where more than 80 percent of the stock of Corporation Y passes to Corporation X in exchange solely for voting stock. The Tax Court presumably would assert that the 50/50 hypothetical posited above can be distinguished from this case, and that its holding implies no view as to the hypothetical. The plurality opinion recognized that the position it adopted creates no small problem with respect to the proper reading of "the acquisition" in the statutory definition. In order to distinguish the 80 percent case from the 50 percent case, it is necessary to read "the acquisition" as referring to at least the amount of stock constituting "control" (80 percent) where related cash purchases are present. Yet the Tax Court recognized that "the acquisition" cannot always refer to the conveyance of an 80 percent bloc of stock in one transaction, since to do so would frustrate the intent of the 1954 amendments to permit so-called "creeping acquisitions."

[The court then reviewed the legislative history of the (B). This portion of the opinion is set out in Sec. 6.2.A.2.]

Besides finding support for the IRS position both in the design of the statute and in the legislative history, we find support in the regulations adopted by the Treasury Department construing these statutory provisions. * * *

Finally, we turn to the body of case law that has developed concerning (B) reorganizations to determine how previous courts have dealt with this question. Of the seven prior cases in this area, all to a greater or lesser degree support the result we have reached, and none supports the result reached by the Tax Court. We recognize that the Tax Court purported to distinguish these precedents from the case before it, and that reasonable persons may differ on the extent to which some of these cases directly control the question raised here. Nevertheless, after carefully reviewing the precedents, we are satisfied that the decision of the Tax Court represents a sharp break with the previous judicial constructions of this statute, and a departure from the usual rule of *stare decisis*, which applies with special force in the tax field where uncertainty and variety are ordinarily to be avoided. * * *

We have stated our ruling, and the reasons that support it. In conclusion, we would like to respond briefly to the arguments raised by the Tax Court, the District Court of Delaware, and the taxpayers in this case against the rule we have reaffirmed today. The principal argument, repeated again and again, concerns the supposed lack of policy behind the rule forbidding cash in a (B) reorganization where the control requirement is met solely for voting stock. It is true that the Service has not pointed to tax loopholes that would be opened were the rule to be relaxed as appellees request. * * *

Possibly, Congress' insertion of the "solely for * * * voting stock" requirement into the 1934 Act was, as one commentator has suggested, an overreaction to a problem which could have been dealt with through more precise and discriminating measures. But we do not think it appropriate for a court to tell Congress how to do its job in an area such as this. * * *

Finally, we see no merit at all in the suggestion that we should permit "boot" in a (B) reorganization simply because "boot" is permitted in some instances in (A) and (C) reorganizations. Congress has never indicated that these three distinct categories of transactions are to be interpreted in *pari materia*. In fact, striking differences in the treatment of the three subsections have been evident in the history of the reorganization statutes. We see no reason to believe a difference in the treatment of "boot" in these transactions is impermissible or irrational. * * *

Notes

1. In May 1981 the IRS and ITT settled this litigation with ITT paying $28.5 million and the IRS agreeing not to pursue claims against the Hartford shareholders. *See* Daily Tax Report, 5/8/81, p. G-5.

2. In Rev. Rul. 72-354, 1972-2 C.B. 216, the Service ruled that a prior purchase by an acquiring corporation of the shares of a target will not violate the "solely for voting stock" requirement of the (B) if, prior to the offer to the target's shareholders in the (B), the acquiring corporation "unconditionally sells such shares to a third party." The ruling reasons:

Under the facts presented the unconditional sale of the Y shares to X is accorded independent significance for tax purposes since it was neither transitory nor illusory and in no way dependent or conditional upon the subsequent reorganization.

3. For the impact of an acquiror's purchase of a target's stock on the continuity of interest requirement, *see* Sec. 6.2.E.

C. Contemporaneous Acquisition of Target's Securities in a (B)

1. Purchase of Target's Convertible Debentures

In Rev. Rul. 69-91, 1969-1 C.B. 106, the Service held that (1) the convertible debentures of a target do not constitute stock, citing *Southwest Consolidated, supra* Sec. 6.4. and (2) the purchase by an acquiring corporation of the target's debentures is not additional consideration paid in the acquisition of the target's stock in a (B) reorganization.

2. Exchange of Securities in a (B) Reorganization
Revenue Ruling 98-19
I.R.B. 1998-10 (March 9, 1998)

Issue Where a stock for stock acquisition otherwise qualifying under § 368(a)(1)(B) of the Internal Revenue Code is accompanied by an exchange of securities, how should the transaction be treated?

Facts The facts are substantially similar to the facts in Rev. Rul. 69-142, 1969-1 C.B. 107.

Corporation X acquires all of the outstanding capital stock of Corporation Y in exchange for voting stock of X. Corporation Y is a solvent corporation. Prior to the exchange, Y has an issue of six percent fifteen-year debentures outstanding. Pursuant to the plan of reorganization, X acquires all the outstanding debentures of Y in exchange for an equal principal amount of new six percent fifteen-year debentures of X. Some of the debentures of Y are held by its shareholders, but a substantial proportion of the Y debentures are held by persons who own no stock.

X is in control of Y immediately after the acquisition of the Y stock. The X and Y debentures constitute "securities" within the meaning of § 354(a)(1) and, thus, do not represent an equity interest. Disregarding the exchange of debentures, the transaction meets the requirements of § 368(a)(1)(B).

Law and Analysis Section 368(a)(1)(B) provides that a reorganization includes the acquisition by one corporation, in exchange solely for all or a part of its voting stock, of stock of another corporation if, immediately after the acquisition, the acquiring corporation has control of such other corporation.

Section 1.368-2(c) of the Income Tax Regulations provides:

In order to qualify as a "reorganization" under section 368(a)(1)(B), the acquisition by the acquiring corporation of stock of another corporation must be in exchange solely for all or a part of the voting stock of the acquiring corporation…, and the acquiring corporation must be in control of the other corporation immediately after the transaction. If, for example, Corporation X in one transaction exchanges nonvoting preferred stock or bonds in addition to all or a part of its voting stock in the acquisition of stock of Corporation Y, the transaction is not a reorganization under section 368(a)(1)(B).

Section 354(a)(1) provides that no gain or loss will be recognized if stock or securities in a corporation a party to a reorganization are, in pursuance of the plan of reorganization, exchanged solely for stock or securities in another corporation a party to a reorganization.

In the circumstances set forth above, the Y shareholders receive exclusively voting stock of X as consideration for the exchange of their Y stock. The fact that a substantial proportion of the Y debentures is held by bondholders who own no stock in Y has the effect of ensuring that the value of the debentures issued by X in exchange for the debentures of Y realistically reflects the value of the Y debentures alone and does not constitute indirect nonqualifying consideration for the Y stock. Because the Y shareholders, in their capacity as shareholders, receive only X voting stock, the transaction constitutes a reorganization within the meaning of § 368(a)(1)(B).

Although the acquisition by X of the debentures of Y in exchange for debentures of X occurs as part of the overall transaction, it is not a part of the stock-for-stock exchange which qualifies as a reorganization. It is, however, an exchange of securities in parties to a reorganization which occurs in pursuance of the plan of reorganization, and, therefore, meets all the conditions of § 354(a)(1). Accordingly, any gain or loss realized by the debenture holders of Y as a result of their exchange of their Y debentures for an equal principal amount of debentures of X will not be recognized. Section 354(a)(1). If, under different facts, the principal amount of the debentures of X was greater than the principal amount of the debentures of Y, §§ 354(a)(2) and 356(d) would apply to require the debenture holders of Y to recognize some or all of any gain realized.

Holding The exchange of Y stock for X stock is a reorganization described in § 368(a)(1)(B); and any gain or loss realized by the shareholders of Y as a result of the exchange will not be recognized. Section 354(a)(1).

The separate exchange of Y debentures for X debentures is an exchange in pursuance of the plan of reorganization described in § 368(a)(1)(B). Thus, any gain or loss realized by the debenture holders of Y as a result of their exchange of their Y debentures for an equal principal amount of debentures of X will not be recognized. Section 354(a)(1).

In certain cases, rights to acquire stock of a party to a reorganization are "securities" for purposes of § 354. *See* § 1.354-1(e) (as amended by T.D. 8752, 1998-9 I.R.B. 4, effective for exchanges occurring on or after March 9, 1998). An exchange of such rights, although separate from a § 368 exchange, may also be in pursuance of the plan of reorganization. In such cases, any gain or loss realized by the holder of such rights as a result of the exchange will not be recognized. Section 354(a)(1).

Effect on Other Revenue Rulings Rev. Rul. 69-142, which dealt with substantially identical facts, is modified and superseded.

Rev. Rul. 70-41, 1970-1 C.B. 77, deals with a stock-for-stock exchange accompanied by an exchange of Acquired debentures for Acquiring stock. It is modified such that §354 applies to the exchange of debentures for stock.

Rev. Rul. 78-408, 1978-2 C.B. 203, deals with a stock-for-stock exchange accompanied by a warrant-for-warrant exchange. It is modified such that §354 applies to the exchange of warrants provided that the warrants constitute securities. *See* §1.354-1(e).

Rev. Ruls. 68-637, 1968-2 C.B. 158, and 70-269, 1970-1 C.B. 82, similarly deal with reorganization exchanges accompanied by exchanges of warrants or options. Each is amplified such that §354 applies to the exchange of warrants or options, provided that, as in Rev. Rul. 78-408 above, the warrants or options constitute securities. * * *

3. Exchange of Warrant

In Rev. Rul. 78-408, 1978-2 C.B. 56, an acquiror acquired, in exchange for its voting stock, the target's voting stock and also acquired, in exchange for its warrants, the target's outstanding warrants. Following Rev. Rul. 69-142, above, the ruling holds that the transaction is a good (B). Although the ruling holds that the exchange of the warrants is taxable, both because the exchange is outside the (B) and because warrants are not stock or securities under §354, this result would seem to be changed by both (1) the amendments to the regulations under §354 relating to the treatment of warrants (*see* §1.354-3(b) and (e) and Sec. 6.9.B), and (2) the treatment in Rev. Rul. 98-19, Sec. 8.2.C.2., of a securities exchange as part of a (B).

4. Acquisition of Target's Debentures in Exchange for Acquiror's Voting Stock

Revenue Ruling 70-41
1970-1 C.B. 77

Corporation *X* acquired all of the outstanding capital stock of corporation *Y* in exchange for voting stock of *X*. As part of the same plan *X* also acquired all of the outstanding six percent ten-year debentures of *Y* in exchange for voting stock of *X*. Most of the debentures of *Y* were held by persons who were not shareholders of *Y*.

Held, the acquisition of the debentures of *Y* in exchange for stock of *X* was not part of the reorganization for purposes of sections 368(a)(1)(B) and 354(a)(1) of the Internal Revenue Code of 1954. Section 368(a)(1)(B) of the Code and section 1.368-2(c) of the Income Tax Regulations in defining a reorganization refer only to an acquisition of stock of another corporation. The exchange of the debentures is governed by section 1001 of the Code and any gain or loss realized by the debenture holders of *Y* will be recognized as provided by section 1002 of the Code.

Questions

What is the basis for the holding in Rev. Rul. 70-41? From a policy standpoint, why should the exchange of target's securities for the acquiror's stock not receive non-recognition treatment where there is a (B) reorganization? What is the effect of Rev. Rul. 98-19, *supra* Sec. 8.2.c? What result on an exchange of the target's securities for the acquiror's stock in an (A) or (C) reorganization?

5. Purchase of Target's Unissued Stock Simultaneously with the (B)

In Rev. Rul. 72-522, 1972-2 C.B. 215, the target needed additional working capital. Consequently, the acquiror purchased the target's unissued stock "[a]t the time of" and "as part of the overall plan" under which the acquiror acquired, in exchange for its voting stock, the target's voting stock. The ruling holds that the solely for voting stock requirement is satisfied and that the transaction qualifies as a (B).

6. Substitution of Qualified Stock Options

In Rev. Rul. 70-269, 1970-1 C.B. 82, the Service held that the substitution of the acquiror's qualified stock options for the target's qualified stock options would not break the (B) transaction. The ruling says that "[s]ince the options contained the same terms * * * no additional benefits inured to the shareholders upon the substitution of the options."

D. Shareholder of Acquiring Corporation Purchases Stock of Target Prior to the (B)

Revenue Ruling 68-562

1968-2 C.B. 157

Advice has been requested whether the requirements of section 368(a)(1)(B) of the Internal Revenue Code of 1954 have been met in the transaction described below.

An individual owned 90 percent of the outstanding stock of corporation X. In January 1968 he purchased for cash 50 percent of the outstanding stock of corporation Y. Two months later X acquired 100 percent of the outstanding stock of Y solely in exchange for its voting common stock.

The principal shareholder was acting as an individual and not as a representative of X when he purchased 50 percent of the stock of Y. He was under no obligation to surrender the Y stock to X. X made no reimbursement to its principal shareholder for the purchase price of the Y stock. * * *

Since the principal shareholder of X purchased the stock solely for his own account and in his own behalf, X is not considered the purchaser of the 50 percent interest in Y. Therefore, the acquisition by X of all of the outstanding stock of Y solely in exchange for its voting stock is a reorganization under section 368(a)(1)(B) of the Code. Thus, no gain or loss will be recognized to the shareholders of Y on the exchange of their stock of Y solely for shares of X voting stock as provided by section 354 of the Code.

Note

For the impact of this type of transaction on the continuity of interest requirement, *see* Sec. 6.2.E.

E. Subsidiary of Acquiror Purchases Target's Stock

Revenue Ruling 85-139

1985-2 C.B. 123

Issue Whether the transaction described below qualifies as a reorganization under section 368(a)(1)(B) of the Internal Revenue Code.

Facts *P* corporation owned all the stock of *S* corporation. *P* desired to obtain control of *X* corporation by acquiring all the shares of the one outstanding class of stock of *X* solely in exchange for *P* voting stock. Certain shareholders of *X*, owning ten percent of its stock, insisted, however, on receiving cash for their stock. Since *P* wanted to eliminate any possible adverse minority interest in *X*, and pursuant to one overall plan to acquire the stock of *X*, *P* acquired ninety percent of the stock of *X* solely in exchange for *P* voting stock, and *P* caused *S* to purchase for cash the remaining ten percent of the *X* stock. The cash paid by *S* for *X*'s stock was not obtained directly or indirectly from *P*. *S* retained ownership of the *X* stock it had purchased.

Law and Analysis * * * The "solely for voting stock" requirement applies to the entire transaction in which stock of a corporation is acquired, not just to the acquisition of a block of stock constituting control. Therefore, the acquisition by a corporation of eighty percent of the stock of a corporation in exchange for its voting stock and the remaining twenty percent in exchange for cash violates "solely for voting stock."

Accordingly, if *P* had acquired all the stock of *X* in exchange for its voting stock and cash, the acquisition would not have qualified as a reorganization under section 368(a)(1)(B). *P*'s structuring of the transaction to have its wholly owned subsidiary acquire some of the *X* stock for cash does not produce a different result. Compare Rev. Rul. 69-48, 1969-1 C.B. 106, which holds that the purchase for cash by *P* of stock of corporation *X* as part of a plan for *P*'s wholly-owned subsidiary, *S*, to acquire substantially all the assets of *X* for *P* voting stock, violates the "solely for voting stock" requirement of section 368(a)(1)(C).

Holding The purchase by *S* of ten percent of *X*'s stock for cash violates the "solely for voting stock" requirement of section 368(a)(1)(B) of the Code. *Compare* Rev. Rul. 85-138, wherein it was held that a similar transaction does not qualify as a reorganization under section 368(a)(1)(C).

Note

For the impact of this type of transaction on the continuity of interest requirement, *see* Sec. 6.2.E.

F. Boot Flowing Directly from Acquiror to Target's Shareholders

1. Purchase of Fractional Shares

Revenue Ruling 66-365
1966-2 C.B. 116

In *Mills, et al. v. Commissioner,* 331 F.2d 321 (1964), reversing 39 T.C. 393 (1962), the United States Court of Appeals for the Fifth Circuit held that the "solely for voting stock" requirement of section 368(a)(1)(B) of the Code was satisfied where the acquiring corporation received all of the stock of several corporations and distributed in return for such stock, shares of its voting common stock and a small amount of cash in lieu of fractional shares. After finding that the cash given in lieu of fractional shares was simply a mathematical rounding-off for the purpose of simplifying the corporate and accounting problems which would have been caused by the actual issuance of fractional shares, the Court concluded that the receipt of the stock of the acquired corporations was for all practical purposes "solely in exchange for voting stock".

The Internal Revenue Service will follow the decision of the Court of Appeals in *Mills, et al. v. Commissioner* in similar factual situations. Accordingly, the "solely for voting stock" requirement of section 368(a)(1)(B) and (C) of the Code will not be violated where the cash paid by the acquiring corporation is in lieu of fractional share interests to which the shareholders are entitled, representing merely a mechanical rounding-off of the fractions in the exchange, and is not a separately bargained-for consideration. * * *

[W]here the cash payment made by the acquiring corporation is not bargained for, but is in lieu of fractional share interests to which the shareholders are entitled, such cash payment will be treated under section 302 of the Code as in redemption of the fractional share interests. * * *

2. Cost of Registering Acquiring Corporation's Stock

Revenue Ruling 67-275
1967-2 C.B. 142

Pursuant to a plan of reorganization which qualified under section 368(a)(1) of the Internal Revenue Code of 1954, an acquiring corporation paid the costs necessary to register with the Securities and Exchange Commission the stock issued to the shareholders in the reorganization. The registration of the shares served to promote the orderly marketing of the acquiring corporation's stock by enabling the shareholders of the acquired corporation to deal with such stock in the same manner as other shareholders of the corporation.

Held, the costs of registering its own stock are properly attributable to the acquiring corporation and are not other property received in the reorganization by the shareholders of the acquired corporation.

3. Acquiring Corporation Pays Reorganization Expenses of Target and Its Shareholders

Revenue Ruling 73-54
1973-1 C.B. 187

* * * As part of the reorganization [under § 368(a)(1)(C)] *Y* [the acquiror] agrees to pay or assume certain expenses. These expenses are legal and accounting expenses; appraisal fees; administrative costs of the acquired corporation directly related to the reorganization such as those incurred for printing, clerical work, telephone and telegraph; security underwriting and registration fees and expenses; transfer taxes, and transfer agents' fees and expenses. These expenses are solely and directly related to the reorganization.

* * * [I]t is held that the payment or assumption by the acquiring corporation of the valid reorganization expenses in the instant case will not prevent the plan from satisfying the definition of a reorganization under the above provision of the Code.

* * * The principles of this Revenue Ruling are equally applicable to such valid reorganization expenses that are paid or assumed by an acquiring corporation in a reorganization described in section 368(a)(1)(B) of the Code. * * *

4. Stock for Services

Revenue Ruling 77-271
1977-2 C.B. 116

A owned all of the outstanding stock of *X* corporation. *X* was engaged in the home construction business. *A* was the president of *X* and was actively involved in the business. Pursuant to a plan of reorganization, *Y* corporation, whose stock is widely held, acquired all of the *X* stock from *A* in exchange solely for shares of *Y* voting stock in an amount equal to the fair market value of the *X* stock received from *A* in exchange therefore. As part of the agreement between *A* and *Y*, *A* entered into an employment contract under which *A* was to continue as president of *X* for a specified period of time and at a specified salary. As consideration for *A* entering into the employment contract, *Y* issued additional shares of its voting stock to *A*.* * *

[T]he exchange of *X* stock for *Y* voting stock of equal value was a reorganization within the meaning of section 368(a)(1)(B) of the Code and, under section 354, no gain or loss was recognized to *A*. The *Y* voting stock received by *A* as consideration for the employment contract was includible in *A's* gross income as ordinary income in the amount of its fair market value on the date of issuance.

5. Acquiror Issues Its Voting Convertible Preferred with Right to Buy Additional Stock

Revenue Ruling 70-108

1970-1 C.B. 78

Advice has been requested whether convertible preferred stock incorporating rights to purchase additional shares of stock upon conversion, qualifies as "solely voting stock" for purposes of section 368(a)(1)(B) of the Internal Revenue Code of 1954. * * *

If rights were separately issued as part of the consideration along with the convertible preferred stock, it is clear that under the rationale of the *Southwest Consolidated Corporation* decision such rights would constitute property other than voting stock. Whether the rights to purchase stock are issued separately or are incorporated in a stock certificate, the nature of such rights remains the same. Furthermore, the fact that such rights are incorporated in a certificate that otherwise represents stock having an equity interest will not alter this conclusion.

Accordingly, the right to purchase stock constitutes property other than voting stock. Therefore, it is held that the acquisition by *Y* of the stock of *X* is not a reorganization within the meaning of section 368(a)(1)(B) of the Code. Gain or loss is recognized to the shareholders of *X* on the exchange of *X* stock for *Y* voting convertible preferred stock.

Questions

Is it possible to structure a (B) reorganization in which the target's shareholders also receive warrants to buy other stock of the acquiror? What about an (A) or (C)? What result if the target's shareholders have the right to "put" a specified portion of the acquiror's stock back to the acquiror in exchange for cash?

6. Right of Target Shareholders to Have Acquiror Stock Redeemed

IRS General Counsel Memorandum 38844

(April 27, 1982)

Issue Is the solely for voting stock requirement of I.R.C. §368(a)(1)(B) violated when stock of one corporation is acquired by another corporation in exchange for its voting preferred stock if the terms of the preferred stock include a right granting the holder of that stock the option to have it redeemed, for a three year period commencing five years after the date of the original exchange, for a fixed cash price equal to the fair market value of the preferred stock on the date of the original exchange?

Conclusion We concur in your conclusion that the right of redemption at a fixed cash price equal to the value of the stock on the date of the original exchange in the instant case cannot be meaningfully distinguished from the conversion right under consideration in situation two of Rev. Rul. 69-265, 1969-1 C.B. 109, which we concluded did not constitute property in addition to the preferred stock in question. Accordingly, G.C.M. 36712 is revoked. * * *

G. Pre-Reorganization Payments by Target to Its Shareholders

1. Dividend Before (B)

Revenue Ruling 70-172

1970-1 C.B. 77

Corporation X acquired all of the stock of corporation S from S's sole shareholder, corporation P, in exchange for voting stock of X. Immediately prior to this exchange, S distributed certain property to P.

The specific question presented is whether the distribution by S to P of property is to be taken into account in determining whether the acquisition by X of the S stock is solely for voting stock of X.

In the circumstances set forth above, the consideration given by X and received by P in exchange for S stock consisted exclusively of voting stock of X. The distribution of property by S to P was not part of the consideration given by X in connection with the exchange of stock.

Accordingly, since only voting stock of X was utilized by X as consideration in the acquisition of the stock of S, the "solely for voting stock" requirement contained in section 368(a)(1)(B) of the Code was met. This exchange of stock is a reorganization within the meaning of section 368(a)(1)(B) of the Code. * * *

2. Redemption Before (B)

a. Redemption of Dissenting Shareholders Pursuant to State Law Requirements

Revenue Ruling 68-285

1968-1 C.B. 147

Advice has been requested whether there can be a reorganization under section 368(a)(1)(B) of the Internal Revenue Code of 1954 if the corporation to be acquired established an escrow account from its own funds to pay dissenting shareholders who elect to accept cash for their stock in the acquired corporation according to the provisions of a state banking law, rather than exchange their stock for stock in the acquiring corporation. * * *

[T]he acquisition of the outstanding stock of Y in exchange for voting stock of X is a reorganization under section 368(a)(1)(B) of the Code even though, in accordance with state banking law, an escrow account was established in order to pay dissenting shareholders for their stock and even though the stock of some dissenting shareholders was not redeemed until after the consummation of the exchange. Thus, no gain or loss will be recognized to the shareholders of Y who exchanged their stock in Y solely for X voting stock, under section 354(a) of the Code.

However, it should be noted that section 368(a)(1)(B) of the Code does not treat as a reorganization any transaction in which the acquiring corporation pays the dissenting shareholders or reimburses the acquired corporation for its payment to the dissenting shareholders.

b. Redemption in Order to Shrink Target's Size
Revenue Ruling 75-360
1975-2 C.B. 110

The purpose of this Revenue Ruling is to explain the position of the Internal Revenue Service with respect to the decision of the Tax Court of the United States in *Arthur D. McDonald*, 52 T.C. 82 (1969). Furthermore, this Revenue Ruling is being published in lieu of the publication of an acquiescence or nonacquiescence in the McDonald decision.

In that decision, the Tax Court held that a redemption of the petitioner's stock pursuant to a plan for acquisition of the redeeming corporation by another corporation was not essentially equivalent to a dividend within the meaning of section 302(b)(1) of the Internal Revenue Code of 1954, and therefore qualified for exchange treatment under section 302(a).

As more fully stated in the Tax Court's opinion, the petitioner owned all the outstanding preferred stock of E & M Enterprises, Inc. ("E & M") and ten of the eleven shares of its outstanding common stock. Borden Company ("Borden") made an initial verbal offer to exchange 5,500 shares of its common stock for all the preferred and common shares of E & M. In the next month Borden submitted a substitute offer in the form of a proposed "Plan of Reorganization." This plan, which was executed, provided that E & M would redeem all of the petitioner's preferred stock for $43,500 in cash and that Borden would acquire all of the common stock of E & M in exchange for 4,839 shares of Borden voting common stock. The difference between the 5,500 shares of Borden common stock originally offered for the business and the 4,839 shares agreed on in the plan represented the amount of $43,500 to be paid to the petitioner by E & M in redemption of his preferred stock. Upon the recommendation of Borden, E & M acquired the cash to carry out the redemption by obtaining a short-term bank loan. A week later E & M common stock was exchanged for Borden stock, and Borden, on the same day, paid E & M $96,000, a portion of which was used by E & M to pay off the bank loan.

Before the Tax Court the Commissioner incorrectly treated the redemption of the petitioner's stock and the exchange of E & M stock for Borden stock as separate transactions, and therefore conceded that the exchange constituted a tax-free reorganization within the meaning of section 368(a)(1)(B) of the Code. Thus, there was presented for determination by the Tax Court only the issue of whether the redemption, when viewed as a separate transaction, was substantially pro rata and should be treated as a distribution subject to section 301 of the Code. The Tax Court correctly found a single integrated transaction, stating, "The record in this case establishes clearly that the redemption was merely a step in the plan of Borden for the acquisition of E & M, so that it is the results of the plan that are significant to us."

Viewing the redemption and reorganization together, the court concluded that the petitioner's interest in E & M had been substantially changed, so that the redemption was not essentially equivalent to a dividend. In reaching this conclusion, the court refrained from comment concerning the propriety of treating the exchange as tax-free because that issue was not before it.

The Service recognizes it was in error in arguing the various steps were separate transactions thereby affording tax-free treatment on the stock exchange. Accordingly, since the acquisition was not solely for voting stock of the acquiring corporation but partly for cash, it is the position of the Service that the acquisition of stock of E & M did not constitute a reorganization. Therefore, under the factual situation presented in *McDonald*, the entire transaction is considered a taxable sale or exchange. In view of this conclusion, the redemption issue dealt with by the Tax Court in *McDonald* was not the correct issue for decision. Therefore, the Service does not consider *McDonald* to be an appropriate precedent.

Questions and Note

1. Does Rev. Rul. 75-360 mean that any stock redemption before a (B) reorganization will break the (B)? If not, what test is to be applied in determining whether a redemption will break a (B)? Why should a prior redemption break a (B), whereas according to Rev. Rul. 70-172, a prior dividend will not?

2. For the impact of redemptions on the continuity of interest requirement, *see* Sec. 6.2.F.

H. The Hybrid Subsidiary (B)

1. Introduction

The materials in this section are concerned with the issue of whether a triangular subsidiary merger may qualify as a constructive straight (B) reorganization.

2. Reverse Subsidiary Merger May Constitute a (B)

Revenue Ruling 67-448

1967-2 C.B. 144

Corporation *P* and Corporation *Y*, incorporated in the same state, are publicly owned corporations. Corporation *P* wanted to acquire the business of Corporation *Y* but could do so with an effective result only if the corporate entity of *Y* were continued intact due to the necessity of preserving its status as a regulated public utility. *P* also desired to eliminate the possibility of minority shareholders in the event less than all of the shareholders of *Y* agreed to the transaction. Since an outright acquisition of stock pursuant to a reorganization as defined in section 368(a)(1)(B) of the Code would not achieve this result, the plan of reorganization was consummated as follows:

(a) *P* transferred shares of its voting stock to its newly formed subsidiary, *S*, in exchange for shares of *S* stock.

(b) S (whose only asset consisted of a block of the voting stock of *P*) merged into *Y* in a transaction, which qualified as a statutory merger under the applicable state law.

(c) Pursuant to the plan of reorganization and by operation of state law, the *S* stock owned by *P* was converted into *Y* stock. At the same time the *Y* stock held by its shareholders was exchanged for the *P* stock received by *Y* on the merger of *S* into *Y*. The end result of these actions was that *P* acquired from the shareholders of *Y* in exchange for its own voting stock more than 95 percent of the stock of *Y*.

(d) *Y* shareholders owning less than five percent of the stock of *Y* dissented to the merger and had the right to receive the appraised value of their shares paid solely from the assets of *Y*. No funds, or other property, have been or will be provided by *P* for this purpose.

Thus, upon the consummation of the plan of reorganization *Y* became a wholly owned subsidiary of *P*.

At the time of the transaction *P* had no plan or intention to liquidate *Y* or to merge it into any other corporation.

The transaction described above does not constitute a reorganization within the meaning of either section 368(a)(1)(A) or section 368(a)(1)(C) of the Code because no assets of *Y* were transferred to nor acquired by another corporation in the transaction but rather all assets (except for amounts paid to dissenting shareholders) were retained in the same corporate entity. * * *

It is evident that the shortest route to the end result described above would have been achieved by a transfer of *P* voting stock directly to the shareholders of *Y* in exchange for their stock. This result is not negated because the transaction was cast in the form of a series of interrelated steps. The transitory existence of the new subsidiary, *S*, will be disregarded. The effect of all the steps taken in the series is that *Y* became a wholly owned subsidiary of *P*, and *P* transferred solely its voting stock to the former shareholders of *Y*.

Accordingly, the transaction will be treated as an acquisition by *P*, in exchange solely for part of its voting stock, of stock of *Y* in an amount constituting control (as defined in section 368(c) of the Code) of *Y*, which qualifies as a reorganization within the meaning of section 368(a)(1)(B) of the Code.

Questions

Does Rev. Rul. 67-448 make § 368(a)(2)(E) superfluous? Would the result change at all if the acquiring corporation provided the cash to pay the dissenting shareholders? What would the treatment have been in Rev. Rul. 67-448 if prior to the reverse subsidiary merger, *P* had purchased 10% of the stock of *Y* for cash? *See* Rev. Rul. 73-427, *supra* Sec. 5.2.A.3.

3. Forward Subsidiary Merger Cannot Constitute a (B)

Bercy Industries, Inc. v. Commissioner

Tax Court of the United States, 1978

70 T.C. 29 (First Issue)

[The target corporation (Old Bercy) was merged into a subsidiary (Beverly Manor) of an acquiring parent (Beverly) with the shareholders of Old Bercy receiving stock of Beverly. Beverly argued that the acquisition qualified as a (B) and therefore § 381(b)(3), was not applicable. Section 381(b)(3) prohibits the carryback of NOLs to a prior year of a target that is acquired in an asset reorganization. *See* Sec. 7.8.]

[The court here discussed Rev. Rul. 67-448, *supra.*] We note that the (B) subsidiary reverse merger technique was codified, liberalized and qualified as a hybrid (A) reorganization in January 1971 with the enactment of section 368(a)(2)(E), Pub.L. 91-693, sec. 1(a).

Respondent contends that the above revenue ruling is not applicable herein and the transaction cannot be classified as a (B) reorganization. He asserts that, pursuant to Article I of the agreement of merger, petitioner did not acquire Old Bercy stock in exchange for its parent stock. At the date of merger all outstanding shares of Old Bercy were canceled and petitioner did not receive the stock of a viable corporation. Therefore immediately after the acquisition, petitioner did not have control of Old Bercy within the meaning of section 368(a)(1)(B). Moreover, in Rev. Rul. 67-448, *supra,* the subsidiary corporation, *S*, had a transitory existence; it was formed solely for the purpose of effectuating an exchange of *P* stock for *Y* stock. Herein petitioner had been in existence since 1968 and continued to exist, receiving Old Bercy's assets and assuming all its liabilities.

We agree with respondent that the transaction is not a (B) reorganization although we disagree, somewhat, with his reasoning. We are unable to see any difference, in substance, between (1) Old Bercy transferring its stock to petitioner in exchange for Beverly stock followed by cancellation of said Old Bercy stock, and (2) cancellation of Old Bercy stock prior to its shareholders receiving Beverly stock.

The decisive element disqualifying the transaction as a (B) reorganization is the fact that, after the dust had settled, the acquired corporation (Old Bercy) and its stock were no longer in existence. Old Bercy had disappeared into petitioner and its stock had been canceled. Thus, instead of acquiring stock, what petitioner acquired were assets and that simply is not a (B) reorganization. * * *

The transaction in the instant case, a triangular merger is, also, a hybrid (A) reorganization pursuant to section 368(a)(2)(D). * * * We believe there are substantial differences between a triangular merger and a reverse triangular merger. In this respect, we note that the House Ways and Means Committee report on section 368(a)(2)(E) stated that a triangular merger in either direction would be tax free and indicated its awareness that a reverse triangular merger was more than formally distinguishable from the triangular merger. * * *

I. Push Up of Target's Assets after a (B)

Revenue Ruling 74-35

1974-1 C.B. 85

Advice has been requested as to the Federal income tax consequences of the acquisition by one corporation, solely for shares of its voting stock, of all of the outstanding stock of another corporation, followed by a distribution by the acquired corporation of a part of its assets under the circumstances described below.

X and Y were unrelated corporations, each of which was engaged in a separate business. Pursuant to a plan of reorganization and for valid business reasons, Y acquired all of the outstanding stock of X solely in exchange for 10,000 shares of voting common stock of Y, representing 20 percent of the Y stock outstanding after the transaction. As part of the plan, X then distributed to Y, its sole shareholder, appreciated investment assets (not constituting an active trade or business within the meaning of sections 346 and 355 of the Internal Revenue Code of 1954) amounting to 30 percent in value of the X assets.

At issue is whether the principle set forth in *Kimbell-Diamond Milling Co.,* [Chapter 2] properly should be invoked when Y, pursuant to the overall plan, acquired direct ownership of some, but not all, of X's assets. If this principle does apply, the transaction will be recast for Federal income purposes into (1) a constructive sale by X to Y of the assets "distributed" in exchange for an amount of the Y stock received of equivalent value, followed by a constructive taxable distribution of such stock by X to its shareholders, and (2) a concurrent exchange by the X shareholders of their X stock solely for the remainder of the Y stock qualifying as a reorganization under section 368(a)(1)(B).

Section 368(a)(1)(B) of the Code provides, in pertinent part, that the term "reorganization" means the acquisition by one corporation, in exchange solely for shares of its voting stock, of the outstanding stock of another corporation if, immediately after the transaction, the acquiring corporation has control of such other corporation. Under section 368(c), "control" means ownership of stock possessing at least 80 percent of the total combined voting power of all classes of stock entitled to vote and at least 80 percent of the total number of shares of all other classes of stock of the corporation.

In *Kimbell-Diamond Milling Co.* and Rev. Rul. 67-274, 1967-2 C.B. 141, one corporation acquired all of the stock of another corporation pursuant to a prearranged plan the essential nature of which was the acquisition of the assets of that corporation by immediately liquidating it. In each, effect was given to the intent, purpose and result of this plan such that the acquiring corporation was treated as if it had actually acquired assets rather than stock. Although Rev. Rul. 67-274 makes no reference to *Kimbell-Diamond,* the holding that the initial acquisition of stock is to be disregarded as transitory and that the transaction is to be treated as an acquisition of assets represents an application of the *Kimbell-Diamond* principle.

Under that principle, whenever a corporation acquires all the stock of another corporation pursuant to a prearranged plan to liquidate that corporation in order to acquire its assets, the transaction is treated, as to the acquiring corporation, as an acquisition of assets.

The *Kimbell-Diamond* principle, as illustrated by Rev. Rul. 67-274, does not support a recast of a portion of a transaction, such as in the instant case, because *Y* does not acquire substantially all the property of *X*. *Y* continues its stock interest in *X*, which retains all of its operating assets and 70 percent in value of all the assets it owned prior to the transaction.

Accordingly, the acquisition by *Y*, in exchange solely for its voting stock, of the outstanding stock of *X* qualifies as a reorganization within the meaning of section 368(a)(1)(B) of the Code. No gain or loss is recognized to the *X* shareholders upon the exchange of their stock for the *Y* stock under section 354(a), nor to *Y* upon receipt of the *X* stock in exchange for the *Y* stock under section 1032(a). The distribution of assets by *X* to *Y* is a distribution of property under section 301.

J. Section 305 and 306 Issues Arising in (B) Reorganization

See Secs. 6.17 and 6.18, for a discussion of issues under §§ 305 and 306 arising in acquisitive reorganizations.

§ 8.3 The Triangular (B) Reorganizations

A. Legislative History of the Triangular (B) Reorganization

In 1964, the parenthetical clause was added to § 368(a)(1)(B), allowing the triangular (B) reorganization. Also, § 368(a)(2)(C) was amended to allow the stock of a target acquired in a triangular (B) to be dropped into a subsidiary of the acquiring subsidiary. Conforming amendments were made to the definition of party to a reorganization in § 368(b). The following discussion from the Senate Report explains the operation of these amendments:

> [T]he 1954 code permits tax-free reorganizations in the case of the exchange of the parent's stock for the assets of a corporation acquired by the subsidiary. However, a similar result is denied where the subsidiary acquires the stock of the other corporation in exchange for the stock of its parent corporation. Since Congress has considered the "continuity of interest" rule satisfied in the case of asset acquisitions, there seems to be no reason for not applying the same rule to stock acquisitions, since there is little in substance to distinguish an asset acquisition from a stock acquisition.
>
> As a result, your committee has concluded that it is desirable to treat these two types of acquisitions in the same manner. For that reason, it has provided tax-free status for the stock-for-stock reorganization in the same manner that present law provides a tax-free status for stock-for-assets reorganizations.

General explanation of provision. — This provision amends the definition of a stock-for-stock reorganization (known as a (B) reorganization) to qualify as a tax-free reorganization a transaction in which a subsidiary corporation acquires the stock of another corporation (and after that is in control of the corporation) in exchange solely for the voting stock of its parent corporation. Present law is also amended to permit the subsidiary corporation acquiring the stock of another corporation in the "(B) reorganization" to transfer all or part of this stock to another corporation which it controls. In addition, conforming changes have been made to the definition of the term "party to the reorganization".

B. Introductory Note

The issues that arise in a triangular (B) under the parenthetical clause of § 368(a)(1)(B) are essentially the same as those that arise in a straight (B). *See* Sec. 8.2. The principal concern is ensuring that the solely for voting stock requirement is not violated. If the stock the subsidiary uses in making the acquisition was contributed to it by the parent, there is a potential zero basis problem. Also. there is a potential recognition problem for the subsidiary. *See* Sec. 8.3.D.

C. Reverse Subsidiary Merger of Second Tier Subsidiary into Target

In both Rev. Rul. 74-564, 1974-2 C.B. 124, and Rev. Rul. 74-565, 1974-2 C.B. 125, a newly formed second tier subsidiary (*S-2*) that was owned 100% by the first tier subsidiary (*S-1*) merged into the target (*T*), with the target's shareholder receiving stock of the parent (*P*). Following Rev. Rul. 67-448, both rulings hold that the transaction is a triangular (B), reasoning that "the net effect of the steps taken" was that *S-2*, acquired solely for voting stock of *P* (which was in control of *S-2*) stock of *T* amounting to control.

In Rev. Rul. 74-565, *P* merely transferred its shares to *S-1* which in turn transferred the shares to *S-2*. In Rev. Rul. 74-564, however, *P* formed *S-2*, contributed its stock to *S-2* and then contributed *S-2* stock to *S-1*. Thus, the *P* stock can be transferred to *S-2* in a variety of ways without altering the results.

D. Zero Basis Problem

See Reg. §§ 1.1032-2 and 1.358-6(b), and Sec. 7.4.F.

See the discussion of the background of the issue in Sec. 7.4.F.1.

§ 8.4 Representations Required in a Ruling Request under § 368(a)(1)(B): Straight and Triangular

Revenue Procedure 86-42

§ 7.04, 1986-2 C.B. 722

[Although as noted in Sec. 6.2.A.6, the IRS generally does not issue private letter rulings on reorganization transactions, the following ruling guidelines can be helpful in structuring a deal.]

[In addition to the following representations, taxpayers are also required to submit representations which are essentially the same as those in paragraphs 1–3, 6, 7, and 9 of the portion of this Rev. Proc. governing the (A) reorganization. *See* Sec. 7.2.L.]

.04 Section 368(a)(1)(B) reorganizations:

Legend: Acquiring   =   The acquiring corporation

                          =   The corporation whose stock is acquired

* * *

3. TARGET HAS NO PLAN OR INTENTION TO ISSUE ADDITIONAL SHARES OF ITS STOCK THAT WOULD RESULT IN ACQUIRING LOSING CONTROL OF TARGET WITHIN THE MEANING OF SECTION 368(c) OF THE INTERNAL REVENUE CODE.

4. ACQUIRING HAS NO PLAN OR INTENTION TO LIQUIDATE TARGET; TO MERGE TARGET INTO ANOTHER CORPORATION; TO CAUSE TARGET TO SELL OR OTHERWISE DISPOSE OF ANY OF ITS ASSETS, EXCEPT FOR DISPOSITIONS MADE IN THE ORDINARY COURSE OF BUSINESS; OR TO SELL OR OTHERWISE DISPOSE OF ANY OF THE TARGET STOCK ACQUIRED IN THE TRANSACTION, EXCEPT FOR TRANSFERS DESCRIBED IN SECTION 368(a)(2)(C) OF THE INTERNAL REVENUE CODE. * * *

7. ACQUIRING WILL ACQUIRE TARGET STOCK SOLELY IN EXCHANGE FOR ACQUIRING VOTING STOCK. FOR PURPOSES OF THIS REPRESENTATION, TARGET STOCK REDEEMED FOR CASH OR OTHER PROPERTY FURNISHED BY ACQUIRING WILL BE CONSIDERED AS ACQUIRED BY ACQUIRING. FURTHER, NO LIABILITIES OF TARGET OR THE TARGET SHAREHOLDERS WILL BE ASSUMED BY ACQUIRING, NOR WILL ANY OF THE TARGET STOCK BE SUBJECT TO ANY LIABILITIES.

8. AT THE TIME OF THE TRANSACTION, TARGET WILL NOT HAVE OUTSTANDING ANY WARRANTS, OPTIONS, CONVERTIBLE SECURITIES, OR ANY OTHER TYPE OF RIGHT PURSUANT TO WHICH ANY PERSON COULD ACQUIRE STOCK IN TARGET THAT, IF EXERCISED OR CONVERTED, WOULD AFFECT ACQUIRING'S ACQUISITION OR RETEN-

TION OF CONTROL OF TARGET, AS DEFINED IN SECTION 368(c) OF THE INTERNAL REVENUE CODE.

9. ACQUIRING DOES NOT OWN, DIRECTLY OR INDIRECTLY, NOR HAS IT OWNED DURING THE PAST FIVE YEARS, DIRECTLY OR INDIRECTLY, ANY STOCK OF TARGET.

12. TARGET WILL PAY ITS DISSENTING SHAREHOLDERS THE VALUE OF THEIR STOCK OUT OF ITS OWN FUNDS. NO FUNDS WILL BE SUPPLIED FOR THAT PURPOSE, DIRECTLY OR INDIRECTLY, BY ACQUIRING, NOR WILL ACQUIRING DIRECTLY OR INDIRECTLY REIMBURSE TARGET FOR ANY PAYMENTS TO DISSENTERS.

   (Alternatively) THERE WILL BE NO DISSENTERS TO THE TRANSACTION.

13. ON THE DATE OF THE TRANSACTION, THE FAIR MARKET VALUE OF THE ASSETS OF TARGET WILL EXCEED THE SUM OF ITS LIABILITIES PLUS THE LIABILITIES, IF ANY, TO WHICH THE ASSETS ARE SUBJECT.

§ 8.5 Section 368(a)(2)(E) Reverse Subsidiary Mergers

A. Legislative History of the Reverse Subsidiary Merger

The reverse triangular (or subsidiary) merger provision, § 368(a)(2)(E), was added in 1970. The operation of this provision was discussed as follows in the Senate Report:

Summary This bill amends the tax law to permit a tax-free statutory merger when stock of a parent corporation is used in a merger between a controlled subsidiary of the parent and another corporation, and the other corporation survives—here called a "reverse merger."

The Treasury Department has indicated that it has no objection to the enactment of this bill.

Reasons for the Bill * * * [U]nder existing law, corporation X (an unrelated corporation) may be merged into corporation S (a subsidiary) in exchange for the stock in corporation P (the parent of S) in a tax-free statutory merger. [*See* § 368(a)(2)(D).] However, if for business and legal reasons (wholly unrelated to Federal income taxation) it is considered more desirable to merge S into X (rather than merging X into S), so that X is the surviving corporation—a "reverse merger"—the transaction is not a tax-free statutory merger. * * *

The committee agrees with the House, that there is no reason why a merger in one direction (S into X in the above example) should be taxable, when the merger in the other direction (X into S), under identical circumstances, is tax-free. Moreover, it sees no reason why in cases of this type the acquisition needs to be made solely for stock. For these reasons the amendment makes statutory mergers tax-free in the circumstances described above.

Explanation of the Bill* * * Under the new provision (sec. 368(a)(2)(E)) * * * a statutory merger may be a tax-free reorganization if it meets several conditions.

First, the corporation surviving the merger must hold substantially all of its own properties and substantially all of the properties of the merged corporation (except stock of the controlling corporation distributed in the transaction).

Second, in the transaction, former shareholders of the surviving corporation must receive voting stock of the controlling corporation in exchange for an amount of stock representing control in the surviving corporation. Control for this purpose (defined in sec. 368(c)) means that the amount of stock in the surviving corporation surrendered for voting stock of the controlling corporation must represent stock possessing at least 80 percent of the total combined voting power (in the surviving corporation), and also stock amounting to at least 80 percent of the total number of shares of all other classes of stock (in the surviving corporation). If voting stock of the controlling corporation is used in the exchange to the extent described, additional stock in the surviving corporation may be acquired for cash or other property (whether or not from the shareholders who received voting stock). Of course, this additional stock in the surviving corporation need not be acquired by the controlling corporation.

The amendment applies not only when the only assets of the merged corporation are the nominal capital required to organize it and the stock of its parent which is to be used in the merger exchange but also when the corporation has substantial properties.

B. Introductory Note

In order to qualify as a reverse subsidiary merger, the transaction must satisfy the following requirements:

(1) The acquiring subsidiary must merge into the target corporation in a transaction that would otherwise qualify as an (A);

(2) After the merger, the target must hold "substantially all" of its properties and substantially all of the acquiring subsidiary's properties, other than stock of the acquiring parent distributed in the transaction; and

(3) The former shareholders of the target must exchange for an amount of voting stock of the acquiring parent, an amount of stock in the target that constitutes control of the target.

The "substantially all" requirement is the same as the one that applies to the (C). *See* Sec. 7.3.C. The (a)(2)(E) has a voting stock requirement, whereas the (a)(2)(D) does not. The (a)(2)(E) is similar to a (B); however, up to 20% of the consideration paid in an (a)(2)(E) can be boot. If the target's shareholders receive solely voting stock of the acquiring corporation, the transaction may also constitute a (B). *See* Rev. Rul. 67-448, *supra* Sec. 8.2.H.

The following materials amplify the (a)(2)(E).

C. The Final Regulations

Preamble to Final Regulations under § 368(a)(2)(E)

Treasury Decision 8059 (October 21, 1985)

Summary of Public Comments and Changes to Proposed Regulations Control requirement. Section 368(a)(2)(E)(ii) of the Code requires that, in the transaction, former shareholders of the surviving corporation (hereinafter "T") exchange, for voting stock of the controlling corporation (hereinafter "P"), an amount of stock which constitutes control of T (as defined in section 368(c) of the Code). Section 1.368-2(j)(3)(i) of the proposed regulations provides that the amount of T stock surrendered in the transaction by T shareholders in exchange for P voting stock must itself constitute control. Accordingly, if P owns more than 20 percent of T, the transaction does not qualify under section 368(a)(2)(E). Example (3) of proposed § 1.368-2(j)(7) illustrates that result. Numerous commenters suggested that, instead, the regulations provide that the requirement of section 368(a)(2)(E)(ii) is satisfied if, in the transaction, T shareholders surrender in exchange for P voting stock an amount of T stock which, when added to P's prior stock ownership in T, constitutes control.

After careful consideration, it is concluded that the statute does not permit the interpretation advanced by the commenters. Section 1.368-2(j)(3)(i) and example (4) of § 1.368-2(j)(7) of the final regulations retain the rule set forth in the proposed regulations. Examples (6) and (7) of § 1.368-2(j)(7) of the final regulations clarify, however, that the control requirement of section 368(a)(2)(E)(ii) may be satisfied despite the fact that, in the transaction, P contributes money or other property to T in exchange for additional T stock, or P receives T stock in exchange for its prior interest in the merged corporation (hereinafter "S"). However, as illustrated in example (9) of § 1.368-2(j)(7) of the final regulations, the receipt of such T stock will not contribute to satisfaction of that control requirement.

Section 1.368-2(j)(3)(i) of the proposed regulations also provides that, for purposes of the control requirement, T's outstanding stock is measured immediately before the transaction. Further, as illustrated in examples (2) and (4) of proposed § 1.368-2(j)(7), payments to T's shareholders other than P voting stock (such as cash payments to dissenters or payments in redemption of T stock), as part of the transaction, could prevent satisfaction of that requirement. Several commenters suggested that, similar to reorganizations under section 368(a)(1)(B), payments to T's shareholders could be disregarded for purposes of the control requirement, provided the consideration was furnished by T and not by P. In response, § 1.368-2(j)(3)(i) of the final regulations, reflecting an interpretation of the statute which looks to the consideration furnished by P rather than that received by the T shareholders, provides that such payments by T and not by P may be disregarded for purposes of section 368(a)(2)(E)(ii). As with reorganizations under section 368(a)(1)(B), the facts and circumstances of each case will determine whether the payments came from T or P. Examples (2) and (3) of § 1.368-2(j)(7) of the final regulations illustrate that result. However, § 1.368-2(j)(3)(i) and (iii) also clarify that those payments are treated as a reduction of T's properties for purposes of section 368(a)(2)(E)(i), which requires that, after the transaction, *T* hold substantially all of its properties. In addition, receipt of consideration other than *P* stock by *T* shareholders in the transaction could prevent satisfaction of the continuity of interest requirement.

Section 1.368-2(j)(3)(i) of the proposed regulations defines control under section 368(c). Since current law is sufficiently clear as to the definition of control under section 368(c), the final regulations do not contain such a definition.

Section 1.368-2(j)(3)(ii) of the proposed regulations provides that *P* must acquire control of *T* in the transaction. Section 1.368-2(j)(3)(ii) of the final regulations clarifies this rule to provide that *P* must be in control of *T* immediately after the transaction. Thus, any disposition by *P* of the *T* stock acquired (other than a transfer described in section 368(a)(2)(C)), or any new issuance of stock by *T* to persons other than *P*, as part of the transaction, which causes *P* not to be in control of *T* will prevent the transaction from qualifying under section 368(a)(2)(E). Example (8) of § 1.368-2(j)(7) of the final regulations illustrates this rule.

"Substantially all" requirement Section 368(a)(2)(E)(i) of the Code requires generally that, after the transaction, *T* hold substantially all of its properties and substantially all of the properties of *S*. Section 1.368-2(j)(4) of the proposed regulations indicates that this requirement will not be satisfied where, as part of the transaction, *T* transfers assets to a corporation controlled by *T*, notwithstanding section 368(a)(2)(C) of the Code. Several commenters suggested that section 368(a)(2)(C) permits assets of *T* to be transferred to a controlled corporation without violating the "substantially all" requirement. In response, § 1.368-2(j)(4) of the final regulations provides that such transfers do not violate the "substantially all" requirement.

Section 1.368-2(j)(3)(iii)(E) of the final regulations clarifies that money transferred from *P* to *S* to satisfy minimum state capitalization requirements, which eventually is returned to *P* as part of the transaction, is not taken into account in applying the "substantially all" test to the assets of *S*.

Assumption of liabilities; exchange of securities Section 1.368-2(j)(5) of the proposed regulations provides that *P* may assume liabilities of *T* without disqualifying the transaction under section 368(a)(2)(E). Commenters requested that the regulations clarify the treatment of such liability assumption by *P*. Accordingly, § 1.368-2(j)(5) of the final regulations clarifies that liability assumption is a contribution to the capital of *T* by its shareholder *P*. In addition, § 1.368-2(j)(5) of the final regulations clarifies that where, pursuant to the plan of reorganization, securities of *T* are exchanged for securities of *P*, or for other securities of *T* which, for example, are convertible into *P* stock, that exchange is subject to the otherwise applicable provisions of sections 354 and 356.

Relation to section 368(a)(1)(B) A few commenters suggested that the regulations confirm that a transaction which fails to qualify under section 368(a)(2)(E) may, under appropriate circumstances, qualify as a reorganization described in section 368(a)(1)(B), as in Rev. Rul. 67-448, 1967-2 C.B. 144. Examples (4) and (5) of § 1.368-2(j)(7) of the final regulations confirm this result.

Merged corporation Finally, in response to comments, § 1.368-2(j)(6) of the final regulations clarifies that *S* can be an existing corporation as well as a corporation formed for purposes of the section 368(a)(2)(E) transaction.

D. Creation of a Holding Company

See Revenue Ruling 77-428, Sec. 7.6.E.

E. Meaning of "Substantially All" of the Acquiring Subsidiary's Assets

Revenue Ruling 77-307

1977-2 C.B. 117

P corporation formed *S* as a wholly owned subsidiary corporation solely for the purpose of effectuating a merger of *S* with and into *T* corporation in a transaction intended to qualify as a reorganization under section 368(a)(1)(A) and (a)(2)(E) of the Internal Revenue Code of 1954. As part of the plan of reorganization, *P* contributed to *S* sufficient cash so *T* (after *S* merged into it) could purchase the *T* stock of those minority *T* shareholders who would not want to exchange their *T* stock for *P* stock, and so *T* could pay cash in lieu of issuing fractional shares of *P* stock to those *T* shareholders who would exchange their *T* stock for *P* stock. The cash to be received by the *T* shareholders in lieu of fractional shares was not separately bargained for but was merely a mechanical rounding off of the fractions which would result from the exchange. In addition, *P* contributed sufficient cash to *S* so *S* could pay its expenses attributed solely to the merger. * * *

After the merger, without taking into account the cash contributed by *P* to *S* for the above stated purposes, *T* held all of the properties held separately by *T* and *S* immediately before the transaction. The transaction otherwise qualified as a reorganization under section 368(a)(1)(A) and (a)(2)(E) of the Code.

Held, in the instant case, *T* held substantially all of its properties and the properties of *S* after the transaction within the meaning of section 368(a)(2)(E) of the Code. The cash contributed by *P* to *S* and used by *S* and *T* for the purposes described above is not taken into account in determining whether the "substantially all" requirement of section 368(a)(2)(E) has been met. Therefore, the transaction qualifies as a reorganization under section 368(a)(1)(A) and (a)(2)(E).

Question

The ruling permits the acquiring corporation to, in effect, pay off the target's dissenters in an (a)(2)(E) reverse subsidiary merger. What result if the target paid the dissenters from its own assets prior to the reorganization?

F. Two-Step Reverse Subsidiary Mergers: Exchange Offer Followed by Merger

Revenue Ruling 2001-26

2001-1 C.B. 1297

Issue On the facts described below, is the control-for-voting-stock requirement of § 368(a)(2)(E) of the Internal Revenue Code satisfied, so that a series of integrated steps constitutes a tax-free reorganization under §§ 368(a)(1)(A) and 368(a)(2)(E) and § 354 or § 356 applies to each exchanging shareholder?

Facts *Situation 1.* Corporation P and Corporation T are widely held, manufacturing corporations organized under the laws of state A. T has only voting common stock outstanding, none of which is owned by P. P seeks to acquire all of the outstanding stock of T. For valid business reasons, the acquisition will be effected by a tender offer for at least 51 percent of the stock of T, to be acquired solely for P voting stock, followed by a merger of a subsidiary of P into T. P initiates a tender offer for T stock conditioned on the tender of at least 51 percent of the T shares. Pursuant to the tender offer, P acquires 51 percent of the T stock from T's shareholders for P voting stock. P forms S and S merges into T under the merger laws of state A. In the statutory merger, P's S stock is converted into T stock and each of the T shareholders holding the remaining 49 percent of the outstanding T stock exchanges its shares of T stock for a combination of consideration, two-thirds of which is P voting stock and one-third of which is cash. Assume that under general principles of tax law, including the step transaction doctrine, the tender offer and the statutory merger are treated as an integrated acquisition by P of all of the T stock. Also assume that all nonstatutory requirements for a reorganization under §§ 368(a)(1)(A) and 368(a)(2)(E) and all statutory requirements of § 368(a)(2)(E), other than the requirement under § 368(a)(2)(E)(ii) that P acquire control of T in exchange for its voting stock in the transaction, are satisfied.

Situation 2. The facts are the same as in *Situation 1*, except that S initiates the tender offer for T stock and, in the tender offer, acquires 51 percent of the T stock for P stock provided by P.

Law and Analysis Section 368(a)(1)(A) states that the term "reorganization" means a statutory merger or consolidation. Section 368(a)(2)(E) provides that a transaction otherwise qualifying under § 368(a)(1)(A) will not be disqualified by reason of the fact that stock of a corporation (the "controlling corporation") that before the merger was in control of the merged corporation is used in the transaction, if (1) after the transaction, the corporation surviving the merger holds substantially all of its properties and of the properties of the merged corporation (other than stock of the controlling corporation distributed in the transaction), and (2) in the transaction, former shareholders of the surviving corporation exchanged, for an amount of voting stock of the controlling corporation, an amount of stock in the surviving corporation that constitutes control of such corporation (the "control-for-voting-stock requirement"). For this purpose, control is defined in § 368(c).

In *King Enterprises, Inc. v. United States*, [Sec. 7.2.C.], as part of an integrated plan, a corporation acquired all of the stock of a target corporation from the target corporation's shareholders for consideration, in excess of 50 percent of which was acquiring corporation stock, and subsequently merged the target corporation into the acquiring corporation. The court held that, because the merger was the intended result of the stock acquisition, the acquiring corporation's acquisition of the target corporation qualified as a reorganization under § 368(a)(1)(A).

Section 354(a)(1) provides that no gain or loss will be recognized if stock or securities in a corporation a party to a reorganization are, in pursuance of the plan of reorganization, exchanged solely for stock or securities in another corporation a party to the reorganization.

Section 356(a)(1) provides that, if § 354 would apply to the exchange except for the receipt of money or property other than stock or securities in a corporate party to the reorganization, the recipient shall recognize gain, but in an amount not in excess of the sum of the money and the fair market value of the other property.

Section 1.368-1(c) of the Income Tax Regulations provides that a plan of reorganization must contemplate the bona fide execution of one of the transactions specifically described as a reorganization in § 368(a) and the bona fide consummation of each of the requisite acts under which nonrecognition of gain is claimed. Section 1.368-2(g) provides that the term plan of reorganization is not to be construed as broadening the definition of reorganization as set forth in § 368(a), but is to be taken as limiting the nonrecognition of gain or loss to such exchanges or distributions as are directly a part of the transaction specifically described as a reorganization in § 368(a).

As assumed in the facts, under general principles of tax law, including the step transaction doctrine, the tender offer and the statutory merger in both *Situations 1 and 2* are treated as an integrated acquisition by P of all of the T stock. The principles of *King Enterprises* support the conclusion that, because the tender offer is integrated with the statutory merger in both *Situations 1 and 2*, the tender offer exchange is treated as part of the statutory merger (hereinafter the "Transaction") for purposes of the reorganization provisions. *Cf. J.E. Seagram Corp. v. Commissioner*, 104 T.C. 75 (1995) (treating a tender offer that was an integrated step in a plan that included a forward triangular merger as part of the merger transaction). Consequently, the integrated steps, which result in P acquiring all of the stock of T, must be examined together to determine whether the requirements of § 368(a)(2)(E) are satisfied. *Cf.* § 1.368-2(j)(3)(i) ; § 1.368-2(j)(6), Ex. 3 (suggesting that, absent a special exception, steps that are prior to the merger, but are part of the transaction intended to qualify as a reorganization under §§ 368(a)(1)(A) and 368(a)(2)(E), should be considered for purposes of determining whether the control-for-voting-stock requirement is satisfied).

In both situations, in the Transaction, the shareholders of T exchange, for P voting stock, an amount of T stock constituting in excess of 80 percent of the voting stock of T. Therefore, the control-for-voting-stock requirement is satisfied. Accordingly, in both *Situations 1 and 2*, the Transaction qualifies as a reorganization under § 368(a)(1)(A) and 368(a)(2)(E).

Under §§ 1.368-1(c) and 1.368-2(g), all of the T shareholders that exchange their T stock for P stock in the Transaction will be treated as exchanging their T stock for P stock in pursuance of a plan of reorganization. Therefore, T shareholders that exchange their T stock only for P stock in the Transaction will recognize no gain or loss under § 354. T shareholders that exchange their T stock for P stock and cash in the Transaction will recognize gain to the extent provided in § 356. In both *Situations 1* and *2*, none of P, S, or T will recognize any gain or loss in the Transaction, and P's basis in the T stock will be determined under § 1.358-6(c)(2) by treating P as acquiring all of the T stock in the Transaction and not acquiring any of the T stock before the Transaction.

Holding On the facts set forth in *Situations 1* and *2*, the control-for-voting-stock requirement is satisfied in the Transaction, the Transaction constitutes a tax-free reorganization under § 368(a)(1)(A) and 368(a)(2)(E), and § 354 or § 356 applies to each exchanging shareholder.

G. Sale of 32% of Stock of Acquiring Parent after a Purported § 368(a)(2)(E)

Technical Advice Memorandum 8702003

(September 24, 1986)

[The stock of the Target was acquired in what purported to be a reorganization under § 368(a)(2)(E). Shortly after the merger, the target's shareholders sold 32% of the stock of the acquiring parent (Parent) in a previously planned firm commitment underwriting.] * * *

Issue Was the "control" requirement of section 368(a)(2)(E)(ii) of the Internal Revenue Code satisfied when the Target shareholders exchanged their Target common stock and preferred stock for Parent voting common stock on October 12, 1981, or was it violated because the merger was preconditioned on a firm commitment underwriting agreement pursuant to which the Target shareholders sold 32 percent of the Parent stock they received on October 12, 1983, to Underwriters on October 20, 1983?

Law and Analysis * * * By preconditioning the merger on a firm commitment underwriting, the Target shareholders established the predicate for the application of all three step-transaction tests since selling the Parent stock was the end result, the steps were interdependent and the precondition established a binding commitment. If the Target shareholders had sold all of their stock, then this case would be right on point with the *McDonald*'s case and the continuity of interest requirement (*see* regulation section 1.368-1(b)) would have been violated. [This position has now been reversed in the regulations dealing with consolidated returns. *See* Sec. 6.2.F.] * * *

In analyzing this issue, GCM 32421 is helpful. That GCM involved the question of whether the "solely for voting stock" requirement of a "B" reorganization was satisfied even though a shareholder ("SH") of the target corporation sold 50 percent of the stock transferred by the acquiring corporation ("A") in the exchange to an underwriter in a public offering in which the acquiring corporation also sold some of its own stock. In concluding that the "solely for voting stock" requirement had not been violated, the GCM stated:

We are satisfied that A exchanged solely voting stock for the stock of [Target]. Any cash received by SH was acquired as a result of the sale of his stock to the underwriter, and was not received from A. The cash was obtained by virtue of the transaction at the shareholder level, and flowed directly from an underwriter to SH. Such cash was never received by A for the purpose of a distribution to SH in redemption of part of his stock.

The GCM further concluded that as to the possible application of the step transaction doctrine:

Even were the exchange and the sale to the underwriters telescoped and considered as part of some integrated transaction, it still could not be said that the acquiring corporation exchanged cash in addition to the voting stock for the stock of SH. There is ample precedent to support the view that where the source of cash to the transferor shareholder is other than from the acquiring company, that the exchange will be regarded as solely for voting stock [citations omitted].

Finally, the GCM concludes:

We believe there is no real basis for attempting to recast the transaction in such a form [*i.e.* as the acquiring corporation issuing all of the stock in the public offering and then transferring the cash to the target shareholder]. * * *

In the present case, Parent had no binding commitment to dispose of any Target stock acquired in the transaction, let alone an amount that would cause it to lose control of Target. Rather, it was the Target shareholders who established the binding commitment. After the transaction, Parent had control of Target and the Target shareholders retained a sufficient equity ownership interest in Parent to satisfy the continuity of interest requirement. The cash received by the Selling Shareholders was obtained from the Underwriters, not from Parent.

Conclusion Consistent with the interpretation of the "control" requirement of section 368(a)(2)(E)(ii) contained in the final regulations section 1.368-2(j), the Step Transaction Doctrine is not applicable to hold that the cash received by the Selling Shareholders from the Underwriters came from Parent and, therefore, we conclude that the control requirement of section 368(a)(2)(E)(ii) was satisfied in this transaction.

H. Effect of Poison Pill Rights in a Reverse Subsidiary Merger under § 368(a)(2)(E)

Private Letter Ruling 8808081

(December 3, 1987)

* * * Parent is a widely held and publicly traded State X corporation which is the common parent of an affiliated group that files a consolidated return. Parent has outstanding several classes of stock including approximately 37,484,933 shares of voting common stock.

On June 11, 1987, the Board of Directors of Parent declared a dividend of one preferred share purchase right ("Right") with respect to each share of Parent's voting stock including its common stock. Until the happening of certain specified events, the Rights will be transferred with and only with the underlying shares.

Sub 1 is a State Y corporation formed solely for the purpose of accomplishing the proposed transaction. All of Sub 1's outstanding stock is held by Parent. Sub 1 is included in Parent's consolidated return. * * *

(i)   Pursuant to the Agreement and Plan of Merger, (Plan), Sub 1 will merge with and into Target in accordance with applicable law.

(ii) The shareholders of Target will receive common stock of Parent (including the Rights attached thereto) in exchange for all the stock of Target, voting and nonvoting, according to a formula stated in the Plan. No fractional shares of Parent stock will be issued in the exchange. Instead, fractional shares will be rounded to the nearest whole share.

(iii) Parent will * * * receive and hold the Target stock from Sub 1 * * *.

Based solely on the information submitted and on the representations set forth above, it is held as follows:

(1) Provided that (i) the proposed merger of Sub 1 with and into Target qualifies as a statutory merger under applicable law, (ii) after the transaction Target holds substantially all of its assets and substantially all of the assets of Sub 1 and, (iii) in the transaction, Target shareholders exchange solely for Parent voting stock an amount of stock constituting "control" of Target within the meaning of section 368(c) of the Internal Revenue Code, the proposed transaction will constitute a reorganization within the meaning of section 368(a)(1)(A). The reorganization is not disqualified by reason of the fact that Parent voting stock is used in the transaction (section 368(a)(2)(E)). For purposes of this ruling, "substantially all" means at least 90 percent of the fair market value of the net assets and at least 70 percent of the fair market value of the gross assets of each of Target and Sub. 1. Parent, Sub. 1, and Target will each be "a party to a reorganization" within the meaning of section 368(b). * * *

(5) Gain, if any, will be recognized by each Target shareholder on the receipt of both Parent stock and other property (the Rights) in exchange for Target stock, but in an amount not in excess of the fair market value of the other property received (section 356(a)(1)). If the exchange has the effect of the distribution of a dividend, then the amount of gain recognized that is not in excess of each Target shareholder's ratable share of the undistributed earnings and profits of Target will be treated as a dividend. The remainder, if any, of the gain will be treated as gain from the exchange of property. The determination of whether the exchange has the effect of the distribution of a dividend will be made with respect to each shareholder in accordance with the principles set forth in Rev. Rul. 74-515, 1974-2 C.B. 118, and Rev. Rul. 75-83, 1975-1 C.B. 112, and with the application of section 318(a). No loss will be recognized on the exchange pursuant to section 356(c). * * *

Question

What is the fair market value of the right? Is it zero? *See* Rev. Rul. 90-11, Sec. 2.9.C.

I. Reverse Subsidiary Merger Followed by a Liquidation Is Not a Reorganization

Revenue Ruling 2008-25

2008-21 I.R.B. 986

ISSUE

What is the proper Federal income tax treatment of the transaction described below?

FACTS

T is a corporation all of the stock of which is owned by individual A. T has 150x dollars worth of assets and 50x dollars of liabilities. P is a corporation that is unrelated to A and T. The value of P's assets, net of liabilities, is 410x dollars. P forms corporation X, a wholly owned subsidiary, for the sole purpose of acquiring all of the stock of T by causing X to merge into T in a statutory merger (the "Acquisition Merger"). In the Acquisition Merger, P acquires all of the stock of T, and A exchanges the T stock for 10x dollars in cash and P voting stock worth 90x dollars. Following the Acquisition Merger and as part of an integrated plan that included the Acquisition Merger, T completely liquidates into P (the "Liquidation"). In the Liquidation, T transfers all of its assets to P and P assumes all of T's liabilities. The Liquidation is not accomplished through a statutory merger. After the Liquidation, P continues to conduct the business previously conducted by T.

LAW

Section 368 (a) (1) (A) of the Internal Revenue Code provides that the term "reorganization" means a statutory merger or consolidation. Section 368 (a) (2) (E) provides that a transaction otherwise qualifying under § 368 (a) (1) (A) shall not be disqualified by reason of the fact that stock of a corporation in control of the merged corporation is used in the transaction, if (i) after the transaction, the corporation surviving the merger holds substantially all of its properties and of the properties of the merged corporation (other than stock of the controlling corporation distributed in the transaction), and (ii) in the transaction, former shareholders of the surviving corporation exchanged, for an amount of voting stock of the controlling corporation, an amount of stock in the surviving corporation which constitutes control of the surviving corporation. Further, § 1.368-2 (j) (3) (iii) of the Income Tax Regulations provides that "[i]n applying the 'substantially all' test to the merged corporation, assets transferred from the controlling corporation to the merged corporation in pursuance of the plan of reorganization are not taken into account."

Section 368 (a) (1) (C) provides in part that a reorganization is the acquisition by one corporation, in exchange solely for all or part of its voting stock, of substantially all of the properties of another corporation, but in determining whether the exchange is solely for stock, the assumption by the acquiring corporation of a liability of the other shall be disregarded. Section 368 (a) (2) (B) provides that if one corporation acquires substantially all of the properties of another corporation, the acquisition would qualify under § 368 (a) (1) (C) but for the fact that the acquiring corporation exchanges money or other property in addition to voting stock, and the acquiring corporation acquires, solely for voting stock described in § 368 (a) (1) (C), property of the other corporation having a fair market value which is at least 80 percent of the fair market value of all of the property of the other corporation, then such acquisition shall (subject to § 368 (a) (2) (A)) be treated as qualifying under § 368 (a) (1) (C). Section 368 (a) (2) (B) further provides that solely for purposes of determining whether its requirements are satisfied, the amount of any liabilities assumed by the acquiring corporation shall be treated as money paid for the property.

Section 1.368-1 (a) generally provides that in determining whether a transaction qualifies as a reorganization under § 368 (a), the transaction must be evaluated under relevant provisions of law, including the step transaction doctrine.

Section 1.368-2 (k) provides, in part, that a transaction otherwise qualifying as a reorganization under § 368 (a) shall not be disqualified or recharacterized as a result of one or more distributions to shareholders (including distribution (s) that involve the assumption of liabilities) if the requirements of § 1.368-1 (d) are satisfied, the property distributed consists of assets of the surviving corporation, and the aggregate of such distributions does not consist of an amount of assets of the surviving corporation (disregarding assets of the merged corporation) that would result in a liquidation of such corporation for Federal income tax purposes.

Rev. Rul. 67-274, 1967-2 C.B. 141, holds that an acquiring corporation's acquisition of all of the stock of a target corporation solely in exchange for voting stock of the acquiring corporation, followed by the liquidation of the target corporation as part of the same plan, will be treated as an acquisition by the acquiring corporation of substantially all of the target corporation's assets in a reorganization described in § 368 (a) (1) (C). The ruling explains that, under these circumstances, the stock acquisition and the liquidation are part of the overall plan of reorganization and the two steps may not be considered independently of each other for Federal income tax purposes. See also, Rev. Rul. 72-405, 1972-2 C.B. 217.

Rev. Rul. 2001-46, 2001-2 C.B. 321, holds that, where a newly formed wholly owned subsidiary of an acquiring corporation merged into a target corporation, followed by the merger of the target corporation into the acquiring corporation, the step transaction doctrine is applied to integrate the steps and treat the transaction as a single statutory merger of the target corporation into the acquiring corporation. Noting that the rejection of step integration in Rev. Rul. 90-95, 1990-2 C.B. 67, and § 1.338-3 (d) is based on Congressional intent that § 338 replace any nonstatutory treatment of a stock purchase as an asset purchase under the Kimbell-Diamond doctrine, the Service found that the policy underlying § 338 is not violated by treating the steps as a single statutory merger of the target into the acquiring corporation because such treatment results in a transaction that qualifies as a reorganization in which the acquiring corporation acquires the assets of the target corporation with a carryover basis under § 362, rather than receiving a cost basis in those assets under § 1012. (In *Kimbell-Diamond Milling Co. v. Commissioner*, 14 T.C. 74, *aff'd per curiam*, 187 F.2d 718 (1951), *cert. denied*, 342 U.S. 827, 72 S. Ct. 50, 96 L. Ed. 626 (1951), the court held that the purchase of the stock of a target corporation for the purpose of obtaining its assets through a prompt liquidation should be treated by the purchaser as a purchase of the target corporation's assets with the purchaser receiving a cost basis in the assets.)

Section 338 (a) provides that if a corporation makes a qualified stock purchase and makes an election under that section, then the target corporation (i) shall be treated as having sold all of its assets at the close of the acquisition date at fair market value and (ii) shall be treated as a new corporation which purchased all of its assets as of the beginning of the day after the acquisition date. Section 338 (d) (3) defines a qualified stock purchase as any transaction or series of transactions in which stock (meeting the requirements of § 1504 (a) (2)) of one corporation is acquired by another corporation by purchase during a 12-month acquisition period. Section 338 (h) (3) defines a purchase generally as any acquisition of stock, but excludes acquisitions of stock in exchanges to which § 351, § 354, § 355, or § 356 applies.

Section 338 was enacted in 1982 and was "intended to replace any nonstatutory treatment of a stock purchase as an asset purchase under the Kimbell-Diamond doctrine." H.R. Conf. Rep. No. 760, 97th Cong, 2d Sess. 536 (1982), 1982-2 C.B. 600, 632. Stock purchase or asset purchase treatment generally turns on whether the purchasing corporation makes or is deemed to make a § 338 election. If the election is made or deemed made, asset purchase treatment results and the basis of the target assets is adjusted to reflect the stock purchase price and other relevant items. If an election is not made or deemed made, the stock purchase treatment generally results. In such a case, the basis of the target assets is not adjusted to reflect the stock purchase price and other relevant items.

Rev. Rul. 90-95 (Situation 2), holds that the merger of a newly formed wholly owned domestic subsidiary into a target corporation with the target corporation shareholders receiving solely cash in exchange for their stock, immediately followed by the merger of the target corporation into the domestic parent of the merged subsidiary, will be treated as a qualified stock purchase of the target corporation followed by a § 332 liquidation of the target corporation. As a result, the parent's basis in the target corporation's assets will be the same as the basis of the assets in the target corporation's hands. The ruling explains that even though "the step-transaction doctrine is properly applied to disregard the existence of the [merged subsidiary]," so that the first step is treated as a stock purchase, the acquisition of the target corporation's stock is accorded independent significance from the subsequent liquidation of the target corporation and, therefore, is treated as a qualified stock purchase regardless of whether a § 338 election is made. Thus, in that case, the step transaction doctrine was not applied to treat the transaction as a direct acquisition by the domestic parent of the assets of the target corporation because such an application would have resulted in treating a stock purchase as an asset purchase, which would be inconsistent with the repeal of the Kimbell-Diamond doctrine and § 338.

Section 1.338-3 (d) incorporates the approach of Rev. Rul. 90-95 into the regulations by requiring the purchasing corporation (or a member of its affiliated group) to treat certain asset transfers following a qualified stock purchase (where no § 338 election is made) independently of the qualified stock purchase. In the example in § 1.338-3 (d) (5), the purchase for cash of 85 percent of the stock of a target corporation, followed by the merger of the target corporation into a wholly owned subsidiary of the purchasing corporation, is treated (other than by certain minority shareholders) as a qualified stock purchase of the stock of the target corporation followed by a § 368 reorganization of the target corporation into the subsidiary. As a result, the subsidiary's basis in the target corporation's assets is the same as the basis of the assets in the target corporation's hands.

ANALYSIS

If the Acquisition Merger and the Liquidation were treated as separate from each other, the Acquisition Merger would be treated as a stock acquisition that qualifies as a reorganization under § 368 (a) (1) (A) by reason of § 368 (a) (2) (E), and the Liquidation would qualify under § 332. However, as provided in § 1.368-1 (a), in determining whether a transaction qualifies as a reorganization under § 368 (a), the transaction must be evaluated under relevant provisions of law, including the step transaction doctrine. In this case, because T was completely liquidated, the § 1.368-2 (k) safe harbor exception from the application of the step transaction doctrine does not apply. Accordingly, the Acquisition Merger and the Liquidation may not be considered independently of each other for purposes of determining whether the transaction satisfies the statutory requirements of a reorganization described in § 368 (a) (1) (A) by reason of § 368 (a) (2) (E). As such, this transaction does not qualify as a reorganization described in § 368 (a) (1) (A) by reason of § 368 (a) (2) (E) because, after the transaction, T does not hold substantially all of its properties and the properties of the merged corporation.

In determining whether the transaction is a reorganization, the approach reflected in Rev. Rul. 67-274 and Rev. Rul. 2001-46 is applied to ignore P's acquisition of the T stock in the Acquisition Merger and to treat the transaction as a direct acquisition by P of T's assets in exchange for 10x dollars in cash, 90x dollars worth of P voting stock, and the assumption of T's liabilities.

However, unlike the transactions considered in Rev. Rul. 67-274, 72-405 and 2001-46, a direct acquisition by P of T's assets in this case does not qualify as a reorganization under § 368 (a). P's acquisition of T's assets is not a reorganization described in § 368 (a) (1) (C) because the consideration exchanged is not solely P voting stock and the requirements of § 368 (a) (2) (B) are not satisfied. Section 368 (a) (2) (B) would treat P as acquiring 40 percent of T's assets for consideration other than P voting stock (liabilities assumed of 50x dollars, plus 1 0x dollars cash). See Rev. Rul. 73-102, 1973-1 C.B. 186 (analyzing the application of § 368 (a) (2) (B)). P's acquisition of T's assets is not a reorganization described in § 368 (a) (1) (D) because neither T nor A (nor a combination thereof) was in control of P (within the meaning of § 368 (a) (2) (H) (i)) immediately after the transfer. Additionally, the transaction is not a reorganization under § 368 (a) (1) (A) because T did not merge into P. Accordingly, the overall transaction is not a reorganization under § 368 (a).

Additionally, P's acquisition of the T stock in the Acquisition Merger is not a transaction to which § 351 applies because A does not control P (within the meaning of § 368 (c)) immediately after the exchange.

Rev. Rul. 90-95 and § 1.338-3 (d) reject the step integration approach reflected in Rev. Rul. 67-274 where the application of that approach would treat the purchase of a target corporation's stock without a § 338 election followed by the liquidation or merger of the target corporation as the purchase of the target corporation's assets resulting in a cost basis in the assets under § 1012. Rev. Rul. 90-95 and § 1.338-3 (d) treat the acquisition of the stock of the target corporation as a qualified stock purchase followed by a separate carryover basis transaction in order to preclude any nonstatutory treatment of the steps as an integrated asset purchase.

In this case, further application of the approach reflected in Rev. Rul. 67-274, integrating the acquisition of T stock with the liquidation of T, would result in treating the acquisition of T stock as a taxable purchase of T's assets. Such treatment would violate the policy underlying § 338 that a cost basis in acquired assets should not be obtained through the purchase of stock where no § 338 election is made. Accordingly, consistent with the analysis set forth in Rev. Rul. 90-95, the acquisition of the stock of T is treated as a qualified stock purchase by P followed by the liquidation of T into P under § 332.

HOLDING

The transaction is not a reorganization under § 368 (a). The Acquisition Merger is a qualified stock purchase by P of the stock of T under § 338 (d) (3). The Liquidation is a complete liquidation of a controlled subsidiary under § 332.

J. Section 305 and 306 Issues Arising in (B) Reorganizations

See Secs. 6.17 and 6.18 for a discussion of §§ 305 and 306 in the context of acquisitive reorganizations.

K. Zero Basis Problem

1. Background

See the discussion of the background of the issue in Sec. 7.4.F.1. *See also* Reg. §§ 1.1032-2 and 1.358-6.

2. Proposed Regulations Relating to Basis in a Reverse Subsidiary Merger
Preamble to Proposed Regulations under §§ 1032 and 358
C0-993-71 (December 27, 1994)

In addition to the materials set out in Sec. 7.4.F., the preamble to the proposed regulations also provided:

> *Merger of Subsidiary into Surviving Corporation* Proposed § 1.358-6 also provides rules for determining the basis of T stock acquired by P in the case of the merger of S into T in a reorganization that qualifies under section 368(a)(1)(A) by reason of the application of section 368(a)(2)(E). In general, the rules provide for the same results that would occur if P acquired T's property in exchange for P stock and then transferred the acquired property and any assumed liabilities back to T in a tax-free transfer. Under these rules, P will have a uniform basis in the T stock (of each class) owned by it after the reorganization (including any T stock owned by P before the reorganization). This treatment is consistent with the results that would occur if P had acquired T's property in the merger and then transferred the property back to T. These rules are designed to parallel the basis rules on forward triangular reorganizations. In addition, by providing for an asset basis they avoid the problems that are inherent in determining the basis of stock held by T's previous shareholders. * * *

3. Final Regulations Relating to Basis in a Reverse Subsidiary Merger
Preamble to Final Regulations
Treasury Decision 8648 (December 20, 1995)

Overlap of Reverse Triangular Merger and Other Transactions The proposed regulations provided that if a transaction qualified as both a reverse triangular merger and a stock acquisition under section 368(a)(1)(B), P adjusted its basis in its T stock based either on T's net asset basis or on the aggregate basis of the T stock surrendered in the transaction (as if the transaction were a reorganization under section 368(a)(1)(B).

One comment noted that a reverse triangular merger might overlap with a section 351 transfer and therefore requested that this rule also apply to such a case. The final regulations adopt this suggestion.

MANNER OF MAKING ELECTIONS The proposed and final regulations provide P with elections for its basis adjustments when P owns stock of T and when a reverse triangular merger also qualifies as a section 351 transaction or B reorganization. In these situations, P does not have to declare how it will compute its basis. Rather, P must simply retain appropriate records. *See* 1.368-3. * * *

4. No Regulations under § 1032

There are no regulations under § 1032 dealing with the reverse subsidiary merger under § 368(a)(2)(E). Why not? Should there be? What purpose could the regulations serve?

L. Representations Required in a Ruling Request under § 368(a)(2)(E)

Rev. Proc. 86-42

§ 7.04, 1986-2 C.B. 722

[Although as noted in Sec. 6.2.A.6, the IRS generally does not issue private letter rulings on reorganization transactions, the following ruling guidelines can be helpful in structuring a deal.]

[In addition to the following representations, taxpayers are required to submit representations which are essentially the same as those in paragraphs 1 and 2, 6, 7 and 9 of the portion of this Rev. Proc. governing the (A) reorganization. *See* Sec. 7.2. L.]

Legend: Parent   =   the controlling corporation
          Sub   =   the merged corporation
          Target   =   the surviving corporation

3. FOLLOWING THE TRANSACTION, TARGET WILL HOLD AT LEAST 90 PERCENT OF THE FAIR MARKET VALUE OF ITS NET ASSETS AND AT LEAST 70 PERCENT OF THE FAIR MARKET VALUE OF ITS GROSS ASSETS AND AT LEAST 90 PERCENT OF THE FAIR MARKET VALUE OF SUB'S NET ASSETS AND AT LEAST 70 PERCENT OF THE FAIR MARKET VALUE OF SUB'S GROSS ASSETS HELD IMMEDIATELY PRIOR TO THE TRANSACTION. FOR PURPOSES OF THIS REPRESENTATION, AMOUNTS PAID BY TARGET OR SUB TO DISSENTERS, AMOUNTS PAID BY TARGET OR SUB TO SHAREHOLDERS WHO RECEIVE CASH OR OTHER PROPERTY, AMOUNTS USED BY TARGET OR SUB TO PAY REORGANIZATION EXPENSES, AND ALL REDEMPTIONS AND DISTRIBUTIONS (EXCEPT FOR REGULAR, NORMAL DIVIDENDS) MADE BY TARGET WILL BE INCLUDED AS ASSETS OF TARGET OR SUB, RESPECTIVELY, IMMEDIATELY PRIOR TO THE TRANSACTION.

4. PRIOR TO THE TRANSACTION, PARENT WILL BE IN CONTROL OF SUB WITHIN THE MEANING OF SECTION 368(c) OF THE INTERNAL REVENUE CODE.

5. TARGET HAS NO PLAN OR INTENTION TO ISSUE ADDITIONAL SHARES OF ITS STOCK THAT WOULD RESULT IN PARENT LOSING CONTROL OF TARGET WITHIN THE MEANING OF SECTION 368(c) OF THE INTERNAL REVENUE CODE. * * *

7. PARENT HAS NO PLAN OR INTENTION TO LIQUIDATE TARGET; TO MERGE TARGET WITH OR INTO ANOTHER CORPORATION; TO SELL OR OTHERWISE DISPOSE OF THE STOCK OF TARGET EXCEPT FOR TRANSFERS OF STOCK TO CORPORATIONS CONTROLLED BY PARENT; OR TO CAUSE TARGET TO SELL OR OTHERWISE DISPOSE OF ANY OF ITS ASSETS OR OF ANY OF THE ASSETS ACQUIRED FROM SUB, EXCEPT FOR DISPOSITIONS MADE IN THE ORDINARY COURSE OF BUSINESS OR TRANSFERS OF ASSETS TO A CORPORATION CONTROLLED BY TARGET.

8. THE LIABILITIES OF SUB ASSUMED BY TARGET AND THE LIABILITIES TO WHICH THE TRANSFERRED ASSETS OF SUB ARE SUBJECT WERE INCURRED BY SUB IN THE ORDINARY COURSE OF ITS BUSINESS.

(Alternatively) SUB WILL HAVE NO LIABILITIES ASSUMED BY TARGET, AND WILL NOT TRANSFER TO TARGET ANY ASSETS SUBJECT TO LIABILITIES, IN THE TRANSACTION. * * *

12. IN THE TRANSACTION, SHARES OF TARGET STOCK REPRESENTING CONTROL OF TARGET, AS DEFINED IN SECTION 368(c) OF THE CODE, WILL BE EXCHANGED SOLELY FOR VOTING STOCK OF PARENT. FOR PURPOSES OF THIS REPRESENTATION, SHARES OF TARGET STOCK EXCHANGED FOR CASH OR OTHER PROPERTY ORIGINATING WITH PARENT WILL BE TREATED AS OUTSTANDING TARGET STOCK ON THE DATE OF THE TRANSACTION.

13. AT THE TIME OF THE TRANSACTION, TARGET WILL NOT HAVE OUTSTANDING ANY WARRANTS, OPTIONS, CONVERTIBLE SECURITIES, OR ANY OTHER TYPE OF RIGHT PURSUANT TO WHICH ANY PERSON COULD ACQUIRE STOCK IN TARGET THAT, IF EXERCISED OR CONVERTED, WOULD AFFECT PARENT'S ACQUISITION OR RETENTION OF CONTROL OF TARGET, AS DEFINED IN SECTION 368(c) OF THE INTERNAL REVENUE CODE.

§ 8.6 Summary Problems on Straight and Triangular Acquisitive Stock Reorganization

The facts for the following questions are set out in Sec. 7.7.

What are the tax consequences to each of the parties under each of the following basic stock transactions and the modifications thereof?

AC issues $100K of its voting common stock to *A*, *B* and *X* in exchange for all of their *TC* stock? What if *AC* issues its voting preferred? Also, *AC* issues its debentures with a face amount and value of $30K to *A* and *Y* in exchange for *TC*'s debentures? There is no OID on AC's debentures.

Consider each of the following modifications separately.

a. Suppose *B* insists upon being paid in cash, and *AC* pays him $20K cash for his stock?

b. Suppose *B* refuses to go along, and *AC* acquires only *A*'s and *X*'s stock?

c. Suppose that immediately after the transaction in b., *AC* liquidates *TC* in a transaction in which *B* receives $20K of cash from *TC,* and *AC* receives the operating assets and assumes *TC*'s liabilities by issuing to *A* and *Y* $30K of *AC* debentures? Suppose instead, that *TC* is merged upstream, with *B* receiving $20K of cash and *A* and *Y* receiving *AC* debentures?

d. Suppose that prior to the acquisition, *TC* redeems *B*'s stock for $20K in cash?

e. Suppose *AC* forms a new subsidiary (*AC-S*) and contributes to *AC-S* (1) $80K of *AC* voting common stock, (2) $20K of cash, and (3) $30K of *AC* debentures. *AC-S* then acquires (1) *A*'s and *X*'s stock in exchange for the *AC* stock, (2) *B*'s stock in exchange for the cash and (3) the *TC* debentures in exchange for the *AC* debentures? Suppose, instead, that *AC-S* merges into *TC* with the parties receiving the same consideration? Suppose, instead, that *TC* merges into *AC-S*?

f. Suppose that in the basic transaction above, *AC* agrees to pay all the expenses of registering the *AC* stock, and *AC* also agrees to pay to *A* an additional $10K of *AC* nonvoting stock as an inducement for *A* to enter into a long-term employment agreement?

g. Suppose that (1) on January 1 of 2017, *AC* acquires *X*'s *TC* stock for *AC* voting common stock, (2) on October 1, 2017, *AC* acquires *B*'s *TC* stock for *AC* voting common stock, and (3) on January 31, 2018, *AC* acquires *A*'s *TC* stock in exchange for *AC* voting common? What if *TC* is merged upstream immediately after *AC* acquires all the stock of *TC*? What if *TC* is liquidated into *AC*?

§ 8.7 Impact of § 382, the Consolidated Return Regulations, and § 269 on the Utilization of the Target's Net Operating Losses

A. Introduction

In each of the forms of acquisitive stock reorganization, the target's net operating loss carryovers continue in the target after the acquisition. The ability of the target to utilize those losses, however, is subject to the § 382 loss limitation rules. The § 382 rules applicable to taxable stock acquisitions of a loss corporation (*see* Sec. 5.8) also apply to the acquisition of a loss corporation in an acquisitive stock reorganization. The applicability of § 382 in the context of a (B) reorganization is examined in the next section.

Because of the overlap rule in the consolidated return regulations, if § 382 applies, the SRLY rules generally will not apply. *See* Sec. 5.8. In addition, the reverse acquisition rule of the consolidated return regulations that applies to acquisitive asset reorganizations (*see* Sec. 7.10.B) also applies to acquisitive stock reorganizations.

Finally, § 269 could apply to acquisitive stock reorganizations because control of the target is acquired. Sec. 5.10.

B. Acquisitive Stock Reorganizations as Equity Structure Shifts

As pointed out in Sec. 7.9.B., *Equity Structure Shifts* under § 382(g)(3) encompass acquisitive stock and asset reorganizations. If an *Equity Structure Shift* results in an *Ownership Change* of a *Loss Corporation*, the losses are limited under § 382. The Conference Report to the TRA 1986 (179) gives the following illustration of an *Ownership Change* that results from a combination of a sale of stock of a *Loss Corporation* followed by an acquisition of other stock of the *Loss Corporation* in a stock for stock (B) reorganization:

> *Example 12.* On July 12, 1989, L corporation is owned 45 percent by P, a publicly traded corporation (with no 5-percent shareholders), 40 percent by individual A, and 15 percent by individual B. All of the L shareholders have owned their stock since L's organization in 1984. Neither A nor B owns any P stock. On July 30, 1989, B sells his entire 15-percent interest to C for cash. On August 13, 1989, P acquires A's entire 40-percent interest in exchange for P stock representing an insignificant percentage of the outstanding P voting stock in a "B" reorganization. [This is a creeping (B), *see* Sec. 8.2.A.]
>
> There is an ownership change immediately following the B reorganization, because the percentage of L stock held (through attribution, as described below) by P shareholders (all of whom are less-than-5-percent shareholders who are treated as one 5-percent shareholder) and C (100 percent-P shareholders-85 percent; C-15 percent) has increased by more than 50 percentage points over the lowest percentage of stock owned by P shareholders and C at any time during the testing period (45 percent held constructively by P shareholders prior to August 13, 1989).

An illustration of an acquisitive asset reorganization that results in *Ownership Changes* is given in Sec. 7.9.B.

§ 8.8 Impact of § 384 on Utilization of Acquiring Corporation's Pre-Acquisition NOLs against Target's Pre-Acquisition Built-In Gains

Section 384 prevents the use of the pre-acquisition NOLs of an acquiring corporation to offset income from the pre-acquisition built-in gains of an acquired target.

Section 384 applies to taxable and tax-free stock acquisitions and to acquisitive asset reorganizations. It does not apply to taxable asset acquisitions. The same rules apply to both taxable stock acquisitions and acquisitive stock reorganizations. Therefore, the materials on § 384 in Sec. 5.11., which deal with taxable stock acquisitions, are equally applicable to acquisitive stock reorganizations. The applicability of § 384 to acquisitive asset reorganizations is addressed in Sec. 7.12.

§ 8.9 Summary Problems on the Utilization of NOLs after an Acquisitive Stock Reorganization

A. Statement of Facts

The facts are the same as those set forth in Sec. 7.13.

1. PC Acquires LC in a Stock for Stock (B) Reorganization or Reverse Subsidiary Reorganization

Prior to the transaction described below, individual *A* owned all of the stock of *LC*. As of the close of business on December 31, 2016, *PC* acquires all the stock of *LC* from *A* in a stock for stock reorganization under § 368(a)(1)(B). In the alternative, *PC* forms *PC-S*, a wholly-owned subsidiary, and *PC-S* either (1) merges into *LC* in a reverse subsidiary merger under § 368(a)(2)(E), or (2) acquires the stock of *LC* from *A* in exchange for stock of *PC* in a triangular (B). In all cases, the consideration paid by *PC* and *PC-S* is solely voting stock of *PC* with a value of $250K. After the transaction, *PC* and *LC* file consolidated returns.

   a. What is the impact, if any, of § 382?

   b. What is the impact, if any, of § 269?

   c. What is the impact, if any, of § 381? Suppose that after the (B), *LC* is liquidated into *PC*. *See* Rev. Rul. 67-274, *supra* Sec. 7.3.B.

   d. What is the impact, if any, of the consolidated return provisions?

   e. What is the impact, if any, of § 384?

2. Over and Down Triangular (A), (B) or (C) Reorganization

Prior to the transaction described below, *LC*'s stock was owned by individual *A*. As of December 31, 2016, *PC* acquires either the assets or stock of *LC* in a § 368(a)(1)(A), (B) or (C) reorganization and immediately thereafter contributes the assets or stock of *LC* to *PC-S* (a newly-formed subsidiary of *PC*) in a § 368(a)(2)(C) reorganization. *PC* issues $250K of its stock in the acquisition.

   a. What is the impact, if any, of § 382?

   b. What is the impact, if any, of § 269?

   c. What is the impact, if any, of § 381?

d. What is the impact, if any, of the consolidated return provisions on these transactions?

e. What is the impact, if any, of § 384?

§ 8.10 Sample Merger Agreement for a Reverse Subsidiary Merger: Time's Initial Proposal to Acquire Warner

Agreement and Plan of Merger among Time Incorporated (Time), TW Sub, Inc., a Wholly-Owned Subsidiary of Time, and Warner Communications Inc. (Warner)[*]

March 3, 1989

AGREEMENT AND PLAN OF MERGER dated as of March 3, 1989, as amended and restated as of May 19, 1989, among TIME INCORPORATED, a Delaware corporation (Time), TW SUB Inc, a Delaware corporation and a wholly owned subsidiary of Time (Sub), and WARNER COMMUNICATIONS INC., a Delaware corporation (WCI).

WHEREAS the respective Boards of Directors of Time, Sub and WCI have approved the merger of WCI and SUB;

WHEREAS, to effect such transaction, the respective Boards of Directors of Time, Sub and WCI, and Time acting as the sole stockholder of Sub, have approved the merger of WCI and Sub (the Merger), pursuant and subject to the terms and conditions of this Agreement, whereby each issued and outstanding share of Common Stock, par value $1 per share, of WCI (WCI Common Stock) not owned directly or through a wholly-owned Subsidiary by Time or directly by WCI will be converted into the right to receive Common Stock, par value $1.00 per share, of Time (Time Common Stock) and each issued and outstanding share of Preferred Stock, par value $1 per share, of WCI (WCI Preferred Stock) not owned directly or through a wholly-owned Subsidiary by Time or WCI will be converted into the right to receive Preferred Stock, par value $1.00 per share, of Time all as provided herein [This transaction is a reverse subsidiary merger under § 368(a)(2)(D)];

WHEREAS Time, Sub and WCI desire to make certain representations, warranties and agreements in connection with the Merger and also to prescribe various condition to the Merger;

* * *

NOW, THEREFORE, pursuant to Section 7.3 of the March Agreement and in consideration of the premises and the representations, warranties and agreements herein

---

[*] This agreement is adapted from Appendix A of Thompson, *Statutory Supplement and Documentary Appendices to Business Planning for Mergers and Acquisitions* (2nd Ed. 2001).

contained, the March Agreement, as amended by Amendment No. 1, is hereby amended and restated in its entirety to read as follows:

Article I
The Merger

1.1 *Effective Time of the Merger.* Subject to the provisions of this Agreement, a certificate of merger (the Certificate of Merger) shall be duly prepared, executed and acknowledged by the Surviving Corporation (as defined in Section 1.3) and thereafter delivered to the Secretary of State of the State of Delaware, for filing, as provided in the Delaware General Corporation Law (the DGCL), as soon as practicable on or after the Closing Date (as defined in Section 1.2). The Merger shall become effective upon the filing of the Certificate of Merger with the Secretary of State of the State of Delaware or at such time thereafter as is provided in the Certificate of Merger (the Effective Time).

* * *

1.2 *Closing.* The closing of the Merger (the Closing) will take place at 10:00 a.m. on a date to be specified by the parties, which shall be no later than the second business day after satisfaction of the latest to occur of [certain specified] conditions***.

1.3 *Effects of the Merger.* (a) At the Effective Time, (i) the separate existence of Sub shall cease and Sub shall be merged with and into WCI (Sub and WCI are sometimes referred to herein as the "Constituent Corporations" and WCI is sometimes referred to herein as the "Surviving Corporation), (ii) the Certificate of Incorporation of WCI shall be amended so that Article FOURTH of such Certificate of Incorporation reads in its entirety as follows: "The total number of shares of all classes of stock which the Corporation shall have authority to issue is 1,000, all of which shall consist of Common Stock, par value $1 per share.", and, as so amended, such Certificate shall be the Certificate of Incorporation of the Surviving Corporation and (iii) the By-laws of WCI as in effect immediately prior to the Effective Time shall be the By-laws of the Surviving Corporation.

Comment

This section describes the reverse subsidiary merger of Sub into WCI. The amendment of WCI's certificate to reduce the number of its authorized shares reduces the amount of franchise tax WCI has to pay the state of Delaware.

* * *

(b) At and after the Effective Time, the Surviving Corporation shall possess all the rights, privileges, powers and franchises of a public as well as of a private nature, and be subject to all the restrictions, disabilities and duties of each of the Constituent Corporations; and all and singular rights, privileges, powers and franchises of each of the Constituent Corporations, and all property, real, personal and mixed, and all debts due to either of the Constituent Corporations on whatever account, as well as for stock subscriptions and all other things in action or belonging to each of the Constituent Corporations, shall be vested in the Surviving Corporations; ***.

Article II
Effect of the Merger on the Capital Stock of the Constituent Corporations; Exchange of Certificates

2.1 *Effect on Capital Stock.* As of the Effective Time, by virtue of the Merger and without any action on the part of the holder of any shares of WCI Common Stock, WCI Preferred stock or capital stock of Sub:

(a) *Capital Stock of Sub.* Each issued and outstanding share of the capital stock of Sub shall be converted into and become one fully paid and nonassessable share of Common Stock, par value $1 per share, of the Surviving Corporation.

(b) *Cancellation of Treasury Stock and Time-Owned Stock.****

(c) *Exchange Ratio for WCI Common Stock.* Subject to Section 2.2(e), each issued and outstanding share of WCI Common Stock (other than shares to be canceled in accordance with Section 2.1(b) shall be converted into the right to receive, .465, subject to adjustment in accordance with Section 2.1(f) (the Conversion Number), of a fully paid and nonassessable share of Time Common Stock including the corresponding percentage of a right (the Right) to purchase shares of Series A Participating Preferred Stock of Time (the Time Series A Preferred) pursuant to the Rights Agreement dated as of April 29, 1986, between Time and Morgan Shareholder Services Trust Company of New York, as Rights Agent *** (the Rights Agreement). Prior to the Distribution Date (as defined in the Rights Agreement) all references in this Agreement to the Time Common Stock to be received pursuant to the Merger shall be deemed to include the Rights. All such shares of WCI Common Stock shall no longer be outstanding and shall automatically be canceled and retired and shall cease to exist, and each holder of a certificate representing any such shares shall cease to have any rights with respect thereto, except the right to receive the shares of Time Common Stock to be issued in consideration therefore upon the surrender of such certificate in accordance with Section 2.2, without interest.

(d) *Exchange of Preferred Stock.* Each share of Series B Variable Rate Cumulative Convertible Preferred Stock, par value $1 per share (the WCI Series B Preferred), of WCI outstanding immediately prior to the Effective Time (except shares of WCI Series B Preferred held by persons who object to the Merger and comply with all provisions of the DGCL concerning the right of such holders to dissent from the Merger and demand appraisal of their share (Dissenting Holders)) shall be converted into the right to receive one share of Series BB Variable Rate Cumulative Convertible Preferred Stock of Time, par value $1.00 per share (Time Series BB Preferred), such Time Series BB Preferred to have the terms set forth on Exhibit 2.1(d). All such shares of WCI Series B Preferred, other than share shares held by Dissenting Holders, shall no longer be outstanding and shall automatically be canceled and retired and shall cease to exist, and each holder of a certificate representing any such shares of WCI Series B Preferred shall cease to have any rights with respect thereto, except the right to receive the shares of Time Series BB Preferred to be issued in consideration therefore upon the surrender of such certificate in accordance with Section 2.2, without interest.

(e) *Shares of Dissenting Holders.* Any issued and outstanding shares of WCI Series B Preferred held by a Dissenting Holder shall not be converted as described in Section 2.1(d) but shall from and after the Effective Time represent only the right to receive such consideration as may be determined to be due to such Dissenting Holder pursuant to the DGCL; ***.

2.2 *Exchange of Certificates.* (a) *Exchange Agent.* As of the Effective Time, Time shall deposit with Manufacturers Hanover Trust Company or such other bank or trust company designated by Time (and reasonably acceptable to WCI) (the Exchange Agent), for the benefit of the holders of shares of WCI Common Stock and WCI Series B Preferred, for exchange in accordance with this Article II, through the Exchange Agent, certificates representing the shares of Time Common Stock and Time Series BB Preferred (such share of Time Common Stock and Time Series BB Preferred, together with any dividends or distributions with respect thereto, being hereinafter referred to as the "Exchange Fund) issuable pursuant to Section 2.1 in exchange for outstanding shares of WCI Common Stock and WCI Series B Preferred. ***

Article III
Representations and Warranties

3.1 *Representations and Warranties of WCI.* WCI represents and warrants to Time and Sub as follows: * * *

(h). *Taxes.* To the best of WCI's knowledge, WCI and each of its Subsidiaries has filed all tax returns required to be filed by any of them and has paid*** or has set up an adequate reserve for the payment of, all taxes required to be paid as shown on such returns and the most recent financial statements contained in the WCI SEC Documents reflect an adequate reserve for all taxes payable by WCI and its Subsidiaries accrued through the date of such financial statements. No material deficiencies for any taxes aggregating in excess of $300,000,000 have been proposed, asserted or assessed against WCI or any of its Subsidiaries. Except with respect to claims for refund, the Federal income tax returns of WCI and each of its Subsidiaries consolidated in such returns have been examined by and settled with the United States Internal Revenue Service (the IRS), or the statute of limitations with respect to such years has expired, for all years through 1976. The Federal income tax returns of WCI and each of its Subsidiaries consolidated in such returns for the 1977–84 are currently under examination by the IRS. For the purpose of this Agreement, the term "tax" (including, with correlative meaning, the terms "taxes" and "taxable) shall include all Federal, state, local and foreign income, profits, franchise, gross receipts, payroll, sales, employment, use, property, withholding, excise and other taxes, duties or assessments of any nature whatsoever, together with all interest, penalties and additions imposed with respect to such amounts.

Comment

This representation is subject to a "knowledge" qualification. It deals with, among other things, (1) the "filing" of all returns, (2) the "payment" of, or adequate "reserve" for, all taxes shown on the returns, and (3) the "reserve" for all taxes otherwise accrued.

3.2 *Representations and Warranties of Time and Sub.* Time and Sub represent and warrant to WCI as follows: [The representations and Warranties set forth here are similar to those set forth by WCI in Section 3.1.]

* * *

Article IV
Covenants Relating to Conduct of Business

4.1 *Covenants of WCI and Time.* During the period from the date of this Agreement and continuing until the Effective Time, WCI and Time each agree as to itself and its Subsidiaries that (except as expressly contemplated or permitted by this agreement, the Share Exchange Agreement, or to the extent that the other party shall otherwise consent in writing***):

(a) *Ordinary Course.* Each party and their respective Subsidiaries shall carry on their respective businesses in the usual, regular and ordinary course in substantially the same manner as heretofore conducted and use all reasonable efforts to preserve intact their present business organizations, keep available the services of the present officers and employees and preserve their relationships with customers, suppliers and others*** to the end that their goodwill and ongoing businesses shall not be impaired in any material respect at the Effective Time.

Comment

Both parties here want assurances that the other party will operate its business in the normal and ordinary course between the date of signing the Merger Agreement and the date of closing.

Article V
Additional Agreements

5.1 *Preparation of S-4 and the Proxy Statement.* Time and WCI shall promptly prepare and file with the SEC the Proxy Statement and Time shall prepare and file with the SEC the S-4 in which the Proxy Statement will be included as a prospectus. * * *

5.5 *Stockholder Meetings.* WCI and Time each shall call a meeting of its respective stockholders to be held as promptly as practicable for the purpose of voting upon this Agreement and related matters in the case of WCI and the Time Vote Matter and the New Time Stock Plan in the case of Time. WCI and Time will, through their respective Boards of Directors, recommend to their respective stockholders approval of such matters. WCI and Time shall coordinate and cooperate with respect to the timing of such meetings and shall use their best efforts to hold such meetings on the same day and as soon as practicable after the date hereof.

5.6. *Legal Conditions to Merger.* Each of WCI, Time and Sub will take all reasonable actions necessary to comply promptly with all legal requirements which may be imposed on itself with respect to the Merger or the Share Exchange Agreement (including furnishing all information required under the HSR Act, in connection with the FCC Approvals and the Local Approvals and in connection with approvals of or filings with any other Governmental Entity) and will promptly cooperate with and furnish information to each other in connection with any such requirements imposed upon any of them or any of their Subsidiaries in connection with the Merger. ***

Article VI
Conditions Precedent

6.1 *Conditions to Each Party's Obligation To Effect the Merger.* The respective obligation of each party to effect the Merger shall be subject to the satisfaction prior to the Closing Date of the following conditions:

(a) *Stockholder Approval.* This Agreement shall have been approved and adopted by the affirmative vote of a majority of the votes that the holders of the outstanding shares of WCI Common Stock and WCI Series B Preferred, voting together as a class, are entitled to cast, and the Time Vote Matter shall have been approved by the affirmative vote of the holders of a majority of the outstanding shares of Time Common Stock. * * *

6.2. *Conditions of Obligations of Time and Sub.* The obligations of Time and Sub to effect the Merger are subject to the satisfaction of the following conditions unless waived by Time and Sub:

(a) *Representations and Warranties.* The representations and warranties of WCI set forth in this Agreement shall be true and correct in all material respects as of the date of this Agreement and (except to the extent such representations and warranties speak as of an earlier date) as of the Closing Date as though made on and as of the Closing Date, except as otherwise contemplated by this Agreement, and Time shall have received a certificate signed on behalf of WCI by the chief executive officer or a member of the Office of the President and by the chief financial officer of WCI to such effect. * * *

(d) *Tax Opinion.* The opinion of Cravath, Swaine & Moore, counsel to Time to the effect that the Merger will be treated for Federal income tax purposes as a reorganization within the meaning of Section 368(a) of the Code, and that Time, Sub and WCI will each be a party to that reorganization within the meaning of Section 368(b) of the Code, dated on or about the date that is two business days prior to the date the Proxy Statement is first mailed to stockholders of WCI and Time, shall not have been withdrawn or modified in any material respect.

Comment

This transaction was designed to be a tax-free reorganization under § 368(a)(2)(E) of the Code.

* * *

6.3. *Conditions of Obligations of WCI.* The obligation of WCI to effect the Merger is subject to the satisfaction of the following conditions unless waived by WCI: [The conditions set forth here are similar to the conditions set forth in Section 6.2.]

Article VII
Termination and Amendment

* * *

Article VIII
General Provisions

8.1 *Nonsurvival of Representation, Warranties and Agreements.* None of the representations, warranties and agreements in this Agreement or in any instrument delivered pursuant to this Agreement shall survive the Effective Time, except for the agreements contained in Sections 2.1, [relating to capital stock], 2.2 [relating to exchange of certificates], 5.9 through 5.17 [relating to certain additional agreements], the last sentence of Section 7.3 [relating to amendments], and Article VIII [relating to termination], and the agreements of the "affiliates" of WCI delivered pursuant to Section 5.7 [relating to restrictions on sales of stock by affiliates.]

Comment

Since the representations, warranties and other agreements do not survive the merger, Time has no recourse against the Warner shareholders. In acquisitions of closely-held corporations, the representations and warranties typically survive the acquisition and in many cases the selling shareholders provide the acquiror with a separate indemnification. (*See* the Sample Asset Acquisition Agreement in Sec. 4.8, and the Sample Stock Acquisition Agreement in Sec. 5.15.)

Chapter 9

Spin-Offs under Section 355 and Their Use in Acquisitions

§9.1 Scope

This chapter introduces tax-free spin-off transactions under §355 and §368(a)(1)(D). These are transactions in which a parent corporation distributes to its shareholders the stock of a subsidiary. The subsidiary can be either (1) an existing subsidiary, in which case only §355 is implicated in the transaction, or (2) a newly formed corporation, in which case both §368(a)(1)(D) and §355 are implicated. If a spin-off qualifies under §355, both the distributing corporation and the shareholders of the distributing corporation receive tax-free treatment with respect to the stock of the controlled corporation distributed in the transaction. Thus, the distributing corporation gets relief from the gain recognition rule in §311(b), which reflects the repeal of *General Utilities*, and the shareholders get relief from dividend taxation under §301 that would otherwise apply.

Sec. 9.2 introduces the statutory structure governing spin-offs: §355 and the (D) reorganization. Sec. 9.3 sets out the legislative background of these provisions, including the impact of the recently enacted limitations on acquisitions in connection with spin-offs. Sec. 9.4 introduces the regulations, rulings and cases under §355, including the treatment of (1) the business purpose requirement, (2) the device clause, (3) the continuity of business requirement, and (4) the active conduct of a trade or business requirement. Sec. 9.5 addresses the issue of whether boot distributed in a §355 transaction is treated as a dividend. Sec. 9.6 looks at transactions in which spin-offs are followed by an acquisitive reorganization. Sec. 9.7 provides illustrations of a spin-off transaction. Finally, Sec. 9.8 presents summary problems.

Because the tax stakes in a §355 transaction are so high, public corporations almost always seek a favorable private letter ruling from the IRS before proceeding. The IRS has set out a "checklist" of information to be provided in a request for a private letter ruling. *See* Rev. Proc. 98-30, 1996-1 C.B. 696. This "check list" was modified by Rev. Proc. 2003-48, 2003-29 I.R.B. 86. Portions of both of these Revenue Procedures are referred to in this chapter. As indicated previously, a tax attorney dealing with any issue should always consult the IRS's current "no ruling" revenue procedure, which is normally the third revenue procedure issued each year, such as Rev. Proc. 2016-3.

For more detailed discussion on the issues covered here, *see* Bittker and Eustice, *Corporations, supra* Sec. 1.12; and Ginsburg and Levin, *Mergers, supra* Sec. 1.12. *See also* the most recent edition of *Tax Strategies, supra* Sec. 1.12; and Thompson, *Mergers, Acquisitions, and Tender Offers, supra* Sec. 1.12 at Chapter 15.

§ 9.2 Statutory Structure Governing Spin-Offs

Section 355 sets out the requirements for qualifying as a spin-off, which are certain tax-free transactions in which a parent corporation distributes to its shareholders the stock of a subsidiary. Section 355 provides the treatment to both the distributing corporation and the shareholders of the distributing corporation participating in a spin-off. If the subsidiary that is being spun off, which is referred to as the controlled corporation, is a preexisting corporation and no properties are transferred to it by the parent corporation, which is referred to as the distributing corporation, then only § 355 is implicated. On the other hand, if the transaction involves the transfer by the distributing corporation of property to a newly formed controlled corporation, the transaction is governed by both § 368(a)(1)(D) and § 355.

For instance, § 368(a)(1)(D) encompasses a transaction in which a distributing corporation transfers a long-operated division to a newly formed controlled corporation in exchange for stock of the controlled corporation, and the distributing corporation then transfers the stock of the controlled corporation to the shareholders of the distributing corporation in a transaction that qualifies under § 355. This is known as a divisive (D) reorganization and is to be distinguished from the nondivisive (D) reorganization, which was introduced in Chapter 3 and addressed in the context of the asset acquisition in Sec. 4.2.B. Section 355 also encompasses a transaction in which the stock of a subsidiary that has been engaged in the active conduct of business for many years is distributed by the controlled corporation to its shareholders. This transaction is not, however, governed by § 368(a)(1)(D), because the distributing corporation does not transfer property to the controlled corporation.

There are three types of § 355 transactions: spin-offs, split-offs and split-ups. In a spin-off, the stock of the controlled corporation is distributed to the shareholders of the distributing corporation. If the transaction does not qualify under § 355, the distribution is a dividend. In a split-off, the shareholders of the distributing corporation surrender a portion of their stock in exchange for stock of the controlled corporation. If the transaction does not qualify under § 355, the shareholder receives either sale or exchange treatment or dividend treatment. The shareholder has sale or exchange treatment if the transaction satisfies any of the paragraphs in § 302(b). In a split-up, the distributing corporation makes a liquidating distribution of the stock of two or more controlled corporations. If the transaction does not qualify under § 355, the shareholders generally have a taxable exchange under § 331. For ease of reference, the use of the term spin-off here encompasses each of these three types of § 355 transactions.

Four basic statutory requirements must be satisfied for a transaction to fit within § 355(a):

(1) The distributing corporation must distribute (either pro rata or non-pro rata) to its shareholders or security holders "solely" stock or securities of the controlled corporation (*see* §§ 355(a)(1)(A), (a)(2) and (a)(3)). If boot is distributed, § 356 will apply (*see* §§ 356(a) and (b)). Boot includes (1) an excess principal amount of securities, (2) stock of a controlled corporation acquired

by the distributing corporation in a wholly or partially taxable transaction within five years of the distribution, and (3) nonqualified preferred stock (*see* § 355(a)(3));

(2) The transaction must not be a "device" for the distribution of E & P (*see* § 355(a)(1)(B) and Sec. 9.4.C);

(3) A separate active trade or business that has been conducted for at least five years must continue to be conducted after the distribution by both the distributing and the controlled corporations (*see* § 355(a)(1)(C) and (b) and Sec. 9.4.E); and

(4) The distributing corporation must distribute all of the stock or securities of the controlled corporation or an amount of stock of the controlled corporation amounting to control, provided that in the latter case it is established that the retention of stock or securities of the controlled corporation is not for tax avoidance purposes (*see* § 355(a)(1)(D)).

If the above conditions are satisfied, then under § 355(a), the shareholders of the distributing corporation receive nonrecognition treatment on receipt of the stock of the controlled corporation. Thus, § 355(a) provides treatment analogous to § 354(a), which provides, for example, for nonrecognition treatment for a target's shareholders in an acquisitive reorganization. Also, under § 355(c), subject to certain exceptions discussed below, the distributing corporation receives nonrecognition treatment on the distribution of the stock of the controlled corporation. Thus, § 355(c) continues the nonrecognition treatment at the corporate level that was otherwise available under the *General Utilities* doctrine. To summarize, in a distribution of stock of a preexisting controlled corporation in a transaction satisfying the conditions of § 355(a), the shareholders of the distributing corporation receive nonrecognition under § 355(a), and the distributing corporation receives nonrecognition treatment under § 355(c).

To qualify as a divisive § 368(a)(1)(D) reorganization, three requirements must be satisfied. First, the distributing corporation must transfer all or a part of its assets to the controlled corporation. Second, immediately after the transfer, the distributing corporation, or one or more of its shareholders, or any combination thereof, must control, within the meaning of § 368(c), the controlled corporation. Finally, the stock or securities of the controlled corporation must be distributed in a transaction that qualifies under §§ 355 or 356. The tax treatment to the parties in the transaction is as follows. Under § 361(a), the distributing corporation receives nonrecognition on the transfer of its assets in exchange for stock and securities of the controlled corporation. Therefore, the distributing corporation takes a § 358 substituted basis for the stock or securities received. Section 351 also applies to this part of the transaction. The controlled corporation has nonrecognition under § 1032 and § 1.61-12(c) upon the issuance of its stock and securities and takes a carryover basis for the assets received under § 362. Subject to certain exceptions noted below, the distributing corporation has nonrecognition under § 361(c) upon the distribution of the stock and securities of the controlled corporation, thus, continuing the *General Utilities* doctrine. Thus, § 361(c) provides analogous nonrecognition treatment to that provided in § 355(c).

The shareholders of the distributing corporation have nonrecognition treatment under §355(a)(1) if they receive solely stock and no boot. *See* §355(a)(3).

If the shareholders of the distributing corporation exchange stock in the distributing corporation for stock in the controlled corporation plus boot, the boot gain and boot dividend rules of §356(a) apply. If, however, they receive a distribution of stock of the controlled corporation plus boot, without exchanging stock of the distributing corporation, the boot is treated as a §301 dividend. *See* §356(b). Under §358, the shareholders of the distributing corporation divide the basis of their shares of the distributing corporation before the distribution between the stock of the distributing corporation and the stock of the controlled corporation in accordance with the relative fair market values of the two. *See* §§358(b) and (c).

Under the disqualified distribution rule of §355(d) or the distribution in connection with an acquisition rule of §355(e) (*see* Sec. 9.6), the distributing corporation will recognize gain on the distribution of the stock of the controlled corporation.

Finally, §§351(c)(2) and 368(a)(2)(H)(ii) provide that where the requirements of §355 are met the following shall not be taken into account in determining control for purposes of §351 or of the divisive (D): "the fact that the shareholders of the distributing corporation dispose of part or all of the distributed stock, or the fact that the corporation whose stock was distributed issues additional stock * * *" This applies with respect to §351 "solely for purposes of determining the tax treatment of the transfers of property to the controlled corporation by the distributing corporation." In the case of the divisive (D), this applies in the case of a transaction with respect to which the requirements of §355 are met. These provisions, in essence, allow the shareholders of the distributing corporation to dispose of the stock of the controlled corporation without adversely affecting the spin-off. These provisions are important in *Morris Trust* transactions. *See* Sec. 9.6.

§9.3 Legislative Background on the (D) Reorganization under §§355 and 354(b)

A. Legislative Developments through 1954

1. Mrs. Gregory's Transaction under the 1924 Act

The (D) was first added to the tax law by the Revenue Act of 1924. As demonstrated in *Gregory v. Helvering*, Sec. 2.11.B., this provision was used by Mrs. Gregory in her attempt to receive capital gains rather than ordinary dividends and to avoid the corporate tax upon the disposition of Monitor securities held by her wholly owned corporation, United Mortgage. Mrs. Gregory caused United Mortgage to form Averill corporation and to transfer the Monitor securities to Averill. Averill was then spun-off to Mrs. Gregory, who promptly liquidated it, receiving and then selling the Monitor shares. She argued that the transaction was a tax-free spin-off, followed by a taxable liquidation that produced capital gain to her and a fair market value basis for the

Monitor shares. The Supreme Court held that, because the transaction was devoid of a business purpose, it was not a reorganization.

The provision Mrs. Gregory relied on in claiming tax-free treatment upon the receipt of the Averill securities in the "distribution" from Monitor was repealed in the 1934 Act. The (D) transaction remained a part of the law, but only for exchange transactions in which stock or securities of the distributing corporation were exchanged for stock or securities of the controlled corporation.

2. The 1951 Act

In 1951, Congress added to the 1939 Code § 112(b)(11), the initial predecessor to § 355. This provision permitted the traditional *Gregory* spin-off so long as it did not "appear" that (1) any of the corporations would fail to continue the active conduct of a trade or business, and (2) the transaction was used principally as a "device" for the distribution of E & P.

3. The 1954 Act

In 1954 Congress carried over from the 1939 Code the basic definition of the (D) reorganization. The Senate Report to the 1954 Code (273–274) explains:

> Subparagraph (D) of [§ 368(a)(1)] restates the definition of existing law appearing in section 112(g)(1)(D) of the Internal Revenue Code of 1939. Under this definition the term "reorganization" includes a transfer by a corporation of all or a part of its assets to another corporation if immediately after such transfer the transferor corporation, or its shareholders, or both, are in control of the transferee. Your committee's bill has altered the definition to provide that if the control of the transferee corporation is in the transferor corporation or in persons who were shareholders of the transferor, or any combination thereof, the transfer will, nevertheless, qualify as a reorganization under section 368(a)(1)(D), the control owned by these persons need not be in the same proportion as it was before the transfer. For example, corporation A owns only properties connected with a drug store and a hardware store. Corporation A transfers the drug store properties to corporation D in exchange for all the stock of D and transfers the hardware store properties to corporation H in exchange for all the stock of H. Immediately thereafter, corporation A distributes all the stock in corporation D to X, one of the two shareholders in A, in exchange for all of X's stock and distributes all the stock in corporation H to Y, the other shareholder in A, in exchange for all his stock. The distributions qualify under section 355. The transfer of the properties by A is a reorganization under subparagraph (D). It should be noted, however, that in the event that the values of the properties transferred to corporations D and H are disproportionate to the value of the stock in A held by shareholders X and Y, the transaction at the shareholder level may have the effect of a gift or a compensation. See section 355.

Subparagraph (D) also explicitly states that a transaction of the type described is only to be considered a reorganization when the stock and securities of the transferee corporation or corporations are distributed to the shareholders and security holders under the terms of section 354, 355, or 356. However, where there is no such distribution, the transaction may, nevertheless, result in nonrecognition of gain or loss to the transferor corporation under the terms of section 351.

Paragraph (2) of [§ 368(a)] lists three special rules which modify existing law. It is provided that if a transaction meets the description, both of an acquisition of assets for stock (subsec. (a)(1)(C)) and also meets the description of a transfer to a controlled corporation (subsec. (a)(1)(D)) it shall be treated as described only in subsection (a)(1)(D).

Your committee intends by this rule to insure that the tax consequences of the distribution of stocks or securities to shareholders or security holders in connection with divisive reorganizations will be governed by the requirements of section 355 relating to distribution of stock of a controlled corporation.

B. Legislative Developments Since 1954

1. 1987 Act: Prevention of Use of § 355 as Surrogate for a Mirror Transaction

See § 355(b)(2)(D).

House Report to the Revenue Act of 1987

1080–1084 (1987)

Present Law Gains on certain distributions to a controlling U.S. corporate shareholder (an 80-percent distributee) are not taxed to the distributing corporation in a liquidation (sec. 337). [*See* § 337(a).] * * *

Certain divisive distributions of corporate stock are also tax-free to the distributing corporation, provided that certain statutory and other constraints are met, including a condition that the transaction not be a device for the distribution of earnings and profits and certain other requirements (sec. 355). * * *

Reasons for Change The Tax Reform Act of 1986 changed the prior-law rules for the treatment of the distributing corporation on liquidating distributions. Such distributions are generally treated in the same manner as nonliquidating distributions, that is, as if the distributing corporation had sold the distributed property to the recipient at fair market value. * * *

The committee understands that some taxpayers take the position that an appreciated subsidiary may be sold or distributed outside the affiliated group without the current recognition of gain on the appreciation by the selling or distributing corporation.

Some of such taxpayers apparently take the position that the so-called "mirror" subsidiary transaction was not curtailed by the 1986 Act. * * *

The committee is also aware that some taxpayers take the position that certain other provisions of the Code may permit the creation of structures said to allow the sale or distribution of an appreciated corporate subsidiary without the recognition of current corporate level tax on the appreciation, or structures that have the effect of permitting one or more acquirors to acquire or resell corporate subsidiaries or other assets with more favorable tax results than the original owners could obtain. Such provisions include * * * the provisions of section 355 of the Code that, together with section 358 of the Code, permit a substituted basis when stock of one corporation is distributed by another corporation. Such provisions might be used to claim a stepped-up, fair market value basis when a subsidiary of an acquired corporation is distributed to the acquiring corporation. The committee believes that the requirements of section 355 of the Code should generally prevent the use of that section to accomplish a sale of a recently distributed subsidiary (or its recently acquired parent) without corporate level tax, or effectively to accomplish a sale of a subsidiary to any significant shareholder by a distribution with respect to recently purchased stock. * * *

Explanation of Provision * * * The bill provides that a distribution of stock will not qualify for nonrecognition under section 355 of the Code if control of a corporation which was conducting such business was acquired in a taxable transaction within the 5 year period ending on the date of the distribution through one or more corporations, including the distributing corporation. [*See* § 355(b)(2)(D).]

2. 1988 Act Amendment to § 355(c) Relating to Treatment of Distributing Corporation

House Report to Miscellaneous Revenue Act of 1988
371–373 (1988)

Present Law * * * The 1986 Act made a series of amendments to the reorganization provisions attempting to conform those provisions with changes made by the 1984 Act. However, numerous technical problems with the 1986 amendments have arisen. The bill responds to these technical problems with a complete revision of the 1986 amendments.

Explanation of Provision * * * *Treatment of section 355 distributions, etc.* * * * [G]ain (but not loss) will be recognized on the distribution of property other than the stock or securities in the controlled corporation in a transfer to which section 355 (or so much of section 356 as relates to section 355) applies. [*See* § 355(c).] * * *

3. 1990 Act: Potential Recognition of Gain in Certain Disqualified Distributions

See § 355(d).

Conference Report to Revenue Reconciliation Act of 1990

82–92 (1990)

Present Law A corporation generally must recognize gain on the sale or distribution of appreciated property, including stock of a subsidiary. However, corporate distributions of subsidiary stock that meet the requirements of section 355 of the Code are tax-free both to the distributing corporation and to the distributee shareholders.

Present law imposes a 5-year holding period requirement for any corporate distributee that has acquired 80 percent of the stock of a corporation ("target"), unless the stock was acquired solely in nontaxable transactions. If the 5-year holding period is not met, distributions of subsidiaries by the target corporation are not tax-free under section 355. [*See* § 355(b)(2)(D).] * * *

Conference Agreement * * * *In general* The conference agreement generally requires recognition of corporate-level gain (but does not require recognition by the distributee shareholders) on a distribution of subsidiary stock or securities qualifying under section 355 (whether or not part of a reorganization otherwise described in section 361(c)(2)) if, immediately after the distribution, a shareholder holds a 50-percent or greater interest in the distributing corporation or a distributed subsidiary that is attributable to stock or securities that were acquired by purchase (as defined in the provision) within the preceding 5-year period. [*See* § 355(d)(1) and (2).] Thus, for example, under the provision, the distributing corporation will recognize gain on the distribution of subsidiary stock and securities if a person purchases distributing corporation stock or securities, and within 5 years, 50 percent or more of the subsidiary stock is distributed to that person in exchange for the purchased stock or securities. The distributing corporation will recognize gain as if it had sold the distributed subsidiary stock and securities to the distributee at fair market value. * * *

Disqualified distribution A disqualified distribution is any section 355 distribution if, immediately after the distribution, any person holds disqualified stock in either the distributing corporation or any distributed controlled corporation constituting a 50-percent or greater interest in such corporation. [*See* § 355(d)(2).]

Disqualified stock The conference agreement defines disqualified stock to include any stock in the distributing corporation or any controlled corporation acquired by purchase (as defined) after October 9, 1990 and during the 5-year period ending on the date of the distribution. * * *

Assume that after the effective date individual A acquires by purchase a 20-percent interest in corporation P and P redeems stock of other shareholders so that A's interest in P increases to a 30 percent interest. Within 5 years of A's purchase, P distributes 50 percent of the stock of its subsidiary, S, to A in exchange for his 30 percent interest in P (the remainder of the stock of S distributed in the section 355 transaction is distributed to other shareholders). P recognizes gain on the distribution of the stock of S because all 50 percent of the stock of S held by A is disqualified stock.

Fifty percent or greater interest The conference agreement provides that a 50-percent or greater interest means stock possessing at least 50 percent of the total combined voting power of all classes of stock entitled to vote or at least 50 percent of the total value of all shares of all classes of stock. [*See* §355(d)(4).] * * *

Acquisition by purchase Stock or securities are generally considered acquired by purchase for purposes of the provision if they are acquired in any transaction in which the acquiror's basis of the stock or securities is not determined in whole or in part by reference to the adjusted basis of such stock or securities in the hands of the person from whom acquired and is not determined under section 1014(a). [*See* §355(d)(5).] * * *

Five-year period Gain is recognized under the provision in the case of a section 355 distribution within 5 years after a shareholder acquires stock or securities by purchase (if the shareholder meets the 50-percent or more ownership test immediately after the distribution). [*See* §335(d)(2) and (3).] * * *

Regulatory authority The Treasury Department has general regulatory authority (1) to prevent the avoidance of the purposes of the provision through any means, including through the use of related persons, intermediaries, pass-through entities, options, or other arrangements; and (2) to exclude from the provision transactions that do not violate the purposes of this provision. [*See* §355(d)(9).] * * *

Note and Question

On December 20, 2000 the Treasury issued final regulations under §355(d). *See* T.D. 8913 and Reg. §1.355-6.

How would the transaction in the *Esmark* case, *supra* Sec. 2.11.C., be taxed assuming that the redemption by Esmark of Mobile's stock in exchange for stock of Esmark's subsidiary, Vickers, qualified under §355?

4. The 1997 Act, Potential Recognition of Gain under §355(e) by Distributing Corporation on a Distribution in Connection with an Acquisition: Introduction to the Morris Trust Issue

As will be seen in Sec. 9.6, under the *Morris Trust* doctrine, it is possible to follow a spin-off with an acquisitive reorganization. However, under §355(e), which was added to the Code in 1997, a distributing corporation recognizes gain on the distribution of the stock of a controlled corporation if the distribution is "part of a plan (or series of related transactions) pursuant to which 1 or more persons acquire directly or indirectly stock representing a 50-percent or greater interest in the distributing corporation or any controlled corporation." *See* §355(e)(2)(A). Thus, for example, if pursuant to a preexisting plan, after a distribution of the stock of a controlled corporation in a §355 spin-off, an acquiring corporation acquired (for less than 50%

of its stock) in an acquisitive reorganization all of the stock of either the distributing corporation or the controlled corporation, the distributing corporation would be taxed on any gains inherent in the stock of the controlled corporation. Section 355(e), which significantly curtails the ability to utilize the *Morris Trust* doctrine, is examined below after a more in depth look at some of the basic provisions of § 355 that are applicable in conventional spin-offs.

5. The 2004 Act, Modification of Treatment of Creditors in Divisive Reorganizations by the American Jobs Creation Act of 2004

Conference Committee Report to the American Jobs Creation Act of 2004

H.R. Conf. Rep. No. 108-755(October 2004)
Conference Agreement followed the Senate Bill,
Senate Committee Report, S. Rep. No. 108-192

Present Law. Section 355 of the Code permits a corporation ("distributing") to separate its businesses by distributing a controlled subsidiary ("controlled") tax-free, if certain conditions are met. In cases where the distributing corporation contributes property to the controlled corporation that is to be distributed, no gain or loss is recognized if the property is contributed solely in exchange for stock or securities of the controlled corporation (which are subsequently distributed to distributing's shareholders). The contribution of property to a controlled corporation that is followed by a distribution of its stock and securities may qualify as a reorganization described in section 368(a)(1)(D). That section also applies to certain transactions that do not involve a distribution under section 355 and that are considered "acquisitive" rather than "divisive" reorganizations.

The contribution in the course of a divisive section 368(a)(1)(D) reorganization is also subject to the rules of section 357(c). That section provides that the transferor corporation will recognize gain if the amount of liabilities assumed by controlled exceeds the basis of the property transferred to it.

Because the contribution transaction in connection with a section 355 distribution is a reorganization under section 368(a)(1)(D), it is also subject to certain rules applicable to both divisive and acquisitive reorganizations. One such rule, in section 361(b), states that a transferor corporation will not recognize gain if it receives money or other property and distributes that money or other property to its shareholders or creditors. The amount of property that may be distributed to creditors without gain recognition is unlimited under this provision.

Reasons for Change. The Committee is concerned that taxpayers engaged in section 355 transactions can effectively avoid the rules that require gain recognition if the controlled corporation assumes liabilities of the transferor that exceed the basis of the assets transferred to such corporation. This could occur because of the rules of section 361(b), which state that the transferor can receive money or other property from the transferee without gain recognition, so long as the money or property is distributed to creditors of the transferor. For example, a transferor corporation could receive money from the transferee corporation (e.g., money obtained from a borrowing by the transferee) and use that money to pay the transferor's creditors, without gain recognition. Such a transaction is economically similar to the actual assumption by the transferee of the transferor's liabilities, but is taxed differently under present law because section 361(b) does not contain a limitation on the amount that can be distributed to creditors.

The Committee also believes that it is appropriate to liberalize the treatment of acquisitive reorganizations that are included under section 368(a)(1)(D). The Committee believes that in these cases, the transferor should be permitted to assume liabilities of the transferee without application of the rules of section 357(c). This is because in an acquisitive reorganization under section 368(a)(1)(D), the transferor must generally transfer substantially all its assets to the acquiring corporation and then go out of existence. Assumption of its liabilities by the acquiring corporation thus does not enrich the transferor corporation, which ceases to exist and whose liability was limited to its assets in any event, by corporate form. The Committee believes that it is appropriate to conform the treatment of acquisitive reorganizations under section 368(a)(1)(D) to that of other acquisitive reorganizations.

Explanation of Provision. [§§ 357 and 361] The bill limits the amount of money plus the fair market value of other property that a distributing corporation can distribute to its creditors without gain recognition under section 361(b) to the amount of the basis of the assets contributed to a controlled corporation in a divisive reorganization. In addition, the bill provides that acquisitive reorganizations under section 368(a)(1)(D) are no longer subject to the liabilities assumption rules of section 357(c).

6. Modification of the Active Trade or Business Test by the 2006 Act

See § 355(b)(3).

Amendments to Section 355 by the Tax Increase Prevention and Reconciliation Act of 2005 Signed into Law on May 10, 2006

House Committee Report (H.R. REP. NO. 109-304)

* * *

Reasons for Change

Prior to a spin-off under section 355 of the Code, corporate groups that have conducted business in separate corporate entities often must undergo elaborate restructurings to place active businesses in the proper entities to satisfy the five-year active business requirement. If the top-tier corporation of a chain that is being spun off or retained is a holding company, then the requirements regarding the activities of its subsidiaries are more stringent than if the top-tier corporation itself engaged in some active business. The Committee believes that it is appropriate to simplify planning for corporate groups that use a holding company structure to engage in distributions that qualify for tax-free treatment under section 355.

Explanation of Provision

Under the bill [*see* § 355(b)(3)], the active business test is determined by reference to the relevant affiliated group. For the distributing corporation, the relevant affiliated group consists of the distributing corporation as the common parent and all corporations affiliated with the distributing corporation through stock ownership described in section 1504(a)(1)(B) (regardless of whether the corporations are includible corporations under section 1504(b)), immediately after the distribution. The relevant affiliated group for a controlled corporation is determined in a similar manner (with the controlled corporation as the common parent).

7. Treatment of Disqualified Investment Companies under the 2006 Act

See § 355(g).

Amendments to Section 355 by the Tax Increase Prevention and Reconciliation Act of 2005 ("TIPRA") and Signed into Law on May 10 2006

Conference Committee Report (H.R. CONF. REP. NO. 109-455)

Senate Amendment

[The basic provisions provide:] [T]he Senate amendment contains [a] provision that denies section 355 treatment if either the distributing or distributed corporation is a disqualified investment corporation immediately after the transaction (including any series of related transactions) and any person that did not hold 50 percent or more of the voting power or value of stock of such distributing or controlled corporation immediately before the transaction does hold such a 50 percent or greater interest immediately after such transaction. The attribution rules of section 318 apply for purposes of this determination.

A disqualified investment corporation is any distributing or controlled corporation if the fair market value of the investment assets of the corporation is [two-thirds] or more of the fair market value of all assets of the corporation. Except as otherwise provided, the term "investment assets" for this purpose means (i) cash, (ii) any stock or securities in a corporation, (iii) any interest in a partnership, (iv) any debt instrument or other evidence of indebtedness[.] * * *

The term "investment assets" does not include any asset which is held for use in the active and regular conduct of [*inter alia*] (i) a lending or finance business (as defined in section 954(h)(4)); (ii) a banking business through a bank (as defined in section 581)[.] * * *

8. Restrictions on Spin-Offs of REITs (Real Estate Investment Trust) by the 2015 Act

Joint Committee on Taxation, Technical Explanation of the Protecting Americans from Tax Hikes Act of 2015, House Amendment #2 to the Senate Amendment to H.R. 2029 (Rules Committee Print 114-40)

December 17, 2015

Restriction on tax-free spin-offs involving REITs (sec. 311 of the bill and sec. 355 of the Code)

Present Law * * *

The IRS has ruled that a REIT [a real estate investment trust, which is generally a pass-through] may satisfy the active business requirement through its rental activities. * * *

Explanation of Provision

The provision makes a REIT generally ineligible to participate in a tax-free spin-off as either a distributing or controlled corporation under section 355. * * *

§ 9.4 Elaboration on the Regulations, Rulings and Cases

A. Introduction to the 1989 Regulations

Preamble to the § 355 Regulations

Treasury Decision 8238 (January 4, 1989)

* * * Section 355 provides that, under certain conditions, a corporation may distribute stock, or stock and securities, of a subsidiary without recognition of gain or loss to its shareholders or security holders. The proposed regulations made two major changes to the existing regulations under section 355. First, the regulations under section 355(a)(1)(B) (requiring that the transaction not be used principally as a device for the distribution of earnings and profits) were revised to specify factors to be taken into account in determining whether a transaction was used principally as such a device. Second, the regulations under section 355(b) (relating to active businesses) were revised to permit the separation of a single business, thereby conforming them to the holdings of *Commissioner v. Coady*, 289 F.2d 490 (6th Cir.1961), *aff'g* 33 T.C. 771 (1960), and *United States v. Marett*, 325 F.2d 28 (5th Cir.1963). The proposed regulations also proposed to clarify the business purpose requirement under section 355. * * *

B. The Business Purpose Requirement

1. The Regulations

See § 1.355-2(b).

Preamble to the § 355 Regulations

Treasury Decision 8238 (January 4, 1989)

Business Purpose (1) *Independent requirement.* Section 1.355-2(b)(1) of the proposed regulations expressed the business purpose requirement as an independent requirement under section 355. Commentors objected to the treatment of the business purpose requirement as a separate requirement and suggested that the existence of a corporate business purpose should be considered only in determining whether a transaction was used principally as a device for the distribution of earnings and profits within the meaning of section 355(a)(1)(B).

Treasury and the Internal Revenue Service acknowledge that there is a very close relationship between the business purpose requirement and the requirement that the transaction not be used principally as a device for the distribution of earnings and profits. Accordingly, the final regulations clarify that the corporate business purpose is evidence that the transaction was not used principally as such a device. See § 1.355-2(d)(3)(ii) in this document. This new provision is discussed below under the heading "Evidence of Nondevice."

However, Treasury and the Internal Revenue Service believe that, as held in *Commissioner v. Wilson,* 353 F.2d 184 (9th Cir.1965), a transaction that is not carried out for a corporate business purpose should not qualify under section 355, even if it was not used principally as a device for the distribution of earnings and profits. Accordingly, the final regulations retain the independent business purpose requirement. See § 1.355-2(b)(1) in this document.

(2) *Corporate business purpose.* Section 1.355-2(b)(1) of the proposed regulations provided that a distribution qualifies under section 355 only if it is carried out for one or more corporate business purposes. Corporate business purposes were identified as "real and substantial non-tax reasons germane to the business of the corporations."

Commentors objected to the "real and substantial" standard on the grounds that it is not useful and is confusing. However, Treasury and the Internal Revenue Service continue to believe that the "real and substantial" standard provides a useful description of the type of corporate business purpose required under section 355. Accordingly, the final regulations retain that standard. See § 1.355-2(b)(2) in this document.

Commentors requested reconsideration of the "non-tax" standard. The Internal Revenue Service has ruled that reduction of state and local capital taxes is a corporate business purpose. Rev. Rul. 76-187, 1976-1 C.B. 97. That rule will remain in effect. However, Treasury and the Internal Revenue Service continue to believe that reduction of Federal taxes should not be regarded as a corporate business purpose. Accordingly, the final regulations replace the "non-tax" standard with a "non Federal tax" standard.

Commentors wondered whether the potential reduction of Federal taxes will offset or negate the existence of a non-Federal tax business purpose. In response, the final regulations clarify that only a transaction motivated in whole or in substantial part by a corporate business purpose will satisfy the corporate business purpose requirement. Further, the final regulations clarify that the potential reduction of Federal taxes by the distributing or controlled corporations (or a corporation controlled by either) is relevant in determining whether a corporate business purpose motivated the distribution. The final regulations also provide that a purpose of reducing non Federal taxes is not a corporate business purpose if (i) the transaction will effect a reduction in both Federal and non Federal taxes because of similarities between Federal tax law and the tax law of the other jurisdiction and (ii) the reduction of Federal taxes is greater than or substantially coextensive with the reduction of non Federal taxes. See § 1.355-2(b)(1) and (2) in this document. Three examples are also added in § 1.355-2(b)(5). The first illustrates that a distribution which is made to enable the distributing and/or controlled corporation to make an election to be an S corporation does not meet the corporate business purpose requirement. The second example illustrates that the result is the same if the distribution is made to enable the distributing and/or controlled corporation to elect to become an S corporation both for Federal tax purposes and for purposes of a state that has tax law provisions similar to Subchapter S of the Internal Revenue Code of 1986. The third example illustrates that the magnitude of the potential reduction of Federal taxes is relevant to the determination of whether the distribution is motivated by a corporate business purpose.

(3) *Shareholder purpose.* Section 1.355-2(b)(1) of the proposed regulations provided that a distribution qualifies under section 355 only if it is carried out for purposes "germane to the business of the corporations." It further provided that "a shareholder purpose for a transaction may be so nearly coextensive with a corporate business purpose as to preclude any distinction between them. In such a case, the transaction is carried out for purposes germane to the business of the corporations." Some cementers complained that the proposed regulations did not adequately acknowledge that, in a closely held corporation, the purposes of the shareholders cannot be distinguished from those of the corporation. Other cementers complained that the proposed regulations addressed cases in which the shareholder purposes are totally coextensive with the corporate business purposes, but failed to address the more common cases in which there is only partial overlap.

In response, the final regulations revise example (2) of § 1.355-2(b)(2) of the proposed regulations to present a disproportionate distribution that satisfies the business purpose requirement without a shareholder disagreement. *See* example (2) of § 1.355-2(b)(5) in this document. * * *

(4) *Business purposes for distribution.* The final regulations provide that the distribution of the stock, or stock and securities, of the controlled corporation to the shareholders must be carried out for one or more corporate business purposes. In example (3) of § 1.355-2(b)(2) of the proposed regulations, the distribution is not carried out for a corporate business purpose. The alleged corporate business purpose for the trans-

action is protection of a business from the risks of another business. Because that purpose is satisfied as soon as the risky business is dropped down to a subsidiary, the distribution of the stock of the subsidiary is not carried out for that purpose. * * *

(5) *Availability of alternative arrangement.* Example (4) of § 1.355-2(b)(2) of the proposed regulations involves a transfer by the distributing corporation of one of its two businesses to a new controlled corporation and a distribution of the stock of the controlled corporation where the transfer and the distribution are required by a lender as a condition on additional loans. The example concludes that the distribution was carried out for one or more corporate business purposes. Cementers asked whether the distribution in example (4) would be carried out for one or more corporate business purposes if the lender would have been satisfied to have the distributing corporation transfer its two businesses to two new controlled corporations and continue as a holding company.

Treasury and the Internal Revenue Service believe that a distribution satisfies the business purpose requirement only if the distributing corporation cannot achieve its corporate business purpose through a nontaxable transaction that does not involve a distribution of the stock of a subsidiary and that is neither impractical nor unduly expensive. Thus, if such an alternative transaction is available, the distribution is not carried out for a corporate business purpose. Accordingly, example (4) is replaced by new examples illustrating this aspect of the business purpose requirement. *See* examples (4) and (5) of § 1.355-2(b)(5) in this document.

2. Illustration of Corporate Business Purpose That Also
Serves a Shareholder Purpose

Revenue Ruling 2004-23
I.R.B. 2004-11, February 13, 2004

ISSUE. Whether a distribution that is expected to cause the aggregate value of the stock of a distributing corporation and the stock of a controlled corporation to exceed the pre-distribution value of the distributing corporation's stock satisfies the corporate business purpose requirement of § 355 of the Internal Revenue Code and § 1.355-2(b) of the Income Tax Regulations when the increased value is expected to serve a corporate business purpose of either the distributing corporation or the controlled corporation (or both), even if it benefits the shareholders of the distributing corporation.

FACTS. D is a corporation that indirectly conducts Business 1 and Business 2 through its subsidiaries. Some subsidiaries engage only in Business 1 and others only in Business 2. D's common stock is widely held and publicly traded.

The two businesses attract different investors, some of which are averse to investing in D because of the presence of the other business. Therefore, D believes, and D's investment banker has advised D, that if each business were conducted in a separate and independent corporation, the stock of the two corporations likely would trade publicly for a higher price, in the aggregate, than the stock of D if it continued to represent an interest in both businesses. The expected increase in the aggregate trading price of the stock of D and C over the pre-distribution trading price of D would not, however, derive in any significant respect from any Federal tax advantage made available to either D or C by the transaction.

With the intent and expectation of increasing the aggregate trading price of the common stock representing Business 1 and Business 2, D transfers the subsidiaries that engage in Business 2 to a newly formed corporation, C, in exchange for all of the C stock and distributes the C stock to its common shareholders, pro rata. D's remaining subsidiaries will continue to conduct Business 1.

Increasing the aggregate trading price of the D and C common stock over the trading price of the pre-distribution D common stock is expected to confer a benefit to existing shareholders. In deciding whether to undertake the distribution, D's directors consider this expected benefit to the shareholders, as well as the expected benefits to the corporation described below. However, D's directors do not effect the distribution to facilitate any particular shareholder's disposition of the stock of either D or C.

Apart from the issue of whether the business purpose requirement of § 1.355-2(b) is satisfied, the distribution meets the requirements of §§ 368(a)(1)(D) and 355.

Situation 1. D uses equity-based incentives as a significant part of its program to compensate a significant number of employees of both Business 1 and Business 2. D's directors wish to enhance the value of employee compensation and have considered either granting additional equity-based incentives or making cash payments in lieu of additional equity incentives. However, granting additional equity-based incentives would unacceptably dilute D's existing shareholders' interests, and making cash payments would be unduly expensive. Therefore, D undertakes the separation of Business 2 from Business 1 with the expectation that its stock value will increase and such increase will enhance the value of its equity-based compensation, providing D with a real and substantial benefit.

Situation 2. As part of its overall strategic planning, D has expanded both Business 1 and Business 2 through acquisitions of assets and the stock of other corporations. In some of these acquisitions, D has used its stock, either in whole or in part, as consideration. D's directors expect to continue expanding Business 1 as appropriate acquisition opportunities are identified in the future. D expects to offer its common stock as consideration, either in whole or in part, in connection with future acquisitions. Therefore D undertakes the separation of Business 2 from Business 1 with the expectation that its stock value will increase and such increase may permit D to effect such acquisitions in a manner that preserves capital with significantly less dilution of the existing shareholders' interests, providing D with a real and substantial benefit. * * *

LAW.* * *

HOLDING. A distribution that is expected to cause the aggregate value of the stock of a distributing corporation and the stock of a controlled corporation to exceed the pre-distribution value of the distributing corporation's stock satisfies the corporate business purpose requirement of § 355 and § 1.355-2(b) when the increased value is expected to serve a corporate business purpose of either the distributing corporation or the controlled corporation (or both), even if it benefits the shareholders of the distributing corporation. * * *

C. Device for Distribution of Earnings and Profits

1. The Regulations

See § 1.355-2(b).

Preamble to the § 355 Regulations

Treasury Decision 8238 (January 4, 1989)

In General Section 1.355-2(c) of the proposed regulations interpreted the requirement of section 355(a)(1)(B) that the transaction not be used principally as a device for the distribution of earnings and profits of the distributing corporation, the controlled corporation, or both (a "device"). That interpretation consisted of a description of the tax avoidance that could be achieved through the use of a device, a specification of factors ("device factors") whose presence is evidence that the transaction was used principally as a device ("evidence of device"), and a specification of certain transactions that ordinarily would not be considered to be a device for the distribution of earnings and profits. The final regulations generally retain these provisions. At the request of cementers, they also specify factors ("nondevice factors") whose presence is evidence that the transaction was not used principally as a device ("evidence of non-device"). See § 1.355-2(d) in this document.

Section 1.355-2(c)(1) of the proposed regulations explained that a corporate separation can present potential for the avoidance of the dividend provisions of the Code. The final regulations make clear that avoidance potential is presented by the substitution of stock interests in two or more corporations for a stock interest in a single corporation. In particular, avoidance potential can be presented by distributions in which the distributing corporation liquidates as well as by distributions in which the distributing corporation does not liquidate. The final regulations also replace the reference to sales or liquidations with a reference to sales, exchanges, or transactions that are treated as exchanges under the Code, thus making clear that redemptions as well as liquidations are covered by the rules. They also limit the rules to transactions involving stock on the grounds that sections 355(a)(3) and 356(d)(2)(C) generally render transactions involving securities incapable of use to avoid the dividend provisions of the Code. At the request of cementers, the final regulations clarify that the determination whether a transaction was used principally as a device depends on all of the facts and circumstances, and that the presence of the device factors specified in § 1.355-2(d)(2) is not alone controlling. See § 1.355-2(d)(1) in this document. The final regulations also make clear that a device can include a transaction that effects a recovery of basis.

The provision in § 1.355-2(c)(1) of the proposed regulations regarding pro rata distributions is clarified and made a separate provision in the final regulations. See § 1.355-2(d)(2)(ii) in this document. Certain transactions that are ordinarily considered not to have been used principally as a device are specified in a separate provision in the final regulations. As suggested by cementers, that provision clarifies that these transactions are ordinarily considered not to have been used principally as a device, notwithstanding the presence of any of the device factors specified in § 1.355-2(d)(2). See § 1.355-2(d)(5) in this document.

Nature And Use Of Assets. Assets not used in a qualifying trade or business. Section 1.355-2(c)(3)(iii) of the proposed regulations provided that the transfer or retention of cash or liquid assets in excess of the reasonable needs of the post-distribution business of the transferee or the retaining corporation ("excess liquid assets") is evidence of device. Some cementers agreed that the transfer of excess liquid assets should be evidence of device, but asserted that the retention of excess liquid assets should be a neutral factor. Other cementers noted that, because liquid assets must either be transferred or retained, the proposed regulations appeared to find evidence of device whenever excess liquid assets are present.

Section 1.355-2(c)(3)(ii) of the proposed regulations provided that, if a substantial portion of the post-distribution assets of the distributing or the controlled corporation consists of a trade or business acquired during the five-year period preceding the distribution in a transaction in which the basis of the assets was not determined in whole or in part by reference to the transferor's basis, this fact is evidence of device (the "new trade or business device factor"). Some cementers objected to this device factor on the grounds that the acquisition of a trade or business should be treated under the active business requirements of section 355(b) instead of the device clause of section 355(a)(1)(B). They pointed out that section 355(b)(2)(C) denies qualification under section 355 to a distribution after which the only trade or business of the distributing or the controlled corporation is a trade or business that was acquired during the five-year period preceding the distribution in a transaction in which the basis of the assets was not determined in whole or in part by reference to the transferor's basis. Other cementers objected to this device factor on the grounds that the presence of operating assets, even if newly acquired, should not be evidence of device. They argued that operating assets are not suitable for use in a device.

Treasury and the Internal Revenue Service believe that the presence of excess liquid assets permits avoidance of the dividend provisions of the Code, regardless of the corporation that holds them. Treasury and the Internal Revenue Service also believe that the active business requirements of section 355(b) do not render unnecessary the principle of the new trade or business device factor of § 1.355-2(c)(3)(ii) of the proposed regulations. * * *

Accordingly, the final regulations provide that the existence of assets that are not used in a trade or business that satisfies the requirements of section 355(b) is evidence of device. * * *

Related function. Section 1.355-2(c)(3)(iv) of the proposed regulations provided that the continued integration of a function with the business from which it has been separated is evidence of device. Cementers objected to this device factor on the grounds that the specified conditions present no compelling evidence of device.

Treasury and the Internal Revenue Service believe that the continued integration of a function with the business from which it has been separated should be evidence of device. This belief is based on the interpretation of section 355(a)(1)(B) expressed in § 1.355-2(c)(1) of the proposed regulations. Under certain circumstances, continued integration indicates a likelihood of avoidance of the dividend provisions of the Code. * * *

Evidence Of Nondevice Section 1.355-2(c)(1), (2), and (3) of the proposed regulations specified device factors whose presence is evidence of device. At the request of cementers, the final regulations specify several nondevice factors whose presence is evidence of nondevice. See § 1.355-2(d)(3) in this document. * * *

The final regulations provide that the corporate business purposes for a transaction present evidence of nondevice. In accordance with the facts and circumstances standard of § 1.355-2(c)(1) of the proposed regulations, the strength of this evidence depends on all of the facts and circumstances. The final regulations adopt a sliding scale approach. Thus, the greater the evidence of device, the stronger the corporate business purpose necessary to outweigh that evidence. Evidence of device presented by a disproportionate allocation of assets not used in a trade or business that satisfies the requirements of section 355(b) can be outweighed by the presence of a strong corporate business purpose for that allocation. The final regulations also specify nonexclusive factors to be taken into account in assessing the strength of a corporate business purpose. See § 1.355-2(d)(3)(ii) in this document.

The final regulations specify other nondevice factors. One of these nondevice factors is that the distributing corporation is publicly traded and has no shareholders who hold large blocks of stock. See § 1.355-2(d)(3)(iii) in this document. Another nondevice factor is that all of the distributees are domestic corporations that would be entitled to the deduction under section 243(a)(1) available to corporations meeting the stock ownership requirements of section 243(c), 243(a)(2), 243(a)(3), or 245(b) if the distribution were taxable as a dividend. See § 1.355-2(d)(3)(iv) in this document.

Examples In light of the changes made to the device rules in the final regulations, the examples in § 1.355-2(c)(4) of the proposed regulations are replaced by new examples. The examples illustrate the application of the facts and circumstances device standard of § 1.355-2(d)(1) and the balancing of the evidence of device presented by the device factors specified in § 1.355(d)(2) against the evidence of nondevice presented by the corporate business purpose nondevice factor specified in § 1.355-2(d)(3)(ii). See § 1.355-2(d)(4) in this document.

Example (1) illustrates that the transaction will be considered to have been used principally as a device if there is a subsequent sale of stock by a shareholder to a key employee that is negotiated or agreed upon before the distribution, even though the employee could have acquired an equivalent amount of stock directly from the corporation. * * *

Transactions Ordinarily Not A Device Section 1.355-2(c)(1) of the proposed regulations specified two transactions that are ordinarily not considered to be a device for the distribution of earnings and profits. The final regulations specify those trans-actions in a separate provision. As suggested by cementers, that provision clarifies that such a transaction is ordinarily considered not to have been used principally as a device, notwithstanding the presence of any of the device factors specified in § 1.355-2(d)(2). See § 1.355-2(d)(5)(i) in this document.

Section 1.355-2(c)(1) of the proposed regulations accorded a presumption against device to a distribution if, in the absence of section 355, no part of a distribution of money by the distributing corporation, the controlled corporation, or any corporation controlled, directly or indirectly, by either of those corporations would be taxable as a dividend because of the absence of earnings and profits.

Cementers questioned the relevance of the earnings and profits of the corporations other than the distributing corporation. They argued that the dividend avoidance interpretation of section 355(a)(1)(B) expressed in § 1.355-2(c)(1) of the proposed regulations made only the earnings and profits of the distributing corporation relevant. Treasury and the Internal Revenue Service, however, believe that the earnings and profits of both the distributing and controlled corporations must be taken into account, and the final regulations so provide. See § 1.355-2(d)(5)(ii) in this document. Also, the application of the presumption must take into account the possibility that a distribution by the distributing corporation would create earnings and profits if section 355 did not apply. * * *

The final regulations also clarify that a transaction to which section 302(a) or 303(a) would apply if section 355 did not is not accorded the presumption against device if it involves the distribution of the stock of more than one controlled corpo-ration and facilitates the avoidance of the dividend provisions of the Code through the subsequent sale or exchange of the stock of one corporation and the retention of the stock of another. The final regulations also add an example of a transaction that is not accorded the presumption because it presents such tax avoidance potential. See example (2) of § 1.355-2(d)(5)(v) in this document.

2. Illustration: Non-Pro Rata Split-Off

Revenue Ruling 71-383

1971-2 C.B. 180

Advice has been requested as to the Federal income tax consequences of a non-pro rata distribution by a corporation of stock of a controlled corporation to certain of its shareholders in exchange for 85 percent of their stock in the distributing cor-poration, under the circumstances described below.

In 1968, *X,* a widely held corporation, acquired all of the outstanding stock of *Y* corporation, which was owned by two shareholders (*A* and *B*), in a transaction qualifying as a reorganization within the meaning of section 368(a)(1)(B) of the Internal Revenue Code of 1954. No gain or loss was recognized in whole or in part in that transaction. Both corporations had been engaged in the active conduct of their respective business for more than five years. *X* corporation was engaged in the business of developing and manufacturing custom components for high technology industries. *Y* was engaged in the business of designing and manufacturing of microwave instrumentation.

In 1970, for valid business reasons, *X* distributed all of the stock of *Y* to *A* and *B* in exchange for 85 percent of the *X* stock of each which was equal in fair market value to the *Y* stock received. Immediately prior to the exchange a substantial capital contribution was made by *X* to *Y* in order to reduce the disparity in the market values of the respective stocks. The capital contribution did not cause a change in the character of *Y's* business. The *X* stock owned by *A* and *B*, was less than five percent of the outstanding *X* stock and consisted solely of the stock received pursuant to the reorganization in 1968. *A* and *B* were completely unrelated to the other shareholders of *X*. * * *

A substantial capital contribution made to a subsidiary by its parent prior to a distribution of the subsidiary's stock to the parent's shareholders may be considered evidence of a device under section 355(a)(1)(B) of the Code. However, in the instant case, if the distribution were considered taxable, it would not result in dividend income to the two shareholders receiving *Y* stock because the exchange of their *X* stock as to each would have been a substantially disproportionate redemption under section 302(b)(2) of the Code and thus would have been treated as a distribution in part or full payment in exchange for such stock under section 302(a) of the Code. Consequently, the transaction is not a device to distribute earnings and profits (that is, to convert dividend income into capital gains) * * *.

Accordingly, no gain or loss is recognized to *A* and *B* upon the receipt of the *Y* stock in exchange for their *X* stock under section 355(a) of the Code.

D. Continuity of Interest Requirement: The Regulations

See § 1.355-2(c).

Preamble to the § 355 Regulations

Treasury Decision 8238 (January 4, 1989)

Continuity Of Interest Section 1.355-2(b)(1) of the proposed regulations provided that section 355 contemplates a continuity of interest in all or part of the business enterprise on the part of those persons who, directly or indirectly, were the owners of the enterprise prior to the distribution or exchange. There was concern it could be argued that the phrase "all or part" meant a transaction could qualify even if none of the owners of the enterprise before the separation had, after the distribution, an interest in the business enterprise of one of the separated corporations. The final regulations make clear that the separation must effect only a readjustment of continuing interests in the property of the distributing and controlled corporations. In this regard, section 355 requires that one or more persons who, directly or indirectly, were the owners of the enterprise prior to the distribution or exchange own, in the aggregate, an amount of stock establishing a continuity of interest in each of the modified corporate forms in which the enterprise is conducted after the separation.

These rules have been relocated in a new § 1.355-2(c). Four examples illustrating the continuity of interest requirement are added, the principles of which are based on previously published revenue rulings. See Rev. Rul. 69-293, 1969-1 C.B. 102 and Rev. Rul. 79-293, 1979-2 C.B. 125.

E. Active Conduct of a Trade or Business Requirement

1. The Regulations

See § 1.355-3.

Preamble to the § 355 Regulations

Treasury Decision 8238 (January 4, 1989)

Active Conduct of a Trade or Business (1) *In general.* Section 1.355-3 of the proposed regulations interpreted the active business requirements of section 355(b). The final regulations retain those provisions and make clarifying revisions to § 1.355-3(b)(2)(iii) (the "active conduct" requirement of section 355(b)(2)(A)) and § 1.355-3(b)(3) (the "five-year active conduct" requirement of section 355(b)(2)(B)).

Section 1.355-3(b)(2)(iii) of the proposed regulations provided that the active conduct of a trade or business requires the performance of active and substantial management and operational functions. Cementers inquired whether a corporation may satisfy that requirement if some or all of its activities are performed by independent contractors. In response, the final regulations clarify that, in determining whether a corporation is actively conducting a trade or business, the activities performed by persons outside the corporation, including independent contractors, generally will not be taken into account. However, a corporation may satisfy that requirement through the activities that it performs directly, even though other activities are performed by independent contractors. See § 1.355-3(b)(2)(iii) in this document.

The final regulations slightly revise examples (1), (2), and (3) of § 1.355-3(c) of the proposed regulations to explain why the described activities do not satisfy the active business requirements. Example (1) illustrates that the holding of investment securities is not the active conduct of a trade or business. See § 1.355-3(b)(2)(iv)(A) in this document. This example is consistent with Rev.Rul. 66-204, 1966 C.B. 113, which holds that activity generated by trading in stock and securities held for one's own account is an investment function and is not the active conduct of a trade or business within the meaning of section 355. Examples (2) and (3) illustrate that the activities relied upon to satisfy the active business requirements must have been actively conducted throughout the five-year period preceding the distribution. See § 1.355-3(b)(3) in this document.

(2) *Separation of a single business.* The proposed regulations provided for the separation of a single business in § 1.355-1(a). They interpreted the five-year active conduct requirement accordingly in § 1.355-3(b)(3). The final regulations retain these provisions. They redesignate example (10) of § 1.355-3(c) of the proposed regulations, which was based on *Commissioner v. Coady,* 289 F.2d 490 (6th Cir.1961), *aff'g* 33 T.C. 771 (1960), as example (4). They redesignate example (11) of § 1.355-3(c) of the pro-

posed regulations, which was based on *United States v. Marett,* 325 F.2d 28 (5th Cir.1963), as example (5) and revise it to conform more closely to the facts of that case. See examples (4) and (5) of § 1.355-3(c) in this document.

(3) *Single or multiple businesses.* In reexamining the active business requirements, Treasury and the Internal Revenue Service recognized that it is often difficult to determine whether a corporation is conducting a single business, which may be separated under section 355 if it has been actively conducted for five years, or multiple businesses, which may be separated from each other under section 355 only if each has been actively conducted for five years. Correlatively, they recognized that it is difficult to determine whether a corporate expenditure for a new activity constitutes the acquisition or creation of a new business or the expansion of an existing business. Accordingly, it is considered to be appropriate to simplify these determinations.

As in *Estate of Lockwood v. Commissioner,* 350 F.2d 712 (8th Cir.1965), the final regulations provide that, for purposes of the five-year active conduct requirement, a new activity in the same line of business as an activity that has been actively conducted by the distributing corporation for the five-year period preceding the distribution ordinarily will not be considered a separate business. As a result, the distribution of a new activity will more easily satisfy the five-year active conduct requirement. See § 1.355-3(b)(3)(ii) in this document.

In example (12) of § 1.355-3(c) of the proposed regulations, a department store that was constructed within the preceding five years is separated from a department store business that has been actively conducted for nine years. The separation satisfies the five-year active conduct requirement because the newly constructed department store became part of the existing business. The final regulations revise example (12) and redesignate it as example (7). Example (7) illustrates that the five-year active conduct requirement is met, whether or not the new and old stores are operated as a single unit prior to the separation. The final regulations also add a new example (8) to illustrate that the same result obtains, whether the new activity results from internal corporate expansion or is purchased as a going concern. See examples (7) and (8) of § 1.355-3(c) in this document.

(4) *Functional separations.* The proposed regulations provided for the separation of a single business in § 1.355-1(a). They interpreted the five-year active conduct requirement accordingly in § 1.355-3(b)(3). Examples (8), (9), and (14) of § 1.355-3(c) of the proposed regulations presented separations of businesses along functional lines satisfying the active business requirements. These examples are grouped together as examples (9), (10), and (11) in the final regulations. Example (14) of the proposed regulations presented the separation of a research department from a business engaged in the manufacture and sale of household products. The final regulations redesignate example (14) as example (9) and revise it to illustrate that the separation satisfies the active business requirements, whether the research department subsequently provides services only to the business from which it was separated or also to others. See examples (9), (10), and (11) of § 1.355-3(c) in this document. It should be noted that functional separations may present evidence of device under § 1.355-2(d)(2)(iv)(C).

(5) *Owner-occupied real estate.* The proposed regulations interpreted the active business requirements to permit functional separations. Cementers noted that, in appropriate cases, the separation of real estate occupied by its owner prior to the distribution ("owner-occupied real estate") should satisfy those requirements. Treasury and the Internal Revenue Service recognize that the separation of owner-occupied real estate may satisfy the active business requirements, but they also recognize that such a separation presents significant tax avoidance opportunities. Accordingly, the final regulations revise §1.355-3(b)(2)(iv)(B) of the proposed regulations to provide that the separation of owner-occupied real estate will be subject to careful scrutiny under the active business requirements. Also, such a separation may be subject to close examination under the related function device factor of §1.355-2(d)(2)(iv)(C). * * *

2. The Anti Yahoo Spin-Off of Alibaba Notice and Revenue Ruling

[This Notice and Rev. Proc. apparently were issued in response to the IRS's decision not to issue Yahoo a private letter ruling on its planned spin-off of it very valuable stock position in Alibaba in a transaction in which there would have been a very small active trade of business in the company that was spun off.]

Notice 2015-59

Internal Revenue Bulletin: 2015-40 (October 5, 2015)

Request for Comments; Areas under Study Relating to §§337(d) and 355 of the Internal Revenue Code

SECTION 1. PURPOSE

The Treasury Department and the Internal Revenue Service (Service) are studying issues under §§337(d) [*see* Chapter 2 and 355 of the Internal Revenue Code (Code) relating to transactions having one or more of the following characteristics: (i) ownership by the distributing corporation or the controlled corporation of investment assets, within the meaning of §355(g)(2)(B), with modifications (Investment Assets), having substantial value in relation to (a) the value of all of such corporation's assets and (b) the value of the assets of the active trade(s) or business(es) on which the distributing corporation or the controlled corporation relies to satisfy the requirements of §355(b) (a Qualifying Business or Qualifying Business Assets); (ii) a significant difference between the distributing corporation's ratio of Investment Assets to assets other than Investment Assets and such ratio of the controlled corporation; (iii) ownership by the distributing corporation or the controlled corporation of a small amount of Qualifying Business Assets in relation to all of its assets; and (iv) an election by the distributing corporation or the controlled corporation (but not both) to be a regulated investment company (RIC), within the meaning of §851, or a real estate investment trust (REIT), within the meaning of §856 [The concerns with RICs and REITs "conversion transactions" is not discussed further here.]

Concurrently with the issuance of this notice, the Service is issuing Rev. Proc. 2015-43, page 467, this Bulletin, which supplements Rev. Proc. 2015-3, 2015-1 I.R.B. 129, by adding certain of these transactions to the list of no-rule areas. This notice describes transactions that concern the Treasury Department and the Service, including transactions on which, while the relevant areas are under study, the Service ordinarily will not rule under sections 4.01(57) and (58) of Rev. Proc. 2015-3 (section 3.01 of Rev. Proc. 2015-43) and transactions on which the Service will not rule under section 5.01(26) of Rev. Proc. 2015-3 (section 3.02 of Rev. Proc. 2015-43). [As indicated previously, a tax attorney dealing with any issue should always consult the IRS's current "no ruling" revenue procedure, which is normally the third revenue procedure issued each year, such as Rev. Proc. 2016-3.] This notice also requests comments concerning the transactions described in this notice.

SECTION 2. DISCUSSION

Background. Section 355 of the Code generally provides that, if certain requirements are satisfied, a distributing corporation may distribute the stock (or stock and securities) of a controlled corporation to its shareholders and security holders without the distributing corporation, its shareholders, or its security holders recognizing income, gain, or loss on the distribution. However, § 355 does not apply to a distribution if the transaction is used principally as a device for the distribution of the earnings and profits of the distributing corporation or the controlled corporation or both (a device). Section 355(a)(1)(B). Numerous other requirements also must be satisfied for § 355 to apply to a distribution.

One such requirement is that the distributing corporation and the controlled corporation each be engaged in the active conduct of a trade or business immediately after the distribution (active trade or business requirement). Section 355(a)(1)(C) and (b)(1)(A). For this purpose, § 355(b)(3)(A) provides that all members of a corporation's separate affiliated group are treated as one corporation. Another such requirement is that the transaction must be carried out for one or more corporate business purposes (business purpose requirement). Section 1.355-2(b)(1).

The Treasury Department and the Service have become aware, in part through requests for letter rulings [*e.g.*, the Yahoo letter ruling regarding its planned Alibaba spin-off], that some taxpayers are taking the position that certain distributions that have one or more of the characteristics described in section 1 of this notice satisfy the requirements of § 355. The Treasury Department and the Service believe that these transactions may present evidence of device for the distribution of earnings and profits, may lack an adequate business purpose or a Qualifying Business, or may violate other § 355 requirements. In addition, these transactions may circumvent the purposes of Code provisions intended to repeal the Supreme Court's decision in *General Utilities & Operating Co. v. Helvering*, 296 U.S. 200 (1935) (*General Utilities repeal*) [*see* Chapter 2]. See, e.g., §§ 311(b), 337(d), 367(a)(5), and 367(e); H.R. Rep. No. 100-391, at 1080–1084 (1987).

Nature of Assets of Distributing Corporation and Controlled Corporation. The Treasury Department and the Service are most concerned about transactions that result in (i) the distributing corporation or the controlled corporation owning a substantial amount of cash, portfolio stock or securities, or other Investment Assets, in relation to the value of all of its assets and its Qualifying Business Assets, and (ii) one of the corporations having a significantly higher ratio of Investment Assets to Non-Investment Assets than the other corporation. While these matters are under study, the Service will not rule on any issue that relates to the qualification of a distribution under § 355 and related provisions and is presented in a distribution described in section 5.01(26) of Rev. Proc. 2015-3. [Section 5.01(26) says that the Service will not rule on "[A]ny issue relating to the qualification, under § 355 and related provisions, of a distribution, or another distribution which is part of the same plan or series of related transactions, if, immediately after any such distribution, all of the following conditions exist: (i) the fair market value of the investment assets of the distributing corporation or the controlled corporation is two-thirds or more of the total fair market value of its gross assets; (ii) the fair market value of the gross assets of the trade(s) or business(es) on which the distributing corporation or the controlled corporation relies to satisfy the active trade or business requirement of § 355(b) is less than 10 percent of the fair market value of its investment assets; and (iii) the ratio of the fair market value of the investment assets to the fair market value of the assets other than investment assets of the distributing corporation or the controlled corporation is three times or more of such ratio for the other corporation (*i.e.*, the controlled corporation or the distributing corporation, respectively)."]

Small Amounts of Qualifying Business Assets. The Treasury Department and the Service are also concerned about transactions in which the distributing corporation or the controlled corporation owns a small amount of Qualifying Business Assets compared to its other assets (non-Qualifying Business Assets). Before enactment of § 355(b)(3), such transactions were common due to the restrictive nature of the "holding company" rule (§ 355(b)(2)(A) prior to its amendment by the Technical Corrections Act of 2007, Pub. L. No. 110-172, § 4(b)(1), 121 Stat. 2473, 2476 (2007)). The Treasury Department and the Service have concluded that, under current law, distributions involving small Qualifying Businesses may have become less justifiable. Accordingly, the Service ordinarily will not rule on any issue that relates to the qualification of a distribution under § 355 and related provisions and is presented in a distribution described in section 4.01(58) of Rev. Proc. 2015-3, but will consider ruling in unique and compelling circumstances. [Section 4.01(58) says that the IRS ordinarily will not rule if "the fair market value of the gross assets of the trade(s) or business(es) on which the distributing corporation or the controlled corporation relies to satisfy the active trade or business requirement of § 355(b) is less than five percent of the total fair market value of the gross assets of such corporation.]

In determining whether unique and compelling circumstances exist to justify the issuance of a ruling or determination letter, the Service will consider all facts and circumstances, including whether a substantial portion of the non-Qualifying Business Assets would be Qualifying Business Assets but for the five-year requirement of § 355(b)(2)(B) and whether there is a relationship between the business purpose for the distribution and the Qualifying Business of the distributing corporation or the controlled corporation.

Exception for Certain Intra-Group Distributions. The Treasury Department and the Service generally are more concerned about transactions in which the stock of a controlled corporation is distributed outside an affiliated group (within the meaning of § 243(b)(2)(A)), including a distribution which is part of a series of related transactions in which the stock of a controlled corporation (including, for example, a controlled corporation that was a distributing corporation with respect to a lower-tier distribution) is distributed outside an affiliated group. * * *

Pro Rata Distributions and Non-Pro Rata Exchanges of Stock Treated Similarly. The Treasury Department and the Service understand that, in many instances, a publicly traded corporation may structure a distribution intended to qualify under § 355 as either a pro rata distribution with respect to its stock or a non-pro rata exchange of the stock of the controlled corporation for some shareholders' stock in the distributing corporation. If the distribution is structured as a pro rata distribution, § 355(g) will not disqualify the distribution from nonrecognition treatment. Furthermore, in most instances, even if the distribution is structured as a non-pro rata exchange, § 355(g) will not disqualify the distribution from nonrecognition treatment because no single shareholder or group of related shareholders will own 50 percent or more of the stock of either the distributing corporation or the controlled corporation after the distribution. In this regard, the Treasury Department and the Service have considered § 1.355-2(d)(3)(iii) ("The fact that the distributing corporation is publicly traded and has no shareholder who is directly or indirectly the beneficial owner of more than five percent of any class of stock is evidence of nondevice.") and § 1.355-2(d)(5)(iv) ("A distribution is ordinarily considered not to have been used principally as a device, if, in the absence of section 355, with respect to each shareholder distributee, the distribution would be a redemption to which section 302(a) applied.").

The Treasury Department and the Service believe, however, that certain characteristics of a transaction may overcome both the nondevice factor of public trading and the non-pro rata structure of a distribution. These characteristics include, as described above, (i) the distributing corporation or the controlled corporation owning Investment Assets with substantial value in relation to the value of all of the corporation's assets and the value of its Qualifying Business Assets, together with a disparity of such relationships between the distributing corporation and the controlled corporation (see § 1.355-2(d)(2)(iv), relating to the nature and use of assets); (ii) in certain situations, the distributing corporation or the controlled corporation owning a small amount of Qualifying Business Assets in relation to all of its assets; and (iii) a prompt or planned RIC or REIT election by the distributing corporation or the controlled corporation. In addition, the Treasury Department and the Service believe that these characteristics may make it less likely that a nontax business purpose for the distribution will satisfy the independent business purpose requirement set forth in § 1.355-2(b) or will qualify as a strong corporate business purpose constituting a nondevice factor. See § 1.355-2(d)(3)(ii) (relationship between business purpose and device). Thus, sections 4.01(57), 4.01(58), and 5.0571(26) of Rev. Proc. 2015-3 do not distinguish between transactions involving distributing corporations the stock of which is or is not publicly traded or between pro rata and non-pro rata distributions.

SECTION 3. REQUEST FOR COMMENTS * * *

F. Is Retention by Distributing Corporation of Stock or Securities of Controlled Corporation Not for Tax Avoidance within § 355(a)(1)(D)(ii)?

Revenue Ruling 75-321

1975-2 C.B. 123

For valid business purposes, *X* intends to distribute to its shareholders, with respect to their stock, 95 percent of the stock of *Y* corporation, one of its wholly owned subsidiaries. *Y* is engaged in the business of banking and is *X*'s only subsidiary so engaged. *Y*, as well as each of the other subsidiary corporations of *X*, has been actively engaged in business for more than 5 years. The business purpose behind the proposed distribution is involuntary in nature in that the applicable Federal banking laws require *X* to qualify as a bank holding company or to limit its stock ownership in any bank to no more than a 5 per cent interest. *X* could not readily qualify as a bank holding company because under banking laws *X* would be required to divest itself of all of its subsidiaries other than *Y*. Therefore, *X* was required to divest itself of 95 percent of its stock interest in its wholly owned subsidiary, *Y*. The proposed distribution will accomplish that result. The business purpose behind the retention of 5 percent of the *Y* stock by *X* is to enable *X* to have assets of sufficient value (the *Y* stock) to serve as collateral so as to enable *X* to obtain needed short-term financing for its remaining business enterprise. * * *

In the instant case the facts show that (1) a genuine separation of the corporate entities will be effected since the distributing corporation will distribute 95 percent of the stock of the controlled corporation; (2) retention of a 5 percent stock interest will not enable the distributing corporation to maintain practical control since several shareholders of the controlled corporation, following the distribution, will each own nearly as much stock in the controlled corporation as will be owned by the distributing corporation; and (3) a sufficient business purpose for the retention of the 5 percent interest is shown to exist. Therefore, the facts establish, in the instant case, that the retention by *X* of 5 percent of the *Y* stock was not in pursuance of a plan having as one of its principal purposes the avoidance of Federal income tax. The facts also establish that the transaction is not a device for the distribution of earnings and profits within the meaning of section 355(a)(1)(B) of the Code.

Accordingly, in the instant case, since all of the requirements of section 355(a) of the Code will be satisfied, no gain or loss will be recognized to (and no amount will be includible in the income of) the shareholders of *X* on the receipt of 95 percent of the *Y* stock.

Note

For a similar result dealing with the retention of debentures, *see* Rev. Rul. 75-469, 1975-2 C.B. 126.

G. Distributions of Hot Stock under § 355(a)(3)(B)

Final Regulations on Hot Stock

Treasury Decision 9435, October 20, 2011

SUMMARY: This document contains final regulations regarding the distribution of stock of a controlled corporation acquired in a transaction described in section 355(a)(3)(B) of the Internal Revenue Code (Code) [*i.e.*, hot stock, which is treated as boot]. * * *

Background

This document contains amendments to 26 CFR part 1 regarding section 355(a)(3)(B). * * *

Section 355(a)(3)(B) provides that for purposes of section 355 (other than section 355(a)(1)(D)) and so much of section 356 as relates to section 355, stock of controlled acquired by distributing by reason of any transaction (i) which occurs within five years of the distribution of such stock, and (ii) which is a taxable transaction, shall not be treated as stock of controlled, but as other property. * * *

The temporary regulations were intended to harmonize the application of section 355(a)(3)(B) with section 355(b). Generally, the temporary regulations: (1) disregarded transfers of controlled stock between members of the distributing corporation's [separate affiliated group] SAG (DSAG), (2) did not treat controlled stock as other property if controlled became a DSAG member, and (3) retained the exception of prior regulation § 1.355-2(g) * * * for acquisitions from affiliates described in § 1.355-3(b)(4)(iii). * * *

Summary of Comment and Guidance * * *

These final regulations adopt the substantive rules of the temporary regulations without change. [These the preamble to the temporary regulations explained, in part:

> [T]hese temporary regulations generally provide that controlled stock acquired by the DSAG within the pre-distribution period in a taxable transaction constitutes hot stock, except if controlled is a DSAG member at any time after the acquisition (but prior to the distribution of controlled). Accordingly, each of Rev. Rul. 76-54 (1976-1 CB 96) and Rev. Rul. 65-286 (1965-2 CB 92) is obsolete.

Transfers Among DSAG Members

Consistent with the SAG regime, which treats the DSAG as a single corporation, transfers of controlled stock owned by DSAG members immediately before and immediately after the transfer are disregarded and are not treated as acquisitions for purposes of the hot stock rule. Compare proposed section 1.355-3(b)(1)(ii) (applying a similar rule for purposes of the ATB requirement).

H. Carryover of Tax Attributes in a Divisive § 355

Section 381, which provides for the carryover of certain assets, such as NOLs, in certain asset reorganizations, is not applicable to § 355 divisive transactions. However, § 312(h)(2) and the regulations thereunder set forth the rules for allocating E & P between the controlled corporation and the distributing corporation. *See* § 1.312-10. In general, in the case of a newly formed controlled corporation, the E & P is allocated in accordance with the relative fair market values of the business retained by the distributing corporation and that contributed to the controlled corporation. *See* § 1.312-10.

§ 9.5 Determination of Whether Boot Is Treated as a Dividend

Revenue Ruling 93-62

1993-2 C.B. 118

Issue Whether gain recognized on the receipt of cash in an exchange of stock that otherwise qualifies under section 355 of the Internal Revenue Code is treated as a dividend distribution under section 356(a)(2).

Facts Distributing is a corporation with 1,000 shares of a single class of stock outstanding. Each share has a fair market value of $1x. A, one of five unrelated individual shareholders, owns 400 shares of Distributing stock. Distributing owns all of the outstanding stock of a subsidiary corporation, Controlled. The Controlled stock has a fair market value of $200x.

Distributing distributes all the stock of Controlled plus $200x cash to A in exchange for all of A's Distributing stock. The exchange satisfies the requirements of section 355 but for the receipt of the cash.

Law and Analysis Section 355(a)(1) of the Code provides, in general, that the shareholders of a distributing corporation will not recognize gain or loss on the exchange of the distributing corporation's stock or securities solely for stock or securities of a controlled subsidiary if the requirements of section 355 are satisfied.

Section 356(a)(1) of the Code provides for recognition of gain on exchanges in which gain would otherwise not be recognized under section 354 (relating to tax-free acquisitive reorganizations) or section 355 if the property received in the exchange consists of property permitted to be received without gain recognition and other property or money ("boot"). The amount of gain recognized is limited to the sum of the money and the fair market value of the other property.

Under section 356(a)(2) of the Code, gain recognized in an exchange described in section 356(a)(1) that "has the effect of the distribution of a dividend" is treated as a dividend to the extent of the distributee's ratable share of the undistributed earnings and profits accumulated after February 28, 1913. Any remaining gain is treated as gain from the exchange of property.

Determinations of whether the receipt of boot has the effect of a dividend are made by applying the principles of section 302 of the Code. *Commissioner v. Clark,* 489 U.S. 726 (1989), 1989-2 C.B. 68. Section 302 contains rules for determining whether payments in redemption of stock are treated as payments in exchange for the stock or as distributions to which section 301 applies.

Under section 302(a) of the Code, a redemption will be treated as an exchange if it satisfies one of the tests of section 302(b). Section 302(b)(2) provides exchange treatment for substantially disproportionate redemptions of stock. A distribution is substantially disproportionate if (1) the shareholder's voting stock interest and common stock interest in the corporation immediately after the redemption are each less than 80 percent of those interests immediately before the redemption, and (2) the shareholder owns less than 50 percent of the voting power of all classes of stock immediately after the redemption.

In *Clark,* the Supreme Court determined whether gain recognized under section 356 of the Code on the receipt of boot in an acquisitive reorganization under section 368(a)(1)(A) and (a)(2)(D) should be treated as a dividend distribution. In that case, the sole shareholder of the target corporation exchanged his target stock for stock of the acquiring corporation and cash. In applying section 302 to determine whether the boot payment had the effect of a dividend distribution, the Court considered whether section 302 should be applied to the boot payment as if it were made (i) by the target corporation in a pre-reorganization hypothetical redemption of a portion of the shareholder's target stock, or (ii) by the acquiring corporation in a post-reorganization hypothetical redemption of the acquiring corporation stock that the shareholder would have received in the reorganization exchange if there had been no boot distribution.

The Supreme Court stated that the treatment of boot under section 356(a)(2) of the Code should be determined "by examining the effect of the exchange as a whole," and concluded that treating the boot as received in a redemption of target stock would improperly isolate the boot payment from the overall reorganization by disregarding the effect of the subsequent merger. Consequently, the Court tested whether the boot payment had the effect of a dividend distribution by comparing the interest the taxpayer actually received in the acquiring corporation with the interest the taxpayer would have had if solely stock in the acquiring corporation had been received in the reorganization exchange.

Prior to the decision in *Clark,* the Service considered the facts and issue presented in this revenue ruling in Rev. Rul. 74-516, 1974-2 C.B. 121. The determination of whether the exchange of Distributing stock for Controlled stock and boot under section 355 of the Code had the effect of a dividend distribution under section 356(a)(2) was made by comparing A's interest in Distributing prior to the exchange with the interest A would have retained if A had not received Controlled stock and had only surrendered the Distributing stock equal in value to the boot. The Court's decision in *Clark* does not change the conclusion in Rev. Rul. 74-516, because, like *Clark,* the ruling determined whether the exchange in question had the effect of a dividend distribution based on an analysis of the overall transaction.

The exchange of A's Distributing stock for stock of Controlled qualifies for non-recognition treatment under section 355 of the Code in part because the overall effect of the exchange is an adjustment of A's continuing interest in Distributing in a modified corporate form. *See* section 1.355-2(c) of the Income Tax Regulations. The Controlled stock received by A represents a continuing interest in a portion of Distributing's assets that were formerly held by A as an indirect equity interest. The boot payment has reduced A's proportionate interest in the overall corporate enterprise that includes both Distributing and Controlled. Thus, the boot is treated as received in redemption of A's Distributing stock, and A's interest in Distributing immediately before the exchange is compared to the interest A would have retained if A had surrendered only the Distributing shares equal in value to the boot.

Under the facts presented here, before the exchange, A owned 400 of the 1,000 shares, or 40 percent, of the outstanding Distributing stock. If A had surrendered only the 200 shares for which A received boot, A would still hold 200 of the 800 shares, or 25 percent, of the Distributing stock outstanding after the exchange. This 25 percent stock interest would represent 62.5 percent of A's pre-exchange stock interest in Distributing. Therefore, the deemed redemption would be treated as an exchange because it qualifies as substantially disproportionate under section 302(b)(2) of the Code.

Holding In an exchange of stock that otherwise qualifies under section 355 of the Code, whether the payment of boot is treated as a dividend distribution under section 356(a)(2) is determined prior to the exchange. This determination is made by treating the recipient shareholder as if the shareholder had retained the distributing corporation stock actually exchanged for controlled corporation stock and received the boot in exchange for distributing corporation stock equal in value to the boot.

§ 9.6 Spin-Offs Followed by Acquisitive Reorganizations: *Morris Trust* Issues

A. Subsequent Sale or Exchange of Stock: Impact on the Device Clause

Revenue Ruling 55-103
1955-1 C.B. 31

The X Corporation is engaged in the manufacture of paper products. It also owns 80 percent of the stock of Y, a foreign corporation, which operates a lumber business. The Y Corporation's stock has greatly appreciated in value and constitutes a large proportion of the total asset value of X Corporation. The X Corporation has common stock of 120x dollars and an earned surplus of 100x dollars. For the past several years, the X Corporation has suffered severe operating losses and its stockholders have received no dividends. For that reason the stockholders of X have voted to liquidate and start dissolution proceedings on a specified date, unless negotiations to sell their stock have been completed on or before such date.

The Z Corporation is interested in buying all of the outstanding common stock of X Corporation and has made an offer to purchase such stock which has not yet been acted upon by X or its stockholders. However, the Z Corporation's offer does not contemplate payment for the value of the Y Corporation's stock as an asset of X Corporation.

Since the Z Corporation has no interest in Y stock held by X Corporation, the latter corporation proposes to distribute this stock to its shareholders, prior to the completion of the sale negotiations. * * *

In the instant case, subsequent to the proposed distribution of Y stock by X, the stock of X Corporation may be sold by the present stockholders pursuant to an arrangement negotiated immediately prior to the distribution. The sale of stock of the distributing corporation immediately subsequent to a distribution of stock of a controlled corporation, when negotiations for such a sale are already in process, is generally considered sufficient evidence that the distribution of stock was used principally as a device for the distribution of earnings and profits of the distributing corporation. The purpose of the requirement that the transaction not be used principally as a device for the distribution of earnings and profits is to limit the application of section 355 of such Code to those cases in which the distribution of stock of the controlled corporation effects only a readjustment of continuing interests in property under modified corporate forms.

In the instant case, the purpose in distributing the Y stock is to facilitate the sale of stock of X Corporation. No continuing interest in X on the part of any of the present stockholders is contemplated. The distribution of the Y stock is merely a device to give to the X stockholders certain assets for which the prospective purchaser of their stock is unwilling to pay. Therefore, it is an arrangement for distributing the earnings and profits of X Corporation and section 355 of the Code is not applicable to such a transaction.

Accordingly, it is held that the amount and taxability of the distribution of the stock of Y Corporation to the stockholders of X Corporation will be determined in accordance with the provisions of section 301(c)(1) of the Internal Revenue Code of 1954. The portion of the distribution constituting a dividend will be determined under the provisions of section 316 of such Code.

B. Spin-Off of Controlled Corporation Followed by Merger of Distributing Corporation into Acquiring Corporation

Commissioner v. Morris Trust

United States Court of Appeals, Fourth Circuit, 1966
367 F.2d 794

HAYNSWORTH, CHIEF JUDGE:

Its nubility impaired by the existence of an insurance department it had operated for many years, a state bank divested itself of that business before merging with a national bank. The divestiture was in the form of a traditional "spin-off," but, because it was a preliminary step to the merger of the banks, the Commissioner treated their receipt of stock of the insurance company as ordinary income to the stockholders of the state bank. We agree with the Tax Court, that gain to the stockholders of the state bank was not recognizable under § 355 of the 1954 Code.

In 1960, a merger agreement was negotiated by the directors of American Commercial Bank, a North Carolina corporation with its principal office in Charlotte, and Security National Bank of Greensboro, a national bank. * * *

For many years, American had operated an insurance department. This was a substantial impediment to the accomplishment of the merger, for a national bank is prohibited from operating an insurance department except in towns having a population of not more than 5000 inhabitants. To avoid a violation of the national banking laws, therefore, and to accomplish the merger under Security's national charter, it was prerequisite that American rid itself of its insurance business.

The required step to make it nubile was accomplished by American's organization of a new corporation, American Commercial Agency, Inc., to which American transferred its insurance business assets in exchange for Agency's stock which was immediately distributed to American's stockholders. At the same time, American paid a cash dividend fully taxable to its stockholders. The merger of the two banks was then accomplished.

Though American's spin-off of its insurance business was a "D" reorganization, as defined in § 368(a)(1), provided the distribution of Agency's stock qualified for nonrecognition of gain under § 355, the Commissioner contended that the active business requirements of § 355(b)(1)(A) were not met, since American's banking business was not continued in unaltered corporate form. He also finds an inherent incompatibility in substantially simultaneous divisive and amalgamating reorganizations.

Section 355(b)(1)(A) requires that both the distributing corporation and the controlled corporation be "engaged immediately after the distribution in the active conduct of a trade or business." There was literal compliance with that requirement, for the spin-off, including the distribution of Agency's stock to American's stockholders, preceded the merger. The Commissioner asks that we look at both steps together, contending that North Carolina National Bank was not the distributing corporation and that its subsequent conduct of American's banking business does not satisfy the requirement. * * *

The Commissioner, indeed, concedes that American's stockholders would have realized no gain had American not been merged into Security after, but substantially contemporaneously with, Agency's spin-off. Insofar as it is contended that § 355(b)(1)(A) requires the distributing corporation to continue the conduct of an active business, recognition of gain to American's stockholders on their receipt of Agency's stock would depend upon the economically irrelevant technicality of the identity of the surviving corporation in the merger. Had American been the survivor, it would in every literal and substantive sense have continued the conduct of its banking business. * * *

There is no distinction in the statute between subsequent amalgamating reorganizations in which the stockholders of the spin-off transferor would own 80% or more of the relevant classes of stock of the reorganized transferor, and those in which they would not. The statute draws no line between major and minor amalgamations in prospect at the time of the spin-off. Nothing of the sort is suggested by the detailed control-active business requirements in the five-year pre-distribution period, for there the distinction is between taxable and nontaxable acquisitions, and a tax free exchange within the five-year period does not violate the active business-control requirement whether it was a major or a minor acquisition. Reorganizations in which no gain or loss is recognized, sanctioned by the statute's control provision when occurring in the five years preceding the spin-off, are not prohibited in the post-distribution period.

As we have noticed above, the merger cannot by any stretch of imagination be said to have affected the continuity of interest of American's stockholders or to have constituted a violation of the principle underlying the statutory control requirement. The view is the same whether it be directed to each of the successive steps severally or to the whole.

Nor can we find elsewhere in the Code any support for the Commissioner's suggestion of incompatibility between substantially contemporaneous devisive and amalgamating reorganizations. The 1954 Code contains no inkling of it; nor does its immediate legislative history. The difficulties encountered under the 1924 Code and its successors, in dealing with formalistic distortions of taxable transactions into the spin-off shape, contain no implication of any such incompatibility. Section 317 of the Revenue Act of 1951 and the Senate Committee Report, to which we have referred, did require an intention that the distributing corporation continue the conduct of its active business, but that transitory requirement is of slight relevance to an interpretation of the very different provisions of the 1954 Code and is devoid of any implication of incompatibility. If that provision, during the years it was in effect, would have resulted in recognition of gain in a spin-off if the distributing corporation later, but substantially simultaneously, was a party to a merger in which it lost its identity, a question we do not decide, it would not inhibit successive reorganizations if the merger preceded the spin-off.

The Congress intended to encourage six types of reorganizations. * * * The "D" reorganization has no lesser standing. It is on the same plane as the others and, provided all of the "D" requirements are met, is as available as the others in successive reorganizations. * * *

Our conclusion that gain was not recognizable to American's stockholders as a result of the spin-off, therefore, is uninfluenced by the fact that the subsequent merger was under the National Banking Act. It would have been the same if the merger had been accomplished under state laws. * * *

While we reject the technical provision of the National Banking Act as a basis for decision, therefore, it is important to the result that, as in every merger, there was substantive continuity of each constituent and its business. In framing the 1954 Code, the Congress was concerned with substance, not formalisms. Its approach was that of the courts in the *Gregory v. Helvering* series of cases. Ours must be the same. The technicalities of corporate structure cannot obscure the continuity of American's business, its employees, its customers, its locations or the substantive fact that North Carolina National Bank was both American and Security.

A decision of the Sixth Circuit[16] appears to be at odds with our conclusion. In *Curtis*, it appears that one corporation was merged into another after spinning-off a warehouse building which was an unwanted asset because the negotiators could not agree upon its value. The Court of Appeals for the Sixth Circuit affirmed a District Court judgment holding that the value of the warehouse company shares was taxable as ordinary income to the stockholders of the first corporation.

A possible distinction may lie between the spin-off of an asset unwanted by the acquiring corporation in an "A" reorganization solely because of disagreement as to its value and the preliminary spin-off of an active business which the acquiring corporation is prohibited by law from operating. We cannot stand upon so nebulous a distinction, however. We simply take a different view. The reliance in *Curtis* upon the Report of the Senate Committee explaining § 317 of the Revenue Act of 1951, quite dissimilar to the 1954 Code, reinforces our appraisal of the relevant materials. * * *

For the reasons which we have canvassed, we think the Tax Court, which had before it the opinion of the District Court in *Curtis*, though not that of the affirming Court of Appeals, correctly decided that American's stockholders realized no recognizable taxable gain upon their receipt in the "D" reorganization of the stock of Agency.

Affirmed.

C. The Service Accepts *Morris Trust*

Revenue Ruling 68-603

1968-2 C.B. 148

The Internal Revenue Service will follow the decision of the United States Court of Appeals for the Fourth Circuit in the case of *Commissioner v. Mary Archer W. Morris Trust*, § 367 F.2d 794 (1966), to the extent it holds that (1) the active business requirements of section 355(b)(1)(A) of the Internal Revenue Code of 1954 were satisfied

---

16. *Curtis v. United States*, 6 Cir., 336 F.2d 714 [16 AFTR 2d 5685].

even though the distributing corporation immediately after the spin-off merged into another corporation, (2) the control requirement of section 368(a)(1)(D) of the Code implies no limitation upon a reorganization of the transferor corporation after the distribution of stock of the transferee corporation, and (3) there was a business purpose for the spin-off and the merger.

D. The Regulations under the Basic § 355 Provisions

See § 1.355-2(d)(2)(iii).

Preamble to the § 355 Regulations

Treasury Decision 8238 (January 4, 1989)

Subsequent Sale or Exchange of Stock (1) *Per se rule.* Section 1.355-2(c)(2) of the proposed regulations provided that a subsequent sale or exchange of 20 percent or more of the stock of either the distributing or the controlled corporation, negotiated or agreed upon before the distribution, is conclusive evidence of device. Commenters objected to this rule on the grounds that it is arbitrary, that it has no case law support, and that it is inconsistent with the facts and circumstances standard mandated by the Code and expressed in § 1.355-1(c)(1) of the proposed regulations.

Upon reconsideration, Treasury and the Internal Revenue Service continue to believe that a subsequent sale or exchange of stock of either the distributing or the controlled corporation, negotiated or agreed upon before the distribution, is substantial evidence of device. However, they agree with the commenters that section 355(a)(1)(B) does not require that this evidence be treated as conclusive, and that taxpayers should not be denied the opportunity to prove that, despite the sale or exchange, the transaction was not used principally as a device. Accordingly, the *per se* rule is eliminated in the final regulations.

The final regulations provide that a subsequent sale or exchange of stock of either the distributing or the controlled corporation, negotiated or agreed upon before the distribution, is substantial evidence of device. Generally, the greater the percentage of stock sold or exchanged, the stronger the evidence of device. *See* § 1.355-2(d)(2)(iii)(A) in this document. In addition, the shorter the period of time between the distribution and the sale or exchange, the stronger the evidence of device.

(2) *Negotiated or agreed upon before the distribution.* The final regulations retain the rules of the proposed regulations concerning whether a sale or exchange is considered to be negotiated or agreed upon before the distribution. *See* § 1.355-2(d)(2)(iii)(D) in this document.

(3) *Subsequent reorganizations.* The final regulations retain the provision in § 355-2(c)(2) of the proposed regulations that an exchange of stock pursuant to a plan of reorganization in which either no gain or loss or only an insubstantial amount of gain is recognized is not evidence of device. The final regulations provide that for this purpose, gain treated as a dividend pursuant to sections 356(a)(2) and 316 shall be disregarded. They also add a provision that any stock received in a reorganization

exchange excepted from the subsequent sale rules will be treated, for purposes of those subsequent sale rules, as the stock surrendered. Thus, any sale or exchange of the stock received will be subject to the subsequent sale rules. *See* § 1.355-2(d)(2)(iii)(E) in this document.

E. Potential Recognition of Gain under § 355(e) by Distributing Corporation on Distribution in Connection with an Acquisition

1. Gain Recognition on Certain Distributions of Controlled Corporation Stock Followed by Acquisition of Either Controlled Corporation or Distributing Corporation: Impact of Taxpayer Relief Act of 1997

See §§ 355(e) and (f), 351(c), 358(g) and 368(a)(2)(H)

a. Senate Report

Revenue Reconciliation Act of 1997 Senate Finance Committee Report No. 105-33

139-142 (June 19, 1997)

Present Law A corporation generally is required to recognize gain on the distribution of property (including stock of a subsidiary) as if such property had been sold for its fair market value. [§§ 311 and 336] The shareholders generally treat the receipt of property as a taxable event as well. [§§ 301 and 331.] Section 355 of the Internal Revenue Code provides an exception to this rule for certain "spin-off" type distributions of stock of a controlled corporation, provided that various requirements are met, including certain restrictions relating to acquisitions and dispositions of stock of the distributing corporation ("distributing") or the controlled corporation ("controlled") prior and subsequent to a distribution. * * *

Reasons for Change The Committee believes that section 355 was intended to permit the tax-free division of existing business arrangements among existing shareholders. In cases in which it is intended that new shareholders will acquire ownership of a business in connection with a spin off, the transaction more closely resembles a corporate level disposition of the portion of the business that is acquired.

The Committee also believes that the difference in treatment of certain transactions following a spin-off, depending upon whether the distributing or controlled corporation engages in the transaction, should be minimized.

The Committee also is concerned that spin-off transactions within a single corporate group can have the effect of avoiding other present law rules that create or recapture excess loss accounts in affiliated groups filing consolidated returns.

Such intra-group distributions also can have the effect of permitting possibly inappropriate basis increases (or preventing basis decreases) following a distribution, due to the differences between the basis allocation rules that govern spin-offs and those that apply to other distributions. In the case of an affiliated group not filing a consolidated return, it is also possible that section 355 distributions could in effect permit similar inappropriate basis results.

Explanation of Provision The bill adopts additional restrictions under section 355 on acquisitions and dispositions of the stock of the distributing or controlled corporation. Under the bill, if either the controlled or distributing corporation is acquired pursuant to a plan or arrangement in existence on the date of distribution, gain is recognized by the other corporation as of the date of the distribution. [This rule was modified by the Conference agreement as indicated below.] * * *

Whether a corporation is acquired is determined under rules similar to those of present law section 355(d), except that acquisitions would not be restricted to "purchase" transactions. Thus, an acquisition occurs if one or more persons acquire 50 percent or more of the vote or value of the stock of the controlled or distributing corporation pursuant to a plan or arrangement. [§ 355(e)(2)(A)] For example, assume a corporation ("P") distributes the stock of its wholly owned subsidiary ("S") to its shareholders. If, pursuant to a plan or arrangement, 50 percent or more of the vote or value of either P or S is acquired by one or more persons, the bill proposal requires gain recognition by the corporation not acquired. Except as provided in Treasury regulations, if the assets of the distributing or controlled corporation are acquired by a successor in a merger or other transaction under section 368(a)(1)(A), (C) or (D) of the Code, the shareholders (immediately before the acquisition) of the corporation acquiring such assets are treated as acquiring stock in the corporation from which the assets were acquired. [§ 355(e)(3)(B). Noted that this type of transaction occurred in *Morris Trust*.] Under Treasury regulations, other asset transfers also could be subject to this rule. However, in any transaction, stock received directly or indirectly by former shareholders of distributing or controlled, in a successor or new controlling corporation of either, is not treated as acquired stock if it is attributable to such shareholders' stock in distributing or controlled that was not acquired as part of a plan or arrangement to acquire 50 percent or more of such successor or other corporation.

Acquisitions occurring within the four-year period beginning two years before the date of distribution are presumed to have occurred pursuant to a plan or arrangement. [§ 355(e)(2)(B)] Taxpayers can avoid gain recognition by showing that an acquisition occurring during this four-year period was unrelated to the distribution.

The bill does not apply to distributions that would otherwise be subject to section 355(d) of present law, which imposes corporate level tax on certain disqualified distributions. The bill does not apply to a distribution pursuant to a title 11 or similar case.

The Treasury Department is authorized to prescribe regulations as necessary to carry out the purposes of the proposal, including regulations to provide for the application of the proposal in the case of multiple transactions. [§ 355(e)(5)] * * *

The bill also modifies certain rules for determining control immediately after a distribution in the case of certain divisive transactions in which a controlled corporation is distributed and the transaction meets the requirements of section 355. In such cases, under section 351 and modified section 368(a)(2)(H) with respect to certain reorganizations under section 368(a)(1)(D), those shareholders receiving stock in the distributed corporation are treated as in control of the distributed corporation immediately after the distribution if they hold stock representing a greater than 50 percent interest in the vote and value of stock of the distributed corporation. [?This provision was amended in 1998 to provide that in certain cases, the post distribution disposition of stock of the controlled corporations is not taken into account. *See* §§ 368(a)(2)(H)(ii) and 351(c)(2)]

The bill does not change the present-law requirement under section 355 that the distributing corporation must distribute 80 percent of the voting power and 80 percent of each other class of stock of the controlled corporation. It is expected that this requirement will be applied by the Internal Revenue Service taking account of the provisions of the bill regarding plans that permit certain types of planned restructuring of the distributing corporation following the distribution, and to treat similar restructurings of the controlled corporation in a similar manner. Thus, the 80-percent control requirement is expected to be administered in a manner that would prevent the tax-free spin-off of a less-than-80-percent controlled subsidiary, but generally would not impose additional restrictions on post-distribution restructurings of the controlled corporation if such restrictions would not apply to the distributing corporation. * * *

b. Conference Report

Statement of Managers on Taxpayer Relief Act of 1997 Conference Report (HR 2014)
BNA pp. S-102-104 (July 31, 1997)

Conference Agreement The conference agreement follows the Senate amendment with additional modifications.

Amount and timing of gain recognition under section 355(e) Under the conference agreement, in the case of an acquisition of either the distributing corporation or the controlled corporation, the amount of gain recognized is the amount that the distributing corporation would have recognized had the stock of the controlled corporation been sold for fair market value on the date of the distribution. Such gain is recognized immediately before the distribution. As under the House bill and Senate amendment, no adjustment to the basis of the stock or assets of either corporation is allowed by reason of the recognition of the gain.[17] [§ 355(e)]

Acquisitions resulting in gain recognition Under the conference agreement, as under the House bill and Senate amendment, the gain recognition provisions of section 355(e) apply when one or more persons acquire 50 percent or more of the voting power or value of the stock of either the distributing corporation or the controlled corporation, pursuant to a plan or series of related transactions. [§ 355(e)(2)(A)]

---

17. There is no intention to limit the otherwise applicable Treasury regulatory authority under section 336(e) of the Code. There is also no intention to limit the otherwise applicable provisions of section 1367 with respect to the effect on shareholder stock basis of gain recognized by an S corporation under this provision.

The conference agreement provides certain additions and clarifications to identify cases that do not cause gain recognition under the provisions of section 355(e).

Single affiliated group Under the conference agreement, a plan (or series of related transactions) is not one that will cause gain recognition if, immediately after the completion of such plan or transactions, the distributing corporation and all controlled corporations are members of a single affiliated group of corporations (as defined in section 1504 without regard to subsection (b) thereof). [§ 355(e)(2)(C)]

Example 1: P corporation is a member of an affiliated group of corporations that includes subsidiary corporation S and subsidiary corporation S1. P owns all the stock of S. S owns all the stock of S1. P corporation is merged into unrelated X corporation in a transaction in which the former shareholders of X corporation will own 50 percent or more of the vote or value of the stock of surviving X corporation after the merger. As part of the plan of merger, S1 will be distributed by S to X, in a transaction that otherwise qualifies under section 355. After this distribution, S, S1, and X will remain members of a single affiliated group of corporations under section 1504 (without regard to whether any of the corporations is a foreign corporation, an insurance company, a tax exempt organization, or an electing section 936 company). [*See* § 1504(b).] Even though there has been an acquisition of P, S, and S1 by X, and a distribution of S1 by S that is part of a plan or series of related transactions, the plan is not treated as one that requires gain recognition on the distribution of S1 to X. This is because the distributing corporation S and the controlled corporation S1 remain within a single affiliated group after the distribution (even though the P group has changed ownership).

Continuing direct or indirect ownership The conference agreement clarifies that an acquisition does not require gain recognition if the same persons own 50 percent or more of both corporations, directly or indirectly (rather than merely indirectly, as in the House bill and Senate amendment), before and after the acquisition and distribution, provided the stock owned before the acquisition was not acquired as part of a plan (or series of related transactions) to acquire a 50-percent or greater interest in either distributing or controlled. [§ 355(e)(3)]

Example 2: Individual A owns all the stock of P corporation. P owns all the stock of a subsidiary corporation, S. Subsidiary S is distributed to individual A in a transaction that otherwise qualifies under section 355. As part of a plan, P then merges with corporation X, also owned entirely by individual A. There is not an acquisition that requires gain recognition under the provision, because individual A owns directly or indirectly 100 percent of all the stock of both X, the successor to P, and S before and after the transaction.[18] The same result would occur if P were contributed to a holding company, all the stock of which is owned by A. The example assumes that A did not acquire his or her stock in P as part of a plan or series of related transactions that results in the direct or indirect ownership of 50 percent or more of S or P sep-

---

18. The example assumes that A did not acquire his or her stock in P as part of a plan or series of related transactions that results in the direct or indirect ownership of 50 percent of more of S or P separately by A. If A's stock in P was acquired as part of such a plan, the transaction would be one requiring on the spin-off of 5.

arately by A. If A's stock in P was acquired as part of such a plan, the transaction would be one requiring gain recognition on the spin-off of S.

The conference agreement, following the House bill and Senate amendment, continues to provide that except as provided in Treasury regulations, certain other acquisitions are not taken into account. For example, under section 355(e)(3)(A), the following other types of acquisitions of stock are not subject to the provision, provided that the stock owned before the acquisition was not acquired pursuant to a plan or series of related transactions to acquire a 50-percent or greater ownership interest in either distributing or controlled:

First, the acquisition of stock in the controlled corporation by the distributing corporation (as one example, in the case of a drop-down of property by the distributing corporation to the corporation to be distributed in exchange for the stock of the controlled corporation);

Second, the acquisition by a person of stock in any controlled corporation by reason of holding stock or securities in the distributing corporation (as one example, the receipt by a distributing corporation shareholder of controlled corporation stock in a distribution-including a split-off distribution in which a shareholder that did not own 50 percent of the stock of distributing owns 50 percent or more of the stock of controlled); and

Third, the acquisition by a person of stock in any successor corporation of the distributing corporation or any controlled corporation by reason of holding stock or securities in such distributing or controlled corporation (for example, the receipt by former shareholders of distributing of 50 percent or more of the stock of a successor corporation in a merger of distributing).

As under the House bill and Senate amendment, a public offering of sufficient size can result in an acquisition that causes gain recognition under the provision.

Attribution The conference agreement also modifies the attribution rule for determining when an acquisition has occurred. Rather than apply section 355(d)(8)(A), which attributes stock owned by a corporation to a corporate shareholder only if that shareholder owns 10 percent of the corporation, the conference agreement provides that, except as provided in regulations, section 318(a)(2)(C) applies without regard to the amount of stock ownership of the corporation. [§ 355(e)(4)(C)]

Example 3: Assume the facts are the same as in the immediately preceding example except that corporations P and X are each owned by the same 20 individual 5-percent shareholders (rather than wholly by individual A). The transaction described in the previous example, in which S is spun off by P to P's shareholders and P is acquired by X, would not cause gain recognition, because the same shareholders would own directly or indirectly 50 percent or more of the stock of each corporation both before and after the transaction.

Section 355(f) The conference agreement follows the Senate amendment in providing that, except as provided in Treasury regulations, section 355 (or so much of section 356 as relates to section 355) shall not apply to the distribution of stock from one member of an affiliated group of corporations (as defined in section 1504(a)) to another member of such group (an "intragroup spin-off") if such distribution is part of a plan (or series of related transactions) described in subsection (e)(2)(A)(ii), pursuant to which one or more persons acquire directly or indirectly stock representing a 50-percent or greater interest in the distributing corporation or any controlled corporation.

Example 4: P corporation owns all the stock of subsidiary corporation S. S owns all the stock of subsidiary corporation T. S distributes the stock of T corporation to P as part of a plan or series of related transactions in which P then distributes S to its shareholders and then P is merged into unrelated X corporation. After the merger, former shareholders of X corporation own 50 percent or more of the voting power or value of the stock of the merged corporation. Because the distribution of T by S is part of a plan or series of related transactions in which S is distributed by P outside the P affiliated group and P is then acquired under section 355(e), section 355 in its entirety does not apply to the intragroup spin-off of T to P, under section 355(f). Also, the distribution of S by P is subject to section 355(e). * * *

Treasury regulatory authority under section 358(c) As under the Senate amendment, the conference agreement provides that in the case of any distribution of stock of one member of an affiliated group of corporations to another member under section 355 ("intragroup spin-off'), the Secretary of the Treasury is authorized under section 358(c) to provide adjustments to the basis of any stock in a corporation which is a member of such group, to reflect appropriately the proper treatment of such distribution. It is understood that the approach of any such regulations applied to intragroup spin-offs that do not involve an acquisition may also be applied under the Treasury regulatory authority to modify the rule of section 355(f) as may be appropriate.

c. Final Regulations under Section 355(e)

Preamble to Final Regulations under Section 355(e), Treasury Decision 9198

April 19, 2005

See Treas. Reg. § 1.355-7.

Summary: This document contains final regulations under section 355(e) of the Internal Revenue Code relating to the recognition of gain on certain distributions of stock or securities of a controlled corporation in connection with an acquisition. Changes to the applicable law were made by the Taxpayer Relief Act of 1997. [This excerpt introduces some of the principal concepts in these very complex and detailed regulations.] * * *

BACKGROUND AND EXPLANATION OF PROVISIONS.

This document contains amendments to 26 CFR part 1 under section 355(e) of the Internal Revenue Code (Code). Section 355(e) provides that the stock of a controlled corporation will not be qualified property under section 355(c)(2) or 361(c)(2) if the stock is distributed as "part of a plan (or series of related transactions) pursuant to which 1 or more persons acquire directly or indirectly stock representing a 50-

percent or greater interest in the distributing corporation or any controlled corporation." * * *

The 2002 temporary regulations provide guidance concerning the interpretation of the phrase "plan (or series of related transactions)." * * *

The 2002 temporary regulations provide that whether a distribution and an acquisition are part of a plan is determined based on all the facts and circumstances and set forth a nonexclusive list of factors that are relevant in making that determination. The 2002 temporary regulations also provide that a distribution and a post-distribution acquisition not involving a public offering can be part of a plan only if there was an agreement, understanding, arrangement, or substantial negotiations regarding the acquisition or a similar acquisition at some time during the two-year period preceding the distribution (the post-distribution acquisition rule). Finally, the 2002 temporary regulations set forth seven safe harbors. The satisfaction of any one of these safe harbors confirms that a distribution and an acquisition are not part of a plan. * * *

Pre-Distribution Acquisitions Not Involving a Public Offering. The 2002 temporary regulations include a safe harbor, Safe Harbor IV, that may be available for a pre-distribution acquisition. That safe harbor provides that an acquisition and a distribution that occurs more than two years after the acquisition are not part of a plan if there was no agreement, understanding, arrangement, or substantial negotiations concerning the distribution at the time of the acquisition or within six months thereafter. In addition to Safe Harbor IV, the 2002 temporary regulations identify a number of factors that are relevant in determining whether a distribution and a pre-distribution acquisition not involving a public offering are part of a plan. Among the factors tending to show that a distribution and a pre-distribution acquisition not involving a public offering are not part of a plan is the absence of discussions by the distributing corporation (Distributing) or the controlled corporation (Controlled) with the acquirer regarding a distribution during the two-year period before the acquisition (the no-discussions factor). The absence of such discussions, however, will not tend to show that a distribution and an acquisition are not part of a plan if the acquisition occurs after the date of the public announcement of the planned distribution (the public announcement restriction). * * *

The IRS and Treasury Department believe that it is desirable to provide for additional bright-line rules for determining whether a distribution and a pre-distribution acquisition not involving a public offering are part of a plan. Accordingly, these final regulations amend Safe Harbor IV, add a new safe harbor for acquisitions of Distributing prior to a pro rata distribution, and amend the no-discussions factor. * * *

New Safe Harbor for Acquisitions Before a Pro Rata Distribution. The IRS and Treasury Department believe that acquisitions of Distributing not involving a public offering that occur before a pro rata distribution are not likely to be part of a plan including the distribution where there has been a public announcement of the distribution prior to the acquisition, there were no discussions regarding the acquisition prior to the public announcement, and the acquirer did not have the ability to participate in or influence the distribution decision. The facts that the distribution was publicly announced prior to discussions regarding the acquisition and that the acquisition was small in size suggest that the distribution would have occurred regardless of the acquisition. Moreover, the fact that a pre-distribution shareholder of Distributing has the same interest in both Distributing and Controlled, directly or indirectly, both immediately before and immediately after a pro rata distribution reduces the likelihood that the acquisition and the distribution were part of a plan. Accordingly, these final regulations include a new safe harbor, Safe Harbor V, that applies to acquisitions of Distributing not involving a public offering that occur prior to a pro rata distribution. That safe harbor provides that a distribution that is pro rata among the Distributing shareholders and a pre-distribution acquisition of Distributing not involving a public offering will not be considered part of a plan if the acquisition occurs after the date of a public announcement regarding the distribution and there were no discussions by Distributing or Controlled with the acquirer regarding a distribution on or before the date of the first public announcement regarding the distribution. * * *

No-Discussions Factor. As discussed above, the IRS and Treasury Department believe that the occurrence of a public announcement of a distribution before the discussion of an acquisition not involving a public offering suggests that the distribution would have occurred regardless of the acquisition. Therefore, these final regulations amend the no-discussions factor to remove the public announcement restriction.

Public Offerings. The 2002 temporary regulations distinguish between acquisitions not involving a public offering and acquisitions involving a public offering. A number of commentators have suggested that it is difficult to apply the 2002 temporary regulations to acquisitions involving public offerings and have requested (1) clarification of the definition of public offering, (2) additional safe harbors for acquisitions involving public offerings, and (3) guidance regarding when an acquisition is similar to a potential acquisition involving a public offering. These final regulations address these requests. * * *

Agreement, Understanding, or Arrangement. Throughout the 2002 temporary regulations reference is made to the phrase "agreement, understanding, or arrangement." The 2002 temporary regulations provide that whether an agreement, understanding, or arrangement exists depends on the facts and circumstances. * * * The IRS and Treasury Department believe that the activities of those who have the authority to act on behalf of Distributing or Controlled as well as the activities of the controlling shareholders of Distributing and Controlled are relevant to the determination of whether a distribution and an acquisition are part of a plan. Therefore, these final regulations provide that an agreement, understanding, or arrangement generally requires either (1) an agreement, understanding, or arrangement by one or more officers or directors acting on behalf of Distributing or Controlled, by a controlling shareholder of Distributing or Controlled, or by another person with the implicit or explicit permission of one or more of such persons, with the acquirer or with a person or persons with the implicit or explicit permission of the acquirer; or (2) an agreement, understanding, or arrangement by an acquirer that is a controlling shareholder of Distributing or Controlled immediately after the acquisition that is the subject of the agreement, understanding, or arrangement, or by a person or persons with the implicit or explicit permission of such acquirer, with the transferor or with a person or persons with the implicit or explicit permission of the transferor. These final regulations also make conforming changes to the rules related to when an option will be treated as an agreement, understanding, or arrangement to acquire stock, and the definition of substantial negotiations.

Substantial Negotiations and Discussions. Under the 2002 temporary regulations, the presence or absence of "substantial negotiations" or "discussions" regarding an acquisition or a distribution is relevant to the determination of whether a distribution and an acquisition are part of a plan. The 2002 temporary regulations provide that, in the case of an acquisition other than a public offering, substantial negotiations generally require discussions of significant economic terms by one or more officers, directors, or controlling shareholders of Distributing or Controlled, or another person or persons with the implicit or explicit permission of one or more officers, directors, or controlling shareholders of Distributing or Controlled, with the acquirer or a person or persons with the implicit or explicit permission of the acquirer. In addition, the 2002 temporary regulations provide that (i) discussions by Distributing or Controlled generally require discussions by one or more officers, directors, or controlling shareholders of Distributing or Controlled, or another person or persons with the implicit or explicit permission of one or more officers, directors, or controlling shareholders of Distributing or Controlled; and (ii) discussions with the acquirer generally require discussions with the acquirer or a person or persons with the implicit or explicit permission of the acquirer.

Commentators have requested that final regulations clarify that, where the acquirer is a corporation, substantial negotiations and discussions must involve one or more officers, directors, or controlling shareholders of the acquirer, or another person or persons with the implicit or explicit permission of one or more of such officers, directors, or controlling shareholders. These final regulations reflect those clarifications. * * *

2. Illustration of the Limits of Section 355(e)

Revenue Ruling 2005-65

2005 IRB LEXIS 362

ISSUE. Under the facts described below, is a distribution of a controlled corporation by a distributing corporation part of a plan pursuant to which one or more persons acquire stock in the distributing corporation under § 355(e) of the Internal Revenue Code and § 1.355-7 of the Income Tax Regulations?

FACTS. Distributing is a publicly traded corporation that conducts a pharmaceuticals business. Controlled, a wholly owned subsidiary of Distributing, conducts a cosmetics business. Distributing does all of the borrowing for both Distributing and Controlled and makes all decisions regarding the allocation of capital spending between the pharmaceuticals and cosmetics businesses. Because Distributing's capital spending in recent years for both the pharmaceuticals and cosmetics businesses has outpaced internally generated cash flow from the businesses, it has had to limit total expenditures to maintain its credit ratings. Although the decisions reached by Distributing's senior management regarding the allocation of capital spending usually favor the pharmaceuticals business due to its higher rate of growth and profit margin, the competition for capital prevents both businesses from consistently pursuing development strategies that the management of each business believes are appropriate.

To eliminate this competition for capital, and in light of the unavailability of nontaxable alternatives, Distributing decides and publicly announces that it intends to distribute all the stock of Controlled pro rata to Distributing's shareholders. It is expected that both businesses will benefit in a real and substantial way from the distribution. This business purpose is a corporate business purpose (within the meaning of § 1.355-2(b)). The distribution is substantially motivated by this business purpose, and not by a business purpose to facilitate an acquisition.

After the announcement but before the distribution, X, a widely held corporation that is engaged in the pharmaceuticals business, and Distributing begin discussions regarding an acquisition. There were no discussions between Distributing or Controlled and X or its shareholders regarding an acquisition or a distribution before the announcement. In addition, Distributing would have been able to continue the successful operation of its pharmaceuticals business without combining with X. During its negotiations with Distributing, X indicates that it favors the distribution. X merges into Distributing before the distribution but nothing in the merger agreement requires the distribution.

As a result of the merger, X's former shareholders receive 55 percent of Distributing's stock. In addition, X's chairman of the board and chief executive officer become the chairman of the board and chief executive officer, respectively, of Distributing. Six months after the merger, Distributing distributes the stock of Controlled pro rata in a distribution to which § 355 applies and to which § 355(d) does not apply. At the time of the distribution, the distribution continues to be substantially motivated by the business purpose of eliminating the competition for capital between the pharmaceuticals and cosmetics businesses.

LAW. Section 355(c) generally provides that no gain or loss is recognized to the distributing corporation on a distribution of stock in a controlled corporation to which § 355 (or so much of § 356 as relates to § 355) applies and which is not in pursuance of a plan of reorganization. Section 355(e) generally denies nonrecognition treatment under § 355(c) if the distribution is part of a plan (or series of related transactions) (a plan) pursuant to which one or more persons acquire directly or indirectly stock representing a 50-percent or greater interest in the distributing corporation or any controlled corporation.

Section 1.355-7(b)(1) provides that whether a distribution and an acquisition are part of a plan is determined based on all the facts and circumstances, including those set forth in § 1.355-7(b)(3) (plan factors) and (4) (non-plan factors). The weight to be given each of the facts and circumstances depends on the particular case. The determination does not depend on the relative number of plan factors compared to the number of non-plan factors that are present.

Section 1.355-7(b)(3)(iii) provides that, in the case of an acquisition (other than involving a public offering) before a distribution, if at some time during the two-year period ending on the date of the acquisition there were discussions by Distributing or Controlled with the acquirer regarding a distribution, such discussions tend to show that the distribution and the acquisition are part of a plan. The weight to be accorded this fact depends on the nature, extent, and timing of the discussions. In addition, the fact that the acquirer intends to cause a distribution and, immediately after the acquisition, can meaningfully participate in the decision regarding whether to make a distribution, tends to show that the distribution and the acquisition are part of a plan.

Section 1.355-7(b)(4)(iii) provides that, in the case of an acquisition (other than involving a public offering) before a distribution, the absence of discussions by Distributing or Controlled with the acquirer regarding a distribution during the two-year period ending on the date of the earlier to occur of the acquisition or the first public announcement regarding the distribution tends to show that the distribution and the acquisition are not part of a plan. However, this factor does not apply to an acquisition where the acquirer intends to cause a distribution and, immediately after the acquisition, can meaningfully participate in the decision regarding whether to make a distribution.

Section 1.355-7(b)(4)(v) provides that the fact that the distribution was motivated in whole or substantial part by a corporate business purpose (within the meaning of §1.355-2(b)) other than a business purpose to facilitate the acquisition or a similar acquisition tends to show that the distribution and the acquisition are not part of a plan.

Section 1.355-7(b)(4)(vi) provides that the fact that the distribution would have occurred at approximately the same time and in similar form regardless of the acquisition or a similar acquisition tends to show that the distribution and the acquisition are not part of a plan.

Section 1.355-7(h)(6) provides that discussions with the acquirer generally include discussions with persons with the implicit permission of the acquirer.

Section 1.355-7(h)(9) provides that a corporation is treated as having the implicit permission of its shareholders when it engages in discussions.

ANALYSIS. Whether the X shareholders' acquisition of Distributing stock and Distributing's distribution of Controlled are part of a plan depends on all the facts and circumstances, including those described in §1.355-7(b). The fact that Distributing discussed the distribution with X during the two-year period ending on the date of the acquisition tends to show that the distribution and the acquisition are part of a plan. See §1.355-7(b)(3)(iii). In addition, X's shareholders may constitute acquirers who intend to cause a distribution and who, immediately after the acquisition, can meaningfully participate (through X's chairman of the board and chief executive officer who become D's chairman of the board and chief executive officer) in the decision regarding whether to distribute Controlled. See id. However, the fact that Distributing publicly announced the distribution before discussions with X regarding both an acquisition and a distribution began suggests that the plan factor in §1.355-7(b)(3)(iii) should be accorded less weight than it would have been accorded had there been such discussions before the public announcement.

With respect to those factors that tend to show that the distribution and the acquisition are not part of a plan, the absence of discussions by Distributing or Controlled with X or its shareholders during the two-year period ending on the date of the public announcement regarding the distribution would tend to show that the distribution and the acquisition are not part of a plan only if X's shareholders are not acquirers who intend to cause a distribution and who, immediately after the acquisition, can meaningfully participate in the decision regarding whether to distribute Controlled. See § 1.355-7(b)(4)(iii). Because X's chairman of the board and chief executive officer become the chairman and chief executive officer, respectively, of Distributing, X's shareholders may have the ability to meaningfully participate in the decision whether to distribute Controlled. Therefore, the absence of discussions by Distributing or Controlled with X or its shareholders during the two-year period ending on the date of the public announcement regarding the distribution may not tend to show that the distribution and the acquisition are not part of a plan.

Nonetheless, the fact that the distribution was substantially motivated by a corporate business purpose (within the meaning of § 1.355-2(b)) other than a business purpose to facilitate the acquisition or a similar acquisition, and the fact that the distribution would have occurred at approximately the same time and in similar form regardless of the acquisition or a similar acquisition, tend to show that the distribution and the acquisition are not part of a plan. See § 1.355-7(b)(4)(v), (vi). The fact that the public announcement of the distribution preceded discussions by Distributing or Controlled with X or its shareholders, and the fact that Distributing's business would have continued to operate successfully even if the merger had not occurred, evidence that the distribution originally was not substantially motivated by a business purpose to facilitate the acquisition or a similar acquisition. Moreover, after the merger, Distributing continued to be substantially motivated by the same corporate business purpose (within the meaning of § 1.355-2(b)) other than a business purpose to facilitate the acquisition or a similar acquisition (§ 1.355-7(b)(4)(v)). In addition, the fact that Distributing decided to distribute Controlled and announced that decision before it began discussions with X regarding the combination suggests that the distribution would have occurred at approximately the same time and in similar form regardless of Distributing's combination with X and the corresponding acquisition of Distributing stock by the X shareholders.

Considering all the facts and circumstances, particularly the fact that the distribution was motivated by a corporate business purpose (within the meaning of § 1.355-2(b)) other than a business purpose to facilitate the acquisition or a similar acquisition, and the fact that the distribution would have occurred at approximately the same time and in similar form regardless of the acquisition or a similar acquisition, the acquisition and distribution are not part of a plan under § 355(e) and § 1.355-7(b).

HOLDING. Under the facts described above, the acquisition and the distribution are not part of a plan under § 355(e) and § 1.355-7(b).

3. Practical Impact of § 355(e)

It is important to focus on the reach of § 355(e). First, § 355(e) has no impact on the tax-free treatment otherwise available to the shareholders of the distributing corporation under § 355(a).

Second, if § 355(e) applies, it imposes a tax on the gains realized by the distributing corporation on the distribution, thereby eliminating the benefits the distributing corporation would otherwise receive from the continuation of the *General Utilities* nonrecognition treatment under § 355(c). This corporate level tax, in most cases, will be a deterrent to effectuating a transaction that falls within § 355(e).

Third, § 355(e) does not apply if the acquisitive reorganization was part of a plan negotiated completely after the spin-off. Thus, as long as the acquisitive reorganization was not part of a plan conceived before the spin-off, § 355(e) is not applicable. The 2002 Temporary Regulations give helpful guidance for determining whether there was a pre-spin-off plan.

Fourth, § 355(e) does not apply if in the acquisitive reorganization the shareholders of the distributing corporation end up with more than 50% of the stock of the acquiror. This is the type of structure used in several large notable transactions, including the acquisition in 2002 by Comcast Corporation of the cable properties of AT&T after a spin-off by AT&T of those properties. This transaction is discussed in Sec. 9.7.B. below.

G. Applicability of Step Transaction Doctrine in Spin-Off Followed by Reorganization

Revenue Ruling 98-27

1998-22 I.R.B. 4

Purpose This revenue ruling obsoletes Rev. Ruls. 96-30, 1996-1 C.B. 36, and 75-406, 1975-2 C.B. 125, modified by Rev. Rul. 96-30. This revenue ruling also modifies Rev. Rul. 70-225, 1970-1 C.B. 80.

Background Rev. Rul. 96-30 applies the principles of *Commissioner v. Court Holding Co.*, 324 U.S. 331 (1945), to a distribution of controlled corporation stock by a publicly traded parent, followed by a merger of the controlled corporation into an unrelated acquiring corporation. The former shareholders of the controlled corporation receive a 25 percent interest in the acquiring corporation. Based on all the facts and circumstances, the ruling concludes that the transaction satisfies the requirements of § 355 of the Internal Revenue Code. Rev. Rul. 96-30 also modifies the factually similar Rev. Rul. 75-406 [dealing with a spin-off of a controlled corporation followed by a merger of the controlled corporation into an acquiring corporation] by eliminating the implication that an independent, post-distribution shareholder vote to approve the acquisition of a controlled corporation is, by itself, enough to prevent application of the step transaction doctrine.

Section 1012(c) of the Taxpayer Relief Act of 1997 (the "Act"), Pub. L. No. 105-34, 111 Stat. 788, 916–17, amended the control requirements of §§ 351 and 368(a)(1)(D) to provide that, generally for transactions seeking qualification after August 5, 1997 under either provision and § 355, the shareholders of the distributing corporation must own stock possessing more than 50 percent of the voting power and more than 50 percent of the total value of the controlled corporation's stock immediately after the distribution. Sections 351(c) and 368(a)(2)(H). In addition, § 1012(a) of the Act amended § 355 by adding subsection (e), which provides rules for the recognition of gain on certain distributions of stock or securities of a controlled corporation in connection with acquisitions of stock representing a 50 percent or greater interest in the distributing corporation or any controlled corporation. Section 1012(a) of the Act generally applies to distributions after April 16, 1997, pursuant to a plan (or series of related transactions) that involves an acquisition described in § 355(e)(2)(A)(ii) occurring after such date.

The Conference Report accompanying the legislation states, in part, that:

> The House bill does not change the present-law requirement under section 355 that the distributing corporation must distribute 80 percent of the voting power and 80 percent of each other class of stock of the controlled corporation. It is expected that this requirement will be applied by the Internal Revenue Service taking account of the provisions of the proposal regarding plans that permit certain types of planned restructuring of the distributing corporation following the distribution, and to treat similar restructurings of the controlled corporation in a similar manner. Thus, the 80-percent control requirement is expected to be administered in a manner that would prevent the tax-free spin-off of a less-than-80-percent controlled subsidiary, but would not generally impose additional restrictions on post-distribution restructurings of the controlled corporation if such restrictions would not apply to the distributing corporation.

H.R. Rep. No. 105-220, at 529–30 (1997).

Analysis The application of *Court Holding* principles to determine whether the distributed corporation was a controlled corporation immediately before the distribution under 355(a) imposes a restriction on postdistribution acquisitions or restructurings of a controlled corporation that is inconsistent with § 1012 of the Act. See § 1012(c) of the Act and H.R. Rep. No. 105-220, at 529–30. Accordingly, the Service will not apply *Court Holding* (or any formulation of the step transaction doctrine) to determine whether the distributed corporation was a controlled corporation immediately before the distribution under § 355(a) solely because of any postdistribution acquisition or restructuring of the distributed corporation, whether prearranged or not. In otherwise applying the step transaction doctrine, the Service will continue to consider all facts and circumstances. See, e.g., Rev. Rul. 63-260, 1963-2 C.B. 147. An independent shareholder vote is only one relevant factor to be considered.

Holding Based on the enactment of § 1012 of the Act, the Service will not apply *Court Holding* (or any formulation of the step transaction doctrine) to determine whether the distributed corporation was a controlled corporation immediately before the distribution under § 355(a) solely because of any postdistribution acquisition or restructuring of the distributed corporation, whether prearranged or not.

Effect on Other Revenue Rulings Rev. Ruls. 96-30 and 75-406 are obsoleted. Rev. Rul. 70-225 is modified to the extent inconsistent with this revenue ruling. * * *

Note

In Rev. Rul. 98-44, 1998-37 I.R.B. 1, the Service declared obsolete (in view of the enactment of § 355(e)) Rev. Rul. 70-225, 1970-1 C.B. 80. This ruling held that a spin-off of a controlled corporation followed by the disposition of the controlled corporation in a (B) reorganization did not qualify under § 355, because the shareholders of the distributing corporation were not in control of the controlled corporation immediately after the spin-off.

H. Elaboration on *Morris Trusts* Transactions

1. Use of *Morris Trust* in Direct (A) Reorganizations, (B) Reorganizations, and Section 351 Transactions

The acquisitive reorganization used in a *Morris Trust* transaction can be a direct merger, which was used in the case, a (B) reorganization, or a § 351 transaction. However, the (C), the triangular (C), the (a)(2)(D) forward subsidiary merger, and the (a)(2)(E) reverse subsidiary merger generally cannot be used because each of these reorganizations has a requirement that "substantially all" the assets be acquired. *See Elkorn Coal*, Sec. 7.3.D.1.

There are four basic types of *Morris Trust* transactions in which the spin-off is followed by a direct merger under § 368(a)(1)(A):

1. Spin-off of unwanted assets followed by a merger of the distributing corporation into the acquiror (*a la Morris Trust*);

2. Spin-off of unwanted assets followed by a merger of a target into the distributing corporation;

3. Spin-off of wanted assets followed by merger of controlled corporation into the acquiror; and

4. Spin-off of wanted assets followed by merger of a target into the controlled corporation.

The transaction in paragraph (1) above is answered by *Morris Trust*. The Service has issued Revenue Rulings dealing with the transactions in paragraphs (2) through (4), and these rulings are set out below in Secs. 9.6.H.2, 3, and 4. The one Revenue Ruling dealing with the use of a *Morris Trust* type transaction in a (B) reorganization is set out in Sec. 9.6.H.5. below.

2. Spin-Off of Controlled Corporation Followed by Merger of Target Into Distributing Corporation

Revenue Ruling 72-530

1972-2 C.B. 212

Advice has been requested regarding the application of the "business purpose requirement" prescribed by section 1.355-2(c) of the Income Tax Regulations to a distribution of stock of a controlled corporation that otherwise qualifies under section 355 of the Internal Revenue Code of 1954.

X corporation and *Y* corporation had been engaged in the active conduct of a warehousing business and a transportation business, respectively, for the last five years. *X* had owned all the outstanding capital stock of *Y* since *Y* was organized. The value of *X's* net assets was evenly divided between the *Y* stock and the warehousing business. *Z* was an unrelated corporation engaged in the warehousing business. *Z's* business was equal in value to *X's* warehousing business. *X* would be substantially strengthened in its competitive position with other warehousing businesses by the acquisition of the assets of *Z*. It was not practical to transfer the *X* and *Z* warehousing businesses to a new corporation because the new corporation would have to apply for a new state warehousing license and comply with conditions applicable to new but not existing warehousing businesses. This would have constituted a severe encumbrance to the new corporation. *X, Z* and the *Z* shareholders entered into negotiations with respect to the merger of *Z* into *X* with the *Z* shareholders receiving solely *X* stock. The terms of the merger agreement were acceptable in all respects to the parties involved except that the shareholders of *Z* were unwilling to accept an amount of stock in *X* representing only a one-third equity interest. Negotiations were stalemated solely because of this objection by the *Z* shareholders.

In order to permit the *Z* shareholders to have a one-half equity interest in *X* after the merger, *X* distributed all the outstanding *Y* stock pro rata to the *X* shareholders. *Z* then merged into *X* and the shareholders of *Z* received a one-half equity interest in *X* as a result of the merger. * * *

The improvement of *X's* position with its competitors in the warehouse business is germane to its corporate business and the acquisition of *Z* will accomplish this purpose. * * * A distribution by *X* to its shareholders of the *Y* stock was the only practical means for *Z* to merge into *X* and for the *Z* shareholders to be able to acquire a one-half equity interest in *X*.

Accordingly, the distribution to the *X* shareholders of the *Y* stock met the "business purpose requirement" of [former] section 1.355-2(c) of the regulations and since all the other requirements under section 355 of the Code and the regulations thereunder have been met, the distribution qualifies under section 355 of the Code.

3. Spin-Off of Controlled Corporation Followed by Merger of Controlled Corporation into Acquiring Corporation

See Revenue Ruling 98-27, Sec. 9.6.G.

Rev. Rul 98-27, Sec. 9.6.G., made Rev. Rul. 75-406 obsolete. In Rev. Rul. 75-406, the service required that the shareholders of the controlled corporation that became a target in a merger reorganization be free to vote their stock in the controlled corporation for or against the merger. Rev. Rul. 98-27 permits a pre-spin-off vote on the merger as is the case in the ATT-Comcast transaction, Sec. 9.7.B.

4. Spin-Off of Controlled Corporation Followed by Acquisition by Controlled Corporation of Target Corporation in Acquisitive Reorganization

Revenue Ruling 76-527

1976-2 C.B. 103

Advice has been requested whether the "business purpose" requirement of section 1.355-2(c) of the Income Tax Regulations is satisfied in the following transaction, which is otherwise qualified under section 355 of the Internal Revenue Code of 1954 and the regulations thereunder.

X corporation and *Y* corporation have been engaged in the active conduct of a construction materials production business and a television broadcasting business, respectively, for the last five years. The stock of *X* is widely held by the public. *X* has owned all the outstanding stock of *Y* since it was organized. The construction materials production business accounts for 80 percent of the combined revenue and profits of *X* and *Y*. Based upon advice from its investment analysts, management of *X* believes that the investment community considers *X* to be only a construction materials producer. Management of *Y* has been actively negotiating for the acquisition of the television broadcasting properties of an unrelated corporation, *Z*. *Z*'s management, however, has indicated an unwillingness to accept *Y* stock as consideration, since *Y* is controlled by a corporation whose business is unrelated to television broadcasting.

Thus, *X* proposes to distribute all of the *Y* stock, pro rata, to the *X* shareholders. This distribution will enable the television broadcasting business to use its own stock to make acquisitions in its expansion efforts. * * *

In order to allow *Y* to use its own stock in the acquisition of the assets of *Z* it was necessary to separate the television broadcasting business of *Y* from the dominant reputation of the construction materials production business of *X* in the investment community.

Therefore, the pro rata distribution by *X* of the *Y* stock to the *X* shareholders will be considered to be carried out for purposes germane to the business of the corporations within the contemplation of [former] section 1.355-2(c) of the regulation.

5. Spin-Off of Controlled Corporation Followed by Disposition of Controlled Corporation in a (B)

Revenue Ruling 70-225

1970-1 C.B. 80

[This ruling is modified to the extent that it is inconsistent with Rev. Rul. 98-27, Sec. 9.6.G.]

Advice has been requested whether the transactions described below qualify as (1) a reorganization under section 368(a)(1)(D) of the Internal Revenue Code of 1954, (2) a distribution of stock of a controlled corporation under section 355 of the Code, and (3) a reorganization under section 368(a)(1)(B) of the Code.

R, a corporation with one shareholder, *A*, for many years has operated a taxicab business and a car rental business. *T*, an unrelated widely held corporation, desired to acquire *R*'s car rental business. Pursuant to a plan, *R* transferred the assets of its car rental business to a newly formed corporation, *S*, in exchange for all the stock of *S* and distributed the stock of *S* to its sole shareholder (*A*) in a transaction intended to qualify under sections 368(a)(1)(D) and 355 of the Code. As part of the prearranged plan, *A* immediately exchanged all his *S* stock for some of the outstanding voting stock of *T* in an exchange intended to meet the requirements of section 368(a)(1)(B) of the Code. * * *

[I]n the instant case, the transfer by *R* of part of its assets to *S* in exchange for all the stock of *S* followed by the distribution of the *S* stock to *A* and by the transfer of the *S* stock to *T* by *A* in exchange for *T* stock is a series of integrated steps which * * * may not be considered independently of each other. Accordingly, neither *R* nor its sole shareholder *A* is in control of *S* after the transfer and the transaction does not constitute a reorganization under section 368(a)(1)(D) of the Code nor a transfer under section 351 of the Code. Section 368(a)(1)(B) of the Code is not applicable to the transaction, since in effect *R* transferred part of its assets to *T* in exchange for a part of the *T* stock, rather than *T* having acquired all the stock of a previously existing corporation solely in exchange for its own voting stock.

Accordingly, the receipt by *A* of the stock of *T* is not a distribution to which section 355 of the Code applies. The fair market value of the stock of *T* is taxable to *A* as a distribution by *R* under section 301 of the Code. In addition, gain or loss is recognized to *R* on the transaction.

Questions

What are the precise holdings in Rev. Rul. 70-225? What is the basis of the holding that the distributing corporation, *R*, recognizes gain?

6. Spin-Off of Controlled Corporation Followed by Disposition of Distributing Corporation in a (B)

Revenue Ruling 70-434
1970-2 C.B. 83

Corporation *X* had been engaged in the active conduct of two businesses (toy manufacturing and hand tool manufacturing) for over five years. Corporation *Z*, an unrelated corporation, desired to acquire the stock of *X* but was only interested in having *X* conduct the hand tool manufacturing business. This was accomplished pursuant to a plan under which *X* transferred its toy manufacturing business, representing 23 percent of the assets of *X*, to a newly created corporation, *Y*, in exchange for all of the stock of *Y* which was distributed pro rata to the *X* shareholders in a transaction that qualified as a reorganization within the meaning of section 368(a)(1)(D) of the Internal Revenue Code of 1954 since the distribution of the *Y* stock met all of the requirements of section 355 of the Code. *Z* then acquired all of the outstanding stock of *X* in exchange solely for voting common stock of *Z*. *X* remained in existence as a wholly owned subsidiary.

Held, the exchange of the *X* stock for the *Z* stock is a reorganization within the meaning of section 368(a)(1)(B) of the Code, which defines as a "reorganization" the acquisition by one corporation, in exchange solely for its voting stock, of stock of another corporation if, immediately after the acquisition, the acquiring corporation has control of such other corporation. The *Y* stock previously distributed to the *X* shareholders is not considered property received from *Z* in connection with the exchange of *X* stock for *Z* stock.

§ 9.7 Illustration of Spin-Off Transaction: Spin-Off Pursuant to a Previously Existing Plan: The Comcast-AT&T Transaction

Excerpts from S-4 Prospectus and Proxy Statements for AT&T Comcast Spin-Off and Merger and AT&T Tracking Stock Filed May 14, 2002

A Merger Proposal—Your Vote Is Very Important

Comcast and AT&T have agreed to combine Comcast and AT&T's broadband business. As a result, AT&T shareholders will have shares of both AT&T and the new corporation—AT&T Comcast. We are proposing the transaction because we believe the combination of Comcast and AT&T Broadband will create the world's premier broadband communications company. The new corporation will be named AT&T Comcast Corporation and will be headquartered in Philadelphia.

When the transaction is completed,

– Comcast shareholders will receive one share of a corresponding class of AT&T Comcast common stock in exchange for each Comcast share they own; and

– AT&T shareholders will receive a number of shares of AT&T Comcast common stock determined pursuant to a formula described in this joint proxy statement/prospectus for each AT&T share they own. If the AT&T exchange ratio were determined as of the date of this joint proxy statement/prospectus, each AT&T shareholder would receive approximately 0.35 of a share of AT&T Comcast common stock for each of their AT&T shares, although the actual exchange ratio may differ. AT&T shareholders will also continue to hold their shares of AT&T common stock.

THE BOARDS OF DIRECTORS OF BOTH COMCAST AND AT&T HAVE UNANIMOUSLY APPROVED THE TRANSACTION AND RECOMMEND THAT THEIR RESPECTIVE SHAREHOLDERS VOTE FOR THE PROPOSAL TO APPROVE AND ADOPT THE MERGER AGREEMENT AND THE TRANSACTIONS CONTEMPLATED BY THE MERGER AGREEMENT. * * *

SUMMARY AND OVERVIEW OF THE TRANSACTIONS QUESTIONS AND ANSWERS ABOUT THE TRANSACTIONS

* * *

Q: What proposals am I being asked to vote upon and what vote is required to approve each proposal?

A: If you are a Comcast shareholder, you are being asked to vote upon the following proposals:

– Approval and adoption of the merger agreement and the transactions contemplated by the merger agreement. The Comcast transaction proposal requires the affirmative vote of a majority of the votes cast by holders of shares of Comcast Class A common stock and Comcast Class B common stock, voting together as a single class. Approval of this proposal is assured because Sural LLC, which holds approximately 86.7% of the combined voting power of the Comcast stock, has agreed to vote its shares in favor of the Comcast transaction proposal. * * *

– Approval of the AT&T Comcast charter. The AT&T Comcast charter proposal requires the affirmative vote of a majority of the votes cast by holders of shares of Comcast Class A common stock and Comcast Class B common stock, voting together as a single class. Approval of this proposal is assured because Sural LLC has agreed to vote its shares in favor of it. * * *

– Approval and adoption of an amendment to the Comcast charter to allow the implementation of the Preferred Structure. * * *

APPROVAL OF THE COMCAST TRANSACTION PROPOSAL AND THE AT&T COMCAST CHARTER PROPOSAL IS NOT CONDITIONED ON APPROVAL OF THE PREFERRED STRUCTURE PROPOSAL.

If you are an AT&T shareholder, you are being asked to vote upon the following proposals:

– Approval and adoption of the merger agreement and the transactions contemplated by the merger agreement, including the AT&T Broadband spin-off. The AT&T transaction proposal requires the affirmative vote of a majority of outstanding shares of AT&T common stock. * * *

– Approval of the AT&T Comcast charter. The AT&T Comcast charter proposal requires the affirmative vote of a majority of the votes cast by holders of shares of AT&T common stock. * * * Approval of the AT&T Comcast charter proposal, including the corporate governance provisions contained in the AT&T Comcast charter, is a condition to completion of the AT&T Comcast transaction. THEREFORE, IF AT&T SHAREHOLDERS WISH TO APPROVE THE AT&T COMCAST TRANSACTION, THEY MUST ALSO APPROVE THE AT&T COMCAST CHARTER PROPOSAL. * * *

Q: What percentage of AT&T Comcast's economic interest and voting power will AT&T shareholders hold upon completion of the AT&T Comcast transaction?

A: AT&T shareholders will own approximately 54.8% of AT&T Comcast's economic interest upon completion of the AT&T Comcast transaction. If the preferred capital structure is implemented, AT&T shareholders will own approximately 60.6% of AT&T Comcast's voting power upon completion of the AT&T Comcast transaction. If the alternative capital structure is implemented, AT&T shareholders will own approximately 56.6% of AT&T Comcast's voting power upon completion of the AT&T Comcast transaction. [Since the AT&T shareholders will end up with more that 50% of AT&T Comcast, § 355(e) will not apply to the spin-off.]

Q: What percentage of AT&T Comcast's economic interest and voting power will Comcast shareholders hold upon completion of the AT&T Comcast transaction?

A: Comcast Class A shareholders, Comcast Class B shareholders and Comcast Class A Special shareholders, who presently own approximately 2.3%, 1.0% and 96.7%, respectively, of Comcast's economic interest, will own approximately 1.0%, 0.4% and 38.6%, respectively, of AT&T Comcast's economic interest upon completion of the AT&T Comcast transaction. * * *

Q: Who will hold the remaining percentage of AT&T Comcast's economic interest and voting power upon completion of the AT&T Comcast transaction?

A: If the transaction with Microsoft Corporation described in this document is completed, Microsoft will hold AT&T Comcast's remaining approximately 5.3% economic interest and 4.95% voting power upon completion of the AT&T Comcast transaction. * * *

SUMMARY

This summary highlights selected information from this document and may not contain all of the information that is important to you. * * *

THE COMPANIES

COMCAST CORPORATION * * *

Comcast is a Pennsylvania corporation incorporated in 1969. Comcast is involved in three principal lines of business:

– Cable — through the development, management and operation of broadband communications networks;

– Commerce — through QVC, its electronic retailing subsidiary; and

– Content — through its consolidated subsidiaries Comcast Spectacor, Comcast SportsNet, Comcast SportsNet Mid-Atlantic, Comcast Sports Southeast, E! Entertainment Television, The Golf Channel and Outdoor Life Network, and through its other programming investments.

AT&T CORP. * * *

AT&T is a New York corporation incorporated in 1885. AT&T currently consists primarily of AT&T Broadband Group, AT&T Consumer Services Group and AT&T Business Services Group. These AT&T groups are not separate companies, but, rather, are parts of AT&T.

The transactions proposed in this document would:

– separate and spin off AT&T Broadband into a separate company that immediately would be combined with and become a part of AT&T Comcast, and

– establish a tracking stock for AT&T Consumer Services Group.

AT&T BROADBAND GROUP

AT&T Broadband Group is one of the nation's largest broadband communications businesses, providing cable television, high-speed cable Internet services and communications services over one of the most extensive broadband networks in the country. * * *

AT&T COMCAST CORPORATION * * *

AT&T Comcast is a newly formed Pennsylvania corporation that has not, to date, conducted any activities other than those incident to its formation, the financing and other matters contemplated by the merger agreement and the preparation of this document. Upon completion of the AT&T Comcast transaction, Comcast and AT&T Broadband will each become a wholly owned subsidiary of AT&T Comcast. The business of AT&T Comcast will be the combined businesses currently conducted by Comcast and AT&T Broadband Group.

THE AT&T COMCAST TRANSACTION REASONS FOR THE AT&T COMCAST TRANSACTION

Comcast and AT&T believe that the combined strengths of Comcast and AT&T's broadband business will enable them to create the world's premier broadband communications company. * * *

THE STRUCTURE OF THE AT&T COMCAST TRANSACTION

The AT&T Comcast transaction will occur in several steps. First, AT&T will transfer the assets and liabilities of AT&T's broadband business to AT&T Broadband, a holding company formed for the purpose of effectuating the AT&T Comcast transaction. Second, AT&T will spin off AT&T Broadband to its shareholders. [This transfer to AT&T Broadband and the spin-off of its stock should qualify as a divisive (D) reorganization under §§ 368(a)(1)(D) and 355.] Third, Comcast and AT&T Broadband will each merge with a different, wholly owned subsidiary of AT&T Comcast. In the AT&T Comcast transaction, Comcast and AT&T shareholders will receive the consideration described below. The merger agreement provides for all of the steps described above to occur on the closing date for the mergers. [This is permissible as a result of Rev. Rul. 98-27, Sec. 9.6.F. As will be seen below the mergers are structured as reverse subsidiary mergers that are designed to qualify as a single § 351 transaction.] * * *

WHAT COMCAST SHAREHOLDERS WILL RECEIVE
IN THE COMCAST MERGER

Comcast shareholders will receive one share of the corresponding class of AT&T Comcast common stock in exchange for each of their shares of Comcast common stock.

Upon completion of the AT&T Comcast transaction, assuming that the Microsoft transaction described below is completed and AT&T Comcast is not required to make any of the additional payments of AT&T Comcast common stock described below, Comcast shareholders will own approximately

- 40.0% of AT&T Comcast's economic interest and
- if the Preferred Structure is implemented, 34.4% of AT&T Comcast's voting power or, if the Alternative Structure is implemented, 38.5% of AT&T Comcast's voting power.

Upon completion of the AT&T Comcast transaction, regardless of which capital structure is implemented and whether or not the Microsoft transaction described below is completed or AT&T Comcast is required to make any of the potential additional payments of AT&T Comcast common stock described below, Sural LLC, which is controlled by Brian L. Roberts, President of Comcast, and currently holds approximately 86.7% of Comcast's voting power, will hold approximately 33 1/3% of AT&T Comcast's voting power, including all of the outstanding AT&T Comcast Class B common stock.

WHAT AT&T SHAREHOLDERS WILL RECEIVE IN THE
AT&T COMCAST TRANSACTION

The precise number of shares of AT&T Comcast common stock that each holder of AT&T common stock will receive in the AT&T Comcast transaction will depend upon the number of shares of AT&T common stock outstanding and the value of the employee stock options and stock appreciation rights held by current AT&T Broadband employees and former AT&T and AT&T Broadband employees, in each case at the time the AT&T Comcast transaction is completed, and the number of shares, if any, of AT&T common stock held by Comcast immediately prior to the record date for the AT&T Broadband spin-off.

If the exchange ratio were determined as of the date of this document, assuming AT&T Comcast is not required to make any of the additional payments of AT&T Comcast common stock described below, AT&T shareholders will receive with respect to each of their shares of AT&T common stock:

- if the Preferred Structure is implemented, approximately 0.35 of a share of AT&T Comcast Class A common stock or

- if the Alternative Structure is implemented, approximately 0.35 of a share of AT&T Comcast Class C common stock.

Upon completion of the AT&T Comcast transaction, assuming the Microsoft transaction described below is completed and AT&T Comcast is not required to make any of the additional payments of AT&T Comcast common stock described below, AT&T shareholders will own approximately

- 54.8% of AT&T Comcast's economic interest and

- if the Preferred Structure is implemented, 60.6% of AT&T Comcast's voting power or, if the Alternative Structure is implemented, 56.6% of AT&T Comcast's voting power.

The actual exchange ratio may vary from the 0.35 estimate calculated as of the date of this document. * * *

CONDITIONS TO THE COMPLETION OF THE AT&T COMCAST TRANSACTION

The completion of the AT&T Comcast transaction is subject to the satisfaction or waiver of several conditions, including:

- approval by AT&T shareholders of the AT&T transaction proposal and the AT&T Comcast charter proposal;

- approval by Comcast shareholders of the Comcast transaction proposal and the AT&T Comcast charter proposal; * * *

- receipt of all required regulatory approvals other than those the failure of which to be obtained would not reasonably be expected to have a material adverse effect on either Comcast or AT&T Broadband Group; * * *

- receipt and continuing effectiveness of an Internal Revenue Service ruling or rulings, or an opinion from tax counsel acceptable to Comcast and AT&T, to the effect that, for U.S. federal income tax purposes, the AT&T Broadband spin-off will be tax-free to AT&T and its shareholders, the mergers will not cause the AT&T Broadband spin-off to fail to be qualified as a tax-free transaction, and the AT&T Broadband spin-off will not cause the distributions by AT&T of the common stock of AT&T Wireless Services, Inc. or of Liberty Media Corporation to fail to qualify as tax-free transactions; * * *

[SUMMARY OF] MATERIAL FEDERAL INCOME TAX CONSEQUENCES

It is a condition to the AT&T Broadband spin-off and to the mergers that AT&T receive a private letter ruling from the Internal Revenue Service, or an opinion of counsel, to the effect that AT&T, AT&T Broadband and holders of AT&T common stock who receive shares of AT&T Broadband common stock in the AT&T Broadband spin-off will not recognize gain or loss for U.S. federal income tax purposes in connection with the AT&T Broadband spin-off. AT&T has filed a private letter ruling request in respect of this matter with the IRS. It is a condition to the mergers that AT&T and Comcast each receive an opinion of counsel to the effect that AT&T Broadband, Comcast and their respective shareholders who exchange their shares for shares of AT&T Comcast common stock in the mergers will not recognize gain or loss for U.S. federal income tax purposes in connection with the mergers, except for gain or loss with respect to cash received instead of fractional shares. The receipt of this opinion by AT&T is also a condition to the AT&T Broadband spin-off.

Subject to the limitations and qualifications described in "The AT&T Comcast Transaction—Material Federal Income Tax Consequences," it is the opinion of Wachtell, Lipton, Rosen & Katz, counsel to AT&T, that the AT&T Broadband spin-off will qualify as a tax-free reorganization. As a result, (1) no gain or loss will be recognized by AT&T or AT&T Broadband upon the separation and the AT&T Broadband spin-off (other than gains related to certain intercompany transactions that will be triggered by the AT&T Broadband spin-off) and (2) no gain or loss will be recognized by U.S. holders of AT&T common stock upon their receipt of shares of AT&T Broadband common stock in the AT&T Broadband spin-off.

Subject to the limitations and qualifications described in "The AT&T Comcast Transaction—Material Federal Income Tax Consequences," it is the opinion of Wachtell, Lipton, Rosen & Katz, counsel to AT&T, and Davis Polk & Wardwell, counsel to Comcast, that the mergers will constitute an exchange to which Section 351 of the Internal Revenue Code applies. As a result, (1) no gain or loss will be recognized by Comcast, AT&T Broadband, the AT&T Broadband merger subsidiary, or the Comcast merger subsidiary upon the mergers and (2) except for gain or loss with respect to cash received instead of fractional shares, no gain or loss will be recognized by U.S. holders of AT&T Broadband common stock or Comcast common stock on the exchange of such stock for AT&T Comcast common stock. * * *

MATERIAL FEDERAL INCOME TAX CONSEQUENCES

Subject to the limitations and qualifications described herein, the following discussion constitutes the opinion of Wachtell, Lipton, Rosen & Katz, counsel to AT&T, as to the material U.S. federal income tax consequences of the AT&T Broadband spin-off and the mergers to United States Holders of AT&T common stock and AT&T Broadband common stock and the opinion of Davis Polk & Wardwell, counsel to Comcast, as to the material U.S. federal income tax consequences of the mergers to United States Holders of Comcast common stock. This discussion is based on the Code, the Treasury Regulations promulgated thereunder, judicial opinions, published positions of the Internal Revenue Service, and all other applicable authorities as of the date of this document, all of which are subject to change (possibly with retroactive effect).

As used in this document, the term "United States Holder" means:

- a citizen or resident of the United States;

- a corporation, or other entity taxable as a corporation for U.S. federal income tax purposes, created or organized in or under the laws of the United States or of any political subdivision thereof; or

- an estate or trust the income of which is subject to United States federal income taxation regardless of its source.

The term United States Holder also includes certain former citizens and residents of the United States.

This discussion does not describe all of the tax consequences that may be relevant to a holder in light of his particular circumstances or to holders subject to special rules, such as:

- certain financial institutions;

- insurance companies;

- tax-exempt organizations;

- dealers in securities or foreign currencies;

- persons holding AT&T common stock, AT&T Broadband common stock or Comcast common stock as part of a hedge;

- United States Holders whose functional currency is not the U.S. dollar;

- partnerships or other entities classified as partnerships for U.S. federal income tax purposes;

- persons subject to the alternative minimum tax;

- shareholders who acquired their AT&T common stock, AT&T Broadband common stock or Comcast common stock through the exercise of options or otherwise as compensation or through a tax-qualified retirement plan; or

- holders of options granted under any AT&T or Comcast benefit plan.

In addition, this summary is limited to shareholders that hold their AT&T common stock, AT&T Broadband common stock or Comcast common stock as capital assets. This discussion also does not address any tax consequences arising under the laws of any state, local or foreign jurisdiction.

Accordingly, each AT&T, AT&T Broadband and Comcast shareholder is strongly urged to consult with a tax adviser to determine the particular federal, state, local or foreign income or other tax consequences to him of the AT&T Broadband spin-off and the mergers.

It is assumed for purposes of the following discussion that the private letter ruling (or an opinion of counsel) on the AT&T Broadband spin-off and the opinions of counsel on the mergers which are discussed below under "—Conditions to Closing" have been received.

MATERIAL FEDERAL INCOME TAX CONSEQUENCES OF THE SEPARATION AND THE AT&T BROADBAND SPIN-OFF

The tax consequences of the separation and the AT&T Broadband spin-off are as follows:

- no gain or loss will be recognized by, and no amount will be included in the income of, AT&T or AT&T Broadband upon the separation and the AT&T Broadband spin-off other than gains related to certain intercompany transactions that will be triggered by the AT&T Broadband spin-off;

- no gain or loss will be recognized by, and no amount will be included in the income of, United States Holders of AT&T common stock upon their receipt of shares of AT&T Broadband common stock in the AT&T Broadband spin-off;

- a United States Holder of AT&T common stock will apportion the tax basis of such holder's AT&T common stock on which AT&T Broadband common stock is distributed between AT&T common stock and the AT&T Broadband common stock received in the AT&T Broadband spin-off in proportion to the fair market values of such AT&T common stock and AT&T Broadband common stock on the date of the AT&T Broadband spin-off; and

- the holding period of the shares of AT&T Broadband common stock received by a United States Holder of AT&T common stock in the AT&T Broadband spin-off will include the period during which such holder held the AT&T common stock on which the AT&T Broadband common stock is distributed.

Current Treasury Regulations require each holder of AT&T common stock who receives AT&T Broadband common stock pursuant to the AT&T Broadband spin-off to attach to his or her federal income tax return for the year in which the AT&T Broadband spin-off occurs, a detailed statement setting forth such data as may be appropriate in order to show the applicability of Section 355 of the Code to the AT&T Broadband spin-off. AT&T will provide the appropriate information to each of its shareholders of record.

MATERIAL FEDERAL INCOME TAX CONSEQUENCES OF THE MERGERS

Subject to the discussion below relating to the receipt of cash instead of fractional shares, for U.S. federal income tax purposes, the tax consequences of the mergers will be as follows:

- the mergers will constitute an exchange to which Section 351 of the Code applies;

- no gain or loss will be recognized by Comcast, AT&T Broadband, the AT&T Broadband merger subsidiary, or the Comcast merger subsidiary as a result of the mergers;

- no gain or loss will be recognized by:

—United States Holders of AT&T Broadband common stock on the exchange of their AT&T Broadband common stock for AT&T Comcast common stock; or

—United States Holders of Comcast common stock on the exchange of their Comcast common stock for AT&T Comcast common stock;

- the aggregate adjusted basis of the AT&T Comcast common stock received in the mergers by:—a United States Holder of AT&T Broadband common stock will be equal to the aggregate adjusted basis of the United States Holder's AT&T Broadband common stock exchanged for that AT&T Comcast common stock, reduced by any tax basis allocable to the fractional share interests in AT&T Comcast common stock for which cash is received; and

—a United States Holder of Comcast common stock will be equal to the aggregate adjusted basis of the United States Holder's Comcast common stock exchanged for that AT&T Comcast common stock; and

- the holding period of the AT&T Comcast common stock received in the mergers by:

—a United States Holder of AT&T Broadband common stock will include the holding period of the United States Holder's AT&T Broadband common stock exchanged for that AT&T Comcast common stock; and

—a United States Holder of Comcast common stock will include the holding period of the United States Holder's Comcast common stock exchanged for that AT&T Comcast common stock. Cash Instead of Fractional Shares. AT&T Comcast will not issue any fractional shares in the AT&T Broadband merger. Instead, any fractional interests AT&T Broadband shareholders otherwise would have been entitled to receive will be sold and the proceeds will be paid to those shareholders. The receipt of cash instead of a fractional share of AT&T Comcast common stock by a United States Holder of AT&T Broadband common stock will result in taxable gain or loss to such United States Holder for U.S. federal income tax purposes based upon the difference between the amount of cash received by such United States Holder and the United States Holder's adjusted tax basis in the fractional share as set forth above. The gain or loss will constitute capital gain or loss and will constitute long-term capital gain or loss if the United States Holder's holding period is greater than one year as of the date of the mergers. The deductibility of capital losses is subject to limitations. * * *

CONDITIONS TO CLOSING

It is a condition to both the AT&T Broadband spin-off and the mergers that AT&T has obtained one or more private letter rulings from the Internal Revenue Service, which will continue in effect at the time of the AT&T Broadband spin-off and mergers, to the effect that:

- the separation and the AT&T Broadband spin-off will be tax-free to AT&T and its shareholders under Sections 355 and 368(a) of the Code,

- the mergers will not cause the separation and the AT&T Broadband spin-off to fail to be qualified as a tax-free transaction pursuant to Section 355 of the Code, and

- the separation and the AT&T Broadband spin-off will not cause the distribution by AT&T of all of the common stock of AT&T Wireless or of Liberty Media to fail to qualify as tax-free transactions pursuant to Sections 355 and 368(a) of the Code.

AT&T has filed a private letter ruling request in respect of the matters described in the immediately preceding bullet points with the Internal Revenue Service. The private letter ruling condition may be waived if AT&T and Comcast mutually agree to obtain an opinion to the same effect from tax counsel of a nationally recognized reputation mutually acceptable to AT&T and Comcast. The receipt of such private letter ruling or opinion of counsel and its continuing validity are subject to factual representations and assumptions. Neither AT&T nor AT&T Broadband nor Comcast is aware of any facts or circumstances that would cause such representations and assumptions to be untrue. An opinion of counsel represents counsel's best legal judgment and is not binding on the Internal Revenue Service or any court.

It is a condition to the Comcast merger that Comcast receive an opinion from Davis Polk & Wardwell, dated the date of the mergers, and it is a condition to the AT&T Broadband merger that AT&T receive an opinion from Wachtell, Lipton, Rosen & Katz, dated the date of the mergers, each to the effect that, on the basis of the facts, representations and assumptions set forth in such opinion, the mergers will constitute an exchange to which Section 351 of the Code applies. Any change in currently applicable law, which may or may not be retroactive, or the failure of any factual representations or assumptions to be true, correct and complete in all material respects, could affect the validity of the Davis Polk & Wardwell and Wachtell, Lipton, Rosen & Katz tax opinions.

An opinion of counsel represents counsel's best legal judgment and is not binding on the Internal Revenue Service or any court. No ruling has been or will be sought from the Internal Revenue Service as to the U.S. federal income tax consequences of the mergers and, as a result, there can be no assurance that the Internal Revenue Service will not disagree with, or challenge, any of the conclusions described below.

AT&T does not intend to waive the receipt of a private letter ruling (or an opinion of counsel) on the AT&T Broadband spin-off and its counsel's opinion on the mergers as a condition to its obligation to complete the AT&T Broadband spin-off and the AT&T Broadband merger, and will not waive the receipt of such ruling and opinion(s) as a condition to its obligation to complete the AT&T Broadband spin-off and AT&T Broadband merger without recirculating this document in order to resolicit shareholder approval. Comcast does not intend to waive the receipt of a private letter ruling (or an opinion of counsel) on the AT&T Broadband spin-off and its counsel's opinion on the mergers as a condition to its obligation to complete the Comcast merger, and will not waive the receipt of such ruling and opinion(s) as a condition to its obligation to complete the Comcast merger without recirculating this document in order to resolicit shareholder approval.

Both counsel intend to deliver, at the date of the mergers, an opinion on the mergers that satisfies the requirements described above. * * *

§ 9.8 Summary Problems on Spin-Offs

Target corporation (TC) has 100 common shares outstanding (its only stock), which is owned as follows:

	No. of Shares	Adjusted Basis
Individual A	40	20K
Corporation X	40	20K
Individual B	20	10K

TC has two different divisions: (1) a widget division, which has plant and equipment with a value of $55K and a basis of $35K, and (2) a wodget division, which has plant and equipment with a value of $55K and a basis of $75K. TC has cash of $20K and liabilities of $30K, represented by 10-year debentures. There is no OID on the debentures. A owns $10K of the debentures and the balance is owned by a bank (Y). A has a basis of $9K for his debentures and Y has a basis of $18K. The debentures have a fair market value of $30K.

The total fair market value of TC's assets is $130K and the net value is $100K, as follows:

Assets	Fair Market Value	Adjusted Basis
Cash	$20K	$20K
Widget Division	$55K	$35K
Wodget Division	$55K	$75K
Total Assets	$130K	
Liabilities		
Debentures	$30K	
	$100K	

The value of TC's stock is also $100K. TC has accumulated E & P of $50K.

Acquiring corporation (AC) is a large conglomerate whose stock is traded on the New York Stock Exchange. AC wants to acquire TC principally for the purpose of getting into the widget business, which AC thinks is about to take off.

What are the tax consequences to each of the parties under each of the following basic asset transactions and the modifications thereof?

TC merges into AC with the shareholders of TC receiving in exchange for their TC stock on a pro rata basis $100K of AC nonvoting common stock. AC issues its debentures with a face and value of $30K, which do not have OID, in exchange for the TC debentures held by A and Y?

Consider each of the following modifications separately.

a. Suppose that prior to the acquisition, *TC* contributes the wodget division to a new subsidiary (*S*) in exchange for stock and $15K of *S* debentures, and *TC* then distributes (1) the stock of *S* to *X* in redemption of the *TC* stock held by *X,* and (2) the $15K of *S* debentures in exchange for $15K of the *TC* debentures? *TC* then merges into *AC* with *A* and *B* receiving solely voting common stock of *AC*? Suppose instead *AC* acquires *TC*'s remaining assets solely for *AC* voting stock? Suppose instead, *AC* then acquires the stock of *TC* from *A* and *B* in exchange for *AC* voting common stock?

b. Suppose that prior to the acquisition, *TC* contributes the widget division plus the cash to a new subsidiary (*S*), in exchange for stock and $15K of *S* debentures, and *TC* then distributes (1) the *S* stock to *A* and *B* in redemption of their stock, and (2) the $15K of *S* debentures in exchange for $15K of *TC* debentures? *S* then merges into *AC* with *A* and *B* receiving solely voting stock of *AC* and the *S* debenture holders receiving *AC* debentures of an equal principal amount? Suppose instead that *AC* acquires *S*'s assets solely for *AC* voting stock? Suppose instead, *AC* acquires the stock of *S* from *A* and *B* in exchange for *AC* voting preferred?

Chapter 10

Introduction to Cross Border Acquisitive Reorganizations (including Inversions) and Spin-Offs

§ 10.1 Scope

This chapter focuses on the impact of Section 367 on cross border tax-free acquisitive reorganizations and spin-offs. Before proceeding with this chapter it is crucial to have a fundamental understanding of the manner in which the reorganization provisions, which are addressed in Chapters 6–9, operate.

After laying the groundwork, this chapter focuses first on outbound acquisitive reorganizations, which are acquisitions in which a foreign acquiror acquires the stock or assets of a U.S. target in a transaction that, subject to Section 367, qualifies for tax-free treatment under Section 354 or Section 361. Also, included in these transactions are outbound acquisitive Section 351 transactions. These transactions include, for example, the acquisition by DaimlerChrysler, a newly formed German holding company, of the stock of Chrysler, a U.S. corporation. As will be seen below, outbound reorganizations are also subject to Section 7874, the anti-inversion statute that was enacted by the Jobs Creation Act of 2004.

The chapter then focuses on inbound acquisitive reorganizations, which are transactions in which a U.S. acquiror acquires the stock or assets of a foreign target. Next, the chapter focuses on Foreign-to-Foreign acquisitive reorganizations, which are transactions in which both the acquiror and target are foreign, but the target has U.S. shareholders, such as in the acquisition by DaimlerChrysler of Daimler Benz, a German operating company that was listed through ADRs on the New York Stock Exchange. Finally, the chapter focuses on tax-free spin-offs to U.S. and foreign shareholders.

The emphasis here is on transactions involving publicly held corporations that are unrelated and have no significant overlapping shareholders. Thus, this chapter generally does not address the impact of Section 367 on transfers within a group of commonly controlled or related corporations and for that reason does not examine (1) the nondivisive (D) reorganization under Sections 368(a)(1)(D) and 354(b), (2) recapitalizations under Section 368(a)(1)(E), (3) mere changes in form under Section 368(a)(1)(F), and (4) Section 304 related company redemptions. As would be expected, the tax treatment of the transactions addressed here is very complex, and this chapter focuses only on the basic principles.

Sec.10.2 introduces the impact of Section 367 on acquisitive reorganizations. Sec.10.3 elaborates on the structure and purpose of Section 367, and Sec.10.4 discusses the forms of outbound, inbound, and Foreign-to-Foreign acquisitive reorganizations involving U.S. shareholders of the target. Sec.10.5 introduces the regulations under Section 367 governing transfers of stock of domestic corporations in outbound reorganizations. Sec. 10.6 discusses the impact of the recently enacted anti-inversion provision, Section 7874, on outbound transactions. Sec.10.7 addresses the impact of Sections 367 and 7874 on the direct outbound transfer of the stock of a domestic target in a (B) stock-for-stock reorganization and in acquisitive Section 351 incorporation transactions. Sec.10.8 focuses on the impact of Sections 367 and 7874 on indirect outbound stock reorganizations, which involve the acquisition by foreign acquirors of the stock of U.S. targets in triangular reorganizations. Sec.10.9 deals with the applicability of Section 367 and 7874 on the direct outbound transfer of the assets of a domestic target to a foreign acquiror; in these transactions, the assets of the domestic target are leaving the U.S. taxing jurisdiction. Sec.10.10 presents summary problems on outbound reorganizations. Sec. 10.11 provides an introduction to New Inversions, including the Treasury's 2016 proposed regulations dealing with both (1) general inversion issues, and (2) debt-equity under Section 385 involving inversions and related transactions. Sec. 10.12 presents a policy perspective on these transactions.

Turning to inbound and Foreign-to-Foreign reorganizations, Sec.10.13 provides an introduction to Section 367(b), which applies to such transactions, and Sec.10.14 sets out the legislative background to Section 367(b). Sec.10.15 discusses general principles underlying the Section 367(b) regulations. Sec. 10.16 addresses the impact of Section 367 on the spin-off by a domestic parent to foreign shareholders in a Section 355 transaction. Finally, Sec. 10.17 focuses on the impact of Section 1248 on a Section 355 distribution by a domestic corporation of stock of a CFC.

For a further discussion of the issues addressed in this chapter, *see Kuntz and Peroni, supra* Sec. 1.11 at Chapters B.5 and B.6; *Isenbergh, supra* Sec. 1.11 at Chapter 32; *Dolan, supra* Sec. 1.11 at Part III. *See also* Thompson, *Mergers, Acquisitions, and Tender Offers, supra* Sec. 1.11 at Chapter 22. This chapter is similar to Chapter 15 of Thompson, *U.S. International Tax Planning and Policy* (2016).

§ 10.2 Impact of Section 367 on Acquisitive Reorganizations

A. Introduction

If a foreign corporation is involved in a reorganization transaction described in Section 368 or a distribution described in Section 355, the effect of Section 367 must be considered. This section can cause gain to be recognized on an exchange even if that exchange is otherwise a nonrecognition transaction under Sections 332, 351, 354, 355, 356 or 361.

A reorganization governed by Section 367 can take the form of an outbound transfer, an inbound transfer or a completely foreign transfer. Examples of outbound reorganization transfers are the transfer by a U.S. person of stock of a domestic target corporation to a foreign acquiring corporation in a stock for stock reorganization under Section 368(a)(1)(B), or the acquisition by a foreign acquiring corporation of the assets of a domestic target corporation in exchange solely for voting stock of the foreign corporation in a transaction that qualifies as a reorganization under Section 368(a)(1)(C). Also, as a result of a 2006 amendment to the definition of the "(A)" reorganization under Section 368(a)(1)(A) to permit mergers involving foreign entities to qualify as a "merger or consolidation," an outbound reorganization could also encompass a merger of a domestic target corporation into a foreign acquiror corporation. These 2006 amendments are examined immediately below. This chapter focuses on all types of acquisitive reorganizations in which a foreign acquiring corporation acquires the stock or assets of a domestic target. Also, the chapter discusses the use of Section 351 in cross border M&A transactions

Inbound reorganization transfers include, for example, the acquisition by a domestic acquiring corporation of the assets of a foreign target corporation in a transaction that qualifies as a Section 368(a)(1)(C) stock for asset reorganization or, as a result of the 2006 regulations, as a Section 368(a)(1)(A) merger reorganization.

Completely foreign reorganization transactions include, for example, the acquisition by a foreign acquiring corporation of the assets of a foreign target corporation in a Section 368(a)(1)(C) stock for stock reorganization or, as a result of the 2006 regulations, in a Section 368(a)(1)(A) merger reorganization.

Outbound transfers are governed by Section 367(a) and inbound and Foreign-to-Foreign transactions are governed by Section 367(b).

B. Introduction to the 2006 Final Regulations Permitting a Merger Involving a Foreign Corporation to Qualify as an "A" Reorganization

1. Preamble to the 2006 Final Regulations Relating to the Definition of the "A" Reorganization

Preamble to Final Regulations on Statutory Mergers and Consolidations, Treasury Decision 9242

January 26, 2006

See § 1.368-2(b)(ii).

SUMMARY: This document contains final regulations that define the term *statutory merger or consolidation* as that term is used in section 368(a)(1)(A) of the Internal Revenue Code, concerning corporate reorganizations. * * *

Background. The Internal Revenue Code of 1986 (Code) provides for general non-recognition treatment for reorganizations described in section 368 of the Code.

Section 368(a)(1)(A) provides that the term reorganization includes *a statutory merger or consolidation.* * * *

As described above, under the 2003 temporary regulations, a transaction can only qualify as a statutory merger or consolidation if the transaction is effected "pursuant to the laws of the United States, or a State or the District of Columbia." Given that many foreign jurisdictions have merger or consolidation statutes that operate in material respects like those of the states, on January 5, 2005, the IRS and Treasury Department proposed regulations (the 2005 proposed regulations) containing a revised definition of statutory merger or consolidation that allows transactions effected pursuant to the statutes of a foreign jurisdiction or of a United States possession to qualify as a statutory merger or consolidation (70 FR 746). Simultaneously with the publication of the 2005 proposed regulations, the IRS and Treasury Department published a notice of proposed rulemaking proposing amendments to the regulations under sections 358, 367, and 884 to reflect that, under the 2005 proposed regulations, a transaction involving a foreign entity and a transaction effected pursuant to the laws of a foreign jurisdiction may qualify as a statutory merger or consolidation (the foreign regulations).

Explanation of Provisions. * * * This Treasury decision adopts the 2005 proposed regulations as final regulations, with certain technical changes. The foreign regulations are adopted as final regulations in a separate Treasury decision. * * *

2. Excerpts from the 2006 Final Regulations; Basic Principles, Foreign Mergers and Amalgamations

Reg. § 1.368-2(b)(1)(ii) addresses the concepts of a "statutory merger" and "consolidation" as follows:

(ii) *Statutory merger or consolidation generally.* For purposes of section 368(a)(1)(A), a statutory merger or consolidation is a transaction effected pursuant to the statute or statutes [note the statutes need not be domestic corporation statutes] necessary to effect the merger or consolidation, in which transaction, as a result of the operation of such statute or statutes, the following events occur simultaneously at the effective time of the transaction—

(A) All of the assets (other than those distributed in the transaction) and liabilities (except to the extent such liabilities are satisfied or discharged in the transaction or are nonrecourse liabilities to which assets distributed in the transaction are subject) of each member of one or more combining units (each a transferor unit) become the assets and liabilities of one or more members of one other combining unit (the transferee unit); and

(B) The combining entity of each transferor unit ceases its separate legal existence for all purposes; provided, however, that this requirement will be satisfied even if, under applicable law, after the effective time of the transaction, the combining entity of the transferor unit (or its officers, directors, or agents) may act or be acted against, or a member of the transferee unit (or its officers, directors, or agents) may act or be acted against in the name of the combining entity of the transferor unit, provided that such actions relate to assets or obligations of the combining entity of the transferor unit that arose, or relate to activities engaged in by such entity, prior to the effective time of the transaction, and such actions are not inconsistent with the requirements of paragraph (b)(1)(ii)(A) of this section.

Reg. § 1.368-2(b)(1)(ii) contains the following illustration of a foreign transactions that qualifies as a statutory merger for the purposes of the (A) reorganization under Section 368(a)(1)(A):

> *Example 13. Transaction effected pursuant to foreign statutes.* (i) *Facts.* Z and Y are entities organized under the laws of Country Q and classified as corporations for Federal income tax purposes. Z and Y combine. Pursuant to statutes of Country Q the following events occur simultaneously: all of the assets and liabilities of Z become the assets and liabilities of Y and Z's separate legal existence ceases for all purposes.
>
> (ii) *Analysis.* The transaction satisfies the requirements of paragraph (b)(1)(ii) of this section because the transaction is effected pursuant to statutes of Country Q and the following events occur simultaneously at the effective time of the transaction: all of the assets and liabilities of Z, the combining entity [*i.e.,* a business entity that is a corporation and not a disregarded entity] of the transferor unit, become the assets and liabilities of Y, the combining entity and sole member of the transferee unit, and Z ceases its separate legal existence for all purposes. Accordingly, the transaction qualifies as a statutory merger or consolidation for purposes of section 368(a)(1)(A).

3. Overlap between (A) and (C)

Even though as a result of the 2006 amendments to the 367 regulations, a foreign corporation can now engage in a merger reorganization, under prior law, which continues in effect, a merger between a domestic and a foreign corporation, or between two foreign corporations that for some reason still does not qualify as an (A), may be treated as a (C) reorganization if all the conditions under Section 368(a)(1)(C) are satisfied[1] or as a nondivisive (D) reorganization if all the conditions of Sections 368(a)(1)(D) and 354(b) are satisfied.

---

1. *See e.g.,* Rev. Rul. 67-326, 1967-2 C.B. 143.

§ 10.3 Elaboration on Impact of Section 367 on Acquisitive Reorganizations, Section 351 Transactions and Spin-Offs*

A. In General

Section 367 can cause gain to be recognized even if the exchange is otherwise a nonrecognition transaction under, among other provisions:

- Section 354, relating to the tax-free exchange of stock or securities of a target corporation for stock or securities of an acquiring corporation pursuant to a reorganization defined in Section 368;

- Section 361, relating to a tax-free transfer by a target corporation of its assets to an acquiring corporation in exchange for stock or securities of the acquiror pursuant to a reorganization defined in Section 368;

- Section 351, relating to, for example, the transfer of the stock of an acquiror and a target to a new holding company; and

- Section 355, relating to the distribution by a parent corporation of the stock of a controlled subsidiary in a spin-off that is tax free to both the parent and its shareholders.

B. Purpose of Section 367 and Controlled Foreign Corporation and Related Provisions

1. Section 367

The United States taxes nonresident aliens and foreign corporations only on (1) certain "fixed or determinable" items of passive income (*e.g.*, interest) from sources within the U.S.,[2] and (2) income that is "effectively connected" with the conduct of a trade or business within the U.S.[3] This system of taxation, combined with certain nonrecognition provisions of the Code, could allow a U.S. resident to avoid U.S. taxation on the sale of appreciated property. These nonrecognition provisions include Sections 354 and 361, which provide nonrecognition treatment to a target's shareholders and the target in acquisitive reorganizations under Section 368.

By way of example, U.S. Target could transfer its assets to Foreign Acquiror, which is organized in a tax haven country such as Bermuda, in a (C) reorganization under Section 368(a)(1)(C). Section 361 would give U.S. Target nonrecognition treatment, and Section 354 would give the shareholders of U.S. Target nonrecognition treatment on receipt of stock of Foreign Acquiror. Foreign Acquiror could

---

* This section is based on Thompson, *Section 367: A "Wimp" for Inversions and a "Bully" for Real Cross Border Acquisitions*, 94 Tax Notes 1505 (March 18, 2002).

2. I.R.C. §§ 871 and 881.

3. I.R.C. §§ 872 and 882.

then sell the assets received from U.S. Target in a transaction that would not be subject to taxation in the tax haven or in the U.S. Consequently, there would be no U.S. tax on the sale proceeds until the proceeds are repatriated to the U.S. in the form of dividends or liquidation payments. This absence of U.S. tax until earnings of a foreign corporation are repatriated to the U.S. is referred to as the deferral principle.

A myriad of transactions involving foreign corporations could give rise to potential avoidance or deferral of U.S. taxation. Many of these transactions involve a non-recognition transaction under (1) Sections 354 and 361, which provide for nonrecognition treatment for corporate reorganizations under Section 368, (2) Section 351, which provides for nonrecognition on the transfers of property to a controlled corporation, and (3) Section 332, which allows nonrecognition treatment on the liquidation of controlled subsidiaries. To deter tax avoidance schemes involving international corporate transactions that are otherwise accorded nonrecognition treatment, Congress enacted the predecessor of Section 367 in 1932. Section 367 has been substantially amended on numerous occasions since its enactment.

The General Explanation of the Tax Reform Act of 1984 gives the following general overview of the operation of the current Section 367(a), which governs outbound transactions, that is, transfers of stock or property outside the taxing jurisdiction of the U.S.:

> The Act restructures the rules governing outbound transfers. [*See* § 367(a).] Under the general rule [of Section 367(a)(1)], a foreign corporation is not considered a corporation for purposes of determining the extent to which gain is recognized on an outbound transfer. A general exception is provided for transfers of property for use in the active conduct of a trade or business outside of the United States. [*See* § 367(a)(3).] Transfers of stock, securities, or partnership interests may qualify for the exception. [*See* §§ 367(a)(2) and (4).] The Secretary of the Treasury, however, by regulations, may provide for recognition of gain in cases of transfers of property for use in the active conduct of a trade or business outside the United States. [*See* 367(a)(3)(A).] It was intended that the Secretary use this regulatory authority to provide for recognition in cases of transfers involving potential tax avoidance. The Act also authorizes the Secretary to designate other transfers that are excepted from the general rule of recognition. [*See* § 367(a)(6).][4]

The General Explanation of the Tax Reform Act of 1976 gives the following description of Section 367(b), which governs non-outbound transactions:

> The Act establishes separate treatment under section 367(b) for a second group of transfers which consists of exchanges described in sections 332, 351, 354, 355, 356, and 361 that are not treated as transfers out of the United States [under Section 367(a).] With respect to these other transactions ... a foreign corporation will not be treated as a corporation to the extent that

---

4. General Explanation of the Tax Reform Act of 1984, at 420 (1984).

the Secretary of the Treasury provides in regulations that are necessary or appropriate to prevent the avoidance of Federal income taxes. * * *

Transfers covered in these regulations are to include transfers constituting a repatriation of foreign earnings. Also included are transfers that involve solely foreign corporations and shareholders (and involve a U.S. tax liability of U.S. shareholders only to the extent of determining the amount of any deemed distribution under the Subpart F rules [*see* Section 4.7]). It is anticipated that in this latter group of exchanges, the regulations will not provide for any immediate U.S. tax liability but will maintain the potential tax liability of the U.S. shareholder.[5]

2. Controlled Foreign Corporation and Related Provisions

In addition to Section 367, the Code also contains other provisions designed to prevent the avoidance of U.S. tax through the use of foreign corporations. Since a foreign corporation is only subject to U.S. taxation on its U.S. source income, it would be possible for U.S. shareholders to avoid U.S. taxation by conducting business or investments through a foreign corporation. Also, little or no tax would be paid if the foreign corporation operated in a tax haven country.

For example, an individual, Sam, could transfer $100,000 of cash to Tax Haven, Inc., a newly formed corporation organized in a tax haven country, and Tax Haven, Inc. could invest in non-U.S. investments. Under the general rules governing foreign corporations, neither Sam nor Tax Haven, Inc. would be subject to U.S. tax on the foreign income earned by Tax Haven, Inc.

The Code, however, contains several provisions designed to prevent this type of avoidance of U.S. tax. These include:

First, the controlled foreign corporation (CFC) provisions,[6] which impute certain types of tax haven income, which is known as subpart F income, to the 10% or more U.S. shareholders of a foreign corporation that is controlled (*i.e.*, more than 50% ownership) by five or fewer 10% U.S. shareholders. *See* Section 4.7.

Second, Section 956, which treats as a dividend to a U.S. parent of a CFC (1) loans made by the CFC to the parent corporation, and (2) certain other U.S. investments by the CFC. *See* Section 4.7.

Third, Section 1248, which treats the gain recognized by a 10% U.S. shareholder on the sale of the stock of a CFC as dividend income (rather than capital gain) to the extent the gain is attributable to earnings of the CFC that have not been subject to U.S. taxation.

Fourth, the passive foreign investment company (PFIC) rules under Sections 1291 to 1298 pursuant to which U.S. investors in foreign investment funds

---

5. General Explanation of the Tax Reform Act of 1976, at 263 (1976).

6. I.R.C. §§ 951–960.

are subject to immediate tax on their shares of the earnings or are subject to an interest charge on the benefit received from the deferral of tax. The PFIC rules apply without respect to the level of U.S. ownership of foreign corporations that have substantial passive assets or income.

The above provisions—the controlled foreign corporation provisions, Section 956, Section 1248, and the PFIC provisions—are designed to eliminate or mitigate the benefits of deferral from U.S. taxation that otherwise are available for the foreign operations of a foreign corporation. Thus, these provisions are backstops to the general worldwide taxation principle that applies in the U.S. The CFC provisions, however, do not apply, for example, to active income earned by a CFC from operations in the country of its incorporation.

C. Elaboration on Structure of Section 367 as Applicable to Acquisitive Reorganizations and Acquisitive Section 351 Transactions

1. Section 367(a)(1) Gain Recognition Rule for Outbound Transfers

Section 367(a)(1) provides:

> If in connection with an exchange provided in section 351 [relating to tax-free contributions to corporations], Section 354 [relating to tax-free treatment for a shareholder of a target who exchanges target stock for stock of an acquiror pursuant to a reorganization as defined in Section 368] ... or Section 361 [relating to tax-free treatment for a target that exchanges its assets for stock of an acquiror pursuant to a reorganization as defined in Section 368], a United States person transfers property to a foreign corporation, such foreign corporation shall not, for purposes of determining the extent to which gain shall be recognized on such transfer, be considered a corporation.

If Section 367(a)(1) applies to a transfer of property to a foreign corporation in what would otherwise be a Section 351 transaction or reorganization, the foreign corporation is not treated as a corporation. Consequently, the transaction will not give rise to tax-free treatment of gain under Sections 351, 354 or 361, all of which require that the transferor receive stock in a corporation. This is referred to here as the gain recognition rule.[7]

This chapter focuses on the impact of Section 367 in situations in which Section 351 is used to effectuate the combination of an acquiror corporation and a target corporation.

As will be seen below, Section 7874, an anti-inversion provision enacted by the Jobs Creation Act of 2004 must also be taken into account in examining outbound transfers.

---

7. Section 367 only provides recognition treatment for gains, not losses.

2. Section 367(a)(6) Exceptions to Gain Recognition Rule for Outbound Transactions Described in Regulations

Notwithstanding the broad sweep of the gain recognition rule of Section 367(a)(1), under Section 367(a)(6), the Treasury may promulgate regulations making Section 367(a)(1) inapplicable to certain transfers of property to foreign corporations.

3. Section 367(a)(2) Exception to Gain Recognition Rule for Transfer of Stock or Security of Foreign Corporations

Section 367(a)(2) provides that the gain recognition rule of Section 367(a)(1) does not apply, except as provided in regulations, to "the transfer of stock or securities of a foreign corporation which is a party to the exchange or a party to the reorganization." The 1998 Section 367 Regulations promulgated rules under this provision,[8] and these rules are examined below.

4. Section 367(a)(3) Exception to Gain Recognition Rule for Certain Outbound Incorporations

Section 367(a)(3) provides an exception to the gain recognition rule of Section 367(a)(1) for certain transfers of property to a foreign corporation to be used in the active conduct by the corporation of a trade or business. This exception principally applies to incorporation transactions under Section 351, in which tangible property is transferred to a controlled foreign corporation in exchange for stock. This provision does not apply to the transfer of stock to a foreign holding company in an acquisitive Section 351 transaction.

5. Section 367(a)(5) Exception to the Section 367(a)(2) and (3) Exceptions

Section 367(a)(5) provides that neither (1) Section 367(a)(2), relating to the exception for the transfer of stock or securities of a foreign corporation, nor (2) Section 367(a)(3), relating to the transfer of an active trade or business, shall "apply in the case of an exchange described in section (a) or (b) of section 361." Section 361 would apply, for example, to the transfer by a U.S. Target of its assets to a Foreign Acquiror in exchange for stock of the Foreign Acquiror pursuant to (1) a (C) reorganization under Section 368(a)(1)(C), or (2) an (A) reorganization under Section 368(a)(a)(A), as a result of the 2006 regulations. Thus, Section 367(a)(5) provides for gain recognition for this type of transaction. However, Section 367(a)(5) also provides an exception to this gain recognition exception "if the transferor corporation [*i.e.*, the U.S. target] is controlled (within the meaning of Section 368(c) [*i.e.*, at least 80%]) by 5 or fewer domestic corporations." Since this chapter deals only with acquisitive reorganizations involving publicly-held targets and acquirors, this rule is not addressed further.

---

8. Treas. Reg. § 1.367(a)-3(a) and (b).

6. Section 367(b) Rules for Non-Outbound Transfers

Section 367(b) governs exchanges described in Sections 354 and 361 in connection with which there is a non-outbound transfer of property. These non-outbound cases involve the following reorganization transactions: (1) the acquisition of a Foreign Target by a U.S. Acquiror (*i.e.*, an inbound reorganization), and (2) the acquisition by Foreign Acquiror of Foreign Target (*i.e.*, Foreign-to-Foreign reorganizations). In these reorganizations, Section 367(b)(1) provides that "a foreign corporation shall be considered to be a corporation except to the extent provided in regulations ... which are necessary or appropriate to prevent the avoidance of Federal income taxes." In elaborating on the scope of these regulations Section 367(b)(2) provides:

> The regulations prescribed pursuant to [Section 367(b)(1)] shall include (but shall not be limited to) regulations dealing with the sale or exchange of stock or securities in a foreign corporation by a United States person, including regulations providing:

> (A) the circumstances under which — (i) gain shall be recognized currently, or amounts included in gross income currently as a dividend, or both, or (ii) gain or other amounts may be deferred for inclusion in the gross income of a shareholder (or his successor in interest) at a later date, and

> (B) the extent to which adjustments shall be made to earnings and profits, basis of stock or securities, and basis of assets.

§ 10.4 Forms of Outbound, Inbound, and Foreign-to-Foreign Acquisitive Reorganization Transactions Involving U.S. Shareholders*

A. Applicability of Section 367 to Outbound Reorganizations and Certain Foreign-to-Foreign Reorganizations

As indicated, a reorganization governed by Section 367 can take the form of an outbound transfer, an inbound transfer or a completely Foreign-to-Foreign transfer. The following sections illustrate outbound reorganizations and the type of Foreign-to-Foreign reorganization that occurred in the DaimlerChrysler acquisition, which involved an acquisition of a foreign corporation with U.S. shareholders.

---

* This section is based on Thompson, *Section 367: A "Wimp" for Inversions and a "Bully" for Real Cross Border Acquisitions*, 94 Tax Notes 1505 (March 18, 2002).

B. Direct Outbound Transfers of Stock or Assets

The principal types of acquisitive reorganization transactions involving direct outbound transfers that could be subject to Section 367(a) are:

- The acquisition by Foreign Acquiror (or its foreign subsidiary) of substantially all of the assets of U.S. Target in exchange for voting stock of Foreign Acquiror in a transaction that qualifies as a reorganization under Section 368(a)(1)(C) (*i.e.*, an outbound (C) reorganization).

- The acquisition by Foreign Acquiror (or its foreign subsidiary) of the stock of U.S. Target in exchange solely for voting stock of the Foreign Acquiror in a transaction that qualifies as a stock for stock reorganization under Section 368(a)(1)(B) (*i.e.*, an outbound (B) reorganization).

- As a result of the 2006 amendments to the definition of the (A) reorganization under Section 368(a)(1)(A), the acquisition by Foreign Acquiror (or its foreign subsidiary) of U.S. Target in exchange for stock of Foreign Acquiror in a transaction that qualifies as (i) a reorganization under Section 368(a)(1)(A) (*i.e.*, a direct outbound (A)) reorganization, or (ii) a forward subsidiary merger reorganization under Section 368(a)(2)(D).

Also, the use of an acquisitive Section 351 transaction in which the stock of U.S. Target is acquired by Foreign Holding Company is a direct outbound transaction.

C. Indirect Outbound Transfers of Stock of a Domestic Target

In addition to the above forms of outbound acquisitive reorganizations, the regulations under Section 367(a) treat certain acquisitive triangular reorganizations in which a subsidiary of Foreign Acquiror merges with U.S. Target as an indirect outbound transfer.[9] In these transactions, the stock or assets of a U.S. Target are acquired in a triangular reorganization in which U.S. Acquiring Subsidiary is a domestic subsidiary of Foreign Acquiring Parent. Thus, in these transactions U.S. Target enters into a triangular reorganization with U.S. Acquiring Subsidiary of Foreign Acquiror, and the shareholders of U.S. Target end up with stock of Foreign Acquiror.

Prior to the 2006 amendments to the Section 367 regulations, for this provision to apply, Acquiring Subsidiary had to be a domestic corporation. Now, as will be discussed below, depending on the circumstances, Acquiring Subsidiary may be either a domestic or foreign corporation.

D. Inbound Acquisitions of Stock or Assets

In these transactions a U.S. Acquiring Corporation acquires either the stock or assets of a Foreign Target. The regulations under Section 367(b) apply to these transactions.

---

9. Treas. Reg. § 1.367(a)-3(d).

E. Foreign-to-Foreign Transfers of Stock or Assets

The principal types of acquisitive Foreign-to-Foreign reorganizations examined here are subject to both Section 367(b) and Section 367(a):

- The acquisition by Foreign Acquiror (or its foreign subsidiary) of the stock of Foreign Target in an exchange that qualifies as a stock for stock reorganization under Section 368(a)(1)(B) (*i.e.*, a foreign (B) reorganization).

- The acquisition by Foreign Acquiror (or its foreign subsidiary) of the assets of Foreign Target in a stock for asset reorganization under Section 368(a)(1)(C) (*i.e.*, a foreign (C) reorganization) or in a nondivisive (D) reorganization under Section 368(a)(1)(D).

- As a result of the 2006 amendments to the Section 367 regulations, the merger of Foreign Target into Foreign Acquiror (or its foreign subsidiary) or the merger of a the foreign subsidiary into Foreign Target in an (A) reorganization under Section 368(a)(1)(A) (*i.e.*, a foreign direct merger reorganization), Section 368(a)(2)(D) (*i.e.*, a foreign forward subsidiary merger reorganization), or Section 368(a)(2)(E) (*i.e.*, a foreign reverse subsidiary merger reorganization).

Also, Foreign Target could be acquired by Foreign Holding Company in an acquisitive Section 351 transaction.

The shareholders of the Foreign Targets in these transactions may include U.S. persons who own stock in the Foreign Target either directly or through American Depositary Receipts (ADRs) traded on a U.S. exchange. For these U.S. shareholders, the transactions have an outbound feature and, therefore, are subject to the rules of Section 367(a).

F. Summary of Outbound and Foreign-to-Foreign Acquisitive Reorganizations and Section 351 Acquisitive Transactions Governed by Section 367

For purposes of analyzing in the following sections the impact of Section 367 and Section 7874, the anti-inversion provision, on the above forms of reorganizations, the transactions are separated into the following categories:

- *Outbound stock for stock reorganizations.* These transactions involve direct and triangular outbound stock for stock (B) reorganizations, in which U.S. persons transfer stock of U.S. Target to Foreign Acquiror or Foreign Acquiror Subsidiary in exchange solely for voting stock of Foreign Acquiror. These transactions are subject to the regulations under Section 367(a) and to Section 7874, the anti-inversion statute. *See* Sec.10.7.

- *Outbound acquisitive Section 351 transaction.* These transactions involve the transfer by the shareholders of U.S. Target of their target stock to Foreign Holding Company in exchange for common stock of the Holding Company in a transaction that qualifies under Section 351. These transactions are subject to the regulations under Section 367(a) and to Section 7874. *See* Sec.10.7.

• *Indirect outbound triangular reorganizations.* These transactions involve the acquisition by Foreign Acquiror of the stock of U.S. Target in exchange for stock of Foreign Acquiror by (1) the domestic subsidiary of Foreign Acquiror in a triangular reorganization, and (2) the foreign subsidiary of Foreign Acquiror in a reverse subsidiary merger under Section 368(a)(2)(E) or a triangular (B) under Section 368(a)(1)(B). These transactions are subject to the regulations under Section 367(a) and to Section 7874. *See* Sec.10.8.

• *Outbound asset reorganizations.* These transactions encompass direct and triangular outbound (C) reorganizations in which U.S. Target transfers its assets to Foreign Acquiror or Foreign Acquiror Subsidiary in exchange for stock of Foreign Acquiror, which is distributed to the shareholders of U.S. Target. These transactions are subject to the regulations under Section 367(a) and to Section 7874. Also, as a result of the 2006 amendments to Section 367, an outbound asset reorganization can be effectuated as (1) a direct merger of U.S. Target into Foreign Acquiror, or (2) a forward subsidiary merger of U.S. Target into a foreign subsidiary of Foreign Acquiror. *See* Sec.10.9.

• *Spin-offs by Domestic Parents of Domestic Subs to Domestic and Foreign Shareholders.* In virtually every spin-off by a publicly held domestic parent of its domestic sub, there will be some foreign shareholders receiving stock of the sub. The regulations under Section 367(b) give these transactions a pass. *See* Sec 10.16. This chapter does not discuss the spin-off by a domestic parent of a controlled foreign corporation, or spin-offs of foreign subs or by foreign corporations.

Other cross-border reorganizations not discussed here include:

• *Inbound asset reorganizations.* These transactions involve the acquisition by a U.S. Acquiring Corporation of the assets of a Foreign Target in a (C) reorganization or in a direct or forward subsidiary merger under Section 368(a)(1)(A) or Section 368(a)(2)(D).

• *Inbound stock reorganizations.* These transactions involve the acquisition by a U.S. Acquiring Corporation of the stock of a Foreign Target in a (B) reorganization or in a reverse subsidiary merger under Section 368(a)(2)(E).

• *Foreign-to-Foreign asset and stock reorganizations.* These transactions encompass Foreign Targets and Foreign Acquirors involved in (1) direct and triangular (B) reorganizations, (2) direct and triangular (C) reorganizations, and (3) direct and triangular (A) reorganizations. These transactions are subject to the concurrent application of Section 367(b) and Section 367(a) if there are U.S. shareholders of the Foreign Targets.

• *Foreign-to-Foreign acquisitive Section 351 transactions.* In these transactions the stock of Foreign Target is transferred to Foreign Holding Company in an acquisitive Section 351 transaction. These transactions are subject to the rules of concurrent application of Section 367(b) and Section 367(a) if there are U.S. shareholders of Foreign Target.

§ 10.5 Introduction to the Outbound Regulations under Section 367 Relating to Transfers of Stock of Domestic Corporations

A. The Final Section 367 Inversion Regulations Relating to Direct Transfers of Stock of U.S. Targets

Preamble to Treasury Decision 8702
See § 1.367(a)-3(c), December 30, 1996.

Explanation of Provisions. Section 367(a)(1) generally treats a transfer of property (including stock or securities) by a U.S. person to a foreign corporation in connection with an exchange described in section 332, 351, 354, 356 or 361 as a taxable exchange unless the transfer qualifies for an exception to this general rule.

Rules that address transfers of stock or securities of domestic corporations are contained in the final regulations described herein. Rules that address transfers of stock or securities of foreign corporations under section 367(a) are contained in Notice 87-85.

The final regulations retain the general rules set forth in the temporary regulations, which provide that a U.S. person that exchanges stock or securities in a U.S. target company (UST) for stock of a foreign corporation (the transferee foreign corporation (or TFC)) in an exchange described in section 367(a) will qualify for nonrecognition treatment if certain reporting requirements are satisfied and each of the following conditions is met:

(i) U.S. transferors must receive no more than 50 percent of the voting power and value of the stock of the TFC in the transfer (i.e., the 50-percent ownership threshold is not exceeded);

(ii) U.S. officers, directors and 5-percent or greater shareholders of the U.S. target must not own, in the aggregate, more than 50 percent of the voting power and value of the TFC immediately after the transfer (i.e., the control group case does not apply);

(iii) The U.S. person (exchanging U.S. shareholder) either must not be a 5-percent transferee shareholder immediately after the transfer or, if the U.S. person is a 5-percent transferee shareholder, must enter into a 5-year gain recognition agreement (GRA) with respect to the UST stock or securities it exchanged. (Without such GRA, the transfer by the 5-percent transferee shareholder will not qualify for nonrecognition treatment; however, transfer by other U.S. transferors not subject to the GRA requirement may qualify if all other requirements are met.); and

(iv) The active trade or business requirement must be satisfied.

If one or more of the foregoing requirements is not satisfied, the transfer by the U.S. person of stock or securities of a domestic corporation in exchange for stock of a TFC is taxable under section 367(a).

In response to suggestions from commentators, however, the final regulations make a number of modifications to the temporary regulations, principally in two areas: (i) the treatment of transfers of "other property" in the context of the 50-percent ownership threshold requirement, and (ii) the active trade or business requirement. * * *

Active Trade or Business Test: In General. [§ 1.367(a)-3(c)(3)] The final regulations modify the "active trade or business" requirement that must be satisfied for a U.S. transferor to qualify for an exception to the general rule of taxability under section 367(a)(1).

Under the requirement contained in the temporary regulations, no exception under section 367(a)(1) is available unless (i) the TFC or an affiliate was engaged in an active trade or business for the entire 36-month period prior to the exchange (the 36-month test), and (ii) such business was substantial in relation to the business of the U.S. target company (the substantiality test). For this purpose, an affiliate is generally defined by reference to the rules in section 1504(a) [*i.e.*, an 80% owned sub] (without the exclusion of foreign corporations).

The active trade or business test under the final regulations includes (i) a modified 36month test, (ii) a new anti-avoidance rule requiring that the transaction not be undertaken with an intention that the TFC cease its active trade or business, and (iii) a modified substantiality test. The final regulations make a number of other modifications and clarifications to the active trade or business test. For example, the final regulations permit the TFC to consider only an 80-percent owned foreign subsidiary (referred to as a "qualified subsidiary"), and not an affiliate, to satisfy the active trade or business test on its behalf.

Active Trade or Business Test: 36-Month Test and Intent Test. Under the 36-month test contained in the temporary regulations, the TFC or an affiliate is required to be engaged in an active trade or business for the entire 36 months immediately preceding the date of the transfer. Under the final regulations, this test can be satisfied by acquired businesses that have a 36-month operating history, unless they are acquired with the principal purpose of satisfying the active trade or business test.

In addition to the 36-month test, the active trade or business test in the final regulations contains a requirement that the transaction not be undertaken with an intention that the TFC cease its active business. The IRS and the Treasury Department believe that if a TFC with a 36-month active business history does not intend to maintain such business, but is only used as a vehicle to acquire the UST, an "inversion" transaction rather than a synergy of two businesses has been effected. * * *

Active Trade or Business Test: Qualified Subsidiaries. The final regulations permit a TFC to take into account only qualified subsidiaries, rather than affiliates, to satisfy the active trade or business test. This aspect of the active trade or business test has been narrowed because the IRS and the Treasury Department do not believe that a TFC should satisfy the active trade or business exception merely because its parent company (or an affiliate of the parent company) is engaged in an active trade or business. * * *

Active Trade or Business Test: Partnership Interests. The temporary regulations did not address whether the TFC could satisfy the active trade or business requirement by taking into account an interest in a partnership engaged in an active trade or business.

The final regulations permit a TFC (or a qualified subsidiary) to take into account the active trade or business engaged in outside the United States by any qualified partnership as there defined.

Active Trade or Business Test: Substantiality Test [§ 1.367(a)-3(c)(3)(iii)]. Under the temporary regulations, the second prong of the active trade or business requirement is the substantiality test. The active trade or business of the TFC is required to be "substantial" vis-à-vis the active trade or business of the UST, but the temporary regulations do not define substantiality.

The final regulations modify the substantiality requirement. Under the final regulations, the substantiality test no longer compares the active trade or business of the TFC vis-à-vis the UST. Instead, it requires that the entire value of the TFC be at least equal to the entire value of the UST at the time of the transaction. However, for this purpose, the value of the TFC may include the value of assets (including stock) acquired within the 36month period prior to the transaction only if (i) such assets were acquired in the ordinary course of business, or (ii) such assets (or their proceeds) do not produce and are not held for the production of passive income (as defined under section 1296(b)), and were not acquired with the principal purpose of satisfying the active trade or business test. A special rule applies if the asset acquired by the TFC in the 36-month period prior to the exchange is stock of a qualified subsidiary or qualified partnership engaged in an active trade or business. In such case, the value of the stock or partnership interest may be taken into account, but must be reduced in accordance with the principles described above. * * *

GRA Term [§ 1.367(a)-(3)(c)(1)(iii) and § 1.367(a)-8]. Under the temporary regulations, a 5-percent transferee shareholder is required to file a GRA. * * *

[T]he final regulations provide that any 5-percent transferee shareholder that is required to file a GRA upon the transfer of domestic stock or securities is required to file a 5-year GRA; 10year GRAs will no longer be required in the case of 5-percent transferee shareholders who transfer domestic stock or securities. * * *

PLR Option in Limited Instances. The final regulations provide that, in limited instances, the IRS may consider issuing private letter rulings to taxpayers that (i) satisfy all of the requirements contained in these regulations, with the exception of the active trade or business test, or (ii) make a good faith effort, but are unable to establish nonadverse applicability of the ownership attribution rules. The IRS and the Treasury Department are aware that the active trade or business test is mechanical in nature and, thus, in limited instances, a taxpayer may demonstrate an ongoing and substantial active trade or business even though it fails to meet the test set forth in the final regulations. However, in no event will the IRS rule on the issue of whether a TFC acquired an active business with the principal purpose of satisfying the 36-month test and/or the substantiality test. * * *

B. Summary of the Five Non-Recognition Requirements of the Section 367(a) Gain Recognition Regulations Applicable to Direct Outbound Transfers

The conditions for non-recognition treatment discussed above in Treas. Reg. § 1.367(a)-1(c) can be summarized as follows: To qualify for tax-free treatment under this regulation, the following conditions must be satisfied: (1) the 50% U.S. Shareholder Limitation, (2) the 50% Control Group Limitation, (3) either the Less Than 5% Shareholder Rule or the 5% Shareholder GRA Requirement, (4) the Active Trade or Business Test, and (5) the Reporting Requirements. The Active Trade or Business Test has the following three requirements: (1) the 36-Month Active Business Requirement, (2) the No Intention to Sell Requirement, and (3) the Substantiality Test. Several examples discussed below illustrate the application of these non-recognition requirements.

C. The Final Section 367 Inversion Regulations Relating to Indirect Transfers of Stock of U.S. Targets

As explained previously, Treas. Reg. § 1.367(a)-3(d) addresses "indirect stock transfers in certain nonrecognition transfers." These transactions include triangular reorganizations where, for example, a foreign acquiror forms a domestic sub that merges into a domestic target with the shareholders of the target receiving stock of the foreign acquiror in a reverse subsidiary merger reorganization under Section 368(a)(2)(E). This type of transaction is substantively the same as a direct outbound transfer of the stock of a domestic target to a foreign acquiror in a (B) reorganization under Section 368(a)(1)(B) or an acquisitive Section 351 exchange.

These indirect outbound transfers are subject to the same five non-recognition requirements discussed above that apply to direct outbound reorganizations under § 1.367(a)-3(c). The indirect transfers set out in the § 1.367(a)-3(d) include:

1. The forward subsidiary merger under Section 368(a)(2)(D), § 1.367(a)-3(d)(1)(i);

2. The reverse subsidiary merger under Section 368(a)(2)(E), § 1.367(a)-3(d)(1)(ii);

3. The triangular B reorganization under Section 368(a)(1)(B), § 1.367(a)-3(d)(1)(iii);

4. The triangular C reorganization under Section 368(a)(1)(C), § 1.367(a)-3(d)(1)(iv);

The application of these indirect outbound transfer rules is illustrated below.

§ 10.6 2004 Anti-Inversion Legislation, Section 7874

A. Introduction to Inversions Generally

Before considering the impact of Section 367 on these cross border transactions, it is first necessary to examine the scope of Section 7874, the anti-inversion legislation enacted by the Jobs Creation Act of 2004. In typical inversion transactions, publicly held U.S. corporations become subsidiaries of publicly held holding companies located in tax haven jurisdictions, such as Bermuda. Prior to the enactment of Section 7874, many U.S. companies were entering into these transactions; for example, during the week of May 14, 2002, the shareholders of both Coopers Industries, Inc. and Leucadia National Corp. approved inversion transactions. As will be seen below, Section 367 has for many years applied to certain outbound inversion transactions, but because the Section 367 anti-inversion rules proved ineffective (*i.e.*, Section 367 was a "wimp" when it came to dealing with inversions), Congress enacted Section 7874 in the Jobs Creation Act of 2004. Thus, inversions are now subject to the rules of both Section 367 and Section 7874. As will be seen below, even Section 7874 has become a "wimp" when dealing with inversions, and there are proposals to strengthen it.

B. Introduction to the "Old Inversion" Problem

Excerpt from Thompson, Treasury's Inversion Study Misses the Mark: Congress Should Shut Down Inversions Immediately

26 Tax Notes Int'l 969 (May 27, 2002)

The prototypical [pre-Section 7874, or "Old Inversion"] transaction is illustrated by the Coopers Industries transaction. Coopers Industries is a New York Stock Exchange corporation that is incorporated in Ohio (Coopers Ohio) and has its head office in Houston. Through the use of a reverse subsidiary merger reorganization under Section 368(a)(2)(E) of the Internal Revenue Code, Coopers Ohio would become a subsidiary of a newly formed publicly held Bermuda holding company (Coopers Bermuda). In this transaction, the public shareholders of Coopers Ohio would become public shareholders of Coopers Bermuda. The Coopers Ohio shareholders would have the same proportionate interests in Coopers Bermuda that they had in Coopers Ohio. The operating headquarters of Coopers Ohio would continue to be located in Houston, and the shares of Coopers Bermuda would be listed on the New York Stock Exchange, where the shares of Coopers Ohio had been listed.

Even though the transaction was a reverse subsidiary merger under Section 368(a)(2)(E), as will be seen below, under the Section 367 regulations, the transaction was a taxable capital gain transaction to the Coopers Ohio shareholders. Notwithstanding this tax treatment, the shareholders voted for the transaction because Coopers estimated that after the reorganization, its worldwide effective tax rate would be reduced from approximately 32% to approximately 20% to 25%, which translates into an annual tax savings of approximately $55 million.

The tax benefits from inversions arise from, *inter alia*, the avoidance of the (CFC) provisions of the Internal Revenue Code (*see* Section 4.7). The purpose of these provisions is to protect the integrity of the worldwide system of taxation the U.S. generally follows. In an inversion transaction, the avoidance of the CFC provisions is achieved when the inverted U.S. corporation (*e.g.*, Coopers Ohio) transfers its foreign subsidiaries to the foreign holding company (*e.g.*, Coopers Bermuda), which as a public corporation is not subject to the CFC provisions even though most of its shareholders are U.S. persons. In addition, in the absence of the applicability of the Treasury's 2016 proposed regulations under Section 385, discussed in Sec. 10.11.F, inversions can be used to strip or divert U.S. taxable income from the inverted corporation to a related foreign corporation through interest payments. With this interest stripping, income tax on U.S. earnings is avoided by merely shifting income from a controlled U.S. corporate pocket (*e.g.*, Coopers Ohio) to a controlled foreign corporate pocket (*e.g.*, the Luxembourg sub of Coopers Bermuda). This is possible because the foreign corporation (*i.e.*, the Luxembourg sub) that receives the interest income from Coopers Ohio is not a CFC, and therefore, although the interest income is passive income, it is not subject to imputation under the CFC provisions, which are not applicable. This transaction, however, would likely be subject to the anti-interest stripping rules of Section 163(j). *See* Section 5.14.

Other transactions can have a similar effect, such as the initial incorporation of Accenture, Ltd., the former consulting arm of Arthur Andersen, as a Bermuda holding company in an initial public offering.

Inversion and related transactions approximate *de facto* territorial taxation. In contrast to the U.S. worldwide system, a territorial system exempts from taxation all of a domestic corporation's foreign income, whether earned directly or indirectly through foreign subsidiaries, until the income is paid out to the ultimate shareholders.

As seen below, the Old Inversion in Coopers is prevented by the enactment of Section 2004 in Section 7874. As seen in the next section, under this provision Coopers Bermuda would be treated as a domestic corporation. After examining the application of Section 7874 and the Section 367(a) regulations to several prototypical inversions or inversion-like transactions, the discussion will turn to "New Inversions."

C. Anti-Inversion Provision Enacted by the American Jobs Creation Act of 2004, Section 7874

Conference Committee Report to the American Jobs Creation Act of 2004

H.R. Conf. Rep. No. 108-755 (October 2004)

Conference Agreement

The conference agreement follows the House bill and Senate amendment with modifications.

In general. The provision [Code Section 7874] defines two different types of corporate inversion transactions and establishes a different set of consequences for each type. Certain partnership transactions also are covered.

Transactions involving at least 80 percent identity of stock ownership. The first type of inversion is a transaction in which, pursuant to a plan or a series of related transactions: (1) a U.S. corporation becomes a subsidiary of a foreign-incorporated entity or otherwise transfers substantially all of its properties to such an entity in a transaction completed after March 4, 2003; (2) the former shareholders of the U.S. corporation hold (by reason of holding stock in the U.S. corporation) 80 percent or more (by vote or value) of the stock of the foreign-incorporated entity after the transaction; and (3) the foreign-incorporated entity, considered together with all companies connected to it by a chain of greater than 50 percent ownership (*i.e.*, the "expanded affiliated group"), does not have substantial business activities in the entity's country of incorporation, compared to the total worldwide business activities of the expanded affiliated group. The provision denies the intended tax benefits of this type of inversion by deeming the top-tier foreign corporation to be a domestic corporation for all purposes of the Code.

In determining whether a transaction meets the definition of an inversion under the proposal, stock held by members of the expanded affiliated group that includes the foreign incorporated entity is disregarded. For example, if the former top-tier U.S. corporation receives stock of the foreign incorporated entity (e.g., so-called "hook" stock), the stock would not be considered in determining whether the transaction meets the definition. Similarly, if a U.S. parent corporation converts an existing wholly owned U.S. subsidiary into a new wholly owned controlled foreign corporation, the stock of the new foreign corporation would be disregarded. Stock sold in a public offering related to the transaction also is disregarded for these purposes.

Transfers of properties or liabilities as part of a plan a principal purpose of which is to avoid the purposes of the proposal are disregarded. In addition, the Treasury Secretary is granted authority to prevent the avoidance of the purposes of the proposal, including avoidance through the use of related persons, pass-through or other non-corporate entities, or other intermediaries, and through transactions designed to qualify or disqualify a person as a related person or a member of an expanded affiliated group. Similarly, the Treasury Secretary is granted authority to treat certain non-stock instruments as stock, and certain stock as not stock, where necessary to carry out the purposes of the proposal.

Transactions involving at least 60 percent but less than 80 percent identity of stock ownership. The second type of inversion is a transaction that would meet the definition of an inversion transaction described above, except that the 80-percent ownership threshold is not met. In such a case, if at least a 60-percent ownership threshold is met, then a second set of rules applies to the inversion. Under these rules, the inversion transaction is respected (*i.e.*, the foreign corporation is treated as foreign), but any applicable corporate-level "toll charges" for establishing the inverted structure are not offset by tax attributes such as net operating losses or foreign tax credits. Specifically, any applicable corporate-level income or gain required to be recognized under sections 304, 311(b), 367, 1001, 1248, or any other provision with respect to the transfer of controlled foreign corporation stock or the transfer or license of other assets by a U.S. corporation as part of the inversion transaction or after such transaction to a related foreign person is taxable, without offset by any tax attributes (e.g., net operating losses or foreign tax credits). This rule does not apply to certain transfers of inventory and similar property. These measures generally apply for a 10-year period following the inversion transaction.

Under the proposal, inversion transactions include certain partnership transactions. Specifically, the proposal applies to transactions in which a foreign-incorporated entity acquires substantially all of the properties constituting a trade or business of a domestic partnership, if after the acquisition at least 60 percent of the stock of the entity is held by former partners of the partnership (by reason of holding their partnership interests), provided that the other terms of the basic definition are met. For purposes of applying this test, all partnerships that are under common control within the meaning of section 482 are treated as one partnership, except as provided otherwise in regulations. In addition, the modified "toll charge" proposals apply at the partner level. * * *

Effective Date. The provision applies to taxable years ending after March 4, 2003.

Note

The American Jobs Creation Act of 2004 also (1) added a provision requiring enhanced reporting by an acquiring corporation that acquires the stock or assets of a target corporation in a taxable acquisition, including in an inversion transaction (Section 6043A), and (2) added an excise tax on the value of certain stock compensation received by insiders in inversion transactions (Section 4985).

D. Elaboration on the Structure of Section 7874

Preamble to Treasury Decision 9238

December 27 2005

Background. * * *

Section 7874 provides rules for expatriated entities and their surrogate foreign corporations. An expatriated entity is defined in section 7874(a)(2)(A) as a domestic corporation or partnership with respect to which a foreign corporation is a surrogate foreign corporation and any U.S. person related (within the meaning of section 267(b) or 707(b)(1)) to such domestic corporation or partnership. Generally, a foreign corporation is a surrogate foreign corporation under section 7874(a)(2)(B), if, pursuant to a plan or a series of related transactions—

(i) The foreign corporation directly or indirectly acquires substantially all the properties held directly or indirectly by a domestic corporation, or substantially all the properties constituting a trade or business of a domestic partnership;

(ii) After the acquisition at least 60 percent of the stock (by vote or value) of the foreign corporation is held by (in the case of an acquisition with respect to a domestic corporation) former shareholders of the domestic corporation by reason of holding stock in the domestic corporation, or (in the case of an acquisition with respect to a domestic partnership) by former partners of the domestic partnership by reason of holding a capital or profits interest in the domestic partnership (ownership percentage test); and

(iii) The expanded affiliated group [EAG] that includes the foreign corporation does not have business activities in the foreign country in which the foreign corporation was created or organized that are substantial when compared to the total business activities of such group. [The regulations provide that for the EAG to have substantial business activities in the relevant foreign country it must have at least 25 percent of its group employees, group assets, and group income located or derived in the relevant foreign country. *See* § 1.7874-3 Substantial business activities.]

The tax treatment of expatriated entities and surrogate foreign corporations varies depending on the level of owner continuity. If the percentage of stock (by vote or value) in the surrogate foreign corporation held by former owners of the domestic entity by reason of holding an interest in the domestic entity is 80 percent or more, the surrogate foreign corporation is treated as a domestic corporation for all purposes of the Code. If such ownership percentage is 60 percent or more (but less than 80 percent) by vote or value, the surrogate foreign corporation is treated as a foreign corporation but any applicable corporate-level income or gain required to be recognized by the expatriated entity under section 304, 311(b), 367, 1001, 1248 or any other applicable provision with respect to the transfer or license of property (other than inventory or similar property) cannot be offset by net operating losses or credits (other than credits allowed under section 901). This treatment of an expatriated entity generally applies from the first date properties are acquired pursuant to the plan through the end of the 10-year period following the completion of the acquisition.

Section 7874(c)(2) provides that stock held by members of the expanded affiliated group which includes the foreign corporation is not taken into account for purposes of the ownership percentage test (affiliate-owned stock rule). Section 7874(c)(1) defines the term expanded affiliated group as an affiliated group defined in section 1504(a) but without regard to the exclusion of foreign corporations in section 1504(b)(3) and with a reduction of the 80 percent ownership threshold of section 1504(a) to a more-than-50 percent threshold.

The statute provides the Secretary of the Treasury significant regulatory authority. Section 7874(c)(6) authorizes the Secretary of the Treasury to prescribe such regulations as may be appropriate to determine whether a corporation is a surrogate foreign corporation, including regulations to treat warrants, options, contracts to acquire stock, convertible debt interests, and other similar interests as stock, and to treat stock as not stock. Section 7874(g) authorizes the Secretary of the Treasury to provide such regulations as are necessary to carry out the section.

The legislative history of section 7874 indicates that it was intended to apply to so-called inversion transactions in which a U.S. parent corporation of a multinational corporate group is replaced by a foreign parent corporation without significant change in the ultimate ownership of the group. See H.R. Conf. Rep. No. 108-755, 108th Cong., 2d Sess., at 568 (Oct. 7, 2004). The statute was also intended to apply to similar transactions in which a trade or business of a domestic partnership is transferred to a foreign corporation at least 60 percent of which is owned by former partners.

A key feature of section 7874 is the rule, in section 7874(c)(2)(A), that disregards affiliate-owned stock for purposes of the ownership percentage test. Congress intended to accomplish two objectives by this rule. See Joint Committee on Taxation, General Explanation of Tax Legislation Enacted in the 108th Congress, at 344. First, Congress intended that the ownership percentage test should be applied without regard to so-called hook stock, which frequently results from inversion transactions. In this context, hook stock is stock of the acquiring foreign corporation held by an entity that is at least 50 percent owned (by vote or value) directly or indirectly by the acquiring foreign corporation. If hook stock were respected as stock of the foreign corporation for purposes of section 7874(a)(2)(B)(ii), a taxpayer might implement an inversion and take the position that section 7874 was not applicable by ensuring that hook stock accounted for over 40 percent of the value and voting power of the foreign corporation's stock.

Second, Congress intended that the affiliate-owned stock rule would prevent the section from applying to certain transactions occurring within a group of corporations owned by the same common parent corporation before and after the transaction, such as the conversion of a wholly owned domestic subsidiary into a new wholly owned controlled foreign corporation. *Id.* In the absence of this rule, section 7874 could apply to internal group restructuring transactions involving the transfer of a wholly owned domestic corporation (or its assets) to a wholly owned foreign corporation, without a change in the parent corporation of the group.

The IRS and Treasury Department have concluded that the affiliate-owned stock rule should not operate in a manner that would result in section 7874 applying to transactions that are outside the intended scope of the section. For example, the type of concerns that Congress meant to address in enacting section 7874 do not result from certain internal group restructuring transactions involving the transfer to a foreign corporation of the stock or assets of a domestic corporation where minority shareholders have a relatively small percentage interest in such stock or assets before and after the transaction.

The IRS and Treasury Department also believe that the affiliate-owned stock rule was not intended to cause section 7874 to apply to certain acquisitive business transactions, such as the acquisition of stock or assets of a domestic corporation by an unrelated foreign corporation where the former owners of the domestic entity do not own 60 percent or more of the acquiring foreign corporation after the acquisition. For example, the contribution of a domestic entity or its assets to a foreign joint venture corporation in exchange for a minority interest in the joint venture corporation should not result in the joint venture corporation's being treated, for purposes of the ownership percentage test, as wholly owned by the former owners of the domestic entity by operation of the affiliate-owned stock rule. In contrast, section 7874 may properly apply to the acquisition of an existing domestic joint venture entity by a foreign corporation which is at least 60 percent owned, after the acquisition, by the former owners of the acquired domestic entity. Congress intended the section to apply to transactions (other than internal group restructurings, as discussed above) that effectively replace a domestic corporation or partnership with a foreign corporation at least 60 percent of which is held by former owners of the domestic entity.

Explanation of Provisions. The IRS and Treasury believe that guidance is necessary to ensure that the ownership percentage test is satisfied only in the case of transactions that Congress intended to be within the scope of section 7874. To avoid unintended results, clarification is needed with respect to the treatment of certain affiliate-owned stock for purposes of the ownership percentage test. * * *

§ 10.7 Impact of Sections 367 and 7874 on Direct Outbound Transfer of Stock of Domestic Target to a Foreign Acquiror in a (B) Reorganization and in an Acquisitive Section 351 Transaction[*]

A. General Principles under Section 367

Treas. Reg. § 1.367(a)-3(c) deals with, *inter alia*, the treatment under Section 367 of the transfer by a U.S. person of the stock of U.S. Target to Foreign Acquiror in an outbound (B) reorganization under Section 368(a)(1)(B) and in an outbound acquisitive Section 351 transaction.[10]

Treas. Reg. Section 1.367(a)-3(c)(1) provides that a transfer of stock of U.S. Target by a U.S. person to Foreign Acquiror in these outbound transactions is not subject to the gain recognition rule of Section 367(a)(1) if the following five conditions are satisfied.

50% U.S. Shareholder Limitation. First, the stock of Foreign Acquiror received by the U.S. shareholders of U.S. Target does not exceed in the aggregate 50% of the total voting power or the total value of the stock of Foreign Acquiror.[11] There is a rebuttable presumption that any person who transfers stock of U.S. Target to Foreign Acquiror is a U.S. person.[12] The regulations set out precise rules regarding ownership statements from U.S. Target's shareholders needed to rebut the presumption.[13] Thus, the amount of stock received by the shareholders of U.S. Target cannot exceed this 50-percent ownership threshold.[14] This is referred to here as the 50% U.S. Share-

---

[*] Part of this section is based on Thompson, *Section 367: A "Wimp" for Inversions and a "Bully" for Real Cross Border Acquisitions*, 94 Tax Notes 1505 (March 18, 2002).

10. Treas. Reg. § 1.367(a)-3 also deals with transfers of stock to a foreign corporation under Section 361 (relating to a transfer of a target's assets in a reorganization). The applicability of the regulations in this context is not addressed here.

11. Treas. Reg. § 1.367(a)-3(c)(1)(i).

12. Treas. Reg. § 1.367(a)-3(c)(2).

13. Treas. Reg. § 1.367(a)-3(c)(7).

14. Treas. Reg. § 1.367(a)-3(c)(1)(i).

holder Limitation. The rationale for this limitation is set out in Notice 94-46, which is discussed above.

Notice 94-46 indicates that the Treasury was concerned with the possible use of inversion transactions (*i.e.*, converting a U.S. corporation to a subsidiary of a foreign corporation) for the purpose of avoiding the controlled foreign corporation provisions.

In particular the Notice was issued to address the Helen of Troy inversion transaction.[15] In this transaction the stock of Helen of Troy Corporation, a publicly held Texas corporation, was to be exchanged for stock of Helen of Troy Limited, a Bermuda corporation. The Prospectus/Proxy Statement indicated that the transaction would be tax-free to the shareholders of the Texas corporation under Section 354 because the transaction would constitute a (B) reorganization under Section 368(a)(1)(B).[16] After the exchange, the former shareholders of the Texas corporation would have the same "relative equity and voting interest" in the Bermuda corporation that they had in the Texas corporation.[17] Also, after the exchange there would be a restructuring designed to minimize taxes. The Prospectus/Proxy Statement made it clear that the exchange and restructuring would reduce the company's tax exposure under the subpart F anti-deferral rules. This was possible because the Bermuda corporation, as a foreign corporation, would not be a "United States shareholder" (*i.e.*, a 10% or more U.S. shareholder) with respect to its direct and indirect foreign subsidiaries, which in turn would not be CFCs.[18] On the other hand, the Texas corporation was a "United States shareholder" with respect to its direct and indirect foreign subsidiaries, which were therefore CFCs.

Since the shareholders of the Texas corporation ended up with the same percentage ownership in the Bermuda company, the transaction was fully taxable to the shareholders under the approach of Notice 94-46, which treated any such inversion transaction in which U.S. shareholders receive more than 50% of the stock of the foreign acquiror as taxable. As indicated above, this 50% limitation in Notice 94-46 is continued in the 1998 Regulations as the 50% U.S. Shareholder Limitation. As a practical matter in order for any acquisition by Foreign Acquiror of U.S. Target to be tax-free Foreign Acquiror must be larger than U.S. Target.

50% Control Group Limitation. The second condition under Treas. Reg. § 1.367(a)-3(c)(1) provides that not more than 50% of the total voting power and total value of the stock of Foreign Acquiror is owned, in the aggregate, immediately after the transfer by U.S. persons who are (1) either officers or directors of U.S. Target, or (2) 5% or more shareholders of U.S. Target.[19] Thus, the officers, directors and 5% or more shareholders of U.S. Target cannot constitute a "control group" with respect to Foreign Acquiror immediately after the transaction.[20] In applying this rule all stock of Foreign Acquiror held

---

15. Helen of Troy Limited, Prospectus/Proxy Statement, January 5, 1994.

16. *Id.* at Tax Consequences to Shareholders, The Exchange.

17. *Id.* at Summary, Change of Domicile, General.

18. I.R.C. Section 957.

19. Treas. Reg. § 1.367(a)-3(c)(1)(ii).

20. *Id.*

by U.S. insiders is counted, not just the stock of Foreign Acquiror received in the transaction. This rule is referred to here as the 50% Control Group Limitation.

Less Than 5% Shareholder Rule and the 5% Shareholder GRA Requirement. The third condition in Treas. Reg. § 1.367(a)-3(c)(1) relates to shareholders of U.S. Target who qualify for tax-free treatment under the first two conditions. To qualify under this third condition, each individual shareholder of U.S. Target, either (1) must not become a 5% or more shareholder of Foreign Acquiror, or (2) if such shareholder becomes a 5% or more shareholder of Foreign Acquiror, the shareholder must enter into a five year gain recognition agreement with respect to the stock of Foreign Acquiror.[21] Both the stock of Foreign Acquiror received in the transaction and such stock held before the transaction are counted for purposes of determining whether the 5% threshold is satisfied.[22] A gain recognition agreement (GRA) is a binding agreement pursuant to which a former shareholder of U.S. Target who becomes a 5% or more shareholder of Foreign Acquiror agrees to recognize gain upon Foreign Acquiror's later disposition of the stock of U.S. Target.[23] These alternative requirements for the less than 5% shareholder and the 5% or more shareholder are referred to here as the Less Than 5% Shareholder Rule and the 5% Shareholder GRA Requirement.

A GRA is triggered if prior to the close of the fifth taxable year following the taxable year of the transaction, Foreign Acquiror disposes of the stock of U.S. Target (or U.S. Target disposes of a substantial portion of its assets). In such case, the transferor shareholder must file an amended return for the year of the (B) reorganization or Section 351 transaction and recognize thereon the gain realized but not recognized in the transaction.[24] At the time of the filing of the GRA, the taxpayer can elect to include the gain in "the year of the triggering event rather than in the year of the initial transfer."[25] If this election is made and gain is triggered, interest must be paid on the tax due from the year of the transfer.[26] This election was added by the 1998 Section 367 Regulations.

The purpose of this provision is to allow nonrecognition treatment for certain substantial shareholders of U.S. Target who, as a result of the (B) reorganization or Section 351 transaction, become substantial shareholders of Foreign Acquiror, only if Foreign Acquiror does not dispose of the stock of U.S. Target and U.S. Target does not dispose of its assets within five years of the reorganization.

The preamble to the regulations explains:

> Without such GRA, the transfer by the 5-percent transferee shareholder will not qualify for nonrecognition treatment; however, transfers by other

---

21. Treas. Reg. § 1.367(a)-3(c)(1)(iii)(A) and (B).
22. Treas. Reg. § 1.367(a)-3(c)(5)(ii).
23. Treas. Reg. § 1.367(a)-8.
24. Treas. Reg. § 1.367(a)-8(b)(3).
25. Treas. Reg. § 1.367(a)-8(b)(1)(vii).
26. Treas. Reg. § 1.367(a)-8(b)(3)(iii).

U.S. transferors not subject to the GRA requirement may qualify if all other requirements are met.[27]

Active Trade or Business Test. Under a fourth requirement in Treas. Reg. § 1.367(a)-3(c)(1), an Active Trade or Business Test must be satisfied.[28] This is a three-part test. Under the first part of this test, Foreign Acquiror or any qualified subsidiary or qualified partnership must have been engaged, directly or indirectly, in an active trade or business outside the U.S. for the entire 36-month period immediately before the reorganization (the 36-month Active Business Requirement).[29] A qualified subsidiary is an 80% or more owned foreign sub of Foreign Acquiror that was not acquired during such 36-month period for the "principal purpose of satisfying the active trade or business test."[30]

Under the second part of this test, neither the shareholders of U.S. Target nor Foreign Acquiror must have an intention to "substantially dispose of or discontinue such trade or business" (the No Intention to Sell Requirement).[31]

Under the third part of the Active Trade or Business Test, at the time of the (B) reorganization or Section 351 transaction, the "substantiality test" must be satisfied (the Substantiality Test).[32] Under the Substantiality Test, the fair market value of Foreign Acquiror must be at least equal to the fair market value of U.S. Target.[33] The regulations do not specify how the fair market value determination is to be made. However, in the private letter ruling issued in the Vodafone-AirTouch transaction, the Service focused on "market capitalization" in determining the value of AirTouch and Vodafone.[34] It appears from the ruling that the Service was focusing only on the market capitalization or aggregate value of the stock of the firms; however, the concept of market capitalization could also include the value of a firm's outstanding tradable debt. This issue will be discussed further in the critique of these regulations.

Under special rules relating to the Substantiality Test, the value of any assets acquired by the Foreign Acquiror outside of the ordinary course of business within the 36-month period preceding the exchange will be taken into account in determining the value of Foreign Acquiror only in the following circumstances. First, the assets do not produce passive income as defined in § 1296(b), and the assets were not acquired for the principal purpose of satisfying the Substantiality Test.[35] Thus, assets recently acquired outside of the ordinary course of business will not count for purposes of the Substantiality Test if such assets are either (1) passive assets, or (2) operating assets that were acquired for purposes of satisfying the Substantiality Test. Second,

---

27. Preamble to Treasury Decision 8702 (Dec. 27, 1996).

28. Treas. Reg. § 1.367(a)-3(c)(1)(iv).

29. Treas. Reg. § 1.367(a)-3(c)(3)(i)(A).

30. Treas. Reg. § 1.367(a)-3(c)(5)(vii). For the definition of qualified partnership, *see* Treas. Reg. § 1.367(a)-3(c)(5)(viii).

31. Treas. Reg. § 1.367(a)-3(c)(3)(i)(B).

32. Treas. Reg. § 1.367(a)-3(c)(3)(i)(C).

33. Treas. Reg. § 1.367(a)-3(c)(3)(i)(C) and -3(c)(3)(iii).

34. Priv. Ltr. Rul. 199929039 [hereinafter *Vodafone Ruling*].

35. Treas. Reg. § 1.367(a)-3(c)(3)(iii)(B).

the assets consist of the stock in a qualified subsidiary or an interest in a qualified partnership.[36] However, assets acquired within the 36-month period from U.S. Target or its affiliates cannot be taken into account.[37]

Thus, the assets of a newly acquired qualified subsidiary or qualified partnership count towards determining if the Substantiality Test is satisfied. Also, the regulations provide that for purposes of determining if the Active Trade or Business Test is satisfied, Foreign Acquiror will be "considered to be engaged in an active trade or business for the entire 36-month period preceding the exchange if it acquires at the time of, or any time prior to, the exchange, a trade or business that has been active throughout the 36-month period preceding the exchange."[38] This rule does not apply, however, if the principal purpose of the acquisition was to satisfy the active trade or business test.[39]

The purpose of these rules is to permit, for example, a newly formed joint venture corporation (JV Holding Company) to satisfy the Substantiality Test. This will be the case as long as at the time of the (B) reorganization or Section 351 transaction JV Holding Company holds stock of a qualified subsidiary or an interest in a qualified partnership that causes the "fair market value of the [JV Holding Company to be] at least equal to the fair market value of the U.S. target company." As discussed below, the qualified subsidiary provision was utilized in the DaimlerChrysler transaction.

Pursuant to Treas. Reg. § 1.367(a)-3(c)(9), the Service may issue a "private letter ruling to permit a taxpayer to qualify for an exception to the general rule of section 367(a)(1)." This option is available, *inter alia*, if the taxpayer is unable to meet all of the requirements of the Active Trade or Business Test but satisfies all the other requirements and is in substantial compliance with the active trade or business rules. As discussed further below, this private letter ruling option was followed in DaimlerChrysler and in Vodafone-AirTouch.

Reporting Requirements. Finally, to qualify under Treas. Reg § 1.367(a)-3(c), a U.S. Target must comply with certain reporting requirements designed to police compliance with the above four conditions (the Reporting Requirements).[40]

Summary of Five Requirements. To summarize: To qualify for tax-free treatment under this regulation, the following conditions must be satisfied: (1) the 50% U.S. Shareholder Limitation, (2) the 50% Control Group Limitation, (3) either the Less Than 5% Shareholder Rule or the 5% Shareholder GRA Requirement, (4) the Active Trade or Business Test, and (5) the Reporting Requirements. The Active Trade or Business Test has the following three requirements: (1) the 36-Month Active Business Requirement, (2) the No Intention to Sell Requirement, and (3) the Substantiality Test.

The application of these requirements can be illustrated as follows. Assume that in a (B) reorganization or Section 351 transaction (1) the shareholders of U.S. Target

---

36. *Id.*
37. Treas. Reg. § 1.367(a)-3(c)(3)(iii)(B)(3).
38. Treas. Reg. § 1.367(a)-3(c)(3)(ii)(A).
39. *Id.*
40. Treas. Reg. § 1.367(a)-3(c)(1) and (6).

end up owning, in the aggregate, less than 50% of the stock of Foreign Acquiror, (2) none of the shareholders of U.S. Target end up owning 5% or more shares of Foreign Acquiror, (3) the Active Trade or Business Test is satisfied, and (4) the Reporting Requirements are complied with. In such case, the shareholders of U.S. Target will receive nonrecognition treatment under Sections 351 or 354 upon the exchange of their stock in U.S. Target for stock in Foreign Acquiror.

This type of tax-free (B) reorganization can be diagramed as follows:

Tax-Free Outbound (B) Reorganization under Section 368(a)(1)(B)

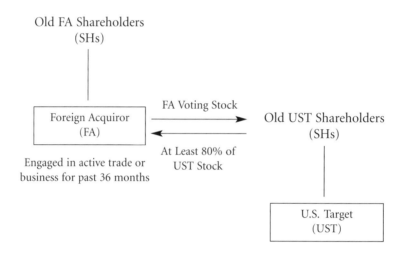

When the Dust Settles

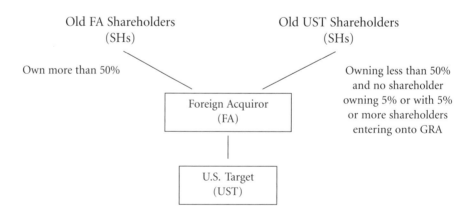

B. General Principles under Section 7874

In addition to Section 367, consideration must also be given to the impact of Section 7874. If Foreign Acquiror and its "expanded affiliated group" (§ 7874(c)(1)) do not have "substantial business activities" in the foreign country in which Foreign Acquiror is incorporated, Section 7874 would apply to the Outbound (B) Reorganization in which Foreign Acquiror acquired directly or indirectly "substantially all the properties" of U.S. Target (§ 7874(a)(2)(B)(i)) in two different cases. First, if the shareholders of U.S. Target end up with at least 80% of the stock measured by vote or value of Foreign Acquiror, then Foreign Acquiror is deemed to be a "surrogate foreign corporation" (§ 7874(a)(2)(B)) and is treated as a domestic corporation. (§ 7874(b)) Consequently, there would be no potential recognition of gain by the shareholders of U.S. Target under the Section 367 Regulations, because the transfer would not be to a foreign corporation.

Second, if the shareholders of U.S. Target ended up with more than 60% but less than 80% of Foreign Acquiror's stock measured by vote or value, then Foreign Acquiror is also deemed to be a "surrogate foreign corporation" (§ 7874(a)(2)(B)), and U.S. Target is deemed to be an "expatriated entity" (§ 7874(a)(2)(A)). As an expatriated entity, for a period of 10 years after the transaction, U.S. Target could not offset any "inversion gain" (§ 7874(d)(2)) with NOLs or other tax attributes, such as foreign tax credits. (§ 7874(a)(1)) Consequently, U.S. Target could not use any NOLs or other tax attributes to offset the gain realized, for example, on the transfer of stock of a foreign subsidiary to Foreign Acquiror. Such a transfer would cause the sub to no longer be a CFC. Inventory gains are not subject to this limitation.

If the shareholders of U.S. Target end up with less than 60% of the stock of Foreign Acquiror or the expanded affiliated group of Foreign Acquiror has substantial business activities in the foreign country in which Foreign Acquiror is incorporated, then Section 7874 is not applicable. (§ 7874(a)(2)) As indicated above, the Senate has proposed to reduce the stock ownership rule in Section 7874 from 60% to 50%.

C. Summary of U.S. Tax Results under Section 367 Regulations and Section 7874

- The transaction constitutes a (B) reorganization under Section 368(a)(1)(B).

- Since all of the conditions of Treas. Reg. § 1.367(a)-3(c) are satisfied, the gain recognition rule of Section 367(a)(1) does not apply to the transfer. Consequently, under Section 354, the shareholders of U.S. Target receive nonrecognition treatment on the exchange of their stock of U.S. Target for stock of Foreign Acquiror.

- Under Section 358, the shareholders of U.S. Target take a substituted basis for the shares of Foreign Acquiror received.

- Since none of the shareholders of U.S. Target becomes a 5% or more shareholder of Foreign Acquiror, a GRA is not required, and therefore, there are no limitations on the period during which Foreign Acquiror must hold the shares of U.S. Target or U.S. Target must conduct its business.

- Since the shareholders of U.S. Target receive less that 60% of the stock of Foreign Acquiror, Section 7874 is not applicable.

- If the shareholders of U.S. Target end up owning, in the aggregate, more than 50% of the stock of Foreign Acquiror, the transaction is completely taxable to all shareholders under the Section 367 Regulations, unless they end up with at least 80% of the stock of Foreign Acquiror, in which case Foreign Acquiror would be treaded as a domestic corporation under Section 7874, assuming Foreign Acquiror did not have substantial business assets in its country of incorporation. If the shareholders of U.S. Target ended up with at least 60% but less than 80% of the stock of U.S. Acquiror, U.S. target could not offset inversion gains with tax attributes for a period of ten years.

- The same results would apply if U.S. Target were acquired by Foreign Acquiror in an acquisitive Section 351 transaction. Also, as demonstrated in the discussion below of indirect stock acquisitions, the same results would obtain for the shareholders of U.S. Target if the stock of U.S. Target were acquired by a subsidiary of Foreign Acquiror in a triangular (B) reorganization.

D. The DaimlerChrysler Acquisition of Chrysler as a (B) Reorganization or an Acquisitive Section 351 Transaction

Daimler Benz, a German corporation, and Chrysler were combined in a transaction in which DaimlerChrysler, a newly formed German holding company, acquired (1) Chrysler in a reverse subsidiary merger in exchange for stock of DaimlerChrysler, and (2) Daimler Benz in an exchange offer for stock of DaimlerChrysler. The acquisition by DaimlerChrysler of Chrysler in a reverse subsidiary merger could potentially qualify for tax-free treatment under any or all of the following provisions. First, it might qualify as a reorganization under Section 368(a)(2)(E), the reverse subsidiary merger reorganization. Second, it might qualify as a stock for stock (B) reorganization under Section 368(a)(1)(B) under the view that the reverse subsidiary merger is ignored and the transaction is merely an exchange of DaimlerChrysler voting stock for control (at least 80%) of the stock of Chrysler.[41] Third, it might be integrated with the exchange offer DaimlerChrysler made for the shares of Daimler-Benz and thereby be treated as a Section 351 transaction. In its private ruling request, Chrysler represented that the transaction will qualify as a reorganization "and/or" a Section 351 transaction.[42]

This section discusses the transaction as a (B) reorganization and as a Section 351 transaction, which are the two direct outbound stock transactions. As will be seen below, the consequences would be the same if the transaction were treated as a reverse subsidiary merger under Section 368(a)(2)(E). This section does not analyze in detail all of the ramifications of this transaction.

---

41. *See, e.g.*, Rev. Rul. 67-448, 1967-2 C.B. 144.
42. Priv. Let. Rul. 9849014 (Sept. 4, 1998) [hereinafter *Chrysler Ruling*].

The Chrysler Ruling says that Chrysler represented that it would satisfy the Reporting Requirement, the 50% U.S. Shareholder Limitation, and the 50% Control Group Limitation. In connection with the three-part Active Trade or Business Test, Chrysler represented that it would satisfy the No Intention to Sell Requirement and the 36-Month Active Business Requirement.

With respect to this 36-Month Requirement, Chrysler represented that Daimler-Benz or "one or more of [its] qualified subsidiaries or qualified partnerships" will have been engaged in the active conduct of a trade or business outside of the United States "for the entire 36-month period immediately preceding the exchange of [Chrysler] stock." Chrysler was relying on the exchange offer by DaimlerChrysler for Daimler-Benz to satisfy the 36-Month Active Trade or Business Requirement even though it was possible that DaimlerChrysler would receive less than 80% of the Daimler-Benz shares in the exchange offer and that the second step merger could be delayed.

If DaimlerChrysler failed to get at least 80% of the shares of Daimler-Benz in the exchange offer, then Daimler-Benz would not have been a qualified subsidiary at the time of the Chrysler merger, and the assets of Daimler-Benz would not have counted for the Active Trade or Business Test. Chrysler asked for a ruling to the effect that it was in substantial compliance with the Active Trade or Business Test even though DaimlerChrysler might not receive 80% of Daimler-Benz's shares in the exchange offer. Also, Chrysler sought a ruling to the effect that it was in substantial compliance with the Active Trade or Business Test "notwithstanding that the Substantiality Test may not be met due to the acquisition by [DaimlerChrysler] or any qualified subsidiary or qualified partnership of [DaimlerChrysler] of certain passive assets not undertaken for a purpose of satisfying the Substantiality Test." Thus, it was possible that when these recently acquired passive assets were excluded the "fair market value of [DaimlerChrysler may not have been] at least equal to the fair market value of [Chrysler]."[43]

Without setting out any reasoning, the Service ruled that the transaction qualified for an exception to Section 367(a)(1). This shows that the Service apparently takes a generous view in responding to requests that the Active Trade or Business Test is met. Also, the Service ruled that any 5% transferee shareholder would qualify for the exception to Section 367(a) only upon entering a GRA.

---

43. The Chrysler Ruling excludes passive assets from value only if such assets were acquired for a stuffing purpose.

§ 10.8 Impact of Sections 367 and 7874 on Indirect Outbound Stock Transactions: Reorganizations Involving the Acquisition of Stock of a Domestic Target by a Foreign Acquiror in a Triangular Reorganization Involving a Subsidiary of the Foreign Acquiror[*]

A. General Principles

1. Introduction

Certain triangular reorganizations in which the stock or assets of a U.S. Target are acquired by a domestic subsidiary (U.S. Sub) and in some cases a foreign sub (For. Sub) of a Foreign Acquiror are treated as indirect outbound transfers of property by U.S. persons to a foreign corporation and are, therefore, subject to Section 367(a). The 1998 Section 367 Regulations replaced prior Temporary Regulations addressing these transactions,[44] and the 2006 Section 367 regulations broadened the reach of these principles in view of the amendments to the Section 368 Regulations permitting mergers between domestic and foreign corporations. Each of these indirect outbound transactions is a reorganization that involves the issuance of stock of Foreign Acquiror to U.S. persons.

The following four triangular reorganizations are treated as indirect outbound stock transactions under this regulation. The treatment of these transactions under the gain recognition rules of Section 367 and the rules of Section 7874 is discussed after an examination of each of the transactions.

2. Indirect Outbound Forward Subsidiary Merger of U.S. Target into U.S. Sub of Foreign Acquiror: The Aborted British Telcom-MCI Merger

An indirect outbound stock transaction includes a merger of U.S. Target into a domestic corporation that is a subsidiary (U.S. Sub) of Foreign Acquiror in a transaction that qualifies as a forward subsidiary merger under Section 368(a)(2)(D).[45] The shareholders of U.S. Target receive stock of Foreign Acquiror. In this transaction, the merger takes place between two domestic corporations, although the stock of U.S. Sub is wholly owned by Foreign Acquiror.[46]

---

[*] Part of this section is based on Thompson, *Section 367: A "Wimp" for Inversions and a "Bully" for Real Cross Border Acquisitions*, 94 Tax Notes 1505 (March 18, 2002).

44. *See* Treas. Reg. § 1.367(a)-3(d), added by the 1998 Section 368 Regulations.

45. Treas. Reg. § 1.367(a)-3(d)(1)(i). *See* Rev. Rul. 74-297, 1974-1CB 84 (holding that this type of transaction qualifies as a reorganization under Section 368(a)(2)(D) even though the parent of the acquiring subsidiary is a foreign corporation). For a general discussion of forward subsidiary mergers under Section 368(a)(2)(D), *see* Chapter 12.

46. Treas. Reg. § 1.367(a)-3(d)(1)(i) and (3), Example 1.

This transaction should be contrasted with a merger of U.S. Target into a Foreign. Sub of Foreign Acquiror. Although such transactions are now permissible in view of the amendments to the Section 368 regulations, the transaction would be an outbound asset transfer because assets are leaving the U.S. taxing jurisdiction, as well as an outbound indirect stock transfer. As noted below, outbound asset transfers generally will produce taxable gain at the U.S. Target level; a nasty result.

The transaction involving the merger of U.S. Target into U.S. Sub may be diagramed as follows:

Indirect Outbound Forward Subsidiary Merger under Section 368(a)(2)(D)

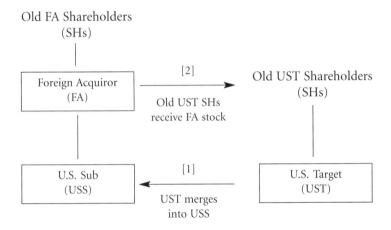

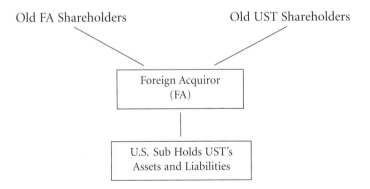

This is the type of transaction in which British Telecommunications plc (BT), a publicly-held U.K. corporation, planned to acquire MCI Communications Corporation, a Delaware corporation. In the transaction, MCI was going to merge into a wholly-owned Delaware subsidiary of BT (Merger Sub), with the shareholders of

MCI receiving both (1) stock in BT represented by American Depository Receipts, which were to be traded on the New York Stock Exchange, and (2) cash.[47] Although the transaction was aborted, the forward subsidiary merger under Section 368(a)(2)(D) is a common structure for effectuating such an acquisition. Another and possibly even more common method is the reverse subsidiary merger under Section 368(a)(2)(E) as discussed in the next section.

One major difference between the forward subsidiary merger under Section 368(a)(2)(D) and the reverse subsidiary merger under Section 368(a)(2)(E) is that only 20% boot can be used in the reverse subsidiary merger, whereas up to 50% (and possibly more) boot can be used in a forward subsidiary merger. (*See* Chapters 4 and 5.)

In the MCI acquisition, the cash to be paid by BT could, depending upon the trading price of BT on the date of the merger, have exceeded 20% of the consideration. This may have been the reason the transaction was structured as a forward rather than as a reverse subsidiary merger.

3. Indirect Outbound Reverse Subsidiary Merger: The Vodafone-AirTouch Merger

An indirect outbound transfer includes the merger of U.S. Sub or a For. Sub that is a subsidiary of Foreign Acquiror into U.S. Target in a reverse subsidiary merger under Section 368(a)(2)(E).[48] The shareholders of U.S. Target receive stock of Foreign Acquiror, and Foreign Acquiror ends up owning all the stock of U.S. Target. Although as a result of the 2006 amendments to the Section 368 regulations, mergers between domestic and foreign corporations are now permissible, it can be expected that most of these transactions will still involve a U.S. Sub[49] and that is the transaction diagramed here:

---

47. *See* MCI Communications Corporation Proxy Statement/Prospectus (March 3, 1997).
48. Treas. Reg. § 1.367(a)-3(d)(1)(ii). For a general discussion of reverse subsidiary mergers under Section 368(a)(2)(E), *see* Chapter 12.
49. *See* Treas. Reg. § 1.367(a)-3(d)(3), Example 2.

Indirect Outbound Reverse Subsidiary Merger under Section 368(a)(2)(E)

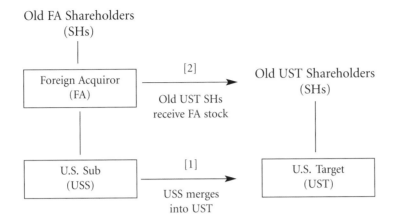

When the Dust Settles

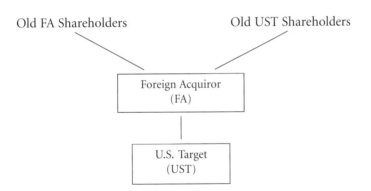

In the Vodafone-AirTouch transaction, Vodafone, a U.K. company, acquired AirTouch, a U.S. company, in a reverse subsidiary merger. The shareholders of AirTouch received five Vodafone shares and $9 cash for each of their AirTouch shares. The cash portion of the consideration could not constitute more than 20% of the merger consideration.

4. Indirect Outbound Triangular (B) Reorganization

An indirect outbound transaction includes an acquisition by U.S. Sub or For. Sub of Foreign Acquiror of a controlling stock interest (*i.e.*, at least 80%) in U.S. Target in exchange solely for voting stock of Foreign Acquiror in a (B) reorganization under Section 368(a)(1)(B).[50] The transaction with the use of a U.S. Sub may be diagramed as follows:

---

50. Treas. Reg. § 1.367(a)-3(d)(1)(iii)(A). For a general discussion of triangular stock for stock reorganizations under Section 368(a)(1)(B), *see* Chapter 12.

Indirect Outbound Triangular (B) Reorganization under Section 368(a)(1)(B)

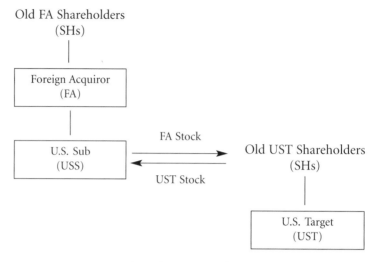

When the Dust Settles

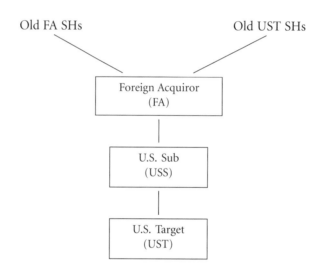

5. Indirect Outbound Triangular (C) Reorganization

The final indirect outbound reorganization is the triangular (C) under Section 368(a)(1)(C) in which U.S. Sub of Foreign Acquiror acquires substantially all of the assets of U.S. Target in exchange solely for voting stock of Foreign Acquiror, and U.S. Target liquidates, distributing the stock to its shareholders.[51] As discussed below, if this transaction is effectuated with a Foreign Sub, the transaction is both an outbound transfer of assets, which generally will be taxable to U.S. Target, and

---

51. Treas. Reg. § 1.367(a)-3(d)(1)(iv). For a general discussion of triangular stock for asset reorganizations under Section 368(a)(1)(C), *see* Chapter 12.

an indirect outbound transfer of stock. The transaction with the use of U.S. Sub may be diagramed as follows:

Indirect Outbound Triangular (C) Reorganization under Section 368(a)(1)(C)

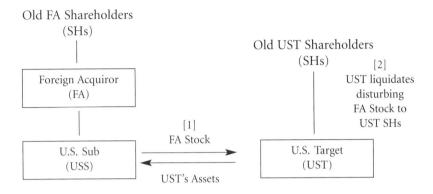

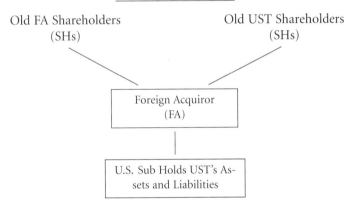

6. Economic Effect of Indirect Outbound Triangular Reorganizations and Impact of Sections 367 and 7874

The economic effect of each of the above triangular reorganizations is essentially the same. First, after completion of the transaction, the assets of U.S. Target continue to be held by a domestic corporation, that is, either by U.S. Target itself in a reverse subsidiary merger and in a triangular (B) or by U.S. Sub in a forward subsidiary merger and in a triangular (C). Thus, the assets of U.S. Target continue to be subject to U.S. taxation.

Second, the shareholders of U.S. Target end up as shareholders of Foreign Acquiror; as a consequence, the transaction is the substantial economic equivalent of a direct outbound transfer of stock of U.S. Target in a direct (B) reorganization as addressed above.

The economic impact of these indirect outbound triangular reorganizations is essentially the same as the economic impact of a direct outbound (B) reorganization.

Consequently, the tax treatment of these transactions under Sections 367 and 7874 should be the same. From the perspective of Section 367, the regulations make it clear that the shareholders of U.S. Target who receive only voting stock of Foreign Acquiror will receive non-recognition treatment under Section 354 provided the following conditions that apply to direct outbound transactions are satisfied: (1) the 50% U.S. Shareholder Limitation; (2) the 50% Control Group Limitation; (3) either the Less Than 5% Shareholder Rule or the 5% Shareholder GRA Requirement; (4) the Active Trade or Business Test; and (5) the Reporting Requirements.

From the perspective of Section 7874, to the extent the shareholders of U.S. Target receive at least 80% of the stock of Foreign Acquiror, Section 7874 would treat Foreign Acquiror as a Domestic Corporation, assuming Foreign Acquiror did not have substantial business assets in its country of incorporation. In such case there would be no gain recognition under Section 367. If the shareholders of U.S. Target received at least 60% of the stock of Foreign Acquiror but less than 80%, U.S. Target could not offset its inversion gains with tax attributes.

§ 10.9 Impact of Section 367 and Section 7874 on Outbound Transfer of Domestic Target's Assets to Foreign Acquiror in an Outbound Asset Reorganization

A. Scope of Transactions

The transactions discussed in this section involve the transfer by U.S. Target of its assets to (1) Foreign Acquiror in an outbound stock for asset direct (C) reorganization under Section 368(a)(1)(C), (2) a subsidiary of Foreign Acquiror in a stock for asset triangular (C) reorganization under Section 368(a)(1)(C), (3) Foreign Acquiror in a direct merger under Section 368(a)(1)(A), and (4) a subsidiary of Foreign Acquiror in a forward subsidiary merger under Section 368(a)(2)(D). As indicated, the latter two reorganizations are now possible as a result of the 2006 amendments to the definition of the term "reorganization." Only the basic principles are covered.

In each of these transactions, the assets of U.S. Target are transferred to a foreign corporation, and the shareholders of U.S. Target end up with shares of Foreign Acquiror. These transactions are referred to here as "Outbound Asset Reorganizations;" the direct (C) and (A) reorganizations are referred to as Direct Outbound Asset Reorganizations, and the triangular (C) and the forward subsidiary merger are referred to a Triangular Outbound Asset Reorganizations. The nondivisive (D) under Section 368(a)(1)(D) and Section 354(b) could also be included as a Direct Outbound Asset Reorganization, but it is not discussed here because it does not involve an acquisition of an unrelated corporation.

B. General Principles under Section 367

1. Treatment of U.S. Target

Subject to the rules of Section 367(a), in each of these transactions, U.S. Target has nonrecognition treatment under Section 361 upon the receipt and distribution of the stock of Foreign Acquiror. The shareholders of U.S. Target have nonrecognition under Section 354 on the exchange of their stock in the target for stock of Foreign Acquiror.

Prior to the repeal of the *General Utilities* doctrine by the Tax Reform Act of 1986, the gain recognition rule of Section 367(a)(1) did not apply to these Outbound Asset Reorganizations if the transaction qualified for the active business exception of Section 367(a)(3) or the stock and security exception of Section 367(a)(2). Thus, the rules that applied to outbound transfers of business assets in Section 351 transactions also applied to Outbound Asset Reorganizations.

In each of these transactions, the Section 367(a)(1) gain recognition rule overpowers Section 361 and requires the target to recognize gain, if any, in its transferred assets. However, subject to such basis adjustments as provided in the regulations, the exceptions in Section 367(a)(2) and (a)(3) apply if the transferee foreign corporation is controlled by five or fewer domestic corporations.[52] This provision is not examined here because it will not apply when U.S. Target is publicly-held, which is the focus of the discussion here.

The 1988 House Report says that new Section 367(a)(5) "clarifies that a transfer of property to a foreign corporation in a transaction that would otherwise qualify as a tax free reorganization is treated in the same manner as a liquidating transfer [under Section 367(e)(2)] of such property to an 80 percent foreign corporate distributee."[53] Section 367(e)(2) provides that, except as provided in regulations, a U.S. subsidiary that liquidates into an 80% controlling foreign parent corporation in a transaction that would otherwise be tax-free under Section 332 and 337, has full recognition of gain on the distribution of its property to the controlling foreign parent corporation. However, the regulations under Section 367(e)(2) provide an exception to the general gain recognition rule if the property distributed is used in a United States trade or business and if the following two basic conditions are satisfied. First, the distributee Foreign Parent Corporation uses the property in the conduct of a U.S. trade or business for the ten-year period beginning on the date of the distribution. Second, both the U.S. subsidiary and the Foreign Parent corporation file a statement requiring recog-

---

52. This provision contemplates that the controlling corporate shareholder or shareholders will take as the basis for the stock of Foreign Acquiror received, the basis that U.S. Target had for its assets. Thus, the gain inherent in U.S. Target's assets is locked into the stock of Foreign Acquiror held by the controlling shareholder or shareholders. In the absence of this rule, the basis to the controlling shareholder or shareholders for the stock of Foreign Acquiror would be a substituted basis under Section 358 (*i.e.*, the basis of U.S. Target stock surrendered), and, thus, the built-in-gain inherent in the assets of U.S. Target may or may not be locked into the stock of Foreign Acquiror held by the controlling shareholder or shareholders.

53. 1988 House Report at 60.

nition of the gain on the distribution by the U.S. subsidiary as of the date of the initial distribution if the property is not used in a U.S. trade or business for the ten-year period.[54]

The Treasury has not promulgated regulations under Section 367(a)(5), and therefore, there is no similar exception for outbound asset reorganizations.

To summarize, in all forms of Outbound Asset Reorganizations, U.S. Target, as a publicly held corporation, is subject to full recognition of gain on the transfer of its assets to Foreign Acquiror, because Section 367(a)(5) overrides the nonrecognition treatment that would otherwise have been provided under Section 361.

2. Treatment of Shareholders of U.S. Target

Subject to the rules of Section 367(a), in each of these transactions, the shareholders of U.S. Target have nonrecognition under Section 354 on the exchange of their stock in the target for stock of Foreign Acquiror. Although Section 367(a)(5) gives U.S. Target recognition in an Outbound Asset Reorganizations, the shareholders of U.S. Target are not impacted by Section 367(a)(5). But here is where different treatment arises for the shareholders of U.S. Target depending on whether the transaction is a Direct Outbound Asset Reorganization or a Triangular Outbound Asset Reorganization. For Direct Outbound Asset Reorganizations, the shareholders are not impacted by Section 367; however, Triangular Outbound Asset Reorganizations are treated as indirect stock acquisitions under Treas. Reg. § 1.367(a)-3(d) at the shareholder level and therefore the inversion gain rules of Section 367(a) are applicable. This result for the shareholders of U.S. Target is confirmed in the 2006 amended Section 367 Regulations, which provide:

> [I]f, in an exchange described in section 354 or 356, a U.S. person exchanges stock or securities of a * * * a domestic * * * corporation pursuant to an asset reorganization that is not treated as an indirect stock transfer under paragraph (d) of this section [indirect stock transfers are examined above], such section 354 or 356 exchange is not a transfer to a foreign corporation subject to section 367(a). See paragraph (d)(3) Example 16 of this section. For purposes of this section, an asset reorganization is defined as a reorganization described in section 368(a)(1) involving a transfer of assets under section 361.[55]

The preamble to the 2006 Section 367(a) Regulations elaborates:

> *Exceptions to the Application of Section 367(a). Exchanges of stock or securities in certain triangular asset reorganizations.* A U.S. person recognizes gain under section 367(a) on the transfer of property to a foreign corporation in an exchange described in section 351, 354, 356, or 361, unless an exception applies. Under § 1.367(a)-3(a), section 367(a) does not apply if, pursuant to a section 354 exchange, a U.S. person transfers stock of a domestic or foreign corpo-

---

54. Treas. Reg. § 1.367(e)-2(b)(2).
55. Treas. Reg. § 1.367(a)-3(a) as amended in 2006.

ration "for stock of a foreign corporation" in an asset reorganization described in section 368(a)(1) that is not treated as an indirect stock transfer.[56]

Example 16 of Treas. Reg. § 1.367(a)-3(d) makes it clear that the shareholders are not affected in a Direct Outbound Asset Acquisition. On the other hand, Example 8B, which is set out below, makes it clear that in a Triangular Outbound Asset Reorganization both (1) the Section 367(a)(5) taxable rule applies at the target level, and (2) the Section 367(a)(1) inversion gain rules apply at the target shareholder level:

> *Example 8B. Concurrent application with individual U.S. shareholder — (i) Facts.* The facts are the same as in Example 8, except that V is an individual U.S. citizen. [Thus, V owns all of the stock of Z, a domestic target corporation. F, a foreign acquiror parent corporation, owns all of the stock of R, its foreign sub. In a transaction otherwise qualifying as a forward subsidiary merger under Section 368(a)(2)(D). Z, the domestic target, merges into R, the foreign sub, with V the U.S. shareholder of Z, receiving 30% of the stock of F, the foreign acquiror parent.]

> (ii) *Result.* Section 367(a)(5) would prevent the application of the active trade or business exception under section 367(a)(3). Thus, Z's transfer of assets to R would be fully taxable under section 367(a)(1). Z would recognize $100 of income. V's basis in its stock of Z is not increased by this amount. V is taxable with respect to its indirect transfer of its Z stock unless V enters into a gain recognition agreement in the amount of the $100, the gain realized but not recognized with respect to its Z stock.

§ 10.10 Summary Problems on Outbound Acquisitive Reorganizations under Section 367

The following problems are designed to illustrate the basic operation of the reorganization provisions and Section 367.

Individuals A and B each own 50% of the outstanding stock of Domestic Target Corporation (DTC). A's basis for his stock is $50K, and B's basis is $150K. The value of DTC's stock is $200K, and, consequently, A's and B's shares are each worth $100K. The fair market value of DTC's assets is $220K, and the adjusted basis thereof is $100K. DTC has liabilities of $20K and E & P of $50K. Foreign Acquiring Corporation (FAC), a publicly held corporation, is interested in acquiring DTC.

(a) What result to A, B, DTC and FAC if DTC merges into FAC in a transaction in which A and B each receive 3% of the voting common stock of FAC with a fair market value of $100K? *See* Sections 331, 336, 368(a)(1)(A), 368(a)(1)(C), 368(b), 354, 356, 357, 358, 361, 362, 367, and 1032. What result if A and B each receive 20% of FAC's voting common stock? 30%?

---

56. Treasury Decision 9243, January 26, 2006.

(b) What if FAC forms a domestic subsidiary (AC-S) by transferring FAC voting common stock to it, and DTC merges into AC-S with A and B receiving the FAC stock (as outlined in Question (a))? Focus only on the treatment of A and B and AC-S's basis for the DTC assets. What if AC-S merges into DTC? Focus only on the treatment of A and B. *See* Sections 368(a)(1)(A), 368(a)(2)(D), 368(a)(2)(E), 368(b), 368(c), 354, 357, 358, 361, 362, 367, and 1032. What result if A and B each receive 20% of FAC's voting stock? 30%?

(c) What result for A, B, DTC and FAC, if FAC acquires the stock of DTC from each of A and B in exchange for 3% of the voting common stock of FAC with a fair market value of $100K? What result if AC-S makes the acquisition using FAC voting common stock? Focus only on the treatment of A and B and AC-S's basis for the DTC stock. *See* Sections 368(a)(1)(B), 368(b), 368(c), 354, 357, 358, 361, 362, 367, and 1032. What result if A and B each receive 20% of FAC's voting common stock? 30%?

(d) What results to A, B, DTC and FAC if FAC acquires the assets and liabilities of DTC in exchange for 6% of the voting common stock of FAC with a fair market value of $200K? DTC is then liquidated? Suppose AC-S makes the acquisition using $200K of FAC voting common stock? *See* Sections 368(a)(1)(C), 368(a)(2)(B), 368(b), 354, 356, 357, 358, 361, 362, and 1032. What result if A and B each receive 20% of FAC's voting common stock? 30%?

§ 10.11 Introduction to the New Inversions

A. Background

Notwithstanding the gain recognition regulations under Section 367(a) and the inversion gain rules of Section 7874, some U.S. companies have recently enter into inversion transactions with the principal purpose (or one of the principal purposes) of reducing tax on ongoing operations through, *inter alia*, earnings stripping from the U.S. These transactions are sometimes referred to as "New Inversions," and may be executed notwithstanding the imposition of (1) the taxable gain under the Section 367(a) regulations, and (2) the application of the 60%–80% inversion gain rules under Section 7874. New Inversions are more tax motivated than the cross border mergers discussed above, such as the Daimler-Chrysler deal.

The Treasury has taken, and continues to take, steps in attempting to curtail these transactions, including the issuance of Notices in 2014 and 2015 and proposed regulations in 2016 that are designed to "rein in" these New Inversions. These complex Notices and proposed regulations are introduced below.

After the discussion of the Notices and proposed regulations, the discussion turns to the following two New Inversions both of which were completed prior to the issuance of the proposed regulations: (1) the Endo-Paladin inversion; and (2) the Burger King-Tim Horton's inversion. Sec. 10.12 presents a policy perspective on New Inversions.

B. Treasury's September 2014 Notice on Actions to Rein in Inversions

I.R.S and Treasury Fact Sheet: Treasury Actions to Rein in Corporate Tax Inversions: [Announcing Notice 2014-52, 2014 I.R.B. LEXIS 576 (Sept 24, 2014), Rules Regarding Inversions and Related Transactions]

September 22, 2014

[The Fact Sheet set out in this section provides an introduction to Notice 2014-52. For a detailed analysis of the Notice, *see* Thompson, *Mergers, Acquisitions, and Tender Offers, supra* Sec. 1.11 at Section 22:7.]

Actions under sections 304(b)(5)(B), 367, 956(e), 7701(l), and 7874 of the Code

What is a corporate inversion?

A corporate inversion is a transaction in which a U.S. based multinational restructures so that the U.S. parent is replaced by a foreign parent, in order to avoid U.S. taxes. Current law subjects inversions that appear to be based primarily on tax considerations to certain potentially adverse tax consequences, but it has become clear by the growing pace of these transactions that for many corporations, these consequences are acceptable in light of the potential benefits.

An inverted company is subject to potential adverse tax consequences if, after the transaction: (1) less than 25 percent of the new multinational entity's business activity is in the home country of the new foreign parent, and (2) the shareholders of the old U.S. parent end up owning at least 60 percent of the shares of the new foreign parent. If these criteria are met for an inverted company, the tax consequences depend on the continuing ownership stake of the shareholders from the former U.S. parent. If the continuing ownership stake is 80 percent or more, the new foreign parent is treated as a U.S. corporation (despite the new corporate address), thereby nullifying the inversion for tax purposes. If the continuing ownership stake is at least 60 but less than 80 percent, U.S. tax law respects the foreign status of the new foreign parent but other potentially adverse tax consequences may follow. The current wave of inversions involves transactions in this continuing ownership range of 60 to 80 percent.

Genuine cross-border mergers make the U.S. economy stronger by enabling U.S. companies to invest overseas and encouraging foreign investment to flow into the United States. But these transactions should be driven by genuine business strategies and economic efficiencies, not a desire to shift the tax residence of the parent entity to a low-tax jurisdiction simply to avoid U.S. taxes.

Today, Treasury is taking action to reduce the tax benefits of—and when possible, stop—corporate tax inversions. This action will significantly diminish the ability of inverted companies to escape U.S. taxation. For some companies considering mergers, today's action will mean that inversions no longer make economic sense.

Specifically, the Notice eliminates certain techniques inverted companies currently use to access the overseas earnings of foreign subsidiaries of the U.S. company that inverts without paying U.S. tax. Today's actions apply to deals closed today or after today.

This notice is an important initial step in addressing inversions. Treasury will continue to examine ways to reduce the tax benefits of inversions, including through additional regulatory guidance as well as by reviewing our tax treaties and other international commitments. Today's Notice requests comments on additional ways that Treasury can make inversion deals less economically appealing.

Specifically, today's Notice will:

Prevent inverted companies from accessing a foreign subsidiary's earnings while deferring U.S. tax through the use of creative loans, which are known as "hopscotch" loans(*Action under section 956(e) of the code*)

- Under current law, U.S. multinationals owe U.S. tax on the profits of their controlled foreign corporations (CFCs) although they don't usually have to pay this tax until those profits are repatriated (that is, paid to the U.S. parent firm as a dividend). Profits that have not yet been repatriated are known as deferred earnings.

- Under current law, if a CFC, tries to avoid this dividend tax by investing in certain U.S. property — such as by making a loan to, or investing in stock of its U.S. parent or one of its domestic affiliates — the U.S. parent is treated as if it received a taxable dividend from the CFC.

- However, some inverted companies get around this rule by having the CFC make the loan to the new foreign parent, instead of its U.S. parent. This "hopscotch" loan is not currently considered U.S. property and is therefore not taxed as a dividend.

- Today's notice removes benefits of these "hopscotch" loans by providing that such loans are considered "U.S. property" for purposes of applying the anti-avoidance rule. The same dividend rules will now apply as if the CFC had made a loan to the U.S. parent prior to the inversion.

Prevent inverted companies from restructuring a foreign subsidiary in order to access the subsidiary's earnings tax-free (*Action under section 7701(l) of the tax code*)

- After an inversion, some U.S. multinationals avoid ever paying U.S. tax on the deferred earnings of their CFC by having the new foreign parent buy enough stock to take control of the CFC away from the former U.S. parent. This "de-controlling" strategy is used to allow the new foreign parent to access the deferred earnings of the CFC without ever paying U.S. tax on them.

- Under today's notice, the new foreign parent would be treated as owning stock in the former U.S. parent, rather than the CFC, to remove the benefits of the "de-controlling" strategy. The CFC would remain a CFC and would continue to be subject to U.S. tax on its profits and deferred earnings.

Close a loophole to prevent inverted companies from transferring cash or property from a CFC to the new parent to completely avoid U.S. tax (*Action under section 304(b)(5)(B) of the code*)

- These transactions involve the new foreign parent selling its stock in the former U.S. parent to a CFC with deferred earnings in exchange for cash or property of the CFC, effectively resulting in a tax-free repatriation of cash or property bypassing the U.S. parent. Today's action would eliminate the ability to use this strategy.

Make it more difficult for U.S. entities to invert by strengthening the requirement that the former owners of the U.S. entity own less than 80 percent of the new combined entity:

- Limit the ability of companies to count passive assets that are not part of the entity's daily business functions in order to inflate the new foreign parent's size and therefore evade the 80 percent rule — known as using a "cash box. (*Action under section 7874 of the code*) Companies can successfully invert when the U.S. entity has, for example, a value of 79 percent, and the foreign "acquirer" has a value of 21 percent of the combined entity. However in some inversion transactions, the foreign acquirer's size is inflated by passive assets, also known as "cash boxes," such as cash or marketable securities. These assets are not used by the entity for daily business functions. Today's notice would disregard stock of the foreign parent that is attributable to passive assets in the context of this 80 percent requirement. This would apply if at least 50 percent of the foreign corporation's assets are passive. Banks and other financial services companies would be exempted.

- **Prevent U.S. companies from reducing their size pre-inversion by making extraordinary dividends.** (*Action under section 7874 of the code*) In some instances, a U.S. entity may pay out large dividends pre-inversion to reduce its size and meet the 80 percent threshold, also known as "skinny-down" dividends. Today's notice would disregard these pre-inversion extraordinary dividends for purposes of the ownership requirement, thereby raising the U.S. entity's ownership, possibly above the 80 percent threshold.

  ○ **Prevent a U.S. entity from inverting a portion of its operations by transferring assets to a newly formed foreign corporation that it spins off to its shareholders, thereby avoiding the associated U.S. tax liabilities, a practice known as "spinversion."** (*Action under section 7874 of the code*) In some cases a U.S. entity may invert a portion of its operations by transferring a portion of its assets to a newly formed foreign corporation and then spinning-off that corporation to its public shareholders. This transaction takes advantage of a rule that was intended to permit purely internal restructurings by multinationals. Under today's action, the spun-off foreign corporation would not benefit from these internal restructuring rules with the result that the spun off company would be treated as a domestic corporation, eliminating the use of this technique for these transactions.

C. Treasury's November 2015 Notice Announcing Additional Actions to Rein in Inversions

IRS and Treasury Fact Sheet: Additional Treasury Actions to Rein in Corporate Tax Inversions

[Announcing Notice 2015-79, 2015-49 I.R.B. ___ (Dec. 7, 2015).]

[The Fact Sheet set out in this section provides an introduction to Notice 2015-79. For a detailed analysis of the Notice, *see* Thompson, *Mergers, Acquisitions, and Tender Offers, supra* Sec. 1.11 at Section 22:7.4.]

* * * The notice being issued today involves transactions in [the] continuing ownership range of 60 to 80 percent.

Only legislation can decisively stop inversions. The Administration has been working together with Congress for several years in an effort to reform our business tax system, make it simpler and more pro-growth, and address the incentives that encourage companies to engage in inversions.

In the absence of legislative action, on September 22, 2014, Treasury announced guidance that both made it more difficult for U.S. companies to invert and reduced the tax benefits of doing so by eliminating techniques used by inverted companies to access overseas earnings without paying U.S. tax. Today, Treasury is taking additional actions to make it more difficult for U.S. companies to invert and to further reduce the tax benefits of inversions.

[SECTION 2] Specifically, today's notice makes it more difficult for U.S. companies to invert by:

Strengthening the requirement that the former owners of a U.S. company own less than 80 percent of the new combined entity

Limit the ability of U.S. companies to combine with foreign entities when the new foreign parent is located in a "third country" (Action under section 7874 of the code)

• In certain inversion transactions, a U.S. company combines with a smaller existing foreign corporation using a new foreign parent whose tax residence is different from that of the existing foreign corporation. In other words, the new foreign parent will be a tax resident of a "third country." The third country chosen generally will have a favorable tax system and income tax treaty with the United States. The decision to locate the tax residence of the new foreign parent outside of both the United States and the jurisdiction in which the existing foreign corporation is a tax resident generally is made to facilitate U.S. tax avoidance after the inversion transaction.

• Today's notice provides that in certain cases when the foreign parent is a tax resident of a third country, stock of the foreign parent issued to the shareholders of the existing foreign corporation is disregarded for purposes of the ownership requirement, thereby raising the ownership at-

tributable to the shareholders of the U.S. entity, possibly above the 80per-
cent threshold.

• The rule addressing "third country" inversions will prevent U.S. firms
from essentially cherry-picking a tax-friendly country in which to locate
their tax residence.

Limit the ability of U.S. companies to inflate the new foreign parent corporation's size and therefore avoid the 80-percent rule. (Action under section
7874 of the code)

• Companies can successfully invert when a U.S. company has, for example, a value of 79 percent, and the foreign "acquirer" has a value of
21 percent of the combined group. However, in some inversion transactions, the foreign acquirer's size may be inflated by "stuffing" assets into
the foreign acquirer as part of the inversion transaction in order to avoid
the 80-percent rule.

• Current law disregards the stock of the foreign parent corporation that
is attributable to such assets, thereby raising the U.S. entity's ownership,
possibly above the 80-percent threshold. However, certain taxpayers may
be narrowly interpreting the anti-stuffing rules to apply only to passive
assets.

• Today's notice clarifies that the anti-stuffing rules apply to any assets acquired with a principal purpose of avoiding the 80-percent rule, regardless
of whether the assets are passive assets.

**Strengthening the substantial business activities exception (Action under section
7874 of the code)**

• Under current law, a U.S. company can successfully invert if, after the transaction, at least 25 percent of the combined group's business activity is in the
foreign country in which the new foreign parent is created or organized. This
is the case regardless of whether the new foreign parent is a tax resident of
that foreign country.

• The standard for determining tax residence of a corporation for U.S. income
tax purposes is where the entity is created or organized. Thus, a corporation
is treated as domestic if it is created or organized under the law of the United
States or of any State and as foreign if it is created or organized under the
law of a foreign country. This standard, however, may not align with standards of foreign countries, which, for example, may be based on criteria
such as the location in which the entity is managed or controlled.

• Today's notice provides that the combined group cannot satisfy the 25-
percent business activities exception unless the new foreign parent is a tax
resident in the foreign country in which it is created or organized. Thus, this
rule will limit the ability of a U.S. multinational to replace its U.S. tax residence with tax residence in another country in which it does not have substantial business activities.

[SECTION 3] Specifically, today's notice reduces the tax benefits of inversions by: Preventing inverted companies from transferring foreign operations "out from under" the U.S. tax net without paying current U.S. tax

Expand the scope of inversion gain for which current U.S. tax must be paid (Action under section 7874 of the code)

• Under current law, U.S. multinationals owe U.S. tax on the profits of their controlled foreign corporations (CFCs), although they do not usually have to pay the tax until those profits are paid to the U.S. parent as a dividend. Profits that have not yet been repatriated are known as deferred earnings. However, to the extent a CFC has passive income the U.S. parent is treated as if it received a taxable deemed dividend from the CFC.

• Under current law, an inverted company must pay current U.S. tax on inversion gain (the gain recognized when the inverted company transfers stock in its CFCs or other property to the new foreign parent) without the benefit of otherwise applicable tax attributes (such as net operating loss carryovers) to offset the gain. Thus, these rules impose penalties on post-inversion transactions that are designed to remove income from foreign operations from the U.S. taxing jurisdiction.

• Today's notice expands the scope of inversion gain to include certain taxable deemed dividends recognized by an inverted company. Specifically when that dividend is attributable to passive income recognized by a CFC when the CFC that transfers foreign operations to the new foreign parent.

Require that all built-in gain in CFC stock be recognized, without regard to the amount of deferred earnings, upon a restructuring of the CFC (Action under section 367 of the code)

• After an inversion transaction, the new foreign parent may acquire CFC stock held by the former U.S.-parented group, with the result that the CFC is no longer under the U.S. tax net. Under current law, the former U.S. parent must recognize built-in gain in the CFC stock as a result of the transfer, but not in excess of the deferred earnings of the CFC.

• Today's notice provides that all the built-in gain in the CFC stock must be recognized as a result of the post-inversion transfer, regardless of the amount of the CFC's deferred earnings, thereby potentially increasing the amount of current U.S. tax paid as a result of the transfer.

[SECTION 4] Additional actions

Make corrections to the rules in Notice 2014-52 that limit the ability of U.S. companies to invert:

Limit the ability of companies to count passive assets that are not part of the entity's daily business functions in order to inflate the new foreign parent's size and therefore evade the 80percent rule—known as using a "cash box." (Action under section 7874 of the code)

• Today's notice corrects the "cash box" rule that disregards stock of the foreign parent that is attributable to existing passive assets in the context of the 80-percent threshold. The correction ensures that assets used in an active insurance business are not treated as passive assets.

Prevent U.S. companies from reducing their size by making extraordinary dividends. (Action under section 7874 of the code)

• Today's notice corrects the rule that would disregard certain pre-inversion extraordinary dividends for purposes of the ownership requirement. The correction ensures that the extraordinary dividend rule does not apply when a foreign corporation acquires a U.S. company in an all-cash or mostly cash acquisition.

D. Introduction to the 2016 Treasury Regulations: (1) Implementing the 2014 and 2015 Treasury Notices, and (2) Promulgating Regulations under Section 385[57]

As discussed in Sec. 10.11.B, in September 2014, the Treasury and IRS issued a notice on inversions (the 2014 Inversion Notice), and as discussed in Sec. 10.11.C, in December 2015, the Treasury and IRS issued an additional notice on inversions (the 2015 Inversion Notice), which supplements and modifies this 2014 Inversion Notice.

In April 2016, the Treasury issued two sets of regulations addressing inversions. One set of regulations implements the concepts discussed in the 2014 and 2015 notices, and the basic principles in this set of regulations are discussed in Sec. 10.11.E. This set of temporary regulations is titled *Inversions and Related Transactions* (the 2016 General Inversion Regs.),[58] and is generally effective as of the date the provision was first announced either in the 2014 or 2015 Notices or on April 4, 2016, the date of the publication of the regulations in the Federal Register.

The second set of regulations is in proposed form and is issued under Sec. 385, which authorizes the Treasury to issue regulations dealing with debt-equity issues. Among other things, this set of regulations, which is titled *Treatment of Certain Interest in Corporations as Stock or Indebtedness* (the 2016 Section 385 Regs),[59] treats as stock certain debt instruments issued to related parties in transactions, including inversions, which can be used for interest stripping. These 2016 Section 385 Regs are discussed in Sec. 10.11.F.

---

57. This and subsequent sections dealing with the Treasury's 2016 inversion and Section 385 regulations are based on Sections 22:7.5 and 22:7.6 of Thompson, *Mergers, Acquisitions and Tender Offers* (PLI 2010, Updated semiannually) (with permission).

58. TD 9761, Inversions and Related Transactions, Final and Temporary Regulations (April 8, 2016) [the 2016 General Inversion Regs].

59. REG-108060-15, Treatment of Certain Interests in Corporations as Stock or Indebtedness, Notice of Proposed Rulemaking (April 8, 2016) [the 2016 Section 385 Regs.].

For a more detailed discussion of these Notices and the proposed regulations, see Thompson, *Mergers, Acquisitions, and Tender Offers*, *supra* Sec. 1.11 at Sec.s 22:7.3 to 22:7.6.

E. Introduction to the 2016 General Inversion Regulations

1. In General

The Summary of the 2016 General Inversion Regs. gives the following guidance on the scope of the regulations:

> This document contains temporary regulations that address transactions that are structured to avoid the purposes of sections 7874 and 367 of the Internal Revenue Code (the Code) and certain post-inversion tax avoidance transactions. These regulations affect certain domestic corporations and domestic partnerships whose assets are directly or indirectly acquired by a foreign corporation and certain persons related to such domestic corporations and domestic partnerships. The text of the temporary regulations also serves as the text of the proposed regulations[.]

This section discusses these regulations in the order in which the particular sections of the regulations are discussed in the preamble to the regulations. The preamble and the regulations run for over 200 pages; therefore, this discussion merely touches on the basic principles.

2. Introduction to the Significance of the Ownership Percentage, Right Sizing, and Pfizer's Abandoned Inversion with Allergan

As indicated previously, under Section 7874, the "Ownership Percentage," is the percentage of the stock (by vote or value) of the foreign acquiring corporation that is held by former shareholders of the domestic corporation by reason of holding stock in the domestic corporation (the "Domestic Shareholders' by-Reason-of-Stock"). The fraction used to calculate the Ownership Percentage is referred to at times as the "Ownership Fraction."

The numerator of the Ownership Fraction is the Domestic Shareholders' by-Reason-of-Stock in the foreign acquiring corporation, and the denominator is all of the outstanding stock of the foreign acquiring corporation. Thus, for example,

1. if the Ownership Percentage is 80% or more, the foreign acquiring corporation is treated as a domestic corporation under Section 7874(b);

2. if the Ownership Percentage is at least 60% and less than 80%, then (a) the Inversion Gain Rule under Section 7874(a) applies, which subjects certain transactions to tax without regard to the availability of net operating losses and credits, and (b) the Anti-Hop Scotch Loan Rule, discussed above and below, applies;

3. if the Ownership Percentage is more than 50% but less than 80% the Section 367(a) Gain Recognition Rule, which requires the shareholders of the domestic corporation to recognize gain but not loss, applies; and

4. if the Ownership Percentage is 50% or less, none of the above rules applies.

Thus, in order to receive any benefit from an inversion, the Ownership Percentage must be less than 80%, because otherwise the foreign acquiring corporation is treated as a domestic corporation. And, in order to avoid the Inversion Gain Rule and the Anti-Hop Scotch Loan Rule, the Ownership Percentage must be less than 60%. And, to avoid the Section 367(a) Gain Recognition Rule, the Ownership Percentage must be not more than 50%.

Since these Ownership Percentage rules are dependent on the relative sizes of the domestic corporation and the foreign acquiring corporation and its foreign subs, it can be expected that companies contemplating an inversion will take measures before the inversion to get the domestic corporation and the foreign acquiring corporation in the "right relative size." This type of "right sizing" will normally involve either (1) reducing the size of the domestic corporation (*i.e.,* slimming down the domestic corporation), or (2) increasing the size of the foreign corporation (*i.e.,* bulking up the foreign acquiring corporation). Many aspects of both the 2014 and 2015 Inversion Notices address this right sizing issue, and the 2016 Temporary Regulations also address the issue. As noted below, one surprising "right sizing" aspect of the 2016 Temporary Regulations caused Pfizer to abandon its inversion with Ireland's Allergan, just two days after the issuance of these regulations.

Although the regulations deal with acquisitions of both corporations and partnerships, this section focuses only on inversions involving the acquisition of domestic corporations.

3. Clarification of the Calculation of the Ownership Percentage: Implementing the Anti-Stuffing Provisions of the 2015 Notice, Section 1.7874-4T

The preamble of the 2016 General Inversion Regs provides the following background and description to the clarification of § 1.7874-4T on the calculation of the ownership percentage, which implements an Anti-Stuffing provision of the 2015 Inversion Notice:

> Under section 7874(c)(2)(B) (statutory public offering rule), stock of a foreign acquiring corporation that is sold in a public offering related to a domestic entity acquisition described in section 7874(a)(2)(B)(i) is excluded from the denominator of the ownership fraction. The statutory public offering rule furthers the policy that section 7874 is intended to curtail domestic entity acquisitions that "permit corporations and other entities to continue to conduct business in the same manner as they did prior to the inversion." S. Rep. No. 192, 108th Cong., 1st. Sess., at 142 (2003); JCT Explanation, at 343.
>
> Section 1.7874-4T modifies the statutory public offering rule. The preamble to § 1.7874-4T provides that "the IRS and the Treasury Department believe that stock of the foreign acquiring corporation transferred in exchange for certain property in a transaction related to the acquisition, but not through a public offering, presents the same opportunity to inappropriately reduce

the ownership fraction." … Accordingly, § 1.7874-4T(b) provides that, subject to a *de minimis* exception, "disqualified stock" is not included in the denominator of the ownership fraction. Disqualified stock generally includes stock of the foreign acquiring corporation that is transferred to a person (other than the domestic entity) in exchange for "nonqualified property." The term "nonqualified property" means (i) cash or cash equivalents, (ii) marketable securities, (iii) certain obligations (for example, obligations owed by members of the EAG [Expanded Affiliated Group]), or (iv) any other property acquired in a transaction (or series of transactions) related to the domestic entity acquisition with a principal purpose of avoiding the purposes of section 7874. This preamble refers at times to the property described in clauses (i), (ii), and (iii) of the preceding sentence collectively as "specified nonqualified property" and to the property described in clause (iv) as "avoidance property." …

b. Clarification

Section 2.03(b) of the 2015 notice provides that § 1.7874-4T will be clarified in certain respects. The temporary regulations implement these clarifications. Accordingly, with respect to the definition of nonqualified property, the temporary regulations clarify that avoidance property means any property (other than specified nonqualified property) acquired with a principal purpose of avoiding the purposes of section 7874, regardless of whether the transaction involves an indirect transfer of specified nonqualified property. See § 1.7874-4T(j), Example 3. Second, the temporary regulations remove the phrase "in a transaction (or series of transactions) related to the acquisition" from the definition of avoidance property. See § 1.7874-4T(i)(7)(iv). Third, the temporary regulations remove the phrase "unless a principal purpose for acquiring such stock or partnership interest is to avoid the purposes of section 7874" from the definition of "marketable securities." See § 1.7874-4T(i)(6). Finally, the temporary regulations clarify Example 1 and Example 2 of § 1.7874-4T(j) by including a reference to section 7874(c)(4).

In addition, the temporary regulations update the *de minimis* exception in § 1.7874-4T(d)(1) to reflect the passive assets rule (described in Section 2 of this Part I.B) and the NOCD [Non-Ordinary Course Distribution] rule (described in Section 5 of this Part I.B), and to also conform the exception to the *de minimis* exceptions in §§ 1.7874-7T(c) and 1.7874-10T(d).[60]

4. Calculation of the Ownership Percentage: The Passive Asset Rule, which is the Anti-Cash Box Rule of the 2014 Notice, Section 1.7874-7T

The preamble to the 2016 General Inversion Regs sets forth as follows the background of the "passive assets rule," which is based on the Anti-Cash Box rule of the 2014 Notice, which is discussed above:

---

60. The 2016 General Inversion Regs , *supra* at 21-23.

Section 2.01(b) of the 2014 notice announced that future regulations would include a rule (the passive assets rule) that would exclude from the denominator of the ownership fraction stock of a foreign acquiring corporation that is attributable to certain passive assets, but only if, after the domestic entity acquisition and all related transactions are complete, more than 50 percent of the gross value of all foreign group property constitutes certain passive assets (referred to in the notice and temporary regulations as "foreign group nonqualified property"). * * * The temporary regulations implement the passive assets rule described in the 2014 notice, subject to [certain] modifications[.]

The 2014 notice provides that the amount of stock that will be excluded under the passive assets rule is equal to the product of (i) the value of the stock of the foreign acquiring corporation, other than stock that is described in section 7874(a)(2)(B)(ii) (that is, by-reason-of stock) and stock that is excluded from the denominator of the ownership fraction under either § 1.7874-1(b) (because it is held by a member of the EAG) or § 1.7874-4T(b) (because it is disqualified stock); and (ii) the foreign group nonqualified property fraction. The numerator of the foreign group nonqualified property fraction is the gross value of all foreign group nonqualified property, and the denominator is the gross value of all foreign group property.[61]

Subject to a *de minimis* exception, section 1.7874-7T(b) implements the above rule with the following general rule:

(b) *General rule.* If, on the completion date [*i.e.*, the date the domestic corporation is acquired], more than fifty percent of the gross value of all foreign group property constitutes foreign group nonqualified property [*i.e.*, certain passive assets], then stock of the foreign acquiring corporation is excluded from the denominator of the ownership fraction in an amount equal to the product of—

(1) The value of [subject to certain exceptions] the stock of the foreign acquiring corporation ... ; and

(2) The foreign group nonqualified property fraction [*i.e.*, the nonqualified property over all property].

5. Calculation of the Ownership Percentage: The Acquisition of Multiple Domestic Entities Rule, the Pfizer Rule, Section 1.7874-8T

Section 1.7874-8T of the 2016 General Inversion Regs, which has no comparable part in the 2014 and 2015 Notices, is directed at transactions like the Pfizer-Allergan inversion. Allergan, which is based in Ireland, was the "right size" so that the merger with Pfizer would give the Pfizer shareholders an Ownership Percentage of approximately 53% of the stock of the resulting firm, thereby avoiding Section 7874, although still subject to the Gain Recognition Rule of Section 367(a).

---

61. *Id.* at 23-24.

Allergan had grown to be the "right size" for a merger with Pfizer through the acquisition of U.S. corporations in inversions. As a result of the rule in § 1.7874-8T, which is titled "Disregard of certain stock attributable to multiple domestic entity acquisitions," the stock issued by Allergan in the prior inversions was not included in the denominator of the Ownership Fraction. Consequently, Allergan was no longer the "right size." Rather, the Pfizer shareholders would have an Ownership Percentage of approximately 70%, and as a consequence, both the inversion gain rule and the Anti-Hop Scotch rule, discussed below, would apply. Also, even without § 1.7874-8T, the 2016 Section 385 Regs, also discussed below, would have applied to any efforts by Pfizer to enter into interest stripping transactions. Thus, as a result of the issuance on April 4 of the 2016 General Inversion Regs and the 2016 Section 385 Regs, Pfizer terminated the inversion on April 6, 2016. The Pfizer press release announcing the termination stated:

> Pfizer Inc. (NYSE: PFE) today announced that the merger agreement between Pfizer and Allergan plc (NYSE: AGN) has been terminated by mutual agreement of the companies. The decision was driven by the actions announced by the U.S. Department of Treasury on April 4, 2016, which the companies concluded qualified as an "Adverse Tax Law Change" under the merger agreement.

The preamble to the 2016 General Inversion Regs discusses as follows the background of § 1.7874-8T:

3. Acquisitions of Multiple Domestic Entities

a. Transactions at issue

The Treasury Department and the IRS are concerned that a single foreign acquiring corporation may avoid the application of section 7874 by completing multiple domestic entity acquisitions over a relatively short period of time, in circumstances where section 7874 would otherwise have applied if the acquisitions had been made at the same time or pursuant to a plan (or series of related transactions). In these situations, the value of the foreign acquiring corporation increases to the extent it issues stock in connection with each successive domestic entity acquisition, thereby enabling the foreign acquiring corporation to complete another, potentially larger, domestic entity acquisition to which section 7874 will not apply. In some cases, a substantial portion of the value of a foreign acquiring corporation may be attributable to its completion of multiple domestic entity acquisitions over the span of just a few years, with that value serving as a platform to complete still larger subsequent domestic entity acquisitions that avoid the application of section 7874. That is, the ownership percentage determined with respect to a subsequent domestic entity acquisition may be less than 60, or less than 80, if the shares of the foreign acquiring corporation issued in prior domestic entity acquisitions are respected as outstanding (thus, included in the denominator but not the numerator) when determining the ownership fraction.

Section 7874 is intended to address transactions in which a domestic parent corporation of a multinational group is replaced with a foreign parent corporation while "permit[ting] corporations and other entities to continue to conduct business in the same manner as they did prior to the inversion." S. Rep. No. 192, at 142 (2003); JCT Explanation, at 343. To further this policy, various rules under section 7874 exclude from the denominator of the ownership fraction stock of the foreign acquiring corporation that otherwise would inappropriately reduce the ownership fraction. For example, the statutory public offering rule of section 7874(a)(2)(B) excludes from the denominator of the ownership fraction stock of the foreign acquiring corporation that is sold for cash in a public offering related to the domestic entity acquisition. For the same reason, rules under §§ 1.7874-4T and 1.7874-7T exclude from the denominator of the ownership fraction certain stock of the foreign acquiring corporation that is transferred in exchange for, or otherwise attributable to, passive assets or other nonqualified property.

The Treasury Department and the IRS have concluded that it is not consistent with the purposes of section 7874 to permit a foreign acquiring corporation to reduce the ownership fraction for a domestic entity acquisition by including stock issued in connection with other recent domestic entity acquisitions. Moreover, the Treasury Department and the IRS do not believe that the application of section 7874 in these circumstances should depend on whether there was a demonstrable plan to undertake the subsequent domestic entity acquisition at the time of the prior domestic entity acquisitions. Therefore, and consistent with the policies underlying the other stock exclusion rules under section 7874, the Treasury Department and the IRS have determined that stock of the foreign acquiring corporation that was issued in connection with certain prior domestic entity acquisitions occurring within a 36-month look-back period should be excluded from the denominator of the ownership fraction.[62]

The basic rule is set out as follows in § 1.7874-8T(a) and (b), which became effective on April 8, 2016:

§ 1.7874-8T Disregard of certain stock attributable to multiple domestic entity acquisitions (temporary).

(a) *Scope.* This section identifies stock of a foreign acquiring corporation that is disregarded in determining an ownership fraction by value because it is attributable to certain prior domestic entity acquisitions. Paragraph (b) of this section sets forth the general rule regarding the amount of stock of a foreign acquiring corporation that is excluded from the denominator of the ownership fraction by value under this section[.]

   (b) *General rule.* This paragraph (b) applies to a domestic entity acquisition (relevant domestic entity acquisition) [*i.e.*, an acquisition of a domestic corporation "that occurred within the 36-month period ending on the signing date of the relevant domestic entity acquisition"] when the foreign acquiring

---

62. *Id.* at 31-33.

corporation ... has completed one or more prior domestic entity acquisitions. When this paragraph (b) applies, then, for purposes of determining the ownership percentage by value (but not vote) described in section 7874(a)(2)(B)(ii), stock of the foreign acquiring corporation is excluded from the denominator of the ownership fraction in an amount equal to the sum of the excluded amounts computed separately with respect to each prior domestic entity acquisition and each relevant share class.

Example 1 of § 1.7874-8T(h) provides the following illustration of the basic rule:

Example 1. Application of general rule—(i) *Facts.* Individual A wholly owns DT1, a domestic corporation. Individual B owns all 100 shares of the sole class of stock of FA, a foreign corporation. In Year 1, FA acquires all the stock of DT1 solely in exchange for 100 shares of newly issued FA stock (DT1 acquisition). On the completion date with respect to the DT1 acquisition, the fair market value of each share of FA stock is $1x. In Year 3, FA enters into a binding contract to acquire all the stock of DT2, a domestic corporation wholly owned by Individual C. Thereafter, FA acquires all the stock of DT2 solely in exchange for 150 shares of newly issued FA stock (DT2 acquisition). On the completion date with respect to the DT2 acquisition, the fair market value of each share of FA stock is $1.50x. FA did not complete the DT1 acquisition and DT2 acquisition pursuant to a plan (or series of related transactions) for purposes of applying § 1.7874-2(e). In addition, there have been no redemptions of FA stock subsequent to the DT1 acquisition.

(ii) *Analysis.* The DT1 acquisition is a prior domestic entity acquisition with respect to the DT2 acquisition (the relevant domestic entity acquisition) because the DT1 acquisition occurred within the 36-month period ending on the signing date with respect to the DT2 acquisition. Accordingly, paragraph (b) of this section applies to the DT2 acquisition. As a result, and because there were no redemptions of FA stock, the excluded amount is $150x (calculated as 100, the total number of prior acquisition shares, multiplied by $1.50x, the fair market value of a single class of FA stock on the completion date with respect to the DT2 acquisition). Accordingly, the numerator of the ownership fraction by value is $225x (the fair market value of the stock of FA that, with respect to the DT2 acquisition, is described in section 7874(a)(2)(B)(ii)). In addition, the denominator of the ownership fraction is $375x (calculated as $525x, the fair market value of all shares of FA stock as of the completion date with respect to the DT2 acquisition, less $150x, the excluded amount). Therefore, the ownership percentage by value is 60.[**Consequently, the transaction is subject to Section 7874.**]

While some observers will question whether the Treasury has the authority to issue these regulations, in my view there is more than ample authority in section 7874(g), which provides, in part:

The Secretary shall provide such regulations as are necessary to carry out this section, including regulations providing for such adjustments to the application of this section as are necessary **to prevent the avoidance of the purposes of this section....**

6. Calculation of the Ownership Percentage: The Third Country Rule, Section 1.7874-9T

The preamble to the 2016 General Inversion Regs introduces as follows the Third Country Rule, which first appeared in the 2015 Notice and is reflected in § 1.7874-9T:

4. Third-Country Rule

a. Background

Section 2.02(b) of the 2015 notice announces that the Treasury Department and the IRS intend to issue regulations providing a rule (the third-country rule) that will apply to certain domestic entity acquisitions in which a domestic entity combines with an existing foreign corporation under a foreign parent corporation that is a tax resident of a "third country" (that is, a foreign country other than the foreign country of which the existing foreign corporation is subject to tax as a resident). The 2015 notice provides that the third-country rule will apply when four requirements are satisfied. First, in a transaction (referred to in the 2015 notice as a "foreign target acquisition" but in this preamble and the temporary regulations as a "foreign acquisition") related to the domestic entity acquisition, the foreign acquiring corporation directly or indirectly acquires substantially all of the properties held directly or indirectly by another foreign corporation (the acquired foreign corporation). Second, the gross value of all property directly or indirectly acquired by the foreign acquiring corporation in the foreign acquisition exceeds 60 percent of the gross value of all foreign group property, other than foreign group nonqualified property, held by the EAG on the completion date (the gross value requirement). Third, the tax residence of the foreign acquiring corporation is not the same as that of the acquired foreign corporation, as determined before the foreign acquisition and any related transaction (the tax residency requirement). And fourth, the ownership percentage, determined without regard to the third-country rule, must be at least 60 but less than 80 (the domestic entity ownership requirement).... [T]he temporary regulations retain the first, third, and fourth requirements described in the 2015 notice but replace the second requirement with [the following new requirement: "[A] continuity of interest requirement (referred to as the "foreign ownership percentage"), ... [which generally] is satisfied if at least 60 percent of the stock (by vote or value) of the foreign acquiring corporation is held by former shareholders of the acquired foreign corporation by reason of holding stock in the acquired foreign corporation[.]].[63]

---

63. *Id.* at 37-38.

7. Calculation of the Ownership Percentage: The Non-Ordinary Course Distributions (NOCD) Rule, Section 1.7874-10T

While all of the provisions discussed thus far dealing with the "Calculation of the Ownership Percentage" have addressed the "right sizing" or bulking up of the foreign acquiror, this Non-Ordinary Course Distributions (NOCD) Rule deals with the "right sizing" or slimming down of the U.S. firm. This concept was first set forth in the 2014 Notice. The preamble to the 2016 General Inversion Regs gives the following introduction to the issue and general description of the approach of this very elaborate set of regulations:

5. Non-Ordinary Course Distributions (NOCD) Rule

a. Overview

The 2014 notice announced that the Treasury Department and the IRS intend to include in future regulations under section 7874 a rule (the NOCD rule) that disregards certain distributions made by a domestic entity before being acquired by a foreign acquiring corporation that otherwise would reduce the numerator of the ownership fraction. Specifically, section 2.02(b) of the 2014 notice provides that, for purposes of applying section 7874(c)(4), NOCDs made by the domestic entity ... during the 36-month period ending on the completion date will be treated as part of a plan a principal purpose of which is to avoid the purposes of section 7874.

The 2014 notice defines NOCDs as the excess of all distributions made during a taxable year by the domestic entity with respect to its stock ... over 110 percent of the average of such distributions during the thirty-six month period immediately preceding such taxable year. The 2014 notice defines distribution, in relevant part, to mean any distribution, regardless of whether it is treated as a dividend or whether, for example, it qualifies under section 355.

Section 4.02(b) of the 2015 notice provides that the future regulations incorporating the NOCD rule will include a *de minimis* exception....

The 2015 notice provides that, when a domestic entity acquisition satisfies the requirements of the *de minimis* exception, no distributions will be treated as NOCDs that are disregarded under the NOCD rule....

Further, the 2014 notice provides that § 1.367(a)-3(c) (concerning outbound transfers of stock or securities of a domestic corporation) will be modified to include a rule that incorporates the principles of the NOCD rule for purposes of the substantiality test, which, in general, requires that the value of the foreign acquiring corporation be equal to or greater than the value of the domestic target corporation.

b. Regulations implementing the NOCD rule

Section 1.7874-10T sets forth the NOCD rule as described in the 2014 notice and the 2015 notice, subject to certain modifications, in part, to address comments received. Section 1.367(a)-3T(c)(3)(iii)(C) sets forth a similar rule for purposes of the substantiality test under § 1.367(a)-3(c).[64]

8. Application of the EAG Rules When There is a Related Transfer of Stock of the Foreign Acquiring Corporation, Section 1.7874-6T

This highly complex provision is only introduced here. The preamble to the 2016 General Inversion Regs gives the following general description of the rule, which is based on a provision of the 2014 Notice:

> Section 2.03(b) of the 2014 notice provides a rule concerning the interaction of § 1.7874-5T and the EAG [Expanded Affiliate Group] rules. Subject to two exceptions, the 2014 notice provides that certain stock, referred to as "transferred stock," is not treated as held by a member of the EAG for purposes of applying the EAG rules. As a result, transferred stock generally is included in both the numerator and the denominator of the ownership fraction. See § 1.7874-5T(a). For this purpose, transferred stock is stock of a foreign acquiring corporation described in section 7874(a)(2)(B)(ii) (that is, by-reason-of stock) that is received by a former domestic entity shareholder ... that is a corporation (transferring corporation), and, in a transaction (or series of transactions) related to the domestic entity acquisition, is subsequently transferred.
>
> The 2014 notice also described two exceptions to this rule: the U.S.-parented group [an affiliated group that has a domestic corporation as a common parent] exception and the foreign-parented group [an affiliated group that has a foreign corporation as a common parent] exception. When either of these exceptions applies, transferred stock is treated as held by members of the EAG for purposes of applying the EAG rules. In these cases, transferred stock is excluded from the numerator of the ownership fraction and, depending on the application of § 1.7874-1(c), may be excluded from the denominator of the ownership fraction. See § 1.7874-1(b) and (c).
>
> The U.S.-parented group exception applies if: (i) before and after the domestic entity acquisition, the transferring corporation (or its successor) is a member of a U.S.-parented group, and (ii) after the domestic entity acquisition, both the person that holds the transferred stock after all related transfers of the transferred stock are complete and the foreign acquiring corporation are members of the U.S.-parented group referred to in (i).
>
> The foreign-parented group exception applies if: (i) before the domestic entity acquisition, the transferring corporation and the domestic entity are members of the same foreign-parented group, and (ii) after the domestic entity acquisition, the transferring corporation is a member of the EAG, or would be a member of the EAG absent the subsequent transfer of any stock of the foreign acquiring corporation by a member of the foreign-parented

---

64. *Id.* at 40-41.

group in a transaction related to the domestic entity acquisition (but taking into account all other transactions related to such acquisition).

The 2014 notice defines a U.S.-parented group as an affiliated group that has a domestic corporation as the common parent corporation, and a foreign-parented group as an affiliated group that has a foreign corporation as the common parent corporation.

For this purpose, the term "affiliated group" means an affiliated group as defined in section 1504(a) [*i.e.,* an 80% owned controlled group] but without regard to section 1504(b)(3) [which excludes foreign corporations], except that section 1504(a) is applied by substituting the term "more than 50 percent" for the term "at least 80 percent" each place it appears. Finally, the 2014 notice provides that, except as provided in the foreign-parented group exception, all transactions related to the domestic entity acquisition must be taken into account for purposes of determining an EAG, a U.S.-parented group, and a foreign-parented group.

3. Regulations Implementing the Rule

Section 1.7874-6T sets forth the rule concerning the interaction of § 1.7874-5T and the EAG rules, as described in the 2014 notice, subject to [certain] modifications[.][65]

9. The Substantial Business Activities Test, The Subject to Tax Rule, Section § 1.7874-3T(b)(4)

The preamble to the 2016 General Inversion Regs gives the following description of this substantial business activities test and the Subject-to-tax rule, which was added by the 2015 Notice:

D. The substantial business activities test

1. The Subject-to-Tax Rule

Section 2.02(a) of the 2015 notice provides a rule (the subject-to-tax rule) that addresses domestic entity acquisitions in which a taxpayer asserts that its EAG has substantial business activities in the relevant foreign country when compared to the EAG's total business activities even though the foreign acquiring corporation is not subject to tax as a resident of the relevant foreign country. Under the subject-to-tax rule, an EAG cannot have substantial business activities in the relevant foreign country when compared to the EAG's total business activities unless the foreign acquiring corporation is subject to tax as a resident of the relevant foreign country.

The temporary regulations implement the subject-to-tax rule described in the 2015 notice without making any substantive changes. See § 1.7874-3T(b)(4).[66]

---

65. *Id* at 58-60.
66. *Id.* at 63.

10. The Anti-Hopscotch Loan Rule, Section § 1.956-2T(a)(4)

The preamble to the 2016 General Inversion Regs gives the following introduction to the basic principles of the Anti-Hop Scotch Loan provisions under Section 956:

A. United States property rule

1. Overview

As described in section 3.01(a) of the 2014 notice, an inversion transaction may permit the new foreign parent of the inverted group, a group still principally comprised of United States shareholders and their CFCs, to avoid section 956 by accessing the untaxed earnings and profits of the CFCs without a current U.S. federal income tax to the United States shareholders. This is a result that the United States shareholders could not achieve before the inversion transaction. The ability of the new foreign parent to access deferred CFC earnings and profits would in many cases eliminate the need for the CFCs to pay dividends to the United States shareholders, thereby circumventing the purposes of section 956.

In order to prevent this avoidance of section 956, section 3.01(b) of the 2014 notice announces that future regulations will include a rule (the United States property rule) providing that, solely for purposes of section 956, any obligation or stock of a non-CFC foreign related person (generally, either the foreign acquiring corporation or a foreign affiliate of the foreign acquiring corporation that is not an expatriated foreign subsidiary) is United States property within the meaning of section 956(c)(1) to the extent such obligation or stock is acquired by an expatriated foreign subsidiary [*i.e.*, a CFC whose U.S. parent has been acquired in an inversion] during the applicable period [the 10 year period after the inversion]....

2. Regulations Implementing the United States Property Rule

These temporary regulations include the rules described in the 2014 notice, with certain modifications, in part, to address comments received.[67]

There are several exceptions to the rule that are not addressed here. The basic principles are illustrated in Example (1) of § 1.956-2T(a)(4)(iv). For purposes of the example the following is a description of the parties:

FA, a foreign corporation, wholly owns DT, a domestic corporation, which, in turn, wholly owns FT, a foreign corporation that is a controlled foreign corporation. FA also wholly owns FS, a foreign corporation. FA acquired DT in an inversion transaction that was completed on January 1, 2015.[**Note that there was an inversion.**]

The example is as follows:

Example 1. (A) *Facts.* FT [a CFC] acquired an obligation of FS [a wholly owned sub of FA, a foreign corporation; FS is not a CFC] on January 31, 2015.

---

67. *Id.* at 65-66.

(B) *Analysis.* Pursuant to § 1.7874-12T, DT is a domestic entity, FT is an expatriated foreign subsidiary, and FS is a non-CFC foreign related person. In addition FT acquired the FS obligation during the applicable period. Thus, as of January 31, 2015, the obligation of FS is United States property with respect to FT for purposes of section 956(a) and § 1.956-2(a).[**Consequently, under Section 956, FT has made a constructive dividend to DT in the amount of the obligation acquired from FS.**]

It should be noted that this rule only applies where there is an inversion within the meaning of section 7874. Thus, in an acquisition by a foreign corporation of a U.S. target in a non-inversion transaction there is no prohibition against the making of Hopscotch Loans. I think the Treasury should extend this anti-Hopscotch Loan rule to all acquisitions by foreign corporations of U.S. targets that own CFCs.

11. The Section 7701(l) Recharacterization Rule, Section § 1.7701(l)-4T

The following is a short excerpt from the discussion of the recharacterization rule under Section 7701(l) that is set out in the preamble to the 2016 General Inversion Regs:

1. Section 7701(l) Recharacterization Rule

a. Overview

As described in the 2014 notice, after an inversion transaction, the inverted group may cause an expatriated foreign subsidiary to cease to be a CFC using certain transactions that do not give rise to U.S. federal income tax, so as to avoid U.S. federal income tax on the CFC's pre-inversion transaction earnings and profits. Additionally, even if the foreign acquiring corporation were to acquire less stock of an expatriated foreign subsidiary, such that the expatriated foreign subsidiary remained a CFC, it could nevertheless substantially dilute a United States shareholder's ownership of the CFC. As a result, the United States shareholder could avoid U.S. federal income tax on the CFC's pre-inversion transaction earnings and profits[.]

In order to prevent the use of these transactions to avoid U.S. federal income tax, the 2014 notice announces that the Treasury Department and the IRS intend to issue regulations under section 7701(l) that will recharacterize specified transactions completed during the applicable period (the section 7701(l) recharacterization rule). A specified transaction is defined in section 3.02(e)(i) of the 2014 notice as a transaction in which stock in an expatriated foreign subsidiary (specified stock) is transferred (including by issuance) to a specified related person. A specified related person [includes] a non-CFC foreign related person[.]

Section 3.02(e)(i)(A) of the 2014 notice provides that a specified transaction is recharacterized for all purposes of the Code, as of the date on which the specified transaction occurs, as an arrangement directly between the specified related person and one or more section 958(a) U.S. shareholders of the expatriated foreign subsidiary. * * *

b. Regulations implementing the section 7701(l) recharacterization rule

These temporary regulations implement the section 7701(l) recharacterization rule described in the 2014 notice, subject to certain modifications[.][68]

These regulations are designed to prevent the post-inversion de-control of CFCs, and any such transaction will have to run the gauntlet set out in these very complicated regulations.

12. The Section 367(b) Stock Dilution Rule, Section § 1.367(b)—4T(e)

The 2016 General Inversion Regs contain a "Section 367(b) Stock Dilution Rule." As discussed Secs. 10.13 through 10.15, under Section 367(b), the Treasury is authorized to write regulations providing for recognition of gain in certain inbound and foreign-to-foreign reorganizations. The preamble to The 2016 General Inversion Regs sets out the following description of the basic rules:

a. Overview

Section 3.02(e)(ii) of the 2014 notice provides a rule (the section 367(b) stock dilution rule) that addresses certain post-inversion transaction exchanges that dilute the interest of a United States shareholder in a CFC and, absent the rule, could allow the United States shareholder to avoid U.S. federal income tax on earnings and profits of the CFC that exist at the time of the exchange. Specifically, the section 367(b) stock dilution rule, as described in the 2014 notice, provides that when certain requirements are satisfied with respect to an exchange…, the exchanging shareholder is generally required to include in income as a deemed dividend the section 1248 amount with respect to the stock exchanged.…

b. Application of the section 367(b) stock dilution rule to unrealized appreciation

The 2015 notice expands the consequences of being subject to the section 367(b) stock dilution rule. The 2015 notice provides that, when an exchanging shareholder is required under the section 367(b) stock dilution rule to include in income as a deemed dividend the section 1248 amount (if any) with respect to the stock exchanged, the exchanging shareholder must also, after taking into account any increase in basis provided in § 1.367(b)-2(e)(3)(ii) resulting from the deemed dividend, recognize all realized gain with respect to the stock that is not otherwise recognized. The 2015 notice explains that this result is necessary to prevent a United States shareholder of a CFC from potentially avoiding U.S. federal income tax on net unrealized built-in-gain in property held by the CFC at the time of the exchange of the stock of the CFC. See section 3.02(b) of the 2015 notice.

The 2015 notice also states that a conforming change will be made to the regulations described in section 3.02(e)(i) of the 2014 notice. * * *

---

68. *Id.* at 73-77.

c. Regulations implementing the section 367(b) stock dilution rule

The temporary regulations implement the section 367(b) stock dilution rule as described in the 2014 notice and the 2015 notice, subject to certain modifications.[69]

13. The Section 367(b) Asset Dilution Rule, Section § 1.367(b)—4T(f)

The 2016 General Inversion Regs also contain a "Section 367(b) Asset Dilution Rule." As indicated above, under Section 367(b), the Treasury is authorized to write regulations providing for recognition of gain in certain inbound and foreign-to-foreign reorganizations. The preamble to the 2016 General Inversion Regs sets out the following description of the basic rules:

3. Section 367(b) Asset Dilution Rule

a. Transactions at issue

For reasons similar to those discussed in section 3.02(d) of the 2014 notice and section 3.02(b) of the 2015 notice, the Treasury Department and the IRS have determined that, upon a transfer by an expatriated foreign subsidiary [*i.e.*, a CFC after an inversion] of property ... to a transferee foreign corporation in certain section 351 exchanges, the expatriated foreign subsidiary should be required to recognize all realized gain in the property that is not otherwise recognized. Absent such a rule, the transfer could dilute a United States shareholder's indirect interest in the property and, as a result, could allow the United States shareholder to avoid U.S. federal income tax on realized gain that is not recognized at the time of the transfer. * * *

b. Regulations implementing the section 367(b) asset dilution rule

The temporary regulations provide a rule (the section 367(b) asset dilution rule) that applies when an expatriated foreign subsidiary transfers specified property to a foreign transferee corporation in an exchange described in section 351 that occurs within the applicable period. § 1.367(b)-4T(f)(1). When the section 367(b) asset dilution rule applies, the expatriated foreign subsidiary must recognize all realized gain (but not loss) with respect to the specified property that is not otherwise recognized, unless an exception applies. § 1.367(b)-4T(f)(1). For this purpose, specified property means any property other than stock of a lower-tier expatriated foreign subsidiary. § 1.367(b)-4T(g)(5).[70]

14. The Section 304 Rules, Section § 1.304—7T

The 2016 General Inversion Regs contain an amendment to the section 304 regulations, which deal with purchases by a corporation of the stock of a related corporation. The preamble to the 2016 General Inversion Regs sets out the following description of the basic rules:

---

69. *Id.* at 86-87.
70. *Id.* at 90-91.

The Section 304 Rules

a. Transactions at issue

Section 3.03(b) of the 2014 notice explains how taxpayers may be engaging in certain transactions following an inversion transaction that reduce the earnings and profits of a CFC to facilitate repatriation of cash and other property of the CFC. The Treasury Department and the IRS understand that taxpayers may interpret section 304(b)(5)(B) to not apply when more than 50 percent of the dividend arising upon application of section 304 is sourced from the domestic corporation, even though, for example, pursuant to an income tax treaty there may be no (or a reduced rate of) U.S. withholding tax imposed on a dividend sourced from the domestic corporation. Under this position, the dividend sourced from earnings and profits of the CFC would never be subject to U.S. federal income tax.

b. Overview

To address [these] concerns * * * section 3.03(b) of the 2014 notice provides rules (the section 304 rules) that apply for purposes of section 304(b)(5)(B). In particular, the section 304 rules provide that the determination of whether more than 50 percent of the dividends that arise under section 304(b)(2) is subject to tax or includible in the earnings and profits of a CFC is made by taking into account only the earnings and profits of the acquiring corporation (and therefore excluding the earnings and profits of the issuing corporation)....

c. Regulations implementing the section 304 rules

Section 1.304-7T sets forth regulations implementing the section 304 rules as described in the 2014 notice.[71] * * *

15. The Inversion Gain Rule, Section § 1.7874-11T

The 2016 General Inversion Regs contain the following discussion of the treatment of inversion gains under § 1.7874-11T:

C. Inversion gain rule

1. In General

Section 7874(a)(1), together with section 7874(e)(1) (which prevents the use of certain credits to offset U.S. federal income tax on inversion gain), ensures that an expatriated entity [*i.e.,* the domestic parent that is acquired in the inversion] generally pays current U.S. federal income tax with respect to inversion gain. These rules are intended to ensure that an appropriate "toll charge" is paid on transactions that accompany or follow an inversion transaction and are designed to "remove income from foreign operations from the U.S. taxing jurisdiction." *See* H.R. Conf. Rep. No. 755, at 568, 574 (2004); JCT Explanation, at 342, 345.

---

71. *Id.* at 92-93.

Section 3.01(b) of the 2015 notice announces that the Treasury Department and the IRS intend to issue regulations that will provide a rule (the inversion gain rule) to address certain indirect transfers by an expatriated entity that, absent the rule, could have the effect of removing foreign earnings from the U.S. taxing jurisdiction while avoiding current U.S. federal income tax. As described in the 2015 notice, the inversion gain rule provides that inversion gain includes income or gain recognized by an expatriated entity from an indirect transfer or license of property, such as an expatriated entity's section 951(a)(1)(A) gross income inclusions taken into account during the applicable period that are attributable to a transfer of stock or other properties or a license of property, either: (i) as part of the acquisition, or (ii) after such acquisition if the transfer or license is to a specified related person. However, clause (ii) of the preceding sentence generally does not apply to transfers or licenses of property that is inventory in the hands of the transferor or licensor. * * *

2. Regulations Implementing the Inversion Gain Rule

Section 1.7874-11T sets forth the inversion gain rule as described in the 2015 notice, subject to [a] modification.[72]

F. The 2016 Treasury Interest Stripping Regulations under Section 385

1. In General

As discussed in Sec. 10.11.D, in September 2014, the Treasury and IRS issued a notice on inversions (the 2014 Inversion Notice) and in December 2015, the Treasury and IRS issued an additional notice on inversions (the 2015 Inversion Notice), which supplements and modifies this 2014 Inversion Notice.

In April 2016, the Treasury issued two sets of regulations addressing inversions. One set of regulations implements the concepts discussed in the 2014 and 2015 notices, and this set of regulations, which is titled *Inversions and Related Transactions*, is discussed in Section 10.11.E. The second set of regulations, which is discussed in this Sec. 10.11.F, is issued under Section 385, which authorizes the Treasury to issue regulations dealing with debt-equity issues. Among other things, this set of regulations, which is titled "*Treatment of Certain Interest in Corporations as Stock or Indebtedness*" (the 2016 Section 385 Regs)[73] treats as stock certain debt instruments issued to related parties in transactions, including inversions, which can be used for interest stripping. This regulation is generally applicable as of the date of issuance, April 4, 2016. This section explores the basic principles in these proposed section 385 regulations.

---

72. *Id.* at 94-95.

73. REG-108060-15, *Treatment of Certain Interests in Corporations as Stock or Indebtedness*, Notice of Proposed Rulemaking (April 8, 2016) [the 2016 Section 385 Regs.].

2. The Words of Section 385

Before starting the analysis it is helpful to look at the words of section 385:

(a) *Authority to prescribe regulations*

The Secretary is authorized to prescribe such regulations **as may be necessary or appropriate** to determine whether an **interest in a corporation is to be treated for purposes of this title as stock or indebtedness (or as in part stock and in part indebtedness).**

(b) *Factors* The regulations prescribed under this section shall set forth factors which are to be taken into account in determining with respect to a particular factual situation whether a debtor-creditor relationship exists or a corporation-shareholder relationship exists. The factors so set forth in the regulations **may include among other factors:**

> (1) whether there is a written unconditional promise to pay on demand or on a specified date a sum certain in money in return for an adequate consideration in money or money's worth, and to pay a fixed rate of interest,
>
> (2) whether there is subordination to or preference over any indebtedness of the corporation,
>
> (3) the ratio of debt to equity of the corporation,
>
> (4) whether there is convertibility into the stock of the corporation, and
>
> (5) **the relationship between holdings of stock in the corporation and holdings of the interest in question.**

(c) *Effect of classification by issuer*

(1) *In general*

The characterization (as of the time of issuance) by the issuer as to whether an interest in a corporation is stock or indebtedness shall be binding on such issuer and on all holders of such interest (but shall not be binding on the Secretary).

(2) *Notification of inconsistent treatment*

Except as provided in regulations, paragraph (1) shall not apply to any holder of an interest if such holder on his return discloses that he is treating such interest in a manner inconsistent with the characterization referred to in paragraph (1).

(3) *Regulations*

The Secretary is authorized to require **such information as the Secretary determines to be necessary** to carry out the provisions of this subsection.

(1) issue debt-equity regulations that "**may be necessary or appropriate;**"

(2) **treat instruments as** "in part stock and in part indebtedness," **which is one of the approaches taken in these proposed regulations, and**

(3) require "**such information as the Secretary determines to be necessary,**" which is the approach taken with the documentation requirement.

While lawyers generally try to see both sides of a story, frankly, in view of the words of Section 385, I cannot see an argument that the Treasury does not have the authority to issue the 2016 Section 385 Regs.

3. Introduction to the 2016 Section 385 Regs

The Summary of the 2016 Section 385 Regs gives the following guidance on the scope of the regulations:

> SUMMARY: This document contains proposed regulations under section 385 of the Internal Revenue Code (Code) that would authorize the Commissioner to treat certain related-party interests in a corporation as indebtedness in part and stock in part for federal tax purposes, and establish threshold documentation requirements that must be satisfied in order for certain related-party interests in a corporation to be treated as indebtedness for federal tax purposes. The proposed regulations also would treat as stock certain related-party interests that otherwise would be treated as indebtedness for federal tax purposes. The proposed regulations generally affect corporations that issue purported indebtedness to related corporations or partnerships.

Although the effective date provisions of these 2016 Section 385 Regs is complex, as a general matter the document requirement provisions are not effective until the final regulations become effective, but the other provisions of the regulations are generally effective on the date the regulations were published in the Federal Register, that is. April 4, 2016.

> The following is a summary of the sections of these proposed regulations:
>
> 1. § 1.385-1 General provisions;
>
> 2. § 1.385-2 Treatment of certain interests between members of an expanded group [*i.e.*, the Documentation Requirement];
>
> 3. § 1.385-3 Certain distributions of debt instruments and similar transactions; and
>
> 4. § 1.385-4 Treatment of consolidated groups.

This section discusses these regulations in the order in which the particular sections of the regulations are discussed in the preamble to the regulations. The preamble and the regulations run for over 130 pages; therefore, this discussion merely touches on the basic principles.

4. Overview of the 2016 Section 385 Regs

The preamble to the 2016 Section 385 Regs gives the following "Overview" of these proposed regulations:

> *Overview*
>
> The proposed regulations provide guidance regarding substantiation of the treatment of certain interests issued between related parties as indebtedness

for federal tax purposes, the treatment of certain interests in a corporation as in part indebtedness and in part stock, and the treatment of distributions of debt instruments and similar transactions that frequently have only limited non-tax effects. More specifically, the proposed regulations are set forth in four sections. First, proposed § 1.385-1 prescribes definitions and operating rules applicable to the regulations under section 385 generally including a rule treating members of a consolidated group, as defined in § 1.1502-1(h), as one corporation. Proposed § 1.385-1(d) also provides that the Commissioner has the discretion to treat certain interests in a corporation for federal tax purposes as indebtedness in part and stock in part. Second, proposed § 1.385-2 addresses the documentation and information [i.e., the Documentation Requirement] that taxpayers must prepare and maintain within required timeframes to substantiate the treatment of an interest issued between related parties as indebtedness for federal tax purposes. Such substantiation is necessary, but not sufficient, for a purported debt interest that is within the scope of these rules to be characterized as indebtedness; general federal income tax principles also apply in making such a determination. Third, if the application of proposed § 1.385-2 and general federal income tax principles otherwise would result in treating an interest issued to a related party as indebtedness for federal tax purposes, proposed § 1.385-3 provides additional rules that may treat the interest, in whole or in part, as stock for federal tax purposes if it is issued in a distribution or other transaction that is identified as frequently having only limited non-tax effect, or is issued to fund such a transaction. Finally, proposed § 1.385-4 provides operating rules for applying proposed § 1.385-3 to interests that cease to be between members of the same consolidated group or interests that become interests between members of the same consolidated group.[74]

5. The Substantiation of Related-Party Indebtedness Requirement, Proposed Reg. § 1.385-2

The preamble to the 2016 Section 385 Regs provides the following basic description of the Documentation Requirement:

> Proposed § 1.385-2 reflects the importance of contemporaneous documentation in identifying the rights, obligations, and intent of the parties to an instrument that is purported to be indebtedness for federal tax purposes. Such documentation is particularly important to the analysis of instruments issued between related parties. In recognition of this importance, the Treasury Department and the IRS are exercising authority granted under section 385(a) to treat the timely preparation and maintenance of such documentation as necessary factors to be taken into account in determining whether certain interests are properly characterized as stock or indebtedness. Accordingly, the proposed regulations first prescribe the nature of the documentation nec-

---

74. *Id.* at 31–32.

essary to substantiate the treatment of related-party instruments as indebtedness and, second, require that such documentation be timely prepared and maintained. The proposed regulations further provide that, if the specified documentation is not provided to the Commissioner upon request, the Commissioner will treat the preparation and maintenance requirements as not satisfied and will treat the instrument as stock for federal tax purposes. The type of stock (for example, common stock or preferred stock, section 306 stock, stock described in section 1504(a)(4)) that the instrument will be treated as for federal tax purposes is determined by taking into account the terms of the instrument (for example, voting and conversion rights and rights relating to dividends, redemption, liquidation, and other distributions).

Satisfaction of the requirements of the proposed regulations does not establish that a related-party instrument is indebtedness. Rather, satisfaction of the proposed regulations acts as a threshold test for allowing the possibility of indebtedness treatment after the determination of an instrument's character is made under federal tax principles developed under applicable case law. If the requirements of the proposed regulations are not satisfied, the purported indebtedness would be recharacterized as stock. In such a case, any federal tax benefit claimed by the taxpayer with respect to the treatment of the interest as indebtedness will be disallowed.[75]

As indicated above, this Documentation Requirement would not become effective until the regulations are published as final regulations.

6. Certain Distributions of Debt Instruments and Similar Transactions, Proposed Reg. § 1.385-3

The most revolutionary and potentially effective anti-interest stripping initiative is taken in Prop. Regs. § 1.385-3. The preamble to the 2016 Section 385 Regs provides the following summary of these rules:

Proposed §§ 1.385-3 * * * provide[s] rules that treat as stock certain interests that otherwise would be treated as indebtedness for federal income tax purposes. Proposed § 1.385-3 applies to debt instruments that are within the meaning of section 1275(a) and § 1.1275-1(d)[*i.e.*, "**a bond, debenture, note, or certificate or other evidence of indebtedness**"], as determined without regard to the application of proposed § 1.385-3. Section 1275(a) and § 1.1275-1(d) generally define a debt instrument as any instrument or contractual arrangement that constitutes indebtedness under general principles of federal income tax law. Thus, the term debt instrument for purposes of proposed §§ 1.385-3 and 1.385-4 means an instrument that satisfies the requirements of proposed §§ 1.385-1 and 1.385-2 [*i.e.*, the Documentation Requirement] and that is indebtedness under general principles of federal income tax law. * * *

---

75. *Id.* at 35-36.

Specifically, proposed § 1.385-3 treats as stock certain debt instruments issued by one member of an expanded group[*i.e.*, an "expanded group" is basically a consolidated group (e.g., parent and its 80% owned subs) plus foreign and tax-exempt corporations, as well as corporations held indirectly, for example, through partnerships] to another member of the same group (expanded group debt instrument) in the [following three circumstances:] * * * ,

(1) in a distribution[*e.g.*, a domestic sub of a foreign parent, distributes to the parent a debt instrument of the sub as a dividend];

(2) in exchange for expanded group stock, other than in an exempt exchange * * *[*e.g.*, a domestic sub of a foreign parent, transfers its debt instrument to the parent in exchange for parent stock]; or

(3) in exchange for property in an asset reorganization, but only to the extent that, pursuant to the plan of reorganization, a shareholder that is a member of the issuer's expanded group immediately before the reorganization receives the debt instrument with respect to its stock in the transferor corporation.[76]

The preamble to the 2016 Section 385 Regs elaborates as follows on these three prongs (*i.e.*, distribution, exchange, and reorganization prongs) of the debt-treated-as-stock rules:

> For purposes of the first prong of the general rule, the term distribution is broadly defined as any distribution by a corporation to a member of the corporation's expanded group with respect to the distributing corporation's stock, regardless of whether the distribution is treated as a dividend within the meaning of section 316. Thus, a debt instrument issued in exchange for stock of the issuer of the debt instrument (that is, in a redemption under corporate law) is a distribution that is covered by the first prong of the general rule and an acquisition of expanded group stock covered by the second prong of the general rule.

> The second prong of the general rule—addressing debt instruments issued in exchange for expanded group stock—applies regardless of whether the expanded group stock is acquired from a shareholder of the issuer of the expanded group stock, or directly from the issuer. * * *

> For purposes of the second prong of the general rule, the term exempt exchange means an acquisition of expanded group stock in which the transferor and transferee of the stock are parties to a reorganization that is an asset reorganization, and either (i) section 361(a) or (b) applies to the transferor of the expanded group stock and the stock is not transferred by issuance; or (ii) section 1032 or § 1.1032-2 applies to the transferor of the expanded group stock and the stock is distributed by the transferee pursuant to the plan of reorganization. As a result, the second prong of the general rule generally does not apply to a debt instrument that is issued in exchange for expanded

---

76. *Id.* at 44-46.

group stock when section 361(a) or (b) applies to the transferor of such stock. This limitation has the effect of causing exchanges of expanded group stock that are part of an asset reorganization to be covered only by the third prong of the general rule, which, as discussed in the next paragraph, imposes limitations on the application of the general rule to exchanges that are part of an asset reorganization.

The third prong of the general rule applies to asset reorganizations among corporations that are members of the same expanded group. An asset reorganization is a reorganization within the meaning of section 368(a)(1)(A), (C), (D), (F), or (G). Specifically, the third prong of the general rule applies to a debt instrument issued in exchange for property in an asset reorganization, but only to the extent that, pursuant to the plan of reorganization, a shareholder that is a member of the issuer's expanded group immediately before the reorganization receives the debt instrument with respect to its stock in the transferor corporation. The second step receipt of the debt instrument by the expanded group shareholder could be in the form of a distribution of the debt instrument to shareholders of the distributing corporation in a divisive asset reorganization, or in redemption of the shareholder's stock in the transferor corporation in an acquisitive asset reorganization. Because the third prong of the general rule applies only to a debt instrument that is received by a shareholder with respect to its stock in the transferor corporation, that debt instrument would, absent the application of § 1.385-3, be treated as "other property" within the meaning of section 356.

The third prong of the general rule is limited to debt instruments distributed to shareholders pursuant to the reorganization, and does not apply to debt instruments exchanged for securities or other debt interests because, in that latter case, the newly issued debt instrument is exchanged for existing debt interests and thus no additional debt is incurred by the parties to the reorganization.[77]

Detailed operating rules regarding the recharacterization are provided, and a rule prevents taxpayers from affirmatively using proposed §§ 1.385-3 and 1.385-4. The preamble further explains:

> To the extent proposed § 1.385-3 treats an interest as stock, the interest is treated as stock for all federal tax purposes. Consistent with the traditional case law debt-equity analysis, when a debt instrument is treated as stock under proposed § 1.385-3, the terms of the debt instrument (for example, voting rights or conversion features) are taken into account for purposes of determining the type of stock resulting from the recharacterization, including whether such stock is preferred stock or common stock.[78]

Example 3 of § 1.385-3(g)(3), illustrates as follows the basic principles in the exchange prong of this regulation:

---

77. *Id.* at 47-48.
78. *Id.* at 45-46.

Example 3. *Issuance of a note in exchange for expanded group stock.* (i) *Facts.* On Date A in Year 1, USS1[**a domestic wholly owned sub of FP, a foreign corporation**] issues USS1 Note to FP in exchange for 40 percent of the FS[**a wholly owned foreign sub of FP**] stock owned by FP[**note that because USS1 is acquiring stock of a sister sub, section 304 would normally apply**].

(ii) *Analysis.* (A) Because USS1 and FP are both members of the FP expanded group, USS1 Note is treated as stock when it is issued by USS1 to FP in exchange for FS stock on Date A in Year 1 under paragraphs (b)(2)(ii)[**an exchange for expanded group stock**] and (d)(1)(i)[**the debt instrument is treated as stock when issued**] of this section.

The exchange of USS1 Note for FS stock is not an exempt exchange within the meaning of paragraph (f)(5) of this section because USS1 and FP are not parties to a reorganization.

(B) Because USS1 Note is treated as stock for federal tax purposes when it is issued by USS1, USS1 Note is not treated as property for purposes of section 304(a) because it is not property within the meaning specified in section 317(a). Therefore, USS1's acquisition of FS stock from FP in exchange for USS1 Note is not an acquisition described in section 304(a)(1).

(C) Because USS1 Note is treated as stock for federal tax purposes when it is issued by USS1, USS1 Note is not treated as indebtedness for purposes of applying paragraph (b)(3) of this section.

7. Exception for Real but Not False Fundings, Proposed Reg. § 1.385-3

The rules do not apply to a funding transaction where, for example, a foreign parent sets up a new domestic sub and contributes to the sub cash in exchange for stock and debt of the sub. In such case, the section 163(j) interest stripping limitation could apply to the debt instrument. However, under an anti-abuse "Funding rule" in § 1.385-3(b)(3), "an expanded group debt instrument that is issued with a principal purpose of funding a transaction described in the general rule[*e.g.*, **a distribution**] (principal purpose debt instrument)" is treated as stock. This funding rule would apply where, for example, (1) a domestic sub of a foreign parent issues a note to a sister foreign sub in exchange for cash in what appears to be a funding transaction that would not be covered by § 1.385-3 , and (2) the domestic sub then distributes the cash to the common foreign parent. In such case, the note would be a principal purpose debt instrument, and as a consequence, the note would be treated as stock.

8. General Anti-Abuse Rule

Proposed § 1.385-3(b)(4) sets out a general anti-abuse rule which "provides that a debt instrument is treated as stock if it is issued with a principal purpose of avoiding the application of the proposed regulations."[79]

---

79. *Id.* at 55.

9. Exceptions to the General Rule

The proposed regulations set out three exceptions to the application of the general rule that treats certain distributed and related debt as equity. The preamble to the 2016 Section 385 Regs gives the following basic description of these three exceptions:

1. Exception for Current Year Earnings and Profits

[P]roposed § 1.385-3(c)(1) includes an exception pursuant to which distributions and acquisitions described in proposed § 1.385-3(b)(2) (the general rule) or proposed § 1.385-3(b)(3)(ii) (the funding rule) that do not exceed current year earnings and profits (as described in section 316(a)(2)) of the distributing or acquiring corporation are not treated as distributions or acquisitions for purposes of the general rule or the funding rule.…

2. Threshold Exception

A second exception provides that an expanded group debt instrument will not be treated as stock if, when the debt instrument is issued, the aggregate issue price of all expanded group debt instruments that otherwise would be treated as stock under the proposed regulations does not exceed $50 million (the threshold exception). If the expanded group's debt instruments that otherwise would be treated as stock later exceed $50 million, then all expanded group debt instruments that, but for the threshold exception, would have been treated as stock are treated as stock, rather than only the amount that exceeds $50 million.…

3. Exception for Funded Acquisitions of Subsidiary Stock by Issuance

An acquisition of expanded group stock will not be treated as an acquisition described in the second prong of the funding rule if (i) the acquisition results from a transfer of property by a funded member (the transferor) to an issuer in exchange for stock of the issuer, and (ii) for the 36-month period following the issuance, the transferor holds, directly or indirectly, more than 50 percent of the total combined voting power of all classes of stock of the issuer entitled to vote and more than 50 percent of the total value of the stock of the issuer.[80]

While I in general support the (1) Threshold Exception, and (2) the Exception for Funded Acquisitions of Subsidiary Stock by Issuance, I do not understand the reasons for the current E&P exception. For example, I do not understand why a domestic corporation should be able to distribute a note to its foreign parent and not be subject to the § 1.385-3 regulations because the domestic corporation has current E&P equal to or in excess of the principal amount of the note, while a note distributed by a similarly situated domestic corporation without current E&P is subject to the § 1.385-3 regulations?

---

80. *Id.* at 58-60

10. Treatment of Notes Issued within a Consolidated Group, Proposed Reg. § 1.385-4

Under the consolidated return provisions, only domestic corporations can file a joint consolidated return, which will include the income and loss of the separate corporations in one return. Under section 1504, at least 80%, measured by vote and value, of a subs stock must be held by the parent in order for the sub and the parent to be in a consolidated group.

The preamble to the 2016 Section 385 Regs points out that "many of the concerns regarding related-party indebtedness are not present in the case of indebtedness between members of a consolidated group."[81] The preamble goes on to explain:

> Accordingly, the proposed regulations under section 385 do not apply to interests between members of a consolidated group, although general federal tax principles continue to apply. Proposed § 1.385-1(e) achieves this result by treating a consolidated group as one corporation.[82]

Of course, a debt instrument that is held by a member of a consolidated group one day, will not be held by a member of the consolidated group the next day if for some reason the member leaves the consolidated group. Prop. Reg. § 1.385-4 addresses this and related issues by setting out "rules for applying § 1.385-3 to consolidated groups when an interest ceases to be a consolidated group debt instrument or becomes a consolidated group debt instrument."[83]

11. My Take on the 2016 Section 385 Regs

I commend the Treasury for proposing the 2016 Section 385 Regs. The heart of the regulations, § 1.385-3, is a revolutionary approach to dealing with debt-equity issues in that it does not rely on some "facts and circumstances" analysis of transactions, which was at the center of the prior proposed regulations under section 385, which were withdrawn.

Rather, § 1.385-3 takes a bright line approach to one of the most vexing issues in international tax: how to curtail interest stripping. If finally adopted, I believe that these regulations will to a substantial extent curtail abuse of the system not just for inversions but for all situations in which a foreign parent controls a U.S. sub. There will obviously be a need for refinements as creative tax professionals seek ways around the general rule.

If these regulations had been in effect at the time of the Endo inversion, which is discussed Section 10.11.G, the note that was issued by Endo U.S. for stock of the Irish inversion parent would have been treated as stock and could not have been used to set up an interest stripping play.

---

81. *Id*. at 35.
82. *Id*.
83. Prop. Reg. § 1.385-4(a).

This approach is consistent with an approach I argue for in discussing the need for the Treasury to take action under Section 385, where I say:

> By focusing on inversions, the regulations would be primarily concerned with artificial debt instruments issued in an inversion or related transaction by a U.S corporation to its new foreign parent or related party, and not "a [situation where a] long-term foreign parent [has] made a real loan of funds to [its] U.S. subsidiary and therefore [is] entitled to repayment with interest."

Indeed, the 2016 Section 385 regulations properly take aim not only at debt issued in inversions but at all debt issued by U.S. subs to foreign parents in transactions that are not real loans. For the reasons stated above I think it is clear that the Treasury has the authority under Section 385 to issue these regulations.

G. Illustration of a New Inversion that Turned Off the Section 367(a) Gain Recognition Regulations through the Use of the Killer B Regulations — The Endo Inversion

Introduction to the New Inversions.[84] New Inversions involve the combination of real U.S. firm, which is the actual acquirer, with real foreign firm, which is the target. The old inversions generally did not involve a combination with a real foreign firm, but rather with a newly formed holding company.

An example of this type of New Inversion is the combination in 2014 of Endo, a publicly held U.S. corporation, with Paladin, a publicly held Canadian corporation.

In the Endo transaction, Endo and Paladin were acquired by a newly formed Irish holding corporation, New Endo. The balance of this section addresses (1) the basic structure of the Endo transaction; (2) the discussion in the Endo Proxy/Prospectus of the impact of Sections 7874 and Section 367(a)(1) on the basic transaction; (3) the efforts to turn off the Section 367(a)(1) Gain Recognition Rule through Endo's "Joe Frazier Left Hook" in the "Killer B" regulations; (4) some summary observations on Endo's "Joe Frazier Left Hook;" and (5) some concluding remarks on whether Ali (a.k.a, IRS) can counter Endo's "Joe Frazier Left Hook."

Note on the Impact of the Treasury's 2016 Section 385 Regs on the Endo Transaction. The Endo transaction took place prior to the issuance by the Treasury of the 2016 Section 385 Regs. If the Endo transaction had been subject to those regulations, the note issued in that transaction would have been treated as stock, thereby eliminating the interest stripping part of the transaction and presumably also eliminating the Joe Frazier Left Hook part of the transaction. However, if cash were issued in place of the note, the Joe Frazier Left Hook part of the transaction could still have worked for Endo.

---

84. This section is based on Thompson, *New Inversions, the 'Joe Frazier Left Hook,' the IRS Notice, and Pfizer*, Tax Notes, 1413 (June 23, 2014). *See also* Thompson, *Mergers, Acquisitions, and Tender Offers*, *supra* Sec. 1.11 at Chapter 22.

The Basic Structure of the Endo Transaction. The Arrangement Agreement between Endo and Paladin provided for the acquisition by a newly formed Irish holding company (IrishCo *a.k.a.* New Endo) of:

(1) Paladin pursuant to an "arrangement" under Canadian law, and

(2) Endo through a triangular B reorganization under the parenthetical language of Section 368(a)(1)(B).

The "arrangement," which is set out in Section 2.1 of the Arrangement Agreement, is similar to the scheme of arrangement under U.K. law. Pursuant to the arrangement, the public shareholders of Paladin received approximately 23% of the stock of New Endo. This part of the transaction is not discussed further here.

The triangular B reorganization was implemented by Section 2.2 of the Arrangement Agreement, which is entitled "Merger." Under this provision, the stock of Endo was acquired by DE,Inc. (*a.k.a.* Endo U.S. Inc.), a Delaware corporation and wholly owned sub of New Endo. The acquisition of Endo by Endo U.S. Inc was effectuated by a reverse subsidiary merger in which Merger Sub, a Delaware LLC that is wholly owned by Endo U.S. Inc., merged into Endo with (1) the public shareholders of Endo receiving for their Endo shares voting shares of New Endo, and (2) Endo U.S. Inc. holding all of the shares of Endo. Thus, when the dust settled on the Endo side of the transaction, (1) Endo became a wholly-owned subsidiary of Endo U.S. Inc., which is a wholly-owned subsidiary of New Endo, the Irish holding company, and (2) the public shareholders of Endo ended up owning approximately 77% of the stock of New Endo. The transaction presumably qualified as a triangular (B) because the consideration paid by Endo U.S. Inc. in the merger of Merger Sub, an LLC, into Endo was solely voting stock of New Endo, the parent of Endo U.S. Inc.

The Endo Proxy/Prospectus gives the following explanation of the reasons for incorporating in Ireland:

A   Incorporating New Endo in Ireland is expected to result in significant benefits to New Endo. These benefits include enhanced global cash management flexibility and associated financial benefits to the combined enterprise, as well as increased global liquidity and cash flow among the various entities of the combined enterprise. In addition, Ireland is a beneficial location for establishing a differentiated platform for further international expansion through an operating base in Ireland and a strong financial profile to support expansion into international markets. Also, Endo estimates that New Endo is expected to realize $75 million of post-tax synergies on a twelve-month basis at some point following the close of the transactions.

The reference to "increased global liquidity and cash flow among the various entities of the combined enterprise" apparently is referring to the increased flexibility as a result of the prospective avoidance of the CFC provisions in the U.S. The reference to the annual "$75 million of post-tax synergies" is addressed below.

The Discussion in the Endo Proxy/Prospectus of the Impact of Sections 7874 and Section 367(a) on the Basic Transaction. *Section 7874.* The basic Endo transaction presents issues under both Section 7874 and Section 367(a) (1). These issues are addressed here followed by a discussion of Endo's "Joe Frazier Left Hook" coming out of the "Killer B" regulations.

The first question under Section 7874 is whether New Endo will be treated as a U.S. corporation. Since the Endo shareholders received less than 80% of the stock of New Endo, Section 7874 should not treat New Endo as a domestic corporation. The Endo Proxy/Prospectus discusses as follows this issue:

> Under Section 7874, a corporation created or organized outside the United States (i.e., a non-U.S. corporation) will nevertheless be treated as a U.S. corporation for U.S. federal income tax purposes (and, therefore, a U.S. tax resident subject to U.S. federal income tax on its worldwide income) if each of the following three conditions are met: (1) the non-U.S. corporation directly or indirectly acquires substantially all of the assets held directly or indirectly by a U.S. corporation (including through the acquisition of all of the outstanding shares of the U.S. corporation), (2) the non-U.S. corporation's expanded affiliated group does not have substantial business activities in the non-U.S. corporation's country of organization or incorporation relative to the expanded affiliated group's worldwide activities, and (3) the shareholders of the acquired U.S. corporation hold at least 80% (by either vote or value) of the shares of the non-U.S. acquiring corporation after the acquisition by reason of holding shares in the U.S. acquired corporation (which includes the receipt of the non-U.S. corporation's shares in exchange for the U.S. corporation's shares), which is referred to in this proxy statement/prospectus as the "ownership test."

> At the merger effective time, New Endo will acquire all of Endo's assets through the indirect acquisition of all of Endo's outstanding shares, but New Endo, including its expanded affiliated group, is not expected to have substantial business activities in Ireland. As a result, New Endo will be treated as a U.S. corporation for U.S. federal income tax purposes under Section 7874 unless, after the merger, the former shareholders of Endo are treated as owning (within the meaning of Section 7874) less than 80% (by both vote and value) of New Endo's ordinary shares by reason of holding shares in Endo.

> Based on the rules for determining share ownership under Section 7874 and certain factual assumptions, after the merger, Endo shareholders are expected to be treated as holding less than 80% (by both vote and value) of the New Endo ordinary shares by reason of their ownership of Endo common stock. However, whether the ownership test has been satisfied must be finally determined after the closing of the merger, by which time there could be adverse changes to the relevant facts and circumstances. * * *

> Endo's obligation to effect the transactions is conditional upon its receipt of the Section 7874 opinion from Skadden, dated as of the closing date and subject to certain qualifications and limitations set forth therein, to the effect that Section 7874 of the Code and the regulations promulgated thereunder should not

apply in such a manner so as to cause New Endo to be treated as a U.S. corporation for U.S. federal income tax purposes from and after the closing date.

The second consideration under Section 7874 is the applicability of the inversion gain rule, which applies because the shareholders of Endo end up with at least 60% but less than 80% of the shares of New Endo. The Endo Proxy/Prospectus discusses as follows this issue:

> Following the acquisition of a U.S. corporation by a non-U.S. corporation, Section 7874 may limit the ability of the acquired U.S. corporation and its U.S. affiliates to utilize certain U.S. tax attributes (including net operating losses and certain tax credits) to offset U.S. taxable income resulting from certain transactions. Specifically, if the shareholders of the acquired U.S. corporation hold at least 60% (but less than 80%), by either vote or value, of the shares of the non-U.S. acquiring corporation by reason of holding shares in the U.S. corporation, the taxable income of the U.S. corporation (and any person related to the U.S. corporation) for any given year, within a ten-year period beginning on the last date the U.S. corporation's properties were acquired, will be no less than that person's "inversion gain" for that taxable year. A person's inversion gain includes gain from the transfer of shares or any other property (other than property held for sale to customers) and income from the license of any property that is either transferred or licensed as part of the acquisition, or, if after the acquisition, is transferred or licensed to a non-U.S. related person.

> Pursuant to the arrangement agreement, the Endo shareholders are expected to receive at least 60% (but less than 80%) of the vote and value of the New Endo ordinary shares by reason of holding Endo common stock. As a result, Endo and its U.S. affiliates would be limited in their ability to utilize certain U.S. tax attributes to offset their inversion gain, if any. However, neither Endo nor its U.S. affiliates expects to recognize any inversion gain as part of the merger, nor do they currently intend to engage in any transaction in the near future that would generate inversion gain. If, however, Endo or its U.S. affiliates were to engage in any transaction that would generate any inversion gain in the future, such transaction may be fully taxable to Endo or its U.S. affiliates (notwithstanding that it may have certain deductions and other U.S. tax attributes which, but for the application of Section 7874, it would be able to use to offset some or all of such gain) and thus Endo may pay U.S. federal income tax sooner than it otherwise would have.

This statement seems to indicate that Endo did not plan to transfer stock of any of its CFCs to New Endo, because any such transfers would produce inversion gain if the CFC stock is appreciated. New Endo could presumably conduct any additional non-Irish business through subsidiaries of New Endo that were not also subs of Endo. Such non-Endo subs would not be subject to the U.S. CFC provisions.

Section 367. As indicated in the previous discussion, the regulations under Section 368(a)(1) provide for gain but not loss recognition on any outbound reorganization like the Endo transaction where the shareholders of the U.S. corporation end up with more than 50% of the stock of the foreign corporation. Also, even if the 50% condition is not satisfied, any 5% or more shareholder recognizes gain unless the shareholder enters into a gain recognition agreement (GRA). The Endo Proxy/Prospectus discusses as follows the general gain recognition rule under Section 367(a)(1):

> In the merger, (i) Merger Sub [an LLC] will merge with and into Endo with Endo surviving, and (ii) for U.S. federal income tax purposes, Endo share-holders will exchange their Endo common stock for New Endo ordinary shares received from both New Endo and Endo U.S. Inc. in the Endo share exchange. Endo expects to receive the reorganization opinion from Skadden dated as of the closing date and subject to certain qualifications and limitations set forth therein, to the effect that, among other things, the merger should qualify as a "reorganization" within the meaning of Section 368(a) of the Code. [Pre-sumably the reorganization opinion will express the view that the reverse sub-sidiary merger is a triangular (B) reorganization.] However, neither the obligation of Endo nor the obligation of New Endo to complete the merger is conditioned upon the receipt of such opinion. See "—*Opinion Regarding the U.S. Federal Income Tax Treatment of the Merger to Endo Shareholders*" below.

> Although shareholders generally do not recognize gain or loss on an exchange of their stock pursuant to a reorganization, with respect to cross-border re-organizations, Section 367(a) of the Code and regulations promulgated there-under generally require U.S. shareholders to recognize gain (but not loss) if stock of a U.S. corporation is exchanged for stock of a non-U.S. corporation and the U.S. shareholders receive more than 50% (by vote or value) of the stock of the non-U.S. corporation. Endo shareholders will receive more than 50% of the New Endo ordinary shares; consequently, absent an applicable exception, U.S. holders of Endo common stock will be required to recognize gain (but not loss) on their exchange of Endo common stock for New Endo ordinary shares in the merger in an amount equal to the excess of the fair market value of the New Endo ordinary shares received over the adjusted tax basis of the Endo common stock exchanged therefor.

Turning Off the Section 367(a)(1) Gain Recognition Rule through Endo's "Joe Frazier Left Hook" Coming Out of the "Killer B" Regulations. In the first fight between Joe Frazier and Muhammad Ali, Joe's "vicious left hook" knocked Ali to the canvas, and Joe won the fight, taking all of the marbles. Imbedded in the Endo transaction is Endo's "vicious left hook" that is designed to (1) knock-out the Section 367(a)(1) gain recognition rule, and (2) take all of the marbles by setting up an interest stripping transaction.

Endo's "vicious left hook" is executed by first, the purchase by Endo U.S. Inc., in exchange for its note, of the stock of New Endo, and second, the transfer by Endo U.S. Inc. of the purchased New Endo stock in exchange for the Endo stock held by the public shareholders of Endo. To understand why this is a "vicious left hook," it is first necessary to understand the Treasury's concern with the "Killer B" transaction, which was principally designed to repatriate foreign income without tax.

The Service first expressed concern with the "Killer B" transaction in Notice 2006-85, I.R.B 2006-41, issued on October 10, 2006.[85] The Notice was directed primarily at the use of a triangular (B) reorganization to avoid what would otherwise be a taxable repatriation of income from a foreign sub. The Notice described the tax-free repatriation transaction as follows:

> The IRS and Treasury are aware that certain taxpayers are engaging in triangular reorganizations involving foreign corporations that result in a tax-advantaged transfer of property from S [a foreign sub] to P [a U.S. parent]. The transaction is often structured as a triangular B reorganization, but could also be structured as a triangular C reorganization or another type of triangular reorganization. For example, assume P, a domestic corporation, owns 100 percent of S, a foreign corporation, and S1, a domestic corporation. S1 owns 100 percent of T, a foreign corporation. S purchases P stock for either cash or a note, and provides the P stock to S1 in exchange for all the T stock in a triangular B reorganization.

> Taxpayers take the position that (i) when P sells its stock to S for cash or a note, P recognizes no gain or loss on the sale under section 1032, (ii) S takes a cost basis in the P shares under section 1012, and (iii) S recognizes no gain under § 1.1032-2(c) upon the transfer of the P shares immediately thereafter because the basis and fair market value of the shares are equal. Thus, taxpayers take the position that the cash or note used by S to acquire the P stock does not result in a distribution under section 301. Furthermore, taxpayers do not include in income amounts under section 951(a)(1)(B) because S acquires and disposes of the P stock before the close of a quarter of the taxable year, which is the time at which to measure P's share of the average amount of United States property held by S. See section 956(a)(1)(A). Finally, under § 1.367(b)-4(b)(1)(ii), S1 does not include in income as a deemed dividend the section 1248 amount attributable to the T stock that S1 exchanges.

In this transaction, P, the domestic parent, receives cash from its CFC, that is, S, in what amounts to a tax-free repatriation transaction. Thus, in this repatriation transaction P is a domestic parent corporation, and this is not the case in the Endo transaction, where the parent, New Endo, is a foreign corporation.

Notice 2006-85 also expressed concern with the possible avoidance of the U.S. gross basis tax and interest stripping through the use of a "Killer B" transaction in which the parent was a foreign corporation. The Notice described this transaction as follows:

> [W]here P is foreign and S is domestic, the transaction could have the effect of repatriating S's U.S. earnings to its foreign parent in a manner that is not subject to U.S. withholding tax. This variation of the transaction also raises U.S. earnings stripping issues where S uses a note to purchase all or a portion of the P stock.

---

85. For a recent discussion of Killer Bs, see Jasper Cummings, 'Killer B" and Tax Policy, 142 Tax Notes 343 (Jan. 20, 2014).

Here the concern is with the use of a "Killer B" to (1) avoid of the gross basis with-holding tax on the payment of what would otherwise be a dividend from the U.S. sub to its foreign parent, and (2) facilitate interest stripping through interest payments by the U.S. sub to the foreign parent on the note the sub gives to the parent in exchange for the parent's stock. This is precisely the concern with the Endo transaction because, in the absence of regulations: (1) there would be no gross basis tax on the purchase by Endo U.S. Inc. of the stock of New Endo, and (2) the note issued by Endo U.S. Inc. to New Endo would facilitate interest stripping from the U.S.

On June 13, 2011, the Treasury issued T.D. 9526, *Treatment of Property Used to Acquire Parent Stock or Securities in Certain Triangular Reorganizations Involving Foreign Corporations*. These regulations, which are principally set out in Reg. § 1.367(b)-10, address "Killer Bs" used for both (1) Tax-Free Repatriations, and (2) Avoidance of Gross Basis Tax together with Interest Stripping. The scope of the regulations is set out in Reg. § 1.367(b)-10(a)(1) which, subject to three exceptions discussed below, provides:

> [T]his section applies to a triangular reorganization if P [parent] or S [sub] (or both) is a foreign corporation and, in connection with the reorganization, S acquires in exchange for property all or a portion of the P stock or P securities (P acquisition) that are used to acquire the stock, securities or property of T [target] in the triangular reorganization.

Thus, the regulation applies to a "Killer B" that is (1) a tax-free repatriation where P is a domestic corporation and S in a foreign corporation, and (2) used to facilitate the avoidance of gross basis tax together with interest stripping where P is a foreign corporation and S is a domestic corporation.

Where the regulation applies, Reg. § 1.367(b)-10(b) converts the purchase of the parent's stock in the "Killer B" into a deemed distribution by the sub and a deemed contribution by the parent as follows:

> (b) General rules — (1) Deemed distribution. If this section applies, adjustments shall be made that have the effect of a distribution of property (with no built-in gain or loss) from S to P under section 301 (deemed distribution). The amount of the deemed distribution shall equal the sum of the amount of money transferred by S ... and the fair market value of other property transferred by S [such as a note of S] in the P acquisition in exchange for the P stock ... received by T shareholders ... in [a reorganization] exchange....
>
> (2) Deemed contribution. If this section applies, adjustments shall be made that have the effect of a contribution of property (with no built-in gain or loss) by P to S in an amount equal to the amount of the deemed distribution from S to P under paragraph (b)(1) of this section (deemed contribution).

Thus, under this general rule, in a "Killer B" used for a tax-free repatriation, the purchase by the foreign sub of the domestic parent's stock is treated as (1) a distribution by the sub to the parent, and (2) a contribution by the parent to the sub. Thus, the distribution is a repatriation of the sub's deferred income. And in a "Killer B" used for the avoidance of gross basis tax together with interest stripping, the note transferred by the domestic sub to the foreign parent is treated as (1) a distribution by the sub, and (2) a contribution by the foreign parent. Thus, the distribution will be subject to the gross basis tax subject to reduction by tax treaty.

Reg. § 1.367(b)-10(a)(2) provides that this section does not apply to the following three situations:

(i) P and S are foreign corporations and neither P nor S is a [CFC];

(ii) S is a domestic corporation, P's stock in S is not a United States real property interest (within the meaning of section 897(c)), and P would not be subject to U.S. tax on a dividend (as determined under section 301(c)(1)) from S under either section 881 (for example, by reason of an applicable treaty) or section 882 [thus, there would be no gross basis or other tax on the outbound distribution]; or

(iii) In an exchange under section 354 or 356, one or more U.S. persons exchange stock or securities of T and the amount of gain in the T stock or securities recognized by such U.S. persons under section 367(a)(1) is equal to or greater than the sum of the amount of the deemed distribution that would be treated by P as a dividend under section 301(c)(1) and the amount of such deemed distribution that would be treated by P as gain from the sale or exchange of property under section 301(c)(3) if this section would otherwise apply to the triangular reorganization. See § 1.367(a)-3(a)(2)(iv) (providing a similar rule that excludes certain transactions from the application of section 367(a)(1)).

The exceptions in (i) and (ii) are not implicated in the Endo transaction and, therefore, are not considered further here. On the other hand, the exception in (iii) is a specific issue in Endo and is explored further below.

Reg. § 1.367(a)-3(a)(2)(iv), referred to in the third exception provides that "the following exchanges are not subject to section 367(a)(1) and therefore gain is not recognized under section 367(a)(1):"

(iv) Certain triangular reorganizations described in § 1.367(b)-10. If, in an exchange under section 354 or 356, one or more U.S. persons exchange stock or securities of T (as defined in § 1.358-6(b)(1)(iii)) in connection with a transaction described in § 1.367(b)-10 (applying to certain acquisitions of parent stock or securities for property in triangular reorganizations), section 367(a)(1) shall not apply to such U.S. persons with respect to the exchange of the stock or securities of T if the condition specified in this paragraph (iv) is satisfied. The condition specified in this paragraph (iv) is that the amount of gain in the T stock or securities that would otherwise be recognized under section 367(a)(1) (without regard to any exceptions thereto) pursuant to the indirect stock transfer rules of paragraph (d) of this section is less than the sum of the amount of the deemed distribution under § 1.367(b)-10 treated as a dividend under section 301(c)(1) and the amount of such deemed distribution treated as gain from the sale or exchange of property under section 301(c)(3). See § 1.367(b)-10(a)(2)(iii) (providing a similar rule that excludes certain transactions from the application of § 1.367(b)-10).

Thus, the third exception to the applicability of Reg. § 1.367(b)-10(a) and the fourth exception to the applicability to the Section 367(a)(1) gain recognition rule are designed to apply one of the rules, but not both of the rules, in a transaction covered by both sections. Thus, these exceptions apply a "no duplication" rule.

Under both of these exceptions, the regulation that produces the largest amount of income applies, with:

> (1) the potential income in under Section 367(a)(1) equaling "the amount of gain in the T stock … that would otherwise be recognized under section 367(a)(1)," which is referred to in the Endo Proxy/Prospectus as the "U.S. shareholders gain amount;" and

> (2) the potential income under Reg. § 1.367(b)-10(b) equaling "the sum of the amount of the deemed distribution under § 1.367(b)-10 treated as a dividend under section 301(c)(1) and the amount of such deemed distribution treated as gain from the sale or exchange of property under section 301(c)(3), which is referred to in the Endo Proxy/Prospectus as the "New Endo income amount."

Reg. § 1.367(b)-10(d) sets out an anti-abuse rule that provides that "[a]ppropriate adjustments shall be made … if, in connection with a triangular reorganization, a transaction is engaged in with a view to avoid the purpose of this section."

As indicated previously, in the Endo transaction, the sub, Endo U.S. Inc., is domestic, and the parent, New Endo, is foreign. Consequently, the "Killer B" regulations applied in this transaction with a view to (1) preventing the avoidance of gross basis tax, and (2) not facilitating interest stripping. The Endo transaction is also governed by the Section 367(a)(1) gain recognition regulations, and consequently, under the "no duplication" rule, the regulation that produces the largest income amount applies. As seen from the discussion below from the Endo Proxy/Prospectus, that transaction is going to be managed in such a way as to have the "Killer B" regulations, and not the Section 367(a) gain recognition regulations, apply.

The Endo Proxy/Prospectus introduces the potential applicability of the "Killer B" exception to the Section 367(a)(1) gain recognition as follows:

> An exception promulgated in Treasury regulations [Reg. § 1.367(b)-10(a)(2)(iii) and Reg. § 1.367(a)-3(a)(2)(iv)] provides that Section 367(a) will not apply to certain triangular reorganizations (including those like the merger) if certain specified conditions (discussed in detail below) are satisfied. It is currently uncertain whether the specified conditions will be satisfied and whether, as a result, Endo shareholders would recognize gain or loss on the Endo share exchange. There is risk that Endo shareholders will be required to recognize gain (but not loss) on the Endo share exchange because, as described below, non-recognition treatment depends on the application of new and complex provisions of U.S. federal income tax law as well as certain facts that are subject to change, that could be affected by actions taken by Endo and other events beyond Endo's control, are subject to change and that cannot be known prior to the end of the year in which the merger is completed. For example, increases

in the Endo stock price following signing of the arrangement agreement and prior to the Endo share exchange may increase the U.S. shareholders gain amount (as defined below) and make it more likely that Endo shareholders will be required to recognize gain (but not loss) on the Endo share exchange. See "—*Detailed Discussion of the Exception to Section 367(a) of the Code for Certain Outbound Stock Transfers*" beginning on page 107.

Following the completion of the merger, New Endo intends to notify Endo shareholders via one or more website announcements regarding whether the specified conditions have been satisfied. These announcements will be updated once actual year-end information becomes available.

The Endo Proxy/Prospectus provides the following "Detailed Discussion of the Exception to Section 367(a) of the Code for Certain Outbound Stock Transfers [Governed by Reg. § 1.367(b)-10]:"

As noted, Section 367(a) of the Code and regulations promulgated thereunder generally require U.S. shareholders to recognize gain (but not loss) if stock of a U.S. corporation is exchanged for stock of a non-U.S. corporation in an otherwise non-taxable reorganization and the U.S. shareholders receive more than 50% (by vote or value) of the stock of the non-U.S. corporation. However, under Treasury regulations, if certain specified conditions (discussed below) are satisfied, Section 367(a) generally will not apply to a reorganization in which a U.S. subsidiary of a non-U.S. corporation purchases stock of the non-U.S. corporation in exchange for cash, debt, or other non-stock property and uses the purchased stock to acquire another corporation from such corporation's shareholders. Pursuant to the arrangement agreement, (i) Endo U.S. Inc., a U.S. corporation and subsidiary of New Endo, will be treated as acquiring New Endo ordinary shares from New Endo, a non-U.S. corporation, in exchange for a promissory note and (ii) such New Endo ordinary shares will be used by Endo U.S. Inc. in the Endo share exchange to acquire Endo in the merger. Accordingly, if the conditions discussed below are satisfied, Section 367(a) should not apply and the Endo shareholders should not recognize any gain or loss on the Endo share exchange.

Under the applicable Treasury regulations, the acquisition of the New Endo ordinary shares by Endo U.S. Inc. in exchange for the promissory note is treated as a deemed distribution by Endo U.S. Inc. to New Endo (referenced herein as the "deemed distribution") in an amount equal to the fair market value of the promissory note. The deemed distribution is subject to Section 301 of the Code [i.e., dividend to the extent of E&P, capital gain, to the extent no dividend distribution exceeds basis of stock]. The specified conditions referenced above are satisfied if, as a factual and legal matter: (1) a portion of the deemed distribution to New Endo is treated as a dividend under Section 301(c)(1) of the Code (which is determined based on the current and accumulated earnings and profits of Endo U.S. Inc. (as determined for U.S. federal income tax purposes)), (2) New Endo is subject to U.S. withholding tax on such amount in accordance with the U.S.-Ireland Tax Treaty, and (3) the sum of (a) the portion of the deemed distribution to New Endo that is treated as a dividend and (b) the portion of the deemed distribution that is treated as gain under Section 301(c)(3) of the Code (such sum referenced herein as the "New Endo income amount"), exceeds the aggregate built-in gain (generally, fair market value minus adjusted tax basis) in the Endo common stock transferred to Endo U.S. Inc. by all U.S. shareholders in the Endo share exchange (such built-in gain is referenced herein as the "U.S. shareholders gain amount.")

Whether Endo U.S. Inc. will have positive earnings and profits for the taxable year that includes the merger (which is expected to be the 2014 calendar year) will depend on overall business conditions and the overall tax position of Endo U.S. Inc. for such taxable year. Such earnings and profits, if any, will take into account, among other things, taxable operating income and loss as well as taxable non-operating income and loss (including dispositions outside the ordinary course of business and extra-ordinary items), subject to certain adjustments, and cannot be determined until the end of the year in which the merger is completed. If Endo U.S. Inc. has positive earnings and profits, New Endo will be subject to withholding on the deemed dividend received from Endo U.S. Inc.

It is uncertain whether the New Endo income amount will exceed the U.S. shareholders gain amount, because the U.S. shareholders gain amount cannot be known with certainty until after the closing date. The U.S. shareholders gain amount will depend on the trading price of the Endo common stock and the tax basis of such stock at the time of the Endo share exchange, neither of which can be predicted with certainty. In particular, increases in the Endo stock price following signing of the arrangement agreement and prior to the Endo share exchange may increase the U.S. shareholders gain amount and make it more likely that Endo shareholders will be required to recognize gain (but not loss) on the Endo share exchange. Moreover, because Endo is a public company, information as to the tax basis of the Endo common stock may not be determinable with certainty or obtainable from all U.S. shareholders and is subject to change based on trading activity in the shares. Following closing, New Endo will undertake a study to estimate the tax basis of the shares of Endo common stock at the time of the Endo share exchange in order to assist New Endo in evaluating whether Endo shareholders will be required to recognize gain (but not loss) on the Endo share exchange. Further, the sampling methodology used to determine the U.S. shareholders gain amount or the amount of gain so determined may be challenged by the IRS, and if the IRS were to make such a challenge, there is no assurance that a court would not agree with the IRS.

The Endo Proxy/Prospectus provides the following discussion of the tax treatment under the U.S.-Irish tax treaty of the deemed distribution under Reg. § 1.367(b)-10:

The deemed distribution for U.S. tax purposes will be treated as a taxable dividend to the extent of Endo U.S. Inc.'s current and accumulated earnings and profits for the year of the deemed distribution and such dividend will be subject to U.S. withholding tax (at a rate of 5%) in accordance with the Convention between Ireland and the United States of America with Respect to Taxes on Income and Capital Gains, signed July 28, 1997, as amended, which is referenced in this proxy statement/prospectus as the "Ireland-U.S. Tax Treaty."

As discussed previously at the outset of this section, the Treasury's 2016 Section 385 Regs would treat the note issued in Endo as stock thereby eliminating the interest stripping component of the transaction and presumably eliminating the Joe Frazier Left Hook. As indicated, if cash were issued in place of the note, the Joe Frazier Left Hook part of the transaction could still have life.

Some Observation's on Endo's "Joe Frazier Left Hook." To summarize, it would appear that to the extent possible, Endo will manage its post-acquisition operations in such a way as to cause the New Endo income amount to exceed the U.S. shareholders' gain amount so that the Section 367(a)(1) gain recognition rule will not apply to the Endo shareholders, and they will, therefore, receive tax free treatment in the transaction. In using the Reg. § 1.367(b)-10 regulations in this manner Endo is rendering a "Joe Frazier left hook" to the Treasury.

The left hook not only makes the Section 367(a) gain recognition rule inapplicable, but it facilitates a large interest stripping game that Endo is playing by having the note issued by Endo U.S. Inc. to New Endo treated as a dividend under the "Killer B" regulations. As the Endo Proxy/Prospectus points out, the deemed dividend would only be subject to a 5% withholding tax under the U.S.-Irish Tax Treaty. This is a small price to pay for the interest stripping benefit associated with the note.

This potential interest stripping benefit can be illustrated as follows. The value of the New Endo stock that went to the Paladin shareholders was $1.6 billion, and presumably the note was in that amount. Assuming the full $1.6 billion note is treated as a dividend under Section 301(c)(1), the 5% withholding tax on the dividend as provided for in the U.S.-Irish Tax Treaty would amount to $276 million. Assuming (1) the interest on the note is 4.5% (a reasonable rate) or $72 million per year, (2) all of the interest is fully deductible because the interest stripping limitation in Section 163(j) does not apply, and (3) New Endo avoids tax on the receipt of the interest, then within less than four years the tax savings from the interest stripping would exceed the withholding tax on the deemed dividend. On a present value basis, the interest stripping benefit would far exceed the withholding tax on the dividend.

This $72 billion estimated annual savings from interest stripping is consistent with the following statement in the Endo Proxy/Prospectus: "New Endo is expected to realize $75 million of post-tax synergies on a twelve-month basis at some point following the close of the transaction."

Notice 2014-32 Takes Some of the Force out of the " Joe Frazier Left Hook"[86] On April 25, 2014 the IRS issued Notice 2014-32,[87] which weakens, but does not block (*i.e.*, eliminate), the "Joe Frazier Left Hook" in the "Killer B" regulations. This section briefly discusses this Notice.

As discussed previously, prior to the issuance of Notice 2014-32, corporations engaged in inversions were paying a very small price for the benefit of having the Section 367(b) regulations take priority.

First, although the Taxable Dividend Amount of the Section 367(b) Income paid by the domestic sub to the foreign parent is subject to the 30% withholding tax under the gross basis tax under Section 881, the 30% withholding is subject to reduction by an applicable tax treaty. For example, in the case of Endo, the deemed Section 367(b) dividend was only subject to a 5% withholding tax under the U.S.-Irish Tax Treaty. Thus, the actual tax on the deemed dividend could be very low as in the Endo inversion.

Second, the Capital Gain Amount of the Section 367(b) Income may or may not be subject to U.S. tax. Capital gain of a foreign corporation that is not realized from a U.S. real property interest is subject to U.S. tax under Section 882 only if such gain is effectively connected with the conduct by the foreign corporation of a trade or business in the U.S. It would appear that in the prototypical inversion, like the Endo inversion, the stock of the inverted corporation is not a U.S. real property interest and the foreign parent is not engaged in a U.S. trade or business. Therefore, there is no tax on capital gains.

Because of these two factors, an inverter would have to pay a *de minimis* price in the form of a small withholding tax for the benefit of having the Section 367(b) regulations take priority over the shareholder level tax in Section 367(a). Notice 2014-32 elaborates on this point as follows:

> The IRS and the Treasury Department ... are aware that the priority rules may facilitate certain transactions designed to avoid recognizing gain under § 1.367(a)-3(c). For example, FP, a foreign corporation, intends to acquire all the stock of UST, a domestic corporation owned by U.S. persons, in exchange for FP stock in a reorganization described in section 368(a)(1)(B) [i.e., a voting stock for voting stock reorganization]. FP forms USS, a domestic corporation. USS generates a small amount of earnings and profits. USS acquires FP stock from FP in exchange for a note and uses the FP stock to acquire all the stock of UST. The shareholders of UST receive 75 percent of the outstanding FP stock. The stock in USS is not a United States real property interest (within the meaning of section 897(c)), and FP would not be subject to U.S. tax under section 882 on a disposition of the stock of USS. The transaction is structured to result in a small amount of dividend income that would be subject to U.S. withholding tax on a distribution and

---

in a significant amount of section 367(b) income in the form of section 301(c)(3) gain. The taxpayer takes the position that the transaction avoids the application of the no-U.S.-tax exception because of the small amount of dividend income. In addition, the taxpayer takes the position that the section 367(b) priority rule applies because the section 367(b) income recognized by FP by reason of the application of § 1.367(b)-10 exceeds the amount of gain that would be recognized by shareholders of UST under section 367(a)(1) with respect to the UST stock. This position is taken even though the section 301(c)(3) gain that FP recognizes by reason of the application of § 1.367(b)-10 (and therefore takes into account in determining section 367(b) income) is not subject to U.S. tax. Finally, the taxpayer takes the position that the anti-abuse rule [discussed below] does not apply with respect to the earnings and profits of UST.

Notice 2014-32 explains that in addressing the glaring defect in the situation (iii) exception, the following modification will be made to the Section 367(b) Priority Rule:

> The section 367(a) priority rule under § 1.367(b)-10 will be modified by adjusting the amount of income or gain that is considered section 367(b) income for this purpose. Regulations will provide that section 367(b) income includes a section 301(c)(1) dividend or section 301(c)(3) gain that would arise if § 1.367(b)-10 applied to the triangular reorganization only to the extent such dividend income or gain would be subject to U.S. tax or would give rise to an income inclusion under section 951(a)(1)(A) that would be subject to U.S. tax. A conforming change will be made to the section 367(b) priority rule under § 1.367(a)-3(a)(2)(iv).

Thus, by providing that Section 367(b) income includes only "such dividend income or gain [or Section 951 inclusion that] would be subject to U.S. tax" (the U.S. Tax Requirement), Notice 2014-32 has increased the price inverters must pay to have the Section 367(b) regulations take priority over the Section 367(a) regulations,. However, the Notice does not eliminate the Section 367(b) Priority Rule. In other words, the Notice has weakened but not blocked the "Joe Frazier Left Hook." As will be discussed subsequently, I believe the Treasury should completely block the "Left Hook."

Also, even with the U.S. Tax Requirement, an inverter likely could ensure that there was sufficient E&P so that the Section 367(b) Income would exceed the Aggregate Section 367(a) Taxable Gain, and consequently, the Section 367(b) rules would take priority. And, if the foreign parent is organized in a country like Ireland, which has a 5% withholding rate on dividends, the tax cost of securing Section 367(b) priority treatment would not be that great particularly when compared to the 23.8% combined capital gains and net investment income tax rate that is likely to apply to the Section 367(a) capital gains of the target's shareholders. The bottom line is that while Notice 2014-32 has increased the cost of giving priority to the Section 367(b) regulations, the Notice would not seem to be a significant deterrent to inverters.

Reg. § 1.367(b)-10(d) sets out an anti-abuse rule that provides that "[a]ppropriate adjustments shall be made … if, in connection with a triangular reorganization, a transaction is engaged in with a view to avoid the purpose of this section." Notice 2014-32 sets out the following extension of the anti-abuse rule:

> The anti-abuse rule in § 1.367(b)-10(d) will be clarified to provide that S's acquisition of P stock or securities in exchange for a note may invoke the anti-abuse rule. In addition, § 1.367(b)-10(d) will be clarified to provide that the earnings and profits of a corporation (or a successor corporation) may be taken into account for purposes of determining the consequences of the adjustments provided in the final regulations, as modified by the rules announced in this notice, regardless of whether such corporation is related to P or S before the triangular reorganization. Thus, the earnings and profits of T (or a successor to T) or a subsidiary of S or T may be taken into account for purposes of determining the consequences of the adjustments provided in the final regulations, as modified by the rules announced in this notice.

This interpretation of the anti-avoidance provision could work to the advantage of inverters, because it would make it more likely that an inverter could generate enough E&P so that the Section 367(b) Income would exceed the Aggregate Section 367(a) Taxable Gain, thereby giving priority to the Section 367(b) "Killer B" regulations.

Can Ali (*a.k.a.* IRS) Counter Endo's "Joe Frazier Left Hook"? In Ali's rematch with Frazer in the "Thrilla in Manila," Ali avoided Frazier's Left Hook and won the fight. The question here is: Can the IRS, like Ali, avoid Endo's Joe Frazer Left Hook and win the Section 367 fight?

First, it is clear from the history of the "Killer B" issue and from common sense that the purpose of the "Killer B" regulations is not to facilitate the type of game Endo is playing with those regulations. For example, it seems clear from Notice 2006-85, discussed *supra*, that the Avoidance of Gross Basis Tax provision of the "Killer B" rules was directed at the tax-free distribution of earnings from a U.S. sub to a long term foreign parent, and not the type of transaction in which the foreign parent is newly formed as is the case with New Endo. Unlike New Endo, a long term foreign parent may have made a real loan of funds to the U.S. sub and, therefore, may in fact be entitled to repayment and to interest. On the other hand, the note going from Endo U.S. Inc. to New Endo is not issued for funds that Endo U.S. Inc. has received.

Second, in this circumstance, the note-for-stock transaction is artificial on its face, lacks a true business purpose, and arguably should be treated as a constructive dividend without respect to the "Killer B" regulations. Further, as noted previously, Reg. § 1.367(b)-10(d) sets out an anti-abuse rule, and the IRS might use that rule to make both (1) the Section 367(a) gain recognition rule, and (2) the deemed dividend rule or a similar constructive dividend rule applicable to the Endo transaction. Finally, it would appear that this type of approach would be consistent with the codification of the economic substance doctrine in Section 7701(o), which provides:

> In the case of any transaction to which the economic substance doctrine is relevant, such transaction shall be treated as having economic substance only if—

(A) the transaction changes in a meaningful way (apart from Federal income tax effects) the taxpayer's economic position, and

(B) the taxpayer has a substantial purpose (apart from Federal income tax effects) for entering into such transaction.

So, the answer is that the IRS, like Ali, can come back and overcome the Endo's Joe Frazer Left Hook. And, to take pressure off tax professionals who are reluctant to engage in Endo type transactions, but are pushed by the competition for clients to do so, the IRS should quickly address the issue.

H. Potential Use of the UPREIT Structure to Turn Off the Section 367(a) Gain Recognition Rule[88]

Introduction. This section discusses the potential use of what is known as an UP-REIT structure, which involves the use of a partnership, for the purpose of giving a target's shareholders nonrecognition treatment in an otherwise taxable acquisition, including a transaction that is subject to the Section 367(a) gain recognition rule.

In an August 26, 2014 press release,[89] Burger King, a publicly held Delaware corporation, and Tim Hortons, a publicly held Canadian corporation, announced an inversion transaction in which Burger King and Tim Hortons would become subsidiaries of a new publicly traded Canadian holding company (Holdings).[90] In the transaction, which has been completed, the shareholders of Tim Hortons received cash and stock of Holdings representing a 22% interest in Holdings. The shareholders of Burger King received at their election either (1) stock of Holdings, or (2) Exchangeable Partnership Units in a partnership that is controlled by Holdings (BK Partnership). The Exchangeable Partnership Units are publicly traded.

The Press Release stated that (1) 3G Capital, the private equity firm that is the principal shareholder of Burger King, will "retain all of its investment in Burger King by converting its roughly 70% equity stake in Burger King into equity of the new company," and (2) "3G Capital is expected to own approximately 51% of the new company with the balance of the common shares to be held by current public shareholders of Burger King and Tim Hortons."

The Press Release described the Exchangeable Partnership Units as follows:

The Exchangeable Partnership Units will be convertible on a 1:1 basis into common shares of the new parent company [Holdings], however, the units may not be exchanged for common shares for the first year following the closing of the transaction. Holders of partnership units will participate in the votes of shareholders of the new parent company on a pro-rata basis as

---

88. This section is based on Samuel C. Thompson, Jr. *The Cat-and-Mouse Inversion Game with Burger King*, 144 Tax Notes 1317 (Sept. 15, 2014).

89. Exhibit 99-1 to Burger King's SEC Form 8-K filed August 26, 2014.

90. For a discussion of various aspects of the transaction see Andrew Velarde, *Burger King to Buy Tim Hortons and Invert to Canada*, 144 Tax Notes 1003 (Sept. 1, 2014) [Velarde, *Burger King*].

though the units had been converted. 3G Capital has committed to elect to receive only partnership units.

The Press Release goes on to explain that (1) the transaction is "expected to be taxable, for U.S. federal income tax purposes, to the shareholders of Burger King, other than with respect to the BK Partnership units received by them in the transaction," and (2) the transaction is "expected to be taxable to shareholders of Tim Hortons in the U.S and Canada."

In responding to a question during the Investor Conference concerning the reason for the use of BK Partnership, an executive of Burger King explained: "Having [BK Partnership units] will defer taxes [under Section 721] [91] until an ultimate sale."[92] It can be expected that tax-indifferent holders of Burger King stock, such as IRAs that hold such stock, will be the principal electors of shares of Holdings. Since 3G is taking Exchangeable Partnership Units, it would appear that 3G is not tax-indifferent. This BK Partnership is the latest gimmick in the "Cat and Mouse" game the Treasury and taxpayers have been playing with inversions.[93] However, if this gimmick works, it is likely to be employed in acquisition transactions generally, and not just inversions.

As noted below, the Exchangeable Partnership Units have all of the economic characteristics of a stock interest in Holdings, and the only discernable purpose of utilizing BK Partnership is the attempted avoidance of the impact of:

(1) the Section 367(a) gain recognition regulations that would apply if the shareholders of Burger King were to receive stock in Holdings in a reorganization or Section 351 transaction[94] because their direct stock interest in Holdings would exceed 50%,[95] or

(2) the taxable gain and loss rule that would apply to the Burger King shareholders if the transaction is not a reorganization or Section 351 transaction.

This section argues first that the Treasury should carefully examine the structure of the transaction to determine if it qualifies as a non-recognition transfer to BK Partnership under Section 721. Second, and more importantly, if the transaction is a Section 721 transfer, the Treasury should vigorously assert (under the authorities discussed below, and perhaps others) that the Exchangeable Partnership Units are the equivalent of shares in Holdings for purposes of, *inter alia*, (1) determining the applicability of the gain recognition rule of Section 367(a) if the transaction qualifies

---

91. Section 721 provides for non-recognition treatment on the transfer of property to a BK Partnership. Section 721 and related partnership tax rules are discussed in Chapter 24, which deals with joint ventures.

92. Velarde, *Burger King, supra.*

93. *See e.g.,* Samuel C. Thompson, Jr., *New Inversions, the 'Joe Frazier Left Hook,' the IRS Notice, and Pfizer,* Tax Notes 1413 (June 23, 2014) [Thompson, *New Inversions*].

94. This section does not take a position on whether the transaction is or is not a reorganization or Section 351 exchange; however, if it is such an exchange under the approach taken here, only gain, and not loss, would be recognized under the Section 367(a) gain recognition rule.

95. For a discussion of the Section 367(a) gain recognition rule, *see* Chapter 22 and Thompson, *New Inversions, supra.*

as a reorganization or Section 351 exchange, and (2) applying the taxable gain or loss rule that would apply if the transaction does not qualify as a reorganization or Section 351 exchange.

If the Treasury does not challenge this transaction, this structure could be used in all types of acquisition transactions, both cross border and purely domestic.

Does Section 721 Non-Recognition Apply to the Transaction? Section 2.3(e)(i) of the Merger Agreement, relating to the Effect on Capital Stock, provides as follows with respect to the Conversion of Merger Sub Common Stock that takes place in Step 2 of the transaction:

> At the Merger Effective Time ... each share of [outstanding] common stock of Merger Sub ... held by Holdings and [BK Partnership], respectively, ... shall forthwith be cancelled ... and be converted into one ... share of common stock of [Burger King], which shall be held directly or indirectly by Holdings and *[Burger King] shall further issue its shares to Holdings and to [BK Partnership] in consideration of Holdings' issuing the Holdings Consideration and [BK Partnership] issuing the Exchangeable Security Consideration[.]* (emphasis added)

The apparent purpose of the italicized language is to set the stage for the argument that as a result of the merger, the Burger King shareholders who will receive Exchangeable Partnership Units in effect will be transferring their shares of Burger King to BK Partnership in exchange for such Units. This construct could be the basis of an assertion that such Burger King shareholders have made a contribution to BK Partnership in exchange for a BK Partnership interest, thereby giving rise to non-recognition treatment under Section 721, which provides for such treatment on a contribution of property to a partnership in exchange for a partnership interest.

One potential problem with this assertion is that it is Burger King (and not the Burger King shareholders) that issues the Burger King stock to BK Partnership as a result of the merger. On the other hand, on the basis of several rulings that hold that a reverse subsidiary merger is a stock acquisition,[96] it might be appropriate to treat the BK Partnership part of the transaction as a Section 721 transfer. But, apparently none of the revenue rulings or regulations dealing with this type of reverse subsidiary merger involve a transfer of part of the target's stock to one entity and part to another entity. In any event, the Treasury should carefully scrutinize this transaction to determine if it falls within the letter and purposes of Section 721. The non-applicability of Section 721 would make the issuance of the Exchangeable Partnership Units a taxable transaction.

If Section 721 Is Applicable, the Treasury Should Treat an Exchangeable Partnership Unit as a Share of Holdings. If the Treasury were to find that Section 721 does apply to the transaction, there are at least three theories that the Treasury should apply to treat the receipt of an Exchangeable Partnership Unit as the receipt of a share of Holdings thereby triggering (1) the Section 367(a) gain recognition rule if the

---

96. *See e.g.*, Rev. Rul. 90-95, 1990-2 C.B. 67.

transaction qualifies as a reorganization or Section 351 exchange, or (2) the general taxable gain or loss rule if the transaction is not a reorganization or Section 351 exchange. These theories are:

- The common law business purpose doctrine, which should apply in view of the lack of a business purpose for forming BK Partnership.
- The codified economic substance doctrine under Section 7701(o), which provides, in part:

  In the case of any transaction to which the economic substance doctrine is relevant, such transaction shall be treated as having economic substance only if—

  (A) the transaction changes in a meaningful way (apart from Federal income tax effects) the taxpayer's economic position, and

  (B) the taxpayer has a substantial purpose (apart from Federal income tax effects) for entering into such transaction.

- The partnership anti-abuse regulations under Treas. Reg. section 1.701-2(a).[97]

In the event any of these theories are applied, (1) if the transaction is a reorganization or Section 351 exchange, because the shareholders of Burger King would end up with more than 50% of the stock of Holdings, under the gain recognition rule of Section 367(a), all of those shareholders would be required to recognize gain, if any, on the transaction; and (2) if the transaction is not a reorganization or Section 351 exchange, the shareholders of Burger King would have a taxable transaction.

After-Thought on the UPREIT Example in the Partnership Anti-Abuse Regulations. In a Letter to the Editor of Tax Notes regarding my *The Cat-and-Mouse* article,[98] I responded as follows to a post by Monte Jackle who criticized me for not discussing the partnership UPREIT example in the partnership anti-abuse regulations (Example 4 of reg. 1.701-2(d)). He says that this example "approves a transaction that is *not unlike*" the BK Partnership, which I conclude should be challenged by the Treasury. Monte is right: I should have discussed the UPREIT example, but not for the proposition that it lends support for the BK Partnership. I should have cited the example for the proposition that it makes it clear that the BK Partnership should be ignored under the anti-abuse regulations.

Let me give a few of the reasons I come to this conclusion: First, the UPREIT example has a contribution of a real business to the partnership, and the partnership operates the business. Here there is no business being contributed to the BK Partnership. Second, in the UPREIT example, the partnership interests are not tradable like the stock of the REIT. On the other hand, in the BK Partnership, the partnership interests are structured to trade just like the stock of the New Holding Company will trade because each partnership interest has the same dividend and voting rights as a

---

97. Treas. Reg. section 1.701-2 was adopted by Treasury Decision 8588 (December 29, 1994), 1995-7 I.R.B. 5.

98. Professor Responds to Criticism of Recent Article. Tax Notes, Sept. 22, 2014, p. 1470

share of stock of the New Holding Company. Thus, in the UPREIT example there is an economic difference between a partnership interest and a share of stock of the REIT, but there is no such economic difference with the BK Partnership. Third, in the UPREIT transaction there is a business purpose for bringing together for the purpose of conducting a business (1) the contributors of the real property to the partnership, and (2) the purchasers of shares of the REIT. There is no such business purpose in the BK deal. As one of the executives of BK explained in the investor conference, the purpose of the BK Partnership is to give tax-free treatment to electing BK shareholders.

The bottom line is that the BK Partnership is very much "not like" the UPREIT example, and for that reason should be challenged by the Treasury. Also, as I point out above, this BK Partnership is challengeable under other grounds, including the codified economic substance doctrine.

§ 10.12 Policy Perspectives on Inversions

A. The Obama Administration's 2015 Legislative Proposal on Inversions

U.S. Treasury, General Explanations of the Administration's Fiscal Year 2017 Revenue Proposals

February 2016

LIMIT THE ABILITY OF DOMESTIC ENTITIES TO EXPATRIATE

Current Law

Section 7874 applies to certain transactions (known as "inversion transactions") in which a U.S. corporation is replaced by a foreign corporation ("foreign acquiring corporation") as the parent company of a worldwide affiliated group of companies in a transaction where (1) substantially all of the assets of a domestic corporation are acquired by a foreign acquiring corporation; (2) the historical owners of the domestic corporation retain at least a 60-percent ownership interest in the foreign acquiring corporation; and (3) the foreign acquiring corporation, together with the expanded affiliated group (EAG) that includes the foreign acquiring corporation, does not conduct substantial business activities in the country in which it is created or organized. Similar provisions apply if a foreign acquiring corporation acquires substantially all of the property constituting a trade or business of a domestic partnership.

The tax consequences of an inversion transaction depend on the level of shareholder continuity. If the continuing ownership of historical shareholders of the domestic corporation in the foreign acquiring corporation is 80 percent or more (by vote or value), the new foreign parent corporation is treated as a domestic corporation for all U.S. tax purposes (the "80-percent test"). If the continuing shareholder ownership is at least 60 percent but less than 80 percent, the foreign status of the acquiring corporation is respected but certain other adverse tax consequences apply, including the inability to use tax attributes to reduce certain corporate-level income or gain ("inversion gain") recognized by the expatriated group (the "60-percent test").

Reasons for Change

In order to reduce their U.S. taxes, domestic entities have with greater frequency been combining with smaller foreign entities such that the level of continued ownership of the historical shareholders of the domestic entity is less than 80 percent (although above the 60-percent threshold). The combination is typically structured so that the domestic entity and the foreign entity will be subsidiaries of a newly formed foreign parent company located in a low-tax jurisdiction. The domestic entities engaging in these transactions often emphasize that the transaction is expected to substantially reduce the U.S. tax liability of the multinational group with only minimal changes to its operations. Inversion transactions raise significant policy concerns because they facilitate the erosion of the U.S. tax base through deductible payments by the remaining U.S. members of the multinational group to the non-U.S. members and through aggressive transfer pricing for transactions between such U.S. and non-U.S. members. The inverted group also may reduce its U.S. taxes by causing its foreign subsidiaries to cease to qualify as controlled foreign corporations in order to avoid U.S. taxation under subpart F of the Code on passive and other highly mobile income that is shifted to the foreign subsidiaries.

The adverse tax consequences under current law of 60-percent inversion transactions have not deterred taxpayers from pursuing these transactions. There is no policy reason to respect an inverted structure when the owners of a domestic entity retain a controlling interest in the group, only minimal operational changes are expected, and there is potential for substantial erosion of the U.S. tax base. Furthermore, an inverted structure should not be respected when the structure results from the combination of a larger U.S. group with a smaller entity or group and, after the transaction, the EAG is primarily managed and controlled in the United States and does not have substantial business activities in the relevant foreign country, even if the shareholders of the domestic entity do not maintain control of the resulting multinational group.

Concerns about inversions have led to the enactment of statutory rules that require certain Federal agencies not to contract with multinational groups that have inverted. Federal agencies, however, generally do not have access to the identity of such groups. To the extent the IRS has or is authorized to collect this information, the IRS would be restricted under section 6103 from sharing it with other Federal agencies.

Proposal

To limit the ability of domestic entities to expatriate, the proposal would broaden the definition of an inversion transaction by reducing the 80-percent test to a greater than 50-percent test, and eliminating the 60-percent test. The proposal also would add a special rule whereby, regardless of the level of shareholder continuity, an inversion transaction would occur if (1) immediately prior to the acquisition, the fair market value of the stock of the domestic entity is greater than the fair market value of the stock of the foreign acquiring corporation, (2) the EAG is primarily managed and controlled in the United States, and (3) the EAG does not conduct substantial business activities in the country in which the foreign acquiring corporation is created or organized.

Additionally, the proposal would expand the scope of acquisitions described in section 7874 so that an inversion transaction could occur if there is a direct or indirect acquisition of substantially all of the assets of a domestic corporation or domestic partnership, substantially all of the trade or business assets of a domestic corporation or domestic partnership, or substantially all of the U.S. trade or business assets of a foreign partnership.

In addition, the proposal would provide the IRS with authority to share tax return information with Federal agencies for the purpose of administering an agency's anti-inversion rules. Federal agencies receiving this information would be subject to the safeguarding and recordkeeping requirements under section 6103.

The proposals that would limit the ability of domestic entities to expatriate would be effective for transactions that are completed after December 31, 2016. The proposal providing the IRS with the authority to share information with other Federal agencies to assist them in identifying companies that were involved in an inversion transaction would be effective after December 31, 2016, without regard to when the inversion transaction occurred.

Does Congress Need to Enter the Fight? But the potential punches from the IRS will not end the story. Congress should reenter the fight against inversions that it undertook with Section 7874. Specifically, Congress should throw even more forceful punches at inversions. Such congressional punches could include:

(1) lowering the threshold in Section 7874 for treating a foreign holding company as a U.S. company from the present 80% to 60%, and

(2) providing that any inversion in which the shareholders of a U.S. firm end up with from 50% to 60% of the stock of the foreign holding company the following three rules will apply: (a) the current Section 367(a)(1) gain recognition rule; (b) the current inversion gain rule in Section 7874; (c) a new rule which would at the time of the inversion treat the U.S. firm as if it had disposed of each of its CFCs in a taxable transaction, thereby ending the deferral benefit; and (d) a strengthened Section 163(j) interest stripping rule that would operate in a similar manner to the provision of the Senate Finance Committee's 2013 *International Business Tax Reform Discussion Draft* that is entitled: "Denial of deductions for related party payments arising in a base erosion arrangement."[99]

In my view, these more forceful punches against inversions would make for good tax policy by further deterring a firm from taking advantage of the great business opportunities this country offers and then using an inversion to undermine our tax sys-

---

99. Joint Committee on Taxation, Technical Explanation of the Senate Committee on Finance Chairman's Staff Discussion Draft of Provisions to Reform International Business Taxation 80 (JCX-15-13) (Nov. 19, 2013), available at: https://www.jct.gov/publications.html?func=startdown&id=4530).

tem. It would also reduce the amount of time deal and tax lawyers spend on artificial transactions that are merely designed to beat the Treasury out of a dollar.

B. My Take on the Policy Aspects of Inversions

1. Introduction

This section principally contains excerpts from a letter on inversions I sent to the Secretary of Treasury in August 2014. In the letter, I outline both legislative and administrative steps I recommend in the fight against inversions.

2. Issues Addressed in My August 12, 2014 Letter to the Secretary of Treasury regarding Inversions

After discussing the reasons for my long-term interest in, and writings about the policy issues raised by inversions, the letter addresses the following topics:

1. Treasury's Current Legislative Proposal: *Inverter Treated as a U.S. Corporation Rule*;

2. Proposed Additional Legislative Initiative by Treasury: *The CFC Taxable Disposition Rule*;

3. Administrative Action: *As Proposed by Professor Shay, Regulations under Section 385 for Future Inversions*;

4. Administrative Action: *Challenging the "Note-for-Stock" Part of Current and Past Inversions*;

5. Administrative Action: *Fixing the "Joe Frazier Left Hook" in the Current Section 367 Regulations*;

6. Administrative Action: *Preventing Avoidance of the Purposes of Section 956 through Hop-Scotch Loans*;

7. Administrative Action: *Addressing the Gross-Ups of the Section 4985 Excise Tax; and*

8. *A Word on the Merits of a Territorial Regime.*

Each of these topics is explored below.

This section was prepared prior to the issuance by the Treasury of its 2016 regulations on inversions and debt/equity issues under Section 385. *See* Secs. 10.11.D. E. and F. Where applicable, the impact of these regulations is noted at the end of the discussion of the particular issue.

3. Treasury's Current Legislative Proposal: Inverter Treated as a U.S. Corporation Rule

The Treasury should be commended for its legislative proposal for curtailing inversions set out most recently in the 2016 legislative proposal of the Obama Administration discussed above. If enacted this proposal would (1) reduce the 80 percent threshold in section 7874 to 50 percent and eliminate the 60 percent test (the *50% Inverter Test)*, and (2) without regard to the level of shareholder continuity, prevent a U.S. company from shifting its tax residence to a foreign jurisdiction if the corporation is managed and controlled in the United States and has significant business operations there (the *U.S. Managed Inverter Test)*. I refer to the *50% Inverter Test* and the *U.S. Managed Inverter Test* as the *Inverter Treated as a U.S. Corporation Rule* legislative proposal.

4. Proposed Additional Legislative Initiative by Treasury: The CFC Taxable Disposition Rule

In addition to the *Inverter Treated as a U.S. Corporation Rule* legislative proposal, as initially proposed in my *New Inversions* article,[100] I suggest that the Treasury also propose a new legislative rule that would treat a U.S. corporation as having disposed in a taxable transaction of the stock of its controlled foreign corporations (CFCs) whenever the U.S. corporation becomes a more than 50% subsidiary of a foreign corporation and the *Inverter Treated as a U.S. Corporation Rule* does not apply. I refer to this rule as the *CFC Taxable Disposition Rule*.

This rule would apply where a foreign corporation acquires a U.S. corporation and neither the *50% Inverter Test* nor the *U.S. Managed Inverter Test* is satisfied. This could happen if, for example, a foreign acquirer purchased for cash all of the stock of a U.S. target and the *U.S. Managed Inverter Test* did not apply. In such case, under the proposed *CFC Taxable Disposition Rule*, at the time of the acquisition of the U.S. target, the target would be treated as disposing of each of its CFCs in a taxable transaction, thereby ending the deferral benefit.

The purpose of the *CFC Taxable Disposition Rule* is to prevent a foreign acquirer from using various techniques to deploy the earnings of the U.S. target's CFCs in a way that would avoid the purposes of Section 956. Thus, this rule would prevent the abuse of Section 956 with regard to the deferred earnings of such CFCs.

This *CFC Taxable Disposition Rule* would address the problem discussed in an article entitled *An Inversion in All but Name*,[101] which was in the New York Times on August 8, 2014. The article discusses the acquisition for cash by a Dutch company of SafeNet, a U.S. company with significant foreign operations. In explaining the difference between the SafeNet transaction and inversions, the article states:

> [Unlike inversions], [s]ales of American companies to overseas buyers ... are not in the cross-hairs. Yet SafeNet's deal could have a similar effect to an inversion. Presumably its tax home can shift from Baltimore to Amsterdam, where its new $8 billion parent company is located. Over half of SafeNet's sales last year were generated outside the United States ... and would therefore be eligible for a reduced tax rate under a new domicile.

---

100. *Id.* at 1421.
101. Jeffrey Goldfarb, *An Inversion in All but Name*, Deal Book, New York Times (Aug. 8, 2014).

The *CFC Taxable Disposition Rule* should also apply, for example, when a U.S. controlled foreign investment firm acquires a U.S. company. This type of transaction was discussed as follows in an article in the Merger & Acquisition Law Report:[102]

> Consider the business founded in 1916 as General Plate Co., a maker of sensors and controls for everything from Fords and Frigidaires to the spaceship that first carried Americans to the moon. While its top executives are still based in Attleboro, Mass., it's now known as Sensata Technologies Holding NV of the Netherlands.
>
> Sensata didn't become Dutch by using the strategy [an] "inversion[.]" ... Instead, Sensata is one of at least 14 firms that have left the U.S. tax system through a sale to an investment fund[.] Although these companies have a combined market value of about $75 billion, this tax-avoidance strategy has gotten less attention in Washington than inversions and may be harder to discourage.
>
> These buyouts mean profits for the U.S. private equity firms like Boston-based Bain Capital LLC that orchestrated them. Bain earned more than $3 billion after it took Sensata public as a Dutch company in 2010, with an effective tax rate about one-tenth of some competing manufacturers.[103]

To be clear, the *CFC Taxable Disposition Rule* would not prevent a foreign acquirer from structuring its post-acquisition foreign operations in its foreign subsidiaries that were not CFCs, thereby avoiding on a prospective basis the U.S.'s CFC rules. It would, however, prevent the tax-free use of the CFC's pre-acquisition deferred earnings. Also, it should be noted that the adoption of this *CFC Taxable Disposition Rule* would make unnecessary the application of the *Preventing Avoidance of the Purposes of Section 956 through Hop-Scotch Loan*s rule. 5

5. Administrative Action: As Proposed by Professor Shay, Regulations under Section 385 for Future Inversions

I agree with Professor Shay's opinion, which he expressed in a Tax Notes article entitled *Mr. Secretary, Take the Tax Juice Out of Corporate Expatriations*.[104] In the article, Professor Shay argues that the Treasury has the authority under Section 385 to curtail some of the interest stripping abuses that inverters are engaging in. I urge the Treasury to follow Professor Shay's suggestion and quickly issue proposed regulations, with an early effective date, reflecting the principles of his "*Related-party debt-to-equity limitation*" proposal.

From my prior study and analysis of the Treasury's proposed but withdrawn regulations under Section 385,[105] I am confident that the Treasury has the authority to

---

102. Zachary R. Mider, *Tax Dodge Used by Bain Shifts U.S. Companies Abroad*, Bloomberg BNA, 17 Mergers & Acquisitions Law Report 1262 (Aug. 1, 2014).

103. Id.

104. Stephen E. Shay, *Mr. Secretary, Take the Tax Juice Out of Corporate Expatriations*, 144 Tax Notes 473 (July 28, 2014) [Shay, *Take the Juice Out of Inversions*].

105. See e.g., Samuel C. Thompson, Jr. et al., Federal Taxation of Business Enterprises (1994), at Sections 4:05–4.17.

adopt regulations under Section 385 that are targeted at inversion and related trans-actions. Indeed, one of the problems with the previously proposed regulations was that they were attempting to deal with the universe of debt-to-equity issues, whereas regulations along the lines of those proposed by Professor Shay would be more focused and manageable and, therefore, more effective. Consequently, I strongly disagree with Robert Willens, "an influential tax commentator,"[106] who has apparently said that because the prior Section 385 regulations were "unworkable" Professor's Shay's proposal is merely "interesting reading with little, if any, practical significance."[107] By focusing on inversions, the regulations would be primarily concerned with artificial debt instruments issued in an inversion or related transaction by a U.S. corporation to its new foreign parent or related party, and not to "a [situation where a] long-term foreign parent [has] made a real loan of funds to [its] U.S. subsidiary and therefore [is] entitled to repayment and interest."[108]

The Treasury's 2016 Section 385 Regs go even further than what Professor Shay proposed by adopting a bright line rule for treating notes issued in inversions and other related party transactions as stock (*see* Sec. 10.11.F). In my opinion, this is a brilliant approach.

6. Administrative Action: Challenging the "Note-for-Stock" Part of Current and Past Inversions

As I have explained in my *New Inversion* article, the note-for-stock transactions which sets up the interest stripping opportunity in inversions is an artificial transaction that is vulnerable to attack under the business purpose doctrine and the codified economic substance doctrine. In the article, I state:

> [T]he note-for-stock transaction is artificial on its face, lacks a true business purpose, and arguably should be treated as a constructive dividend regardless of the Killer B regulations. Moreover, the note-for-stock transaction is not essential for qualifying the transaction as a triangular reorganization because (1) the parent could transfer its stock directly to the target's shareholders, or (2) the parent could contribute the stock to the subsidiary, which could then transfer the stock to the target's shareholders. In both cases, the transaction would qualify as a reorganization.[109]

Thus, I believe that without regard to the potential prospective application of the Section 385 regulations to these transactions, the IRS should quickly state publicly that it will challenge the note portion of any inversion transaction under the business purpose and codified economic substance doctrines. Without the direct or indirect issuance of a note to the new foreign parent or one of its controlled subsidiaries, interest stripping likely would not be possible.

---

106. Victor Fleischer, How Obama Can Stop Corporate Expatriations, for Now, Deal Book New York Times (Aug. 7, 2014).

107. *Id.*

108. Thompson, *New Inversions, supra* note 2, at 1421.

109. *Id.*

7. Administrative Action: Fixing the "Joe Frazier Left Hook" in the Current Section 367 Regulations

For the reasons discussed above in the examination of the Endo inversion, the Treasury should eliminate the "Joe Frazier Left Hook" in the Section 367 regulations by immediately announcing that the Section 367 regulations will be amended to (1) treat all inversions where the target's shareholders end up with between 50% and 80% of the foreign acquirer's stock as being subject to the Section 367(a) Gain Recognition rule, and (2) treat all notes issued in inversion transactions as constructive dividends. I discuss the technical issues involving these proposals as follows in my *New Inversion* article:

> [A]lthough the scope of the antiabuse rule in reg. section 1.367(b)-10(d) is not completely clear, Treasury might use that rule to make both the section 367(a) gain recognition rule and the deemed dividend rule (or a similar constructive dividend rule) apply in inversions. Indeed, it is curious that Treasury treats the note-for-stock part of an inversion transaction as a non-outbound transaction under the section 367(b) regulations. The note-for-stock part of the transaction is clearly part of a larger outbound transaction (that is, the exchange by the U.S. shareholders of their stock in the U.S. target for stock in the foreign holding company). And because the larger outbound transaction is governed by the section 367(a) regulations, the note-for-stock part of the transaction should also be subject to section 367(a). This type of change could be accomplished by providing under the section 367(a) regulations [or the Section 367(b) regulations] that the note-for-stock part of an inversion transaction is a deemed distribution.

> [P]ossibly the most direct approach would be for the IRS and Treasury to issue a notice saying that the section 367 regulations would be changed, effective on the date of the notice, to expressly bring these transactions back under section 367(a) as well as under section 367(b).[110]

The Treasury's 2016 Section 385 Regs, which treat notes issued in inversions and related transactions as stock, presumably will eliminate the Joe Frazier Left Hook in inversions where notes are issued. However, this presumably is not the case if cash is issued for stock of the new parent holding company. In any event, any possibility of the survival of the Left Hook should be eliminated.

8. Administrative Action: Preventing Avoidance of the Purposes of Section 956 through Hop-Scotch Loans

In the part of Professor Shay's article entitled *Protecting Deferred U.S. Ttaxation of CFC Eearnings*, he says:

> Regulatory authority could be used to ensure that the inversion is not used to gain access to earnings that should be subject to deferred U.S. tax in com-

110. *Id.*

panies that are not owned by the expatriated U.S. companies. This would protect the deferred U.S. taxation of untaxed CFC earnings and the integrity of section 956 rules for investments in U.S. property.[111]

I make the same point in my *New Inversion* article, except I suggest that the Treasury can take steps under the current law to curtail avoidance of Section 956. I make this point as follows:

A Word on Avoidance of Section 956

Sections 951(a)(1)(B) and 956 apply to certain indirect repatriations of deferred foreign income. For example, if a CFC made a 10-year loan to its U.S. parent, the loan would be treated as a dividend distribution from the CFC to the U.S. parent, thereby eliminating the deferral benefit.

Some taxpayers may attempt to use inversions as a way around sections 951(a)(1)(B) and 956. For example, after an inversion, a long-time CFC of the U.S. parent could make a 10-year loan to the new foreign holding company, which in turn could make a similar loan to the U.S. parent, which is a sub of the foreign holding company. By using these back-to-back loans, the parties could argue that the indirect repatriation rules are not applicable. Treasury should make it clear that this and similar transactions (including acquisitions of U.S. corporations in non-inversion transactions) do not avoid those rules.[112]

As discussed above, Notice 2014-52 says that the Treasury is going to issue regulations prohibiting "hop-scotch" loans.

In April 2016, the Treasury issued regulations that treat "hop-scotch" loans made after an inversion as a constructive dividend under Section 956. *See* Sec 10.11.E.10. In my view, this rule should apply generally and not just in inversions.

9. Administrative Action: Addressing the Gross-Ups of the Section 4985 Excise Tax

As explained in my *New Inversion* article, Section 4985 imposes a 15 percent excise tax on certain "specified [unrealized] stock compensation held (directly or indirectly) by or for the benefit of" certain high-level executives of an inverted corporation. The purpose of the tax is to impose a tax penalty on the high-level executives of the inverted corporation, thereby reducing the incentives to invert.

As it turns out, some corporations engaging in inversions have been "grossing up" their high-level executives so that they do not bear the burden of the excise tax. Thus, these inverters are shifting to the shareholders of the inverted corporation the cost of the excise tax. Also, the inverted corporations may be claiming "ordinary and necessary" business deductions under Section 162 for the gross-up payments.

---

111. Shay, *Take the Juice Out of Inversions, supra* note 9.
112. Thompson, *New Inversions, supra,* at 1423.

These gross-ups undermine the law and are unseemly. At a minimum, the Treasury should publicly state that it will deny any business deduction under Section 162 or otherwise for these payments. These payments clearly can't possibly meet the "ordinary and necessary" standard under Section 162.

Also, the Treasury may want to consult with the SEC about possible action under the securities laws to prohibit publicly held companies from undermining the purposes of the law in this manner.

10. A Word on the Merits of a Territorial Regime and Its Effect on Inversions

The points made in this section of my letter to the Treasury are made more comprehensively addressed in my subsequently published Tax Notes article entitled *Territoriality Would Make All U.S. Companies De Facto Inverters*, which is set out here

Thompson, Territoriality Would Make All U.S. Companies *De Facto* Inverters

Tax Notes, Dec. 14, 2015, at 1403

Introduction. Inversions have again been thrust into the tax policy spotlight as a result of the following two recent announcements: (1) the Treasury's announcement on November 19, 2015 of a new Inversion Notice,[113] and (2) Pfizer's announcement on November 23, 2015 of its merger with Allergan, an Irish company, in the largest inversion to date.[114]

As an indication of the tax policy significance of inversions, in a press release commenting on the Treasury's new Inversion Notice, Senator Orin Hatch, the Chairman of the Senate Finance Committee said: "[T]he best way to resolve [the inversion] issues would be through a comprehensive tax overhaul that lowers the corporate tax rate and shifts the U.S. to a territorial tax system[.]"[115]

In a territorial system, active income of foreign subsidiaries of U.S. corporations would be exempt from U.S. tax both at the time earned and at the time repatriated. Under our current deferral system, the active income of foreign subs is not subject to U.S. tax at the time earned but is subject to U.S. tax at the time of repatriation.

Senator Hatch's statement is consistent with Republican orthodoxy on this issue, as all of the Republican presidential candidates who have addressed the issue, except for Donald Trump,[116] have proposed moving to a territorial regime, and many have mentioned that such a move would eliminate inversions. For example, Jeb Bush, who has

---

113. IRS, Notice 2015-79 (Nov. 19, 2015).
114. Pfizer Inc., SEC Form 8-K (Nov 23, 2015).
115. Senate Finance Committee, *Hatch Statement on Latest Anti-Inversion Tax Guidance from Treasury* (Nov. 19, 2015).
116. Samuel C. Thompson, Jr. *Hooray for Trump's Proposal to End Deferral*, 149 Tax Notes 157 (Oct. 5, 2015) [hereinafter "*Hooray for Trump*"].

one of the most detailed tax plans, says: "We will end the practice of world-wide taxation on U.S. businesses, which fosters the insidious tactic called corporate 'inversions.'"[117]

Two Corporate Tax Cuts. This Republican orthodoxy of proposing (1) a move to a territorial regime, with (2) a reduction in the corporate tax rate, has two tax cuts for U.S. corporations. The first tax cut is the obvious cut in the corporate tax rate, which, for example, Jeb Bush would reduce from the 35% current rate to 20%. In addition to cutting the corporate tax rate, Jeb Bush would allow for full expensing of capital investment,[118] and there are no significant revenue offsets. This is also generally the case with the other plans of the Republican presidential candidates for cutting the corporate tax rate.

The Explicit Corporate Tax Cut. The rationale for the explicit corporate rate cut without revenue offsets is the conviction of the Republican presidential candidates that merely cutting the corporate tax rate will lead to greater economic growth, which in turn will result in increased tax revenue. However, there is significant economic evidence that has discredited this "Supply Side" theory.[119]

At least Bobby Jindal, the governor of Louisiana, who has dropped out of the race for president, acknowledged that his tax plan, which would reduce the corporate tax rate to zero "chooses to starve Washington."[120] Thus, a more cynical view of these proposals for cutting the explicit corporate rate without revenue offsets may be a surreptitious effort to "Starve the Beast."

The Territoriality, Stealth Corporate Tax Cut. The second corporate tax cut would come from the adoption of territoriality itself. This would arise because income earned by U.S. controlled foreign subs in low tax countries would be subject to tax only in those countries. Under our current system, the deferral of this income from immediate U.S. taxation is our largest corporate tax expenditure, and adoption of territoriality would make permanent the exemption of this tax expenditure from U.S. tax. In addition, there would be a huge incentive for moving income out of the U.S. and into low tax jurisdictions.

This incentive for off-shoring of income is what the OECD's BEPS project is all about. Countries with territorial regimes, which most OECD countries employ, especially have been seeing an erosion of their tax bases through base erosion (BE) and profit shifting (PS). The BEPS project, which was adopted at the November 2015 G-20 meeting in Turkey,[121] is designed to cut back on BEPS.

---

117. Jeb Bush, Presidential Website, Taxes: Reform and Growth, available at https://jeb2016.com/?lang=en, visited on Oct. 28, 2015. Jeb Bush proposes to assess a one-time tax of 8.75% payable over 10 years, on the more than $2 trillion in corporate profits sitting overseas. The other Republican candidates have made similar proposals.

118. *Id.*

119. See e.g., Paul Krugman, *Fantasies and Fictions at G.O.P. Debate*, New York Times (Sept. 18, 2015).

120. Paul C. Barton, *Tax Plans Show Supply Side's Still-Formidable Grip on GOP*, 149 Tax Notes 361 (Oct. 19, 2015).

121. White House Fact Sheet: The 2015 G-20 Summit in Antalya, Turkey, *A Modern, Fair International Tax System* (Nov. 16, 2015).

As an illustration of the magnitude of the BEPS problem, the Introduction to the final BEPS report explains: "The affiliates of [Multinational Enterprises] in low tax countries report almost twice the profit rate (relative to assets) of their global group, showing how BEPS can cause economic distortions."[122]

To be clear, embedded in our current deferral system is an incentive for engaging in BEPS, but there is even a greater incentive for engaging in BEPS in a territorial system. Further, a move to a territorial system with the inherent increase in the problem with BEPS effectively would be bestowing on American business a large *stealth* corporate tax cut.

For example, under our current deferral system, State College, Inc. (SCI), a fictious corporation operating in State College, PA and subject to a corporate tax rate of 35%, has an incentive to divert its taxable income to its foreign subsidiary (FS) operating in a country with a low tax rate, say 10%. For every dollar of taxable income SCI can divert to FS, SCI saves 25 cents in immediate tax. However, if SCI repatriates FS's 90 cents of after-tax income, there would be a U.S. tax of 25 cents, thus bringing the total tax to 35%.[123]

On the other hand, under a territorial system, if SCI can successfully divert the dollar of income to FS, SCI can bring the dollar back to state college without any additional U.S. tax, thus getting a stealth corporate tax cut. It should be obvious to policy makers that with the adoption of territoriality, in the search of the stealth tax cut, tax advisers would be advising their clients to pursue even more aggressive BEPS schemes than are currently utilized under our deferral system.

Purpose of Actual or De Jure Inversions. A major purpose of actual or *de jure* inversions, like the Pfizer-Allergan inversion, is to give Pfizer the benefit of Ireland's territorial regime so that it can avoid the U.S deferral system on future income earned by its non-Irish foreign subs.[124] Thus, it is not as though Pfizer is going to have significant amounts of its income taxed in Ireland; rather, it is using Ireland so that it can have significant amounts of its foreign income (including income diverted from the U.S. through BEPS) taxed only in other low tax foreign jurisdictions, many with lower tax rates than Ireland's.

Territoriality Would Create De Facto Inverters. The argument that territoriality would eliminate actual or *de jure* inversions is absolutely accurate. This is because

---

122. OECD/G20 Base Erosion and Profit Shifting Project, *Explanatory Statement*, 2015 Final Reports (Nov. 2015), at Introduction, paragraph 2.

123. As a general matter, under the foreign tax credit and related provisions, upon receipt of the 90 cents from FS, SCI would (1) include in its income $1 (*i.e.*, the 90 cents, plus the gross-up of the 10 cents foreign tax); (2) be subject to U.S. tax on the $1 at 35%, or 35 cents; and (3) be allowed a foreign tax credit of 10 cents against the 35 cents U.S. tax, which results in a U.S. tax of 25 cents.

124. Prior to the issuance of the Treasury's 2014Inversion Notice (IRS Notice 2014-52, I.R.B. 2014-42 (Oct. 14, 2014)), U.S. inverters were avoiding the U.S. tax on repatriation of previously deferred foreign income through "hop scotch loans" made from the controlled foreign subs of the U.S. parent corp to the new post inversion foreign parent. The 2014 Notice states the Treasury position that such loans result in a repatriation tax in the U.S. As a consequence, it can be expected that inverters will avoid "hop scotch loans."

territoriality would grant the benefits of a *de jure* inversion to every U.S. business, including large publicly held corporations, small closely held corporations, partnerships, and LLCs. With territoriality, every U.S. owned business would automatically have the benefits that come with a *de jure* inversion without going through the mechanics of such an inversion; thus every U.S. firm could become a *de facto* inverter.

This principal benefit offered to *de facto* inverters is the same benefit offered to current *de jure* inverters, like Pfizer: the ability, through the use of BEPS and other tax avoidance techniques to take advantage of lower tax rates offered by certain countries, particularly tax havens. With territoriality every U.S. business, whether large or small would have an incentive to deflect income to foreign subs operating in tax havens, so that in the words of the BEPS report, the foreign subs operating in "low tax countries [have a significantly higher] profit rate (relative to assets) [than that] of their global group[.]"

The Imputation Alternative to Territoriality and the Impact on De Jure Inversions. I have argued in several Tax Notes articles, the latest in my *Hooray for Trump* article,[125] that we should move to an imputation system for taxing foreign income of U.S. corporations. Under an imputation system, the income of a foreign sub of a U.S. parent corporation would be taxed on a current basis, with a foreign tax credit for foreign taxes paid by the foreign sub. Thus, in the example above of SCI and its foreign sub, FS, the $1 of income of FS would be included in SCI's taxable income and would be subject to a 35% tax, with a tax credit for the 10 cents of foreign tax paid by FS.

One of the principal benefits of an imputation system is that it would preserve the U.S. tax base by significantly reducing, if not completely eliminating, the problem with BEPS in the context of foreign investment by U.S. firms. Also, adoption of an imputation system would generate significant revenue, because as discussed previously, the deferral of foreign income is the largest corporate tax expenditure. The increased revenues from the elimination of deferral could be used to significantly reduce the corporate tax rate for all corporations on a revenue neutral basis.

Although under an imputation system, it would be necessary to retain anti-inversion provisions to address *de jure* inversions like the Pfizer-Allergan transaction, this result is far superior to giving every U.S. firm the potential of becoming a *de facto* inverter, which would happen with the adoption of a territorial system. Also, the lowered corporate tax rate that could accompany adoption of an imputation system would decrease the incentive for entering *de jure* inversions.

Continuing Anti-Inversion Measures. Without respect to whether or not an imputation system is adopted, as long as a territorial system is not adopted, it is wise tax policy to adopt the following policies regarding *de jure* inversions:

---

125. *Hooray for Trump, supra,* and Thompson, "Logic Says No to Options Y, Z, and C, but Yes to Imputation," Tax Notes, May 5, 2014, p. 579 (2014 TNT 87-4); Thompson, "An Imputation System for Taxing Foreign-Source Income," and Tax Notes, Jan. 31, 2011, p. 567 (2011 TNT 21-6); and Thompson, supra note 2.

1. Congress should adopt the anti-inversion provisions suggested by the Obama Administration in the 2015 Green Book, which would significantly narrow the types of transactions that could be treated as *de jure* inversions;

2. The anti-"hop scotch loan" provisions in the 2014 Inversion Notice should be expanded to apply to any foreign acquisition of a U.S. firm, which at the time of the acquisition or at a later time has controlled foreign subs with deferred income; and

3. The Treasury should quickly adopt interest stripping and related anti-BEPS rules that are specifically applicable after the acquisition by a foreign acquirer of a U.S. target, whether or not in an inversion.

C. Potential Impact of Integration of Corporate and Individual Taxes on Inversions

As this book goes to press in March 2016, legislators are considering the possibility of moving to a system of corporate integration, which would integrate the corporate and individual taxes. Integration is briefly discussed in Chapter 13, which deals with policy generally.

In this connection, some tax professionals have been suggesting that adoption of integrated system could be an "antidote" to inversions. *See e.g.*, Mindy Herzfeld, *Could Integration Be the Antidote to Inversions?* 81 Tax Notes Int'l 711 (Feb. 29, 2016). Ms. Herzfeld provides the following basic guidance to the issue:

> In the early 1990s, Treasury issued a report on corporate integration that recommended a dividend exclusion as the preferred method of establishing an integration system in the United States. [Under a dividend exclusion method, the shareholder is not taxed on receipt of the dividend.] ... The American Law Institute, in a 1993 report, also recommended integration, but through a shareholder credit for corporate taxes paid, similar to the method used by Australia.... While other proposals would allocate corporate income and taxes paid to shareholders, similar to how pass-throughs are taxed today, or tax shareholders on a mark-to-market basis, the integration method being considered most seriously today is the dividends paid deduction....

> Integration has been discussed as a possible solution to many distortions created by the corporate income tax system, including unequal tax treatment of debt versus equity and the double taxation of corporate earnings. But depending on how an integration system applied to foreign taxes and foreign investors, it could also provide solutions to many of the most pressing international tax issues, including [inversions].

> Inversions

> Inversions are the most obvious sign of the pressure multinational companies face as a result of the divergence between the U.S. corporate tax rate and cor-

porate tax rates in the rest of the world, and because the United States taxes corporations on their worldwide income....

Could moving to a corporate integration system be the solution? Advocates of integration—whose numbers are increasing—say yes. Much depends on the details of how integration would apply to foreign taxes paid, foreign investors in the United States, and foreign corporations.

While at this time, I have not had the opportunity to carefully study this issue, my tentative analysis leads me to conclude that even though it may be good policy to adopt an integrated corporate-shareholder system, such a system by itself would not likely significantly deter inversions. It should be noted that the integration system discussed by Ms. Herzfeld is different from the imputation system I have proposed above, which, unlike an integration system, would not apply at the ultimate shareholder level.

§ 10.13 Introduction to Section 367(b)

As discussed above, Section 367(a) governs outbound nonrecognition transactions under Sections 332, 351, 354, 356 and 361. These transactions include the transfer of assets by a U.S. person to a foreign corporation in a tax-free incorporation transaction under Section 351, the acquisition by a foreign acquiring corporation (FAC) of the stock of a domestic target in exchange for voting common stock of FAC in a tax-free reorganization under Section 368(a)(1)(B) (*see* above), and the liquidation of a U.S. subsidiary into its foreign parent corporation in a tax-free liquidation under Section 332. Each of these transactions is outbound because stock or assets are being transferred by a U.S. person to a foreign corporation. The general rule for such transactions is that gain is recognized under the gain recognition rule of Section 367(a)(1). Exceptions to the gain recognition rule are provided for, *inter alia,* transfers of property used in the active conduct of a trade or business and certain reorganization transfers in which the transferee shareholders receive a limited interest.

Section 367(b) deals with tax-free exchanges under Sections 332, 351, 354, 355, 356 and 361 in connection with which there is no transfer of property described in Section 367(a)(1). Thus, Section 367(b) reaches non-outbound transfers. Section 367(b)(1) provides that a foreign corporation participating in such an exchange shall be considered to be a corporation, except to the extent provided in regulations. Thus, the general rule of Section 367(b) provides for nonrecognition treatment, whereas the general rule of Section 367(a) provides for recognition. Section 367(b) deals with, for example, the acquisition by a domestic acquiring corporation (DAC) of the stock or assets of a foreign target in an acquisitive reorganization.

Section 367(b)(2) provides that the regulations dealing with the sale or exchange by a U.S. person of stock or securities in a foreign corporation are to include rules regarding:

(A) The circumstances under which (i) gain shall be recognized currently, or amounts included in gross income currently as a dividend, or both, or

(ii) gain or other amounts may be deferred for inclusion in the gross income of a shareholder (or his successor in interest) at a later date, and

(B) The extent to which adjustments shall be made to earnings and profits, basis of stock or securities, and basis of assets.

This section briefly introduces the Section 367(b) regulations. For a more detailed discussion of these rules *see* Thompson, *Mergers, Acquisitions, and Tender Offers, supra* Sec. 1.11 at Sections 22:9–22:14.

§ 10.14 Legislative Background to Section 367(b)

General Explanation of the Tax Reform Act of 1976

263–265 (1976)

Other transfers. — The Act establishes separate treatment under section 367(b) for a second group of transfers which consists of exchanges described in sections 332, 351, 354, 355, 356, and 361 that are not treated as transfers out of the United States [under Section 367(a).] With respect to these other transactions * * * a foreign corporation will not be treated as a corporation to the extent that the Secretary of the Treasury provides in regulations that are necessary or appropriate to prevent the avoidance of Federal income taxes. * * *

Transfers covered in these regulations are to include transfers constituting a repatriation of foreign earnings. Also included are transfers that involve solely foreign corporations and shareholders (and involve a U.S. tax liability of U.S. shareholders only to the extent of determining the amount of any deemed distribution under the subpart F rules). It is anticipated that in this latter group of exchanges, the regulations will not provide for any immediate U.S. tax liability but will maintain the potential tax liability of the U.S. shareholder.

It is intended that the regulations promulgated with respect to this group of transactions will enable taxpayers to determine the extent (if any) to which there will be any immediate U.S. tax liability resulting from any transaction. The Act provides (sec. 367(b)(2)) that the regulations promulgated with respect to this group will include (but shall not be limited to) regulations dealing with the sale or exchange of stock or securities in a foreign corporation by a U.S. person, including regulations providing the circumstances under which (i) gain is recognized currently or is included in income as a dividend, or both, or (ii) gain or other amounts may be deferred for inclusion in the gross income of a shareholder (or his successor in interest) at a later date. The regulations may also provide the extent to which adjustments are to be made to the earnings and profits of any corporation, the basis of any stock or securities, and the basis of any assets.

Examples of transfers into the United States which are to be treated within this group (sec. 367(b)(1)) include: (i) the liquidation of a foreign corporation into a domestic parent; (ii) the acquisition of assets of a foreign corporation by a domestic corporation in a type "C" or "D" reorganization; and (iii) the acquisition of stock in a foreign corporation by a domestic corporation in a type "B" reorganization. With respect to transfers which exclusively involve foreign parties (*i.e.,* where no U.S. persons are parties to the exchange), examples of situations coming within section 367(b)(1) include: (i) the acquisition of stock of a controlled foreign corporation by another foreign corporation; (ii) the acquisition of stock of a controlled foreign corporation by another foreign corporation which is controlled by the same U.S. shareholders as the acquired corporation; (iii) the acquisition of the assets of a controlled foreign corporation by another foreign corporation; (iv) the mere recapitalization of a foreign corporation (type "E" reorganization); and (v) a transfer of property by one controlled foreign corporation to its foreign subsidiary. For these exclusively foreign transactions, it is anticipated that regulations will provide for no immediate U.S. tax liability.

The Secretary's authority to prescribe regulations relating to the sale or exchange of stock in a foreign corporation includes authority to establish rules pursuant to which an exchange of stock in a second tier foreign corporation for other stock in a similar foreign corporation will result in a deferral of the toll charge which otherwise would be imposed based on accumulated earnings and profits. This deferral could be accomplished by designating the stock received as stock with a deferred tax potential in a manner similar to section 1248 without reference to the December 31, 1962, date; the amount includable as foreign source dividend income upon the subsequent disposition of the stock in question results in dividend income only to the extent of the gain realized on the subsequent sale or exchange. In addition, if a second tier foreign subsidiary is liquidated into a first tier foreign subsidiary, the regulations may provide that the tax which would otherwise be due in the absence of a ruling is deferred until the disposition of the stock in the first tier foreign subsidiary.

§ 10.15 Introduction to the General Principles Underlying the Regulations under Section 367(b)

Preamble to Notice of Proposed Rulemaking

(INTL-054-91, INTL-178-86) (August 26, 1991)

The following are the general principles that were taken into account in developing the proposed regulations under section 367(b).

Prevention of the repatriation of earnings or basis without tax. The United States generally does not tax a foreign corporation on its foreign source earnings and profits. If the foreign corporation is owned in whole or in part, directly or indirectly, by a United States person, in certain circumstances the United States does not tax the United States person on the foreign corporation's earnings and profits until those earnings and profits are repatriated (for example, through the payment of dividends) or the United States person disposes of an interest in the foreign corporation. One of the principles of the proposed regulations under section 367(b) is that the repatriation of a United

States person's share of earnings and profits of a foreign corporation through what would otherwise be a nonrecognition transaction (for example, a liquidation of a foreign subsidiary into its domestic parent in a transaction described in section 332, or an acquisition by a domestic corporation of the assets of a foreign corporation in a reorganization described in section 368) should generally cause recognition of income by the foreign corporation's shareholders. A domestic acquirer of the foreign corporation's assets should not succeed to the basis or other tax attributes of the foreign corporation except to the extent that the United States tax jurisdiction has taken account of the United States person's share of the earnings and profits that gave rise to those tax attributes.

Prevention of material distortion in income. Another objective of the regulations under section 367(b) is to prevent the occurrence of a material distortion in income. For this purpose, a material distortion in income includes a distortion relating to the source, character, amount or timing of any item, if such distortion may materially affect the United States tax liability of any person for any year. Thus, for example, the regulations generally operate to prevent the avoidance of provisions such as section 1248 (which requires inclusion of certain gain on the disposition of stock as a dividend). For this purpose, the concept of "avoidance" includes a transaction that results in a material distortion in income even if such distortion was not a purpose of the transaction.

Minimization of complexity. The regulations under section 367(b) also generally attempt to minimize complexity to the extent not inconsistent with principles (1) and (2) described above, in order to reduce taxpayer compliance burdens and the Treasury's administrative costs, and to improve enforcement of the tax laws. * * *

Permissibility of deferral. To the extent not inconsistent with principles (1), (2) and (3) described above, the regulations under section 367(b) generally do not operate to accelerate the recognition of income that is realized but which would not otherwise be recognized by reason of a nonrecognition provision of the Internal Revenue Code.

§ 10.16 Section 355 Spin-Offs by Domestic Corporations to Foreign Shareholders

A. In General

As discussed in Chapter 9, in a (D) reorganization, a corporation (the "distributing corporation") transfers all or part of its assets to another corporation (the "controlled corporation"), and immediately after the transfer, the distributing corporation or its shareholders or a combination thereof are in control of the controlled corporation. The distribution by the distributing corporation to its shareholders of stock or securities of the controlled corporation must qualify under Section 354, 355 or 356. (D) reorganizations can be either nondivisive or divisive. Section 354(b) deals with the nondivisive (D).

Section 355 encompasses divisive (D) reorganizations in which there is a breakup of a corporation into two or more corporations. Divisive (D) reorganizations generally fall into three broad categories: spin-offs, split-offs and split-ups. In a spin-off, a distributing corporation transfers part of its assets to a controlled corporation and then distributes to its shareholders the stock of the controlled corporation in a pro rata distribution. Thus, the shareholders continue their same pro rata interest but in two corporations rather than one. In a split-off, stock of the distributing corporation is redeemed in exchange for stock of the controlled corporation. In the split-up, the distributing corporation contributes its assets to two or more controlled corporations and then liquidates, distributing the stock to its shareholders. Section 355 applies not only to (D) reorganizations; it also applies to distributions of the stock of existing subsidiaries. In order for a transaction to fit within Section 355, the following requirements must be satisfied:

- The distributing corporation must distribute to its shareholders or security holders "solely" stock or securities of the controlled corporation (*see* §§ 355(a)(1)(A) and 355(a)(2)); the distribution need not be pro rata. If boot is distributed, Section 356 will apply (*see* §§ 356(a) and (b));

- The transaction must not be a "device" for the distribution of E & P (*see* § 355(a)(1)(B));

- A separate active trade or business that has been conducted for at least five years must continue to be conducted after the distribution by each of the distributing and controlled corporations (*see* §§ 355(a)(1)(C) and (b)); and

- The distributing corporation must distribute all of the stock or securities of the controlled corporation or an amount of stock of the controlled corporation amounting to control, provided that in the latter case it is established that the retention of stock or securities of the controlled corporation is not for tax avoidance purposes (*see* § 355(a)(1)(D.)).

For transactions that fall within Section 355, the shareholders or security holders of the distributing corporation receive nonrecognition treatment on receipt of the stock or securities of the controlled corporation. *See* § 355(a). Thus, Section 355 is analogous to Section 354, which gives nonrecognition treatment for reorganizations other than the divisive (D). In the event boot is distributed in a Section 355 transaction, gain is recognized to the extent of the boot. *See* § 356(a)(1). The gain recognized is generally treated as a dividend. *See* §§ 356(a)(2) and (b).

The distributing corporation generally has tax-free treatment on the distribution. *See* § 355(c) with respect to distributions of preexisting subs and § 361(c) with respect to the distribution of the stock of subs formed in (D) reorganizations.

This section addresses only spinoffs by domestic corporations of the stock of a domestic sub to both domestic and foreign shareholders. It does not address spinoffs by domestic corporations of stock of foreign subs or spinoffs by foreign corporations. For a more detailed discussion of the impact of Section 367 on cross-border spinoffs *see* Thompson, *Mergers, Acquisitions, and Tender Offers, supra* Sec. 1.11 at Section 22:15.

B. Spin-Off by Domestic Distributing Corporation of a Domestic Sub to both Domestic and Foreign Shareholders

1. Introduction

Section 367(e)(1) provides that if a domestic parent corporation (DP) distributes the stock of a controlled corporation (CC), whether domestic or foreign, to a foreign shareholder of DP, then to the extent provided in regulations, gain is recognized by DP "under principles similar to the principles of this section." The purpose of Section 367(e)(1) is to prevent the removal of the stock of CC out of the hands of a taxpayer that is subject to the U.S. taxing jurisdiction. The preamble to the regulations under Section 367(e)(1) is set out below.

2. Final Regulations on Spin-Offs under Section 367(e)(1)

Preamble to Treasury Decision 8834

August 9, 1999

Explanation of Revisions and Summary of Comments *Overview.* These final regulations address the tax consequences of a distribution by a domestic corporation of its subsidiary's stock to foreign shareholders in a transaction described in section 355 (outbound section 355 distribution). * * *

Details of Provisions. *Outbound Section 355 Distributions.* The final regulations * * * do not require gain recognition on an outbound section 355 distribution of the stock or securities of a domestic corporation. [§ 1.367(e)-1(c)]

§ 10.17 Impact of Sections 1248(a) and (f) on Spinoffs by Domestic Corporations of CFCs

If gain is recognized by a distributing corporation under the above rules under Section 367, then the gain may be treated as a dividend under Section 1248 and thereby qualify for the analogue to the Section 902 indirect foreign tax credit under the Section 1248 regulations.

In addition to the above rules under Section 367, Section 1248(f) applies to a domestic corporation that distributes in a Section 355 distribution (as well as certain other tax-free distributions) stock of a CFC. In such case, the distributing domestic corporation is required to include in its income as a dividend its ratable share of the CFC's E&P that was accumulated during the period the distributing corporation was a 10% or greater shareholder of the CFC. The amount of the dividend cannot exceed the gain realized on the distribution of the stock. There is an exception in Section 1248(f)(2) for certain distributions to corporate shareholders. Thus, the gain recognition rules under Section 367 discussed above apply to the gain not recognized as a dividend under Section 1248(f).

Section 1248 has no impact on the distributee shareholders.

Chapter 11

Use of Partnerships, Including LLCs, and S Corporations in Mergers and Acquisitions

§ 11.1 Scope

This chapter briefly introduces some of the issues that can arise when (1) a partnership, or a limited liability company (LLC) that is treated as a partnership for Federal income tax purposes, is the acquisition vehicle in a taxable acquisition of the stock or assets of a C corporation, and (2) an S corporation either acquires a C corporation or is acquired by a C corporation in a taxable or tax-free transaction. As pointed out in Sec. 1.3.B., partnerships are not subject to taxation, and as pointed out in Sec. 1.3.C., an S corporation is not subject to taxation, except in certain cases such as when it was previously a C corporation and had appreciated property at the time of conversion to S status. Secs. 1.3.B. and C. should be reviewed before proceeding with the materials in this chapter. This chapter does not present a comprehensive treatment of the taxation of partnerships and S corporations. For a casebook treatment (1) of partnerships and S corporations, *see Taxation of Business Entities*, *supra* Sec. 1.12, and for a textual treatment of partnerships *see* the current edition of McKee, Nelson, and Whitmire, *Federal Taxation of Partnerships and Partners*, and (2) of S corporations *see* Bittker and Eustice, *Corporations*, *supra*, Sec. 1.12.

Sec. 11.2 deals with the taxable acquisition of a C corporation's assets by a partnership, and Sec. 11.3 addresses the taxable acquisition of a C corporation's stock by a partnership. A partnership may not participate in a corporate reorganization.

Sec. 11.4 first discusses several provisions of subchapter S that are particularly relevant to mergers and acquisitions involving S corporations. The balance of the chapter then looks at various types of stock or asset acquisitions in which an S corporation acquires a C corporation or a C corporation acquires an S corporation.

In addressing taxable acquisitions involving S corporations, Sec. 11.5 deals with the taxable acquisition by an S corporation of the assets of a C corporation, and Sec. 11.6 addresses the taxable acquisition by an S corporation of the stock of a C corporation. Sec. 11.7 deals with the taxable acquisition by a C corporation of the assets of an S corporation. Sec. 11.8 examines the taxable acquisition by a C corporation of the stock of an S corporation and, thus, considers the use of § 338(h)(10) in an acquisition of an S corporation.

In addressing tax-free reorganizations involving S corporations, Sec. 11.9 examines the tax-free acquisition by an S corporation of the assets of a C corporation in connection with the following asset reorganizations addressed in Chapter 7: the (A), the (C), the triangular (C), and the forward subsidiary merger under § 368(a)(2)(D). Sec. 11.10 looks at the tax-free acquisition by an S corporation of the stock of a C corporation in connection with the following stock reorganizations examined in Chapter 8: the (B), the triangular (B), and the reverse subsidiary merger under § 368(a)(2)(E). Sec. 11.11 considers the tax-free acquisition by a C corporation of the assets of an S corporation, and Sec. 11.12 examines the tax-free acquisition by a C corporation of the stock of an S corporation. Finally, Sec. 11.13 deals with spin-offs involving S corporations.

Various considerations that can arise in the taxable disposition of the stock or assets of an S corporation are considered in Chapter 19 of *Taxation of Business Entities*, *supra* Sec. 1.12.

For a more detailed discussion of the issues discussed in this chapter, see Ginsburg and Levin, *Mergers*, *supra* Sec. 1.12. *See also* the most recent edition of PLI, *Tax Strategies*, *supra* Sec. 1.12 and Thompson, *Mergers, Acquisitions, and Tender Offers, supra* Sec. 1.11 at Chapter 9.

§ 11.2 Taxable Acquisition by Partnership of a C Corporation's Assets

A. Treatment of the C Corporation

Javaras, Acquisition Techniques and Financing Considerations for Partnerships and S Corporations

Taxes 741, 756 (OCTOBER, 1988), with permission

If a partnership acquires the assets of a corporation in a taxable transaction, the target corporation will pay a tax on the gain in the assets (the *General Utilities* tax on the assets sold). [*See* Chapter 2.] * * *

The target corporation's tax attributes, including net operating losses, could be used to offset the gain. The shareholders of the target would be taxed on a liquidation or other distribution with respect to their shares. [§ 331]

If the purchase is for notes, the corporate tax may be deferred under the installment method, subject to the exceptions [generally applicable under the installment sale provisions]. [*See* Chapter 2.] * * *

If the corporation liquidates, a tax will be triggered on any deferred gain at the corporate level. [§ 453B] If the corporation liquidates promptly (i.e., within 12 months of the sale) and the shareholders would have been entitled to use the installment method on a sale of their stock, they should be able to use the installment method to report gain recognized on the liquidation under Section 453(h).

Interest income earned on the installment note could make the target corporation a personal holding company, if the stock ownership requirements were met. * * *

B. Treatment of the Partnership

The partnership takes a fair market value basis for the acquired assets and must allocate the purchase price among the assets in accordance with § 1060. *See* Sec. 4.3.D. If all of the partners are individuals there will be only one level of tax on the income generated by the assets. Any losses will flow through to the partners subject to limitation under §§ 704(d), 465 and 469. *See* Chapter 14 of *Taxation of Business Entities, supra* Sec. 1.12. Consequently, it could be beneficial to use a partnership (or an S corporation) in an asset acquisition. Under § 752, partnership liabilities are included in the bases of the partners's interests, thereby allowing them to take deductions in excess of their actual contributions to the partnership. This is not the case with an S corporation.

§ 11.3 Taxable Acquisition by Partnership of C Corporation's Stock

Javaras, Acquisition Techniques and Financing Considerations for Partnerships and S Corporations

Taxes 771, 756–757 (October 1988), with permission

If the partnership acquires the stock of a corporation in a taxable transaction, the corporation's shareholders would be taxed on the sale of their stock. [T]he installment method might apply to defer tax in the case of a sale for notes.

If the partnership does not liquidate the corporation, the income of the corporation would be subject to the double tax and any losses would be trapped in the corporation. The corporation would retain its basis in its assets and there would be no immediate corporate-level tax on any gain or recapture. Interest incurred to purchase the corporation's stock might be investment interest, the deduction of which would be limited by Section 163(d).

If the partnership buys the stock of the corporation directly, it would not be entitled to make a Section 338 election or a Section 338(h)(10) election if one were desirable. It is possible that if the purchased corporation was a member of an affiliated group, an election could be made by the seller to treat the transaction as an asset sale under Section 336(e). [This could happen, however, only under regulations that have not been issued.] [*See* Chapter 2.]

Although the scope of Section 336(e) is not clear, it appears that a step-up in basis should be available to the acquiring partnership. In some cases the seller's gain on its stock in the target corporation may be approximately the same as its gain would be on an asset sale. In such case, the stepped-up basis would be achieved at little or no cost. The partnership could then liquidate the target corporation without tax cost (if it did so soon after the purchase of the stock) since it should essentially have a fair market value basis in the stock and the corporation should have a fair market value basis in its assets.

The partnership could form a corporation (Newco) to be used to make the purchase of the target stock if an election under Section 338 is desirable. In order for the Section 338 election to work, it would be necessary to keep Newco in existence for a certain amount of time. An immediate liquidation of Newco could cause the corporate purchaser to be disregarded. However, the up-front cost of a section 338 election will generally exceed the benefits of any step-up flowing therefrom. A step-up under Section 338 may be desirable in some cases. * * * For example, when the target corporation has NOLs; or when it is possible to make a Section 338(h)(10) election.

The partnership could liquidate the corporation, at the cost of recognizing gain at the corporate level. [*See* § 336 and Chapter 2.] The cost of the liquidation would be similar to the cost of a regular Section 338 election. The partnership's exchange of its stock in the target would be taxable [under § 331], but if the liquidation were done soon after the acquisition, there would presumably be little gain. A liquidation would remove the assets from corporate solution.

Note that Section 279 [*see* Sec. 5.3.A.2] does not generally apply to acquisitions made by partnerships. However, the deductibility of interest on partnership debt could be affected by the passive loss rules or the investment interest rules.

Note

There generally will not be a tax reason for using a partnership to acquire a corporation's stock because the earnings of the corporation will continue to be subject to a double tax. On the other hand, there may be a compelling tax reason for using a partnership to acquire a target's assets because on a going forward basis, the double tax can be avoided.

§ 11.4 Introduction to Subchapter S and Elaboration on Provisions of Particular Significance in Mergers and Acquisitions

A. Introduction

This section introduces the provisions of subchapter S and then discusses in some detail certain provisions that are of particular importance in mergers and acquisitions involving S corporations. Subsequent sections of this chapter refer to, and build on, the concepts discussed in this section. Sec. 11.4.B. introduces the basic administrative provisions relating to such issues as the qualifications for electing to be an S corporation, and the effect of an election. Sec. 11.4.C. briefly reviews the provisions that govern the tax treatment of S corporations.

B. The Basic Administrative Provisions: §§ 1361, 1362 and 1363

Section 1361 sets out the requirements that must be satisfied to permit a corporation to elect to operate as an S corporation, and these requirements are examined further in this section. Section 1362 sets out the procedures for electing to be an S corporation, and § 1362(e), which is examined below in Sec. 11.4.F., sets out rules regarding the termination of an S election, such as when the stock of an S corporation is acquired by a C corporation.

Under § 1363(a), which sets out the effect of an S election, an S corporation is not subject to income tax except as otherwise provided in the Code. The two exceptions to this rule are (1) the tax under § 1375 on passive income on certain S corporations that were previously C corporations, and (2) the tax under § 1374 on built-in gains, which applies to certain S corporations that were previously C corporations or that acquired assets of a C corporation in a carryover basis transaction, such as an (A) reorganization. The § 1374 tax on built-in-gains is designed to protect the repeal of the *General Utilities* doctrine through transactions that move built-in-gain assets held by a C corporation to an S corporation. This tax can be of significant importance in certain acquisitions involving S corporations, and for that reason is examined in greater detail in Sec. 11.4.G. below.

Section 1361(b) sets out six requirements that a corporation must satisfy to be considered a "small business corporation" and, therefore, eligible to elect, under § 1362, to be an S corporation.

(1) The corporation must be a domestic (*i.e.,* U.S.) corporation. *See* § 1361(b)(1). Thus, a foreign corporation cannot qualify as an S corporation, but there is no prohibition against an S corporation conducting foreign operations. Also, there is no size limitation on an S corporation.

(2) Under § 1361(b)(1), the corporation cannot be an "ineligible corporation," which § 1361(b)(2) defines to include, for example, an insurance company. As noted below in Sec. 11.4.D., as a result of the 1996 Act, S corporations can own stock of subsidiaries, and this liberalization can be important in planning acquisition transactions.

(3) The corporation can have no more than 75 shareholders. *See* § 1361(b)(1)(A). Thus, for example, if an S corporation makes an acquisition for its stock, it must be sure that this 75 shareholder limitation is not exceeded by the issuance. Congress is considering increasing the limit to 100 shareholders.

(4) All shareholders must be individuals, except for certain types of estates, trusts and tax exempt entities. *See* § 1361(b)(1)(B). Thus, if an S corporation issues its stock in an acquisition, it will have to ensure that all of the target's shareholders are individuals or qualifying entities.

(5) No shareholder can be a nonresident alien. *See* § 1361(b)(1)(C). Thus, for example, if an S corporation issues its stock in an acquisition, it will have to ensure that none of the target's shareholders is a nonresident alien.

(6) The corporation can have only one class of stock. *See* § 1361(b)(1)(D). Thus, for example, an S corporation can only issue common stock in an acquisition; however, nonvoting stock can be issued without violating this requirement. *See* § 1361(c)(4).

C. Introduction to Provisions Governing Operations

The starting point for determining the tax consequences of the operations of an S corporation is § 1366, which in general provides that all income, gain, loss, and credit (income items) of an S corporation passes through to the shareholders. Section 1377(a), requires that the income items be allocated among the shareholders on a pro-rata basis in accordance with their ownership percentages on each day during the taxable year. A shareholder of an S corporation may deduct losses only to the extent of the basis of the shareholder's stock and debt in the corporation. *See* § 1366(d). Unlike the rule for partnerships, debt incurred by the corporation is not included in the shareholder's basis for her shares. Losses also may be limited by the "at risk" requirements of § 465 and the passive loss requirements of § 469.

The shareholder increases the basis for her shares by her allocable share of income and gain, and decreases basis by her allocable share of losses. *See* § 1367. Distributions of cash or property by an S corporation are generally tax-free to the shareholder if (1) the distributions come out of income accumulated while the corporation was an S corporation, and (2) the shareholder reduces the basis of her shares by the amount of the distribution. *See* § 1368. The treatment of other distributions under § 1368 is beyond the scope of this chapter.

Section 1371(a), which is discussed further below in Sec. 11.4.E., provides that the rules of subchapter C apply to an S corporation except to the extent otherwise provided in subchapter S. As a consequence, the gain recognition rule for current distributions in § 311(b) and for liquidating distributions in § 336 applies to S corporations. Thus, if an S corporation distributes appreciated property, the corporation recognizes gain and such gain passes through to the shareholders.

D. S Corporations Permitted to Hold Subsidiaries: Effect of the Small Business Job Protection Act of 1996

Joint Committee on Taxation, General Explanation of Tax Legislation Enacted in the 104th Congress

(JCS-12-96) (December 18, 1996)

Prior Law A small business corporation could not be a member of an affiliated group of corporations (other than by reason of ownership in certain inactive corporations). Thus, an S corporation could not own 80 percent or more of the stock of another corporation (whether an S corporation or a C corporation).

In addition, a small business corporation could not have as a shareholder another corporation (whether an S corporation or a C corporation).

Reasons for Change The Congress understood that there were situations where taxpayers wished to separate different trades or businesses in different corporate entities. The Congress believed that, in such situations, shareholders should be allowed to arrange these separate corporate entities under parent-subsidiary arrangements as well as brother-sister arrangements.

Explanation of Provision *C corporation subsidiaries* An S corporation is allowed to own 80 percent or more of the stock of a C corporation. [§ 1361(b)] The C corporation subsidiary can elect to join in the filing of a consolidated return with its affiliated C corporations. An S corporation is not allowed to join in such election. [§ 1504(b)(8)] Dividends received by an S corporation from a C corporation in which the S corporation has an 80 percent or greater ownership stake are not treated as passive investment income for purposes of sections 1362 and 1375 to the extent the dividends are attributable to the earnings and profits of the C corporation derived from the active conduct of a trade or business. [§ 1362(d)(3)(E)]

S corporation subsidiaries In addition, an S corporation is allowed to own a qualified subchapter S subsidiary. [§ 1361(b)(3)] The term "qualified subchapter S subsidiary" means a domestic corporation that is not an ineligible corporation (i.e., a corporation that would be eligible to be an S corporation if the stock of the corporation were held directly by the shareholders of its parent S corporation) if (1) 100 percent of the stock of the subsidiary is held by its S corporation parent and (2) the parent elects to treat the subsidiary as a qualified subchapter S subsidiary. For this purpose, the term "qualified subchapter S subsidiary" is intended to include a subsidiary, the stock of which is held by a qualified subchapter S subsidiary (i.e., the election is available to chains of qualified corporations as well as brother-sister subsidiaries of an S corporation). The election need not be made for all subsidiaries eligible for treatment as qualified subchapter S subsidiaries.

If a subsidiary ceases to be a qualified subchapter S subsidiary (either because the subsidiary fails to qualify or the parent revokes the election) another such election (or a subchapter S election) may not be made for the subsidiary by the parent (or its shareholders) for five years without the consent of the Secretary of the Treasury. * * *

Under the election, the qualified subchapter S subsidiary is not treated as a separate corporation and all the assets, liabilities, and items of income, deduction, loss, and credit of the subsidiary are treated as the assets, liabilities, and items of income, deduction, loss, and credit of the parent S corporation. Thus, transactions between the S corporation parent and qualified subchapter S subsidiary are not taken into account and items of the subsidiary (including accumulated earnings and profits, passive investment income, built-in gains, etc.) are considered to be items of the parent. In addition, if a subsidiary ceases to be a qualified subchapter S subsidiary (e.g., fails to meet the wholly-owned requirement), the subsidiary will be treated as a new corporation acquiring all of its assets (and assuming all of its liabilities) immediately before such cessation from the parent S corporation in exchange for its stock.

Under the Small Business Act, if an election is made to treat an existing corporation (whether or not its stock was acquired from another person or previously held by the S corporation) as a qualified subchapter S subsidiary, the subsidiary will be deemed to have liquidated under sections 332 and 337 immediately before the election is effective. [*See* Chapter 2.] The built-in gains tax under section 1374 * * * may apply where the subsidiary was previously a C corporation. [*See* Sec. 11.4.F.] Where the stock of the subsidiary was acquired by the S corporation in a qualified stock purchase, an election under section 338 with respect to the subsidiary may be made. [*See* Sec. 11.6.] * * *

E. Treatment of S Corporations under Subchapter C: Impact of the Small Business Job Protection Act of 1996

Joint Committee on Taxation, General Explanation of Tax Legislation Enacted in the 104th Congress
(JCS-12-96) pp. 124–125 (December 18, 1996)

Present And Prior Law * * * [U]nder prior law, an S corporation in its capacity as a shareholder of another corporation was treated as an individual for purposes of subchapter C (sec. § 1371(a)(2)). In 1988, the IRS took the position that this rule prevents the tax-free liquidation of a C corporation into an S corporation because a C corporation cannot liquidate tax-free when owned by an individual shareholder. In 1992, the IRS reversed its position, stating that the prior ruling was incorrect.

Reasons For Change The Congress wished to clarify that the position taken by the IRS in 1992 that allows the tax-free liquidation of a C corporation into an S corporation represented the proper policy.

Explanation Of Provision The Small Business Act repeals the rule that treats an S corporation in its capacity as a shareholder of another corporation as an individual. [§ 1371(a)] Thus, the provision clarifies that the liquidation of a C corporation into an S corporation will be governed by the generally applicable subchapter C rules, including the provisions of sections 332 and 337 allowing the tax-free liquidation of a corporation into its parent corporation. [*See* Chapter 2.] Following a tax-free liquidation, the built-in gains of the liquidating corporation may later be subject to tax under section 1374 upon a subsequent disposition. [*See* Sec. 11.4.F.] An S corporation also will be eligible to make a section 338 election (assuming all the requirements are otherwise met), resulting in immediate recognition of all the acquired C corporation's gains and losses (and the resulting imposition of a tax). [*See* Sec. 11.6.]

The repeal of this rule does not change the general rule governing the computation of income of an S corporation. For example, it does not allow an S corporation, or its shareholders, to claim a dividends received deduction with respect to dividends received by the S corporation. * * *

F. Rules Regarding Termination of S Status

1. The Subchapter S Revision Act of 1982

See §§ 1362(d) and (e).

Senate Finance Report on the Subchapter S Revision Act of 1982

Termination Of Election (Secs. 1362(d), (e), and (g)) Generally, specific events during the taxable year which cause a corporation to fail to meet the definition of a small business corporation will result in a termination of the election as of the date on which the event occurred (rather than as of the first day of the taxable year, as under present law). [*See* § 1362(d)(2).] The events causing disqualification will be: (1) exceeding the maximum allowable number of shareholders; (2) transfer of stock to a corporation, partnership, ineligible trust, or nonresident alien; [and] (3) the creation of a class of stock other than the voting and nonvoting common stock allowed. * * *

The day before the day on which the terminating event occurs will be treated as the last day of a short subchapter S taxable year, and the day on which the terminating event occurs will be treated as the first day of a short regular (i.e., subchapter C) taxable year. [*See* § 1362(e)(1).] There will be no requirement that the books of a corporation be closed as of the termination date. Instead the corporation will allocate the income or loss for the entire year (i.e., both short years) on a proration basis. [*See* § 1362(e)(2).]

The corporation can elect, with the consent of all persons who were shareholders at any time during the year, to report the taxable income or loss on each return (subchapter S and subchapter C) on the basis of income or loss shown on the corporation's permanent records (including work papers). [*See* § 1362(e)(3).] Under this method, items will be attributed to the short subchapter S and subchapter C years according to the time they were incurred or realized, as reflected in such records. [The Tax Reform Act of 1984 amends this provision to provide that the election to close the books may be made if all the shareholders owning stock during the short S year and all shareholders owning stock on the first day of the short C year consent.]

The short subchapter S and subchapter C taxable years will be treated as one year for purposes of carrying over previous subchapter C losses. [*See* § 1362(e)(6)(A).] The income allocated to the subchapter C taxable year will be subject to annualization for purposes of applying the corporate rate brackets. [*See* § 1362(e)(5).] The return for the short subchapter S year will be due on the same date as the return for the short subchapter C year is due. [*See* § 1362(e)(6)(B).] * * *

2. Modification of Termination Provisions: Impact of Small Business Job Protection Act of 1996

Joint Committee on Taxation, General Explanation of Tax Legislation Enacted in the 104th Congress

(JCS-12-96) pp. 116–119, 131–132 (December 18, 1996)

Agreement To Terminate Year

Present And Prior Law In general, each item of S corporation income, deduction and loss is allocated to shareholders on a per-share, per-day basis. [§ 1377(a)(1)] However, if any shareholder terminated his or her interest in an S corporation during a taxable year, the S corporation, with the consent of all its shareholders, could elect to allocate S corporation items by closing its books as of the date of such termination rather than applying the per-share, per-day rule. [§ 1377(a)(2).]

Reasons For Change The Congress believed that the election to close the books of an S corporation did not need the consent of shareholders whose tax liability is unaffected by the election.

Explanation Of Provision The Small Business Act provides that, under regulations to be prescribed by the Secretary of the Treasury, the election to close the books of the S corporation upon the termination of a shareholder's interest is made by all affected shareholders and the corporation, rather than by all shareholders. [§ 1377(a)(2)] The closing of the books applies only to the affected shareholders. [§ 1377(a)(2)] For this purpose, "affected shareholders" means any shareholder whose interest is terminated and all shareholders to whom such shareholder has transferred shares during the year. If a shareholder transferred shares to the corporation, "affected shareholders" includes all persons who were shareholders during the year. [§ 1377(a)(2)(B)]

3. Final Regulations under § 1377

Preamble to Treasury Decision 8696

(December 20, 1996)

When a post-termination transition period arises [Under § 1371(e), a former S corporation can make a tax-free distribution of its prior undistributed S earnings during the post-termination transition period. The post-termination transition period is defined in § 1377(b) to generally mean the one-year period after the termination of the S election.] The proposed regulations provide that a post-termination transition period (PTTP) arises following the termination under section 1362(d) of a corporation's S election. By example, the proposed regulations state that a PTTP arises when a C corporation acquires the assets of an S corporation in a transaction to which section 381(a) (2) applies. Several commentators requested clarification concerning whether the example results in a termination under section 1362(d) of the corporation's election to be an S corporation or merely the cessation of the S corporation's taxable year. The final regulations clarify that, pursuant to the rule in section 1377(b)(1), a PTTP arises the day after the last day that an S corporation was in existence if a C corporation acquires the assets of an S corporation in a transaction to which section 381(a)(2) applies. * * *

G. Section 1374 Built in Gains Tax

1. Introduction and Purpose of § 1374

Announcement 86-128

1986-51 I.R.B. 22 (Dec. 22, 1986)

The Tax Reform Act of 1986 (the Act) modifies the treatment of S corporations that were formerly C corporations by imposing a corporate-level tax under section 1374 of the Internal Revenue Code on certain "built-in" gains (gains arising prior to the conversion to S corporation status) that are recognized by the corporation (built-in gain tax). This built-in gain tax is applicable to S corporations for taxable years beginning after December 31, 1986, but only if the S election for the corporation is made after December 31, 1986. * * * [The Protecting Americans from Tax Hikes Act of 2015 reduced the recognition period from 10 years to 5 years.] The built-in gain tax is intended both to complement the amendments to the Code made by the Act that repeal the *General Utilities* doctrine and to prevent the circumvention of the purposes of those amendments.

2. Legislative History of § 1374

a. The Tax Reform Act of 1986

See § 1374.

General Explanation of the Tax Reform Act of 1986

344–345 (1986)

The Act modifies the treatment of an S corporation that was formerly a C corporation. A corporate-level tax is imposed on any gain that arose prior to the conversion ("built-in" gain) and is recognized by the S corporation, through sale, distribution or other disposition within ten years after the date on which the S election took effect. [*See* §§ 1374(a) and (d)(7).] The total amount of gain that must be recognized by the corporation, however, is limited to the aggregate net built-in gain of the corporation at the time of conversion to S corporation status. [*See* §§ 1374(c)(2) and (d)(1).] Congress expected that the Treasury Department could prevent avoidance of the built-in gain rule by contributions of built-in loss property prior to the conversion for the purpose of reducing the net built-in gain. [*See* § 1374(e).]

Gains on sales or distributions of assets by the S corporation are presumed to be built-in gains, except to the extent the taxpayer establishes that the appreciation accrued after the conversion, such as where the asset was acquired by the corporation in a taxable acquisition after the conversion. [*See* § 1374(d)(3).] Built-in gains are taxed at the maximum corporate rate applicable to the particular type of income (i.e., the maximum rate on ordinary income under section 11 or, if applicable, the alternative rate on capital gain income under section 1201) for the year in which the disposition occurs. [*See* § 1374(b)(1).] The corporation may take into account all of its subchapter C tax attributes in computing the amount of the tax on recognized built-in gains. [*See* § 1374(b)(2).] Thus, for example, it may use unexpired net operating losses, capital loss carryovers, and similar items to offset the gain or the resulting tax.

b. The Technical and Miscellaneous Revenue Act of 1988

House Report to the Technical and Miscellaneous Revenue Act of 1988

62–64 (1988)

Explanation Of Provision * * * The bill clarifies that the built-in gain provision applies not only when a C corporation converts to S status but also in any case in which an S corporation acquires an asset and the basis of such asset in the hands of the S corporation is determined (in whole or in part) by reference to the basis of such asset (or any other property) in the hands of the C corporation. [*See* § 1374(d)(8).] In such cases, each acquisition of assets from a C corporation is subject to a separate determination of the amount of net built-in gain, and is subject to the provision for a separate [5]-year recognition period. The bill clarifies that the Treasury Department has authority to prescribe regulations providing for the appropriate treatment of successor corporations—for example, in situations in which an S corporation engages in a transaction that results in carryover basis of assets to a successor corporation pursuant to subchapter C of the Code. [*See* § 1374(c).] * * *

3. Treatment of Installment Sales under § 1374

Notice 90-27

1990-1 C.B. 336

* * * Section 1374(e) of the Code provides that regulations shall be issued as may be necessary to carry out the purposes of section 1374. In addition, section 337(d), in part, provides that regulations shall be issued as may be necessary or appropriate to carry out the purposes of the amendments under the Act made to section 1374, including regulations to ensure that such purposes not be circumvented through the use of any provision of law or regulation. The Service has determined that the purposes underlying the repeal of the *General Utilities* doctrine and the related amendments to section 1374 would fail to be carried out in certain cases if an S corporation disposes of an asset either prior to or during the recognition period in an installment sale reported under the installment method.

Accordingly, the Service will issue regulations governing the treatment of installment sales under section 1374 of the Code, including regulations providing that, in certain cases, section 1374 will continue to apply to income recognized under the installment method during a taxable year ending after the expiration of the recognition period. Under the regulations, if a taxpayer sells an asset either prior to or during the recognition period and recognizes income (either during or after the recognition period) from the sale under the installment method, the income will, when recognized, be taxed under section 1374 to the extent it would have been so taxed in prior taxable years if the selling corporation had made the election under section 453(d) not to report the income under the installment method. * * *

4. Final Regulations under § 1374 Relating to Acquisition by S Corporation of Assets of a C Corporation in a Reorganization

Preamble to Final Regulations under § 1374, Treasury Decision 8579

(DEC 27, 1994)

* * * *Section 1374(d)(8) Transactions* Section 1374(d)(8) imposes a section 1374 tax if an S corporation acquires assets in a transaction where the S corporation's basis in the assets is determined by reference to their basis in the hands of a C corporation (a section 1374(d)(8) transaction) and, thereafter, the S corporation disposes of the assets. The proposed regulations provide that a separate determination of tax under section 1374 must be made for the assets acquired in each section 1374(d)(8) transaction. Thus, an S corporation's section 1374 attributes held on the day it became an S corporation may only be used to reduce a section 1374 tax imposed on dispositions of assets the S corporation held on that day. Similarly, section 1374 attributes acquired by an S corporation in a section 1374(d)(8) transaction may only be used to reduce a section 1374 tax imposed on dispositions of assets the S corporation acquired in the same transaction.

Commentators argue that restrictions on the use of section 1374 attributes acquired by an S corporation in a section 1374(d)(8) transaction should not be greater than the restrictions that would apply if the attributes were acquired by a C corporation in a similar transaction. For example, commentators contend that an S corporation's net operating loss carryforwards when it changed from C to S status should be allowed to reduce a section 1374 tax imposed on assets the S corporation acquires in a section 1374(d)(8) transaction, subject to all statutory limits on their use including the anti-trafficking rules of sections 382, 383, and 384.

The final regulations retain the rules in the proposed regulations. Section 1374(d)(8) imposes a section 1374 tax on the "net recognized built-in gain attributable to" the assets acquired in a particular transaction. The legislative history under section 1374 states that "each acquisition of assets from a C corporation is subject to a separate determination of the amount of net built-in gain * * *." H.R. Rep. No. 795, 100th Cong., 2d Sess. 63 (1988).

5. Reduction of Income by Amount of § 1374 Tax

Under § 1366(f)(2), any tax imposed by § 1374 is treated as a deductible loss sustained by the S corporation. Thus, only the income of the corporation after deduction of the § 1374 tax is passed through to shareholders under § 1366(a).

§ 11.5 Taxable Acquisition by an S Corporation of the Assets of a C Corporation

In this transaction an S corporation acquires the assets of a C corporation and the C corporation is liquidated, distributing the consideration to its shareholders. The tax treatment to the C corporation and its shareholders is the same as the treatment in any taxable asset acquisition. *See* Chapter 4. Basically, the corporation has taxable gain or loss, and the shareholders have taxable gain or loss, subject to the possibility of receiving installment sale treatment under § 453(h).

The tax treatment of the actual acquisition to the acquiring S corporation is essentially the same as the tax consequences to an acquiring C corporation. *See* Chapter 4. Basically, the S corporation (1) takes a cost basis for the assets acquired, (2) allocates the purchase price among the assets acquired under the rules of § 1060, and (3) amortizes the cost of goodwill and other intangibles over a period of 15 years under § 197.

On a going forward basis, the income, gain, or loss from operating the acquired assets will pass through to the shareholders of the S corporation as demonstrated in Sec. 1.3.C. Any debt financing incurred or assumed by the S corporation generally will not be included in the bases of the shareholders' shares and, therefore, the shareholders' deductions may be limited. This issue, which is beyond the scope of this chapter, is explored in Chapter 15 of *Taxation of Business Entities, supra*, Sec. 1.12. Since the assets are acquired in a taxable acquisition, there is no issue under the built-in-gain provision. *See* § 1374 and Sec. 11.4.G.

It is important to ensure that the acquisition does not result in the loss of S status for the acquiring S corporation. This could happen, for example, if the S corporation issued its stock or some other type of equity interest as part of the consideration and thus violated the one class of stock rule or the individual shareholder rule. As long as the acquisition consideration is cash or *bona fide* debt instruments, the acquiring corporation's S status should not be jeopardized. In issuing its debt, the S corporation may want to take advantage of the straight debt safe harbor under § 1361(c)(5), pursuant to which debt is treated as debt and not equity. This straight debt issue, which is beyond the scope of this chapter, is explored in Chapter 6 of *Taxation of Business Entities, supra*, Sec. 1.12.

§ 11.6 Taxable Acquisition by an S Corporation of the Stock of a C Corporation

In this transaction an S corporation acquires in a taxable acquisition the stock of a C corporation. The transaction may be effectuated in a taxable reverse subsidiary merger, which is discussed in Chapter 5. This section focuses on an acquisition of all of the stock of a C corporation in one transaction. Prior to the 1996 Act an S corporation could not own more than 80% of the stock of another corporation. Now, under § 1361(b), an S corporation can generally hold more than 80% of the stock of a corporation, and in this section we are addressing situations where the S corporation owns all of the stock of another corporation.

The tax consequences to the selling shareholders are generally the same as the tax consequences on the sale of stock to a C corporation. *See* Chapter 5. If a parent corporation is selling the stock of a subsidiary, a § 338(h)(10) election may be filed by the selling parent and the acquiring S corporation. Under § 1371, *see* Sec. 11.4.E., there is no doubt that an S corporation can make a § 338 election.

In the acquisition of a stand-alone target, the S corporation could make a § 338 election, but probably would not for the reasons discussed in Chapter 5. The acquiring S corporation has three principal options for dealing with its newly acquired sub. First, it could continue to operate it as a C corporation, in which case the sub's earnings are subject to tax under § 11 and the S corporation's shareholders are subject to tax on dividends distributed by the sub. The S corporation does not get a dividends received deduction. Second, the S corporation could liquidate the sub in a tax-free liquidation under §§ 332 and 337. Since under § 334(b), the S corporation would take a carry over basis for the sub's assets, the § 1374 built in gains tax would apply. *See* Sec. 11.4.G. Third, the S corporation could elect to treat the sub as a qualified subchapter S subsidiary, which would mean that the assets and liabilities of the sub would be deemed owned by the S corporation. *See* Sec. 11.4.D. In such case, the Q sub is treated as a division of the S corporation. The § 1374 built-in gains tax would also apply if this election were made. *See* Sec. 11.4.G.

§ 11.7 Taxable Acquisition by a C Corporation of the Assets of an S Corporation

In this transaction, an acquiring C corporation acquires for cash the assets of an S corporation. The transaction may be effectuated as a taxable forward subsidiary merger, which is discussed in Chapter 4. From the perspective of the acquiring C corporation, the tax consequences of this transaction are essentially the same as in the acquisition by a C corporation of the assets of another C corporation. *See* Chapter 4.

From the perspective of the target S corporation, many of the principles discussed in Chapter 4, such as the allocation rules of § 1060 also apply to the S corporation. In addition, the gain realized on the transaction by the S corporation passes through to the shareholders under § 1366, and the shareholders receive an increase in their bases for their stock under § 1367. *See* Sec. 1.3.C. Under § 1366(b), the character of the gain or loss realized by the corporation on the sale of its assets passes through to the shareholders.

Assuming that before the sale, the bases of each shareholder's shares equals the proportionate bases of the corporation's assets (this would normally be the case for corporations that have always been S corporations and for shareholders who acquired their shares by making contributions to the corporation), then after the sale by the S corporation, the bases of the shareholders' shares should equal the amount of cash held by the S corporation. Thus, on the liquidating distribution of the cash, the share-holders would not have further gain under § 331. *See* Chapter 19 of *Taxation of Business Entities, supra,* Sec. 1.12.

§ 11.8 Taxable Acquisition by a C Corporation of the Stock of an S Corporation: Impact of § 338(h)(10)

A. Introduction

In this transaction a C corporation acquires in a taxable acquisition the stock of an S corporation. The transaction may be effectuated as a taxable reverse subsidiary merger, which is discussed in Chapter 5. This section focuses on an acquisition of all of the stock of an S corporation for cash or notes. Other issues can arise in the acquisition of part of the stock of an S corporation. *See* Chapter 19 of *Taxation of Business Entities, supra,* Sec. 1.12.

The first question that needs to be addressed in this transaction is whether a § 338(h)(10) election should be filed. If this election is filed, the transaction is treated like an asset acquisition transaction discussed above, with one level of taxation. However, whereas the shareholders of an S corporation receive all capital gain on the sale of their stock, in both a direct sale of assets and in a § 338(h)(10) sale of assets, any ordinary gain at the S level passes through to the shareholders. If the corporation does not have substantial appreciation in ordinary income assets, and if the shareholders' bases are the same as the bases of the corporation's assets, then the selling shareholders may be indifferent between a stock sale without a § 338(h)(10) election and a stock sale with such an election. The § 338(h)(10) option, including the installment sales rules, is explored further immediately below in Sec. 11.8.B.

If a § 338(h)(10) election is not filed, the selling shareholders will have taxable gain and installment sale treatment under § 453 as discussed in Chapter 5. Also, in general, the acquiring C corporation will not make a regular § 338 election for S because as a result of the acquisition the S corporation becomes a C corporation, and assuming the S's assets are appreciated, there would be the standard heavy tax costs with the § 338 election.

At the time of the acquisition, under § 1362(e), the S status will come to an end. If the acquisition takes place during a taxable year as opposed to at the end of a taxable year and a § 338 election is not filed, the income of the S target must be allocated between the S part of the year and the C part of the year under the rules of § 1362(e), which are discussed above in Sec. 11.4.F. If the S corporation becomes a member of the consolidated group of the acquiring C corporation, special consolidated return rules apply. *See* Sec. 11.8.C.

B. The § 338(h)(10) Election for an S Target

1. The 1999 Proposed Regulations: The § 338(h)(10) for an S Corporation

Preamble to Proposed Regulations

August 10, 1999, 64 F.R. 43462 [Treasury Decision 8940, Feb. 13, 2001, finalized these regulations substantially in the form discussed here.]

Under the proposed regulations, old target is treated as transferring all of its assets by sale to an unrelated person. Old target recognizes the deemed sale gain while * * * owned by the S corporation shareholders (both those who actually sell their shares and any who do not). Old target is then treated as transferring all of its assets to the * * * S corporation shareholders and ceasing to exist. * * * [T]he deemed asset sale and deemed liquidation are considered as occurring while [the target] is still an S corporation. The proposed regulations treat all parties concerned as if the fictions the section 338(h)(10) regulations deem to occur actually did occur, or as closely thereto as possible. The structure of this model should help taxpayers answer any questions not explicitly addressed by the proposed regulations. Also, old target generally is barred by the proposed regulations from obtaining any tax benefit from the section 338(h)(10) election that it would not obtain if it actually sold its assets and liquidated.

The treatment of S corporation targets which own one or more qualified subchapter S subsidiaries (as defined in section 1361(b)(3)) is also addressed * * *.

Deemed Liquidation. The current regulations provide that, when a section 338(h)(10) election is made, old target is deemed to sell all of its assets and distribute the proceeds in complete liquidation. The term complete liquidation is generally considered to be a term of art in tax law. The proposed regulations instead provide that old target transferred all of its assets to the * * * S corporation shareholders and ceased to exist, making it clear that the transaction following the deemed asset sale does not automatically qualify as a distribution in complete liquidation under either section 331 or 332. * * *

Special S Corporation Issues. The current regulations provide that, notwithstanding the purchase of 80 percent of the shares of an S corporation by a purchasing C corporation, the S corporation continues to be considered an S corporation for purposes of determining the tax effects of the section 338(h)(10) election to old target and its S corporation shareholders. For example, old target reports to its shareholders under section 1366 the tax effects of its deemed asset sale, and the shareholders adjust their stock basis pursuant to section 1367. The proposed regulations clarify that when the target itself is an S corporation immediately before the acquisition date, any direct and indirect subsidiaries of target with respect to which qualified subchapter S subsidiary elections are in effect are considered to remain qualified subchapter S subsidiaries for purposes of target's and its S corporation shareholders' reporting the effects of target's deemed sale of assets and deemed liquidation. No similar rule applies when a qualified subchapter S subsidiary, as opposed to the S corporation that is its owner, is the target corporation. The IRS and Treasury request comments as to whether it would be beneficial to make section 338(h)(10) elections available for acquisitions of qualified subchapter S subsidiaries and as to how the section 338(h)(10) regulations should be modified to accommodate the unique taxation of these entities.

The proposed regulations clarify the effects of the section 338(h)(10) election on both selling and non-selling S corporation shareholders. For example, the proposed regulations clarify that all S corporation shareholders, selling or not, must consent to the making of the section 338(h)(10) election, particularly because the non-selling shareholders have to include their proportionate share of the deemed sale gain under section 1366. Form 8023 will be corrected to reflect this requirement. * * *

2. The 2001 Final Regulations: The § 338(h)(10) for an S Corporation
Preamble to Final Regulations
February 13, 2001, 66 F. R. 9925

Forms 8023 * * *. The current temporary regulations provide that a section 338(h)(10) election for an S corporation target must be made jointly by the purchaser and the S corporation shareholders. These regulations specifically require nonselling S corporation shareholders to consent to the election. *See* § 1.338(h)(10)-1T(c)(2). However, the instructions for the election form (Form 8023) do not clearly require the nonselling shareholders to sign the election form. * * * The IRS will revise Form 8023 to make clear that nonselling S corporation shareholders must also sign. * * * The IRS will recognize the validity of otherwise valid elections made on the current version of the form even if not signed by the nonselling shareholders, provided that the S corporation and all of its shareholders (including nonselling shareholders) report the tax consequences consistently with the results under section 338(h)(10). *See* § 1.338(i)-1(b). * * *

C. Acquisition of Stock of S Corporation by a Consolidated Group
Preamble to Proposed Regulation, Reg-1006219
December 17, 1998, Finalized by Treasury Decision 8842, November 10, 1999

Background This document contains proposed amendments to the Income Tax Regulations (26 CFR part 1) under section 1502 of the Internal Revenue Code of 1986 (the consolidated return regulations). The amendments apply to acquisitions by a consolidated group of at least eighty percent of the stock of an S corporation. When a consolidated group acquires an S corporation, the interaction of the consolidated return regulations and the subchapter S rules requires the filing of a separate return for the day of the acquisition. In most situations, complying with this requirement results in an unnecessary administrative burden for taxpayers. * * *

The IRS and Treasury have determined that the compliance burdens associated with filing a separate return for the day that an S corporation is acquired by a consolidated group are not necessary to achieve the separate goals of section 1362(e) and the consolidated return regulations. The proposed regulations will eliminate this requirement in most situations, while preserving the purpose and effect of the rules under section 1362(e). These proposed regulations will not apply, however, if an S corporation becomes a member of a consolidated group in a qualified stock purchase for which an election under section 338(g) is made. If the common parent of the consolidated group and the shareholders of the S corporation jointly make a section 338(h)(10) election, the administrative relief provided by these proposed regulations is unnecessary because the S corporation election of the old target corporation does not terminate. *See* § 1.338(h)(10)-1(e)(2)(iv).

Under the proposed regulations, an S corporation will become a member of the consolidated group at the beginning of the day that includes the acquisition, and its tax year will end for all Federal income tax purposes at the end of the day preceding the acquisition. Thus, instead of three short taxable years, the corporation will have two short taxable years as a result of the acquisition: (1) the period ending on the day before the S corporation joins the consolidated group, which will be treated as a taxable year in which the corporation was an S corporation, and (2) the period during which the corporation is a member of the consolidated group. The termination of an S corporation election under section 1362(d)(2) continues to become effective on the day of the acquisition. However, because the consolidated return regulations create a separate taxable year for the corporation, the first day of which is the day on which the S corporation election terminates, there is no S termination year within the meaning of section 1362(e)(4). Consequently, section 1362(e) technically does not apply to the corporation. * * *

§ 11.9 Tax-Free Acquisition by an S Corporation of the Assets of a C Corporation in an Asset Reorganization

A. Illustration of an (A) Reorganization Prior to the Current § 1371

Revenue Ruling 69-566

1969-2 C.B. 165

An electing small business corporation, as defined in section 1371(b) of the Internal Revenue Code of 1954, [now § 1361(a)] acquired the assets of another corporation, not an electing small business corporation, in a statutory merger within the meaning of section 368(a)(1)(A) of the Code. The electing small business corporation was the surviving corporation, and the stock of the other corporation was cancelled.

Held, the statutory merger in and of itself, did not terminate the corporation's election as an electing small business corporation. *Held further,* the merger did not terminate the electing small business corporation's taxable year.

B. Elaboration

The validity of Revenue Ruling 69-566 above is codified under current law by § 1371. *See* Sec. 11.4.E. Even though the transaction qualifies as an (A), the S status of the acquiring corporation would terminate if, for example, in the merger, its stock was issued to a corporate shareholder of the target.

The principle in this ruling also applies to the acquisition by an S corporation of the assets of a target in a (C) reorganization, and the acquisition by a subsidiary of an S corporation of the assets of a target in either a triangular (C) or a forward subsidiary merger under § 368(a)(2)(E). As indicated in Sec. 11.4.D., an S corporation can have controlled subsidiaries, so there is nothing to prevent an S corporation from using triangular reorganizations.

Care will have to be taken to ensure that the S corporation's status does not terminate as a result of the acquisition. For example, in the (C) and triangular (C) reorganizations, to preserve the S status of the acquiring S corporation, it is necessary that the target immediately liquidate so that there is no corporate shareholder of the stock of such corporation.

As indicated in Sec. 11.4.G., since the target's assets are acquired in a carryover basis transaction, the § 1374 built-in gains tax will apply to those assets unless they are held by a subsidiary that is a C corporation.

§ 11.10 Tax-Free Acquisition by an S Corporation of the Stock of a C Corporation in a Stock Reorganization

This section deals with the acquisition by an S corporation of the stock of a target that is a C corporation in a direct (B) stock for stock reorganization, a triangular (B) reorganization, and a reverse subsidiary merger under § 368(a)(2)(E). In each of these reorganizations, which are explored in Chapter 8, the S corporation or in the case of a triangular (B) a subsidiary of the S, ends up owning more than 80% of the stock of the target. Provided the conditions for these reorganizations are satisfied, there is no problem with the fact that the acquiror is an S corporation. Of course, the acquiring S corporation will have to ensure that its status as an S does not terminate as a result of the transaction, such as by transferring stock to a corporate shareholder.

If after the acquisition, the acquiring corporation keeps the target as a C subsidiary, the sub will be subject to tax under § 11. If the acquiror either liquidates the sub or makes a qualified subchapter S subsidiary election, then the transaction would likely be examined as a (C) reorganization under the principles of Rev. Rul. 67-274, Sec. 7.3.B. Thus, in such case, care would have to be taken to ensure that the transaction satisfied all of the conditions of a (C), including the substantially all requirement. If such an election is made or the sub is liquidated, the § 1374 built-in gains tax will apply. *See* Sec. 11.4.G.

§ 11.11 Tax-Free Acquisition by a C Corporation of the Assets of an S Corporation

This section deals with the acquisition by a C corporation of the assets of a target that is an S corporation in a direct (A) merger reorganization, a stock for assets (C) reorganization, a triangular (C) reorganization, or a forward subsidiary merger under § 368(a)(2)(D). In these transactions, the S status terminates as a result of the acquisition, and the termination rules discussed in Sec. 11.4.F. apply. The shareholders of the S target may want to cause the S corporation to make a tax-free distribution of its S earnings under § 1368 prior to the acquisition. Any such pre-reorganization distribution would have to pass muster under the continuity of interest regulations discussed in Chapter 6 (*see* Sec. 6.2.F.3) and could not be so large as to cause a failure of the substantially all requirement that applies in the (C) and forward subsidiary mergers.

Also, as indicated in Sec. 11.4.F.4., under § 1371(e), a former S corporation can make a tax-free distribution of its prior undistributed S earnings during the post-termination transition period, which generally means the one-year period after the termination of the S election. This provision can presumably apply to distributions made to the former S shareholders one year after the acquisition.

§ 11.12 Tax-Free Acquisition by a C Corporation of the Stock of an S Corporation

This section deals with the acquisition by a C corporation of the stock of a target that is an S corporation in a direct (B) stock for stock reorganization, a triangular (B) reorganization, and a reverse subsidiary merger under § 368(a)(2)(E). In these transactions the S status terminates as a result of the acquisition, and the termination rules discussed in Sec. 11.4.F. apply.

As in the case of the asset reorganizations discussed above, the shareholders of the S target may want to cause the S corporation to make a tax-free distribution of its S earnings under § 1368 prior to the acquisition. Any such pre-reorganization distribution would have to pass muster under the continuity of interest regulations discussed in Chapter 6 and could not be so large as to cause a failure of the substantially all requirement that applies in the reverse subsidiary merger. *See* 6.2.F.3. Also, the distribution would have to be structured so that it did not give rise to boot in a (B). *See* Sec. 8.2.G.

§ 11.13 Spin-Offs Involving S Corporations

There is no prohibition against an S corporation engaging in a spin-off transaction under § 355, which is explored in Chapter 9.

Chapter 12

Introduction to Bankruptcy Restructurings and Related Transactions

§ 12.1 Scope

This chapter introduces several issues that can arise in bankruptcy restructurings and similar transactions. Sec. 12.2 deals with the treatment of the holder of a corporate debt instrument on the swap of the instrument for stock or debt of the corporation. Sec. 12.3 introduces the concept of cancellation of indebtedness (COD) income and the structure of § 108, which provides an exclusion for certain COD income. Sec. 12.4 deals with the relationship between § 108 and the OID provisions on the swap of debt for debt. Sec. 12.5 examines the regulations under § 1.1001-3 dealing with the treatment of the modification of debt instruments. These regulations were issued in response to the *Cottage Savings* decision, and in certain cases under these regulations, a modification may be treated as an exchange, which could give rise to COD income for the issuer and a realization event for the holder. Sec. 12.6 introduces the bankruptcy reorganization under § 368(a)(1)(G), which includes a transaction in which an acquiring corporation acquires a bankrupt corporation. Sec. 12.7 deals with the impact of § 382 in bankruptcy and insolvency acquisitions. As will be seen below, there is a relationship between the exclusion of COD income in § 108 and the impact of § 382. Sec. 12.8 examines the impact of § 269 in bankruptcy reorganizations. Finally, Sec. 12.9 sets out excerpts from the discussion of the tax consequences in the WorldCom bankruptcy, one of the largest bankruptcies in history.

For a more detailed discussion of the issues raised in this chapter, *see* the current editions of Henderson and Goldring, *Tax Planning for Troubled Companies*, and PLI, *Tax Strategies, supra* Sec. 1.12. *See also* Thompson, *Mergers, Acquisitions, and Tender Offers, supra* Sec. 1.11 at Chapter 16.

§ 12.2 Treatment of Corporate Creditor on Swap of Debt Instrument for Stock or Debt

When a creditor of a corporation swaps a security in the corporation for stock or another security in the corporation, the transaction likely will qualify as a recapitalization under § 368(a)(1)(E). *See* Chapter 23 of *Taxation of Business Entities, supra* Sec. 1.12. As a consequence, the security holder may qualify for nonrecognition treatment under §354. *See* Sec. 6.8. If the creditor swaps a debt instrument that is not a security for stock or debt, the transaction is taxable. *See Neville Coke, supra,* Sec. 6.8.A. The modification of a debt instrument may be treated as an exchange of instruments. *See* Sec. 12.3.

§ 12.3 Introduction to Cancellation of Indebtedness Income (COD) and to the Structure of § 108: Dealing with of the Corporate Creditor

A. Introduction to COD Income and to the Basic Rules under § 108

1. Legislative History

Senate Report to the Bankruptcy Tax Act of 1980
8–20 (1980)

Present Law *In general* Under present law, income is realized when indebtedness is forgiven or in other ways cancelled (sec. 61(a)(12) of the Internal Revenue Code). For example, if a corporation has issued a $1,000 bond at par which it later repurchases for only $900, thereby increasing its net worth by $100, the corporation realizes $100 of income [that is cancellation on indebtedness (COD) income] in the year of repurchase (*United States v. Kirby Lumber Co.,* 284 U.S. 1 (1931)).

There are several exceptions to the general rule of income realization. Under a judicially developed "insolvency exception," no income arises from discharge of indebtedness if the debtor is insolvent both before and after the transaction; and if the transaction leaves the debtor with assets whose value exceeds remaining liabilities, income is realized only to the extent of the excess. * * *

A debtor which otherwise would be required to report current income from debt cancellation under the preceding rules instead may elect to reduce the basis of its assets in accordance with Treasury regulations (Code secs. 108 and 1017). * * *

Explanation of Provision *Overview* * * * The committee's bill provides tax rules in the Internal Revenue Code applicable to debt discharge in the case of bankrupt or insolvent debtors, and makes related changes to existing Code provisions applicable to debt discharge in the case of solvent debtors outside bankruptcy.

The rules of the bill concerning income tax treatment of debt discharge in bankruptcy are intended to accommodate bankruptcy policy and tax policy. To preserve the debtor's "fresh start" after bankruptcy, the bill provides that no income is recognized by reason of debt discharge in bankruptcy, so that a debtor coming out of bankruptcy (or an insolvent debtor outside bankruptcy) is not burdened with an immediate tax liability. [*See* § 108(a)(1).] The bill provides that the debt discharge amount thus excluded from income is applied to reduce the taxpayer's net operating losses and certain other tax attributes, unless the taxpayer elects to apply the debt discharge amount first to reduce basis in depreciable assets (or in realty held as inventory). [*See* §§ 108(b) and 1017.]

In the case of solvent debtors outside bankruptcy, [the 1986 Act repealed] the election (under Code secs. 108 and 1017) permitting such debtors to reduce assets basis in lieu of reporting ordinary income from debt cancellation, as on repurchase of bonds at a discount. [*See* former § 108(c).] * * *

Stock-for-debt rules to encourage reorganizations The committee bill generally does not change the present law rule developed by the courts governing whether income is recognized if a corporation issues its own stock to its creditor for outstanding debt (whether or not the debt constitutes a security for tax purposes). Therefore, no attribute reduction generally will be required where such stock is issued to discharge the debt. * * * [As indicated in Sec. 12.3.B., the stock for debt exception has been repealed.] * * *

Capital Contributions The bill provides that the discharge of indebtedness rules apply to the extent that the amount of debt transferred to a corporation as a contribution to capital exceeds the shareholder's basis in the debt. [*See* § 108(e)(6).] Thus, the discharge of indebtedness rules apply when a cash-basis taxpayer contributes to the capital of an accrual-basis corporation a debt representing an accrued expense previously deducted by the corporation.

2. Elective Basis Reduction under § 1017 for COD Income Realized under § 108

a. Proposed Regulations

Proposed Regulations Reg-208172-91

62 F.R. 955, January 7, 1991

Summary: This document contains proposed regulations that provide ordering rules for the reduction of bases of property under sections 108 and 1017 of the Internal Revenue Code of 1986. The regulations will affect taxpayers that exclude discharge of indebtedness from gross income under section 108.

Explanation of Provisions *Overview* The legislative history of the Bankruptcy Tax Act states that the exclusion of discharge of indebtedness (COD income) from gross income under section 108 is intended to promote a debtor's fresh start. * * * The exclusion provided by the statute generally operates, however, to defer, rather than eliminate, income from discharge of indebtedness.

The deferral of income provided by statute is generally achieved by requiring a taxpayer to reduce specified tax attributes (including adjusted bases of property) under section 108(b) by an amount equal to the COD income excluded from gross income under section 108(a). Section 108(b)(2) requires a taxpayer to reduce tax attributes in the following order: (A) net operating loss; (B) general business credit; (C) minimum tax credit; (D) capital loss carryovers; (E) adjusted bases of property; (F) passive activity loss and credit carryovers; and (G) foreign tax credit carryovers. If the excluded COD income exceeds the sum of the taxpayer's tax attributes, the excess is permanently excluded from the taxpayer's gross income.

When basis reductions are necessary, section 1017(a) requires the taxpayer to reduce the adjusted bases of property held on the first day of the following tax year. Section 1017(b)(1) provides that the amount of the basis reduction required under section 1017(a), and the particular properties the bases of which are to be reduced, shall be determined under regulations.

General Rules for Basis Reduction Consistent with the legislative history of the Bankruptcy Tax Act, the proposed regulations generally retain the "tracing" approach of the existing regulations issued under prior law. Thus, the proposed regulations require a taxpayer to reduce the adjusted basis of the property that secured the discharged indebtedness before reducing the adjusted bases of other property.

In addition, the proposed regulations modify the categories in the existing regulations to simplify the process of basis reduction. First, the distinction between purchase-money indebtedness and other secured indebtedness is eliminated. Second, the order of basis reduction for property that secured discharged indebtedness is changed. Thus, the first category of the general ordering rule is real property used in the taxpayer's trade or business or held for the production of income (other than section 1221(1) real property) that secured the discharged indebtedness, and the second category is personal property used in the taxpayer's trade or business or held for the production of income (other than inventory, accounts receivable, and notes receivable) that secured the discharged indebtedness. Therefore, if an indebtedness secured by a building, a parcel of land used in the taxpayer's trade or business, office equipment, and office furniture is discharged, the taxpayer proportionately reduces the adjusted bases of the building and the parcel of land, based upon their relative adjusted bases, to the full extent of the excluded COD income before reducing the adjusted bases of the office equipment and the office furniture. The IRS and Treasury Department believe that this modification of the current regulations will simplify the process of basis reduction for many taxpayers.

Special Rules for Depreciable Properties Instead of reducing tax attributes in the order specified by section 108(b)(2), a taxpayer may elect under section 108(b)(5) first to reduce the adjusted bases of depreciable property (real and personal) to the extent of the excluded COD income. If the adjusted bases of depreciable property are insufficient to offset the entire amount of excluded COD income, the taxpayer must reduce any remaining tax attributes in the order specified in section 108(b)(2). Section 108(c) requires that excluded COD income from the cancellation of qualified real property business indebtedness must be applied against depreciable real property. * * *

b. Final Regulations

Treasury Decision 8787

63 Fed Register 56559, October 22 1988

Background This final regulation contains amendments to the income tax regulations (26 CFR Parts 1 and 301) under sections 108 and 1017 of the Internal Revenue Code of 1986 (Code). The amendments conform the regulations to amendments to sections 108 and 1017 made by the Bankruptcy Tax Act of 1980 [and other acts]. * * *

Explanation of Revisions and Summary of Comments *Basis Reduction Limited to Fair Market Value* One commentator requested that basis reduction be limited to fair market value as provided by § 1.1016-7(a) (as removed by this regulation). The final regulations do not adopt this recommendation. Section 1017, as enacted by the Bankruptcy Tax Act, fundamentally changed the rules relating to basis reduction where discharge of indebtedness income (cancellation of debt (COD) income) is excluded from gross income. The revised statute, in section 1017(b)(2), provides only one limitation on basis reduction for insolvent and bankrupt taxpayers who do not make an election under section 108(b)(5). Under that rule, the basis reduction may not exceed the excess of the aggregate of the bases of the property held by the taxpayer immediately after the discharge over the aggregate of the liabilities of the taxpayer immediately after the discharge. The fair market value limitation found in the regulations removed by this Treasury decision is not reflected in section 1017. Accordingly, the IRS and Treasury Department do not believe that a rule limiting basis reduction to fair market value would be appropriate. * * *

Allocation of Basis Reduction of Multiple Properties Within the Same Class The proposed regulations incorporated the limitation described in section 1017(b)(2) which provides that the basis reduction for bankrupt and insolvent taxpayers may not exceed the excess of the aggregate of the bases of the property held by the taxpayer immediately after the discharge over the aggregate of the liabilities of the taxpayer immediately after the discharge. A commentator suggested that this limitation be applied on a class by class basis, so that when a basis reduction applied within a single class of properties described in § 1.1017-1(a) exceeds the amount of basis over the debt secured by the properties in that class, the basis reduction in excess of that amount should default to the next class.

The final regulations do not adopt this comment.

The overall limitation on basis reduction is determined by reference to the adjusted basis of property and the amount of money held by the taxpayer over the liabilities of the taxpayer "immediately after the discharge." By contrast, under the basis reduction rules applicable for purposes of section 108(b)(2)(E), the taxpayer must reduce the adjusted basis of property "held by the taxpayer at the beginning of the taxable year following the year in which the discharge occurs." Section 1017(a). Given the difference in the relevant time for applying the basis limitation and the basis reduction rules, and the relative complexity of the calculations necessary to implement the proposal, the IRS and Treasury Department believe that the suggested limitation is not workable. Accordingly, the final regulations continue to apply the limitation based on the aggregate bases and liabilities of the taxpayer consistent with section 1017(b)(2). * * *

3. Introductory Problems on §§ 108 and 1017

Debtor Corporation (*DC*) has outstanding common stock and debentures. The debentures have a principal amount of $100K. There is no OID on the debentures.

DC is not in bankruptcy, is not insolvent, and has always been profitable. Because of an increase in interest rates, the debentures have a fair market value of $90K.

    a. *DC* purchases its $100K of outstanding debentures for $90K in cash. What result to *DC*?

    b. Suppose *DC* issues its new debentures with an issue price, principal, and fair market value of $90K in exchange for the old debentures?

    c. What result in *(a)* and *(b)* if *DC* is in bankruptcy and has substantial NOLs?

    d. What result in *(a)* and *(b)* if *DC* is insolvent and has substantial NOLs?

B. Modification of the Stock-for-Debt Exception

See § 108(e)(8).

1. The Revenue Reconciliation Act of 1993

Conference Report to the Revenue Reconciliation Act of 1993

141–142 (1984)

Present Law Gross income generally includes cancellation of indebtedness (COD) income. Taxpayers in title 11 cases and insolvent taxpayers, however, generally exclude COD income from gross income but reduce tax attributes by the amount of COD income. The amount of COD income that an insolvent taxpayer excludes cannot exceed the amount by which the taxpayer is insolvent.

The amount of COD income generally is the difference between the adjusted issue price of the debt being canceled and the amount of cash and the value of any property used to satisfy the debt. Thus, for purposes of determining the amount of COD income of a debtor corporation that transfers stock to a creditor in satisfaction of its indebtedness, the corporation generally is treated as realizing COD income equal to the excess of the adjusted issue price of the debt over the fair market value of the stock. However, if the debtor corporation is in a title 11 case or is insolvent, the excess of the debt discharged over the fair market value of the transferred stock generally does not constitute COD income (the "stock-for-debt exception"). Thus, a corporate debtor that qualifies for the stock-for-debt exception is not required to reduce its tax attributes as a result of the debt discharge. The stock-for-debt exception does not apply to the issuance of certain preferred stock, nominal or token shares of stock, or stock issued to unsecured creditors on a relatively disproportionate basis. In the case of an insolvent debtor not in a title 11 case, the exception applies only to the extent the debtor is insolvent.

House Bill No provision.

Senate Amendment The Senate amendment repeals the stock-for-debt exception. Thus, regardless of whether a debtor corporation is insolvent or in bankruptcy, the transfer of its stock in satisfaction of its indebtedness is treated as if the corporation satisfied the indebtedness with an amount of money equal to the fair market value of the stock that had been transferred. Under the Senate amendment, an insolvent corporation or a corporation in a title 11 case may exclude from income all or a portion of the COD income created by the transfer of its stock in satisfaction of indebtedness by reducing tax attributes. * * *

Conference Agreement The conference agreement follows the Senate amendment with the following modifications.

The conference agreement provides authority to the Treasury Department to promulgate such regulations as are necessary to coordinate the present-law rules regarding the acquisition by a corporation of its debt from a shareholder as a contribution to capital (sec. 108(e)(6)) with the repeal of the stock-for-debt exception. * * *

2. Introductory Problems on Stock-for-Debt Exceptions

The facts are the same as in Sec. 12.3.A.3.

a. What result if *DC* acquires its outstanding debentures for its common stock with a value of $90K? The common stock amounts to 10% of *DC*'s outstanding common stock after issuance. What if it issues preferred stock with a value of $90K?

b. What result in a, if *DC* is bankrupt?

c. What result in a, if *DC* is insolvent?

§ 12.4 Debt-for-Debt Swaps: Relationship between COD Provisions of § 108 and the OID Provisions of § 1274

A. Legislative History

House Report to the Revenue Reconciliation Act of 1990
175–179 (1990)

Income from the cancellation of indebtedness In general. Gross income includes income from the cancellation of indebtedness (COD). Taxpayers in title 11 cases and insolvent debtors generally exclude COD from income but reduce tax attributes by the amount of COD created on the discharge of debt. The amount of COD excluded from income by an insolvent debtor not in a title 11 case cannot exceed the amount by which the debtor is insolvent. For all taxpayers, the amount of COD generally is the difference between the adjusted issue price of the debt being cancelled and the amount used to satisfy such debt. The COD rules generally apply to the exchange of an old obligation for a new obligation, including a modification of the old debt that is treated as an exchange (a debt-for-debt exchange). * * *

Original issue discount rules The issuer of a debt instrument with original issue discount (OID) generally accrues and deducts the discount, as interest, over the term of the instrument on an economic accrual basis. The holder of an OID instrument also includes the amount of OID in income on an economic accrual basis. Original issue discount is the excess of the stated redemption price at maturity over the issue price of a debt instrument. For purposes of the OID rules, the issue price of a debt instrument that is issued for property generally is determined by reference to fair market value if either the debt instrument or the property for which it was issued is publicly traded. (Sec. 1273(b)(3)). If neither the debt instrument nor the property for which it is issued is publicly traded, the issue price of the instrument generally is its stated principal amount, provided the instrument has adequate stated interest. If the debt instrument lacks adequate stated interest, the issue price of the instrument generally is determined by using the applicable Federal rate to discount all payments due under the instrument. (Sec. 1274). Finally, for debt-for-debt exchanges in a reorganization, the issue price of a new debt instrument is not less than the adjusted issue price of the old debt instrument. (Sec. 1275(a)(4)). In certain other cases, issue price is equal to stated redemption price at maturity (Sec. 1273(b)(4)).

Reasons for Change The committee is aware that taxpayers take various positions as to whether and how these OID and other rules apply for purposes of determining COD. With respect to exchanges that qualify as reorganizations, taxpayers with net operating losses, or in title 11 or similar proceedings, may take the position that the OID rules do not apply, so that COD is created. * * *

The committee believes that the rules for determining the amount of COD created on a debt-for-debt exchange need to be clarified in order to provide guidance to taxpayers, to ensure similar treatment for taxpayers undertaking similar transactions, and to prevent taxpayers from selectively choosing the tax treatment for a transaction. The committee further believes that the amount of COD created on a debt-for-debt exchange is properly determined by comparing the adjusted issue price of the old obligations being discharged to the issue price of the new obligations, and that the OID rules, as modified by the bill, provide the appropriate framework for determining the issue price of a new obligation. * * *

Explanation of Provisions *Debt-for-debt exchanges Treatment of issuers.* The provision provides explicit rules for determining the amount of COD created in a debt-for-debt exchange and how the OID rules apply in such a situation. * * *

Under the provision, for purposes of determining the amount of COD of a debtor that issues a new debt instrument in satisfaction of an old debt, such debtor will be treated as having satisfied the old debt with an amount of money equal to the issue price of the new debt.[1] For this purpose, the issue price of the new obligation will be

---

1. In any case in which an old debt instrument is exchanged by the holder for a new debt instrument, or in which the terms of an old debt instrument are modified so as to constitute an exchange by the holder, the debtor is treated as having issued a new debt instrument in satisfaction of an old debt instrument.

determined under the general rules applicable to debt instruments issued for property (i.e., secs. 1273(b) and 1274). For debt instruments subject to section 483 (rather than section 1274), the issue price as determined under section 1273(b)(4) is reduced to exclude unstated interest for purposes of determining COD.

In addition, the reorganization exception in section 1275(a)(4) of the OID rules is repealed. Thus, either or both COD or OID may be created in a debt-for-debt exchange that qualifies as a reorganization, so long as the exchange qualifies as a realization event under section 1001 for the holder. The provision does not change the present-law rules of sections 354, 355, or 356 regarding the amount of gain or loss recognized or not recognized in a reorganization.

Thus, if either the old or the new obligation in a debt-for-debt exchange is publicly traded, the issue price of the new obligation will be the fair market value of the publicly-traded obligation. If neither obligation is publicly traded, the issue price of the new obligation will be its stated principal amount, unless the new obligation does not have adequate stated interest. [*See* § 1274.] In such case, the issue price generally is determined by using the applicable Federal rate to discount all payments due under the new obligation.

Example 1.—A corporation issued for $1000 a bond that provided for annual coupon payments based on a market rate of interest. The bond is publicly traded. Some time later, when the old bond is worth $600, the corporation exchanges the old bond for a new bond that has a stated redemption price at maturity of $750. The exchange is treated as a realization event under section 1001. Under the bill, the new bond will have an issue price of $600 (the fair market value of the old bond) [*see* § 1273] and deductible OID of $150 ($750 stated redemption price at maturity less $600 issue price) [*see* § 1272] and the corporation will have COD of $400 ($1000 adjusted issue price of the old bond less $600 issue price of the new bond). Such results will occur whether or not the exchange qualifies as a reorganization.

Treatment of the holder.—The repeal of section 1275(a)(4) will be applicable to the holder as well as the issuer of the new debt instrument for purposes of determining the issue price of the new debt instrument received in a debt-for-debt exchange.

Example 2.—Assume the holder of the old bond in Example 1 above had recently purchased such bond for $600. Even if the debt-for-debt exchange qualifies as a reorganization, the holder will have an issue price of $600 and includible OID of $150 with respect to the new bond. * * *

B. Introductory Problems on Debt-for-Debt Swaps

The facts are the same as in Sec. 12.3.A.3., except *DC*'s outstanding debentures were issued with OID. The debentures are publicly traded. The adjusted issue price is $90K and the stated principal amount is $100K. The fair market value of the debentures is $70K. In exchange for the old debentures, *DC* issues its new debentures with a fair market value and issue price of $70K and a stated principal amount of $80K. What is the treatment to *DC* and the debenture holders?

§ 12.5 Treatment of Modifications of Debt Instruments

See Reg. § 1.1001-3.

Preamble to Proposed Regulations under § 1.1001-3

FI-31-92 (Dec. 2, 1992) These regulations have been adopted.

Explanation of Provisions Section 1.1001-1(a) of the regulations provides that gain or loss is realized on the sale of property or on the "exchange of property for other property differing materially either in kind or in extent." This rule has applied not only to actual exchanges of properties between owners, but also to deemed exchanges arising from the modification of the terms of debt instruments.

With the exception of the mortgage swap transaction discussed below, § 1.1001-1(a) of the regulations has resulted in relatively little controversy in the case of actual exchanges between holders of debt instruments. Taxpayers and the Service generally have agreed that, absent unusual facts, an actual exchange gives rise to gain or loss. Uncertainty exists, however, with respect to whether particular types of modifications result in deemed exchanges of debt instruments. This uncertainty has resulted in a great deal of controversy between taxpayers and the Service and has produced a substantial body of administrative and judicial precedents.

The decision of the Supreme Court in *Cottage Savings Ass'n v. Commissioner,* 111 S.Ct. 1503 (1991), [*see* Sec. 2.2.B. of *Taxation of Business Entities, supra* Sec. 1.12], has generated additional controversy regarding the treatment of modifications. In *Cottage,* a savings and loan association engaged in a series of purchases and sales of mortgage participation interests. In each transaction, the taxpayer sold mortgage participation interests to another financial institution and purchased substantially identical mortgage participation interests from the other institution. Although cast as sales and purchases, the holders exchanged mortgage participation interests. The taxpayer treated the exchanges as realization events under section 1001 of the Code and claimed losses. The Service sought to disallow the losses on the ground that the exchanged properties were economically equivalent and thus did not differ materially within the meaning of § 1.1001-1(a) of the regulations.

The Court held that the taxpayer had realized a loss. After concluding that § 1.1001-1 of the regulations is a reasonable interpretation of section 1001(a) of the Code, the Court determined that, because the participation interests exchanged by the taxpayer were derived from loans made to different obligors and secured by different homes, the exchanged interests embodied legally distinct entitlements and therefore were materially different. Thus, the transaction resulted in a sale or disposition under section 1001 of the Code.

Cottage did not involve the modification of an instrument, but an actual exchange between holders. Questions have arisen, however, concerning the Court's interpretation of the material difference standard and its possible application to modifications of debt instruments by issuers and holders. It has been suggested that the parties to a debt instrument should be able to adjust certain terms of their instrument without the modification rising to the level of a deemed exchange.

In response to the issues raised by the *Cottage* decision, and in an effort to provide certainty, the Service proposes to expand the regulations under section 1001 of the Code to deal explicitly with the modification of debt instruments. The proposed regulations define when a modification will be deemed to be an exchange of the original instrument for a modified instrument that differs materially either in kind or in extent.

Even if a modification results in a deemed exchange under the proposed regulations, the holder and issuer may not realize gain or loss. * * * The realization by the issuer of income from discharge of indebtedness under section 108(e)(11) of the Code will depend on whether the adjusted issue price of the original instrument is less than or greater than the issue price of the new instrument, which is determined under sections 1273 and 1274 of the Code. The realization of gain or loss by the holder generally will depend on whether the issue price of the new instrument is less than or greater than the holder's basis in the original instrument. In addition, even if a gain or loss is realized, certain nonrecognition provisions of the Code may apply. [*See* § 368(a)(1)(E) and Chapter 23 of *Taxation of Business Entities, supra* Sec. 1.12.] * * *

The proposed regulations are found in new § 1.1001-3. Paragraph (a) provides the general rule that, for purposes of § 1.1001-1(a) of the regulations, a significant modification of a debt instrument under these regulations is treated as an exchange of the original instrument for a modified instrument that differs materially either in kind or extent. Modifications that are not significant modifications are not exchanges.

Paragraph (b) provides that these regulations apply to all modifications of debt instruments regardless of the form of the modification. The regulations do not apply to exchanges of instruments between holders unless such an exchange effects an indirect modification.

Paragraph (c) defines the term "modification" and paragraph (e) defines the term "significant modification." In applying the regulations, the first step is to determine whether the original instrument has been modified. Only if there has been a modification under paragraph (c) is there a need to consider the rules of paragraph (e) to determine whether the modification is significant.

The general rule of paragraph (c) is that an alteration of a legal right or obligation of the holder or the issuer is a modification. Alterations that occur by operation of the original terms of an instrument, however, generally are not modifications. An alteration that occurs through the exercise or waiver of a right under an instrument is by operation of the instrument only if the exercise or waiver is unilateral. Another exception to the general rule provides that a temporary failure of the issuer to perform its obligations under the instrument, including a delay in payment, is not a modification. * * *

The rules of paragraph (e) set standards for determining whether the more common types of modifications are significant. In some cases, the rules provide a bright-line test. For example, in determining whether a change in yield is significant, paragraph (e)(1) prescribes a 1/4 of one percent rule. In other cases, the rules are more general.

The Service invites comments on all the specific rules of paragraph (e). Suggestions for additional bright-line tests or for rules governing other types of modifications are welcome. * * *

§ 12.6 Introduction to the Bankruptcy Reorganization under § 368(a)(1)(G)

A. Introduction

Many bankruptcy reorganizations involve the restructuring of a single corporation; others involve a merger or acquisition involving two or more companies. To preserve the loss corporation's NOLs in any merger or acquisition and to provide for tax-free treatment to the exchanging shareholders and security holders, if tax-free treatment is desired, the loss corporation must be acquired in a reorganization or a § 351 transaction.

An acquisiton of a bankrupt corporation might be structured to qualify as a (G) reorganization under § 368 (a)(1)(G), which is discussed below. The principal benefit of qualifying as a (G) is the carry over of the bankrupt corporations NOLs under § 381.

B. Legislative History of § 368(a)(1)(G)

Senate Report to the Bankruptcy Act of 1980

33–39 (1980)

Present Law *Definition of reorganization* A transfer of all or part of a corporation's assets, pursuant to a court order in a proceeding under chapter X of the Bankruptcy Act (or in a receivership, foreclosure, or similar proceeding), to another corporation organized or utilized to effectuate a court-approved plan may qualify for tax-free reorganization treatment under special rules relating to "insolvency reorganizations" (secs. 371–374 of the Internal Revenue Code).[2]

These special rules for insolvency reorganizations generally allow less flexibility in structuring tax-free transactions than the rules applicable to corporate reorganizations as defined in section 368 of the Code. Also, the special rules for insolvency

---

2. Under present law, it is not clear to what extent creditors of an insolvent corporation who receive stock in exchange for their claims may be considered to have "stepped into the shoes" of former shareholders for purposes of satisfying the nonstatutory "continuity of interest" rule, under which the owners of the acquired corporation must continue to have a proprietary interest in the acquiring corporation. Generally, the courts have found the "continuity of interest" test satisfied if the creditors' interests were transformed into proprietary interests prior to the reorganization (e.g., *Helvering v. Alabama Asphaltic Limestone Co.*, 315 U.S. 179 (1942) [*see* Sec. 6.2.B.7]; Treas. Reg. § 1.371-1(a)(4)). It is unclear whether affirmative steps by the creditors are required or whether mere receipt of stock is sufficient.

reorganizations do not permit carryover of tax attributes to the transferee corporation, and otherwise differ in important respects from the general reorganization rules. * * *

Reasons for Change The committee believes that the provisions of existing Federal income tax law which are generally applicable to tax-free corporate reorganizations should also apply to reorganizations of corporations in bankruptcy or similar proceedings, in order to facilitate the rehabilitation of financially troubled businesses. * * *

Explanation of Provisions Section 4 of the bill generally conforms the tax rules governing insolvency reorganizations with the existing rules applicable to other corporate reorganizations. * * *

Definition of reorganization [*See* §§ 368(a)(1)(G) and (a)(2)(C).] In general The bill adds a new category—"G" reorganizations—to the general Code definition of tax-free reorganizations (sec. 368(a)(1)). The new category includes certain transfers of assets pursuant to a court-approved reorganization plan in a bankruptcy case under new title 11 of the U.S. Code, or in a receivership, foreclosure, or similar proceeding in a Federal or State court. * * *

In order to facilitate the rehabilitation of corporate debtors in bankruptcy, etc., these provisions are designed to eliminate many requirements which have effectively precluded financially troubled companies from utilizing the generally applicable tax-free reorganization provisions of present law. To achieve this purpose, the new "G" reorganization provision does not require compliance with State merger laws (as in category "A" reorganizations), does not require that the financially distressed corporation receive solely stock of the acquiring corporation in exchange for its assets (category "C"), and does not require that the former shareholders of the financially distressed corporation control the corporation which receives the assets (category "D").

The "G" reorganization provision added by the bill requires the transfer of assets by a corporation in a bankruptcy or similar case, and the distribution (in pursuance of the court-approved reorganization plan) of stock or securities of the acquiring corporation in a transaction which qualifies under section 354, 355, or 356 of the Code. This distribution requirement is designed to assure that either substantially all of the assets of the financially troubled corporation, or assets which consist of an active business under the tests of section 355, are transferred to the acquiring corporation.

"Substantially all" test [*See* § 354(b).] The "substantially all" test in the "G" reorganization provision is to be interpreted in light of the underlying intent in adding the new "G" category, namely, to facilitate the reorganization of companies in bankruptcy or similar cases for rehabilitative purposes. * * *

Relations to other provisions * * * A transaction in a bankruptcy or similar case which does not satisfy the requirements of new category "G" is not thereby precluded from qualifying as a tax-free reorganization under one of the other categories of section 368(a)(1). For example, an acquisition of the stock of a company in bankruptcy, or a recapitalization of such a company, which transactions are not covered by the new "G" category, can qualify for nonrecognition treatment under sections 368(a)(1)(B) or (E), respectively.

Continuity of interest rules The "continuity of interest" requirement which the courts and the Treasury have long imposed as a prerequisite for nonrecognition treatment for a corporate reorganization must be met in order to satisfy the requirements of new category "G". Only reorganizations—as distinguished from liquidations in bankruptcy and sales of property to either new or old interests supplying new capital and discharging the obligations of the debtor corporation—can qualify for tax-free treatment.

It is expected that the courts and the Treasury will apply to "G" reorganizations continuity-of-interest rules which take into account the modification by P.L. 95-598 of the "absolute priority" rule. As a result of that modification, shareholders or junior creditors, who might previously have been excluded, may now retain an interest in the reorganized corporation.

For example, if an insolvent corporation's assets are transferred to a second corporation in a bankruptcy case, the most senior class of creditor to receive stock, together with all equal and junior classes (including shareholders who receive any consideration for their stock), should generally be considered the proprietors of the insolvent corporation for "continuity" purposes. * * *

Thus, short-term creditors who receive stock for their claims may be counted toward satisfying the continuity of interest rule, although any gain or loss realized by such creditors will be recognized for income tax purposes. [*See Neville Coke,* Sec. 6.8.A.]

Triangular reorganizations [*See* § 368(a)(2)(C).] The bill permits a corporation to acquire a debtor corporation in a "G" reorganization in exchange for stock of the parent of the acquiring corporation rather than for its own stock.

In addition, the bill permits an acquisition in the form of a "reverse merger" of an insolvent corporation (i.e., where no former shareholder of the surviving corporation receives any consideration for his stock) in a bankruptcy or similar case if the former creditors of the surviving corporation exchange their claims for voting stock of the controlling corporation which has a value equal to at least 80 percent of the value of the debt of the surviving corporation. * * *

Carryover of tax attributes [*See* § 381(a)(2).] Under the bill, the statutory rule generally governing carryover of tax attributes in corporate reorganizations (Code sec. 381) also applies in the case of a "G" reorganization. This eliminates the so-called "clean slate" doctrine.

"Principal amount" rule; "boot" test [*See* § 354(a)(2).] Under the bill, "G" reorganizations are subject to the rules governing the tax treatment of exchanging shareholders and security holders which apply to other corporate reorganizations.

Accordingly, an exchanging shareholder or security holder of the debtor company who receives securities with a principal amount exceeding the principal amount of securities surrendered is taxable on the excess, and an exchanging shareholder or security holder who surrenders no securities is taxed on the principal amount of any securities received. Also, any "boot" received is subject to the general dividend-equivalence test of Code section 356.

Treatment of accrued interest [*See* § 354(a)(2)(B).] Under the bill, a creditor exchanging securities in any corporate reorganization described in section 368 of the Code (including a "G" reorganization) is treated as receiving interest income on the exchange to the extent the security holder receives new securities, stock, or any other property attributable to accrued but unpaid interest (including accrued original issue discount) on the securities surrendered. This provision, which reverses the so-called *Carman* rule, applies whether or not the exchanging security holder realizes gain on the exchange overall. Under this provision, a security holder which had previously accrued the interest (including original issue discount) as income recognizes a loss to the extent the interest is not paid in the exchange. * * *

C. The "Net Value Requirement" in the 2005 Proposed Regulations

Preamble to the Proposed Regulations Addressing "No Net Value" Reorganizations and Other Transactions

March 11, 2005

SUMMARY:

This document contains proposed regulations providing guidance regarding corporate formations, reorganizations, and liquidations of insolvent corporations. These regulations provide rules requiring the exchange (or, in the case of section 332, a distribution) of net value for the nonrecognition rules of subchapter C to apply to the transaction. * * *

GENERAL BACKGROUND.

The IRS and the Treasury Department believe that there is a need to provide a comprehensive set of rules addressing the application of the nonrecognition rules of subchapter C of the Internal Revenue Code (Code) to transactions involving insolvent corporations and to other transactions that raise similar issues. The proposed regulations provide three sets of rules, the principal one of which is that the nonrecognition rules of subchapter C do not apply unless there is an exchange (or, in the case of section 332, a distribution) of net value (the "net value requirement"). * * *

EXPLANATION OF PROVISIONS. EXCHANGE OF NET VALUE REQUIREMENT. BACKGROUND.

In subchapter C, each of the rules described below that provides for the general nonrecognition of gain or loss refers to a distribution in cancellation or redemption of stock or an exchange for stock. Section 332 provides, in part, that "[n]o gain or loss shall be recognized on the receipt by a corporation of property distributed in complete liquidation of another corporation … only if … the distribution is by such other corporation in complete cancellation or redemption of all its stock." Section 351 provides, in part, that "[n]o gain or loss shall be recognized if property is transferred to a corporation by one or more persons solely in exchange for stock in such corporation." Section 354 provides, in part, that "[n]o gain or loss shall be recognized if stock or securities in a corporation a party to a reorganization are … exchanged solely for stock or securities … in another corporation a party to the reorganization." Finally, section 361 provides that "[n]o gain or loss shall be recognized to a corporation if such corporation is a party to a reorganization and exchanges property … solely for stock or securities in another corporation a party to the reorganization."

The authorities interpreting section 332 have consistently concluded that the language of the statute referring to a distribution in complete cancellation or redemption of stock requires a distribution of net value. * * *

Rev. Rul. 59-296 holds that the principles relevant to liquidations under section 332 also apply to reorganizations under section 368. * * *

EXPLANATION OF RULES. *Net Value Requirement.*

For potential liquidations under section 332, the net value requirement is effected by the partial payment rule in section 1.332-2(b) of the current regulations. The proposed regulations make no modifications to this rule, except, as discussed below, for transactions in which the recipient corporation owns shares of multiple classes of stock in the dissolving corporation. The proposed regulations also make minor changes to other sections of the regulations under section 332 to conform those regulations to changes in the statute.

For potential transactions under section 351, the proposed regulations add section 1.351-1(a)(1)(iii)(A), which requires a surrender of net value and, in paragraph (a)(1)(iii)(B), a receipt of net value. This rule is similar to that for potential asset reorganizations, discussed below. The proposed regulations make minor changes to other sections of the regulations under section 351 to conform those regulations to changes in the statute.

For potential reorganizations under section 368, the proposed regulations modify section 1.368-1(b)(1) to add the requirement that there be an exchange of net value. Section 1.368-1(f) of the proposed regulations sets forth the rules for determining whether there is an exchange of net value. These rules require, in paragraph (f)(2)(i) for potential asset reorganizations and paragraph (f)(3)(i) for potential stock reorganizations, a surrender of net value and, in paragraph (f)(2)(ii) for potential asset reorganizations and paragraph (f)(3)(ii) for potential stock reorganizations, a receipt of net value. * * *

D. Preamble to the Final Regulations Addressing Creditor Continuity of Interest in Reorganizations

Preamble to Final Regulations

Treasury Decision 9434, December 12, 2008

SUMMARY: This document contains final regulations providing guidance regarding when and to what extent creditors of a corporation will be treated as proprietors of the corporation in determining whether continuity of interest ("COI") is preserved in a potential reorganization. * * *

Explanation of Provisions

These final regulations provide that, in certain circumstances, stock received by creditors may count for continuity of interest purposes both inside and outside of bankruptcy proceedings. The expansion of the application of the G reorganization rules to reorganizations of insolvent corporations outside of bankruptcy is consistent with Congress' intent to facilitate the rehabilitation of troubled corporations. S. Rep. No 96-1035, 96th Sess. 35 (1980). Accordingly, the final regulations adopt the rules proposed for creditors of an insolvent target corporation outside of a title 11 or similar case in new § 1.368-1(e)(6) with only minor modifications and clarifications. The final regulations treat claims of the most senior class of creditors to receive a proprietary interest in the issuing corporation and claims of all equal classes of creditors (together, the senior claims) differently from the claims of classes of creditors junior to the senior claims (the junior claims). The final regulations treat such senior claims as representing proprietary interests in the target corporation. * * *

§ 12.7 Impact of § 382 in Bankruptcy and Insolvency Cases

See § 382(l)(5) and (6).

A. Introduction to § 382

Section 382 is discussed in detail in Chapter 5, *supra*. As indicated there, the limitation in Section 382 applies if there is a change of control of a corporation that has a net operating loss (NOL), that is, a loss corporation. A change of control includes, for example, the purchase by an acquiring corporation of more than 50% of the stock of the loss corporation. In such case, the NOLs are limited in each year after the acquisition to an amount determined by multiplying the value of all the stock of the corporation by the long-term tax-exempt rate. This limitation could significantly limit the ability of a new investor to take advantage of a bankrupt or insolvent corporation's NOLs. In this regard, § 382(l)(1) generally excludes capital contributions from consideration in determining the value of the loss corporation. Sections 382(l)(5) and (6), which are discussed below, provide relief from the harsh rules of § 382 in certain bankruptcy and insolvency transactions.

B. Legislative History of §§ 382(l)(5) and (6)

General Explanation of the Tax Reform Act of 1986

321–322 (1986)

Bankruptcy proceedings The special limitations [under § 382, *see* Sec. 5.8] do not apply after any ownership change of a loss corporation if (1) such corporation was under the jurisdiction of a bankruptcy court in a Title 11 or similar case immediately before the ownership change, and (2) the corporation's historic shareholders and creditors (determined immediately before the ownership change) own 50 percent of the value and voting power of the loss corporation's stock immediately after the ownership change (new sec. 382(l)(5)). The 50-percent test is satisfied if the corporation's shareholders and creditors own stock of a controlling corporation that is also in bankruptcy (new sec. 382(l)(5)(A)(ii).) [Thus, if the requirements of § 382(l)(5) are satisfied, the limitation on the utilization of losses otherwise applicable under § 382 will not apply. To fall within § 382(l)(5), the exchange of stock for debt must be pursuant to a plan of bankruptcy.]

This special rule applies only if the stock-for-debt exchange, reorganization, or other transaction is ordered by the court or is pursuant to a plan approved by the court. [Thus, the transaction encompassed by § 382(l)(5) includes a single firm stock-for-debt exchange, a (G) bankruptcy reorganization, and a § 351 transaction.] For purposes of the 50-percent test, stock of a creditor that was converted from indebtedness is taken into account only if such indebtedness was held by the creditor for at least 18 months before the date the bankruptcy case was filed or arose in the ordinary course of the loss corporation's trade or business and is held by the person who has at all times held the beneficial interest in the claim. [*See* § 382(l)(5)(E).] [Thus, it is important that the historic debt holders, with an 18-month test of historic, and ordinary course creditors, receive stock for their debt. These are referred to as qualified creditors. To prevent trading after the bankruptcy announcement that may cause this condition not to be satisfied, the bankrupt corporation may apply for a stay against trading, at least by 5% shareholders within the meaning of § 382, in its debt. *Cf. Prudential*, Sec. 12.7.E.] Indebtedness will be considered as having arisen in the ordinary course of the loss corporation's business only if the indebtedness was incurred by the loss corporation in connection with the normal, usual, or customary conduct of its business. [*See* § 382(l)(5)(E)(ii).] It is not relevant for this purpose whether the debt was related to ordinary or capital expenditures of the loss corporation. In addition, stock of a shareholder is taken into account only to the extent such stock was received in exchange for stock that was held immediately before the ownership change. [§ 382(l)(5)(A)(ii)] [It is important to note the interrelationship between § 382(l)(5) and § 108. A transaction covered by § 382(l)(5) will give rise to COD income, which is excluded from income under § 108(a), but gives rise to a reduction in NOLs or other attributes under § 108(b). Thus, the transaction that overrides the general § 382 limitation may result in a reduction in the NOLs otherwise available to be carried forward.]

If the exception for bankruptcy proceedings applies, several special rules are applicable. * * * Second, the loss corporation's pre-change NOL carryforwards are reduced by the interest on the indebtedness that was converted to stock in the bankruptcy proceeding and paid or accrued during the period beginning on the first day of the third taxable year preceding the taxable year in which the ownership change occurs and ending on the change date. [*See* § 382(l)(5)(B).]

[This limitation could significantly reduce the amount of the NOLs that would otherwise be available after the bankruptcy reorganization. Section 382(l)(5)(C) provides that "[i]n applying section 108(e)(8) [relating to COD income arising from the issuance of stock for debt] to any case to which subparagraph (A) applies [relating to the bankruptcy exception to the § 382 limitation], there shall not be taken into account any indebtedness for interest described in subparagraph (B) [relating to the nondeductibility of interest paid within the last three years].]

Finally, after an ownership change that qualifies for the bankruptcy exception, a second ownership change during the following two-year period will result in the elimination of NOL carryforwards that arose before the first ownership change. [*See* § 382(l)(5)(D).] [To prevent this potential loss of the NOLs, restrictions may be placed on the transferability of the debtor's shares.]

The Act provides an election, subject to such terms and conditions as the Secretary may prescribe, to forgo the exception for title 11 or similar cases (new sec. 382(l)(5)(H)). If this election is made, the general rules [of § 382] will apply except that [pursuant to § 382(l)(6)] the value of the loss corporation will reflect any increase in value resulting from any surrender or cancellation of creditors' claims in the transaction (for purposes of applying new section 382(e) [relating to the value of the loss corporation]). [*See* §§ 382(l)(5)(H) and (6). *See also* Sec. 12.7.D., relating to the determination of the value of the loss corporation under § 382(l)(6), which overrides the anti-stuffing rules of § 382(l)(1).] [The parties may make the § 382(l)(5)(H) election if, for example, the denial under § 382(l)(5)(B) of deductions for interest paid within the last three years would result in a greater limitation on the utilization of NOLs than the regular § 382 limitation. The second ownership change rule under § 382(l)(5)(D) is not applicable if this election is made.] * * *

C. Determining Whether Stock of a Loss Corporation Is Owned by Reason of Being a Qualified Creditor within § 382(l)(5)(E)

1. Proposed Regulations under § 382(l)(5)(E)

Proposed Regulation RIN 1545-AQ08

58 FR 27498, May 10, 1993

Background This document proposes amendments to the Income Tax Regulations (26 CFR part 1) under section 382 of the Internal Revenue Code (Code). Section 382 limits the amount of income earned by a corporation after an ownership change that can be offset by losses incurred prior to the ownership change. In general, an ownership change is an increase of more than 50 percentage points in stock ownership by 5-percent shareholders over a three-year period. Section 382(l)(5) provides special rules for ownership changes resulting from bankruptcy proceedings. A loss corporation that qualifies for the special rules can use its loss carryforwards, after certain reductions, against its post-change income without limitation by section 382. A loss corporation qualifies only if its pre-change shareholders and creditors own at least 50 percent of its stock after the ownership change.

Section 382(l)(5)(E) provides that stock issued in exchange for indebtedness counts toward the 50 percent threshold of section 382(l)(5) only if the indebtedness (1) was held by the creditor at least 18 months before the bankruptcy filing, or (2) arose in the ordinary course of the trade or business of the loss corporation and was held at all times by the same beneficial owner. * * *

Explanation of Provisions *Definitions of Qualified Creditor and Qualified Indebtedness* Section 1.382-9(b)(2) of the regulations provides generally that section 382(l)(5) of the Code does not apply to an ownership change unless the pre-change shareholders and qualified creditors of the old loss corporation own (after the ownership change and as a result of being pre-change shareholders or qualified creditors immediately before the ownership change) at least 50 percent of the stock of the new loss corporation. The amendments proposed in this document, following the 1991 proposed regulations, provide that a qualified creditor is the beneficial owner, immediately before the ownership change, of qualified indebtedness of the loss corporation. Indebtedness of a loss corporation is qualified indebtedness if it (1) has been owned by the same beneficial owner since the date that is 18 months before the date of the filing of the title 11 or similar case, or (2) arose in the ordinary course of the trade or business of the loss corporation and has been owned at all times by the same beneficial owner.

Ordinary Course Indebtedness The 1991 proposed regulations provided that ordinary course indebtedness is indebtedness incurred by the loss corporation in connection with the normal, usual or customary conduct of business, determined without regard to whether the indebtedness funds ordinary or capital expenditures of the loss corporation. This definition closely followed the language of the relevant legislative history. See H.R. Rep. No. 841, 99th Cong., 2d Sess. II-192 (1986). The 1991 proposed regulations also provided specific examples of ordinary course indebtedness. The provisions regarding ordinary course indebtedness included in these proposed amendments are virtually identical to those of the 1991 proposed regulations. * * *

Treatment of Certain Indebtedness as Continuously Owned by the Same Owner The 1991 proposed regulations contained special rules intended to simplify the determination of whether the holders of widely-held indebtedness met the continuous ownership requirement of section 382(l)(5)(E). As the preamble to the 1991 proposed regulations explained, tracking the ownership of widely-held indebtedness can be costly and difficult, because, for example, the indebtedness is often held in street name. To alleviate these difficulties, the 1991 proposed regulations generally would have allowed a loss corporation to treat all or a portion of each class of its widely-held indebtedness as always having been owned by the same beneficial owners. The amount that could have been so treated was the amount owned by less-than-5-percent beneficial owners on either the plan date or the date of the ownership change, whichever amount was lower. The plan date was defined generally as the date of approval of a plan of reorganization. The 1991 proposed regulations would have required measurement of ownership of widely-held indebtedness on the plan date to preclude the application of the special rule for widely-held indebtedness to indebtedness accumulated by speculative investors and sold, prior to the change date, to purchasers who each own less than 5 percent of the class of indebtedness.

The 1991 proposed regulations provided optional procedures to determine ownership of widely-held indebtedness on the plan date and the change date. These optional procedures were intended to simplify the determination of the portion of indebtedness held in street name owned by one or more less-than-5-percent beneficial owners.

Based on comments on the 1991 proposed regulations, the Service determined that the rules of the proposed regulations can be simplified, thereby further reducing the administrative difficulties involved in the application of section 382(l)(5), and facilitating planning regarding the application of that section. In particular, the amendments proposed in this document include a *de minimis* rule that allows a loss corporation to treat indebtedness as always having been owned by the beneficial owner of the indebtedness immediately before the ownership change if the beneficial owner is not, immediately after the ownership change, either a 5-percent shareholder or an entity through which a 5-percent shareholder owns an indirect ownership interest in the loss corporation (a 5-percent entity). * * *

Finally, the proposed amendments do not require a loss corporation applying the *de minimis* rule to determine the ownership of its indebtedness on any date other than the change date. The Service determined that the possibility of purchases and sales of indebtedness by speculative investors do not justify the additional burdens involved in requiring loss corporations to measure the ownership of their indebtedness on the plan date as well as the change date.

As noted above, the *de minimis* rule applies only if the owner of the indebtedness prior to the ownership change is not, thereafter, either a 5-percent shareholder or a 5-percent entity. * * *

Special Rule if Indebtedness Is a Large Portion of a Beneficial Owner's Assets The 1991 proposed regulations included a special rule under which indebtedness of a loss corporation generally would not have been qualified indebtedness if (1) the beneficial owner of the indebtedness itself had had an ownership change during a prescribed period and (2) the indebtedness represented more than 25 percent of the beneficial owner's gross assets on the change date. This special rule would not have applied, however, if, immediately before the ownership change of the loss corporation, the beneficial owner owned less than $100,000 of the loss corporation's indebtedness, or the beneficial owner owned widely-held indebtedness that was less than 5 percent of its class. As stated in the preamble to the 1991 proposed regulations, this special rule was considered necessary to prevent the creation of special purpose entities to hold corporate indebtedness so that, if the debtor became financially troubled, ultimate economic ownership of the indebtedness could be transferred by selling interests in the entity without adversely affecting the debtor's ability to qualify under section 382(l)(5). The amendments proposed in this document include a special rule that is similar to that of the 1991 proposed regulations. Consistent with the de minimis rule described in Part (C), however, the special rule applies only if the beneficial owner of the indebtedness is a 5-percent entity.

Tacking Rules The preamble to the 1991 proposed regulations included a request for comments on whether, in certain circumstances, a transferee of debt should be treated as having owned the debt during the period that it was held by the transferor for the purpose of determining whether the debt meets the continuous ownership requirement of section 382(l)(5)(E). Based in part on comments on the 1991 proposed regulations, the amendments proposed in this document include tacking rules that provide such treatment.

In general, under the proposed amendments, a transferee of indebtedness in a qualified transfer is treated as having owned the indebtedness for the period that it was owned by the transferor for the purpose of determining whether the indebtedness is qualified indebtedness. A transfer is a qualified transfer if (1) the transfer is between related parties, (2) the transfer is pursuant to a customary loan syndication, (3) the transfer is by an underwriter pursuant to an underwriting, (4) the transferee's basis in the indebtedness is determined under section 1014 or 1015 or with reference to the transferor's basis in the indebtedness, (5) the transfer is in satisfaction of a right to receive a pecuniary bequest, (6) the transfer is pursuant to a divorce or separation instrument, or (7) the transfer is by reason of subrogation. A transfer of indebtedness is not a qualified transfer, however, if the transferee acquired the indebtedness for a principal purpose of benefiting from the losses of the loss corporation.

The proposed amendments provide a special rule for cases in which a loss corporation satisfies its indebtedness with new indebtedness, either through an exchange of new indebtedness for old indebtedness or a change in the terms of indebtedness that results in an exchange under section 1001. Under this rule, the owner of the new indebtedness is treated as having owned the new indebtedness for the period that it owned the old indebtedness. In addition, the new indebtedness is treated as having arisen in the ordinary course of the trade or business of the loss corporation if the old indebtedness so arose.

2. Final Regulations under § 382(l)(5)(E)

Treasury Decision 8529

59 FR 12844, March 18, 1994

Background This document contains final regulations to be added to the Income Tax Regulations (26 CFR part 1) under section 382 of the Internal Revenue Code (Code). The final regulations provide rules relating to the determination of whether stock of a loss corporation is owned as a result of being a qualified creditor for purposes of section 382(l)(5)(E) of the Code. * * *

Explanation of Provisions * * *The final regulations adopt the proposed regulations with several changes to respond to comments. The changes, as well as certain comments that were not adopted in the final regulations, are discussed below.

Treatment of Certain Indebtedness As Continuously Owned by the Same Owner The proposed regulations include a de minimis rule that allows a loss corporation to treat indebtedness as always having been owned by the beneficial owner of the indebtedness immediately before the ownership change if the beneficial owner is not, immediately after the ownership change, either a 5-percent shareholder or an entity through which a 5-percent shareholder owns an indirect ownership interest in the loss corporation (a 5-percent entity). The de minimis rule does not apply to indebtedness owned by a person whose participation in formulating a plan of reorganization makes evident to the loss corporation that the person has not owned the indebtedness for the requisite period. This exception applies regardless of whether the participant exchanges the indebtedness for stock pursuant to the plan or transfers the indebtedness to other persons prior to the effective date of the plan. * * *

The final regulations retain the exception to the *de minimis* rule. The loss corporation should not be able to disregard the fact that a creditor has not held its debt for the period required by section 382(l)(5)(E) if that fact is made evident by the creditor's participation in the formulation of the plan of reorganization. The need for the requirement that the loss corporation take these facts into account outweighs any potential difficulty the loss corporation may have in applying the requirement if the creditor that participates in formulating the plan transfers its debt prior to the effective date of the plan. * * *

Treatment of Accrued Interest on Qualified Indebtedness The proposed (and final) regulations generally provide that stock received by a creditor counts toward the 50 percent threshold of section 382(l)(5) only to the extent that the creditor receives the stock in full or partial satisfaction of qualifying indebtedness held for the requisite period. In response to a comment, the final regulations clarify that such indebtedness held by a creditor includes interest accrued thereon. * * *

D. Determining the Value of a Loss Corporation under § 382(l)(6)

Treasury Decision 8530
59 FR 12840, March 18, 1994

Summary This document contains final regulations that provide guidance on determining the value of a loss corporation following an ownership change to which section 382(l)(6) of the Internal Revenue Code of 1986 applies. * * *

Explanation of Provisions Section 382(l)(6) of the Code provides a special valuation rule for certain ownership changes that result from a title 11 or similar case to which section 382(l)(5) does not apply. Under this special valuation rule, the value of the loss corporation reflects any increase in value resulting from any surrender or cancellation of creditors' claims in the bankruptcy transaction. The proposed regulations provide rules regarding the application of this special valuation rule and the coordination of that rule with other statutory rules related to the value of a loss corporation. * * *

The proposed regulations provide that the value of a loss corporation under the special valuation rule of section 382(l)(6) of the Code is the lesser of the value of its stock immediately after the ownership change, or the value of its assets (determined without regard to liabilities) immediately before the ownership change. The proposed regulations further provide that the value of the loss corporation's pre-change assets is reduced by the amount of any capital contribution to which section 382(l)(1) applies. The proposed regulations could be read to require such a reduction even in cases in which the value of the pre-change assets would not reflect the value of the contributed assets, as would be the case, for example, when the contribution is con-current with the ownership change. To avoid this possibility, the final regulations provide that the value of the pre-change assets of the loss corporation is determined without regard to any capital contribution to which section 382(l)(1) applies. * * *

A commenter suggested that the final regulations clarify that a loss corporation need not use liquidation value in determining the value of its gross assets, and that the corporation may take into account the value of any intangible assets, such as goodwill and going concern value. The Treasury and the Service have determined that the proposed clarification is unnecessary. The valuation rule refers to "the value of the loss corporation's pre-change assets," without limitation to either liquidation value or tangible assets. Therefore, if a loss corporation is able to establish the existence and value of any intangible assets, that value may be taken into account.

The proposed regulations provide that the amount received by a loss corporation for the issuance of debt is treated as a capital contribution that must be excluded from the value of its pre-change assets if the issuance of the debt is part of a plan a principal purpose of which is to increase the value of the loss corporation under the rules of the proposed regulations. A commenter questioned the appropriateness of treating an issuance of debt as a capital contribution. The commenter also suggested that, if the proposed rule is retained, it should be subject to an exception for cases in which the loss corporation uses the proceeds of the debt to fund operating expenses.

The final regulations retain the rule of the proposed regulations regarding the treatment of certain debt issuances as capital contributions. The Treasury and the Service believe that this rule effectuates the principles of section 382(l)(1) of the Code. The Treasury and the Service will consider possible exceptions to this rule in the context of providing general guidance under section 382(l)(1).

Section 382(l)(5)(D) of the Code provides that, if a second ownership change occurs within two years after an ownership change to which section 382(l)(5) applies, the section 382 limitation with respect to the second ownership change is zero. A commenter suggested that the final regulations provide that the zero limitation applies only to losses incurred prior to the first ownership change. The final regulations do not provide such a rule because it would be inconsistent with the language of section 382(l)(5)(D).

The proposed regulations provide that the value of the stock of a loss corporation does not include stock issued with a principal purpose of increasing the section 382 limitation without subjecting the investment to the entrepreneurial risks of corporate business operations. A commenter requested that the final regulations provide further guidance regarding the stock subject to this rule. The Treasury and the Service believe that additional guidance is not necessary because the test sufficiently limits the scope of this anti-abuse provision.

The proposed regulations provide that the value of any stock issued in connection with the ownership change cannot exceed the value of the property received by the loss corporation in consideration for the stock. A commenter questioned the appropriateness of this limitation. The final regulations, however, retain the limitation to preclude any claims that the stock is worth more than what was paid for it. The limitation avoids the valuation disputes that would result from these claims. Further, the limitation on losses provided by section 382(a) of the Code is intended to measure the earnings power of the corporation. When a loss corporation issues stock, it increases its earnings power by the value of the property it receives, regardless of whether that value represents a fair price for the stock.

E. Introductory Problems on Impact of § 382 in Bankruptcy

Debtor Corporation (*DC*) has both common stock and debentures outstanding. The debentures have a principal amount of $100K, and there is no OID on the debentures. $30K of interest was paid on the debentures within the last three years. *DC* is in bankruptcy, and it has $200K of NOLs. Pursuant to a plan of bankruptcy, *DC* issues its common stock with a value of $40K in exchange for its old debentures. The newly issued common stock amounts to 90% of the outstanding common stock after issuance, so the old common shareholders end up with 10% of the stock. What is the impact on the debenture holders and *DC,* including the impact of §§ 108 and 382? What if an investor purchased the debentures six months before the exchange? What if a year and a half after the transaction, a third party purchases on the open market 75% of the stock of *DC*?

§ 12.8 Impact of § 269 on Utilization of NOLs after a Bankruptcy Reorganization

Preamble to Final Regulations under § 269

Treasury Decision 8388 (January 6, 1992)

Ownership Changes to Which Section 382(l)(5) Applies Section 1.269-7 of the proposed regulations clarifies that section 269 of the Code may be applied to disallow a deduction, credit or other allowance even though the acquisition of control or property of a corporation occurs in connection with an ownership change to which section 382 applies. Section 1.269-3(d) of the proposed regulations provides that, absent strong evidence to the contrary, a requisite acquisition of control or property in connection with an ownership change to which section 382(l)(5) [relating to bankruptcy, *see* Sec. 12.7] applies is considered to be made for the principal purpose of tax evasion or avoidance unless the corporation carries on more than an insignificant amount of an active trade or business during and subsequent to the title 11 or similar case. * * *

[T]he Service has made certain changes to clarify that the determination of whether a corporation carries on more than an insignificant amount of an active trade or business is made without regard to continuity of business enterprise under § 1.368-1(d) and that a corporation may satisfy this requirement even if all of the corporation's business activities temporarily cease for a period of time in order to address business exigencies. * * *

Section 269 of the Code should play only a residual role, applying only to transactions to which the rules of sections 382 and 383 technically do not apply, but which violate the purposes of those sections. [Section 382 is examined in Secs. 6.8. and 12.7.] These commentators believe that the acquisition of control of a bankrupt corporation by its qualified creditors in a section 382(l)(5) ownership change does not violate the purposes of section 382 regardless of the corporation's level of business activity because the creditors have borne the economic losses reflected in the tax attributes.

Relegating section 269 of the Code to a residual role is inconsistent with the intent of Congress, expressed in the Conference Report to the Tax Reform Act of 1986, that the amendment of sections 382 and 383 not alter the continuing application of section 269. The rules of section 269 and other provisions of the Code that prohibit or limit deductions, credits, or other allowances are not mutually exclusive. *See* § 1.269-2(b). The application of section 269 to loss corporations that do not carry on more than an insignificant amount of a trade or business is consistent with interpretations of existing law that prevent taxpayers from trafficking in tax attributes of corporations carrying on minimal business activities. * * *

§ 12.9 Disclosure Statement in WorldCom Bankruptcy

In re WorldCom, Inc.

United States Bankruptcy Court
Southern District Of New York, April 14, 2003

Debtors' Disclosure Statement Pursuant to Section 1125 of the Bankruptcy Code

INTRODUCTION. WorldCom, Inc. and certain of its direct and indirect subsidiaries, as debtors and debtors in possession (collectively, "WorldCom" or the "Debtors"), submit this Disclosure Statement pursuant to section 1125 of title 11 of the United States Code (the "Bankruptcy Code") to holders of Claims against and Equity Interests in the Debtors. * * *

SUMMARY OF CLASSIFICATION AND TREATMENT OF CLAIMS AND EQUITY INTERESTS UNDER THE PLAN.[The following is a summary of much of the plan of distribution. Administrative Expense Claims, Priority Tax Claims, and certain Other Priority Claims are paid in full in cash or remain Unimpaired. Certain Convenience Claims (*i.e.*, small claims) are paid in cash to the extent of 40%. WorldCom Senior Debt Claims are entitled to, at the option of the holder, Common Stock or New Notes. WorldCom General Unsecured Claims receive a distribution of Common Stock and Cash. On the other hand, WorldCom Subordinated Claims and Equity receive no distribution.]

GENERAL INFORMATION. OVERVIEW OF CHAPTER 11. Chapter 11 is the principal business reorganization chapter of the Bankruptcy Code. Under chapter 11 of the Bankruptcy Code, a debtor is authorized to reorganize its business for the benefit of itself, its creditors and its equity interest holders. In addition to permitting the rehabilitation of a debtor, another goal of chapter 11 is to promote equality of treatment for similarly situated creditors and similarly situated equity interest holders with respect to the distribution of a debtor's assets.

The commencement of a chapter 11 case creates an estate that is comprised of all of the legal and equitable interests of the debtor as of the commencement date. The Bankruptcy Code provides that the debtor may continue to operate its business and remain in possession of its property as a "debtor in possession."

The consummation of a plan of reorganization is the principal objective of a chapter 11 reorganization case. A plan of reorganization sets forth the means for satisfying claims against and interests in a debtor. Confirmation of a plan of reorganization by the bankruptcy court binds the debtor, any issuer of securities under the plan, any person acquiring property under the plan, and any creditor or equity interest holder of a debtor. * * *

Certain holders of claims against and interests in a debtor are permitted to vote to accept or reject the plan. Prior to soliciting acceptances of the proposed plan, section 1125 of the Bankruptcy Code requires a debtor to prepare a disclosure statement containing adequate information of a kind, and in sufficient detail, to enable a hypothetical reasonable investor to make an informed judgment regarding the plan. The Debtors are submitting this Disclosure Statement to holders of Claims against and Equity Interests in the Debtors to satisfy the requirements of section 1125 of the Bankruptcy Code pursuant to that provision. * * *

CERTAIN FEDERAL INCOME TAX CONSEQUENCES OF THE PLAN. The following discussion summarizes certain federal income tax consequences of the implementation of the Plan to the Debtors and certain holders of Claims. * * *

The federal income tax consequences of the Plan are complex and are subject to significant uncertainties. The Debtors have not requested a ruling from the IRS or an opinion of counsel with respect to any of the tax aspects of the Plan. * * *

Consequences to the Debtors. The WorldCom Group files a consolidated federal income tax return, which takes into account the operations of all of the Debtors (some of which are treated as partnerships or disregarded entities for federal income tax purposes). The WorldCom Group reported consolidated NOL carryforwards for federal income tax purposes of approximately$6.6 billion as of December 31, 2001, a portion of which is subject to certain existing limitations. In addition, the Debtors expect to incur additional losses during the taxable year ending December 31, 2002. The amount of the Debtors' losses and NOL carryforwards are currently under examination by the IRS and remain subject to adjustment. * * *

Cancellation of Debt. The Tax Code provides that a debtor in a bankruptcy case must reduce certain of its tax attributes—such as NOL carryforwards, current year NOLs, tax credits and tax basis in assets—by the amount of any cancellation of debt ("COD"). COD is the amount by which the indebtedness discharged (reduced by any unamortized discount) exceeds any consideration given in exchange therefor, subject to certain statutory or judicial exceptions that can apply to limit the amount of COD (such as where the payment of the cancelled debt would have given rise to a tax deduction). To the extent the amount of COD exceeds the tax attributes available for reduction, the remaining COD is simply forgiven. However, to the extent that nonrecourse debt is satisfied with the underlying collateral, generally the debtor recognizes a gain from the disposition of property based on an amount realized equal to the nonrecourse debt satisfied, as opposed to COD.

It is unclear whether the reduction in tax attributes occurs on a separate company basis even though the Debtors file a consolidated federal income tax return. * * *

As a result of the discharge of Claims pursuant to the Plan, the Debtors will suffer substantial COD. The extent of such COD and resulting tax attribute reduction will depend, in principal part, on the value of the New Common Stock distributed. Based on the estimated reorganization value of the Reorganized Debtors (see Article X), it is anticipated that the Reorganized Debtors will incur COD of upwards of $19 billion or more. The extent to which NOLs and certain tax credits survive tax attribute reduction, and the extent of any basis reduction, will depend upon the manner of applying the attribute reduction rules in the context of a consolidated group.

Limitations on NOL Carryforwards and Other Tax Benefits. Following the implementation of the Plan, any remaining NOL and tax redit carryforwards and, possibly, certain other tax attributes of the Reorganized Debtors allocable to periods prior to the Effective Date (collectively, "pre-change losses") may be subject to limitation under section 382 of the Tax Code as a result of the change in ownership of the Reorganized Debtors.

Under section 382, if a corporation undergoes an "ownership change" and the corporation does not qualify for (or elects out of) the special bankruptcy exception discussed below, the amount of its pre-change losses that may be utilized to offset future taxable income is subject to an annual limitation. Such limitation also may apply to certain losses or deductions that are "built-in" (i.e., economically accrued but unrecognized) as of the date of the ownership change and that are subsequently recognized.

The issuance of the New Common Stock of Reorganized WorldCom to holders of Allowed Claims pursuant to the Plan will constitute an ownership change of the Reorganized Debtors.

General Section 382 Limitation. In general, the amount of the annual limitation to which a corporation (or consolidated group) would be subject is equal to the product of (i) the fair market value of the stock of the corporation (or, in the case of a consolidated group, the common parent) immediately before the ownership change (with certain adjustments) multiplied by (ii) the "long term tax exempt rate" in effect for the month in which the ownership change occurs (4.58% for ownership changes occurring in April 2003). For a corporation (or consolidated group) in bankruptcy that undergoes the change of ownership pursuant to a confirmed plan, the stock value generally is determined immediately after (rather than before) the ownership change, and certain adjustments that ordinarily would apply do not apply.

Any unused limitation may be carried forward, thereby increasing the annual limitation in the subsequent taxable year. However, if the corporation (or the consolidated group) does not continue its historic business or use a significant portion of its assets in a new business for two years after the ownership change, the annual limitation resulting from the ownership change is zero.

Built In Gains and Losses. If a loss corporation (or consolidated group) has a net unrealized built-in loss at the time of an ownership change (taking into account most assets and items of "built-in" income and deduction), then any built-in losses recognized during the following five years (up to the amount of the original net unrealized built-in loss) generally will be treated as pre-change losses and similarly will be subject to the annual limitation. Conversely, if the loss corporation (or consolidated group) has a net unrealized built-in gain at the time of an ownership change, any built-in gains recognized during the following five years (up to the amount of the original net unrealized built-in gain) generally will increase the annual limitation in the year recognized, such that the loss corporation (or consolidated group) would be permitted to use its pre-change losses against such built-in gain income in addition to its regular annual allowance. Although the rule applicable to net unrealized built-in losses generally applies to consolidated groups on a consolidated basis, certain corporations that join the consolidated group within the preceding five years may not be able to be taken into account in the group computation of net unrealized built-in loss. Such corporations would nevertheless still be taken into account in determining whether the consolidated group has a net unrealized built-in gain. In general, a loss corporation's (or consolidated group's) net unrealized built-in gain or loss will be deemed to be zero unless it is greater than the lesser of (i) $10 million or (ii) 15% of the fair market value of its assets (with certain adjustments) before the ownership change. The Debtors anticipate that the WorldCom Group will be in a net unrealized built in loss position as of the Effective Date.

Special Bankruptcy Exception. An exception to the foregoing annual limitation rules generally applies where qualified (so-called "old and cold") creditors of a debtor receive, in respect of their claims, at least 50% of the vote and value of the stock of the reorganized debtor (or a controlling corporation if also in bankruptcy) pursuant to a confirmed chapter 11 plan. Under this exception, a debtor's pre-change losses are not limited on an annual basis but, instead, are required to be reduced by the amount of any interest deductions claimed during the three taxable years preceding the effective date of the reorganization, and during the part of the taxable year prior to and including the reorganization, in respect of all debt converted into stock in the bankruptcy proceeding. Moreover, if this exception applies, any further ownership change of the debtor within a two-year period after the consummation of the chapter

11 plan will preclude the debtor's future utilization of any pre-change losses existing at the time of the subsequent ownership change.

The receipt of the New Common Stock by holders of Claims pursuant to the Plan may qualify for this exception. Neither the statute nor the regulations address, however, whether this exception can be applied on a consolidated basis or only on a separate company basis. * * * Even if the Debtors qualify for this exception, the Debtors may, if they so desire, elect not to have the exception apply and instead remain subject to the annual limitation described above. Such election would have to be made in the Debtors' federal income tax return for the taxable year in which the change occurs. For purposes of the Projected Financial Information, the Debtors have taken the position that their pre-change losses will not be limited on an annual basis under Section 382 of the Tax Code due to the special exception applicable to certain ownership changes in bankruptcy.

The Reincorporation of WorldCom, Inc. The Debtors anticipate, and the discussion herein assumes, that the reincorporation of WorldCom, Inc. as a Delaware corporation pursuant to the Plan should qualify as a reorganization under section 368(a)(1)(G) of the Tax Code (a "G" reorganization) for federal income tax purposes. In addition to other statutory and non-statutory requirements common to tax-free reorganizations, for a merger of a corporation in bankruptcy to qualify as a "G" reorganization, (i) the debtor corporation must transfer substantially all of its assets to the acquiring corporation and distribute all stock and securities received of such corporation or its parent, including to at least one stockholder or security holder of the debtor corporation, and (ii) the historic shareholders and creditors of the debtor corporation must receive, collectively, a sufficient percentage of the acquiring corporation's stock relative to the amount of non-stock consideration received. The Debtors believe that all of these requirements will be satisfied. Accordingly, WorldCom, Inc. should not recognize any gain or loss as a result of the reincorporation.

The Intermedia Merger. The Debtors anticipate, and the discussion herein assumes, that the merger of Intermedia with and into another first-tier subsidiary of WorldCom, Inc. pursuant to the Plan in exchange for New Common Stock should qualify as a reorganization under section 368(a)(1)(G) of the Tax Code (a "G" reorganization) for federal income tax purposes. * * *

Consequences to Holders of Certain Claims. Pursuant to and in accordance with the Plan, holders of Allowed WorldCom General Unsecured Claims and Allowed Intermedia General Unsecured Claims will receive New Common Stock and cash in satisfaction of their Claims, holders of Allowed WorldCom Senior Debt Claims, Allowed Intermedia Senior Debt Claims and Allowed Intermedia Subordinated Debt Claims will receive New Common Stock and/or New Notes in satisfaction of their Claims, * * *. Holders of Allowed Convenience Claims will receive cash in satisfaction of their Claims.

The federal income tax consequences of the Plan to holders of Claims (other than Convenience Claims) against WorldCom, Inc. and Intermedia depend, in part, on whether such holders' Claims, and whether the New Notes, constitute "securities" for federal income tax purposes. The term "security" is not defined in the Tax Code or in the Treasury Regulations issued thereunder and has not been clearly defined by judicial decisions. The determination of whether a particular debt constitutes a "security" depends on an overall evaluation of the nature of the debt. One of the most significant factors considered in determining whether a particular debt is a security is its original term. In general, debt obligations issued with a weighted average maturity at issuance of five (5) years or less (e.g., trade debt and revolving credit obligations) do not constitute securities, whereas debt obligations with a weighted average maturity of ten (10) years or more constitute securities. For example, the Debtors believe that the Intermedia Senior Debt Claims (each having an original ten-year maturity) constitute "securities" of Intermedia for federal income tax purposes. Each holder is urged to consult its tax advisor regarding the status of its Claim, or any portion thereof, and the New Notes as "securities" for federal income tax purposes.

The following discussion does not necessarily apply to holders who have Claims in more than one Class relating to the same underlying obligation (such as where the underlying obligation is classified as partially secured and partially unsecured). Such holders should consult their tax advisor regarding the effect of such dual status obligations on the federal income tax consequences of the Plan to them.

Consequences to Holders of Convenience Claims. In general, holders of Allowed Convenience Claims will recognize gain or loss in an amount equal to the difference between (i) the amount of cash received by such holder in satisfaction of its Claim (other than any Claim for accrued but unpaid interest) and (ii) the holder's adjusted tax basis in its Claim (other than any Claim for accrued but unpaid interest). * * *

Consequences to Holders of Allowed Claims that Do Not Constitute "Securities" of WorldCom, Inc. or Intermedia. The receipt of New Common Stock, New Notes and/or cash in satisfaction of Allowed Claims (other than Convenience Claims) that do not constitute "securities" of WorldCom, Inc. or Intermedia will be a fully taxable transaction. * * *

Where gain or loss is recognized by a holder, the character of such gain or loss as long term or short term capital gain or loss or as ordinary income or loss will be determined by a number of factors. * * *

Consequences to Holders of Claims that Constitute "Securities" of WorldCom, Inc. and Intermedia. In general, a holder of an Allowed Claim that constitutes a "security" of WorldCom, Inc. or Intermedia will not recognize loss upon the receipt of New Common Stock, New Notes and/or cash, but will recognize gain (computed as described in the preceding section), if any, to the extent of the "issue price" of any New Notes (see "Ownership and Disposition of the New Notes—Interest and Original Issue Discount on New Notes") if the New Notes do not constitute "securities" or the amount of any cash received in satisfaction of its Claim (other than any Claim for accrued but unpaid interest). * * *

However, the receipt by a holder of solely New Notes will be a fully taxable transaction (with the same consequences as described in the preceding section) unless the New Notes constitute "securities" for federal income tax purposes.

If the New Notes do not constitute "securities," then (i) a holder'saggregate tax basis in any New Common Stock received in satisfaction of its Claim will equal the holder's aggregate adjusted tax basis in its Claim (including any Claim for accrued but unpaid interest) and decreased by any deductions claimed in respect of any previously accrued interest and (ii) a holder's aggregate tax basis in any New Notes received will equal the "issue price" of such notes. If the New Notes constitute "securities," then a holder's aggregate tax basis in any New Common Stock and New Notes received will equal such holder's adjusted tax basis in its Claim (including any Claim for accrued but unpaid interest) and decreased by any deductions claimed in respect of any previously accrued interest. In such case, the tax basis will be allocated between such New Common Stock and New Notes based on relative fair market value. In general, the holder's holding period for any New Common Stock received and any New Notes (if the New Notes constitute "securities") will include the holder's holding period for the Claim except to the extent issued in respect of a Claim for accrued but unpaid interest. If the New Notes do not constitute "securities," a holder's holding period for any New Notes received will begin the day following the issuance of such notes.

Distributions in Discharge of Accrued Interest. In general, to the extent that any distribution to a holder of an Allowed Claim (whether paid in New Common Stock or New Notes) is received in satisfaction of accrued interest or amortized original issue discount ("OID") during its holding period, such amount will be taxable to the holder as interest income (if not previously included in the holder's gross income). * * *

Ownership and Disposition of the New Notes. Interest and Original Issue Discount on the New Notes. * * * [U]nder certain circumstances, the New Notes may be treated as issued with OID. In general, a debt instrument is treated as having OID to the extent its "stated redemption price at maturity" exceeds its "issue price" by more than a de minimis amount. * * *

Acquisition and Bond Premium * * *

Market Discount * * *

Subsequent Sale of New Common Stock. * * * Any gain recognized by a holder upon a subsequent taxable disposition of New Common Stock received in satisfaction of a Claim directly against WorldCom, Inc. or a first-tier subsidiary of WorldCom, Inc. pursuant to the Plan (or any stock or property received for it in a later tax free exchange) will be treated as ordinary income to the extent of (i) any bad debt deductions (or additions to a bad debt reserve) claimed with respect to its Claim and any ordinary loss deductions incurred upon satisfaction of its Claim, less any income (other than interest income) recognized by the holder upon satisfaction of its Claim, and (ii) with respect to a cash basis holder, any amount that would have been included in its gross income if the holder's Claim had been satisfied in full but that was not included by reason of the cash method of accounting.

In addition, as discussed in the preceding section, a holder that receives its New Common Stock in exchange for a Claim that constitutes a "security" of WorldCom, Inc. or Intermedia for federal income tax purposes maybe required to treat all or a portion of any gain recognized as ordinary income under the market discount provisions of the Internal Revenue Code.

Information Reporting and Withholding * * *

ALTERNATIVES TO CONFIRMATION AND CONSUMMATION OF THE PLAN. If the Plan is not confirmed and consummated, the Debtors' alternatives include (i) liquidation of the Debtors under chapter 7 of the Bankruptcy Code and (ii) the preparation and presentation of an alternative plan or plans of reorganization.

LIQUIDATION UNDER CHAPTER 7. If no chapter 11 plan can be confirmed, the Chapter 11 Cases may be converted to cases under chapter 7 of the Bankruptcy Code in which a trustee would be elected or appointed to liquidate the assets of the Debtors. * * * The Debtors believe that liquidation under chapter 7 would result in, among other things, (i) smaller distributions being made to creditors and Equity Interest holders than those provided for in the Plan because of additional administrative expenses attendant to the appointment of a trustee and the trustee's employment of attorneys and other professionals, (ii) additional expenses and claims, some of which would be entitled to priority, which would be generated during the liquidation and from the rejection of leases and other executory contracts in connection with a cessation of the Debtors' operations and (iii) the failure to realize the greater, going concern value of the Debtors' assets. * * *

Chapter 13

Tax Policy Aspects of Mergers and Acquisitions

§ 13.1 Scope

This chapter deals with tax policy aspects of mergers and acquisitions. Sec. 13.2 discusses the proposed repeal of the acquisitive reorganization provisions. Sec. 13.3 presents a proposal for the comprehensive revision of the merger, acquisition, and LBO provisions of the Code. Sec. 13.4 provides an analysis of the conceptual foundations of the reorganization provisions, and Sec. 13.5 examines a proposal for federalizing the (A) merger. Sec. 13.6 provides a comparison of the corporate nonrecognition provisions in the U.S. with those in Canada. Sec. 13.7 examines various options that Congress has considered for dealing with LBO transactions. Sec. 13.8 presents some policy perspective on domestic and international business tax reform generally. These general reforms, including the possibility of lowering the corporate tax rate, would have an impact on M&A activity and transactions. Finally, Sec. 13.8 refers to Chapter 10, which deals with cross border reorganizations, for a policy analysis of the treatment of inversion transactions and the possibility of moving to a territorial or imputation system. Inversions are transactions in which a publicly held U.S. corporation becomes a subsidiary of a publicly held foreign holding company. The impact of §§ 367 and 7874 on these transactions is examined in Chapter 10.

In addition to the materials included in this chapter, *see ALI 1980 Subchapter C Study, supra* Sec. 1.12; *ALI 1989 Subchapter C Study, supra* Sec. 1.12; *ALI 1993 Integration Study, supra* Sec. 1.12; *Treasury Integration Study, supra* Sec. 1.12; and the articles and other sources cited in Chapter 1 of Thompson, *Reform of the Taxation of Mergers, Acquisitions and LBOs, supra* Sec. 1.12.

§ 13.2 Proposal for Repeal of the Reorganization Provisions

Report of Staff of Senate Finance Committee on Subchapter C Revision Bill of 1985

37–54 (1985)

[The proposals set out below are based on and are substantially the same as proposals made by The American Law Institute. *See ALI 1980 Subchapter C Study, supra* Sec. 1.12.]

Reasons for Change *General reasons for change* * * * The current law of Subchapter C is seriously flawed. The "law" consists of a series of rules, some statutory and others of judicial origin, which, when taken together, lack consistency, are unnecessarily complex, and are often subject to manipulation. By providing uncertain and often capricious tax consequences to business transactions, the law inadequately addresses the needs of businessmen, their corporations, and their investors. Moreover, by being inconsistent and subject to manipulation, the law is biased, at times encouraging tax-motivated transactions, and at times discouraging or making less efficient legitimate business dealings. * * *

The inadequacy of current law presents three interrelated principal reasons for change. First, current law needs to be made more rational and consistent, thereby providing greater certainty and less complexity in the area. For example, under current law, an "A" reorganization (statutory merger or consolidation) may involve a significant amount of cash consideration, a "B" reorganization (stock-for-stock acquisition) cannot have any cash consideration, and a "C" reorganization (stock-for-assets acquisition) may involve a small amount of cash consideration. No policy justification can be found for these and other distinctions. The bill would propose to eliminate artificial distinctions of that sort. * * *

Detailed reasons for change Problems relating to the definition of "reorganization" As outlined below, the different definitional requirements for a "reorganization" create much of the complexity in current law. Some of these requirements are based on statutory rules, and others are of judicial origin. There are persuasive arguments for standardizing and making uniform these rules, as well as the rules prescribing the various forms of taxable acquisitions.

Boot as consideration. No consideration other than voting stock is permitted in a B reorganization. A C reorganization permits a limited amount of boot (up to 20 percent of the total consideration). No specific statutory rule limits the amount of boot in an A reorganization, although the continuity of interest doctrine imposes some limitation. In certain cases, the assumption of liabilities may be treated as boot and in certain other cases, it may not be. No policy justification can be found for maintaining these disparate rules in what are essentially economically equivalent transactions.

Voting stock as consideration. The qualifying consideration in a B or C reorganization, or a reverse triangular merger, must be *voting* stock. No such limitation applies in an A reorganization or a forward triangular merger.

Stock of corporation in control of acquiring corporation as consideration. If structured correctly, as many as three tiers of acquiring corporations may be involved in an acquisitive transaction without affecting reorganization status. It is unclear from the statute whether reorganization status can be preserved if the structuring is not proper and, for example, the acquiring corporation is in the third tier of corporations, although the IRS has ruled favorably on the question. It is also questionable whether stock of a corporation involving more remote ownership may be used. This introduces unnecessary rigidity when a target corporation is acquired by one or more members of an affiliated group.

Subsidiary mergers. Different rules apply depending upon the direction of a subsidiary merger under section 368(a)(2)(D) or 368(a)(2)(E). Further, the "substantially all" limitation (discussed below) applies to subsidiary mergers even though they are nominally classified as A reorganizations. Thus, the requirements for a subsidiary merger are closer to C reorganizations than A reorganizations. The different, inconsistent, and complex requirements applicable to an acquisition through a subsidiary have been described as impossible to justify.

"Substantially all" requirement. As noted, C reorganizations and subsidiary mergers impose a "substantially all" limitation. Certain D reorganizations have the same requirement. No such limitation is contained in an A reorganization. Thus, for example, a predisposition of assets prior to an acquisition may cause the transaction to fail as a C reorganization, [*see Elkhorn Coal, supra* Sec. 7.3.D.1] but as an A reorganization. [*See Morris Trust, supra* Chapter 9.]

Furthermore, the exact meaning of "substantially all" is unclear. Ruling guidelines applicable to C reorganizations and subsidiary mergers establish a 70 percent of gross assets and 90 percent of net assets standard. [*See* Rev. Proc. 77-37 in Sec. 6.2.C.] Case law in the D reorganization area has permitted a much smaller percentage of assets to qualify as "substantially all."

Predisposition of assets. As described above, a predisposition of assets prior to an acquisition may affect qualification as a C reorganization or a subsidiary merger. No such problem generally occurs in an A or B reorganization.

Overlap issues. With the exception of a transaction qualifying as both a C and D reorganization where D reorganization status is mandated, the statute does not provide rules settling overlap questions between and among reorganization provisions. This creates substantial uncertainty where the tax consequences of the transaction depend upon the specific category of reorganization that is satisfied.

Continuity of interest requirement. This judicial doctrine is of uncertain application. The portion of total consideration consisting of an equity interest must be a "material part" of the consideration for the transferred assets. [*See Minnesota Tea, supra* Sec. 6.2.B.2.] However, where 38 percent of the consideration consisted of callable preferred stock, this requirement has been considered satisfied. [*See John A. Nelson, supra* Sec. 6.2.B.3.]

Moreover, the assumption underlying the limitation is that preferred treatment should be provided to consideration in the form of stock because stock represents a continuing commitment by the shareholders of the target corporation in the risks of the target business after the acquisition. This policy goal may not be effectively implemented where, for example, preferred stock subject to early redemption is provided tax-free treatment whereas a long-term creditor interest is not. In that case, the preferred stock may represent much less of a continuing commitment in the business risks of the target corporation than the long-term creditor interest.

Further, the IRS has indicated for ruling purposes that continuity of interest is important both before and after an acquisition. As noted, at least one case has held that continuity of interest is not present if the target corporation shareholders dispose of the stock received in the transaction pursuant to a prearranged plan. [This position has been reversed in the new continuity of interest regulations, *See* Chapter 6.] [Prior to the new continuity of interest regulations,] it is unclear whether significant preacquisition arbitrage activity will preclude tax-free treatment of the subsequent acquisition.

Finally, the existence of continuity of interest may depend upon the nature of the interest in the target corporation surrendered by the target investor. For example, in a merger of a stock savings and loan association into a mutual savings and loan association, where the former shareholders of the target corporation received passbook savings accounts and certificates of deposit of the acquiring entity (the only form of "equity" available in the acquiring entity), the Supreme Court held that the continuity of interest requirement was not satisfied. [*See Paulsen, supra* Sec. 6.2.B.10.] In contrast, where interests in a mutual savings and loan association were exchanged for interests in an acquiring mutual savings and loan association, the IRS held that continuity of interest was satisfied.

Continuity of business enterprise and business purpose doctrines. Two other non-statutory requirements for a corporate reorganization are the business purpose and continuity of business enterprise doctrines. The regulations were recently amended to provide that the trade or business of the target corporation must be continued, or a "significant portion" of the target company's historic business assets must be used in a trade or business following the acquisition, in order to satisfy the continuity of business enterprise requirement. Some uncertainty surrounds the exact parameters of these tests.

Linking of shareholder level consequences to corporate level consequences and to tax treatment of other shareholders. Current law links the shareholder level consequences of a reorganization to the corporate level consequences and to the tax treatment of other shareholders in the transaction. This produces a number of anomalous results.

For example, a transaction that fails reorganization status at the corporate level (*e.g.,* because a predisposition of assets causes failure of the "substantially all" requirement) will therefore be fully taxable at the shareholder level, even though the shareholders of the target corporation all receive stock in the acquiring corporation. This is contrary to the policy decision that stock in an acquiring corporation should entitle a target shareholder to tax-free treatment.

As another example, failure to satisfy a shareholder level requirement (*e.g.,* continuity of interest) will make a transaction completely taxable at the corporate level. This recently occurred in the case of *Paulsen v. Commissioner* [*see* Sec. 6.2.B.10] where, because of failure of continuity of interest, a merger of a stock savings and loan association into a mutual savings and loan association was a taxable transaction. A more rational system would permit the corporate merger to be tax-free so long as the acquiring entity obtained only a carryover basis in the assets transferred.

A final example is illustrated by *May B. Kass v. Commissioner.* [*See* Sec. 7.2.E.] In that case, a single minority target shareholder who received solely stock in the acquiring corporation in an acquisition, was required to treat the exchange as a taxable one because of failure of the overall transaction to satisfy continuity of interest. No apparent policy reason can be found to justify linking the tax consequences for one shareholder of a target corporation to the tax treatment of other such shareholders. Furthermore, as described earlier, the well-advised may, in any event, be able to obtain nonrecognition treatment for the minority shareholder through the formation of a holding company. [*See* Rev. Rul. 84-71, *supra* Sec. 6.19.D.] * * *

Summary of Proposals The principal proposals contained in the bill are described below. A more detailed description of the proposals is set forth in the Technical Explanation accompanying the bill.

Definition of qualified acquisition (new section 364 of the Code) In general, the bill consolidates, simplifies, and makes uniform the rules classifying corporate mergers and acquisitions, whether treated under current law as a "reorganization", a liquidating sale * * * or a section 338 stock acquisition.

New section 364 defines "qualified acquisition" as meaning any "qualified stock acquisition" or any "qualified asset acquisition." A qualified stock acquisition is defined as any transaction or series of transactions during the 12-month acquisition period in which one corporation acquires stock representing control of another corporation. A qualified asset acquisition means (1) any statutory merger or consolidation, or (2) any other transaction in which one corporation acquires at least 70 percent of the gross fair market value and at least 90 percent of the net fair market value of the assets of another corporation held immediately before the acquisition, and the transferor corporation distributes, within 12 months of the acquisition date, all of its assets (other than assets retained to meet claims) to its shareholders or creditors.

For these purposes, the definition of "control" is conformed to that contained in section 1504(a)(2) of the Code. * * *

The common-law doctrines of continuity of interest, continuity of business enterprise, and business purpose would have no applicability in determining whether a transaction qualifies as a qualified acquisition.

The bill repeals section 368. Acquisitive reorganizations ("A", "B" and "C" reorganizations and subsidiary mergers) under current law would be replaced by the rules for qualified acquisitions. The "D" reorganization rules would be replaced by special rules (described below) relating to qualified acquisitions between related parties. Transactions qualifying under current law as an "E" reorganization (a recapitalization) and an "F" reorganization (a mere change in identity, form, or place of organization of one corporation) are conformed to the definition of qualified acquisitions. Finally, the "G" reorganization rules (bankruptcy reorganizations), developed largely in response to continuity of interest problems in those types of transactions, are no longer needed and therefore are repealed.

Elective tax treatment of qualified acquisitions (new section 365 of the Code) The corporate level tax consequences of a qualified acquisition are explicitly made elective. Under new section 365, all qualified acquisitions are treated as "carryover basis acquisitions" unless an election to be treated as a "cost basis acquisition" is made.

In general, elections may be made on a corporation-by-corporation basis. Thus, for example, if an acquiring corporation makes a qualified stock acquisition of both a target corporation and a target subsidiary, a cost basis election may be made for the target corporation but, if desired, no such election need be made for the target subsidiary. * * *

Corporate level tax consequences of qualified acquisitions (sections 361, 362 and 381 of the Code) The corporate level tax consequences of a qualified acquisition result directly from the election made at the corporate level. For example, in the case of a carryover basis acquisition, no gain or loss is recognized by the target corporation and the acquiring corporation obtains a carryover basis in any assets acquired. Attributes carry over under section 381.

In the case of a cost basis acquisition, the target corporation recognizes gain or loss and the acquiring corporation obtains a basis in any assets acquired determined under section 1012. Attributes do not carry over. Where the cost basis acquisition is a qualified stock acquisition, the target corporation is deemed to have sold all of its assets for fair market value at the close of the acquisition date in a transaction in which gain or loss is recognized, and then is treated as a new corporation which purchased all of such assets as of the beginning of the day after the acquisition date. * * *

Shareholder level tax consequences of qualified acquisitions (sections 354, 356, and 358 of the Code) In general, shareholder level tax consequences of a qualified acquisition are determined independent of the corporate level tax consequences and independent of the election made at the corporate level. Thus, even if a transaction is treated as a cost basis acquisition at the corporate level, it may be wholly or partly taxfree at the shareholder level. In addition, shareholder level consequences are generally determined shareholder-by-shareholder, and the consequences to one shareholder do not affect the tax treatment of other shareholders or investors of the target corporation.

As a general rule, nonrecognition treatment is provided to shareholders or security holders of the target corporation upon receipt of "qualifying consideration," *i.e.,* stock or securities of the acquiring corporation and, where the acquiring corporation is a member of an affiliated group, of the common parent of such group and any other member of such group specified in regulations. [*See* § 354(a).] The nonrecognition rule applies to the receipt of securities only to the extent the issue price of any securities received does not exceed the adjusted basis of any securities surrendered. [*See* § 354(a)(2).] * * *

Receipt of "nonqualifying consideration" (*i.e.,* any consideration other than qualifying consideration) generally results in recognition of gain to the shareholder or security holder. Such gain is treated as gain from the sale or exchange of property unless the receipt of nonqualifying consideration has the effect of a distribution of a dividend. [*See* § 356(a)(2).] The determination of dividend effect is made by treating the shareholder as having received only qualifying consideration in the exchange, and then as being redeemed of all or a portion of such qualifying consideration (to the extent of the non-qualifying consideration received). For these purposes, earnings and profits of both the target and acquiring corporations are generally taken into account. * * *

§ 13.3 Proposal for Comprehensive Revision of the Merger, Acquisition and LBO Provisions of the Code

Samuel C. Thompson, Jr., Reform of the Taxation of Mergers, Acquisitions and LBOs

12–21 (Carolina Academic Press 1993)

* * * Part 2 [of this book] sets out an alternative approach to the portion of the ALI 1989 Study that deals with the tax treatment (basically taxable or tax-free) of the parties to an acquisitive transaction. Specific proposals are made here for revising the provisions of the Code dealing with acquisitive reorganizations and taxable acquisitions.

This book rejects the ALI's suggestion that the reorganization concept be repealed and replaced with what is, in essence, a "like kind exchange" approach at the shareholder level and an express codification of the mirror transaction at the corporate level. Part 2 accepts, although in a more limited form, the ALI's suggestion for elective carryover basis treatment of the target's assets in certain asset acquisitions. Under this carryover basis regime, a target does not have taxable gain on the disposition of its assets, and the acquiring corporation takes as its basis for those assets the target's old basis for the assets (*i.e.,* takes a carryover basis). Thus, the price of tax-free treatment to the target is a carryover basis for the assets in the hands of the acquiring corporation.

Five basic tax policy questions are addressed in part 2. First, should Congress adopt the ALI's suggestion that the shareholder level consequences in a corporate acquisition be separated from the corporate level consequences? That is, should (as the ALI has proposed) the acquisitive reorganization concept be eliminated? In this connection, should the continuity of interest doctrine be eliminated, retained, or strengthened? Also, should the "substantially all" concept apply uniformly to all forms of acquisitive reorganizations? Under the "substantially all" concept, which applies to four of the seven forms of acquisitive reorganizations, the acquiring corporation must acquire "substantially all" of the target's assets to qualify the acquisition as a reorganization. With uniformity, tax-free treatment would be available only in an acquisitive transaction in which substantially all of the target's assets are either acquired in an asset reorganization, or held by the target after the acquisition of the target in a stock reorganization.

Second, should a carryover basis rule be provided for taxable asset acquisitions? With the repeal of *General Utilities,* a very heavy tax burden applies when a target sells its assets and then distributes the proceeds to its shareholders in liquidation. Both the target and its shareholders are fully taxed on such transactions. This high tax cost effectively eliminates the use of taxable asset acquisitions, even though such transactions serve a useful business purpose. A carryover basis rule would allow the target to escape taxation on such transactions, but the acquiring corporation would take the target's basis for the assets (*i.e.,* a carryover basis) and not a fair market value basis. There would only be a shareholder level tax. * * *

Third, should there be an exception to the repeal of the *General Utilities* doctrine for taxable acquisitions involving the liquidating sale or distribution of goodwill in which the parties do not choose the carryover basis rule discussed above. If an exception for goodwill applied, the target would be taxable on the liquidating sale of all of its assets, except goodwill and other non-amortizable intangibles. The target's shareholders would be fully taxed on the receipt of the liquidating proceeds. Also, should this elective nonrecognition treatment apply even if Congress provides an amortization deduction for goodwill, as is currently proposed?

Fourth, assuming the adoption of a carryover basis election for a limited class of taxable asset acquisitions, should parity in the treatment of taxable stock acquisitions be adopted? Parity could be obtained by imposing mandatory target level taxation (*i.e.,* a mandatory § 338 election) for a stock acquisition that could not have been structured as a carryover basis asset acquisition. Under this rule, in certain circumstances a target would automatically be deemed to have sold its assets after an acquisition of the target's stock.

Fifth, what needs to be done in order to curtail the mischaracterization of purchase price as deductible payments in both acquisitive reorganizations and taxable acquisitions? With the current small capital gains preference, taxpayers have been allocating significant portions of what is in economic reality purchase price of stock to deductible payments, such as covenants not to compete. This is a clear abuse and needs to be stopped. * * *

Chapter 4 sets out proposals regarding reorganizations, which encompass various types of tax-free acquisitions. These proposals are premised on the judgment that the central themes of the reorganization provisions reflect correct tax policy:

> An exception to the general recognition (*i.e.,* taxation) rule of Section 1001 should apply at the corporate and shareholder levels for corporate acquisitions in which for a good business purpose the acquiring corporation acquires the target's historic assets and a significant portion of the consideration received by the target's historic shareholders is stock of the acquiring corporation.

Thus, the position taken in Chapter 4 is that the business purpose, continuity of business enterprise, and continuity of interest doctrines of present law are consistent with proper tax policy. If the spirit of these doctrines is satisfied in a corporate acquisition, the transaction is not analogous to a sale or taxable exchange because the target's shareholders have a continuing interest in the historic assets of the target through their ownership of stock of the acquiring corporation. Consequently, it is appropriate in such cases to provide nonrecognition treatment for both the target corporation and its shareholders. This position is directly contrary to that taken in the ALI 1989 Study.

If the reorganization concept is reformed as proposed here, there would be uniformity in the application of both (1) the continuity of interest requirement, and (2) the substantially all requirement. Under present law, the continuity of interest requirement differs for the various types of reorganizations, and the substantially all requirement applies only in the stock for asset reorganization [*See* § 368(a)(1)(C).] and in the forward and reverse subsidiary merger reorganizations. [*See* §§ 368(a)(1)(D) and (E).] Consequently, under the proposals here there would be consistency in the treatment of acquisitive reorganizations, manipulation would be prevented, and the operation of these provisions would be reflective of the underlying policy rationale.

In striving for consistency, Chapter 4 attempts to eliminate many of the needless traps in the reorganization provisions, such as the *Bausch & Lomb* doctrine, [which has now been eliminated, *see* Sec. 7.3.H.] and to codify those principles in the case law and rulings that are consistent with the fundamental concept of a reorganization, such as the *McDonald* decision. [In adopting the new continuity of interest regulations, *see* Chapter 6, the Treasury rejected the *McDonald* decision, and in retrospect, this was an excellent policy judgment, because of the significant simplification in the application of this doctrine.] * * *

The proposals made here regarding taxable acquisitions are contained in Chapters 5, 6, and 7 and arise out of the repeal by the TRA 1986 of the *General Utilities* doctrine. As a result of the repeal of this doctrine, a target corporation is fully taxed on the liquidating sale or distribution of its assets. Also, the target's shareholders are taxed under general principles upon receipt of the liquidation proceeds. Thus, today there is a double level of tax on liquidating sales; prior to the repeal of the *General Utilities* doctrine, only a tax at the shareholder level generally applied.

Chapter 5 would eliminate the current barrier to taxable asset acquisitions of stand-alone target corporations by providing for carryover basis treatment for a taxable acquisition of the assets of a nonsubsidiary target. With carryover basis treatment, the target would not be subject to tax and the acquiring corporation would take the target's assets with the target's basis (*i.e.,* a carryover basis). The target's shareholders would be taxed upon receipt of the liquidating proceeds. Thus, there would be only one level of tax.

This carryover basis treatment would be available only if the acquisition would have qualified as an acquisitive reorganization under the proposals contained in Chapter 4, but for the failure to satisfy the continuity of interest requirement. Thus, carryover basis treatment would be allowed only if the acquiring corporation acquires substantially all of the target's historic assets. This carryover basis proposal provides a limited exception to the repeal of the *General Utilities* doctrine. This basic concept of a carryover basis for taxable acquisitions was first introduced in the ALI 1982 Study and is also present in the ALI 1989 Study, although different from that proposed here.

Chapter 6 proposes tax-free treatment in a liquidating sale by a nonsubsidiary target corporation of goodwill and going concern value. This exception would apply only if the parties do not treat the transaction under the carryover basis rule set forth in Chapter 5. A special rule would apply if Congress enacts currently proposed legislation that would provide an amortization deduction for goodwill and going concern value. As is the case for carryover basis treatment, this nonrecognition rule for goodwill would be available only if the transaction would have qualified for acquisitive reorganization treatment under the proposals contained in Chapter 4, but for the failure to satisfy the continuity of interest requirement. Thus, this exception to the repeal of the *General Utilities* doctrine is available only if the acquiring corporation acquires "substantially all" of the target's historic assets. This proposal is similar to a proposal contained in the ALI 1989 Study. The circumstances in which nonrecognition is available, however, are more limited under the proposal here. Also, the ALI would require the acquiring corporation to take a carryover basis for goodwill acquired in a nonrecognition transaction, but under the proposal here the purchaser would take a cost basis.

The carryover basis rule in Chapter 5 and the goodwill nonrecognition rule in Chapter 6 are mutually exclusive. Thus, in any liquidating taxable sale of substantially all of a target's historic assets, the parties would have two options: (1) a carryover basis acquisition in which the target is not subject to tax and the acquiring corporation takes a carryover basis for the target's assets; or (2) taxable treatment for the target, except for goodwill and other non-amortizable intangibles. In both cases, the target's shareholders would be taxed upon receipt of the liquidating proceeds.

Chapter 7 provides a rule requiring mandatory target level taxation (*i.e.,* a mandatory Section 338 election) for certain stock purchases in which the target's assets could not have been acquired in a carryover basis asset acquisition. The effect of this mandatory Section 338 election is to treat the target as if it had sold and repurchased its assets in a taxable transaction. This mandatory Section 338 election applies if, at the time of the acquisition of at least 80 percent of the target's stock by an acquiring corporation, the target does not hold substantially all of its historic assets. The purpose of this provision is to prevent the use of a stock acquisition for the purpose of acquiring only a portion of the target's assets in a carryover basis transaction. The carryover basis proposal and the mandatory Section 338 proposal should provide neutrality in the treatment of taxable stock and asset acquisitions.

Chapter 8 proposes the adoption of a statutory limit on the amount of consideration that can be allocated to a covenant not to compete or similar deductible item. This provision applies in both taxable acquisitions and acquisitive reorganizations. This provision will curtail the misallocation of purchase price. * * *

Part 3 of this book sets out an alternative to the portions of the ALI 1989 Study dealing with LBOs and related transactions. Thus, the proposals here are offered as alternatives to the ALI's proposals for (1) a minimum tax on distributions, and (2) an absolute prohibition on the deduction for interest on debt issued in an equity conversion transaction.

For the reasons discussed below, this book suggests changes in the tax rules governing the deduction of interest in LBOs and related transactions involving publicly held corporations; no changes are suggested for such transactions involving privately held firms and divisions and subsidiaries of publicly held firms.

This book is not motivated by a belief that LBOs are bad for the economy and should be discouraged or penalized. An underlying theme of this book is that although LBOs and related transactions are on balance good for the economy, in that they move assets into the hands of those who can put those assets to their highest and best use, the deduction for interest under the present tax system has resulted in excessively leveraged LBOs and related transactions involving publicly held corporations. The excessive leverage is inconsistent with sound tax policy because such leverage erodes the corporate tax base and has a great potential for being economically harmful. This harm results because such transactions (1) increase bankruptcy risk above acceptable levels, and (2) put an unacceptable damper on expenditures for investment and research and development, thereby reducing opportunities to exploit value maximizing strategies. If the suggestions made here were to be adopted, there would be a prudent level of equity in these transactions, the bankruptcy risk would be reduced, and the equity base would give the firm greater opportunities to invest, conduct R & D, and grow.

Although concerns with excessive leverage can arise in a variety of contexts, it appears that the principal concern is with excessively leveraged LBOs and related transactions involving publicly held corporations. Although similar problems can exist with acquisitions of privately held corporations and acquisitions of divisions and subsidiaries of publicly held corporations, the current concern with LBOs arose out of acquisitions of publicly held firms. Also, there does not appear to be a problem with the issuance of debt for the purpose of internal corporate expansion by the purchase of bricks and mortar. For this reason, the proposals contained in part 3 would merely eliminate the tax incentive for excessively leveraged acquisitions and related transactions of publicly held corporations. * * *

Chapter 12 sets out the proposal here for the denial of the deductibility of interest in certain equity conversion transactions involving publicly held corporations. The proposals here would get at the core of the problem of LBOs and other equity conversion transactions of publicly held corporations by disallowing the deduction for interest on the following debt issued by such corporations: (1) debt issued as a dividend; (2) debt issued for the purpose of directly or indirectly paying an extraordinary dividend or making an extraordinary redemption, such as a leveraged recapitalization; and (3) all junk debt and any excessive nonjunk debt issued for the purpose of acquiring either control stock or substantially all the assets of a publicly held corporation. Thus, the rules here would apply to both LBOs and various types of leveraged recapitalizations involving publicly held corporations.

Junk debt includes, for example, zero coupon bonds and payment in kind bonds issued in the acquisition of a publicly held corporation. Also, under the junk debt rule, interest above a stated level on straight junk debt is not deductible; there is no effect on the interest below the stated level. The excessive debt rule prevents the use of excessive debt in LBOs involving publicly held corporations.

The rule regarding junk debt applies to tax-free reorganizations as well as to taxable acquisitions. There could not be excessive debt in a reorganization, and therefore, the excessive debt rule has no application to reorganizations. The rules disallowing interest on debt issued as a dividend, in a redemption, or in a leveraged recapitalization are designed to eliminate a needless tax incentive for excessive leveraging and to prevent a corporation from avoiding the effect of the disallowance rule that applies in acquisition transactions. * * *

Although there has been both a decrease in the number of highly leveraged acquisitions of publicly held firms and an increase in the amount of equity in the transactions that are completed, this does not mean that the day of the overly leveraged transaction will not return. Rather than waiting for such a possible return and the attendant increases in bankruptcy risk, it would be prudent for Congress to adopt the LBO proposals now. * * *

§ 13.4 An Analysis of the Conceptual Foundations for the Reorganization Provisions

Steven Bank, Mergers, Taxes and Historical Realism

75 Tulane Law Review 1 (November, 2000)

* * * The adoption of the tax-free reorganization provisions must be considered in the context of [the] debate over realization. Before the Supreme Court ever established a realization requirement, upheld the taxation of capital gains, and struck down the taxation of stock dividends, Congress and Treasury instituted provisions to tax property exchanges while providing an exception for reorganizations, mergers, and consolidations. The chronology of these events evidenced a compromise between the two extremes in the realization debate. Although realization became a precondition to the recognition of income, recognition was not delayed until the point at which consumption took place. This compromise appeared to spring in part from Congress's desire to tax savings and investments while responding to concerns about the taxation of paper gains. Although Congress was unwilling to completely adopt the cash flow concept urged by the consumption tax model, it was sympathetic to the worry that tax would be imposed on a continuing investment. Thus, it enacted the realization concept in modified form. As with most compromises, it was neither wholly consistent nor rationally applied in all respects. Despite the enduring dissatisfaction with it, the resulting system of realization has remained remarkably faithful to this original compromise.

The thesis of this Article is that the tax-free reorganization provisions originated, and arguably continue to exist, as a part of this realization compromise. Thus, the argument that nonrecognition treatment has no current conceptual or theoretical basis is unfounded. Until an accretion or consumption tax model is fully embraced by Congress and integrated into the Code, the tax-free reorganization will remain a logical part of the realization compromise. * * *

Under the [1918] Act and the accompanying Treasury Regulations, property exchanges were classified into one of three categories: (1) taxable exchanges; (2) nontaxable exchanges; and (3) reorganizations, mergers, and consolidations. By enacting this scheme before the Court had a chance to decide the capital gains or stock dividend issues, Congress sought to limit the most extreme, and embrace the most desirable, features of each of the respective models. The goal was to defer paper gains while taxing real gains.

Taxable Exchanges

The 1918 Act enacted the general rule that property exchanges are taxable transactions. Under section 202(b) of the Act, when property is exchanged for other property, the property received is treated as the equivalent of cash to the extent of its fair market value. This position constituted an official rejection of the consumption tax model's view that the receipt of property does not constitute taxable income. * * * Establishing the general rule that a receipt of property constituted income was important because it prevented the indefinite deferral possible through a barter economy. Moreover, this rule recognized that a gain could be real or effectively locked-in without being converted to cash.

Nontaxable Exchanges

Although the 1918 Act established a general rule that property exchanges are taxable, the statutory language that property will be treated as "the equivalent of cash to the amount of its fair market value, if any" suggested that there could be nontaxable exchanges. Treasury accordingly interpreted the statute so as to provide an exception to the general rule. Under Article 1563 of the Regulations, gain is realized on a property exchange if property is received "(a) that is essentially different from the property disposed of and (b) that has a market value." "In other words," the Regulations continued, "both (a) a change in substance and not merely in form, and (b) a change into the equivalent of cash, are required to complete or close a transaction from which income may be realized." This was the forerunner of the modern like-kind exchange provisions.

This Regulation provided a test by which property exchanges could seek to be excluded as technical rather than actual realizations. According to the examples provided by Treasury, an exchange of publicly traded stock for a voting trust certificate would not be taxable because it would be a mere change in form, while an exchange of the same stock for stock in a closely held corporation would not be taxable because of the absence of a market for the stock received. * * * When an investment continues, as it would in an exchange of like-kind property, there is no closed transaction, and any gain is still paper or uncertain because of this continuing quality. Only an exchange of the stock for different property, such as a bond or a piece of real estate, would be taxable under the Regulations. * * *

In contrast to the exemption in the Treasury Regulations, the reorganization provision was a *per se* exemption. Thus, it did not leave room for the fine distinctions between reorganizations that were open transactions, and therefore gave rise to paper gains, and reorganizations that constituted decisions to cash out investments and realize actual gains. As long as the stockholder in a reorganization, merger, or consolidation received, in place of his or her stock, new stock of "no greater aggregate par or face value," the transaction would not give rise to taxable income. * * *

In reality, the reorganization provision was a product of the realization compromise. By deferring recognition of gain or loss on a reorganization, merger, or consolidation, Congress tempered the impact of capital gains taxation without excepting such transactions altogether. Adopting a realization requirement was the first step in this process. * * * The reorganization provision broadened the general effect of a realization requirement by declaring that reorganizations, mergers, and consolidations constituted *per se* nontaxable property exchanges.

There were two features meriting *per se* nonrecognition treatment for reorganizations, mergers, and consolidations. First, the stockholders in such transactions continued their investments, rather than cashing them out, to the extent that they received stock in the combined venture. In both a merger and a consolidation, the resulting entity was considered to be a combination of the assets and liabilities of the constituent parties. Stock in this entity would thus represent the former target shareholder's continuing investment in the property of the disappearing corporation.

While a general property exchange may or may not, depending upon the underlying facts, involve a continuing investment, a shareholder receiving stock in a reorganization, merger, or consolidation by definition continued his or her investment.

There were, of course, transactions that appeared to test this general principle. For example, a shareholder of a corner grocery store "may feel, quite rightly, that he has 'sold out' for the near-equivalent of cash" when the store is merged into a large national grocery chain, but this is not precisely true. After all, if the transaction occurred in the reverse, so that the large publicly traded corporation merged into the closely held corporation, the private market for the closely held corporation's shares would no doubt improve considerably. Few, however, within the confines of a realization-based system, would suggest that added liquidity alone should be a taxable event for the closely held corporation's pre-existing shareholders.

Moreover, even if receiving a publicly traded interest in the national grocery chain were considered to be the equivalent of selling out, the shareholders would still hold an interest in the assets of the corner grocery store. This interest, of course, has been diluted to some extent because the former corner grocery store shareholders no longer hold an exclusive interest in the assets of the store. To measure the extent to which the shareholders have truly sold out their investment, however, the government would have to look through the stock to the assets. This would be a difficult task in any event, but practically impossible in the case of a large public corporation. Instead of measuring such partial implicit disinvestments, Congress chose an "all-or-nothing approach." Unless former target shareholders received cash or other property not constituting an equity interest in the surviving or resulting corporation, they were treated as if they had continued their investment in its entirety.

Second, reorganizations not only posed a high risk of taxing paper or theoretical gains, but also posed a substantial risk that such gains were based on "fictitious" or inaccurate values. In the closely held corporation context, this problem was readily apparent as a practical matter. There is no easy reference for determining the fair market value of the stock of the acquiring corporation. * * *

These conceptual difficulties would not be overcome by limiting the taxation of reorganizations, mergers, and consolidations to exchanges of publicly traded stocks and securities. While isolated exchanges of public stocks and securities fail to cause even a ripple in a stock's trading price, mergers and acquisitions often involve wholesale changes in ownership of a corporation's stock. Such massive changes may produce intense fluctuations in the prices of the respective stocks. At the time the reorganization provision was first adopted, it was not always clear that even publicly traded stock or securities could be sold after the transaction for the listed price. Soon after the reorganization provision was enacted, Robert Montgomery, a prominent tax practitioner, concluded that it may be improper to impose a tax on the participants in reorganizations "even if there were a market value" for the securities received. The problem is that, while a public market may exist after a reorganization, it "is usually a temporary, excited, manipulated market." Any value obtained may be artificially inflated, and it becomes difficult as a conceptual matter to distinguish between the real gain and the temporary gain in the stock's value. This problem was readily evident to contemporary legislators. * * *

Even today, reorganizations and other similar transactions routinely produce pre- and post-merger fluctuations in even the most widely traded of shares. These wide swings were shaky evidence of profit or taxable income for contemporary courts. Robert Montgomery noted that, because "[t]he courts are reluctant to impose a tax upon values established by widely fluctuating quotations," it may be better to treat all stocks and securities the same under a broad reorganization provision. The alternative was to end up with some transactions being taxed and others being deferred, depending upon a court's view of the state of the market for the corporation's shares.

Thus, the reorganization provision was enacted in 1918 in a compromise over two competing models of the taxation of capital investments. The accretion model suggested annual taxation of increases in value, while the consumption model favored no taxation at all on increases in value or on proceeds that were reinvested rather than consumed. Observers feared the taxation of paper gains under the former and the indefinite deferral of taxes under the latter. At a time when the legal outcome of the taxation of capital gains and stock dividends was still uncertain, Congress struck a compromise that exempted capital gains from taxation until the occurrence of a definite realization event. While a realization event was relatively easy to spot when property was sold for cash, it was more difficult in the case of property exchanges. As a result, Congress taxed property exchanges as a general rule, while exempting those, such as like-kind exchanges or reorganizations, that were most likely not to represent the termination of the taxpayer's investments and therefore the taxation of which would most likely measure only paper rather than real gains. There may be other transactions that pose similar problems, and, as with all compromises, logical consistency was stretched to some degree. On the whole, however, the reorganization provision was important in securing the popular and legal acceptance of the realization compromise.

The Realization Compromise Today

The tax-free reorganization has been attacked on the grounds that the passage of time and the change of circumstances have diminished the force of the traditional rationales for its existence. The question is whether this Article's alternative explanation for the origin of the reorganization provisions fares any better as a continuing justification for nonrecognition treatment.

Many will likely attack the modern relevance of any rationale that relies on the understanding of concepts such as realization and the taxation of capital appreciation. * * * The realization concept, while strongly supported by the legislature in the 1918 Act and later by the Court in *Eisner v. Macomber*, was scaled back considerably in the reorganization cases decided during the 1920s. Eventually, it was stripped of its status as a constitutional requirement. Subsequent judicial decisions have further eroded the realization requirement by permitting seemingly minor changes to trigger gain or loss. While such decisions do not preclude the legislative reaffirmation of a strong realization requirement, no such action appears to be forthcoming. In fact, an accretion-based or, as it is more often called, "mark-to-market," approach has been adopted in several statutory provisions covering the securities industry.

Moreover, any uncertainty about the taxation of capital gains has long since dissipated. When the 1918 Act was enacted, anti-capital gains taxation sentiments combined with sympathetic judicial precedent to form an effective argument against taxing such gains. In *Eisner v. Macomber*, the Court fueled the debate by declaring that income included the "profit gained through a sale or conversion of capital assets," while later appearing to contradict itself with the statement that "enrichment through increase in value of capital investment is not income." Around the same time, a federal district court issued an opinion holding that the taxation of gain on the sale of a capital asset was unconstitutional. By 1921, however, the Supreme Court had resolved the question by declaring, in a series of four cases, that income included capital appreciation. While subsequent legislatures have differed over the application of special reduced rates to the taxation of capital gains, few currently dispute the government's power to tax such gains to the full extent of other income. * * *

Just as reform proposals reflect the divide between the accretion and consumption tax systems, recent tax legislation reflects the continuing influence of the realization compromise. Despite the advent of provisions leaning toward one or the other of these alternative systems, the realization principle has remained remarkably dominant. The explicit mark-to-market provisions inserted in the Code in the last few years, for example, have not spread outside of their limited application to the taxation of financial instruments. * * * Similarly, the explicit consumption tax provisions available for retirement and education savings have not been extended to other forms of general purpose savings. Nor do these provisions cover an unlimited amount of savings or apply to all income groups.

§ 13.5 Proposal for Federalizing the (A) Merger

Steven Bank, Federalizing the Tax-Free Merger: Towards an End to the Anachronistic Reliance on State Corporation Laws

77 N.C.L. Rev. 1307 (April 1999)

Introduction

[T]he Code's failure to apply a uniform tax standard for all reorganizations has been widely criticized as arbitrary, complex, and overly formalistic. This criticism appears to be faithful to some of the original concerns of the legislative drafters because the Code defines a number of economically similar transactions as "reorganizations" so that the same tax consequences should be applied to each. * * * Because of the concern over disparate treatment, many proposals to collapse the various types of reorganizations and requirements have been submitted over the years, but no wholesale changes have been made.

What reformers have ignored in their quest to rid the overall system of disparity, however, is that an even more arbitrary and formalistic disparity exists within "the oldest of, and the prototype for, the various reorganization forms"—the A reorganization. Under the A reorganization's statutory merger requirement, economically and substantively identical transactions are treated differently not because of Congress's decision to apply a different set of requirements, but merely because of differences in state corporation laws. * * *

Recent developments in state corporation law and federal tax law have exacerbated the disparities in treatment for parties seeking A reorganization status and have obliterated any notion that state corporation laws continue to provide a check against tax avoidance. The adoption of the new check-the-box regulations, which de-emphasize the Code's reliance on state corporation law and permit single-member limited liability companies to elect to be treated as divisions of their parent, has the ironic potential to magnify the disparity caused by the A reorganization's reliance on state corporation laws. Because an acquiring corporation need not directly assume the liabilities of its target under state law, a single member limited liability company eliminates one obstacle to the use of the A reorganization. The statutory merger requirement, however, may limit tax-free treatment for such a deserving merger when the state corporation laws do not provide for the merger of corporate and non-corporate entities or do not recognize the existence of single member limited liability companies. [*See* Sec. 7.2.I. regarding mergers with disregarded unities.] Moreover, as a gatekeeper, the reliance on state corporation laws for the determination of whether a transaction qualifies as an A reorganization has become both over- and under-inclusive. The reliance on state corporation laws is over-inclusive because the advent of increasingly liberal state corporation laws has moved the concept of a merger or consolidation farther and farther from the common law definitions. While it has long been apparent that the statutory merger requirement cannot be depended upon to prevent an abuse of the reorganization provisions, a state merger statute that permits a sale to be classified as a merger turns the A reorganization provision on its head. The reliance on state corporation laws also is under-inclusive because it is difficult to justify the exclusion of statutory transactions that are not defined as mergers, but provide many of the shareholder and creditor protections originally used to justify nonrecognition treatment for reorganizations. These developments highlight the need to focus on the disparity and inequity that is caused by the continued reliance on the statutory merger requirement for A reorganizations.

This Article argues that a merger's eligibility for A reorganization treatment should not depend upon whether it has satisfied the requirements imposed by a state's corporation laws. * * *

The Case for Removing the Statutory Merger Requirement Congress should eliminate the statutory merger requirement from the reorganization provisions. While the requirement has never been a particularly useful part of the reorganization provisions, recent developments suggest that now is the time to remove it altogether. The statutory merger requirement is out of step with recent congressional efforts to reduce the Code's reliance on historic and formalistic differences among state statutes. Moreover, the statutory merger requirement's reliance on state corporation laws as a guard against tax avoidance has become both over-inclusive and under-inclusive. * * *

Options for Federalizing the Tax-Free Merger To the extent that nonrecognition treatment for mergers and consolidations is still justified, and thus that any gain from stock and securities received in reorganizations should continue to be tax-deferred, it makes little sense to maintain a statutory merger requirement as a condition of a tax-free reorganization. There are at least three alternatives: (1) Congress could itself decide on a uniform set of common law criteria for mergers that could be imposed on parties seeking A reorganization treatment; (2) the A reorganization could be eliminated from the Code altogether; or (3) the statutory merger requirement could be excised from the Code and the definition of the phrase "merger or consolidation" could be left to the IRS and the courts.

Redraft Section 368(a)(1)(A) to Include Certain Common Law Requirements The statutory merger requirement can be replaced with more directed language that replicates the type of state law features now thought to be inherent in the statutory merger. This result could be accomplished by redrafting the provision to capture explicitly certain fundamental features of a merger, such as requirements that: (1) the target shareholders receive stock consideration; (2) the merging entity dissolves; and (3) the surviving corporation assumes all liabilities. The belief that such requirements were intrinsic to a statutory merger led the drafters of the Revenue Act of 1934 to consider it as a separate category. Although there may be some disagreement in identifying and defining the fundamental elements of a merger or consolidation, it would not be an insurmountable obstacle.

Imposing an explicit stock consideration requirement for A reorganizations has both statutory precedent in the existing "solely for voting stock" rule for B reorganizations and judicial precedent in the continuity of interest requirement. * * *

Remove the A Reorganization from the Code Altogether Although replacing the statutory merger requirement with common law requirements for mergers or consolidations would address the disparity in results for parties seeking A reorganization status, it would not satisfy critics. The overall disparity among the various reorganization alternatives would remain. Eliminating the A reorganization from the Code altogether, however, would help reduce the disparity caused by the A reorganization's status as "the most lenient type of reorganization in terms of requirements that must be satisfied." While the conditions to A reorganization treatment that develop in the absence of the statutory merger requirement are likely to minimize this overall disparity, preserving the A reorganization is clearly a second-best solution to the disparity that exists between the state law and non-state law types of reorganizations.

Removing the A reorganization has been proposed several times before. In 1958, an America Law Institute Tax Project and an ABA Subcommittee proposed to eliminate the A reorganization as a separate manner of obtaining nonrecognition treatment:

(1) Two basic categories of tax-free unifying corporation reorganizations should be recognized—asset acquisitions and stock acquisitions. The rules for these acquisitions should be essentially the same. Statutory mergers and consolidations should be eliminated as a separate category with different rules, but instead, should be subsumed within the asset acquisition and specifically mentioned as such in the statutory language. * * * During the consideration of the Tax Reform Act of 1986, Congress directed Treasury to study the proposals outlined by the Senate Finance Committee and report back on their desirability. As with the earlier reform efforts, however, the basic structure of reorganization provisions was never significantly altered. * * *

The various proposals to collapse the reorganization provisions, and thus eliminate the A reorganization, have never become law in part because of the complexity of the suggested alternatives. The elimination of the A reorganization alternative has generally been proposed, not as a stand-alone measure, but as part of an overall effort to reform the reorganization provisions. * * *

Even if proposals to eliminate the A reorganization are separated from the larger reform efforts, they also face conceptual and practical opposition. First, eliminating the A reorganization faces practical opposition from participants to statutory mergers that would not otherwise qualify as B or C reorganizations. The B reorganization's zero tolerance for non-stock consideration and the C reorganization's "substantially all the properties" requirement each would serve to deny nonrecognition treatment to transactions that would have formerly qualified as A reorganizations. While there may be sound reasons for such an outcome, the exclusion of a pre-existing exit strategy or the loosening of a current requirement would necessitate political strength that may not be present on this issue.

Second, proposals to eliminate the A reorganization altogether may never be fully embraced because of the commonly held belief that a merger is the prototypical reorganization provision. * * *

Leave the Definition to the IRS and the Courts The simplest solution to implement is to remove the word "statutory" from 368(a)(1)(A) and let the courts and the IRS resolve the issue. As a practical matter, qualification as a merger under state law would continue to serve as highly probative evidence of the existence of a merger for tax purposes. However, eliminating the requirement that mergers be effected pursuant to state law would negate the notion that qualification under state law was either necessary or sufficient for A reorganization treatment. The IRS would attempt to provide guidance for the definition of the terms "merger" and "consolidation" through the issuance of administrative pronouncements, while the courts would monitor the outer boundaries of the terms on a case-by-case basis. This flexible approach structured around general principles was advocated by T.S. Adams and the Treasury Department in 1924, but cast aside by Congress in favor of the detailed treatment recommended by A.W. Gregg in the Gregg Statement. * * *

[L]eaving the definition of merger or consolidation to the IRS and the courts would resolve the A reorganization's internal inequities without suffering from either the complexity or the conceptual difficulties of the other alternatives. This modest solution essentially acknowledges the preexisting judicial and administrative role in the definition of the terms "merger and consolidation." The innovation is to remove the limits to that interpretive role that have contributed to the A reorganization's demise as a useful standard for nonrecognition treatment.* * *

Finally, the removal of the statutory merger requirement is more than a mere technical fix in the underbrush of a larger reform of corporate taxation. It is symbolically connected with the check-the-box regulations in de-linking the Code from the historical and formalistic requirements of state law. This general trend toward the "federalization" of the Code evidences an intent to base federal decisions to tax on uniform criteria that are, whenever possible, independent from non-tax local law concerns. For example, one of the primary concerns involved in the decision to change from an individual taxpaying unit system to a marital taxpaying unit system was to reconcile differences in treatment between community property and common law states. Closer to home, the addition of non-merger reorganizations was designed to unify the treatment of mergers in states with and without merger statutes. Viewed in this context, the removal of the statutory merger requirement is necessary on grounds independent of those used to justify the reform of corporate taxation. It is an attempt to lessen the Code's anachronistic reliance on state corporation laws.

§ 13.6 Comparison of Corporate Nonrecognition Provisions in Canada and the U.S.

Brown and Manolakas, The United States and Canada: A Comparison of Corporate Nonrecognition Provisions

30 Case Western Reserve Journal of International Law (1998)

Introduction Under both the Canadian and United States tax systems, income realized from the disposition of property is recognized for tax purposes. Nevertheless, both tax systems allow for nonrecognition of gain in transactions where the investment of the taxpayer in the transferred assets remains unliquidated. Not surprisingly, the corporate tax provisions of both countries contain many such nonrecognition provisions. * * * This Article provides a detailed discussion of the Canadian corporate nonrecognition provisions and provides important parallels between these and U.S. corporate nonrecognition provisions. * * *

Transfers of Property to a Corporation I.R.C. section 351 and I.T.A. section 85 provide for nonrecognition on the transfer of property to a corporation in exchange for its stock. Absent these sections, an exchange of property for stock would constitute dispositions of property at fair market value. Tax deferment reflects a policy decision by both countries that a transfer of property to a corporation for stock represents a continuation of investment in a modified form, rather than a liquidation of the investment in the assets transferred. I.R.C. section 351 is a mandatory nonrecognition provision applicable to the transfer of property to a new or existing corporation, if the transferors have control of the corporation immediately after the transfer. By way of comparison, I.T.A. section 85 is elective and does not contain a "control" requirement. As continuity of interest is not a factor, I.T.A. section 85 applies to a wider range of circumstances. * * *

The I.T.A. section 85 rollover is available to any taxpayer, whether resident or non-resident, who disposes of eligible property to a taxable Canadian corporation. * * * "Eligible property" includes capital property but does not include the following:

1. real property which is inventory (for example, land owned by a dealer in real estate), or any interests in or options in respect of real property which form part of the inventory of the taxpayer; and

2. real property including interests and options in respect of real property owned by a non-resident, unless the property is used during the year by the taxpayer in a business carried on in Canada.

I.T.A. section 85 requires the taxpayer transferring the assets and the corporation receiving the assets to jointly elect tax deferment treatment. The election allows the transferor and the transferee corporation to specify an amount, within the parameters of I.T.A. section 85, which will be deemed to be the proceeds received on the disposition of the property and the cost basis to the taxpayer and the corporation of the assets received in the exchange. For example, a taxpayer transferring land with a basis of $50 and a value of $100 can elect jointly with the transferee corporation $50 as the deemed proceeds on disposition and, thereby, defer all gain recognition. The taxpayer's basis in the shares received from the corporation and the transferee corporation's basis in the asset received from the taxpayer is $50. If the taxpayer and the corporation jointly elected $75 as the deemed proceeds on disposition, a $25 capital gain would be recognized by the taxpayer and the resulting basis of the shares to the transferor and the land to the transferee corporation would be $75.

Generally, upper and lower limits exist on the amount that may be agreed upon by the transferor and the transferee corporation as the deemed proceeds on disposition. First, the amount elected with respect to an asset cannot exceed its fair market value. Second, the elected amount cannot be less than the value of any nonshare consideration received from the corporation. Where the elected amount is less than the value of the nonshare consideration received, the value of the boot is deemed to be the elected amount. This places a lower limit on the election. The purpose of this lower limit is to prevent a taxpayer from actually realizing and extracting the economic value of a gain without recognizing the gain for tax purposes. Thus, the election can range from between the fair market value of the property transferred to the corporation and the value of the boot received from the transferee corporation where that value exceeds the asset's cost basis. If the consideration received from the corporation exceeds this range, further tax consequences will follow either in the form of a shareholder benefit under I.T.A. section 15 or a deemed dividend under I.T.A. section 84. * * *

The amount of consideration received by the transferor from the transferee corporation in an I.T.A. section 85 exchange is fundamental to an effective rollover. If the transferor is not the sole shareholder and related persons hold shares, the shares received by the taxpayer on the rollover must be structured to ensure avoidance of a constructive gift. * * *

Similarly, under the U.S. tax system, when a relationship exists between parties to a transaction, the terms of the agreement are closely scrutinized; however, under I.R.C. section 351, the method of recharacterizing the transaction has not been formalized. Nevertheless, if the stock and boot received by the transferor is disportionate to the value of the property transferred to the transferee corporation, the entire transaction will be effectively taxed in accordance with its true nature. For example, the transfer may be recharacterized as in part a gift, compensation for services, or satisfaction of an obligation.

Corporate Divisions Tax-deferred corporate divisions are available under both the U.S. and Canadian tax systems. I.R.C. section 355 allows a tax-free division of a corporate enterprise into two separate corporations owned by the shareholders of the original corporation. * * *

A divisive corporate reorganization is also possible for Canadian tax purposes provided there is significant continuity of interest in the property of the distributing corporation. As previously mentioned, such divisive reorganizations in Canada are commonly referred to as butterfly transactions. The essence of a butterfly transaction is that property of a corporation is transferred to one or more corporate shareholders in proportion to their share interest in that corporation in a tax-deferred exchange for shares under I.T.A. section 85. Subsequently, shares of the transferee corporations owned by the transferor corporation are redeemed and the shares of the transferor corporation owned by a subsidiary of the transferees are redeemed, thereby triggering deemed intercorporate dividends pursuant to I.T.A. subsection 84(3). These dividends are deductible pursuant to I.T.A. subsection 112(1) provided the tax avoidance provisions in I.T.A. subsection 55(3) are not offended. As a result, a transaction which would otherwise give rise to a capital gain is instead executed using a combination of a nonrecognition provisions and the integration mechanism which permits the tax-free flow of intercorporate dividends.

The policy reason for permitting a distribution of property free of capital gains tax in certain circumstances is that there is no true economic disposition of the property. The shareholders still retain their proportionate beneficial interest in the assets of the corporation, but in a different form. As in the United States, the characterization of a distribution to a corporate shareholder as a dividend is preferred to a capital gain because of the intercorporate dividend deduction. * * *

Stock-for-Stock Exchanges Under both the U.S. and Canadian tax systems, stock-for-stock exchanges are given nonrecognition treatment. I.R.C. § 368(a)(1)(B) defines a B reorganization as the acquisition of stock of one corporation in exchange solely for the voting stock of the acquiring corporation, or its parent, provided the acquiring corporation has control of the acquired corporation immediately after the transaction, whether or not the acquiring corporation had control immediately before the acquisition. * * *

Under the Canadian tax system, I.T.A. section 85.1 allows shareholders who exchange the shares of a taxable Canadian corporation, the target corporation, for the shares of a Canadian corporation, the acquiring corporation, to receive tax-deferred treatment. In the absence of this rollover provision, the target corporation shareholder would be considered to have disposed of the shares of the target corporation for proceeds equal to the fair market value of the shares received from the acquiring corporation. The exchange must be solely for shares of a single class of the acquiring corporation's treasury stock. No nonshare consideration may be received on the transaction. In order to qualify for nonrecognition, the parties to the exchange must be dealing at arm's length before and after the exchange. * * * The rollover is not mandatory and the shareholder may recognize any amount of gain or loss realized on the transaction. If gain or loss is not recognized, the basis of the shareholder's old shares is rolled over into the basis of the new shares, thus, preserving any unrecognized gain or loss on the exchange. The basis in the target shares to the acquiring corporation is the lesser of the fair market value of the shares or their PUC immediately before the exchange. [The PUC is the paid up capital, which represents an amount a corporation can return to its shareholders as a tax-free return of capital. PUC is similar to capital on financial statements.] As a result, the acquiring corporation will inherit the PUC of the target corporation shares as its cost basis in the target shares. In consequence, the new cost basis to the acquiring corporation will generally be less than the fair market value of the exchanged shares. * * *

[M]any significant differences exist between a B reorganization and an I.T.A. section 85.1 share-for-share exchange. Both provisions require that the consideration for the target corporation's stock be solely stock of the acquiring corporation, however, I.T.A. section 85.1 does not require voting stock but does require a single class of acquiring corporation stock. Control immediately after the exchange is an important part of the rationale for nonrecognition in a B reorganization while the I.T.A. section 85.1 share-for-share exchange requires that the target shareholders be at arm's length with the acquiring corporation both before and after the exchange. Finally, a I.T.A. section 85.1 share-for-share exchange is not mandatory and the shareholders may recognize any amount of gain or loss on the exchange. * * *

Mergers or Amalgamations Both the U.S. and the Canadian tax systems contain provisions allowing the combination of two or more corporations without recognition of gain or loss. I.R.C. section 368(a)(1)(A) defines an A reorganization as a statutory merger or consolidation. Typically, under a state merger statute, the assets and liabilities of the target corporation are transferred to the acquiring corporation and the target corporation dissolves by operation of law. The shareholders of the target corporation receive stock or debt instruments of the acquiring corporation, cash or other property, or a any combination of these types of consideration. A consolidation involves a similar transfer of assets and liabilities of two or more corporations to a newly created corporate entity and the shareholders of the transferor corporations become shareholders of the new corporation by operation of law. A merger and a consolidation are both classified as A reorganizations.

I.T.A. section 87 allows for the tax-free fusion of two or more corporations into an amalgamated corporate entity. The shareholders and the creditors of the transferor corporations become the shareholders and creditors of the amalgamated corporation. To qualify as an amalgamation under this provision, no new corporate entity can result from the exchange. Therefore, in comparison to an A reorganization, only a transaction similar to a consolidation, and not a merger, is possible. * * *

For Canadian income tax purposes, an amalgamation is a merger of two or more taxable Canadian corporations which results in the amalgamating corporations continuing as one amalgamated corporation. No new corporate entity is created. Instead, all of the property and liabilities of the amalgamating corporations become the property of the amalgamated corporation and all of the shareholders of the amalgamating corporations receive stock in the amalgamated corporation. The most common patterns are vertical and horizontal amalgamations. In a vertical amalgamation, a parent corporation merges with one or more subsidiary corporations to form the amalgamated corporation. Thus, a vertical amalgamation is similar in effect to the winding-up of a subsidiary into its parent corporation. A horizontal amalgamation is the merger of two or more corporations to form the amalgamated corporation. The corporate entity resulting from either form of amalgamation carries forward the tax attributes of the merged corporations. The shareholders of the target corporations receive an exchange basis in the shares in the amalgamated corporation and the amalgamated corporation receives a transferred basis in the assets received from the target corporations.

In addition, I.T.A. section 87 deems certain corporate transactions to be amalgamations for tax purposes. A deemed amalgamation occurs, for example, where a corporation and one or more of its wholly-owned subsidiaries, or two or more corporations each of which is a wholly-owned subsidiary of the same corporate parent, are merged and no shares are issued by the amalgamated corporation. * * *

I.T.A. subsection 87(2) provides detailed rules for the rollover of particular types of property that may be acquired by the amalgamated corporation. For example, under I.T.A. paragraph 87(2)(e) if capital property is acquired by the amalgamated corporation by virtue of the amalgamation, the cost of that property to the amalgamated corporation is simply the adjusted cost basis of that property to the predecessor corporation. An additional provision provides for a flow-through of the property and tax accounts to the new corporation. * * *

Corporate Dissolutions. In both the United States and Canada, the dissolution of a corporation results in recognition of gain or loss at the shareholder and corporate levels. In the United States, with the repeal of the *General Utilities* Doctrine, the distributing corporation is treated as if it sold its assets to the shareholders at fair market value. * * * The shareholders of the distributing corporation are considered to have exchanged their stock for an amount equal to the fair market value of the property received from the corporation. Similarly, assets distributed by a Canadian corporation to its shareholders on winding-up are deemed to have been disposed of by the corporation at fair market value. A shareholder is entitled to receive in cash or property an amount equal to its PUC without any tax consequences. However, if a shareholder receives cash or property in excess of PUC, the excess will be treated as a deemed dividend. In addition, the shareholder will be deemed to have disposed of its shares. Proceeds of disposition, however, are reduced by the amount of any deemed dividend received in the transaction. The result, where the PUC and cost basis of the share are the same, is no capital gain or loss realized on the winding-up. Comparing the two provisions, it is important to note that, in Canada, corporate distributions of dividends are preferable to capital gains as Canada has an integrated corporate tax system. In the United States, unless the shareholder is a corporate shareholder, capital gains treatment is generally preferred over dividend treatment.

Both Canada and the United States provide exceptions to recognition upon the liquidation of a subsidiary corporation by a parent corporation. * * *

I.T.A. subsection 88(1) provides that a taxable Canadian corporation, which is at least 90%, owned by another taxable Canadian corporation can be wound up into its parent on a tax-free basis. * * *

§ 13.7 House Ways and Means List of Options for Dealing with LBOs

Ways and Means Press Release Announcing Hearings on LBO Issues and Setting Forth Options List on LBOs

Reprinted in Tax Notes, 349 (April 17, 1989)

Options Modifying the Current Tax Treatment of Corporate Interest

1. Interest deductions could be denied on debt incurred or continued to purchase 20 percent, or more, of the stock of a corporation in a hostile tender offer, or to purchase assets of a corporation following such a stock purchase (H.R. 158). A hostile tender offer would be defined as one disapproved by a majority of the independent members of the board of directors of the target corporation. In addition, all gain would be recognized at the corporate level in the case of an acquisition of 80 percent, or more, of the stock of a corporation where a significant portion of the stock was purchased pursuant to a hostile tender offer.

2. The deduction for interest could be denied for debt incurred to finance mergers determined not to be in the public interest, specifically those transactions that result in a significant loss of jobs (H.R. 679). If the merger is expected to reduce employment

by more than 100 employees in the location of the establishment, the Federal Trade Commission would determine (i) the economic reasons for the proposed reduction in employment, (ii) the extent of economic losses to those employed by the establishment in which the reduction will occur, (iii) the extent of any economic loss, including a decline in the tax base, of any local government unit and any person in the geographic area in which such establishment is located, and (iv) other findings. If the Federal Trade Commission finds that the proposed merger would have a substantial adverse effect on employment in a county, city or other jurisdiction, the interest deduction limitations would apply.

3. The deduction for interest payments on certain high-yield or so-called "junk bond" debt could be denied above a specified threshold amount. The threshold exemption would be provided for a certain dollar limit of debt, such as $50 million, on an issue-by-issue or aggregate basis. A junk bond could be defined as an instrument that possesses one, or more, of several characteristics, such as an excessively high interest rate (as measured by some number of percentage points over the prime rate or the applicable Federal rate (AFR)), significant subordination to other debt of the issuer, convertibility into equity, or a noninvestment grade bond rating. Such restrictions could be applied to junk bonds used in a broad class of stock or asset acquisitions, including stock buybacks, or such restrictions could be limited to a narrower class of circumstances, such as hostile takeovers.

4. The deduction for corporate interest could be reduced by a specified percentage. Under the proposal, the revenues raised by such modification would be utilized to provide a percentage deduction for dividend payments made by corporations. The percentage deduction allowed for corporate interest would be the same as the percentage deduction allowed for dividend payments. This percentage would be determined on a revenue-neutral basis.

5. The deduction for corporate interest expense could be fully repealed and replaced with a credit to shareholders representing the corporate taxes paid on the earnings distributed to shareholders as a dividend. Depending upon the revenue consequences of such a proposal, the scope of these rules could be modified for companies whose shares are not publicly owned.

6. A corporate taxpayer's deduction for interest in excess of a specified rate of interest could be disallowed in whole, or in part. The rate above which the interest deduction would be disallowed would be selected by reference to some number of percentage points over the AFR. For example, disallowance could apply to interest in excess of three, six, or nine percentage points over the AFR at the time the instrument was issued. This option would not affect the characterization of an obligation as debt or equity under present law. Special antiavoidance rules could address issues such as the possible ability of taxpayers to issue debt qualifying under the option for full deductibility, which debt subsequently is securitized into a combination of lower-rate instruments, plus higher-rate instruments that would not have qualified for full deductibility if issued directly by the corporation.

7. A normative level of debt to equity of a corporation could be established, such as 80 percent. Any transaction which results in debt to equity levels above this percentage would be penalized, for example, through the imposition of a 50-percent reduction in the deductibility of interest on the debt incurred. The option might also be designed with a different ratio, such as debt to net worth, not counting junk bonds.

8. The deduction for corporate interest expense could be replaced with an annual percentage deduction based upon the overall capitalization of a company. The percentage deduction for capital would be established on a revenue-neutral basis, according to revenues raised by the denial of the current law deduction for corporate interest. For nonfinancial corporations, overall capitalization would include the sum of recorded shareholders' equity, plus the average of any loans for which the interest rate paid is greater than the percentage rate set for capital deductions. For financial corporations, only equity would be counted toward overall capitalization, but such corporations would be allowed to offset interest expense against interest income, so long as net interest income would be positive.

9. Corporate interest deductions for interest expense that is not actually paid currently could be deferred with respect to original issue discount (OID) obligations in transactions in which debt replaces corporate equity, until such time as interest amounts were actually paid. The amount of the ultimate deduction could be increased to reflect the time value of the deferral of the deduction. The proposal could be tailored to only apply to OID obligations held by tax-exempt entities and foreign persons.

As an alternative to postponing interest deductions of the issuer, OID from obligations which result in the replacement of corporate equity with debt could be treated as unrelated business income for tax-exempt entities. In addition, foreign holders of such obligations could be subject to full current taxation. Antiavoidance rules would govern situations in which such OID obligations are held through intermediaries.

Options Modifying the Current Tax Treatment of Equity
Distributions Made by Corporations

1. A shareholder-level credit could be provided in an amount equal to the corporate tax paid with respect to a percentage of dividends paid by a corporation. Shareholders would include in income the total amount of the dividend and the credit, and then would offset income tax liability by the amount of the credit. In this manner, a portion of the corporate-level tax on earnings distributed as dividends would be relieved.

2. Shareholders could be provided an exclusion from income for a percentage of dividend income.

3. Corporations could be provided a deduction for a percentage of dividends paid to shareholders. This option could be modified to reduce the deduction to the extent of holdings by foreign and tax-exempt shareholders, or, alternatively, to impose a compensating tax on such shareholders.

Each of the above options could apply only to equity raised by a corporation after the enactment of the proposal, or could be applied to both existing and newly raised equity. * * *

§ 13.8 Policy Perspective on Domestic and International Business Tax Reform Generally

A. Congressional Research Service Discussion of Issues in Corporate Tax Reform

Jane G. Gravelle and Thomas L. Hungerford, Corporate Tax Reform: Issues for Congress

Congressional Research Service
December 16, 2011

Potential Revisions in the Corporate Tax

There are a variety of potential revisions that could be made to the corporate tax to permit lowering the rate. The revisions discussed here include (1) broadening the corporate tax base and using the revenues to reduce the rate or to provide investment incentives, (2) correcting interest deductions and income for inflation, and (3) increasing the individual level tax to permit a lower tax at the firm level or taxing large unincorporated firms as corporations.

Eliminating Corporate Tax Preferences

One type of revision that would probably be supported by many economic analysts is to eliminate certain corporate preferences in exchange for a lower statutory corporate tax rate. The 2007 Treasury Study estimated that eliminating corporate preferences (e.g., accelerated depreciation and deferral of income of controlled foreign corporations would allow the tax rate to be lowered to 27%. * * *

The largest preference in the list is expensing and accelerated depreciation ($41 billion) and the second largest is the production activities deduction ($21 billion)[.] * * * Other significant provisions (worth over $10 billion each in these years) include the exclusion of interest on state and local bonds, the research and experimentation tax credit, and the deferral of income from foreign sources, which is probably responsible for much of the international distortions.

Over several Congresses, Senator Wyden [former Democrat Chair of the Senate Finance Committee], along with co-sponsors, has introduced a broad tax reform proposal. His proposal for the 111th Congress, S. 3018 (co-sponsored with Senator Gregg, a Republican) * * * would also eliminate a range of corporate tax preferences and lower the rate to 24%. This legislation would [also] index corporate debt for inflation[.] * * * [Further,] a major revenue raiser in that study was a provision * * * to provide a per country foreign tax credit limit rather than an overall limit) for foreign source income[.]

The Fiscal Commission proposed a measure very similar to the Wyden Gregg bill except that they did not include the deferral and per country foreign tax credit limit. Rather, they included a territorial tax that would raise somewhat less revenue than repealing deferral alone. * * *

President Obama's annual budgets have also included corporate tax reform provisions, concentrated in a few areas: international provisions, insurance provisions, inventory accounting, and fossil fuels. * * *

The Congressional Budget Office includes revenue raising corporate and business tax options in their budget options study[.] * * * Their options include a more limited proposal to restrict depreciation that raises less than half the revenue as replacing accelerated depreciation with the alternative depreciation system (which is the standard against which the tax expenditure is measured).

The options also consider a different foreign tax return which would combine allocation of deductions rules with an exemption for active income, a territorial type of tax treatment. * * *

How much could corporate tax rates be cut while maintaining revenue neutrality? Proposals discussed above have indicated rate reductions to 27% (Treasury 2007), to 24% (S. 3018, although there was a small corporate revenue loss), and to 30.5% for a more limited proposal.

Two important determinants of this potential rate reduction are whether to use revenues associated with unincorporated businesses which are included in these revenue raising options and how to treat provisions that arise largely from timing differences. * * * Although calculations vary slightly given the particular year of estimation, the largest tax expenditure, accelerated depreciation, would allow a rate reduction of almost 5 percentage points using standard scoring approaches and allowing revenues from both corporate and noncorporate businesses to be used to reduce the corporate tax rate. It would be one percentage point smaller if only corporate revenues were used. * * *

Recently, the Joint Committee on Taxation has estimated that relying solely on elimination of corporate tax expenditures, the rate could be reduced to 28%, although this proposal did not include the repeal of deferral. * * *

The Treasury Study also discussed the possibility of using this base broadening to provide an investment incentive, such as a partial expensing. Such a provision would lower the tax rate on new investment. It is difficult, however, to design investment subsidies in a fashion that is both neutral across types of assets and generates an even revenue loss pattern over time. Historically, investment subsidies have been restricted to equipment. The provision used most frequently in the past is the investment tax credit which, if allowed at a flat rate, favors short-lived assets. Partial expensing is neutral across investments if allowed for all types but its revenue loss is very large in the short run. Accelerated depreciation can be designed to be neutral, but it also has an uneven revenue loss pattern and cannot be applied to non-depreciable assets, such as inventories.

A benefit of lowering the statutory rate is that it reduces the incentive to shift profits abroad to tax havens, although that incentive would probably be considerably lessened in any case if deferral of taxation of foreign source income were ended, as proposed in H.R. 3018.

Although there are large potential gains from taxing foreign source income, as in H.R. 3018, and there are economic justifications for taxing foreign source income the same as domestic source income, and a lesser amount through ending deferral, international reforms are controversial. Indeed some pressure has been exerted to move in the other direction, toward a territorial tax.[1] Both the Chairman of the Ways and Means Committee and the Fiscal Commission proposed a territorial tax. There are, however, some more limited approaches. For example, the President's advisory panel proposed to exempt dividends of active businesses but disallow costs such as interest to the extent income is exempt. And, as proposed in H.R. 3970 and the President's proposals, one could also defer interest deductions associated with deferred income without making any other changes, or direct restrictive rules to tax havens.

Conclusion

Is there an urgent need to lower the corporate tax rate, as some recent discussions and analyses have suggested? On the whole, many of the new concerns expressed about the tax appear not to stand up under empirical examination. The claims that behavioral responses could cause revenues to rise if rates were cut does not hold up on both a theoretical basis and an empirical basis. Studies that purport to show a revenue maximizing tax rate of 30% contain econometric errors that produce biased and inconsistent results; when those problems are corrected the results disappear. Cross-country studies to provide direct evidence showing that the burden of the corporate tax actually falls on labor in some cases yield unreasonable results and prove to suffer from econometric flaws that also lead to a disappearance of the results when corrected. Similarly, claims that high U.S. tax rates will create problems for the United States in a global economy suffer from a misrepresentation of the U.S. tax rate compared to other countries and are less important when capital is imperfectly mobile, as it appears to be.

While these new arguments appear to rely on questionable data, the traditional concerns about the corporate tax appear valid. While many economists believe that the tax is still needed as a backstop to individual tax collections, it does result in some economic distortions. These economic distortions, however, have declined substantially over time as corporate rates and shares of output have fallen. There are a number of revenue-neutral changes that could reduce these distortions, allow for a lower corporate statutory tax rate, and lead to a more efficient corporate tax system. At the same time, the amount of rate reduction that could be achieved with a long run, revenue neutral corporate tax reform seems limited to a few percentage points.

---

1. A territorial tax system is one where the tax is imposed only in the country where business activity occurs and not in the country of ownership. While the present international tax system results in distortions, it is not clear how moving to a territorial tax would reduce these distortions, and even less clear how it would improve tax compliance and profit shifting. For a more detailed discussion, see CRS Report RL34115, *Reform of U.S. International Taxation: Alternatives*, by Jane G. Gravelle.

B. The Obama Administration's Business Tax Reform Proposals

The President's Framework for Business Tax Reform

February 2011

The President's Framework would eliminate dozens of different tax expenditures and fundamentally reform the business tax base to reduce distortions that hurt productivity and growth. It would reinvest the savings in reducing the rate from 35 percent to 28 percent. This combination of a broader base and a lower rate would alleviate a number of the significant economic distortions identified above that cause businesses to base investment decisions on tax rules rather than economic returns. Furthermore, this would encourage greater investment here at home and reduce incentives for U.S. companies to move their operations abroad or to shift profits to lower-tax jurisdictions. Where appropriate, the changes would allow adequate transition periods to permit affected parties to adjust to the new permanent tax rules. Finally, this reform would bring certainty to a business tax code that annually features the expiration of dozens of business tax incentives. Many of these temporary provisions would be eliminated and those that remain would be made permanent—helping to improve incentives to allocate capital efficiently and to simplify the tax code.

Specifically, the President's Framework would:

• Reduce the corporate tax rate from 35 percent to 28 percent. This reduction in the rate would put the United States in line with other advanced countries, help encourage greater investment in the United States, and reduce the tax-related economic distortions discussed above.

• Eliminate dozens of business tax loopholes and tax expenditures. The President's plan would start from a presumption that we should eliminate all tax expenditures for specific industries, with the few exceptions that are critical to broader growth or fairness. The following are a few examples of specific reductions in tax expenditures and loophole closers that should be part of any reform:

Eliminate "last in first out" accounting. * * *

Eliminate oil and gas tax preferences. * * *

Reform treatment of insurance industry and products. * * *

Taxing carried (profits) interests as ordinary income. Currently, many hedge fund managers, private equity partners, and other managers in partnerships are able to pay a 15 percent capital gains rate on their labor income (on income that is known as "carried interest"). This tax loophole is inappropriate and allows these financial managers to pay a lower tax rate on their income than other workers. The Framework would eliminate the loophole for managers in investment services partnerships and tax carried interest at ordinary income rates.

Eliminate special depreciation rules for corporate purchases of aircraft. * * *

• Reform the corporate tax base to invest savings in cutting the tax rate and reducing harmful distortions. This Framework lays out a menu of options that should be under consideration in reform. At least several of these would be necessary to get the rate down to 28 percent:

Addressing depreciation schedules. Current depreciation schedules generally overstate the true economic depreciation of assets. Although this provides an incentive to invest, it comes at the cost of higher tax rates for a given amount of revenue. In an increasingly global economy, accelerated depreciation may be a less effective way to increase investment and job creation than reinvesting the savings from moving towards economic depreciation into reducing tax rates.

Reducing the bias toward debt financing. A lower corporate tax rate by itself would automatically reduce but not eliminate the bias toward debt financing. Additional steps like reducing the deductibility of interest for corporations should be considered as part of a reform plan. This is because a tax system that is more neutral towards debt and equity will reduce incentives to overleverage and produce more stable business finances, especially in times of economic stress. In addition, reducing the deductibility of interest for corporations could finance lower tax rates and do more to encourage investment in the United States than keeping rates higher or paying for the rate reductions in other ways.

Establishing greater parity between large corporations and large non-corporate counterparts. Establishing greater parity between large corporations and their large non-corporate counterparts should be considered as a way to help improve equity, reduce distortions in how businesses organize themselves, and finance lower tax rates. A variety of ways to do this have been proposed, including ones discussed in the 2005 report of President Bush's Advisory Panel on Tax Reform, and in reform options developed by President Obama's Economic Recovery Advisory Board in 2010. It is essential that any changes in this area should not affect small businesses.

• Improve transparency and reduce accounting gimmicks. Corporate tax reform should increase transparency and reduce the gap between book income, reported to shareholders, and taxable income, reported to the IRS. These reforms could include greater disclosure of annual corporate income tax payments.

§ 13.9 Policy Perspective on Inversion Transactions and Changing to a Territorial or Imputation System for Taxing Foreign Income

See Sec. 10.12.

Index